Y0-BWV-286

AFRICAN BOOKS IN PRINT

LIVRES AFRICAINS DISPONIBLES

AFRICAN BOOKS IN PRINT

An Index by Author, Subject and Title

LIVRES AFRICAINS DISPONIBLES

Index par Auteurs, Matières et Titres

SECOND EDITION   DEUXIÈME ÉDITION

EDITED BY   ÉDITÉE PAR

HANS M. ZELL

VOLUME

I

MANSELL, LONDON
MECKLER BOOKS, WESTPORT, CONNECTICUT
ÉDITIONS FRANCE EXPANSION, PARIS
UNIVERSITY OF IFE BOOKSHOP, ILE-IFE

1978   LACo   1

ISBN 0 7201 0810 1 Volume I
0 7201 0811 X Volume II
0 7201 0798 9 Set of two volumes

Mansell Information/Publishing Limited, 3 Bloomsbury Place, London WC1A 2QA

First published 1975
Second edition 1978 revised and greatly enlarged

British Library Cataloguing in Publication Data
African books in print.
    1978–79: 2nd ed.
    1. Africa – Imprints
    I. Title II. Zell, Hans Martin
    015'.6   Z3501
    ISBN 0-7201-0798-9

The Editor has made every effort to include information submitted
directly by publishers and institutions, but the Publisher
cannot assume, and hereby disclaims, any liability to any party
for any loss or damage caused by omissions in *African books in print*,
whether such errors or omissions result from negligence, accident or
any other cause.

L'éditeur s'est efforcé d'inclure la totalité des informations transmises
par les éditeurs et institutions concernés. Ces informations sont
toutefois données sans garanties, et ne peuvent engager en aucune
façon sa responsabilité.

Meckler Books, 520 Riverside Avenue, P.O. Box 405 Saugatuck Station,
Westport, Ct. 06880
ISBN 0 930466 09 8

Library of Congress Cataloging in Publication Data
Zell, Hans M
    African books in print.
    1. Africa—Imprints. I. Title.
    Z3501.Z44 1978 [DT3] 015'.96   78-5618
    ISBN 0-930466-09-8

Éditions France Expansion, 15 Square de Vergennes, 75015 Paris
ISBN 2 229 00651 7 Volume I
2 229 00652 5 Volume II

University of Ife Bookshop Limited, Ile-Ife, Nigeria

Preliminary material photoset by Preface Limited,
Salisbury, United Kingdom, Indexes computer generated
and typeset in the USA, printed and bound in the
United Kingdom by The Scolar Press, Ilkley, Yorkshire

Contents

Table des Matières

Introduction to the second edition

This second edition of *African Books in Print* lists over 12,000 titles, twice the number that were included in the first edition, published in 1975. The objective of *ABIP* is to provide a systematic, reliable and functional reference tool and buying guide to African published materials currently in print.

Revisions to the new edition have been very extensive, both in terms of overall organization as well as in scope and comprehensiveness. However, the original idea to publish *African Books in Print* in two parts, with English/African and French language volumes to be issued in alternating years, has been abandoned, and the second edition now covers English and African languages publications as well as material from francophone Africa. It includes (i) books, still in print, listed in the first edition; (ii) a cumulation of all titles listed in volumes I (1975) to III (1977) of the quarterly journal the *African Book Publishing Record* (see also p. xlvii) totalling 4,644 records; plus (iii) new data, largely appertaining to pre-1973 imprints, not previously listed either in *ABIP* or in *ABPR*. The substantial number of new records has necessitated publication in two volumes, volume I providing an index by author, and volume II indexes by subject and by title. As elsewhere in the world, inflation is rampant in most African countries and over 4,000 records have had to be corrected as a result of price increase notifications received from publishers. Inevitably, the considerable costs of changing all these records in the computer file are reflected in the retail price of *ABIP*'s second edition.

Other features of the second edition are the introduction of a substantial number of new subject headings and the addition of many new cross-references, which should make it both more functional and easier to use.

Three hundred and ninety-six publishers, and research institutions and other organizations with publishing programmes, from thirty-seven African nations are represented in the second edition of *African Books in Print*. This compares with 188 publishers from nineteen African countries who had titles listed in the first edition. A breakdown by country of the number of publishers follows:

Country	No. of publishers represented	Country	No. of publishers represented
Algeria	2	Egypt (Engl. lang. publ. only)	2
Benin	–	Equatorial Guinea	–
Botswana	1	Ethiopia	10
Burundi	2	Gabon	–
Cameroun	7	Gambia	1
Central African Empire	–	Ghana	22
Chad	1	Guinea	–
Congo, People's Republic	–	Guinea Bissau	–
		Ivory Coast	8
Djibouti	–	Kenya	31

Introduction à la deuxième édition

Cette seconde édition de *Livres Africains Disponibles* répertorie plus de 12,000 titres, soit le double de la première édition, publiée en 1975. L'objectif de ce répertoire est de fournir un instrument de référence systématique, fonctionnel et sûr, et un guide pour l'acquisition des publications africaines courantes.

L'organisation générale de la nouvelle édition, ainsi que son plan et sa portée, ont fait l'objet de révisions approfondies. Nous avons abandonné notre idée première de publier le répertoire en deux éditions annuelles, l'une consacrée aux ouvrages anglais et africains, l'autre aux ouvrages français. La seconde édition couvre désormais aussi bien les publications en anglais que les ouvrages en français. Elle comprend (i) les livres encore disponibles répertoriés dans la première édition; (ii) le catalogue récapitulatif des titres mentionnés dans les volumes I (1975) à III (1977) de la revue trimestrielle *African Book Publishing Record* (*ABPR*) (voir p. xlvii), ce qui représente 4,644 notices; (iii) des entrées nouvelles qui se rapportent pour une grande part aux notices bibliographiques antérieures à 1973, qui n'étaient pas précédemment répertoriées. Le nombre important de ces nouvelles entrées nous a amenés à la publication de deux volumes: le premier contient l'index-auteurs, et le second les index-matières et titres. Comme partout, l'inflation gagne la plupart des pays africains et plus de 4,000 notices ont dû être corrigées à la suite des augmentations de prix communiquées par les éditeurs.

Nous avons par ailleurs introduit dans cette seconde édition un nombre important de vedettes-matières et de nombreux renvois, qui devraient la rendre plus fonctionnelle.

Trois cent quatre-vingt-six éditeurs, instituts de recherche et autres organisations à vocation d'édition, issus de trente-sept pays africains, sont représentés dans cette seconde édition contre 188 éditeurs de dix-neuf pays africains dans la première. La répartition des éditeurs par pays est la suivante:

Pays	Nombre d'éditeurs représentés	Pays	Nombre d'éditeurs représentés
Afrique du Sud	73	Ethiopie	10
Algérie	2	Guinée équatoriale	–
Bénin	–	Gabon	–
Botswana	1	Gambie	1
Burundi	2	Ghana	22
Cameroun	7	Guinée	–
Congo, République populaire	–	Guinée Bissau	–
Côte d'Ivoire	8	Haute Volta	1
Djibouti	–	Kenya	31
Egypte (publications de langue anglaise seulement)	2	Lesotho	4
		Libéria	2
Empire Centrafricain	–	Libye	–
		Madagascar	5
		Malawi	10
		Mali	1

Country	No. of publishers represented	Country	No. of publishers represented	Pays	Nombre d'éditeurs représentés	Pays	Nombre d'éditeurs représentés
Lesotho	4	Senegal	6	Maroc	3	Sierra Leone	6
Liberia	2	Seychelles	—	Mauritanie	—	Somale, République de	—
Libya	—	Sierra Leone	6	Maurice (Ile)	2	Soudan (publication en langue anglaise seulement)	3
Madagascar	5	Somali Republic	—	Namibie (Afrique du S.O.)	2		
Malawi	10	South Africa	73	Niger	4	Swaziland	2
Mali	1	Sudan (Engl. language publ. only)	3	Nigéria	96	Tanzanie	25
Mauritania	—	Swaziland	2	Ouganda	7	Tchad	1
Mauritius	2	Tanzania	25	Réunion, Ile de la	2	Togo	—
Morocco	3	Togo	—	Rhodésie (Zimbabwe)	14	Tunisie	2
Namibia (South West Africa)	2	Tunisia	2	Rwanda	3	Zaïre, République du	14
Niger	4	Uganda	7	Sénégal	6	Zambie	22
Nigeria	96	Upper Volta	1	Seychelles	—		
Réunion	2	Zaire Republic	14				
Rhodesia (Zimbabwe)	14	Zambia	22				
Rwanda	3						

The table indicates that although there is good coverage of most countries in West, East and Southern Africa, the coverage of some areas of francophone Africa and the Maghreb nations, particularly Morocco, is still unsatisfactory. In one country, Algeria, most publishing is in the hands of a state monopoly, which explains the fact that only two publishers are represented. In certain other francophone nations, such as Benin, Gabon, Guinea, the Central African Empire and the Congo Popular Republic, indigenous publishing, other than the production of government and official publications, is virtually non-existent. In Egypt, and in North Africa, the bulk of publishing output is in Arabic, not covered by *ABIP*, hence the small number of publishers. However, one state-sponsored publisher, the General Egyptian Organization for Publishing and Printing, does publish some books in English and French, but we have been unable to obtain details of their titles despite repeated requests. Elsewhere, too, there are still several publishers (as listed on page lxxi) who continue to ignore all requests for information — whether written to in English or in French, either by way of circular letters or personal follow-up requests. Their continued silence points to three conclusions: (1) the companies are no longer in business; (2) they have an apparent indifference to supplying the information required and in the designated form; (3) they are determined *not* to bring their titles to the attention of librarians, booksellers, and other bookbuyers in all parts of the world where *ABIP* is used as a reference and acquisitions tool!

Problems in securing information will no doubt continue for quite some time, and whilst the ultimate goal of providing truly comprehensive coverage is still somewhat distant, this second edition indicates considerable progress in achieving that aim. Many African publishers are supplying information promptly, meticu-

Ce tableau montre que, alors que la plupart des pays d'Afrique de l'Ouest, de l'Est et du Sud sont bien représentés, certaines zones d'Afrique francophone et du Maghreb — le Maroc en particulier — le sont de façon encore peu satisfaisante. En Algérie, la majeure partie de l'édition est confiée à un monopole d'état; de ce fait deux éditeurs seulement sont représentés. Dans d'autres nations francophones, comme le Bénin, le Gabon, la Guinée, l'Empire Centrafricain et la République populaire du Congo, l'édition locale, à l'exception des publications gouvernementales et officielles, est presque inexistante. En Egypte et en Afrique du Nord, la plupart des publications sont en arabe, que nous ne répertorions pas, d'où le petit nombre d'éditeurs retenus. Cependant, l'Organisation Générale Egyptienne d'Edition et d'Imprimerie (G.E.O.P.P.), éditeur subventionné par l'Etat, publie quelques livres en anglais et en français, mais nous n'avons pas pu obtenir les informations voulues sur leurs titres malgré de multiples rappels. Ailleurs encore, plusieurs éditeurs (voir page lxxi) continuent à 'ignorer toutes nos demandes d'information — qu'elles soient écrites en anglais ou en français, sous forme de circulaires ou de lettres personnelles pressantes. Leur silence prolongé nous amène a trois conclusions: (1) ces maisons d'édition ne travaillent plus; ou bien (2) elles sont apparemment indifférentes à nos demandes de renseignements; ou, (3) elles sont déterminées à *ne pas* porter leurs titres à l'attention des bibliothécaires, libraires et autres clients dans toutes les parties du globe où notre répertoire est utilisé comme instrument de référence et d'acquisition!

Les problèmes liés à la collecte des informations dureront sans doute encore longtemps. Bien que le but final — assurer la plus large couverture — soit difficile à atteindre, cette seconde édition dénote cependant l'effort considérable qui est fait dans ce sens. De nombreux éditeurs africains fournissent, il est vrai, les renseignements voulus avec rapidité et précision; le succès et la publication des futures éditions de *Livres Africains*

lously and comprehensively, but the successful continuation and publication of future biennial editions of *African Books in Print* will depend very largely on the active cooperation of all sectors of the African book world.

Approximately 7,400 titles or 62% of all records in this edition are in English, some 2,200 or 17% are in French, and about 2,500 records or 21% are in African languages. A few of the reviewers of *ABIP*'s first edition called for increased coverage of publications in the African languages. A survey recently conducted among subscribers to *African Book Publishing Record*, however, indicated that only a small proportion of librarians (3%) made frequent use of listings of titles in the African languages. Another 49% stated that occasional use was made of them, and the remaining 48% indicated that they were never consulted. In view of this, and because of the considerable data input costs per title, African language materials have been included only selectively, with the emphasis on most recently published titles. Nevertheless, more than double the number of titles in the first edition are included in this volume, representing a total of eighty-three African languages. This covers the output of the various Literature Bureaux, where they exist, with the exception of that in Sierra Leone (Mende, Temne, etc.) which unfortunately has not responded to any requests for data. There are weaknesses of representation in a few other languages, among them Zulu, Xhosa and Amharic, but other major languages such as Shona or Ndebele, or the various Ghanaian languages, are now represented in strength in this edition.

Oxford   H.M.Z.

January 1978

Disponibles (tous les deux ans) dépendront malgré tout largement de la coopération active de tous les secteurs du monde du livre africain.

Près de 7,400 titres, soit 62% des notices signalées dans cette édition, sont en anglais; 2,200, soit 17%, sont en français et 2,500 (environ 21%) sont dans des langues africaines. Quelques lecteurs de la première édition nous ont demandé une plus forte représentation des publications dans les langues africaines. Une enquête effectuée récemment parmi les abonnés de l'*African Book Publishing Record* montre pourtant qu'un petit nombre de bibliothécaires (3% seulement) utilise fréquemment les répertoires de titres publiés en langues africaines; 49% d'entre eux déclarent qu'ils les utilisent occasionnellement et les 48% restant, qu'ils ne les consultent jamais. C'est pourquoi, et en raison aussi du coût considérable d'enregistrement des données par titre, les ouvrages en langue africaine ont été introduits de façon sélective — l'accent étant mis sur les titres publiés récemment. Ils représentent néanmoins plus du double du nombre des titres contenus dans la première édition, soit au total quatre-vingt trois langues africaines. Cela couvre la production des différents Bureaux du Livre, là où ils existent, exception faite de celui de Sierra Leone (Mende, Temne, etc.) qui n'a malheureusement pas répondu à nos demandes de renseignements. Certaines langues sont encore faiblement représentées dans cette édition, parmi elles, le Zoulou, le Xhosa et l'Amharique, mais d'autres langues plus importantes telles que le Shona, le Ndebele ou les différentes langues Ghanéennes y occupent maintenant une large place.

Oxford   H.M.Z.

Janvier 1978

Acknowledgements

I am indebted to all those publishers and research institutions in Africa represented in this volume and without whose active cooperation this new edition of *African Books in Print* could not have materialized.

Very special thanks to Mary Madden, Vice President, Computer Systems, Blackwell North America, Inc., Beaverton, Oregon, and her staff, for their excellent data processing and computer services. A word of thanks also to my publishers, Mansell Information/Publishing Ltd., particularly to my former editor David Millett, and its current editorial director David Powell, for their continued interest and support of the *ABIP* project. I am also grateful to Nadine Chenu for having translated the main part of the preliminary pages into French and to Roland Ducasse and Alain Ricard for having checked the translation. Finally, I wish to acknowledge editorial help provided by Kathryn Weiskel.

H.M.Z.

Remerciements

Ma reconnaissance va à tous les éditeurs et instituts de recherche africains qui sont représentés dans ce volume. Sans leur active coopération, cette nouvelle édition de *Livres Africains Disponibles* n'aurait pu être réalisée.

Je remercie particulièrement Mary Madden, Vice-Présidente de Computer Systems, Blackwell North America, Inc., Beaverton (Oregon) et son personnel pour leur excellent service d'informatique. Je remercie également mes éditeurs, Mansell Information/Publishing Ltd., particulièrement mon ancien rédacteur, David Millett, et son directeur actuel, David Powell, pour l'intérêt et l'appui qu'ils accordent à notre projet. Je remercie aussi Nadine Chenu, qui a traduit en français la partie principale des pages préliminaires, ainsi que Roland Ducasse et Alain Ricard, qui ont revu la traduction. Je remercie enfin Kathryn Weiskel pour le concours qu'elle m'a apporté au plan éditorial.

H.M.Z.

Publishing progress in black Africa 1973-1977

This short introductory essay aims to provide a round-up of publishing activities in black Africa (South Africa excepted) since the publication of the first edition of *African Books in Print*, and to report on a number of significant developments in the African book world over the past five years.[1]

There is no doubt that over the past decade indigenous publishing has become an established reality in many African countries. Despite the lack of precise and up to date statistics, total output is clearly increasing substantially, perhaps by as much as 50% annually. The total figures are still modest in comparison with those of Western countries; the 1977 edition of *British Books in Print*, lists 282,706 books from 8,872 publishers, compared with 12,000 in this volume from just under 400 publishers, and throughout an entire continent. Much of the publishing also continues to come from research institutions attached to, or affiliated with, the various universities, though their specialized output will not concern us here.

Several new imprints have been launched during the period in East, West and Southern Africa, with many of them, however, having only small publishing programmes primarily devoted to producing self-study or "cram" books and revision texts. Sadly, too, a number of indigenous publishers, some with innovative and promising publishing programmes, have apparently ceased to exist or have become dormant. This may be attributed to several factors: sometimes it is chronic undercapitalization of publishing ventures, the low rate of literacy and the consequent lack of a sufficient readership at home, above all for enjoyment reading, or inadequate distribution systems and retail outlets. Frequently, however, these publishing failures are also due to financial management which is not very sound, or promotion and marketing which is not very effective. The acquisition by overseas librarians of books from a number of African publishers continues to be a problem[2] and it would appear that some firms are in fact determined *not* to bring their new publications to the attention of a wide audience of librarians and book buyers overseas. In addition, they are apparently unable to fill orders from major British or American booksellers. In one case the situation has deteriorated to such a level that a prominent Oxbridge firm of booksellers now actually refuses to handle orders for a particular African publisher.[3]

Ife publishing conference

A significant event for the African book industry was the international conference on publishing and book development held at the University of Ife, Nigeria, in December 1973. The conference was attended by well

Les progrès de l'édition en Afrique noire 1973-1977

Ce court essai liminaire tente de donner un panorama des activités de l'édition en Afrique noire (hormis l'Afrique du sud) depuis la publication de la première édition de *African Books in Print*, (Livres africains disponibles), et de rendre compte de plusieurs événements importants qui se sont déroulés dans le monde du livre africain pendant ces cinq dernières années.[1]

Il est indéniable qu'au cours de la dernière décennie, la publication d'ouvrages autochtones est devenue une réalité bien établie dans nombre de pays africains. Malgré l'absence de statistiques précises et à jour, il est évident que la production totale s'accroît considérablement, peut-être même de 50% par an. Bien sûr, les chiffres totaux restent modestes par rapport aux pays occidentaux: l'édition de 1977 de *British Books in Print* (Livres anglais disponibles) cite 282,706 titres publiés par 8,872 éditeurs, alors que celle-ci réunit 12,000 volumes provenant d'un peu moins de 400 éditeurs, et ceci pour le continent africain tout entier. La plupart du matériel édité continue de venir des instituts de recherche attachés ou affiliés aux diverses universités, mais nous ne nous occuperons pas ici de leur production.

Plusieurs nouvelles maisons d'édition ont été créés au cours de cette période en Afrique orientale, occidentale et australe, la plupart avec de petits programmes de publication composés principalement de livres pour étudier seul, d'"aide-mémoire" pour les examens ou de textes de révision. Malheureusement, il faut aussi signaler que certains éditeurs autochtones, dont plusieurs présentaient des programmes originaux et s'annonçaient bien, ont disparu ou arrêté leurs activités. Il y a probablement plusieurs raisons à cela: c'est parfois dû à une sous-capitalisation chronique des opérations, au faible taux d'alphabétisation et par conséquent à l'insuffisance de lecteurs lisant chez eux pour leur plaisir, ou encore à la carence des réseaux de diffusion et des points de vente au détail. Toutefois, il arrive souvent que les échecs du monde de l'édition soient aussi dûs à une gestion financière malsaine ou à la médiocrité de la promotion des ventes ou de la commercialisation. Il est encore difficile aux bibliothécaires étrangers d'acquérir des livres de plusieurs éditeurs africains[2] et certaines entreprises semblent résolues à *ne pas* faire connaître leurs nouvelles publications à un large auditoire de bibliothécaires et de libraires de l'étranger. Par ailleurs, elles semblent incapables de répondre aux commandes émanant des principales librairies britanniques ou américaines. Dans un cas précis, la situation s'est détériorée au point qu'une importante société de libraire d'Oxbridge refuse maintenant de prendre des commandes pour les ouvrages d'un éditeur africain particulier.[3]

over a hundred delegates who came from several African countries as well as from Europe and the United States, and forty-two papers were presented. The conference proceedings and the numerous resulting recommendations were published by the University of Ife Press in 1975.[4] The solutions offered in the proceedings are possibly neither practical nor immediate enough to satisfy the individual indigenous publisher, but the conference did achieve a measure of success in coming to grips with fundamental problems, the solutions to which are a necessary precursor to the effective functioning of individual publishers within the system.

The conference was also unique since it provided, for the first time, a platform for a get-together of professionals from all areas of the book world in Africa today to exchange views and ideas. In general terms, conference participants reconfirmed their belief — as some had done at an earlier UNESCO-sponsored conference on book development held in Ghana in 1968 — that books are an indispensable cornerstone in education; that a lively and flourishing publishing industry is vital for the development of the reading habit; to foster and preserve a country's culture; to produce inexpensive books which meet local needs; and that a nation's book industry must be considered essential in terms of national development. It was one of the aims of the Ife conference to again draw the attention of African governments to the unsatisfactory state of the book. While most African governments realize its importance to nation-building, few have thus far taken positive action to help and actively support their indigenous book industries. It remains to be seen whether government action will follow as a result of the Ife meeting — five years later there are not many noticeable signs. Happily, however, at least two recommendations put forward at the Ife conference have materialized, one being the launching of an African book trade journal in the form of the quarterly bibliography and trade organ, the *African Book Publishing Record* (*ABPR*),[5] and the other an annual African book fair, the Ife Book Fair, held at the same location as the conference. Also in Nigeria, the Nigerian Publishers' Association is now increasingly active in sponsoring training workshops and seminars for personnel in the local book industries.

Book development centres

The setting-up of the Centre Régional de Promotion du Livre en Afrique (Regional Book Promotion Centre) in Yaoundé, Cameroun, was also endorsed by the Ife conference, and it is now fully operational. The UNESCO co-sponsored Centre aims to encourage the production of books by Africans, to conduct research into the problems of the book industries, to help to develop means for the promotion of the reading habit,

Conférence de l'édition à Ifé

En décembre 1973, la conférence internationale de l'édition et de la promotion du livre, qui s'est tenue à l'Université d'Ifé, au Nigéria, a été un grand événement pour l'industrie du livre africain. Plus de cent représentants y ont pris part, provenant de plusieurs pays africains aussi bien que d'Europe, et des Etats-Unis, et quarante-deux communications ont été présentées. Les actes de la conférence et les recommandations nombreuses qui en ont résulté ont été publiés par les Presses de l'Université d'Ifé en 1975.[4] Les solutions présentées dans ces actes ne sont peut-être ni pratiques ni assez immédiates pour satisfaire chaque éditeur autochtone, mais la conférence n'en a pas moins réussi dans une certaine mesure à aborder les problèmes fondamentaux qui devront être résolus avant que les éditeurs puissent chacun de leur côté opérer avec efficacité dans le cadre du système.

La conférence a également présenté la particularité de fournir pour la première fois une tribune où un ensemble de professionnels appartenant à toutes les branches du monde actuel du livre en Afrique ont pu échanger idées et points de vue. En termes généraux, les délégués ont à nouveau affirmé leur conviction, comme certains l'avaient déjà fait à l'occasion d'une conférence tenue sous l'égide de l'UNESCO sur l'essor du livre au Ghana en 1968, que le livre est la pierre angulaire de l'éducation; qu'une industrie du livre énergique et florissante est essentielle si l'on veut développer des habitudes de lecture, encourager et préserver la culture d'un pays, produire des livres bon marché répondant aux besoins locaux, et enfin que l'industrie du livre d'un pays doit être considérée comme un élément fondamental du développement national. L'un des objectifs de la conférence d'Ifé a été d'appeler une fois de plus l'attention des gouvernements africains sur la situation déplorable dans laquelle se trouve l'édition. Si la plupart de ces gouvernements apprécient son importance, s'agissant de la construction de la nation, peu d'entre eux ont jusqu'à présent pris des mesures positives pour aider et soutenir activement les industries du livre de leur pays. Reste à voir si des mesures gouvernementales résulteront de la réunion d'Ifé: cinq ans après, on n'en voit guère de signe perceptible. Toutefois, au moins deux des recommandations présentées à la conférence d'Ifé se sont heureusement concrétisées: il s'agit tout d'abord du lancement d'un magazine professionnel du livre africain sous la forme d'une bibliographie trimestrielle et d'un bulletin professionnel intitulé *African Book Publishing Record* (*ABPR*);[5] et ensuite, d'une foire du livre africain, la "Foire du livre d'Ifé" qui se tient à l'emplacement même de la conférence. Au Nigéria également, l'association des éditeurs nigérians s'occupe activement de réunir des colloques et des séminaires de formation

and to organize workshops and seminars for book publishing personnel, the first of which was a course in publishing management held between 24 May and 12 June 1976 which brought together participants from five francophone African countries. The Centre will be particularly concerned in the future with the production of children's books relevant to the environment of an African child, and Jean Dihang of Editions CLE outlined this project in the April 1976 issue of *ABPR*.[6] A quarterly *Information Bulletin* is also promised by the Centre.[7]

National book development councils now exist in several African countries, including Ghana, Kenya, and Nigeria, and one is shortly to be established in Zambia. Unfortunately there is not much evidence at this stage of their impact and their activities seem to be rather low-key. The most feasible explanation for this is that all of them are government controlled and administered — unlike the Book Development Council in Britain which serves as the export arm of the Publishers' Association — and therefore badly hampered by the slow-grinding machinery of government bureaucracy. However, in at least one country, Nigeria, the Book Development Council, after long delays leading up to its formal launching, now looks set to assume a much more active role in the country's development of its book industries, as well as its library network. The Nigerian Book Development Council will also work closely with a new National Publishing and Printing Company, whose establishment was announced by the Nigerian Federal Military Government in 1977. The government intends to provide infrastructural facilities for the printing industries, and on the publishing side the company will undertake the publication of worthy manuscripts — particularly in the indigenous languages — which do not attract profit-oriented commercial publishers. Few specific details are available as yet on the government's precise intentions and they are largely speculative. The indications are, however, that there seems to be no cause for foreign firms with subsidiaries in Nigeria to be alarmed that their operations will be curtailed, or that the government will create a state-owned monopoly.

In Ghana, a recently inaugurated new book development project will involve teachers in the writing of school textbooks and the production of other teaching aids through a series of workshops. The project is jointly sponsored by the Ghana National Association of Teachers, the Canadian Teachers' Federation, and the Ghana National Book Development Council. An important seminar on the writing and production of literature for children was held at the University of Ghana, Legon, in April 1967, and the organizer of the seminar, Sam Kotei, wrote about it, and the recommendations that were put forward, in the *ABPR* October 1976 issue.[8]

pour le personnel employé dans les industries locales du livre.

Centre de promotion du livre

La création du Centre Régional de Promotion du livre en Afrique, à Yaoundé, Cameroun, a été entérinée à la conférence d'Ifé et le Centre fontionne activement à l'heure actuelle. Dépendant aussi de l'UNESCO, il vise à encourager la production de livres par les africains, à conduire des travaux de recherche destinés à apporter des solutions aux problèmes que rencontrent les industries du livre, à aider à mettre au point des méthodes d'incitation à la lecture, et à organiser des colloques et des séminaires pour le personnel de l'édition. Le premier de ceux-ci, portant sur la gestion de l'édition, s'est déroulé du 24 mai au 12 juin 1976, et a rassemblé des participants provenant de cinq pays d'Afrique francophone. A l'avenir, le Centre s'occupera notamment de la production de livres pour enfants en harmonie avec l'environnement d'un enfant africain, projet dont Jean Dihang, des Editions C.L.E., a donné un aperçu dans le numéro d'avril 1976 de *ABPR*.[6] Le Centre a également promis de publier un *Bulletin d'information* trimestriel.[7]

Des "Conseils nationaux de promotion du livre" existent maintenant dans plusieurs pays africains (Ghana, Kenya, Nigéria) et un autre sera bientôt établi en Zambie. Malheureusement, on manque jusqu'à présent d'indications quant à leur influence, et leurs activités semblent plutôt modestes. L'explication la plus plausible est que tous sont contrôlés et administrés par les gouvernements, (à la différence du Conseil de promotion du livre de Grande-Bretagne qui joue le rôle d'exportateur de l'Association des éditeurs) et par conséquent leur action est fortement entravée par le poids de la machine bureaucratique gouvernementale. Toutefois, au moins dans un pays, le Nigéria, le Conseil de promotion du livre, dont le lancement officiel a été retardé pendant longtemps, semble maintenant capable d'assumer un rôle beaucoup plus actif dans la promotion nationale des industries du livre aussi bien que des réseaux de bibliothèques. Le Conseil de promotion du livre nigérian travaillera également en étroite collaboration avec une nouvelle Société nationale d'édition et d'imprimerie, dont la création a été annoncée par le gouvernement militaire fédéral nigérian en 1977. Le gouvernement a l'intention de fournir les installations d'infrastructure pour les imprimeries, et en ce qui concerne l'edition, cette société entreprendra la publication de manuscrits de valeur, notamment dans les langues autochtones qui n'intéressent pas les éditeurs commerciaux plutôt motivés par la réalisation de bénéfices. On ne possède à ce jour que peu de détails sur les intentions précises du gouvernement qui paraissent fort théoriques. Toutefois, il semble que les entreprises

Union of African writers

A Union of Writers of the African Peoples (Union des Ecrivains Négro-Africains) was formed in Accra in June 1975, and has subsequently held two meetings.[9] The proceedings of the first full congress of the Union, held in Dakar in February 1976, are shortly to be published under the title *African world alternatives*. The Union's president is the Congolese poet Felix Tchikaya U'Tamsi, and its general secretary is Wole Soyinka who is living again in Nigeria. Among the aims and objectives of the Union are "to establish a cooperative publishing house in Africa to which all members would be encouraged to cede publishing rights for African readership" and to "translate all such published works into Kiswahili, thus promoting the continental use of the language". The favoured location of such a cooperative publishing house, that would seek to establish a continent-wide distribution and sales network, would appear to be Dakar.

Book promotional events

Another event of major significance for the African book world was the first Ife Book Fair, held in Nigeria in March 1976, which brought to a realization one of the recommendations put forward at the Ife conference on publishing. It is now already firmly established in the calendar of international book trade events, and the third Fair is to be held between 5 and 9 March 1978. The man behind the Ife Book Fair is the energetic 'Wunmi Adegbonmire, managing director of the University of Ife Bookshop, which officially sponsors the Fair in association with the various professional groups representing the book industries in Nigeria, as well as the Nigerian Book Development Council. The Fair features a supporting programme of lectures and seminars with distinguished speakers from the fields of education, publishing, and the literary world. The Fair is attracting wider and wider international participation each year, but indigenous African publishers, other than those from Nigeria, have been notably absent in 1976 and 1977. One hopes that they will be present in larger numbers in 1978. The Ife Book Fair is, after all, an *African* book trade event, and it is vital that the Ife initiatives gain the fullest possible support from African publishers, as indeed from the entire African book world.

To celebrate their twenty-fifth anniversary, the Ghana Library Board also sponsored an international book fair in Accra, in October 1975. Twenty-six publishers from Ghana, Nigeria and Britain participated with exhibits.

Another welcome development was the first "Book Fare" sponsored by the Text Book Centre Ltd. in association with the Kenyan Booksellers', Publishers' and Library associations, which was held in Nairobi in

étrangères ayant des filiales au Nigéria n'ont aucune raison de craindre ni une réduction du volume de leurs opérations ni l'institution d'un monopole d'état par le gouvernement.

Au Ghana, un nouveau projet de promotion du livre récemment adopté fera participer les professeurs à la rédaction de manuels scolaires et à la production d'autres éléments éducatifs dans le cadre d'une série de colloques. Ce projet est financé conjointement par l'Association nationale des professeurs du Ghana, la Fédération des professeurs canadiens et le Conseil national ghanéen de promotion du livre. Un séminaire important sur la rédaction et la production de livres pour enfants s'est tenu à l'Université du Ghana, à Legon, en avril 1967, et Sam Kotei, organisateur du séminaire, a rendu compte de cet événement et des recommandations présentées à cette occasion dans un article publié dans le numéro d'octobre 1976 de *ABPR*.[8]

Union des écrivains africains

L'Union des Ecrivains Négro-Africains a été créée à Accra en juin 1975 et s'est réunie deux fois depuis.[9] Les actes du premier Congrès de l'Union qui a eu lieu à Dakar en février 1976 seront publiés sous peu sous le titre *African world alternatives* [Solutions de rechange pour le monde africain]. La présidence de l'Union a été confiée à Felix Tchikaya U'Tamsi, poète congolais, et le secrétariat général à Wole Soyinka, qui vit en ce moment au Nigéria. Les objectifs de l'Union sont, notamment, "d'établir une coopérative d'édition en Afrique à laquelle tous les membres seraient invités à céder leurs droits de publication pour les lecteurs africains" et de "traduire tous les ouvrages ainsi publiés en kiswahili, afin de promouvoir l'utilisation de la langue à travers tout le continent." Il semble que Dakar soit l'emplacement choisi pour la création d'une coopérative d'édition qui s'efforcerait d'établir un réseau de diffusion et de points de vente dans tout le continent.

Evénements de promotion du livre

Un autre événement d'importance pour le monde du livre africain a été la première Foire du livre d'Ifé, qui s'est tenue au Nigéria en mars 1976, en application de l'une des recommandations présentées à la Conférence d'Ifé sur l'édition. Elle a maintenant une place bien établie au calendrier des événements internationaux du monde de l'édition. La troisième Foire a eu lieu du 5 au 9 mars 1978. L'homme dynamique de cette Foire, c'est 'Wunmi Adegbonmire, directeur-gérant de la librairie de l'Université d'Ifé, qui patronne officiellement la Foire, avec les divers groupes professionnels des industries du livre au Nigéria, ainsi que le Conseil nigérian de promotion du livre. Cette Foire comporte un

August 1976. Some 3,000 paperbacks were on display, and the five-day exhibition attracted over 15,000 people from all walks of life. A second exhibition took place in Mombasa and Kisumu in 1977, and it is now likely to become an annual event. The original idea of an open-air exhibition under canvas is being retained, and the fair is supplemented by daily talks, lectures, and debates.

Developments in the publishing world

English-speaking West Africa

Inevitably, in any survey of publishing activities in West Africa, **Nigeria** must come first and it is the country that probably presents the liveliest publishing scene in the whole of black Africa. The bulk of the market is still very much dominated by the British multinationals, mainly six companies: Longman, Oxford University Press, Heinemann, Evans, Macmillan, and Thomas Nelson. All of them have extensive local publishing programmes catering primarily for the school-book market, but they also produce a wide range of scholarly and general interest titles, children's books, and creative writing by Nigerian authors. With the introduction in Nigeria of free universal primary education (U.P.E.), likely to become compulsory in the 1980s, the market for school-books has taken on enormous proportions, and many publishers are struggling to cope with the staggering demand for books for the scheme. The first of these was a series of government-commissioned texts for teacher-training, the various subject areas being allocated among the six large British multinationals, with Longman getting the largest share. Some indigenous companies did submit tenders to produce some of the texts but apparently failed to persuade the authorities that they had the capacity to produce them, an indication of a somewhat unfortunate lack of confidence by the government in their indigenous book industries.

Longman (Nigeria) Ltd. more than doubled their turnover in 1976, and a sizeable capital investment programme has been authorized for the Nigerian subsidiary which will provide it with much-needed additional warehousing and office space at Ikeja, and this will be funded from local resources. (Overall turnover of the Pearson Longman group in Africa in 1976 was a staggering £13,886,000, with profit before taxation amounting to £3,868,000.)[10] For other British publishers, too, Nigeria has in recent years grown vastly in importance — after the United States, it is Oxford University Press's second largest overseas market, and their Ibadan-based operation employs 170 people. The chief executives of all the Nigerian companies of British publishers are now Nigerian, and the Nigerian Enterprises Promotion Decree of February 1972 has ensured that the majority of the equity is in Nigerian hands.

programme de conférences et de séminaires donnés par d'éminents orateurs appartenant à l'enseignement, à l'édition et au monde littéraire. Chaque année, la Foire attire de plus en plus de participants venus du monde entier. Malheureusement les éditeurs africains autochtones autres que ceux du Nigéria, ont brillé par leur absence en 1976 et 1977. On souhaite qu'ils seront venus en grand nombre en 1978. La foire d'Ifé est un événement du monde de l'édition *africaine* et il est essentiel que les initiatives d'Ifé obtiennent le soutien le plus complet de la part des éditeurs africains et aussi du monde du livre africain tout entier.

Pour célébrer son vingt-cinquième anniversaire, le Bureau des bibliothèques du Ghana a financé une Foire internationale du livre à Accra en octobre 1975 à laquelle ont exposé vingt-six éditeurs du Ghana, du Nigéria et de Grande-Bretagne.

Un autre événement heureux a eu lieu à Nairobi, en août 1976. Il s'agit de la première "Foire du livre" lancée conjointement par le Text Book Centre Ltd et par les associations des libraires, éditeurs et bibliothécaires kényans. Plus de 3,000 livres de poche y ont été présentés et l'exposition a attiré en cinq jours 15,000 personnes de tous les horizons. Une seconde exposition s'est déroulée à Mombasa et à Kisumu en 1977 et cette foire deviendra sans doute maintenant un événement annuel. On a maintenu l'idée initiale d'une exposition en plein air sous une tente et la foire est accompagnée d'entretiens, de conférences et de débats quotidiens.

Evolution du monde de l'édition

Afrique occidentale anglophone

Naturellement, dans toute étude portant sur les activités de l'édition de l'Afrique occidentale, il faut tout d'abord s'arrêter au **Nigéria** car c'est là que se trouve le monde de l'édition le plus actif de toute l'Afrique noire. L'ensemble du marché est toujours dominé par les multinationales britanniques, principalement six sociétés: Longman, Oxford University Press, Heinemann, Evans, Macmillan et Thomas Nelson. Toutes présentent d'importants programmes d'édition locaux s'adressant surtout au marché du manuel scolaire, mais elles produisent également une large gamme d'ouvrages d'érudition ou d'intérêt général, de livres pour enfants et de créations littéraires d'auteurs nigérians. Avec l'introduction au Nigéria de l'enseignement primaire universel et gratuit (U.P.E.), qui deviendra vraisemblablement obligatoire vers les années 80, le marché des manuels scolaires s'est accru considérablement et nombre d'éditeurs luttent pour faire face à la demande énorme de livres nécessaires pour ce projet. Sa première partie est constituée par une série de textes commandés par le gouvernement pour la formation de professeurs. Les diverses matières ont été réparties entre les six grandes

Among the multinationals, it is perhaps the Nigerian branch of Oxford University Press that, in addition to their extensive school-book publishing programme, has the most diversified list of books published under its local imprint. Among recent OUP-Nigeria scholarly books are *Ifa: an exposition of Ife literary corpus* by Wande Abimbola, on this most important genre of Yoruba oral literature; a book on *Ayo*, the popular Yoruba board game, by Chief A. O. Odeleye; Professor Dupe Olatunbosun's perceptive analysis of *Nigeria's neglected rural majority; Black people in Britain 1555-1833* by Folarin Shyllon; and *University development in Africa: the Nigerian experience* by the current Registrar of the West African Examinations Council, Chukuemeka Ike. Oxford University Press have also published a locally produced edition of Wole Soyinka's play *Madmen and specialists*, and other new drama has included works by Zulu Sofola and Sunny Oti. What originally was a series of local radio broadcasts has been brought together under the title *Discovering Nigeria's past* edited by Thurstan Shaw; it provides an introduction to Nigerian archaeology for the general public. Longman Nigeria have launched an attractive new series of stories aimed at school children in the upper classes of primary school and lower form secondary schools, the "Palm Library": among the first titles to appear were two books by the popular novelist Cyprian Ekwensi. A scholarly title from Macmillan Nigeria was *A complete course in Igbo grammar* by M. N. Okonkwo; and it has been announced that Macmillan intend to enter the field of African popular fiction "believing that well-written novels in English, written in simple style, will help to promote reading fluency" and that the production of books at this level "may help to encourage creative writing generally."[11] Macmillan's affiliated company in Zaria, the Northern Nigerian Publishing House, continues to produce educational books for the market in the north of Nigeria, primarily in Hausa. The Nigerian affiliates of Heinemann Educational Books and Evans Brothers are active in the field of law in addition to school-book publishing (Heinemann is particularly strong in the sciences); Evans produces a series of law texts on behalf of the University of Lagos Press.

An innovative step was taken in Nigeria with the launching of the "Onibonoje Book Club" in December 1973 — the first ever in black Africa — sponsored by the pioneering and perhaps most enterprising indigenous African publisher, Onibonoje Press and Book Industries Ltd. It is claimed that the book club now enjoys a membership of several thousand. Coinciding with this development came the release of the first titles of two new Onibonoje series, one the "African Literature Series" aimed at the adult trade market including novels, short story collections and drama; the other a "Junior African Literature Series" for young readers. Both series have

multinationales britanniques, parmi lesquelles Longman s'est taillé la part du lion. Des sociétés autochtones ont bien présenté des offres pour la production de certains de ces manuels, mais apparemment elles n'ont pas réussi à persuader les autorités qu'elles en étaient capables, ce qui indique un certain manque de confiance regrettable de la part du gouvernement à l'égard des industries du livre du pays.

En 1976, la société Longman (Nigéria) Ltd. a plus que doublé son chiffre d'affaires. Un important programme d'investissement a été accordé à sa filiale nigérianne, ce qui lui permettra d'agrandir ses entrepôts, qui en ont bien besoin, et d'étendre ses bureaux d'Ikeja. Ce programme sera financé par des ressources locales. (En 1976, le chiffre d'affaires total du Groupe Pearson Longman en Afrique a atteint 13,886,000 de livres sterling, avec un bénéfice avant impôts de 3,868,000 de livres.)[10] Pour d'autres éditeurs britanniques également le Nigéria est devenu ces dernières années un marché plus important: pour Oxford University Press, le Nigéria est, après les Etats-Unis, le second marché étranger, et à Ibadan la société emploie 170 personnes. Les principaux cadres de toutes les filiales nigériannes d'éditeurs britanniques sont maintenant nigérians et la Loi sur la promotion des entreprises nigériannes de février 1972 a fait en sorte que la majorité des actions sont maintenant aux mains des Nigérians. De toutes les multinationales, c'est peut-être la filiale nigérianne de Oxford University Press qui, en plus de son programme étendu de publication de manuels scolaires, offre la liste de titres la plus variée. Les livres d'érudition récemment publiés par OUP-Nigéria, comprennent *Ifa: an exposition of Ife literary corpus*, de Wande Abimola, sur ce genre très important de littérature orale yorouba; un livre sur l'*Ayo*, jeu populaire yorouba, du Chef A. O. Odeleye; une analyse pénétrante du professeur Dupe Olatunbosun: *Nigeria's neglected rural majority; Black people in Britain 1555–1833* de Folarin Shyllon; et *University development in Africa: the Nigerian experience* de Chukuemeka Ike, secrétaire actuel du Conseil des examens de l'Afrique de l'ouest. L'O.U.P. a également publié localement une édition de la pièce de Wole Soyinka intitulée *Madmen and specialists*, ainsi que d'autres pièces de théâtre récentes, notamment des œuvres de Zulu Sofola et Sunny Oti. Ce qui, à l'origine était une série d'émissions de la radio locale a été rassemblé sous le titre: *Discovering Nigeria's past*, préparé par Thurstan Shaw, introduction à l'archéologie nigérianne destinée au grand public. Longman Nigéria a lancé une nouvelle série intéressante d'histoires pour le jeune public des grandes classes de l'école primaire et les premières classes du secondaire intitulée "Palm Library": parmi les premiers titres parus se trouvent deux livres du romancier populaire Cyprian Ekwensi. Macmillan Nigéria a publié un ouvrage d'érudition, *A complete*

had many new titles added during the past five years. Onibonoje Press also continues to publish new school texts, one major project being a primary course in social studies, as well as examination and study guides. It was in fact with the publication of numerous "cram" or self-study books that Gabriel Onibonoje first gained a reputation in the 1960s, and he has had much scorn heaped on him in the past by other publishers and by academics. Mr. Onibonoje has nevertheless gone from strength to strength thanks to his drive and dynamics in approaching and settling problems.

Onibonoje's fiercest indigenous competitor is probably Aromolaran Publishers (formerly Progresso Publishers), also with headquarters at Ibadan, largely with a list of school-books and revision texts. A new imprint with a similar list, launched in 1976, was that of Cross Continent Press in Lagos, with an initial programme comprising mainly school-books and readers, examination guides, and children's books. Another new imprint is New Horn Press in Ibadan, set up by a consortium of writers and headed by the former chairman of Ethiope Publishing Corporation, Professor Abiola Irele, who to date has published two small paperbacks: one is a satrical novel by the gifted young Nigerian writer Femi Osofisan, entitled *Kolera koleji*, which centres round the outbreak of a cholera epidemic on the campus of an imaginary university somewhere in Nigeria; the other is a play, *The curse*, by the prolific Kole Omotoso. A further enterprising new publishing company is Deto Deni Educational Productions at Ibadan, whose first book is by the former ombudsman of the Nigerian *Daily Times*, Tola Adeniji. Entitled *The lunatic, epitome of our golden age*, it is a lively collection of essays and articles, and is being promoted very aggressively — ". . . corruption, detention, greed, grab, graft . . . all in *The lunatic* . . . it's only N1.00, less than the cost of two bottles of beer" said a poster. And surely with the way inflation is going in Nigeria it will soon be only the price of *one* bottle of beer!

West African Book Publishers Limited in Lagos, an affiliate of one of Nigeria's major printers, Academy Press Ltd., is another recent arrival on the scene. Initial titles have included books on health, motherhood and child care, as well as an extremely well produced *Guide to Lagos* written and compiled by E. Seriki and E. Pullybank. A new children's series in Yoruba and English, "Atoka Books", will be launched by them in 1978. Yet another new imprint, that would appear to specialize in academic works on geology, yet goes under the somewhat unlikely name of Elizabethan Publishing Company, has produced a major volume, *The geology of Nigeria*, edited by C. A. Kogbe, as well as E. O. Osinsanya's small illustrated booklet on *Nigerian traditional and cultural hairstyles*.

A privately owned indigenous publishing house which

course in Igbo Grammar, de M. N. Okonkwo, et l'éditeur a annoncé son intention d'entrer dans le domaine du roman populaire africain "parce que, à son avis, de bons romans écrits en anglais dans un style simple, aideront au developpement de la lecture", et que la production de livres de ce niveau "pourra encourager la création littéraire en général".[11] La société filiale de Macmillan à Zaria, Northern Nigerian Publishing House, continue à produire des livres éducatifs pour le marché du nord du Nigéria principalement en hausa. Les filiales nigériannes de Heinemann Educational Books et de Evans Brothers sont très actives dans le domaine du droit et de la publication de livres scolaires (celle de Heinemann étant spécialisée en sciences). Evans produit une série d'ouvrages de droit pour University of Lagos Press.

En décembre 1973 une innovation en Afrique noire: le lancement au Nigéria du "Onibonoje Book Club" financé par un des pionniers des éditeurs africains autochtones, et peut-être le plus entreprenant, Onibonoje Press and Book Industries Ltd. On prétend que ce club du livre a maintenant plusieurs milliers de membres. En même temps que cette innovation, ont été publiés les premiers titres de deux collections de Onibonoje Press, l'une, "African Literature Series" orientée vers le marché des adultes, comprenant des romans, des recueils de nouvelles et des pièces de théâtre; l'autre, intitulée "Junior African Literature Series", pour les jeunes lecteurs. De nombreux titres ont été ajoutés aux deux séries au cours de ces cinq dernières années. Les Presses Onibonoje continuent également la publication de nouveaux manuels de classe: un projet important est un cours élémentaire de sciences sociales, ainsi que des guides pour les examens et les études. C'est en publiant tout d'abord de nombreux aide-mémoires et livres pour autodidactes pendent les années 60 que Gabriel Onibonoje a construit sa réputation et s'est attiré le mépris, dans le passé, des autres éditeurs et des universitaires. Monsieur Onibonoje n'en a pas moins affermi progressivement sa position grâce au dynamisme et à l'énergie qu'il a déployés en abordant et en réglant les problèmes.

Sur place, le concurrent autochtone le plus féroce d'Onibonoje est sans doute Aromolaran Publishers (anciennement Progresso Publishers), dont le siège est aussi à Ibadan, et qui produit principalement des manuels scolaires et des textes de révision. Un nouvel éditeur offrant un choix semblable s'est installé à Lagos en 1976: Cross Continent Press, dont le programme initial comprend principalement des manuels scolaires et des recueils de morceaux choisis, des guides pour les examens et des livres pour enfants. New Horn Press est une nouvelle maison d'édition créée par un groupe d'écrivains et dirigée par le professeur Abiola Irele, ancien président de la Société d'édition Ethiope Publish-

was much in the limelight when it started operations in 1971, Nwamife Publishers in Enugu, has experienced a transitional period over the past few years and the original emphasis on literary and political works — not, apparently, very successful in terms of financial returns — has been shifted to a much wider and more balanced programme of scholarly studies, law texts, books on agricultural development, and school texts. A severe setback, however, was the sudden announcement by the Nigerian government of the abolition of the teaching of modern mathematics in all primary and post-primary institutions, which left Nwamife with a warehouse full of books in their "Modern mathematics for primary and secondary schools" series. This is clearly the kind of disastrous setback from which a much under-capitalized small indigenous publisher finds it much more difficult to recover and to recoup their losses than would any of the large multi-nationals.

One of the founders of Nwamife Publishers, Arthur Nwankwo, has now set up his own new imprint, Fourth Dimension Publishers, also in Enugu, with the first titles expected in 1978. It is an impressive initial list: it includes two children's tales by Chinua Achebe; first novels by Kalu Uka, Labo Yaro, Ogali A. Ogali, Ben Gbulie; new verse by Mamman Vatsa and Lari Williams; a major new study on Igbo history by C. Xrydz-Eyutchae; and a new book that is likely to be not only topical but also controversial, Okay Achike's *Groundwork of military law and rule in Nigeria*.

After the highly promising start of the Ethiope Publishing Corporation in Benin in the early seventies, little has been heard of this company recently. Operational difficulties and a large turnover of staff have meant that only a handful of titles have been published: among these were Fidelis Nwadialo's *The criminal procedure of the southern states of Nigeria*; a study guide and introduction to Ferdinand Oyono's novel *Une vie de boy* by K. Britwum; and a collection of essays by the distinguished South African writer in exile Lewis Nkosi, entitled *The transplanted heart*.

Several Nigerian publishers produced special books as a contribution to the Second World Black and African Festival of the Arts and Culture, held in Lagos and elsewhere in the country between 15 January and 12 February 1977. These included *Lagos: the development of an African city*, a collection of essays edited by A. B. Aderidigbe published by Longman Nigeria; *The living culture of Nigeria*, a lavishly illustrated volume on the arts in Nigeria edited by Saburi Biobaku and published by Thomas Nelson; and *Mbari: Art as sacrifice*, a book on Igbo religious mud sculpture by John Okparocha and produced by that lively Christian publisher, Daystar Press. Two new Daystar series launched recently were "Documents of Nigerian Church History" and "Nigerian Names"; and a highlight of 1975 was the publication of

ing Corporation, qui a déjà publié deux petits livres de poche; l'un est un roman satirique intitulé *Kolera koleji*, du jeune écrivain d'avenir Femi Osofisan, qui traite de l'épidémie de choléra dans le campus d'une université imaginaire au Nigéria; l'autre est une pièce de théâtre, *The curse*, écrite par un écrivain fécond, Kole Omotoso. Deto Deni Educational Productions est une nouvelle maison d'édition entreprenante d'Ibadan dont le premier livre a été écrit par Tola Adeniji, l'ancien ombudsman du *Daily Times* nigérian. *The lunatic, epitome of our golden age* est un recueil vivant d'essais et d'articles qui font l'objet d'une publicité agressive: ". . . corruption, détention, avarice, rapacité, pots-de-vin . . . vous trouverez tout cela dans *The lunatic* . . . qui coûte 1 N. seulement, soit moins que deux bouteilles de bière" déclare une affiche. Et il est certain qu'au rythme actuel d'accroissement de l'inflation au Nigéria, cela sera bientôt le prix d'une seule bouteille de bière!

A Lagos, West African Book Publishers Limited, filiale de l'un des éditeurs les plus importants du Nigéria, Academy Press Ltd., est un nouvel arrivant. Parmi les premiers titres, des livres sur la santé, la maternité et les soins aux enfants, ainsi que d'un *Guide to Lagos* extrêmement bien réalisé, écrit et compilé par E. Seriki et E. Pullybank. En 1978, cet éditeur projette de lancer une nouvelle collection pour enfants en yorouba et en anglais, les livres "Atoka". Une autre maison d'édition qui semble vouloir se spécialiser en ouvrages universitaires de géologie et dont le nom surprendra peut-être, Elizabethan Publishing Company, a produit un volume remarquable intitulé *The geology of Nigeria*, présenté par C. A. Kogbe, et également une brochure illustrée sur *Nigerian traditional and cultural hairstyles* de E. O. Osinsanya.

A Enugu, Nwamife Publishers est une maison d'édition appartenant à des autochtones qui a tenu le devant de la scène à ses débuts en 1971. Elle a connu une période de transition au cours de ces dernières années: au lieu de s'intéresser surtout comme au début aux ouvrages littéraires et politiques, pas très rémunérateurs, elle est passée à un programme plus étendu et plus équilibré composé d'études érudites, de manuels de droit, de livres sur le développement agricole et de manuels scolaires. Mais l'annonce soudaine par le gouvernement nigérian de l'abolition de l'enseignement des mathématiques modernes dans toutes les écoles primaires et post primaires a porté un coup dur à Nwamife qui s'est retrouvé avec un entrepôt rempli de livres appartenant à leur série "Modern mathematics for primary and secondary schools". C'est là bien sûr un coup désastreux, dont cette petite maison d'édition qui ne dispose que d'un capital insuffisant, a du mal à se remettre; et les pertes seront plus difficiles à récupérer que s'il s'agissait de l'une quelconque des grandes sociétés multinationales.

Ambassador of Christ and Caesar, by the Reverend William Fitzjohn, at one time Sierra Leone's Ambassador in Washington, which includes the story of the snubbing Rev. Fitzjohn received at a Howard Johnson restaurant in Hagerstown, Maryland. The episode ended with breakfast with President Kennedy, a civic reception by the Mayor of Hagerstown, and finally a confrontation with Howard Johnson himself on board the *Queen Mary*!

A publisher of a rather different nature is Di Nigro Press whose titles tend to be fairly racy and have included *Sex is a nigger, God is a racist* and *Fires of Africa*, all by self-styled revolutionary and pragmatic socialist Naiwu Osahon. Di Nigro's original handout claimed that it was established for "top-quality black authors disillusioned by their treatment at the hands of the dominant white publishing houses [who] are to be encouraged through commissions and sponsorships to write the absolute truth about the Blacks and to re-educate the world." However, judging from the company's record during the past few years, it would appear that it is only Mr. Oshahon who is a "top quality black author". The only other black author who has been published by Di Nigro thus far is Obi Egbuna, with a small booklet entitled *The ABC of black power thought*.

Pilgrim Books in Lagos, and its affiliated imprint African Universities Press who pioneered the popular children's series "African Readers Library", have launched a new drama series, the first title of which was *Kiriji* by Wale Ogunyemi, a historical drama on the Ekiti Parapo war in the nineteenth century. Another Lagos publisher, Islamic Publications Bureau, published in 1976 an important study by A. B. Balogun, *The life and works of Utham Dan Fodio*, which retells the story of this Muslim reformer and scholar of West Africa.

The bulk of scholarly publishing output continues to come from Ibadan University Press, and recently this has included two important collections of papers on industrial and economic development and regional planning both in Nigeria and in Africa as a whole, studies on Nigerian internal politics and foreign policy, Nigerian indigenous entrepreneurship, literary criticism, and bibliographies. Of particular note was *Issues in the development of tropical Africa*, by the current Vice-Chancellor of the University of Ife, Prof. O. Aboyade, which provides an analysis of the major development issues and of viable policy choices for African nations. In the field of bibliography Ibadan University Press published the valuable *Bibliography of literary contributions to Nigerian periodicals, 1946–1972*, compiled by Bernth Lindfors, which cites over 4,000 references, and *Nigerian publications 1950–1970*, compiled by O. G. Tamuno and G. A. Alabi, which presents a twenty-year cumulation of books deposited at the Ibadan University Library. An I.U.P. book that provoked much debate was Professor

L'un des fondateurs de Nwamife Publishers, Arthur Nwankso, a maintenant créé sa propre maison, Fourth Dimension Publishers, également à Enugu, et les premiers titres paraîtront en 1978. Cette première liste est impressionante: elle comprend deux contes pour enfants de Chinua Achebe, de premiers romans de Kalu Uka, Labo Yaro, Ogali A. Ogali, Ben Gbuile, de nouveaux poèmes de Mamman Vatsa et Lari Williams, une nouvelle étude importante sur l'histoire Igbo par C. Xrydz-Eyutchae, et un nouvel ouvrage qui sera non seulement d'actualité mais aussi très controversé, *Groundwork of military law and rule in Nigeria* de Okay Achike.

Apres les débuts hautement prometteurs de Ethiope Publishing Corporation, au Bénin au début des années 70, on a peu entendu parler de cette maison dernièrement. Les difficultés rencontrées et la rotation élevée de personnel ont fait qu'une poignée de titres seulement a été publiée parmi lesquels se trouvent *The criminal procedure of the southern states of Nigeria*, de Fidelis Nwadialo; un guide pour l'introduction à l'étude du roman de Ferdinand Oyono, *Une vie de boy*, préparé par K. Britwum; et *The transplanted heart*, recueil d'essais de l'éminent Lewis Nkosi, auteur sudafricain en exil.

Plusieurs éditeurs nigérians ont produit des livres spéciaux pour commémorer le second Festival mondial négro-africain des arts et de la culture qui s'est tenu à Lagos et dans d'autres parties du pays entre le 15 janvier et le 12 février 1977. Il s'agit notamment de *Lagos: the development of an African city*, recueil d'essais présentés par A. B. Aderidigbe et publié par Longman Nigeria; *The living culture of Nigeria*, volume somptueusement illustré sur les arts au Nigéria présenté par Saburi Biobaku et publié par Thomas Nelson, et *Mbari: Art as sacrifice*, livre sur la sculpture religieuse en terre cuite de John Okparocha et produit par le dynamique éditeur chrétien, Daystar Press. Deux nouvelles séries Daystar ont été lancées récemment: "Documents of Nigerian Church History" et "Nigerian Names"; et un des grands moments de l'année 1975, ce fut la publication de *Ambassador of Christ and Caesar*, par le révérend William Fitzjohn, jadis ambassadeur de Sierra Leone à Washington, qui conte l'histoire de l'affront qu'il reçut dans un restaurant Howard Johnson à Hagerstown, dans le Maryland. Cet épisode s'est terminé par un petit déjeuner avec le président Kennedy, une réception municipale donnée par le maire de Hagerstown, et finalement par une confrontation avec Howard Johnson en personne à bord du *Queen Mary*!

Les Presses Di Nigro sont un peu différentes et présentent des titres un peu corsés, notamment *Sex is a nigger, God is a racist* et *Fires of Africa*, sous la signature de Naiwu Osahon, révolutionnaire au style personnel et socialiste pragmatique. La brochure originale des

A. A. Ayandele's *The educated elite in the Nigerian society*, a series of lectures delivered as part of the University of Ibadan's twenty-fifth anniversary celebrations.

From the University of Ife Press has come a most attractive and liberally illustrated volume on *Nigerian handcrafted textiles* put together by Joanne Eicher; and an Ife title which appeared at an opportune time and which also enjoyed excellent reviews was Itse Sagay's *The legal aspects of the Namibian dispute*. Of particular interest to librarians is a comprehensive bibliography of *Nigerian government publications* which was published in 1976. Compiled by Janet Stanley, the bibliography covers official publications of the federal government, the former four regional governments and the twelve state governments, for the period 1966 to the end of 1973. The University of Ife Press was making publishing history in Africa by the release early in 1975 of the initial titles in their "Ife Music Editions", the first of its kind in Africa, and now numbering over ten titles, with the prominent Nigerian composer and musicologist Akin Euba serving as series editor.

The third active scholarly press is the Ahmadu Bello University Press in Zaria which, in conjunction with the Nigerian branch of Oxford University Press produced its first title, *A celebration of Black and African writing* edited by Kolawole Ogunbesan and Bruce King. Five new A.B.U. Press titles are scheduled to appear during the first half of 1978, and include books on law, history, and agriculture.

In **Ghana**, the Ghana Publishing Corporation has embarked upon an intensive production drive to provide new textbooks for Ghana's expanding educational programme. They now have over three hundred titles in print, including school and university level texts, scholarly monographs, creative writing by Ghanaian authors, as well as numerous children's books. One of the most attractive, a picture story book entitled *Tawia goes to sea* by Mesack Asare, has been translated and published in Japanese by Holp Shuppan. It is believed to be the first book from an African publisher to be translated into Japanese. Among many new G.P.C. children's titles were Nimoh Mercy's *The walking calabash*, D. K. Essandoh's *Happy birthday and other stories*, and *Rookie the unlucky hen* by Michael Asiedu. A reissue of an early African novel by R. E. Obeng, *Eighteenpence* — in fact the first novel in English written by a Ghanaian — was published in 1974, as was a new volume of verse by Atukwei Okai, *Lorgorligi logarithms* (Okai's earlier volume of poetry was published by Simon & Schuster in New York), and an anthology of *Ghanaian writing today* edited by B. S. Kwakwa. Additions to the academic list have included a study in medical sociology, *Medical systems in Ghana* by P. A. Thumasi; and *Girls'*

Presses Di Nigro affirme que la maison a été créée pour que "les auteurs noirs de haute qualité déçus par la manière dont ils ont été traités par les importantes maisons d'édition blanches soient encouragés au moyen de commandes et de parrainages à écrire la vérité absolue sur les Noirs pour rééduquer le monde". Jusqu'à présent les Presses Di Nigro n'ont publié qu'un seul autre écrivain noir: Obi Egbuna, auteur d'un petit livre intitulé *The ABC of black power thought*.

A Lagos, Pilgrim Books et sa filiale African Universities Press, pionnier des séries populaires pour enfants, "African Readers Library", viennent de lancer une nouvelle série d'œuvres théâtrales dont le premier volume *Kiriji*, de Wale Ogunyemi raconte un drame historique qui traite de la guerre Ekiti Parapo du dix-neuvième siècle. Un autre éditeur de Lagos, Islamic Publications Bureau, a publié en 1976 une étude considérable de A. B. Balogun, *The life and works of Utham Dan Fodio*, qui conte l'histoire de ce musulman réformateur et érudit d'Afrique occidentale.

La plupart des publications continuent à provenir d'Ibadan University Press, qui a récemment publié deux importants recueils d'articles sur le développement industriel et économique et sur la planification régionale à la fois au Nigéria et dans l'ensemble de l'Afrique, des études sur la politique intérieure et étrangère nigérianne, sur le dynamisme des entreprises autochtones, des ouvrages de critique littéraire et des bibliographies. Il faut noter en particulier l'ouvrage du vice-chancelier actuel de l'Université d'Ifé, Prof. O. Aboyade *Issues in the development of tropical Africa*, qui analyse les principales questions que pose le développement, et les choix politiques possibles offerts aux nations africaines. Dans le domaine de la bibliographie, I.U.P. a publié la remarquable *Bibliography of literary contributions to Nigerian periodicals, 1946–1972*, établie par Bernth Lindfors et qui répertorie plus de 4,000 références; et *Nigerian publications 1950–1970*, établie par O. G. Tamuno et G. A. Alabi, qui comprend tous les livres réunis depuis vingt ans à la bibliothèque de l'Université d'Ibadan. L'ouvrage très controversé du professeur A. A. Ayandele, *The educated elite in the Nigerian society*, publié aux Presses universitaires d'Ibadan, rassemble une série de conférences données à l'occasion de la commémoration du vingt-cinquième anniversaire de l'Université d'Ibadan.

On doit aux Presses universitaires d'Ifé un volume très agréable et abondamment illustré sur les *Textiles artisanaux nigérians* de Joanne Eicher. Un autre titre des Presses d'Ifé qui a paru au bon moment et a fait l'objet de commentaires très favorables est *The legal aspects of the Namibian dispute*, de Itse Sagay. La bibliographie complète des *Nigerian government publications* publiée en 1976 est d'un grand intérêt pour les bibliothé-caires. Etablie par Janet Stanley, cette bibliographie

nubility rites in Ashanti, which provides an insight into an important social institution of the Ashanti people, by the Reverend Peter Sarprong, the Catholic Bishop in Kumasi, who also produced *Ghana in retrospect*, an examination of the religious and social life of Ghanaians and aspects of their culture and traditions. *The history of education in Ghana* by Charles Kwesi Graham, published in 1976, traces the growth and development of a European-type of education in Ghana from the early days of her contact with Europeans in 1839 through to independence in 1957. GPC also publish in Twi and Ewe, but the widest range of books, both fiction and non-fiction and materials for adult literacy education, comes from the government-sponsored Ghana Bureau of Languages.

The Ghana Universities Press now publish about a dozen new books each year, including a series of in-augural lectures. Among notable scholarly titles which have appeared during the course of the past few years were *African entrepreneurship and economic growth* by Rowena Lawson and Eric Kwei, which focused on Ghana's fishing industry, how it responded to economic growth, modern methods of production and marketing, and the problems this indigenous industry encountered in its attempt to introduce rapid structural changes; S. K. B. Asante's *Property law and social goals 1855-1966* was concerned with the philosophical, social and economic implications of Ghanaian property concepts and institutions; another important GUP title was *Sickle stages: clinical features in West Africans*, by Roger A. Lewis, an account of the inherited abnormalities of haemoglobin structure common in West Africa.

Two of Ghana's commercial publishers, Anowuo Educational Publications owned by novelist Asare Konadu, and Moxon Paperbacks run by Anglo-Ghanaian honorary Chief James Moxon, have been dormant for several years now. This is regrettable, for both were innovative and promising publishing ventures. Moxon, for example, had earlier started a splendid series of African detective novels, had published *Who's who in Ghana* and a set of "Ghanaian cookery cards". He has abandoned book publishing for the present to concentrate on magazine publishing and, presumably, to devote himself to the culinary arts and the running of his excellent restaurant "The Black Pot"!

One new imprint, Sam Woode's Afram Publications, however, has been very active; the directors include Ghanaian musicologist Professor J. H. K. Nketia, and playwright and novelist Efua Sutherland. For the moment the list covers mainly O-level texts, and a magazine, *Students' World*, was launched in 1977. Afram has also taken on the distribution of an important study about the pioneers of Ghana's press, *History, politics and the early press in Ghana* by the late Professor K. A. B. Jones-Quartey. The volume is illustrated with

englobe toutes les publications officielles du gouvernement fédéral, des quatre anciens gouvernements régionaux et des gouvernements des douze états pour la période 1966-1973. Les Presses d'Ifé ont apporté leur contribution à l'histoire de l'édition en Afrique en publiant au début de 1975 les premiers titres de "Ife Music editions", première collection de cette nature en Afrique, qui réunit maintenant plus de dix titres publiés sous la direction de Akin Euba, compositeur et musicologue nigérian.

Une troisième maison d'édition de livres d'érudition, Ahmadu Bello University Press, de Zaria, a produit, en collaboration avec la filiale nigérianne de Oxford University Press, son premier ouvrage: *A celebration of Black and African writing*, annoté par Kolawole Ogunbesan et Bruce King. Au cours de la première moité de 1978, A.B.U. Press fera paraître cinq nouveaux ouvrages portant notamment sur le droit, l'histoire et l'agriculture.

A Ghana, Ghana Publishing Corporation s'est lancé dans une production intensive pour fournir les nouveaux manuels nécessaires au programme d'enseigement en plein essor de ce pays. Trois cents ouvrages sont actuellement parus, notamment des livres scolaires et universitaires, des monographies de haut niveau, des œuvres originales d'auteurs ghanéens ainsi que de nombreux livres pour enfants. L'un des plus remarquables de ceux-ci est un livre d'images intitulé *Tawia goes to sea*, de Mesack Asare, qui a été traduit en japonais et publié au Japon par Holp Shuppan. On pense que c'est le premier ouvrage publié en Afrique qui ait été traduit en japonais. Parmi les nombreux nouveaux titres pour enfants de G.P.C., il faut noter *The walking calabash*, de Nimoh Mercy, *Happy birthday and other stories*, de D. K. Essandoh, et *Rookie the unlucky hen*, de Michael Asiedu. La réimpression d'un ancien roman africain de R. E. Obeng, *Eighteenpence*, premier ouvrage en anglais écrit par un ghanéen, a paru en 1974 ainsi qu'un nouveau livre de poésie de Atukwei Okai *Lorgorligi lorgarithms* (le précédent volume de poèmes de Okai avait été publié par Simon & Schuster, à New York), et une anthologie, *Ghanaian writing today*, annotée par B. S. Kwakwa. Il faut ajouter à la liste d'ouvrages universitaires une étude de sociologie médicale, *Medical systems in Ghana*, de P. A. Thumasi; et *Girls' nubility rites in Ashanti*, étude en profondeur d'une institution sociale importante du peuple ashanti, réalisée par le réverend Peter Sarprong, évêque catholique de Kumasi, qui est également l'auteur de *Ghana in retrospect*, analyse de la vie religieuse et sociale des ghanéens et de certains aspects de leur culture et de leurs traditions. *The history of education in Ghana*, de Charles Kwesi Graham, parue en 1976, retrace l'essor et la mise au point d'un système éducatif de style européen

several facsimile reproductions and provides a valuable inventory of all newspapers ever published in Ghana.

Active Christian publishers in Ghana are the African Christian Press in Achimota and the Waterville Publishing House, a division of the Presbyterian Book Depot. In addition to Christian literature, Waterville also produce fiction, short story collections, and children's books both in English and in several of the Ghanaian languages. They have released Twi translations of Sophocles' *Antigone* and Plato's *Apology*, and the third volume of Dr. J. B. Danquah's diaries and letters, *Journey to independence and after* by H. K. Akyeampong. An important biography of Danquah — who died in prison in February 1965, a year before the fall of Nkrumah, and who is generally regarded as the doyen of Ghanaian politicians — was *The life and times of J. B. Danquah* by Professor Ofosu-Appiah, also published by Waterville. Professor Ofosu-Appiah is also the director of the "Encyclopaedia Africana" project which has its headquarters in Accra. Publication of the first titles was repeatedly postponed, but the initial volume of the *Dictionary of African biography* finally appeared in 1977. It did not, however, come from an African press, but from an American company, Reference Publications, Inc. of New York, although there are plans to sell to publishers in Africa rights to produce subsidized and inexpensive editions for the African markets. A total of 146 Ethiopian and 138 Ghanaian biographies, living persons not included, by more than seventy contributors comprise the first volume of the planned twenty-volume work.

Very little can be reported about **Liberia, Sierra Leone** and the **Gambia**. A recent development in Liberia was the establishment of an organization called Liberian Literary and Educational Publications, who announced that they intended to issue works of Liberian creative writing, including reprints of early novels, but these plans do not in fact appear to have materialized to date. Publishing activities at the Sierra Leone University Press are virtually at a standstill, due to a severely restricted flow of money coming into the university and hence to the press. There is no shortage of good manuscripts, only funds, and one book in the pipeline is Arthur Abraham's *Mende government and politics* which will probably be published jointly with O.U.P. Long awaited, but also experiencing delay due to insufficient finance, is a Krio dictionary compiled and edited by Clifford Fyle and Eldred Jones. Other plans include a Krio series consisting of a handbook, a popular dictionary, and actual texts. A new imprint sponsored by the Institute of African Studies at Fourah Bay College is Leone Publishers, and its first title was *Topics in Sierra Leone history* by Arthur Abraham. The Fourah Bay College Bookshop has a small programme of occasional publications, and has also issued a new revised edition of its

au Ghana depuis les premiers jours des relations avec les Européens en 1839 jusqu'à l'indépendance en 1957. G.P.C. a également publié en twi et ewe, mais la gamme la plus étendue de livres, à la fois de fiction et d'autres genres, ainsi que le matériel pour l'alphabétisation des adultes, provient du Bureau of Language du Ghana pris en charge par le gouvernement.

La Ghana Universities Press publie maintenant une douzaine de nouveaux ouvrages chaque année y compris une série de conférences inaugurales. Parmi les titres savants importants de ces dernières années, *African entrepreneurship and economic growth* de Rowena Lawson et Eric Kwei, traite notamment de l'industrie de la pêche du Ghana, à la manière dont elle a réagi à la croissance économique, aux méthodes modernes de production et de commercialisation, et des problèmes rencontrés par cette industrie locale lorsqu'elle a tenté d'introduire des changements structurels rapides; *Property Law and social goals 1855–1966* de S. K. B. Asante se penche sur les conséquences philosophiques, sociales et économiques découlant des concepts et des institutions de la propriété au Ghana; un autre titre important *Sickle stages: clinical features in West Africans* de Roger A. Lewis décrit les anomalies héréditaires de la structure de l'hémoglobine qui se rencontrent souvent en Afrique de l'Ouest.

Depuis plusieurs années, deux éditeurs commerciaux ghanéens ont interrompu leurs activités: Anuwuo Educational Publications, appartenant au romancier Asare Konadu, et Moxon Paperbacks, dirigé par le Chef honoraire anglo-ghanéen James Moxon. C'est très regrettable car il s'agissait de deux affaires innovatrices et qui s'annonçaient bien. Moxon, par exemple, avait entamé une série splendide de romans policiers africains et publié un *Who's who in Ghana* ainsi qu'une série de "Ghanaian cookery cards". Il a abandonné pour l'instant la publication de livres pour s'occuper de la publication de revues, et sans doute aussi pour se consacrer à l'art culinaire et à la direction de son excellent restaurant "The Black Pot"!

Sam Woode's Afram Publications est une nouvelle maison très active: parmi les administrateurs se trouvent le professeur J. H. K. Nketia musicologue ghanéen et le romancier et auteur dramatique Efua Sutherland. Pour l'instant, le catalogue comprend surtout des textes pour les O-level (équivalent britannique du baccalauréat) et un magazine, *Student's World*, lancé en 1977. Afram a également entrepris la diffusion d'une importante étude sur les pionniers de la presse du Ghana, *History, politics and the early press in Ghana*, du professeur décédé K. A. B. Jones-Quartey. Ce volume est illustré de plusieurs reproductions en fac-simile et fournit un inventaire précieux de tous les journaux jamais publiés au Ghana.

Parmi les éditeurs chrétiens actifs du Ghana, on compte African Christian Press à Achimota et the

popular illustrated *Birds of the Freetown area* by Geoffrey Field.

Francophone West Africa

Publishing activities in French-speaking West Africa are concentrated in two countries, **Cameroun** and **Senegal**. Editions C.L.E. in Yaoundé is the first full-scale publishing house in francophone Africa. Its name is somewhat misleading — Centre de Littérature Evangélique — since it publishes a great deal more than Christian literature, and the lead title in 1976 was undoubtedly the new novel by Francis Bebey, *Le roi Albert d'Effidi.* Several other C.L.E. writers have now gained reputations throughout francophone Africa and beyond; they include the Congolese writer Guy Menga whose popular *La palabre stérile* is being reprinted repeatedly, and Guillaume Oyono-Mbia whose new play *Le train spécial de Son Excellence* came out in 1975. A successful and pioneering CLE venture is their low-priced series entitled "Pour Tous", brief novelettes based either on the oral tradition or on contemporary African life, that aim to reach a wide audience and promote leisure reading among the general public. A new series, "Grandes Figures Africaines", consisting of short biographical volumes of outstanding leaders from Africa's past is being co-published with Les Nouvelles Editions Africaines in Dakar.

Another successful C.L.E. author, René Philombe, has revived his own press, Editions Semences Africaines, and expects to publish several works, both his own and by other authors. One is a volume of epic poetry by Théophile Bikoula Abessola, which has the emancipation of African women as its theme.

The most significant publishing development in francophone Africa, however, was the founding in Dakar in 1972 of Les Nouvelles Editions Africaines. It is a joint undertaking by the governments of Senegal and the Ivory Coast and French publishing interests, including Fernand Nathan, Editions du Seuil, Présence Africaine, Armand Colin and Librairie Hachette. The aims of N.E.A. are to foster African authorship, to publish books in the indigenous languages for literacy development and adult education, and to produce school-books adapted to African, rather than European realities and experience. The company has progressed rapidly to a position where it is now one of the leading publishers of school-books for the whole of French-speaking Africa. Many familiar and distinguished names from the literary as well as the academic world now appear on the N.E.A. list of almost 200 titles: Bernard Dadié, Birago Diop, Cheikh Anta Diop, Ibrahim Sall, Amadou Hampate Ba, Edouard Maunick, Mamadou N'Diaye, and, not surprisingly, Senegalese President Léopold Senghor. In 1974, N.E.A. published Senghor's first ever complete collection of poetry, previously dispersed in several

Waterville Publishing House, section du Presbyterian Book Depot. Waterville produit, outre des ouvrages chrétiens, des romans, des recueils de nouvelles, et des livres pour enfants en anglais et dans les diverses langues ghanéennes. Cette maison a publié deux traductions en twi de l'*Antigone* de Sophocle et l'*Apologie* de Platon, ainsi que le troisième volume du journal et des lettres de J. B. Danquah, *Journey to independence and after*, de H. K. Akyeampong. Waterville a également publié une importante biographie de Danquah, mort en prison en février 1965, (soit un an avant la chute de Nkrumah, et considéré généralement comme le doyen des hommes politiques ghanéens), intitulée *The life and times of J. B. Danquah*, par le professeur Ofosu-Appiah, qui est aussi le directeur du projet "Encyclopaedia Africana" dont le siège est à Accra. La publication des premiers titres a été différée plusieurs fois, mais le volume initial du *Dictionary of African biography* a finalement paru en 1977, non pas chez un éditeur africain mais aux Etats-Unis chez Reference Publications, Inc., New York. Toutefois, on prévoit de vendre à des éditeurs africains les droits pour la production d'éditions subventionnées et bon marché destinées aux marchés africains. Ce premier volume d'une série de vingt qui reunit les biographies de 146 Ethiopiens et de 138 Ghanéens, à l'exclusion de toute personne vivante, est l'œuvre de 70 collaborateurs.

On possède peu de données sur le **Libéria**, la **Sierra Leone** et la **Gambie**. Une organisation s'est créée dernièrement au Libéria sous le titre Liberian Literary and Educational Publications. Elle a annoncé la parution d'ouvrages littéraires d'auteurs libériens, ainsi que la réimpression de romans, mais ces projets sont restés lettre morte pour l'instant. Les activités des Presses universitaires de la Sierra Leone sont virtuellement arrêtées en raison d'une restriction sévère du budget alloué à l'université, et partant aux Presses. Ce sont les fonds qui manquent et non les bons manuscrits. En préparation, un ouvrage d'Arthur Abraham intitulé *Mende government and politics*, qui sera probablement publié en collaboration avec l'O.U.P. Attendue depuis longtemps, mais toujours différée en raison du manque de fonds, la publication d'un dictionnaire krio établi et annoté par Clifford Fyle et Eldred Jones. Les autres projets comprennent une collection en krio composée d'un manuel, d'un dictionnaire populaire et de textes. Leone Publishers est une nouvelle maison d'édition prise en charge par l'institut d'études africaines du Collège Fourah Bay, dont le premier ouvrage est *Topics in Sierra Leone history* d'Arthur Abraham. La librairie du Collège Fourah Bay a un programme restreint de publications occasionnelles et a également fait paraître une nouvelle édition revue et corrigée de l'ouvrage populaire illustré *Birds of the Freetown area*, de Geoffrey Field.

earlier volumes. President Senghor has also written *La parole chez Paul Claudel et chez les Négro-Africains*. Among many other notable scholarly works were *La désertification au sud du Sahara*, the proceedings of the 1973 Nouakchott conference on drought; Mamadou Dia's *Islam, sociétés africaines et culture industrielle*; Yves Person's *Samori, fondateur de l'empire mandique*; and what is probably the first book on atomic theory to be published in Black Africa, *Physique nucléaire et chronologie absolue* by Cheikh Anta Diop. N.E.A. has also set itself the goal of cultural and tourist promotion and this is reflected in the publication of guide books such as the richly illustrated catalogue to the Dakar Museum of traditional African art, *Musée de Dakar, témoin de l'art nègre* by Michel Renaudeau (co-published with Editions Delroisse in Paris); and Richard Bonneau's *Ecrivains, cinéastes et artistes ivoiriens* which provides a valuable bibliographic inventory of the literature on the arts in the Ivory Coast. It is difficult to single out any particular title in the area of literature, but some books that have attracted especially critical attention were Lamine Diakhate's new novel *Prisonnier du regard*; a lyrical collection by the poetess Kine Kirama entitled *Chants de la rivière fraîche*; an epic novel by Mamadou Seyni Mbengue — at present Senegalese Ambassador to the Soviet Union — *Le royaume de sable* — which recounts a popular uprising in Senegal before World War I. Philippe Touzard, commercial director at N.E.A., provided fuller details on his company's operations, as well as on other publishing activities in Senegal, in the October 1975 issue of *African Book Publishing Record*.[12]

Les Nouvelles Editions Africaines maintains a subsidiary in Abidjan, which perhaps is a reason for the paucity of other commercial publishing activity in the **Ivory Coast**. Although the country has been represented for the past few years with a combined book exhibit at the Frankfurt Book Fair, it is difficult to obtain information from the sponsoring organization, the Centre d'Edition et de Diffusion Africaines. The same can be said about Editions Populaires du **Mali**, who have a list of some forty titles in print largely devoted to history and Mali oral tradition, and who were represented at the Frankfurt Book Fair for the first time in 1975. It is somewhat paradoxical that while some francophone African publishers go to the considerable expense of exhibiting at Frankfurt, they subsequently ignore all requests for information on their books.

Elsewhere in French-speaking West Africa (in **Gabon**, **Guinea**, **Niger**, **Upper Volta**, **Benin**, and in **Chad**) evidence of indigenous publishing, other than occasional books from research institutes and government publications, is virtually non-existent for the time being. So far,

Afrique occidentale francophone

Les activités du monde de l'édition de l'Afrique francophone se limitent à deux pays: Le **Cameroun** et le **Sénégal**. Les Editions C.L.E. à Yaoundé constituent la maison d'édition la plus importante de l'Afrique francophone. Son nom est un peu trompeur: Centre de Littérature Evangélique, car il publie bien d'autres choses que des œuvres chrétiennes et en 1976 le titre le plus important a sans aucun doute été le roman de Francis Bebey: *Le roi Albert d'Effidi*. Plusieurs autres écrivains du C.L.E. sont maintenant célèbres dans toute l'Afrique francophone et au-delà. Il s'agit notamment de l'écrivain congolais Guy Menga, dont le fameux ouvrage *La palabre stérile* est réimprimée régulièrement, et de Guillaume Oyono-Mbia auteur de la nouvelle pièce *Le train spécial de Son Excellence*, parue en 1975. La collection bon marché intitulée "Pour tous" est une opération pilote réussie offrant de courtes nouvelles fondées sur la tradition orale ou sur la vie africaine contemporaine, et dont l'objectif est de toucher un grand auditoire et de promouvoir le plaisir de lire dans le grand public. Publiée en collaboration avec les Nouvelles Editions Africaines de Dakar, une nouvelle série "Grandes figures africaines" offre des opuscules biographiques sur des dirigeants éminents du passé africain.

René Philombe, autre auteur célèbre du C.L.E., a ressuscité sa propre maison d'édition, Editions Semences Africaines, et espère publier plusieurs ouvrages écrits par lui et par d'autres écrivains. L'un de ces ouvrages est un volume de poésie épique de Théophile Bikoula Abessola, qui a pour thème l'émancipation des femmes africaines.

L'événement le plus important du monde de l'édition d'Afrique francophone a été la fondation en 1972 à Dakar des Nouvelles Editions Africaines. Il s'agit d'une entreprise réalisée grâce à la collaboration des gouvernements du Sénégal et de la Côte d'Ivoire, de maisons d'édition françaises, comme Fernand Nathan, les Editions du Seuil, Présence Africaine, Armand Colin et la Librairie Hachette. Les objectifs des N.E.A. sont de promouvoir les auteurs africains pour qu'ils publient des livres dans les langues autochtones, de manière à favoriser le développement de l'alphabétisation et de l'éducation des adultes, et à produire des livres scolaires adaptés à la réalité et au vécu africain. La société a rapidement progressé pour devenir l'une des éditeurs de livres scolaires les plus importants de toute l'Afrique francophone. Dans la liste des 200 titres parus aux N.E.A., figurent nombre de noms familiers et éminents du monde littéraire et universitaire: Bernard Dadié, Birago Diop, Cheikh Anta Diop, Ibrahim Sall, Amadou Hampate Ba, Edouard Maunick, Mamadou N'Diaye et, bien entendu, celui du président sénégalais Léopold Senghor. En 1974, a paru aux N.E.A. pour la première fois en un recueil unique les œuvres poétiques complètes

publishing in francophone Africa has flourished mainly with the help of government or church support, and its book industries are beset by many obstacles and still lag far behind their anglophone counterparts. However, the impressive beginnings of Les Nouvelles Editions Africaines in Dakar can perhaps be viewed as an indication of the emergence soon of a lively book industry in other parts of French-speaking Africa.

Eastern Africa

Addis Ababa University Press (formerly Haile Selassie I University Press) in **Ethiopia** has been struggling with limited budgets and has published only a handful of books over the past few years. These have included one published jointly with Heinemann, *The survival of Ethiopian independence* by Sven Rubenson, an introduction to environmental health practice; *Water supply — Ethiopia* by Gabre-Emanuel Teka; and Sue Edward's *Some wild flowering plants of Ethiopia*, a colour-keyed booklet for botanists, teachers and tourists. When the situation looks more optimistic in terms of funds the Press hopes to publish a series of biographies in Amharic as well as early Amharic writing; and another book currently in preparation is Wolde Aregay's *Southern Ethiopia and the Christian Kingdom, 1508-1708.*

There has been a very noticeable increase in local publishing activities in **Kenya**, not least in the area of popular mass paperbacks. These books are similar to the Nigerian Onitsha market literature, but are rather more sophisticated, more elitist, and better produced. There are now about half a dozen popular series available which include "Comb books" (Comb Book Publishers), "Spear Books" (Heinemann East Africa), "Afromances" (Transafrica) and the "Longman Crime Series" and "African Leisure Library" (Longman Kenya). They have familiar popular topics such as love and romance, sex, crime, or espionage, and are generally aimed at the African middle-class reader who may be looking for alternative forms of entertainment to nightclubs, cinemas or TV. One book in the new "Longman Crime Series" which attained something of a bestseller status — and it is said it is to be translated into several languages — was Hilary Ng'weno's *The men from Pretoria* which follows the exploits of a tough Nairobi crime reporter "Scoop" Nelson Nacta and his confrontation with the feared South African Bureau of State Security. Perhaps the most successful new popular fiction, however, comes from David Maillu's "Comb Books", with titles such as *My dear bottle, The flesh: diary of a prostitute, The kommon man, Dear Monica,* etc. Some books have come under fire because of their cheap morality — several of them have already been banned in Tanzania — but surely the increasing number of such popular paper-

de Léopold Sédar Senghor, jusqu'alors dispersées dans plusieurs volumes. Le président Senghor a également écrit *La parole chez Paul Claudel et les Négro-africains.* On peut également trouver parmi de nombreux autres ouvrages d'érudition *La désertification au sud du Sahara*, travaux de la conférence de Nouakchott de 1973 sur la sécheresse; *Islam, sociétés africaines et culture industrielle* de Mamadou Dia, *Samori, fondateur de l'empire mandique* de Yves Person, et *Physique nucléaire et chronologie absolue* de Cheikh Anta Diop, probablement le premier ouvrage sur la théorie atomique publiée en Afrique noire. Les N.E.A. se sont également fixé pour objectif de promouvoir la culture et le tourisme, comme le montre la publication de guides tels le catalogue richement illustré sur l'art africain traditionnel intitulé *Musée de Dakar, témoin de l'art nègre*, de Michel Renaudeau (publié en collaboration avec les Editions Delroisse de Paris); et enfin *Ecrivains, cinéastes et artistes ivoiriens*, de Richard Bonneau, qui fait l'inventaire bibliographique des œuvres portant sur les arts en Côte d'Ivoire. Dans le domaine littéraire, il est difficile d'isoler un titre en particulier, mais certains livres ont retenu l'attention des critiques, par exemple, le nouveau roman de Lamine Diakhate *Prisonnier du regard*; un recueil lyrique de la poétesse Kine Kirama intitulé *Chants de la rivière fraîche*; un roman épique de Mamadou Seyni Mbengue, actuellement ambassadeur du Sénégal en Union soviétique: *Le royaume de sable* qui conte le soulèvement populaire du Sénégal avant la Première Guerre Mondiale. Philippe Touzard, directeur commercial de N.E.A. a donné une vue d'ensemble détaillée et complète des opérations de sa société ainsi que sur les autres activités du monde de l'édition au Sénégal dans le numéro d'octobre 1975 de *African Book Publishing Record.*[12]

Les Nouvelles Editions Africaines ont une filiale à Abidjan, ce qui explique sans doute pourquoi il y a si peu d'autres activités dans l'édition en **Côte d'Ivoire**. Bien que ce pays ait exposé avec d'autres à la Foire du livre de Francfort ces dernières années, il est difficile d'obtenir des renseignements sur l'organisation responsable, le Centre d'Edition et de Diffusion Africaines. On peut dire la même chose des Editions Populaires du **Mali** qui ont une liste de quelque quarante titres parus, consacrés pour la plupart à l'histoire et à la tradition orale du Mali, et qui étaient présentes à la Foire du livre de Francfort pour la première fois en 1975. Il est paradoxal de noter que bien que les éditeurs africains francophones prennent la peine d'exposer à Francfort, ils omettent de répondre aux demandes de renseignements concernant leurs livres.

Partout ailleurs en Afrique occidentale francophone, que ce soit au **Gabon**, en **Guinée**, au **Niger** en **Haute**

back series must be a welcome development. As Heinemann's Henry Chakava has aptly commented in an article in *ABPR* "whatever their weaknesses may be, these novels are clearly helping in the cultivation of the reading habit amongst Kenyans, and, in any case, it is better to read local trash than imported trash."[13]

David Maillu has also come up with a novel idea: the insertion of a detailed and wide-ranging questionnaire into all his books asking readers whether or not they enjoyed the book, whether it was "stupid" or "extraordinarily interesting" (two of the nine choices). Readers are also invited to offer candid comment on, and criticism of, the book's weaknesses, whether it was easy to comprehend, to what sort of person it could be recommended, etc. The responses, together with details about the reader's age, marital status, number of children, sex, educational or professional background, hobbies, and more, surely could form the basis of a most interesting analysis of readership attitudes in one part of Africa.

Among the crop of newly established indigenous Kenyan publishers is Transafrica Publishers Limited, founded in 1974 by John Nottingham, former director of the East African Publishing House. In addition to its "Afromances" popular series, it has launched a most attractively produced series of children's books called "Bush Babes": the first title was Sally Syokabi's *The chameleon who couldn't stop changing his mind*. Transafrica has also published new fiction by Rebeka Njau and Grace Ogot, and a particularly important new book, *Letters from Salisbury Prison* by one of the Zimbabwe nationalist leaders, Ndabaningi Sithole. In a co-published venture with the popular Kenyan monthly magazine *Joe*, Transafrica recently issued a highly amusing paperback, *Field Marshal Abdulla Salim Fisi (or how the hyena got his!)* by Alimidi Osinya, a pseudonym for a Ugandan now living in Nairobi. It is a traditional African satire on a modern political situation; the drift towards an apolitical military dictatorship and its horrific consequences. It includes some delightful illustrations by Terry Hirst, managing editor of *Joe*, who has several more titles lined up for publication but faces the usual struggle of financing them. Says Terry Hirst: "the Kenya economy is too buoyant with regard to property and coffee for much money to be attracted to speculative publishing unconnected with mammoth school-book orders. So the market for general readership is held back enormously."[14] Nevertheless, the first edition of 5,000 copies sold out a few months after publication in March 1977.

Another new company, also established in 1974, is Foundation Books, run by Fred Okwanya, the current President of the Kenyan Publishers' Association. Its main objective is to promote Kiswahili, the medium of mass communication throughout East Africa, and now rapidly gaining ground in other parts of Africa as well.

Volta, au **Bénin** et au **Tchad**, il n'y a pratiquement pas pour le moment d'ouvrages autochtones, hormis quelques livres émanant d'instituts de recherche et des publications gouvernementales. Jusqu'à présent, l'édition en Afrique francophone n'a pu se développer que grâce à l'aide du gouvernement ou de l'église, et les industries du livre doivent faire face à de nombreux obstacles qui les empêchent d'atteindre le rayonnement de leurs équivalents d'Afrique anglophone. Toutefois, les débuts impressionants des Nouvelles Editions Africaines de Dakar peuvent être considérés comme le signe qu'une industrie du livre vigoureuse naîtra bientôt dans d'autres parties de l'Afrique francophone.

Afrique orientale

En **Ethiopie**, Addis Ababa University Press (ancienne Hailé Sélassié I University Press) ne dispose que d'un budget réduit et a seulement publié une poignée de livres au cours de ces dernières années. Il s'agit de *The survival of Ethiopian independence* de Sven Rubenson, publié en collaboration avec Heinemann, d'une introduction à la pratique de l'hygiène de l'environnement, *Water supply — Ethiopia*, de Gabre-Emanuel Teka; et de *Some wild flowering plants of Ethiopia* de Sue Edward, livre en couleurs destiné aux botanistes, aux enseignants et aux touristes. Quand sa situation financière s'améliorera, l'éditeur espère publier une série de biographies en amharique ainsi que des œuvres en amharique, et un autre livre actuellement en préparation *Southern Ethiopia and the Christian Kingdom, 1508-1708*, de Wolde Aregay.

Au **Kenya**, on a noté une augmentation notable des publications locales, notamment dans le domaine des livres de poche. Semblables aux ouvrages du marché nigérian, ces livres sont plus complexes, plus élitistes et mieux produits. Il existe maintenant environ une demi-douzaine de collections populaires, notamment "Comb Books" (Comb Book Publishers), "Spear Books" (Heinemann East Africa), "Afromances" (Transafrica) et la série "Longman Crime Series" et "African Leisure Library" (Longman Kenya). Ces collections traitent de thèmes populaires et familiers comme l'amour, les aventures romanesques, l'érotisme, le crime ou l'espionnage et sont susceptibles d'intéresser en général le lecteur africain à la recherche d'autres formes de distraction que les boîtes de nuits, le cinéma ou la télévision. L'un des titres de la série "Longman Crime series" est devenu un best-seller (on dit qu'il sera même traduit en plusieurs langues): il s'agit de *The men from Pretoria*, de Hilary Ng'weno, qui retrace les exploits énergiques d'un reporter d'affaires criminelles, "Scoop" Nelson Nacta, aux prises avec le terrible Bureau sud-africain de la sécurité d'Etat. Toutefois, les œuvres les plus populaires en ce moment appartiennent probablement à la série "Comb Series" de David Maillu, par

Among initial titles released were novels in Kiswahili, two booklets of proverbs, plus several popular readers and children's books. Foundation's other main area of activity is devoted to a programme of books on adult education, again in Kiswahili, particularly in the field of agriculture, health, and family life. Recently published was a bio-bibliography of President Nyerere, *Mwalimu Julius Kambarage Nyerere* by H. A. K. Mwenegoha, produced in conjunction with the Tanzania Library Service.

The activities of the above-mentioned enterprises notwithstanding, the bulk of the indigenous publishing output in Kenya has come from two major concerns: the East African Publishing House and the East African Literature Bureau, the latter being the publishing arm of the now disintegrated East African Community. Operations of the Literature Bureau came to a standstill when the Community finally collapsed early in 1977. The Bureau is at present in a transitional period and it is not clear what will happen in the future. Non-Kenyan staff have moved to the Community's former headquarters in Arusha and the Tanzanian section of the Bureau plans to continue operations there, and also to become instrumental in the setting-up of a university press at the University of Dar es Salaam, whereas the Kenyan branch has been taken over by the Ministry of Education. A substantial number of books are in various stages of production and others have been printed but not released by the printers due to the outstanding debts of the Community. Until the complex problem of sharing the assets and liabilities of the Community has been resolved between the governments of the former partner states, one can only sympathize with the many authors who now find themselves casualties of a political tug of war and their books held up midway through production.

Prior to the current difficulties, the East African Literature Bureau produced about fifty new titles annually, and also published no less than twenty journals. A sizeable proportion of the books covered adult education and literacy materials and books in Kiswahili and other East African languages. However, the Bureau also produced an increasing amount of scholarly books and creative writing in English by new East African authors. The E.A.L.B. academic list is wide and covers books in the social sciences, economics, humanities, law, agriculture and medicine. Among more recently published titles are J. H. Binhammer's *The development of a financial infrastructure in Tanzania*, a study in the development of the monetary economics of Tanzania and an analysis of the country's banking system; an evaluation of U.N.D.P. special fund projects in two East African countries, *Multilateral aid for national development and self-reliance* by Susan Gitelson; a case study on the contribution of religion to the political debate in Uganda during 1952–1962, *Issues*

exemple *My dear bottle, The flesh: diary of a prostitute, The kommon man, Dear Monica*, etc. Certains livres ont été attaqués en raison de leur faible moralité, plusieurs ont déjà été interdits en Tanzanie, mais il est certain que l'accroissement des titres de collections populaires de cet ordre est un développement heureux. Comme Henry Chakava, de Heinemann, l'a fait remarquer dans un article publié dans l'ABPR, "quelles que soient leurs faiblesses, ces romans aident à cultiver l'habitude de la lecture chez les Kényans, et dans nombre de cas, il vaut mieux lire une littérature de pacotille locale que de la camelote importée."[13]

David Maillu vient d'avoir également une nouvelle idée: l'insertion d'un questionnaire détaillé et étendu dans tous ses livres, demandant aux lecteurs s'ils ont aimé le livre ou non, s'il était à leur avis "stupide" ou "extraordinairement intéressant" (deux de neuf choix possibles). Les lecteurs sont également invités à fournir leurs opinions sincères et leurs critiques sur les faiblesses du livre, à dire s'il était facile à comprendre, à qui on pourrait le recommander, etc. Les réponses ainsi que les détails concernant l'âge des lecteurs, leur état-civil, le nombre d'enfants, leur sexe, leurs études ou leur profession, leurs passe-temps et autres détails, pourraient certainement constituer une base de départ pour une analyse passionnante des attitudes des lecteurs dans cette partie de l'Afrique.

Parmi la floraison de nouveaux éditeurs autochtones kényans, on compte Transafrica Publishers Limited, fondé en 1974 par John Nottingham, ancien directeur de East African Publishing House. En plus de sa collection populaire "Afromances", il a lancé une série très bien présentée de livres pour enfants intitulée "Bush Babes" avec comme premier titre *The chameleon who couldn't stop changing his mind* de Sally Syokabi. Transafrica a également publié de nouveaux romans de Rebeka Njau et de Grace Ogot, ainsi qu'un livre important, *Letters from Salisbury Prison* de Ndabaningi Sithole, leader nationaliste zimbabwen. Dans une opération conjointe avec le magazine *Joe*, mensuel populaire africain, Transafrica a récemment publié un livre de poche très amusant, *Field Marshal Abdulla Salim Fisi (or how the hyena got his!)* d'Alimidi Osinya, pseudonyme d'un Ougandais vivant actuellement à Nairobi. Il s'agit d'une satire africaine traditionnelle sur une situation politique moderne: le glissement vers une dictature militaire apolitique et ses horribles conséquences. On y trouve de délicieuses illustrations de Terry Hirst, rédacteur en chef de *Joe*, qui a en préparation plusieurs autres ouvrages à publier mais qui se trouve aux prises avec les habituelles difficultés. De l'avis de Terry Hirst: "l'economie kényanne est trop active dans le domaine de l'immobilier et du café pour que les capitaux s'intéressent à l'édition hasardeuse d'œuvres n'ayant aucun rapport avec les énormes commandes de livres scolaires. Alors le

in pre-independence politics in Uganda by A. G. G. Gingyera-Pinycwa; a collection of papers devoted to the theme of social change in East Africa, *Hadith 6: history and social change in East Africa*, edited by Bethwell Ogot; and two profusely illustrated volumes about the fifteenth-century Kenyan coastal town of Lamu by Usman Ghaidan, *Lamu: A study in conservation* and *Lamu: A study of the Swahili town*. Additions to the increasingly impressive law list included a major contribution on the legal system in East Africa, *Introduction to the legal system in East Africa* by William Burnett Harvey; a massive 1,200-page *The law of business organizations in East and Central Africa* by J. W. Katende and others; and the papers of a workshop on the teaching of population dynamics in African law schools, *Law and population change in Africa* edited by U. U. Uche. Among new medical titles were J. O. Kokwaro's *Medicinal plants in East Africa*; and the proceedings of the twentieth annual scientific conference of the East African Medical Research Council which was devoted to the topic "The use and abuse of drugs and chemicals in tropical Africa". New creative writing has included a lively collection of stories, poems and thoughts by the controversial East African writer Taban lo Liyong, *Ballads of underdevelopment*; two radio plays by Peter Nazareth; new fiction by Bediako Asare, Godfrey Kalimugogo, Billy Ogana, and Chris Wanjala; as well as verse collections by Micere Githae Mugo, Joy Higiro and Mauri Yambo. Finally, an attractive colouring book for children was Ray Prather's *A is for Africa*, which has forty full-page drawings depicting the various peoples of Africa, accompanied by small maps showing their geographical location.

The East African Publishing House now has well over 500 titles in print, and a major publishing event for them was the publication of Ayi Kwei Armah's new novel *Two thousand seasons* — significant not least for the fact that this is the first novel by this distinguished African writer (a Ghanaian, now living in Tanzania) actually published in Africa. His previous three works were published, to much acclaim, in the U.S.A. by Doubleday and Houghton Mifflin and in the UK by Heinemann. E.A.P.H. will also shortly publish his next book, a historical novel entitled *The healers*. Early in 1973, E.A.P.H. published the second novel by Charles Mangua, who is probably Kenya's most popular prose writer, *A tail in the mouth*, subsequently awarded the Kenyatta Prize for Literature. His previous *Son of woman* was already a best-seller and according to E.A.P.H. his second novel is now proving to be the fastest selling work of fiction ever to bear its imprint. Other new fiction came from Kenneth Watene, David Sebukima, Jacqueline Pierce (an Afro-American living in Tanzania); and additions to the "African Theatre" series included new plays by Uganda's Robert Serumaga,

développement du marché des ouvrages destinés au lecteur ordinaire est considérablement freiné."[14] Néanmoins, une première édition de 5 000 exemplaires a été épuisée quelques mois après sa publication en mars 1977.

Foundation Books, fondé en 1974, est dirigé par Fred Okwanya, président actuel de l'Association des éditeurs kényans. Son principal objectif est de promouvoir le kiswahili, moyen de communication de masse de toute l'Afrique orientale, qui gagne également du terrain en ce moment dans d'autres parties de l'Afrique. Parmi les premiers titres publiés, on trouve des romans en kiswahili, deux opuscules de proverbes, et plusieurs livres de lectures populaires et livres pour enfants. Foundation Books se consacre aussi principalement à un programme de livres, toujours en kiswahili, sur l'enseignement pour adultes, notamment dans le domaine de l'agriculture, de la santé et de la vie de famille. Cet éditeur vient de publier une bio-bibliographie du président Nyerere, *Mwalimu Julius Kambarage Nyerere* de H. K. A. Mwenegoha, produite en collaboration avec Tanzania Library Service.

A l'exception des entreprises mentionnées ci-dessus, la majorité de la production des éditeurs autochtones kényans est le fait de deux groupes principaux: East African Publishing House et East African Literature Bureau, ce dernier étant l'éditeur de la Communauté de l'Afrique Orientale, organisation maintenant dissoute. Les opérations du Literature Bureau se sont arrêtées lorsque la Communauté a finalement disparu au début de 1977. Le Bureau est actuellement en pleine transition et on ne voit pas très bien dans quelle direction il va s'orienter. Le personnel non-kényan a été déplacé vers l'ancien siège de la Communauté à Arusha, et la section tanzanienne du Bureau projette de continuer ses opérations là-bas, ainsi que de prendre part à la création de presses universitaires à l'Université de Dar-es-Salaam, tandis que la section kényanne a été reprise par le Ministère de l'Education. Un nombre important de livres se trouvent à des stades divers de production, et d'autres ont été imprimés mais non mis sur le marché par les imprimeurs parce que la Communauté laisse des dettes. Tant que les problèmes complexes de la liquidation du bilan de la Communauté n'auront pas été résolus par les gouvernements des anciens états membres, on ne peut que s'apitoyer sur le sort des auteurs qui paient le prix d'une rivalité politique et voient leurs livres arrêtés au beau milieu de la production.

Avant l'apparition des difficultés actuelles, le East African Literature Bureau sortait environ cinquante titres par an et ne publiait pas moins de vingt périodiques. Une partie assez importante de la production de livres avait trait à l'enseignement pour adultes et aux livres et aux fournitures pour l'alphabétisation en kiswahili et autres langues de l'Afrique orientale.

Elvania Zirimu, and John Ruganda's *Black mamba*, a satrical play about racial tensions at a university campus. A new volume in the splendid series of children's picture storybooks, the "Lioncubs", was a special East African edition of Chinua Achebe's and John Iroaganachi's *How the leopard got his claws*, originally published by Nwamife Publishers in Nigeria. E.A.P.H. also continues to publish a wide range of academic books and monographs, among them Ann Seidmann's *Ghana's development experience; Kenya before 1900*, a collection of eight regional studies on pre-colonial Kenya edited by Bethwell Ogot and the first volume of the "History of Kenya" project which has been conducted by the Department of History of the University of Nairobi since 1966; *Socialism in Tanzania*, a two-volume reader on the socialist experience in Tanzania edited by Lionel Cliffe and John Saul; and *Federalism and higher education in East Africa* by Roger Southall, the first title in a new series entitled "East African Specials" which aims to replace the now defunct *East Africa Journal*. Another new E.A.P.H. book that has been in the limelight was *Kwacha: an autobiography* by Kanyama Chiume, who was one of the six ministers dismissed from Dr. Hastings Banda's cabinet in 1964 for voicing their opposing views on Malawi's future development policies. It recounts his progress from Makerere University via a journalistic career to become Malawi's Minister of External Affairs.

Kenya's major school-book publishers are the Jomo Kenyatta Foundation, and the multinational companies. Like their counterparts in Nigeria these concentrate mainly on the school-book market, but here, too, three — Oxford, Longman and Heinemann — are active in other areas and have published scholarly books, creative writing, and general interest titles. For example, Heinemann Educational Books (East Africa) Ltd., has an imaginative local publishing programme both in English and Kiswahili and its joint managing director, Henry Chakava, has described some of the problems of publishing in a multilingual situation in a recent article in *ABPR*.[15] Heinemann has published translations into Kiswahili of major African literary works by Chinua Achebe, Ferdinand Oyono, Ayi Kwei Armah and Ngugi wa Thiong'o, among others, and has also recently launched the "Heinemann Study Guides", which provide notes and examination guidelines for the study of books by major African writers. One of Heinemann's general interest titles was an *African cookery book* by M. Ominde; and for railway enthusiasts there was Kevin Patience's *Steam in East Africa*, a photographic volume which traces the eventful history of the building and expansion of railways in East Africa between 1893 and 1976.

The East African branch of Oxford University Press has published a Kiswahili translation of Wole Soyinka's play *The trials of brother Jero* [Masaibu ya Ndugu Jero],

Toutefois, cet éditeur produisait également une quantité croissante de livres d'érudition et de création littéraire en anglais écrites par de nouveaux auteurs est-africains. La longue liste d'ouvrages universitaire de E.A.L.B. comprend des livres de sciences sociales, économie politique, litterature classique, droit, agriculture et médecine. Parmi les ouvrages publiés récemment il faut signaler *The development of a financial infrastructure in Tanzania* de J. H. Binhammer, étude du développement de l'économie monétaire de la Tanzanie et analyse du système bancaire du pays; *Multilateral aid for national development and self reliance* de Susan Gitelson, est une évaluation de projets pour des fonds spéciaux (P.D.N.U. dans deux pays est-africains); une monographie sur la contribution de la religion au débat politique en Ouganda, de 1952 à 1962, intitulée *Issues in pre-independence politics in Uganda* de A. G. G. Gingyera-Pinycwa; un recueil d'articles consacrés au thème de l'évolution sociale en Afrique orientale, *Hadith 6: history and social change in East Africa*, sous la signature de Bethwell Ogot; et deux volumes abondamment illustrés sur Lamu, ville du littoral kényan au quinzième siècle, de Usman Ghaidan, intitulés *Lamu: A study in conservation* et *Lamu: A study of the Swahili town*. A cette liste impressionante, il faut ajouter une contribution importante sur le système juridique en Afrique de l'est, *Introduction to the legal system in East Africa* de William Burnett Harvey; un ouvrage massif de 1200 pages, *The law of business organisations in East and Central Africa*, par J. W. Katende et divers auteurs; et enfin les articles d'un colloque sur l'enseignement de la dynamique de la population dans les facultés de droit africaines, *Law and population change in Africa*, établi par U. U. Uche. Parmi les nouveaux ouvrages de médecine, il faut compter *Medicinal plants in East Africa*, de J. O. Kokwaro, et les actes de la vingtième conférence scientifique annuelle du Conseil est-africain de la recherche médicale qui sont consacrés au thème 'The use and abuse of drugs and chemicals in tropical Africa'. Parmi les créations littéraires, notons un recueil vivant de nouvelles, poésies et pensées de l'écrivain est-africain controversé Taban lo Liyong, intitulé *Ballads of underdevelopment*; deux pièces pour la radio de Peter Nazareth; de nouveaux romans de Bediako Asare, Godfrey Kalimugogo, Billy Ogana, et Chris Wanjala; ainsi que des recueils de poésies de Micere Githae Mugo, Joy Higiro et Mauri Yambo. Enfin, un joli album à colorier pour enfants, *A is for Africa*, de Ray Prather, avec quarante pages de dessins représentant les divers peuples africains avec de petites cartes pour indiquer leur situation géographique.

East African Publishing House a maintenant publié plus de 500 ouvrages, et la publication du nouveau roman de Ayi Kwei Armah, *Two Thousand seasons*, est un événement important pour cet éditeur car c'est la

and has added four children's books by the prolific Barbara Kimenye to its list. One of them is *Martha the millipede* which recounts the story of Martha who was fed up with getting sore feet and decided it was about time to get herself some shoes! Important recent academic titles from O.U.P. were a new volume of articles and speeches by President Julius Nyerere, *Freedom and development*, covering the period from 1968 to January 1973; *An African dilemma* by Joeal D. Barkan, an analysis of the roles African university students play, and are likely to play, in society following the completion of their studies, and the significance of these studies for economic development and political change; and a book which examines in depth the nature of the industrialization process which has taken place in Tanzania, the institutional framework in which this process has occurred and the consequences for a future industrial strategy, entitled *Underdevelopment and industrialization: a study of perverse capitalist development* by Justinian F. Rweyemamu, who is head of the Economics department at the University of Dar es Salaam.

The two major religious publishers are the Evangel Publishing House in Nairobi and G.A.B.A. Publications in Eldoret which has a particularly lively publishing programme. Two recent titles in G.A.B.A.'s "Spearheads" series were Laurenti Magesa's *The church and liberation in Africa*, and *Ujamaa and Christian communities* by Bishop Christopher Mwoleka and Father Joseph Healy, which represents a radical re-interpretation of the church's role in the community in Africa.

Tanzania is a country where publishing activities tend to be somewhat restricted due to foreign exchange regulations. The government-sponsored Tanzania Publishing House produces materials in accordance with the theme "education for self-reliance" and the original emphasis on primary school-book publishing is shifting gradually to a comprehensive publishing programme both in English and Kiswahili. This is reflected in the range of some of the new books published recently, including several additions to the "Tanzanian Studies Series", such as *Cooperatives in Tanzania* edited by Goran Hyden and A. Z. Mutaha, *Tourism and socialist development* by I. G. Shivji, and an *Adult education handbook* compiled by the staff of the Institute of Adult Education at the University of Dar es Salaam. Among new novels were Hamza Sokko's *The gathering storm* and W. E. Mkufy's *The wicked walk*. A highly topical forthcoming TPH title is Ann Seidman's *U.S. multinationals in Southern Africa*, but possibly the best-selling title in the overseas market was Walter Rodney's *How Europe underdeveloped Africa*, a paperback published in 1973.

Other than the largely school-book programme of

première fois qu'une oeuvre de cet écrivain africain réputé, un ghanéen vivant en ce moment en Tanzanie, est publiée en Afrique. Ses trois œuvres précédentes ont été publiées aux Etats-Unis par Doubleday et Houghton Mifflin, et au Royaume-Uni par Heinemann. E.A.P.H. va publier prochainement son prochain ouvrage, un roman historique intitulé *The healers*. Au début de 1973, E.A.P.H. a publié le second roman de Charles Mangua, le prosateur kényan sans doute le plus populaire, intitulé *A tail in the mouth*, qui a reçu le Prix Kenyatta de Littérature. Son œuvre précédente, *Son of woman*, était déjà un succès commercial et selon l'éditeur son second roman détient en ce moment le record des ventes de tous les titres jamais publiés par E.A.P.H. Les nouveaux romans de Kenneth Watene, Davis Sebukima, Jacqueline Piere (une afro-américaine vivant en Tanzanie) sont également publiés par E.A.P.H., ainsi que des compléments à la collection "African Theatre" avec les nouvelles pièces de l'ougandais Robert Serumaga, de Elavnia Zirimu, et *Black Mamba*, de John Ruganda, satire des tensions raciales sur un campus universitaire. *How the leopard got his claws* de Chinua Achebe et John Iroaganachi est un nouveau volume de la splendide collection de livres d'images pour enfants "Lioncubs", édité spécialement en Afrique orientale après avoir paru chez Nwamife Publishers, au Nigéria. E.A.P.H. poursuit la publication d'une gamme étendue de livres universitaires et de monographies, parmi lesquels il faut noter *Ghana's development experience* de Ann Seidmann; *Kenya before 1900*, recueil de huit études régionales sur le Kenya pré-colonial présentées par Bethwell Ogot, qui constitue le premier volume d'un projet d'"Histoire du Kenya" entamé en 1966 sous l'égide de la faculté d'histoire de l'Université de Nairobi; *Socialism in Tanzania*, morceaux choisis en deux volumes sur l'expérience socialiste en Tanzanie présentés par Lionel Cliffe et John Saul; et *Federalism and higher education in East Africa* de Roger Southall, premier ouvrage d'une nouvelle collection intitulée "East African Specials", destinée à remplacer le défunt *East Africa Journal*. *Kwacha: an autobiography*, est un autre livre publié par E.A.P.H., qui a retenu également l'attention: l'auteur, Kanyama Chiume, est l'un des six ministres du cabinet du Dr Hastings Banda limogés en 1964 pour avoir élevé des objections à la future politique du développement du Malawi. Le livre raconte comment, parti de l'Université de Makerere, il a fait carrière dans le journalisme, et est devenu Ministre des Affaires étrangères du Malawi.

Au Kenya, les principaux éditeurs de livres scolaires sont Jomo Kenyatta Foundation et les entreprises multi-nationales. De même que leurs équivalents du Nigéria, ces dernières s'occupent surtout du marché du livre scolaire, mais ici aussi, trois multinationales, Oxford, Longman et Heinemann, sont très actives dans d'autres

Longman Tanzania Ltd., there is very little commercial publishing output. A number of mission publishers, Inland Publishers in Mwanza, the Tanzania Mission Press in Tabora, and the Central Tanganyika Press, produce a wide range of Christian literature, school texts and books for adult education in Kiswahili. A recent title in English from the Central Tanganyika Press that ought to find a market well beyond Tanzania was *The church in East Africa 1840–1974*, by W. B. Anderson.

Very little reliable information is available about publishing activities in **Uganda**: the Uganda Publishing House, formerly in partnership with Macmillan but whose share-holding is now exclusively held by the National Trust of Uganda, was one of the few African publishers with an exhibit at the Frankfurt Book Fair in 1974, but it appears to have been dormant for the past three years.

English-speaking Central Africa

The development of publishing and the booktrade in **Zambia** is being influenced by geo-political considerations, the decline in the price of copper (which comprises over 90% of Zambia's exports), and the resultant scarcity of foreign exchange. Geoffrey Williams described in depth the state of the current Zambian publishing scene in the January 1977 issue of *ABPR*.[16] The largest publisher is the National Educational Company of Zambia whose main activity is school-book publishing, especially the comprehensive "Zambia Primary Course". N.E.C.Z.A.M. also produces a wide range of general interest books and academic titles, and it maintains an active programme devoted to creative writing by Zambians, though a really outstanding literary figure from Zambia has yet to emerge. An important recent title was *Fundamentals of Zambian humanism* by T. Kandeke, in which the author outlines Zambia's reasoning in opting for humanism as her national philosophy; among others were P. B. Mushindo's *A short history of the Bemba*, and *The Kapelwa Musonda file*, in which one of Zambia's best known and most outspoken journalists brings together a collection of his newspaper articles. N.E.C.Z.A.M.'s extensive publishing programme in the numerous Zambian languages has produced new titles, both fiction and non-fiction, in seven different languages.

In **Rhodesia** it is to be hoped that new indigenous imprints reflecting African aspirations will emerge soon after independence. At the present time there are few publishers, apart from school-book publishers, that cater for the African majority, with the exception of the sizeable output of the Rhodesia Literature Bureau and Mambo Press in Gwelo, which have publishing programmes of books largely in Shona and Ndebele. Two new series in English were launched by Mambo

domaines tels les livres d'érudition, les nouveautés littéraires, et les ouvrages d'intérêt général. La société Heinemann Educational Books (East Africa) offre par exemple un programme imaginatif de publications locales en anglais et en kiswahili, et son co-directeur général, Henry Chakava, a publié récemment dans *ABPR*[15] un article sur les problèmes de l'édition dans un contexte multilingue. Heinemann a publié des traductions en kiswahili d'œuvres maîtresses de la littérature africaine, notamment de Chinua Achebe, Ferdinand Oyono, Ayi Kwei Armah et Ngugi wa Thiong'o, et a aussi lancé récemment les "Heinemann Study Guides", collection de notes et conseils en vue des examens pour faciliter l'étude des œuvres des principaux auteurs africains. En ce qui concerne les livres d'intérêt général publiés par Heinemann, signalons *African cookery book* de M. Ominde, et pour les fanatiques des chemins de fer, *Steam in East Africa*, de Kevin Patience, album de photos retraçant l'histoire mouvementée de la construction et de l'essor des chemins de fer en Afrique orientale, de 1893 à 1976.

La filiale est-africaine d'Oxford University Press a publié une traduction en kiswahili de la pièce de Wole Soyinka *The trials of brother Jero* [Massaibu ya Ndugu Jero] ainsi que quatre nouveaux livres pour enfants de l'auteur fécond Barbara Kimenye. L'un d'eux, *Martha the millipede*, raconte l'histoire de Martha qui en avait assez d'avoir mal aux pieds et décide qu'il est temps de s'acheter des souliers! Dans la catégorie des ouvrages universitaires importants, O.U.P. a publié dernièrement un nouveau volume d'articles et de discours du président Julius Nyerere, intitulé *Freedom and development*, portant sur la période 1968 — janvier 1973; *An African dilemma*, de Joeal D. Barkan, qui analyse les rôles joués par les étudiants des universités africaines et ceux qu'ils seront amenés à jouer dans la société, une fois leurs études achevées, ainsi que l'influence qu'auront ces études sur le développement économique et l'évolution politique; enfin, un ouvrage qui examine en profondeur la nature du processus d'industrialisation qui a eu lieu en Tanzanie, le cadre institutionnel dans lequel ce processus s'est déroulé et ses conséquences sur la stratégie industrielle à venir, ouvrage intitulé: *Underdevelopment and industrialization: a study of perverse capitalist development*, de Justinian F. Rweyemamu, doyen de la faculté des sciences économiques de l'Université de Dar es Salaam.

Evangel Publishing House, à Nairobi, et G.A.B.A. Publications, à Eldoret, sont les deux principaux éditeurs religieux offrant un programme de publications particulièrement intéressant. Deux récents ouvrages de la série "Spearheads", de G.A.B.A: *The church and liberation in Africa*, de Laurenti Magesa, et *Ujamaa and Christian communities*, de Monseigneur Christopher Mwoleka et du Père Joseph Healy, qui donne une ré-

Press: "Zambeziana", the first volume of which was *A service to the sick* by Michael Gelfand, a history of the health services for Africans in Southern Rhodesia from 1890–1953; and "Shona Heritage Series", volume one being *The Shona peoples* by B. Boudillon, and volume two *Tsumo-Shumo*, a collection of 1,600 proverbs in Shona with English translations and explanations, compiled by M. A. Hamutyinei and Albert Plangger.

Longman Rhodesia, a multi-racial publishing organization, cooperates with the Rhodesia Literature Bureau on a number of projects, but its chief activity is the publication of an extensive, integrated primary school course. For some time now Longman Rhodesia has also published a successful "Bundu Series", each title dealing with a local natural history subject, with the accent on attractive presentation and colour plates. Other school-books and general trade titles come primarily from the College Press and its affiliated imprint, Galaxie Press. Books of Rhodesia Publishing Company at Bulawayo is best known as publishers of facsimile reprints of Rhodesiana and Africana. Its "Rhodesiana Reprint Library — Silver Series" was launched in 1975, following on the earlier thirty-six-volume "Gold Series". The books are designed to appeal to both the historian and the general reader, and for the most part cover scarce works on the pioneering, growth, and military history of Rhodesia. The series has already reached volume 15 and among the most recently published titles are a biography, *Matabele Thompson* edited by Nancy Rouillard, and the two-volume *The war history of Southern Africa, 1939–1945* by J. F. MacDonald, which describes the Rhodesian contribution to the Allied war effort. A non-series book is a pictorial narrative of Rhodesia's sporting endeavours, a reprint of J. de L. Thompson's *The story of Rhodesian sport, 1889–1935*. Another Books of Rhodesia title was a most useful guide to Zimbabwe nationalist leaders, with biographical information, career details, etc., *African nationalist leaders in Rhodesia: who's who* edited by Robert Cary and Diana Mitchell.

M. O. Collins in Salisbury publish mainly scholarly and cartographic works, and have also served as publishers to the Rhodesia Scientific Association. An important new title issued in 1976 was L. K. A. Chippindal's *240 common grasses of Southern Africa*. This comes in loose-leaf form, with individual descriptions of eighty grasses in four binders, plus an index. A new series, "The Environment of the Rhodesian People", so far consists of five titles covering land and water resources, agriculture, mining and industry, and social services.

Francophone Central Africa

Substantial publishing output comes from the **Zaire Republic**, but the bulk of it is produced by various

interprétation radicale du rôle de l'église au sein de la communauté en Afrique.

En **Tanzanie**, l'activité éditoriale est plus reduite en raison des restrictions de devises. Tanzania Publishing House, financé par le gouvernement, a une production conforme au thème "Education for Self-Reliance" [L'enseignement comme moyen d'accéder à l'indépendance], et l'accent qui était à l'origine placé sur les publications destinées à l'école primaire s'est déplacé progressivement au bénéfice d'un programme global de publications en anglais et en kiswahili, comme le prouve la gamme des nouveaux ouvrages publiés dernièrement, notamment plusieurs nouveautés de la collection "Tanzanian Studies Series", telles que *Cooperatives in Tanzania* établi par Goran Hyden et A. Z. Mutaha, *Tourism and socialist development* de I. G. Shivji, et un *Adult education handbook* établi par le personnel de l'Institut d'enseignement aux adultes de l'Université de Dar es Salaam; plusieurs romans, notamment *The gathering storm*, de Hamza Sokko, et *The wicked walk*, de W. E. Mkufy. Prochainement, un titre d'actualité attendu: *U.S. multi nationals in Southern Africa* de Ann Seidman; mais l'ouvrage sans doute le mieux vendu sur les marchés étrangers, c'est *How Europe underdeveloped Africa*, de Walter Rodney, livre de poche paru en 1973.

Exception faite du programme principalement orienté vers les livres scolaires de Longman Tanzania Ltd, la production de livres commerciaux est faible. Plusieurs éditeurs des missions, Inland Publishers à Mwanza, Tanzania Mission Press à Tabora, et Central Tanganyika Press produisent une gamme variée d'ouvrages chrétiens, de manuels scolaires et de livres pour l'enseignement aux adultes en kiswahili. Central Tanganyika Press a publié récemment en anglais un titre qui devrait trouver un marché plus large que la seule Tanzanie, il s'agit de *The church in East Africa 1840–1974* de W. B. Anderson.

On ne possède guère de renseignements sûrs à propos de l'édition en **Ouganda**: Uganda Publishing House, anciennement associé à Macmillan et dont les actions sont maintenant en totalité aux mains du National Trust of Uganda, était l'une des rares maisons d'édition à avoir exposé à la Foire du livre de Francfort, en 1974, mais il semble qu'elle ait cessé ses activités depuis ces trois dernières années.

Afrique centrale anglophone

Les progrès de l'édition et de l'industrie du livre en **Zambie** subissent les conséquences des considérations géopolitiques, de la chute du prix du cuivre (qui constitue plus de 90% des exportations de la Zambie) et de la rareté des devises qui en résulte. Geoffrey Williams a décrit en détail la situation actuelle dans laquelle se trouve le

research institutions and the Presses Universitaires du Zaïre. Specialist recent monographs from P.U.Z. have included *La religion traditionelle des Bantous et leur vision du monde* by Mulago Gwa Cikala; *Autour de la philosophie africaine* by A. J. Smet; *Les réformes administratives au Zaïre* by K. Mpinga and J. S. Gould; and Malu wa Kalenga's *Les utilisations de l'énergie nucléaire: cas de l'Afrique*. The Press has currently over a hundred titles in print, some of which are undergraduate texts. A welcome development was the founding in 1972 of Les Editions du Mont-Noir. Although created on the initiative of a Belgian clergyman who continues to be associated with the venture, it is directed by the novelist V. Y. Mudimbe and is staffed by a group of African intellectuals. In addition to several traditional texts in Lingala, Editions du Mont-Noir produces verse, short stories, novels, literary criticism and essays in French, mainly by Zaire authors. Among these were a new verse collection by Zaire's premier poet Jean Baptiste Tati-Loutard, *Les normes du temps*; Mwilambwe Kahoto's philosophical study, *Muntu, animisme et possessions*; and *L'oeuvre romanesque de Jacques-Stephen Alexis* by Mudimbe-Boyi Mbulamwanza, which provides a critical introduction to the work of this Haitian writer. Another small press is Mwamba-di Mbuyi's Les Presses Africaines, which has a list of general interest titles and fiction. Also active in the literary arena is the church-sponsored Centre Protestant d'Edition et de Diffusion which, in association with the Centre Africain de Littérature pour l'Afrique Francophone, publishes a series of inexpensively produced booklets covering new fiction by Zaire writers.

Editions St. Paul Afrique has a publishing programme of books in French, Kiswahili and Lingala, most of them Christian tracts and books aimed at children and young adults, but with some creative writing also.

There is no evidence of any significant publishing activities in the neighbouring **People's Republic of the Congo** and there is little to report on **Rwanda**, **Burundi** and the **Central African Empire**. An important exception, however, is a bibliographic volume which was published by the Press of the Université Nationale du Rwanda in Butare, *Contribution à la Bibliographie du Rwanda 1965–1970* edited by A. Levesque. Issued late in 1974, it is unfortunately already out of print. Elsewhere in Rwanda there is some publishing output from Editions Rwandaises, affiliated with Caritas Rwanda, which consists at the present time of books exclusively in Kinyarwanda.

In **Madagascar**, book production is largely in the national language, Malagasy. Among the country's publishers of fiction and general books in Malagasy are Editions Takariva and Editions/Librairie Ambozontany

monde de l'édition en Zambie dans le numéro de janvier 1977 de *ABPR*.[16] L'éditeur le plus important est National Educational Company of Zambia, qui se consacre principalement à la publication de manuels scolaires, notamment l'ensemble "Zambia Primary Course". N.E.C.Z.A.M. produit également une gamme variée de livres d'intérêt général et d'ouvrages universitaires, sans oublier son programme dynamique consacré aux créations littéraires des auteurs zambiens, bien qu'aucun écrivain d'envergure n'ait déjà été découvert. *Fundamentals of Zambian humanism* de T. Kandeke est un ouvrage important dans lequel l'auteur donne un aperçu des raisons pour lesquelles la Zambie a choisi l'humanisme comme philosophie nationale. Parmi les autres ouvrages il faut noter *A short history of the Bemba* de P. B. Mushindo, et *The Kapelwa Musonda file*, dans lequel l'un des journalistes les plus éminents et les plus honnêtes de Zambie rassemble une série d'articles de journaux. N.E.C.Z.A.M. possède un programme étendu pour les nombreuses langues parlées en Zambie et a sorti de nouveaux ouvrages, à la fois romans et essais, en sept langues différentes.

En **Rhodésie**, on espère que de nouvelles maisons d'edition reflétant les aspirations africaines verront le jour peu de temps après l'indépendance. Pour le moment, il n'y a que quelques éditeurs, à part ceux qui publient des manuels scolaires, qui offrent des livres à la majorité africaine, exception faite de la production importante de Rhodesia Literature Bureau and Mambo Press à Gwelo, qui ont mis au point des programmes de publication de livres principalement en shona et en ndebele. Deux nouvelles collections en anglais ont été lancées par Mambo Press: "Zambeziana", dont le premier volume, *A service to the sick* de Michael Gelfand, conte l'histoire des services de santé destinés aux Africains en Rhodésie du Sud, de 1890 à 1953; et dans la collection "Shona Heritage Series", le premier volume, *The Shona peoples* de B. Bourdillong, et le second volume, *Tsumo-Shumo*, recueil de 1600 proverbes en shona avec leurs traductions et des explications en anglais, rassemblés par M. A. Hamatyinei et Albert Plangger.

Longman Rhodesia, maison d'édition multiraciale, a entrepris plusieurs projets en collaboration avec Rhodesia Literature Bureau, mais son activité principale est la publication d'un important cours intégré pour école primaire. Depuis un certain temps, Longman Rhodesia publie une collection appréciée, "Bundu Series", dont chaque titre traite d'un sujet d'histoire naturelle locale et dont la présentation et les planches en couleurs sont particulièrement soignées. D'autres livres scolaires et d'intérêt général paraissent principalement chez College Press et sa filiale Galaxie Press. A Bulawayo, Books of Rhodesia Publishing Company est

whose retail outlet issues a useful new bibliographic tool, *Vao Niseho* [Just published] which provides a quarterly classified listing of new books and periodicals from Madagascar. The Lutheran Church-sponsored Trano Printy Loterana has a publishing programme of educational and religious books in Malagasy.

Southern Africa

A most welcome development in **Malawi**, a country which had lacked any indigenous publishing apart from the efforts of various mission presses, was the launching of the "Malawian Writers Series" by Popular Publications in Limbe, in association with Montfort Press. Three collections of folklore, short stories, and drama have already appeared and several more volumes are in the pipeline. It is one of the aims of Popular Publications to encourage creative writing in the country, both in English and in Malawi's main indigenous language, Chichewa. The major school-book publisher in the country until September 1977 was Longman Malawi, when its interests were taken over by a new indigenous company, Dzuka Publishing, headed by the previous general manager of Longman Malawi. Its publishing programme will not alter dramatically, but the new company hopes to produce increasingly more fiction, drama, and poetry in Chichewa in addition to maintaining its extensive school-book list. An attractive existing series taken over from Longman Malawi is "Malawians to Remember", short biographical volumes on outstanding leaders from Malawi's past. Several church-supported organizations in Malawi have publishing programmes, and these include the Christian Literature Association in Malawi (C.L.A.I.M.), the Malamulo Publishing House, and the Likuni Press and Publishing House. A comprehensive survey about the development of printing presses and publishing in Malawi, by Steve S. Mwiyeriwa, Government Archivist at the National Archives of Malawi, appeared in the April 1978 issue of *ABPR*.[17]

The scale of publishing in **Botswana**, **Lesotho**, and **Swaziland** is still limited, even though Swaziland, for example, now has its first indigenous publisher in the form of Mabiya Publications (Pty.) Ltd., which will shortly publish its first book, *Our Swazi way of life* by Sishayi Simon Nxumalo. One organization that is active in Lesotho is the Mazenod Institute, which also maintains a retail outlet, the Mazenod Book Centre. In addition to educational and religious books in Sesotho and original creative writing in that language, it has published a *Basic economics for Lesotho* by W. B. S. Trimble, a text based on a book originally published in Canada but entirely revised and adapted for use in Lesotho. Other recent Mazenod titles were Martha Schmitz's *Flowering plants of Lesotho*; the first book in

surtout connu pour la publication de réimpressions en facsimilé d'œuvres rhodésiennes et africaines. Sa collection "Rhodesiana Reprint Library — Silver Series" a été lancée en 1975, après la "Gold Series" qui compte trente-six volumes. Ces livres sont destinés aux historiens et au grand public et pour la plupart regroupent des ouvrages rares sur les pionniers, le développement et l'histoire militaire de la Rhodésie. Cette série en est déjà à son quinzième volume, et parmi les derniers titres parus, il faut signaler une biographie *Matabele Thompson*, présentée par Nancy Rouillard, et les deux volumes de J. F. MacDonald, *The war history of Southern Africa, 1939–1945*, qui décrit la contribution rhodésienne à l'effort de guerre des Alliés. *The story of Rhodesian sport, 1889–1935*, de J. de L. Thompson, qui n'appartient à aucune collection, raconte en images les grands moments du sport rhodésien. Autre titre paru chez Books of Rhodesia, *African nationalist leaders in Rhodesia: Who's who,* établi par Robert Cary et Diana Mitchell, guide très utile sur les leaders nationalistes du Zimbabwe, comportant des renseignements biographiques et des détails sur leurs carrières.

A Salisbury, M. O. Collins publie principalement des ouvrages d'érudition et de cartographie, ainsi que les œuvres de l'Association scientifique de Rhodésie. En 1976, un titre important a paru, *240 common grasses of Southern Africa*, de L. K. A. Chippindal, sous forme de feuillets détachables, donnant la description de quatre-vingts sortes d'herbes, réunies en quatre classeurs accompagnés d'une table alphabétique. "The Environment of the Rhodesian People" est une collection comprenant jusqu'ici cinq titres sur les ressources du sol, l'hydrologie, l'agriculture, les mines, l'industrie et les services sociaux.

Afrique centrale francophone

Il existe en **République du Zaïre** une production importante dont la majeure partie est assurée par des institutions diverses de recherche et par les Presses Universitaires du Zaïre. Des monographies récentes sur des sujets spéciaux ont paru récemment aux Presses sous les titres: *La religion traditionnelle des Bantous et leur vision du monde* de Mulago Gwa Cikala; *Autour de la philosophie africaine* de A. J. Smet; *Les réformes administratives au Zaïre* de K. Mpinga et J. S. Gould; et *Les utilisations de l'énergie nucléaire: cas de l'Afrique*, de Malu wa Kalenga. Les Presses ont sorti à l'heure actuelle une centaine de titres dont certains sont destinés aux étudiants des universités. En 1972, les Editions du Mont-Noir ont été créés. Bien que sa création soit due à l'initiative d'un prêtre belge qui continue à être associé aux opérations, cette entreprise est dirigée par le romancier V. Y. Mudimbe, secondé d'un groupe d'intellectuels africains. A côté des textes traditionnels en lingala, les Editions du Mont-Noir publient des ouvrages

a new primary school series *The earth and its wonders — for the children of Africa* by E. Butler and T. Dylak; and A. C. A. van der Wiel's *Migratory wage labour*, which analyses the export of labour to the employment centres in the Republic of South Africa.

Although not covered in this survey, the situation in the **South African** publishing industry merits a brief mention: despite the restrictions imposed by the country's Publications Control Board, which is empowered to declare any book, film, or object "undesirable", there has been a marked increase in publishing activities during the past years, accompanied by a sustained output by local writers, both black and white. Several small independent companies have sprung up, many of which are prepared to publish socially committed literature or new creative writing by black South Africans. The firms of Adriaan Donker, David Philip, James Matthews' B.L.A.C. Publishing House, the recently founded Quagga Press, and Ravan Press in Johannesburg in particular, are among these.[18]

Ravan Press was founded in 1974, having had its origins in the Study Project on Christianity in Apartheid Society (Spro-Cas). This body, which was sponsored by the South African Council of Churches and the now banned Christian Institute of Southern Africa, was set up to analyse the South African political order and to propose radical alternatives pointing in the direction of a just, free, and non-discriminatory society. Subsequently, Ravan's editorial scope has widened and the company has published relevant books on many contemporary Southern African issues, with emphasis on literary and socio-political topics. Inevitably, a number of titles have fallen foul of the South African censors and Ravan's editorial editor, Peter Randall, was one of the individuals recently served with a banning order by the South African government, along with Dr. Beyers Naudé, Director of the Christian Institute. After the mass bannings in South Africa of 19 October 1977 it remains to be seen what the future holds for Ravan Press and other small "liberal" publishing companies trying to survive in a repressive society.

Notes and references

1 Some of the material in this article has previously appeared in two papers (i) "Publishing Progress in Africa 1973–74", Standing Conference on Library Materials on Africa (S.C.O.L.M.A.) seminar, Institute of Commonwealth Studies, London, 7 February 1975; and, (ii) "Publishing Progress in Africa 1975–6: problems in securing information and the role of the *African Book Publishing Record*", Progress in African Bibliography conference, organized by the Standing Conference on Library Materials on Africa (S.C.O.L.M.A.), Commonwealth Institute, London, 17–18 March 1977.

2 Problems of acquisitions of African publications were discussed and analysed at the S.C.O.L.M.A. Progress in African Bibliography conference, Commonwealth Institute, London, 17 and 18 March 1977. The conference proceedings are available at £5/$13 from the Librarian,

de poésie, des nouvelles, des romans, des ouvrages de critique littéraire et des essais en français, écrits pour la plupart par des auteurs zaïrois. Parmi ces ouvrages, il faut compter une nouvelle collection de poèmes du premier poète zaïrois, Jean-Baptiste Tati-Loutard, intitulé *Les normes du temps*; l'étude philosophique *Muntu, animisme et possession* de Mwilambwe Kahoto; et *L'œuvre romanesque de Jacques-Stephen Alexis*, de Mudimbe-Boyi Mbulamwanza, qui donne une introduction critique de l'œuvre de cet écrivain haïtien. Les modestes Presses Africaines, dirigées par Mwamba-di Mbuyi, publient des livres d'intérêt général et des romans. Le Centre Protestant d'Edition et de Diffusion, pris en charge par l'Eglise, est également très actif dans le domaine littéraire et publie, en association avec le Centre Africain de Littérature pour l'Afrique Francophone, une collection de nouvelles œuvres romanesques d'auteurs zaïrois en opuscules bon marché.

Les Editions St-Paul Afrique ont un programme pour la publication de livres en français, kiswahili et lingala, pour la plupart des documents et des livres chrétiens destinés aux enfants et aux jeunes adultes, mais éditent aussi des nouveautés littéraires.

On ne peut discerner aucun signe d'activité importante dans ce domaine dans la **République Populaire du Congo** et il y a peu de choses à dire sur le **Rwanda**, le **Burundi** et l'**Empire Centrafricain**. Exception notable toutefois, le volume bibliographique publié aux Presses de l'Université Nationale du Rwanda, à Butare, en 1974, *Contribution à la bibliographie du Rwanda, 1965–1970*, présenté par A. Levesque. Malheureusement cet ouvrage est déjà épuisé. Au Rwanda, par ailleurs, les Editions Rwandaises, filiale de Caritas Rwanda, n'éditent que des livres en kinyarwanda.

A **Madagascar**, on édite essentiellement des livres en malgache. Parmi les éditeurs de romans et de livres d'intérêt général, on trouve les Editions Takariva et les Editions/Librairie Ambozontany dont le point de vente au détail édite un nouvel instrument bibliographique utile *Vao Niseho* [Vient de paraître], qui donne tous les trimestres une liste par catégorie des nouveaux livres et périodiques de Madagascar. Trano Printy Loterana, pris en charge par l'Eglise luthérienne, a inscrit à son programme la publication d'ouvrages éducatifs et religieux en langue malgache.

Afrique australe

Au **Malawi**, pays qui manquait de publications autochtones, exception faite des efforts déployés par les diverses presses des missions, on a bien accueilli la venue de la série "Malawian Writers Series", aux Popular Publications de Limbe, en association avec Montfort Press. Trois collections pour le folklore, les nouvelles et le

Institute of Commonwealth Studies, University of London, 27 Russell Square, London WC1B 5DS.

3 See Anon, "A Hausa hiatus", *West Africa*, 25 October 1976, and "Letters to the Editor", *West Africa*, 20 December 1976.

4 *Publishing in Africa in the Seventies*, Proceedings of an International Conference on Publishing and Book Development held at the University of Ife, Ile-Ife, Nigeria, 16–20 December 1973, edited by Edwina Oluwasanmi, Eva McLean, and Hans Zell. Ile-Ife: University of Ife Press, 1975. ix + 377 pp. cloth N9 in Nigeria, £7/$16.50 elsewhere.

5 *African Book Publishing Record*, vol. I, no. 1, January 1975, published quarterly. £18/$40 annually.

6 Jean Dihang, "Vers un programme de co-publication, en Afrique, de livres pour les jeunes", *African Book Publishing Record*, Vol. II, no. 2, April 1976, p. 93.

7 Available from Centre Régional de Promotion du Livre en Afrique, BP 1646, Yaoundé, Cameroun.

8 S.I.A. Kotei and Colin Ray, "The Legon Seminar on Writing and Production of Literature for Children, 5–10 April 1976", *African Book Publishing Record*, vol. II, no. 4, October 1976, pp. 227–9.

9 Union of Writers of the African Peoples/Union des Ecrivains Négro-Africains, P.O. Box 2838, Accra, Ghana.

10 Source: *Pearson Longman Ltd. Report and Accounts for 1976*.

11 Elizabeth Paren, "The Multinational Publishing Firm in Africa: the Macmillan perspective", *African Book Publishing Record*, vol. IV, no. 1, January 1978, p. 17.

12 Philippe Touzard, "Panorama de l'Edition au Sénégal", *African Book Publishing Record*, vol I, no. 4, October 1975, pp. 301–5.

13 Henry Chakava, "Publishing in a Multi-lingual Situation: the Kenya case", *African Book Publishing Record*, vol. III, no. 2, April 1977, p. 87.

14 Terry Hirst, personal communication.

15 Chakava, pp. 83–90.

16 Geoffrey J. Williams, "The Zambian Publishing Scene: a commentary", *African Book Publishing Record*, vol. III, no. 1, January 1977, pp. 15–22.

17 Steve S. Mwiyeriwa, "Printing Presses and Publishing in Malawi", *African Book Publishing Record*, vol. IV, no. 2, April 1978, pp. 87–97.

18 See also, Peter Randall, "Minority Publishing in South Africa", *African Book Publishing Record*, vol. I, no. 3, July 1975, pp. 219–22.

théâtre ont déjà paru, et d'autres volumes sont en préparation. L'un des objectifs de Popular Publications est d'encourager la création littéraire locale non seulement en anglais mais aussi en chichewa, principale langue du Malawi. Longman Malawi a été le principal éditeur de livres scolaires du pays jusqu'à septembre 1977, date à laquelle ses intérêts ont été repris par une nouvelle société autochtone, Dzuka Publishing, dirigée par l'ancien directeur général de Longman Malawi. Son programme de publications ne changera pas beaucoup, mais la nouvelle société espère publier plus de romans, de pièces de théâtre et de poésie en chichewa, tout en conservant une liste étendue de manuels scolaires. L'une des collections agréables héritées de Longman Malawi, "Malawians to Remember", réunit de courtes bibliographies de héros de l'histoire malawi. Plusieurs organisations financées par l'Eglise du Malawi ont des programmes de livres, notamment Christian Literature Association in Malawi (CLAIM), Malamulo Publishing House, et Likuni Press and Publishing House. Une étude exhaustive retraçant l'essor des imprimeries et des maisons d'édition au Malawi est parue sous la signature de Steve S. Mwiyeriwa, archiviste du gouvernement aux Archives Nationales du Malawi, dans le numéro d'avril 1978 de *ABPR*.[17]

Les maisons d'édition du **Botswana, Lesotho** et de **Swaziland** sont encore en nombre réduit, bien que le Swaziland ait maintenant son premier éditeur autochtone, Mabiya Publications (Pty.) Ltd., qui sortira bientôt son premier livre, *Our Swazi way of life* de Sishayi Simon Nxumalo. Le Mazenod Institute est une organisation active du Lesotho avec un point de vente, le Centre du livre Mazenod. En plus des livres éducatifs et religieux et des créations littéraires en sesotho, il a publié *Basic economics for Lesotho* de W. B. S. Trimble, texte se fondant sur un livre publié d'abord au Canada, mais entièrement revu et adapté pour être utilisable au Lesotho. Parmi les autres récents titres de Mazenod on trouve *Flowering plants of Lesotho* de Martha Schmitz; le premier livre d'une nouvelle collection pour l'école primaire, *The earth and its wonders — for the children of Africa* de E. Butler et T. Dylak; et *Migratory wage labour* de A. C. A. van der Wiel, qui analyse l'exportation de main d'œuvre vers les centres d'emploi de la République Sud-africaine.

Bien que l'édition **sud-africaine** ne soit pas du ressort de cette étude, elle mérite cependant qu'on s'y arrête un bref instant: en dépit des restrictions imposées par le Bureau de contrôle des publications du pays, qui a le pouvoir de déclarer que tout livre, film ou objet est "indésirable", l'activité s'est accrue au cours de ces dernières années, et elle s'accompagne d'une production soutenue de la part des écrivains locaux, noirs comme

blancs. Plusieurs petites maison indépendantes ont surgi, pour la plupart disposées à publier des ouvrages engagés socialement ou des nouveautés littéraires d'auteurs sud-africains noirs. Par exemple, Adriaan Donker, David Philip, B.L.A.C. Publishing House, dirigée par James Matthews, Quagga Press, fondée récemment, et Ravan Press à Johannesbourg.[18] Ravan Press a été fondée en 1974 grâce à un Projet d'étude sur le Christianisme dans une société d'apartheid (Spro-Cas). Cette organisation, prise en charge par le Conseil Sud-africain des églises et par l'Institut chrétien d'Afrique du Sud, maintenant interdit, avait été créée pour analyser l'ordre politique sud-africain et proposer des solutions radicales pour l'instauration d'une société plus juste, plus libre et non discriminatoire. Par la suite, la maison Ravan a élargi son domaine et publié des livres se faisant l'écho des problèmes sud-africains contemporains, en insistant sur les sujets d'actualité littéraire ou socio-politique. Il était inévitable qu'un certain nombre de titres aient été refusés par les censeurs sud-africains et le rédacteur Peter Randall fut l'une des victimes de la loi d'interdiction promulguée par le gouvernement sud-africain, de même que Dr. Beyers Naudé, directeur de l'Institut chrétien. Après les interdictions massives d'octobre 1977 en Afrique du Sud, on ne sait ce que l'avenir réserve à Ravan Press et aux autres maisons d'édition "libérales" qui s'efforcent de survivre dans une société répressive.

Notes et références

1 Une partie du contenu de cet article a déjà paru dans deux articles, (i) "Publishing Progress in Africa 1973–74", séminaire de la Conférence permanente sur les matériaux de bibliothèques sur l'Afrique (S.C.O.L.M.A.) Institute of Commonwealth Studies, Londres, 7 février 1975; et (ii) "Publishing Progress in Africa 1975–6: problems in securing information and the role of *African Book Publishing Record*", conférence sur les progrès bibliographiques africains, organisée par la conférence permanente sur les matériaux de bibliothèques sur l'Afrique (S.C.O.L.M.A.), Institute of Commonwealth Studies, Londres, 17 et 18 mars 1977.

2 Les problèmes d'acquisitions des publications africaines ont été examinés et analysés à la conférence sur les progrès bibliographiques africains de la S.C.O.L.M.A. Commonwealth Institute, Londres 17 et 18 mars 1977. Les actes de la conférence sont disponibles au prix de £5/$13 auprès de la Bibliothécaire de l'Institute of Commonwealth Studies, Université de Londres, 27 Russell Square, Londres WC1B 5DS.

3 Voir "A Hausa hiatus", *West Africa*, 25 octobre 1976 et "Letters to the Editor", *West Africa*, 20 décembre 1976, tous deux par des auteurs anonymes.

4 *Publishing in Africa in the Seventies*, actes d'une Conférence internationale sur l'édition et le développement du livre, qui s'est tenue à l'Université d'Ifé. Ilé-Ifé, Nigéria, du 16 au 20 décembre 1973, annotés par Edwina Oluwasanmi, Eva McLean et Hans Zell. Ilé-Ifé: University of Ife Press. 1975, ix + 377 p. broché N9 au Nigéria, £7/$16.50 ailleurs.

5 *African Book Publishing Record*, vol. I, no. 1, January 1975, trimestriel. £18/$40 par an.

6 Jean Dihang, "Vers un programme de co-publication, en Afrique, de livres pour les jeunes", *African Book Publishing Record*, vol. II, no. 2, April 1976, p. 93.

7 Disponible au Centre Régional de Promotion du Livre en Afrique, BP 1646, Yaoundé, Cameroun.

8 S.I.A. Kotei et Colin Ray, "The Legon Seminar on Writing and Production of Literature for Children, 5–10 Avril 1976", *African Book Publishing Record*, vol. II, no. 4, octobre 1976, pp. 227–9.

9 Union of Writers of the African Peoples/Union des Ecrivains Négro-Africains, P.O. Box 2838, Accra, Ghana.

10 Source: *Pearson Longman Ltd. Report and Accounts for 1976*.

11 Elizabeth Paren, "The Multinational Publishing Firm in Africa: the Macmillan perspective", *African Book Publishing Record*, vol. IV, no. 1, janvier 1978, p. 17.

12 Philippe Touzard, "Panorama de l'Edition au Sénégal", *African Book Publishing Record*, vol. I, no. 4, octobre 1975, pp. 301–5.

13 Henry Chakava, "Publishing in a Multilingual Situation: the Kenya case", *African Book Publishing Record*, vol. III, no. 2, avril 1977, p. 87.

14 Terry Hirst, communication personnelle.

15 Chakava, pp. 83–90.

16 Geoffrey J. Williams, "The Zambian Publishing Scene: a commentary", *African Book Publishing Record*, vol. III, no. 1, janvier 1977, pp. 15–22.

17 Steve S. Mwiyeriwa, "Printing Presses and Publishing in Malawi", *African Book Publishing Record*, vol. IV, no. 2, avril 1978, pp. 87–97.

18 Voir aussi Peter Randall, "Minority Publishing in South Africa", *African Book Publishing Record*, vol. I, no. 3, juillet 1975, pp. 219–22.

Scope and Arrangement

Based exclusively on data supplied by African publishers, *African Books in Print* provides an index to African published material currently in print — by author, subject, and title. It covers titles in English and French and in numerous African languages. In addition to books from commercial and state-sponsored publishers, it includes publications from research institutions, learned societies, and professional associations, as well as publications available from university libraries or bookshops acting as distributors on behalf of university departments, institutes, etc. The sole criterion for inclusion of a title in *ABIP*, regardless of content, is that it must have been published on the African continent. The titles of the various British multinational firms operating in Africa are also included, but are confined to those books *published* under the imprint of a local African subsidiary; titles merely *distributed* by expatriate publishers are *not* included, even though the books may be written by African authors. *ABIP* lists books, pamphlets, reports and series (including irregular series), but not periodical publications other than yearbooks or annuals. This edition covers titles published, and still in print, in late 1977; the details of some 1977 publications are tentative, with bibliographic data incomplete or subject to change.

Three major indexes are provided — author (volume I) and subject and title (volume II). Arrangement throughout is alphabetical. In the author index, entries with multiple authors appear in full under the main author and are cross-referenced to the co-author(s). The index of subject and area headings, with form divisions as applicable, also appears in a straightforward alphabetical sequence including cross-references.

How data are collected and processed

Information, both for *ABIP* and *African Book Publishing Record* (*ABPR*), is collected by means of regular circular mailings (in English and French) to a roster of publishers and research institutions which currently consists of over 500 names and addresses. These are accompanied by a series of "Fact sheets for publishers", which outline requirements in terms of bibliographic details needed, closing dates for submitting entries, etc. The circular letters are supplemented by individual and personal follow-up letters to publishers who fail to reply, submit incomplete data, or who do not meet copy deadlines. Data are then edited, transcribed on to an entry slip, classified, and thereafter converted to machine-readable form via a mini-computer data entry system which generates a tape for processing on a large mainframe computer, an IBM 360/65. The machine-readable format is a modified Library of Congress MARC format. Initial processing includes error checking and the generation of a proof list. Corrections

Plan de l'ouvrage et Domaines Couverts

Exclusivement fondé sur les renseignements fournis par les éditeurs africains, *Livres Africains Disponibles* comporte un classement par auteurs, matières et titres. Il comprend des titres en anglais, en français et dans de nombreuses langues africaines. Outre la production des éditeurs publics ou privés, il recense les publications des instituts de recherche, sociétés savantes, associations professionnelles, ainsi que celles qui sont seulement disponibles dans les bibliothèques universitaires ou chez les libraires jouant un rôle de distributeur pour les sections universitaires, les instituts, etc. Le seul critère d'insertion d'un titre, quel que soit son contenu, est d'avoir été édité sur le continent africain. Les publications proposées par les nombreuses entreprises multinationales britanniques qui éditent en Afrique sont également indiquées, mais elles sont classées parmi les ouvrages de leur filiale locale africaine; les titres des éditeurs étrangers simplement *distribués* localement ne sont *pas* inclus, même s'ils sont écrits par des auteurs africains. Le répertoire recense les livres, les brochures, les rapports et les collections (y compris les collections irrégulières), mais non les publications périodiques à l'exception des annuaires. Cette édition comprend les ouvrages édités, ainsi que ceux qui étaient en cours de publication en 1977; pour ceux-ci certaines indications bibliographiques sont provisoires ou incomplètes.

Les ouvrages apparaissent dans l'ordre alphabétique sous trois classements: auteurs (volume I), matières et titres (volume II). Dans l'index des auteurs, les ouvrages collectifs sont indiqués de façon complète sous l'auteur principal, et sous forme de renvois à chacun des co-auteurs. L'index des matières est organisé par rubriques avec des renvois.

Collecte et traitement des données

Les renseignements destinés à notre répertoire et à *African Book Publishing Record* sont réunis grâce à des circulaires régulières (en anglais et en français) qui sont envoyés à une liste de 500 éditeurs et instituts de recherche. Ces circulaires sont accompagnées d'une série de " Conseils aux editeurs" qui rapellent la nécessité des renseignements bibliographiques, précisent les dates limites pour leur enregistrement dans le catalogue, etc. Les circulaires sont complétées par des lettres personnelles aux éditeurs qui n'ont pas répondu, qui ont fourni des informations incomplètes, ou encore qui n'ont pas respecté les dates limites. Les données sont ensuite rédigées, transcrites sur un bordereau, classées, puis enregistrées par les terminaux d'une unité centrale qui produit des bandes. Ces bandes son traitées par un ordinateur IBM 360/65. Le format de lecture est un format *MARC* de la *Library of Congress* modifié. Le traitement de base comprend la correction des erreurs et la sortie d'une épreuve. Les corrections sont ensuite

are subsequently keyed and processed until all errors are eliminated. When it is time to produce camera-ready copy for either *ABPR* or *ABIP*, titles are selected by date of entry, or the entire file is processed for *ABIP* or *ABPR*.

Early in 1977 all publishers were mailed individual computer print-out edit lists, including all titles on file from the first edition of *African Books in Print*, plus all those cumulated from *African Book Publishing Record* to vol. III, no. 2, (records from issue nos. 3 and 4 of vol. III were added to the file later). Publishers were requested to check the edit lists for accuracy, delete out-of-print titles, indicate price changes and new editions, and add any missing titles. By previous standards, the response rate to the mailing of publishers' print-outs was encouragingly good; approximately 75% of publishers contacted responded and returned the corrected edit lists, many of them also submitting a considerable amount of new information. There were, nevertheless, some publishers (about 25%) who failed to return the edit lists, despite duplicate copies and up to three reminders being sent. All these are indicated by a dagger symbol in the directory of publishers (see page liii). It must follow that the availability status of the titles from these publishers and institutions is uncertain, and that information provided may be neither entirely up to date nor complete. Sadly, two of the larger publishers who failed to return the edit lists despite numerous reminders are Editions CLE in Yaoundé, Cameroun, and the Société Nationale d'Edition et de Diffusion (SNED) in Algeria. Among those from English-speaking Africa who did not respond are Pilgrim Books in Lagos, Transafrica Publishers in Nairobi, and a number of South African companies. It is hoped that these companies can be persuaded to cooperate in the future for later editions of *ABIP*.

Deletions and availability

A total of 1,274 titles listed in the first edition have been deleted from this edition, as publishers indicated they were out-of-print, or unlikely to be available by the time the second edition of *ABIP* is published. However, the editor and the publishers cannot guarantee availability of any of the titles listed in the second edition.

Government and official publication

Government and official publications are not included, except for titles from certain quasi-autonomous government bodies with publishing programmes, e.g., Geological Survey Departments, Chambers of Commerce, Museums, Central Statistical Offices, etc., who distribute books *independently* and not through government printers and publications agencies. A full

effectuées, puis vérifiées jusqu'à l'élimination de toutes les erreurs.

Au début de 1977, tous les éditeurs ont reçu individuellement les listes dressées par l'ordinateur; elles comprenaient tous les titres du fichier depuis la première édition de *Livres africains disponibles*, auxquels s'ajoutent les titres cumulés de l'*African Book Publishing Record* jusqu'au vol. III, no. 2, (les notes des nos. 3 et 4 du vol. III ont été intégrées ultérieurement au fichier). Nous avons demandé aux éditeurs de corriger les listes pour plus de précision, de rayer les titres épuisés, d'indiquer les changements de prix et les nouvelles éditions, enfin d'ajouter tout titre manquant. Environ 75% des éditeurs ont répondu et renvoyé les listes corrigées, bon nombre d'entre eux ont aussi apporté une quantité considérable de nouveaux renseignements. Notons cependant que 25% environ des éditeurs n'ont pas restitué les listes, malgré un double envoi et de nombreuses lettres de rappel. Ces éditeurs sont indiqués d'une croix dans le répertoire des éditeurs (voir p. liii). Il résulte de ces manquements que la disponibilité de leurs titres est incertaine et que les notices correspondantes ne sont peut-être plus tout-à-fait à jour ou complètes. Nous regrettons évidemment beaucoup que des éditeurs tels que les Editions CLE, à Yaoundé, au Cameroun, et la Société Nationale d'Edition et de Diffusion (S.N.E.D.), en Algérie, figurent parmi ceux qui ont négligé de nous retourner nos listes malgré nos nombreuses lettres de rappel. On compte aussi parmi les éditeurs d'Afrique anglophone qui n'ont pas répondu: Pilgrim Books à Lagos, Transafrica Publishers à Nairobi et de nombreuses sociétés d'Afrique du Sud. Nous espérons toujours arriver à persuader ces sociétés de coopérer dans l'avenir aux éditions ultérieures de ce répertoire.

Suppressions et disponibilité

Au total 1,274 titres mentionnés dans la première édition ont été écartés de cette édition, les éditeurs les ayant signalés comme épuisés ou susceptibles de n'être pas disponibles au moment de la publication de notre seconde édition. Cela ne signifie pas bien entendu que les éditeurs et nous-mêmes garantissons la disponibilité de tous les titres catalogués dans la seconde édition.

Les publications nationales et officielles

Les publications nationales et officielles ne sont pas comprises, sauf les titres de certains organismes nationaux quasi-autonomes qui ont des programmes de publication, par exemple, les Services de Relevé Géologique, les Chambres de Commerce, les Musées, les Bureaux Centraux de Statistiques, etc., qui distribuent leurs ouvrages *indépendamment* sans passer par les imprimeries nationales et les organismes de publication.

listing of the names and addresses of government printers throughout Africa is provided as an appendix to the directory of publishers on page lxxiii.

Classification and subject index

The *Sears List of Subject Headings* is used as the main thesaurus of classification of titles, modified and expanded to suit the particular needs of *ABIP*. Without actual examination of each book, and with no further guidance other than the publishers' original information or descriptive data when available, classification can present difficulties. Inevitably, therefore, there are still a small number of entries the classification of which in the subject index may not be absolutely correct or entirely consistent.

Sears provides no definite rules on subdividing by place or by subject, but the following classification policies generally apply:

(i) *Entries under subject, subdivided by place and/or form:*

Agricultural sciences and industries
Agricultural development
Archaeology
Architecture, Housing and urban planning
Business, Management, Industry, Labour, Trade unions, Employment
Church history, Christianity in Africa, Christian Missions
Economics, Finance, Economic development
Geology, Mining, Mines and mineral resources
Health education, Public health, Nutrition
Languages and linguistics
Law (all areas)
Leisure and entertainment
Library sciences (other than bibliographies)
Medicine, Life sciences, Natural history
Philosophy
Pure sciences
Sports
Technology, and applied sciences
Wildlife and conservation

(ii) *Entries under place (i.e., geographic division, country, area, etc.) subdivided by subject and/or form:*

Administration, Local government, Rural development
Bibliographies, national
Demography
Education
Geography
History
Politics and government
Religion (other than Missions, Christian and Church history)

Une liste complète des noms et adresses des Imprimeries nationales en Afrique est donnée en appendice du répertoire des éditeurs page lxxiii.

Classement et index des matières

C'est la *liste des vedettes-matière Sears*, modifiée et développée pour répondre aux exigences du répertoire, qui a été utilisée comme principal thésaurus pour le classement des ouvrages. Faute de pouvoir examiner chaque livre et sans autres indications que celles des éditeurs, le classement a présenté quelques difficultés. Il est inévitable qu'un petit nombre de classifications de l'index des matières soit incorrect ou quelque peu incomplet.

Sears ne donne pas de règles absolues pour la subdivision des lieux et des matières, mais, en général, nous avons appliqué la classification suivante:

(i) *Entrées-matières, subdivisées par lieu et/ou forme:*

Agriculture,
Archéologie
Architecture, Logement et urbanisme
Bibliothéconomie (autre que les bibliographies)
Commerce, Gestion, Industrie, Syndicats, Travailleurs
Développement agricole
Droit (toutes disciplines)
Economie, Finances, Développement économique
Faune et conservation
Géologie, Exploitation minière, Mines et ressources minières
Histoire de l'Eglise, Christianisme en Afrique, Missions chrétiennes
Hygiène, Santé publique, Nutrition
Linguistique
Loisirs
Médecine, Histoire naturelle
Philosophie
Sciences appliquées et Technologie
Sciences pures
Sport

(ii) *Entrées par lieu (division géographique, pays, zone, etc.) subdivisées par matière et/ou forme:*

Administration, Gouvernement local, Développement rural
Bibliographies nationales
Démographie
Enseignement
Géographie
Histoire
Politique et Gouvernement
Religion (autre que Missions, Histoire chrétienne et de l'Eglise)

Social sciences
Travel and guide books

It should be noted that general works on African topics are always classified under subject first, regardless of their nature: for example, a book entitled *Education in Africa today* will appear under

>   Education — Africa
> and *not*
>   Africa — Education

whereas a title on the Nigerian educational system, for example, will be listed under place first, i.e.

>   Nigeria — Education

The following *form* divisions are used in addition to subject or place headings:

Addresses and essays	Fiction
Atlases and maps	Folklore
Autobiography	Grammar
Bibliography	Guide books
Bio-bibliography	History
Biography	Indexes
Cartoons	Periodical indexes
Catalogues	Pictorial works
Collections	Poetry
Conversation and phrase books	Social life and customs
Conversion tables	Statistics
Diaries, letters	Study and teaching
Dictionaries	Study and teaching (Elementary)
Directories	Study and teaching (Secondary)
Drama	
Economic aspects	Theatre
Encyclopedias	
Examinations, questions	Yearbooks

Biographical and autobiographical titles in the subject index appear in the direct form under the name of the person treated. Titles in the African languages are classified in a simplified form as explained below. A French translation of the major subject headings is provided on page vii of Volume II.

Cross references

An extensive system of cross references is included in the subject thesaurus, using the following:

>   *See also* reference made to related form
>   *See* reference made from unused form

In general, *see also* references are made from the general subject to more specific parts of it, and not from the specific to the general. *See also* cross references under country headings guide the user to individual ethnic

Sciences sociales
Voyages et Guides

Il faut remarquer que les ouvrages généraux sur les questions africaines sont toujours classés au premier rang selon la matière, quelle qu'elle soit: par exemple, un livre intitulé *L'Education en Afrique aujourd'hui* apparaîtra à:

>   Education — Afrique
> et *non* à
>   Afrique — Education

alors qu'un titre sur le système d'éducation nigérian, par exemple, sera répertorié au premier rang selon le lieu, i.e.:

>   Nigéria — Education

Les divisions suivantes de *forme* sont employées en plus des vedettes-matière et de lieux:

Annuaires	Folklore
Atlas et cartes	Grammaire
Autobiographie	Guides
Bandes dessinées	Histoire
Bibliographie	Index
Bio-bibliographie	Index des périodiques
Biographie	Journal, lettres
Catalogues	Livres de conversation et de citations
Collections	
Dictionnaires	Ouvrages illustrés
Discours et essais	
Economie	Poésie
Encyclopédies	
Etude et Enseignement	Répertoire
Etude et Enseignement (élémentaire)	Statistiques
Etude et Enseignement (secondaire)	Tables de conversion Théâtre
Examens, questions	
Fiction	Vie sociale et coutumes

Les titres biographiques et autobiographiques dans l'index des matières apparaissent directement au nom de la personne traitée. Les titres en langues africaines sont classés sous une forme simplifiée comme il est indiqué ci-après. Une traduction en français des principales vedettes matière est donnée page vii de Volume II.

Les renvois

Un vaste système de renvois est inclus dans le thesaurus des matières, sous la forme:

>   *Voir aussi*, qui renvoie à une notion voisine et complémentaire
>   *Voir*, qui renvoie à la vedette matière effectivement utilisée

groups of each country. Users of *ABIP* must also look for additional cross references not only under general subject headings, but also under individual countries.

African literature and creative writing

This group appears subdivided by the following form headings: *Bibliography, Folklore, History and criticism, Collections, Fiction, Drama* and *Poetry*. Francophone African literature is listed separately under these headings, as *African literature in French*. There are several interpretations and definitions of just what is African literature and what makes an African writer. In *ABIP* the sections on African literature include not only Black African writing, but also fiction, drama, and poetry by white South African writers and what is generally termed as "South African English literature." In some cases works by North African authors writing in French have been classified, somewhat arbitrarily, as "African" literature, rather than Arabic literature, for which there is also a separate heading.

Children's books

These are listed under the general heading *Children's literature* and *Children's literature in French*, with the majority appearing under *Children's literature, African* or *Children's literature in French, African*. The rule has been to classify, as far as ascertainable, all those children's books as "African" whose stories include an African setting.

Educational books, textbooks, and school-books

Most texts and educational books are identified, as far as possible, by the form heading *Study and teaching (Secondary)* and *Study and teaching (Elementary)*. (It should be noted, however, that certain educational courses overlap in level between final year of elementary education and first-year secondary courses.) Entries under these two headings are strictly school-books, whereas those which appear with the form heading *Study and teaching* only may not be specifically school texts, or are of an advanced level or academic nature. Another form heading, *Examinations, questions* is also used frequently and identifies self-study or "cram" books, of which there are a great many.

Titles of school texts can be ambiguous; for example, a series of books entitled *Secondary economics for West Africa* may not be specifically *about* West Africa, but merely designed for West African Examinations Council syllabus requirements. A textbook of this nature would appear under the general *Economics—Study and teaching (Secondary)* heading, and not under *Economics–Africa, West, Study and teaching (Secondary)*.

En général, les renvois *voir aussi* vont du sujet général à des éléments plus spécifiques, et non du particulier au général. Les renvois *voir aussi* des vedettes pays guident l'usager vers les groupes ethniques individuels de chaque pays. Les lecteurs doivent aussi rechercher les renvois non seulement au niveau des vedettes matière générales, mais à celui de chaque pays.

La littérature africaine

Ce groupe est subdivisé de la façon suivante: *Bibliographie, Folklore, Histoire et critique, Collections, Romans, Théâtre* et *Poésie*. La littérature d'Afrique francophone est classée séparément selon ces vedettes à *Littérature africaine de langue française*. Il existe plusieurs interprétations et définitions de ce qu'est exactement la littérature africaine et de ce que fait un auteur africain. Nos sections sur la littérature africaine comprennent non seulement la production d'Afrique noire, mais aussi le roman, le théâtre et la poésie des Africains blancs d'Afrique du Sud, ce qui est généralement désigné par "Littérature d'Afrique du Sud de langue anglaise". Dans certains cas, les ouvrages des auteurs Nord-africains qui écrivent en français ont été classés, de façon quelque peu arbitraire, comme littérature "africaine" plutôt que comme littérature arabe pour laquelle il existe une vedette propre.

Livres d'enfants

Ceux-ci sont classés sous la vedette générale *Littérature pour la jeunesse* et *Littérature pour la jeunesse en langue française* dont la plus grande partie apparaît à *Littérature africaine pour la jeunesse* ou *Littérature africaine pour la jeunesse en langue française*. La règle a été de classer, autant que possible, tous ces livres d'enfants comme "africains" lorsque le cadre de leurs histoires est africain.

Livres d'enseignement, manuels et livres scolaires

La plupart des textes et des livres d'enseignement sont signalés, autant que possible, par la vedette *Etude et enseignement (secondaire)* et *Etude et enseignement (élémentaire)*. (On notera cependant que le niveau des cours de la dernière année d'enseignement élémentaire fait double emploi avec celui des cours de la première année du secondaire.) Seuls les livres scolaires ont des entrées sous ces deux vedettes. Ceux qui n'apparaissent qu'à la vedette *Etude et enseignement* ne sont pas toujours spécifiquement des textes scolaires ou sont alors d'un niveau avancé, universitaire. La vedette *Examens, questions* est aussi fréquemment employée; elle signale les mémentos, livres d'exercices qui existent en grand nombre.

African languages

Works (in English or French) about the various African languages — dictionaries, grammars, etc. — appear under the direct expression with form headings as appropriate, for example:

> Amharic language—Dictionaries

or

> Hausa language—Grammar

African Books in Print provides details of books in over seventy African language groups. African languages and African language classification are complex subjects and *ABIP* users may be interested in two new reference books on this topic: David Dalby, Director of the International African Institute in London, has recently published a provisional version of his *Language map of Africa* (London: International African Institute, 1977); and *African languages: a genetic and decimalized classification for bibliographic and general reference* by Derek Fivaz and Patricia E. Scott (Boston: G. K. Hall, 1977) meets a long-felt need for a comprehensive index to African languages.

African ethnic groups

Books dealing with aspects of the life, customs, etc., of specific African ethnic groups or "tribes" appear under the direct expression, with the words *African people* added in parentheses, plus form headings where applicable. For example:

> Yoruba (African people) — Social life and customs

or

> Luo (African people) — Law, customary

ABIP lists books on almost one hundred African ethnic groups.

Books in the African languages

Titles in the African languages (as opposed to books, in English or French, *about* African languages) are listed *selectively* only, with the emphasis on most recently published materials. Books in over eighty languages are listed, a total of about 2,500 titles, those most heavily represented being Swahili (Kiswahili), Yoruba, Hausa, Igbo, Zulu, Twi, Luganda, Shona, and Ndebele. In the alphabetical subject index, and within the author and title indexes, entries in any of the African languages are identified by their MARC language code. A key to MARC language codes appears on page l. Unlike materials in English or French, titles in the African languages are not classified by subject, except for a simplified form of sub-divisions as follows:

> General and Non-fiction (this includes literacy primers and adult education material)

Les titres des textes scolaires sont parfois ambigus, par exemple: une série de livres intitulés *Economie secondaire pour l'Afrique de l'Ouest* peut ne pas traiter précisément de l'Afrique de l'Ouest mais avoir pour objet l'énumération des sugets choisis par le Conseil des Examens pour l'Afrique de l'Ouest. Un manuel de cette sorte devrait apparaître sous la vedette générale *Economie — Etude et enseignement (secondaire)* et non à *Economie — Afrique, de l'Ouest — Etude et enseignement (secondaire)*.

Les langues africaines

Les ouvrages (en anglais ou en français) sur les différentes langues africaines — dictionnaires, grammaires, etc. — apparaissent aux vedettes appropriées, par exemple:

> Amharique (langue) — Dictionnaires

ou

> Hausa (langue) — Grammaire

Livres Africains Disponibles donne des renseignements sur des livres écrits en plus de soixante-dix groupes de langues africaines. Les langues africaines et leur classification sont des matières complexes aussi nos lecteurs seront-ils intéressés par deux nouveaux ouvrages de référence sur ce sujet: David Dalby, Directeur de l'Institut Africain International à Londres a récemment publié une version provisoire de sa *Language map of Africa* (Londres: International African Institute, 1977). D'autre part, *African languages: a genetic and decimalized classification for bibliographic and general reference* de Derek Fivaz et Patricia E. Scott (Boston: G. K. Hall, 1977) répond au besoin depuis longtemps ressenti d'un vaste index des langues africaines.

Groupes ethniques africains

Les livres ayant trait aux aspects de la vie, coutumes, etc., des groupes ethniques d'Afrique apparaissent sous l'expression directe, suivie des mots *peuple d'Afrique* entre parenthèses et de la vedette de forme si nécessaire. Par exemple:

> Yorouba (peuple d'Afrique) — Vie sociale et coutumes

ou

> Louo (peuple d'Afrique) — Droit coutumier

Nous recensons des livres de près de cent groupes ethniques d'Afrique.

Les livres en langues africaines

Les titres en langues africaines (par opposition aux livres, en anglais ou en français, sur les langues africaines) sont répertoriés de façon sélective, l'accent étant mis sur les ouvrages publiés récemment. Plus de quatre-vingts langues sont représentées, environ 2,500 titres. Le plus fort pourcentage revient au Swahili

School-books, Readers, Children's literature
Fiction, Drama, Poetry

It has not always been easy to distinguish clearly between the first two groups, but the sub-divisions should provide a basic guide.

Translations of titles in the African languages are provided [in square brackets] whenever possible. Occasionally publishers have failed to provide translations despite follow-up requests. It should also be noted that some publishers have tended to give *descriptive* rather than literal translations, since literal English translations are frequently difficult to provide.

For technical reasons, it has not been possible to print intonation marks and diacritic signs for titles in certain African languages.

Bibliographic data

A complete entry may include the following bibliographic information:

1 Author(s), Editor(s) or Compiler(s) with initials
2 Title and subtitle
3 Translated title
4 Translator note
5 Edition, if other than first
6 Series (given in parentheses, where available; mainly confined to *numbered* series)
7 Book, volume or part number, and total number of books, etc., in set (where known)
8 Number of pages
9 Details of illustrations, etc.
10 Binding (if other than paper)
11 Price
12 Publisher (in abbreviated form)
13 Year of publication
14 MARC country code for place of publication
15 MARC language code

The following are selected entries:

Amharic—General and Non-fiction
Assegé, W.G.[1]
    Mesfinu Merkonya. [Story of the young son of Emperor Tewodros who died in England.][3] 162pp. ill. photo.[9] Eth.$2.00 Bookshop Supply Org 1973 ET AMH
Beyene, T.
    Lisan. [Tongue] 208pp.[8] Eth.$10.00 Bible Churchmen's Miss Soc 1972 ET AMH
Last, G. Pankhurst, R.
    Ye Ethiopa Tank Besil. [A history of Ethiopia in pictures] tr. fr. eng. S. Muluneh[4] 56pp. ill. Eth.$2.75 OUP-Addis 1972 ET AMH[15]

Anatomy
Tobias, P.V. Arnold, M.
    Man's anatomy: a study in dissection.[2] 2nd ed.[5] 3 v.[7] ill. cl. R20.00 Witwatersrand UP 1967 SA

(Kiswahili), Yorouba, Hausa, Ibo, Zoulou, Twi, Louganda, Shona et au Ndebele. Dans l'index alphabétique des matières et à l'intérieur de l'index des auteurs et des titres, les entrées dans n'importe quelle langue africaine sont identifiées par leur code MARC de langue. Une liste des codes MARC des langues est donné page 1. Contrairement aux ouvrages en anglais ou en français, les titres dans les langues africaines ne sont pas classés par sujet, sauf pour les formes simplifiées de subdivision. Par example:

Ouvrages généraux (ceci inclut les premiers éléments de littérature et les ouvrages d'enseignement pour adultes)
Livres scolaires, Manuels, Littérature pour la jeunesse
Roman, Théâtre, Poésie

Il n'a pas été toujours facile de distinguer clairement les deux premiers groupes, mais les subdivisions devraient servir de base.

Les traductions en anglais des titres en langues africaines sont fournies [entre crochets] chaque fois que cela est possible. Les éditeurs n'ont pas toujours fourni les traductions. Il faut aussi noter que certains éditeurs ont tendance à donner une traduction plus descriptive que littérale, car il est souvent difficile de traduire en anglais.

Pour des raisons techniques, il n'a pas été possible d'imprimer les marques d'intonation et les signes diacritiques pour les titres publiés dans certaines langues africaines.

Les données bibliographiques

Une entrée complète peut comprendre les renseignements bibliographiques suivants:

1 Auteur(s), Editeur(s) ou Compilateur(s) avec initiales
2 Titre et sous-titre
3 Titre traduit en anglais
4 Nom du traducteur
5 Quantième d'édition (si elle est différente de la première)
6 Collection (donnée entre parenthèses. Ceci est limité surtout aux collections *numérotées*)
7 Numéro de tome ou de chapitre et nombre total de volumes, etc.
8 Nombre de pages
9 Illustrations, etc.
10 Reliure (pour les ouvrages non brochés)
11 Prix
12 Editeur (en abrégé)
13 Année d'édition
14 Code MARC du pays pour le lieu d'édition
15 Code MARC de la langue

Angas language—Study and teaching
Burquest, D.A.
   A preliminary study of Angas phonology. 52pp. N1.50
   ($2.60/£1.00) (Studies in Nigerian languages, 1)[6] Inst
   Ling-ABU 1971 NR

Animals—Africa, Southern
Miller, W.T.
   The flesh-eaters: a guide to the carnivorous animals in
   Southern Africa. 100pp. photos. maps. hd.[10] R7.50[11]
   Purnell[12] 1972[13] SA[14]

All bibliographic data and prices given are subject to change and availability cannot be guaranteed. All books are paperbound (soft-cover) unless otherwise indicated. Prices are given in the country's own currency, and a key to abbreviations is provided on page xlviii along with approximate US dollar and British sterling equivalents. Overseas prices, where established, are given in parentheses. A key to MARC language and country codes appears on pages l to li. Details of deluxe editions are not included, and listings are confined to standard editions only for titles which are also published in special limited editions.

Whilst every effort has been made to give full information for each title, bibliographic data are unfortunately incomplete for a small proportion of entries, due to publishers' failure to supply full bibliographic details in accordance with our requirements.

Directory of publishers

The majority of publishers' names appear in abbreviated form and a directory of publishers represented, with full names and addresses and a key to the abbreviations used, appears on page liii. More information about publishers, the nature of their publishing programmes, executive personnel, areas of specialization, etc., may also be found in *The African Book World and Press: a directory/Répertoire du Livre et de la Presse en Afrique*, (Oxford: Hans Zell Publishers Ltd., 1977; US edition: Gale Research Company, Detroit; French edition: France Expansion, Paris; German edition: Verlag Dokumentation, Munich). This directory also provides extensive information about libraries, bookshops, magazines and periodicals, and major newspapers throughout Africa. Its listings of the retail book trade indicate, amongst other information, whether each bookseller listed is willing to handle export orders and provide standing order services for locally published material.

A small number of entries covers books published privately by the authors. The ordering addresses for these do not appear in the directory of publishers, but are given as part of the bibliographic data provided with the listing.

voici quelques entrées types:

Amharic—General and Non-fiction
Assegé, W.G.[1]
   Mesfinu Merkonya. [Story of the young son of Emperor
   Tewodros who died in England.][3] 1962pp. ill. photo.[9]
   Eth.$2.00 Bookshop Supply Org 1973 ET AMH
Beyene, T.
   Lisan. [Tongue] 208pp.[8] Eth.$10.00 Bible Churchmen's
   Miss Soc 1972 ET AMH
Last, G. Pankhurst, R.
   Ye Ethiopia Tank Besil. [A history of Ethiopia in pictures]
   tr. fr. eng. S. Muluneh[4] 56pp. ill. Eth.$2.75 OUP-Addis
   1972 ET AMH[15]
Anatomy
Tobias, P.V. Arnold, M.
   Man's anatomy: a study in dissection.[2] 2nd ed.[5] 3 v.[7] ill.
   cl. R20.00 Witwatersrand UP 1967 SA
Angas language—Study and teaching
Burquest, D.A.
   A preliminary study of Angas phonology. 52pp. N1.50
   ($2.60/£1.00) (Studies in Nigerian languages, 1)[6] Inst
   Ling-ABU 1971 NR
Animals—Africa, Southern
Miller, W.T.
   The flesh-eaters: a guide to the carnivorous animals in
   Southern Africa. 100pp. photos. maps. hd.[10] R7.50[11]
   Purnell[12] 1972[13] SA[14]

Toutes les données bibliographiques et les prix sont sujets à modifications et la disponibilité ne peut pas être garantie. Tous les livres sont brochés sauf indication contraire. Les prix sont donnés dans la monnaie du pays et une liste des abréviations est fournie page xlviii avec les équivalents en Dollar U.S. et Livre Sterling britannique. Lorsque des prix étrangers sont établis, ils sont indiqués entre parenthèses. Une liste des codes MARC de langue et de pays est donnée pages l à li. Les renseignements sur les éditions de luxe ne sont pas inclus. Pour les livres qui sont egalement publiés dans des éditions spéciales et limitées, les notices couvrent seulement les éditions normales.

Bien que nous ayons fait tous nos efforts pour fournir des renseignements complets pour chaque titre, les données bibliographiques sont malheureusement incomplètes pour un petit nombre d'entrées; la responsabilité en incombe aux éditeurs qui ne nous ont pas transmis les informations bibliographiques voulues.

Répertoire des éditeurs

La majorité des noms d'éditeurs sont abrégés. Un répertoire des éditeurs représentés avec noms et adresses, et un guide des abréviations sont donnés page liii. De plus amples informations sur les éditeurs, la nature de leurs programmes d'édition, le personnel, les zones de spécialisation, etc. peuvent être trouvées dans *The African Book World and Press: a Directory/Répertoire du Livre et de la Presse en Afrique*, (Oxford: Hans Zell

Supplementary and updating service

A supplementary and updating service for *ABIP* is featured in *African Book Publishing Record*, a quarterly trade journal and bibliography which commenced publication in January 1975. This journal provides extensive coverage of new and forthcoming African publications in English and French and significant titles in the African languages. In addition to its bibliographic coverage, *ABPR* also serves as a medium of communication between the African book professions and includes news, reports, and articles about African book trade activities and developments; other features are reviews of new books and periodicals, and a "Preview" section covering forthcoming African publications. Annual subscription rates are £24/$50 by surface mail, or £30/$62 by airmail. More details and sample copies are available from: *African Book Publishing Record*, Hans Zell Publishers Ltd., P.O. Box 56, Oxford OX1 3EL, England.

Publishers Ltd., 1977; édition US: Gale Research Company, Detroit; édition française: France Expansion, Paris; édition allemande: Verlag Dokumentation, München). Ce répertoire donne aussi de nombreux renseignements sur les bibliothèques, librairies, magazines, périodiques et les principaux journaux d'Afrique. Ses listes consacrées au commerce de détail du livre signalent, entre autres informations, les libraires recenées qui acceptent de passer des commandes d'exportation et de fournir les ouvrages édité localement.

Un petit nombre d'entrées couvre les livres publiés à compte d'auteurs. Les adresses de commande pour ceux-ci n'apparaissent pas dans le répertoire des éditeurs, mais elles sont données avec les renseignements bibliographiques.

Annexes et mise à jour

Les annexes et la mise à jour de *Livres Africains Disponibles* sont assurées par *African Book Publishing Record* (*ABPR*), revue bibliographique et professionnelle trimestrielle dont la publication a commencé en janvier 1975. Cette revue fournit un vaste panorama des publications africaines nouvelles et à paraître en anglais et en français ainsi que les nouveaux titres importants dans les langues africaines. Outre son panorama bibliographique, *ABPR* sert aussi de moyen de communication entre les professionnels africains des métiers du livre et présente des rapports et des articles sur l'activité editoriale et commerciale en Afrique. Il comporte aussi des revues de livres et de périodiques nouveaux, et une section consacrée aux publications africaines à paraître. Les tarifs d'abonnement annuel sont de £24/$50 (£30/$62 par avion). Pour obtenir de plus amples détails et un specimen, adressez vous à: *African Book Publishing Record*, Hans Zell Publishers Ltd., P.O. Box 56, Oxford OX1 3EL, Angleterre.

Key to currency abbreviations

country	currency	symbols	approximate £ Sterling value	approximate US dollar value
Algeria	Algerian dinar	DA	0.13	0.25
Benin	CFA franc	CFA	0.21	0.42 (CFA 100)
Botswana	Pula	P	0.62	1.15
Burundi	Burundi france	BF	0.06	0.12 (BF 10)
Cameroun	CFA franc	CFA	0.21	0.42 (CFA 100)
Central African Empire	CFA franc	CFA	0.21	0.42 (CFA 100)
Chad	CFA franc	CFA	0.21	0.42 (CFA 100)
Congo, People's Republic	CFA franc	CFA	0.21	0.42 (CFA 100)
Egypt	Egyptian pound	£E	1.36	2.56
Ethiopia	Birr	B	0.25	0.48
Gabon	CFA franc	CFA	0.21	0.42 (CFA 100)
Gambia	Dalasi	Dal	0.25	0.46
Ghana	Cedi	C & pes.	0.46	0.87
Guinea	Syli	Sy	0.24	0.48 (Sy 10)
Ivory Coast	CFA franc	CFA	0.21	0.42 (CFA 100)
Kenya	Kenya shilling	K.shs.	0.07	0.12
Lesotho	South African rand	R	0.59	1.15
Liberia	U.S. dollar	S & c.	0.52	1.00
Libya	Libyan dinar	DL	1.75	3.75
Madagascar	Malagasy franc	FMG	0.21	0.42 (FMG 100)
Malawi	Kwacha	K & t.	0.60	1.07
Mali	Mali franc	MF	0.11	0.21 (FM 100)
Mauritania	Ugiya	U	0.11	0.22 (U 10)
Mauritius	Rupee	Rs.	0.08	0.15
Morocco	Moroccan dirham	Dir	0.12	0.26
Namibia (South West Africa)	South African rand	R	0.59	1.15
Niger	CFA franc	CFA	0.21	0.42 (CFA 100)
Nigeria	Naira	N & k.	0.79	1.56
Réunion	French franc	FF	0.11	0.21
Rhodesia (Zimbabwe)	Rhodesian dollar	R$	0.78	1.62
Rwanda	Rwanda franc	RF	0.06	0.10 (RF 10)
Senegal	CFA franc	CFA	0.21	0.42 (CFA 100)
Seychelles	Rupee (Seychelles)	Rs.	0.07	0.14

Liste des abréviations de devises

Pays	Devise	Symboles	Valeur approximative £ Sterling	Valeur approximative Dollar EU.
Afrique du Sud	Rand sud africain	R & C	0.59	1.15
Algérie	Dinar algérien	DA	0.13	0.25
Bénin	Franc CFA	CFA	0.21	0.42 (CFA 100)
Botswana	Pula	P	0.62	1.15
Burundi	Burundi france	BF	0.06	0.12 (BF 10)
Cameroun	Franc CFA	CFA	0.21	0.42 (CFA 100)
Congo (République populaire)	Franc CFA	CFA	0.21	0.42 (CFA 100)
Côte d'Ivoire	Franc CFA	CFA	0.21	0.42 (CFA 100)
Egypte	Livre égyptienne	£E	1.36	2.56
Empire Centre-africain	Franc CFA	CFA	0.21	0.42 (CFA 100)
Ethiopie	Birr	B	0.25	0.48
Gabon	Franc CFA	CFA	0.21	0.42 (CFA 100)
Gambie	Dalasi	Dal	0.25	0.46
Ghana	Cedi	C & Pes.	0.46	0.87
Guinée	Syli	Sy	0.24	0.48 (Sy 10)
Haute-Volta	Franc CFA	CFA	0.21	0.42 (CFA 100)
Kenya	Shilling Kenya	K. shs.	0.07	0.12
Lesotho	Rand sud africain	R	0.59	1.15
Libéria	Dollar EU	S & c.	0.52	1.00
Libye	Dinar libyen	DL	1.75	3.37
Madagascar	Franc malgache	FMG	0.21	0.42 (FMG 100)
Malawi	Kwacha	K & t.	0.60	1.07
Mali	Franc Mali	MF	0.11	0.21 (FM 100)
Mauritanie	Ugiya	U	0.11	0.22 (U 10)
Maurice	Roupie	Rs.	0.08	0.15
Maroc	Dirham marocain	Dir	0.12	0.26
Namibie (Afrique du Sud-Ouest)	Rand sud africain	R	0.59	1.15
Niger	Franc CFA	CFA	0.21	0.42 (CFA 100)
Nigéria	Naira	N & k.	0.79	1.56
Ouganda	Shilling ougandais	U. shs.	0.07	0.12
Réunion	Franc CFA	CFA	0.11	0.21
Rhodésie (Zimbabwe)	Dollar rhodésien	R$	0.78	1.62
Rwanda	Franc rwanda	RF	0.06	0.10 (RF 10)
Sénégal	Franc CFA	CFA	0.21	0.42 (CFA 100)
Seychelles	Roupie (Seychelles)	Rs.	0.07	0.14
Sierra Leone	Leone	Le & c.	0.50	0.93

country	currency	symbols	approximate £ Sterling value	approximate US dollar value
Sierra Leone	Leone	Le & c.	0.50	0.93
Somalia Republic	Somali shilling	Sm.shs.	0.08	0.15
South Africa	South African rand	R & c.	0.59	1.15
Sudan	Sudanese pound	£S & pt.	1.48	2.87
Swaziland	Lilangeni	L & c.	0.60	1.15
Tanzania	Tanzania shilling	T.shs.	0.06	0.12
Togo	CFA franc	CFA	0.21	0.42 (CFA 100)
Tunisia	Dinar	D	1.30	2.51
Uganda	Uganda shilling	U.shs.	0.07	0.12
Upper Volta	CFA franc	CFA	0.21	0.42 (CFA 100)
Zaire Republic	Zaire	Z & k.	0.63	1.15
Zambia	Kwacha	K & n.	0.69	1.56

Pays	Devise	Symboles	Valeur approximative £ Sterling	Dollar EU
Somalie (République)	Shilling somalien	Sm.Shs.	0.08	0.15
Soudan	Livre soudanaise	£S & pt.	1.48	2.87
Swaziland	Lilangeni	L & c.	0.60	1.15
Tanzanie	Shilling tanzanien	T. Shs.	0.06	0.12
Tchad	Franc CFA	CFA	0.21	0.42 (CFA 100)
Togo	Franc CFA	CFA	0.21	0.42 (CFA 100)
Tunisie	Dinar	D	1.30	0.64
Zaïre (République)	Zaïre	Z & k.	0.63	1.15
Zambie	Kwacha	K & n.	0.69	1.56

Key to MARC Language Codes
(other than English)

Liste des codes MARC de langues
(autres que l'anglais)

MARC code	Language		MARC code	Language
ABU	Abua		LIN	Lingala
ACH	Acholi		LOZ	Lozi
AKW	Akwapim		LGB	Lugbara
AMH	Amharic		LUG	Luganda
ASA	Asante		LUL	Lulogooli
			LUN	Lunda
BAM	Bamileke		LUO	Luo
BAS	Basaa		LUV	Luvale
BEM	Bemba		LUY	Luyia
BIN	Bini			
			MAS	Maasai
CEW	Cewa		MBU	Mbukushu
CHC	Chichewa		MER	Meru
CHM	Chitumbuka		MLA	Malagasy
			MUL	Multilingual works
DAG	Dangme			
DUA	Duala		NAM	Nama
DYU	Dyula		NDE	Ndebele
			NDO	Ndonga
EDO	Edo		NEM	Membe
EFI	Efik		NIC	Sesotho
EKP	Ekpeye		NYA	Nyanja
ENN	Engenni		NYO	Nyero
EPI	Epie		NZE	Nzema
EWE	Ewe			
EWO	Ewondo		OGB	Ogbia
			OGH	Oghah
FAN	Fante		OKR	Okrika
FRE	French			
			PEN	Pende
GAA	Ga		POK	Pokot
HAU	Hausa		RNY	Runyankore
HER	Herero		RUY	Runyoro
IBA	Ibani		SHO	Shona
IDO	Ido		SIS	Siswati
IGB	Igbo (Ibo)		SOS	Sotho/Southern Sotho
IJO	Ijo		SWA	Swahili
IKW	Ikwerre			
			TES	Teso
KAB	Kalabari		TIR	Tigrinya
KAE	Kasem		TON	Tonga
KAI	Karinnoyong		TSW	Tswana
KAL	Kalenjiu		TUM	Tumbuka
KAM	Kamba		TWI	Twi
KAO	Kaonde			
KHA	Khana		XHO	Xhosa
KIK	Kikuyu			
KIO	Kikongo		YOR	Yoruba
KIT	Kikuba			
KWA	Kwangali		ZUL	Zulu
KWY	Kwanyama			

Code MARC	Langue		Code MARC	Langue
ABU	Abouro		LIN	Lingala
ACH	Acholi		LOZ	Lozi
AKW	Akwapim		LGB	Lugbara
AMH	Amharique		LUG	Luganda
ASA	Asante		LUL	Lulogooli
			LUN	Lunda
BAM	Bamileke		LUO	Luo
BAS	Basaa		LUV	Louvalé
BEM	Bemba		LUY	Luyia
BIN	Bini			
			MAS	Maasai
CEW	Cewa		MBU	Mbukushu
CHC	Chichewa		MER	Meru
CHM	Chitumbuka		MLA	Malgache
			MUL	Ouvrages multilingues
DAG	Dangme			
DUA	Douala		NAM	Nama
DYU	Dioula		NDE	Ndebele
			NDO	Ndonga
EDO	Edo		NEM	Nembe
EFI	Efik		NIC	Sesotho
EKP	Ekpeye		NYA	Nyanja
ENN	Engenni		NYO	Nyero
EPI	Epié		NZE	Nzema
EWE	Ewe			
EWO	Ewondo		OGB	Ogbia
			OGH	Oghah
FAN	Fanti		OKR	Okrika
FRE	Français			
			PEN	Pende
GAA	Ga		POK	Pokot
HAU	Hausa		RNY	Runyankore
HER	Herero		RUY	Runyoro
IBA	Ibani		SHO	Shona
IDO	Ido		SIS	Siswati
IGB	Igbo (Ibo)		SOS	Sotho/Sotho du Sud
IJO	Ijo		SWA	Swahili
IKW	Ikwerré			
			TES	Teso
KAB	Kalabari		TIR	Tigrinya
KAE	Kasem		TON	Tonga
KAI	Karinnoyong		TSW	Tswana
KAL	Kalenjiu		TUM	Tumbuka
KAM	Kamba		TWI	Twi
KAO	Kaondo			
KHA	Khana		XHO	Xhosa
KIK	Kikuyu			
KIO	Kikongo		YOR	Yoruba
KIT	Kikuba			
KWA	Kwangali		ZUL	Zoulou
KWY	Kwanyama			

Key to MARC Country Codes

Liste des codes MARC de pays

MARC code	country	Code MARC	Pays
AE	Algeria	AE	Algérie
DM	Benin	DM	Bénin
BS	Botswana	BS	Botswana
BD	Burundi	BD	Burundi
CM	Cameroun	CM	Cameroun
CX	Central African Empire	CX	Empire centrafricain
CD	Chad	CD	Tchad
CF	Congo (People's Republic)	CF	Congo (République populaire)
UA	Egypt	UA	Egypte
ET	Ethiopia	ET	Ethiopie
GO	Gabon	GO	Gabon
GM	Gambia	GM	Gambie
GH	Ghana	GH	Ghana
GV	Guinea	GV	Guinée
IV	Ivory Coast	IV	Côte d'Ivoire
KE	Kenya	KE	Kenya
LO	Lesotho	LO	Lesotho
LB	Liberia	LB	Libéria
LY	Libya	LY	Libye
MG	Madagascar	MG	Madagascar
MW	Malawi	MW	Malawi
ML	Mali	ML	Mali
MU	Mauritania	MU	Mauritanie
MF	Mauritius	MF	Maurice
MR	Morocco	MR	Maroc
SX	Namibia (South West Africa)	SX	Namibie
NG	Niger	NG	Niger
NR	Nigeria	NR	Nigéria
RH	Rhodesia (Zimbabwe)	RH	Rhodésie (Zimbabwé)
RW	Rwanda	RW	Rwanda
SG	Senegal	SG	Sénégal
SE	Seychelles	SE	Seychelles
SL	Sierra Leone	SL	Sierra Leone
SO	Somali Republic	SO	Somalie (République)
SA	South Africa	SA	Afrique du Sud
SJ	Sudan	SJ	Soudan
SQ	Swaziland	SQ	Swaziland
TZ	Tanzania	TZ	Tanzanie
TG	Togo	TG	Togo
TI	Tunisia	TI	Tunisie
UG	Uganda	UG	Ouganda
UV	Upper Volta	UV	Haute-Volta
ZR	Zaire Republic	ZR	Zaïre (République)
ZA	Zambia	ZA	Zambie

Abbreviations Used   Abréviations

bk., bks.	book/books	bk., bks.	livre/livres
cl.	cloth bound	cl.	relié toile
comp., comps.	compiler/compilers	comp., comps.	compilateur/compilateurs
Dept.	Department	Dept.	Département, service
D. fl.	Dutch florins (guilders)	D.fl.	Florins hollandais (guilders)
distr.	distributor	distr.	distributeur
DM	Deutsche Mark	DM	Deutsche Mark
ed., eds.	editor/edited/edition/editors	ed., eds.	éditeur/édité/édition/éditeurs
enl.	enlarged	enl.	augmenté
ex. only	available on exchange only	ex. only	disponible en échange seulement
F	French francs	F	Francs français
Fac.	Faculty	Fac.	Faculté
FB	Belgian francs	FB	Francs belges
hd.	hardbound	hd.	cartonné ou relié toile
ill., col. ill	illustrations/colour illustrations	ill., col. ill.	illustrations/illustrations en couleur
incl.	including/inclusive	incl.	inclus
Inst.	Institute	Inst.	Institut
lec.	lecture	lec.	conférence
maps, fold. maps	maps/folding maps	maps, fold. maps	cartes/cartes pliantes
mimeo.	mimeographed (duplicated)	mimeo.	miméographié
occas.	occasional	occas.	occasionnel
pp.	pages	pp.	pages
p.	(British) pence (given in overseas prices)	p.	pence britanniques (pour les prix étrangers)
pap.	paperbound (limp, softbound)	pap.	broché (cartonnage souple)
paps.	papers	paps.	papiers
photos.	photographs	photos.	photographies
pl.	plates	pl.	planches
pt., pts.	part/parts	pt., pts;	partie/parties
publ., pubs.	publication/publications	publ., pubs.	publication/publications
rev.	revised	rev.	revu
tr.	translator/translated	tr.	traducteur/traduit
var.	various (paging)	var.	variable (pagination)
v., vol., vols.	volume/volumes	v., vol., vols.	volume/volumes
[?]	queried information	[?]	renseignements demandés
Africa only; No US; etc.	indicates marketing restrictions	Africa only; No US; etc.	Afrique seulement; etc. indique les restrictions de vente

Multi-volume or multi-part entries are listed as follows:

Les éléments comprenant plusieurs volumes ou parties sont indiqués comme suit:

2,6 bks.	indicates that this is book 2 of a publication consisting of six books (applies largely for school-books)	2,6 bks.	il s'agit du second tome d'une publication comprenant 6 tomes (s'applique surtout aux livres scolaires)
1,4v.	indicates that this is volume 1 of a four-volume work.	1,4v.	désigne le volume 1 d'un ouvrage de 4 volumes.

Directory of Publishers and their Abbreviations

The full names and addresses of publishers whose titles are included in the second edition of *ABIP* are provided below. Publishers' abbreviations are indicated in **bold**. Names of distributors in the United States, Great Britain or in Europe are given in parentheses (other than for multi-national firms).

A dagger symbol † indicates a publisher who failed to return the computer print-out edit and proof lists despite reminders. It must follow that the availability status of the titles from these publishers and institutions is uncertain, and that information provided may be neither entirely up to date nor complete.

Répertoire des éditeurs et leurs abréviations

On trouvera ci-dessous les noms et adresses des éditeurs dont les ouvrages sont recensés dans cette édition. Les abréviations utilisées sont indiquées en caractère **gras**. Les noms des distributeurs aux Etats-Unis, en Grande-Bretagne et en Europe apparaissent entre parenthèses (sauf pour les sociétés multinationales).

Le nom des éditeurs qui ne nous ont pas renvoyé les listes dressées par de notre ordinateur et les épreuves est suivi d'une croix(†). Dans ce cas, la disponibilité de leurs titres n'est pas certaine et les notices correspondantes ne sont pas forcément exactes, à notre grand regret.

AAU
Association of African Universities
PO Box 5744
Accra North
Ghana

†ABU Bkshop
Ahmadu Bello University Bookshop
 Ltd
Zaria
Kaduna State
Nigeria

†ABU Lib
Ahmadu Bello University Library
Zaria
Kaduna State
Nigeria

Addis Ababa Univ. Lib
Addis Ababa University Library
PO Box 1176
Addis Ababa
Ethiopia

Addis Ababa UP
Addis Ababa University Press
PO Box 1176
Addis Ababa
Ethiopia

Adebara
Adebara Publishing House
PO Box 1970
Ibadan
Oyo State
Nigeria

†Adult Educ Centre
Adult Education Centre
37/39 Fifth Street
PO Box 7176
Kampala
Uganda

Adult Educ Gen Ext Ser
Adult Education and General
 Extension Services Unit
Ahmadu Bello University
Zaria
Nigeria

Advance
Advance Publishing Co. Ltd.
PO Box 2317
Accra New Town
Ghana

Aegis
Aegis Publishing House
c/o Ravan Press
PO Box 31134
Braamfontein
2017 South Africa

AFAA
Association of Faculties of
 Agriculture in Africa
University of Nairobi
PO Box 30197
Kenya

Afram
Afram Publications (Ghana) Ltd.
Ring Road East
PO Box M18
Accra
Ghana

Africa Bibliographic Centre
Africa Bibliographic Centre
PO Box 35131
Dar es Salaam
Tanzania

African Med Res Found
African Medical and Research
 Foundation
PO Box 30125
Nairobi
Kenya

†African Res Publ. Co.
African Resources Publishing Co.
PMB 5398
Ibadan
Oyo State
Nigeria

African Studies Inst — Wit
African Studies Institute
University of the Witwatersrand
1 Jan Smuts Avenue
Johannesburg
2001 South Africa

African Universities Press *see* **Pilgrim**

Ahmadu Bello UP
Ahmadu Bello University Press
PMB 1094
Zaria
Kaduna State
Nigeria

Al-Arab Bookshop
Al Arab Publishing House
28 Sharia Kamel Sidky
Cairo
Egypt
United Arab Republic

†Alliance
Alliance West African Publishers and
   Co.
Orindingbin Estate
New Aketan Layout
PMB 1039
Oyo
Oyo State
Nigeria

Am Univ
American University in Cairo Press
113 Sharia Kasr El Aini
Cairo
Egypt
United Arab Republic

Africa Book Serv
Africa Book Service (EA) Ltd
PO Box 45245
Nairobi
Kenya

Africa Christian
Africa Christian Press
PO Box 30
Achimota
Ghana

(*distributed outside Ghana by/distribué hors du
Ghana par: Africa Christian Press, 20 Nedford
Road, South Woodford, London E18,
England*)

Africa Inland Church
Africa Inland Church Literature
   Department
PO Box 125
Mwanza
Tanzania

Africa Inst
Africa Institute of South Africa
PO Box 630
Pretoria
0001 South Africa

Africana Book Soc
Africana Book Society Ltd.
PO Box 1071
Johannesburg
2000 South Africa

Africana Educ
Africana Educational Publishers
   (Nigeria) Ltd.
PO Box 83
Aba
Imo State
Nigeria

African Book Co
African Book Co. Ltd.
Akalam House
PO Box 7
Nsukka
Anambra State
Nigeria

†Africani
Africani Agency
98 Emir's Road
PO Box 38
Ilorin
Ondo State
Nigeria

†Aowa
Aowa Press and Publications
PO Box 3090
Ibadan
Oyo State
Nigeria

Aromolaran
Aromolaran Publishers
PO Box 1800
Ibadan
Oyo State
Nigeria

Assoc Publ
Associated Publishers (Nig)
PO Box 1268
Ibadan
Oyo State
Nigeria

†Balkema
A. A. Balkema Publishers
93 Keerom Street
PO Box 3117
Cape Town
8000 South Africa

(*distributed outside South Africa by/distribué
hors de l'Afrique du Sud par: A. A. Balkema,
Postbus 1675, Rotterdam, Netherlands*)

Bateleur
Bateleur Press
c/o Ravan Press
PO Box 31134
Braamfontein
2017 South Africa

(*distributed outside Southern Africa
by/distribué hors de l'Afrique australe par:
Hans Zell Publishers Ltd., PO Box 56, Oxford
OX1 3EL, England*)

Benin Univ
Benin University Library
PMB 1191
Benin City
Bendel State
Nigeria

BERPS
Bureau d'Etudes et de Recherches
   pour la Promotion de la Santé
Kangu-Mayombe
Zaïre Republic

†Bible Churchmen Miss Soc
Bookshop Supply Org.
The Bible Churchmen's Mission
   Society
PO Box 864
Asmara
Eritrea
Ethiopia

Biblio Nat — Iv
Bibliothèque Nationale
BP V180
Abidjan
Ivory Coast

Bibl Nat — Alg
Bibliothèque Nationale
Avenue du Docteur Fanon
Alger
Algeria

BLAC
BLAC Publishing House
PO Box 17
Athlone
Cape
South Africa

Black Academy
Black Academy Press
PO Box 255
Owerri
Imo State
Nigeria

Black Comm Prog
Black Community Programmes Ltd.
86 Beatrice Street
Durban
4001 South Africa

Books for Africa
Books for Africa (Kenya) Ltd.
PO Box 30797
Queensway House
York Street
Nairobi
Kenya

Bookshop Supply Org *see* **Bible Churchmen Miss Soc**

Books of Rhodesia
Books of Rhodesia Co (Pvt.)
137a Rhodes Street
PO Box 1994
Bulawayo
Rhodesia

†**Bosede**
Bosede Business Foundation
12 Broad Street
Akure
Oyo State
Nigeria

Botanical Res Inst
Botanical Research Institute
PB X101
Pretoria
0001 South Africa

Botswana Nat Lib Serv
Botswana National Library Service
PB 0036
Gaborone
Botswana

Brenthurst
Brenthurst Press
PO Box 241
Johannesburg
2000 South Africa

Brit Inst EA
British Institute in East Africa
PO Box 30710
Nairobi
Kenya

Bulpin
T.V. Bulpin
1004 Cape of Good Hope
117 George Street
PO Box 1516
Cape Town
8000 South Africa

Bur Ghana Lang
Bureau of Ghana Languages
PO Box 1851
Accra
Ghana

Bur Market Res
Bureau of Market Research
University of South Africa
Pretoria
0001 South Africa

Bur Res Assess — Tanz
Bureau of Research Assessment and
Land Use Planning
University of Dar es Salaam
PO Box 35097
Tanzania

Bur Stat — Mas
Bureau of Statistics
PO Box 455
Maseru
Lesotho

Butterworth
Butterworth and Co (SA) (Pty.)
Ltd.
152/4 Gale Street
PO Box 792
Durban
4000 South Africa

†**CAFRAD**
Centre Africain de Formation et de
   Recherche Administrative pour le
   Développement
BP 310
Tangier
Morocco

Cape Coast UP
Cape Coast University Bookshop
Private Mail Bag
University Post Office
Cape Coast
Ghana

Caritas
Editions Rwandaises
BP 124
Kigali
Rwanda

†**CEDA**
Centre d'Edition et de Diffusion
   Africaines
BP 4541
Abidjan
Ivory Coast

CEDI
Centre Protestant d'Editions et de
   Diffusion
BP 11398
Kinshasa I
Zaïre Republic

CEEBA
Centre d'Etudes Ethnologiques
   Branche Anthropos
BP 19
Bandundu
Zaïre Republic

*(distributed outside Zaïre by/distribué hors du
Zaïre par: Steyler Verlag, Arnold Janssen Str.
20–22, 5205 St. Augustin 1, Fed. Rep. of
Germany)*

CELRIA
Centre d'Etudes des Littératures
   Africaines
BP 1501
Lubumbashi
Zaïre Republic

CELTA
Centre de Linguistique Théorique
et Appliquée
BP 1607
Lubumbashi
Zaïre Republic

CELTHO
Centre d'Etudes Linguistique que et
Historique par Tradition Orale
BP 78
Niamey
Niger

Central Africa Hist Assoc
The Central Africa Historical
Association
PMB 167
Salisbury
Rhodesia

Central Tanganyika
Central Tanganyika Press
PO Box 15
Dodoma
Tanzania

Centre Africain Litt
Centre Africaine de Littérature pour
l'Afrique francophone
c/o CEDI
BP 11398
Kinshasa I
Zaïre Republic

Centre Cont Educ — Zam
Centre for Continuing Education
University of Zambia
PO Box 2379
Lusaka
Zambia

Centre Cult Coll Libermann
Centre Culturel du Collège
Libermann
BP 5351
Douala-Akwa
Cameroun

Centre Dev Stud
Centre for Development Studies
University of Cape Coast
Cape Coast

Centre Doc Agricole
Centre de Documentation Agricole
BP 7537
Kinshasa I
Zaire Republic

Centre Univ Réunion
Centre Universitaire de la Réunion
Centre d'Etudes Administratives
12 Avenue de la Victoire
97489 Saint-Denis
Réunion

CEPAS
Centre d'Etudes pour l'Action Sociale
BP 3096
Kinshasa Gombe
Zaïre Republic

Challenge
Challenge Publications
PMB 2010
Jos
Plateau State
Nigeria

Chamber Comm — Eth
Ethiopian Chamber of Commerce
POB 517
Addis Ababa
Ethiopia

Chamber Comm — Mal
Chamber of Commerce and
Industry of Malawi
PO Box 258
Blantyre
Malawi

Christ Lit Assoc — Mal
Christian Literature Association in
Malawi
PO Box 503
Blantyre
Malawi

†Christ Lit Dev
Christian Literature Development
Project
PO Box 2248
Addis Ababa
Ethiopia

†Church World
Church World Service
BP 624
Niamey
Niger

CLAD
Centre de Linguistique Appliquée
Université de Dakar
Fann Parc
Daka
Senegal

†CLE
Editions CLE
BP 1501
Yaoundé
Cameroun

(*distributed in France by/distribué en France
par: Librairie Protestante 140 Bd. Saint
Germain, Paris 75006; distributed in Canada by
distribué au Canada par Editions Naaman, CP
733, Sherbrooke, Québec*)

CODESRIA
CODESRIA
BP 3304
Dakar
Senegal

†Cole & Yancy
Cole and Yancy Bookshop Ltd.
PO Box 286
Monrovia
Liberia

College Press *see* **Galaxie**

Comb Books
Comb Books
PO Box 20019
Nairobi
Kenya

†Conch
Conch Magazine Ltd.
Publishers
113 Douglas Road
Owerri
Imo State
Nigeria

CPE
Centre de Publications
    Evangéliques pour l'Afrique
Francophone
BP 8900
Abidjan
Ivory Coast

†**Craft Centre**
Craft Centre
National Museum Compound
Onikan
Lagos
Lagos State
Nigeria

CRIDE
Centre de Rech. interdisciplinaire
    pour le Dévelop. de l'Education
BP 1386
Kisangani
Zaïre Republic

Cross Continent
Cross Continent Press Ltd.
PO Box 282
Yaba
Lagos State
Nigeria

CSIR
Council for Scientific and Industrial
    Research
PO Box 395
Pretoria
0001 South Africa

CSIR — Ghana
Central Reference and Research
    Library
Council for Scientific and Industrial
    Research
PO Box M32
Accra
Ghana

CSS
Agency and Publishing Division
CSS Bookshops
PO Box 174
Lagos
Lagos State
Nigeria

Daily Sketch
Sketch Publishing Co Ltd.
Sketch Buildings
Ibadan
Oyo State
Nigeria

†**Daily Times — Nig**
Daily Times of Nigeria Ltd.
3 Kakawa Street
PO Box 138
Lagos
Lagos State
Nigeria

Daystar
Daystar Press (Publishers)
Daystar House
PO Box 1261
Ibadan
Oyo State
Nigeria

Daystar — Lusaka
Daystar Publishers Ltd
PO Box 2211
Lusaka
Zambia

Dept Adult Educ — Ib
Department of Adult Education
University of Ibadan
Ibadan
Oyo State
Nigeria

Dept African Lang — Rhodes
Department of African Languages
Rhodes University
PO Box 184
Grahamstown
6140 South Africa

Dept Agric Eng — Dar
Department of Agricultural
    Engineering and Land Planning
Faculty of Agriculture and Forestry
University of Dar es Salaam
PO Box 643
Morogoro
Tanzania

Dept Antiquities
Federal Department of Antiquities
Jos Museum
Jos
Plateau State
Nigeria

Dept Antiquities — Mal
Conservator of Antiquities
PO Box 30312
Capital City
Lilongwe 3
Malawi

Dept Bantu Educ *see* **Native Lang Bur**

Dept Biblio Lib & Typo
Department of Bibliography,
    Librarianship and Typography
University of the Witwatersrand
Jan Smuts Avenue
Johannesburg
2001 South Africa

Dept Botany — Dar
Department of Botany
University of Dar es Salaam
PO Box 35060
Dar es Salaam
Tanzania

Dept Econ — Natal
Department of Economics
University of Natal
PO Box 375
Pietermaritzburg
3200 South Africa

Dept Educ — ABU
Department of Education
Ahmadu Bello University
Zaria
Kaduna State
Nigeria

Dept Geog — Mak
Department of Geography
Makerere University
PO Box 7062
Kampala
Uganda

Dept Geol — ABU
Department of Geology
Ahmadu Bello University
Zaria
Kaduna State
Nigeria

†Dept Geol — Ib
Department of Geology
University of Ibadan
Ibadan
Oyo State
Nigeria

†Dept Govt — ABU
Department of Government
Ahmadu Bello University
Zaria
Kaduna State
Nigeria

Dept Lib Stud — Ib
Department of Library Studies
University of Ibadan
Ibadan
Pyo State
Nigeria

Dept Lib Stud — Univ Ghana
Department of Library and Archival
　Studies
University of Ghana
PO Box 60
Legon
Ghana

Dept Math — Dar
Department of Mathematics
University of Dar es Salaam
PO Box 35091
Dar es Salaam
Tanzania

Dept Philosophy — Rhodes
Department of Philosophy
Rhodes University
PO Box 184
Grahamstown
6140 South Africa

Dept Psychology — Zam
Department of Psychology
University of Zambia
PO Box 2379
Lusaka
Zambia

†Dept Rural Econ — Mak
Department of Rural Economy and
　Extension
Makerere University
PO Box 7062
Kampala
Uganda

†Dept Soc — ABU
Department of Sociology
Ahmadu Bello University
Zaria
Kaduna State
Nigeria

Dept Town Poly — Ib
Department of Town Planning and
　Estate Management
The Polytechnic
PMB 5063
Ibadan
Oyo State
Nigeria

†Design Prod
Design Production Nigeria Ltd
1 Hussey Street
PO Box 499
Yaba
Lagos State
Nigeria

Deto Deni
Deto-Deni Educational Productions
PO Box 5411
Lagos
Lagos State
Nigeria

di Nigro
di Nigro Press
10/14 Calcutta Crescent
PO Box 610
Apapa
Lagos State
Nigeria

Directory Publ
Directory Publishers of Zambia Ltd
PO Box 1659
Ndola
Zambia

Donker
Ad Donker/Publisher
Craighall Mews
Jan Smuts Avenue
Craighall Park
PO Box 4102
Johannesburg
2000 South Africa

Dzuka Publishing *see* **Longman Mal**

EALB
East African Literature Bureau
PO Box 30022
Nairobi
Kenya

and at

PO Box 1002
Arusha
Tanzania

(*distributed outside East Africa by/distribué
hors de l'Afrique de l'Est par: Hans Zell
Publishers Ltd., PO Box 56, Oxford OX1 3EL,
England*)

EAPH
East African Publishing House
Lusaka Close
PO Box 30571
Nairobi
Kenya

EBAD
Ecole de Bibliothècaires Archivistes et
　Documentalistes
Université de Dakar
BP 3252
Dakar
Senegal

ECA
Economic Commission for Africa
Documents Section
Room 314 B
PO Box 3001
Addis Ababa
Ethiopia

Ecole Nat Admin — Niger
Ecole Nationale d'Administration
BP 542
Niamey
Niger

Econ Res Bur — Tanz
Economic Research Bureau
University of Dar es Salaam
PO Box 35096
Dar es Salaam
Tanzania

Ecumenical Res Unit
Ecumenical Research Unit
PO Box 17128
Groenkloof
0027 South Africa

Ed La Porte
Editions la Porte
281 Avenue Mohammed V
Rabat
Morocco

Ed Maghreb
Les Editions Maghrebines
5 Rue Soldat Roch
Casablanca
Morocco

Ed Mont Noir
Editions du Mont Noir
BP 1944
Lubumbashi
Zaire Republic

(distributed outside Zaïre by/distribué hors du Zaïre par: Mukala Kadima-Nzuji, 61 Square du Nord, 95500 Gonesse, France)

†Ed Pop — Mali
Edition-Imprimeries du Mali
BP 21
Bamako
Mali

Ed Semences Africaines
Les Editions Semences Africaines
BP 2180
Yaoundé
Cameroun

†Ed Takariva
Edition Imprimerie Takariva
BP 1029
Tananarive
Malagasy Republic

Edit and Publ Serv
Editorial and Publishing Services
PO Box 5743
Accra
Ghana

Educ Res Inst
Educational Research Institute
PO Box 277
Ibadan
Oyo State
Nigeria

Elizabethan
Elizabethan Publishing House
41 Ogunlena Drive
Lagos
Lagos State
Nigeria

†Emotan
Emotan Publishing Co (Nig.) Ltd.
152nd Ire Street
Benin City
Bendel State
Nigeria

Entomological Soc — Nig
Entomological Society of Nigeria
c/o Department of Agricultural
  Biology
University of Ibadan
Ibadan
Oyo State
Nigeria

†Equatorial
Equatorial Publishers
PO Box 47973
Nairobi
Kenya

Ethiope
Ethiope Publishing House
PMB 1332
Benin City
Bendel State
Nigeria

Evangel
Evangel Publishing House
PO Box 28963
Nairobi
Kenya

Evans — Nig
Evans Brothers (Nigeria Publishers)
  Ltd
Jericho Road
PMB 5164
Ibadan
Oyo State
Nigeria

Fac Law — Dar
Faculty of Law
University of Dar es Salaam
PO Box 35091
Dar es Salaam
Tanzania

Foreign Affairs Assoc
Foreign Affairs Association
PO Box 26410
Arcadia
Pretoria
0007 South Africa

Forest Res Inst
Forest Research Institute of Malawi
PO Box 270
Zomba
Malawi

Foundation
Foundation Books Ltd
PO Box 73435
Nairobi
Kenya

Fourah Bay Bkshop
Fourah Bay College Bookshop Ltd
University of Sierra Leone
Freetown
Sierra Leone

Fourah Bay College Lib
Fourah Bay College Library
University of Sierra Leone
Freetown
Sierra Leone

FRDOI
Fondation pour la Recherche et le
  Développement dans l'Océan
  Indien
28 Rue Roland Garros
97400 Saint-Denis
Réunion

Gaba
Gaba Publications
PO Box 908
Eldoret
Kenya

Galaxie
Galaxie Books
The College Press (Pvt.) Ltd
PO Box 3041
Salisbury
Rhodesia

†**Gambia Meth Bkshop**
The Gambia Methodist Bookshop
  Ltd.
PO Box 203
Banjul
The Gambia

†**Gebo**
Gebo and Brothers
Students Own Bookshop
58 Venn Road South
Onitsha
Anambra State
Nigeria

Geol and Min Res — Sudan
Geological and Mineral Resources
  Department
PO Box 410
Khartoum
Sudan

†**Geol Soc — SA**
Geological Society of South Africa
PO Box 61019
Marshalltown,
Transvaal
2107 South Africa

Geol Survey — Mal
Geological Survey Department
PO Box 27
Zomba
Malawi

Geol Survey — Zam
Geological Survey of Zambia
PO Box RW135
Ridgeway
Lusaka
Zambia

Ghana Central Bur Stat
Ghana Central Bureau of Statistics
PO Box 1098
Accra
Ghana

Ghana Lib Assoc
Ghana Library Association
PO Box 5015
Accra
Ghana

Ghana Lib Board
Ghana Library Board
PO Box 663
Accra
Ghana

†**Ghana Museum**
Ghana Museums and Monuments
  Board
Barnes Road
PO Box 3343
Accra
Ghana

Ghana Publ Corp
Ghana Publishing Corporation
Publishing Division
Private Post Bag
Tema
Ghana

Ghana UP
Ghana Universities Press
PO Box 4219
Accra
Ghana

(*distributed in the UK by/distribué au
Royanme Uni par: Coltart & Collings Ltd., 69
Marylebone High Street, London, WIM 3AQ*)

†**Graphic**
Graphic Corporation
Brewery Road
PO Box 742
Accra
Ghana

Haum
Haum Publishers
PO Box 1371
Cape Town
8000 South Africa

Heinemann Educ — Ib
Heinemann Educational Books
  (Nigeria) Ltd.
PMB 5205
Ibadan
Oyo State
Nigeria

Heinemann Educ — Nair
Heinemann Educational Books (East
  Africa) Ltd
PO Box 45314
Nairobi
Kenya

†**Herald**
Herald Books Ltd
80 Awka Road
Onitsha
Anambra State
Nigeria

†**Hist Assoc Tanz**
Historical Association of Tanzania
PO Box 35032
Dar es Salaam
Tanzania

Housing Res Dev Unit
Housing Research Development Unit
University of Nairobi
PO Box 30197
Nairobi
Kenya

Human and Rousseau
Human and Rousseau (Pty.) Ltd,
State House
3–9 Rose Street
PO Box 5050
Cape Town
8000 South Africa

Human Science Res Council
Human Sciences Research Council
Private Bag X41
Pretoria
0001 South Africa

IABL
Inter-African Bureau of Languages
OAU
PO Box 7234
Kampala
Uganda

†**Ibadan Chamber Comm**
Ibadan Chamber of Commerce
Barclay's Bank Building
PMB 5168
Ibadan
Oyo State
Nigeria

Ibadan U Lib
Ibadan University Library
Ibadan
Oyo State
Nigeria

Ibadan UP
Ibadan University Press
University of Ibadan
Ibadan
Oyo State
Nigeria

ICIC
ICIC (Directory Publishers) Ltd.
PO Box 398
Lagos
Lagos State
Nigeria

IFAN
Institut Fondamental d'Afrique
  Noire
BP 206
Dakar
Senegal

Ilesanmi
Ilesanmi Press and Sons (Nig.) Ltd.
PO Box 204
Ilesha
Imo State
Nigeria

INADES
INADES
BP 8008
Abidjan
Ivory Coast

Inst Admin — ABU
Department of Research and
  Consultancy
Institute of Administration
Ahmadu Bello University
Zaria
Kaduna State
Nigeria

Inst Admin — Ife
Institute of Administration
University of Ife
Ile-Ife
Oyo State
Nigeria

Inst Adult Educ — Dar
Institute of Adult Education
University of Dar es Salaam
PO Box 20679
Dar es Salaam
Tanzania

Inst Adult Educ — Ib
Institute of Adult Education
University of Ibadan
Ibadan
Oyo State
Nigeria

Inst Adv Calvinism
Institute for the Advancement of
  Calvinism
Potchefstroom University of Higher
  Education
Potchefstroom
2520 South Africa

Instr Afr Stud — FBC
Institute of African Studies
Fourah Bay College
Freetown
Sierra Leone

†**Inst Afr Stud — Ib**
Institute of African Studies
University of Ibadan
Ibadan
Oyo State
Nigeria

Inst Afr Stud — Lusaka
Institute for African Studies
University of Zambia
PO Box 900
Lusaka
Zambia

†**Inst Afric Stud — Nig**
Institute of African Studies
University of Nigeria
Nsukka
Anambra State
Nigeria

†**Inst Afr Stud — Univ Ghana**
Institute of African Studies
University of Ghana
Legon
Ghana

Inst Agric Res
Institute for Agricultural Research
PMB 1044
Samaru
Zaria
Kaduna State
Nigeria

Inst Agric Res — Addis
Institute of Agricultural Research
  PO Box 2003
Addis Ababa
Ethiopia

Inst Dev Stud
Institute of Development Studies
University of Nairobi
PO Box 30197
Nairobi
Kenya

†**Inst Educ — Dar**
Institute of Education
University of Dar es Salaam
PO Box 35091
Dar es Salaam
Tanzania

†**Inst Educ — Ib**
Institute of Education
University of Ibadan
Ibadan
Oyo State
Nigeria

Inst Ethiop Stud
Institute of Ethiopian Studies
PO Box 1176
Addis Ababa
Ethiopia

†**Inst Ethno-Socio**
Institut d'Ethno-Sociologie
Université d'Abidjan
BP 8865
Abidjan
Ivory Coast

Inst For and Comp Law
Institute of Foreign and
    Comparative Law
University of South Africa
PO Box 392
Pretoria
0001 South Africa

Inst Ichthyology
Smith Institute of Ichthyology
Rhodes University
PO Box 94
Grahamstown
6140 South Africa

Inst Lib — Ib *see* **Dept Lib Stud — Ib**

†**Inst Ling — ABU**
Institute of Linguistics
Ahmadu Bello University
Zaria
Kaduna State
Nigeria

Inst Ling Appliquée
Institut de Linguistique Appliquée
Université d'Abidjan
BP 8887
Abidjan
Ivory Coast

Inst Nat Rwandaise
Institut National de Recherche
    Scientifique
BP 218
Butare
Rwanda

Inst Nat Tchad
Institut National Tchadien pour les
    Sciences Humaines
BP 503
N'Djamena
Chad

Inst Rech Sci Hum
Institut de Recherches en Sciences
    Humaines
BP 318
Niamey
Niger

Inst Sciences Hum — Cam
Institut des Sciences Humaines
BP 193
Yaoundé
Cameroun

Inst Soc & Econ Res
Institute of Social and Economic
    Research
Rhodes University
PO Box 94
Grahamstown
6140 South Africa

Inst Soc Res — Natal
Institute for Social Research
University of Natal
King George V Avenue
Durban
4001 South Africa

Inst Soc Res — Zam *see* **Inst Afr Stud
    — Lusaka**

Inst Study Engl
Institute for the Study of English
Rhodes University
Grahamstown
6140 South Africa

Inst Study of Man
Institute for the Study of Man
c/o Medical School
Hospital Street
Johannesburg
2001 South Africa

Inst Swahili Res
Institute of Kiswahili Research
University of Dar es Salaam
PO Box 35110
Dar es Salaam
Tanzania

Interafrica
Interafrica Publishers Co Ltd.
PO Box 75024
Nairobi
Kenya

Int Lib African Music
International Library of African
    Music
PO Box 138
Roodeport
1725 South Africa

IPMS
Institute of Population and
    Manpower Studies
Faculty of Social Sciences
University of Ife
Ile-Ife
Oyo State
Nigeria

Islamic
Islamic Publications Bureau
PO Box 3881
Lagos
Lagos State
Nigeria

Johannesburg Pub Lib
Johannesburg Public Library
Market Square
Johannesburg
2001 South Africa

Johannesburg Pub Lib
Johannesburg Public Library
Market Square
Johannesburg
2001 South Africa

Jomo Kenyatta Found
The Jomo Kenyatta Foundation
School Book Publishers
PO Box 30533
Nairobi
Kenya

Juta
Juta & Co.
Mercury Crescent
Wetton
PO Box 2
Wynberg
7824 South Africa

*(incomplete listing, largely law list, as publisher
failed to supply full details of general and trade
titles/liste incomplète, principalement titres
légaux, parce que l'éditeur n'a pas fourni tous
les détails de ses titres généraux)*

Kenya Inst Admin
Kenya Institute of Administration
Lower Kabete
Kenya

†Kenya Lib Assoc
Kenya Library Association
PO Box 46031
Nairobi
Kenya

Kenyatta Univ Coll
Kenyatta University College Library
PO Box 43844
Nairobi
Kenya

Khartoum UP
Khartoum University Press
PO Box 321
Khartoum
Sudan

Kwara State Publ Corp
Kwara State Printing and Publishing
   Corporation
PMB 1369
Ilorin
Kwara State
Nigeria

†Lagos City Directory
Lagos City Directory Co.
PO Box 603
Lagos
Lagos State
Nigeria

Lavigerie
Les Presses Lavigerie
BP 1640
Bujumbura
Burundi

Legal And Financial
Legal and Financial Books
Flesh Financial Publications (Pty.)
   Ltd
58 Burg Street
PO Box 3473
Cape Town
8000 South Africa

Leone Publ
Leone Publishers
Institute of African Studies
University of Sierra Leone
Freetown
Sierra Leone

Lib des Volcans
Librarie Les Volcans
22 Avenue President Mobutu
BP 400
Goma
Zaïre Republic

†Liberian Lit
Liberian Literary and Educational
   Publications
PO Box 2387
Monrovia
Liberia

Lib Madagascar
La Librairie de Madagascar
BP 402
Tananarive
Malagasy Republic

Lib Univ Rwanda
Librairie Universitaire
Université Nationale de Rwanda
BP 117
Butare
Rwanda

Longman — Ken
Longman Kenya Ltd
Harambee Avenue
PO Box 18033
Nairobi
Kenya

Longman — Mal
Dzuka Publishing Co Ltd
Private Bag 39
Blantyre
(formerly Longman Malawi)

Longman — Nig
Longman Nigeria Ltd.
52 Oba Akran Avenue
PMB 1036
Ikeja
Lagos State
Nigeria

Longman — Rhod
Longman Rhodesia (Pvt.) Ltd.
PO Box ST125
Salisbury
Rhodesia

Longman — SA
Longman Penguin Southern Africa
   (Pty.) Ltd.
Vrystaat Street
PO Box 1616
Paarden Eiland
Cape Town
8000 South Africa

†Longman — Tanz
Longman Tanzania Ltd
Independence Avenue
PO Box 3164
Dar es Salaam
Tanzania

Lovedale
Lovedale Press
PO Lovedale
5702 South Africa
(*incomplete listing/liste incomplète*)

Lumko Inst
Lumko Institute
Lady Frere
5410 South Africa

Macmillan
Macmillan Nigeria Publishers Ltd
PO Box 1463
Ibadan
Oyo State
Nigeria

Macmillan — SA
Macmillan South Africa Publishers
   (Pty.) Ltd
Total Centre
PO Box 31487
Braamfontein
2017 South Africa

Mahatma Gandhi Inst
The Mahatma Gandhi Institute
Site Office
Moka
Mauritius

Maison Tunis
Maison Tunisiènne d'Edition
54 Avenue de la Liberté
Tunis
Tunisia

Mak Inst Soc Res
Makerere Institute of Social Research
PO Box 16002
Kampala
Uganda

†Mak Univ Lib
Makerere University Library
PO Box 16002
Kampala
Uganda

†Malamulo
Malamulo Publishing House
PO Box 11
Makwasa
Malawi

Mambo
Mambo Press
Senga Road
PO Box 779
Gwelo
Rhodesia

†Maskew Miller
Maskew Miller Ltd
7–11 Bury Street
PO Box 396
Cape Town
8000 South Africa

Mazenod Inst
Mazenod Institute
Mazenod Book Centre
PO Box 18
Mazenod
Lesotho

†McGraw-Hill SA
McGraw-Hill Book Co SA (Pty.) Ltd
PO Box 371
Isando
1600 South Africa

Methodist
Methodist Publishing House
PO Box 708
Cape Town
8000 South Africa

M. O. Collins
M. O. Collins (Pvt.) Ltd,
PO Box 3094
Salisbury
Rhodesia

†Morija
Morija Sesuto Book Depot
PO Box 4
Morija
Lesotho

†Multimedia
Multimedia Zambia
PO Box 8199
Lusaka
Zambia

Nat Archives — Rhod
National Archives of Rhodesia
Private Bag 7729
Causeway
Salisbury
Rhodesia

†Nat Archives — Zam
National Archives of Zambia
PO Box RW10
Ridgeway
Lusaka
Zambia

Nat Arch — Mal
National Archives of Malawi
PO Box 62
Zomba
Malawi

Nat Bank Commerce
The National Bank of Commerce
International Banking Department
Trade Promotion Division
PO Box 1255
Dar es Salaam
Tanzania

Nat Council Res — Sudan
National Council for Research (al-
   Majilis-Qawmi lil-Bihuth)
PO Box 2404
Khartoum
Sudan

Nat Council Scient Res — Zam
National Council for Scientific
   Research
Documentation and Scientific
   Information Centre
PO Box CH158
Lusaka
Zambia

Nat Housing Author — Zam
National Housing Authority
PO Box RW74
Lusaka
Zambia

National Museum — SA
Nasionale Museum
PO Box 266
Bloemfontein
9300 South Africa

National Museum — Tanz
National Museum of Tanzania
PO Box 511
Dar es Salaam
Tanzania

Native Lang Bur
Native Language Bureau
Private Bag 13236
Windhoek
Namibia

Nat Lib — Nig
National Library of Nigeria
Wesley Street
PMB 12626
Lagos
Lagos State
Nigeria

Nat Mon Comm — Zambia
National Monuments Commission
PO Box 124
Livingstone
Zambia

Nat Mus Board — Zam
National Museums Board
Livingstone Museum
PO Box 498
Livingstone
Zambia

Nat Print Co
National Printing Company
PO Box 2320
Dar es Salaam
Tanzania

Nasou
Nasou Ltd,
386 Voortrekker Road
PO Box 105
Parow
7500 South Africa

Ndanda Mission Press
Ndanda Mission Press
PO Box 1004
Ndanda — via Lindi
Tanzania

Neczam
National Educational Co of Zambia
  Ltd
Chishango Road
PO Box 2664
Lusaka
Zambia

(distributed in the UK by/distribué au Royaume Uni par: Third World Publications, 151 Stratford Road, Birmingham B11 1AG, England; distributed in the USA by/distribué aux Etats Unis par: African Imprint Library Services, Guard Hill Road, Bedford, N.Y. 10506)

†**Nelson — Nig**
Thomas Nelson (Nigeria) Ltd.
PO Box 1303
Ikeja
Lagos State
Nigeria

New Horn
New Horn Press Ltd,
PO Box 4138
Ibadan
Oyo State
Nigeria

†**New Kenya**
New Kenya Publishers
PO Box 12336
Nairobi
Kenya

Newspread
Newspread International
PO Box 46854
Nairobi
Kenya

†**Nig Acad Arts Sci**
Nigerian Academy of Arts, Sciences
  and Technology
c/o Faculty of Social Science
University of Ibadan
Ibadan
Oyo State
Nigeria

Nig Bk Suppliers
Nigerian Book Suppliers Ltd
54/56 Bankole Street
PO Box 3870
Lagos
Lagos State
Nigeria

†**Nig Nat Press**
Nigerian National Press
PO Box 1154
Apapa
Lagos
Lagos State
Nigeria

†**Nig Tourist**
Nigerian Tourist Association
47 Marina
PO Box 2944
Lagos
Lagos State
Nigeria

Nigerian Lib Assoc
Nigerian Library Association
PMB 12655
Lagos
Lagos State
Nigeria

†**NISER**
Nigerian Institute of Social and
  Economic Research
University of Ibadan
PMB 5
Ibadan
Oyo State
Nigeria

†**Njogu**
Njogu Gitene Publications
PO Box 72989
Nairobi
Kenya

Northern Nig
Northern Nigerian Publishing Co
  Ltd.
PO Box 412
Zaria
Kaduna State
Nigeria

Nouv Ed Afric
Les Nouvelles Editions Africaines
10 rue Thiers
BP 260
Dakar
Senegal

and at

Avenue Nogues
BP 20615
Abidjan
Ivory Coast

Nwamife
Nwamife Publishers Ltd
10 Ibiam Street
Uwani
PO Box 430
Enugu
Anambra State
Nigeria

OAU
Organization of African Unity
Information Division
PO Box 3243
Addis Ababa
Ethiopia

Oceanographic Res Inst
Oceanographic Research Institute
2 West Street
PO Box 736
Durban
4000 South Africa

Onibonoje
Onibonoje Press and Book
  Industries (Nigeria) Ltd.
PO Box 3109
Ibadan
Oyo State
Nigeria

†**OUP — Addis**
Oxford University Press
PO Box 1024
Addis Ababa
Ethiopia

OUP — Nairobi
Oxford University Press
Eastern Africa Branch
PO Box 72532
Nairobi
Kenya

OUP — Nig
Oxford University Press
Nigerian Branch
PMB 5095
Iddo Gate
Ibadan
Oyo State
Nigeria

OUP — Rhod
Oxford University Press
Roslin House
Baker Avenue
Salisbury
Rhodesia

OUP — SA
Oxford University Press South Africa
11 Buitencingle Street
PO Box 1141
Cape Town
8000 South Africa

†**OUP — Zam**
Oxford University Press
PO Box 2335
Lusaka
Zambia

Paico
Paico Ltd
46 Commercial Avenue
PO Box 3944
Yaba
Lagos
Lagos State
Nigeria

Pan-african
Pan-African Researchers
PO Box 22777
Nairobi
Kenya

†**People's Publ Co**
People's Publishing Co Ltd
Lagos
Lagos State
Nigeria

Philip
David Philip Publisher (Pty.) Ltd.
3 Scott Road
PO Box 408
Claremont
Cape Town
7735 South Africa

†**Pilgrim**
Pilgrim Books Ltd.
305 Herbert Macaulay Street
PO Box 3560
Lagos
Lagos State
Nigeria

Popular Publ
Popular Publications
PO Box 5592
Limbe
Malawi

Precambrian Res Unit
Precambrian Research Unit
Department of Geology
University of Cape Town
Private Bag
Rondebosch
7700 South Africa

Presses Africaines
Les Presses Africaines
Place du 27 Octobre
BP 12924
Kinshasa I
Zaïre Republic

Press Univ Zaire
Presses Universitaires du Zaire
Publications Rectorat
BP 13399
Kinshasa I
Zaïre Republic

Project Time
Project Time
PMB 1140
Yaba
Lagos State
Nigeria

Prometheus
Prometheus Publishing Company
   Ltd.
PO Box 1850
Lusaka
Zambia

†**Publ Central Africa**
Publications Central Africa
PO Box 1027
Bulawayo
Rhodesia

†**Publ Int**
Publications International (Nigeria)
   Ltd.
PO Box 1372
Ibadan
Oyo State
Nigeria

Purnell
Purnell and Sons (SA) (Pty.) Ltd
70 Keerom Street
PO Box 4501
Cape Town
8000 South Africa

Quagga
Quagga Press (Prop.) Ltd.
PO Box 66254
Broadway
2020 South Africa

Ravan
Ravan Press (Pty.) Ltd
Queensbridge
60 Juta Street
PO Box 31910
Braamfontein
2017 South Africa
(*distributed outside Southern Africa
distribué hors de l'Afrique meridionale par: by
Hans Zell Publishers Ltd., PO Box 56, Oxford
OX1 3EL, England*)

Renoster Books *see* **Ravan**

Rhod Christ Press
Rhodesian Christian Press
Byo
Rhodesia

Rhod Lit Bur
Rhodesia Literature Bureau
Ministry of Education
Causeway
PO Box 8137
Salisbury Rhodesia

Rhodes Univ Lib
Rhodes University Library
PO Box 184
Grahamstown
6140 South Africa

Rur Dev Stud Bur — Zam
Rural Development Studies Centre
PO Box 900
Lusaka
Zambia

SAED
Société Africaine d'Etudes et de
   Développement
BP 593
Ouagadougou
Upper Volta

SA Inst Int Affairs
The South African Institute of
   International Affairs
PO Box 31596
Braamfontein
Johannesburg
2017 South Africa

SA Inst Race Relations
South African Institute of Race
   Relations
68 de Korte Street
PO Box 97
Johannesburg
2007 South Africa

SA Missionary Museum
South African Missionary Museum
27 Berkeley Street
King William's Town
5600 South Africa

SAWTRI
South African Wool and Textile
   Research Institute
PO Box 1124
Port Elizabeth
6000 South Africa

School Hum Soc Sci — Zam
School of Humanities and Social
   Science
PO Box 2379
Lusaka
Zambia

Service Geol — Mad
Service Géologique
BP 322
Tananarive
Malagasy Republic

†Shuter
Shuter and Shooter (Ptd.) Ltd.
230 Church Street
PO Box 109
Pietermaritzburg
3200 South Africa

Sierra Leone Lib Board
Sierra Leone Library Board
PO Box 326
Freetown
Sierra Leone

Sierra Leone UP
Sierra Leone University Press
Fourah Bay College
PO Box 67
Freetown
Sierra Leone

SIM
(Sudan Interior Mission) *see/voir*
Challenge

SKEA
Société Kenkoson d'Etudes
   Africaines
BP 4064
Yaoundé
Cameroun

†SNED
Société Nationale d'Edition et de
   Diffusion
3 Bvd Zirout Youcef
BP 49
Alger Strasbourg
Algeria

Soc Africaine
Société Africaine d'Edition
16 bis rue de Thiong
BP 1877
Dakar
Senegal

(*distributed outside Senegal by/distribué hors
du Sénégal par: Société Africaine d'Edition, 32
rue de l'Echiquier, Paris 10, France*)

Soc Malgache
Société Malgache d'Edition
26 rue Béréni
BP 659
Tananarive
Malagasy Republic

SODEMI
Chef de Service de Documentation
SODEMI
BP 2816
Abidjan
Ivory Coast

South Africa Lib
The South African Library
Queen Victoria Street
Cape Town
8001 South Africa

State Lib — SA
The State Library
PO Box 397
Pretoria
0001 South Africa

St. Michael's Mission
St. Michael's Mission
PO Box 25
Roma
Lesotho

St. Paul
Editions St. Paul
Avenue du Commerce 76
BP 8505
Kinshasa
Zaire Republic

Struik
C. Struik (Pty.) Ltd.
PO Box 1144
Cape Town
8000 South Africa

(*distributed in the USA by/distribué aux Eta
Unis par: Lawrence Verry Inc., 16 Holmes
Street, Mystic, Conn. 06355*)

Sugar Res Inst
Sugar Industry Research Institute
Reduit
Mauritius

†**Survival**
Survival Bookshop
81 Upper New Market Road
Onitsha
Anambra State
Nigeria

SWA Scient Soc
South West African Scientific Society
PO Box 67
Windhoek
Namibia

Tafelberg
Tafelberg Publishers Ltd
PO Box 879
Cape Town
8000 South Africa

Tanz Lib Serv
Tanzania Library Service
PO Box 9283
Dar es Salaam
Tanzania

Tanz Mission Press *see/voir* **TMP**

Tanz Publ House
Tanzania Publishing House
PO Box 2138
Dar es Salaam
Tanzania

(*distributed in the UK by/distribué au Royaume Uni par: Third World Publications, 151 Stratford Road, Birmingham B11 1AG, England*)

Tanz Soc Animal Prod
Tanzania Society of Animal
    Production
Faculty of Agriculture and Forestry
University of Dar es Salaam
PO Box 643
Morogoro
Tanzania

Technitrain
Technitrain (Pty.) Ltd.
117 Everite House
20 de Korte Street
PO Box 31648
Braamfontein
Johannesburg
20017 South Africa

TEDRO
Test Development and Research
    Division
West African Examinations Councils
PMB 1076
Yaba
Lagos State
Nigeria

Textbook Ctre
Text Book Centre Ltd.
Kijabe Street
PO Box 47540
Nairobi
Kenya

Thomson
Thomson Newspapers Rhodesia
    (Pvt.) Ltd.
PO Box 1683
Salisbury
Rhodesia

TMP
Tanzania Mission Press
PO Box 399
Tabora
Tanzania

Torch Books *see/voir* **Cole & Yancy**

Town & Gown
Town and Gown Press
4 Kajew Street
PMB 5073
Akoka
Yaba
Lagos State
Nigeria

TPL
Trano Printy Loterana
Avenue Grandidier
BP 588
Tananarive
Malagasy Republic

†**Transafrica**
Transafrica Publishers Ltd
Kenwood House
Kimathi Street
PO Box 42990
Nairobi
Kenya

(*distributed in the UK by/distribué au Royaume Uni par: Coltart & Collings Ltd., 69 Marylebone High Street, London W1M 3AQ*)

†**Uganda Pub House**
Uganda Publishing House
UTA House
Bombo Road
PO Box 2923
Kampala
Uganda

UG Kerk
DR Church Publishers
PO Box 4539
Cape Town
8000 South Africa

†**United Africa**
United Press of Africa Ltd.
PO Box 41237
Nairobi
Kenya

United Pub
United Publishers
PO Box 200
Victoria
Cameroun

Univ Abidjan
Université d'Abidjan
BP 8109
Abidjan
Ivory Coast

Univ Bkshop — Dar
The University Bookshop
University of Dar es Salaam
PO Box 35090
Dar es Salaam
Tanzania

Univ Bots & Swazi
University of Botswana and
    Swaziland Library
Private Bag
Kwaluseni
Swaziland

Univ Bujumbura
Bibliothèque
Université Officielle de Bujumbura
Bujumbura
Burundi

Univ Cameroun
Université de Yaoundé
BP 1312
Yaoundé
Cameroun

Univ Cape Coast Lib
University of Cape Coast Library
University of Cape Coast
Cape Coast
Ghana

Univ Cape Town Lib
University of Cape Town
J. W. Jagger Library
Private Bag
Rondebosch
7700 South Africa

Univ Dar es Salaam
University Publications Office
University of Dar es Salaam
PO Box 35091
Dar es Salaam
Tanzania

Univ Dar es Salaam Lib
University of Dar es Salaam
    Library
PO Box 35091
Dar es Salaam
Tanzania

Univ Durban — Westville
University of Durban—Westville
Private Bag X54001
Durban
4000 South Africa

Univ Ghana Bkshop
University Bookshop
University of Ghana
PO Box 1
Legon
Ghana

Univ Ibadan Bkshop
University Bookshop (Nigeria) Ltd
University of Ibadan
Ibadan
Oyo State
Nigeria

Univ Ife Bkshop
University of Ife Bookshop Ltd
Ile-Ife
Oyo State
Nigeria

Univ Ife Press
University of Ife Press
Ile-Ife
Oyo State
Nigeria

†Univ Lagos Bkshop
University of Lagos Bookshop
Yaba
Lagos
Lagos State
Nigeria

†Univ Lagos Press
University of Lagos Press
Yaba
Lagos State
Nigeria

Univ Malawi Lib
University of Malawi Library
PO Box 280
Zomba
Malawi

Univ Natal
University of Natal Press
PO Box 375
Pietermaritzburg
3200 South Africa

(distributed in the USA by/distribué aux Etats Unis par: Lawrence Verry Inc., 16 Holmes Street, Mystic, Conn. 06355)

†Univ Nigeria Bkshop
University of Nigeria Bookshop Ltd.
Nsukka
Anambra State
Nigeria

Univ of Witwatersrand Lib
University of the Witwatersrand
Johannesburg
2001 South Africa

Univ of Zambia Bkshop
University of Zambia Bookshop
PO Box 2379
Lusaka
Zambia

Univ Press Africa
University Press of Africa Ltd.
Bank House
Government Road
PO Box 3981
Nairobi
Kenya

Univ Publ
University Publishing Company
11 Central School Road
PO Box 386
Onitsha
Anambra State
Nigeria

Univ Rhodesia Lib
University of Rhodesia Library
PO Box MP 45
Mount Pleasant
Salisbury
Rhodesia

Univ South Africa
University of South Africa
PO Box 392
Pretoria
0007 South Africa

Univ Stellenbosch Lib
University of Stellenbosch
University Library
PB 5036
Stellenbosch
7600 South Africa

Univ Tunis
Faculté des Lettres et Sciences
    Humaines de Tunis
BP 1128
Tunis
Tunisia

Univ Zambia Lib
University of Zambia Library
PO Box 2379
Luska
Zambia

Uzima
Uzima Press
PO Box 48127
Nairobi
Kenya

Valiant
Valiant Publishers (Pty.) Ltd.
Sandton City
PO Box 78236
Sandton
2146 South Africa

Van Schaik
J. L. van Schaik (Pty.) Ltd.
Libri Building
Church Street
PO Box 724
Pretoria
0001 South Africa

*(incomplete listing, as publisher has failed to
supply any new data since 1972/liste
incomplète, puisque l'éditeur ne fournit pas de
nouvelles informations depuis 1972)*

Vision
Vision Publications
PO Box 1532
Salisbury
Rhodesia

Waterville
Waterville Publishing House
PO Box 195
Accra
Ghana

Webster's
Webster's (Pty.) Ltd.
West Street
PO Box 292
Mbabane
Swaziland

†West
John West Publications Ltd.
212 Broad Street
Lagos
Lagos State
Nigeria

West African Book
West African Book Publishers Ltd.
PO Box 3445
Lagos
Lagos State
Nigeria

Witwatersrand UP
Witwatersrand University Press
1 Jan Smuts Avenue
Johannesburg
2001 South Africa

Yaba
Yaba College of Technology Library
PMB 2011
Yaba
Lagos State
Nigeria

†Zambia Cult Serv
Zambia Cultural Services
PO Box RW177
Lusaka
Zambia

Zambia Geog Assoc
Zambia Geographical Association
PO Box RW287
Lusaka
Zambia

†Zambia Lib Assoc
Zambia Library Association
PO Box 2389
Lusaka
Zambia

Directory of Publishers Not Appearing in this Edition

Editeurs n'apparaissant pas dans cette édition

The publishers listed below — research institutes, societies, or professional associations *not* included — have chosen to ignore all our requests for details about their publications. Their titles are therefore missing from *African Books in Print* (see also note on p. xxxix).

Les éditeurs cités ci-dessous — instituts de recherche, sociétés ou associations professionnelles *non* répertoriés — n'ont répondu à aucune de nos demandes de renseignements concernant leurs publications. Par conséquent, leurs titres ne figurent pas dans *Livres Africains Disponibles* (voir aussi la note p. xxxix).

Africa Editions
BP 1926
Dakar
Senegal

via Afrika Ltd
PO Box 114
Parrow
7500 South Africa

Anowuo Educational Publications
2R McCarthy Hill
PO Box 3918
Accra
Ghana

Cameroun Printing and Publication Company
PO Box 51
Victoria
Cameroun

Catholic Mission Press
PO Box 60
Cape Coast
Ghana

Central News Agency Ltd.
PO Box 10799
Johannesburg
2000 South Africa

Centre d'Edition et de Production de Manuels et d'Auxiliaires l'Enseignement
BP 808
Yaoundé
Cameroun

Christian Publishing Co.
PO Box 132
Roodeport
1725 South Africa

College of Careers (Pty.) Ltd.
PO Box 2081
Cape Town
8000 South Africa

East African Directory Co. (1975) Ltd.
PO Box 30670
Nairobi
Kenya

Edition des Trois Fleuves
18 Blvd de République
Dakar
Senegal

Editions Afrique-Levant
50 Rue de Grammont
Dakar
Senegal

Editions Clairafrique
2 Rue Sandiniery
BP 2005
Dakar
Senegal

Editions Croix de Sud
1 Barracks Street
Port Louis
Mauritius

Editions Le Progrès
6 Sharia Sherif Pasha
Cairo
Egypt
United Arab Republic

Editions Madprint
BP 953
Tananarive
Malagasy Republic

Editions Nassau
Rue Barclay
Rose Hill
Mauritius

Editogo
BP 891
Lome
Togo

Folktales Educational Books
50 Coates Street
Ebute-Metta
Lagos
Lagos State
Nigeria

Gazelle Books Company
PO Box 21267
Nairobi
Kenya

General Egyptian Book Organization
1117 Corniche El Nil Street
Cairo
Egypt
United Arab Republic

General Press Corporation
PO Box 959
Tripoli
Libya

Howard Timmins (Pty.) Ltd.
45 Shortmarket Street
PO Box 94
Cape Town
8000 South Africa

Hugh Keartland Publishers (Pty.) Ltd.
PO Box 9221
Johannesburg
2000 South Africa

Industrial Publications (1975) Ltd.
PO Box 30670
Nairobi
Kenya

Kola-Sanya Publishers
PO Box 252
Ijebu-Ode
Ogun State
Nigeria

Les Editions Universitaires d'Egypt
32 Abdel Khalek Tharwat
Cairo
Egypt
United Arab Republic

Librairie du Progrès
37 Rue Paul Rafiringa
Tananarive
Malagasy Republic

Likuni Press and Publishing House
PO Box 133
Lilongwe
Malawi

John Malherbe (Pty.) Ltd.
PO Box 1207
Cape Town
8000 South Africa

Mbari Artists' and Writers' Club
PMB 5162
Ibadan
Oyo State
Nigeria

Methodist Book Depot Ltd.
PO Box 100
Cape Coast
Ghana

Moxon Paperbacks Ltd.
Barnes Road
PO Box M160
Accra
Ghana

New World Publications (Pty.) Ltd.
PO Box 4429
Cape Town
8000 South Africa

Njala University Publishing Centre
Njala University
PM Bag
Freetown
Sierra Leone

Office du Livre Malagasy
BP 257
Antananarivo
Malagasy Republic
(information to appear in ABPR as from 1978/information apparaîtront dans ABPR à partir de 1978)

Oudiovista Production (Pty.) Ltd.
PO Box 4429
Cape Town
8000 South Africa

Perskor Publishers
PO Box 845
Johannesburg
2000 South Africa
(information to appear in ABPR as from 1978/ informations apparaîtront dans ABPR à partir de 1978)

Salama Publications Ltd.
PO Box 48009
Nairobi
Kenya

Senouhy Publishers
54 Sharia Abdel-Khalek
Cairo
Egypt
United Arab Republic

Shungwaya Publishers Ltd
PO Box 49162
Nairobi
Kenya

Simondium Publication (Pty.) Ltd.
PO Box 3737
Cape Town
8600 South Africa

Sphinx Publishing House
3 Sharwaby Street
Cairo
Egypt
United Arab Republic

Sudan International Publications
PO Box 7140
Khartoum
Sudan

Success Publications
PO Box 10983
Nairobi
Kenya

Tai Publishers Ltd.
PO Box 46319
Nairobi
Kenya

Thomson Publications (SA) (Pty.)
 Ltd.
PO Box 8308
Johannesburg
2000 South Africa

Trend Publishers Ltd.
PO Box 66319
Nairobi
Kenya

United Christian Council Literature
 Bureau
Bunumbu Press
Bo
Sierra Leone

United Methodist and Lutheran
 Church
PO Box 1010
Monrovia
Liberia

University of Zululand Press
PO Kwa-Dlangezwa
via Empangeni
3886 South Africa

Varia Books
PO Box 3868
Alrode
South Africa

Vipopremo Agencies
Koinange Street
PO Box 47717
Nairobi
Kenya

Vuga Press
PO Box 25
Soni
Tanzania

Appendix: List of Government Printers and Publications Agencies in Africa

Appendice: Maisons d'édition gouvernementales et Organisations officielles d'édition en Afrique

Algeria / Algérie
Imprimerie Officielle
7–13 avenue Abdelkador Benbarek
Alger

Angola / Angola
Imprensa Nacional de Angola
CP 1306
Luanda

Benin / Benin
Imprimerie du Gouvernement
BP 59
Porto-Novo

Botswana / Botswana
Government Printer
BP Box 87
Gaborone

Burundi / Burundi
Imprimerie du Gouvernement
BP 1400
Bujumbura

Cameroun / Cameroun
Imprimerie Nationale du
  Gouvernement
BP 1091
Yaoundé

**Central African Empire /
Empire-Centre-africain**
Imprimerie Centrale d'Afrique
BP 329
Bangui

Chad / Tchad
Imprimerie Nationale du Tchad
BP 69
N'Djamena

**Congo, People's Republic /
République Populaire du Congo**
Imprimerie Officielle
BP 58
Brazzaville

Djibouti / Djibouti
Imprimerie Administrative
BP 268
Djibouti

Ethiopia / Ethiopie
Government Printing Press
PO Box 980
Addis Ababa

Gabon/Gabon
Imprimerie Centrale d'Afrique
BP 154
Libreville

The Gambia / Gambie
Government Press
Banjul

Ghana / Ghana
Government Printing Department
PO Box 124
Accra

Guinea / Guinée
Imprimerie Patrice Lumumba
BP 156
Conakry

Ivory Coast / Côte d'Ivoire
Imprimerie Nationale
BP 1362
Abidjan

Kenya / Kenya
Government Printing Press
PO Box 30128
Nairobi

Lesotho / Lesotho
Mazenod Printing Press
PO Box MZ18
Mazenod

Liberia/Liberia
Government Printing Office
Ashmun Street
Monrovia

Libya / Libye
Agency for Development of
  Publications and Distribution
Printing Division
PO Box 34/35
Tripoli

Madagascar / Madagascar
Imprimerie Nationale
BP 38
Tananarive

Malawi / Malawi
Government Printer
PO Box 37
Zomba

Mali / Mali
Imprimerie Nationale
Avenue Kasse Keita
BP 21
Bamako

Mauritania / Mauritanie
Imprimerie Nationale de la
  République Islamique de
  Mauritanie
BP 618
Nouakchott

Mauritius / Maurice
Government Printing Office
Elizabeth II Avenue
Port Louis

Morocco / Maroc
Imprimerie Officielle
Avenue Jean Mermoz Rabat-Chellah
Rabat

Mozambique / Mozambique
Imprensa Nacional de Moçambique
CP 275
Maputo

Niger / Niger
Imprimerie Générale du Niger
BP 61
Niamey

Nigeria / Nigéria
Government Printer
Federal Printing Division
Ministry of Information
PMB 12530
Lagos
Lagos State

*(each state government also maintains
individual printing divisions/chaque
gouvernement statal maintient aussi une
imprimerie individuelle)*

**Rhodesia (Zimbabwe)/
Rhodésie (Zimbabwé)**
Department of Printing and
   Stationery
Gordon Avenue
PO Box 8062
Causeway
Salisbury

Rwanda / Rwanda
Imprimerie Nationale du Rwanda
BP 124
Kigali

Senegal / Sénégal
Imprimerie du Gouvernement
Rue Fisque
BP 1
Dakar

Seychelles / Seychelles
Government Printing Department
Victoria

Sierra Leone / Sierra Leone
Government Printing Department
George Street
Freetown

Somali Republic / Somalie
Government Printer
Ministry of Information
Mogadishu

South Africa / Afrique du Sud
Government Printer
PB 85
Pretoria 0001

Sudan / Soudan
Government Printing Press
PO Box 38
Khartoum

Swaziland / Swaziland
Swaziland Printing and Publishing
   Co Ltd.
PO Box 28
Mbabane

Tanzania/Tanzanie
Government Printer
PO Box 2483
Dar es Salaam

Togo / Togo
Imprimerie National Editogo
BP 891
Lomé

Tunisia / Tunisie
Imprimerie Officielle
42 rue du 18 Janvier 1952
Tunis

Uganda / Ouganda
Government Printer
PO Box 33
Entebbe

**United Arab Republic /
R.A.U. Egypte**
General Organization for
   Government Press Affairs
22 Kasr El Nil Street
Imbaba
Guiza
Cairo

Upper Volta / Haute Volta
Imprimerie Nationale
BP 558
Ouagadougou

Zaire Republic / République du Zaïre
Imprimerie du Gouvernement
   Central
BP 3021
Kinshasa-Kalina

Zambia / Zambie
Government Printer
PO Box 136
Lusaka

AUTHOR INDEX

INDEX-AUTEURS

A-Ankrah, E.A.N., ed.
Agwasen-wiemci. [Proverbs and maxims.] 2nd ed.
61pp. C1.00 Bur Ghana Lang 1976 GH GAA

Ababio, E.S.T.
Blema kakalci. [Brave men of old.] 3rd ed. 58pp. ill.
80pes. Bur Ghana Lang 1976 GH GAA

Abaelu, J.N. Cook, H.L.
Wages of unskilled workers in agriculture and some
characteristics of the farm labour market in the Western
State of Nigeria. 44pp. N2.00 ($3.75/£1.50) (Univ.
Ife, Faculty of Agriculture Research Bull., 3) Univ Ife
Press 1975 NR

Abba, R.
Principles of Christian worship. 196pp. R2.50 South
Africa only Methodist 1977 SA

Abbiw, D.K.
Ndzemba ahyese. [Stories about the Creation.] 4th ed.
59pp. ill. 30pes. Bur Ghana Lang 1973 GH FAT

Abd-Ul-Masih.
Islam and Christianity: 90 questions and answers. 44pp.
25k Daystar 1965 NR

Abdalla, A.
Sauti ya dhiki. [The voice of agony] 80pp.
K.shs.15.25 OUP - Nairobi 1974 KE SWA

Abdalla, A.
Utenzi wa maisha Ya Adam na Hawaa. [Epic poem on
Adam and Eve] 80pp. K.shs5.25 (Vito Vya Kiswahili
(Swahili Gems), 1) OUP-Nairobi 1972 KE SWA

Abdalla, A.G.M., ed.
Studies in ancient languages of the Sudan. 146pp.
maps. 65pt. ($2.50) Khartoum UP 1974 SJ

Abdallah, H.
Utenzi wa Abdirahamani na Sufiyani. [The history of
Abdurrahaman and Sufiyani] 2nd ed. K.shs.7.00
($2.50/£1.00) (Johari za Kiswahili, 2) EALB 1966 KE
SWA

Abdallah, H.
Utenzi wa Seyyid na Husein bin Ali. [The history of
Prince Hussein's son Ali] 130pp. K.shs.5.75
($2.00/80p) EALB 1965 KE SWA

Abdel Rahman Ali Taha, F.
Settlement of the Sudan-Ethiopia boundary dispute.
37pp. 25pt. ($1.50) Khartoum UP 1975 SJ

Abdelmalek, Z.A.
Standard contemporary Arabic. See: Hana, S.

Abdesselem, A.
Les historiens Tunisiens des XVIIe-XVIIIe et XIXe siècles.
D0.350 (Série IV, Histoire, 11) Univ Tunis 1973 TI FRE

Abdesselem, A.
Ithaf ahl az-Zaman d'Ahmad ibn Abi D. Diaf. Ch. VI
(Régime d'Ahmad Bey). Edition critique avec introduction,
analyse et notes en langue française. 354pp. photos.
D2.300 (Série IV, Histoire, 12) Univ Tunis 1971 TI FRE

Abdessemed, B.
T'Fouda, terre africaine. Ifis, l'illuminé du désert. v. 1
352pp. DA31.50 Author (22 avenue du 1er Novembre
Alger, Algeria) 1975 AE FRE

Abdul, M.O.A.
The classical Caliphate. 192pp. N3.50 Islamic 1975
NR

Abdul, M.O.A.
The historical origin of Islam. With some reference to West
Africa. 134pp. ill. N1.50 Islamic 1973 NR

Abdul, M.O.A.
The holy book of Islam: its contents and value. An
introduction to the study of the Qur'an. 105pp. N1.50
(Studies in Islam, 3) Islamic 1971 NR

Abdul, M.O.A.
Islam as a religion: faith and duties. 101pp. ill. N1.25
(Studies in Islam, 1) Islamic 1970 NR

Abdul, M.O.A.
The prophet of Islam. Life sayings and deeds. An
introduction to the study of the Hadith. 120pp. N1.25
(Studies in Islam, 2) Islamic 1970 NR

Abdul, M.O.A.
The selected traditions of Al Nawawi. 90pp. N1.50
Islamic 1974 NR

Abdulkadir, D.
The poetry, life and opinions of Sa'Adu Zungar. N1.65
Northern Nig 1973 NR

Abdulkadir, D.
The poetry, life and opinions of Sa'Adu Zungur. 109pp.
N1.65 Northern Nig 1974 NR

Abdulla, M.S.
Mke mmoja, waume watutu. [Folktale.] 60pp.
K.shs.9.00 ($3.00) EAPH 1975 KE SWA

Abdulla, M.S.
Mwana wa yungi hulewa. [Folktale.] 139pp.
K.shs.12.50 ($3.50) EAPH 1976 KE SWA

Abdulla, M.S.
Mzimu wa watu wa kale. [Thriller] 4th ed. 86pp.
K.shs7.50 ($2.25/60p.) EALB 1975 KE SWA

Abdullahi, J.
Nagari Na Kowa. [A good man is for all] 110pp.
N1.38 Northern Nig 1970 NR HAU

Abedi, K.A.
Sheria za kitunga mashairi na diwani za Amri. [The
poems of Amri essay on Swahili poetry and the rules of
versification] 4th ed. 130pp. K.shs6.00 ($2.00/70p.)
EALB 1965 KE SWA

Abega, P.
Grammaire ewondo. CFA150 Univ Cameroun 1971
CM FRE

Abega, P.
Lexique ewondo. CFA150 Univ Cameroun 1972 CM
FRE

Abibu, A.
Notes on "Animal farm". 80pp. N1.20 Aromolaran
1970 NR

Abilla, W.D.
The Black Muslims in America. A sociological analysis and
commitment. 106pp. K.shs.15.75 ($2.95/£1.45)
EALB 1977 KE

Abimbola, O.
Eko nipa eda ati ilera. bk. 1 See: Ilesanmi, M.A.

Abimbola, O.
Eko nipa eda ati ilera. bk. 2. See: Ilesanmi, M.A.

Abimbola, O.
Eko nipa eda ati ilera. bk. 3. See: Ilesanmi, M.A.

Abimbola, O.
Eko nipa eda ati ilera. bk. 4. See: Ilesanmi, M.A.

Abimbola, W.
Awon oju odu Mereerindinlogun. [The sixteen odus of Ifa
divination.] 158pp. OUP - Nig 1976 NR YOR

Abimbola, W.
Ifa: an exposition of Ifa literary corpus. 256pp. photos.
cl. & pap. N7.50 cl. N4.00 pap. OUP - Nig 1976
NR

Abimbola, W.
Sixteen great poems of Ifa. 470pp. CFA1,140
CELTHO 1975 NG

Abiodun,
Arofo awon omode. Apa kinni. [Poems for children] pt.
1 58pp. maps. 40k OUP-Nig 1971 NR YOR

Abiri, J.O.O.
Moremi: epic of feminine heroism. 76pp. photos. 80k
Onibonoje 1970 NR

Abiri, J.O.O.
Moremi: Itan akoni obinrin. [Moremi: An epic of feminine
heroism] 63pp. photos. 75k Onibonoje 1970 NR
YOR

Ablorh-Odjidja, J.R.
The adventures of Olatunde in Ghana. 42pp. ill.
45pes. Waterville 1974 GH

Aboaba, F.A.
Engineering in the production of food. N1.00
(Inaugural lecture) Ibadan UP 1977 NR

Aboagye, P.A.K.
Nzema anee ne anwo mgbanyidweke. [History of the
Nzema language.] 59pp. 40pes. Bur Ghana Lang
1973 GH NZE

Abour, C.O.
White highlands no more. A modern political history of
Kenya. v. 1. 440pp. ill. map. K.shs.40.00
Pan-African 1973 KE

Aboyade, O.
Incomes profile. 38pp. ill. 70k Univ Ibadan Bkshop
1973 NR

Aboyade, O.
Issues in the development of tropical Africa. 125pp. cl. &
pap. N7.00 cl. N5.00 pap. Ibadan UP 1976 NR

Aboyade, T. O'Connell, J. Dudley, B.
Nigeria 1965: crisis and criticism. 130pp. N1.20
Ibadan UP 1966 NR

Abraham, A.
The pattern of warfare and settlement among the Mende of
Sierra Leone in the second half of the nineteenth century.
60c. ($1.00) (Inst. of African Studies, occas. paps., 1)
Inst Afr Stud - FBC 1976 SL

Abraham, A.
Topics in Sierra Leone history. ($5.00/£2.50) Leone
Publ 1976 SL

Abraham, J.H.
Technology, politics and value. 22pp. C1.00
($1.00/50p.) (Inaugural lecture) Ghana UP 1970 GH

Abraham, R.C.
The principles of Amharic. 245pp. hd. N2.00 (Inst. of
African Stud. Univ of Ibadan, occas. pub., 9) Inst Afr
Stud-Ibadan 1968 NR

Abraham, R.C.
The principles of Ibo. 154pp. hd. N2.00 (Inst. of
African Stud., Univ. of Ibadan, occas. pub., 4) Inst Afr
Stud-Ibadan 1967 NR

Abrahams, L.
The celibacy of Felix Greenspan. R5.25 ($7.00/£3.75)
Bateleur 1977 SA

Abrahamse, L.
South Africa: the next fifteen years: a microcosm of world
problems. See: Oppenheimer, H.F.

Abrahamson, B.
The nature of modern mathematics. ex. only
(Inaugural lec.) Rhodes Univ Lib 1959 SA

Abruquah, J.W.
The catechist. 2nd ed. 202pp. C1.00 ($1.00)
Ghana Publ Corp 1971 GH

Abu Al-Izz, M.S.
Landforms of Egypt. 281pp. L.E.4.000 ($10.00) Am
Univ 1971 UA

Abudu, M.
Methali za Kiswahili. Maana na matumizi. [Kiswahili
proverbs. Meaning and usage.] 32pp. K.shs.4.50
($2.50) Foundation 1974 KE SWA

Abukutsa, J.L., ed.
The role of books in development. Proceedings of the fifth
biennial conference of the Kenya Library Association
Nairobi, 25-29 September, 1972. 141pp. Kenya Lib
Assoc 1974 KE

Abul-Naga, A.
Recherche sur les termes de théâtre et leur traduction en
Arabe moderne. 303pp. 15,00 DA SNED 1973 AE
FRE

Abul-Naga, A.
Les sources Françaises du théâtre Egyptien. 340pp.
15,00 DA SNED 1973 AE FRE

Abushama, F.T.
A guide to the physiology of terrestrial arthropoda.
See: Cloudsley-Thompson, J.L.

Acaye, M.
Agwata matek ma ma puku. 72pp. K.shs4.00
($3.00/£1.25) EALB 1972 KE ACH

Accam, T.N.
Gbi sitemi. [Introduction to Dangme language] 50pp. ill.
20pes. Waterville 1969 GH DAG

Accam, T.N.
Gbi sitemi setsc. [A sequel to Gbi Sitemi] 62pp. ill.
20pes. Waterville 1970 GH DAG

Accam, T.N.N.
Dangme munyutulc. [Dangme speaker.] 67pp.
40pes. Bur Ghana Lang 1973 GH DAG

Achara, D.N.
Ala Bingo. [A story] 38pp. col. ill. 45k Longman -
Nig 1972 NR IGB

Achara, D.N.
Elelia na ihe o mere. [Elelia and his deeds.] 122pp. ill.
65k Longman - Nig 1974 NR IGB

Achara, D.N.
Elelia na ihe o mere. [Language text.] New ed.
122pp. ill. 65k Longman - Nig 1974 NR IGB

Achebe, C.
Beware soul brother and other poems. 80pp. 75k
Nwamife 1971 NR

Achebe, C.
Eby'edda bisasika. [Things fall apart tr. fr. English B. L.
Walakira] 154pp. K.shs.8.00 (80p.) Heinemann
Educ - Nair 1971 KE LUG

Achebe, C. et al.
The insider: stories of war and peace in Nigeria. 124pp.
75k Nwamife 1971 NR

Achebe, C.
Hamkani: si whwari tena. [No longer at ease] 168pp.
ill. K.shs7.00 ($2.60) EAPH 1972 KE SWA

Achebe, C. Iroaganachi, J.
How the leopard got his claws. 35pp. ill. pap. & cl.
N1.25 cl. 75k pap. Nwamife 1972 NR

Achebe, C. Iroagariachi, J.
How the leopard got its claws. 48pp. col. ill.
K.shs.10.00 ($3.20 East Africa only) EAPH 1976 KE

Achebe, C.
Mshale wa Mungu. [Arrow of God.] 220pp.
K.shs.17.00 (Waandishi wa Kiafrika, 17) Heinemann
Educ - Nair 1977 KE SWA

Achebe, C.
Mwakilishi wa watu. [A man of the people] 142pp.
K.shs.15.00 (Waandishi wa Kiafrika, 16) Heinemann
Educ - Nair 1977 KE SWA

Achike, O.
Nigerian law of contract. 356pp. cl. N11.00 Nwamife
1973 NR

Achinivu, K.
Akwukwo nke mbu [Primary Igbo course book].
[Primary Igbo course book 1] bk. 1 40pp. col. ill.
32k Longman - Nig NR IGB

Achinivu, K.
Akwukwo nke mbu [Primary Igbo course book].
[Primary Igbo course book 3] bk. 3 80pp. 50k
Longman - Nig 1963 NR IGB

Achour, M.
Heliotropes. 196pp. DA8.00 SNED 1973 AE FRE

Achour, M.
Le survivant et autres nouvelles. 306pp. DA7.60
SNED 1971 AE FRE

Ackah, M.K.
Abibile maanle. [History of Africa.] 139pp. map.
85pes. Bur Ghana Lang 1974 GH NZE

Acocks, J.P.H.
Veld types of South Africa. ill. pl. map. R7.20
(R8.70) (Memoirs of the Botanical Survey of South Africa,
40) Botanical Res Inst 1975 SA

Acquah, I.
Accra survey. 2nd ed. 176pp. photos. ill. cl. C4.24
(£2.20/$4.24) Ghana UP 1972 GH

Acsadi, G.T., ed.
Demographic statistics in Nigeria: proceedings of the
symposium on technical and practical problems in the
collection of demographic statistics for reconstructions and
development in Nigeria. See: Igun, A.A., ed.

Adadevoh, B.K.
Sub-fertility and infertility in Africa. Report on an
international workshop on correlates of sub-fertility and
infertility in Africa, held at the Conference Centre,
University of Ibadan, Nigeria, November 26-30, 1973.
114pp. N5.00 (£3.00) ($7.50) Author c/o National
Inst for Medical Research, P.M.B. 2013, Yaba, Lagos
State, Nigeria 1974 NR

Adalemo, I.A.
Marketing of cash crops in the Kainji lake basin.
(N.I.S.E.R. monographs, 1) NISER 1972 NR

Adamolekun, N.K.
Introduction to government. 208pp. N1.70 Macmillan
1971 NR

Adamou, N.N.
Dairou IV. 52pp. CFA250 (Coll. Théâtre) CLE 1973
CM FRE

Adams, L.P.
What is land surveying? 14pp. 30c (Univ. Cape
Town. Inaugural lec., 21) Univ Cape Town Lib 1973 SA

Adams, P.
Grass for the unicorn. R4.20 Juta 1976 SA

Adamson, J.
Simba kaishi na wanadamu. [Born free] 52pp. photos.
K.shs.2.50 ($1.00) EAPH 1966 KE SWA

Adamson, R.S.
Notes on the vegetation of the Kamiesberg. 25c.
(Memoirs of the Botanical Survey of South Africa, 18)
Botanical Res Inst 1938 SA

Adamu, A.A.
The Nigerian statistical system. N5.00 Ibadan UP
1977 NR

Adamu, H.A.
The North and Nigerian unity: some reflections on the
political, social and educational problems of Northern
Nigeria. 74pp. 40k Dept Govt- ABU NR

Adamu, S.O. Johnson, T.
Statistics for beginners. 286pp. ill. N3.25 Onibonoje
1974 NR

Adamu, S.O. Johnson, T.L.
Statistics for beginners: Workbook. 180pp. ill. N2.25
Onibonoje 1975 NR

Adande, A.
Les récades des rois du Dahomey. 104pp. pl.
CFA1200 (Catalogues et Documents, 15) IFAN 1962
SG FRE

Adansi, M.A.
Coconut in Ghana. See: Chona, B.L.

Adaralegbe, A.
Africans in their environment. 2, 3 bks. 292pp. maps.
N1.50 Onibonoje 1964 NR

Adaralegbe, A., ed.
Education in Nigeria - towards better administration and
supervision of instruction: Proceedings of first seminar on
school admin., etc. Ile-Ife, August 24-30, 1969.
See: Fafunwa, A.B., ed.

Adaralegbe, A., ed.
A philosophy for Nigerian education. 347pp. N4.75
Heinemann Educ - Nig 1972 NR

Adaralegbe, A.
Man in his environment. 1, 3 bks. 183pp. maps ill.
N1.50 Onibonoje 1972 NR

Adaye, J.J.
Bere adu. [Now is the hour] rev. ed. 127pp.
60pes. Waterville 1969 GH TWI

Addae, S.K.
The kidney in sickle cell disease. 142pp. pl. hd.
C12.00 ($12.00/£6.00) Ghana UP 1975 GH

Addae, S.K.
Temperature, hormones and the kidney in sickle cell
disease. 11pp. C1.00 ($1.00/50p.) (Inaugural
lecture) Ghana UP 1971 GH

Addo, M.
Ghana's foreign policy in retrospect. 49pp. photos.
maps. 20pes. Waterville 1967 GH

Addo, N.O. et al.
Symposium on implications of population trends for policy
measures in West Africa. 170pp. C3.00 (Univ.
Ghana, Population Studies, 3) Univ Ghana Bkshop; distr.
1969 GH

Addo, N.O. et al.
Symposium on population and socio-economic
development in Ghana. 162pp. C3.00 (C4.50)
(Ghana Population Stud., 2) Univ Ghana Bkshop 1969
GH

Addow, E.R.
Anansesen ne Ayesem. 30pp. ill. 30pes. ($.30)
Ghana Publ Corp 1969 GH TWI

Addow, E.R.
Edin ne mmrane. [Names and appellations.] 2nd ed.
93pp. ill. C1.20 Bur Ghana Lang 1976 GH ASA

Addy, P.L.N.A.
Economics of cocoa production and marketing with special
reference to Ghana. See: Okali, C.

Ade-Ajayi, C.
Ade, our naughty little brother. 65pp. 65k (Junior
African Literature Series, 15) Onibonoje 1975 NR

Ade-Ajayi, C.
The old story teller. 35pp. ill. 55k (Junior African
Literature Series, 14) Onibonoje 1976 NR

Adebara, D.
B'oju ri. [What the eye sees] 113pp. N1.10
Onibonoje 1969 NR YOR

Adebara, D.
Economic atlas of West Africa. 160pp. ill. maps. cl. &
pap. N6.50 cl. N4.00 pap. ($10.00/£5.50 cl.)
($6.20/£3.50 pap.) Adebara 1977 NR

Adebayo, G.A.
Agbeka Yoruba. [Presentation of Yoruba.] 2nd ed.
bk. 1. 97pp. 95k Ilesanmi 1975 NR YOR

Adebayo, G.A.
Agbeka Yoruba. [Presentation of Yoruba.] 2nd ed.
bk. 2. 128pp. 95k Ilesanmi 1975 NR YOR

Adebimpe, S.O.
Revision notes in nature study and hygiene for Nigerian
schools. 2nd rev. ed. 60pp. ill. 50k Macmillan
1966 NR

Adebisi, G.A.
Geography made easy (Northern State) 1, 2 bks 110pp.
maps photos. N1.25 Ilesanmi 1971 NR

Adebisi, G.A.
Geography made easy (Northern State) 2, 2 bks 101pp.
maps photos. N1.25 Ilesanmi 1971 NR

Adebisi, G.A.
Geography made easy (Western State) 2nd ed. 1, 2
bks 99pp. maps photos. ill. N1.35 Ilesanmi 1971
NR

Adebisi, G.A.
Geography made easy (Western State) 2nd ed. 2, 2
bks 101pp. maps photos. N1.35 Ilesanmi 1971 NR

Adebiyi, A.
Lati okunkun si imole. [From darkness into light] 35pp.
10 Daystar 1965 NR YOR

Adebiyi, B.
Bi a se le bori idewo esu. [How to overcome temptation]
26pp. 15k Daystar NR YOR

Adebiyi, B.
Bisobu ayanfe: Itan igbe-aiye Bisobu A.B. Akinyele.
[Beloved bishop: the story of the life of Bishop A.B.
Akinyele] 65pp. 20k Daystar NR YOR

Adebiyi, B.
Danger: easy money. 2nd ed. 37pp. 10k Daystar
1971 NR

Adebiyi, T.A.
The beloved bishop. 102pp. photos. 85k Daystar
1969 NR

Adebiyi, T.A.
Ibere ati idahun l'ori awon itan inu Bibeli. [Bible quiz and
answers] 57pp. 15k Daystar 1969 NR YOR

Adebiyi, T.A.
Two kinds of love. 31pp. 10k Daystar 1967 NR

Adebolu, F.
Objective tests in school certificate biology. 100pp.
N2.00 Armolaran 1970 NR

Adeboyejo, S.
Eto isin ikomojade. [Programme for child-naming]
12pp. 5k Daystar 1969 NR YOR

Adedeji, A., ed.   Hyden, G., ed.
Developing research in African administration. Some
methodological issues. 320pp. cl. & pap. N5.00 pap.
N8.00 cl. ($8.00 pap.) ($12.95 cl.) Univ Ife Press (US
& West Africa only; in East Africa: EALB) 1975 NR

Adedeji, A., ed.   Hyden, G., ed.
Developing research on African administration. Some
methodological issues. 201pp. K.shs.36.75 no West
Africa ($6.60/£3.10) EALB 1974 KE

Adedeji, A., ed.   Rowland, L., ed.
Local government finance in Nigeria - problems and
prospects: the report of the third national conference on
local government, held in Benin City, 9-11 December,
1970. 352pp. N3.80 (£3.50/$8.95) Univ Ife Press
1973 NR

Adedeji, A., ed.   Rowland, L., ed.
Management problems of rapid urbanization in Nigeria: the
challenge to governments and local authorities. 368pp.
hd. N4.95 (£5.00/$12.00) Univ Ife Press 1973 NR

Adedeji, A., ed.
Problems and techniques of administrative training in
Africa. 157pp. N2.50 ($3.60/£1.50) Univ Ife Press
1969 NR

Adedeji, A.
The Tanzania civil service a decade after independence:
progress, problems and prospects. 30pp. 75k
(60p./$1.40) (Univ. of Ife, Inst. of Administration
Monograph Series, 2) Univ Ife Press 1974 NR

Adedeji, R.
The fat woman. 7pp. ill. 35k Onibonoje 1973 NR

Adedeji, R.
Four stories about the tortoise. 25pp. ill. 40k
Onibonoje 1973 NR

Adedeji, R.
It's time for stories. 33pp. ill. 40k Onibonoje 1973
NR

Adedeji, R.
Papa Ojo and his family. 9pp. ill. 35k Onibonoje
1973 NR

Adedun, J.   Omiyale, T.A.
Key (answer book) to Path to common examination I & II.
28pp. 60k Ilesanmi 1970 NR

Adedun, J.A.   Onibokun, E.A.
Comprehension exercises for Nigerian schools. 87pp.
55k Ilesanmi 1971 NR

Adedun, J.A.   Fagbemi, J.O.   Omiyale, T.A.
Path to common entrance examination. 1, 2 pts 123pp.
N1.35 Ilesanmi 1970 NR

Adedun, J.A.   Fagbemi, J.O.   Omiyale, T.A.
Path to common entrance examination. 2, 2pts. 125pp.
N1.35 Ilesanmi 1970 NR

Adegbesan, J.O.
Idoani past and present: the story of one Yoruba kingdom.
See: Asabia, D.O.

Adegbola, A.A.
All flesh is grass. 13pp. 30k (Inaugural lec., 3)
Univ Ife Press 1973 NR

Adegoke, O.S., eds.
The ecology of Lake Kainji. See: Imevbore, A.M.A., eds.

Adejuyigbe, J.O.
Boundary problems in Western Nigeria: a geographical
analysis. 226pp. maps. N6.00 ($10.00/£4.75)
Univ Ife Press 1975 NR

Adejuyigbe, O.   Olagbaiye, A.
Ile-Ife: guide maps. 12pp. fold-out maps. 75k Univ
Ife Bkshop 1975 NR

Adekanla, B.
Notes, questions/answers on "Mayor of Casterbridge".
41pp. N1.20 Aromolaran 1975[?] NR

Adekanla, B.
Revision questions/answers on "Mayor of Casterbridge".
52pp. N1.20 Aromolaran 1975(?) NR

Adekola, A.O.
The art of construction and the science of material.
27pp. ill. 20k Univ Lagos Bookshop 1971 NR

Adekola, D.A.
Bibeli iwe iyanu. [Bible a mysterious book] 32pp.
15k Daystar 1970 NR YOR

Adekoya, O.C.   Vagale, L.R.
Industrial environment of an African city: case study of
Ibadan, Nigeria. 96pp. pl. maps. hd. N6.00 cl. Dept
Town Poly - Ib 1974 NR

Adelaja, S.
Modern primary mathematics. pupils bk. 4. See: Halim,
E.C.

Adelakun, A.A.
Onibonoje modern mathematics for secondary schools.
bk. 2 See: Ojo, J.B.O.

Adelakun, A.A.
Onibonoje modern mathematics for secondary schools.
bk. 3 See: Ojo, J.B.O.

Adelakun, A.A.
Onibonoje modern mathematics for secondary schools.
bk. 4 See: Ojo, J.B.O.

Adelowo, D.
Questions and answers on 'O' level Bible knowledge. (New
Testament) 136pp. N2.00 Aromolaran 1975[?] NR

Adelowo, D.   Dopamu, D.
Revision questions/answers on 'O' level Bible knowledge.
(Old Testament) bk. 1. 157pp. N2.00 Aromolaran
1975[?] NR

Adeloye, A., ed.
Nigerian pioneers of modern medicine: selected writings.
299pp. cl. & pap. N9.00 cl. N7.00 pap. Ibadan UP
1977 NR

Adeloye, A.
Henry Dallimore. 16pp. 15k Daystar 1970 NR

Adelusi, O.
English and verbal aptitude tests. 180pp. N1.25
Onibonoje 1969 NR

Adelusi, O. et al.
Complete objective tests in English language. 234pp.
N1.50 Onibonoje 1969 NR

Adelusi, O.   Dada, S.A.
Hints and solutions to apptitude tests. 32pp. 40k
Onibonoje 1966 NR

Adelusi, O.
"Things Fall Apart": notes. 96pp. 85k Onibonoje 1966 NR

Ademola, F., ed.
Reflections. 120pp. 62k Pilgrim 1962 NR

Ademosun, A.A.
Livestock production in Nigeria: our commission and omission. 24pp. 75k. ($1.40/60p.) Univ Ife Press 1976 NR

Adenadaga, C.
Sensole kukui. [The behaviour of birds and animals.] 18pp. ill. 20pes. Bur Ghana Lang 1973 GH KAE

Adeniji, D.A. et al.
The Oxford arithmetic course for Nigeria. workbook 4. 33pp. ill. 40k. OUP - Nig 1977 NR

Adeniji, D.A. et al.
The Oxford arithmetic course for Nigeria. workbook 5. 33pp. ill. 40k. OUP - Nig 1977 NR

Adeniji, D.A. et al.
The Oxford arithmetic course for Nigeria. workbook 6. 31pp. ill. 40k. OUP - Nig 1977 NR

Adeniji, D.A. et al.
Oxford arithmetic course (Nig.): pupils bk. 3rd ed. 1, 6 bks. 64pp. ill. 60k OUP - Nig 1973 NR

Adeniji, D.A. et al.
Oxford arithmetic course (Nig.): pupils bk. 3rd ed. 2, 6 bks. 64pp. ill. 65 OUP - Nig 1973 NR

Adeniji, D.A. et al.
Oxford arithmetic course (Nig.): pupils bk. 3rd ed. 3, 6 bks. 185pp. N1.00 OUP - Nig 1973 NR

Adeniji, D.A. et al.
Oxford arithmetic course (Nig.): pupils bk. 3rd ed. 4, 6 bks N1.00 OUP - Nig NR

Adeniji, D.A. et al.
Oxford arithmetic course (Nig.): pupils bk. 3rd ed. 5, 6 bks. N1.25 OUP - Nig NR

Adeniyi, E.O.
The North-Western state development plan 1970-1974 a selective appraisal. (N.I.S.E.R. Occas. paps., 1) NISER 1973 NR

Adeniyi, T.
The lunatic and other features. An epitome of our golden age. 77pp. ill. N1.00 Deto Deni 1976 NR

Adeniyi, T.
Soul fire, and other poems. 50pp. 50k Aromolaran 1973 NR

Adenuga, I.J.
Integrated science. See: Maxwell, D.A.

Adeoye, C.L.
Eda omo Odua. [Man: a creation of Odua] 137pp. maps. 75k OUP-Nig 1971 NR YOR

Adeoye, C.L.
Oruko Yoruba. [Yoruba names] 129pp. ill. 75k OUP-Nig 1972 NR YOR

Adeoye, K.B.
A note on the reliability of rainfall at Samaru and Kano, Nigeria. 30k (Samaru misc. pap., 54) Inst Agric Res - Zaria 1976 NR

Adepeju, A.
Vegetable gardening. 24pp. ill. 40k Daystar 1976 NR

Adepoju, A.
Biology revision notes on school certificate. 141pp. N2.00 Ilesanmi 1972 NR

Adepoju, L.
Ladepo omo adanwo. [Ladepo: a child of temptation] 110pp. 90k Onibonoje 1974 NR YOR

Adepoju, O.
Ironu Akewi. [Philosophical thoughts] 66pp. 90k Onibonoje 1972 NR YOR

Adepoju, O.
Sagba di were. [Make the adult mad] 95pp. N1.10 Onibonoje 1972 NR YOR

Aderibigbe, A.B., ed.
Lagos: the development of an African city. 276pp. photos. Longman - Nig 1976 NR

Adesanya, M. O.
Business law in Nigeria. 329pp. hd. N7.50 ($7.50) Univ Lagos Press 1972 NR

Adesanya, S.A.
Laws of matrimonial causes. 294pp. cl. & pap. N8.00 cl. N5.00 pap. Ibadan UP 1973 NR

Adetoro, J.E.
A geography course for junior secondary schools in Nigeria. rev. ed. 1, 3bks ill. N1.20 Macmillan 1969 NR

Adetoro, J.E.
A geography course for junior secondary schools in Nigeria. rev. ed. 2, 3 bks ill. N1.30 Macmillan 1969 NR

Adetoro, J.E.
A geography course for junior secondary schools in Nigeria. rev. ed. 3, 3bks ill. N1.45 Macmillan 1969 NR

Adetoro, J.E.
A history course for junior secondary schools in Nigeria. 1, 3 bks 196pp. ill. maps. N1.20 Macmillan 1964 NR

Adetoro, J.E.
A history course for junior secondary schools in Nigeria. 2, 3 bks 226pp. ill. maps. N1.30 Macmillan 1964 NR

Adetoro, J.E.
A history course for junior secondary schools in Nigeria. rev. ed. 3, 3 bks 208pp. ill. maps. N1.30 Macmillan 1964 NR

Adetoro, J.E.
A national bureau of ideas. 262pp. N2.00 Town & Gown 1974 NR

Adetoro, J.E.
A primary history for Nigeria. 1, 4 bks 48pp. col. ill. N1.15 Macmillan 1965 NR

Adetoro, J.E.
A primary history for Nigeria. 2, 4 bks 64pp. col. ill. N1.30 Macmillan 1965 NR

Adetoro, J.E.
A primary history for Nigeria. 3, 4 bks 80pp. ill. N1.30 Macmillan 1965 NR

Adetoro, J.E.
A primary history for Nigeria. 4, 4 bks 90pp. ill. N1.40 Macmillan 1965 NR

Adetoro, J.E.
Social studies for Nigeria: pupils' bk. 1, 3 bks. N1.15 Macmillan NR

Adetoro, J.E.
Social studies for Nigeria: pupils' bk. 2, 3 bks. N1.00 Macmillan NR

Adetoro, J.E.
Social studies for Nigeria: pupils' bk. 3, 3 bks. N1.30 Macmillan NR

Adetoro, J.E.
Social studies for Nigeria: teacher's bk. 1, 3 bks. 65k Macmillan NR

Adetoro, J.E.
Social studies for Nigeria: teacher's bk. 2, 3 bks. 65k Macmillan NR

Adetoro, J.E.
Social studies for Nigeria: teacher's bk. 3, 3 bks. 68k Macmillan NR

Adetoye, F.
Advanced level economics of West Africa: questions and answers. 158pp. N1.60 Onibonoje 1969 NR

Adetuyi, V.
All is not lost. 80k Ilesanmi 1972 NR

Adetuyi, V.T.
"West African verse": notes. 64pp. 85k Onibonoje 1972 NR

Adewoye, O., ed.
Background to the names of roads and halls at Ibadan University. 24pp. 50k Ibadan UP 1969 NR

Adewumi, A.Y.
Preparing for the school certificate English. 144pp. N1.60 Ilesanmi 1971 NR

Adewuya, B.
Topics in European history, 1415-1715. 101pp. 45k Onibonoje 1970 NR

Adeyanju, D.
Notes on school certificate regional geography. (Northwest Europe and North America) 120pp. N2.00 Aromolaran 1975[?] NR

Adeyanju, D.
Notes on school certificate regional geography. (West Africa) 106pp. N2.00 Armolaran 1970 NR

Adeyemi, O., comp.
National telephone directory of Nigeria. 2nd. ed. 982pp. cl. N15.00 ($30.00) ICIC 1974 NR

Adeyemi, O., ed.
Nigerian yellow pages. 1,000pp. N20.00 ($40.00) ICIC 1976 NR

Adeyemi, O.
The Nigerian Naira and kobo standard reckoner. 424pp. cl. N5.00 ($10.00) ICIC NR

Adeyemi, O.
Nigerian office and residential directory. v. 4, no. 1 750pp. N15.00 ($30.00) ICIC NR

Adeyinka, A.
A'level Old Testament: from monarchy to exile - questions and answers. 139pp. N1.35 Onibonoje 1972 NR

Adeyinka, A.
New Testament: essays on Mark, Matthew and Acts. 104pp. 85k Onibonoje 1970 NR

Adeyinka, A.
O'level essays in New Testament; Luke and the Acts. 91pp. 50k Onibonoje 1966 NR

Adeyinka, A.
O'level textbook on Luke and the Acts. 148pp. N1.50 Onibonoje 1972 NR

Adeyinka, A.
Synoptic gospels: questions and answers for A'level. 114pp. N1.35 Onibonoje 1972 NR

Adeyoju, S.K.
Forestry and the Nigerian economy. 308pp. cl. & pap. N5.00 pap. N8.00 cl. Ibadan UP 1975 NR

Adighibe, J., ed.
Directory and Who's Who in Liberia. 340pp. photos. maps. cl. U.S.$5.00 Cole & Yancy 1971 LB

Adigwe, F.
Essentials of government for West Africa. 390pp. N3.50 OUP - Nig 1974 NR

Adiko, A.
Histoire des peuples noirs. 192pp. ill. maps. cl. CFA770 cl. CEDA 1963 IV FRE

Adimola, A.B.
Lobo Acoli. [A geographical survey of the Acoli District] 37pp. K.shs.1.50 ($1.50/60p.) EALB 1956 KE LUO

Adinyira, F.K.
Tartuif. [Hypocrite.] 2nd ed. 176pp. ill. C1.20 Bur Ghana Lang 1975 GH EWE

Adiuku, T.I.
A handbook of physical education for elementary schools. 148pp. N1.50 Macmillan NR

Adler, F.B.
The South African field artillery in German East Africa and Palestine (1915-1919) R3.00 Van Schaik SA

Adler, T., ed.
Perspectives on Southern Africa. A collection of working papers. 366pp. R3.50 (African Studies Institute, Communications, 4) African Studies Inst - Wit 1977 SA

Adult Education Association of Zambia.
Adult education and development. 38pp. 40n. Neczam 1970 ZA

Adult Education Centre.
Handbook for community development. 114pp. hd. U.shs.5.00 (Social workers manual, 2) Adult Educ Centre 1968 UG

Adult Education Centre.
The press. 27pp. U.shs1.00 Adult Educ Centre 1970 UG

Adult Education Centre.
Teaching adult club groups. 212pp. hd. U.shs.7.50 (Social workers manual, 1) Adult Educ Centre 1968 UG

Adumua, S.T.
Dzen sadzi fa. [Happenings in life are many] 40pp. ill. 15pes. Waterville 1966 GH GAA

Advance Publ. Co. Ltd.
Accra-Tema in pictures. 168pp. pl. C1.00 Advance 1969 GH

Advance Publ. Co. Ltd.
Behold the man. 76pp. ill. 30pes. Advance 1969 GH

Afenyo, G.Y.
200 objective questions in physics with answers and solutions. 54pp. ill. C1.50 Afram 1975 GH

Afenyo, G.Y.
Comprehensive studies in 'O' level statistics. 64pp. C3.00 Afram 1975 GH

Afenyo, G.Y.
Physics for easy reading. 64pp. ill. C3.00 Afram 1975 GH

Afenyo, G.Y.
Revision questions and answers in general science physics. 40pp. C1.20 Afram 1976 GH

Affia, G.B.
Nigerian crisis, 1966-1970. 24pp. 30k Univ Lagos Bookshop 1970 NR

Afia, M.S.
Fodikwan iron ore deposits. See: Kabesh, M.L.

Afia, M.S. Widatalla, A.L.
An investigation of Hofrat en Nahas copper deposits, Southern Darfur. 131pp. maps pl. £S1.30 ($1.47/£1.60) (Bulletin, 10) Geol and Min Res - Sudan 1961 SJ

Afia, M.S.
Manganese ore deposits of the Sudan. See: Kabesh, M.L.

Afia, M.S.
The Wollastonite deposits of Dirbat well. See: Kabesh, M.L.

Afigbo, A.E.
Studies in Igbo history and culture. 400pp. ill. N12.00 Cross Continent 1977 NR

Afolabi, H.
Prospects of planning-programming-budgeting as a management technique in a university organisation. 51pp. 55k (40p./$1.00) Inst Admin - Zaria 1968 NR

Afolabi Ojo, G.J.
Culture and modernization in Nigeria. 23pp. N1.50 ($2.50/£1.10) (Faculty of Arts Lecture Series, 5) Univ Ife Press 1975 NR

Afolalu, R.O.
A.D. 1,000 to the present day. 395pp. ill. maps. N2.20 Onibonoje 1971 NR

Afolalu, R.O.
History of Africa since 1800. 317pp. maps. N2.00 Onibonoje 1972 NR

Author Index

Afonja, Y.A.O., comps.
Small-scale industries: Midwestern State, Kwara State, and Lagos State of Nigeria. See: Aluko, S., comps.

Afre, S.A., comp.
Directory of research in the social sciences and humanities in Ghana, 1974-76. 55pp. C2.00 Cape Coast UP 1975 GH

Africa Bibliographic Centre.
An Africa Bibliographic Centre (ABC) - an outline. 6pp. T.shs.15.00 ($2.00) (Africa Bibliographic Centre, Position Paper, 4) Africa Bibliographic Centre 1975 TZ

Africa Bibliographic Centre.
Status report on progress towards an Africa Bibliographic Centre. 4pp. T.shs.15.00 ($2.00) (Africa Bibliographic Centre, Position Papers, 2) Africa Bibliographic Centre 1975 TZ

Africa Christian Press.
Being sure of salvation. 24pp. 20pes. (6p.) (Way of Life Booklets, 2) Africa Christian 1968 GH

Africa Christian Press.
The Christian and sport. 24pp. ill. 40pes. (12p.) Africa Christian 1967 GH

Africa Christian Press.
Christian witness among Muslims. Popular abbrev. ed. 32pp. 40pes. (10p.) Africa Christian 1972 GH

Africa Christian Press.
Christian witness among Muslims. Standard ed. 96pp. C1.00 (30p.) Africa Christian 1971 GH

Africa Christian Press.
God. 32pp. 25pes. (9p.) (What the Bible Teaches Booklets, 1) Africa Christian 1974 GH

Africa Christian Press.
Growing in the Christian life. 24pp. 20pes. (6p.) (Way of Life Booklets, 3) Africa Christian 1968 GH

Africa Christian Press.
The Holy Spirit. 32pp. 25pes. (9p.) (What the Bible Teaches Booklet, 3) Africa Christian 1974 GH

Africa Christian Press.
Jesus Christ. 32pp. 25pes. (9p.) (What the Bible Teaches Booklets, 2) Africa Christian 1974 GH

Africa Christian Press.
Knowing God's guidance. 24pp. 20pes. (6p.) (Way of Life Booklets, 6) Africa Christian 1969 GH

Africa Christian Press.
Leading a friend to Christ. 24pp. 20pes. (6p.) (Way of Life Booklets, 5) Africa Christian 1969 GH

Africa Christian Press.
Learning to pray. 24pp. 20pes. (6p.) (Way of Life Booklets, 7) Africa Christian 1969 GH

Africa Christian Press.
Let's study the Bible together. 44pp. map. 40pes. (15p.) Africa Christian 1973 GH

Africa Christian Press.
Letters to a student. 48pp. ill. 45pes. (15p.) Africa Christian 1972 GH

Africa Christian Press.
Living songs. 80pp. C1.00 (32p.) Africa Christian 1975 GH

Africa Christian Press.
Living Songs. Music edition. [With melody, guitar chords and tonic solfa.]. 320pp. C5.40 (£1.98) Africa Christian 1975 GH

Africa Christian Press.
More letters to Gabriel. 32pp. ill. 45pes. (15p.) Africa Christian 1973 GH

Africa Christian Press.
Nimekuwa kiumbe kipya. [I became a new person] 56pp. T.shs.2.50 Central Tanganyika 1974 TZ SWA

Africa Christian Press.
Overcoming temptation. 24pp. 20pes. (6p.) (Way of Life Booklets, 4) Africa Christian 1968 GH

Africa Christian Press.
Receiving Christ as saviour. 24pp. 20pes. (6p.) (Way of Life Booklets, 1) Africa Christian 1968 GH

Africa Christian Press.
Réponses à vos questions. 52pp. CFA200 CPE 1973 IV FRE

Africa Christian Press.
The spirits. 32pp. ill. 25pes. (10p.) (What the Bible Teaches Booklets, 5) Africa Christian 1976 GH

Africa Christian Press.
Stephen on holiday. 56pp. ill. 45pes. (15p.) Africa Christian 1969 GH

Africa Christian Press.
This faith works. True stories of changed lives. 48pp. 40pes. (10p.) Africa Christian 1967 GH

Africa Christian Press.
The Trinity. 32pp. 25pes. (9p.) (What the Bible Teaches Booklets, 4) Africa Christian 1974 GH

Africa Christian Press.
Trusting God's word. 24pp. 20pes. (6p.) (Way of Life Booklets, 8) Africa Christian 1969 GH

Africa Christian Press.
What is a Christian? 24pp. 20pes. (6p.) (Way of Life Booklets, 10) Africa Christian 1970 GH

Africa Christian Press.
Work! 64pp. ill. 50pes. (20p.) Africa Christian 1968 GH

Africa Christian Press.
Your exams. 24pp. 20pes. (6p.) (Way of Life Booklets, 9) Africa Christian 1970 GH

Africa Christian Press.
Your questions answered. 40pp. 45pes. (15p.) Africa Christian 1967 GH

Africa Inland Mission.
Nyimbo za Sifa. [The hymns of praise] Reprint of 1964 ed. T.shs.11.00 Africa Inland Church 1972 TZ SWA

Africa Institute of South Africa.
Africa at a glance. R1.50 (R2.00) Africa Inst - Pret 1973 SA

Africa Institute of South Africa.
Africa in the sixties. 329pp. ill. R6.90 (60c) Africa Inst - Pret 1970 SA

Africa Institute of South Africa.
Africa: maps and statistics, cplte. series 1-8. maps. R6.00 Africa Inst - Pret 1964 SA

Africa Institute of South Africa.
Africa wall chart (1,000x640mm) maps. 75c (R1.00) Africa Inst - Pret 1971 SA

Africa Institute of South Africa.
Agriculture and forestry. maps. 75c (R1.00) (Africa: Maps and statistics, 6) Africa Inst - Pret 1963 SA

Africa Institute of South Africa.
Animal husbandry and fisheries. maps. 75c (R1.00) (Africa: Maps and statistics, 7) Africa Inst - Pret 1964 SA

Africa Institute of South Africa.
Countries of Africa: Angola and Mocambique. ill. 50c (60c) Africa Inst - Pret 1969 SA

Africa Institute of South Africa.
Countries of Africa: Madagascar. ill. 50c (60c) Africa Inst - Pret 1968 SA

Africa Institute of South Africa.
Countries of Africa: Mauritius. ill. 50c (60c) Africa Inst - Pret 1968 SA

Africa Institute of South Africa.
Countries of Africa: South West Africa. ill. 50c (60c) Africa Inst - Pret 1970 SA

Africa Institute of South Africa.
Cultural and educational aspects. maps. R1.00 75c (Africa: Maps and statistics, 3) Africa Inst - Pret 1963 SA

Africa Institute of South Africa.
The francophone countries of West and Central Africa. 140pp. ill. R2.50 (60c) Africa Inst - Pret 1973 SA

Africa Institute of South Africa.
Mining, industries and labour. maps. 75c (R1.00)
(Africa: Maps and statistics, 8) Africa Inst - Pret 1964 SA

Africa Institute of South Africa.
Population. maps. 75c (R1.00) (Africa: Maps and
statistics, 1) Africa Inst - Pret 1962 SA

Africa Institute of South Africa.
Southern Africa at a glance. R1.00 (R1.20) Africa
Inst - Pret 1972 SA

Africa Institute of South Africa.
Southern Africa data. [Bilingual series containing statistical
maps and tables. 12 parts published 1969-1974.]. ill.
maps. cl. R18.00 (R21.00) Africa Inst 1974 SA

Africa Institute of South Africa.
Transport and communications. maps. 75c (R1.00)
(Africa: Maps and statistics, 4) Africa Inst - Pret 1963 SA

Africa Institute of South Africa.
Vital and medical aspects. maps. 75c (R1.00)
(Africa: Maps and statistics, 2) Africa Inst - Pret 1962 SA

Africa Institute of South Africa.
Water and power. maps. 75c ($1.00) (Africa: Maps
and statistics, 5) Africa Inst - Pret 1963 SA

African Climatology Unit.
Climatological atlas of Africa. maps. cl. R40.00
Witwatersrand UP 1961 SA

African Education Programme. C.S.S. Bookshops, Lagos.
Entebbe maths. Decimal/metric ed. Pupil's bk. 1
144pp. ill. 60k CSS 1974 NR

African Education Programme. C.S.S. Bookshops, Lagos.
Entebbe maths. Decimal/metric ed. Pupil's bk. 2
171pp. ill. 80k CSS 1974 NR

African Education Programme. C.S.S. Bookshops, Lagos.
Entebbe maths. Decimal/metric ed. Pupil's bk. 3
187pp. ill. 85k CSS 1974 NR

African Education Programme. C.S.S. Bookshops, Lagos.
Entebbe maths. Decimal/metric ed. Pupil's bk. 4
251pp. ill. N1.40 CSS 1974 NR

African Education Programme. C.S.S. Bookshops, Lagos.
Entebbe maths. Decimal/metric ed. Pupil's bk. 5
198pp. ill. N1.40 CSS 1974 NR

African Education Programme. C.S.S. Bookshops, Lagos.
Entebbe maths. Decimal/metric ed. Pupil's bk. 6
304pp. ill. N2.40 CSS 1974 NR

African Education Programme. C.S.S. Bookshops, Lagos.
Entebbe maths. Decimal/metric ed. Teacher's bk. 1
140pp. ill. N2.68 CSS 1974 NR

African Education Programme. C.S.S. Bookshops, Lagos.
Entebbe maths. Decimal/metric ed. Teacher's bk. 2
162pp. N2.68 CSS 1974 NR

African Institute for Economic Development and Planning
Dakar.
Collection of studies on economic and social development,
v. 1 (English version) 68pp. CFA500 (F10.00) Nouv
Ed Afric 1973 SG

African Way of Life Club, Kachebere.
Bantu wisdom. 128pp. K1.40 Neczam 1972 ZA

Africana Museum.
Catalogue of the philatelic collection. gratis
Johannesburg Public Lib 1960 SA

Afuwape, S.O.
Thirty tests in primary six English language. 89pp. 65k
Alliance 1971 NR

Agabani, F.
Scientific and technical potential "STP" in the Sudan.
Summary of results. See: Sammani, A.

Agabani, F.A.
Scientific and technical potential in the Sudan. 'STP'
summary of results. See: Yaquob, E.S.A.

Agabani, Y.
Scientific and technical potential "STP" in the Sudan.
Summary of results. See: Sammani, A.

Agadzi, A.
Akwasi seeks adventure. 54pp. ill. 40pes. Advance
1969 GH

Agadzi, A.
From poverty to prosperity. 25pp. ill. 30pes.
Advance 1969 GH

Agadzi, A.
Spelling made easy. 40pp. 35pes. ($.60) Ghana
Publ Corp 1970 GH

Agar-Hamilton, J.A.I.
Border port: a study of East London, South Africa, with
special reference to the white population. See: Watts,
H.L.

Agbaje, T.A. et al.
Physics objective tests. 108pp. ill. 85k Onibonoje
1966 NR

Agbebi, D.A.
School Certificate objective tests in agricultural science.
See: Komolafe, K.F.

Agbodeka, F.
Achimota in the national setting. A unique educational
experiment in West Africa. 218pp. ill. cl. & pap.
C19.50 cl. C15.00 pap. Afram 1977 GH

Agbodeka, F.
Ghana in the twentieth century. 152pp. maps. C4.00
(£2.00/$4.00) Ghana UP 1972 GH

Agbossahessou.
Les haleines sauvages. 96pp. CFA400 CLE 1972
CM FRE

Agence Novosti.
Vladimire Lenine. 74pp. DA3.00 SNED 1970 AE
FRE

Aggarwal, V.P.
Comprehensive book for junior secondary classes
geography. 130pp. maps. K.shs.12.00 Textbook
Ctre 1977 KE

Aggarwal, V.P.
Comprehensive books for junior secondary classes
general science. 126pp. ill. K.shs12.00 Textbook
Ctre 1977 KE

Aggarwal, V.P.
Comprehensive books for junior secondary classes history.
126pp. K.shs.12.00 Textbook Ctre 1977 KE

Aggarwal, V.P.
The CPE prep book. 124pp. ill. K.shs.25.00
Textbook Ctre 1977 KE

Aggarwall, V.P. Parkash, A.
Certificate health science digest. 208pp. K.shs.10.00
Elimu (Textbook Ctre) 1974 KE

Agnel, J.
La méthode des unités-exercices en matière de formation
professionnelle dans les services publics des pays en voie
de développement. Dir18.00 (Coll. du Centre d'étude
du développement économique et social, 5) Ed La Porte
1962 MR FRE

Agomatanakahn, R.
Introduction à l'anthroponymie Zairoise. 48pp. CELTA
1975 ZR FRE

Agoyun, A.
Yoruba imura idanwo. 80pp. 70k Armolaran 1970
NR

Agricultural and Veterinary Departments, Central Province.
Urimi mwega thiini wa Central Province. [Better farming
in Central Province] 72pp. K.shs.2.50 ($1.50/60p.)
EALB 1962 KE KIK

Aguda, T.A.
Principles of criminal liability in Nigerian law. 368pp.
N7.00 Ibadan UP 1965 NR

Aguessy, C.
Contribution à l'étude de l'histoire de l'ancien royaume de
Porto-Novo. [Reprint of ed. 1953]. See: Akindele, A.

Agunbiade, R.O., comp.
Printed and published in Africa: catalogue of an exhibition of outstanding African materials. 122pp. 50k ($1.00) Univ Ife Bkshop 1973 NR

Agunbiade, R.O., comp.
Printed and published in Africa. Catalogue of an exhibition of outstanding African published materials. Rev. & e enl.ed. 101pp. 50k ($1.00) Univ Ife Bkshop 1974 NR

Agunwa, C.O. Stitt, J.
Primary English workbooks. stage 3. 28pp. ill. 35k Longman - Nig 1974 NR

Agunwa, C.O. Stitt, J.
Primary English workbooks. stage 4. 28pp. ill. 35k Longman - Nig 1974 NR

Agunwa, C.O. Stitt, J.
Primary English workbooks. stage 5. 44pp. ill. 42k Longman - Nig 1974 NR

Agunwa, C.O. Stitt, J.
Primary English workbooks. stage 6. 44pp. ill. 42k Longman - Nig 1974 NR

Agyei-Gyane, L., comp.
Directory of special libraries in Ghana. 71pp. ex. only CSIR-Ghana 1974 GH

Agyemang, F.
Accused in the Gold Coast. 98pp. photos. C1.00 ($1.00) Ghana Publ Corp 1972 GH

Agyemang, F.
A century with boys. 103pp. photos. 30pes. Waterville 1967 GH

Agyemang, F.
School and career. 85pp. ill. 50pes. Waterville 1968 GH

Agyemfra, L.S.G.
Ghana Church union: an opinion. 50pp. 20pes. Waterville 1969 GH

Ahamba, S.M. Osuagwu, B.I.N. Nwoga, D.I.
Ogogo Igbo 4. [Primary Efik course.] pupils bk. 4. 104pp. ill. N1.30 Macmillan 1976 NR IGB

Ahamba, S.M. Osuagwu, B.I.N. Nwoga, D.I.
Ogogo Igbo. [Primary Igbo course.] pupil's bk. 3. 96pp. ill. N1.13 Macmillan 1976 NR IGB

Ahamba, S.M. Nwoga, D.I.
Ogugu Igbo. [Primary Igbo course] pupil's bk. 1 46pp. ill. 85k Macmillan 1974 NR IGB

Ahamba, S.M. Nwoga, D.I.
Ogugu Igbo. Pupil's bk. 2 54pp. ill. N1.10 Macmillan 1975 NR IGB

Ahamba, S.M. Osuagwu, B.I.N. Nwoga, D.I.
Ogugu Igbo. [Primary Igbo course.] pupil's bk. 5. 80pp. N1.10 Macmillan 1977 NR IGB

Ahene-Affoh K.
Twi kasakoa ne kasatomme ahorow bi. 66pp. ($1.50) Ghana Publ Corp 1976 GH TWI

Ahizi, A.P.
Annales de l'université d'Abidjan. L'administration du travail en Côte d'Ivoire. CFA1000 (F20.00) (Série A-Droit, 1) Univ Abidjan 1972 IV FRE

Ahle-s, H.J. Schyff, P.J.v.d.
Senior secondary mathematics for standard 9. 390pp. ill. R5.25 Nasou 1975 SA

Ahlers, H.J., et al.
Junior secondary mathematics for standard 7. (TVL) 278pp. ill. R3.35 Nasou 1974 SA

Ahlers, H.J., et al.
Senior secondary mathematics for standard 8. 321pp. ill. R3.95 Nasou 1974 SA

Ahlers, H.J. Schnell, C.J.W.
Junior secondary mathematics for standard 5. 337pp. ill. R3.50 Nasou 1974 SA

Ahlers, H.J. Bowker, J. Bekker, M.J.
Junior secondary mathematics for standard 6. 312pp. ill. R3.40 Nasou 1974 SA

Ahlers, H.J. Schyff, P.J.v.d.
Senior secondary mathematics, standard 10. 462pp. ill. R6.00 Nasou 1975 SA

Ahmad, K., ed.
Islam: its meaning and message. 279pp. N5.00 Islamic 1977 NR

Ahmadu Bello University. Adult Education and General Extension Services Unit.
First report to the General Extension Services Board, May 1973. 56pp. pl. free Adult Educ Gen Ext Serv 1974 NR

Ahmadu Bello University. Institute for Agricultural Research. Dept. of Agricultural Economics and Rural Sociology.
Cropping scheme meeting 1975: notes on the socioeconomic extension programme. 67pp. Inst Agric Res-Zaria 1975 NR

Ahmed, A.G.M.
Shaykhs and followers: Political struggle in the Rufa'a al-Hoi, nazirate in the Sudan. 170pp. ill. 75pt. ($3.00) Khartoum UP 1974 SJ

Ahmed, R.H.
Critical appraisal to the role of the public service commission in the Sudan (1954-1969) 52pp. 50pt. ($2.00) Khartoum UP 1974 SJ

Ahmed, U. Daura, B.
An introduction to classical Hausa. 136pp. N4.00 Northern Nig 1970 NR

Ahmed, U.B.
Bora Da Mowa. [The loved and the unloved wife] 90pp. N1.00 Northern Nig 1973 NR HAU

Ahmed U.B.
A school certificate Hausa course. N2.45 Northern Nig 1975 NR HAU

Ailloud, J. Ben Said, C.
Essaie d'évaluation comparative de la méthode 'Today's English'. CFA125 (C.L.A.D. Etude, 49) CLAD 1972 SG FRE

Aires, M.A.
Rustenburg magisterial district. 55pp. R2.85 Dept Bibliog, Lib & Typo 1969 SA

Aitken, R.D. Gale, G.W.
Botanical survey of Natal and Zululand. 15c. (Memoirs of the Botanical Survey of South Africa, 2) Botanical Res Inst 1921 SA

Aitken, R.D.
Researches on the vegetation of Natal. See: Bews, J.W.

Aitken, R.D.
Researches on the vegetation of Natal. See: Bews, J.W.

Aiyegbayo, J.T.
Model questions/answers in agricultural science. 100pp. N2.00 Armolaran 1970 NR

Aiyenuro, O.
'O' level commerce. 254pp. ill. N2.10 Onibonoje 1975 NR

Aiyepeku, W.O.
Geography, wars and the Nigerian situation: a bibliographic analysis. 26pp. 50k (Inst. of Librarianship, occas. pap., 4) Inst Lib-Ib 1970 NR

Ajaegbu, H.L. Faniran, A.
A new approach to practical work in geography. 124pp. N3.23 Heinemann Educ - Nig 1973 NR

Ajanaku, F.
Oruko amutorunwa. See: Sowande, F.

Ajayi, E.O. Nwosu, T.C.
Controlled composition exercises for primaries five and six. 96pp. N1.50 Cross Continent 1976 NR

Ajayi, E.O. Nwosu, T.C.
Controlled composition exercises for primary four. 64pp. N1.50 Cross Continent 1976 NR

Ajayi, G.B., et al.
Government and political science for West African students. 1, 2 pts. 280pp. N1.20 Econ Res Bur 1967 NR

Author Index

Ajayi, G.B., et al.
Government and political science for West African Students. 2, 2 pts. 127pp. N1.30 Econ Res Bur NR

Ajayi, G.B. et al.
New English language examination aid series. Rev ed. 263pp. N2.50 Ilesanmi 1972 NR

Ajayi, G.B.
Industrial development in West Africa. 43pp. 40k Econ Res Bur 1969 NR

Ajayi, G.B.   Alawiye, I.A.
Introduction to economics of West Africa: economic analysis, structure and organization and revision notes. 1, 3 pts. 208pp. N1.20 Econ Res Bur 1965 NR

Ajayi, G.B.   Alawiye, I.A.
Introduction to economics of West Africa: economic analysis, structure and organization and revision notes. 2, 3 pts. 266pp. N1.20 Econ Res Bur 1966 NR

Ajayi, G.B.   Alawiye, I.A.
Introduction to economics of West Africa: economic analysis, structure and organization and revision notes. 3, 3 pts. 80pp. 50k Econ Res Bur 1967 NR

Ajayi, G.B.   Akintayo, A.O.   Alawiye, I.A.
Model essays and letters for WASC, GCE and HSE examinations. 263pp. N1.20 (English language aid, 1) Econ Res Bur 1966 NR

Ajayi, G.B.
Model question and answer on economic history for West African students. 152pp. N1.10 Econ Res Bur 1968 NR

Ajayi, G.B.   Alawiye, I.A.
Model questions and answers on government and political science for GCE students and university undergraduates. 206pp. N1.35 Econ Res Bur 1968 NR

Ajayi, G.B.   Akintayo, A.O.   Alawiye, I.A.
Precis, comprehension and grammar. 277pp. N1.20 (English language aid, 2) Econ Res Bur 1966 NR

Ajayi, J.A.
Crowther's attitude to other faiths. OUP-Nig 1973 NR

Ajayi, J.F.A., ed.   Espie, I., ed.
A thousand years of West African history. Rev ed. 549pp. maps. N4.04 Ibadan UP 1969 NR

Ajayi, J.F.A., ed.   Tamuno, T.N., ed.
The University of Ibadan 1948-1973: a history of the first twenty-five years. 436pp. map pl. pap. & hd. N6.00 hd. N6.00 pap. Ibadan UP 1973 NR

Ajayi, J.F.A.   Smith, R.S.
Yoruba warfare in the nineteenth century. 172pp. ill. N3.50 Ibadan UP 1971 NR

Ajayi, V.
A guide to good health a manual for rural workers. 66pp. Ethiope 1975 NR

Ajibola, J.O.
Orin Yoruba-Yoruba songs. 120pp. pap. & cl. N4.25 cl. N1.95 pap (£3.00/$7.50) Univ Ife Press 1973 NR YOR

Ajibola, J.O.
Owe Yoruba. [Yoruba proverbs] 2nd ed. 113pp. 80k OUP-Nig 1971 NR YOR

Ajibola, W.A.
Foreign policy and public opinion: a case study of British foreign policy on the Nigerian Civil War. N6.00 Ibadan UP 1977 NR

Ajuwon, B.
Aditu ijinle ohun enu Ifa. bk. 1 99pp. 85k. Onibonoje 1972 NR YOR

Aka, S.M.O.
The mid-day darkness. 136pp. N1.05 (African Literature series, 4) Onibonoje 1973 NR

Aka, S.M.O.
Stories from an African village. 80pp. ill. N1.00 Longman Nig 1976 NR

Akafia, S.Y., ed.
Ku le xome. [Death from within.] 3rd ed. 178pp. ill. C1.80 Bur Ghana Lang 1976 GH EWE

Akande, O., ed.
Proceedings of the 3rd Nigerian irrigation seminar, Zaria, 13-18 August, 1973. 208pp. free Inst Agric Res-Zaria 1973 NR

Akande, O., ed.
Proceedings of the meeting of Agricultural engineers, Zaria, 4-5 September, 1973. See: Cromer, C.A., ed.

Akande, O., ed.
The role of nutrition in preventive health-care. Report of the 4th home economics in-service training course, Zaria, 5-16, 1973. 52pp. free Inst Agric Res-Zaria 1973 NR

Akande, S.
Tests in physics: with answers. See: Ryan, O.

Akande, S.
Tests in physics: without answers. See: Ryan, O.

Akande, S.T.O.
Common family problems: advice and counsel on eight problems in family life. 24pp. 25k Daystar 1971 NR

Akande, S.T.O.
Marriage and home making in Nigeria society. 79pp. N1.00 Daystar 1971 NR

Akande, S.T.O.
What to do when someone dies. 42pp. 60k Daystar 1976 NR

Akapelwa, S.
Bupilo bwa Sepo. [The life of Sepo] 54pp. 45n. Neczam 1972 ZA LOZ

Akeredolu-Ale, E.
The underdevelopment of indigenous entrepreneurship in Nigeria. 119pp. map. cl. & pap. N4.00 pap. N6.00 cl. Ibadan UP 1975 NR

Akilimali Snow-White, K.H.A.
Diwani ya Akilimali. [Akilimali's poems] 4th ed. K.shs11.00 ($2.90/70p.) (Johari za Kiswahili, 5) EALB 1975 KE SWA

Akinbode, I.A.
Factors associated with adoption of three farm practices in the Western State of Nigeria: N.S.I. maize, cocoa spray and poultry-egg programmes. See: Clark, R.C.

Akindele, A.   Aguessy, C.
Contribution à l'étude de l'histoire de l'ancien royaume de Porto-Novo. [Reprint of ed. 1953]. 168pp. ill. pl. (D.fl.50.00) (Mémoires de l'IFAN, 25) IFAN 1953 SG FRE

Akingba, J.B.
The problem of unwanted pregnancies in Nigeria today. 126pp. 50k Univ Lagos Bookshop 1971 NR

Akinlade, E.K.
Alosi ologo. [The left-handed murderer.] 176pp. ill. N1.60 Longman - Nig 1975 NR YOR

Akinlade, E.K.
Owo eje. 121pp. N1.10 Onibonoje 1976 NR YOR

Akinlade, E.K.
Things that great men do: Chaka the Zulu. 72pp. ill. 70k (Junior African Literature Series, 12) Onibonoje 1973 NR

Akinlade, E.K.
Things that great men do: Ogunmola Basorun. 90pp. ill. 80k (Junior African Literature Series, 11) Onibonoje 1973 NR

Akinlade, K.
Abraham the friend of God. 42pp. ill. 50k. Onibonoje 1977 NR

Akinlade, K.
Mahatma Ghandi. ill. 65k. Onibonoje 1977 NR

Akinlade, K.
Owo te amookunsika. [The evildoer is caught] 128pp. ill. N1.35 Macmillan 1970 NR YOR

Akinlade, K.
Shehu Usman Dan Fodio. ill. 70k. Onibonoje 1977 NR

Akinlade, K.
Tal'o pa omoooba? [Who has killed the prince?] 112pp. ill. N1.30 Macmillan 1970 NR YOR

Akinlade, K.
Things that great men do: Ajayi the bishop. 22pp. ill. 50k (Junior African Literature Series, 9) Onibonoje 1973 NR

Akinlade, K.
Things that great men do: Esther the queen. 61pp. ill. 65k (Junior African Literature Series, 7) Onibonoje 1973 NR

Akinlade, K.
Things that great men do: Oluyole the Basorun. 53pp. ill. 65k (Junior African Literature Series, 8) Onibonoje 1973 NR

Akinola, O.   Fletcher, J.E.
Progressive mathematics: pupils bk. 1, 6 bks 80pp. 55k. Heinemann Educ - Nig 1973 NR

Akinola, O.   Fletcher, J.E.
Progressive mathematics: pupils bk. 2, 6 bks 101pp. 65k. Heinemann Educ - Nig 1973 NR

Akinola, O.   Fletcher, J.E.
Progressive mathematics: pupils bk. 3, 6 bks 75pp. 85k. Heinemann Educ - Nig 1973 NR

Akinola, O.   Fletcher, J.E.
Progressive mathematics: pupils bk. 4, 6 bks 46pp. 50k. Heinemann Educ - Nig 1973 NR

Akinola, O.   Fletcher, J.E.
Progressive mathematics: teachers bk. 1, 6 bks 52pp. 85k. Heinemann Educ - Nig 1973 NR

Akinola, O.   Fletcher, J.E.
Progressive mathematics: teachers bk. 2, 6 bks 73pp. 95k. Heinemann Educ - Nig 1973 NR

Akinola, O.   Fletcher, J.E.
Progressive mathematics: teachers bk. 3, 6 bks 106pp. 50k. Heinemann Educ - Nig 1973 NR

Akinrodoye, A.
Detailed question and answers on School Certificate economics (1966-1971) 193pp. N1.25 Aromolaran 1970 NR

Akinsanya, O.
A mini biography of Chief Obafemi Awolowo. 27pp. 20k People's Publ Co 1972 NR

Akinsanya, S.A.
Mayflower: the school that controversy produced. 68pp. 50k People's Publ Co 1973 NR

Akinsemoyin, K.
Twilight and the tortoise. 64pp. ill. 53k (African Reader's Library, 3) Pilgrim 1963 NR

Akinswmoyin, K.
Twilight tales. 80pp. ill. 45k (African Junior Library, 8) Pilgrim 1965 NR

Akintayo, A.O.
Model essays and letters for WASC, GCE and HSE examinations. See: Ajayi, G.B.

Akintayo, A.O.
Notes, questions/answers on "Anthology of longer poems". 68pp. N1.30 Aromolaran 1975[?] NR

Akintayo, A.O.
Precis, comprehension and grammar. See: Ajayi, G.B.

Akintayo, O.A.
Essential notes on "Mayor of Casterbridge". 46pp. N1.20 Aromolaran 1975[?] NR

Akintoye, S.A.
Ten years of the University of Ife, 1962-1972. 78pp. photos. pap. & hd. N4.00 hd. N2.25 pap. (£3.00/$7.95 hd.) (£1.50/$4.00 pap.) Univ Ife Press 1973 NR

Akinwale, L.O.
A bibliography of Marxism and African economic development, 1952-1968. 72pp. 75k ($1.25) (N.I.S.E.R. indexes and bibliographies, 13) NISER 1968 NR

Akinyele, J.I.
Akebaje. [The spoilt child] 76pp. ill. 60k Ilesanmi 1972 NR YOR

Akinyele, J.I.
Life and teaching of Christ. 166pp. ill. N1.40 Ilesanmi 1971 NR

Akinyele, J.I.
The spoilt child. 76pp. 80k Ilesanmi 1972 NR

Akinyele, O.
West African school certificate history. 151pp. maps. N1.25 Ilesanmi 1971 NR

Akinyemi, A.B.
Foreign policy and federalism. 217pp. cl. & pap. N5.00 pap. N7.50 cl. (Ibadan Political and Administrative Studies, 2) Ibadan UP 1974 NR

Akinyoade, R.O.A. et al.
Biology objective tests. 2nd ed. 117pp. ill. 90k Onibonoje 1968 NR

Akinyotu, A.
Bibliography on development planning in Nigeria, 1955-1968. 133pp. N1.50 ($2.50) (N.I.S.E.R. indexes and bibliographies, 14) NISER 1969 NR

Akivaga, S.K.
Notes on George Orwell's "Animal Farm". 44pp. K.shs.6.00 (Heinemann Student's Guides) Heinemann Educ - Nair 1976 KE

Akiwowo, A.   Basu, A.C.
Tobacco growers in Northern Oyo division and adoption of new farming ideas and practices. N1.25 ($2.00) (N.I.S.E.R. research reports, 1) NISER NR

Akiwumi, A.
Higher education for nurses. 14pp. C1.00 ($1.00/50p.) (Inaugural lecture) Ghana UP 1971 GH

Akkache, A.
L'evasion. 154pp. DA8.00 SNED 1973 AE FRE

Akkache, A.
La résistance Algérienne de 1845 à 1945. DA1.00 SNED 1972 AE FRE

Akkache, A.
Tacfarinas. 87pp. DA4.00 pap. SNED 1968 AE FRE

Akol, J.W.L.
Niemuto A'nikarimojong. 2nd ed. 40pp. K.shs.2.70 ($1.50/60p.) EALB 1966 KE KAI

Akonaay, A.
Hadith za kaka fisi. [Swahili supplementary reader] 24pp. ill. K.shs.1.70 ($1.00) EAPH 1967 KE SWA

Akono, S.
Intendance de l'église et crise financière. 80pp. CFA240 CLE 1973 CM FRE

Akotey, K.
Ku di fo na wo. [Death satisfied them.] 135pp. ill. 90pes. Bur Ghana Lang 1974 GH EWE

Akpatsi, R.S.
Amea deke menya. [The life of a school boy.] 93pp. ill. 60pes. Bur Ghana Lang 1974 GH EWE

Akrofi, C.A.
Twi mmebusem. [Twi proverbs] 173pp. 50pes. Waterville 1970 GH TWI

Akuffo, B.S.
Ahenfi adesua. [African customs.] 112pp. ($3.75) Ghana Publ Corp 1976 GH TWI

Akwa, K.G., ed.
Twer Nyame. [Trust in God.] 2nd ed. 80pp. ill. C1.20 Bur Ghana Lang 1976 GH FAT

Akwisombe, J.B.
Jero sikitu. 84pp. T.shs.9.00 Tanz Publ House 1972 TZ SWA

Akyeampong, H.K.
Journey to independence and after: Dr. J.B. Danquah's letters. 3 v. 141pp. pap. & cl. C1.00 cl. 80pes. pap. Waterville 1971 GH

Akyeampong, H.K.
Tributes to J.B. Danquah. 48pp. photos. 30pes. ($.30) Ghana Publ Corp 1967 GH

al-Hardallo, I.
Antisemitism: a changing concept. 44pp. 10 pt. (50c.) Khartoum UP 1970 SJ

Ala, J.A.
Akomolede Yoruba. bk. 4 See: Aromolàran, A.

Alà, J.A.
Akomolede Yoruba: Iwe atona fun oluko. Bks 1-3 See: Aromolaran, A.

Alá, J.A.
Akomolede Yoruba: Iwe ise-sise ekerin. See: Aromolaran, A.

Alà, J.A.
Akomolede Yoruba: Iwe ise-sise eketa. See: Aromolaran, A.

Alá, J.A.
Akomolede Yoruba: Iwe ise-sise ekinni. See: Aromolaran, A.

Alà, J.A.
Akomolede Yoruba: Iwe kika ekarun. See: Aromolaran, A.

Alà, J.A.
Akomolede Yoruba: Iwe kika ekefa. See: Aromolaran, A.

Ala, J.A.
Akomolede Yoruba: Iwe kika ekeji. See: Aromolaran, A.

Alá, J.A.
Akomolede Yoruba: Iwe kika eketa. See: Aromolaran, A.

Alá, J.A.
Akómólédè Yorùbá: Ìwé sísé ise èkejì. See: Aromolaran, A.

Alabi, E.O.
School certificate mathematics: objective test. 155pp. N1.40 Ilesanmi 1972 NR

Alabi, G.A., comp.
Nigerian publications 1950-1970. [Cumulative volume.]. See: Tamuno, O.G., comp.

Alabi, J.O.
Revision physics. 137pp. ill. 85k Onibonoje 1971 NR

Alade, R.B.
The broken bridge. Reflections and experience of a medical doctor during the Nigerian civil war. 140pp. photos. N2.50 Univ Ibadan Bkshop; distr. 1975 NR

Aladejana, A.
A list of books, articles and government publications on the economy of Nigeria, 1969. 68pp. 75k ($1.25) NISER 1970 NR

Aladejana, A.
The marketing board systems: a bibliography. 78pp. 75k ($1.25) (N.I.S.E.R. indexes and bibliographies, 15) NISER 1971 NR

Aladji, V.
Akossiwa mon amour. 52pp. CFA200 CLE 1971 CM FRE

Aladji, V.
L'équilibriste. 52pp. CFA200 CLE 1972 CM FRE

Alagoa, E.J.
A chronicle of Grand Bonny. 134pp. pl. map. N2.50 Ibadan UP 1972 NR

Alagoa, E.J., ed. Awe, B., ed.
Nigerian antiquities: report of a symposium held at the Institute of African Studies, University of Ibadan, from Thursday 20th April to Sunday 23rd April, 1972. (Special number of African Notes) 99pp. ill. N2.00 Inst Afric Studies-Ibadan 1973 NR

Alagoa, E.J.
A history of the Niger Delta: an introduction to Ijo oral tradition. 231pp. pl. ill. N3.00 Ibadan UP 1972 NG

Alagoa, E.J.
A history of the Niger Delta: an introduction to Ijo oral tradition. 231pp. pl. ill. N3.00 Ibadan UP 1972 NR

Alawiye, I.A.
Introduction to economics of West Africa: economic analysis, structure and organization and revision notes. 1, 3 pts. See: Ajayi, G.B.

Alawiye, I.A.
Introduction to economics of West Africa: economic analysis, structure and organization and revision notes. 2, 3 pts. See: Ajayi, G.B.

Alawiye, I.A.
Introduction to economics of West Africa: economic analysis, structure and organization and revision notes. 3, 3 pts. See: Ajayi, G.B.

Alawiye, I.A.
Model essays and letters for WASC, GCE and HSE examinations. See: Ajayi, G.B.

Alawiye, I.A.
Model questions and answers on government and political science for GCE students and university undergraduates. See: Ajayi, G.B.

Alawiye, I.A.
Precis, comprehension and grammar. See: Ajayi, G.B.

Albert, J. Verheust, T.
Physionomie du corps enseignant des écoles secondaires au Zaire. Année scolaire 1972-1973, enseignant catholique. 41pp. Z3.00 ($2.40) (Cahiers du CRIDE, Nouvelle série, I, 2) CRIDE 1976 ZR FRE

Alberti, L.
Ludwig Alberti's account of the tribal life and customs of the Xhosa in 1807. 132pp. pl. hd. fl. 27.00 Balkema 1968 SA

Alcock, R.N.
Police instruction book. 90pp. 60k Northern Nig 1974 NR

Alderson, E.A.H.
With the mounted infantry and the Mashonaland field force, 1896. [Reprint ed. 1898]. 295pp. ill. photos. maps. cl. R$6.90 cl. (Rhodesiana Reprint Library, Gold Series, 20) Books of Rhodesia 1971 RH

Aldous, L.W.
Commerce and industry in East Africa. K.shs2.50 EALB 1969 KE

Aldrich, D.V.
A comparison of the processing performance of a hand picked and machine picked South African cotton cultivar. 17pp. R2.50 (SAWTRI Technical Reports, 245) SAWTRI 1975 SA

Aldrich, D.V.
The effect of sample preparation on the accuracy of the IIC/Shirley cotton fineness-maturity tester. 15pp. R2.50 (SAWTRI Technical Reports, 272) SAWTRI 1975 SA

Aldrich, D.V.
The processing of blends of cotton and wool on the cotton system, part I: an introductory investigation. 20pp. R2.50 (SAWTRI Technical Reports, 248) SAWTRI 1975 SA

Aldrich, D.V.
A study of the physical properties of some commercial South African cotton blends and resultant carded yarns. 24pp. R2.50 (SAWTRI Technical Reports, 278) SAWTRI 1975 SA

Aldrich, V.
The between bale and between lot variation of South African grown cottons, part I: micronaire, maturity ration, fineness, 2.5% span length, uniformly ratio and trash content. See: Gee, E.

Aldrich, V.
Blending of two cottons differing widely in fibre properties.
15pp.   R2.50   (SAWTRI Technical Reports, 299)
SAWTRI 1976 SA

Aldrich, V.
A comparison of open-end and ring spinning of cotton,
part I: the physical properties of 25 tex yarns spun from
different cottons grown in Southern Africa.   See: Hunter,
L.

Aldrich, V.
The processing of blends of cotton and wool on the cotton
system, part II: yarn and fabric properties of a 67/33
cotton/wool blend.   17pp.   R2.50   (SAWTRI Technical
Reports, 298)   SAWTRI 1976 SA

Aldrich, V.
Some spinning and weaving trials on existing and new
South African cotton cultivars.   17pp.   R2.50
(SAWTRI Technical Reports, 312)   SAWTRI 1976 SA

Aldridge, M.
Some crops we eat.   32pp.   ill.   K.shs.2.25
OUP-Nairobi 1966 KE

Aldridge, M.
Some crops we use.   28pp.   ill.   K.shs.2.25
OUP-Nairobi 1966 KE

Aldridge, M.
Some tropical fruits.   32pp.   ill.   K.shs.2.25
OUP-Nairobi 1966 KE

Aldridge, M.
Sourcebook for an introductory historical study of the
English language: old English.   1, 2 pts.   See: Branford,
W.

Aldridge, M.
Sourcebook for an introductory historical study of the
English language: paradigms and glossary.   2, 2 pts.
See: Branford, W.

Aldridge, M.
Wanyama wakubwa wa Afrika.   [The large animals of
Africa]   32pp.   ill.   K.shs.7.50   OUP-Nairobi 1971 KE
SWA

Aldridge, M.V., ed.
Robert Lowth, "A short introduction to English grammar
(1762)".   R2.50   Inst Study Engl 1973 SA

Aldridge, M.V.   Branford, W.
Rhodes manual of old English.   R2.10   Inst Study Engl
1976 SA

Aldridge, M.V.   Branford, W.
Rhodes manual of old English.   New rev. ed.   125pp.
R2.10   Inst Study Engl 1975 SA

Alemu, G.W., comp.
Results of experiments in animal production (from 1966/67
to 1975). S. Edwards, ed.   See: O'Donovan, P.B.,
comp.

Alencastre, A.
El-Feth (Les Commandos arabes en Palestine)   156pp.
DA7.00   SNED 1970 AE FRE

Alexander, D.
Holiday in Mauritius.   col. ill.   R4.75   Purnell 1976 SA

Alexander, D.
Holiday in Mozambique.   172pp. photos./maps. hd.
R2.75   Purnell 1971 SA

Alexander, D.
Holiday in the islands.   col. ill.   R7.50   Purnell 1975
SA

Alexander, D.J.
Origins and development of university extension in Zambia,
1966-1975.   133pp.   (Univ. Zambia, Centre for
Continuing Education, occas. pap., 3)   Centre Cont Educ -
Zam 1975 ZA

Alexander, F.L.
South African graphic arts and its techniques.   260pp. pl.
R21.00 cl.   Human and Rousseau 1974 SA

Alexander, J.E.
An expedition of discovery into the interior of Africa.
[Reprint of 1838 edition].   2 v.   325 & 320pp. ill. pl. cl.
R12.60 set   (Africana collectanea, 22 & 23)   Struik 1967
SA

Alexander, M.
The comrades marathon story.   cl.   R7.50   Juta 1976
SA

Alexander, S.
The works of Sidney Henry Haughton.   78pp.   R4.65
Dept Bibliog Lib & Typo 1975 SA

Alexandre, R.P.
La langue Moré. [Reprint of ed. 1953].   2 vols   407 &
506pp.   (D.fl.250.00 set)   (Mémoires de l'IFAN, 34)
IFAN 1953 SG FRE

Algazali, A.
British administration and development of Northern Nigeria.
75pp.   65k (50p./$1.25)   Inst Admin - Zaria 1967 NR

Ali, A.I.M.
The British, the slave trade and slavery in the Sudan,
1820-1881.   142pp.   60 pt.   ($2.50)   Khartoum UP
1972 SJ

Ali Bin Nasir, S.A.
Al inkishafi.   [The soul's awakening]   196pp. photos.
K.shs.13.00   OUP-Nairobi 1972 KE SWA

Ali, I.
Man in West Africa.   N4.50   Ethiope 1976 NR

Ali, M.A.R.
Fluctuation and impact of government expenditure in the
Sudan, 1955-1967.   45pp.   75pt. ($3.00)   Khartoum
UP 1974 SJ

Ali, M.A.R.
Government expenditure and economic development.
176pp.   LS1.35 ($6.00)   Khartoum UP 1974 SJ

Alisson, A.A.
Izibalo zanamuhla.   Ibanga, 3   See: Oscroft, E.B.

Aliyu, A.
Fasaha akiliya.   [Hausa poems.]   N1.25   Northern Nig
1976 NR HAU

Aliyu, A.H., et al.
Ka Koyi Karatu Sabuwar Hanya, 1.   [Learn how to read]
1, 6 bks.   49pp.   45k   Northern Nig 1971 NR HAU

Aliyu, A.H.   Boyd, J.   Ingawa, M.
Ka Kara Karatu Sabuwar Hanya, 3.   [Read Again]   3, 6
bks.   47pp. ill.   50k   Northern Nig 1972 NR HAU

Alkaly, K.
Nègres, qu'avez-vous fait?   70pp.   MF770   Ed Pop -
Mali 1972 ML FRE

Alkuin, P.
Pour toi qui reves l'amour.   2nd ed.   128pp. photos.
25k   St. Paul 1970 ZR FRE

Allan, W. et al.
Land holding and land usage among the Plateau Tonga of
Mazabuka district: a reconaissance survey.   192pp.
K2.00 (£1.00)   (Rhodes-Livingstone paps., 14)   Inst
Soc Res - Zam 1945 ZA

Allan, W.
Studies in African land usage.   85pp.   K1.50 (75p.)
(Rhodes-Livingstone paps., 15)   Inst Soc Res - Zam 1949
ZA

Allangba, A.
Education civique. Manuel pour la Côte d'Ivoire.   95pp.
CFA600 (F12.00)   Nouv Ed Afric 1974 SG FRE

Allen, C.J., ed.   Tet, M.R., ed.
Rhodesia and Nyasaland law reports, 1956-1963.
R27.00 per v.   Butterworths SA

Allen, C.P.S.
Ralukya osome.   [Hasten to read]   37pp. ill.
K.shs2.00 ($1.25/50p.)   EALB 1960 KE NYO

Allen, C.P.S.   Kirwan, B.E.R.
Yanguya okusoma.   [Make haste and learn to read]
43pp. ill.   K.shs.2.75 ($1.50/60p.)   EALB 1970 KE
LUG

Allen, J.W.T., ed.
Utendi wa ayubu. 44pp. K.shs3.50 (35p.) (Sanaa Ya Utungo, 4) Heinemann Educ - Nair 1972 KE SWA

Allen, J.W.T., ed.
Utendi wa masahibu. 74pp. K.s5.25 (50p.) (Sanaa Ya Utungo, 2) Heinemann Educ - Nair 1972 KE SWA

Allen, V.
Kruger's Pretoria. 272pp. ill. hd. fl. 56.25 Balkema 1971 SA

Allen, V.L.
Typing for juniors, standard 8. See: Eksteen, F.R.L.N.

Allen, V.L.
Typing for seniors, standard 9. See: Eksteen, F.R.L.N.

Allen, V.L.
Typing for seniors, standard 10. See: Eksteen, F.R.L.N.

Allen, W.E.
Mwanzo wa masomo: kitabu cha kwanza. [Primary reader] 2nd ed. bk. 1 82pp. ill. K.shs.2.00 ($1.25/50p.) EALB 1958 KE SWA

Allen, W.E.
Mwanzo wa masomo: kitabu cha pili. [Primary reader] 4th ed. bk. 2 80pp. ill. K.shs.3.50 ($1.50/50p.) EALB 1975 KE SWA

Allison, A.A.
Guided social studies. Standard 5. See: Brown, S.

Allison, A.A.
Izibalo zanamuhla. Ibanga, 1 See: Oscroft, E.B.

Allison, A.A.
Izibalo zanamuhla. Ibanga, 2 See: Oscroft, E.B.

Allison, A.A.
Izibalo zanamuhla. Ibanga, 4 See: Oscroft, E.B.

Allison, A.A.
Izibalo zanamuhla. Ibanga, 5 See: Oscroft, E.B.

Allison, A.A.
Izibalo zanamuhla. Ibanga, 6 See: Oscroft, E.B.

Allison, P.
Cross River monoliths. 108pp. ill. N1.05 Dept Antiquities 1968 NR

Alloo, C.K.
Otieno achach. [Luo supplementary reader] ill. K.shs.6.00 ($2.30) EAPH 1966 KE LUO

Allsopp, A.H. Olivier, F.G.
General methods of modern education. 168pp. R1.05 Shuter 1955 SA

Alman, S.B.
South African native life and problems. Modern status and conditions 1964-1970. [A supplement to modern status and conditions in L. Schapera, 'A select bibliography of South African native life and problems'.] 39pp. R1.30 (Univ. Cape Town Libraries. Bibl. ser.) Univ Cape Town Lib 1974 SA

Almeida, A. de.
Bushmen and other non-Bantu peoples of Angola. 43pp. ill. maps. cl. R2.00 (ISMA pub., 1) Witwatersrand UP 1964 SA

Almeida, T.
L'Afrique et son médecin. 64pp. CFA400.00 CLE 1974 CM FRE

Alot, M.
A girl cannot go on laughing all the time. 64pp. K.shs.6.00 (45p) (Spear Books, 4) Heinemann Educ - Nair 1975 KE

Alpers, E.A.
The East African slave trade. 26pp. K.shs2.50 ($1.00) EAPH 1967 KE

Alsac, C.
Contribution à l'étude des gisements de barytine de l'Andavakoera. 10pp. pl. photo. FMG105 (F2.10) (Série Documentation, 161) Service Geol - Mad 1963 MG FRE

Alsac, C.
Contribution à l'étude des pouzzolanes de Madagascar. 12pp. pl. photo. FMG100 (F2.00 pap.) (Série Documentation, 160) Service Geol - Mad 1963 MG FRE

Alsac, C.
Etude géologique et prospection de la feuille: Faratsiho. 44pp. pl. map. FMG850 (F17.00) (Travaux du Bureau Géologique, 112) Service Geol - Mad 1963 MG FRE

Alsac, C.
Etude géologique et prospection des feuilles: Miarinarivo-Maroadabo. 21pp. pl. map. FMG741 (F14.82 pap.) (Travaux du Bureau Géologique, 123) Service Geol - Mad 1966 MG FRE

Alsop, M.H.
The population of Natal. $3.75 (Natal regional survey pub., 2) Dept Econ - Natal 1952 SA

Altshuler, A.F.
Uitenhage as a service centre. R2.00 (Inst. for Planning Research, series B, 5) Inst Planning Res 1974 SA

Aluko, J.
Essays on elements of government for 'A' level students. 71pp. N2.00 Aromolaran 1975[?] NR

Aluko, S., comps. Afonja, Y.A.O., comps. Oguntoye, O.A., comps.
Small-scale industries: Midwestern State, Kwara State, and Lagos State of Nigeria. 276pp. N3.50 (£2.75/$6.80) Univ Ife Press 1973 NR

Aluko, S.A.
Christianity and communism: the challenge to our church. 2nd ed. 68pp. 75k Daystar 1966 NR

Aluko, S.A., comp.
Small-scale industries, Western State of Nigeria. 380pp. N3.00 Univ Ife Press 1972 NR

Aluko, S.A.
Money in economic theory. 20pp. 30k (Inaugural lec., 8) Univ Ife Press 1973 NR

Alvord, E.D.
A survey of the food and feed resources of the Union of South Africa. See: Van de Wall, G.

Amadi, E.
Pepper soup and the road to Ibadan. 76pp. N1.00 Onibonoje 1977 NR

Amadi, P.S. et al.
Lively English reading. bk. 4. 142pp. ill. N1.00 OUP - Nig 1977 NR

Amadi, P.S. et al.
Lively English reading. workbook, 4. 77pp. ill. 40k. OUP - Nig 1977 NR

Amali, O.
Selections from the Gospel of Luke. [in Edo]. 19pp. 20k Inst Afr Stud-Ibadan 1972 NR EDO

Amali, S.O.O.
The Benue-Plateau State, a record of a visit. 16pp. 20k Inst Afr Stud-Ibadan 1970 NR

Amali, S.O.O.
The leaders. [A bi-lingual play in Idoma and English] 123pp. N1.00 (Inst of African Stud., Univ. of Ibadan occas. pub., 30) Inst Afr Stud-Ibadan 1972 NR

Amali, S.O.O.
Onugbo mloko: a poetic drama in Idoma. tr. fr. Idoma R.G. Armstrong, S.O.O. Amali 64pp. pap. & hd. 55k pap. N1.15 hd. (Inst. of African Stud., Univ of Ibadan, Bi-lingual literary works, 3) Inst Afr Stud-Ibadan 1972 NR

Amankwa, A.
Mmotafowa adannan ne aduannuro. [Child care] 57pp. 30pes. Waterville 1950 GH TWI

Amann, V.F., ed.
Agricultural employment and labour migration in East Africa. 290pp. U.shs.50.00 ($8.50) Mak Inst Soc Res 1974 UG

Author Index

Amann, V.F., ed.
Agricultural policy issues in East Africa. 341pp.
U.shs.28.00 ($7.00) Mak Inst Soc Res 1973 UG

Amann, V.F., ed.
Essentials of production and farm management economics.
145pp. U.shs.20.00 ($4.00) Mak Inst Soc Res 1975
UG

Amann, V.F., ed.
Financing rural development. See: Wilson, F., ed.

Amann, V.F., ed. Stanfield, J.P., ed. Belshaw, D.G.R.,
ed.
Nutrition and food in an African economy. 1, 2 v.
334pp. photos. ill. U.shs50.00 ($7.25) Dept Rur
Econ - Mak 1972 UG

Amann, V.F., ed.
Project appraisal and evaluation in agriculture.
See: Raikes, P., ed.

Amann, V.F. Stanfield, J.P. Belshaw, D.G.R.
Nutrition and food in an African economy: bibliography.
2, 2v. 246pp. photos. ill. U.shs84.00 ($12.50) Dept
Rur Econ - Mak 1972 UG

Amanquah, S.Y.
A review of Kenaf research with special reference to
Ghana. 17pp. C1.00 ($1.00/50p.) Ghana UP 1968
GH

Amarteifio, Dr. et al.
Ghana recipe book. 140pp. ill. C1.50 ($1.50)
Ghana Publ Corp 1971 GH

Amarteifio, G.W. Whitham, D. Butcher, D.A.P.
Tema Manhean: a study of resettlement. 97pp. photos.
ill. cl. C5.00 (£2.50/$5.00) (Planning research stud.,
3) Ghana UP 1966 GH

Amartey, A.A.
Ga work book pt. 1. Exercises in Ga language. 51pp.
34pes. Waterville 1966 GH GAA

Amartey, A.A.
Ga work book pt. 2. Exercises in Ga language. 60pp.
42pes. Waterville 1966 GH GAA

Amartey, A.A.
Omanye aba. [May goodness come.] 2nd ed. 144pp.
C1.70 Bur Ghana Lang 1976 GH GAA

Amayo, A.
Ynunozedo, Ebe okaro. pupils bk. 1. See: Uwaifo.

Amedekey, E.Y.
The culture of Ghana: a bibliography. 215pp. map. hd.
C6.00 (£3.00/$6.00) Ghana UP 1970 GH

Amegboh, J.
Ossei Toutou. 112pp. CFA250 (F5.00) Nouv Ed
Afric 1976 SG FRE

Amegbon, J.
Behanzin - Roi d'Abomey. 112pp. CFA250 (F5.00)
(Coll. "Grandes figures africaines") Nouv Ed Afric 1975
SG FRE

Amengual, M., ed.
Une histoire de l'Afrique est-elle possible? 256pp.
CFA800 Nouv Ed Afric 1975 SG FRE

Amerasinghe, C.F.
Aspects of the actio iniuriarum in Roman-Dutch law.
R9.00 Juta 1966 SA

Amevor, D.K.H.
Children's delight. See: Doku, C.W.

Amin El-Tom, M.
The rains of the Sudan: mechanism and distribution.
136pp. 95pt. ($4.00) Khartoum UP 1975 SJ

Amin, J.J.
Revision questions in physical science for junior
secondary. 144pp. K.shs.16.00 Heinemann Educ -
Nair 1976 KE

Amin, M.
Kenya's world-beating athletes. 100pp. photos.
K.shs.16.00 ($5.00) EAPH 1972 KE

Amin, M. Moll, P.
Mzee Jomo Kenyatta. [Pictorial biography of Jomo
Kenyatta.] 144pp. pl. col. pl. K.shs.30.00 Transafrica
1974 KE SWA

Amin, M. Moll, P.
One man one vote. 144pp. photos. EAPH 1975 KE

Amin, M.
Tom Mboya: a photographic tribute. 96pp. photos.
K.shs.0.30 cl. K.shs.1.10 pap. ($5.60 cl.) ($3.20
pap.) EAPH 1969 KE

Amir, A.J.
Hadithi zenye mafunzo. [Stories with a moral for primary
schools] 44pp. ill. K.shs.7.50 OUP-Nairobi 1973 KE
SWA

Amir, A.J.
Nahodha Fikirini. [Captain Fikirini] 56pp. ill.
K.shs.5.50 OUP-Nairobi 1971 KE SWA

Amissah, G.H.
Africa speaks aloud. 12pp. 25pes. Univ Ghana
Bkshop; distr. 1975 GH

Amissah, G.M.
The living echoes of Kwame Nkrumah. 12pp. C1.50
Univ Ghana Bkshop; distr. 1975 GH

Amissah, G.M.
On first seeing Achimota. 29pp. C1.50 Univ Ghana
Bkshop; distr. 1977 GH

Ammah, C.
Ga Homowo. 30pp. ill. 30pes. Advance 1968 GH
TWI

Amoako, B.O., ed.
Etire nni safoa. [There is no key to the head.] 2nd ed.
208pp. C2.50 Bur Ghana Lang 1977 GH ASA

Amoako, B.O.
Enne nso bio. [Today again.] 172pp. ill. C2.00 Bur
Ghana Lang 1976 GH ASA

Amoako, B.O.
Etire nni safoa. [The head has no key.] 207pp. ill.
C2.50 Bur Ghana Lang 1975 GH TWI

Amoako, K.
Fie atamfo a. [Sufferings of a young man.] 169pp.
C1.30 Bur Ghana Lang 1974 GH FAT

Amoaku, J.K.
Badu goes to Kumasi. 46pp. ill. 30pes. ($.30)
Ghana Publ Corp 1970 GH

Amoaku, J.K.
The Christmas hut. 27pp. ill. 25pes. ($.40) Ghana
Publ Corp 1970 GH

Amon d'Aby, F.J.
La mare aux crocodiles. Contes et légendes populaires de
Côte d'Ivoire. 128pp. ill. CFA500 (F10.00) Nouv
Ed Afric 1973 SG FRE

Amonoo, E.
The flow and marketing of Cassava in the central region
with special reference to Cape Coast. 47pp. C1.50
(Univ. of Cape Coast, Centre for Development Studies,
Research Report Series, 9) Centre Dev Stud 1972 GH

Amonoo, E.
The focus and concentrate programme in the Somanya
district: evaluation of an extension programme.
See: Dumor, E.

Amonoo, E.
The production, distribution and marketing of rice in the
Bolgatanga district. 38pp. C1.50 (Univ. of Cape
Coast, Centre for Development Studies, Research Report
Series, 8) Centre Dev Stud 1972 GH

Amorin, J.E.K.
Concepts of disease causation throughout the ages.
20pp. C1.00 ($1.00/50p.) (Inaugural lecture) Ghana
UP 1971 GH

Amosu, M.
Creative African writing in the European languages.
35pp. 50k (Inst. of African Stud., Univ of Ibadan,
occas. pub., 1) Inst Afr Stud-Ibadan 1964 NR

Ampene, K.
Atetescm. [Historical stories.] 46pp. ill. 45pes. Waterville 1976 GH TWI

Ampofo, D.A.
The family planning movement in Ghana. 18pp. C1.00 ($1.00/50p.) (Inaugural lecture) Ghana UP 1971 GH

Ampofo, D.D.
Africonism. 48pp. C4.00 Univ Ghana Bkshop; distr. 1977 GH

Amrani, D.
Aussi loin que mes regards se portent. 246pp. DA5.00 SNED 1972 AE FRE

Amrani, D.
Bivouac des certitudes. 120pp. DA4.00 SNED 1969 AE FRE

Amsalem, R.
Climatologie generale. 215pp. photos. DA24.00 SNED 1971 AE FRE

Amuzu-Kpeglo, A.
Xexeame do atsyc. 60pp. ($1.30) Ghana Publ Corp 1975 GH EWE

Anakaa, D.K.
How to know God's guidance. 3rd ed. 20pp. 10k Daystar 1968 NR

Ananaba, W.
Trade union movement in Nigeria. 336pp. N4.00 (NR only) Ethiope 1972 NR

Anande, S.
Estimation of available phosphorus in soils by extraction with sodium bicarbonate. 10pp. 60k (Samaru misc. pap., 36) Inst Agric Res-Zaria 1972 NR

Anane, F.K.
Kofi Mensah. 60pp. ill. 35pes. ($1.00) Ghana Publ Corp 1968 GH

Anang, J.L.
Our United Nations family. 32pp. ill. photos. 30pes. ($.30) Ghana Publ Corp 1968 GH

Andam, F.
Ato Badu's school days. 96pp. ill. C1.00 (40p.) Africa Christian 1975 GH

Andani Vo-Naa, R.I.
Dagbani Yeltcyi. [Dagbani riddles and proverbs.] 21pp. 20pes. Bur Ghana Lang 1973 GH DAB

Andersen, K.B.
African traditional architecture: a study of the housing and settlement patterns of rural Kenya. 256pp. photos. & ill. K.shs.60.00 OUP - Nairobi 1977 KE

Anderson, A.A.
Twenty-five years in a waggon. Sport and travel in South Africa. [Reprint of 1888]. 3rd. ed. 427pp. pl. maps. cl. R10.50 (Africana Collectanea, 48) Struik 1974 SA

Anderson, C., eds. Kilima, V.L., eds.
Parasitosis of man and animals in Africa. 573pp. ill. K.shs.68.00 ($17.50/£8.25) EALB 1974 KE

Anderson, D.
Rock paintings and petroglyphs of South and Central Africa - 1959-1970. 29pp. R1.60 Dept Bibliog, Lib & Typo 1971 SA

Anderson, J.D.C.
Kaa kimya. [The quiet time.] 52pp. T.shs.2.00 Africa Inland Church 1971 TZ SWA

Anderson, J.G.
Common weeds of South Africa. See: Henderson, M.

Anderson, M.
Commerce for Rhodesians. 128pp. R$1.70 Longman - Rhod 1972 RH

Anderson, M.P. McBain, F.C.A.
Beginning geography in Kenya. 88pp. K.shs.11.50 OUP-Nairobi 1966 KE

Anderson, W.W.
Day-care services for pre-school and school-going children in Chatsworth. free (Chatsworth Community and Research Centre, Research Report, 3) Univ of Durban - Westville 1973 SA

Anderson, W.W. Mason, J.
Rental survey. free (Chatsworth Community and Research Centre, Research Report, 1) Univ of Durban - Westville 1972 SA

Andes, B.M.
Agricultural studies for Lesotho. See: Maes, Y.M.

Andrade, M. de. Ollivier, M.
The war in Angola. 160pp. maps. Tanz Publ House 1975 TZ

Andreou, P.
Agricultural development and co-operative marketing in Cyprus. 264pp. K.shs.36.65 ($7.50/£4.50) EALB 1977 KE

Andreou, P.
Contemporary issues in agricultural and economic development of poor nations. 360pp. K.shs.45.65 ($9.10/£5.25) EALB 1977 KE

Andreou, P., ed.
Co-operative institutions and economic development. Some lessons from advanced and developing countries. 564pp. K.shs.65.75 ($12.60/£6.00) EALB 1977 KE

Andrews, G.
A comparison of open-end and ring spinning of cotton, part I: the physical properties of 25 tex yarns spun from different cottons grown in Southern Africa. See: Hunter, L.

Andrews, G.
The relationship between certain properties of wool worsted yarns and their knitting performance, part II: the effect of different levels of some solid lubricants on knitting performance. See: Hunter, L.

Andrianjafy, M.
Orimbaton'ny Fiadanana. 180pp. FMG400 Ed Takariva 1975 MG MLA

Anene, J. C. et al.
Essays in African history, 19th and 20th centuries. 201pp. N2.00 Onibonoje 1966 NR

Anene, J.C., ed. Brown, G., ed.
Africa in the nineteenth and twentieth centuries. 555pp. maps pl. N5.10 Ibadan UP 1966 NR

Angas, G.F.
The Kaffirs illustrated ... [Reprint of ed. 1849]. 152pp. ill. col. pl. cl. R150.00 ($270.00) Balkema 1974 SA

Angas, G.F.
The Kafirs illustrated. (Facsimile edition of orig. 1849 ed., with a new introduction by F.R. Bradlow) 150pp. col. pl. Fl.675.00 Balkema 1974 SA

Angenot, J.P., et al.
Interpretation générative du phenomène de l'emprunt linguistique. 136pp. Z2.00 CELTA 1974 ZR FRE

Angenot, J.P., et al.
Répertoire des vocables Brésiliens d'origine Africaine. 192pp. maps. Z2.00 CELTA 1974 ZR FRE

Angira, J.
Juices. 59pp. K.shs6.00 ($2.40) EAPH 1970 KE

Angira, J.
Soft corals. 156pp. K.shs.10.00 (Poets of Africa, 5) EAPH 1974 KE

Anglars, H.P.
Wana wa Ibrahimu. [Children of Abraham.] 3rd ed. 200pp. T.shs.7.00 ($1.00) TMP 1974 TZ SWA

Anglican Diocese, Lagos.
Eto isin fun orisirisi ajodun l'aarin ebi. [Programme for different festivals within a household] 26pp. 10k Daystar 1969 NR YOR

Angulo, E. Kemijumbi, P.
Uganda recipes. U.shs.5.00 Uganda Pub House 1974 UG

Author Index

Anjorin, J.F.
Students objective maths. 2nd ed. 170pp. ill. N1.00
Ilesanmi 1973 NR

Ankoma, P., ed.
Ehia wo a nwu. [Do not commit suicide because of
poverty.] 2nd ed. 60pp. ill. C1.00 Bur Ghana Lang
1976 GH ASA

Ankrah, E.
Mutinta goes hunting. 24pp. ill. 50n. Neczam 1972
ZA

Annane, L.
Information et calcul économique. 37pp. DA1.00
SNED 1972 AE FRE

Anno, S.W.
We went hunting. 25pp. ill. 20pes. Waterville 1970
GH

Anno, S.W.
Yekoo akotobo. 116pp. ($3.00) Ghana Publ Corp
1976 GH TWI

Annor, S.W.
The honey hunters. 35pp. ill. 35pes. Waterville
1974 GH

Anoka, G.M.K., ed.
Poetry for primary schools. 81pp. N1.00 Nwamife
1976 NR

Anokwu, C.C.
Health science objective tests. See: Nwanevu, S.S.I.

Anoma, G. et al.
Annales de l'université d'Abidjan. 153pp. CFA1500
(F30.00) (Série C-Sciences, 1) Univ Abidjan 1965 IV
FRE

Anozie, S.O., ed.
Nigeria 1975: 2nd World Festival of Black and African Arts
& Cultures. 152pp. maps. N5.50 ($7.00) (Conch
Special editions) Conch 1974 NR

Ansah, W.K.
The denizens of the street. 103pp. C1.25 ($1.25)
Ghana Publ Corp 1971 GH

Ansong, B.F.
Wcaka nea eye akyere mo. [You have been told what is
good] 14pp. 9pes. Waterville 1966 GH TWI

Ansre, G.
Proceedings of the conference on the study of Ghanaian
languages. See: Birnie, J.H.

Anstee, M.J.
Africa and the world. See: Robert, K.A.

Anteh, E.A.
Ga snwemci. [Cultural games.] 2nd ed. 144pp. pl.
C1.70 Bur Ghana Lang 1976 GH GAA

Anthonio, Q.B.O.
Fish marketing survey in the Kainji lake basin: Yelwa area
study. 120pp. N6.50 ($9.00) (N.I.S.E.R. research
reports, 2) NISER 1970 NR

Anthony, K.R.M.
Agricultural change in Geita, Tanzania. A study of
economic, cultural and technical determinants of
agricultural change in tropical Africa. See: Uchendu, V.C.

Anthony, K.R.M.
Agricultural change in Kisii District Kenya.
See: Uchendu, V.C.

Anthony, K.R.M.
Agricultural change in Teso district, Uganda. A study of
economic, cultural and technical determinants of
agricultural change in tropical Africa. See: Uchendu, V.C.

Anti, A.A.
Akwapim Denkyira Akwamu Ashanti in the lives of Osei
Tutu and Okomfo Anokye. 100pp. photos. map.
C1.00 ($1.00) Ghana Publ Corp 1971 GH

Anti, A.A.
Ancient Asante king. 75pp. C2.50 Univ Ghana
Bkshop; distr. 1974 GH

Anwan, O.E.E.
Edikot nwed: pupils book I. See: Udo-Ema, A.J.

Anwan, O.E.E.
Edikot nwed: teacher's book I. See: Udo-Ema, A.J.

Anwanwu, V.A.
Textbook of agriculture for school certificate.
See: Anyanwu, A.C.

Anwar, H.A.
Sabuwar han yar Hausa don makarantu littafi na. 1,
6bks See: Dangambe, A.

Anwar, H.A.
Sabuwar han yar Hausa don makarantu littafi na. 2,
6bks See: Dangambe, A.

Anwar, H.A.
Sabuwar han yar Hausa don makarantu littafi na. 3,
6bks See: Dangambe, A.

Anwar, H.A.
Sabuwar han yar Hausa don makarantu littafi na. 4,
6bks See: Dangambe, A.

Anwar, H.A.
Sabuwar han yar Hausa don makarantu littafi na. 5,
6bks See: Dangambe, A.

Anwar, H.A.
Sabuwar han yar Hausa don makarantu littafi na. 6,
6bks See: Dangambe, A.

Anyanwu, A.C. Anwanwu, V.A. Anyanwu, B.O.
Textbook of agriculture for school certificate. 2nd ed.
320pp. pl. ill. N3.50 Africana Educ 1976 NR

Anyanwu, B.O.
Textbook of agriculture for school certificate.
See: Anyanwu, A.C.

Anywar, R.S.
Acoli ki ker megi. K.shs.2.50 ($1.50/60p.) EALB KE
LUO

Aouchal, L.
Une autre vie. 155pp. DA7.00 SNED 1970 AE FRE

Aoustin, J.
Fés. Dir12.00 (Collection "Découverte", 1) Ed La
Porte 1972(?) MR FRE

Appiah-Kubi, K., ed. Mugambi, J., ed.
African and Black theology. 150pp. K.shs.25.00
Transafrica 1976 KE

Appiah, O.
Eight stories for children. 60pp. ill. ($1.20) Ghana
Publ Corp 1976 GH

Appiah, P.
A dirge too soon. 182pp. ill. ($3.75) Ghana Publ
Corp 1976 GH

Appiah, P.
Gift of the Mmoatia. 112pp. ill. 85pes. Ghana Publ
Corp 1972 GH

Appiah, P.
Why are there so many roads? 64pp. ill. 45k
(African Junior Library, 5) Pilgrim 1971 NR

Appleby, L.
First Luyia grammar. 3rd ed. 132pp. K.shs.12.00
($3.35/£1.30) EALB 1961 KE

Appleyard, M.E.
Dr. David Livingstone. 33pp. 70c. Univ Cape Town
Lib 1970 SA

Apraku, L.D., ed.
Aku Sika. [Aku Sika.] 3rd ed. 69pp. ill. 80pes.
Bur Ghana Lang 1976 GH TWI

Apthorpe, R.H., ed.
Present interrelations in Central African rural and urban life.
175pp. 75n. (35p.) (Rhodes-Livingstone Institute conf.
proc., 11) Inst Afr Stud - Lusaka 1958 ZA

Apthorpe, R.J., ed.
From tribal rule to modern government. 216pp. K1.00
(60p.) (Rhodes-Livingstone Institute conf. proc., 13) Inst
Afr Stud - Lusaka 1960 ZA

Apthorpe, R.J., ed.
Social relations in Central African industry.
See: Matthews, D., ed.

Apthorpe, R.J., ed.
Social research and community development. 173pp. K1.00 (59p.) (Rhodes-Livingstone Institute Conference, 15) Inst Afr Stud - Lusaka 1961 ZA

Arbousset, T.   Daumas, F.
Narrative of an exploratory tour to the Cape of Good Hope [Reprint of 1846 edition]. 338pp. ill. pl. cl. R8.40 (Africana collectanea, 27) Struik 1968 SA

Arbuthnot, A.
The utilization of sugar cane bagasse in the pulp and paper industry - soda and NSSC pulping. See: Venter, J.S.M.

Arbuthnot, A.
The utilization of sugar cane bagasse in the pulp and paper industry - soda semi-chemical pulping. See: Venter, J.S.M.

Archer, A.
New commercial mathematics for standard 8. 215pp. ill. R3.60 Nasou 1976 SA

Archer, A.   de Villiers, G.
New commercial mathematics for standards 9 and 10. 373pp. ill. R3.80 Nasou 1974 SA

Archer, A.A., et al.
Accountancy for standard 9. A logical approach. 356pp. R4.50 Nasou 1974 SA

Archer, A.A., et al.
Accountancy for standard 10. A logical approach. 353pp. pl. R4.85 Nasou 1974 SA

Archer, A.B.   Thomas, H.G.
Abaana omukaaga abomu nsi ezewala. 58pp. K.shs.2.00 ($1.25/50p.) EALB 1963 KE LUG

Archibald, J.E.
The works of Professor Isaac Schapera: a selective bibliography. 62pp. R3.20 Dept Bibliog, Lib & Typo 1969 SA

Archibong, G.
The keen little hunter and other stories. 72pp. Nwamife 1973 NR

Are, L.A.
Cacao in West Africa. See: Gwynne-Jones, G.

Aremu, A.
Asayan oriki. [Collection of Yoruba cognomes.] 66pp. ill. 70k OUP - Nig 1975 NR YOR

Arewa, O.   Shreve, G.M.
The genesis of structures in African narrative. Vol. I: Zande trickster tales. 300pp. cl. N13.50 ($20.00) (Studies in African Semiotics) Conch 1975 NR

Argyle, W.J., ed.   Preston-White, E.M., ed.
Social system and tradition in Southern Africa. 190pp. ill. hd. R7.50 OUP - SA 1977 SA

Arias, A.A.
Iwillimiden. 2nd ed. 155pp. CFA350 CELTHO 1974 NG FRE

Arinze, F.A.
Sacrifice in Ibo religion. 129pp. pl. N3.00 Ibadan UP 1970 NR

Arkin, M.
Economists and economic historians. ex. only (Inaugural lec.) Rhodes Univ Lib 1968 SA

Arkin, M.
Storm in a teacup. The later years of the John Company at the Cape, 1815-36. 272pp. cl. R7.50 Struik 1973 SA

Arku Mensha, D.
Onyifurafo n'awar mu. See: Quartey, J.K.

Arkutu, A.A.
A guide to pregnancy and childbirth. 96pp. ill. pl. C3.00 Afram 1975 GH

Arkwright, R.
Sport and service in South Africa. 104pp. hd. fl. 16.00 Balkema 1971 SA

Armah, A. K.
Wema hawajazaliwa. [Tr. of The beautiful ones are not yet born.] 196pp. K.shs.14.50 (£1.20) Heinemann Educ - Nair 1975 KE SWA

Armah, A.K.
Fragments. 280pp. K.shs.15.00 (Modern African Library, 29) EAPH 1974 KE

Armah, A.K.
Two thousand seasons. 312pp. K.shs.15.00 (Modern African Library, 27) EAPH 1974 KE

Armah, A.K.
Why are we so blest? 260pp. K.shs.14.00 (Modern African Library, 30) EAPH 1974 KE

Armah, E.O.
Objective exercises in biology. 91pp. ill. 85k (NR only) Ethiope 1972 NR

Armand, E.   Thomas, P.   Dachelet, R.
Codage informatique du contenu lexical des programmes télévisuels de français (CP1 - CP2) 74pp. CFA500 (Enseignement du Français, 55) Inst Ling Appliquée 1976 IV FRE

Armar, T.Q.
Objective questions and answers in arithmetic: decimal currency and metric edition. N1.97 Macmillan 1959 NR

Armstrong, R.G.
A comparative wordlist of five Igbo dialects. 127pp. N2.00 (Inst. of African Stud., Univ. of Ibadan, occas. pub.,4v5) Inst Afr Stud-Ibadan 1967 NR

Armstrong, R.G.
The issues at stake: Nigeria,1967. 20pp. 10k Ibadan UP 1967 NR

Armstrong, R.G.
The study of West African languages. [An expanded version of an inaugural lecture.]. 74pp. N1.50 Ibadan UP 1967 NR

Arnheim, J.
Swaziland. 23pp. 60c. Univ Cape Town Lib 1969 SA

Arnold, G.
Kenyatta and the politics of Kenya. 200pp. K.shs.25.00 (Africa only) Transafrica 1975 KE

Arnold, L.M.   Varty, A.E.
English through activity. Fourth year, teacher's manual. 232pp. R2.50 Shuter 1974 SA

Arnold, M.
Man's anatomy: a study in dissection. 3 v. See: Tobias, P.V.

Arnott, B.
Claude Bouscharain. 64pp. ill. col. ill. cl. R9.75 (South African Art Library, 7) Struik 1977 SA

Arnott, B.
Muafangejo. 60pp. pl. col. ill. cl. R18.00 Struik 1977 SA

Arnott, K.
Ayo, msichana wa Kiafrika shuleni kwake. [Ayo, an African schoolgirl] 56pp. ill. K.shs3.00 OUP-Nairobi 1968 KE SWA

Aromolaran, A.
Akomolede ijinle Yoruba 3. pupils bk. 3. See: Mustapha, B.

Aromolaran, A.   Mustapha, B.
Akomolede ijinle Yoruba. [Secondary Yoruba course. Pubils' bk. 1.] bk. 1 172pp. ill. N1.80 Macmillan 1974 NR YOR

Aromolaran, A.   Mustapha, B.
Akomolede ijinle Yoruba. [Secondary Yoruba course. Pubils' bk. 2.] bk. 2 160pp. ill. N1.90 Macmillan 1975 NR YOR

Aromolaran, A.   Oladiji, A.
Akomolede Yoruba. [Primary Yoruba course. Pupils' bk. 1.] Rev. ed. bk. 1. 48pp. ill. 75k Macmillan 1974 NR YOR

Asante, G.S.
Biochemical education in perspective. 23pp. C1.00
($1.00/50p.) (Inaugural lecture series) Ghana UP 1974
GH

Asante, S.A.
Common entrance objective tests in history and civics.
See: Buah, F.K.

Asante, S.K.B.
Property law and social goals in Ghana. 292pp. cl.
C18.00 ($18.00/£9.00) Ghana UP 1975 GH

Asare, B.
Majuto. [Novel]. 145pp. K.shs6.00 ($2.00/80p.)
EALB 1976 KE SWA

Asare, B.
Mwasi. [Rebel tr. fr. English N. Zaidi] K.shs11.25
(85p.) (Waandishi Wa KiAfrika, 5.) Heinemann Educ -
Nair 1972 KE SWA

Asare, B.
The stubborn. 162pp. K.shs.20.90 ($4.70/£2.20)
EALB 1976 KE

Asare, M.
I am Kofi. 16pp. ill. 10pes. ($.20) Ghana Publ
Corp 1972 GH

Asare, M.
Mansa helps at home. 16pp. ill. 10pes. ($.20)
Ghana Publ Corp 1972 GH

Asare, M.
Tawia goes to sea. 31pp. ill. cl. C1.50 ($1.50)
Ghana Publ Corp 1970 GH

Ascadi, G.T., ed. Johnson, G.Z., ed. Igun, A.A., ed.
Surveys of fertility, family and family planning in Nigeria.
306pp. N5.50 (IMPS Publication, 2) Univ Ife Bkshop
1972 NR

Ascough, S.W.
Computation of thermodynamic equilibrium of
heterogeneous reaction systems by minimumization of the
free energy. See: Hamblyn, S.M.L.

Asebiomo, A.J.
Tests in mathematics: with answers. See: Potts, H.

Asebiomo, A.J.
Tests in mathematics: without answers. See: Potts, H.

Ashall, C.
Nzige the desert locust. K.shs0.10 ($1.00/40p.)
EALB 1959 KE

Ashaolu, T. A.
Topics in European history, 1700-1830. 159pp. N1.05
Onibonoje 1969 NR

Ashaolu, T.A. et al.
A.D. 1,000 to the present day: essays. 2nd ed. 221pp.
maps. N2.00 Onibonoje 1967 R

Ashaolu, T.A. et al.
Economic history of West Africa: questions and answers.
257pp. N1.65 Onibonoje 1968 NR

Ashaolu, T.A.
A new college history. 132pp. maps. N1.65
Onibonoje 1967 NR

Ashby, G.W.
Theodoret of Cyrrhus as Exegete of the Old Testament.
158pp. hd. R6.00 Rhodes Univ Lib SA

Asheri, J.
Promise. 96pp. ill. 53k (African Reader's Library,
16) Pilgrim 1969 NR

Ashong-Katai, S.
Confessions of a bastard, and other stories. 122pp.
C3.00 ($3.00) Ghana Publ Corp 1976 GH

Ashton, H.
Problem territories of Southern Africa: Basutoland,
Bechuanaland protectorate, Swaziland. See: Dundas, C.

Ashton, M. Ohene-Asante, G.
God's plan for your life. 24pp. ill. 45pes. (20p.)
Africa Christian 1975 GH

Ashworth, A.E.
School certificate physics objective tests. 137pp. ill.
N2.30 OUP - Nig 1976 NR

Ashworth, A.E.
School certificate revision course: Physics. See: Ryan,
O.

Asiedu Akrofi, K.
An analytical study of teachers' associations in Ghana.
78pp. 75pes. Univ Cape Coast (distr.) 1974 GH

Asiedu-Akrofi, K.
Teachers Associations in Ghana. 78pp. 75pes. Cape
Coast Bkshp 1971 GH

Asihene, E.V.
Asempaka adwuma. [Evangelism] 42pp. 20pes.
Waterville 1965 GH TWI

Asirifi, A.
Common entrance composition. 94pp. C1.00
Advance 1970 GH

Askwith, T.G.
Adult education in Kenya. 57pp. K.shs.6.00 ($3.00)
EALB 1961 KE

Askwith, T.G.
Progress through self-help: principles and practice in
community development. 34pp. ill. K.shs.2.25
($2.00/80p.) EALB 1960 KE

Asrat, T.
Pupil's book. See: Rogers, J.

Assegé, W.G.
Mesfinu Merkonya. [Story of the young son of Emperor
Tewodros who died in England.] 1962pp. ill. photo.
Eth.$2.00 Bookshop Supply Org 1973 ET AMH

Association of African Universities.
Directory of African universities, Anglophone universities.
2nd rev. ed. pt. 1, 2. 278pp. AAU 1976 GH

Association of African Universities.
Directory of African universities, Francophone universities.
[In French.]. 2nd rev. ed. pt. 2, 2. 111pp. ($33.00)
AAU 1976 GH

Association of African Universities.
Report of the second general conference of the
Association of African Universities, Kinshasa 19th-21st
1969. [also available in French.]. 164pp. ($5.00) AAU
GH

Association of African Universities.
Report of the Third General conference of The Association
of African Universities, Ibadan 9th-14th April 1973. [also
available in French.]. 136pp. ($5.00) AAU GH

Astrinsky, A.
South African English novels, 1930-1960. 50pp. 80c.
Univ Cape Town Lib 1970 SA

Atangana, J.
Chemins d'Afrique. 176pp. CFA500.00 (Coll. Point
de Vue) CLE 1973 CM FRE

Atangana, N.
Comment fonctionne notre économie. 3rd ed. 112pp.
CFA360 CLE 1972 CM FRE

Atangana, N.
Travail et développement. 84pp. CFA360 (Point de
vue, 4) CLE 1971 CM FRE

Ater, J.M.
Out of confusion. 32pp. ill. 40pes. (12p.) Africa
Christian 1973 GH

Atieno Odhiambo, E.S.
The paradox of collaboration and other essays. 166pp.
K.shs.18.00 ($3.60/£1.80) EALB 1974 KE

Atigbi, I.A.
Nigeria: cultural safari tours. English and French 44pp.
photos. gratis Nig Tourist 1973 NR

Atigbi, I.A.
Nigeria: traditional festivals - a guide to cultural
amusements. English and French 60pp. photos.
gratis Nig Tourist 1972 NR

Author Index

Atigbi, I.A.
Nigerian tourist guide. English and French 156pp. maps photos. gratis Nig Tourist 1973 NR

Atkinson, D.
General science for tropical schools: workbook, 1. 95k OUP-Nig 1954 NR

Atkinson, N.
Educational co-operation in the Commonwealth. 265pp. R$2.00 (Fac. of Education, Univ. of Rhodesia, Series in Education, 1) Univ Rhodesia Lib 1972 RH

Attipoe, F.E.Y.
The businessman's Cedi reckoner. 146pp. C1.00 Waterville 1967 GH

Attobrah, K.
The kings of Akyam Abuakwa and the ninety-nine wars against Asante. 62pp. photos. ($3.00) Ghana Publ Corp 1976 GH

Attwell, A.F.I.
The Methodist church. 25pp. 50c. Methodist 1976 SA

Attwell, O.H.B.
Index of words and phrases. R6.00 Juta 1951 SA

Aucamp, J.H.
Fitting and turning for standard 9. See: Swartz, W.F.

Audouin, J. Deniel, R.
L'Islam en Haute-Volta à l'époque coloniale. 96pp. maps. CFA700 INADES 1975 IC FRE

Auerbach, F.E.
The ABC of race. Rev. ed. 59pp. maps pl. R1.05 ($1.95) SA Inst of Race Relations 1976 SA

Auerbach, F.E.
South Africa: a fundamentally unjust society? 18pp. 30c. ($1.10) SA Inst of Race Relations 1970 SA

Aurouze, J.
Bibliographie géologique de Madagascar. 14pp. FMG105 (F2.10) (Série Documentation, 152) Service Geol - Mad 1960 MG FRE

Austin, D.
The Commonwealth in eclipse. 38pp. C1.20 ($1.20/60p.) Ghana UP 1972 GH

Awe, B., ed.
Nigerian antiquities: report of a symposium held at the Institute of African Studies, University of Ibadan, from Thursday 20th April to Sunday 23rd April, 1972. (Special number of African Notes) See: Alagoa, E.J., ed.

Awe, O.
Physics in Ibadan: developing physics in a developing country. 28pp. N1.00 (Inaugural lecture) Ibadan UP 1974 NG

Awiti, A.
The development of Ujamaa villages and the peasant question in Iringa district. T.shs.12.00 ($3.00) (Research pap., 71.17) Econ Res Bur - Tanz 1975 TZ

Awokoya, S.O.
A first science course for Nigeria: the science of things above us. 1, 3bks 96pp. col. ill. N1.20 Macmillan NR

Awokoya, S.O.
A first science course for Nigeria: the science of things around us. plants and animals 2, 3bks 96pp. col. ill. N1.40 Macmillan NR

Awokoya, S.O.
A first science course for Nigeria: the science of things around us: their chemical composition. 3, 3bks 124pp. col. ill. N1.60 Macmillan NR

Awolola, M.A.
Thirty tests in primary six arithmetic. 101pp. 65k Alliance 1972 NR

Awolowo, O.
My early life. 125pp. 50k West 1968 NR

Awolowo, O.
The path to economic freedom in developing countries. 1 23pp. 30k Univ Lagos Bookshop 1968 NR

Awolowo, O.
The people's republic. 356pp. hd. N4.50 OUP-Nig 1968 NR

Awolowo, O.
The strategy and tactics of the People's Republic of Nigeria. 144pp. hd., pap. N1.20 pap. N5.50 hd. Macmillan 1970 NR

Awolowo, O.
Thoughts on Nigerian constitution. 196pp. map. 50k OUP-Nig 1966 NR

Awoniyi, T.A.
Aiye kooto. [Truth is spurned] 115pp. N1.10 Onibonoje 1973 NR YOR

Awoniyi, T.A.
Yoruba atata fun ode oni. [Yoruba for today] 128pp. N1.50 Onibonoje 1971 NR YOR

Awoonor-Renner, M.
Ndapi's childhood. 106pp. ill. Pilgrim 1976 NR

Awua-Asamoah, A.K.
Some Akan fables. 68pp. ill. 60pes. Waterville 1975 GH

Awuku, G.O.
Mmere di adannan. [Time changes.] 96pp. ill. 75pes. Waterville 1975 GH TWI

Axelson, E.
Portugal and the scramble for Africa 1875-1891. 318pp. maps pl. cl. R8.00 (Oppenheimer Inst. of Portuguese stud. pub., 3) Witwatersrand UP 1964 SA

Axelson, E.
Portuguese in South-East Africa 1488-1600. 288pp. cl. R7.50 Struik 1973 SA

Axelson, E.
Portuguese in South-East Africa 1600-1700. 226pp. maps/pl. cl. R8.00 (Oppenheimer Inst. of Portuguese stud. pub., 4) Witwatersrand UP 1969 SA

Ayandele, E.A.
The educated elite in the Nigerian society. 177pp. cl. & pap. N3.00 pap. N5.00 cl. Ibadan UP 1974 NR

Ayandele, E.A.
A visionary of the African church. Mogala Agbebi. 31pp. K.shs3.80 ($1.00) EAPH 1971 KE

Ayany, S.
Kar chakruok mar Luo. K.shs.3.00 Equatorial 1973 KE LUO

Ayany, S.G.
A history of Zanzibar: study in constitutional development 1934-1964. 188pp. ill. pap. & cl. K.shs.34.00 cl. K.shs.22.60 pap. ($6.95/£3.40 cl.) EALB 1970 KE

Aye, E.O.
Merehua. [Folk tales] 125pp. 50pes. Waterville 1971 GH TWI

Ayeh, E.F.A.
Wobekc bi ana? [Will you also go?] 2nd ed. 134pp. ill. C1.70 Bur Ghana Lang 1976 GH TWI

Ayeke, K.
Asitsu Atcawo. [Married life of a couple.] 2nd ed. 113pp. ill. 80pes. Bur Ghana Lang 1975 GH EWE

Ayeke, K.
Hlcbiabia. [Retribution.] 97pp. ill. 70pes. Bur Ghana Lang 1974 GH EWE

Ayeni, D.A.
One thousand speed and accuracy. 1st ed. 1, 2bks 51pp. 40k Ilesanmi 1971 NR

Ayeni, D.A.
One thousand speed and accuracy. 1st ed. 2, 2bks 52pp. 40k Ilesanmi 1971 NR

Ayeni, D.A.
One thousand speed and accuracy. Rev. ed. bk. 1. 75pp. ill. 95k Ilesanmi 1973 NR

Ayeni, D.A.
One thousand speed and accuracy. rev. ed. bk. 2. 87pp. ill. 95k Ilesanmi 1973 NR

Ayerst, P.W.
Animal nutrition: A do-it-yourself revision text. 64pp.
K.shs7.00 OUP-Nairobi 1972 KE

Ayida, A.A., ed.
Reconstruction and development in Nigeria. See: Onitiri,
H.M.A., ed.

Ayisi, C.H.
The motivation of human learning. 24pp. 45pes.
(Univ. of Cape Coast, School of Education, Educational
Psychology Monographs, 2) Univ Cape Coast Lib (distr.)
1974 GH

Ayisi, C.H.
The psychology of creativity. 29pp. 50pes.
(Educational psychology monog., 1) Cape Coast Bkshp
1972 GH

Ayisi, O.
Twi mmebusem 750. [750 Twi proverbs] 191pp.
50pes. Waterville 1966 GH TWI

Ayissi, L.M.
Contes et berceuses béti. 2nd ed. 96pp. CFA360
pap. CLE 1972 CM FRE

Ayliff, J.
The journal of John Ayliff, 1821-1830. 136pp. hd. fl.
18.00 (The Graham's Town, 1) Balkema 1971 SA

Ayo, E.B.
Comprehension practice for forms 3-6. See: Gibbs, E.D.

Ayobolu, B.
Native authority finance patterns. See: Fairholm, G.W.

Ayodele, S.
The church is the problem. 68pp. 60k Daystar 1977
NR

Ayorinde, J.A.
Igbesi aiye Oba Akinye. [Biography of the late King of
Ibadan] 84pp. ill. N1.00 OUP - Nig 1973 NR YOR

Ayot, H.O.
Topics in East African history 1000-1970. 152pp.
K.shs.20.50 ($4.60/£2.20 pap.) EALB 1976 KE

Azan, M. M'B.S.
Martin Samba du Cameroun. 112pp. CFA250
(F5.00) Nouv Ed Afric 1976 SG FRE

Azariah, V.S.
Sadaka ya wakristo. 58pp. 30k CEDI 1974 ZR SWA

Azasu, K.
Streams of thought. 105pp. C2.50 Univ Ghana
Bkshop; distr. 1974 GH

Azikiwe, N.
Democracy with Military vigilance. 104pp. N2.00
(£1.50) African Book Co. 1977 NR

Aziz, M.A. Narayan, S.
Biology objective questions for 'A' level students. 130pp.
K.shs.16.50 Textbook Ctre 1975 KE

Aziza, M.
Regards sur le théâtre arabe contemporain. 162pp.
D0.600 Maison Tunis 1970 TI FRE

Aziza, M.
Le théâtre et l'Islam. 80pp. hd. DA20.00 SNED 1970
AE FRE

Azzegah, A.
Chacun son métier. 124pp. DA4.00 SNED 1966 AE
FRE

Ba, A.H.
Jésus vu par un musulman. 64pp. CFA250 Nouv Ed
Afric 1975 SG FRE

Ba, A.H.
Petit Bodiel. 72pp. CFA550 (F11.00) Nouv Ed Afric
1976 SG FRE

Bâ, D.T.
Histoire du Sénégal. Cours elementaire première année.
See: Cissoko, S.M.

Ba, O.
Glossaire des mots étrangers passés en pular du
Fouta-Toro. CFA375 (C.L.A.D. Etude, 46) CLAD
1971 SG FRE

Ba, O.
Glossaire des mots mandé en poular du Fouta-Toro.
CFA375 (C.L.A.D. Etude, 47) CLAD 1972 SG FRE

Ba, O.
La pénétration française au Cayor, du règne de Damel
Birima Ngoné Latyr à l'intronisation de Madiodio Déguène
Codou. Première et deuxième parties 1854-1861.
500pp. ill. pl. maps. ($45.00) Dakar, Author (distr.
outside Senegal and France by African Imprint Library
Services, Guard Hill Road, Bedford, N.Y. 10506, USA)
1975 SG FRE

Ba, O.
Petit lexique Peul-Français de la faune et de la flore du
Fouta Toro. 41pp. CFA250 (C.L.A.D. Etude , 35 bis)
CLAD 1969 SG FRE

Ba, O.
Petit vocabulaire de la langue peul, parlée au Fouta Toro.
55pp. CFA320 (C.L.A.D. Etude, 35 ter) CLAD 1969
SG FRE

Ba, O.
La terminologie géographique du Pulaar. 111pp. CLAD
1975 SG FRE

Ba, T. O.
Histoire du Sénégal. Cours élémentaire deuxième année.
See: Cissoko, S. M.

Babajamu, M.
Nigeria, my beloved country. 99pp. ill. N1.75
Africani 1975 NR

Babalola, A., ed.
Orin ode fún àseye. [Hunter's song for celebrations]
184pp. N2.00 Macmillan 1973 NR YOR

Babalola, A.
Iwe ede Yoruba: Apa keji. [Yoruba language course]
2, 2 bks. 171pp. ill. N1.20 Longman - Nig 1970 NR
YOR

Babalola, A.
Iwe ede Yoruba: Apa kini. [Yoruba language course]
1, 2 bks. 139pp. ill. N1.20 Longman - Nig 1971 NR
YOR

Babalola, A.
Not vernacular, but languages! 42pp. 25k Univ Lagos
Bkshop; distr. 1975 NR

Babalola, E.O.
The advent and growth of Islam in West Africa. 77pp.
80k Publ Int 1973 NR

Babalola, E.O.
Essential stuff for a study of the birth of modern Egypt and
Sudan. 'O'/'A' level. 73pp. N1.50 Publ Int 1973 NR

Babalola, E.O.
Islam in West Africa, 'O'/'A' level. Rev. enl. ed. 94pp.
N1.50 Publ Int 1973 NR

Babalola, E.O.
Model answers in Islam in West Africa and Egypt, Sudan
and Ethiopia in the 19th century. 'O'/'A' level. 115pp.
N1.50 Publ Int 1973 NR

Babalola, S.A.
Akojopo alo ijapa. [Tortoise tales] pt. 1 172pp. ill.
N1.50 OUP - Nig 1973 NR YOR

Babalola, S.A.
Akojopo alo ijapa. [Tortoise tales] pt. 2 180pp. ill.
N1.70 OUP - Nig 1974 NR YOR

Babalola, S.A.
At'oko eru dide. [The rise from slavery] 148pp. maps.
55k OUP-Nig 1966 NR YOR

Babaluba, E.
Uganda n'ensimbi zaayo. [Uganda and its system of
currency] 2nd ed. 20pp. K.shs.0.60 ($1.00/40p.)
EALB 1958 KE LUG

Babatope, E.
Student power in Nigeria, 1960-70. A documentary source
book of student militancy. vol. 1. 51pp. 50k Univ
Lagos Bkshop; distr. 1974 NR

Babatunde, G.M.
Animal production in the tropics. See: Loosli, J.K.

Baccar, M.
Droit international et coopération économique. La C.N.U.C.E.D. 366pp. D2,000 Maison Tunis 1971 TI FRE

Bachrach, S.
Ethiopian folk-tales. 148pp. Eth. $1.75 OUP-Addis 1967 ET

Bachtarzi, M.
Mémoires (1919-1939) 500pp. DA15.00 SNED 1969 AE FRE

Backer, W.
Manpower development. R5.95 McGraw-Hill SA 1976 SA

Bada, S.O.
Owe Yoruba ati isedale won. [Yoruba proverbs and their origin] 69pp. 40k OUP-Nig 1970 NR YOR

Badawi, A.I.
Agricultural zoology for students in Africa.
See: Venkatraman, T.V.

Badenhorst, J.J.
Survey of the Cape Midlands and Karroo regions, vol. 1: a geographical study. 118pp. ill. maps. Inst Soc & Econ Res - SA 1970 SA

Badriah, S.
Kenya animal world A-Z. 32pp. ill. K.shs.9.00 ($5.25) Foundation 1976 KE

Baeta, C.G.
The relationships of Christians with men of other living faiths. 27pp. C1.00 ($1.00/50p.) (Valedictory lecture) Ghana UP 1971 GH

Bagein, P.
Petite grammaire kirundi. 92pp. hd. BF35 cl. Lavigerie 1951 BD FRE

Bagshawe, A.F. Mngola, E.N. Maina, G.
The use and abuse of drugs and chemical in tropical Africa. Proceedings of the 1973 annual scientific conference of the East African Medical Research Council, Nairobi. 693pp. K.shs.195.00 cl. ($42.00/£19.50 cl.) EALB 1975 KE

Bagunywa, A.
Muyizza Akumma. [A visit to Europe] 2nd ed. 67pp. K.shs.3.60 ($1.75/70 p.) EALB 1969 KE LUG

Bahroun, S.
La planification Tunisienne. 136pp. D1,200 Maison Tunis 1968 TI FRE

Bailey, D.K.
Carbonatites of the Rufunsa valley, Feira District. K4.20 (Dept. of Geological Survey, Bulletins, 5) Geol Survey - Zam 1960 ZA

Bailey, H.G.
Pietermaritzburg and the Natal midlands: pen and ink drawings. 40pp. ill. R2.50 Shuter 1975 SA

Bain, S.
Homemakers training manual. 108pp. pl. 50c Rhod Lit Bur 1970 RH

Baines, T.
The gold regions of south eastern Africa. [Reprint ed. 1877]. 240pp. ill. cl. R9.65 cl. (Rhodesiana Reprint Library, Gold Series, 1) Books of Rhodesia 1968 RH

Baines, T.
Shifts and expedients of camp life, travel and exploration. [Reprint of ed. 1878]. See: Lord, W.B.

Baines, T.
The Victoria falls, Zambesi river, sketched on the spot. 20pp. pl. cl. R$40.50 cl. Books of Rhodesia 1969 RH

Baird, M.
Television Baird. The story of the man who invented television. 160pp. photos. R3.00 cl. Haum 1973 SA

Bajah, H.S.T. Samuel, P.S. Ryan, J.O.
Integrated science for tropical schools. Teacher's book 2, 2 bks. 75pp. N2.00 OUP - Nig 1971 NR

Bajah, S.
A-Level volumetric analysis. 72pp. ill. N1.04 Longman - Nig 1974 NR

Bajah, S. Godman, A.
Chemistry: a New Certificate approach. New ed. ill. pl. N4.08 Longman - Nig 1975 NR

Bajah, S.T. Samuel, P.S. Ryan, J.O.
Integrated science for tropical schools. Pupil's bk. 1. 2nd ed. 2 bks. 90pp. ill. N1.50 OUP - Nig 1974 NR

Bajah, S.T. Samuel, P.S. Ryan, J.O.
Integrated science for tropical schools. 2nd ed. Pupil's book 2, 2bks. 121pp. N1.50 OUP - Nig 1974 NR

Bajah, S.T. Samuel, P.S. Ryan, J.O.
Integrated science for tropical schools. Teacher's book 1, 2bks. 63pp. ill. N2.00 OUP - Nig 1974 NR

Bajah, S.T. Samuel, P.S. Ryan, J.O.
Integrated science for tropical schools: workbk. 1, 2 bks. 78pp. N1.00 OUP - Nig 1970 NR

Bajah, S.T. Samuel, P.S. Ryan, J.O.
Integrated science for tropical schools, workbk. 2, 2 bks. 108pp. ill. N1.25 OUP - Nig 1973 NR

Bakaluba, J.J.
Honeymoon for three. 192pp. ill. K.shs.12.00 ($3.50) EAPH 1975 KE

Bakare, C.G.M.
Progressive colouring book. pupils bk. 2, 2 bks. 61pp. ill. 85k. Heinemann Educ - Ib 1976 NR

Bakare, C.G.M.
Progressive colouring book: teacher's guide. 24pp. 50k. Heinemann Educ - Ib 1976 NR

Bakare, C.G.M.
Progressive handwriting workbook. pupils bk. 1, 4 bks. 96pp. ill. 85k. Heinemann Educ - Ib 1977 NR

Bakare, C.G.M.
Progressive handwriting workbook. pupils bk. 2, 4 bks. 96pp. ill. 75k. Heinemann Educ - Ib 1977 NR

Bakare, O.G.M.
Progressive colouring book. pupils bk. 1, 2 bks. 60pp. ill. 75k. Heinemann Educ - Ib 1976 NR

Baker, C., ed. Balogun, M.J., ed.
Ife essays in administration. 240pp. N4.50 (£3.60) ($8.75) Univ Ife Press 1975 NR

Baker, C.
The evolution of local government in Malawi. 62pp. N1.50 (£1.10) ($2.75) (Univ. of Ife, Inst. of Administration Monograph Series, 3) Univ Ife Press 1975 NR

Baker, C.A., ed.
Training for public administration: report of the first Commonwealth Regional Seminar on Training in East, Central and Southern Africa and Mauritius. K.shs.25.00 Kenya Inst Admin 1972 KE

Baker, C.A.
Johnston's administration, a history of the British Central Africa administration 1891-1897. 134pp. pl. maps. K2.50 pap. (Department of Antiquities, 9) Dept Antiquities - Mal 1971 MW

Baker, H.A. Oliver, E.G.H.
Ericas in Southern Africa. 350pp. pl. ill. maps. hd. R15.00 Purnell 1967 SA

Baker, P.M.
Alan John Percival Taylor: English historian and journalist. A bibliography of his works. 38pp. R2.00 Dept Bibliog, Lib & Typo 1970 SA

Baker, P.R.
Environmental influence on cattle marketing in Karamoja. 57pp. U.shs20.00 (Occas. paps., 5) Dept Geog - Mak 1967 UG

Baker, P.W.E.   Farlam, I.G.
Handbook on the magistrates' courts act and rules. [in Afrikaans and English.]. 3rd rev. ed. 314pp. R7.50 Juta 1976 SA

Baker, R.L.
Littafin Malamai teacher's notes. 89pp. 38k OUP - Nig 1963 NR HAU

Baker, R.L.
Oxford Hausa reader: Aliyu da fadimatu. 1, 3 bks 29pp. 35k OUP - Nig 1957 NR HAU

Baker, R.L.
Oxford Hausa reader: Matafiya. 3, 3 bks. 35k OUP - Nig NR HAU

Baker, R.L.
Oxford Hausa reader: Ranar Kasuwa. 2, 3 bks. 32pp. 35k OUP - Nig 1957 NR HAU

Bakhda, S.
Practice tests for C.P.E. mathematics. 56pp. ill. K.shs.10.00 OUP - Nairobi 1977 KE

Bakhda, S.
Teach your child modern mathematics: bk. 1: sets, numbers and operations. 96pp. ill. K.shs.12.50 OUP - Nairobi 1974 KE

Bakhda, S.
Teach your child modern mathematics. bk. 2: Geometry 96pp. ill. K.shs.12.50 OUP - Nairobi 1976 KE

Baktavatsalou, M. et al.
Annales de l'université d'Abidjan. 191pp. CFA1500 (F30.00) (Série C-Sciences, 2) Univ Abidjan 1966 IV FRE

Bakwata.
Tujifunze dini yetu. [Let us learn our religion] bk. 1 56pp. ill. K.shs.5.25 OUP-Nairobi 1972 KE SWA

Bakwata.
Tujufunze dini yetu. Syllabus. [Let us learn our religion] 16pp. OUP-Nairobi 1972 KE SWA

Bal, W.
La comparaison. Son emploi dans 'Gaspard des Montagnes,' d'Henri Peurrat. 60pp. 40k Press Univ Zaire 1958 ZR FRE

Bal, W.
Introduction à la linguistique. 20pp. 30k Press Univ Zaire 1962 ZR FRE

Baldry, P.J.   Jackson, A.F.
Chemistry in Sierra Leone. (Annual) v. 3. 46pp. Le2.00 Fourah Bay Bkshop; distr. 1976 SL

Balewa, A.T.   Epele, S.
Nigeria speaks. 178pp. pl. pap. & cl. N1.58 pap. N3.00 hd. Longman - Nig 1964 NR

Balewa, A.T.
Shaihu Umar. [Professor Umar] 49pp. 70k Northern Nig 1955 NR HAU

Balihuta, K.
Dictionnaire de la langue Swahili. Swahili-Français et Français Swahili. 700pp. Z1300.00 ($12.00) Lib Les Volcans 1975 ZR FRE

Balisidya, N.
Shida. [Problems.] 96pp. K.shs.10.00 ($4.00) Foundation 1975 KE SWA

Balkema, G.H.
Chimerism and diplontic selection: a research project into Arabidopsis and the sunflower to obtain information about sectorial chimerism within the plants, its occurences, distribution and loss. 181pp. pl. fl. 36.00 Balkema 1971 SA

Balkema Publishers.
The Cape sketchbooks of Sir Charles D'Oyly, 1832-1833. 252pp. hd. fl. 67.50 Balkema 1968 SA

Balkema Publishers.
Planning open pit mines. 404pp. ill. hd. fl. 38.25 Balkema 1971 SA

Balkema Publishers.
Proteins and food supply in the Republic of South Africa. 534pp. hd. fl. 90.00 Balkema 1971 SA

Balkema Publishers.
Soil mechanics and foundation engineering. 437pp. ill. hd. fl. 90.00 Balkema 1968 SA

Balkema Publishers.
Tabulae geographicae quibus Colonia Bonae Spei antiqua depingitur. [Eighteenth century cartography of the Cape of Good Hope] 64pp. maps. hd. fl. 135.00 Balkema 1952 SA

Balkind, M., comp.
Index to My Command in South Africa, 1874-1878 by A.T. Cuminghame. gratis Johannesburg Public Lib 1964 SA

Ball, J.
Health science for primary schools. Pupils' bk. 84pp. ill. K.shs.13.50 OUP - Nairobi 1977 KE

Ball, P.H.
A guide to successful selling. 77k Pilgrim 1972 NR

Ball, R.W.
The earlier stone age in Southern Africa. 33pp. 80c. Univ Cape Town Lib 1969 SA

Ballantyne, M.   Shepherd, R.H.W.
Forerunners of modern Malawi. 301pp. R3.50 Lovedale 1968 SA

Balldin, B., et al.
Child health. A manual for medical assistants and other rural health workers. 416pp. ill. K.shs.20.00 (Rural Health Series, 1) African Med Res Found 1975 KE

Ballinger, M.
From union to apartheid. R6.30 Juta SA

Ballinger, R.B.
South Africa and the United Nations: myth and reality. 32pp. 30c. SA Inst Int Affairs 1963 SA

Balmer, P.
Actes et épitres. 64pp. CFA150 (Cahier biblique, enseignement secondaire, 4) CLE 1968 CM FRE

Balogun, F.
Olikperebu et autres contes. N1.00 Ethiope 1975 NR FRE

Balogun, I.A.B.
A brief history of the life of the prophet Muhammad and the growth of Islam. See: El Dessuky, M.A.

Balogun, I.A.B.
The life and works of Uthman Dan Fodio. 72pp. N2.50 Islamic 1975 NR

Balogun, M.J., ed.
Ife essays in administration. See: Baker, C., ed.

Balogun, O.
The tragic years: Nigeria in crisis, 1966-1970. 125pp. photos. 75k Ethiope 1973 NR

Balogun, S.I.
Tobias and the Angel. 35pp. 40k Educ Res Inst 1971 NR

Bamalli, N.
Bala Da Babiya. [Bala and Babiya] 82pp. ill. 95k Northern Nig 1950 NR HAU

Bamfo, G.
Mr Mee escapes. See: Gyane, D.

Bamfo, G.
Mr Mee runs a race. See: Gyane, D.

Bamford, B.R.
The law of partnerships and voluntary associations in South Africa. 2nd ed. R15.00 Juta 1971 SA

Bamford, B.R.
The law of shipping and carriage in South Africa. Cumulative supplement. R5.00 (Main volume and supplement R30.00) Juta 1977 SA

Bamford, B.R.
Newspaper law of South Africa. See: Blackwell, L.

Bamford, B.R.
South African motor law. See: Cooper, W.E.

Bamgbose, A., ed.
The Yoruba verb phrase. 196pp. N3.50 Ibadan UP 1972 NG

Bamgbose, A., ed.
The Yoruba verb phrase (Papers of the seminar on the Yoruba verb phrase held at Ibadan in April, 1971) 196pp. N2.50 Inst Afr Stud-Ibadan 1972 NR

Bamgbose, A.
Linguistics in a developing country. 20pp. N1.00 (Inaugural lecture) Ibadan UP 1973 NG

Bamgbose, A.
The novels of D.O. Fagunwa. 132pp. N2.00 Ethiope 1974 NR

Bamgbose, A.
A short Yoruba grammar. New ed. 63pp. ill. N1.00 Heinemann Educ - Nig 1974 NR

Bamgbose, A.
Yoruba orthography: a linguistic appraisal with suggestions for reform. 33pp. N1.00 Ibadan UP 1969 NR

Bamkole, T.O. Ogunkoya, L.
Introductory organic chemistry. 242pp. ill. pl. N4.50 Daystar 1977 NR

Bamuyeja, I. Dibwe, M.B.
Deux griots de Kamina. 31pp. 50k (CFA250) Centre Africain Litt 1974 ZR

Banach, J.A.
The Cape midlands: its demography (1911-1960) and regional income (1954/55-1959/60) R2.50 (Inst. of Social and Economic Research occas. paps., 14) Inst Soc & Econ Res - SA 1969 SA

Banda, A.A.
Huduma katika utumishi. [Personnel management.] 93pp. K.shs.9.00 ($1.80) (Comb Books in Kiswahili, 2) Comb Books 1975 KE SWA

Bandey, D.W.
Baptism reconsidered. 102pp. R2.10 Methodist 1976 SA

Banfo, G.
Vers la lumière. See: Gyane, D.

Banfo, G.
Vers le but. See: Gyane, D.

Banham, M., ed.
Nigerian student verse, 1959. 33pp. N1.00 Ibadan UP 1960 NR

Bankole, A.
Three part-songs for female choir. 20pp. music. N2.00 (£1.25/$3.00) (Ife Music Editions, 3) Univ Ife Press 1974 NR

Bankole, A.
Three songs for baritone and piano. 15pp. music. N2.00 ($4.00/£1.75) (Ife Music Editions, 6) Univ Ife Press 1976 NR

Banks, A.W.
Mume mmoja, mke mmoja: kwa nini kuwe na desturi ya mwanamume kuoa mke mmoja tu? [Why monogamy?] 2nd ed. 30pp. K.shs.0.75 ($1.25/50p.) EALB 1964 KE SWA

Banks, D.
How to work for God. 16pp. 3k SIM 1968 NR

Bannister, A.
Okavango: sea of land, land of water. [Also available in German.]. See: Johnson, P.

Banzi, A.
Titi la mkwe. [Inlaw's breast.] 88pp. T.shs.8.50 Tanz Publ House 1972 TZ SWA

Baptie, R.
Ackson. 58pp. ill. 75n. (Eagle Readers) Neczam 1974 ZA

Baptie, R.
The drummer of the west and other stories. 110pp. 90n. Neczam 1971 ZA

Baptie, R.
Sakatoni and other stories. 94pp. 90n. Neczam 1971 ZA

Baptie, R.
Vishimo mu Luvale. [Luvale stories] 46pp. 40n. Neczam 1972 ZA LUV

Bar-David, Y. Pairault, C. et al.
Annales de l'université d'Abidjan. 370pp. CFA1000 (F20.00) (Série D-Lettres, 6) Univ Abidjan 1973 IV FRE

Baranowski, A.
Sugar cane in Ghana. 95pp. C3.50 (£1.70/$3.50) Ghana UP 1970 GH

Barat, C.
Pluviologie et aquidimétrie dans la zone intertropicale. 80pp. pl. CFA800 (Mémoires de l'IFAN, 49) IFAN 1957 SG FRE

Barber, H.H.
What is a protestant, an evangelical, a pentecostal? 16pp. K.shs.1.00 Evangel 1967 KE

Barber, J.
Imperial frontier. 221pp. photos. maps. K.shs.45.00 cl. K.shs25.00 pap. ($10.00 cl.) ($5.80 pap.) EAPH 1968 KE

Barbier, A.
Economie domestique. 7th ed. 150pp. ill. 40k St. Paul 1971 ZR FRE

Barbour, J., ed. Simmonds, D., ed.
Adire cloth in Nigeria: the preparation, dyeing of indigo patterned cloths among the Yoruba. 104pp. photos. ill. N1.50 Inst Afr Stud-Ibadan 1971 NR

Barbour, K.M., ed.
Planning for Nigeria: a geographical approach. 228pp. ill. N5.00 Ibadan UP 1972 NR

Barbour, K.M.
Population in Africa. An inaugural lecture. 2nd ed. 40pp. ill. N1.00 Ibadan UP 1966 NR

Barclay, W.
Ahadi ya roho. [The promise of the spirit.] 96pp. T.shs.5.00 Central Tanganyika 1967 TZ SWA

Bardon, P.
Collection des masques d'or baoulé de l'IFAN. 22pp. pl. CFA300 pap. (Catalogues et Documents, 4) IFAN 1949 SG FRE

Barima-Achampong, R.O.
Maths and quantitative aptitude tests. 160pp. C6.00 Afram 1976 GH

Barkan, J.D.
An African dilemma. University students development and politics in Ghana, Tanzania and Uganda. 280pp. cl. & pap. K.shs.70.00 cl. K.shs.40.00 pap. OUP - Nairobi 1975 KE

Barker, A.
Physic and protocol among the Zulus. 40c (ISMA paps., 32) Inst Study of Man 1972 SA

Barker, E.E.
A short history of Nyanza. 5th ed. 28pp. ill. K.shs.5.60 ($1.90/£1.00) EALB 1975 KE

Barker, H.A.F.
Economics of the wholesale clothing industry of South Africa, 1907-1957. R10.00 Juta SA

Barker, J.P.
Industrial development in a border area: facts and figures from East London. R1.85 (Inst. of Social and Economic Research occas. paps., 7) Inst Soc & Econ Res - SA 1966 SA

Barker, P.
Operation cold chop. 210pp. ill. map. 95pes. ($2.50) Ghana Publ Corp 1969 GH

Barker, R. De La Bere.
Visa vya mzee Rufiji: kapteni aliyeshambuliwa na simba. [The adventures of Rufiji] 2nd ed. bk. 5 K.shs.0.75 ($1.25/50p.) EALB 1968 KE SWA

Author Index

Barker, R. De La Bere.
Visa vya mzee Rufiji: safari yetu ya kwenda Rufiji. [The adventures of Rufiji] 2nd ed. bk. 4 K.shs.0.75 ($1.25/50p.) EALB 1968 KE SWA

Barker, R. De La Bere.
Visa vya mzee Rufiji: uchawi na mazingaombue. [The adventures of Rufiji] 2nd ed. bk. 3 ($1.00/40 p.) EALB 1968 KE SWA

Barkhuizen, B.P.
The Cycad garden of UNISA. [Bilingual in English and Afrikaans]. 77pp. col. ill. hd. R8.00 (R9.00) Univ South Africa 1975 SA

Barkhuysen, F.A.
Liquid ammonia mercerisation of cotton, part I: construction of a pilot plant chainless merceriser. See: Hanekom, E.C.

Barkhuysen, F.A.
Liquid ammonia mercerisation of cotton, part II: the influence of anhydrous liquid ammonia on the dimensional stability of cotton fabrics. 19pp. R2.50 (SAWTRI Technical Reports, 286) SAWTRI 1976 SA

Barkhuysen, F.A.
Liquid ammonia mercerisation of cotton, part III: the influence of anhydrous liquid ammonia on the physical properties of cotton fabrics. 28pp. R2.50 (SAWTRI Technical Reports, 289) SAWTRI 1976 SA

Barkhuysen, F.A.
Liquid ammonia mercerisation of cotton, part IV: liquid ammonia mercerisation as a pretreatment for subsequent durable press treatments. 11pp. R2.50 (SAWTRI Technical Reports, 293) SAWTRI 1976 SA

Barkhuysen, F.A.
Liquid ammonia mercerisation of cotton, part V: the influence of anhydrous liquid ammonia on certain chemical properties of cotton. 13pp. R2.50 (SAWTRI Technical Reports, 311) SAWTRI 1976 SA

Barkhuysen, F.A.
Liquid ammonia mercerisation of cotton, part VI: liquid ammonia treatment of 50/50 cotton/polyester fabrics. 9pp. R2.50 (SAWTRI Technical Reports, 329) SAWTRI 1976 SA

Barkhuysen, F.A.
Liquid ammonia mercerisation of cotton, part VII: liquid ammonia treatment of 67/33 cotton/wool blended fabrics. 11pp. R2.50 (SAWTRI Technical Reports, 336) SAWTRI 1977 SA

Barkhuysen, F.A.
The SAWTRI continuous shrink-resist treatment of wool tops. See: Hanekom, E.C.

Barkhuysen, F.A.
Stability of the chlorinating solution used in the SAWTRI chlorination process. See: Hanekom, E.C.

Barlow, T.B.
Digest of the law of murder and culpable homicide. R1.25 Juta 1951 SA

Barlow, T.B.
The life and times of President Brand. 277pp. ill. maps. R10.50 Juta 1972 SA

Barlow, T.B.
Offences under the Insolvency Act. R7.50 Juta 1966 SA

Barnard, A.
The letters of Lady Anne Barnard to Henry Dundas from the Cape and elswhere, 1793-1803: together with her journal of a tour into the interior and certain other letters. 328pp. pl. hd. fl. 45.00 (South African biographical and historical studies, 17) Balkema 1973 SA

Barnard, C.
South Africa - a sharp dissection. R3.00 Tafelberg 1976 SA

Barnard, J.L.
Corrosion of sewers. 16pp. (CSIR research reports, 250) CSIR 1967 SA

Barnard, P. J., et al.
Junior geography for standard 6. 219pp. ill. pl. maps. R2.25 Nasou 1974 SA

Barnard, T.T.
Gladiolus: a revision of the South African species. See: Lewis, G.J.

Barnes, C.
Spontaneous settlement problems in Kenya. See: Mbithi, P.

Barnes, J.A.
Marriage in a changing society: a study in structural change among the Fort Jameson Ngoni. 136pp. K1.50 (63p.) (Rhodes-Livingstone paps., 20) Inst Soc Res - Zam 1951 ZA

Barnes, J.A.
Politics in a changing society. 220pp. ill. photos .maps. hd. K4.20 (£2.10/$8.50) Inst Afr Stud - Lusaka 1954 ZA

Barnes, K.
Economics of Volta River project. 65pp. cl. C4.00 Univ Ghana Bkshop 1966 GH

Barnett, A.M.
Uniform rules of court. [Text in Afrikaans and English.]. See: Nathan, C.J.M.

Barnett, C.
Hitting the lip. Surfing in South Africa. 186pp. ill. photos. col. photos. maps. cl. & pap. R3.75 pap. R7.50 cl. Macmillan - SA 1974 SA

Baroin, C.
Les marques de bétail chez les Azza et Daza du Niger. 276pp. maps photos. CFA1500 (F30.00) (Etudes Nigeriennes, 29) Inst Rech Sci Hum 1972 NG FRE

Barongo, E.B.
Mkiki mkiki wa siasa Tangayika. [The political struggle for independence in Tanganyika] 294pp. K.shs.11.00 ($3.00/£1.20) EALB 1966 KE SWA

Barr, L.I.
A course in Lugbara. 146pp. K.shs.10.00 ($2.75/£1.10) EALB 1965 KE

Barr, M.W.C.
Limestone of the Lusaka South Forest Reserve and adjacent areas. 40n (Dept. of Geological Survey. Economic Reports, 25) Geol Survey - Zam 1970 ZA

Barra, G.
1,000 Kikuyu proverbs: with translations and English equivalents. 2nd ed. 123pp. K.shs.10.00 ($2.70/70p.) EALB 1975 KE

Barratt, I.
A guide to social pensions. Rev. ed. 34pp. 75c ($1.61) SA Inst of Race Relations 1976 SA

Barratt, J., ed. Louw, M., ed.
International aspects of overpopulation: proceedings of a conference held at Jan Smuts House, Johannesburg in 1970. 334pp. hd. R10.90 (£4.50) SA Inst Int Affairs 1972 SA

Barratt, J. et al., eds.
Accelerated development in Southern Africa: proceedings of a conference held at Jan Smuts House, Johannesburg in 1972. SA Inst Int Affairs 1973 SA

Barratt, J.
Southern Africa: intra-regional and international relations. 24pp. 30c. SA Inst Int Affairs 1973 SA

Barrett, D.
African initiatives in religion. 283pp. photos. K.shs27.50 ($10.40) EAPH 1971 KE

Barrett, D.
Graines d'evangile. See: Lamont, V.

Barrett, D.B. et al., eds.
Kenya churches handbook. The development of Kenyan Christianity, 1498-1972. [includes directory of churches and Christian organisations, plus bibliography]. 350pp. col. maps. cl. & pap. K.shs.30.00 pap. K.shs.47.00 cl. ($9.95 cl.) Evangel 1974 KE

Barrett, D.B.
Schism and renewal in East Africa. 386pp. pl. map. cl. K.shs64.25 cl. OUP-Nairobi 1968 KE

Barrett, L.
The state of black desire. New ed. 57pp. ill. N1.25 Ethiope 1974 NR

Barrow, B.
Song of a dry river. ill. R7.95 Purnell 1975 SA

Barrow, B.
South African people. [Also available in Afrikaans.]. ill. photos. maps. cl. R6.75 (The Macdonald Heritage Library series) Purnell 1977 SA

Barry, B.
Bocar Biro. 96pp. CFA250 (F5.00) Nouv Ed Afric 1976 SG FRE

Barry, T.H. et al.
Contributions to the cranial morphology of Agama hispida Linn. 82pp. ill. R1.10 (A v. 29, no 2-3) Univ Stellenbosch, Lib 1953 SA

Bart-Williams, P.J.
The story of St. George's Cathedral. 90pp. 40c. Fourah Bay Bkshp 1973 SL

Bartel, P.R.
Long-term electrocerebral sequelae of kwashiorkor. 151pp. (CSIR Special Report, PERS 244) CSIR 1976 SA

Barthas, M.
France Afrique. Douze contes africains. A French reader for year 2 of secondary schools in West Africa. See: Coomber, A.A.

Bartholomé, P.
The Gore mountain garnet deposit, New York. Structure and petrography. 32pp. ill. pl. 35k Press Univ Zaire 1958 ZR

Bartholomé, P.
Les minérais cuprocobaltifères de Kamoto (Katanga-Ouest). vol. 1. Pétrographie. 40pp. pl. 85k Press Univ Zaire 1962 ZR FRE

Bartholomé, P.
Les minérais cuprocobaltifères de Kamoto (Katanga-Ouest). vol. 2. Paragenèse. 24pp. ill. 25k Press Univ Zaire 1962 ZR FRE

Bartholomé, P.
On the paragenesis of copper ores. 32pp. ill. 30k Press Univ Zaire 1958 ZR

Barton, F.
The press in Africa. 80pp. photos. K.shs5.00 ($2.20) EAPH 1966 KE

Barton, I.M.
Africa in the Roman Empire. 84pp. pl. maps. C2.50 (£1.25/$2.50) Ghana UP 1972 GH

Bartstra, G.J. Casparie, W.A.
Modern quaternary research in Southeast Asia. vol. 2. 81pp. col. pl. photos. maps. cl. ($9.00/£5.50) Balkema 1976 SA

Basri, B.
L'agent d'autorité. Dir30.00 (Coll. Fac. des Sciences juridiques, économiques et sociales, 25) Ed La Porte 1975 MR FRE

Bass, A.J.
Analysis and description of variation in the proportional dimensions of scyliorhinid, carcharhinid and sphyrnid sharks. 28pp. R1.20 (Investigational Reports, 32) Oceanographic Res Inst 1973 SA

Bass, A.J. Kistnasamy, N. D'Aubrey, J.D.
Sharks of the east coast of southern Africa, 1: the genus "Carcharhinus" (Carcharhinidae) 168pp. R2.60 (Investigational Reports, 33) Oceanographic Res Inst 1973 SA

Bass, A.J. Kistnasamy, N. D'Aubrey, J.D.
Sharks of the east coast of southern Africa, 2: the families Scyliorhinidae and Pseudotriakidae. 63pp. R1.20 (Investigational Reports, 37) Oceanographic Res Inst 1975 SA

Bass, A.J. Kistnasamy, N. D'Aubrey, J.D.
Sharks of the east coast of southern Africa, 3: the families Carcharhinidae (excluding Carcharhinus and Mustelus) and Sphyrnidae. 100pp. R2.40 (Investigational Reports, 38) Oceanographic Res Inst 1975 SA

Bass, A.J. Kistnasamy, N. D'Aubrey, J.D.
Sharks of the east coast of southern Africa, 4: the families Odontaspididae, Scapanorhychidae, Isuridae, Cetorhinidae, Alopiidae, Orectolobidae, and Rhiniodontidae. 102pp. R3.40 (Investigational Reports, 39) Oceanographic Res Inst 1975 SA

Basson, I.L.
Hail in the Pretoria-Witwatersrand area 1962-1969. See: Carte, A.E.

Basson, P.
Water-soluble coatings and their application by electrodeposition, 1960-1965: a selective bibliography. 66pp. R3.40 Dept Bibliog, Lib & Typo 1965 SA

Bassori, T.
Les bannis du village. 132pp. CFA500 (F10.00) Nouv Ed Afric 1974 SG FRE

Basu, A.C.
Tobacco growers in Northern Oyo division and adoption of new farming ideas and practices. See: Akiwowo, A.

Bateleur Press.
Bateleur poets, 75. 111pp. R3.75 ($5.25/£2.75) Bateleur 1975 SA

Bateleur Press.
Bateleur poets, 77. 94pp. R3.75 ($5.25/£2.75) Bateleur 1975 SA

Batten, A. Bokelmann, H.
Wild flowers of the Eastern Cape province. pl. ill. R10.00 Bulpin 1966 SA

Baturi, S. Maxwell, E.
Looking at the Old Testament. pt. 4 270pp. K.shs.20.00 ($2.50 pap.) Evangel 1976 KE

Baudet, J. et al.
Annales de l'université d'Abidjan. 247pp. CFA1500 (F30.00) (Série C-Sciences, 3) Univ Abidjan 1967 IV FRE

Baudet, J.B.
Annales de l'université d'Abidjan. See: Proutière A.

Bauer, P.T.
Nigerian development experience: aspects and implications. 34pp. 75k (60p./$1.40) (Univ. of Ife, Inst. of Administration Monograph Series, 1) Univ Ife Press 1974 NR

Bauman, R.A.
The crimen maiestatis in the Roman Republic and Augustan Principate. 330pp. cl. R16.00 Witwatersrand UP 1970 SA

Baumbach, E.J.M. Marivate, C.T.D.
Xironga folk-tales. Swihitari swa Xironga. [Bi-lingual ed. English-Xironga]. 199pp. ill. cl. R7.90 (R8.90) (Documenta 12) Univ South Africa SA

Bawuuba, E.K.
Elizabeth Fry. ill. K.shs.1.00 ($1.25/50p.) EALB 1962 KE LUG

Bax, K.C.
South African attorneys handbook. See: Randell, G.H.

Baxter, T.W., ed. Burke, E.E., ed.
Guide to the historical manuscripts in the National Archives. 527pp. cl. R$8.00 Nat Archives - Rhod 1970 RH

Baxter, T.W., ed.
A guide to the public archives of Rhodesia, 1890-1923. 2nd ed. 1 262pp. cl. R$4.20 Nat Archives - Rhod 1969 RH

Bennett, A.J.
  A survey of river water quality in Northern Nigeria. 17pp. map. 20k (Samaru misc. pap., 17) Inst Agric Res-Zaria 1967 NR

Bennett, F.J., ed. Nsanzumuhite, H., ed. Nhonoli, A.M., ed.
  Degenerative disorders in the African environment. 500pp. K.shs.221.40 cl. K.shs.162.00 pap. (£41.00/£18.50 cl.) EALB 1976 KE

Bennett, F.J., ed. Nsanzumuhire, H., ed. Nhonoli, A.M., ed.
  Degenerative disorders in the African environment. Epidemiology and consequences. 390pp. ill. pl. cl. K.shs.221.40 ($41.00/£18.50) EALB 1976 KE

Bennett, F.J., ed.
  Medicine and social sciences in East and West Africa. 92pp. U.shs.15.00 ($3.00) (M.I.S.R. Nkanga ed. 7) Mak Inst Soc Res 1973 UG

Bennett, J.D.
  The geology and mineral resources of Malawi. See: Carter, G.S.

Bennett, R.
  Deep end of the night. 100pp. 75k Di Nigro 1974 NR

Bennett, T. Phillips, S.
  A bibliography of African law with special reference to Rhodesia. 279pp. R$5.00 (Univ. Rhodesia, Library Bibliographical series, 4) Univ Rhodesia 1975 RH

Benoist, J.
  Pour une connaissance de la Réunion: travaux du Seminaire de recherches en sciences sociales. 108pp. (Documents et recherches, 2) FRDOI 1975 RE FRE

Bensalem, A.
  La nationalité des navires et des aéronefs. Dir30.00 (Coll. Fac. des Sciences juridiques, économiques et sociales, 24) Ed La Porte 1975 MR FRE

Benson, C.W. Irwin, M.P.S.
  A contribution to the ornithology of Zambia. 139pp. pl. maps. R2.50 (Zambia Museum paps. 1) Nat Mus Board - Zam 1967 ZA

Benson, T.G.
  Kikuyu-English dictionary. 275pp. cl. K.shs.42.00 EALB 1962 KE

Bent, J.T.
  The ruined cities of Mashonaland. [Reprint of ed. 1896]. 459pp. ill. cl. R$7.20 cl. (Rhodesiana Reprint Library, Gold Series, 5) Books of Rhodesia 1969 RH

Bentel, L.
  The works of Alan Paton. 29pp. R1.60 Dept Bibliog, Lib & Typo 1969 SA

Bepswa, K.S.
  Ndakamuda dakara afa. [I loved her unto death.] 88pp. 35c Mambo 1960 RH SHO

Bequele, A. Chole, E.
  A profile of the Ethiopian economy. 138pp. map. K.shs.23.50 OUP-Nairobi 1969 KE

Berbain, S.
  Le comptoir français du Juda (Ouidah) au XVIII siècle. [Reprint of ed. Paris, 1942]. 127pp. pl. (D.fl.45.00) (Mémoires de l'IFAN, 3) IFAN 1942 SG FRE

Bercher, L.
  Le statut personnel en droit musulman hanefite. See: Bousquet, G.H.

Bere, R.M.
  The wild mammals of Uganda. 148pp. ill. K.shs.10.50 ($3.00/£1.20) EALB 1962 KE

Bereng, C.T.
  Lithothokise tsa Moshoeshoe. [Praises to Moshoeshoe 1] 76pp. 30c. Morija 1967 LO SOS

Berepiki, C.I.
  Kála. [Kálábari reader, 1] 63pp. ill. 30k (Inst. of African Stud., Univ. of Ibadan, Rivers readers project, 24) Inst Afr Stud-Ibadan 1971 NR KAB

Berger, A.
  Tunisie. Poèmes en couleurs. See: Deflandre, J.

Berger, S.
  Mechanism of arbovirus infections in mosquitoes and their experimental transmission to vertebrate hosts: a bibliography. 32pp. R1.20 Dept Bibliog, Lib & Typo 1970 SA

Berglund, A.I.
  Zulu thought patterns and symbolism. 400pp. ill. R12.00 Philip 1975 SA

Bergsma, H.R.
  Tales Tiv tell. 104pp. ill. 75k OUP - Nig 1969 NR

Berhanu Debele.
  Detailed soil survey and irrigability land classification of Gode agricultural research station. See: Ochtman, L.H.J.

Beriel, M.M.
  Complément à la bibliographie du Tchad. (Sciences humaines) 103pp. ex.only (Etudes et Documents Tchadiens, Série A, 6) Inst Nat Tchad 1975 CD FRE

Berland, L.
  Les Arachnides de l'Afrique noire française. 130pp. ill. CFA600 (Initiations et Etudes Africaines, 12) IFAN 1955 SG FRE

Berman, E.
  The story of South African painting. 272pp. ill. col. ill. cl. R21.00 ($38.00) Balkema 1974 SA

Berman, S., comp.
  Subject headings employed at the Makerere Institute of Social Research library: a select list. 102pp. U.shs.10.00 Mak Univ Lib 1972 UG

Berning, J.M., comp.
  Index to obituary notices of Methodist ministers, 1815-1920. gratis Johannesburg Public Lib 1969 SA

Berning, J.M.
  Manuscripts in libraries: A South African outline of procedures and problems. R1.00 (Dept. of Librarianship, occas. paps., 3) Rhodes Univ Lib 1971 SA

Bernus, E. Bernus, S.
  Du sel et des dattes, introduction à l'étude de la communauté d'In Gall et de Tegidda-n-tesemt. 130pp. maps photos. CFA1250 (F25.00) (Etudes Nigeriennes, 31) Inst Rech Sci Hum 1972 NG FRE

Bernus, E.
  Du sel et des dattes, introduction à l'étude de la communauté d'In Gall et de Tegidda-n-tesemt. See: Bernus, E.

Bernus, S.
  Henri Barth chez les Touaregs de l'Air. Extraits du journal de Barth dans l'Air, juillet-décembre 1850. 195pp. maps photos. CFA1500 (F30.00) (Etudes Nigeriennes, 28) Inst Rech Sci Hum 1972 NG FRE

Berque, J.
  Maghreb, histoire et sociétés. 227pp. DA18.00 pap. SNED 1975 AE FRE

Berrenguer, A.
  Un curé d'Algérie en Amerique Latine. 261pp. DA8.50 SNED 1966 AE FRE

Berron, H. et al.
  Annales de l'université d'Abidjan. 256pp. CFA850 (F17.00) (Série G-Géographie, 3) Univ Abidjan 1971 IV FRE

Berry, L.
  Dodoma population density. 6pp. maps. T.shs.15.00 (Research reports, 42) Bur Re Assess 1971 TZ

Berry, L., ed.
  Studies in soil erosion and sedimentation in Tanzania. See: Rapp, A., ed.

Berry, L. et al.
  Human adjustment to agricultural drought in Tanzania: pilot investigations. 64pp. map. T.shs.15.00 (Research paper, 13) Bur Res Assess - Tanz 1972 TZ

Berry, L. et al.
Water development-Tanzania: a critical view of research.
101pp. ill. T.shs.10.00 (Research paper, 12) Bur
Res Asses - Tanz 1970 TZ

Berry, L. McKay, J.
Kharumwa water supply: final report. 15pp. maps.
T.shs.5.00 (Research report, 24(b)) Bur Res Assess -
Tanz 1971 TZ

Berry, L.
The university in Africa and Tanzania. 23pp. ill.
T.shs.1.00 (Inaugural lecture, 11) Univ Dar es Salaam
1970 TZ

Berry, P.F.
The biology of "Nephrops andamanicus Wood-Mason"
(Decapoda, Reptantia) 55pp. R1.20 Oceanographic
Res Inst 1969 SA

Berry, P.F.
The biology of the spiny lobster "Palinurus delagoae"
Barnard, off the coast of Natal, South Africa. 27pp.
R1.20 (Investigational Reports, 31) Oceanographic Res
Inst 1973 SA

Berry, P.F.
The biology of the spiny lobster "Panulirus homarus"
(Linnaeus) off the east coast of southern Africa. 75pp.
R2.40 Oceanographic Res Inst 1971 SA

Berry, P.F. Heydorn, A.E.F.
A comparison of the spermatophoric masses and
mechanisms of fertilization in southern African spiny
lobsters (Palinuridae) 18pp. R1.10 Oceanographic
Res Inst 1970 SA

Berry, P.F.
Mating behaviour, oviposition and fertilization in the spiny
lobster "Panulirus homarus" (Linnaeus) 16pp. R1.10
Oceanographic Res Inst 1970 SA

Berry, P.F.
Palinurid and scyllarid lobster larvae of the Natal coast,
South Africa. 44pp. R1.20 (Investigational Reports,
34) Oceanographic Res Inst 1974 SA

Berry, P.F.
The spiny lobsters (Palinuridae) of the east coast of
southern Africa: distribution and ecological notes. 23pp.
R1.20 Oceanographic Res Inst 1971 SA

Berry, P.M.
A place for sociology in teacher education. 16pp.
C1.00 ($1.00/50p.) (Inaugural lecture) Ghana UP
1972 GH

Berthoud, J.A. Gardner, C.O.
The sole function. 172pp. cl. R3.50 Univ of Natal
1969 SA

Bertrand, H. et al.
Annales de l'université d'Abidjan. 325pp. CFA1400
(F28.00) (Série E-Ecologie, 2-1) Univ Abidjan 1969 IV
FRE

Besairie, H.
Le bassin charbonnier du sud-ouest de Madagascar.
24pp. pl. FMG210 (F4.20) (Série Documentation,
147) Service Geol - Mad 1960 MG FRE

Besairie, H. Hottin, G.
Bibliographie géologique de Madagascar, 1967-1969.
20pp. FMG145 (F2.90) (Série Documentation, 181)
Service Geol - Mad 1970 MG FRE

Besairie, H.
Contribution à l'étude des bauxites du sud-est de Madag.
11pp. pl. FMG120 (F2.40) (Série Documentation,
159) Service Geol - Mad 1963 MG FRE

Besairie, H.
Description géologique du massif ancien de Madagascar:
a région côtiere orientale entre le Mangoro et
Vangaindrano. 2, 5v. 67pp. FMG575 (F11.50)
(Série Documentation, 177 b) Service Geol - Mad 1969
MG FRE

Besairie, H.
Description géologique du massif ancien de Madagascar:
La région central. Le systeme du Vohibory. Série
schistoquartzo-calcaire, groupe d'Amborompotsy. 4, 5v.
90pp. FMG660 (F13.20) (Série Documentation,
177d) Service Geol - Mad 1970 MG FRE

Besairie, H.
Description géologique du massif ancien de Madagascar:
La région centrale. Le systeme du graphite, group
d'Ambatolampy. 3, 5v. 73pp. FMG630 (F12.60)
(Série Documentation, 177c) Service Geol - Mad 1969
MG FRE

Besairie, H.
Description géologique du massif ancien de Madagascar:
Le sud. 5, 5v. 156pp. pl. FMG1220 (F24.40)
(Série Documentation, 177e) Service Geol - Mad 1970
MG FRE

Besairie, H.
Etude des calcaires et argiles de la région centrale
utilisables pour cimenterie. 21pp. pl. FMG160
(F3.20) (Série Documentation, 165) Service Geol - Mad
1964 MG FRE

Besairie, H.
Géologie du bassin de Majunga à Madagascar. 243pp.
pl. FMG3290 (F65.80) (Série Documentation, 172)
Service Geol - Mad 1966 MG FRE

Besairie, H.
Géologie économique de la préfecture d'Antsirabe.
138pp. pl. photos. maps. FMG2330 (F46.60)
(Série Documentation, 156) Service Geol - Mad 1962
MG FRE

Besairie, H.
Géologie économique de la sous-préfecture
d'Ambatofinan-drahana. 49pp. pl. photos. FMG1135
(F22.70) (Série Documentation, 170) Service Geol -
Mad 1965 MG FRE

Besairie, H.
Les gîtes minéraux de Madagascar. 2 v. 437pp. pl. cl.
FMG3000 cl. (F60.00 cl.) (Annales Géologiques de
Madagascar, 34) Service Geol - Mad 1964 MG FRE

Besairie, H.
Itinéraires géologiques le long des principales routes de
Madagascar. 164pp. pl. FMG1335 (F26.70)
(Série Documentation, 174) Service Geol - Mad 1968
MG FRE

Besairie, H.
Note sommaire sur les gisements de nickel d'oxydation
súperficielle. Types généraux dans le monde et à
Madagascar. 41pp. FMG630 (F12.60) (Série
Documentation, 153) Service Geol - Mad 1961 MG FRE

Besairie, H.
Notice explicative de la carte géologique au 1/2,000,000
(abrégé de géolgie malgache) 104pp. map. FMG1930
(F38.60) (Série Documentation, 184) Service Geol -
Mad 1971 MG FRE

Besairie, H.
Précis de géologie malgache. 185pp. pl. photos.
FMG2400 (F48.00) (Série Documentation, 180)
Service Geol - Mad 1970 MG FRE

Besairie, H.
Prospection aéromagnétique à Madagascar. 16pp. pl.
FMG341 (F6.80) (Série Documentation, 164) Service
Geol - Mad 1964 MG FRE

Besairie, H.
La recherche minière à Madagascar. 17pp. FMG125
(F2.50) (Série Documentation, 169) Service Geol - Mad
1965 MG FRE

Besairie, H.
Recherches de matières premières pour verrerie à
Madagascar. 29pp. pl. FMG203 (F4.06) (Série
Documentation, 157) Service Geol - Mad 1963 MG FRE

Besairie, H.
Les ressources minérales de Madagascar. 335pp. pl. FMG2345 (F46.90) (Série Documentation, 151) Service Geol - Mad 1960 MG FRE

Besairie, H.
Les ressources minérales de Madagascar. 116pp. ill. cl. FMG900 cl. (F18.00 cl.) (Annales Géologiques de Madagascar, 30) Service Geol - Mad 1961 MG FRE

Beshir, M.O.
Education in Africa. 60pp. ($1.50) Khartoum UP 1974 SJ

Beshir, M.O.
Israel and Africa. 48pp. 20pt. ($1.00) Khartoum UP 1974 SJ

Beshir, M.O.
The mercenaries and Africa. 26pp. 10 pt. ($1.00) Khartoum UP 1972 SJ

Besseling, J.L.N.
Information and the paper explosion. 8pp. 30c (Univ. Cape Town. Inaugural lec., 37) Univ Cape Town Lib 1976 SA

Bessey, A.
France Afrique. Douze contes africains. A French reader for year 2 of secondary schools in West Africa. See: Coomber, A.A.

Bessis, A. et al.
Le territoire des Ouled Sidi Ali Ben Aoun. 123pp. pl. D1.275 (Série III, Mémoires du Centre d'Etudes Humaines, 1) Univ Tunis 1956 TI FRE

Best, K., ed.
African challenge. 191pp. K.shs.28.00 Transafrica 1975 KE

Bester, A.B.
The influence of different stacking techniques on the quality of kiln-dried timber. 14pp. R5.00 (CSIR Special Report, HOUT 87) CSIR 1974 SA

Bester, A.B.
Kiln design - a development study. 38pp. R5.00 (CSIR Subject Survey, O/HOUT 17) CSIR 1975 SA

Bethel, M. Owen, W.
Lesson notes for Christian teaching. Standard 1. 260pp. K.shs.22.50 Evangel 1975 KE

Bethel, M. Owen, W.
Lesson notes for Christian teaching. Standard 2. 296pp. K.shs.22.50 Evangel 1973 KE

Bethel, M. Owen, W.
Lesson notes for Christian teaching: standard 3. 208pp. K.shs.16.50 Evangel 1975 KE

Bethel, M. Owen, W.
Lesson notes for Christian teaching. Standard 4. 224pp. K.shs.18.00 Evangel 1973 KE

Bethel, M.
Outline notes for Christian teaching in schools. bk.1 96pp. K.shs4.00 EALB 1963 KE

Bethell, A.J.
Notes on South African hunting. [Reprint of ed. 1887]. 160pp. photos. hd. R$7.75 (Rhodesiana Reprint Library, Silver Series, 7) Books of Rhodesia 1976 RH

Betley, J.A., comp.
The scramble for Africa: documents on the Berlin West African conference and related subjects, 1884-1885. See: Gavin, R.J., comp.

Bettison, D.G.
Cash wages and occupational structure, Blantyre-Limbe, Nyasaland. 19pp. 20n. (10p.) (Rhodes-Livingstone communications, 9) Inst Afr Stud - Lusaka 1958 ZA

Bettison, D.G.
The demographic structure of seventeen villages in the peri-urban area of Blantyre-Limbe, Nyasaland. 16pp. 50n. (25p.) (Rhodes-Livingstone communications, 11) Inst Afr Stud - Lusaka 1958 ZA

Bettison, D.G.
Further economic and social studies, Blantyre-Limbe, Nyasaland. 49pp. 40n. (20p.) (Rhodes-Livingstone communications, 17) Inst Afr Stud - Lusaka 1959 ZA

Bettison, D.G.
Numerical data on African dwellers in Lusaka, Northern Rhodesia. 108pp. K1.00 (50p.) (Rhodes-Livingstone communications, 16) Inst Afr Stud - Lusaka 1959 ZA

Bettison, D.G. Rigby, P.J.
Patterns of income and expenditure, Blantyre-Limbe, Nyasaland. 153pp. K1.05 (52p.) (Rhodes-Livingstone communications, 20) Inst Afr Stud - Lusaka 1961 ZA

Bettison, D.G.
The social and economic structure of a sample of peri-urban villages, Blantyre-Limbe, Nyasaland. 99pp. 75n. (38p.) (Rhodes-Livingstone communications, 12) Inst Afr Stud - Lusaka 1958 ZA

Beuchat, P-D.
The verb in Zulu. 80pp. cl. R3.00 Witwatersrand UP 1966 SA

Beuchat, P.D.
Do the Bantu have a literature? 40c. (Isma pap., 7) Inst Study of Man 1962 SA

Beukes, K.
Omalehita naga teme. 74c. Native Lang Bur 1975[?] SX NDO

Beuthin, R.C.
The range of a company's interests. ex. only (Inaugural lec.) Rhodes Univ Lib 1969 SA

Bevan, E.J.
Mzilikazi, 1790-1868. 39pp. R2.05 Dept Bibliog, Lib & Typo 1969 SA

Bevan, M.
Dr. James Barry (1795?-1865). Inspector-general of military hospitals. 32pp. free Dept Bibliog, Lib & Typo 1966 SA

Beveridge, K.H.
Story, song and rhyme. bk. 1 See: Beveridge, W.M.

Beveridge, K.H.
Story, song and rhyme. bk. 2 See: Beveridge, W.M.

Beveridge.
Sua me ansa: pupils. [A first reader: begin with me first] 35pp. ill. 25pes. Waterville 1969 GH TWI

Beveridge, W.M.
Child study. An introduction to psychology for African teachers. 61pp. N1.60 Aromolaran 1975(?) NR

Beveridge, W.M. Beveridge, K.H.
Story, song and rhyme. bk. 1 45pes. ($.45) Ghana Publ Corp 1974 GH

Beveridge, W.M. Beveridge, K.H.
Story, song and rhyme. bk. 2 32pp. 45pes. ($.85) Ghana Publ Corp 1973 GH

Bews, J.W. Aitken, R.D.
Researches on the vegetation of Natal. 25c. (Memoirs of the Botanical Survey of South Africa, 5) Botanical Res Inst 1923 SA

Bews, J.W. Aitken, R.D.
Researches on the vegetation of Natal. 25c. (Memoirs of the Botanical Survey of South Africa, 8) Botanical Res Inst 1925 SA

Bex, A.
St. Peter's harare. Portrait of an African town parish. 63pp. 65c. (Mambo Missio-Pastoral Series, 7) Mambo 1976 RH

Beyene, T.
Lisan. [Tongue] 208pp. Eth.$10.00 Bible Churmen's Miss Soc 1972 ET AMH

Bezuidenhout, N.S.
Modern course accountancy, stds. 7 & 8. 245pp. R1.85 Shuter 1970 SA

Author Index

Bhagwandeen, S.B.
Schistosomiasis in Durban. 207pp. R4.75 Univ of Natal 1968 SA

Bhengu, K.
African cultural identity and international relations. R4.00 Shuter 1975 SA

Bhengu, K.
Ayikho impunga yehlathi. [Crime does not pay.] 211pp. R1.75 Shuter 1974 SA ZUL

Bhengu, K.
Ubogawula ubheka. [Look out as you fell trees] 130pp. 65c. Shuter 1968 SA ZUL

Bhengu, K.
Unyambose nosinitha. [Nyambose and Zinitha] 172pp. 50c. Shuter 1965 SA ZUL

Bhengu, S.M.E.
Chasing gods not our own. African cultural identity and international relations, analysis of Ghanaian and Nigerian sources 1958-1974. 170pp. R5.25 Shuter 1976 SA

Bhushan, K., ed.
Uhuru 12. Kenya yearbook 1976. 124pp. ill. maps. K.shs.25.00 Newspread 1976 KE

Bhushan, K., ed.
Uhuru 13: Kenya yearbook 1977. 4th ed. 204pp. photos. maps. K.shs.25.00 Newspread 1977 KE

Biarnes, M.
La cuisine Ivoirienne. 64pp. pl. CFA1,000.00 Soc Africaine 1974 SG FRE

Biarnes, M.
La cuisine Sénégalaise. 159pp. CFA750 (CFA1500) Soc Africaine 1972 SG FRE

Biarnès, P. Rondot, P. Decraene, P.
L'année politique Africaine. (Edition 1975) 11th ed. 280pp. pl. maps. CFA15,000.00 (F300.00) Soc Africaine 1975 SG FRE

Bibliothèque Nationale, Alger.
Bibliographie de l'Algérie. Periodiques, livres. (annual) [In French and Arabic]. DA15.00 ($10.00) Bibl Nat - Alg AE FRE

Bibliothèque Nationale.
Bibliographie de la Côte d'Ivoire. 1969. v. 1 56pp. CFA480 (F9.60) Biblio Nat - Iv 1970 IV FRE

Bibliothèque Nationale.
Bibliographie de la Côte d'Ivoire. 1970. v. 2 132pp. CFA850 (F20.00) Biblio Nat - Iv 1971 IV FRE

Bibliothèque Nationale.
Bibliographie de la Côte d'Ivoire. 1972. v. 4 167pp. CFA950 (F23.00) Biblio Nat - Iv 1973 IV FRE

Bibliothèque Nationale.
Bibliographie de la Côte d'Ivoire. 1973, 1. v.5 129pp. CFA950 (F23.00) Biblio Nat - Iv 1974 IV FRE

Bichi, Y.
Wakar Tarihin Rikicin Nijeriya. [The history of the Nigerian crisis] 46pp. 45k Northern Nig. 1970 NR HAU

Bidi Setsoafia, H.K.
Togbui Kpeglo II. [Chief Kpeglo II.] 127pp. C1.50 Bur Ghana Lang 1975 GH EWE

Bienefeld, M.A.
Construction industry in Tanzania. 93pp. T.shs12.00 ($3.00) (Research pap., 70.22) Econ Res Bur - Tanz 1970 TZ

Bienefeld, M.A.
Long-term housing policy for Tanzania. 50pp. T.shs.12.00 ($3.00) (Research pap., 70.9) Econ Res Bur - Tanz 1970 TZ

Bienefeld, M.A.
Manpower planning and the university. 32pp. ill. T.shs.12.00 ($3.00) (Research pap., 70.2) Econ Res Bur - Tanz 1970 TZ

Bienefeld, M.A. Sabot, R.H.
The national urban mobility: employment and income survey of Tanzania. v.1 T.shs.45.00 ($9.00) Econ Res Bur - Tanz 1973 TZ

Bienefeld, M.A.
The perspective performance of the Tanzania construction industry during the 2nd five year plan. T.shs.12.00 ($3.00) (Research pap., 69.32) Econ Res Bur - Tanz 1975 TZ

Bienefeld, M.A. Binhammer, H.
Tanzania housing finance and housing policy. T.shs.12.00 ($3.00) (Research pap., 69.19) Econ Res Bur - Tanz 1969 TZ

Bieniawski, A.M.
Fracture of rock. 64pp. R3.30 Dept Bibliog, Lib & Typo 1965 SA

Bieniawski, Z.T., ed.
Exploration for rock engineering. Proceedings of the symposium on exploration for rock engineering. Johannesburg 1-5 November, 1976. 2 v. 542pp. cl. ($50.00/£31.00) Balkema 1977 SA

Bierbaum, P.
Interaction between ultrasonic surface waves and conduction electrons in thin metal films. 148pp. gratis (CSIR research report, 317) CSIR 1973 SA

Biesheuvel, S.
Black-white wage gap. 12pp. 40c. ($1.10) SA Inst of Race Relations 1972 SA

Biesheuvel, S.
The development of African abilities. 16pp. 50c (Fac. of Education, Univ. of Rhodesia, 8) Univ Rhodesia Lib 1967 RH

Bigalke, R.
What animal is it? 85c Van Schaik SA

Biggs, B.J.
Nigeria in history. See: Fajana, A.

Biggs, P.A.
Use of cotton in raschel outerwear. See: Robinson, G.A.

Bihan, G., ed. Torchar, G., ed.
Dadu à Kumasi. 48pp. ill. ($1.30) Ghana Publ Corp 1976 GH FRE

Billingham, P.A.
NBRI introductory guide to damp in buildings. See: Grobbelaar, C.S.

Binhammer, H.
Tanzania housing finance and housing policy. See: Bienefeld, M.A.

Binhammer, H.H.
Commercial banking in Tanzania. 13pp. ill. T.shs12.00 ($3.00) (Research pap., 69.11) Econ Res Bur - Tanz 1969 TZ

Binhammer, H.H.
The development of a financial infrastructure in Tanzania. 216pp. ill. K.shs.32.05 ($6.60/£3.20) EALB 1976 KE

Binhammer, H.H.
Financial infra-structure and the availability of credit to the rural sector of the Tanzania economy. 28pp. ill. T.shs.12.00 ($3.00) (Research pap., 68.17) Econ Res Bur - Tanz 1968 TZ

Binhammer, H.H.
Financing housing in Tanzania. 15pp. ill. T.shs.12.00 ($3.00) (Research pap., 69.5) Econ Res Bur - Tanz 1969 TZ

Binji, H.
Ibada Da Hukunci. [Rules for worship] 1, 2 bks. 92pp. 95k Northern Nig 1957 NR HAU

Binji, H.
Ibada Da Hukunci. [Rules for worship] 2, 2 bks. 80pp. 95k Northern Nig 1960 NR HAU

Binji, H.
Littafin Addini. [Book of religion] 1, 2 bks. 55pp. 55k Northern Nig 1957 NR HAU

Binji, H.
Littafin Addini. [Book of religion] 2, 2 bks. 63pp. 60k Northern Nig 1957 NR HAU

Binji, H. Wali, N.S.
Mu Koyi Ajami Da Larabci. [Let us learn Ajami and Arabic] 77pp. 65k Northern Nig 1969 NR HAU

Binyon, P.
A workbook of Old Testament history. 90k Macmillan 1973 NR

Binyon, P.
A workbook of the life of Christ and Book of Acts. N1.00 Macmillan 1973 NR

Biobaku, S.
The preservation of culture as a factor in nation building. 10pp. 75k ($1.40/60p) (Univ. Ife, Faculty of Arts Lecture series, 3) Univ Ife Press 1975 NR

Biobaku, S.O., ed.
The living culture of Nigeria. 128pp. N10.00 Nelson - Nig 1976 NR

Bird, J.
Annals of Natal, 1495-1845 [Reprint of 1888 edition]. 2 v. 784, 505pp. ill./pl. cl. R18.00 set (Africana collectanea, 14 & 15) Struik 1965 SA

Bird, W.
State of the Cape of Good Hope in 1822 [Reprint of 1823 edition]. 484pp. ill. pl. cl. R6.30 Struik 1965 SA

Birkinshaw, P.
The Livingstone touch. 200pp. R5.00 Purnell 1974 SA

Birks, J.B.
The nature and development of modern physics. ex. only (Inaugural lec.) Rhodes Univ Lib 1952 SA

Birley, R.
The shaking off of burdens. 17pp. 25c. (University of Cape Town T.B. Davie memorial lecture, 7) Univ Cape Town Lib 1965 SA

Birnie, J.H. Ansre, G.
Proceedings of the conference on the study of Ghanaian languages. 112pp. C2.00 Ghana Publ Corp 1969 GH

Birru, D. Heryui, T. Tsige, H.
The scholarship and other stories. 48pp. ill. 90pes. (28p.) Africa Christian 1975 GH

Bischoff, L.R.
The search for gold in South Africa from 1842-1872: a bibliography. 22pp. R1.60 Dept Bibliog, Lib & Typo 1970 SA

Bishop, J.
Agriculture. 37pp. ill. col. ill. maps. ($1.20) (The Environment of the Rhodesian People, 4) M.O. Collins 1974 RH

Bishop, J.W.S.
How to grow vegetables. See: Turnbull, W.H.

Bishop, J.W.S.
How to look after cattle. See: Turnbull, W.H.

Bishop, J.W.S.
Sheep, goats, pigs and poultry. See: Turnbull, W.H.

Bishops of Tanganyika.
Africans and the Christian way of life. Pastoral letter. 62pp. T.shs.2.00 ($0.30 pap.) TMP 1953 TZ

Bisset, C.B.
The Chilwa series of Southern Nyasaland. See: Dixey, F.

Bivar, A.D.H.
Nigerian panoply: arms and armour of the Northern Region. 68pp. ill. N1.00 Dept Antiquities 1964 NR

Biza, R.T.
Chaitemure chava kuseva. 56pp. 45c. Longman - Rhod 1971 RH SHO

Blachère, J.C. Maubert, J.
Littérature française, classe de lere. 556pp. CFA240 (F48.00) Nouv Ed Afric 1976 SG FRE

Black Community Programmes.
Handbook of Black organizations. 97pp. 60c. Black Comm Prog 1973 SA

Black, M.
Kerry's adventure. 32pp. ill. 35c. Longman SA 1963 SA

Blacking, J.
Process and product in human society. 23pp. R1.40 (Inaugural lec.) Witwatersrand UP 1970 SA

Blacking, J.A.R.
Venda children's songs: a study in ethnomusicological analysis. 211pp. pl. cl. R10.00 Witwatersrand UP 1967 SA

Blackwell, L. Bamford, B.R.
Newspaper law of South Africa. R6.00 Juta 1963 SA

Blaeu, J. Guilj, J.
Aethiopia inferior vel exterior 1635. map. fl. 22.50 Balkema SA

Blair, D.
Negritude: whence and whither? 40c. (Isma paps., 31) Inst Study of Man 1971 SA

Blair Rains, A.
Grassland research in Northern Nigeria, 1952-62. 69pp. map. N1.00 (Samaru misc. pap., 1) Inst Agric Res - Zaria 1963 NR

Blaize, J.P.
Africani latine discunt. 2e année. See: Chaumartin, F.R.

Blaize, J.P.
Africani Latine Discunt. Livre du mâitre. See: Chaumartin, F.R.

Blaize, J.P.
Africani Latine Discunt. Première année. Livre de L'élèeve. See: Chaumartin, F.R.

Blake, E.
From stone axe to space age. See: Haliburton, G.M.

Blake, R.
Mbiri ya kale ya m'Mawu a Mulungu. [Old Testament history] 133pp. ill. 80t. (35c.) Christ Lit Assoc - Mal 1970 MW CHC

Blamey, R. D., et al.
History and geography for standard 7. (Practical course) 173pp. ill. photos. maps. R2.50 Nasou 1974 SA

Blamey, R.D., et al.
History and geography for standard 8. (Practical course) 218pp. ill. photos. R4.45 Nasou 1975 SA

Blanch, S.
It is written. A new approach to the Old Testament. 136pp. map. N1.50 Daystar 1977 NR

Blandé, J.
Langage et textes. Classe de 5e. Livre de l'élève. See: Calvet, L.J.

Blandé, J.
Langage et textes. Classe de 5e. Livre du mâitre. See: Calvet, L.J.

Blay, B.
Emelia's promise and fulfilment. Rev. ed. 134pp. C3.90 Waterville 1967 GH

Blay, B.
Ghana sings. 78pp. 35pes. Waterville 1965 GH

Blay, J.B.
African drums. 51pp. 50pes. Benibengor 1972 GH

Blay, J.B.
Be content with your lot. 5th ed. 28pp. 20pes. Benibengor 1973 GH

Blay, J.B.
Dr. Bengia wants a wife. 3rd ed. 18pp. 20pes. Benibengor 1972 GH

Blay, J.B.
Earlier Poems. 68pp. 50pes. Benibengor 1971 GH

Blay, J.B.
Love in a clinic. 4th ed. 20pp. 20pes. Benibengor 1972 GH

Blay, J.B.
Parted lovers. 3rd ed. 23pp. 20pes. Benibengor 1972 GH

Blay, J.B.
The stay of Tata. 44pp. ill. C1.00 Univ Ghana Bkshop; distr. 1976 GH

Blay, J.B.
Stubborn girl. 3rd ed. 20pp. 20pes. Benibengor 1973 GH

Blay, J.S.
Adawu edodo. [Short stories.] 66pp. ill. C1.25 Bur Ghana Lang 1974 GH NZE

Blay, J.S., ed.
Adawu edodo. [Folktales.] 4th ed. 66pp. ill. C1.25 Bur Ghana Lang 1976 GH NZE

Bleek, W.H.I.
The Natal diaries of Dr. W.H.I. Bleek, 1855-1856. 127pp. ill. hd. fl. 20.25 Balkema 1965 SA

Blege, W.
Jacaranda first atlas for Ghana. 32pp. maps col. maps. 65k Pilgrim 1974 NR

Blegge, W., ed.
Shakespeare fe Makbet. [Shakespeare's Macbeth.] 2nd ed. 128pp. ill. C1.20 Bur Ghana Lang 1976 GH EWE

Bleksley, A.E.H.
The principle of superposition and its application in solid geometry- Euclidian and non-Euclidian. 15pp. 15c. (A v. 7 no. 1) Univ Stellenbosch, Lib 1929 SA

Blennerhasset, R. Sleeman, L.
Adventures in Mashonaland. Reprint of 1893 ed. 348pp. photos. ill. R$9.60 (Rhodesiana Reprint Library, Gold Series, 8) Books of Rhodesia 1969 RH

Blignaut, F.W. Fourie, H.P.
Communication: introductory essays. [Also available in Afrikaans]. 313pp. ill. photos. R2.50 cl. (R3.50 cl.) Univ South Africa 1970 SA

Blocksma, M.
How the earth was satisfied. 47pp. col. ill. 60k OUP - Nig 1971 NR

Blonde, J.
Langage et textes. Méthode complète d'enseignement du français en Afrique, classe de 4e, livre de l'élève. See: Calvet, L.J.

Bloomfield, K. Garson, M.S.
The geology of the Kirk Range-Lisungwe Valley area. 234pp. hd. K4.20 (Geological Survey of Malawi, Bull. 17) Geol Survey - Mal 1965 MW

Bloomfield, K.
The geology of the Nkana Coalfield, Karonga District. 36pp. maps pl. 50t. (Geological Survey of Malawi, Bull. 8) Geol Survey - Mal 1957 MW

Bloomfield, K.
The geology of the Port Herald area. 76pp. map pl. hd. K1.05 (Geological Survey of Malawi, Bull. 9) Geol Survey - Mal 1958 MW

Bloomfield, K.
The geology of the Thambani-Salambidwe area. See: Cooper, W.G.G.

Bloomfield, K.
The geology of the Zomba area. 193pp. map pl. hd. K3.50 (Geological Survey of Malawi, Bull. 16) Geol Survey - Mal 1965 MW

Bloomfield, K.
Infracrustal ring complexes of Southern Malawi. 115pp. pl. hd. K2.50 (Geological Survey of Malawi, Memoir, 4) Geol Survey - Mal 1965 MW

Bloomfield, K.
The Pre-Karroo geology of Malawi. 166pp. hd. K4.00 (Geological Survey of Malawi, Memoir, 5) Geol Survey - Mal 1968 MW

Blumenfeld, J.P.
Survey of the Cape Midlands and Karroo regions, vol. 4: the economic structure. 272pp. ill. Inst Soc & Econ Res - SA 1973 SA

Boadi, L. Nwankwo, B. Grieve, D.W.
Grammatical structure and its teaching. 288pp. pap. & cl. N4.65 cl. N2.75 pap. Pilgrim 1968 NR

Boahen, A.A.
Clio and nation-building in Africa. 22pp. C1.00 (50p) (Inaugural lecture) Ghana UP 1975 GH

Boakye, J.K.A.
Composition of households in some Fante communities (A study of the framework of social integration)
See: Vercruijsse, E.V.W.

Boateng, A.
France Afrique. La famille Tano. French reader for years 2 and 3 of secondary schools in West Africa. 32pp. ill. 70k Macmillan 1975 NR

Boateng, A.
Le village de Papa Mensah. 48pp. C1.70 Afram 1975 GH FRE

Boateng, G.
Rudiments of music. 25pp. 35pes. Waterville 1972 GH

Boberg, P.Q.R. et al., eds.
Annual survey of South African law, 1975. cl. R30.00 Juta 1977 SA

Boberg, P.Q.R.
The law of persons and the family: with illustrative cases. cl. R36.00 Juta 1977 SA

Bobito, J.
Prescription: love. 32pp. K.shs.2.50 (Afromance series, 5) Transafrica 1975 KE

Bobrov, J.
The keeping of attorneys' books. 2nd ed. R10.00 Juta 1971 SA

Bodker, C.
The leopard. 205pp. ill. K.shs.10.00 (African Secondary Readers, 2) EAPH 1974 KE

Boer, H.
A history of the early church. N2.50 Africa only Daystar 1975 NR

Boer, H.R.
The minor prophets. 84pp. 75k (No US) Daystar 1965 NR

Boer, R.H.
A brief history of Islam: a Christian interpretation. 121pp. N1.25 Daystar 1968 NR

Bohannan, P.
Tiv farm and settlement, 1954. 87pp. N2.00 Inst Afr Stud-Ibadan 1969 NR

Boissard, P.
Cuisine malgache, cuisine creole. [Text in French and Malagasy]. 144pp. Lib Madagascar 1976 MG MUL

Bokamba-Bouka Epotu.
Rêves du soir. Poèmes. 32pp. 50k (CFA250) Centre Africain Litt 1973 ZR FRE

Bokelmann, H.
Wild flowers of the Eastern Cape province. See: Batten, A.

Boktor, A.
The development and expansion of education in the United Arab Republic. 182pp. £.E.2.000 ($6.50) Am Univ 1963 UA

Bolaji, S.L.
Anatomy of corruption in Nigeria. 144pp. 75k Daystar 1970 NR

Bolaji, S.L.
Recipe for Nigerian Progress. 28pp. photos. maps. 20k Daily Sketch 1973 NR

Boland, R.G.A.
BOL 450 multi-language learning system: Afrikaans. [Book with cassette tape]. R9.75 Struik 1975 SA

Bolarin, J.K.
Which church should I join? 12pp. 3k SIM 1967 NR

Bolawa, A.
School certificate economics for West African students ('O' level) 144pp. N1.50 pap. Publ Int 1974 NR

Bolling, E.L.
Kwabena. 44pp. photos. 50 pes. Waterville 1968 GH

Bolwig, N.
Animals: their world, our world. 37pp. N1.00 Ibadan UP 1967 NR

Bombay, C.R.
How to read your bible. 32pp. K.shs.2.00 Evangel 1972 KE

Bombay, C.R.
Money, man and God. 20pp. K.shs.3.00 Evangel 1966 KE

Bombay, C.R.
Sin, sickness and God. 24pp. K.shs.2.00 Evangel 1969 KE

Bombay, C.R.
Who is this Jesus? 24pp. K.shs.2.50 Evangel 1970 KE

Bombay, C.R.
The young Christian and the Bible. 2nd rev. ed. 96pp. K.shs.6.50 Evangel 1975 KE

Bon, G. Nicolas, F.J.
Grammaire l'élé; glossaire l'élé-français. 452pp. map. CFA2400 (Mémoires de l'IFAN, 24) IFAN 1953 SG FRE

Bond, C.
Okavango: sea of land, land of water. [Also available in German.]. See: Johnson, P.

Bond, G.
Past climates in Africa. 34pp. 30c pap. Univ Rhodesia Lib 1962 RH

Bond, J.
They were South Africans. 232pp. R2.40 OUP-SA 1971 SA

Bone, R.C.
African education in Rhodesia. 37pp. 50c (Fac. of Education, Univ. of Rhodesia, 9) Univ Rhodesia Lib 1969 RH

Bone, R.C.
The future of teacher education. 17pp. 30c Univ Rhodesia Lib 1970 RH

Bongela, K.S.
Alitshoni lingenandaba. [Every day has its stories] R1.10 Shuter 1972 SA XHO

Bongela, K.S.
Imizabalazo yematriki. [Matriculation tests] 55pp. 70c. Shuter 1969 SA XHO

Boni, D.
Annales de l'université d'Abidjan. Le pays akyé (Côte d'Ivoire): étude de l'économie agricole. 206pp. CFA1150 (F23.00) (Série G-Géographie, 2-1) Univ Abidjan 1970 IV FRE

Bonneau, D. et al.
Annales de l'université d'Abidjan. 200pp. CFA900 (F18.00) (Série D-Lettres, 4) Univ Abidjan 1971 IV FRE

Bonneau, D. et al.
Annales de l'université d'Abidjan. 248pp. CFA1100 (F22.00) (Série D-Lettres, 5) Univ Abidjan 1972 IV FRE

Bonneau, R.
Ecrivains, cinéastes, et artistes ivoiriens. Aperçu bibliographique. 176pp. ill. CFA1200 (F24.00) Nouv Ed Afric 1974 SG FRE

Bonni, F.
Ways with rice. 37pp. ill. 35pes. ($.35) Ghana Publ Corp 1972 GH

Bonsels, W.
Maya okanyushi. [Tr. of the German book "Die Biene Maja und ihre Abenteuer.] 142pp. Native Lang Bur 1974 SX HER

Bonsels, W.
Maya okanyushi. R3.25 Native Lang Bur 1975[?] SX NDO

Bonte, P.
L'élevage et le commerce du bétail dans l'Ader Doutchi-Majya. 2nd ed. 210pp. maps. CFA1250 (F25.00) (Etudes Nigeriennes, 23) Inst Rech Sci Hum 1973 NG FRE

Boobeyer, G.H.
Jesus and the politics of his time. 20pp. Free Univ Rhodesia Lib 1968 RH

Bookers (Malawi) Ltd.
How to run a successful shop. 48pp. ill. pl. 55t Christ Lit Assoc - Mal 1975 MW

Books of Rhodesia.
The southern Rhodesia native affairs department annual. v.1: 1923-1927 600pp. ill. cl. R$21.00 cl. Books of Rhodesia 1972 RH

Boonstra, L.D.
A contribution of the cranial osteology of Pareiasaurus serridens. 18pp. pl. ill. 20c. (A v.8, no.5) Univ Stellenbosch, Lib 1930 SA

Boorman, B.L. Treadaway, J.
East African secondary school atlas. 108pp. maps col. maps photos. K.shs.35.00 Transafrica 1974 KE

Boorman, B.L.
North America; studies for East African students. See: Hayward, R.L.

Boorman, J.
The Nigerian butterflies: an atlas of plates with notes, 2: Pieridae and Danaidae. 12pp. pl. N5.00 Ibadan UP 1973 NR

Boorman, J. Roche, P.
The Nigerian butterflies: an atlas of plates with notes: nymphalidae, 1. 3, 9 pts 16pp. pl. N5.00 Ibadan UP 1965 NR

Boorman, J. Roche, P.
The Nigerian butterflies: an atlas of plates with notes: nymphalidae, 3. 5, 9 pts 19pp. pl. N2.50 Ibadan UP 1959 NR

Boorman, J. Roche, P.
The Nigerian butterflies: an atlas of plates with notes: papilionidae. 1, 9 pts. 7pp. pl. N2.00 Ibadan UP 1957 NR

Boorman, J. Roche, P.
The Nigerian butterflies: an atlas of plates with notes: pieridae and danaidae. 2, 9 pts pl. N5.00 Ibadan UP 1973 NR

Boorman, J. Roche, P.
The Nigerian butterlfies: an atlas of plates with notes: acraeidae. 6, 9 pts 8pp. pl. N2.50 Ibadan UP 1961 NR

Booth, A.R.
The United States experience in South Africa 1784-1870. 256pp. ill. hd. R15.00 cl. (Dfl.45/$17.50/£8.80 cl.) (South African biographical and historical studies, 22) Balkema 1976 SA

Booysen, P. de V.
Common veld and pasture grasses of Natal. See: Tainton, N.M.

Bordinat, P., ed. Thomas, P., ed.
Revealer of secrets. 112pp. ill. (African Reader's Library, 24) Pilgrim 1975 NR

Borowitz, A. Semple, H.
Encounter with age...or how to avoid a nervous breakdown while growing old. 70pp. R2.40 ($2.85/£1.50) Ravan 1976 SA

Borrel, A.
Les pêches sur la côte septentrionale de la Tunisie.
85pp. pl. D0.850 (Série III, Mémoires du Centre
d'Etudes Humaines, 2) Univ Tunis 1956 TI FRE

Boruett, W.K.
Give the devil his due. 53pp. ill. K.shs3.00 ($1.00)
EAPH 1969 KE

Bosa, G.
Finance of small businesses in Uganda. 131pp.
U.shs18.00 (M.I.S.R. occas. paps., 3) Mak Inst Soc Res
1969 UG

Bosch, M.
A guide to the teaching of basic mathematics. See: Dill,
A.W.

Bosdari, C.
Cape Dutch houses and farms. 150pp. pl. fl. 22.50
Balkema 1971 SA

Bosede Business Foundation.
Business winners' memo. 21pp. N1.05 Bosede 1971
NR

Bosede Business Foundation.
The funds raiser. 10pp. ill. 75k Bosede 1972 NR

Bosede Business Foundation.
How to own £1,000,000 or N2 m. business without
capital. 24pp. 75k Bosede 1971 NR

Bosek'Ilolo-Baleka Lima.
Les marais brûlés. Contes. 40pp. 50k (CFA250)
Centre Africain Litt 1973 ZR FRE

Boshoff, M.M.
Juvenile delinquency in South Africa. 48pp. 80c.
Univ Cape Town Lib 1965 SA

Bosman, H.C.
A Bekkersdal marathon. 2nd ed. 170pp. R3.95 cl.
Human and Rousseau 1974 SA

Bosman, H.C.
Bosman at his best. 8th ed. 206pp. ill. R3.25 cl.
Human and Rousseau 1974 SA

Bosman, H.C.
A cask of Jerepigo. 2nd ed. 245pp. R3.95 cl.
Human and Rousseau 1974 SA

Bosman, H.C.
Cold stone jug. A chronicle: being the unimpassioned
record of a somewhat lengthy sojourn in prison. 3rd ed.
220pp. cl. R3.95 Human and Rousseau 1975 SA

Bosman, H.C.
The earth is waiting. 86pp. R3.50 cl. Human and
Rousseau 1974 SA

Bosman, H.C.
Jurie Steyn's post office. 2nd ed. 147pp. R3.95 cl.
Human and Rousseau 1974 SA

Bosman, H.C.
Mafeking road. 7th ed. 116pp. cl. R3.95 Human
and Rousseau 1977 SA

Bosman, H.C.
Unto dust. 5th ed. 181pp. R3.95 cl Human and
Rousseau 1974 SA

Bossert, C.
La Bible et les témoins de Jehovah. 24pp. CFA100
CPE 1972 IV FRE

Bossman, S.A.
Csaman pa. [Good ghost.] 76pp. ill. 75pes. Bur
Ghana Lang 1975 GH ASA

Boston, F.
Preparing for Christian initiation. 90pp. K.shs.8.50
(Gaba Pastoral Papers, 26) Gaba 1973 KE

Boswell, D.
Escorts of hospital patients: a preliminary report on a
social survey undertaken at Lusaka Central Hospital from
July - August 1964. 19pp. 30n. (15p.) (Rhodes-
Livingstone communications, 29) Inst Afr Stud - Lusaka
1965 ZA

Botanical Research Institute.
A guide to botanical survey work. 25c. (Memoirs of
the Botanical Survey of South Africa, 4) Botanical Res
Inst 1922 SA

Botchey, G.L.
Introduction to elementary poultry keeping. 55pp. ill.
50pes. Waterville 1974 GH

Both, E.L.M.
Books and pamphlets published in German relating to
South Africa and South West Africa 1950-1964. 132pp.
R1.20 Univ Cape Town Lib 1969 SA

Botha, C.
Trial of Andries Botha, field-cornet of the upper Blinkwater,
in the Kat River settlement for treason in the Supreme
Court of the colony of the Cape of Good Hope. [Reprint
of ed. Cape Town, 1852] 313pp. ill. R8.50
(Reprints, 19) State - Lib - SA 1969 SA

Botha, C.
A laboratory process for dyeing wool with reactive dyes
from a charged solvent system using a single emulsifier.
See: Roberts, M.B.

Botha, C.
Manuscripts and papers in the Killie Campbell Africana
Collection: a catalogue. 89pp. R4.55 Dept Bibliog,
Lib & Typo 1967 SA

Botha, C.G.
Social life of the Cape Colony in the eighteenth century.
4th ed. 108pp. ill. pl. cl. R4.50 Struik 1976 SA

Botha, J.
Modern revision exercises in biology for standard 8.
See: Fox, H.E.

Botha, L.I.
The Namib Desert. 26pp. 60c. Univ Cape Town Lib
1970 SA

Botha, R.
Source guide for drama, ballet, films and radio plays. v.
I. 252pp. R5.00 Human Science Res Council 1972
SA

Botha, R.
Source guide for drama, ballet, films and radio plays.
New series ed. v. II. 287pp. R4.05 Human Science
Res Council 1974 SA

Botha, R.
Source guide for drama, ballet, films and radio plays.
New series ed. v. III. 314pp. R4.70 Human Science
Res Council 1974 SA

Botuli-Bolumbu Ikole.
Feuilles d'olive. 31pp. 30k (Jeune littérature, 14)
Ed Mont Noir 1972 ZR FRE

Bouabba, Y.
Les Almohades. 40pp. DA1.00 SNED 1971 AE FRE

Bouabba, Y.
Les Turcs au Maghreb central du 16e au 19e siècle.
DA1.00 SNED 1972 AE FRE

Bouali, M.
La sédition permanente en Tunisie. 1, 2v. 256pp.
D0.800 Maison Tunis 1972 TI FRE

Bouayed, M. Khammar, A.
Dix ans de production intellectuelle en Algérie: 1962-1972.
Les écrits en langue arabe. pt. 1 156pp. D5.00
(D10.00) Bibl Nat - Alg 1974 AE FRE

Bouayed, M. Khammar, A.
Dix ans de production intellectuelle en Algérie, 1962-1972.
Première partie: les écrits en langauge arabe. 134pp.
5,00 DA SNED 1974 AE FRE

Bouayed, M.
L'histoire par la bande. Une expérience de la Bibliothèque
Nationale d'Algérie. 80pp. D2.00 pap. (D8.00) Bibl
Nat - Alg 1974 AE FRE

Bouchama, A.
L'arceau qui chante. 75pp. DA2.50 SNED 1966 AE
FRE

Bouchama, A.
Mouvements pensants et matière. 255pp. photos.
DA8.00 SNED 1968 AE FRE

Bouchenaki, M.
Fouilles de la nécropole occidentale de Tipaza (Matarès)
1968-1972. 213pp. pl. D40.00 (D100.00) Bibl Nat
- Alg 1975 AE FRE

Bouchenaki, M.
La monnaie de l'Emir Abd El Kader. 121pp. ill. D6.00
(D12.00) (Notes et documents, 2) Bibliotheque
Nationale 1976 AE FRE

Boucher, M.
The examining board and the examining university. Some
observations on the establishment and development of the
University of Good Hope to 1885. 45pp. 75c.
(R1.25) Univ South Africa 1969 SA

Boucher, M.
Spes in Arduis: a history of the University of South Africa.
[also available in Afrikaans.]. 404pp. photos. cl.
R5.00 (R6.00) Univ South Africa 1973 SA

Boudalia, A.
Les maladies cryptogamiques de la vigne. photos.
DA1.00 SNED 1971 AE FRE

Boudjedra, R.
Pour ne plus rever. 80pp. DA4.00 SNED 1966 AE
FRE

Bouffel, M. Farcy, H. de.
La commercialisation agricole. 4 pts. 125pp.
CFA1200 INADES 1968 IV FRE

Bouffel, M.
L'économie rurale. 5 pts. 164pp. CFA1500 INADES
1969 IV FRE

Boughey, A.S.
The origin of the African flora. 48pp. 30c Univ
Rhodesia Lib 1957 RH

Bouhdiba, A.
A la recherche des normes perdues. 274pp. D1,100
Maison Tunis 1973 TI FRE

Bouillon, A.
Etudes sur les termites africains. Distribution spatiale et la
dispersion des espèces du genre apicotermes
(Termitinae) 35pp. maps. 45k Press Univ Zaire 1962
ZR FRE

Bouillon, A.
La fécondité chez l'araignée latrodectus géometricus C.
Koch. 22pp. ill. 20k Press Univ Zaire 1957 ZR FRE

Bouillon, A.
Les fonctions du cocon chez l'araignée latrodectus C.
Koch. 30pp. ill. 30k Press Univ Zaire 1957 ZR FRE

Bouillon, A.
Introduction à la biologie. 24pp. 30k Press Univ
Zaire 1963 ZR FRE

Bouillon, A. Krumback, G.
La longévité chez l'araignée latrodectus C. Koch. 21pp.
20k Press Univ Zaire 1958 ZR FRE

Bouillon, A.
La sex-ratio chez l'araignée latrodectus C. Koch. 8pp. ill.
10k Press Univ Zaire 1957 ZR FRE

Bouillon, A.
Variations, cycles et rythmes dans l'activité du latrodectus
geometricus C. Koch. 16pp. 20k Press Univ Zaire
1960 ZR FRE

Boulanger, A.
Yambe à l'aube des symboles. Essai d'anthropologie
religieuse. 145pp. map. (DM22.00) (CEEBA. serie II,
Mémoires et Monographies, 21) CEEBA 1975 ZR FRE

Boularès, H.
Murad III. 100pp. D0.200 Maison Tunis 1968 TI FRE

Boulet, J.
Le pays de la Bénoué. 134pp. CFA1,000 Inst
Sciences Hum - Cam 1972 CM FRE

Bouquet, C.
Atlas pratique du Tchad. See: Cabot, J.

Bouquet, C.
Le Tchad. Géographie. See: Cabot, J.

Bourdillon, B.
The Shona peoples. hd. & pap. R$5.40 (Shona
Heritage Series, 1) Mambo 1976 RH

Bourdillon, M., ed.
Christianity south of the Zambezi. v. 2. 219pp.
R$3.00 Mambo 1976 RH

Bourély, M.
Droit public. v. 1: Institutions politiques. Dir40.00 Ed
La Porte 1965 MR FRE

Bourély, M.
Droit public. v. 2: Libertés publiques. Dir30.00 Ed La
Porte 1965 MR FRE

Bourgeade, A. et al.
Annales de l'université d'Abidjan. 232pp. (Série B -
Médecine, 5) Univ Abidjan 1971 IV FRE

Bourges, H.
Information et développement. Conditions actuelles de la
presse en Afrique et perspectives d'avenir. 21pp. Univ
Cameroun 1972 CM FRE

Bourguiba, H.
Discours. D1,800 Maison Tunis 1971 TI FRE

Bourguiba, H.
La Tunisie et la France. 464pp. D0.300 Maison Tunis
1971 TI FRE

Bourouiba, M.
L'art musulman en Algérie. 75pp. photos. maps.
DA3.00 SNED 1972 AE FRE

Bourouiba, R.
Abd al-Mumin, flambeau des almohades. 168pp.
DA18.00 pap. SNED 1975 AE FRE

Bourouiba, R.
L'art religieux musulman en Algérie. 320pp. ill. col. pl.
40,00 DA SNED 1974 AE FRE

Bourouiba, R.
Ibn Tumart. 144pp. DA18.00 pap. SNED 1975 AE
FRE

Bousquet, G.H. Bercher, L.
Le statut personnel en droit musulman hanefite. 271pp.
D1.000 Univ Tunis 1952 TI FRE

Boustany, S.
The journals of Bonaparte in Egypt, 10 vols. 3517pp. cl.
Al-Arab Bookshop 1975[?] UA

Boustead, P.G.
Rainfall at the Jonkershoek Forest hydrological research
station. See: Wicht, C.L.

Bousteyak, L.
Etude pétrographique de formations stannifères dans la
region d'Ihosy. 10pp. pl. FMG369 (F7.38)
(Travaux du Bureau Géologique, 130) Service Geol -
Mad 1968 MG FRE

Boutrais, J.
Etude d'une zone de transhumance. La plaine de Ndop.
164pp. ill. maps. CFA1,000 Inst Sciences Hum - Cam
1974 CM FRE

Bouzaher, H., ed.
Les cinq doigts du jour. 224pp. DA11.40 SNED
1969 AE FRE

Bouzida, A.
L'idéologie de l'instituteur. 254pp. DA10.00 SNED
1976 AE FRE

Bowden, W.
The lady with a lamp. 160pp. ill. 75c. Longman SA
1971 SA

Bowden, W.
"Silas Marner". 288pp. ill. R1.85 Longman SA 1966
SA

Bowen, A.D.
Certificate geography of Swaziland. 112pp. photos.
maps. R2.00 Longman - SA 1975 SA

Bowen, C.
15 essays in halftone. 50c Van Schaik SA

Bowen, R.E.C.
World to world: on Rhodesia's magic carpet. 49pp. ill. 50c. Books of Rhodesia 1974 RH

Bowker, J.
Junior secondary mathematics for standard 6. See: Ahlers, H.J.

Bowler, D.
The treatment of cotton fabrics with dimethyloldihydroxyethylene urea and various catalysts. See: Hanekom, E.C.

Bown, L., ed.
Adult education in Nigeria. The next ten years. Report of the Nigerian National Council for Adult Education first annual conference, held at Abdullahi Bayero College, Kano, March 24 - 28, 1972. pl. N1.00 Adult Educ Gen Ext Serv 1974 NR

Bown, L. Erubu, H.
Second report to the General Extension Services Board on the activities of the unit, April 1973 to December 1974. 58pp. photos. free Adult Educ Gen Ext Serv 1976 NR

Bown, L.
Third report to the General Extension Services Board on the activities of the unit, 1975. 64pp. photos. free Adult Educ Gen Ext Serv 1976 NR

Boxer, C.R.
An African Eldorado, Monomotapa and Mocambique, 1498-1752. 60c. (Local series pamphlets, 2) Central Africa Hist Assoc 1961 RH

Boxer, C.R.
Four centuries of Portuguese expansion, 1415-1825. 96pp. map ill. cl. R3.00 (Oppenheimer Inst. of Portuguese stud. pub., 3) Witwatersrand UP 1968 SA

Boxwell, J.
Jeqe, the body-servant of King Tshaka. tr. fr. Zulu John Dube. 84pp. 50c. Lovedale 1951 SA

Boyce, A.N., ed.
Evaluation in education. R7.50 Maskew Miller 1975 SA

Boyce, W.B.
Notes on South African affairs [Reprint of 1838 edition]. 298pp. cl. R7.50 (Africana collectanea, 39) Struik 1971 SA

Boyd, J.
The battle of Tabkin Kwatto. 8pp. ill. 10k Northern Nig 1967 NR

Boyd, J.
Flame of Islam. 94pp. 75k Northern Nig 1969 NR

Boyd, J.
Ka Kara Karatu Sabuwar Hanya, 3. 3, 6 bks. See: Aliyu, A.H.

Boyd, J.
Ka Koyi Karatu Sabuwar Hanya, 2. 1, 6 bks See: Ingawa, M.

Boyd, J.
Ka Yi Ta Karatu Sabuwar Hanya, 4. 4, 6 bks See: Ingawa, M.

Boyd, R., et al.
Science et bible. Tr. fr. English. 46pp. CFA180 CLE 1967 CM FRE

Boyd, R.L.F. et al.
Scientists look at the Bible. 38pp. 40k Daystar 1969 NR

Boyd, T.A.
An enquiry concerning employment opportunities for secondary school leavers in Ghana. See: French, S.

Boyd, T.A.
An enquiry concerning employment opportunities for secondary school leavers in Ghana. See: French, S.

Boyd, T.A.
Evaluation of an extension programme. Report of a pilot study into the effects of the focus and concentrate programme in the Tamale area. See: Vercruijsse, E.V.W.

Boyd, T.A.
Evaluation of an extension programme: report of a pilot study into the effects of the focus and concentrate programme in the Tamale area. See: Vercruijsse, E.V.W.

Boyd, T.A.
Occupational differentiation in rural areas. A research design. See: Vercruijsse, E.V.W.

Boyd, T.A.
Occupational differentiation in rural areas: a research design. See: Vercruijsse, E.V.W.

Boyd, T.A.
Value orientations influencing decision making in rural communities: an exploratory study. 34pp. C1.00 (Univ. of Cape Coast, Centre for Development Studies, Research Report Series, 5) Centre Dev Stud 1971 GH

Boyd, T.A.
Value orientations influencing decision making in rural communities: an exploratory study. 34pp. (University of Cape Coast, social studies project, research report, 5) Cape Coast Bkshp 1971 GH

Boye, M.A.
Essays and notes on New Testament. 64pp. 80k Ilesanmi 1971 NR

Boyeldieu, P. Palayer, P.
Les langues du groupe Boua. Etudes phonologiques. 220pp. ex. only (Série C, 2) Inst Nat Tchad 1975 CD FRE

Bozzoli, G.R.
Education is the key to change in South Africa. 1977 Hoernlé Memorial Lecture. 14pp. 90c. ($1.80) SA Inst of Race Relations 1977 SA

Bozzoli, G.R.
Technological man in Southern Africa. 40c. (Isma paps., 10) Inst Study of Man 1963 SA

Bracey, D. Lieta, P.
Longman graded reading scheme. Reader 1. 16pp. col. ill. K.shs.3.75 Longman - Ken 1975 KE

Bracey, D. Lieta, P.
Longman graded reading scheme. Reader 2. 28pp. col. ill. K.shs.4.85 Longman - Ken 1975 KE

Bracey, D. Lieta, P.
Longman graded reading scheme. Reader 3. 28pp. col. ill. K.shs.4.85 Longman - Ken 1975 KE

Bracey, D. Lieta, P.
Longman graded reading scheme. Reader 4. 28pp. col. ill. K.shs.3.50 Longman - Ken 1975 KE

Bracey, D. Lieta, P.
Longman graded reading scheme. Teachers bk. col. ill. K.shs.29.75 Longman - Ken 1975 KE

Brachet, M.L.
Deux enfants en vacances. 60pp. ill. 80k Macmillan 1970 NR

Brachet, M.L.
France-Afrique: a French course for Africa: pupil's bk. bk. 4, 5 bks. See: Grandsaigne, J.D.

Bradlow, F.R.
Africana books and pictures. A selection of published papers. 144pp. ill. cl. R14.25 cl. (Dfl.42.75/$17.00/£8.20 cl.) Balkema 1976 SA

Bradlow, F.R.
Baron von Ludwig and the Ludwig's-burg garden. 124pp. ill. hd. fl. 22.50 Balkema 1965 SA

Bradlow, F.R.
Thomas Bowler: his life and work. 318pp. ill. hd. fl. 135.00 Balkema 1967 SA

Bradshaw, B.
The culture plan: world techniques in uniformity. ex. only (Inaugural lec.) Rhodes Univ Lib 1961 SA

Brahimi, C.
Initiation à la préhistoire de l'Algérie. 95pp. DA8.00 SNED 1972 AE FRE

Braimah, J.A.
The Ashanti and the Gonja at war. 63pp. ill. map photos. 60pes. ($.60) Ghana Publ Corp 1970 GH

Branche, P.C.
A survey of the careers of a sample of the 1954 common entrance examination failures in Freetown primary schools. 22pp. Le1.30 (Dept. of Education, Fourah Bay College, Research bull., 1) Fourah Bay Bkshp 1966 SL

Brandt, M.P.
Transmission and scanning electron micrographs of some selected phyllosilicates and inosilicates of Southern Africa. See: Oberholster, R.E.

Branford, W.
Manual of English sentence structure. R2.00 Inst Study Engl 1974 SA

Branford, W.
Manual of English sentence structure. R2.00 Rhodes Univ Lib 1974 SA

Branford, W.
New directions in the study of English. ex. only (Inaugural lec.) Rhodes Univ Lib 1966 SA

Branford, W.
Rhodes manual of old English. See: Aldridge, M.V.

Branford, W.
Rhodes manual of old English. See: Aldridge, M.V.

Branford, W. Aldridge, M.
Sourcebook for an introductory historical study of the English language: old English. 1, 2 pts. 63pp. 50c Inst Study Engl SA

Branford, W. Aldridge, M.
Sourcebook for an introductory historical study of the English language: paradigms and glossary. 2, 2 pts. 78pp. 50c Inst Study Engl SA

Brann, C.M.B., ed.
French curriculum development in Anglophone Africa: a symposium and guide. 206pp. N1.20 (Inst. of Ed. occas. pap., 9) Inst Educ-Ib 1970 NR

Brann, C.M.B.
The training of teachers of French in Anglophone West Africa. 62pp. 75k (Inst. of Ed. occas. pap., 11) Inst Educ-Ib 1970 NR

Bransby, D.I.
Common veld and pasture grasses of Natal. See: Tainton, N.M.

Branton, M. Toly, O. Ranc, O.
Mathématique. Collection I.R.E.M. Dakar, classe de 4e. 318pp. CFA1,600 (F32.00) Nouv Ed Afric 1976 SG FRE

Brasseur, G.
L'A.O.F. 74pp. maps photos. CFA600 pap. (Initiations et Etudes Africaines, 13) IFAN 1957 SG FRE

Brasseur, G.
Porto-Novo et sa palmeraie. See: Brasseur-Marion, P.

Brasseur-Marion, P. Brasseur, G.
Porto-Novo et sa palmeraie. 132pp. pl. CFA1000 (Mémoires de l'IFAN, 32) IFAN 1953 SG FRE

Brasseur, P.
Bibliographie générale du Mali (1961-1970) 285pp. F100.00 (Catalogues et Documents, 16-2) IFAN 1976 SG FRE

Breger, R.A.
Installation of general testing programme for the selection and classification of workers. See: Verster, M.A.

Breger, R.A.
Job grading procedure for selection and placement of workers at the lower levels. See: Lätti, V.I.

Breitenbach, J.J., ed.
South Africa in the modern world (1910-1970) 500pp. pl. maps. cl. R6.00 Shuter 1974 SA

Breitenbach, J.J. et al.
South Africa in the modern world, 1910-1970. 576pp. pl. maps. cl. & pap. R5.50 pap. R8.40 cl. Shuter 1975 SA

Brelsford, W.V.
Aspects of Bemba chieftainship. 57pp. 50n. (25p.) (Rhodes-Livingstone communications, 2) Inst Afr Stud - Lusaka 1944 ZA

Brelsford, W.V.
Fishermen of the Bangweulu swamps: a study of the fishing activities of the Unga tribe. 153pp. K2.50 (£1.25) (Rhodes-Livingstone paps., 12) Inst Soc Res - Zam 1946 ZA

Brenner, Y. Wagenbuur, H.T.M.
Lime farmers: a case study of a cashcrop subsistence economy. 36pp. maps. C1.00 (Univ. of Cape Coast, Centre for Development Studies, Research Report Series, 1) Centre Dev Stud 1969 GH

Bretout, F.
Mogho Naba du royaume Mossi. 96pp. CFA250 (F5.00) Nouv Ed Afric 1976 SG FRE

Brett, E.A., comp.
Tentative list of books and pamphlets on South Africa published in the United States and Canada. gratis Johannesburg Public Lib 1959 SA

Breytenbach, P.P.B.
National documentation centre for performing arts. 9pp. photos. free Human Science Res Council 1972 SA

Breytenbach, W.J.
The black worker. See: Leistner, G.M.E.

Breytenbach, W.J.
Boleswa. 96pp. R3.00 (R3.50) (Communications of the Africa Institute, 31) Africa Inst 1977 SA

Breytenbach, W.J.
Crocodiles and commoners in Lesotho. 136pp. R3.00 (R3.50) Africa Inst - Pret 1975 SA

Brian, R.
Education for development in Southern Africa. See: Hirschmann, D.

Bridge, J.
Plant parasitic nematodes of irrigated crops in the Northern states of Nigeria. 15pp. 60k (Samaru misc. pap., 42) Inst Agric Res-Zaria 1972 NR

Bridger, P., et al.
Encyclopaedia Rhodesia. v. 1 446pp. ill. col. map. R$9.50 College Press 1973 RH

Brigish, U., ed.
The library of Jan Christiaan Smuts. Dept Bibliog, Lib & Typo SA

Brimble, A.R.
The Northern Rhodesia mental ability survey 1963. See: MacArthur, R.S.

Brimer, M.
Utopia unlimited or the complete musician and his world. 11pp. 30c (Univ. Cape Town. Inaugural lec., 30) Univ Cape Town Lib 1975 SA

Brindley, M.
Western Coloured Township. Problems of an urban slum. 110pp. photos. R4.20 ($6.25/£3.25) Ravan 1976 SA

Brink, S.A.
Classification scheme for law books in the University of Rhodesia law library. 36pp. R$5.00 cl. (Univ. Library, Univ. of Rhodesia, New Series, 1) Univ Rhodesia Lib 1971 RH

Brink, V.H.
A genetic study of the vertebral column of the griqua. 77pp. 30c. (A v.9, no.1) Univ Stellenbosch, Lib 1933 SA

Brisbois, P.R. Raymond, Abbe.
Je t'aimerai d'un amour éternel. Manuel et guide pour le sacrement de mariage. 85pp. 28k St. Paul 1968 ZR FRE

The British Council/Thomas Nelson Nigeria Ltd.
Joint English project: cycle one. Pupils' bk. 96pp. 40k Nelson - Nig 1976 NR

British Council/Thomas Nelson Nigeria Ltd.
Joint English project: cycle one. Teachers' bk. 176pp.
N1.50 Nelson - Nig 1976 NR

The British Council/Thomas Nelson Nigeria Ltd.
Joint English project: cycle three. Pupils' bk. 96pp.
40k Nelson - Nig 1976 NR

The British Council/Thomas Nelson Nigeria Ltd.
Joint English project: cycle three. Teachers' bk. 176pp.
N1.50 Nelson - Nig 1976 NR

The British Council/Thomas Nelson Nigeria Ltd.
Joint English project: cycle two. Pupils' bk. 96pp.
40k Nelson - Nig 1976 NR

The British Council/Thomas Nelson Nigeria Ltd.
Joint English project: cycle two. Teachers' bk. 176pp.
N1.50 Nelson - Nig 1976 NR

British Red Cross Society.
Kitabu cha msaada wa kwanza. [Practical first aid]
64pp. ill. K.shs.1.20 ($1.25/50p.) EALB 1958 KE
SWA

British South Africa Company.
The British South Africa Company reports on the native
disturbances in Rhodesia, 1896-97. [Reprint of ed. 1898].
169pp. ill. pl. cl. R$10.00 (Rhodesiana Reprint
Library, Silver series, 2) Books of Rhodesia 1975 RH

Brits, J.P.
Diary of a national scout, P.J. du Toit. 122pp. R5.30
Human Science Res Council 1974 SA

Britwum, K., ed.
Oyono's "Une vie de boy". 133pp. N2.50 Ethiope
1975 NR

Britz, W.J., et al.
Re bala Sesotho. pt. 1. 64pp. ill. R1.10 Nasou
1976 SA SOS

Britz, W.J., et al.
Re bala Sesotho. pt. 2. 63pp. ill. R1.20 Nasou
1976 SA SOS

Britzius, O.
Companies Amendment Act, 1976. (Supplement to
Britzius, South African company secretarial practice.)
R1.00 Juta 1977 SA

Britzius, O.
South African commercial practice. R9.75 Juta 1971
SA

Britzius, O.
South African company secretarial practice. 2nd rev. ed.
970pp. cl. R27.00 [incl. 1976 supplement] Juta 1975
SA

Broadhurst, J.
An analysis of data on Bunaji cattle at Birnin Kudu and
Kabomo, Northern Nigeria. See: Wheat, J.D.

Broadhurst, J.
An analysis of data on Sokoto Gudali cattle at Bulassa and
Dogondaji, Northern Nigeria. See: Wheat, J.D.

Broadley, D.G.   Cock, E.V.
Snakes of Rhodesia. 176pp. col. pl. R$4.75
(Bundu series) Longman - Rhod 1975 RH

Brock, B., ed.
The Bugisu coffee industry: an economic and technical
survey. See: Wallace, I.R., ed.

Brock, B.
Education a la vie. v. 1: periode prenatale. tr. fr.
American 80pp. ill. 20k St. Paul 1974 ZR FRE

Brock, B.B., ed.   Brock, B.G., ed.
Historical Simon's Town. 240pp. ill. col. pl. cl.
R28.35 cl. (Dfl.85.00/$32.00/£16.50 cl.) Balkema
1976 SA

Brock, B.B.
A global approach to geology: the background of a
mineral exploration strategy based on significant form in
the patterning of the earth's crust. 388pp. ill. hd. fl.
67.50 Balkema 1972 SA

Brock, B.G., ed.
Historical Simon's Town. See: Brock, B.B., ed.

Brokensah, D.
Akwapim handbook. 310pp. maps. C6.50 ($6.50)
Ghana Publ Corp 1972 GH

Bromley, J.
The geology of the Ntchisi-Middle Bua area.
See: Bellingham, K.S.

Brookes, E.
A South African pilgrimage. An autobiography. 158pp.
cl. & pap. R4.50 pap. R6.90 cl. ($5.00/£2.95 pap.)
($9.00/£4.75 cl.) Ravan 1977 SA

Brookes, E.H.
The Commonwealth today. 70pp. R1.10 Univ of
Natal 1959 SA

Brookes, E.H.   Webb, C. de B.
A history of Natal. 371pp. ill. R3.30 Univ of Natal
1967 SA

Brookes, E.H.
A history of the University of Natal. 194pp. ill. cl.
R3.00 Univ of Natal 1967 SA

Brookes, E.H.   Hurwitz, N.
The native reserves of Natal. $3.75 (Natal regional
survey pub., 7) Dept Econ, Natal 1957 SA

Brookes, E.H.
White rule in South Africa 1830-1910. Varieties in
governmental policies affecting Africans. 3rd rev. ed.
223pp. cl. R13.50 Univ of Natal 1974 SA

Brooks, K.L.
Basic Bible course. 2nd ed. 44pp. 20k SIM 1970
NR

Brooks, K.L.
The Gospel of John. 2nd ed. 32pp. 20k SIM 1970
NR

Brooks, K.L.
Studies in prophecy. 32pp. 20k SIM 1964 NR

Broome, F.N.
Not the whole truth. 293pp. R2.75 Univ of Natal
1962 SA

Brosens, R.P.
La lettre. 12th ed. 90pp. 20k St. Paul 1970 ZR
FRE

Brosnahan, L.F.
Genes and phonemes. 12pp. 30k Ibadan UP 1957
NR

Brosnahan, L.F.   Spenser, W.
Language and society. 16pp. 50k Ibadan UP 1962
NR

Broster, J.N.   Smit, J.J.
Good news - scripture for standard seven. ill. maps.
R3.95 Maskew Miller 1976 SA

Brou de Biano, K.
Mensonges des soirs d'Afrique. 64pp. CFA150
(Coll. Pour Tous) CLE 1973 CM FRE

Brown, A.G.
Some kyanite deposits around Lusaka. 60n (Dept. of
Geological Survey. Economic Reports, 12) Geol Survey
- Zam 1966 ZA

Brown, B.
A guide to the constitutional development of Kenya.
K.shs.10.00 Kenya Inst Admin KE

Brown, B.A.
Revision arithmetic for common entrance examinations
(with objective test papers) 148pp. ill. N1.45
Longman - Nig 1973 NR

Brown, B.H.M.
Christian unity and joint action in the mission of the church.
50c. (Peter Ainslie Memorial lec. 19) Rhodes Univ Lib
1970 SA

Brown, D.
Evangelism. East African ed. 32pp. T.shs.1.00
Central Tanganyika 1969 TZ

Brown, D.
Uinjilisti. [Evangelism.] 32pp. T.shs.2.50 Central
Tanganyika 1967 TZ SWA

Brown, G., ed.
Africa in the nineteenth and twentieth centuries.
See: Anene, J.C., ed.

Brown, G.N.
All Africa readers: complete set (including free teacher's notes and map) ill. map. N2.00 Pilgrim 1970 NR

Brown, G.N.
All Africa readers: teacher's bk. 16pp. ill. 17k Pilgrim 1970 NR

Brown, G.N.
All Africa readers: Wall map. map. 17k Pilgrim 1970 NR

Brown, G.N.
Botswana: the first man and fire. 16pp. ill. 17k (All Africa readers, 11) Pilgrim 1970 NR

Brown, G.N.
Chad: the beautiful girl and the snake. 16pp. ill. 17k (All Africa readers, 2) Pilgrim 1970 NR

Brown, G.N.
Congo: the mongoose, the buffalo and the crocodile. 16pp. ill. 17k (All Africa readers, 4) Pilgrim 1970 NR

Brown, G.N.
Ethiopia: the tower of baboons. 16pp. ill. 17k (All Africa readers, 12) Pilgrim 1970 NR

Brown, G.N.
Ghana: Ananse. 16pp. ill. 17k (All Africa readers, 3) Pilgrim 1970 NR

Brown, G.N.
Kenya: the jackal and the camel. 16pp. ill. 17k (All Africa readers, 1) Pilgrim 1970 NR

Brown, G.N.
Malagasy: the cardinal bird. 16pp. ill. 17k (All Africa readers, 5) Pilgrim 1970 NR

Brown, G.N.
Nigeria: to see or to walk. 16pp. ill. 17k (All Africa readers, 6) Pilgrim 1970 NR

Brown, G.N.
Senegal: the hare and the termites. 16pp. ill. 17k (All Africa readers, 7) Pilgrim 1970 NR

Brown, G.N.
Sierra Leone: Ee Ar Ee. 16pp. ill. 17k (All Africa readers, 8) Pilgrim 1970 NR

Brown, G.N.
Uganda: the chief of the night. 16pp. ill. 17k (All Africa readers, 9) Pilgrim 1970 NR

Brown, G.N.
Zambia: the clever hare. 16pp. ill. 17k (All Africa readers, 10) Pilgrim 1970 NR

Brown, G.R. Rix, L.B. Chennells, A.J.
Arthur Shearly Cripps. A selection of his prose and verse. 308pp. R$2.75 (Mambo Writers Series, English section, 1) Mambo 1976 RH

Brown, J.
Typewriting examinations: aids to success. 135pp. ill. N2.00 OUP - Nig 1975 NR

Brown, J.A.
A gathering of eagles: the campaigns of the South African Air Force in Italian East Africa 1940-1941. 2 342pp. photos./maps. hd. R5.00 Purnell 1970 SA

Brown, J.A.
Nuka atapon. 3rd ed. ill. K.shs.0.10 EALB 1956 KE LUO

Brown, J.A.
The return. 191pp. hd. R3.50 Purnell 1971 SA

Brown, J.A.
The snare. R6.95 pap. Purnell 1976 SA

Brown, J.A.
South African forces World War II. v.4 Eagles strike. R9.50 Purnell 1976 SA

Brown, L.
East African coasts and reefs. 128pp. col. photos. maps. K.shs.55.00 ($12.00) EAPH 1975 KE

Brown, L.
East African mountains and lakes. 122pp. photos. K.shs21.00 ($10.40) EAPH 1971 KE

Brown, L.
The mystery of the Flamingos. 132pp. K.shs.50.00 EAPH 1974 KE

Brown, L.
The partnership of Christian marriage. K.shs3.00 ($1.50/60p.) EALB 1963 KE

Brown, L.H.
A checklist of the birds of Ethiopia. See: Urban, E.K.

Brown, L.H.
A checklist of the birds of Ethiopia. See: Urban, E.K.

Brown, L.H.
Conservation for survival: Ethiopia's choice. 96pp. maps. ($3.00/£1.20) Addis Ababa UP 1973 ET

Brown, M.
A helping hand. 96pp. 90pes. (25p.) Africa Christian 1969 GH

Brown, M.
Je, naweza kukusaidia? [A helping hand.] 92pp. T.shs.4.50 Central Tanganyika 1976 TZ SWA

Brown, M.J.
Introduction to social group work in Africa. 85pp. K1.75 (£1.00) Inst Afr Stud - Lusaka 1969 ZA

Brown, N.
The last laugh. 51pp. ill. K.shs4.80 ($2.20) EAPH 1970 KE

Brown, N.
Notes on Gogol's "The Government Inspector". 44pp. K.shs.6.00 (Heinemann's Student's Guides) Heinemann Educ - Nair 1974 KE

Brown, N.
Notes on Wole Soyinka's "Kongi's Harvest". 48pp. K.shs.6.00 (Heinemann's Student's Guides) Heinemann Educ - Nair 1973 KE

Brown, N.
The play of the shepherds. 56pp. ill. K.shs4.80 ($2.20) EAPH 1971 KE

Brown, N.
The sacrifice. 44pp. ill. K.shs3.50 ($1.50) EAPH 1972 KE

Brown, R., ed.
The Zambesian past: studies in Central African history. See: Stokes, E.T., ed.

Brown, R.
The Ndebele succession crisis, 1868-1877. 75c. (Local series pamphlets, 5) Central Africa Hist Assoc 1962 RH

Brown, S.
Architects and others: an annotated list of people of South African interest appearing in the Royal Institute of British Architects Journal. 1880-1925. 31pp. R1.65 Dept Bibliog, Lib & Typo 1969 SA

Brown, S. Allison, A.A. Stewart, M.
Guided social studies. Standard 5. 256pp. pl. maps. R1.80 Shuter 1975 SA

Brown, T.M., ed.
Directory of Malawi libraries. See: Made, S.M., ed.

Brown, W.
You and your children: help for Christian parents. K.shs2.00 EALB 1963 KE

Brown, W.H.
On the South African frontier. [Reprint ed. 1899]. 457pp. ill. photos. maps. cl. R$11.55 cl. (Rhodesiana Reprint Library, Gold Series, 12) Books of Rhodesia 1970 RH

Brownlee, F.
Transkeian native territories: historical records. 135pp. R2.80 Lovedale 1923 SA

Brownlee, M.
The lives and work of South African missionaries. 32pp. 80c. Univ Cape Town Lib 1969 SA

Brownlees, W.T.
  Reminiscences of a Transkeian. 156pp. ill. photos.
  maps. hd. R5.50 Shuter 1975 SA
Brownwood, D.O.
  Selected East African cases on commercial law.
  K.shs.17.00 Kenya Inst Admin 1968 KE
Brownwood, D.O.
  Trade unions in Kenya. 34pp. K.shs.6.50 Kenya Inst
  Admin 1969 KE
Bru, G.
  Départ en coopération. 108pp. CFA390 (Point de
  vue, 12) CLE 1972 CM FRE
Bruins, S.
  Catalogue of basic books for a South African natural
  history museum based on the collection in the South
  African Museum. 92pp. R1.00 Univ Cape Town Lib
  1965 SA
Brumfit, C.J., ed.
  A handbook for English teachers. 110pp. T.shs.6.00
  Inst Educ - Dar 1969 TZ
Brundmann, H.E.
  What kind of patent law does Tanzania need? 18pp.
  T.shs12.00 ($3.00) (Research pap., 68.15) Econ Res
  Bur - Tanz 1968 TZ
Bruneau, X.
  Roboa-Nat, le sorcier malgré lui. 72pp. CFA350 CLE
  1972 CM FRE
Brunel, H.
  Mauritius. col. photos. R10.95 Purnell 1976 SA
Bryant, A.T.
  Zulu medicine and medicine-men. 2nd ed. 115pp. cl.
  R3.25 Struik 1970 SA
Bryant, A.T.
  The Zulu people: as they were before the white man
  came. 769pp. cl. R5.25 Shuter 1950 SA
Bryce, V.K.
  Askari wa polisi. [The policeman] 3rd ed. 9pp. ill.
  K.shs.0.50 ($1.00/40p.) (Kazi za wanadamu (The work
  of men), 2) EALB 1967 KE SWA
Bryce, V.K.
  Dreva wa gari la moski. [The railway engine driver] 3rd
  ed. 9pp. ill. K.shs.0.50 ($1.00/40p.) (Kazi za
  wanadamu (The work of men), 3) EALB 1967 KE SWA
Bryce, V.K.
  Mkulima. [The farmer] 3rd ed. 9pp. ill. K.shs.0.50
  ($1.00/40p.) (Kazi za wanadamu (The work of men), 5)
  EALB 1967 KE SWA
Bryce, V.K.
  Mtu wa simu. [The telegraphist] 3rd ed. 9pp. ill.
  K.shs.0.50 ($1.00/40p.) (Kazi za wanadamu (The work
  of men), 1) EALB 1967 KE SWA
Bryce, V.K.
  Mwalimu. [The teacher] 3rd ed. 8pp. ill.
  K.shs.0.50 ($1.00/40p.) (Kazi za wanadamu (The work
  of men), 8) EALB 1967 KE SWA
Bryce, V.K.
  Mwuguzi. [The nurse] m3rd ed. 12pp. ill.
  K.shs.0.50 ($1.00/40p.) (Kazi za wanadamu (The work
  of men), 6) EALB 1967 KE SWA
Bryce, V.K.
  Tarishi. [The messenger] 3rd ed. ill. K.shs.0.50
  ($1.00/40p.) (Kazi za wanadamu (The work of men), 7)
  EALB 1967 KE SWA
Bryer, S.
  Sometimes, suddenly. 112pp. R1.80 (Mantis Poets,
  2) Philip 1973 SA
Bryer, V., comp.
  Professor Percival Robson Kirby. gratis Johannesburg
  Public Lib 1965 SA
Bryer, V.
  Professor Percival Robson Kirby, 1921-1954. A
  bibliography of his works. 70pp. gratis Dept Bibliog,
  Lib & Typo 1965 SA

Buah, F.K.   Asante, S.A.
  Common entrance objective tests in history and civics.
  64pp. ill. 50k Macmillan NR
Buah, F.K.
  History notes -- West Africa since A.D. 1000.Bk. 1: the
  people. 263pp. ill. N1.60 Macmillan 1974 NR
Buah, F.K.
  The world since 1750. 1, 3 bks 183pp. maps photos.
  ill. N1.10 Macmillan 1966 NR
Buah, F.K.
  The world since 1750. 2, 3bks 246pp. maps ill.
  photos. N1.30 Macmillan 1967 NR
Buah, F.K.
  The world since 1750. 2nd rev. ed. 352pp. ill. maps
  photos. N1.70 Macmillan 1975 NR
Buah, F.K.
  The world since 1750. 3, 3 bks 224pp. ill. maps
  photos. N1.70 Macmillan 1969 NR
Buakasu, T.K.M.
  L'impensé du discours, Kindoki et Nkisi en pays Kongo du
  Zaire. 321pp. Z3.50 Press Univ Zaire 1973 ZR FRE
Buchanan, J.L.
  The quantum of damages in bodily and fatal injury cases.
  See: Corbett, M.M.
Buchanan, J.L.
  The quantum of damages in bodily and fatal injury cases.
  1976 Annual Supplement. See: Corbett, M.M.
Buchanan, W.M.
  Bantu siderosis with special reference to Rhodesian
  Africans. 30pp. 50c pap. (Fac. of Medicine, Univ. of
  Rhodesia, Research Lec. Series, 1) Univ Rhodesia Lib
  1967 RH
Buchele, W.F.
  No starving billions: the role of agricultural engineering in
  economic development. 35pp. C1.00 ($1.00/50p.)
  (Inaugural lecture) Ghana UP 1969 GH
Buchell, C.J.
  Art and craft in the primary school. 64pp. ill. pl.
  K.shs.9.50 Longman - Ken 1975 KE
Bugengo, J.   Rwelengera, J.B.K.   Mutangira, J.P.B.
  The Nyarubanja system and Ujamaa villages development
  in West Lake region - Tanzania. 60pp. T.shs.12.00
  ($3.00) (Research pap., 76.1) Econ Res Bur - Tanz
  1976 TZ
Buhriy, H.B.A.
  Utenzi wa vita vya wadachi kutamalaki Mrima. [The
  German conquest of the coast] 2nd ed. 84pp.
  K.shs.4.30 ($1.75/70p.) EALB 1960 KE SWA
Buis, R.
  Religious beliefs and white prejudice. 64pp. R2.40
  ($3.30/£1.75) Ravan 1974 SA
Buitron, A.
  Community development in Latin America: a practical
  guide for community development workers. 42pp.
  K.shs.2.30 ($2.00/80p.) EALB 1966 KE
Bukenya, A.
  The people's bachelor. 176pp. K.shs9.50 ($2.60)
  EAPH 1972 KE
Bullen, P.
  The education and training of land surveyors. 20pp.
  R1.60 Dept Bibliog, Lib & Typo 1968 SA
Bulley, M., comp.
  Literature of sickle-cell and allied hereditary disorders: an
  annotated bibliography. 55pp. C1.50 (Univ. of
  Ghana, Dept. of Library & Archival Studies, occas. paps.
  12) Dept Lib Stud - Univ Ghana 1974 GH
Bulpin, T.V.
  Discovering Southern Africa. 2nd ed. R15.00 Bulpin
  1970 SA
Bulpin, T.V.   Miller, P.
  The great trek. 2nd ed. ill. R3.50 Bulpin 1969 SA
Bulpin, T.V.
  The ivory trail. 7th ed. R5.00 Bulpin 1967 SA

Bulpin, T.V.
Lost trails of the Transvaal. 2nd ed. ill. pl. R9.00
Bulpin 1969 SA

Bulpin, T.V.
Natal and the Zulu country. 3rd ed. 473pp. col. ill.
R9.00 Bulpin 1969 SA

Bulpin, T.V.
Tickey. 242pp. ill. R15.00 Bulpin 1976 SA

Bulteel, S.
Kafue textiles of Zambia. 9pp. 60n. ($1.50)
(Zambia Geographical Assoc, special publ., 3) Zambia
Geog Assoc 1972(?) ZA

Bulundu. Pelende.
Il mit du poison dans le vin de ses frères. Mythes suku.
Textes suku-Français. 152pp. map. (DM26.00)
(CEEBA. série II, Mémoires et Monographies, 30) CEEBA
1976 ZR FRE

Bunduki, K.N.
Essai de lexique linguistique. Français-ciluba. 247pp.
Z2.00 CELTA 1975 ZR FRE

Bunyan, J.
Kristofonyo gbefaa. [Pilgrim's progress] 107pp.
50pes. Waterville 1970 GH GAA

Bunyan, J.
Rugendo rua mugendi. [Pilgrim's progress] 2nd ed.
88pp. K.shs.2.00 ($1.25/50p.) EALB 1960 KE KIK

Burawoy, M.
The colour of class in the copper mines. From African
advancement to Zambianisation. 121pp. K2.50
(£1.44) (Zambian paps., 7) Inst Soc Res - Zam 1972
ZA

Burawoy, M.
Constraint and manipulation in industrial conflict. A
comparison of strikes among Zambian workers in a
clothing factory and the mining industry. 60pp. K1.50
(85p) (Inst. African Studies, Univ. of Zambia,
communications, 10) Inst Afr Stud - Lusaka 1975 ZA

Burchall, J.
An evaluation of primary productivity studies in the
Continental Shelf region of the Agulhas Current near
Durban. (1961-1966) 44pp. R1.20 Oceanographic
Res Inst 1968 SA

Burchall, J.
Primary production studies in the Agulhas Current region
off Natal. 16pp. R1.10 Oceanographic Res Inst 1968
SA

Burchell, E.M. Hunt, P.M.A.
South African criminal law and procedure: general
principles of criminal law. 1, 4v. hd. R20.00 Juta
SA

Bureau INADES. Formation au Zaire.
Boloni mobimba mpe bokoli bibwele. [Agriculture
générale et élevage. Cours par correspondance.] 10 pts.
376pp. Z4.00 CEPAS 1977 ZR LIN

Bureau of Ghana Languages.
Akuapem-Twi language guide. 5th ed. 47pp. map.
50pes. Bur Ghana Lang 1975 GH

Bureau of Ghana Languages.
Ananse akuamoa. [Ananse stories.] 3rd ed. vol. 1
24pp. ill. 35pes. Bur Ghana Lang 1974 GH TWI

Bureau of Ghana Languages.
Ananse akuamoa. [Ananse stories.] 3rd ed. vol. 2
24pp. ill. 35pes. Bur Ghana Lang 1974 GH TWI

Bureau of Ghana Languages.
Asante-Twi language guide. 50pp. map. 50pes. Bur
Ghana Lang 1975 GH

Bureau of Ghana Languages.
Dangme ngmami bc. [Dangme orthography.] 38pp.
C1.00 Bur Ghana Lang 1976 GH DAG

Bureau of Ghana Languages.
Ewe language guide. 4th ed. 53pp. map. 50pes.
Bur Ghana Lang 1974 GH EWE

Bureau of Ghana Languages.
Fante language guide. 4th ed. 52pp. map. 50pes.
Bur Ghana Lang 1975 GH FAT

Bureau of Ghana Languages.
Ga language guide. 5th ed. 49pp. map. 50pes.
Bur Ghana Lang 1974 GH GA

Bureau of Ghana Languages.
Kasem language guide. 3rd ed. 60pp. 50pes. Bur
Ghana Lang 1977 GH

Bureau of Ghana Languages.
Nileegbe 1. [Reading book for primary class 1.] 24pp.
ill. C1.00 Bur Ghana Lang 1976 GH GAA

Bureau of Ghana Languages.
Nileegbe shishijee wolo. [Language primer.] 52pp. ill.
75pes. Bur Ghana Lang 1973 GH GAA

Bureau of Ghana Languages.
Nimdee kwan dwumadi nhoma. [Workbook for primary
class 1.] 40pp. ill. C1.20 Bur Ghana Lang 1976 GH
TWI

Bureau of Ghana Languages.
Yeno chona-boboom tcnc. [Picture book for primary
class 1.] 52pp. ill. C2.50 Bur Ghana Lang 1976 GH
KAE

Bureau of Market Research.
The minimum and supplemented living levels of non-whites
residing in the main and other selected urban areas of the
Republic of South Africa - August 1976. 90pp. R50.00
(Bureau of Market Research, Research Reports, 52) Bur
Market Res 1976 SA

Bureau of Resource Assessment.
Economic report of Kigoma region. 28pp. T.shs.15.00
(Research report, 38) Bur Res Assess - Tanz 1971 TA

Bureau of Resource Assessment.
Economic report of Morogoro region. 31pp.
T.shs.15.00 (Research report, 39) Bur Res Assess -
Tanz 1971 TZ

Bureau of Resource Assessment.
Economic report of Mwanza region. 26pp. T.shs.15.00
(Research report, 37) Bur Res Assess - Tanz 1971 TZ

Bureau of Resource Assessment.
Economic report on Ruvuma region. 34pp.
T.shs.15.00 (Research report, 36) Bur Res Assess -
Tanz 1971 TZ

Bureau of Resource Assessment.
Economic report on Sungida region. 19pp.
T.shs.15.00 (Research report, 34) Bur Res Assess -
Tanz 1971 TZ

Bureau of Resource Assessment.
Economic report on Tanga region. 41pp. T.shs. 15.00
(Research report, 35) Bur Res Assess - Tanz 1971 TZ

Bureau Organisation et Méthodes.
Documents comptables officiels de fin d'exercice.
CFA5,000 (F100.00) Nouv Ed Afric 1976 SG FRE

Bureau Organisation et Méthodes.
Plan comptable Sénégalais. 270pp. CFA7,500
(F150.00) Nouv Ed Afric 1976 SG FRE

Bureau, R.
Initiation africaine - supplément de philosophie et de
sociologie à l'usage de l'Afrique noire. See: Tolra, P.L.

Bureau, R.
Trois etudes sur le Harrisme. 200pp. CFA1,200
(F24.00) Inst Ethno-Socio 1971 IV FRE

Burger, A.P.
Hall on water rights. See: Hall, C.G.

Burger, R. Gonin, C.R.
A proposed method to evaluate sugar-cane bagasse for
useful fibre. 32pp. R5.00 (CSIR Special Report,
HOUT 110) CSIR 1975 SA

Burgers, A.C.J.
Xenopus Laevis: a supplementary bibliography.
See: Zwarenstein, H.

Burgess, Y.
A life to live. 184pp. R5.50 Donker 1973 SA

Burgess, Y.
The strike. A novel. 220pp. cl. R5.50 (£3.50)
Donker 1975 SA

Burke, E.E., ed.
Guide to the historical manuscripts in the National
Archives. See: Baxter, T.W., ed.

Burke, E.E., ed.
The journals of Carl Mauch, 1869-72. tr. F.O. Bernhard
314pp. R$6.30 Nat Archives - Rhod 1969 RH

Burke, R.M.
Pounds and pennies: how to save, spend and give. 5
5thed. 20pp. 10k Daystar 1967 NR

Burki, B.
La case des Chrétiens. 128pp. ill. CFA300.00 (Coll.
Théologique CLE) CLE 1973 CM FRE

Burkill, T.A.
Faith, knowledge and cosmopolitanism. 8pp. 30c
Univ Rhodesia Lib 1971 RH

Burlot, J.
Rabat. Dir12.00 (Collection "Découverte", 2) Ed La
Porte 1973(?) MR FRE

Burman, J. Levin, S.
The Saldanha Bay story. 165pp. ill. pl. R7.50 cl.
Human and Rousseau 1974 SA

Burman, J.
Strange shipwrecks of the southern seas. 245pp. ill.
photos. cl. R4.95 Struik 1968 SA

Burnett, B.B.
Lambeth 1958 and reunion: an Anglican version. 50c.
(Peter Ainslie Memorial lec., 10) Rhodes Univ Lib 1959
SA

Burnett, D.S.
Revision notebook of East African geography. 64pp.
maps. K.shs5.25 OUP-Nairobi 1969 KE

Burney-Nicol, M., ed.
Sierra Leone nursery schools art. 12pp. photos. 75c.
Fourah Bay Bkshp 1966 SL

Burnham, F.R.
Scouting on two continents. [Reprint of ed. 1926].
370pp. pl. cl. R$11.25 (Rhodesiana Reprint Library,
Silver series, 4) Books of Rhodesia 1975 RH

Burnham, W.
Chronology of church history. 132pp. K.shs.17.00
($2.15 pap.) Evangel 1976 KE

Burnton, R.
The work of Dr. Arthur E.H. Bleksley. 47pp. R2.45
Dept Bibliog, Lib & Typo 1970 SA

Burquest, D.A.
A preliminary study of Angas phonology. 52pp. N1.50
($2.60/£1.00) (Studies in Nigerian languages, 1) Inst
Ling-ABU 1971 NR

Burrell, T.D.
South African patent law and practice. 475pp. R27.25
cl. Butterworths 1972 SA

Burrow, J.
Travels in the wilds of Africa. 96pp. ill. hd. fl. 22.50
Balkema 1971 NR

Burrow, P.C.
Johannesburg's coloured community with especial
reference to Riverlea. See: Randall, P.

Burrows, E.H.
A history of medicine in South Africa. 389pp. ill. hd.
fl. 45.00 Balkema 1958 SA

Burrows, E.H.
The Moodies of Melsetter. 204pp. ill. hd. fl. 22.50
Balkema 1960 SA

Bursell, E.
A prospect of tsetse flies. 26pp. 30c Univ Rhodesia
Lib 1968 RH

Burton, A.W.
The highlands of Kaffraria. 2nd ed. 90pp. ill. pl. cl.
R3.90 Struik 1968 SA

Burton, W.F.P.
Teachings from the word of God. 113pp. K.shs.4.00
Evangel 1969 KE

Burtt, B.L.
Streptocarpus: a genus of gesneriaceae. See: Hilliard,
O.M.

Buruga, J.
The abandoned hut. 96pp. K.shs24.00 cl.
K.shs6.00 pap. ($5.80 cl.) ($2.40 pap.) EAPH 1969
KE

Bush, S.F.
Honoris causa. 120pp. cl. R4.20 Univ of Natal 1967
SA

Bushrui, S.B., ed.
W.B. Yeats 1865-1965: centenary essays on the art of
W.B. Yeats. See: Maxwell, D.E.S., ed.

Bussière, P.
Etude géologique et prospection dans les régions de
Mahazoma - Antanimbaritsara - Maevatanana
Minéralisations ferrifères et chronifères. 22pp. pl. photo.
FMG425 (F8.50) (Série Documentation, 154) Service
Geol - Mad 1961 MG FRE

Butcher, D.A.P.
Tema Manhean: a study of resettlement. See: Amarteifio,
G.W.

Butere Girls School.
Loice: high school student. 148pp. ill. K.shs7.50
($2.00) EAPH 1970 KE

Buthelezi, Chief M.G.
White and black nationalism. Ethnicity and the future of the
Homelands. 21pp. 60c ($1.45) (Hoernle Memorial
Lecture) SA Inst of Race Relations 1974 SA

Buthelezi, G.
Isizulu a incwadi yesibili. See: Ndlovu, R.S.

Buthelezi, G.
Isizulu a incwadi yokuqala. See: Ndlovu, R.S.

Buthelezi, G.G.N.C. Made, E.H.A.
Isizula senganyama. [The king's Zulu] Ibanga, 5
116pp. Shuter 1965 SA ZUL

Buthelezi, G.G.N.C. Made, E.H.A.
Isizulu sengonyama. [The king's Zulu] Ibanga, 1
80pp. 35c. Shuter 1965 SA ZUL

Buthelezi, G.G.N.C. Made, E.H.A.
Isizulu sengonyama. [The king's Zulu] Ibanga, 2
96pp. 35c. Shuter 1965 SA ZUL

Buthelezi, G.G.N.C. Made, E.H.A.
Isizulu sengonyama. [The king's Zulu] Ibanga, 3
80pp. 35c. Shuter 1965 SA ZUL

Buthelezi, G.G.N.C. Made, E.H.A.
Isizulu sengonyama. [The king's Zulu] Ibanga, 4
96pp. 45c. Shuter 1965 SA ZUL

Buthelezi, G.G.N.C. Made, E.H.A.
Isizulu sengonyama. [The king's Zulu] Ibanga, 6
128pp. 55c Shuter 1965 SA ZUL

Butler, B.H.
Teach us to pray. 52pp. 20k SIM 1966 NR

Butler, E. Dylak, T.
The earth and its wonders - for the children of Africa. bk.
3 129pp. ill. maps. R1.40 pap. Mazenod Inst 1976
LO

Butler, G., ed.
The 1820 settlers. 366pp. ill. R18.00 cl. Human and
Rousseau 1974 SA

Butler, G., ed.
A book of South African verse. 272pp. R4.20
OUP-SA 1968 SA

Butler, G., ed.
When boys were men. 296pp. maps ill. R2.90
OUP-SA 1969 SA

Butoyi, C.I.
Comprehensive book for junior secondary classes
Kiswahili. 130pp. K.shs.11.00 Textbook Ctre 1977
KE

Butterworths, South Africa.
Butterworths consolidated legal service. [Collection of Acts, full details from publisher.].   R115.00 with binder R110.00 set   Butterworths SA

Butterworths, South Africa.
Butterworths index and noter-up to South African Law Reports, 1947-72. 2 v. 1349pp.   R44.00 Butterworths 1972 SA

Butterworths, South Africa.
Butterworths South African income tax legislation service. R3.00 binder   R15.00   Butterworths SA

Butterworths, South Africa.
Butterworths taxation service for Rhodesia.   R25.50 Butterworths SA

Butterworths, South Africa.
Lawyer's pocketbook.   310pp. hd.   R11.75 Butterworths 1971 SA

Butterworths, South Africa.
Pothier on partnership.   rep. 1854 ed.   156pp.   R6.25 Butterworths 1970 SA

Buttner, J.D.
Account of the Cape/Brief description of Natal/Journal extracts on East Indies. 168pp. hd.   fl. 20.25 Balkema 1970 NR

Butzer, K.W., ed.   Cooke, H.B.S., ed.   Clark, J. D., ed.
The geology, archaeology and fossil mammals of Cornelia, O.F.S. 85pp.   R2.50   (Memoirs van die Nasionale Museum, 9) Nasionale Museum 1974 SA

Buys, J.G.   van Rooyen, A.M.   van der Merwe, J.P.
The dimensional stability of single jersey fabrics from woolrich blends. 10pp.   R2.50   (SAWTRI Technical Reports, 221) SAWTRI 1974 SA

Buys, J.G.   Hunter, L.
The influence of certain machine settings on the knitting performance of all-wool yarn on some double jersey machines. 24pp.   R2.50   (SAWTRI Technical Reports, 233) SAWTRI 1974 SA

Buyu, J.
Certificate Kiswahili digest.   See: Parkar, A.

Buyu, J.O.
A thousand fireflies. 66pp.   K.shs.7.25   Longman - Ken 1974 KE

Bvuma, E.
Shumba yembongoro. [A mule in a lion's skin.] 12pp. pl.   3c Rhod Lit Bur 1976 RH SHO

Bwantsa-Kafungu.
Esquisse grammaticale de lingala.   Z1.40   Press Univ Zaire 1970 ZR FRE

Byamugisha, J.B.
Insurance law in East Africa. 2nd ed. 215pp. cl. & pap. K.shs.40.50 pap.   K.shs.81.00 cl. ($8.10/£3.25 pap.) ($15.50/£7.50 cl.) EALB 1977 KE

Byuma, F.
Ibereho Nkindi. [Sois heureux Nkindi.] 108pp.   RF20 Caritas 1972 RW KIN

C. Struik Publishers.
Cape directory, 1800. 225pp. cl.   R6.75 Struik 1969 SA

C. Struik Publishers.
Durban. [Also available in German.]. 80pp. ill. col. ill. R3.95 (Struik's All-colour Southern Africa series) Struik 1977 SA

C. Struik Publishers.
Images of South Africa. [Also available in German.]. 80pp. ill. col. ill.   R3.95 (Struik's All-colour Southern Africa series) Struik 1977 SA

C. Struik Publishers.
Report of the Select Committee on Aborigines. 2 v. 1145pp. cl.   R47.50 Struik 1966 SA

C. Struik Publishers.
South West Africa. [Also available in German.]. 80pp. ill. col. ill.   R3.95 (Struik's All-colour Southern Africa series) Struik 1977 SA

Cabot, J.   Bouquet, C.
Atlas pratique du Tchad. 77pp. maps col. maps.   ex. only Inst Nat Tchad 1974 CD FRE

Cabot, J.   Bouquet, C.
Le Tchad. Géographie. 96pp.   ex. only Inst Nat Tchad 1974 CD FRE

Cadenat, J.
Noms vernaculaires des principales formes d'animaux marins des côtes de l'Afrique occidentale française. 56pp.   CFA300 (Catalogues et Documents, 2) IFAN 1947 SG FRE

Cahill, A.F.
T.S. Eliot and the human predicament: a study in his poetry. 222pp. cl.   R3.25   Univ of Natal 1968 SA

Cahill, T.
A South African vegetarian cook book. 2nd ed. 80pp. ill. cl.   R3.90 cl. HAUM 1974 SA

Cairns, J.   Munonye, J.
Drills and practice in English language: pupil's bk. 60pp. 47k Pilgrim 1965 NR

Cairns, J.   Munonye, J.
Drills and practice in English language: teacher's bk. 80pp.   60k Pilgrim 1965 NR

Cairns, J.   Scott, A.
Middle forms objective questions in English language: with answers. 80pp.   88k Pilgrim 1967 NR

Cairns, J.   Scott, A.
Middle forms objective questions in English language: without answers. 76pp.   77k Pilgrim 1967 NR

Cairns, J.   Scott, A.   Peterside, P.D.
Objective questions in English language. 96pp.   82k Pilgrim 1966 NR

Cairns, T.   Taylor, I.R.
Cost and management accounting with programmed instruction. 2nd ed.   R14.50 Juta 1976 SA

Cairns, T.   Taylor, I.R.
Graded questions in cost and management accounting. R4.50 Juta 1965 SA

Cairns, T.
Selected questions in accounting, 1 - elementary. See: Wimble, B.J.S.

Cairns, T.
Selected questions in accounting, 2 - intermediate. See: Wimble, B.J.S.

Calburn, S.
Calburn's birds of Southern Africa. 256pp. pl. ill. hd. R10.00 Purnell 1969 SA

Calder, A.
Writers in East Africa.   See: Curr, A.

Calderwood, D.M.
Native housing in South Africa. ill. hd.   R3.00 (CSIR research reports, 124) CSIR 1953 SA

Calderwood, D.M.
Waterkloof primary school. 46pp. (CSIR research reports, 171) CSIR 1966 SA

Caldwell, W.
Meet the healer. 96pp.   K.shs.5.00 Evangel 1971 KE

Caldwell, W.
Pentecostal baptism. 84pp.   K.shs.4.80 Evangel 1971 KE

Caldwell, W.
When the world goes boom. 56pp.   K.shs.3.50 Evangel 1971 KE

Callaway, A.
Nigerian enterprise and the employment of youth: study of 225 businesses in Ibadan. 57pp.   50k (N.I.S.E.R. Monograph, 2) NISER 1973 NR

Callaway, A.C.
Indigenous business enterprise and unemployment. (N.I.S.E.R. monographs, 2) NISER 1973 NR

Callaway, G.
Pioneers in Pondoland. 119pp.   R2.00 Lovedale 1935 SA

Callaway, H.
The religious system of the Amazulu [Reprint of 1884 edition]. 448pp. ill. pl. cl. R8.40 (Africana collectanea, 35) Struik 1970 SA

Calverley, E.E.
Islam: an introduction. 2nd rev. ed. 97pp. $5.75 £E1.25 Am Univ 1974 UA

Calvet, J.L., et al.
Langage et textes. Méthode complète d'enseignement du français en Afrique, classe de 3e, livre de l'élève. CFA1,400.00 (F28.00) Nouv Ed Afric 1976 SG FRE

Calvet, L. Rotman, L. Gazio, J.
Langage et textes. Méthode complète d'enseignement du français en Afrique, classe de 6e, livre de l'élève. 192pp. CFA1,025 (F20.50) Nouv Ed Afric 1974 SG FRE

Calvet, L.J. Wisselman, R. Blandé, J.
Langage et textes. Classe de 5e. Livre de l'élève. CFA1250 Nouv Ed Afric 1975 SG FRE

Calvet, L.J. Wisselman, R. Blandé, J.
Langage et textes. Classe de 5e. Livre du maître. CFA1800 Nouv Ed Afric 1976 SG FRE

Calvet, L.J. Wisselmann, R. Blonde, J.
Langage et textes. Méthode complète d'enseignement du français en Afrique, classe de 4e, livre de l'élève. CFA1,310 (F26.20) Nouv Ed Afric 1976 SG FRE

Calvet, L.J. Rotman, L. Gazio, J.
Langage et textes. Méthode complète d'enseignement du français en Afrique, classe de 6e, livre du professeur. 334pp. CFA1,800 (F36.00) Nouv Ed Afric 1974 SG FRE

Calvet, M.J.
Les 115 mots les plus fréquents de la langue wolof. See: Diop, A.

Calvet, M.J.
De l'oralité à l'écriture. 25pp. CFA200 (C.L.A.D. Etude, 30) CLAD 1969 SG FRE

Calvet, M.J.
Etude phonétique des voyelles du wolof. 30pp. CFA320 (C.L.A.D. Etude, 14) CLAD 1965 SG FRE

Calvet, M.J.
L'expansion du wolof au Sénégal. See: Wioland, F.

Calvet, M.J. Dumont, P.
Le français au Sénégal: Interférences du wolof dans le français des élèves sénégalais. 27pp. CFA250 (C.L.A.D. Etude, 39) CLAD 1969 SG FRE

Calvet, M.J.
Le français parlé. Enquête au lycée de Thiès. 46pp. CFA250 (C.L.A.D. Etude, 4B) CLAD 1964 SG FRE

Calvet, M.J.
Le français parlé. Etude phonétique. Interférences du phonétisme wolof. 19pp. CFA250 (C.L.A.D. Etude, 4A) CLAD 1964 SG FRE

Calvet, M.J.
La transcription des langues du Sénégal. Problèmes théoriques pour le choix d'un alphabet officiel. 82pp. CFA500 pap. (C.L.A.D. Etude, 29 bis) CLAD 1969 SG FRE

Calvet, M.J.
Le wolof fondamental. 5 v. See: Diop, A.

Camara, A. Toly, O. Diouf, M.
Mathématique. Collection I.R.E.M. de Dakar. Class de sixième. 192pp. CFA1325 Africa only Nouv Ed Afric 1974 SG FRE

Camara, C.
Saint Louis du Sénégal. Evolution d'une ville en milieu africain. 292pp. photos. cap. CFA2000 (Initiations et Etudes Africaines, 24) IFAN 1968 SG FRE

Camberg, H.
Daphne Rooke. Her works and selected literary criticism. 16pp. R1.60 Dept Bibliog, Lib & Typo 1969 SA

Camdem, K.R. Nero, R.L.
Graphical work. 192pp. R1.05 Shuter 1964 SA

Cameron, R.W.
Model English tests for school certificate. 144pp. K.shs.12.50 OUP-Nairobi 1972 KE

Campbell, A.A.
'Mlimo. The rise and fall of the Matabele, by 'Mziki. [Reprint of ed. 1926]. 192pp. ill. map. cl. R$3.00 cl. Books of Rhodesia 1972 RH

Campbell, G.
Lonely warrior. 62pp. 60t Christ Lit Assoc - Mal 1975 MW

Campbell, G.H. Msiska, S.K.
Twana Twizenge. [Let the children come] 20pp. ill. 10t. (12c.) Christ Lit Assoc - Mal 1969 MW CHH

Campbell, J.
Travels in South Africa. [Reprint of 1815]. 4th ed. 402pp. pl. maps. cl. R11.50 (Africana Collectanea, 38) Struik 1974 SA

Campbell, M.J.
Development planning in local government. 20pp. 40k ($0.80/30p.) Inst Admin-Zaria 1964 NR

Campbell, M.J.
A word list of government and local government terms: English-Hausa. 23pp. 45k (40p./$0.90) Inst Admin - Zaria NR

Campbell Smith, W.
The Chilwa series of Southern Nyasaland. See: Dixey, F.

Campion, H.
The new Transkei. 158pp. ill. pl. maps. R9.90 Valiant 1976 SA

Candi, R.
Elombe mwindo. (Littérature classique, 4) Ed Mont Noir 1974 ZR FRE

Caney, L.R.
The law of novation in South Africa. 2nd ed. R12.50 Juta 1973 SA

Caney, L.R.
The law of suretyship in South Africa. 2nd ed. R13.75 Juta 1970 SA

Cantey, R.A.
The mystery of a cockcrow: a play in three acts. 47pp. 40pes. ($.65) Ghana Publ Corp 1972 GH

Canu, A., et al.
Français écrit et français parlé dans le second degré, classes de seconde du Lycée Technique d'Abidjan. v.1: analyse typologique d'un corpus écrit et oral. 125pp. CFA600 (Enseignement du français, 44) Inst Ling Appliquée 1973 IV FRE

Canu, A., et al.
Français écrit et parlé dans le second degré, classes de seconde du Lycée Technique d'Abidjan. v.2: exercices de correction et de perfectionnement. 241pp. CFA1,000 (Enseignement du français, 47) Inst Ling Appliquée 1974 IV FRE

Canu, A., et al.
Grammaire essentielle de l'enseignement primaire. 87pp. CFA500 (Enseignement du français, 42) Inst Ling Appliquée 1973 IV FRE

Canu, A., et al.
Vocabulaire essential de l'enseignement primaire, 4ème année. 236pp. CFA1,200 (Enseigement du français, 41) Inst Ling Appliquée 1973 IV FRE

Canu, A.
Vocabulaire des spécialités de l'enseignement primaire. 60pp. (Enseignement du français, 43) Inst Ling Appliquée 1974 IV FRE

Canu, A. Gregoire, H.C. Duponchel, L.
Vocabulaire essentiel de l'enseignement primaire, 5ème et 6ème années. 217pp. CFA1,000 (Enseignement du français, 46) Inst Ling Appliquée 1974 IV FRE

Canu, G.
Contes mossi actuels. Etude ethno-linguistique. 316pp. CFA3800 (Mémoires de l'IFAN, 82) IFAN 1969 SG FRE

Canu, G.
Description synchronique de la langue Mòré (dialecte de Ouagadougou) 673pp. CFA1,500 (Linguistique Africaine, 45) Inst Ling Appliquée 1973 IV FRE

Canu, G. et al.
Annales de l'université d'Abidjan. 267pp. CFA1000 (F20.00) (Série H-Linguistique, 3) Univ Abidjan 1970 IV FRE

Canu, G. et al.
Annales de l'université d'Abidjan. 180pp. CFA880 (F16.60) (Série H-Linguistique, 4) Univ Abidjan 1971 IV FRE

Canu, G.
Le français écrit en classe de sixième. 69pp. CFA500 Univ Cameroun 1969 CM FRE

Canu, G.   Renaud, P.
Initiation à l'enquête linguistique. 146pp. CFA600 Inst Ling Appliquée 1971 IV FRE

Canu, G.   Lamy, A.   Duponchel, L.
Langues négro-africaines et enseignement du français. Conférences et comptes rendus. 85pp. CFA400 (Enseignement du français, 27) Inst Ling Appliquée 1971 IV FRE

Canu, G.
Les systémes phonologiques des principales langues du Sénégal. Etude comparative. 44pp. CFA320 pap. (C.L.A.D. Etude, 13) CLAD 1965 SG FRE

Cap, M.
Brick clays in the Kasama area with particular reference to the Lukashya deposit. See: Maczka, L.

Cap, M.
Brick clays in the Mansa area. See: Legg, C.A.

Cap, M.
The Mkushi river illite clays. See: Maczka, L.

Caprile, J.P.
La dénomination des couleurs chez les mbay de Moissala. 65pp. ex. only (Etudes et Documents Tchadiens, Série C, 1) Inst Nat Tchad 1971 CD FRE

Carney, T.F.
Roman and related foreign coins with descriptions of each coin, plates and an introduction of the monetary history of Rome. Catalogue of the Sir Stephen Courtauld coin collections. 120pp. R$6.00 cl. Univ Rhodesia Lib 1964 RH

Carnochan, J.   Iwuchukwu, B.
Igbo revision course. 168pp. N1.00 OUP - Nig 1963 NR

Carpenter, O.
The development of Southern Rhodesia from the earliest times to the year 1900. 21pp. 50c. Univ Cape Town Lib 1969 SA

Carradine, J.J.
Teacher's notes for book three. 456pp. ill. B6.70 (The New Oxford English Course, 3) OUP-Addis 1971 ET

Carrara, J.
Kijana hodari. [A brave youth.] 49pp. T.shs.3.00 Africa Inland Church 1973 TZ SWA

Carrington, J.
La voix des tambours. Tr. from the English 75pp. ill. 40k CEDI 1974 ZR FRE

Carstens, E.M.J. et al.
Bacteriophage of serratia marcescans as an index of human virus survival during sewage purification. 18pp. (CSIR research reports, 241) CSIR 1965 SA

Cart, H.P.
Conception des rapports politiques au Burundi. 23pp. (Faculté des Sciences Sociales, 8) Univ Bujumbura 1966 BD FRE

Cart, H.P.   Rousson, M.
Prestige et connaissance des professions au Burundi. 25pp. (Faculté des Sciences Sociales, 11) Univ Bujumbura 1968 BD FRE

Carte, A.E.   Basson, I.L.
Hail in the Pretoria-Witwatersrand area 1962-1969. 28pp. (CSIR research reports, 293) CSIR 1969 SA

Carte, A.E.   Held, C.
Hailstorms in 1970/71. 45pp. ill. (CSIR research reports, 312) CSIR 1972 SA

Carte, A.E.
Hailstorms in Johannesburg, Pretoria and surroundings on January 15 and 16, 1964. 26pp. ill. (CSIR research reports, 228) CSIR 1964 SA

Carter, A.
Shaibu. 48pp. ill. 65k Macmillan NR

Carter, G.S.   Bennett, J.D.
The geology and mineral resources of Malawi. 62pp. map. K4.00 (Geological Survey of Malawi, Bull. 6) Geol Survey - Mal 1973 MW

Carter, W.
The home builder's guide for East Africa. 34pp. ill. K.shs.5.00 ($2.00/80p) EALB 1956 KE

Cartwright, A.P.
By the waters of the Letaba. R7.50 Purnell 1976 SA

Cartwright, A.P.
The first South Africa: the life and times of Sir Perry FitzPatrick. 2nd. ed. 256pp. photos. hd. R6.00 Purnell 1971 SA

Cartwright, A.P.
The golden age. 363pp. photos. ill. hd. R5.00 Purnell 1968 SA

Cartwright, J.F.
Maps of Southern Africa in printed books 1750-1856. 50pp. maps. R1.50 (Univ. Cape Town Libraries. Bibliographical series) Univ Cape Town Lib 1976 SA

Cartwright, M.F.
Maps of Africa and Southern Africa in printed books 1550-1750. 46pp. maps. R1.50 (Univ. Cape Town Libraries. Bibliographical series) Univ Cape Town Lib 1976 SA

Cary, R.
Countess Billie: the intriguing story of Fanny Pearson and Edmond, Vicomte de la Panouse. v. 1 216pp. ill. cl. R$5.00 Galaxie 1973 RH

Cary, R.
The Pioneer Corps. History of the Pioneer Corps from 1890 to 1975. 142pp. ill. cl. R$8.00 Galaxie 1975 RH

Cary, R.
The story of Reps: the history of Salisbury repertory players, 1931-1975. v.1. 240pp. ill. cl. & pap. R$5.00 pap. R$9.50 cl. Galaxie 1975 RH

Casalis, A.
English-Sotho vocabulary. 172pp. R. 90c. Morija 1972 LO

Casalis, E.
My life in Basutoland [Reprint of 1889 edition]. 310pp. cl. R6.50 (Africana collectanea, 38) Struik 1971 SA

Casanova, M.
Lat-Dior. 112pp. CFA250 (F5.00) Nouv Ed Afric 1976 SG FRE

Casanova, R. et al.
Annales de l'université d'Abidjan. 112pp. CFA550 (F11.00) (Série C-Sciences, 6) Univ Abidjan 1970 IV FRE

Casparie, W.A.
Modern quaternary research in Southeast Asia. vol. 2. See: Bartstra, G.J.

Cassell, A.B.
Liberian trade and industry handbook. See: Cole, H.B.

Casthelain, J.   Lassort, P.
La langue guerzé; grammaire guerzé. 423pp. CFA2000 (Mémoires de l'IFAN, 20) IFAN 1952 SG FRE

Castle, E.B.
  Principles of education for teachers in Africa.   168pp.
  K.shs.12.50   OUP-Nairobi 1965 KE
Castle, M.
  Guided general science. Standard 5.   See: Pellew, V.
Castle, M.
  Guided general science. Standard 6.   See: Pellew, V.
Castle, P.H.J.
  A contribution to a revision of the Moringuid eels.   29pp.
  ill.   R1.00   (Special publ., 3)   Inst Ichthyology 1968
  SA
Castle, P.H.J.
  Description and osteology of a new eel of the genus
  "Bathymyrus" from off Mozambique.   12pp. ill.   70c.
  (Special publ., 4)   Inst Ichthyology 1968 SA
Castle, P.H.J.
  The eel genera "Congrina" and "Coloconger" off southern
  Mozambique and their larval forms.   10pp. ill.   60c.
  (Special publ., 6)   Inst Ichthyology 1969 SA
Castle, P.H.J.
  Eggs and early larvae of the Congrid eel "Gnathiphis
  capensis" off Southern Africa.   5pp. ill.   60c.
  (Special publ., 5)   Inst Ichthyology 1969 SA
Castle, P.H.J.
  An index and bibliography of eel larvae.   121pp.   R3.00
  (Special publ., 7)   Inst Ichthyology 1969 SA
Castle, P.H.J.   Williams, G.R.
  Systematics and distribution of eels of Muraenesox group
  (Anguilliformes, Muraenesocidae)   R1.00   (Special publ.,
  15)   Inst of Ichthyology 1975 SA
Castle, P.H.J.
  Taxonomic notes on the eel "Muraenesox cinereus"
  (Forsskal, 1775) in the western Indian Ocean.   10pp. pl.
  60c.   (Special publ., 2)   Inst Ichthyology 1967 SA
Castle, P.H.J.
  Two remarkable eel-larvae from off Southern Africa.
  12pp. ill. pl.   70c.   (Special publ., 1)   Inst Ichthyology
  1967 SA
Castle, W.M.
  Gambling aspects of medicine.   20pp.   50c pap.
  (Fac. of Medicine, Univ. of Rhodesia, 1)   Univ Rhodesia
  Lib 1969 RH
Cattareo, H.
  Playing cards with Hildegard.   ill.   R3.90
  ($4.75/£2.50)   Bateleur 1975 SA
Cavvadas, J., ed.
  South African tax cases.   32v.   See: Ogilvie Thompson,
  N.
Cawood, L.
  The churches and race relations.   140pp.   60c.
  ($1.45)   SA Inst of Race Relations 1964 SA
Cawood, M.
  Cotton in fine gauge single jersey, part I: plied yarns.
  See: Robinson, G.A.
Cawood, M.
  Single jersey knitting performance, part I: a comparison of
  the knitting performance at different feeders and of various
  structures.   See: Hunter, L.
Cawood, M.P.
  The effect of atmospheric conditions on the knitting
  performance of wool worsted yards.   See: Hunter, L.
Cawood, M.P.
  Knittability of all-wool yarns on a 28 gauge single jersey
  machine.   See: Robinson, G.A.
Cawood, M.P.
  The relationship between certain properties of wool
  worsted yarns and their knitting performance, part III:
  effect of fabric structure.   See: Hunter, L.
Cawood, M.P.
  The relationship between yarn properties and knitting
  performance for cotton yarns knitted to a constant stitch
  length on single and double jersey machines.
  See: Hunter, L.

Cawood, M.P.   Dobson, D.A.   Robinson, G.A.
  Single jersey knitting performance, part II: the influence of
  machine speed, yarn input tension and yarn linear density
  on the knitting performance of fine worsted yarns knitted
  on a 28 gg single jersey machine.   8pp.   R2.50
  (SAWTRI Technical Reports, 308)   SAWTRI 1976 SA
Cazziol, R.J.
  Revision French. Objective questions with grammar
  revision: with answers.   81pp.   88k   Pilgrim 1970 NR
Cazziol, R.J.
  Revision French. Oobjective questions with grammar
  revision: without answers.   80pp.   82k   Pilgrim 1970
  NR
Cech, F.   Vrana, S.
  A non-metamict allanite from Zambia.   50n   (Dept. of
  Geological Survey. Occas. paps., 46)   Geol Survey -
  Zam 1972 ZA
Central Africa Historical Association.
  Conference on the study and teaching of history.
  R$1.80   (Local series pamphlets, 1)   Central Africa Hist
  Assoc 1960 RH
Central Africa Historical Association.
  Proceedings of the 1966 conference.   pt. 1.   R$1.50
  (Local series pamphlets, 18)   Central Africa Hist Assoc
  1967 RH
Central Africa Historical Association.
  Proceedings of the 1966 conference.   pt. 2.   R$1.20
  (Local series pamphlets, 19)   Central Africa Hist Assoc
  1967 RH
Central Tanganyika Press.
  Africa Sunday school curriculum - masomo ya junior,
  Mwaka wa Kwanza.   144pp. ill.   T.shs.4.50   Central
  Tanganyika 1966 TZ
Central Tanganyika Press.
  Africa Sunday school curriculum - masomo ya junior,
  Mwaka wa Pili.   132pp. ill.   T.shs.4.50   Central
  Tanganyika 1967 TZ
Central Tanganyika Press.
  Africa sunday school curriculum - masomo ya primary,
  Mwaka wa Kwanza.   121pp. ill.   T.shs.5.00   Central
  Tanganyika 1968 TZ
Central Tanganyika Press. .
  African Sunday school curriculum - masomo ya primary,
  Mwaka wa Tatu.   128pp. ill.   T.shs.5.50   Central
  Tanganyika 1971 TZ
Central Tanganyika Press.
  Barua kwa dada. [My sister's letters.]   54pp. ill.
  T.shs.3.50   Central Tanganyika 1945 TZ SWA
Central Tanganyika Press.
  Danieli. [Daniel.]   24pp.   T.shs.1.50   Central
  Tanganyika 1971 TZ SWA
Central Tanganyika Press.
  Daudi. [David.]   32pp. ill.   T.shs.2.00   Central
  Tanganyika 1972 TZ SWA
Central Tanganyika Press.
  Esta. [Stories of Estor, Rebeca and Ruth.]   24pp.
  T.shs.3.00   Central Tanganyika 1969 TZ SWA
Central Tanganyika Press.
  Ewe kijana. [Youth handbook.]   96pp.   T.shs.6.00
  Central Tanganyika 1971 TZ SWA
Central Tanganyika Press.
  Ibrahimu na yusufu. [Bible study guide.]   20pp.
  T.shs.2.00   (Imani Series, 2)   Central Tanganyika 1973
  TZ SWA
Central Tanganyika Press.
  Imani ya mitumenna sala ya bwana.   [Apostles Creed and
  Lord's prayer.]   20pp.   T.shs.2.00   (Imani Series, 3)
  Central Tanganyika 1973 TZ SWA
Central Tanganyika Press.
  Kazi. [Work!]   64pp.   T.shs.2.50   Central Tanganyika
  1972 TZ SWA

Central Tanganyika Press.
Kueni katika imani. [Primary school Christian education series; 16 titles, more details from publisher] T.shs.3.00 T.shs.12.00 Central Tanganyika 1973-1976 TZ SWA

Central Tanganyika Press.
Maisha ya Yesu. [Life of Christ.] T.shs.2.00 (Imani Series, 1) Central Tanganyika 1972 TZ SWA

Central Tanganyika Press.
Maswali ishirini. 24pp. T.shs.2.00 Central Tanganyika 1976 TZ SWA

Central Tanganyika Press.
Mhudumu wa Kristo. [Work of an evangelist.] 26pp. T.shs.2.00 Central Tanganyika 1967 TZ SWA

Central Tanganyika Press.
Mtoto wako anavyozaliwa. [A new child is born.] 32pp. ill. T.shs.2.50 Central Tanganyika 1974 TZ SWA

Central Tanganyika Press.
Mwalimu. [Teaching of Jesus.] 32pp. ill. T.shs.1.00 Central Tanganyika TZ SWA

Central Tanganyika Press.
My sister's letters. ill. T.shs.2.00 Central Tanganyika 1971 TZ

Central Tanganyika Press.
Petro na Paulo. [Bible study guide.] 20pp. T.shs.2.00 (Imani Series, 4) Central Tanganyika 1975 TZ SWA

Central Tanganyika Press.
Sala za nyumbani. [Family prayers.] 34pp. T.shs.2.00 Central Tanganyika 1966 TZ SWA

Central Tanganyika Press.
Tufundishe watoto - Kitabu cha I. [Let's teach children.] bk. 1 105pp. T.shs.7.50 pap. Central Tanganyika 1976 TZ SWA

Central Tanganyika Press.
Tufundishe watoto-watoto wadogo. [Sunday school teachers guide for young children.] 96pp. ill. T.shs.7.50 Central Tanganyika 1973 TZ SWA

Central Tanganyika Press.
Tutege masikio. [Sunday school leaders handbook.] 36pp. ill. T.shs.3.50 Central Tanganyika TZ SWA

Central Tanganyika Press.
Twenty awkward questions. 16pp. T.shs.2.00 Central Tanganyika 1968 TZ

Central Tanganyika Press.
Uchungaji. [Pastoralia.] 154pp. T.shs.8.00 Central Tanganyika 1969 TZ SWA

Central Tanganyika Press.
Uhai sasa. [Teaching of Christ's life.] 40pp. T.shs.1.50 (Layman's Series) Central Tanganyika 1969 TZ SWA

Central Tanganyika Press.
Yusufu. [Children's book.] 32pp. ill. T.shs.2.00 Central Tanganyika 1968 TZ SWA

Centre Africain de Littérature pour l'Afrique francophone.
Quatre poètes du Kivu. 31pp. 50k (CFA250) Centre Africain Litt 1974 ZR FRE

Centre Culturel du College Libermann.
Basogol ba nkal lè. [Recueil de textes de littérature basaa.] CFA900 Centre Cult Coll Libermann 1976 CM BAS

Centre Culturel du College Libermann.
Bwambo bwa duala. [Initiation à la lecture et à l'écriture duala.] CFA300 Centre Cult Coll Libermann 1973 CM DUA

Centre Culturel du College Libermann.
Dictionnaire Basaa-francais. CFA1,450 Centre Cult Coll Libermann 1973 CM FRE

Centre Culturel du College Libermann.
Herméneutique de la littérature orale. Actes du colloque de Yaoundé-Mvolyé 2-4 Septembre 1975. CFA1,250 Centre Cult Coll Libermann 1975 CM FRE

Centre Culturel du College Libermann.
Je parle bamiléké-jo. Manuel d'initiation au bamiléké-jo. CFA400 Centre Cult Coll Libermann 1974 CM FRE

Centre Culturel du College Libermann.
Je parle Basaa. Manuel d'initiation au basaa. 2 v. CFA1,250 Centre Cult Coll Libermann 1975 CM FRE

Centre Culturel du College Libermann.
Les langues africaines facteur de développement. Actes du séminaire pour l'enseignement des langues africaines. Douala 2-14 Juillet 1973. CFA900 Centre Cult Coll Libermann 1974 CM FRE

Centre Culturel du College Libermann.
Lenan. [Documents pour l'etude du bamileke-dschang.] CFA600 Centre Cult Coll Libermann 1973 CM BAI

Centre Culturel du College Libermann.
M'akad nâ. [Manuel d'initiation à l'ewondo en 80 leçons.] CFA850 Centre Cult Coll Libermann 1976 CM EWO

Centre Culturel du College Libermann.
Minkana beti. [Recueil de 300 proverbes en langue ewondo.] CFA900 Centre Cult Coll Libermann 1975 CM EWO

Centre Culturel du College Libermann.
Na ma-topo duala. [Livre d'initiation au duala en 73 leçons.] CFA700 Centre Cult Coll Libermann 1974 CM DUA

Centre Culturel du College Libermann.
Pé Nké. [Manuel d'initiation au bamiléké pour les élèves de 6è et 5è.] CFA325 Centre Cult Coll Libermann 1975 CM BAI

Centre de Documentation Agricole.
Index no. 1: 0001-00660, Agriculture, 1960-1975. 178pp. Centre Doc Agricole 1976 ZR FRE

Centre de Linguistique Appliquée de Dakar.
Afrique, mon Afrique. Cours moyen première année. 256pp. ill. CFA1150 Africa only Nouv Ed Afric 1974 SG FRE

Centre de Linguistique Appliquée de Dakar.
Lexique wolof. A a l. v. 1 180pp. CFA375 (C.L.A.D. Etude, 42) CLAD 1970 SG FRE

Centre de Linguistique Appliquée de Dakar.
Pour parler français. 5e année. Livre du maître 1. 318pp. CFA1,800 (F36.00) Nouv Ed Afric 1976 SG FRE

Centre de Linguistique Appliquée de Dakar.
Pour parler français. 5e année. Livre du maître 2. 272pp. CFA1,800 (F36.00) Nouv Ed Afric 1976 SG FRE

Centre de Linguistique Appliquée de Dakar.
Pour parler français. 5e année. Livre du maître 3. 256pp. CFA1,800 (F36.00) Nouv Ed Afric 1976 SG FRE

Centre de Linguistique Appliquée de Dakar.
Pour parler français. Cahier d'exercices 4ème année. 64pp. CFA255 Africa only Nouv Ed Afric 1973 SG FRE

Centre de Linguistique Appliquée de Dakar.
Pour parler français. Cahier d'exercices graphiques et sensoriels. 64pp. CFA140 Africa only Nouv Ed Afric 1973 SG FRE

Centre de Linguistique Appliquée de Dakar.
Pour parler français. Deuxième année. 2, 4 bks. 128pp. CFA615 Africa only Nouv Ed Afric 1973 SG FRE

Centre de Linguistique Appliquée de Dakar.
Pour parler français. Manuel de langage à l'usage des classes d'initiation et des cours préparatoires lere année. Livre du maître 1. 272pp. CFA900 (F18.00) Nouv Ed Afric 1975 SG FRE

Centre de Linguistique Appliquée de Dakar.
Pour parler français. Manuel de langage à l'usage des classes d'initiation et des cours préparatoires lere année. Livre du maître 2. 251pp. CFA900.00 (F18.00) Nouv Ed Afric 1975 SG FRE

Centre de Linguistique Appliquée de Dakar.
Pour parler français. Manuel de langage à l'usage des cours préparatoires du Sénégal. Livre du maître 3. 250pp. CFA900 (F18.00) Nouv Ed Afric 1975 SG FRE

Centre de Linguistique Appliquée de Dakar.
Pour parler français. Manuel de langage à l'usage des cours préparatoires du Sénégal. Livre du maître 4. 252pp. CFA900 (F18.00) Nouv Ed Afric 1975 SG FRE

Centre de Linguistique Appliquée de Dakar.
Pour parler français. Manuel de langage à l'usage du cours Elementaire. Livre du maître 5. 445pp. CFA1.670 (F23.40) Nouv Ed Afric 1975 SG FRE

Centre de Linguistique Appliquée de Dakar.
Pour parler français. Manuel de lecture à l'usage des cours elementaires lere année. Livre du maître 6. 175pp. CFA900 (F18.00) Nouv Ed Afric 1975 SG FRE

Centre de Linguistique Appliquée de Dakar.
Pour parler français. Première année. 1, 4 bks. 111pp. CFA550 Africa only Nouv Ed Afric 1973 SG FRE

Centre de Linguistique Appliquée de Dakar.
Pour parler français. Quatrième anne. 4, 4 bks. 356pp. CFA950 Africa only Nouv Ed Afric 1974 SG FRE

Centre de Linguistique Appliquée de Dakar.
Pour parler français. Troisième année. 3, 4 bks. 304pp. CFA1025 Africa only Nouv Ed Afric 1973 SG FRE

Centre de Linguistique Appliquée de Dakar.
Today's English. Classe de 2e. 191pp. CFA1,490 (F25.80) Nouv Ed Afric 1975 SG FRE

Centre de Linguistique Appliquée de Dakar.
Today's English. Leading the course. 3, 3 bks. 80pp. CFA900 (F18.00) Nouv Ed Afric 1973 SG FRE

Centre de Linguistique Appliquée de Dakar.
Today's English. Over the fence. 2, 3 bks. 96pp. CFA805 (F16.10) Nouv Ed Afric 1973 SG FRE

Centre de Linguistique Appliquée de Dakar.
Today's English: Ready! Steady! Go! 1, 3 bks. 80pp. CFA640 (F12.80) Nouv Ed Afric 1973 SG FRE

Centre de Linguistique Appliquée de Dakar.
Today's English: transcriptions phonologiques. 1, 3 bks. 24pp. CFA240 (F4.00) Nouv Ed Afric 1973 SG FRE

Centre de Linguistique Appliquée de Dakar.
Today's English: transcriptions phonologiques. 2, 3 bks. 16pp. CFA290 (F4.80) Nouv Ed Afric 1973 SG FRE

Centre de Linguistique Appliquée de Dakar.
Today's English: transcriptions phonologiques. 3, 3 bks. 8pp. CFA260 (F4.20) Nouv Ed Afric 1973 SG FRE

Centre de Littérature Evangelique.
Auprès des malades et le ministère de l'église. 192pp. CFA450 CLE 1968 CM FRE

Centre de Littérature Evangélique.
Culte des enfants pour l'Afrique d'expression française: La promesse - pour les grands. v. 1 96pp. maps photo. CFA80 CLE 1968 CM FRE

Centre de Littérature Evangélique.
Culte des enfants pour l'Afrique d'expression française: La royauté - pour les grands. v. 3 96pp. maps ill. CFA100 CLE 1970 CM FRE

Centre de Litterature Evangélique.
Culte des enfants pour l'Afrique d'expression française: La royaute - pour les petits. v. 3 96pp. map ill. CFA100 CLE 1970 CM FRE

Centre de Litterature Evangélique.
Culte des enfants pour l'Afrique d'expression française: L'alliance - pour les grands. v. 2 96pp. maps ill. CFA80 CLE 1969 CM FRE

Centre de Littérature Evangélique.
Manuel de théologie pratique. Colloque de Yaoundé. 332pp. CFA990 CLE 1971 CM FRE

Centre de Littérature Evangélique.
Programme d'enseignement biblique pour les écoles primaires. v. 3. 272pp. CFA540 CLE 1973 CM FRE

Centre de Littérature Evangélique.
Suis-moi. Catéchisme évangélique. 3rd ed. 40pp. CFA100 CLE 1970 CM FRE

Centre de Littérature Evangéliques pour l'Afrique Francophone.
Cultes des enfants pour l'Afrique d'expression française: L'alliance - pour les petits. v. 2 96pp. ill. CFA80 pap. CLE 1969 CM FRE

Centre de Publications Evangeliques.
Comment progresser dans la vie chretien. 64pp. ill. CFA100 CPE 1975 IV FRE

Centre de Publications Evangeliques.
Paraboles. 20pp. ill. CFA100 CPE 1975 IV FRE

Centre de Publications Evangeliques.
Plus fort que les fetiches. 20pp. CFA50 CPE 1975 IV FRE

Centre de Publications Evangéliques pour l'Afrique Francophone.
Le chrétien et le sport. 24pp. ill. CFA100 CPE 1976 IV FRE

Centre de Publications Evangéliques pour l'Afrique Francophone.
Etudions la Bible ensemble. 72pp. CFA300 CPE 1976 IV FRE

Centre de Publications Evangéliques pour l'Afrique Francophone.
Les héros d'hier nous parlent aujourd'hui. 64pp. CFA300 CPE 1975 IV FRE

Centre de Recherches Interdisciplinaires pour le Développement de l'Education.
Acte du colloque sur l'interdisciplinarité, 17-20 décembre 1974. 146pp. CRIDE 1975 ZR FRE

Centre d'Edition et de Diffusion Africaines.
Education civique et morale. Mémento pratique. 36pp. CFA370 CEDA 1972 IV FRE

Centre d'Edition et de Diffusion Africaines.
Géographie et économie de la Côte-d'Ivoire. 48pp. ill. FF8.80 CEDA 1974 IV FRE

Centre d'Etudes Ethnologiques Branche Anthropos.
Agriculture et élevage dans l'entre Kwango-Kasai. (Rep. du Zaire) 288pp. maps. (DM27.00) (CEEBA. série I, Rapports et Comptes Rendus, 5) CEEBA 1973 ZR FRE

Centre d'Etudes Ethnologiques Branche Anthropos.
Dieu desseécha le fleuve. Rapports du VIIe colloque de Bandundu, République du Zaire. map. (CEEBA. série I, Rapports et Comptes Rendus) CEEBA 1976 ZR FRE

Centre d'Etudes Ethnologiques Branche Anthropos.
Dieu, idoles et sorcellerie dans la région Kwango/Bas-Kwilu. 148pp. (DM16.00) (CEEBA. série I, Rapports et Comptes Rendus, 2) CEEBA 1968 ZR FRE

Centre d'Etudes Ethnologiques Branche Anthropos.
Le mariage, la vie familiale et l'éducation coutumière chez diverses ethnies de la province de Bandundu. 175pp. (DM12.00) (CEEBA. série I, Rapports et Comptes Rendus, 1) CEEBA 1966 ZR FRE

Centre d'Etudes Ethnologiques Branche Anthropos.
Mort, funérailles, deuil et culte des ancêtres chez les populations du Kwango/Bas-Kwilu. 239pp. (DM24.00) (CEEBA. série I, Rapports et Comptes Rendus, 3) CEEBA 1969 ZR FRE

Centre d'Etudes Ethnologiques Branche Anthropos.
L'organisation sociale et politique chez les Yansi, Teke et Boma. 195pp. map. (DM21.00) (CEEBA. série I, Rapports et Comptes Rendus, 4) CEEBA 1970 ZR FRE

Centre d'Etudes pour l'Action Sociale.
Mobutu et le développement, idées-forces, extraites des discours, allocutions et messages 1965-1975. 35pp. Z2.00 CEPAS 1976 ZR FRE

Centre Protestant d'Editions et de Diffusion.
Amitié entre garçons et filles, par un groupe d'écrivains
africains. Tr. from the English 46pp. 25k CEDI
1974 ZR FRE

Centre Protestant d'Editions et de Diffusion.
Vingt questions difficiles et vingt résponses franches.
24pp. 20k CEDI 1974 ZR FRE

Centre Universitaire de la Réunion.
Commentaire des principales decisions du tribunal
administratifs de la Réunion (rendues en 1974) 110pp.
(Dossiers, 3) Centre Univ Reunion 1975 RE FRE

Centres d'Etudes Ethnologiques Branche Anthropos.
Conflits familiaux et reconciliation. Rapport du VIe colloque
de Bandundu (Rep. du Zaire) 149pp. map. (DM21.00)
(CEEBA. série I, Rapports et comptes rendus, 6) CEEBA
1975 ZR FRE

Cervenka, Z.
History of the Nigerian war, 1967-1970. 172pp. maps.
N1.95 Onibonoje 1972 NR

Chacha, G.N.
Historia ya Abakuria na sheria zao. [A history of the
Abakuria and their laws] 64pp. K.shs.8.00
($2.50/£1.00) EALB 1963 KE SWA

Chacko, V.G.
School certificate revision notes: Mathematics. 112pp.
ill. N1.05 Macmillan 1975 NR

Chadha, S.S.
Effect of some climatic factors on the fluctuation of
population of "Antigastra Catalaunalis" Dupon.
(Lepidoptera Pyralidae), a pest of "Sesamum Indicum"L.
23pp. 30k (Samaru misc. pap., 48) Inst Agric
Res-Zaria 1974 NR

Chadhoro, S.J.
Tatizo la kisauni. 46pp. ill. K.shs.3.00 ($1.00)
EAPH 1969 KE SWA

Chadwick , G.
Man through the ages. Standard 7. See: Syphus, E.

Chadwick, O.
Christian unity. 50c. (Peter Ainslie Memorial lec., 14)
Rhodes Univ Lib 1963 SA

Chagula, W.K.
The economics and politics of higher education and
research in East Africa. 24pp. K.shs.2.50
($1.50/70p.) EALB 1972 KE

Chahai, F.
L'aide financière d'obédience américaine et son impact sur
le secteur public au Maroc. 228pp. cl. Dir18.00 cl.
Ed Maghreb 1976 MR FRE

Chahilu, B.P.
The herdsman's daughter. 284pp. K.shs.12.00
(African Secondary Readers, 3) EAPH 1974 KE

Chaibi, A.
Rached. 352pp. D900 Maison Tunis 1975 TI FRE

Chailley, C.
Les grandes missions françaises en Afrique occidentale.
145pp. ill. maps. CFA1200 (Initiations et Etudes
Africaines, 10) IFAN 1953 SG FRE

Chakaipa, P.
Dzasukwa mwana asina hembe. 128pp. 85c.
Longman - Rhod 1967 RH SHO

Chakaipa, P.
Garandichauya. 2nd ed. 104pp. 65c. Longman -
Rhod 1970 RH SHO

Chakaipa, P.
Karikoga gumiremiseve. 72pp. 50c. Longman - Rhod
1958 RH SHO

Chakaipa, P.
Pfumo reropa. 112pp. 60c. Longman - Rhod 1961
RH SHO

Chakaipa, P.
Rudo ibofu. [Love is blind.] 91pp. 38c Mambo
1961 RH SHO

Chakava, H.
Notes on Meja Mwangi's "Kill Me Quick". 50pp.
K.shs.6.00 (Heinemann Student's Guides) Heinemann
Educ - Nair 1976 KE

Chale, E.M.
Mass education by correspondence in Tanzania. 30pp.
T.shs.5.00 (Studies in Adult Education, 26) Inst Adult
Educ - Dar 1976 TZ

Challenge Publications.
Aure de zaman gida. [Marriage and at home.] 45pp.
Challenge 1976 NR HAU

Challenge Publications.
Bayanin Littafi mai Tsarki. [Explaining the Bible: Genesis
to Esther.] 153pp. Challenge 1976 NR HAU

Challenge Publications.
Enikozi be'mi nupe nyi. [Nupe hymn book.] 168pp.
Challenge 1976 NR NUP

Challenge Publications.
Fassarar sabon aikawari. [New Testament commentary:
John Revelation.] 214pp. Challenge 1976 NR HAU

Challenge Publications.
Idi ti mo fi gba Bibeli gbo. [Why I believe in the Bible.]
Challenge 1976 NR YOR

Challenge Publications.
Jiga Jigan littafi mai Tsarki. [Christian doctrine: Genesis -
Esther.] 143pp. Challenge 1976 NR HAU

Challenge Publications.
Littafin wakoki. [Hausa hymn book.] 318pp. Challenge
NR HAU

Challenge Publications.
Steps to baptism. 32pp. Challenge 1976 NR

Challenge Publications.
Taimako ga Fulani. [Handbook on Fulani evangelism.]
59pp. Challenge 1976 NR HAU

Challenge Publications.
Tsarin aikin fastoci. [ECWA Ministers handbook.] 74pp.
Challenge 1976 NR HAU

Challenge Publications.
Tushen bangas kiyar kirita. [Catechism.] 60pp.
Challenge 1976 NR HAU

Chamakh, N.
La santé mère - enfant. See: Hamza, B.

Chamard, P.C.
Geographie du Niger. See: Sidikou, H.A.

Chamard, P.C. Sall, M.
Le Sénégal, Géographie. 92pp. ill. CFA500
(F10.00) Nouv Ed Afric 1973 SG FRE

Chamber of Commerce and Industry of Malawi.
Industrial and trade directory of Malawi, 1976. 2nd ed.
K2.50 Chamber Comm - Mal 1976 MW

Chambre de Commerce d'Industrie et d'Artisanat de la Region
du Cap-Vert.
Le Sénégal, guide économique de l'investisseur. 120pp.
CFA1500 (F30.00) Nouv Ed Afric 1973 SG FRE

Champion, G.
The journal of the Rev. George Champion. 149pp. pl.
cl. R4.25 Struik 1967 SA

Channing, A. Van Dujk, D.E.
A guide to the frogs of South West Africa. 47pp. ill.
R1.50 (R2.00) (Monograph series, 2) Univ
Durban-Westville 1976 SA

Channon. Smith.
New general mathematics for West Africa. (Metric ed.)
bk. 1. 318pp. ill. N2.13 Longman - Nig 1973 NR

Channon. Smith.
New general mathematics for West Africa. (Metric ed.)
bk. 2. 352pp. ill. N2.38 Longman - Nig 1973 NR

Channon. Smith.
New general mathematics for West Africa. (Metric ed.)
bk. 3. 456pp. ill. N2.72 Longman - Nig 1974 NR

Channon. Smith.
New general mathematics for West Africa. (Metric ed.)
bk. 4. 352pp. ill. N2.04 Longman - Nig 1974 NR

Chant, J.F.
Bibliography of recent farm system studies in Tanzania.
T.shs.12.00 ($3.00) (Research pap., 68.31) Econ Res
Bur - Tanz 1975 TZ

Chantoux, A. Prost, A. Gontier, A.
Grammaire gourmantché. 160pp. CFA1000
(Initiations et Etudes Africaines, 23) IFAN 1968 SG FRE

Chantraine, J.
Bibliographie géologique de Madagascar, 1962-1964.
17pp. FMG165 (F3.30) (Série Documentation, 168)
Service Geol - Mad 1965 MG FRE

Chantraine, J.
Bibliographie géologique de Madagascar, 1964-1965.
15pp. FMG115 (F2.30) (Série Documentation, 173)
Service Geol - Mad 1967 MG FRE

Chantraine, J.
Etude géologique de la région d'Ambalavao. 32pp. pl.
FMG950 (F19.00) (Travaux du Bureau Géologique,
132) Service Geol - Mad 1970 MG FRE

Chantraine, J.
Etude géologique et prospection des feuilles
Janjina-Mandrosonoro. 20pp. pl. map. FMG845
(F16.90) (Travaux du Bureau Géologique, 124) Service
Geol - Mad 1966 MG FRE

Chantraine, J.
Géologie et prospection de la région:
Ambohimahasoa-Fianarantsoa-Ifanadiana. 25pp. pl.
maps. FMG1535 (F30.70) (Travaux du Bureau
Géologique, 127) Service Geol - Mad 1968 MG FRE

Chaplin, J.
Adventure with a pen. 168pp. ill. C1.20 (50p.)
Africa Christian 1972 GH

Chaplin, J.
Fiction writing: Africa Christian writers' course. v. 3
87pp. ill. 50t. (58c.) Christ Lit Assoc - Mal 1972
MW

Chapman, Dr.
Dangerous snakes and the treatment of snake bites in
South Africa. See: Visser, J.

Chapman, J.
Travels in the interior of Africa. 2 vols. 540pp. hd. fl.
67.50 (South African biographical and historical studies,
10) Balkema 1971 SA

Charette, J.
Introduction à la physique. 28pp. 45k Press Univ
Zaire 1962 ZR FRE

Charles, E.
Accounts: double entry bookkeeping. bk. 2 256pp.
N1.65 Onibonoje 1966 NR

Charlés, P.
La promotion des travailleurs nationaux à l'intérieur des
entreprises industrielles des pays en voie de
développement. Dir18.00 (Coll. du Centre d'étude du
développement économique et social, 2) Ed La Porte
1961 MR FRE

Charlewood, G.P., ed.
Gynaecology in Southern Africa. 384pp. ill. cl.
R10.00 Witwatersrand UP 1972 SA

Charo, A.K.
Toka kizazi hadi kizasi. 89pp. ill. K.shs.15.00
($3.80/£1.40) EALB 1977 KE SWA

Charsley, S.
The princes of Nyakyusa. 120pp. photos. K.shs16.00
($4.00) EAPH 1969 KE

Charsley, T.J.
Limestone resources of Malawi. (Geological Survey of
Malawi, Memoir, 6) Geol Survey - Mal 1973 MW

Chase, J.C.
The Cape of Good Hope and the Eastern Province of
Algoa Bay [Reprint of 1843 edition]. 380pp. pl. cl.
R6.30 (Africana collectanea, 25) Struik 1967 SA

Chase, J.C.
The Natal papers [Reprint of 1843 edition]. 320pp. cl.
R8.40 (Africana collectanea, 30) Struik 1968 SA

Chateh, P. Eno Belinga, T.
Catalogue des mémoires soutenus à l'Université de
Yaoundé, 1973-1975 Supplément. 34pp. CFA400
Univ Cameroun 1975 CM FRE

Chateh, P., comp. Eno Belinga, T., comp.
Catalogue des mémoires soutenus à l'Université de
Yaoundé 1965-1973. 42pp. CFA400 Univ Cameroun
1974 CM FRE

Chateh, P., comp Mahieu, F., comp. Eno Belinga, T.,
comp.
Guide des bibliothèques et centres de documentation de
Yaoundé. 26pp. CFA400 Univ Cameroun 1973 CM
FRE

Chateh, P.
Conférence permanente des bibliothèques universitaires
africaines, zone occidentale (CPBUAZOC) 43pp.
CFA500 Univ Cameroun 1976 CM FRE

Chateh, P.
Rapport d'un stage en bibliothéconomie au Canada et
d'une visite d'etude en Grande-Bretagne du 23 juillet au 23
août 1972. 33pp. CFA300 Univ Cameroun 1972 CM
FRE

Chateh, P.
Rapport sur la 39è session du congrès de la Fédération
Internationale des Associations de Bibliothécaires. 25pp.
CFA500 Univ Cameroun 1973 CM FRE

Chateh, P.
Rapports de la réunion d'experts sur la planification des
réseaux de services de documentation en Afrique (NATIS)
42pp. CFA500 Univ Cameroun 1976 CM FRE

Chatenay, D. Mathe, G. Jacquet, P.
Abatou Lilié, village Dida. Les jeunes et l'agriculture.
128pp. maps pl. CFA1,000 (F20.00) Inst
Ethno-Socio 1970 IV FRE

Chaudhry, A.
Kenyatta. A man and his people, a photographic tribute.
76pp. ill. K.shs.10.00 ($2.00) Africa Book Serv
1969 KE

Chauke, E. et al.
First Corinthians. 240pp. K.shs.20.00 ($2.50 pap.)
Evangel 1976 KE

Chaulet, C.
La mitidja autogerée. 402pp. DA20.00 SNED 1972
AE FRE

Chaulet, P. Larbaoui, D.
Acquisitions récentes sur la tuberculose en Algérie.
240pp. DA20.00 SNED 1971 AE FRE

Chaumartin, F.R. Blaize, J.P.
Africani latine discunt. 2e année. CFA1000 Nouv Ed
Afric 1975 SG FRE

Chaumartin, F.R. Blaize, J.P. Diara, F.
Africani Latine Discunt. Livre du maître. 72pp.
CFA1000 Nouv Ed Afric 1974 SG FRE

Chaumartin, F.R. Blaize, J.P. Diara, F.
Africani Latine Discunt. Première année. Livre de L'éleeve.
158pp. CFA900 Nouv Ed Afric 1974 SG FRE

Chaumartin, F.R., et al.
Africani Latine Discunt, classe de 4e livre de l'élève.
CFA1,200 (F24.00) Nouv Ed Afric 1976 SG LAT

Chavunduka, D.M.
Inkomo egulayo. [Cattle diseases.] 136pp. pl. 45c
Mambo 1971 RH NDE

Chavunduka, D.M.
Kuchengeta imbwa. [Looking after your dog.] 68pp. pl.
35c Mambo 1970 RH SHO

Chavunduka, G.L.
Social change in a Shona ward. 56pp. R$1.00
(Dept. of Sociology, Univ. of Rhodesia, 4) Univ Rhodesia
Lib 1970 RH

Cheal, C.H.
A young man to remember. 20pp. 10k Daystar 1967 NR

Chebli, H.
Pour une terre de soleil. 66pp. DA4.00 SNED 1972 AE FRE

Chekure, J.
Rudo ndimashingise. [Love is courage.] 96pp. pl. 65c. Mambo 1976 RH SHO

Chele, S.
Hedaya. 120pp. K.shs.12.75 EALB 1977 KE SWA

Chenet, G.
Poèmes du village de Toubab Dyalaw. 38pp. CFA300 (F5.00) (Coll. Woi) Nouv Ed Afric 1974 SG FRE

Chennells, A.J.
Arthur Shearly Cripps. A selection of his prose and verse. See: Brown, G.R.

Cherif, A.F.
Le royaume de Sinaban. 64pp. CFA150 (Coll. Pour Tous) CLE 1973 CM FRE

Cherif, H.
Les aventures de Sindbad. 20pp. D0.350 Maison Tunis 1975 TI FRE

Cherkaoui, A.
Le contrôle de l'Etat sur la commune. Dir35.00 (Coll. Fac. des Sciences juridiques, économiques et sociales, 20) Ed La Porte 1968 MR FRE

Cherry, R.D.
Science and complexity. 14pp. 30c (Univ. Cape Town. Inaugural lec., 13) Univ Cape Town Lib 1972 SA

Chesterman, M.R.
The law of business organisations in East and Central Africa. See: Katende, J.W.

Chheda, H.R.
Plant breeding and the conquest of hunger. N1.00 (Inaugural lecture) Ibadan UP 1977 NR

Chibanza, S.J.
Central Bantu historical texts, I. pt. 2, Kaonde history 137pp. K1.50 (75p.) Inst Afr Stud - Lusaka 1961 ZA

Chibesakunda, K.
Umulabasa. [Broadcasting] 64pp. photos. 75n. Neczam 1971 ZA BEM

Chibesakunda, L.
Teshamo. [A tragic story.] 36pp. ill. 40n. Neczam 1970 ZA BEM

Chibule, A.
The breaking branch. 35pp. ill. K.shs2.50 ($1.00) EAPH 1968 KE

Chick, J.D.
An exploratory investigation of press readership among selected students in Zaria. 49pp. N1.00 (80p./$2.00) Inst Admin - Zaria 1966 NR

Chick, J.K. Johannson, S.K.
English workshop. Pupil's book. 142pp. pl. R3.75 Shuter 1975 SA

Chick, J.K. Johannson, S.K.
English workshop. Teacher's book. 146pp. pl. R4.50 Shuter 1975 SA

Chidwayi, M.S.
Zilengwa zya Batonga. [Tonga customs] 96pp. 45n. Neczam 1972 ZA TON

Chidyausiku, P.
Karumekangu. 96pp. 55c. Longman - Rhod 1970 RH SHO

Chidyausiku, P.
Ndakambokuyambira. [I warned you before.] 63pp. 35c Mambo 1968 RH SHO

Chidyausiku, P.
Nhoroondo dzokuwanana. [Novel] 2nd ed. 64pp. ill. 65c OUP-SA 1969 SA SHO

Chidyausiku, P.
Nyadzi dzinokunda rufu. [Novel] 48pp. ill. 60c OUP-SA 1969 SA SHO

Chidyausiku, P.
Nyadzi dzinokunda rufu. [Death before dishonour.] 47pp. pl. 60c OUP - Rhod 1975 RH SHO

Chief J.B.O.
Ilesanmi modern mathematics for Nigerian schools: teacher's notes. bk. 1. See: Iweama, W.E.

Chief J.B.O.
Ilesanmi modern mathematics for Nigerian schools: teacher's notes. bk. 2. See: Iweama, W.E.

Chiezey, T.
Oji and the hen. 16pp. ill. 22k OUP - Nig 1967 NR

Chike, M.
Count not the dark hours. 68pp. 50pes. Waterville 1976 GH

Chikelu, I.
The hornbill and the tortoise. 16pp. ill. 18k OUP - Nig 1967 NR

Chilamo, S.L.
Imisango isuma ku Babemba. [Good manners in Bemba society.] 34pp. 40n. Neczam 1972 ZA BEM

Chilangwa, W.B.
Sheli. [Sheli, a thriller] 58pp. 50n. Neczam 1971 ZA BEM

Chilayi, M.S.
Chihandilu cha Kabuchi. [The adventures of Kabuchi] 58pp. 60n. Neczam 1971 ZA LUN

Child, D.
Charles Smythe-- Pioneer, premier and administrator of Natal. 288pp. cl. R5.75 Struik 1973 SA

Child, F.C.
Employment, technology and growth - role of the intermediate sector in Kenya. 100pp. K.shs.15.00 (Inst. Development Studies, occas. paps., 19) Inst Dev Stud 1976 KE

Childs, J. Moyo, J.
Ndebele. 2nd ed. Grade 1: Ekhaya lesikolo. 64pp. 60c. Longman - Rhod 1970 RH NDE

Childs, J. Moyo, J.
Ndebele. Grade 2: Zifundele izindaba. 64pp. 55c. Longman - Rhod 1969 RH NDE

Childs, J. Moyo, J.
Ndebele. Teacher's bk. grade 1. 148pp. R$1.15 Longman - Rhod 1968 RH NDE

Childs, J. Moyo, J.
Ndebele. Teacher's bk. grade 2. 96pp. 65c. Longman - Rhod 1968 RH NDE

Chilombo, A.
Iminshoni ya U.M.C.A. [The U.M.C.A. mission] 39pp. 21n. OUP - Lusaka 1957 ZA LOZ

Chiluba, J.Z.B.
Here's how to play netball. 18pp. ill. 15 Multimedia 1972 ZA

Chilver, E.M. Kaberry, P.M.
Western grassfields, linguistic notes (Camerouns) N3.00 Inst Afr Stud - Ib 1974 NR

Chima, R.
The loneliness of a drunkard. 36pp. Neczam 1973 ZA

Chima, R.
The loneliness of a drunkard. 48pp. ill. 25n. Neczam 1973 ZA

Chimulu, F.M.
Student attitudes to the University of Malawi libraries: a pilot survey. 17pp. University of Malawi Lib 1976 MW

Chinde, J.C.
Central Bantu historical texts III. Royal praises and praise names of the Lunda Kazembe of Northern Rhodesia - the meaning and historical background. tr. fr. Bemba 50n. (25p.) (Rhodes- Livingstone communications, 25) Inst Afr Stud - Lusaka 1962 ZA

Chiniquy, C.
Ile karama ya uzima. [That gracious gift of life] 26pp. T.shs.1.50 Africa Inland Church 1972 TZ SWA

Chinnery, D.N.W.
Solar water heating in South Africa. 79pp. ill. (CSIR research reports, 248) CSIR 1967 SA

Chintamunnee, M.
Hindi translation and composition for secondary classes. [Text in English and Hindi.]. Rs.5.00 Mahatma Gandhi Inst 1975 MF

Chipasula, F.
Vision and reflections. 52pp. 25n. Neczam 1972 ZA

Chipimo, E.
Our land and peoples: Summary and comprehension exercises for school certificate. See: Holmes, T.

Chipimo, E.M.
Our land and people: summary and comprehension exercises for school certificate. See: Holmes, T.

Chipinga, C.C.J.
Atambwali sametana. [A humorous play] 36pp. 22c. Shuter SA NYA

Chippindal, L.K.A.
240 common grasses of Southern Africa. [Loose leaf form, 80 grasses in three binders, plus index.]. ill. maps. R$48.00 ($150.00 pap.) M.O. Collins 1976 RH

Chiraghdin, S.
Darasa za Kiswahili. [Swahili lessons.] bk. 1 100pp. K.shs.10.00 OUP-Nairobi 1972 KE SWA

Chiraghdin, S.
Darasa za Kiswahili. [Swahili lessons] bk. 2 100pp. K.shs.11.00 OUP - Nairobi 1974 KE SWA

Chiraghdin, S.
Darasa za Kiswahili. [Swahili exercises] bk. 3 176pp. K.shs.15.00 OUP - Nairobi 1976 KE SWA

Chiraghdin, S. Mnyampala, M.E.
Historia ya Kiswahili. [The history of Kiswahili.] 104pp. K.shs.11.00 OUP - Nairobi 1977 KE SWA

Chiraghdin, S.
Kiswahili. 77pp. K.shs.7.25 (Longman Certificate Notes) Longman - Ken 1974 KE SWA

Chiraghdin, S.
Mapenzi ni kikohozi. [Love is blind.] New ed. 64pp. ill. K.shs.5.70 (Hekaya za kuburudisho) Longman - Ken 1974 KE SWA

Chirwa, C.H., ed.
Five plays from Zambia. 100pp. K2.30 Neczam 1975 ZA

Chittick, H.N.
Kilwa: an Islamic city on the East African Coast. Vol. I: History and archaeology. Vol. II: The finds. 514pp. ill. pl. col. pl. £25.00 set 2 vols. (British Inst. in Eastern Africa, Memoirs, 5) Brit Inst EA 1974 KE

Chiume, M.
Dunia Ngumu. [Difficult world] 48pp. T.shs3.00 Tanz Publ House 1969 TZ SWA

Chiume, M.W.K.
Caro ncinonono. [Historical novel.] 64pp. 55n. Neczam 1977 ZA TUM

Chiume, M.W.K.
Mbutolwe mwana wa umma. [Mbutolwe, child of the people.] 60pp. T.shs.10.00 Tanz Publ House 1973 TZ SWA

Chiume, M.W.K.
Meana wa ngoza. [Novel.] 74pp. 50n. Neczam 1972 ZA TUM

Chiware, C.M.
Mushambarichakwata. [A gluttonous person.] 16pp. pl. 5c Rhod Lit Bur 1974 RH SHO

Chodak, S.
African peasantry - a sociological concept. 14pp. ill. T.shs.1.00 (Inaugural lecture, 7) Univ Dar es Salaam 1968 TZ

Chogo, A.
Kortinimtu huyu. [A play.] 56pp. K.shs.6.50 ($3.50) Foundation 1976 KE SWA

Chogo, A.
Wala mbivu. [Play]. 28pp. K.shs.3.00 EAPH 1974 KE SWA

Chojnacki, S., comp. Ephraim, H., comp.
Ethiopian publications, 1963-64 [Text in Amharic and English.]. 64pp. ($3.00) Inst Ethiop Stud 1965 ET

Chojnacki S., comp. Ephraim, H., comp.
Ethiopian publications, 1965 [Text in Amharic and English.]. 45pp. ($3.00) Inst Ethiop Stud 1966 ET

Chojnacki, S., comp. Ephraim, H., comp.
Ethiopian publications, 1966 [Text in Amharic and English.]. 58pp. ($3.00) Inst Ethiop Stud 1967 ET

Chojnacki, S., comp. Ephraim, H., comp.
Ethiopian publications, 1967 [Text in Amharic and English.]. 50pp. ($3.00) Inst Ethiop Stud 1968 ET

Chojnacki, S., comp. Diro, M., comp.
Ethiopian publications, 1968 [Text in Amharic and English.]. 50pp. ($3.00) Inst Ethiop Stud 1969 ET

Chojnacki, S., comp. Diro, M., comp.
Ethiopian publications, 1969 [Text in Amharic and English.]. 50pp. ($3.00) Inst Ethiop Stud 1970 ET

Chojnacki, S., comp. Diro, M., comp.
Ethiopian publications, 1970 [Text in Amharic and English.]. 60pp. ($3.00) Inst Ethiop Stud 1971 ET

Chojnacki, S., comp. Diro, M., comp.
Ethiopian publications, 1971 [Text in Amharic and English.]. 62pp. ($3.00) Inst Ethiop Stud 1972 ET

Chojnacki, S., comp. Diro, M., comp.
Ethiopian publications, 1973-74. [Text in Amharic and English]. 58pp. ($3.00) Inst Ethiop Stud 1975 ET

Chojnacki, S., comp. Ephraim, H., comp.
List of current periodical publications in Ethiopia. (annual) 32pp. ($3.00) Inst Ethiop Stud ET

Chojnacki, S., comp. Pankhurst, R., comp.
Register of current research on Ethiopia and the Horn of Africa. (annual) 39pp. ($3.00) Inst Ethiop Stud ET

Chojnacki, S., comps Diro, M., comps.
Ethiopian publications., 1972. [Text in Amharic and English]. 60pp. ($5.00) Inst Ethiop Stud 1973 ET

Chojnacki, S., ed.
The dictionary of Ethiopian biography. v. I. See: Belaynesh, M., ed.

Chole, E.
A profile of the Ethiopian economy. See: Bequele, A.

Chona, B.L. Adansi, M.A.
Coconut in Ghana. 20pp. C1.50 ($1.50) (80p.) Ghana UP 1970 GH

Chona, M.M.
Kabuca uleta tunji. [Everyday brings fortune and misfortune] 84pp. 55n. Neczam 1956 ZA TON

Chongo, J.
Fumbi knoboo! [Collection of humorous stories.] 122pp. K1.50 Neczam 1973 ZA NYA

Chosack, H.
The African homelands of South Africa: a list of material held by the Jan H. Hofmeyr library. 35pp. 50c ($1.30) SA Inst of Race Relations 1976 SA

Chosack, H.
Irma Stern. See: Hurwitz, J.

Chrea, H.
Le tombeau de Jugurtha. 141pp. DA6.50 SNED 1968 AE FRE

Christeller, S.
English-Sotho: Sotho-English pocket dictionary. 144pp. 75c. cl. Morija 1966 LO

Christian Council of Nigeria.
Vision for a people. The report of the 6th assembly of the Christian Council of Nigeria August, 1973: speeches and Bible studies. N1.00 Daystar 1974 NR

Christian Council of Tanzania.
Wote wawe na umoja. [That they may be one.] 80pp. T.shs.5.00 Central Tanganyika 1976 TZ SWA

Christian Literature Association in Malawi.
The Blantyre Synod centenary. 20pp. photos. 30t.
Christ Lit Assoc - Mal 1976 MW CHC

Christian Literature Association in Malawi.
Five women. 10t Christ Lit Assoc - Mal 1973 MW

Christian Literature Association in Malawi.
Pocket ready reckoner. 140pp. K1.35 Christ Lit
Assoc - Mal 1975 MW

Christian Literature Association in Malawi.
Ukani. [Wake up!] bk. 1, 3 bks. 48pp. ill. 17t.
Christ Lit Assoc - Mal 1976 MW CHC

Christian Literature Association in Malawi.
Ukani. [Wake up!] bk. 2, 3 bks. 48pp. ill. 17t.
Christ Lit Assoc - Mal 1976 MW CHC

Christian Literature Association in Malawi.
Ukani. [Wake up!] bk. 3, 3 bks. 48pp. ill. 17t.
Christ Lit Assoc - Mal 1976 MW CHC

Christian Literature Bureau.
Maleredwe a ana a Akristu. [Bringing up children in
Christian families] 60pp. 35t. (25c.) Christ Lit Assoc
- Mal 1971 MW CHC

Christie, R.H.
Plain speaking in law. 36pp. 30c Univ Rhodesia Lib
1968 RH

Christie, R.H.
Rhodesian commercial law. 348pp. R10.50 Juta
1961 SA

Christopher, A.J.
Land ownership on the Port Elizabeth rural-urban fringe.
R2.00 (Inst. for Planning Research, series B, 3) Inst
Planning Res 1973 SA

Christopherson, P.
Bilingualism. An inaugural lecture. 16pp. 30k Ibadan
UP 1949 NR

Chubb, L.T.
Ibo land tenure. 2nd ed. 115pp. N2.50 Ibadan UP
1961 NR

Chukuezi, A.B.
Udo Ka Mma [Play]. 94pp. N1.00 OUP - Nig 1974
NR IGB

Chukwukere, B.I.
Cultural resilience: the Asafo company system of the Fanti.
19pp. C1.00 (Univ. of Cape Coast, Centre for
Development Studies, Research Report Series 3) Centre
Dev Stud 1970 GH

Chum, H.
Kilimo cha minazi. See: Magande, B.K.

Chum, H.
Utenzi wa vita vya Uhud. [The epic of the battle of Hud]
2nd ed. 96pp. K.shs.5.75 ($2.00/80p.) EALB 1970
KE SWA

Church, J.
Jesus satisfies. 40pp. 45pes. (15p.) Africa Christian
1969 GH

Churchill, C.H.
La vie de Abd-El-Kader. Tr. fr. English M. Habart.
256pp. DA10.00 SNED 1971 AE FRE

Churchill, R.
Men, mines and animals in South Africa. Reprint of 1893
ed. 339pp. ill. fold-out maps. R$9.60 (Rhodesiana
Reprint Library, Gold Series, 7) Books of Rhodesia 1969
RH

Churchouse, G.
The Reverend Francis McCleland, colonial chaplain to Port
Elizabeth 1825-1853. A family history. 89pp. pl. cl.
R6.65 (Genealogy publ. 4) Human Science Res Council
1976 SA

Cikin, M.
A preliminary report on the geology and ore reserves of
the Hippo mine, Kafue national park. 60n (Dept. of
Geological Survey. Economic Reports, 19) Geol Survey
- Zam 1969 ZA

Cilliers, A.C.
The law of costs. 440pp. cl. R18.50 Butterworths
1972 SA

Cilliers, A.C. Van Wyk, J.H.
A mathematical expression for the growth of trees in their
dependence on time and density of stocking. 36pp.
15c. (A v.16, no.2) Univ Stellenbosch, Lib 1938 SA

Cilliers, H.S. Benade, M.L.
Company law. 2nd ed. 467pp. cl. & pap. R15.50
pap. R20.00 cl. Butterworths 1968 SA

Cilliers, H.S. Rossoun, S. Benade, M.L.
Financial statements under the Draft Companies Bill.
128pp. R7.75 Butterworths 1975 SA

Cilliers, H.S. Faul, M.A. Rossouw, S.
Group statements. cl. & pap. R14.75 cl. R11.25
pap. Butterworths 1974 SA

Cilliers, J. A., et al.
Accountancy for standard 7. A new approach. 137pp.
ill. photos. R1.80 Nasou 1974 SA

Cilliers, J.A., et al.
A practical course in accountancy for standard 6. A new
approach. 112pp. R2.45 Nasou 1974 SA

Cilliers, J.L.R.
Education and the child. R5.25 Butterworths 1975 SA

Cilliers, S.P.
Coloured people: education and status. 28pp. 50c.
($1.30) SA Inst of Race Relations 1971 SA

Cintas, P.
Céramique punique. 685pp. pl. ill. D2.500 (Série I,
Archéologie-Histoire, 3) Univ Tunis 1950 TI FRE

Ciona, G.L.
Namwali wokana amuna. [A beautiful girl who rejects all
suitors.] 66pp. 60n. Neczam 1972 ZA NYA

Cissé, D. Diabaté, M.M.
La dispersion des Mandeka. 112pp. MF585 Ed Pop
- Mali 1970 ML FRE

Cissé, D.
Structure des Malinkés de Kita. 352pp. MF2070 Ed
Pop - Mali 1970 ML FRE

Cissoko, S. M. Ba, T. O.
Histoire du Sénégal. Cours élémentaire deuxième année.
90pp. ill. CFA700 (F14.00) Nouv Ed Afric 1975 SG
FRE

Cissoko, S.M. Bâ, D.T.
Histoire du Sénégal. Cours elementaire première année.
64pp. ill. CFA400 (F8.00) Nouv Ed Afric 1973 SG
FRE

Cissoko, S.M. Sambou, K.
Recueil des traditions orales des Mandingues de Gambie
et de Casamance. 270pp. CFA350 CELTHO 1974
NG FRE

Cissoko, S.M.
Tombouctou et l'empire Songhay. 256pp. CFA600
Nouv Ed Afric 1975 SG FRE

City of Johannesburg Public Library.
Index to South African Periodicals. Annual. R10.00
Johannesburg Public Lib 1976 SA

Civin, L.
Iris Murdoch. 30pp. R1.60 Dept Bibliog, Lib & Typo
1968 SA

Claassens, C.J.
Claassens dictionary of legal words and phrases. 4 v.
R19.75 each Butterworths SA

Claesou, C.-F. Egero, B.
Migration and the urban population. 40pp. maps.
T.shs.15.00 (Research notes, 11.2) Bur Res Assess -
Tanz 1972 TZ

Claesou, C.-F. Egero, B.
Migration in Tanzania. 41pp. maps. T.shs 15.00
(Research notes, 11.3) Bur Res Assess - Tanz 1972 TZ

Claesou, C-F.   Egero, B.
    Movement to towns in Tanzania.   86pp. maps.
    T.shs.15.00   (Research notes, 11.1)   Bur Res Assess -
    Tanz 1971 TZ

Clammer, D.
    The last Zulu warrior.   240pp. ill. pl. col. pl. cl.
    R125.00   Purnell 1977 SA

Clancey, D.A.
    Game birds of South Africa.   120pp. pl. ill. hd.   R8.00
    Purnell 1967 SA

Clarendon Press.
    Oxford atlas for Nigeria.   65pp. maps.   N1.50   OUP -
    Nig 1968 NR

Clark, D.J.
    Reading and writing Ekpeye.   24pp.   10k   (Inst. of
    African Stud., Univ. of Ibadan, Rivers readers project, 20)
    Inst Afr Stud-Ibadan 1971 NR

Clark, E., ed.   Manley, D., ed.
    Poetry.   113pp.   60k   (African Reader's Library, 20)
    Pilgrim 1973 NR

Clark, G.   Wagner, L.
    Potters of Southern Africa.   184pp. photos. col. photos.
    cl.   R12.75   Struik 1974 SA

Clark, G.C.   Dickson, C.G.C.
    Life histories of the South African lycaenid butterflies.
    270pp. pl. hd.   R15. hd.   Purnell 1971 SA

Clark, J. D., ed.
    The geology, archaeology and fossil mammals of Cornelia,
    O.F.S.   See: Butzer, K.W., ed.

Clark, J.
    Natal settler-agent: the career of John Moreland agent for
    the Byrne emigration-scheme of 1849-51.   230pp. pl.
    hd.   fl. 42.75   (South African biographical and historical
    studies, 15)   Balkema 1972 SA

Clark, J.P.
    The Ozidi saga.   [Bi-lingual Ijo/English.]   320pp. cl. &
    pap.   N16.00 cl.   N14.00 pap.   Ibadan UP 1977 NR

Clark, P.G.
    Development planning in East Africa.   153pp.
    K.shs.17.50   ($4.00)   EAPH 1965 KE

Clark, P.M.
    The autobiography of an old drifter. [Reprint ed. 1936].
    272pp. photos. cl.   R$6.95 cl.   (Rhodesiana Reprint
    Library, Gold Series, 26)   Books of Rhodesia 1972 RH

Clark, R.C.   Akinbode, I.A.
    Factors associated with adoption of three farm practices
    in the Western State of Nigeria: N.S.I. maize, cocoa spray
    and poultry-egg programmes.   44pp.   N1.00   (Faculty
    of Agriculture, research bull., 1)   Univ Ife Press 1968 NR

Clark, W.G.C.
    There is a transcendence from science to science.   18pp.
    R1.00   (Raymond Dart lec., 2)   Inst Study of Man 1965
    SA

Clarke, D.A.
    The college library and the community.   22pp.   30c
    Univ Rhodesia Lib 1961 RH

Clarke, D.A.
    Prospecting for brick clay in the Chipata area.   K2.00
    (Dept. of Geological Survey, Technical Reports, 79)   Geol
    Survey - Zam 1976 ZA

Clarke, D.G.
    Agricultural and plantation workers in Rhodesia. A report
    on conditions of labour and subsistence.   300pp. ill.
    R$4.80   (Mambo Socio-economic Series, 6)   Mambo
    1977 RH

Clarke, D.G.
    Contract workers and underdevelopment in Rhodesia.
    132pp.   R$1.40   (Mambo Socio-Economic Series, 3)
    Mambo 1974 RH

Clarke, D.G.
    The distribution of income and wealth in Rhodesia.
    128pp.   R$1.80   (Mambo Socio-economic Series, 7)
    Mambo 1977 RH

Clarke, D.G.
    Domestic workers in Rhodesia. The economics of masters
    and servants.   88pp.   R$1.00   (Mambo
    Socio-Economic Series, 1)   Mambo 1974 RH

Clarke, J.
    Our fragile land. South Africa's environmental crisis.
    134pp. ill. photos. cl.   R5.95   Macmillan - SA 1974 SA

Clarke, J.B.
    Rhodesian map-reading, book 1: an introduction to
    map-reading with exercises.   2nd ed.   40pp. maps.
    $1.95   OUP-SA 1973 SA

Clarke, J.B.
    Rhodesian map-reading, book 2: an introduction to
    map-reading with exercises.   2nd ed.   40pp. maps.
    $1.95   OUP-SA 1973 SA

Clarke, J.B.
    Rhodesian maps and exercises. (for O and M levels)
    maps. $1.95   OUP-SA 1970 SA

Clarke, M.
    My speech book for infants.   2   30c.   Shuter 1952 SA

Clarke, R., eds.
    Teaching adults.   See: Prosser, R., eds.

Clarke, R.F.
    Continuing literacy.   194pp. hd.   U.shs.5.00   Adult
    Educ Centre 1968 UG

Clarke, W.
    Travels and explorations in Yorubaland, 1854-1858.
    297pp. maps ill. cl. & pap.   N4.00 pap.   N6.50 cl.
    Ibadan UP 1972 NR

Clay, G.C.R.
    History of the Mankoya district.   21pp.   K1.00   (50p.)
    (Rhodes-Livingstone communications, 4)   Inst Afr Stud -
    Lusaka 1945 ZA

Clayton, A.
    Counter insurgency in Kenya, 1952-60.   80pp. pl. map.
    K.shs.10.00   (Transafrica Historical papers, 3)
    Transafrica 1975 KE

Clayton, G.H.
    Christian unity: an Anglican view.   50c.   (Peter Ainslie
    Memorial lec., 1)   Rhodes Univ Lib 1949 SA

Clayton, H.
    Sketches. Ed. by A.H. Smith.   See: Stone, I.M.

Clerc, M. et al.
    Annales de l'université d'Abidjan.   268pp.   CFA1000
    (F20.00)   (Série B - Médecine, 7)   Univ Abidjan 1973 IV
    FRE

Clevenger, J.
    Eni va, 1.   See: Urugba, M.

Clevenger, J.
    Eni va, 2.   See: Urugba, M.

Clevenger, J.
    Teachers' notes on Eni va, 1.   93pp.   50k   (Inst. of
    African Stud., Univ of Ibadan, Rivers readers project, 23)
    Inst Afr Stud-Ibadan 1971 NR ENN

Clevenger, J.
    Teachers' notes on Eni va, 2.   (Inst. of African Stud.,
    Univ. of Ibadan, Rivers readers project, 33)   Inst Afr
    Stud-Ibadan 1973 NR ENN

Cliffe, L., ed.
    One party democracy.   465pp. photos. maps.
    K.shs.70.00   ($13.00)   EAPH. 1967 KE

Cliffe, L., ed.
    One party democracy.   470pp. hd.   U.shs25.00
    (M.I.S.R. individual monog., 13)   Mak Inst Soc Res 1967
    UG

Cliffe, L., ed.
    Selections from one party democracy.   143pp.
    U.shs6.00   (M.I.S.R. individual monog., 14)   Mak Inst
    Soc Res 1967 UG

Cliffe, L., eds.   Saul, J., eds.
    Socialism in Tanzania, v. 2.   358pp.   K.shs.55.00
    (Political Studies, 14b)   EAPH 1974 KE

Cliffe, L.
Socialism in Tanzania. v.1. 346pp. K.shs45.00 ($12.00) EAPH 1972 KE

Clifford, G., ed.
Health and disease in Africa: the community approach. 540pp. K.shs.95.00 ($18.00/£8.50) EALB 1972 KE

Clifford, P.
Cancer in Africa. 458pp. photos. maps. K.shs.105.00 ($20.00) EAPH 1968 KE

Clifford, W.
Crime in Northern Rhodesia. 121pp. K1.00 (50p.) (Rhodes-Livingstone communications, 18) Inst Afr Stud - Lusaka 1960 ZA

Clifford, W.
An introduction to African criminology. 240pp. cl. & pap. K.shs.45.00 pap. K.shs.55.00 cl. OUP - Nairobi 1974 KE

Clifford, W.
A primer of social casework in Africa. 94pp. K.shs9.25 OUP-Nairobi 1966 KE

Cloete, C.E.
Bibliography on marine pollution in South Africa. See: Darracott, D.A.

Cloete, C.E. Oliff, W.D.
South African marine pollution survey report 1974-1975. 60pp. (NSPU Report, 8) CSIR 1976 SA

Cloete, E., comps.
Alphabetic index to Major Hook's With Sword and and Statute. See: Rosenthal, E., comps.

Cloete, H.
Five lectures on the emigration of the Dutch farmers from the colony of the Cape of Good Hope, and their settlement in the district of Natal, until their formal submission to Her Majesty's authority, in the year 1843. [Reprint of ed. Cape Town, 1856] 168pp. R4.20 (Reprints, 22) State-Lib-SA 1968 SA

Cloete, J.J.N.
Emergent Africa: political and administrative trends. 53pp. ill. R1.00 (Commun. of the Africa Inst., 4) Africa Inst - Pret 1966 SA

Cloete, S.E. Visser, J.G.J.
The cranial morphology of Rhyacotriton olympicus olympicus (Gaige); The cranial anatomy and kinsesis of the bird snake Thelotornis capensis (Smith) 62pp. ill. R1.20 (A v.36, no.2-3) Univ Stellenbosch, Lib 1961 SA

Cloudsley-Thompson, J.L. Abushama, F.T.
A guide to the physiology of terrestrial arthropoda. 88pp. 14. 65 pt. ($2.50) Khartoum UP 1970 SJ

Clum, A.
Guideposts to learning. 192pp. ill. hd., pap. N2.50 hd. N2.30 pap. Macmillan 1971 NR

Coates, P.R.
Track and trackless. 224pp. ill. pl. cl. R15.00 Struik 1976 SA

Cock, E.V.
Snakes of Rhodesia. See: Broadley, D.G.

Cockburn, H.
The complete East African poultry book. 172pp. photos. K.shs20.00 Textbook Ctre 1976 KE

Cockburn, H.
Poultry keeping in East Africa. 3rd ed. 88pp. K.shs.6.25 ($2.00/80p.) EALB 1975 KE

Cockram, B.
General Smuts and South African diplomacy. 10pp. 30c. SA Inst Int Affairs 1970 SA

Cockram, B.
Problems of Southern Africa. 64pp. 55c. SA Inst Int Affairs 1963 SA

Cockram, B.
Seen from Southern Africa: short studies of current international problems. 73pp. 50c. SA Inst Int Affairs 1962 SA

Cockram, G.M.
Administrative law. R3.50 Juta 1976 SA

Cockram, G.M., ed.
Constitutional law. 96pp. hd. R3.50 cl. Juta 1976 SA

Cockram, G.M., ed.
Interpretation of statutes. 96pp. hd. R3.50 cl. Juta 1976 SA

Cockram, G.M.
South West African mandate. R15.00 Juta 1976 SA

Codere, H.
The biography of an African society: Rwanda 1900-1960. Based on forty-eight Rwandan autobiographies. 399pp. RF2,070 (FB900.00/$22.50) (Institut National de Recherche Scientifique, 12) Inst Nat - Rwandaise 1973 RW

Coertze, T.F.
Bantu divorce courts. See: Kloppers, H.P.

Coetzee, A.
Some folkloristic aspects of Afrikaans folk medicine. 40c. (Isma paps., 5) Inst Study of Man 1962 SA

Coetzee, A.G.
Junior secondary history for standard 6. See: Paynter, B.E.

Coetzee, A.G.
Junior secondary history for standard 7. See: Paynter, B.E.

Coetzee, A.G.
Senior secondary history for standard 8. See: Paynter, B.E.

Coetzee, C.
Candid Cape Town. See: Michaelides, G.G.

Coetzee, C.
Eikestad. [Text in English and Afrikaans]. 88pp. ill. cl. R18.00 Struik 1976 SA

Coetzee, C.J.S. Geggus, C.
Tertiary training outside universities and career opportunities. 234pp. R2.30 Human Science Res Council 1977 SA

Coetzee, J.C.
Annotated bibliography of research in education. 1-2, 5 pts. 182pp. R2.15 Human Science Res Council 1976 SA

Coetzee, J.C.
Annotated bibliography of research in education. 3-4, 5 pts. 263pp. R7.30 Human Science Res Council 1976 SA

Coetzee, J.C.
Annotated bibliography of research in education. 5, 5 pts. R8.70 Human Science Res Council 1976 SA

Coetzee, J.M.
Dusklands. Two nouvellas with an inner connection. 134pp. R3.00 ($4.75/£2.50) Ravan 1974 SA

Coetzee, O.J. et al.
The bacteriological quality of the water resources of small communities. 83pp. ill. (CSIR research reports, 238) CSIR 1966 SA

Coetzee, P.C.
Colendo explorare. 263pp. photos. hd. R8.25 cl. (Contributions to Library Science, 15) State Lib - SA 1975 SA

Coetzee, P.C.
A theory of logistic facet analysis. 31pp. R3.00 (Contributions to Library Science, 9) State-Lib-SA 1968 SA

Coetzee, R.
Traditional cookery in South Africa. 152pp. pl. ill. cl. R9.95 Struik 1977 SA

Cohen, K., comp.
South African English poetry. 851pp. R24.00 Dept Bibliog, Lib & Typo 1974 SA

Cohen, K.
South African English poetry, 1937-1970 in the
Johannesburg Public Library and the Gubbins Collection of
Africana in the University of the Witwatersrand Library. 1,
2v. R25.00 Dept Bibliog Lib & Typo 1975 SA

Cohen, K.
South African English poetry, 1937-1970 in the
Johannesburg Public Library and the Gubbins Collection of
Africana in the University of the Witwatersrand Library. 2,
2v. 362pp. R25.00 Dept Bibliog Lib & Typo 1975 SA

Cohen, L.
Reminiscences of Johannesburg and London. [Reprint ed.
1924]. 316pp. ill. cl. R15.10 (Africana Reprint
Library, 7) Africana Book Soc 1976 SA

Cohic, F.
Annales de l'université d'Abidjan. Contribution à l'étude
des aleurodes africains. 156pp. CFA700 (F14.00)
(Série E-Ecologie, 2-2) Univ Abidjan 1969 IV FRE

Cojeen, R.
Case studies in Nigerian business. 138pp. N1.25
(£1.00/$2.50) Inst Admin - Zaria 1966 NR

Coker, I.H.E.
Landmarks of the Nigerian press. 126pp. photos.
N3.75 Nig Nat Press 1968 NG NR

Coldwell, D.A.L.
Role conflict and job satisfaction: a review with
implications regarding urban employed black workers.
30pp. (CSIR Special Report PERS, 228) CSIR 1975 SA

Cole, D.T.
Contributions to the history of Bantu linguistics.
See: Doke, C.M.

Cole, D.T.
An introduction to Tswana grammar. 512pp. R4.20
Longman SA 1955 SA

Cole, D.T.
Some features of Ganda linguistic structure. 140pp. cl.
R6.00 Witwatersrand UP 1967 SA

Cole, H.B. Cassell, A.B.
Liberian trade and industry handbook. 228pp. photos.
U.S.$5.00 Cole & Yancy 1971 LB

Cole-King, P.A., ed.
Four archaeological articles covering research in Malawi's
southern region. 100pp. pl. maps. K2.00
(Department of Antiquities, 14) Dept Antiquities - Mal
1973 MW

Cole-King, P.A., ed.
Kukumba Mbiri Mu Malawi. A summary of archaeological
research to March 1973. 81pp. pl. maps. K2.50
(Department of Antiquities, 15) Dept Antiquities - Mal
1973 MW

Cole-King, P.A.
Historical guide to Blantyre. 28pp. photos. map.
K1.00 Christ Lit Assoc - Mal 1974 MW

Cole-King, P.A.
Lilongwe. A historical study. 53pp. pl. maps. 75t
(Department of Antiquities, 10) Dept Antiquities - Mal
1971 MW

Cole, S.O.
Elementary psychology and mental health. 120pp. ill.
C1.50 Waterville 1975 GH

Coles, D.
The oil-crushing industry in East Africa. 105pp.
U.shs20.00 (M.I.S.R. occas. paps., 4) Mak Inst Soc Res
1968 UG

Coles, D.M.S.
The vegetable oil crushing industry in East Africa. 131pp.
K.shs.20.00 Africa Book Serv 1970 KE

Coles, R.
Children and political authority. 34pp. 25c (Univ.
Cape Town. T.B. Davie Memorial lec., 15) Univ Cape
Town Lib 1974 SA

Collet, N. Engel, K.
Lively learning. 64pp. ill. T.shs.5.00 Central
Tanganyika 1975 TZ

Collett, N.E.
Ilikuwaje? Maelezo na picha zihusuzo Biblia. [Simplified
Bible dictionary] 120pp. ill. T.shs.6.00 Central
Tanganyika 1974 TZ SWA

Collier, J.
Portrait of Cape Town: deluxe edition. 112pp. ill. hd.
R6.60 Longman SA 1961 SA

Collier, J.
Portrait of Cape Town: standard edition. 112pp. ill. hd.
R2.10 Longman SA 1961 SA

Collier, J.
The purple and the gold. 192pp. ill. hd. R3.25
Longman SA 1965 SA

Collignon, M.
Ammonites néocrétacées du Menabe: les desmoceratidae.
111pp. pl. cl. FMG1800 cl. (F36.00 cl.) (Annales
Géologiques de Madagascar, 31) Service Geol - Mad
1961 MG FRE

Collignon, M.
Atlas des fossiles caractéristiques de Madagascar. v.6:
Tithonique. 136pp. pl. photos. FMG2513 (F50.26)
Service Geol - Mad 1960 MG FRE

Collignon, M.
Atlas des fossiles caractéristiques de Madagascar. v.8:
Berriasien à Barrémien. 96pp. photos. FMG2129
(F42.58) Service Geol - Mad 1962 MG FRE

Collignon, M.
Atlas des fossiles caractéristiques de Madagascar. v.9:
Aptien. 64pp. photos. FMG1319 (F26.38) Service
Geol - Mad 1962 MG FRE

Collignon, M.
Atlas des fossiles caractéristiques de Madagascar. v.10:
Albien. 184pp. photos. FMG4109 (F82.18) Service
Geol - Mad 1963 MG FRE

Collignon, M.
Atlas des fossiles caractéristiques de Madagascar. v.11:
Cénomanien. 152pp. photos. FMG3210 (F64.20)
Service Geol - Mad 1964 MG FRE

Collignon, M.
Atlas des fossiles caractéristiques de Madagascar. v.12:
Turonien. 82pp. photos. FMG2015 (F40.30)
Service Geol - Mad 1965 MG FRE

Collignon, M.
Atlas des fossiles caractéristiques de Madagascar. v.13:
Coniacien. 88pp. photos. FMG2189 (F43.78)
Service Geol - Mad 1965 MG FRE

Collignon, M.
Atlas des fossiles caractéristiques de Madagascar. v.14:
Santonien. 134pp. photos. FMG3198 (F63.96)
Service Geol - Mad 1966 MG FRE

Collignon, M.
Atlas des fossiles caractéristiques de Madagascar. v.15:
Campanien inférieur. 216pp. photos. FMG5030
(F100.60) Service Geol - Mad 1969 MG FRE

Collignon, M.
Atlas des fossiles caractéristiques de Madagascar. v.16:
Campanien moyen et supérieur. 82pp. photos.
FMG3955 (F79.10) Service Geol - Mad 1970 MG FRE

Collignon, M.
La géologie de la province de Diégo-Suarez, terrains
sédimentaires. 181pp. pl. FMG1760 (F35.20)
(Série Documentation, 171) Service Geol - Mad 1965
MG FRE

Collingridge, L.T., ed.
The downfall of Lobengula. [Reprint ed. 1894].
See: Wills, W.A., ed.

Collins, J.
Lusaka: the myth of the garden city. 32pp. 75n.
(43p.) (Zambian Urban stud., 2) Inst Afr Stud - Lusaka
1969 ZA

Collins-Longman.
Atlas for Malawi. 2nd ed. 36pp. maps col. maps. K1.10 (55p) Longman - Mal 1974 MW

Collins, M.M.
Opio kede tottere. [Opio and his mother] 2nd ed. 44pp. ill. K.shs.8.00 ($2.25/60p.) EALB 1970 KE LUO

Collins, M.O.
Bantu education. The republic of South Africa described for schools in simple atlas form. 2nd ed. 32pp. maps. ($2.50 pap.) M.O. Collins 1970 RH

Collins, M.O.
Cape Province. A simple atlas presentation of the Republic of South Africa and the Cape Province in relation to the world. 32pp. col. maps. ($2.50) M.O. Collins 1974 RH

Collins, M.O. et al.
The environment of the Rhodesian people, cplte. series. 199pp. ill. col. ill. maps. ($10.00) M.O. Collins 1974 RH

Collins, M.O.
Junior atlas for African schools. 32pp. col. maps. ($3.00) M.O. Collins RH

Collins, M.O.
Land and water. 20pp. ill. col. ill. maps. ($1.00) (The Environment of the Rhodesian People, 2) M.O. Collins 1974 RH

Collins, M.O.
The people. 24pp. ill. col. ill. maps. ($1.00) (The Environment of the Rhodesian People, 1) M.O. Collins 1974 RH

Collins, M.O.
Rhodesia: its natural resources and economic development. 52pp. maps. hd. R$6.30 cl. ($13.00 cl.) M.O. Collins 1965 RH

Collins, R.
Nigeria in conflict. 215pp. N1.80 West 1970 NR

Collins, R.
Tonga grammar. 182pp. K1.50 Neczam 1970 ZA

Collinson, M.P.
Example of farm survey work directed towards the solution of a policy problem - aromatic or Virginia tobacco on small family farms in Tabora area. 35pp. T.shs.12.00 ($3.00) (Research pap., 70.7) Econ Res Bur - Tanz 1970 TZ

Collison, R.L.
Hotel-keeping for Africans. 32pp. ill. K.shs.0.30 ($1.00/40p.) EALB 1947 KE

Collister, P.
The last days of slavery. ills. cl. K.shs7.50 ($2.20/50p.) EALB 1963 KE

Colloque sur Picasso.
Art nègre et civilisation de l'universel. 160pp. CFA500 pap. Nouv Ed Afric 1975 SG FRE

Colman, G.
Cross-examination. R6.50 Juta 1970 SA

Colombo, S.
Etudes des transcendantes intervenant dans la résolution des équations intégrales de voltera à noyaux logarithmiques. 42pp. ill. 60k Press Univ Zaire 1964 ZR FRE

Colomer, A.
Droit musulman. v. 1: Les personnes. La famille. Dir40.00 Ed La Porte 1963 MR FRE

Colquhoun, A.R.
Matabeleland: the war and our position in South Africa. [Reprint of ed. London] 167pp. R5.10 (Reprints, 40) State-Lib-SA 1969 SA

Colson, E., ed. Gluckman, M., ed.
Seven tribes of British Central Africa. 395pp. ill. photos maps. cl. K4.20 (£2.10/$8.50) Inst Afr Stud - Lusaka 1951 ZA

Colson, E.
Marriage and the family among the Plateau Tonga of Northern Rhodesia. 395pp. ill. hd. K4.50 (£2.40/$8.50) Inst Afr Stud - Lusaka 1958 ZA

Colson, E.
The Plateau Tonga of Northern Rhodesia (Zambia): social and religious studies. 367pp. ill. hd. K.4.00 (£2.00/$7.50) Inst Afr Stud - Lusaka 1966 ZA

Colson, E.
The social consequences of resettlement: the impact of the Kariba resettlement upon the Gwembe Tonga. 277pp. K3.60 (£1.80) (Kariba studs., 4) Inst Afr Stud - Lusaka 1971 ZA

Colson, E.
The social organisation of the Gwembe tribe. 256pp. hd. K3.60 (£1.80/$6.50) (Kariba stud., 1) Inst Afr Stud - Lusaka 1960 ZA

Comaroff, J.L., ed.
The Boer War diary of Sol T. Plaatje: an African at Mafeking. 214pp. photos. map. hd. R6.60 (£5.25) Macmillan, S.A. 1973 SA

Combet, S.
Fatou au pays des Baoulés. 44pp. CFA650 Nouv Ed Afric 1976 SG FRE

Comhaire-Sylvain, S.
Jetons nos couteaux! Contes des garconnets de Kinshasa et quelques parallèles haitiens. Textes lingala-français, creole-français. 223pp. (DM22.00 pap.) (CEEBA. série II, Mémoires et Monographies, 15) CEEBA 1974 ZR FRE

Comhaire-Sylvain, S.
Qui mange avec une femme. Contes zairois et haitiens. Textes lingala-français et créole-français. 310pp. (DM29.00) (CEEBA publications, série II, Mémoires et Monographies, 6) CEEBA 1973 ZR FRE

Comins, D.M.
The vegetation of the districts of East London and King William's Town, Cape Province. R2.40 (Memoirs of the Botanical Survey of South Africa, 33) Botanical Res Inst 1962 SA

Commission d'Experts de la Conférence des Ministres de l'Education Nationale des Etats Africains et Malgache d'expression française.
Litterature africaine, classe de 2e. 447pp. CFA900 (F18.00) Nouv Ed Afric 1973 SG FRE

Commission d'Experts de la Conférence des Ministres de l'Education Nationale des Etats Africains et Malgache d'expression française.
Littérature française, class de 2e. 407pp. CFA900 (F18.00) Nouv Ed Afric 1973 SG FRE

Committee Against Nigeria's Exploitation.
Victim of UAC. 32pp. 50k. di Nigro 1977 NR

Community Development Division, Dodoma.
Ugogo na wilaya zake. 44pp. K.shs.1.00 ($1.25/50p.) EALB 1965 KE SWA

Comoe Krou, B. et al.
Annales de l'université d'Abidjan. 180pp. CFA1400 (F28.00) (Série F-Ethno-Sociologie, 5) Univ Abidjan 1973 IV FRE

Comprehensive High School, Aiyetoro.
Social studies for Nigerian secondary school. 136pp. N1.26 Univ Lagos Bookshop 1968 NR

Comrie, R. G.
South African mercantile and company law.
See: Gibson, J. T. R.

Comte, G.
Askia Mohamed. L'apogée de l'empire Songhay.
See: Kake, I.B.

Conacher, J.R.H.
An initial readership survey of Ethiopia. 100pp. hd. Eth.$25.00 Christ Lit Dev 1969 ET

Condamin, M.
Monographie du genre Bicyclus (Lepidoptera Satyridae)
324pp. ill. col. pl. CFA4800.00 (Memoires de l'IFAN,
88) IFAN 1973 SG FRE

Conde, A.
Sociétés traditionnelles mandingues. 238pp. CFA350
CELTHO 1974 NG FRE

Connah, G.E.
A map of Benin City walls. map. 15k Dept
Antiquities NR

Connah, G.E.
Polished stone axes in Benin. 31pp. ill. 35k Dept
Antiquities NR

Conrad, J.
Kiini cha giza. [Heart of Darkness.] tr. fr. Eng. W.T.
Kisanji. 93pp. T.shs.5.50 Tanz Publ House 1975 TZ
SWA

Conradie, A.L.
The neo-calvinistic concept of philosophy. 219pp. cl.
R3.50 Univ of Natal 1960 SA

Conradie, A.M.
The law of carriage of goods by railway in South Africa.
180pp. hd. R8.25 Butterworths 1964 SA

Conradie, B.
linkoti kondundu. 74c. Native Lang Bur 1975[?] SX
NDO

Conradie, P.J.
The treatment of Greek myths in modern French drama:
study of the "classical" plays of Anouilh, Cocteau,
Giraudoux and Sartre. 100pp. R1.25 (B v.29, no. 2)
Univ Stellenbosch, Lib 1963 SA

Contant, R.B., ed.
Compte rendu de la conference inaugurale, Association
des Facultes Agronomiques d'Afrique (AFAA), Nairobi,
Juillet 1973. Tr. fr. English 210pp. free AFAA 1974
KE FRE

Contant, R.B., ed.
Compte rendu de la deuxième conférence générale,
Association des Facultés Agronomiques d'Afrique (AFAA),
le Caire, 1975. tr. fr. English. free AFAA 1977 KE
FRE

Contant, R.B., ed.
Proceedings of the inaugural conference, Association of
Faculties of Agriculture in Africa (AFAA), Nairobi, 1973.
187pp. free AFAA 1973 KE

Contant, R.B., ed.
Proceedings of the second general conference,
Association of Faculties of Agriculture in Africa (AFAA),
Cairo, 1975. 209pp. free AFAA 1977 KE

Contant, R.B.
Résumé du Compte rendu de la deuxième conférence,
Association des Facultés Agronomiques d'Afrique (AFAA),
le Caire, 1975. tr. fr. English. 64pp. free AFAA
1977 KE FRE

Contant, R.B.
Summary of proceedings of the second general
conference, Association of Faculties of Agriculture in Africa
(AFAA), Cairo, 1975. 58pp. free AFAA 1977 KE

Conyers, D.
Agro-economic zones of Dodoma and Singida. 80pp.
map. T.shs.10.00 (Research report, 47) Bur Res
Assess - Tanz 1971 TZ

Conyers, D.
Agro-economic zones of Sukumaland. 112pp. map.
T.shs.15.00 (Research report, 16) Bur Res Assess -
Tanz 1970 TZ

Conyers, D.
Agro-economic zones of Tanzania. T.shs.40.00
($12.00) (Research pap., 25) Bur Res Assess - Tanz
1973 TZ

Conyers, D.
Agro-economic zones of West Lake region. 42pp. map.
T.shs.7.00 (Research report, 28) Bur Res Assess -
Tanz 1971 TZ

Conyers, D. et al.
Agro-economic zones of Kigoma and Tabora. 64pp.
T.shs.10.00 (Research report, 46) Bur Res Assess -
Tanz 1971 TZ

Conyers, D. et al.
Agro-economic zones of northeastern Tanzania. 123pp.
map. (Research report, 13) Bur Res Assess Tanz 1970
TZ

Conyers, D. et al.
Agro-economic zones of the Southern Highlands. 94pp.
map. T.shs.15.00 (Research report, 23) Bur Res
Assess - Tanz 1971 TZ

Conyers, D.
Forestry in Tanzania. 23pp. maps. T.shs.7.00
(Research notes, 5d) Bur Res Assess - Tanz 1969 TZ

Cook, A.
Assessment of soil erosion in Dodoma region by the
interpretation of photo mosaics. T.shs.20.00
(Research reports, 16) Bur Res Assess - Tanz 1975 TZ

Cook, A.
Land use recommendations for Rufiji district.
T.shs.20.00 (Research reports, new series, 11) Bur Res
Assess - Tanz 1974 TZ

Cook, A.
A photo-interpretation of soils and land use in the Rufiji
Basin. T.shs.15.00 (Research pap., 36) Bur Res
Assess - Tanz 1975 TZ

Cook, A.
A photo-interpretation study of the soils and land use
potential of the lower Wami basin. T.shs.40.00
(Research pap., 40) Bur Res Assess - Tanz 1975 TZ

Cook, A.
A soils bibliography of Tanzania. 56pp. hd. & pap.
T.shs.25.00 pap. T.shs.40.00 hd. ($8.00 pap.)
($12.00 hd.) (Research pap., 39) Bur Res Assess -
Tanz 1975 TZ

Cook, A.
The use of photo-interpretation in the assessment of
physical and biological resources in Tanzania.
T.shs.20.00 ($7.00) (Research pap., 31) Bur Res
Assess - Tanz 1974 TZ

Cook, C.
Good scouting. 88pp. pl. 25c Mambo 1963 RH

Cook, C.W.
Enthusiasm re-visited. ex. only (Inaugural lec.)
Rhodes Univ Lib 1971 SA

Cook, D., ed.
In black and white. Writings from East Africa. 169pp.
K.shs.25.90 pap. (£2.70/$5.50 pap.) EALB 1976 KE

Cook, D.
Literature: the great teaching power of the world.
K.shs.3.50 ($1.75/70p.) EALB 1970 KE

Cook, G.P.
Survey of the Cape Midlands and Karroo regions, vol. 2:
towns of the Cape Midlands and Eastern Karroo. 115pp.
ill. maps. Inst Soc & Econ Res - SA 1971 SA

Cook, H.L.
Big food processors: saints or sinners? 18pp. 45k
(35p./80c) (Univ. of Ife, Inaugural Lecture Series, 11)
Univ Ife Press 1974 NR

Cook, H.L.
Wages of unskilled workers in agriculture and some
characteristics of the farm labour market in the Western
State of Nigeria. See: Abaelu, J.N.

Cooke, B.V. Fairbairn, D.G.
The hospital laundry and linen service: hospital design 8.
16pp. (CSIR research reports, 258) CSIR 1967 SA

Cooke, C.K.
A guide to the rock art of Rhodesia. 64pp. col. ill. maps. R$2.25 Longman - Rhod 1974 RH

Cooke, C.K.
Rock art of Southern Africa. col. pl ill. R3.50 Bulpin 1969 SA

Cooke, H.B.S., ed.
The geology, archaeology and fossil mammals of Cornelia, O.F.S. See: Butzer, K.W., ed.

Cooke, R.
Stephen comes to town. 52pp. ill. 50n. Neczam 1973 ZA

Cooke, R.A.
Stephen and the animals. 44pp. ill. 50n. Neczam 1972 ZA

Cooke, R.A.
The umbrella and the bicycle. 40pp. ill. 90n. (Eagle Readers) Neczam 1974 ZA

Cookey-Gam, S.E.
Beginning history, elementary 4. 96pp. ill. 72k Longman - Nig 1965 NR

Coomber, A.A. Barthas, M. Bessey, A.
France Afrique. Douze contes africains. A French reader for year 2 of secondary schools in West Africa. 56pp. ill. 80k Macmillan 1975 NR FRE

Coon, J.
Biblical foundations for a Christian home. 96pp. (75p.) Africa Christian GH

Coon, J.
Biblical foundations for a Christian home. 96pp. (75p.) Africa Christian 1977 GH

Cooper-Chadwick, J.
Three years with Lobengula, and experiences in South Africa. [Reprint of ed. 1894]. 160pp. ill. pl. map. cl. $7.80 (Rhodesiana Reprint Library, Silver Series, 1) Books of Rhodesia 1975 RH

Cooper, R.
Butterflies of Rhodesia. 138pp. col. ill. R$3.25 Longman - Rhod 1973 RH

Cooper, St. G.C. et al.
Agricultural research in tropical Africa. 248pp. K.shs35.00 cl. K.shs20.00 pap. ($4.50/£1.70 pap.) ($7.25/£3.50 cl.) EALB 1970 KE

Cooper, W.E. Bamford, B.R.
South African motor law. R25.00 Juta 1965 SA

Cooper, W.E.
South African road traffic legislation. 942pp. R32.00 [incl. revision services] Juta 1967 SA

Cooper, W.G.G.
Electrical aids in water finding. 2nd ed. 25pp. pl. K1.25 (Geological Survey of Malawi, Bull. 7) Geol Survey - Mal 1965 MW

Cooper, W.G.G. Habgood, F.
The geology of the Livingstonia Coalfield. 51pp. maps pl. hd. K1.05 (55p.) (Geological Survey of Malawi, Bull. 11) Geol Survey - Mal 1959 MW

Cooper, W.G.G. Bloomfield, K.
The geology of the Thambani-Salambidwe area. 63pp. map pl. hd. K1.05 (Geological Survey of Malawi, Bull. 13) Geol Survey - Mal 1961 MW

Cooray, P.G.
The geological sciences in the service of Nigeria. 14pp. 30k (Inaugural lec., 2) Univ Ife Press 1973 NR

Cope, R.L., ed.
Journals of the Rev. T.L. Hodgson. 423pp. cl. R18.00 Witwatersrand UP 1977 SA

Copeland, R.F., ed.
English teaching in South Africa. R2.00 Inst Study Engl. 1964 A

Copeling, A.J.C.
Casebook on mercantile law. R12.75 Butterworths 1975 SA

Copeling, A.J.C.
Copyright law in South Africa. 394pp. R17.50 cl. Butterworths 1969 SA

Copeling, A.J.C., ed.
Students casebook on mercantile law. R12.75 Butterworths 1975 SA

Copeling, A.J.C.
The nature and object of copyright. 14pp. 40c. (90c.) Univ South Africa 1969 SA

Coque, R.
Nabeul et ses environs. Etude d'une population Tunisienne. 146pp. photos. D1.500 (Série III, Mémoires du Centre d'Etudes Humaines, 9) Univ Tunis 1966 TI FRE

Corbett, M.M. Buchanan, J.L.
The quantum of damages in bodily and fatal injury cases. 2nd ed. R61.50 [incl. annual supplements up to 1976] Juta 1971 SA

Corbett, M.M. Buchanan, J.L.
The quantum of damages in bodily and fatal injury cases. 1976 Annual Supplement. R6.50 Juta 1976 SA

Corbin, H.
Handbook for teachers of social studies. See: Nwosu, S.

Cordor, S.M.H.
The African life. A collection of short stories. 230pp. $3.50 Liberian Lit 1975 LB

Cordor, S.M.H., ed.
An anthology of short stories by writers from the West African Republic of Liberia. 341pp. cl. & pap. $3.95 pap. $5.95 cl. Liberian Lit 1974 LB

Cordor, S.M.H., ed.
The writings of Roland T. Dempster and Edwin J. Barclay. A prose and poetry collection of two leading Liberian poets. 288pp. $5.00 Liberian Lit 1975 LB

Cordor, S.M.H.
Towards the study of Liberian literature. A critical anthology of Liberian literature. 200pp. $3.00 Liberian Lit 1973 LB

Cory, G.E.
The rise of South Africa [Reprint of 1910 edition]. 6 v. 2,642pp. maps ill. cl. R40.00 Struik 1966 SA

Costins, R.A.
Contes africains. Cours moyen deuxième année. 64pp. CFA400 (F8.00) Nouv Ed Afric 1973 SG FRE

Cotton, A.F.
Patterns and principles. See: Hawksworth, W.A.

Cottrell, J.A.
Black eagle fly free. 154pp. pl. hd. R2.50 Purnell 1971 SA

Coulson, A.C.
A simplified political economy of Tanzania. T.shs.12.00 ($3.00) (Research pap., 74.9) Econ Res Bur - Tanz 1975 TZ

Coulson, C.A.
The church in the world. 50c. (Peter Ainslie Memorial lec., 13) Rhodes Univ Lib 1962 SA

Council for Scientific and Industrial Relations.
NBRI film catalogue. 26pp. CSIR 1975 SA

Council for Scientific and Industrial Research.
Economic analysis in road engineering, BENC 03. 35pp. (Computer Information Centre for Transportation, NITRR Manual P3) CSIR 1976 SA

Council for Scientific and Industrial Research.
Economic analysis methods for road engineering projects. 61pp. (Technical Manual, NITRR, K27) CSIR 1976 SA

Council for Scientific and Industrial Research.
Geotechnical and soil engineering mapping for roads and the storage of materials data. 34pp. (Technical recommendations for Highways, NITRR, Draft TRH 2) CSIR 1976 SA

Council for Scientific and Industrial Research.
Medical research centres in Ghana. Current research projects (1973) 43pp. ex. only CSIR-Ghana 1973 GH

Council for Scientific and Industrial Research, Pretoria.
Building in the Cape. v. 1 240pp. R10.00 (CSIR reports, S106) CSIR 1975 SA

Council for Scientific and Industrial Research, Pretoria.
Continuous operators in Lp and generalized random processes a kernel representation. 18pp. (CSIR Special Report WISK, 177) CSIR 1975 SA

Council for Scientific and Industrial Research, Pretoria.
Directory of scientific and technical periodicals published in South Africa, 1975. 50pp. R1.50 CSIR 1975 SA

Council for Scientific and Industrial Research, Pretoria.
Directory of scientific and technical societies in South Africa, 1975. 153pp. R2.50 CSIR 1975 SA

Council for Scientific and Industrial Research, Pretoria.
Directory of scientific research organizations in South Africa, 1975. 300pp. R4.00 CSIR 1975 SA

Council for Scientific and Industrial Research, Pretoria.
Getting more out of our timber resources. 232pp. R15.00 (CSIR reports, S99) CSIR 1974 SA

Council for Scientific and Industrial Research, Pretoria.
NBRI film catalogue, 1975. 26pp. (CSIR reports, K22) CSIR 1975 SA

Council for Scientific and Industrial Research.
Selection and design of hot-mix asphalt surfacings for highways. (Technical Recommendations for Highways, NITRR, Draft TRH 8) CSIR 1976 SA

Council for Scientific and Industrial Research.
Slope stability analysis by Bishop's method (circular slip) SLOP 2. 24pp. (Computer Information Centre for Transportation, NITRR Manual P1) CSIR 1976 SA

Council for Scientific and Industrial Research.
Slope stability analysis by Morgenstern's method (general slip) SLOP 3. 30pp. (Computer Information Centre for Transportation, NITRR Manual P2) CSIR 1976 SA

Council for the Development of Economic and Social Research in Africa.
Africa development research annual. v. 2. 350pp. cl. ($20.00) CODESRIA 1976 SG

Council for the Social Sciences in East Africa.
Proceedings of the Annual Social Science Conference, University of Dar es Salaam, December 18 - 30, 1973. Theme: Rural development. T.shs.200.00 Univ Bkshop - Dar; distr. 1974 TZ

Coupland, R.T. et al.
Annales de l'université d'Abidjan. Colloque PBI Lamto "milieux herbacés.". 311pp. CFA1250 (F25.00) (Série E-Ecologie, 6-2) Univ Abidjan 1973 IV FRE

Courade, J.
The urban development of Buea. An essay in social geography. 27pp. CFA300 Inst Sciences Hum - Cam 1970 CM

Courade, J.
Victoria-Bota. Croissance urbaine et immigration. 135pp. maps. CFA1,000 Inst Sciences Hum - Cam 1975 CM FRE

Court, D.
Education as social control: the response to inequality in Kenya and Tanzania. 40pp. K.shs.7.00 (Inst. Development Studies, Discussion paps., 217) Inst Dev Stud 1975 KE

Court, D. Ghai, D.P.
Education, society and development: new perspectives from Kenya. 356pp. K.shs.40.00 OUP - Nairobi 1974 KE

Courtejoie, J.
La bilharziose: cycle évolutif du parasite et mesures préventives. 130pp. ill. photos. 80k ($3.60) BERPS 1978 ZR FRE

Courtejoie, J.
Comment bien se nourrir? Quelques informations sur les meilleurs aliments. See: Rotsart de Hertaing, I.

Courtejoie, J.
Cours de statistique sanitaire, a l'usage des infirmiers et des techniciens d'assainissement. See: van der Heyden, A.

Courtejoie, J.
Le dispensaire et sa nouvelle orientation: les responsabilités nouvelles du technicien de la santé. See: Rotsart de Hertaing, I.

Courtejoie, J.
Le don du sang. (Quelques informations sur le don du sang et la transfusion sanguine.) See: Rotsart de Hertaing, I.

Courtejoie, J. Rotsart de Hertaing, I.
L'éducateur nutritionnel: comment améliorer l'alimentation des enfants pour l'éducation. 48pp. photos. 90k ($1.08) (Protection et éducation de la jeunesse, 32) BERPS 1975 ZR FRE

Courtejoie, J.
L'éducateur sanitaire! Un enseignant ou un infirmier peut-il devenir un bon éducateur sanitaire? See: Mvuezolo Bagwanga.

Courtejoie, J. Rotsart de Hertaing, I.
L'éducation de la santé à l'école. Expérience pratique de Kangu-Mayumbe. 32pp. photos. 60k ($0.72) (Protection et éducation de la jeunesse, 5) BERPS 1975 ZR FRE

Courtejoie, J.
L'éducation nutritionnelle. Quelques principes de base et recommandations pratiques. See: Rotsart de Hertaing, I.

Courtejoie, J.
L'éducation sanitaire. Quelques principes de base. See: Nzungu Mavinga.

Courtejoie, J. et al.
Santé et maladie. Hygiène - éducation sanitaire: la santé et les maladies. v. 3 140pp. ill. photos. Z1.60 ($1.92) BERPS 1975 ZR FRE

Courtejoie, J. et al.
Santé et maladie. Hygiène - éducation sanitaire: notions élémentaires sur la propreté et notre corps. 86pp. ill. photos. 80k ($0.96) BERPS 1975 ZR FRE

Courtejoie, J. et al.
Santé et maladie. Hygiène - éducation sanitaire: notre corps, le milieu où nous vivons. v. 2 110pp. ill. photos. Z1.20 ($1.44) BERPS 1975 ZR FRE

Courtejoie, J. Rotsart de Hertaing, I.
L'hôpital rural en zone tropicale: pour une orientation nouvelle des hôpitaux vers le progrès de la santé. 32pp. photos. 60k ($.72) (Orientation nouvelle de l'action médicale, 1) BERPS 1975 ZR FRE

Courtejoie, J.
L'infirmier et la santé publique: notions de prophylaxie et de lutte contre les maladies sociales. See: Rotsart de Hertaing, I.

Courtejoie, J.
L'Infirmier face au malade. Comment favoriser la guérison par un contact authentique? See: Thadila Masiala.

Courtejoie, J.
La jeunesse et le problème des naissances désirables. Quelques informations sur les attitudes de la jeunesse en face de la sexualité. See: Mvuezolo Bafwanga.

Courtejoie, J.
La jeunesse et les maladies vénériennes. Quelques informations sur la blennorragie et la syphilis. See: Rotsart de Hertaing, I.

Courtejoie, J.
Laboratoire et sante: techniques usuelles de laboratoire. See: Rotsart de Hertaing, I.

Courtejoie, J.
La lèpre aujourd'hui! Conceptions récentes de la lutte contre la lèpre. See: Rotsart de Hertaing, I.

Courtejoie, J. Rotsart de Hertaing, I.
Lexique médical: le vocabulaire médical à la portée de tous. 136pp. Z1.00 ($1.20) BERPS 1974 ZR FRE

Courtejoie, J.
Ma maison et ma santé. Comment la maison peut-elle favoriser la santé de ma famille? See: Rotsart de Hertaing, I.

Courtejoie, J.
La malaria: cycle évolutif du parasite du paludisme et mesures préventives. See: van der Heyden, A.

Courtejoie, J.
La malnutrition de l'enfant et ses conséquences. See: Rotsart de Hertaing, I.

Courtejoie, J.
La maternité et promotion de la santé. Le rôle de l'infirmière-accoucheuse dans la médecine promotionnelle. See: Rotsart de Hertaing, I.

Courtejoie, J.
Maternité et santé. See: Rotsart de Hertaing, I.

Courtejoie, J.
La médecine à l'école: comment améliorer les contacts entre les écoles, les hôpitaux et les dispensaires. See: Rotsart de Hertaing, I.

Courtejoie, J.
Les médicaments à la maison. Quelques informations sur la pharmacie familiale et son usage. See: Dilayen Dilamutung-a-Ngya.

Courtejoie, J.
Les médicaments et le tabac sont-ils dangereux? Quelques informations sur l'usage des médicaments et leurs abus: l'alcool, la drogue, le tabac. See: Rotsart de Hertaing, I.

Courtejoie, J. Rotsart de Hertaing, I.
Notions de pharmacologie. 204pp. Z4.00 ($4.80) BERPS 1975 ZR FRE

Courtejoie, J.
Nourriture saine, meilleure santé: Cours de diététique à l'usage des infirmiers et des enseignants des régions tropicales. See: Van der Heyden, A.

Courtejoie, J.
La nutrition. L'éducation nutritionnelle dans la pratique journalière. See: Rotsart de Hertaing, I.

Courtejoie, J.
On ne trouve rien au dispensaire...et pourtant, je suis malade. Quelques informations sur les maladies psychosomatiques. See: Nzungu Mavinga.

Courtejoie, J. Rotsart de Hertaing, I.
Petit aide-mémoire pour le dispensaire: quelques médicaments courants et leurs usages. 104pp. Z1.00 ($1.20) BERPS 1974 ZR FRE

Courtejoie, J. Rotsart de Hertaing, I.
Petits problèmes de pharmacologie et d'éducation sanitaire. 40pp. 80k ($0.96) BERPS 1974 ZR FRE

Courtejoie, J.
Peut-on éviter les accidents? Quelques informations sur les accidents et leur prévention. See: Rotsart de Hertaing, I.

Courtejoie, J.
Pour que mon bébé naisse en bonne santé. Quelques informations sur les consultations prénatales et leur importance pour la mère et l'enfant. See: Rotsart de Hertaing, I.

Courtejoie, J.
Pour une authentique éducation sexuelle. La sexualité et les problèmes qu'elle pose aux jeunes. See: Rotsart de Hertaing, I.

Courtejoie, J.
Pourquoi vacciner vox enfants? Quelques informations sur le rôle des vaccins dans la défense contre les maladies. See: Rotsart de Hertaing, I.

Courtejoie, J.
Le sang et l'anémie. Qu'est-ce que l'anémie SS? Quelques informations sur l'importance du sang et les maladies qui peuvent l'abîmer. See: Rotsart de Hertaing, I.

Courtejoie, J.
La santé de vos enfants: comment protéger la santé des enfants depuis la naissance jusqu'à leur entrée à l'école. See: Matundu Nzita.

Courtejoie, J.
Santé et tradition: proverbes et coutumes relatifs à la santé. See: Nzungu Mavinga.

Courtejoie, J.
Santé meilleure, source de progrès! See: Rotsart de Hertaing, I.

Courtejoie, J.
La tuberculose aujourd'hui! Conceptions récentes de la lutte contre la tuberculose. See: Rotsart de Hertaing, I.

Courtejoie, J.
La tuberculose: l'évolution de la maladie et sa prévention par l'éducation sanitaire. See: Rotsart de Hertaing, I.

Courtejoie, J.
Les vers intestinaux à l'école: prise de conscience par la jeunesse. See: Nzungu Mavinga.

Courtejoie, J.
Les vers intestinaux: cycles évolutifs des vers intestinaux et moyens de prévention. See: van der Herden, A.

Courtejoie, J. Rotsart de Hertaing, I.
Vers un éclairage nouveau de quelques problèmes de santé: l'attitude des techniciens de la santé en face de leurs nouvelles responsabilités. 28pp. photos. 50k ($0.60) (Orientation nouvelle de l'action médicale, 3) BERPS 1975 ZR FRE

Coussements, S. et al.
La fumure minérale du caféier d'arabie au Burundi. 51pp. Univ Bujumbura 1971 BD FRE

Coutts, J.J.
Prophètes et rois d'Israel. Tr. fr. English 156pp. maps photos. CFA660 CLE 1971 CM FRE

Cowan, D.
A method of estimating the number of operating theatres required in a general hospital. 8pp. (CSIR research reports, 201) CSIR 1963 SA

Cowden, J.W.
Holmes' local government finance in South Africa. 2 2nded. 552pp. R22.50 cl. Butterworths 1969 SA

Cowen, B.A. Gering, L.
The law of negotiable instruments in South Africa. 4 4thed. R18.50 Juta 1966 SA

Cowie, M.J.
The London Missionary Society in South Africa. 81pp. R1.00 Univ Cape Town Lib 1969 SA

Cowley, C.
Schwikkard of Natal and the old Transvaal. 160pp. ill. cl. R4.50 Struik 1974 SA

Cowley, D. Serour, A.
Cairo: A practical guide. [revised entry]. 160pp. maps. £E3.00 ($7.50) Am Univ 1975 UA

Cowley, D., ed. Magalli, M., ed.
A practical guidebook to Cairo. 90pp. maps. $6.50 £E1.50 Am Univ 1975 UA

Cox, K.M.
Immigration into South Africa 1940-1967. 26pp. 60c. Univ Cape Town Lib 1970 SA

Cox, P.
Why me? 68pp. ill. C1.20 (50p.) Africa Christian 1973 GH

Cozens, A.B.
New biology for West African schools. See: Stone, R.H.

Cozien, M.P.
Wheat farming in Southern Africa. Serials articles 1961-1971. 20pp. R1.00 (Univ. Cape Town Libraries. Bibl. ser.) Univ Cape Town Lib 1974 SA

Crabbe, A.
John Mensah Sarbah: his life and works, 1864-1910. 115pp. photos. C4.00 (£2.00/$4.00) Ghana UP 1971 GH

Cragg, D.G.L.
Christ and liberation. 36pp. 50c. Methodist 1977 SA

Crahay, F.
Humanisme communautaire, idéologie bien portante?
20pp. 30k Press Univ Zaire 1962 ZR FRE

Crahay, H.
La diversité des sciences dans l'unité du savoir. 24pp.
30k Press Univ Zaire 1963 ZR FRE

Craig, B.J.
Rock paintings and petroglyphs of South and Central
Africa. 58pp. 80c. Univ Cape Town Lib 1947 SA

Craig, R.
The church: unity in integrity. 50c. (Peter Ainslie
Memorial lec., 16) Rhodes Univ Lib 1965 SA

Craig, R.
Politics and religion: a Christian view. 23pp. Free
Univ Rhodesia Lib 1972 RH

Craig, R.
Religion - its reality and its relevance. 29pp. 30c
Univ Rhodesia Lib 1965 RH

Cranwell, H.
Let the children play! A beginner's guide to creative play
and playgroups. 32pp. ill. photos. 25t Christ Lit
Assoc - Mal 1975 MW

Crass, R.S.
Freshwater fishes of Natal. 180pp. ill. pl. map. cl.
R2.10 Shuter 1965 SA

Craw, W. Ram, K.
A guide to the Co-operative Societies Act. 136pp.
K.shs.20.00 Kenya Inst Admin 1969 KE

Crawford, C.E.
Stocklam market survey. See: White, M.D.

Crawford, J.
Dieu et votre argent. Tr. from the English 142pp.
Z1.00 CEDI 1974 ZR FRE

Crawford, J.R.
Témoignage protestant au Zaire (1878-1970) 52pp.
35k CEDI 1974 ZR FRE

Crawford, J.R.
Your money and God. 108pp. T.shs.6.50 Central
Tanganyika 1974 TZ

Crawford, M.
Second thoughts on learning science by rote. 21pp.
C1.00 ($1.00/50p.) (Inaugural lecture) Ghana UP
1971 GH

Crayner, J.B.
Yeehyiahyia oo! [Greetings!] 101pp. C1.00 Bur
Ghana Lang 1975 GH FAT

Crealock, J.N.
The road to Ulundi. 48pp. ill. R24.00 Univ of Natal
1969 SA

Creaser, H.
Beginning science in Eastern Nigeria. 1, 2 bks.
See: Onyekwere, A.O.

Creaser, H.
Beginning science in Eastern Nigeria. 2, 2 bks
See: Onyekwere, A.

Creative Writers Association.
Talent for tomorrow: 5th anthology. 233pp. ill. C1.20
($.60) Ghana Publ Corp 1966 GH

Creed, P.
The dimensional stability of all-wool single jersey fabric.
See: Silver, H.M.

Cressman, A.
The letter of James. 32pp. K.shs.3.00 Evangel 1972
KE

Cressman, A.
Marriage and the home. 32pp. K.shs.3.00 Evangel
1965 KE

Cressman, A.
The pastor. 64pp. K.shs.4.00 Evangel 1968 KE

Cressman, A.
Paul's first letter to Corinth. 52pp. K.shs.2.50
Evangel 1972 KE

Cressman, A.
Paul's second letter to Corinth. 36pp. K.shs.2.00
Evangel 1972 KE

Cressman, E.
Marriage and the home. 2nd ed. 40pp. 15k SIM
1969 NR

Creswell, K.A.C.
Bibliography of the Architecture, arts & crafts of Islam.
1,355pp. hd. L.E.20.000 ($57.50) Am Univ 1972 UA

Cretois, L.
Dictionnaire serer-français. 4 v. CFA1250 (C.L.A.D.
Etude, 48) CLAD 1972 SG FRE

Crewe, W. Porter, D. Dallas, D.
Scientific English: a comprehension course. 1, 2 pts.
242pp. 75pt. ($3.00) Khartoum UP 1972 SJ

Crewe, W. Porter, D. Dallas, D.
Scientific English: a comprehension course. 2, 2 pt.
232pp. 80pt. ($3.00) Khartoum UP 1972 SJ

Crewe, W. Porter, D. Dallas, D.
Scientific English: a comprehension course. Answer
book, pt. 1. 73pp. 40pt. ($1.50) Khartoum UP 1972
SJ

Crewe, W. Porter, D. Dallas, D.
Scientific English: a comprehension course. Answer
book, pt. 2. 89pp. 40pt. ($1.50) Khartoum UP 1972
SJ

Crider, D.
Mchungaji na kazi yake. See: Msweli, S.

Crider, D.
The shepherd and his work. See: Msweli, S.

Criper, C.
Language in Uganda. See: Ladefoged, P.

Crippen, D. et al.
God, myself and others. 176pp. ill. K.shs.17.00
($2.15) Evangel 1976 KE

Crippen, D.
New approaches in religious education. 40pp.
K.shs.5.00 Evangel 1974 KE

Cripwell, K.K.R.
Teaching adults by television. 130pp. 50c (Fac. of
Education, Univ. of Rhodesia, 6) Univ Rhodesia Lib 1966
RH

Cristiani, M.
Sainte Marie Goretti. 39pp. 40k St. Paul 1969 ZR
FRE

Croft, J. ed.
Aureol poems. 24pp. 20c. Fourah Bay Bkshp 1970
SL

Croft, P.
General science, Form I. See: Dent, S.R.

Cromer, C.A., ed. Akande, O., ed. Gwarzo, M.A., ed.
Proceedings of the meeting of Agricultural engineers,
Zaria, 4-5 September, 1973. 170pp. free Inst Agric
Res-Zaria 1974 NR

Cronin, J.P., ed.
Ideologies of politics. See: de Crespigny, A., ed.

Cronje, F.J.C., et al.
New history for the OFS standard 3. 115pp. ill. photo.
85c. Nasou 1975 SA

Crossley, J.
Alaye isin Kristi fun musulumi. [The explanation of
Christianity for the Moslems] 19pp. 10k Daystar 1968
NR YOR

Crossley, J.
Awon imale mbere. [The Moslems are asking] 26pp.
10k Daystar 1968 NR YOR

Crowder, M., ed. Ikime, O., ed.
West African chiefs: their changing status under colonial
rule and independence. 453pp. pap. & hd. N6.00 cl.
N3.00 pap. Univ Ife Press (NR only) 1970 NR

Author Index

Crowder, M.
Eze goes to school.   See: Nzekwu, O.

Crowder, M.
A guide map of Ife.   See: Majasan, J.A.

Crowe, N.D.
Growth, yield and economics of Pinus patula in the Natal Midlands. 82pp. map.   R1.70   (A v.42, no.2)   Univ Stellenbosch, Lib 1967 SA

Crowe, T.J.   Tsedeke, A.A.
An annotated list of insect pests of field crops in Ethiopia. 71pp. map. ($5.00) Inst Agric Res - Addis 1977 ET

Crowe, T.J.   Shitaye, G.M.
Crop pest handbook. 3rd rev. ed.   Inst Agric Res - Addis 1977 ET

Crowe, T.J., ed.   Edwards, S., ed.
Holletta - Guenet research station: progress report for the period April 1972 to March 1973.   344pp.   ex. only. Inst Agric Res - Addis 1975 ET

Crowley, D.J.
Folktale research in Africa.   19pp.   C1.00 ($1.00/50p.)   (Inaugural lecture)   Ghana UP 1971 GH

Cruickshank, B.
Potentials in pathology.   39pp.   30c   Univ Rhodesia Lib 1966 RH

Cruickshank, J.G.   Ellis, B.P.B.   Farrell, J.G.
Cholera in the Manicaland Province of Rhodesia, February to May, 1974.   10pp.   R$1.00   (Fac. of Medicine, Univ. of Rhodesia, 6)   Univ Rhodesia Lib 1975 RH

Cruickshank, J.G.
Fundamental approach to the enigmas of virus and disease.   27pp.   30c   Univ Rhodesia Lib 1970 RH

Cruise, S.E.
The place of geometry in university mathematics.   ex. only   (Inaugural lec.)   Rhodes Univ Lib 1963 SA

CSIR National Building Research Institute.
Addendum to Dr. 3: termites wood-borers and fungi in buildings.   ill.   R1.50 cl.   (CSIR research reports, 48) CSIR 1950 SA

CSIR National Building Research Institute.
A guide to special housing for aged people.   54pp. ill. (CSIR research reports, 245)   CSIR 1967 SA

CSIR National Building Research Institute.
Handbook of South African national building stone. 160pp. pl. map. hd.   R7.00   Van Schaik 1967 SA

CSIR National Building Research Institute.
Research studies on the costs of urban Bantu housing. rev ed.   ill.   R1.50   (CSIR research reports, 112A) CSIR 1954 SA

CSIR National Building Research Institute.
A survey of rent paying capacity of urban natives in South Africa.   ill.   R1.50   (CSIR research reports, 175) CSIR 1960 SA

CSIR National Institute for Road Research.
Hot storage of bituminous road-binders in the field. 13pp. ill.   (CSIR research reports, 169)   CSIR 1960 SA

CSIR National Institute for Road Research.
Review of a number of road priming experiments carried out between August 1961 and March 1964.   24pp. ill. (CSIR research reports, 256)   CSIR 1967 SA

CSIR School Buildings Committee.
1200-pupil comprehensive high school: recommendations of the school building committee, report, 14.   48pp. (CSIR research reports, 193)   CSIR 1964 SA

CSIR School Buildings Committee.
Industrial art centres.   35pp. ill.   (CSIR research reports, 192)   CSIR 1962 SA

CSIR School Buildings Committee.
School gymnasia: African, English.   261pp. ill.   (CSIR research reports, 191)   CSIR 1963 SA

CSIR Vocational School Buildings Committee.
Housecraft high schools.   19pp.   (CSIR research reports, 220)   CSIR 1965 SA

CSIR Vocational School Buildings Committee.
Planning commercial high schools.   43pp.   (CSIR research reports, 194)   CSIR 1963 SA

CSIR Vocational School Buildings Committee.
School hostels: English and African.   41pp.   (CSIR research reports, 206)   CSIR 1964 SA

CSIR Vocational School Buildings Committee.
Technical high schools.   67pp.   (CSIR research reports, 207)   CSIR 1964 SA

C.S.S. Bookshops.
Akwukwo ogugu Igbo. [Igbo language text.].   3rd ed. 71pp.   40k   CSS 1974 NR IGB

Cubitt, G.   Richter, J.
South West. [Also available in German].   156pp. photos. cl.   R9.95   Struik 1976 SA

Cubitt, G.S., ed.   Helfet, A., ed.
South Africa. [Also available in German].   208pp. pl. col. pl. maps. cl.   R9.95   Struik 1975 SA

Cubitt, G.S.
Islands of the Indian Ocean. Iles de l'Océan Indien. [English and French text].   176pp. pl. col. pl. maps. cl. R12.95   Struik 1975 SA

Cuisenier, J.
L'Ansarine - contribution à la sociologie du développement.   199pp. ill.   D2.130   (Série III, Mémoires du Centre d'Etudes Humaines, 7)   Univ Tunis 1963 TI FRE

Cullen, A.
Crash strike.   175pp. photos.   K.shs.35.00   ($12.00) EAPH 1971 KE

Cullen, A.
Hamisi's hardest safari.   125pp. ill.   K.shs4.50 ($2.00)   EAPH 1967 KE

Cullen, A.
Hamisi's holiday safari.   111pp. ill.   K.shs4.50   ($2.00) EAPH 1965 KE

Cullen, A.
Hamisi's second safari.   131pp. ill.   K.shs6.00 ($2.00)   EAPH 1966 KE

Cullen, A.
Window onto wilderness.   186pp. photos.   K.shs.42.00 cl.   K.shs.26.50 pap.   ($7.80 cl.) ($4.50 pap.)   EAPH 1969 KE

Cullen, M.E.
The suppression of dust in mines, 1950-1967.   31pp. R1.65   Dept Bibliog, Lib & Typo 1968 SA

Culwick, A.T.
Good out of Africa: a study in the relativity of morals. 44pp.   K1.50   (75p.)   (Rhodes-Livingstone paps., 8) Inst Soc Res - Zam 1942 ZA

Cumpsty, J.S.
Religion in the dynamics of freedom.   10pp.   30c. (U.C.T. inaugural lec. New series, 5)   Univ Cape Town Lib 1970 SA

Cunningham, A.M., comp.
Guide to the archives and papers in the University of the Witwatersrand Library.   3rd ed.   161pp.   R5.00   Univ Witwatersrand Lib 1975 SA

Cunningham, A.M., ed.
J. Howard Pim papers.   52pp.   R2.50   (Historical & Literary Papers: Inventories of Collections, 3)   Univ of the Witwatersrand Lib 1977 SA

Cunningham, A.M., ed.
J.D. Rheinallt Jones papers.   35pp.   R2.50   (Historical & Literary Papers: Inventories of Collections, 4)   Univ of the Witwatersrand Lib 1977 SA

Cunningham, A.M., ed.
Nourse family papers.   31pp.   R2.00   (Historical & Literary Papers: Inventories of Collections, 1)   Univ of the Witwatersrand Lib 1977 SA

Cunningham, A.M., ed.
Schoch family papers. 21pp. R1.75 (Historical & Literary Papers: Inventories of Collections, 2) Univ of the Witwatersrand Lib 1977 SA

Cunnison, I.
History of the Luapula: an essay on the historical notions of a Central African tribe. 42pp. K1.25 (63p.) (Rhodes-Livingstone paps., 21) Inst Soc Res - Zam 1951 ZA

Cunnison, I.
Kinship and local organisation on the Luapula: a preliminary account or some aspects of Luapula social organisation. 32pp. 55n. (27p.) (Rhodes-Livingstone communications, 5) Inst Afr Stud - Lusaka 1950 ZA

Cunnison, I.
The Luapula peoples of Northern Rhodesia: customs and history in tribal politics. 250pp. ill. hd. K4.00 (£2.00/$6.50) Inst Afr Stud - Lusaka 1960 ZA

Curr, A. Calder, A.
Writers in East Africa. 151pp. K.shs.19.50 ($4.00/£1.90) EALB 1974 KE

Curran, C., joint author.
New perspectives in moral theology and on the future. See: Verryn, T.D., joint author.

Currey, R.F.
Rhodes University 1904-1970: a chronicle. 181pp. hd. R2.50 Rhodes Univ Lib 1971 SA

Currey, R.N.
The Africa we knew. 32pp. R1.80 (Mantis Poets, 1) Philip 1973 SA

Currey, R.N.
Letters and other writings of a Natal Sheriff: Thomas Phipson, 1815-76. 280pp. map/ill. R6.50 OUP-SA 1968 SA

Curriculum Development Centre, Ministre of Education, Lusaka.
Zambia Primary Course: English-Primary Mathematics-Social Studies-Zambia Languages-Mathematics; Grades I-VII. [An extensive course in over 400 parts: pupil's books, teacher's handbooks, readers, word cards, flashcards, etc.] Full details from publisher. Neczam 1970 ZA

Currie, D.
South Africa; an address delivered to the fellows of the Royal Colonial Institute at their meeting in London on Tuesday, the 10th April, 1888. 48pp. R3.50 (Reprints, 50) State-Lib-SA SA

Currie, D.
South Africa: an address delivered to the fellows of the Royal Colonial Institute at their meeting in London on Tuesday, the 10th April, 1888. Reprint ed. 1888. ed. 48pp. R3.50 (Reprints, 50) State Lib - SA 1970 SA

Currie, J.C.
Material published during the period 1946-56 on the Indian question in South Africa. 28pp. 60c. Univ Cape Town Lib 1969 SA

Curtin, P.D., ed.
Africa remembered: narratives by West Africans. 364pp. maps ill. N5.00 Ibadan UP 1967 NR

Curtis, A.
Conversation practice. 54pp. K.shs5.50 ($2.00) EAPH 1971 KE

Curtis, A.
Who's afraid of CPE? 248pp. K.shs.15.00 ($4.00) EAPH 1971 KE

Curtis, A.
Write well. 72pp. ill. K.shs.6.50 OUP - Nairobi 1975 KE

Curtis, D.L.
A review of the sorghum breeding programme in Nigeria. 14pp. 20k (Samaru misc. pap., 18) Inst Agric Res-Zaria 1969 NR

Cuthbert, V.
The great siege of Fort Jesus. 148pp. ill. K.shs7.50 ($2.60) EAPH 1970 KE

Cutler, V.F.
Woman power, social imperatives and home science. 19pp. C1.00 ($1.00/50p.) (Inaugural lecture) Ghana UP 1969 GH

Cvetkovic, D.
Sources of feldspar in the Sarenje and Mit Hills areas. K3.00 (Dept. of Geological Survey, Economic Reports, 32) Geol Survey - Zam 1976 ZA

Cywes, S.
The surgeon and the child. 12pp. pl. 30c. (Univ. Cape Town. Inaugural lec., new series, 41) Univ Cape Town Lib 1976 SA

D'Aby, A.
Le problème des chefferies traditionnelles en Côte d'Ivoire. 47pp. photos. pl. CFA250 (F5.00) Inst Ethno-Socio 1968 IV FRE

Dachelet, R.
Codage informatique du contenu lexical des programmes télévisuels de français (CP1 - CP2) See: Armand, E.

Dachs, A., ed.
Christianity south of the Zambezi. v. 1 210pp. R$2.90 Mambo 1973 RH

Dachs, A. J.
Livingstone: missionary explorer. ($1.40) (Local series pamphlets, 28) Central Africa Hist Assoc 1974 RH

Dachs, A.J.
A discussion of the major stone-built ruins of Southern Rhodesia and adjacent territories. 50c. (Local series pamphlets, 9) Central Africa Hist Assoc 1963 RH

Dachs, A.J.
The papers of John Mackenzie. 283pp. cl. R8.00 African Stud Inst - Wit 1975 SA

Dachs, A.J.
The road to the north. The origin and force of a slogan. 60c. (Local series pamphlets, 23) Central Africa Hist Assoc 1969 RH

Dada, G.O.
Onibonoje primary social studies; teacher's guide to bk. I. 65pp. ill. 60k Onibonoje 1976 NR

Dada, G.O.
Onibonoje primary social studies; teacher's guide to bk. II. 78pp. 70k Onibonoje 1976 NR

Dada, S.
Notes, questions/answers on "A Christmas carol". N1.20 Aromolaran 1975[?] NR

Dada, S.
Notes, questions/answers on "The trumpet major". 60pp. N1.20 Aromolaran 1975[?] NR

Dada, S.
Notes, questions/answers on "Weep not child". N1.20 Aromolaran 1975[?] NR

Dada, S.A.
Arithmetic and quantitative aptitude tests. 160pp. N1.25 Onibonoje 1966 NR

Dada, S.A., et al.
Onibonoje primary modern mathematics. bk. 1 82pp. ill. 90k Onibonoje 1974 NR

Dada, S.A., et al.
Onibonoje primary modern mathematics. bk. 2 63pp. ill. N1.10 Onibonoje 1974 NR

Dada, S.A., et al.
Onibonoje primary modern mathematics. bk. 3 107pp. ill. N1.10 Onibonoje 1974 NR

Dada, S.A., et al.
Onibonoje primary modern mathematics. bk. 4. 135pp. ill. N1.30 Onibonoje 1976 NR

Dada, S.A., et al.
Onibonoje primary modern mathematics. bk. 5. 120pp ill. N1.40 Onibonoje 1976 NR

Dada, S.A., et al.
Onibonoje primary modern mathematics. bk. 6. 135pp.
ill. N1.65 Onibonoje 1976 NR

Dada, S.A., et al.
Onibonoje primary modern mathematics. Teacher's bk.
1. 40pp. ill. 65k. Onibonoje 1976 NR

Dada, S.A., et al.
Onibonoje primary modern mathematics. Teacher's bk.
2. 60pp. ill. 70k. Onibonoje 1976 NR

Dada, S.A., et al.
Onibonoje primary modern mathematics. Teacher's bk.
3. 65pp. ill. 75k. Onibonoje 1976 NR

Dada, S.A., et al.
Onibonoje primary modern mathematics. Teacher's bk.
4. 65pp. ill. 85k. Onibonoje 1976 NR

Dada, S.A., et al.
Onibonoje primary modern mathematics. Teacher's bk.
5. 60pp. ill. 95k. Onibonoje 1976 NR

Dada, S.A., et al
Onibonoje primary modern mathematics. Teacher's bk.
6. 65pp. ill. N1.05 Onibonoje 1976 NR

Dada, S.A., et al.
Onibonoje primary modern mathematics. Workbk. 1.
100pp. ill. 65k. Onibonoje 1976 NR

Dada, S.A., et al.
Onibonoje primary modern mathematics. Workbk. 2.
75pp. ill. 75k. Onibonoje 1976 NR

Dada, S.A., et al.
Onibonoje primary modern mathematics. Workbk. 3.
80pp. ill. 85k. Onibonoje 1976 NR

Dada, S.A., et al.
Onibonoje primary modern mathematics. Workbk. 4.
70pp. ill. 95k. Onibonoje 1976 NR

Dada, S.A., et al.
Onibonoje primary modern mathematics. Workbk. 5.
96pp. ill. N1.00 Onibonoje 1976 NR

Dada, S.A., et al.
Onibonoje primary modern mathematics. Workbk. 6.
105pp. ill. N1.10 Onibonoje 1976 NR

Dada, S.A.
Fundamental principles of education. 75pp. N1.20
Onibonoje 1973 NR

Dada, S.A.
General mathematics: objective tests. 141pp. N1.35
Onibonoje 1970 NR

Dada, S.A.
Hints and solutions to apptitude tests. See: Adelusi, O.

Dada, S.A.
Modern mathematics: objective tests. 160pp. N1.35
Onibonoje 1971 NR

Dada, S.A. Josiah, M.O.
Secondary school modern mathematics: pupils bk. 1, 5
bks 202pp. N1.90 Heinemann Educ - Nig 1973 NR

Dada, S.A. Josiah, M.O.
Secondary school modern mathematics: pupils bk. 2, 5
bks 291pp. N2.00 Heinemann Educ - Nig 1973 NR

Dada, S.A. Josiah, M.O.
Secondary school modern mathematics: pupils bk. 3, 5
bks 239pp. N2.25 Heinemann Educ - Nig 1973 NR

Dada, S.A. Josiah, M.O.
Secondary school modern mathematics: pupils bk. 4, 5
bks 259pp. N2.40 Heinemann Educ - Nig 1973 NR

Dada, S.A. Josiah, M.O.
Secondary school modern mathematics: pupils bk. 5, 5
bks 249pp. N2.50 Heinemann Educ - Nig 1973 NR

Dadié, B.
Papassidi maître - excroc. 72pp. CFA600 Nouv Ed
Afric 1975 SG FRE

Daff, K.E.
Mathematics for the practical course, standard 6.
See: de Wet, J.J.

Daff, K.E.
Mathematics for the practical course, standard 7.
See: de Wet, J.J.

Daffalla, H.
The Nubian exodus. 366pp. £S6.00 ($23.00)
Khartoum UP 1975 SJ

Daget, J.
Catalogue de la collection des poissons d'eau douce de
l'IFAN. 59pp. ill. CFA300 (Catalogues et
Documents, 3) IFAN 1949 SG FRE

Daget, J. Iltis, A.
Poissons de Côte d'Ivoire (eaux douces et saumâtres)
385pp. ill. pl. CFA3600 (Mémoires de l'IFAN, 74)
IFAN 1965 SG FRE

Daget, J.
Les poissons du Fouta Dialon et de la Basse Guinée.
210pp. pl. ill. CFA1600 (Mémoires de l'IFAN, 65)
IFAN 1962 SG FRE

Daget, J.
Les poissons du Niger supérieur. [Reprint of ed. 1951].
391pp. ill. (D.fl.110.00) (Mémoires de l'IFAN, 36)
IFAN 1951 SG FRE

Daget, S.
Annales de l'université d'Abidjan. See: Kodjo, N.G.

Dago-Akribi, A.
Annales de l'université d'Abidjan. See: Ette-Battesti, F.

Dagut, J.
Source material on the South African economy,
1860-1899. 1, 3 vols. See: Houghton, D.H.

Dagut, J.
Source material on the South African economy,
1899-1919. 2, 3 vols. See: Houghton, D.H.

Dagut, J.
Source material on the South African economy,
1919-1970. 3, 3vols. See: Houghton, D.H.

Dahal, C.
The adventures of Mr. Hyena. 42pp. K.shs3.60
Equatorial 1972 KE

Dahal, C.
The orange thieves. 72pp. ill. K.shs3.00 ($1.00)
EAPH 1966 KE

Dahlschen, E.
Children in Zambia. 64pp. photos. K2.20 Neczam
1972 ZA

Dahunsi, A.
Jacaranda first atlas for Nigeria. 32pp. maps col. maps.
65k Pilgrim 1974 NR

Dahunsi, A.
Oloyinmomo: Apa kini. 1, 4 bks. See: Jeboda, F.

Dahunsi, A.
Oloyinmomo: Iwe keji. 2, 4 bks. See: Jeboda, F.

Dahunsi, A.
Oloyinmomo: pupils' bk. 3, 4bks. See: Jeboda, F.

Dahunsi, A.
Oloyinmomo: teachers' bk. 4, 4 bks. See: Jeboda, F.

Daily Graphic., ed.
Ghana yearbook, 1975. 152pp. pl. 60pes. Graphic
1975 GH

Daily Times (Nig.) Ltd.
Nigeria Year Book 1973. 22nd ed. 280pp. photos. ill.
maps. 55k Daily Times - Nig 1973 NR

Daily Times (Nig.) Ltd.
Times trade and industrial directory, 1972-1973. 147pp.
hd. N2.10 Daily Times - Nig 1973 NR

Daily Times (Nig.) Ltd.
Who's who in Nigeria: dictionary of prominent
personalities. 2nd ed. 232pp. ill. photos. maps. 50k
Daily Times - Nig 1971 NR

Dak, O.
A geographical analysis of migrants in Uganda. 213pp.
U.shs.30.00 (Occas. paps., 11) Dept Geog - Mak 1969
UG

Dale, D.
A basic English-Shona dictionary. 212pp. pl. hd. & pap. R$1.60 pap. R$1.90 hd. Mambo 1975 RH

Dale, D.
Shona companion. 337pp. R$1.60 Mambo 1974 RH

Dalgalian, G.
Formation des maîtres et didactique des langues. CFA250 (C.L.A.D. Étude, 52) CLAD 1974 SG FRE

Dallas, D.
Scientific English: a comprehension course. 1, 2 pts. See: Crewe, W.

Dallas, D.
Scientific English: a comprehension course. 2, 2 pt. See: Crewe, W.

Dallas, D.
Scientific English: a comprehension course. Answer book, pt. 1. See: Crewe, W.

Dallas, D.
Scientific English: a comprehension course. Answer book, pt. 2. See: Crewe, W.

Dally, A.H.
Geography of North America. 199pp. ill. pl. maps. N1.50 Onibonoje 1974 NR

Damane, M.
Peace, the mother of nations. 56pp. 20c. Morija 1947 LO

Damann, K.E.
Drinking water or sewage: is there a difference? 22pp. 30k (Inaurugal lec., 9) Univ Ife Press 1973 NR

Damant, C.G.
Samuel Makoanyane. 40pp. R.20c. Morija 1957 LO

Damba, A.S.
A teacher's metric system: exercises, problems, activities and projects in metric units. 72pp. U.shs.5.00 Uganda Pub House 1973 UG

Dana, M.
Kufundwa ngamava. [Novel] 2nd ed. 104pp. ill. R1.20 OUP-SA 1971 SA XHO

Dandadzi, J.
Idya Nehama. [Blood is thicker than water.] 13pp. ill. 10c. Rhod Lit Bur 1976 RH SHO

Dandy, A.J.
The B.Sc. examination papers in chemistry. 254pp. hd. K.shs18.00 ($4.25/£1.70) EALB 1971 KE

Daneel, L.
Source guide for art and architecture. 478pp. R11.75 Human Science Res Council 1976 SA

Dangambe, A. Anwar, H.A.
Sabuwar han yar Hausa don makarantu littafi na. [New method of teaching Hausa for schools] 1, 6bks 95k Ilesanmi 1973 NR HAU

Dangambe, A. Anwar, H.A.
Sabuwar han yar Hausa don makarantu littafi na. [New method of teaching Hausa for schools] 2, 6bks N1.00 Ilesanmi NR HAU

Dangambe, A. Anwar, H.A.
Sabuwar han yar Hausa don makarantu littafi na. [New method of teaching Hausa for schools] 3, 6bks N1.10 Ilesanmi NR HAU

Dangambe, A. Anwar, H.A.
Sabuwar han yar Hausa don makarantu littafi na. [New method of teaching Hausa for schools] 4, 6bks N1.20 Ilesanmi NR HAU

Dangambe, A. Anwar, H.A.
Sabuwar han yar Hausa don makarantu littafi na. [New method of teaching Hausa for schools] 5, 6bks N1.40 Ilesanmi NR HAU

Dangambe, A. Anwar, H.A.
Sabuwar han yar Hausa don makarantu littafi na. [New method of teaching Hausa for schools] 6, 6bks N1.45 Ilesanmi NR HAU

Dangambo, A.
Mukoyi Hausa. [Hausa language course.] bk. 1. 74pp. N1.10 Ilesanmi 1976 NR HAU

Dangambo, A.
Mukoyi Hausa. [Hausa language course.] bk. 2. 87pp. N1.25 Ilesanmi 1976 NR HAU

Daniel, F.
General science for tropical schools. 2nd (Metric) ed. workbook 2 79pp. ill. 95k OUP - Nig 1976 NR

Daniel, J.B.M.
The challenge and the response. ex. only (Inaugural lec.) Rhodes Univ Lib 1972 SA

Daniel, J.B.M.
Grahamstown and its environs. 42pp. 50c Rhodes Univ Lib 1974 SA

Daniel, J.B.M.
Survey of the Cape Midlands and Karroo regions. v.5: A geographical analysis of farming. 107pp. maps. Inst Soc & Econ Res - SA 1975 SA

Daniel, W.C.E., ed. Woodman, G.R., ed.
Essays in Ghanaian law: supreme court centenary publication 1876-1976. 273pp. cl. C10.00 Univ Ghana Bkshop; distr. 1976 GH

'Daniel'.
A young man's secrets. 32pp. ill. 45pes. (15p.) Africa Christian 1965 GH

Daniell, S.
African scenery and animals [Reprint of ed. 1805]. 148pp. col. pl. hd. R361.65 cl. (Dfl.1085/$420/£210 cl.) Balkema 1976 SA

Daniels, S.G.H., ed. Freeth, S.J., ed.
Stratigraphy: an interdisciplinary symposium. 56pp. 50k (Inst. of African Stud., Univ. of Ibadan, occas. pub., 19) Inst Afr Stud-Ibadan 1970 NR

Dankoussou, I.
Baaki abim magana. [Contes hawsa.] 180pp. CFA350 CELTHO NG HAU

Dankoussou, I.
Histoire du Dawra. 90pp. CFA350 CELTHO 1970 NG FRE

Dankoussou, I.
Katsina. 465pp. CFA350 CELTHO 1970 NG FRE

Dankwa, J.
Eleven folk plays. 120pp. ill. 60pes. Waterville 1970 GH

Dankwa, J.Y.
Okanni ba. [Cultural play.] 3rd ed. 24pp. ill. 35pes. Bur Ghana Lang 1974 GH TWI

Dankwa, J.Y.
Tete wo bi kyere. [Customs and festivals.] 148pp. ill. 90pes. Bur Ghana Lang 1974 GH TWI

Dankyi, I.M.
Objective exercises in geography. ill./maps. ($6.00) Ghana Publ Corp 1973 GH

Dannenbring, R.
A classification of law books in the University of South Africa library. 65pp. 75c. (R1.25) Univ South Africa 1965 SA

Danquah, M., ed.
Ghana economic review, 1975. hd. ed. 380pp. ill. pl. C10.00 Edit and Publ Serv 1975 GH

Danso.
Okristoni abrabc ho akwankyere. See: Poulton.

Danso, R.O.
Okristoni aboadema ne towyi. [Christian giving] 35pp. 17pes. Waterville 1962 GH TWI

Danziger, C.
Twentieth century South African history in cartoons. 132pp. ill. cl. & pap. R2.95 pap. R5.95 cl. OUP - SA 1976 SA

d'après Ba, T. Diallo, A.W.
Lat Dior. ill. CFA295 Nouv Ed Afric 1976 SG FRE

Dar Tois, P.
   Lexique de droit des affaires zairoises.   See: Nguyen Chanh, T.

Daramola, O.
   Awon asa ati orisa Ile Yoruba.   [Customs and Gods of Yorubaland] 300pp. photos.   N2.50   Onibonoje 1967 NR YOR

Daramola, O.
   Ile ti a fi ito mo.   128pp.   N1.50   Onibonoje 1975 NR YOR

Dare.
   Ilesanmi health course.   1, 6 bks.   See: Omodara.

Dare.
   Ilesanmi health course.   2, 6 bks.   See: Omodara.

Dare.
   Ilesanmi health course.   3, 6 bks.   See: Omodara.

Dare.
   Ilesanmi health course.   4, 6 bks.   See: Omodara.

Dare.
   Ilesanmi health course.   5, 6 bks.   See: Omodara.

Dare.
   Ilesanmi health course.   6, 6 bks.   See: Omodara.

Darkwa, E.N.A.
   Akanfo Anwonsem.   ill.   75pes.   ($.75)   Ghana Publ Corp 1973 GH TWI

Darracott, D.A.   Cloete, C.E.
   Bibliography on marine pollution in South Africa.   131pp. (NSPU Report, 5)   CSIR 1976 SA

Darras, D.
   Index to pictures of South African interest in The Graphic 1915-1932.   65pp.   R3.35   Dept Bibliog, Lib & Typo 1968 SA

Dart, R.A.
   Address.   25c.   (Isma paps., 9)   Inst Study of Man 1963 SA

Dart, R.A.
   Man's evolution.   40c.   (Isma pap., 15)   Inst Study of Man 1964 SA

Dathorne, O.R., comp.
   African poetry for schools and colleges.   168pp.   N1.30 Macmillan 1969 NR

Datoo, B.
   Population density and agricultural systems in the Uluguru mountains, Morogoro district.   T.shs.15.00   ($5.00) (Research pap., 26)   Bur Res Assess - Tanz 1973 TZ

Datoo, B.A.
   Port development in East Africa.   174pp.   K.shs.20.50 pap.   ($4.55/£2.25 pap.)   EALB 1976 KE

D'Aubrey, J.D.
   A carchariid shark new to South African waters.   16pp. R1.10 (Investigational Reports, 9)   Oceanographic Res Inst 1964 SA

D'Aubrey, J.D.
   Regression analysis as an aid to shark taxonomy. See: Steffens, F.E.

D'Aubrey, J.D.   Davies, D.H.
   Shark attack off the east coast of South Africa, 1st February 1961.   5pp.   R1.10 (Investigational Reports, 5) Oceanographic Res Inst 1961 SA

D'Aubrey, J.D.
   Shark attack off the east coast of South Africa, 6 January 1961.   See: Davies, D.H.

D'Aubrey, J.D.
   Shark attack off the east coast of South Africa, 24 December 1960, with notes on the species of shark responsible for the attack.   See: Davis, D.H.

D'Aubrey, J.D.
   Sharks of the east coast of southern Africa, 1: the genus "Carcharhinus" (Carcharhinidae)   See: Bass, A.J.

D'Aubrey, J.D.
   Sharks of the east coast of southern Africa, 2: the families Scyliorhinidae and Pseudotriakidae.   See: Bass, A.J.

D'Aubrey, J.D.
   Sharks of the east coast of southern Africa, 3: the families Carcharhinidae (excluding Carcharhinus and Mustelus) and Sphyrnidae.   See: Bass, A.J.

D'Aubrey, J.D.
   Sharks of the east coast of southern Africa, 4: the families Odontaspididae, Scapanorhychidae, Isuridae, Cetorhinidae, Alopiidae, Orectolobidae, and Rhiniodontidae.   See: Bass, A.J.

D'Aubrey, J.D.
   Two new scyliorhinid sharks from the east coast of Africa with notes on related species.   See: Springer, S.

Daumas, F.
   Narrative of an exploratory tour to the Cape of Good Hope [Reprint of 1846 edition].   See: Arbousset, T.

Daura, B.
   Hausa customs.   See: Madauchi, I.

Daura, B.
   An introduction to classical Hausa.   See: Ahmed, U.

Daura, S.A.
   Mu Kyautata Al'Adun Auren Mu 2.   [Let us improve our marital customs] 16pp.   20k   Northern Nig 1973 NR HAU

Daura, S.A.
   Tauraruwar Hamada.   [The star of the desert] 72pp. 85k   Northern Nig 1970 NR HAU

Daveau, S.
   Recherches morphologiques sur la région de Bandiagara. 120pp. ill. maps pl.   CFA1800   (Mémoires de l'IFAN, 56)   IFAN 1959 SG FRE

Davellex, B.
   Chimie générale.   See: Ouahes, R.

Davenport, T.R.H.
   The Afrikaner bond: the history of a South African political party, 1880-1911.   436pp. pl. maps.   R3.00 pap R8.10 hd.   OUP-SA 1966 SA

Davenport, T.R.H.
   The beginnings of urban segregation in South Africa: the Natives (urban areas) Act of 1923 and its background. 80c   (Inst. of Social and Economic Research occas. paps., 15)   Inst Soc & Econ Res - SA 1971 SA

Davenport, T.R.H., ed.   Hunt, K.S., ed.
   The right to the land. (Documents on Southern African History) 96pp. photos. maps. cl. & pap.   R7.50 cl. R4.50 pap.   Philip 1974 SA

Davenport, T.R.H., ed.
   Studies in local history. Essays in honour of Winifred Maxwell.   107pp. hd.   R7.50 cl.   OUP - SA 1976 SA

Davey, T.H.
   Disease and population pressure in the tropics.   22pp. 30k   Ibadan UP 1958 NR

David, A.S., et al.
   Interdisciplinary approaches to population studies proceedings on the West Africa science on population studies. University of Ghanna, Legon 30th November-4th December 1972.   333pp.   C6.00   (Univ. Ghana, Population Studies, 4)   Univ Ghana Bkshop; distr. 1975 GH

David, M., ed.
   Summary report of a workshop on a food and nutrition strategy for Kenya.   See: Westley, S.B., ed.

David Philip Publisher/Anglican Church.
   Liturgy 1975: The holy eucharist, morning and evening prayer: presentation edition.   80pp. cl.   R6.00 cl. Philip 1976 SA

Davids, J.
   Searching for words.   32pp.   R1.80   (Mantis Poets, 3) Philip 1974 SA

Davidson, E.
   Pietersburg magisterial district.   69pp.   R1.75   Dept Bibliog, Lib & Typo 1968 SA

Davidson, L.
Res medica - a personal philosophy. 26pp. 30c pap. Univ Rhodesia Lib 1965 RH

Davies, C.S.
Shona. Grade 1: Go go goi (Manyika) 64pp. 65c. Longman - Rhod 1969 RH SHO

Davies, C.S.
Shona. Grade 1: Svikai (Zezuru). 64pp. 55c. Longman - Rhod 1969 RH SHO

Davies, C.S.
Shona. Grade 2: Pindai (Manyika). 64pp. 65c. Longman - Rhod 1969 RH SHO

Davies, C.S.
Shona. Grade 2: Tambirwai (Zexuru). 64pp. 60c. Longman - Rhod 1969 RH SHO

Davies, C.S.
Shona. Grade 3. Farai (Zezuru) 96pp. 60c. Longman - Rhod 1970 RH SHO

Davies, C.S.
Shona. Grade 3: Garai (Manyika). 96pp. 60c. Longman - Rhod 1970 RH SHO

Davies, C.S.
Shona. Grade 4: Nakirwai. 116pp. 65c. Longman - Rhod 1970 RH SHO

Davies, C.S.
Shona. Grade 5: Nzwisisai. 128pp. 70c. Longman - Rhod 1970 RH SHO

Davies, C.S.
Shona. Teacher's bk. grade 1. 140pp. R$1.40 Longman - Rhod 1968 RH SHO

Davies, C.S.
Shona. Teacher's bk. grade 2. 96pp. 85c. Longman - Rhod 1968 RH SHO

Davies, C.S.
Shona. Teacher's bk. grade 3. 64pp. 70c. Longman - Rhod 1970 RH SHO

Davies, C.S.
Shona. Teacher's bk. grade 4. 64pp. 60c. Longman - Rhod 1971 RH SHO

Davies, C.S.
Shona. Teacher's bk. grade 5. 44pp. 60c. Longman - Rhod 1972 RH SHO

Davies, D.A.
East Africa's weather service: the work of E.A. meteorological development. ill. K.shs.2.50 ($1.50/60p.) EALB 1968 KE

Davies, D.H.
Land use in central Cape Town. 128pp. photo. hd. R5.00 Longman SA 1965 SA

Davies, D.H.
The miocene shark fauna of the southern St. Lucia area. 16pp. R1.10 (Investigational Reports, 10) Oceanographic Res Inst 1964 SA

Davies, D.H.
The Penaeid prawns of the St. Lucia Lake system. See: Joubert, L.E.S.

Davies, D.H. Smith, E.D. Lochner, J.P.A.
Preliminary investigations on the hearing of sharks. 10pp. R1.10 (Investigational Reports, 7) Oceanographic Res Inst 1963 SA

Davies, D.H.
Shark attack and its relationship of temperature, beach patronage and the seasonal abundance of dangerous sharks. 43pp. R1.20 (Investigational Reports, 6) Oceanographic Res Inst 1963 SA

Davies, D.H.
Shark attack off the east coast of South Africa, 1st February 1961. See: D'Aubrey, J.D.

Davies, D.H. D'Aubrey, J.D.
Shark attack off the east coast of South Africa, 6 January 1961. 7pp. R1.10 (Investigational Reports, 3) Oceanographic Res Inst 1961 SA

Davies, D.H.
Shark attack off the east coast of South Africa, 22nd January 1961. 6pp. R1.10 (Investigational Reports, 4) Oceanographic Res Inst 1961 SA

Davies, D.H.
Shark attack on fishing boat in South Africa. 4pp. R1.10 (Investigational Reports, 1) Oceanographic Res Inst 1961 SA

Davies, D.H. Joubert, L.E.S.
Tag evaluation and shark tagging in South African waters. 36pp. R1.10 (Investigational Reports, 12) Oceanographic Res Inst 1966 SA

Davies, H.R.J.
Town and country in North Central State, Nigeria. N1.00 (Samaru misc. pap., 63) Inst Agric Res - Zaria 1976 NR

Davies, M.B.
The novels of Benjamin Disraeli. 20pp. C1.00 ($1.00/50p.) (Inaugural lecture) Ghana UP 1969 GH

Davies, O.
Natal archaeological studies. 44pp. ill. 55c. Univ of Natal 1952 SA

Davies, R.J.
Of cities and societies: a geographer's viewpoint. 20pp. 30c. (Univ. Cape Town. Inaugural lec., new series, 38) Univ Cape Town Lib 1976 SA

Davies, W.J.
Patterns of non-white population distribution in Port Elizabeth with special reference to the application of the group areas act. R2.80 (Inst. for Planning Research, series B, 1) Inst Planning Res 1971 SA

Davies, W.J.
Urban Bantu retail activities, consumer behaviour, and shopping patterns: a study of Port Elizabeth. R2.00 (Inst. for Planning Research, series B, 2) Inst Planning Res 1972 SA

Davis, A.G.
The university college farm in the agriculture of Rhodesia and Nyasaland. 43pp. 30c pap. Univ Rhodesia Lib 1960 RH

Davis, D.H. D'Aubrey, J.D.
Shark attack off the east coast of South Africa, 24 December 1960, with notes on the species of shark responsible for the attack. 10pp. R1.10 (Investigational Reports, 2) Oceanographic Res Inst 1961 SA

Davis, E.
Introduction to modern English usage. 3rd ed. 40pp. 45c. OUP-SA 1972 SA

Davis, E.
Yeat's contacts with French poetry. 63pp. 60c. (R1.10) Univ South Africa 1961 SA

Davis, M.A.G.
Incorporation in the Union of South Africa or self-government: Southern Rhodesia's choice, 1922. 82pp. 85c. (R1.35) Univ South Africa 1965 SA

Davis, N.E.
Africa: the making of the modern world. bk. 3 120pp. maps. K.shs.13.50 OUP-Nairobi 1973 KE

Davis, O.
The archaeology of the flooded Volta Basin. 24pp. 70pes. (Occas. pap in Archaeology, 1) Univ Ghana Bkshop 1971 GH

Davis, R.
Prospects for joint production of livestock and wildlife on East African rangeland: the case of Kenya. 21pp. T.shs.7.00 Bur Res Assess - Tanz 1969 TZ

Davis, S.
The decipherment of the Minoan Linear A and pictographic scripts. 342pp. ill. cl. R20.00 Witwatersrand UP 1970 SA

Davis, S.
Sumerograms and akkadograms in Minoan Hittite. 45pp. R5.00 cl. Witwatersrand UP 1969 SA

Author Index

Davison, R.B.
West African Institute of Social and Economic Research: The study of industrial relations in West Africa. N1.00 ($2.00) (W.A.I.S.E.R., 2nd annual conference pap., 1) NISER 1953 NR

Dawe, H.
Philosophy in South Africa 1950-1962. 32pp. 60c. Univ Cape Town Lib 1964 SA

Dawodu, W.
Lagos city directory. 8th ed. 135pp. N1.25 Nig Trade Rev NR

Dawodu, W.
Nigeria trade review. 12th ed. 140pp. N1.55 ($8.00) Nig Trade Rev NR

Dawson, A.L.   Kirkpatrick, I.M.
The geology of the Cape Maclear Peninsula and Lower Bwanje valley. 71pp. pl. map. hd. K2.00 (Geological Survey of Malawi, Bull. 28) Geol Survey - Mal 1968 MW

Dawson, A.L.
The geology of the Lake Chiuta area. 36pp. hd. K2.50 (Geological Survey of Malawi, Bull. 34) Geol Survey - Mal 1970 MW

Day, J.H.
A guide to marine life on South African shores. 308pp. pl. hd. fl.54.00 Balkema 1974 SA

Daystar Press.
Awon aditu ibere ati idahun fun awon odo. [Questions and answers for children] 22pp. 10k Daystar NR YOR

Daystar Press.
Christian concern in the Nigerian civil war. 136pp. 75k Daystar 1969 NR

Daystar Press.
Discussions in preparation for marriage. 47pp. 20k Daystar 1968 NR

Daystar Press.
Discussions on love and sex. 36pp. 20k Daystar 1966 NR

Daystar Press.
Discussions on marriage problems in African society. 36pp. 20k Daystar 1966 NR

Daystar Press.
Family planning in Christian marriage. 3rd ed. 58pp. 40k Daystar 1972 NR

Daystar Press.
Getting married? 48pp. ill. 20k Daystar 1964 NR

Daystar Press.
Justice and peace in Nigeria: there can be no peace where justice is denied. 164pp. N1.00 Daystar 1971 NR

Daystar Press.
Ore l'aarin awon odo. [Friendship between children] 24pp. 10k Daystar 1967 NR YOR

Daystar Press.
Take care of your baby. rev. ed. 56pp. Daystar 1967 NR

Daystar Press.
Twenty awkward questions and twenty frank answers. 2nd ed. 16pp. 10k Daystar 1968 NR

Dazana, S.
Oxford Xhosa grammars/Ulwimi Iwakowethu: standard 3 (Sisagaga) and 4 (Sesigingaa) See: Pahl, H.W.

Dazana, S.
Oxford Xhosa grammars/Ulwimi Iwakowethu: standard 5 (Masisus' Unyawo) See: Pahl, H.W.

Dazana, S.
Oxford Xhosa grammars/Ulwimi Iwakowethu: standard 6 (Phambili) See: Pahl, H.W.

de Baulny, V.
The ideal husband. A study in adolescent psychology. See: Joinet, B.

de Beaumont, P.
L'ancien testament. Essai de traduction moderne des textes essentiels aux hommes d'aujourd'hui. 222pp. map. CFA140 CEDA 1967 IV FRE

de Beaumont, P.
L'évangile selon saint Jean aux hommes d'aujourd'hui. 126pp. CFA110 CEDA 1967 IV FRE

de Bekker, E.   Taylor, G.
Marriage cases and the parish priest. Declaration of nullity cases possession and good faith cases. bk.2 160pp. T.shs.8.00 ($1.20 pap.) TMP 1966 TZ

de Bruyn, R.
Pressure drop in air flow across banks of fin tubes with varying tube pitch and fin spacing. 20pp. (CSIR Report CENG, 119) CSIR 1976 SA

De Coning, C.
The regional distribution of purchasing power in the Transvaal. 61pp. ill. 50c. (R1.00) Univ South Africa 1959 SA

de Crespigny, A., ed.   Cronin, J.P., ed.
Ideologies of politics. 160pp. R2.95 OUP - SA 1976 SA

de Crespigny, A.R.C.
The general theory of revolution. 16pp. 30c (Univ. Cape Town. Inaugural lec., 32) Univ Cape Town Lib 1975 SA

de Epalza, M.
Islam, christianisme et incroyance. 420pp. D0.150 Maison Tunis 1973 TI FRE

de Graft-Hansen, J.O.
Papa Ewusi and the magic marble. 48pp. ill. 75pes. ($.65) Ghana Publ Corp 1973 GH

de Graft Hanson, J.O.
The fetish hideout. 100pp. ill. C1.20 ($1.20) Ghana Publ Corp 1975 GH

de Graft, J.
Muntu. 104pp. K.shs.10.00 Heinemann Educ - Nair 1977 KE

de Jager, E.J., comp.
Select bibliography of the anthropology of the Cape Nguni tribes. gratis Johannesburg Public Lib 1966 SA

de Jager, E.J.
Contemporary African art in South Africa. 168pp. pl. col. pl. R10.00 Struik 1973 SA

De Jager, E.S., ed.
Man: anthropological essays. 276pp. photos. cl. R8.75 Struik 1971 SA

De Jesus, A.S.M.
The manufacture of germanium (lithium) detectors. 15pp. (CSIR research reports, 283) CSIR 1969 SA

de Jongh, D.C.
Structure and prediction in "The limits to growth". 18pp. (CSIR Special Report, WISK 219) CSIR 1976 SA

de Jongh, S.J.
Encylopedia of South African wines. R14.95 McGraw-Hill SA 1976 SA

De Klerk, C.
The profitability of occupations pursued by highly qualified persons. 59pp. Human Science Res Council 1976 SA

De Kock, A.
Industrial laws of South Africa. 2nd ed. 770pp. R50.00 [including six revision services up to 1976] Juta 1970 SA

de Kock, J.M.   Fouries, S.
The cranial morphology of sturnis vulgaris vulgaris linnacus; A contribution to the cranial morphology of Nyctisyrigmus pectoralis pectoralis with special reference to the palate and cranial kinesis. 63pp. ill. R1.20 (A v. 31, no.3-4) Univ Stellenbosch, Lib 1955 SA

De L. Thompson, J.
  The story of Rhodesian sport. v. I, 1889-1935. [Reprint of ed. 1935; 'History of sport in Southern Rhodesia, 1889-1935']. 1, 3 v. 423pp. cl. R$17.00 ($12.00) Books of Rhodesia 1976 RH

De la Roche, H.
  Etude géologique de l'extrême sud de Madagascar. 183pp. pl. photo. cl. FMG1800 cl. (F36.00 cl.) (Annales Géologiques de Madagascar, 28) Service Geol - Mad 1963 MG FRE

de Leeuw, P.N.
  Bunaji cattle at the Shika research station, North Central State, Nigeria. See: Wheat, J.

de Leusse, H.
  Des "Poèmes" au "Lettres d'hivernage". 96pp. CFA400 (F8.00) Nouv Ed Afric 1976 SG FRE

de Mist, J.P.A.U.
  Diary of a journey to the Cape of Good Hope and the interior of Africa in 1802 and 1803. 59pp. pl. hd. fl. 11.25 Balkema 1970 SA

De Muizon, J.
  Faune des brenthides d'Afrique. 256pp. ill. CFA2000 (Mémoires de l'IFAN, 59) IFAN 1960 SG FRE

de Ngouma, O.S.
  La guerre entre Ndje Far Ndje et Hambodedjo Hammadi. 190pp. CFA350 CELTHO 1975 NG FRE

De Ploey, J.
  Quelques indices sur l'évolution morphologique et paléoclimatique des environs du Stanley Pool (Congo) 16pp. 35k Press Univ Zaire 1963 ZR FRE

de Pury, J.M.S.
  Crop pests of East Africa. 244pp. ill. K.shs30.00 OUP-Nairobi 1968 KE

de Pury, P.
  Comment élever des moutons. 312pp. CFA270 CLE 1969 CM FRE

de Pury, P.
  Comment élever des poules. 3rd ed. 240pp. CFA390 CLE 1972 CM FRE

de Rauville, C.
  Chazal des antipodes. Approches et anthologie. 120pp. ill. CFA500 (F10.00) Nouv Ed Afric 1974 SG FRE

De Rop, A.
  Eléments de phonétique historique du lomongo. 60pp. 40k Press Univ Zaire 1958 ZR FRE

De Rop, A.
  Théâtre nkundo. 59pp. 65k Press Univ Zaire 1958 ZR FRE

de Rosny, E.
  Ndimsi, ceux qui soignent dans la nuit. 328pp. CFA1,200 CLE 1975 CM FRE

De Sa, B.
  This strange universe. 17pp. C1.00 ($1.00/50p.) (Inaugural lecture) Ghana UP 1971 GH

de Saint Moulin, R.P.
  L'atlas des collectivités du Zaire. 64pp. Z5.30 Press Univ Zaire 1976 ZR FRE

de Saint Ours, J.
  Campagne 1959 de recherches hydrogéologiques dans le sud de Madagascar. 84pp. pl. FMG590 (F11.80) (Série Documentation, 149) Service Geol - Mad 1960 MG FRE

de Swardt, A.M.J. et al.
  The petrography of the Karoo Dolerite sill and Dyke at Paardekop. 360pp. photos. maps. R1.05 (A v.22, no. 1-14) Univ Stellenbosch, Lib 1944 SA

de Swardt, A.M.J. Simpson, J.G. Garrard, P.
  Major zones of transcurrent dislocation and superposition of orogenic belts in part of central Africa. 14pp. 10n (Dept. of Geological Survey. Occas. paps., 37) Geol Survey - Zam 1965 ZA

De Swardt, A.M.J. Drysdall, A.R.
  Precambrian geology and structure in central Northern Rhodesia. K6.30 (Dept. of Geological Survey, Memoirs, 2) Geol Survey - Zam 1964 ZA

de Turville, J.R.P.D. Schomberg, A.C.B.
  Guide for teachers of English. 60pp. 60k Pilgrim 1968 NR

de Villiers, C.
  The "African-American Manifesto" - a guideline to double standards. 19pp. R1.00 (FAA Focus, 4) Foreign Affairs Assoc - SA 1977 SA

de Villiers, C.
  South Africa - a changing society. 27pp. R1.00 (FAA Focus, 5) Foreign Affairs Assoc - SA 1977 SA

de Viller, A.
  Paul was here. 72pp. photos. map. R3.00 Shuter 1976 SA

De Villier, J.M.
  Molism, agriculture and natural resources. 15pp. 30c Univ of Rhodesia Lib 1974 RH

de Villiers, A., ed.
  English speaking South Africa: an assessment. 365pp. R12.00 OUP - SA 1976 SA

de Villiers, A.
  In the land of the Book. 88pp. pl. maps. R2.50 Shuter 1974 SA

de Villiers, A.
  That you may believe. 120pp. maps. R2.40 Shuter 1975 SA

de Villiers, A.
  Where the Master trod. 84pp. pl. maps. R1.50 Shuter 1973 SA

de Villiers, C.C.
  Genealogies of the old families of South Africa. 3 vols. 1268pp. hd. fl. 112.50 Balkema 1966 SA

De Villiers, D.Z.
  The prism of memory. ex. only (Inaugural lec.) Rhodes Univ Lib 1968 SA

de Villiers, G.
  Modern revision exercises in general science for standard 6. See: Fox, H.E.

de Villiers, G.
  Modern revision exercises in physical science for standard 8. See: Fox, H.E.

de Villiers, G.
  New commercial mathematics for standards 9 and 10. See: Archer, A.

De Villiers, H.
  The skull of the South African Negro: a biometrical and morphological study. 208pp. cl. R24.00 Witwatersrand UP 1968 SA

De Villiers, J.
  The Transvaal. [Reprint of ed. London, 1896] 88pp. ill. R3.60 (Reprints, 49) State-Lib-SA 1969 SA

De Villiers, J.E. Knight, D.B. Macintosh, J.C.
  The law of agency in South Africa. 2nd ed. R10.50 Juta 1956 SA

de Villiers, R., ed.
  Better than they knew. 239pp. photos. hd. R4.50 Purnell 1972 SA

De Villiers, S.A.
  Otto Landsberg, 19th Century South African artist. 152pp. photos. col. photos. cl. R12.50 Struik 1974 SA

De Vleeschauwer, H.J.
  Plan d'études au XVIIe siécle, 1, Le plan d'études de René Descartes. 60pp. 80c. (R1.30) Univ South Africa 1962 SA FRE

De Vleeschauwer, H.J.
  Le plan d'études d'Arnold Geulincx. 72pp. 80c. (R1.20) Univ South Africa 1964 SA FRE

De Vleeschauwer, H.J.
  Le problème du suicide dans la morale d'Arnold Geulincx.
  80pp.   70c.   (R1.20)   Univ South Africa 1965 SA FRE
De Vleeschauwer, H.J.
  Three centuries of Geulincx research.   72pp.   50c.
  (R1.00)   Univ South Africa 1957 SA
de Vletter, D.R.
  Zambia's mineral industry and its position amongst the
  world's major copper producers.   50n   (Dept. of
  Geological Survey. Occas. paps., 51)   Geol Survey -
  Zam 1972 ZA
de Vos, M.P.
  Cytological studies in genera of the mesembryanthemeae.
  26pp. ill.   35c.   (A v.25, no. 1)   Univ Stellenbosch, Lib
  1947 SA
De Vos, T.J.
  An analysis of building and construction industry
  expenditure in the Republic, 1959 and 1960.   18pp.
  (CSIR research reports, 221)   CSIR 1964 SA
De Vos, T.J.
  Housing requirements in South Africa.   See: Evenwell,
  J.K.
De Vos, T.J.   Miners, T.W.   Evenwel, J.K.
  Mechanization in the building industry.   72pp. ill.   (CSIR
  research reports, 265)   CSIR 1968 SA
De Vos, T.J.
  Survey of building statistics.   See: Beard, L.A.
de Vries, C.M.
  The basket among the reeds: Moses.   tr. fr. Dutch.
  16pp. ill.   40c.   (Rainbow series, 4)   United Protestant
  1971 SA
de Vries, C.M.
  The boy with the beautiful coat: Joseph.   tr. fr. Dutch.
  16pp. ill.   40c.   (Rainbow series, 3)   United Protestant
  1971 SA
de Vries, C.M.
  The child of Bethlehem: Christ.   tr. fr. Dutch.   16pp. ill.
  40c.   (Rainbow series, 6)   United Protestant 1971 SA
de Vries, C.M.
  The shepherd who became a king: David.   tr. fr. Dutch.
  16pp. ill.   40c.   (Rainbow series, 5)   United Protestant
  1971 SA
de Vries, C.M.
  To the unknown land: Abraham.   tr. fr. Dutch.   16pp. ill.
  40c.   (Rainbow series, 1)   United Protestant 1971 SA
de Vries, C.M.
  The two brothers: Jacob and Esau.   tr. fr. Dutch.   16pp.
  ill.   40c.   (Rainbow series, 2)   United Protestant 1971
  SA
de Waal, D.C.
  With Rhodes in Mashonaland. [Reprint of ed. 1896.].
  356pp. ill. cl.   R$8.95   (Rhodesiana Reprint Library,
  Gold Series, 36)   Books of Rhodesia 1974 RH
de Waal, J.S.
  Mathematics 6 answers/Wiskune 6 antwoorde. [Bilingual
  in English and Afrikaans.].   See: Griesel, P.O.
de Waal, J.S.
  Mathematics 7.   See: Griesel, P.O.
De Waal, J.S.
  My mathematics books. My fifth mathematics/arithmetic
  book.   See: Levinsohn, S.
De Waal, J.S.
  My mathematics books. My first mathematics/arithmetic
  book.   See: Levinsohn, S.
De Waal, J.S.
  My mathematics books. My fourth mathematics/arithmetic
  book.   See: Levinsohn, S.
De Waal, J.S.
  My mathematics books. My third mathematics/arithmetic
  book.   See: Levinsohn, S.
de Waal, S.
  My mathematics books. My sixth mathematics/arithmetics
  book.   See: Levinsohn, J.S.

de Wet, B.X.
  Learning Greek through the New Testament.   R10.75
  Butterworths 1975 SA
de Wet, E. P.   Wessels, S. A.   Monk, O.
  Bookbinding projects, standard 2.   21pp. ill.   70c
  Nasou 1974 SA
de Wet, E. P.   Wessels, S. A.   Monk, O.
  Bookbinding projects, standard 3.   20pp. ill.   70c
  Nasou 1974 SA
de Wet, E. P.   Wessels, S. A.   Monk, O.
  Bookbinding projects, standard 4.   13pp. ill.   70c
  Nasou 1974 SA
de Wet, E. P.
  General handwork for standard 5.   60pp. pl.   R1.35
  Nasou 1974 SA
de Wet, E.P.   Love, J.W.
  Woodwork, standard 5.   132pp. ill. photo.   R2.75
  Nasou 1975 SA
de Wet, E.P.   Love, J.W.
  Woodwork, standards 9-10.   231pp. ill. photo.   R5.25
  Nasou 1975 SA
de Wet, J.J.   Daff, K.E.
  Mathematics for the practical course, standard 6.   153pp.
  ill.   R2.75   Nasou 1975 SA
de Wet, J.J.   Daff, K.E.
  Mathematics for the practical course, standard 7.   140pp.
  ill.   R3.25   Nasou 1975 SA
de Wet, J.J.
  Mathematics for the practical course, standard 8.   185pp.
  ill.   R3.60   Nasou 1976 SA
de Wet, M.
  South African stapelieae.   97pp.   R1.10   Univ Cape
  Town Lib 1964 SA
de Wet, S.M., comp.
  Sulphur and phosphorous in the production of steel and
  ferroalloys.   231pp.   R10.00   Dept Bibliog, Lib & Typo
  1974 SA
Dean, E.
  Plan implementation in Nigeria, 1962-1966.   294pp. hd.
  N5.50   OUP-Nig 1973 NR
Dean, J.
  Standards of practice for West African libraries:
  proceedings of a seminar held at the Institute of
  Librarianship, University of Ibadan.   116pp.   N2.00
  (Inst. of Librarianship, occas. pap., 1)   Inst Lib-Ib 1969
  NR
Dean, W.H.B.
  Whither the constitution?   23pp.   30c   (Univ. Cape
  Town. Inaugural lec., 35)   Univ Cape Town Lib 1975 SA
Dearlove, P.
  Mining in Rhodesia, 1976.   100pp. photos. 266. maps.
  R$5.00   ($8.10)   Thomson (annual) RH
Debrunner, H.
  Biography: Owura Nico.   79pp.   20pes.   Waterville
  1965 GH
Debrunner, H.
  Biography: Sampson Opong.   30pp.   10pes.
  Waterville 1965 GH
Debrunner, H.
  History of Christianity in Ghana.   382pp. photos. maps.
  hd.   C7.50   Waterville 1967 GH
Decle, L.
  Three years in savage Africa. [Reprint of ed. 1900].
  594pp. ill. col. maps. cl.   R$10.25   (Rhodesiana
  Reprint Library, Gold Series, 35)   Books of Rhodesia
  1974 RH
Decloitre, L.
  Recherches sur les rhizopodes thécamoebiens d' A.O.F.
  249pp. ill.   CFA2000   (Mémoires de l'IFAN, 31)   IFAN
  1953 SG FRE
Decraene, P.
  L'année politique Africaine. (Edition 1975)   See: Biarnès,
  P.

Decraene, P.
Lettres de l'Afrique Atlantique. 28pp. CFA1300 pap.
Nouv Ed Afric 1976 SG FRE

Decroux, P.
Droit privé. v. 1: Sources du droit. Dir20.00 Ed La
Porte 1963 MR FRE

Dedeke, D.
Orin ma gbagbe ile. [Melody edition.] 63pp. ill. 45k
OUP - Nig 1963 NR YOR

Dedeke, D.
Orin ma gbagbe ile: piano edition. 113pp. music. cl.
N1.38 OUP - Nig 1963 NR YOR

Dederick, R.
Bi-focal. Poems. 48pp. R2.85 Philip 1974 SA

Dederick, S.
Tickey. 144pp. ill. R2.10 OUP-SA 1965 SA

Deed, F.
Giryama-English dictionary. 114pp. K.shs.8.20
($2.50/£1.00) EALB 1964 KE

Deflandre, J. Berger, A.
Tunisie. Poèmes en couleurs. col. pl. D0,300
Maison Tunis 1973 TI FRE

Degife, G.T., comp. Diro, M., comp.
Ethiopian publications, 1975. [Text in Amharic and
English]. 53pp. ($5.00) Inst Ethiop Stud 1976 ET

deGraft-Hansen, J.O.
The little Sasabonsam. 64pp. ill. 75pes. ($.65)
Ghana Publ Corp 1973 GH

deGraft-Hansen, J.O.
Papa and the animals. 20pp. ill. 50pes. ($.50)
Ghana Publ Corp 1973 GH

deHeer, A.N., ed.
Symposia on problems of communication between the
library and its user, Accra, 10th-12th July, 1972. 100pp.
C3.50 ($4.50) (Communication series, 2) Ghana Lib
Assoc 1977 GH

DeHeer, A.N., ed.
Workshop on introduction of international standard
bibliographic description (ISBD) to Ghana. 59pp.
C2.50 ($4.00) (Communications series, 1) Ghana Lib
Assoc 1976 GH

Dei-Anang, M.F.
Ghana resurgent. 248pp. photos. maps. C3.00
Waterville 1964 GH

Dei-Anang, M.F.
Ghana semitones. 28pp. 20pes. Waterville 1964 GH

Dekeyser, P.L. Villiers, A.
Contribution à l'étude du peuplement de la Mauritanie.
Notations écologiques et biogéographiques sur la faune de
l'Adrar. 222pp. pl. CFA1600 (Mémoires de l'IFAN,
44) IFAN 1956 SG FRE

Dekeyser, P.L. Derivot, J.
Etude d'un type d'oiseau ouest-africain: corvus albus.
Généralités - ostéologie. 58pp. ill. CFA400
(Initiations et Etudes Africaines, 16) IFAN 1958 SG FRE

Dekeyser, P.L. Derivot, J.H.
Les oiseaux de l'Ouest africain. Guide d'indentification
illustré, traitant de 1.160 especes. [Atlas.] 1 & 2, 3pts.
507pp. ill. maps. CFA5000 (Initiations et Etudes
Africaines, 19) IFAN 1966 SG FRE

Dekeyser, P.L. Derivot, J.H.
Les oiseaux de l'Ouest africain. Sources bibliographiques,
notes critiques. 3, 3pts. 112pp. CFA1000
(Initiations et Etudes Africaines, 19) IFAN 1968 SG FRE

Dekeyser, P.L. Villiers, A.
Récolte et préparation des collections zoologiques.
44pp. CFA200 (Instructions Sommaires, 1) IFAN
1948 SG FRE

Delamarquise, P.E.
Ilay tana-mihoson-drà. [La main ensanglantée.] 120pp.
FMG400 Ed Takariva 1975 MG MLA

Delannoy.
La formation des agents de l'etat au Zaïre.
See: Gatarayima.

Delano, I.O.
Conversation in Yoruba and English. 81pp. 51k
Heinemann Educ - Nig 1963 NR YOR

Delano, I.O.
Josiah Ransome Kuti. 71pp. ill. 45k (Makers of
Nigeria, 1) OUP - Nig 1968 NR

Delano, I.O.
Oba Ademola II. 54pp. ill. 40k (Makers of Nigeria,
2) OUP - Nig 1969 NR

Delano, I.O.
Owe l'esin oro. [Yoruba proverbs] 209pp. map. hd.,
pap. 80k pap. N1.20 hd. OUP - Nig 1958 NR YOR

Delbos, L. Rantoanina, M.
Les gisements fer-nickel des environs de Moramanga.
61pp. pl. FMG1920 (F38.40) (Travaux du Bureau
Géologique, 106) Service Geol - Mad 1961 MG FRE

Delcourt, A.
La France et les établissements français au Sénégal entre
1713 et 1763. 432pp. maps. CFA2000 (Mémoires
de l'IFAN, 17) IFAN 1952 SG FRE

Delius, A.
Border. 408pp. hd. R9.60 Philip 1975 SA

Delubac, C. Rantoanina, M.
Etude géologique et prospection des feuilles:
Itermo-Ambatofinandrahana. 43pp. map. FMG820
(F16.40) (Travaux du Bureau Géologique, 113) Service
Geol - Mad 1963 MG FRE

Delubac, C. Rakotoarison, W.
Etude géologique et prospection des feuilles
Kiranomena-Mahasambo-Analabe. 38pp. pl. map.
FMG433 (F8.66) (Travaux du Bureau Géologique, 117)
Service Geol - Mad 1964 MG FRE

Delubac, C. Rantoanina, M. Rakotoarison, W.
Etude géologique et prospection des feuilles
Tananarive-Manjakandriana. 49pp. map. FMG680
(F13.60) (Travaux du Bureau Géologique, 114) Service
Geol - Mad 1963 MG FRE

Delubac, C. Rakotonanahary. Rakotoarison, W.
Etue géologique et prospection des feuilles:
Miarinarivo-Arivonimamo. 26pp. map. FMG702
(F14.04) (Travaux du Bureau Géologique, 120) Service
Geol - Mad 1964 MG FRE

Delvaux, J.P.
L'examen de l'intelligence des écoliers de Kinshasa.
220pp. Z2.50 Press Univ Zaire 1970 ZR FRE

Dembo, U.
Tauraruwa Mai Wutsiya. [The rocket] 56pp. 90k
Northern Nig 1969 NR HAU

Dembo, U.
Wasannin Yara. [Plays for children] 46pp. 90k
Northern Nig 1972 NR HAU

Demeerseman, A.
La famille Tunisienne et les temps nouveaux. 438pp.
photos. D1,300 Maison Tunis 1972 TI FRE

Demerseman, A.
Là-bas à Zarzis et maintenant. 320pp. D0.600
Maison Tunis 1969 TI FRE

Democratic Republic of the Sudan, Geological and Mineral
Resource Department.
Gravity studies in the Sudan. pt. 1. 48pp. ill.
£S1.50 ($4.00/£1.80) (Bulletin, 26) Geol and Min
Res - Sudan 1972 SJ

Democratic Republic of the Sudan, Geological and Mineral
Resource Department.
Mining and oil exploration laws in the Sudan. 103pp.
£S2.00 ($5.88/£2.48) (Bulletin, 25) Geol and Min
Res - Sudan 1974 SJ

Democratic Republic of the Sudan, Geological and Mineral
Resource Department.
Outlines of the geology of the Nuba mountains and vicinity
Southern Kordofan Province. 30pt. (89c./39p.)
(Bulletin, 23) Geol and Min Res - Sudan 1973 SJ

Democratic Republic of the Sudan, Geological and Mineral
Resource Department.
Quantitative interpretation of secondary dispersion pattern
of gold deposit in the Red Sea Hills, Sudan. 63pp. pl.
50pt. ($1.47/62p.) (Bulletin, 24) Geol and Min Res -
Sudan 1973 SJ

Democratic Republic of the Sudan, Geological and Mineral
Resources Department.
Geology of the Third Cataract-Halfa district, Northern
Province, Sudan. 30pt. (89c./39p.) (Bulletin, 22)
Geol and Min Res - Sudan 1973 SJ

Democratic Republic of the Sudan, Geological and Mineral
Resources Department.
Guide to oil exploration in Sudan. 20pt. ($0.56c./25p.)
(Bulletin, 20) Geol and Min Res - Sudan 1972 SJ

Democratic Republic of the Sudan, Geological and Mineral
Resources Department.
Hydrogeology of Kassala district, Kassala Province.
70pt. ($2.01/86p.) (Bulletin, 21) Geol and Min Res -
Sudan 1972 SJ

Demougeot, A.
Notes sur l'organisation politique et administrative du
Labéavant et depuis l'occupation français. [Reprint of ed.
Paris, 1944]. 85pp. (D.fl.25.00) (Mémoires de l'IFAN
6) IFAN 1944 SG FRE

Deniel, R.
L'Islam en Haute-Volta à l'époque coloniale.
See: Audouin, J.

Deniel, R.
Religions dans la ville: croyances et changements sociaux
à Abidjan. 211pp. CFA1,500 INADES 1975 IV FRE

Deniel, R.
Une société paysanne de Côte d'Ivoire: les Ano. Traditions
et changement. 228pp. ill. CFA1,600 INADES 1976
IV FRE

Denman, P.D. Money, N.J.
The coal resources of the Zambezi valley. v.5:
Siankondobo - the northeastern area - a preliminary report
40n (Dept. of Geological Survey. Economic Reports, 23)
Geol Survey - Zam 1969 ZA

Denman, P.D.
Some aspects of the geology of the Siankondobo coalfield.
See: Drysdall, A.R.

Denoon, D.
A history of Kigezi in South-West Uganda. 302pp. hd.
U.shs.10.00 Adult Educ Centre 1971 UG

Dent, A.G.
Izibalo zanamuhla. Ibanga, 1 See: Oscroft, E.B.

Dent, A.G.
Izibalo zanamuhla. Ibanga, 2 See: Oscroft, E.B.

Dent, A.G.
Izibalo zanamuhla. Ibanga, 3 See: Oscroft, E.B.

Dent, A.G.
Izibalo zanamuhla. Ibanga, 4 See: Oscroft, E.B.

Dent, A.G.
Izibalo zanamuhla. Ibanga, 5 See: Oscroft, E.B.

Dent, A.G.
Izibalo zanamuhla. Ibanga, 6 See: Oscroft, E.B.

Dent, G.R. Nyembezi, C.L.S.
Compact Zulu dictionary (English/Zulu, Zulu/English) 3rd
rev. ed. 146pp. 70c. Shuter 1959 SA

Dent, G.R. Kolbe, G.A.
Ezemvelo. [Nature study] Ibanga, 3 87pp. ill. 50c.
Shuter 1957 SA ZUL

Dent, G.R. Kolbe, G.A.
Ezemvelo. [Nature study] Ibanga, 4 84pp. ill. 50c.
Shuter 1957 SA ZUL

Dent, G.R. Kolbe, G.A.
Ezemvelo. [Nature study] Ibanga, 5 75pp. ill. 50c.
Shuter 1957 SA ZUL

Dent, G.R. Kolbe, G.A.
Ezemvelo. [Nature study] Ibanga, 6 82pp. ill. 75c.
Shuter 1957 SA ZUL

Dent, G.R.
General science, Forms II & III. See: Dent, S.R.

Dent, G.R.
Izincwadi ezintsha zezempilo. Ibanga, 3 See: Dent,
S.R.

Dent, G.R.
Izincwadi ezintsha zezempilo. Ibanga, 4 See: Dent,
S.R.

Dent, G.R.
Izincwadi ezintsha zezempilo. Ibanga, 5 See: Dent,
S.R.

Dent, G.R.
Scholar's Zulu dictionary (English and Zulu)
See: Nyembezi, C.L.S.

Dent, G.R. Dent, S.R.
Studies of life. 395pp. ill. R1.80 Shuter 1968 SA

Dent, S.R. et al.
Ezezwe nezalo. [Studies concerning the world] rev. ed.
4 216pp. ill. R1.00 Shuter 1961 SA ZUL

Dent, S.R. et al.
Ezezwe nezalo. [Studies concerning the world] rev. ed.
5 212pp. ill. R1.10 Shuter 1961 SA ZUL

Dent, S.R. et al.
Ezezwe nezalo. [Studies concerning the world] 6
261pp. ill. R1.20 Shuter 1961 SA ZUL

Dent, S.R. Croft, P.
General science, Form I. 4th rev. ed. 168pp. ill.
R1.05 Shuter 1957 SA

Dent, S.R. Dent, G.R.
General science, Forms II & III. 320pp. R1.95 Shuter
1971 SA

Dent, S.R. Nyembezi, L.S. Dent, G.R.
Izincwadi ezintsha zezempilo. [New health books]
Ibanga, 3 72pp. ill. 45c. Shuter 1971 SA ZUL

Dent, S.R. Dent, G.R. Nyembezi, L.S.
Izincwadi ezintsha zezempilo. [New health books]
Ibanga, 4 70pp. ill. 45c. Shuter 1971 SA ZUL

Dent, S.R. Dent, G.R. Nyembezi, L.S.
Izincwadi ezintsha zezempilo. [New health books]
Ibanga, 5 55c. Shuter 1971 SA ZUL

Dent, S.R. Nyembezi, L.S.
Izincwadi ezintsha zezempilo. [New health books]
Ibanga, 6 72pp. 55c. Shuter 1971 SA ZUL

Dent, S.R.
Life: a biology for senior certificate. 2nd. rev. ed. v. 2
420pp. ill. R3.45 Shuter 1967 SA

Dent, S.R.
Life: a biology for the secondary school. 4th ed. v. 1
356pp. ill. R1.55 Shuter 1959 SA

Dent, S.R. Hallowes, E.E.
Social studies for junior certificate, Form 1. 5th rev. ed.
210pp. maps ill. 95c. Shuter 1957 SA

Dent, S.R. Hallowes, E.E.
Social studies for junior certificate, Forms 2 & 3. 3rd rev.
ed. 360pp. maps ill. R1.35 Shuter 1958 SA

Dent, S.R.
Studies of life. See: Dent, G.R.

Denteh, A.C.
Akwasi Mahuw. [Akwasi Mahuw.] 2nd ed. 38pp. ill.
70pes. Bur Ghana Lang 1976 GH ASA

Denteh, A.C.
Ehwene a eye ha (Asante) [The nose that hunts (Asante
version)] 19pp. ill. 30pes. Waterville 1964 GH TWI

Denyssen, A.J.W.
Needlework and clothing manual, standards 9-10. v. 1.
See: Louw, W.A.

Department of Commerce, Uganda.
Benge. [The Bank. How it will help Africans] ill.
K.shs.0.50 ($1.50/60p.) EALB 1955 KE LUO

Department of Commerce, Uganda.
Kutumia hesabu. [Using the accounts] 39pp.
K.shs.2.50 ($1.25/50p.) EALB 1956 KE SWA

Department of Commerce, Uganda.
Using accounts. 40pp. ill. K.shs2.50 EALB 1956 KE

Department of Library Studies.
Education for librarianship in Ghana. 13pp. 40pes.
($1.00) Dept Lib Stud - Univ Ghana 1973 GH

Depestre, R.
Cancate d'octobre. 88pp. DA4.00 SNED 1970 AE
FRE

Deppe, R.K.
A comparative study of the motives observed in selected
pictorial advertisements directed at the Bantu. 86pp.
R30.00 (Bureau of Market Research, Research Reports,
39) Bur Market Research 1974 SA

Deppe, R.K.
A study of the attitudes of urban Blacks to advertising.
82pp. R50.00 (Bureau of Market Research, Research
Reports, 48) Bur Market Research 1975 SA

Depuydt, G.
Fiscalité Algérienne: 1973. See: Garelik, J.

Depuydt, G.
Fiscalité algérienne (mise à jour) 142pp. DA10.00
SNED 1972 AE FRE

Depuydt, G.
Précis de fiscalité algérienne. 213pp. DA7.00 SNED
1972 AE FRE

Depuydt, G.
Précis de fiscalité algérienne. Supplement. DA2.00
SNED 1972 AE FRE

Deregowska, E.L.
Some aspects of social change in Africa south of the
Sahara 1959-66: a bibliography. 93pp. 75n. (38p.)
(Communications, 3) Inst Soc Res - Zam 1967 ZA

Deregowski, J.B.
Drawing ability of Zambian rural primary school children.
Results of an 'art competition' in a single school. 10pp.
free (Human Development Research Unit Report, 6)
Dept Psychology - Zam 1968 ZA

Deregowski, J.B.
Frames of reference for copying orientation: a
cross-cultural study. See: Serpell, R.

Deregowski, J.B.
The role of symmetry in pattern reproduction in African
school children. 15pp. free (Human Development
Research Unit Report, 20) Dept Psychology - Zam 1971
ZA

Deregowski, J.B.
Teaching pictorial depth perception: a classroom
experiment. See: Serpell, R.

Derine, R.
Le droit de propriété en France et en Belgique au 19e
siècle: droit absolu et quasi illimité? 68pp. 55k Press
Univ Zaire 1959 ZR FRE

Derive, M.J.
Chroniques de grandes familles d'Odienné. 228pp.
CFA1,000 (Linguistique Africaine, 57) Inst Ling
Appliquée 1976 IV FRE

Derivot, J.
Etude d'un type d'oiseau ouest-africain: corvus albus.
Généralités - ostéologie. See: Dekeyser, P.L.

Derivot, J.H.
Les oiseaux de l'Ouest africain. Guide d'indentification
illustré, traitant de 1.160 especes. 1 & 2, 3pts.
See: Dekeyser, P.L.

Derivot, J.H.
Les oiseaux de l'Ouest africain. Sources bibliographiques,
notes critiques. 3, 3pts. See: Dekeyser, P.L.

Derksen, R.
Civics for Tanzania. 152pp. ill. K.shs.14.00
OUP-Nairobi 1969 KE

Derrett, J., ed.
Studies in the laws of succession in Nigeria. 293pp.
N5.00 ($7.50) NISER 1965 NR

Derricourt, R.
Beyond the Cape frontier. See: Saunders, C.

Derricourt, R.M., comp.
A supplementary bibliography of the archaeology of
Zambia, 1967-1973. 15pp. 50n ($1.00) Nat Mon
Comm - Zambia 1975 ZA

Derricourt, R.M., ed.
A classified index of archaeological and other sites in
Zambia. 169pp. K5.00 (Research publication, 3)
Nat Mon Comm - Zambia 1976 ZA

Derricourt, R.M.
Prehistoric man in the Ciskei and Transkei. 368pp. ill.
R18.00 Struik 1977 SA

Desai, N.C. Forland, K.S.
Elementary chemical calculations. 59pp. K.shs3.30
($1.50/60p.) EALB 1968 KE

Desai, Yunus.
From 'coolie location' to group area: a brief account of
Johannesburg's Indian community. See: Randall, P.

Descoings, B. et al.
Annales de l'université d'Abidjan. 605pp. CFA1850
(F37.00) (Série E-Ecologie, 5-1) Univ Abidjan 1972 IV
FRE

Despois, J.
La Tunisie orientale: Sahel et basse steppe. 554pp. pl.
maps. D3.400 (Série II, Géographie, 1) Univ Tunis
1955 TI FRE

Dessauvagie, T.F.J., ed. Whiteman, A.J., ed.
African geology: proceedings of the conference on African
geology held at the University of Ibadan from 7-14
December 1970, in commemoration of the tenth
anniversary of the founding of the geology department.
668pp. maps pls. N20.00 Dept Geol-Ib 1972 NR

Deuse, P.
Contribution à étude des tourbières du Rwanda et du
Burundi. 65pp. photos. (Faculté des Sciences, 12)
Univ Bujumbura 1966 BD FRE

Deuse, P.
Marais et tourbières au Rwanda et au Burundi. 14pp.
(Faculté des Sciences, 6) Univ Bujumbura 1963 BD FRE

d'Ewes, D.R.
A guide to gardening in Southern Africa. 104pp. col. pl.
R4.95 Struik 1975 SA

Dhlomo, H.I.E.
The girl who killed to save. 46pp. 50c. Lovedale
1935 SA

Dhlomo, R.R.R.
Dingane kasenzangakhona. [Dingane son of
Senzangakhona] 144pp. 50c. Shuter 1936 SA ZUL

Dhlomo, R.R.R.
Indlela yababi. [The path of the wicked] 142pp. 75c.
Shuter 1946 SA ZUL

Dhlomo, R.R.R.
Ucetshwayo. [Cetshwayo] 135pp. 70c. Shuter
1953 SA ZUL

Dhlomo, R.R.R.
Udinuzulu. [Dinuzulu] photos. 65c. Shuter 1968
SA ZUL

Dhlomo, R.R.R.
Unomalanga kandengezi. [Nomalanga daughter of
Ndengezi] 120pp. 70c. Shuter 1947 SA ZUL

Dhlomo, R.R.R.
Ushaka. [Shaka] 170pp. 60c. Shuter 1937 SA
ZUL

Dia, M.
Islam et humanisme. 144pp. CFA900 (F18.00)
Nouv Ed Afric 1976 SG FRE

Author Index

Dietrich, B.C.
Catalogue and handbook on Classics department antiquities. 13pp. R1.00 Rhodes Univ Lib 1966 SA

Dietrich, B.C. Dietrich, A.C.
Rhodes vases [Fascicles I-III]. Catalogue and handbook on Classics Department antiquities. R2.00 Rhodes Univ Lib 1966 SA

Dietrich, B.C.
The semantics of the soul. ex. only (Inaugural lec.) Rhodes Univ Lib 1964 SA

Digweed, M.
Worry and tension. 34pp. 20k Daystar 1969 NR

Dike, K.O.
Origins of the Niger Mission. 21pp. 50k Ibadan UP 1962 NR

Dilayen Dilamutung-a-Ngya. Courtejoie, J. Rotsart de Hertaing, I.
Les médicaments à la maison. Quelques informations sur la pharmacie familiale et son usage. 28pp. photos. 50k ($0.60) (Protection maternelle et infantile, 15) BERPS 1975 ZR FRE

Dilke, O.A.W.
Lucan: poet of freedom. ex. only (Inaugural lec.) Rhodes Univ Lib 1961 SA

Dill, A.W. Bosch, M.
A guide to the teaching of basic mathematics. 128pp. ill. R3.75 Longman - SA 1976 SA

Dinizulu.
The trial of Dinizulu on charges of high treason at Greytown, Natal, 1908-9. [Reprint of ed. Pietermaritzburg, 1910]. 103pp. R4.70 (Reprints, 48) State-Lib-SA 1969 SA

Dintenfass, M.P.
How to adapt and use reading materials. 96pp. K.shs.6.50 OUP-Nairobi 1968 KE

Dinwiddy, C L.
Elementary mathematics for economists. 370pp. K.shs.12.00 OUP-Nairobi 1967 KE

Diocese of Central Tanganyika Mother's Union.
Wakina mama tujifunze. [Bible lessons for mothers' union groups.] 96pp. ill. T.shs.6.50 Central Tanganyika 1975 TZ SWA

Diop, A. Dia, O. Calvet, M.J.
Les 115 mots les plus fréquents de la langue wolof. 51pp. CFA375 (C.L.A.D. Etude, 41) CLAD 1970 SG FRE

Diop, A. et al.
Lexique analytique du Wolof. 68pp. (C.L.A.D. Étude, 59) CLAD 1975 SG FRE

Diop, A. Galdin, J.C. Dia, O.B.K.
Jukib tanneefu baat-yu-sax. Receuil de textes choisis. Les langues africaines au Sénégal. 85pp. CLAD 1975 SG FRE

Diop, A.
Test d'audiométrie vocale en wolof. 65pp. CFA625 (C.L.A.D. Etude, 20) CLAD 1966 SG FRE

Diop, A. Dia, O. Calvet, M.J.
Le wolof fondamental. 5 v. 1500pp. CFA3125 (C.L.A.D. Etude, 40) CLAD 1969 SG FRE

Diop, A.B.
Société toucouleur et migration (enquête sur l'immigration toucouleur à Dakar) 232pp. maps. CFA1200 (Initiations et Etudes Africaines, 18) IFAN 1965 SG FRE

Diop, B.
L'Os de Mor Lam. 72pp. CFA600 (F12.00) Nouv Ed Afric 1976 SG FRE

Diop, C.A.
L'Antiquité africaine par l'image. 68pp. CFA1,000 (F20.00) Nouv Ed Afric 1976 SG FRE

Diop, C.A.
Le laboratoire de radiocarbone de l'IFAN. 110pp. CFA1000 (Catalogues et Documents, 21) IFAN 1968 SG FRE

Diop, C.A.
Physique nucleaire et chronologie absolue. 160pp. CFA3,000 (F60.00) Nouv Ed Afric 1976 SG FRE

Diop, M.T.
Mon Dieu est noir. 32pp. CFA300 (F6.00) Nouv Ed Afric 1975 SG FRE

Diouf, M. Toly, O.
Mathématique. Collection I.R.E.M. Dakar, classe de 5e. 192pp. CFA1,480 (F25.60) Nouv Ed Afric 1976 SG FRE

Diouf, M.
Mathematique. Collection I.R.E.M. de Dakar. Class de sixième. See: Camara, A.

Diouldé, L.
La tradition orale. 200pp. CFA800 CELTHO 1972 NG FRE

Directory Publishers of Zambia Limited.
Zambia directory, 1977. (Annual) 350pp. K10.00 Directory Publ 1977 ZA

Directory Publishers of Zambia Limited.
Zambia/Malawi/Botswana and neighbouring districts directory, 1977. (annual) 1,000pp. K25.00 Directory Publ 1977 ZA

Diro, M., comp.
Ethiopian publications, 1968 [Text in Amharic and English.]. See: Chojnacki, S., comp.

Diro, M., comp.
Ethiopian publications, 1969 [Text in Amharic and English.]. See: Chojnacki, S., comp.

Diro, M., comp.
Ethiopian publications, 1970 [Text in Amharic and English.]. See: Chojnacki, S., comp.

Diro, M., comp.
Ethiopian publications, 1971 [Text in Amharic and English.]. See: Chojnacki, S., comp.

Diro, M., comp.
Ethiopian publications, 1973-74. [Text in Amharic and English]. See: Chojnacki, S., comp.

Diro, M., comp.
Ethiopian publications, 1975. [Text in Amharic and English]. See: Degife, G.T., comp.

Diro, M., comps.
Ethiopian publications., 1972. [Text in Amharic and English] See: Chojnacki, S., comps

Disney, C.
The Shell history of the East African Safari. 126pp. photos. K.shs12.50 ($3.60) EAPH 1966 KE

Dissogi, L.A.G., comp.
Botany bibliography of the Sudan up to 1975. 109pp. ill. Nat Council Res 1975 SJ

Dittebrandt, H.
The African elephant: a selective bibliography. 36pp. R1.90 Dept Bibliog, Lib & Typo 1970 SA

Divaris, C.
Silke on South African income tax. 1976/77 supplement. See: Silke, A.S.

Divenuti, B.
A text book writing guide for teacher organisation in Africa. 35pp. K.shs.6.50 Africa Book Serv 1968 KE

Dixey, F. Bisset, C.B. Campbell Smith, W.
The Chilwa series of Southern Nyasaland. 70pp. pl. K1.25 (Geological Survey of Malawi, Bull. 5) Geol Survey - Mal 1955 MW

Djebar, A.
Poèmes pour l'Algérie heureuse. 84pp. DA4.00 SNED 1969 AE FRE

Djebar, A.
Rouge l'aube. 102pp. DA5.00 SNED 1969 AE FRE

Djedidi, T.L.
La poésie amoureuse des arabes: le cas des 'udrites. Contribution à une sociologie de la littérature arabe. 163pp. DA12.00 SNED 1974 AE FRE

Djelid, M.
Plaies. 60pp. DA4.00 SNED 1968 AE FRE

Djibo Hamani.
Contribution a l'etude de l'histoire des etats hausa: l'Adar precolonial. 277pp. maps photos. CFA2250 (F45.00) (Etudes Nigeriennes, 38) Inst Rech Sci Hum 1975 NG FRE

Djoleto, S.A.A.
English practice for the African student. 192pp. N1.05 Macmillan 1967 NR

Dliwayo, E.
Inggamu yenhlazi. [A fish's knife.] 16pp. pl. 6c Rhod Lit Bur 1973 RH NDE

Dobrska, Z.
Criteria for public investment in manufacturing: five Tanzania case studies. T.shs.12.00 ($3.00) (Research pap., 68.28) Econ Res Bur - Tanz 1975 TZ

Dobrska, Z.
Criteria for public investment in manufacturing industry. T.shs.12.00 ($3.00) (Research pap., 68.18) Econ Res Bur - Tanz 1968 TZ

Dobson, D.A.
Cotton in fine gauge single jersey, part I: plied yarns. See: Robinson, G.A.

Dobson, D.A.
The effect of atmospheric conditions on the knitting performance of wool worsted yards. See: Hunter, L.

Dobson, D.A.
Knittability of all-wool yarns on a 28 gauge single jersey machine. See: Robinson, G.A.

Dobson, D.A.
A proposed method of assessing the knittability of a yarn. See: Robinson, G.A.

Dobson, D.A.
The relationship between certain properties of wool worsted yarns and their knitting performance, part III: effect of fabric structure. See: Hunter, L.

Dobson, D.A.
The relationship between yarn properties and knitting performance for cotton yarns knitted to a constant stitch length on single and double jersey machines. See: Hunter, L.

Dobson, D.A.
Single jersey knitting performance, part I: a comparison of the knitting performance at different feeders and of various structures. See: Hunter, L.

Dobson, D.A.
Single jersey knitting performance, part II: the influence of machine speed, yarn input tension and yarn linear density on the knitting performance of fine worsted yarns knitted on a 28 gg single jersey machine. See: Cawood, M.P.

Dobson, D.E.
Building regulations: a review of the position in some Western countries. 163pp. (CSIR research reports, 269) CSIR 1968 SA

Dock, S.
Dambanavana. [Play with children.] 45pp. 35c pap. Rhod Lit Bur 1973 RH SHO

Dodd, A.D., ed.
More short stories by South African writers. R1.45 Juta SA

Dodd, A.D., ed.
Short stories by South African writers. R1.30 Juta SA

Dodu, S.R.A.
Our heritage: the traditional medicine of mankind. 14pp. C1.00 ($1.00/50p.) (Inaugural lecture) Ghana UP 1972 GH

Doerksen, E.
Mu rera waka. [Chorus book.] 48pp. Challenge NR HAU

Dogbe, Y.E.
La crise de l'éducation. 112pp. CFA550 (F11.00) Nouv Ed Afric 1976 SG FRE

Dogbeh, R.
Voyage au pays de Lenine. 96pp. CFA360 CLE 1967 CM FRE

Doi, A.R.I.
The cardinal principles of Islam. 201pp. ill. N2.50 Islamic 1972 NR

Doi, A.R.I.
Introduction to the Hadith. 155pp. N2.00 Islamic 1971 NR

Doi, A.R.I.
Introduction to the Qur'an. 134pp. N1.75 Islamic 1971 NR

Dokali, R.
Les mosquées de la période turque à Alger. 128pp. ill. DA35.00 SNED 1974 AE FRE

Doke, C.M.
A comparative study in Shona phonetics. 298pp. photos. maps. cl. R25.00 Witwatersrand UP 1931 SA

Doke, C.M. Cole, D.T.
Contributions to the history of Bantu linguistics. 129pp. cl. R6.00 Witwatersrand UP 1969 SA

Doke, C.M. Sikakana, J.M.A. Malcolm, D.M.
English and Zulu dictionary. 1, 2 pts. cl. R6.00 Witwatersrand UP 1971 SA

Doke, C.M.
English-Lamba vocabulary. 2nd rev. ed. 179pp. cl. R5.00 Witwatersrand UP 1963 SA

Doke, C.M. Sikakana, J.M.A. Malcolm, D.M.
English-Zulu dictionary. 2, 2 pts. 572pp. R4.00 Witwatersrand UP 1971 SA

Doke, C.M.
The phonetics of the Zulu language. 310pp. cl. R16.00 Witwatersrand UP 1969 SA

Doke, C.M.
A textbook of Southern Sotho grammar. 508pp. R6.90 Longman SA 1957 SA

Doke, C.M.
Textbook of Zulu grammar. 400pp. R3.50 Longman SA 1927 SA ZUL

Doke, C.M. Vilakazi, B.W.
Zulu-English dictionary. 2nd rev. ed. 918pp. cl. R12.00 Witwatersrand UP 1972 SA

Doke, C.M. Sikakana, J.M.A. Malcolm, D.M.
Zulu-English vocabulary. 342pp. R4.00 Witwatersrand UP 1971 SA

Doku, C.W. Amevor, D.K.H.
Children's delight. 18pp. ill. C1.80 Univ Ghana Bkshop; distr. 1973 GH

Doku, E.V.
Cassava in Ghana. 57pp. photos. map ill. C1.00 ($1.00) (50p.) Ghana UP 1969 GH

Doku, G. et al.
The cowrie girl and other stories. 100pp. 75pes. ($.75) Ghana Publ Corp 1971 GH

Dominy, P.
Looking at the Old Testament. pt. 1. 224pp. K.shs.19.00 Evangel 1975 KE

Donaint, P.
Les cadres géographiques à travers les langues du Niger. Contribution à la pédagogie de l'étude du milieu. 289pp. ill. hd. (Etudes Nigériennes, 37) Inst Rech Sci Hum 1975 NG FRE

Donald, D.G.M.
Fundamental studies to improve nursery production of Pinus radiata and other pines. 180pp. photos. map. R4.00 (A v.43, no.1) Univ Stellenbosch, Lib 1968 SA

Donald, D.G.M.
A study of the history, practice and economics of forest nurseries in South Africa. 107pp. photos. R1.75 (A v.40, no. 1) Univ Stellenbosch, Lib 1965 SA

Donaldson, D.
Essential diagnostic tests. See: Lascelles, P.T.

Donaldson, G.W.
Foundation problems experienced in Africa. $3.00 (Publication, 81) OAU 1962 ET

Donaldson, M.
Minors in Roman law. 134pp. R6.50 cl. Butterworths 1955 SA

Doneux, J.
Pour parler wolof (livre de l'étudiant.) pt. 2 CFA375 (C.L.A.D. Etude, 43 bis) CLAD 1970 SG FRE

Doneux, J.
Pour parler wolof (livre du maîtres, 1ère partie.) pt. 1 CFA375 (C.L.A.D. Etude, 43) CLAD 1970 SG FRE

Doneux, J.
Les systèmes phonologiques des langues de Casamance. 100pp. CFA625 pap. (C.L.A.D. Etude, 28) CLAD 1969 SG FRE

Doneux, J.L. N'Dao, M.
Fréquences des graphes et des structures syllabiques en Wolof. 33pp. (C.L.A.D. Étude, 60) CLAD 1975 SG FRE

Donges, T.E.
The liability for safe carriage of goods in Roman-Dutch law. R5.50 Juta 1928 SA

Donkoh, C.E.
Aduse-Poku Kcnkcnko. [Abuse-Puku.] 88pp. photos. 65pes. Bur Ghana Lang 1973 GH TWI

Donkoh, C.E.
Nkraboc. [Messages through letters.] 54pp. 40pes. Bur Ghana Lang 1974 GH TWI

Donkor, W.
A stab in my heart. 72pp. ill. C2.00 Univ Ghana Bkshop; distr. 1977 GH

Donohew, G.
Rita mende abaawabwe. [Rita and her family] 2nd ed. 121pp. ill. K.shs.2.50 ($1.50/60p.) EALB 1969 KE LUY

Doorndos, M.R.
Regalia galore. The decline and eclipse of Ankole kingship. 158pp. K.shs.23.50 ($5.10/£2.50) EALB 1975 KE

Dopamu, D.
Revision questions/answers on 'O' level Bible knowledge. (Old Testament) bk. 1. See: Adelowo, D.

Dorey, A.
The Victoria incident and the Anglo-Matabele war of 1893. R$1.00 (Local series pamphlets, 16) Central Africa Hist Assoc 1966 RH

Dorner, H.H.T.
A dictionary of English usage in Southern Africa. See: Beeton, D.R.

Dorsinville, R.
Dans un peuple de dieux. 94pp. DA7.00 SNED 1971 AE FRE

Dosekun, F.O.
The place of physiological sciences in medicine. 8pp. 10k Univ Lagos Bookshop 1971 NR

Dosunmu, J.A., ed.
Nigerian books in print 1968. 78pp. N1.00 (N3.00) (National Library pubs, 19) Nat Lib Nig 1970 NR

Dotse, J.M.
Practical geography (Map work). Model questions and answers (Advanced level) 161pp. C3.00 Univ Cape Coast (distr.) 1974 GH

Dottin, O.
Bibliographie géologique de Madagascar: 1958-1959. See: Noizet, G.

Dottin, O.
Etude géologique et prospection de la haute Betsiboka. 27pp. pl. FMG356 (F7.12) (Travaux du Bureau Géologique, 105) Service Geol - Mad 1961 MG FRE

Dottin, O.
Etude géologique et prospection des feuilles Longozabe, Antanandehibe-Mahanoro. 61pp. pl. maps. FMG1367 (F27.34) (Travaux du Bureau Géologique, 102) Service Geol - Mad 1960 MG FRE

Douaouri, B.
Ampelographie algérienne. See: Levadoux, L.

Doucoure, L.
Légende de la dispersion des Kusa (épopée soninke) See: Meillassoux, C.

Dougall, I.
Life for God's people. See: Kiongo, C.

Dougall, I.C.
Imani ya mkristo. See: Kiongo, C.

Dougall, I.C.
What I believe. See: Kiongo, C.

Douglas, P.
Television today. 208pp. hd. R11.10 Philip 1975 SA

Doumbe-Moulongo, M.
Les coutumes et le droit au Cameroun. 150pp. CFA660 CLE 1972 CM FRE

Douwes Dekker, L.C.G.
Are works committees trade unions? 26pp. 40c Title banned in SA SA Inst of Race Relations 1974 SA

Douwes Dekker, L.C.G.
Workers' participation as an important part in the institutionalisation of an open plural society. 39pp. 60c Title banned in SA SA Inst of Race Relations 1976 SA

Dovlo, C.K.
Christianity and family life in Ghana. 55pp. 20pes. Waterville 1962 GH

Dowdle, E.B.D.
Science and humanism in medicine. 10pp. 30c. (U.C.T. Inaugural lec. New series, 8) Univ Cape Town Lib 1971 SA

Downes, L.W. Paling, D.
Oxford arithmetic course (Nig): pupils bk. 3rd ed. 6, 6 bks. N1.30 OUP - Nig NR

Downes, L.W. Paling, D. Smithies, A.
Oxford arithmetic course (Nig.): teacher's bk. 3rd ed. 1, 6 bks. 142pp. ill. N1.60 OUP - Nig 1973 NR

Downes, L.W. Paling, D. Smithies, A.
Oxford arithmetic course (Nig.): teacher's bk. 3rd ed. 2, 6 bks. 136pp. ill. N1.75 OUP - Nig 1973 NR

Downes, L.W. Paling, D. Smithies, A.
Oxford arithmetic course (Nig.): teacher's bk. 3rd ed. 3, 6 bks. 185pp. N1.75 OUP - Nig 1973 NR

Downes, L.W. Paling, D. Smithies, A.
Oxford arithmetic course (Nig.): teacher's bk. 3rd ed. 4, 6 bks. N1.75 OUP - Nig NR

Downes, L.W. Paling, D. Smithies, A.
Oxford arithmetic course (Nig.): teacher's bk. 3rd ed. 5, 6 bks. N1.75 OUP - Nig NR

Downes, L.W. Paling, D. Smithies, A.
Oxford arithmetic course (Nig.): teacher's bk. 3rd ed. 6, 6 bks. N1.75 OUP - Nig NR

Downes, L.W.
Oxford modern mathematics for Nigerian primary schools. pupil's bk. 1, 6 bks. See: Lassa, P.N.

Downes, L.W.
Oxford modern mathematics for Nigerian primary schools. pupil's bk. 2, 6 bks. See: Lassa, P.N.

Downes, L.W.
Oxford modern mathematics for Nigerian primary schools. pupil's bk. 3, 6 bks. See: Lassa, P.N.

Downes, L.W.
Oxford modern mathematics for Nigerian primary schools. pupil's bk. 4, 6 bks. See: Lassa, P.N.

Downes, L.W.
Oxford modern mathematics for Nigerian primary schools. pupil's bk. 5, 6 bks. See: Lassa, P.N.

Downes, L.W.
Oxford modern mathematics for Nigerian primary schools. pupil's bk. 6, 6 bks. See: Lassa, P.N.

Downes, L.W.
Oxford modern mathematics for Nigerian primary schools. teacher's bk. 1, 6 bks. See: Lassa, P.N.

Downes, L.W.
Oxford modern mathematics for Nigerian primary schools. teacher's bk. 2, 6 bks. See: Lassa, P.N.

Downes, L.W.
Oxford modern mathematics for Nigerian primary schools. teacher's bk. 3, 6 bks. See: Lassa, P.N.

Downes, L.W.
Oxford modern mathematics for Nigerian primary schools. teacher's bk. 4, 6 bks. See: Lassa, P.N.

Downes, L.W.
Oxford modern mathematics for Nigerian primary schools. teacher's bk. 5, 6 bks. See: Lassa, P.N.

Downes, L.W.
Oxford modern mathematics for Nigerian primary schools. teacher's bk. 6, 6 bks. See: Lassa, P.N.

Downes, L.W.
Oxford modern mathematics for Nigerian primary schools. workbook 1, 5 bks. See: Lassa, P.N.

Downes, L.W.
Oxford modern mathematics for Nigerian primary schools. workbook 2, 5 bks. See: Lassa, P.N.

Downes, L.W.
Oxford modern mathematics for Nigerian primary schools. workbook 3, 5 bks. See: Lassa, P.N.

Downes, L.W.
Oxford modern mathematics for Nigerian primary schools. workbook 4, 5 bks. See: Lassa, P.N.

Downes, L.W.
Oxford modern mathematics for Nigerian primary schools. workbook 5, 5 bks. See: Lassa, P.N.

Downes, L.W.   Paling, D.
Revision, objective and aptitude tests for Oxford primary mathematics course. 98pp. ill. 85k OUP - Nig 1974 NR

Downes, R.M.
Tiv religion. 102pp. pl. N2.50 Ibadan UP 1971 NR

Doxey, M.
South Africa's external economic relations: new initiatives in a changing environment. 18pp. 35c. SA Inst Int Affairs 1969 SA

Doyle, A.C.
The great Boer war. [Reprint of 18th enl. ed.]. 776pp. foldout maps. cl. R17.50 (Anglo Boer War Reprint Library, 1) Struik 1976 SA

Doyle, M.S.
Lease valuation tables. R5.00 Juta 1975 SA

Dracopoli, J.L.
Sir Andries Stockenstrom, 1792-1864: the origins of the racial conflict in South Africa. 223pp. hd. fl. 33.75 (South African biographical and historical studies, 4) Balkema 1969 SA

Dransfield, M.
Seed dressing trials on cotton in Northern Nigeria. 22pp. 20k (Samaru misc. pap., 26) Inst Agric Res - Zaria 1968 NR

Draper, P.L.
When Christ comes back. 64pp. hd. 22k SIM 1966 NR

Dresang, D.
Zambia civil service. 188pp. K.shs.52.00 ($13.00) EAPH 1976 KE

Drew, J.D.C.
Malawi national bibliography. List of publications deposited in the Library of the National Archives, 1967. 10pp. Nat Arch - Mal 1968 MW

Drew, J.D.C.
Malawi national bibliography. List of publications deposited in the Library of the National Archives, 1968. 12pp. Nat Arch - Mal 1969 MW

Drew, J.D.C.
Malawi national bibliography. List of publications deposited in the Library of the National Archives, 1969. 8pp. Nat Arch - Mal 1971 MW

Drew, J.D.C.
Malawi national bibliography. List of publications deposited in the Library of the National Archives, 1970. 14pp. Nat Arch - Mal 1973 MW

Dreyer, C.
Exponents and logarithms. 38pp. ill. R2.00 Technitrain 1974 SA

Dreyer, J.J.
My mathematics books. My fifth mathematics/arithmetic book. See: Levinsohn, S.

Dreyer, J.J.
My mathematics books. My first mathematics/arithmetic book. See: Levinsohn, S.

Dreyer, J.J.
My mathematics books. My fourth mathematics/arithmetic book. See: Levinsohn, S.

Dreyer, J.J.
My mathematics books. My sixth mathematics/arithmetics book. See: Levinsohn, J.S.

Dreyer, J.J.
My mathematics books. My third mathematics/arithmetic book. See: Levinsohn, S.

Drummond, R., et al.
Common trees of the highveld. 99pp. col. ill. R$2.50 Longman - Rhod 1973 RH

Drummond, R.B., ed.
Trees of southern Africa. See: Palgrave, C.K., ed.

Dryden, S.
Local administration in Tanzania. 251pp. K.shs.56.00 cl. K.shs.24.00 pap. ($10.40 cl.) ($7.80 pap.) EAPH 1968 KE

Drysdall, A.R.
The alluvial gold of the Msidza river, Lundazi District. See: Simpson, J.G.

Drysdall, A.R.
The clays of Central Brickfields, Broken Hill. K1.50 (Dept. of Geological Survey. Economic Reports, 8) Geol Survey - Zam 1965 ZA

Drysdall, A.R., et al.
Coal resources of the Zambezi valley. v.2: Siankondobo - the Kazinze basin: geology of the shafts 75n (Dept. of Geological Survey. Economic Reports, 14) Geol Survey - Zam 1967 ZA

Drysdall, A.R., et al.
Coal resources of the Zambezi valley. v.3: Siankondobo - the northern part of the Kazinze basin. K1.00 (Dept. of Geological Survey. Economic Reports, 15) Geol Survey - Zam 1967 ZA

Drysdall, A.R., et al.
Coal resources of the Zambezi valley. v.4: Siankondobo - the Izuma basin. K1.50 (Dept. of Geological Survey. Economic Reports, 16) Geol Survey - Zam 1967 ZA

Drysdall, A.R., et al.
Outline of the geology of Zambia. 50n (Dept. of Geological Survey. Occas. paps., 50) Geol Survey - Zam 1972 MW

Drysdall, A.R.   Utting, J.
Fossils of Zambia. 30n (Dept. of Geological Survey, occas. paps., 57) Geol Survey - Zam 1973 ZA

Drysdall, A.R.
The geological survey of Zambia: a geological survey in a developing environment. K1.00 (Dept. of Geological Survey. Occas. paps., 49) Geol Survey - Zam 1973 ZA

Author Index

Drysdall, A.R.
The Geological Survey of Zambia: its role in the social and economic development of the country. K2.15 (Dept. of Geological Survey, occas. paps., 70) Geol Survey - Zam 1974 ZA

Drysdall, A.R. Simpson, J.G.
The Kankomo clay deposit, Kitwe District. 75n (Dept. of Geological Survey. Economic Reports, 11) Geol Survey - Zam 1966 ZA

Drysdall, A.R. Weller, R.K.
Karroo sedimentation in Northern Rhodesia. 50n (Dept. of Geological Survey. Occas. paps., 39) Geol Survey - Zam 1966 ZA

Drysdall, A.R.
The limestone of Morton limeworks, Lusaka. 25n (Dept. of Geological Survey. Economic Reports, 3) Geol Survey - Zam 1964 ZA

Drysdall, A.R. Langevad, E.J.
The mines and minerals act, 1969, and the mineral tax act, 1970. 75n (Dept. of Geological Survey. Economic Reports, 26) Geol Survey - Zam 1970 ZA

Drysdall, A.R.
The Njoka graphite deposit, Lundazi District. See: Simpson, J.G.

Drysdall, A.R.
Precambrian geology and structure in central Northern Rhodesia. See: De Swardt, A.M.J.

Drysdall, A.R. Kitching, J.W.
A re-examination of the Karroo succession and fossil localities of part of the upper Luangwa valley. K3.00 (Dept. of Geological Survey, Memoirs, 1) Geol Survey - Zam 1963 ZA

Drysdall, A.R. Money, N.J. Denman, P.D.
Some aspects of the geology of the Siankondobo coalfield. 20n (Dept. of Geological Survey. Occas. paps., 40) Geol Survey - Zam 1967 ZA

Drysdall, A.R.
The tin belt of the Southern Province: a summary report. 2nd ed. K1.15 (Dept. of Geological Survey. Economic Reports, 1) Geol Survey - Zam 1967 ZA

Drysdall, A.R.
The tin mineralisation of Chimwami mine, Choma district. See: Newman, D.

Du Bois, W.E.B.
Selected poems. 42pp. C1.00 ($1.00/50p.) Ghana UP 1964 GH

du Plessis, A., ed.
The conservation of our heritage. 296pp. ill. R9.75 cl. Human and Rousseau 1974 SA

du Plessis, J.
The Brezhnev doctrine and South Africa. 18pp. R1.00 (FAA Study Report, 5) Foreign Affairs Assoc - SA 1976 SA

du Plessis, J.
Soviet strategy towards Southern Africa. 10pp. (FAA Study Report, 1) Foreign Affairs Assoc - SA 1976 SA

du Plessis, J.
Virus diseases and some symptomologically related abnormalities of the swine. 33pp. photos. 50c. Univ Stellenbosch, Lib 1950 SA

Du Plessis, J.C.
Invariance properties of variational principles in general relativity. 83pp. R2.75 (R3.75) (Studia, 1) Univ South Africa 1968 SA

du Preez, H.E., comp.
The poetry of Conrad Ferdinand Meyer. 30pp. R2.10 Dept Bibliog, Lib & Typo 1974 SA

du Preez, J.L.
Post primary arithmetic, Forms II & III. See: Stone, S.

Du Preez, J.P.A.
Religious education. 128pp. map ill. R2.10 Longman - SA 1976 SA

Du Ry, C.J.
Wandering in western culture. 12pp. 30c. (Univ. Cape Town. Inaugural lec., new series, 39) Univ Cape Town Lib 1976 SA

Du Toit, A.E.
The earliest British document on education for the coloured races. 40pp. 40c. (90c.) Univ South Africa 1962 SA

Du Toit, A.E.
The earliest South African documents on the education and civilization of the Bantu. 91pp. 80c. (R1.30) Univ South Africa 1963 SA

du Toit, A.J.W.
Needlework and clothing manual for standards 9-10. vol.2. See: van der Walt, W.A.

Du Toit, A.S. Maharaj, M.D.
Socio-economic study of Chatsworth. free (Chatsworth Community and Research Centre, Research Report, 2) Univ of Durban - Westville 1973 SA

du Toit, B.M.
Akuna. A New Guinea village community. 398pp. ill. maps. cl. & pap. R11.00 pap. R15.50 cl. ($15.50 pap.) ($21.50 cl.) Balkema 1975 SA

Du Toit, B.M.
Configurations of cultural continuity. 159pp. R8.35 (Dfl.25/$9.50/£4.85) Balkema 1976 SA

Du Toit, B.M., ed.
Drugs, rituals and altered states of consciousness. 300pp. photos. cl. ($16.00/£9.50) Balkema 1977 SA

du Toit, B.M.
People of the valley. An isolated valley community of Afrikaners in South Africa. 144pp. pl. maps. R4.50 ($8.25) Balkema 1974 SA

du Toit, J.J., et al.
Senior biology for standards 9-10. v. 2. 569pp. ill. photo. R3.65 Nasou 1976 SA

du Toit, J.J.D.P.
Senior biology for standards 9-10. v. 1. 313pp. ill. photos. R3.95 Nasou 1975 SA

du Toit, M.A.
South African trade unions. R7.95 McGraw-Hill SA 1976 SA

du Toit, P., et al.
Senior biology for standard 8. 274pp. ill. R3.15 Nasou 1974 SA

du Toit, S.
The Bible and evolution. 40c. (Isma pap., 17) Inst Study of Man 1964 SA

Dubb, A.A.
Community of the saved: an African revivalist church in the East Cape. 175pp. pl. R7.00 cl. (African Stud. Inst. pub.) Witwatersrand UP 1976 SA

Dubb, A.A., ed. Schutte, A.G., ed.
Black religion in South Africa, ['African Studies' special number, v. 33, no. 2]. 49pp. R2.40 African Studies Inst - Wit 1974 SA

Dubb A.A., ed.
The multitribal society. 147pp. (Rhodes-Livingstone Institute conf. proc., 16) Inst Afr Stud - Lusaka 1962 ZA

Dubb, A.A., ed.
Myth in modern Africa. 156pp. K1.00 (59p.) (Rhodes-Livingstone Institute conf. proc., 14) Inst Afr Stud -Lusaka 1960 ZA

Dubb, A.A.
Jewish South Africans: a sociological view of the Johannesburg community. R5.50 (Inst. of Social and Economic Research, occas. paps., 21) Inst Soc & Econ Res 1977 SA

Dube, B.J.
Inkinga yomendo. [The riddle of marriage] 94pp. 65c. Shuter 1961 SA ZUL

Dube, B.J.
Uthemi. [Themi] 130pp. 75c. Shuter 1968 SA ZUL

Dunlop, A.
A practical rancher's ramblings. ill. R$1.50 ($3.00)
M.O. Collins 1974 RH

Dunlop, H.
The development of European agriculture in Rhodesia
1945-1965. 73pp. R$1.00 (Dept. of Economics, Univ.
of Rhodesia, 5) Univ Rhodesia Lib 1971 RH

Dupire, M.
Les facteurs humains de l'économie pastorale. 2nd ed.
93pp. maps photos. CFA1250 (F25.00) (Etudes
Nigeriennes, 6) Inst Rech Sci Hum 1972 NG FRE

Duponchel, L.
L'alladian: phonologie et enquête lexicale. 661pp.
CFA1;500 (Linguistique Africaine, 50) Inst Ling
Appliquée 1974 IV FRE

Duponchel, L.
Contribution à l'étude lexicale du français de Côte d'Ivoire.
Problèmes de néologie et enseignement du vocabulaire.
168pp. CFA600 (Enseignement du français, 35) Inst
Ling Appliquée 1972 IV FRE

Duponchel, L.
Dictionnaire du Français de Côte-d'Ivoire. 277pp.
CFA1,100 (Enseignement du Français, 52) Inst Ling
Appliquée 1975 IV FRE

Duponchel, L. et al.
Annales de l'université d'Abidjan. 245pp. CFA1250
(F25.00) (Série H-Linguistique, 6) Univ Abidjan 1973 IV
FRE

Duponchel, L.
Langues négro-africaines et enseignement du français.
Conférences et comptes rendus. See: Canu, G.

Duponchel, L.
Proverbes de Cote-d'Ivoire, fascicule 1: abey, avikam.
See: Dumestre G.

Duponchel, L.
Vocabulaire essentiel de l'enseignement primaire, 5ème et
6ème années. See: Canu, A.

Durand, P.
Géographie du Niger. 58pp. maps. Ecole Nat Admin -
Niger 1976 NG FRE

Durand, P.P.
Evidence for magistrates. 2 v. 219pp. K.shs.42.00
Kenya Inst Admin 1969 KE

Durand, P.P.
Working with the laws of Kenya and law reports in East
Africa. 42pp. K.shs.15.00 Kenya Inst Admin 1969
KE

Durhan, B.
Here's how to write better letters. 17pp. 15n
Multimedia 1971 ZA

Durojaiye, A.
Gbekude ati ise abe. ill. 50k OUP - Nig 1971 NR
YOR

Durojaiye, S.M.
Practical methods for nursery schools. 156pp. ill.
N2.70 OUP - Nig 1977 NR

Durr, H.J.R.
A host plant index of South African plant lice (Aphididae)
See: Potgieter, J.T.

Duteil, P.A.   Sarazin, S.
Jeune fille prépare. 77pp. 45k St. Paul 1976 ZR
FRE

Duthie, A.V.
Contribution to our knowledge of the genus eriospermum.
64pp. pl. 30c. (A v.18, no. 2) Univ Stellenbosch, Lib
1940 SA

Duthie, A.V.
Contribution to our knowledge of the Stellenbosch flora.
New or little known flowering plants of the Stellenbosch
Flats. 8pp. pl. 15c. (A v.4, no. 3) Univ
Stellenbosch, Lib 1928 SA

Duthie, A.V.
Contribution to our knowledge of the Stellenbosch flora:
The species of Anthericum and Chlorophytum of the
Stellenbosch Flats. 23pp. pl. 15c. (A v.4, no. 1)
Univ Stellenbosch, Lib 1926 SA

Duthie, A.V.
Contribution to our knowledge of the Stellenbosch flora.
The species of Urginea of the Stellenbosch Flats. 16pp.
pl./ill. 15c. (A v. 4, no. 2) Univ Stellenbosch, Lib
1928 SA

Duthie, A.V.
The eriospermums of the Stellenbosch Flats. 22pp. ill.
15c. (A v.2, no. 3) Univ Stellenbosch, Lib 1924 SA

Dutkiewicz, R.K.
Bridges from the ivory tower. 8pp. 30c (Univ. Cape
Town. Inaugural lec., 22) Univ Cape Town Lib 1973 SA

Dutto, C.A.
Nyeri townsmen Kenya. 296pp. K.shs.39.75
($9.10/£4.40) EALB 1975 KE

Duviard, D. et al.
Annales de l'université d'Abidjan. 315pp. CFA1200
(F24.00) (Série E-Ecologie, 3) Univ Abidjan 1970 IV
FRE

Duyile, D.
FESTAC '77 souvenir. 48pp. photo. 50k Daily
Sketch 1977 NR

Duze, M., ed.   Menakaya, J.C., ed.
Nigeria school atlas. 18pp. maps. N1.10 Macmillan
1972 NR

Duze, M.
Primary atlas for Lagos state. 45pp. maps. N1.10
Macmillan 1965 NR

Duze, M.
Primary atlas for Oyo, Ogun and Ondo states of Nigeria.
33pp. maps. N1.10 Macmillan 1965 NR

Duze, M.
Primary atlas for the Bendel state of Nigeria. 41pp.
maps. N1.10 Macmillan 1965 NR

Duze, M.
A primary geography for Nigeria. 1, 2bks 112pp. maps
ill. N1.10 Macmillan 1963 NR

Duze, M.
A primary geography for Nigeria. 2, 2bks maps ill.
N1.30 Macmillan 1963 NR

Duze, M.
A primary geography for Nigeria: teacher's bk, 1. 48pp.
maps ill. 50k Macmillan 1963 NR

Dye, N.
Knit-de-Knit in a polyester/cotton blend. See: Robinson,
G.A.

Dyer, R.A.
The vegetation of the divisions of Albany and Bathurst.
(Memoirs of the Botanical Survey of South Africa, 17)
Botanical Res Inst 1937 SA

Dylak, T.
The earth and its wonders - for the children of Africa. bk.
3 See: Butler, E.

Dyson, R.H.
Reproducibility of measurements of solute recovery in pilot
scale rotary vaccum filtration using a tritium tracer.
See: Rushton, A.

Dzobo, N.K.
African marriage -- right or wrong? 60pp. cl. & pap.
80pes. pap. C1.20 cl. Waterville 1975 GH

Dzobo, N.K.
African proverbs: guide to conduct. (The moral value of
Ewe proverbs) v. 1, pt. 1. 115pp. C3.00 Univ Cape
Coast (distr.) 1973 GH

Dzobo, N.K.
African proverbs: guide to conduct. v. 2. 136pp.
C2.50 Waterville 1975 GH

Dzoro, S.T.
Chakabaya chikatyokera. [Beyond redemption.] 74pp.
70c Longman - Rhod 1973 RH SHO

Dzoro, S.T.
Mbodza inozvimbira. [Despising something that is of
great value.] 16pp. pl. 10c Rhod Lit Bur 1976 RH
SHO

East African Community. East African Natural Resources
Research Council.
Approved research programmes, 1975/80. 26pp. EALB
1976 KE

East African Community.
Review of economic integration activities within the East
African Community, 1973-74. 166pp. K.shs.30.00
($2.65/£1.20) EALB 1974 KE

East African Dental Association.
East African dental and medical directory 1973. 200pp.
cl. K.shs.50.00 ($9.80/£4.50) EALB 1974 KE

East African Literature Bureau.
Barua ya Mgendi. [Mgendi's letter] 20pp. ill.
K.shs.2.00 ($1.25/50p.) EALB 1971 KE SWA

East African Literature Bureau.
Bed bugs and flies. ills. K.shs.0.20 (85c./50p.)
(Red Cross booklet, 9) EALB 1963 KE

East African Literature Bureau.
Birth of baby in the home. 21pp. ill. K.shs.0.50
($1.00/40p) (Red Cross booklet, 11) EALB 1963 KE

East African Literature Bureau.
Care of aged and crippled. ill. K.shs.0.40
($1.00/40p) (Red Cross booklet, 10) EALB 1961 KE

East African Literature Bureau.
Child welfare. ill. K.shs.0.50 ($1.00/40p.) (Red
Cross booklet, 12) EALB 1963 KE

East African Literature Bureau.
Consumption. 11pp. ill. K.shs.0.25 ($1.00/40p.)
(Red Cross booklet, 2) EALB 1963 KE

East African Literature Bureau.
Dare to die. K.shs15.00 ($5.00/£3.50) EALB 1972
KE

East African Literature Bureau.
The fourth trial: kisses of fate. K.shs9.50
($2.75/£1.10) EALB 1972 KE

East African Literature Bureau.
How to keep healthy. 3rd ed. 12pp. ill. K.shs.0.40
($1.00/40p.) (Red Cross booklet, 8) EALB 1968 KE

East African Literature Bureau.
How to keep well: a health booklet of general interest.
60pp. ill. K.shs.2.00 ($1.00/40p.) EALB 1955 KE

East African Literature Bureau.
Jiendeleze. bk.1 56pp. K.shs.0.50 EALB 1968 KE
SWA

East African Literature Bureau.
Keeping a shop: a handbook for Africans in the trade
business. 34pp. K.shs1.50 ($1.25/50p.) EALB KE

East African Literature Bureau.
Kielelezo cha mafunzo. [Reader's guide] 2nd ed.
20pp. K.shs.1.75 ($1.00/40p.) EALB 1971 KE SWA

East African Literature Bureau.
Kifua kikuu. [Tuberculosis: its causes and how to
prevent it from spreading] 2nd ed. ill. K.shs.0.10
($1.00/40p.) EALB 1961 KE SWA

East African Literature Bureau.
Kila mwaka wa tano. [Every fifth year] 26pp. ill.
K.shs.2.20 ($1.25/50p.) EALB 1971 KE SWA

East African Literature Bureau.
Kuanza kusoma: usomaji wa watu wazima. [Beginning
to read. adult literacy primer] 5th ed. bk.7 28pp. ill.
K.shs.1.25 ($1.25/50p.) EALB 1964 KE SWA

East African Literature Bureau.
Kuiyura nda tikuo guthondeka mwiri. [Feeding the body
is more than filling the stomach] 16pp. K.shs.0.35
($1.00/60p.) EALB 1950 KE KIK

East African Literature Bureau.
Leprosy. 2nd ed. ill. K.shs.0.20 ($1.00/40p.)
(Red Cross booklet, 1) EALB 1961 KE

East African Literature Bureau.
Maendeleo ya jumuia: haya ni maendeleo ya jumuia katika
Kenya. [Community development: this is community
development in Kenya] ill. K.shs.1.00 ($1.25/50p.)
EALB 1965 KE SWA

East African Literature Bureau.
Matunda ya kuishi kijamaa. [Fruits of socialistic living]
20pp. ill. K.shs.2.20 ($1.25/50p.) EALB 1971 KE
SWA

East African Literature Bureau.
Moto. [Fire] 20pp. ill. K.shs.2.00 ($1.25/50p.)
EALB 1971 KE SWA

East African Literature Bureau.
Murutanire wa ibuku ria mbere ria gikuyu ria guthoma.
[Teacher's manual for adult literacy classes] K.shs.1.25
EALB KE KIK

East African Literature Bureau.
Musau, mundu mui. [Ways with health] 3rd ed. 57pp.
ill. K.shs.1.50 ($1.25/50p.) EALB 1968 KE KAM

East African Literature Bureau.
Ng'ano ikumi na ithano cia Ugikuyu. [Fifteen Kikuyu
fables] 4th ed. 39pp. ill. K.shs.5.10 ($1.90/50p.)
EALB 1970 KE KIK

East African Literature Bureau.
Nuru ya nyumgani. [Motherhood and child care] 178pp.
K.shs.35.50 ($6.50/£2.60) EALB 1974 KE SWA

East African Literature Bureau.
Occasional papers on community development. 75pp.
K.shs.3.00 ($2.00/80p.) (Occasional papers, 1) EALB
1962 KE

East African Literature Bureau.
Ongesoman. 4th ed. 23pp. ill. K.shs.1.00
($1.25/50p.) EALB 1964 KE KAL

East African Literature Bureau.
Pesa matumizi na utunzaji. [Money: its use and care]
13pp. K.shs.1.50 ($2.25/90p.) EALB 1950 KE SWA

East African Literature Bureau.
Prevention of eye troubles and blindness. 13pp. ill.
K.shs.0.30 ($1.00/40p.) (Red Cross booklet, 7) EALB
1963 KE

East African Literature Bureau.
Safari ya kwenda Mwanza. [A journey to Mwanza]
20pp. ill. K.shs.2.20 ($1.25/50p.) EALB 1971 KE
SWA

East African Literature Bureau.
Scabies. 2nd ed. 8pp. ill. K.shs.0.30 ($1.00/40p.)
(Red Cross booklet, 5) EALB 1966 KE

East African Literature Bureau.
Tanzania kabla na baada ya uhuru. [Tanzania before
and after independence] 2nd ed. 20pp. K.shs.5.25
($2.00/80p.) EALB 1971 KE SWA

East African Literature Bureau.
Tuandike barua. [Letter writing] 22pp. ill. K.shs.1.00
($1.25/50p.) EALB 1963 KE SWA

East African Literature Bureau.
Twimanyisyei kusoma. [Let us learn how to read] 2
2nded. 24pp. ill. K.shs.0.90 ($1.25/50p.) EALB
1969 KE KAM

East African Literature Bureau.
Ulcers and sores. 2nd ed. 8pp. ill. K.shs.0.30
($1.00/40p.) (Red Cross booklet, 6) EALB 1966 KE

East African Literature Bureau.
Usiku wa mashaka. [The troublesome night] 20pp. ill.
K.shs2.00 ($1.25/50p.) EALB 1971 KE SWA

East African Literature Bureau.
Usiku wa ngoma. [The dancing night] 20pp. ill.
K.shs2.00 ($1.25/50p.) EALB 1971 KE SWA

East African Literature Bureau.
Uwindaji haramu. [Poaching] 20pp. ill. K.shs.2.00
($1.25/50p.) EALB 1971 KE SWA

East African Literature Bureau.
Wafinyanzi wa Tanzania. [Potters of Tanzania] 20pp. ill.
K.shs.2.00 ($1.25/50p.) EALB 1971 KE SWA

East African Literature Bureau.
Wilaya yetu ya Njombe. [Our Njombe district] 28pp.
K.shs.0.75 ($1.25/50p.) EALB 1963 KE SWA

East African Literature Bureau.
The work of an African chief in Kenya. 5th ed. 49pp.
K.shs.1.50 EALB 1960 KE

East African Literature Bureau.
Worms. 2nd ed. 8pp. ill. K.shs.0.30 ($1.00/40p.)
(Red Cross booklet, 3) EALB 1966 KE

East African Medical Research Council.
The child in the African environment. 472pp. ill.
K.shs.196.50 cl. K.shs.92.50 pap. ($36.20/£16.00
cl.) ($17.20/£6.90 pap.) EALB 1975 KE

East African Medical Research Council.
Myocardiology in Africa. East African Medical Research
Council. Proceedings of the international symposium -
preventive myocardiology and cardiac metabolism. v.2
174pp. pl. cl. & pap. K.shs.94.50 cl. K.shs.55.75
pap. (£8.50/$17.80 cl.) (£4.40/$10.85 pap.) EALB
1976 KE

East African Medical Research Council.
Myocardiology in Africa. Proceedings of the international
symposium - preventive mycardiology and cardiac
metabolism. v. 1 332pp. cl. & pap. K.shs.98.00 pap.
K.shs.165.00 cl. ($18.00/£7.40 pap.) ($30.30/£14.50
cl.) EALB 1974 KE

East African Publishing House.
Elections. 12pp. ill. K.shs.4.20 (Primary Civics
series) EAPH 1974 KE

East African Publishing House.
Kenya: an official handbook. 205pp. photos.
K.shs.36.00 EAPH 1974 KE

East African Publishing House.
Kenya's wild life. 22pp. ill. pl. K.shs.7.50 EAPH
1976 KE

East African Publishing House.
Learning about our country. 12pp. ill. K.shs.4.00
(Primary Civics series) EAPH 1974 KE

East African Publishing House.
Our national anthem. 12pp. ill. K.shs.4.90 (Primary
Civics series) EAPH 1974 KE

East African Publishing House.
Our national flag and court of arms. 12pp. ill.
K.shs.4.20 (Primary Civics series) EAPH 1974 KE

East African Publishing House.
Our national holidays. 12pp. ill. K.shs.4.20 (Primary
Civics series) EAPH 1974 KE

East African Publishing House.
A visit to parliament. 10pp. ill. K.shs.4.20 (Primary
Civics series) EAPH 1974 KE

East African Publishing House.
Wall map of East Africa. K.shs.60.00 ($15.00) EAPH
1975 KE

East African Publishing House.
The work of the District Commissioner. 12pp. ill.
K.shs.4.00 (Primary Civics series) EAPH 1974 KE

Easterbrook, R.
Discovering Rhodesian geography. Pupil's grade 5.
96pp. 90c. Longman - Rhod 1969 RH

Easterbrook, R.
Discovering Rhodesian geography. Teacher's grade 5.
128pp. 95c. Longman - Rhod 1968 RH

Ebeling, D.H.
The greatest book. 146pp. T.shs5.00 Africa Inland
Church TZ

Ebersohn, J. J.
Systematic typing for the senior secondary course.
See: Geldenhuys, A.

Ebrahim, G.J.
Childcare for tropical mothers. 48pp. ill. K.shs.9.50
($2.75/£1.30) EALB 1970 KE

Ebrahim, G.J.
A handbook of tropical pediatrics. 104pp. K.shs.19.95
($4.50/£2.20) EALB 1975 KE

Ebrahim, G.J.
The newborn in tropical Africa. 111pp. ill. K.shs.9.00
($2.50/£1.20) EALB 1969 KE

Ebrahim, G.J.
Practical mother and child health in developing countries.
2nd rev. ed. 108pp. ill. K.shs.18.00 ($4.60/£2.20)
EALB 1974 KE

Eby, O.
News writing: Africa Christian writers' course. v. 1
47pp. 35t. (40c.) Christ Lit Assoc -Mal 1972 MW

Echard, N.
L'experience du passé: histoire de la société paysanne
hausa de l'Ader. 232pp. ill. hd. (Etudes Nigériennes,
36) Inst Rech Sci Hum 1975 NG FRE

Echebima, G.N. Lucas, B.O.
Model answers on "Macbeth". 74pp. N1.60
Aromolaran 1975[?] NR

Echeruo, M.J.C.
Poets, prophets and professors. N1.00 (Inaugural
lecture) Ibadan UP 1977 NR

Ecole Superieure Internationale de Journalisme de Yaoundé.
Une semaine à Bandjoum. 104pp. CFA300 Univ
Cameroun 1972 CM FRE

Economic Commission for Africa.
A critique of conventional planning in Africa in relation to
the unified approach. 24pp. (E/CN.14/CAP.6/5) ECA
1976 ET

Economic Commission for Africa.
The data base for discussion on the interrelations between
the integration of women in development, their situation
and population factors in Africa. 86pp.
(E/CN.14/SW/37) ECA 1975 ET

Economic Commission for Africa.
ECA activities in the field of economic research and
planning, July 1974 to October 1976. 8pp.
(E/CN./CAP.6/7) ECA 1976 ET

Economic Commission for Africa.
Follow-up decisions taken at the fifth session of the
Conference, Addis Ababa, 19-20 June, 1974. 2pp.
(E/CN.14/CAP.6/6) ECA 1976 ET

Economic Commission for Africa.
Pharmaceuticals in Africa. 79pp. (E/CN.14/INR/217)
ECA 1976 ET

Economic Commission for Africa.
Public works programmes and integrated rural
development for the alleviation of mass poverty,
unemployment and underemployment. 26pp.
(E/CN.14/CAP.6/2) ECA 1976 ET

Economic Commission for Africa.
Recent decisions of interest to the Commission adopted by
the General Assembly and the Economic and Social
Council. 24pp. (E/CN.14/598/Add.6) ECA 1975 ET

Economic Commission for Africa.
Report on the first meeting on the Trans-East African
Highway. (Addis Ababa, 15-17 June 1976) 16pp.
(E/CN.14/TRANS/129) ECA 1976 ET

Economic Commission for Africa.
Social development planning in Africa within the framework
of the principles of the unified approach to development
analysis and planning. 17pp. (E/CN.14/CAP.6/3)
ECA 1976 ET

E.C.W.A.
Minister's handbook. 80pp. 50k SIM 1972 NR

Edet, M.J.
Obufa Edikot nwed 1. [Primary Efik course.] pupils bk.
1. 36pp. ill. 73k. Macmillan 1976 NR EFI

Edet, M.J.
Obufa Edikot nwed 2. [Primary Efik course.] pupils bk.
2. 56pp. ill. 90k. Macmillan 1976 NR EFI

Edet, M.J.
Obufa Edikot nwed 3. [Primary Efik course.] pupils bk.
3. 78pp. ill. N1.05 Macmillan 1976 NR EFI

Edet, M.J.
Obufa Edikot nwed 4. [Primary Efik course.] pupils bk.
4. 80pp. ill. N1.10 Macmillan 1976 NR EFI

Edet, M.J.
Obufa edikot nwed. Nwed-andikpep. [Teachers' guide to
primary Efik. Course bks. 1-3] 48pp. N1.30
Macmillan 1975 NR EFI

Edet, M.J.
Obufa edikot nwed. Nwed-utom ndito. [Primary Efik
course. Workbook 2.] bk. 2 32pp. ill. 65k
Macmillan 1973 NR EFI

Edewor, S.A.
Acts of the Apostles. 2nd ed. 78pp. 20k SIM 1972
NR

Edewor, S.A.
What the Bible teaches. 3rd ed. 68pp. 20k SIM
1971 NR

Edgang, E.
Sidibe [Play]. 56pp. 72k OUP - Nig 1974 NR EFI

Edge, W. Loening, W. Wallace, H.
Your child. R4.75 Juta 1976 SA

Editions du Mont Noir.
Poésie vivante. v. 2 30k Ed Mont Noir 1973 ZR FRE

Editions St. Paul Afrique.
André et Monique se marient. 72pp. 10k St. Paul
1961 ZR FRE

Editions St. Paul Afrique.
André et Monique sont fiancés. 2nd ed. 80pp. photos.
20k St. Paul 1969 ZR FRE

Editions St. Paul Afrique.
Annoncer l'évangile. Exhortation apostolique de Paul VI du
8 décembre 1975. 94pp. 40k St Paul 1976 ZR FRE

Editions St. Paul Afrique.
Enjili takatifu. [Gospels of the Bible.] 351pp. 15k
St. Paul 1968 ZR SWA

Editions St. Paul Afrique.
La main dans la main. 64pp. photos. St. Paul 1971
ZR FRE

Editions St. Paul.
Un enfant vient au monde. 48pp. ill. 10k St. Paul
1974 ZR FRE

Editions St. Paul.
Jesus des jeunes. 32pp. 10k St. Paul 1974 ZR FRE

Editions St. Paul.
Mpo na yo elenge mwasi. [For you, young mother.]
48pp. ill. col. ill. 15k St. Paul 1974 ZR LIN

Editions St. Paul.
Nous avons un enfant. 80pp. ill. 20k St. Paul 1974
ZR FRE

Editions St. Paul.
Reconciliation et renovation, 1975. L'année sainte dans
l'église du Zaire. 32pp. 10k St. Paul 1974 ZR FRE

Editions St. Paul.
A toi jeune maman. 48pp. ill. col. ill. 15k St. Paul
1974 ZR FRE

Edmunds, A.
Ama-Efese. [A commentary on Ephesians.] 2nd ed.
154pp. 95c Methodist 1974 SA XHO

Edney, E.G.
The survival of animals in hot deserts. 32pp. 30c
Univ Rhodesia Lib 1957 RH

Edorhe, P.F.
"Weep not Child": notes. 48pp. 70k Onibonoje 1970
NR

Edwards, D.
A plant ecological survey of the Tugela River Basin.
R5.30 (Memoirs of the Botanical Survey of South Africa,
36) Botanical Res Inst 1967 SA

Edwards, J.
Church and state relationships in South Africa. A list of the
material held by the Jan H. Hofmeyr Library. 22pp.
35c ($1.30/55p) SA Inst of Race Relations 1975 SA

Edwards, J., comp.
Migrant labour: a select bibliography. 35pp. 50c
($1.45/85p) SA Inst of Race Relations 1975 SA

Edwards, J., comp. Horner, D., comp.
A select bibliography on the poverty datum line in South
Africa. 22pp. 35 ($1.30/55p) SA Inst of Race
Relations 1975 SA

Edwards, J.
A select bibliography on the question of foreign investment
in South Africa. 15pp. 20c ($0.80) SA Inst of Race
Relations 1975 SA

Edwards, S., ed.
Angar-Gutin sub-station progress report for the period
March 1975 to March 1976. See: Kohler, P., ed.

Edwards, S., ed.
Annual report April 1973 to March 1974, Institute of
Agricultural Research. See: Saunders, J.H., ed.

Edwards, S., ed.
Bako research station: progress report for the period April
1973 to March 1974. See: Zschintzsch, J., ed.

Edwards, S., ed.
Bako research station progress report for the period April
1974 to March 1975. 172pp. ill. ex. only Inst Agric
Res - Addis 1976 ET

Edwards, S., ed.
Gambella experiment station: progress report for the
period April 1973 to March 1974 and April 1974 to March
1975 and April 1975 to March 1976. See: Saunders,
J.H., ed.

Edwards, S., ed.
Holletta - Guenet research station: progress report for the
period April 1972 to March 1973. See: Crowe, T.J., ed.

Edwards, S., ed.
IAR/EPID cooperative programme - Nedjo progress report
1974-1975. 35pp. ill. ex. only Inst Agric Res - Addis
1976 ET

Edwards, S., ed.
IAR/EPID cooperative programme Woretta (Begemdir)
progress report 1974-1975. See: Pinto, F.F., ed.

Edwards, S., ed.
IAR/EPID cooperative research programme, Chencha:
progress report for the period April 1974 to March 1975.
See: Grundy, G.M.F., ed.

Edwards, S., ed.
Jimma research station, Melko: progress report for the
period April 1973 to March 1974. See: Fernie, L.M., ed.

Edwards, S., ed.
Mekele station: progress report for the period April 1974
to March 1975. See: Erickson, B., ed.

Edwards, S., ed.
Melka Werer research station: progress report for the
period April 1973 to March 1974. See: Saunders, J.H.,
ed.

Edwards, S., ed.
Melka Werer research station progress report for the
period April 1974 to March 1975. See: Saunders, J.H.,
ed.

Edwards, S., ed.
National crop improvement committee: results of the
national crop trials and others 1974. 250pp. ex. only.
Inst Agric Res - Addis 1976 ET

Edwards, S., ed.
National horticultural centre, Nazareth research station:
progress report for the period April 1973 to March 1974.
See: Jackson, T.H., ed.

Edwards, S., ed.
Preliminary findings of integrated research in field crops at Kobo, 1973-1975. See: Pinto, F.F., comp.

Edwards, S., ed.
Proceedings: fifth annual research seminar, 30 October to 1 November 1974. 248pp. ex. only. Inst Agric Res - Addis 1975 ET

Edwards, S., ed.
Results of the IAR/DDA field trials and demonstration project in the highlands 1973-1976. See: Haile, A., ed.

Edwards, S.
Some wild flowering plants of Ethiopia: an introduction. 80pp. col. pl. maps. B5.00 ($3.60/£1.50) Addis Ababa UP 1976 ET

Edwards, S.J.
Zambezi odyssey. 230pp. ill. R10.50 Bulpin 1975 SA

Edyau, J.P.
Spatial relations of local markets in Kaberamaido county, Teso. 46pp. U.shs.30.00 (Occas. paps., 19) Dept Geog - Mak 1971 UG

Efebo, L.A.
Nembe language made easy. [Mie lokomote Nembebibi] 116pp. 50k (Inst of African Stud., Univ of Ibadan, occas. pub., 6) Inst Afr Stud - Ibadan 1967 NR

Efue, J.D.
Handbook to the Synoptic Gospels. 240pp. N1.25 Macmillan 1971 NR

Egan, E.N., ed.
Ordinances of the Cape Province: the consolidated Cape ordinances, 1910-1962. binder R125.00 [including all annual revision services up to 1976] Juta 1970 SA

Egan, E.N.
Index to the appellate division reports, 1933-46. R10.00 Juta SA

Egberipou, O.A.   Williamson, K.
Bolou izon go fun. [Ijo reader, 1] 63pp. ill. 30k (Inst. of African Stud., Univ. of Ibadan, Rivers readers project, 1) Inst Afr Stud-Ibadan 1969 NR IJO

Egberipou, O.A.   Kay, W.
Bolou Izua Egberi fun. [Ijo tales, bk, 1] 20pp. ill. 20k (Inst. of African Stud., Univ. of Ibadan, occas. pub., 15) Inst Afr Stud-Ibadan 1968 NR IJO

Egberipou, O.A.   Williamson, K.
Teacher's notes on Bolou izon go fun. 25pp. N1.00 (Inst. of African Stud., Univ. of Ibadan, Rivers readers project, 2) Inst Afr Stud-Ibadan 1969 NR IJO

Egblewogbe, E.Y.
Games and songs as education media: a case study among the Ewes of Ghana. 112pp. C3.50 ($3.50) Ghana Publ Corp 1975 GH

Egblewogbe, E.Y.
Victims of greed. 120pp. C3.00 ($3.00) Ghana Publ Corp 1975 GH

Egblewogbe, E.Y.
The wizard's pride and other poems. 40pp. 95pes. ($.95) Ghana Publ Corp 1975 GH

Egbuna, O.B.
The ABC of Black Power thought. 35pp. 30k Di Nigro 1973 NR

Egero, B.
The 1967 population census of Tanzania. A demographic analysis. See: Henin, R.

Egero, B., ed.   Henin, R., ed.
The population of Tanzania. Census volume 6. T.shs.40.00 ($12.00) Bur Res Assess - Tanz 1973 TZ

Egero, B.
Migration and economic development South of Lake Victoria. T.shs.15.00 ($5.00) (Research pap., 32) Bur Res Assess - Tanz TZ

Egero, B.
Migration and the urban population. See: Claesou, C.-F.

Egero, B.
Migration in Tanzania. See: Claesou, C.-F.

Egero, B.
Movement to towns in Tanzania. See: Claesou, C-F.

Egero, B.
Population movement and the colonial history of Tanzania. T.shs.15.00 ($5.00) (Research pap., 35) Bur Res Assess - Tanz 1975 TZ

Egharevba, J.
Itan edagbon mwe. [Autobiography] 92pp. N1.25 Ibadan UP 1972 NR EDO

Egharevba, J.U.
A short history of Benin. 4th ed. 100pp. pl. N2.00 Ibadan UP 1968 NR

Eglington, C.B.
Under the horizon. The collected verse of Charles Beaumont Eglington, 1918-1970. 144pp. cl. R30.00 Purnell 1977 SA

Egudu, R.   Nwoga, D.
Poetic heritage: Igbo traditional verse. 137pp. hd. N2.50 Nwamife 1972 NR

Ehret, C.
Ethiopians and East Africans. 96pp. K.shs.18.00 (Nairobi Historical Studies, 3) EAPH 1974 KE

Eicher, J.
Nigerian handcrafted textiles. 200pp. col. ill. photos. hd. & pap. N18.00 cl. N10.50 pap. ($28.00/£12.50 cl.) ($17.25/£7.25 pap.) Univ Ife Press 1976 NR

Eiselen, W.
Initiation rites of the Bamasemola. 35pp. 30c (B v.10, no.2) Univ Stellenbosch, Lib 1932 SA

Ejiofor, L.U.
Controversy in education: government take-over of schools in Nigeria. 92pp. N1.00 Black Academy 1974 NR

Ekanem, I.I.
The 1963 Nigerian census: a critical appraisal. 217pp. map. cl. N8.00 Ethiope 1972 NR

Ekechukwu, R.M., ed.
Akpa uche. [An anthology of modern Igbo verse.] 102pp. N1.10 OUP - Nig 1975 NR IGB

Ekpe, O.
"Julius Caesar", essays. 63pp. N1.00 Univ Publ 1973 NR

Ekperigin, N.I.   Uti, J.O.
A handbook of physical education. 128pp. ill. N1.20 Macmillan 1971 NR

Ekpiken, A.N.
A bibliography of the Efik-Ibibio speaking peoples of the old Calabar Province of Nigeria, 1668-1964. 96pp. map. N3.50 Ibadan UP 1970 NR

Eksteen, F.R.L.N.
Business economics for standard 10. 321pp. ill. maps. R3.85 Nasou 1974 SA

Eksteen, F.R.L.N.   Naude, C.H.B.
Business methods for standard 8 (Practical course) 200pp. ill. photo. R3.40 Nasou 1976 SA

Eksteen, F.R.L.N., et al.
Salesmanship for standard 8. (Practical course.) 164pp. ill. photo. R3.05 Nasou 1975 SA

Eksteen, F.R.L.N., et al.
Typing for beginners, standard 7. 161pp. ill. R4.30 Nasou 1976 SA

Eksteen, F.R.L.N.
Salesmanship for standard 7. (Practical course) 105pp. ill. R1.40 Nasou 1974 SA

Eksteen, F.R.L.N.   Geldenhuys, J.P.   Allen, V.L.
Typing for juniors, standard 8. 208pp. ill. R5.00 Nasou 1976 SA

Eksteen, F.R.L.N.   Allen, V.L.
Typing for seniors, standard 9. 271pp. ill. R6.00 Nasou 1976 SA

Eksteen, F.R.L.N.   Allen, V.L.
    Typing for seniors, standard 10.   294pp. ill.   R6.50
    Nasou 1976 SA

Ekundare, R.O.
    Marriage and divorce under Yoruba customary law.
    90pp.   N2.00   Univ Ife Press 1969 NR

Ekwensi, C.
    An African night's entertainment.   96pp. ill.   53k
    (African Reader's Library, 1)   Pilgrim 1962 NR

Ekwensi, C.
    Coal camp boy.   64pp. col. ill.   62k   (English supp.
    readers, 2)   Longman - Nig 1973 NR

Ekwensi, C.
    Juju rock.   110pp. ill.   53k   (African Reader's Library,
    11)   Pilgrim 1965 NR

Ekwensi, C.
    The rainmaker and other stories.   80pp. ill.   53k
    (African Reader's Library, 6)   Pilgrim 1965 NR

Ekwensi, C.
    Tafrija ya Usiju.   80pp. ill.   K.shs.5.00   ($2.30)   EAPH
    1966 KE SWA

Ekwensi, C.O.D.
    Coal camp boy.   66pp. ill.   62k   (Palm Library for
    Younger Readers)   Longman - Nig 1973 NR

Ekwensi, C.O.D.
    Samankwe in the strange forest.   58pp. ill.   67k
    (Palm Library for Younger Readers)   Longman - Nig 1973
    NR

El Attar, M.S.
    Le Yemen.   352pp. maps.   DA25.00   SNED 1965 AE
    FRE

El Berini, M.
    Chaines du passé.   144pp. cl.   Dir6.00 cl.   Ed
    Maghreb 1976 MR FRE

El-Busaidy, H.B.S.
    Ndoa na talaka.   [Marriage and divorce]   45pp.
    K.shs.2.60   ($1.50/60p.)   EALB 1968 KE SWA

El Bushra.   el Sayed.
    An atlas of Khartoum conurbation.   100pp.   £S1.50
    ($6.00)   Khartoum UP 1976 SJ

El Dessuky, M.A.   Balogun, I.A.B.
    A brief history of the life of the prophet Muhammad and
    the growth of Islam.   112pp.   N1.25   Islamic 1976 NR

El Din, F.T.
    Flies, mosquitoes and disease.   79pp.   85pt.   ($4.00)
    Khartoum UP 1974 SJ

El Fatih El-Badawi, Z.
    The Muslim woman.   20pp.   30pt.   ($1.50)   Khartoum
    UP 1975 SJ

El Habaschi, M.O.
    Aden: l'évolution politique, économique et sociale de
    l'Arabie du Sud.   475pp. maps.   DA18.00   SNED
    1966 AE FRE

El Hassan, A.M., ed.
    An introduction to the Sudan economy.   244pp.
    £S1.60   ($6.00)   Khartoum UP 1976 SJ

El-Ibrahimi, A.T.
    Lettres de prison.   261pp.   DA8.00   SNED 1966 AE
    FRE

El Jack, A.H.
    The Sudan management development and productivity
    centre.   56pp.   45pt.   ($2.00 pap.)   Khartoum UP
    1973 SJ

el Mahdi, S.M.A.
    A guide to land settlement and registration in the Sudan.
    92pp.   20 pt.   ($1.00)   Khartoum UP 1971 SJ

El Mehairy, T.
    Adjustment to Egypt: somatopsychic health guide.   55pp.
    £.E.1.00   ($1.50)   Am Univ 1975 UA

el Naqar, U.
    The pilgrimage tradition in West Africa.   192pp. cl. &
    pap.   77pt. pap.   LS2.25 cl.   ($4.00 pap.)   ($9.50
    cl.)   Khartoum UP 1972 SJ

El Nasrie, A.R.
    Theses on the Sudan.   64pp.   ($2.00)   Khartoum UP
    1974 SJ

El Rashidi, L.
    Cours de la fonction publique.   92pp.   Ecole Nat Admin -
    Niger 1976 NG FRE

El Saaty, H.   Hirabayashi, G.K.
    Industrialization in Alexandria: some ecological and social
    aspects.   198pp. maps.   £.E.O.750   ($5.00)   Am
    Univ 1959 UA

el Saeed, T.M.
    Groundwater appraisal of the Gash River Basin at
    Kassanal, Kassala Province.   80pt.   ($2.30/99p.)
    (Bulletin, 17)   Geol and Min Res - Sudan 1969 SJ

el Sayed.
    An atlas of Khartoum conurbation.   See: El Bushra.

El-Tayeb, A.
    Heroes of Arabia.   64pp.   40pt.   ($1.50)   Khartoum UP
    1976 SJ

el Tayeb, G.E.
    Forestry and land use in the Sudan.   80pp.   25pt.
    ($1.50)   Khartoum UP 1972 SJ

el Tayeb, S.
    The students' movement in the Sudan 1940-1970.   76pp.
    25 pt.   ($1.50)   Khartoum UP 1972 SJ

Ela, J.M.
    La plume et la pioche: réflexion sur l'enseignement et la
    société dans le développement.   96pp.   CFA450
    (Point de vue, 9)   CLE 1971 CM FRE

Elebe, P.
    Rythmes.   36pp.   20k pap.   (Jeune Littérature, 5)   Ed
    Mont Noir 1972 ZR FRE

Elgie, I. D., ed.
    Zambia Geographical Association. Conference handbook,
    Chipata 1973.   188pp.   K2.00   ($5.00)   Zambia Geog
    Assoc 1974 ZA

Elgie, I.D., comp.
    A bibliography of the Zambia Geographical Association.
    August 1967 to July 1974.   50n.   ($1.00)   (Zambia
    Geographical Assoc., Bibliographic series, 1)   Zambia
    Geog Assoc 1974 ZA

Elgie, J.D., ed.
    Kitwe and its hinterland.   168pp.   K2.00   (Handbook
    series, 3)   Zambia Geog Assoc 1974 ZA

Elias, T.O., ed.
    The Nigerian magistrate and offender.   130pp.   N1.75
    (Ethiope law series, 1)   Ethiope 1972 NR

Elias, T.O., ed.
    Papers of the third annual conference of the Nigerian
    Society of International Law.   104pp.   N1.50   Ethiope
    1972 NR

Elias, T.O.
    Law and social change in Nigeria.   292pp. pap. & cl.
    N7.50 cl.   N4.25 pap.   Univ Lagos Press 1972 NR

Elias, T.O.
    Law in a developing society.   26pp.   30k   Univ Lagos
    Bookshop 1969 NR

Elias, T.O.
    Law in a developing society.   208pp.   N3.50   (Ethiope
    Law, series, 3)   Ethiope 1973 NR

Élias, T.O.
    Law in a developing society.   New ed.   208pp. cl. &
    pap.   N3.50 pap.   N6.00 cl.   Ethiope 1973 NR

Eliovson, S.
    The complete gardening book.   297pp. photos. col.
    photos. cl.   R12.50   Macmillan - SA 1974 SA

Eliovson, S.
    Namaqualand in flower.   184pp. col. ill. hd.   R9.60
    Macmillan SA 1972 SA

Eliovson, S.
    Proteas for pleasure.   3rd ed.   329pp. col. pl. photos.
    hd.   R9.60   Macmillan SA 1973 SA

Author Index

Eliovson, S.
Shrubs, trees and climbers.   320pp. col. pl. cl.
R19.50   Macmillan - SA 1975 SA

Eliovson, S.
South African wildflowers for the garden.   5th ed.
306pp. col. ill. photos. hd.   R16.50   Macmillan SA
1973 SA

Elisa, J.A.
Mazoezi ya hesabu.   [Exercises in mathematics]
Longman Tanz 1973 TZ SWA

Ellenberger, V.
A century of mission work in Basutoland.   380pp. cl.
R.80c.   Morija 1938 LO

Ellingworth, P.
Pour une théologie africaine.   See: Dickson, K.

Elliot, J.
An inquiry into staffing and organisation of secondary
schools in Zambia.   150pp.   K1.50   (84p.)   (Inst.
African Studies, Univ. Zambia, communications, 8)   Inst
Afr Stud - Lusaka 1972 ZA

Elliot, J.
Let's discuss education.   211pp. photos.   N1.35   OUP
- Nig 1968 NR

Elliott, C.
Constraints on the economic development of Zambia.
426pp. maps.   K.shs.52.75   OUP-Nairobi 1969 KE

Elliott, G.
The long grass whispers.   120pp. ill. cl.   60c.   Shuter
1959 SA

Elliott, R.C.
Elliott's legal forms.   5th ed.   R12.50   Juta 1972 SA

Elliott, R.C.
The South African notary.   5th ed.   R21.00   Juta 1977
SA

Ellis, A.B.
The Yoruba-speaking peoples of West Africa. Their
religion, manners, customs, laws, language, etc.   2
2nd.ed.   412pp. maps. cl.   N7.50 Africa only
(Academic Reprints Series)   Pilgrim 1974 NR

Ellis, B.L.
Religion among the Bantu in South Africa since 1956: a
list of works.   18pp.   R1.60   Dept Bibliog, Lib & Typo
1968 SA

Ellis, B.P.B.
Cholera in the Manicaland Province of Rhodesia, February
to May, 1974.   See: Cruickshank, J.G.

Ellis, E.J.
Two missionary visits to Ijebu country, 1892.
See: Johonson, J.

Ellis, G.F.R.
On understanding the world and the universe.   18pp.
30c (Univ. Cape Town. Inaugural lec., 27)   Univ Cape
Town Lib 1974 SA

Ellis, J.O.
Linguistics in a multilingual society.   26pp.   C1.00
($1.00/50p.)   (Inaugural lecture)   Ghana UP 1971 GH

Ellis, R.
Incorporation of leno weave units into lightweight all-wool
worsted fabric.   See: Robinson, G.A.

Ellis, R.
Incorporation of small percentage of leno using continuous
filament yarns in lightweight wool worsted fabrics.
See: Robinson, G.A.

Ellis, R.
Production of mohair yarns on the repco spinner, part II:
the spinning of wrapped core-spun mohair yarns and their
use in lightweight mohair suiting fabrics.   See: Robinson,
G.A.

Ellis, R.
Some novel methods for producing mohair blankets.
See: Robinson, G.A.

Ellis, R.
Some novel methods for producing mohair blankets.
See: Robinson, G.A.

Ellis, R.
The use of leno in all-wool lightweight shirting and safari
suiting fabrics.   See: Robinson, G.A.

Ellison, P.A.
The Indian domestic budget.   See: Pillay, P.N.

Ellman, A.O.
Agricultural improvements through cooperative farming in
Tanzania.   10pp.   T.shs12.00   ($3.00)   (Research
pap., 69.23)   Econ Res Bur - Tanz 1969 TZ

Els, W.J.
Contributions to the morphology and histology of the
genital system of the pulmonate cochicella ventricosa
(Draparnaud) 31pp. pl.   R1.40   (Univ. Stellenbosch,
Annals, vol. 48, A.1)   Univ Stellenbosch Lib 1973 SA

Emenanjo, E.N., ed.   Ogbalu, F.C., ed.
Igbo language and culture.   232pp. cl. & pap.   N3.20
pap.   N4.50 cl.   OUP - Nig 1975 NR

Emiola, A.
Nigerian labour law.   cl. & pap.   N11.00 cl.   N9.00
pap.   Ibadan UP 1977 NR

Endicott, J.
New method English dictionary.   See: West, M.

Ene, J.C.
Insects and man in West Africa.   58pp. ill.   N1.00
Ibadan UP 1963 NR

Engberg, L.E., ed.
Family welfare and planning.   252pp.   C5.00   (Legon
Family Research paps. 4)   Inst Afr Stud - Univ Ghana
1975 GH

Engel, K.
Lively learning.   See: Collet, N.

Engel, K.F.   Wyatt, J.
Ilinde Amana. Historia ya Biblia.   [How we got our Bible]
64pp. ill.   T.shs.4.50   Central Tanganyika 1974 TZ
SWA

Engelbrecht, D.v.Z. et al.
Contributions to the cranial morphology of the chamaelcon
Microsaura pumila Daudin.   165pp. ill.   R1.50   (A v.
27, no. 1-5)   Univ Stellenbosch, Lib 1951 SA

Engelbrecht, F.M.
The pathogenesis of experimental silicotic fibrosis.   25pp.
photos.   45c.   (v.30, no.2)   Univ Stellenbosch, Lib
1954 SA

Engelbrecht, J.A.
Swazi customs relating to marriage.   25pp.   20c   (B
v.8, no.3)   Univ Stellenbosch, Lib 1930 SA

Engelbrecht, J.A.
Swazi texts with notes.   21pp.   20c   (B v.8 no.2)   Univ
Stellenbosch, Lib 1930 SA

Engelbrecht, S.P.
Centenary album of Pretoria.   R1.50   van Schaik SA

Engelbrecht, S.W.H.
Report of the committee for differentiated education and
guidance in connection with a national system for
handicapped pupils...etc.   pt. 3, v. 1   90pp.   R1.35
Human Science Res Council 1975 SA

Eni, H.D.
The Ujari people of Awka district.   77pp.   N1.00   Univ
Publ 1974 NR

Enin, T.Y.
Seidu drives his father's cow.   74pp. ill.   (95c.)   Ghana
Publ Corp 1975 GH

Ennulat, H.
Fali, description phonologique.   See: Ennulat, J.

Ennulat, J.   Ennulat, H.
Fali, description phonologique.   61pp.   CFA500   Univ
Cameroun 1972 CM FRE

Eno Belinga, T.
Catalogue des mémoires soutenus à l'Université de
Yaoundé, 1973-1975 Supplément.   See: Chateh, P.

Eno Belinga, T., comp.
Catalogue des mémoires soutenus à l'Universite de Yaoundé 1965-1973. See: Chateh, P., comp.

Eno Belinga, T., comp.
Guide des bibliothèques et centres de documentation de Yaoundé. See: Chateh, P., comp

Enobakhare, G.N.I.
How shall we educate? 53pp. 45k Macmillan 1972 NR

Enslin, M.D.
Problem drivers: the effects and after effects of alcohol on driver proficiency. 58pp. (CSIR Special Report PERS, 222) CSIR 1975 SA

Enslin, N.C. de V.
Should scientists and engineers call a halt to research? 6pp. 30c. (U.C.T. Inaugural lec. New series, 6) Univ Cape Town Lib 1971 SA

Epalza, M.
Ecrits relatifs à l'histoire de l'Espagne publiés en Algérie de 1962 à 1973. 64pp. D4.00 (D10.00) (Bibliographies et catalogues, 3) Bibliotheque Nationale 1974 AE FRE

Epée, V.
Transatlantic blues. 64pp. CFA300 CLE 1972 CM FRE

Epele, S.
Nigeria speaks. See: Balewa, A.T.

Ephraim, E.
God over my shoulder. 32pp. 40pes. (12p.) Africa Christian 1968 GH

Ephraim, H., comp.
Ethiopian publications, 1963-64 [Text in Amharic and English.]. See: Chojnacki, S., comp.

Ephraim, H., comp.
Ethiopian publications, 1965 [Text in Amharic and English.]. See: Chojnacki S., comp.

Ephraim, H., comp.
Ethiopian publications, 1966 [Text in Amharic and English.]. See: Chojnacki, S., comp.

Ephraim, H., comp.
Ethiopian publications, 1967 [Text in Amharic and English.]. See: Chojnacki, S., comp.

Ephraim, H., comp.
List of current periodical publications in Ethiopia. (annual) See: Chojnacki, S., comp.

Ephson, I.S.
Murder at the palace. 179pp. C5.00 Univ Ghana Bkshop; distr. 1976 GH

Eppstein, J.
The cult of revolution in the church. 134pp. hd. R9.60 Africa only Valiant 1975 SA

Epstein, A.L.
Juridicial techniques and the judicial process: a study in African customary law. 45pp. 75n. (38p.) (Rhodes-Livingstone paps., 23) Inst Soc Res - Zam 1954 ZA

Epstein, A.L.
Politics in an urban African community. 283pp. photos. maps. hd. K3.60 (£1.80/$7.50) Inst Afr Stud - Lusaka 1958 ZA

Equilbecq, F.
La Légende de Samba Guélâdio Diêgui prince du Fouta. 351pp. CFA1000 (F20.00) Nouv Ed Afric 1974 SG FRE

Erapu, L.
Notes on John Ruganda's "The Burdens". 36pp. K.shs.6.00 (Heinemann Student's Guides) Heinemann Educ - Nair 1977 KE

Erapu, L.
Notes on Wole Soyinka's "The Lion and the Jewel". 44pp. K.shs.6.00 (45p) (Heinemann's Student's Guides) Heinemann Educ - Nair 1975 KE

Erasmus, P.F.
A survey of the literature on Bantu personality with particular reference to TAT and depth perception investigations. 62pp. ill. R2.20 (Human Sciences Research Council, P-series, 10) Human Science Res Council 1975 SA

Erbe, H.
The violet in the crucible: on translating poetry. ex. only (Inaugural lec.) Rhodes Univ Lib 1964 SA

Erebinulu, S.O.
Kokoro isiro owo. [Numeration of money] 40pp. 45k Pilgrim 1966 NR YOR

Erickson, B., ed. Edwards, S., ed.
Mekele station: progress report for the period April 1974 to March 1975. 62pp. ex. only. Inst Agric Res - Addis 1975 ET

Ericsson, E. Mauma, R.
Elimu ya siasa utangulizi. [A study on radio programmes] 20pp. T.shs.2.00 (Studies in Adult Education, 9) Inst Adult Educ - Dar 1973 TZ

Erikson, E.H.
Insight and freedom. 18pp. 25c. (University of Cape Town T.B. Davie memorial lecture, 9) Univ Cape Town Lib 1968 SA

Erneholm, N.
Agriculture for schools: a textbook for the East African certificate. 192pp. K.shs.30.00 Heinemann Educ - Nair 1976 KE

Erneholm, N.
Agriculture in East Africa. 192pp. pl. K.shs.30.00 (£1.50) Heinemann Educ - Nair 1975 KE

Erubu, H.
Second report to the General Extension Services Board on the activities of the unit, April 1973 to December 1974. See: Bown, L.

Esan, O.
Esin atiroja. 40pp. ill. 45k OUP - Nig 1966 NR YOR

Esan, O.
Orekelewa. 52pp. ill. 40k OUP - Nig 1965 NR YOR

Esan, O.
Teledalase. 50pp. ill. 50k OUP - Nig 1965 NR YOR

Esan, S.O.
K'a s'oto k'a ku. [Plato's Krito] 10pp. 20k Ibadan UP 1964 NR YOR

Esezobor, J.E.
Selected list of scientific and technical serials in Libraries in Mid-western State of Nigeria. 63pp. Benin Univ Lib 1971 NR

Eshun, J.O.
The adventures of the Kapapa. 116pp. ill. C3.00 ($3.00) Ghana Publ Corp 1976 GH

Eshun, R.C.
Kotoka and Ghana. 56pp. photos. 40pes. ($.40) Ghana Publ Corp 1968 GH

Espie, I., ed.
A thousand years of West African history. See: Ajayi, J.F.A., ed.

Espitalie, J. Sigal, J.
Contribution à l'étude des foraminifères du jurassique supérieur et du néocomien du bassin de Majunga. 2 v. 100pp. pl. photo. cl. FMG1800 cl. (F36.00 cl.) (Annales Geologiques de Madagascar, 32) Service Geol - Mad 1963 MG FRE

Essaïd, M.J.
La présomption d'innocence. Dir54.00 (Coll. Fac. des Sciences juridiques, économiques et sociales, 22) Ed La Porte 1971 MR FRE

Essang, S. Olayide, S.
Intermediate economics analysis. 350pp. N5.00 Aromolaran 1975[?] NR

Essen, A.J.A.
School certificate English literature. 130pp. 85k
Paico 1966 NR

Essien, E.S.
The teaching of mathematics in elementary schools:
decimal currency and metric edition. 1, 2bks 172pp.
N1.20 Macmillan 1967 NR

Essien, E.S.
The teaching of mathematics in elementary schools:
decimal currency and metric edition. 2, 2bks 220pp.
N1.20 Macmillan 1967 NR

Essienne, D.
Annals de l'université d'Abidjan: Le ministère des affaires
étrangères de Côte d'Ivoire. CFA1000 (F20.00 pap.)
(Série A- Droit, 2) Univ Abidjan 1973 IV FRE

Essomba, H.G.A.
Le fruit défendu. 145pp. CFA540 CLE 1975 CM
FRE

Esterhuysen, M.
South Africa's first gold coin. R12.50 Purnell 1976 SA

Esuruoso, O.F.   Samuel, P.S.
New biology for 'O' level. bk. 1 134pp. ill. N1.15
Macmillan 1974 NR

Eteffa, M.
Pupil's book. See: Rogers, J.

Eteki'a Mbumua, W.
Démocratiser la culture. 96pp. CFA490.00 CLE 1974
CM FRE

Etherington, D.M.
An economic analysis of smallholder tea production in
Kenya. 152pp. cl. & pap. K.shs.52.00 cl.
K.shs.20.00 pap. ($10.20/£4.80 cl.) ($5.00/£2.50
pap.) EALB 1973 KE

Etherton, D., et al.
Mathare Valley, a case study of uncontrolled settlement in
Nairobi. 96pp. K.shs.61.50 Housing Res Dev Unit
1971 KE

Ethiopian Chamber of Commerce.
Directory of industry, 1976. B5.00 ($2.50) Chamber
Comm - Eth 1976 ET

Ethiopian Chamber of Commerce.
Investment guide to Ethiopia, 1976. B3.00 Chamber
Comm - Eth 1976 ET

Ethiopian Chamber of Commerce.
Statistical digest. ($2.50) Chamber Comm - Eth 1977
ET

Ethiopian Chamber of Commerce.
Trade directory and guide book to Ethiopia, 1976.
B8.00 ($4.83) Chamber Comm - Eth 1976 ET

Etian, E.E.
Qui es-tu Jesus? 58pp. CFA240.00 CLE 1973 CM
FRE

Etokakpan, E.
Force of superstition. 94pp. ill. 80k OUP-Nig 1970
NR

Ette, A.
Annales de l'université d'Abidjan. See: Loubiere, R.

Ette, A.I.I.
On lightning, thunder and rain. N1.00 (Inaugural
lecture) Ibadan UP 1977 NR

Ette-Battesti, F.   Dago-Akribi, A.
Annales de l'université d'Abidjan. 205pp. CFA1,300
(F26.00) (Série B-Médecine, 9) Univ Abidjan 1975 IV
FRE

Etubi, S.U.
Otakada ukoche alu Igala. pupils bk. 1. See: Okwoli,
P.E.

Etubi, S.U.
Otakada ukoche alu Igala. pupils bk. 2. See: Okwoli,
P.E.

Etuk-Udo, J.S.
Principles of accounts for West Africa. 2nd Metric ed.
bk. 1. 334pp. ill. N2.75 OUP - Nig NR

Etuk-Udo, J.S.
Principles of accounts for West Africa. Metric ed. bk. 2
332pp. N4.35 OUP - Nig 1970 NR

Euba, A.
Scenes from traditional life, for piano. 18pp. music.
N2.00 (£1.25/$3.00) (Ife Music Editions, 1) Univ Ife
Press 1974 NR

Euba, A.
Six Yoruba songs, arranged for voice and piano. 14pp.
music. N2.00 (£1.25/$3.00) (Ife Music Editions, 2)
Univ Ife Press 1974 NR

Evangel Publishing House.
The beginning of people - a study course for Muslims.
32pp. K.shs.6.50 (85c.) Evangel 1977 KE

Evangel Publishing House.
Effective witnessing. 40pp. K.shs.3.00 Evangel 1970
KE

Evangel Publishing House.
Evangel sunday school register. [1 year]. K.shs.2.00
pap. Evangel 1965 KE

Evangel Publishing House.
God loves people. Study course for Muslims. 48pp.
K.shs.7.50 (95c.) Evangel 1977 KE

Evangel Publishing House.
God's covenant with the people of Israel. Study course for
Muslims. 40pp. K.shs.7.50 (95c.) Evangel 1977 KE

Evangel Publishing House.
Learning God's truth. 40pp. K.shs.3.00 Evangel
1968 KE

Evangel Publishing House.
Minister's service book. 20pp. K.shs.2.50 Evangel
1969 KE

Evangel Publishing House.
The people of faith. Study course for Muslims. 40pp.
K.shs.7.00 (90c.) Evangel 1977 KE

Evangel Publishing House.
Sermons of Africa. 48pp. K.shs.4.00 (Seed-Bed
Series, 2) Evangel 1975 KE

Evangel Publishing House.
Speaking with other tongues. 28pp. K.shs.2.00
Evangel 1970 KE

Evangel Publishing House.
Standard of faith and fellowship. 32pp. K.shs.2.00
Evangel 1969 KE

Evangel Publishing House.
Worship the king. 106pp. K.shs.5.00 Evangel 1972
KE

Evans, C.M.
Project geography. Work bk. 1. 108pp. ill. EAPH
1976 KE

Evans, D.S., et al., ed.
Herschel at the Cape. 436pp. pl. hd. fl. 27.00 No US
(South African biographical and historical studies, 3)
Balkema 1969 SA

Evans, E.V.
The world of food and nutrition. 31pp. C1.00
($1.00/50p.) (Inaugural lecture) Ghana UP 1970 GH

Evans, H.G.J.
Culture and civilization. 22pp. N1.00 (Inaugural
lecture) Ibadan UP 1976 NR

Evans, M.J.
Index to pictures of South African interest in The Graphic
1875-1895. 162pp. R8.10 Dept Bibliog Lib & Typo
1966 SA

Evans-Pritchard, J.J.
Some aspects of marriage and the family among the Nuer.
70pp. K1.80 (90p.) (Rhodes-Livingstone paps., 11)
Inst Soc Res - Zam 1945 ZA

Evans, R.K.
The geology of the Shire highlands. 54pp. pl. maps.
hd. K1.50 (Geological Survey of Malawi, Bull. 18)
Geol Survey - Mal 1965 MW

Evans, S.
New management committees in local government. R5.75   Juta SA

Evenden, D.
Andrew Geddes Bain.   32pp.   R1.70   Dept Bibliog Lib & Typo 1971 SA

Evenwel, J.K.
Mechanization in the building industry.   See: De Vos, T.J.

Evenwell, J.K.   De Vos, T.J.
Housing requirements in South Africa.   20pp.   R2.00 CSIR 1969 SA

Evenwell, J.K.
Modern building methods.   183pp. hd.   R3.00   CSIR 1971 SA

Everard, A.C.J.
Guidelines for the safe custody of equipment.   58pp. ill. K.shs1.00   ($1.25/50p.)   EALB 1966 KE

Everett, J.
Obstetric emergencies. A manual for rural health workers. 29pp. ill.   K.shs.3.50   (Rural Health Series, 4)   African Med Res Found 1976 KE

Evraed, M.T.
Le savoir-vivre en société moderne.   40pp. ill.   20k St. Paul 1969 ZR FRE

Ewart, J.
James Ewart's journal.   pl. cl.   R15.00   Struik 1970 SA

Ewer, D.W.
Zoology: should it exist?   24pp.   C1.00   ($1.00/50p.) (Inaugural lecture)   Ghana UP 1969 GH

Ewing, A.
Studies in the development of African resources: Industry. 64pp. pl.   N1.50   (Studies in the Development of African Resources, 2)   OUP - Nig 1975 NR

Eygelaar, J.
Climatic aspects of design, material selection, and constructions methods of rural housing.   15pp. K.shs.7.50   Housing Res Dev Unit 1975 KE

Eygelaar, J.
Cost of softwoods related to sawn sizes.   26pp. K.shs.15.00   Housing Res Dev Unit 1974 KE

Eygelaar, J.
Foundations for low-cost houses.   15pp.   K.shs.7.50 Housing Res Dev Unit 1976 KE

Eygelaar, J.
Housing by-laws in the Kenya building code.   12pp. K.shs.7.50   Housing Res Dev Unit 1975 KE

Eygelaar, J.
Roof slopes for low cost structures.   4pp.   K.shs.5.00 Housing Res Dev Unit 1975 KE

Eygelaar, J.
Roof structures for low-cost housing cost comparison for various roofing materials.   19pp. ill.   K.shs.15.00 Housing Res Dev Unit 1975 KE

Eygelaar, J.
Roofing tiles for low-cost structures.   7pp.   K.shs.5.00 Housing Res Dev Unit 1975 KE

Eyidi, N.
Comment élever des porcs.   80pp. ill.   CFA300.00 CLE 1973 CM FRE

Eyo, E.
2000 years of Nigerian art.   ill. pl. col.pl. cl.   N30.00 Dept Antiquities 1977 NR

Eyo, E.
Guide to Nigerian museum.   60pp. ill.   N1.50   Dept Antiquities NR

Eyo, E.
Highlights from 2,000 years of Nigerian art.   37pp. ill. 50k   Dept Antiquities 1973 NR

Eze, E.
The cassava ghost. A play in three acts.   147pp. N1.35   Ethiope 1974 NR

Ezeh, J.E.
An approach to unseen English literature.   60pp.   N1.40 Aromolaran 1970 NR

Ezeh, J.E.
Notes, questions/answers on "Julius Caesar".   62pp. N1.30   Aromolaran 1970 NR

Ezeh, J.E.
Notes, questions/answers on "Merchant of Venice". 40pp.   N1.60   Aromolaran 1975(?) NR

Ezeh, J.E.
Notes, questions/answers on "West African verse". 60pp.   N1.60   Aromolaran 1975[?] NR

Ezempilo, A.
A guide to health [in Zulu].   20c.   Shuter 1955 SA ZUL

Faba, R.A.
Notes on "Anthology of Longer Poems".   124pp.   90k Onibonoje 1968 NR

Faber, M.
Economic structuralism and its relevance to Southern Rhodesia's future.   50pp.   85n. (43p.) (Rhodes-Livingstone paps., 36)   Inst Soc Res - Zam 1965 ZA

Fabian, B.C.
The ultrastructure of the gill of "Monodactylus argenteus" (a Euryhaline teleost fish) with particular reference to morphological changes associated with changes in salinity. See: Fearnhead, E.A.

Fabunmi, M.A.
Ayajo ijinle ohun ife.   96pp.   85k   Onibonoje 1972 NR YOR

Fabunmi, M.A.
Ife shrines.   28pp. maps pl.   50k   Univ Ife Press 1969 NR

Fabunmi, M.A.
Yoruba idioms.   76pp.   72k   Pilgrim 1969 NR

Faculty of Agriculture, University of Ife.
Fifth Annual research report, 1969/70.   56pp.   80k Univ Ife Press 1972 NR

Faculty of Agriculture, University of Ife.
Fourth annual research report, 1968/69.   47pp.   80k Univ Ife Press 1972 NR

Faculty of Agriculture, University of Ife.
Ninth annual research report.   41pp.   N1.50 ($2.50/£1.10)   Univ Ife Press 1975 NR

Faculty of Agriculture, University of Ife.
Second annual research report, 1966/67.   36pp.   50k Univ Ife Press 1968 NR

Faculty of Agriculture, University of Ife.
Sixth annual research report 1970/71.   56pp.   80k Univ Ife Press 1972 NR

Faculty of Agriculture, University of Ife.
Third annual research report, 1967/68.   36pp.   50k Univ Ife Press 1969 NR

Faculty of Law, Univ. Ife.
Integration of customary and modern legal systems in Africa.   461pp.   N8.40 NR only   Univ Ife Press 1971 NR

Faculty of Law, University of Natal.
Legal aid in South Africa. Proceedings of a conference held in the Faculty of Law, University of Natal, Durban, from 2nd-6th July, 1973.   272pp. cl.   R5.00   Fac Law - Univ Natal 1974 SA

Fadeiye, D.
Egypt and Nile. Questions and answers.   235pp. N2.00   Ilesanmi 1976 NR

Fadeiye, D.
Ilesanmi social studies for Nigerian schools.   bk. 1. 36pp. ill.   95k   Ilesanmi 1974 NR

Fadeiye, D.
Ilesanmi social studies for Nigerian schools.   bk. 2. 55pp. ill.   N1.10   Ilesanmi 1975 NR

Fadeiye, D.
Ilesanmi social studies for Nigerian schools. bk. 3.
100pp. ill. N1.15 Ilesanmi 1975 NR

Fadeiye, D.
Ilesanmi social studies for Nigerian schools. bk. 4.
111pp. ill. N1.25 Ilesanmi 1975 NR

Fadeiye, D.
Ilesanmi social studies for Nigerian schools. bk. 5.
115pp. ill. N1.30 Ilesanmi 1975 NR

Fadeiye, D.
Ilesanmi social studies for Nigerian schools. bk. 6.
99pp. ill. N1.35 Ilesanmi 1975 NR

Fadeiye, D.
Ilesanmi social studies for Nigerian schools. teacher's
notes, bk. 1. 19pp. 95k. Ilesanmi 1977 NR

Fadeiye, D.
Ilesanmi social studies for Nigerian schools. teacher's
notes, bk. 2. 32pp. 90k. Ilesanmi 1977 NR

Fadeiye, D.
Ilesanmi social studies for Nigerian schools. teacher's
notes, bk. 3. 27pp. 90k. Ilesanmi 1977 NR

Fadeiye, D.
Ilesanmi social studies for Nigerian schools. teacher's
notes, bk. 4. 40pp. 95k. Ilesanmi 1977 NR

Fadeiye, D.
Ilesanmi social studies for Nigerian schools. teacher's
notes, bk. 5. 45pp. 95k. Ilesanmi 1977 NR

Fadeiye, D.
Ilesanmi social studies for Nigerian schools. teacher's
notes, bk. 6. 33pp. 95k. Ilesanmi 1977 NR

Fadeyi, D.
Questions/answers on history of West Africa 100 A.D. -
present day. 102pp. N2.00 Armolaran 1970 NR

Fadipe, N.A.
The sociology of the Yoruba. 354pp. map pl. N7.50
Ibadan UP 1970 NR

Fadli, M.
L'opération-Labour. Dir18.00 (Coll. du Centre d'étude
du développement économique et social, 4) Ed La Porte
1961 MR FRE

Faerber, D.J.
The development of education aids for industrial training of
adult Africans. 39pp. R2.05 Dept Bibliog, Lib & Typo
1971 SA

Fafunwa, A.B., ed. Adaralegbe, A., ed.
Education in Nigeria - towards better administration and
supervision of instruction: Proceedings of first seminar on
school admin., etc. Ile-Ife, August 24-30, 1969. 198pp.
N3.00 ($4.00/£1.75) Inst Educ Ife 1971 NR

Fafunwa, A.B.
A history of Nigerian higher education. 320pp. hd., pap.
N3.00 pap. N6.00 hd. Macmillan 1971 NR

Fafunwa, A.B.
New perspectives in African education. 170pp. hd., pap.
N2.00 pap. N2.50 hd. Macmillan 1967 NR

Fagan, B.M.
A short history of Zambia. rev. ed. 165pp. K2.07
(£1.03) OUP - Lusaka 1970 ZA

Fagbemi, J.O.
Path to common entrance examination. 1, 2 pts
See: Adedun, J.A.

Fagbemi, J.O.
Path to common entrance examination. 2, 2pts.
See: Adedun, J.A.

Fagbulu, A.M., et al.
Universal primary mathematics. [In Hausa.]. Pupils' bk.
1 80k (43p) Evans - Nig 1976 NR HAU

Fagbulu, A.M., et al.
Universal primary mathematics. [In Hausa.]. Pupils' bk.
2 N1.35 (73p) Evans - Nig 1976 NR HAU

Fagbulu, A.M., et al.
Universal primary mathematics. Pupils' bk. 1 80k
(43p) Evans - Nig 1976 NR

Fagbulu, A.M., et al.
Universal primary mathematics. Pupils' bk. 2 N1.35
(73p) Evans - Nig 1976 NR

Fagbulu, A.M., et al.
Universal primary mathematics. Pupils' bk. 3 N1.50
(81p) Evans - Nig 1976 NR

Fagbulu, A.M., et al.
Universal primary mathematics. Teacher's guide. bk. 1
N2.50 (£1.35) Evans - Nig 1976 NR

Fagbulu, A.M., et al.
Universal primary mathematics. Teacher's guide. bk. 2
N3.00 (£1.60) Evans - Nig 1976 NR

Fage, J.D.
States and subjects in sub-Saharan Africa. 24pp.
R1.60 (Raymond Dart lec., 10) Inst Study of Man 1974
SA

Fage, J.D.
States and subjects in sub-Saharan African history.
24pp. R2.00 (Raymond Dart Lectures, 10)
Witwatersrand UP 1974 SA

Fagunwa, D.O. Solaru, T.T.
Taiwo ati Kehinde: Belo ati Bintu. Teacher's book. 2, 6
bks. 84pp. 60k OUP - Nig 1969 NR YOR

Fagunwa, D.O. Solaru, T.T.
Taiwo ati kehinde: Joke ati Femi: pupils bk. 3rd ed. 4,
6 bks. 139pp. 85k OUP - Nig 1971 NR YOR

Fagunwa, D.O. Solaru, T.T.
Taiwo ati Kehinde: Joke ati Femi: teacher's bk. 4, 6 bks.
74pp. 70k OUP - Nig 1972 NR YOR

Fagunwa, D.O. Solaru, T.T.
Taiwo ati Kehinde: Kola ati Kemi. pupil's bk. 3, 6 bks.
119pp. 80k OUP - Nig 1970 NR YOR

Fagunwa, D.O. Solaru, T.T.
Taiwo ati Kehinde Kola ati Kemi: teacher's bk. 3, 6 bks.
63pp. 45k OUP - Nig 1970 NR YOR

Fagunwa, D.O. Solaru, T.T.
Taiwo ati Kehinde: picture cards. 35k OUP - Nig NR
YOR

Fagunwa, D.O. Solaru, T.T.
Taiwo ati Kehinde: pupils bk. 1, 6 bks. col. ill. 65k
OUP - Nig 1968 NR YOR

Fagunwa, D.O. Solaru, T.T.
Taiwo ati Kehinde: teacher's bk. 1, 6 bks. 60k OUP
- Nig 1969 NR YOR

Fagunwa, D.O. Solaru, T.T.
Tawio ati Kehinde: Belo ati Bintu. pupil's bk 2, 6 bks.
139pp. ill. 80k OUP - Nig 1969 NR YOR

Faik, S., et al.
Le Zaire, deuxième pays francophone du monde? 35pp.
CELTA 1975 ZR FRE

Fair, T.J.D.
Development in Africa: a study in regional analysis with
special reference to Southern Africa. See: Green, L.P.

Fair, T.J.D. Jones, H.M. Murdoch, G.
Development in Swaziland: a regional analysis. 155pp.
maps/pl. cl. R8.00 Witwatersrand UP 1969 SA

Fair, T.J.D.
The distribution of population in Natal. $3.00 (Natal
regional survey pub., 3) Dept Econ, Natal 1955 SA

Fairbairn, D.G.
Brick veneer construction for South Africa. See: Scott,
T.W.

Fairbairn, D.G.
A design concept for housing aged people. 13pp.
(CSIR research reports, 170) CSIR 1960 SA

Fairbairn, D.G.
The hospital laundry and linen service: hospital design 8.
See: Cooke, B.V.

Fairbairn, W.J.
The accounts of executors and administrators. 3rd ed.
R13.50 Juta 1974 SA

Farrell, D.
The Charlie Manson, false bay, talking rock blues.
R1.45 ($1.80/95p.) Bateleur 1974 SA

Farrell, J.G.
Cholera in the Manicaland Province of Rhodesia, February
to May, 1974. See: Cruickshank, J.G.

Farsi, S.
Swahili idioms. 60pp. K.shs.5.00 EAPH 1974 KE

Farsy, M.S.
Kurwa na doto. 4th ed. 61pp. K.shs3.50
($1.52/50p.) EALB 1970 KE SWA

Farsy, M.S.A.
Ada za harusi katika Unguja. [Marriage customs in
Zanzibar] 2nd ed. 50pp. ill. K.shs.2.55
($1.50/60p.) EALB 1965 KE SWA

Farsy, S.S.
Swahili sayings from Zanzibar: Proverbs. 8th ed. bk. 1
52pp. K.shs.5.50 ($1.25/60p.) EALB 1970 KE

Farsy, S.S.
Swahili sayings from Zanzibar: riddles and superstitions.
7th ed. bk. 2 32pp. K.shs.2.50 ($1.25/60p.) EALB
1970 KE

Fatoki, S., ed.
Sketch Annual, 1973. 240pp. maps photos. 50k
Daily Sketch 1973 NR

Fatoki, S., ed.
Sketch annual, 1974. 128pp. photos. 50k Daily
Sketch 1974 NR

Fatubarin, A.R.
Basic practical biology. 152pp. ill. N1.75 Ilesanmi
1976 NR

Faturoti, A.
New chemistry for 'O' level. See: Oyewole, F.

Faturoti, A.
School certificate organic chemistry. 65pp. photos.
40k Educ Res Inst 1970 NR

Faucett, I.W.
Lotino dano ma kulica ki ododo mukene. See: Faucett,
M.G.M.

Faucett, M.G.M. Faucett, I.W.
Lotino dano ma kulica ki ododo mukene. [The good little
men and other stories] 32pp. ill. K.shs.0.90
($1.25/50p.) EALB 1957 KE LUO

Faul, M.A. Pistorius, A.W.I. van Vuuren, L.M.
Accounting: an introduction. R19.25 Butterworths
1975 SA

Faul, M.A.
Group statements. See: Cilliers, H.S.

Faure, M.
Hery. 44pp. ill. FMG1090 Soc Malgache 1976 MG
FRE

Fawehinmi, G.
Digest of Western State Court of Appeal: civil cases
1967-1969. 125pp. N5.00 West 1973 NR

Fawehinmi, G.
People's right to free education at all levels. 92pp.
N1.00 West 1974 NR

Fawole, F.B., comp.
Theses and dissertations accepted for higher degrees in
Nigerian universities, 1966-1967. 13pp. 50k (N1.00)
(National Library pubs, 13) Nat Lib-Nig 1969 NR

Fawole, F.B., comp.
Theses and dissertations accepted for higher degrees in
Nigerian universities, 1967-1968. 20pp. 50k (N1.00)
(National Library pubs, 16) Nat Lib-Nig 1970 NR

Fawole, F.B., comp.
Theses and dissertations accepted for higher degrees in
Nigerian universities, 1968-1969. 16pp. 50k (N1.00)
(National Library pubs, 22) Nat Lib-Nig 1970 NR

Fawole, S.L.
Essentials of Bible knowledge. 162pp. N1.75 Daystar
1968 NR

Fayemi, A.A.A.
Problems of agricultural production in Nigeria and how to
solve them. 10pp. 25k Univ Ibadan Bkshop 1973
NR

Fearnhead, E.A. Fabian, B.C.
The ultrastructure of the gill of "Monodactylus argenteus"
(a Euryhaline teleost fish) with particular reference to
morphological changes associated with changes in salinity.
39pp. R1.20 Oceanographic Res Inst 1971 SA

Fearns, M.
How are you today? (Prayers for use in hospital) 30pp.
60c Methodist 1973 SA

Federal Department of Antiquities.
Proceedings of the third International Conference held at
Ibadan, 1949. 479pp. maps. N4.20 Dept Antiquities
1956 NR

Fédération du Français Universel.
Le français hors de France. 380pp. CFA1,500
(F30.00) Nouv Ed Afric 1976 SG FRE

Feldberg, M.
Business profits and social responsibility. 15pp. 30c.
(U.C.T. Inaugural lec. New series, 10) Univ Cape Town
Lib 1972 SA

Feldberg, M.
Organizational behaviour. R14.50 Juta 1975 SA

Feldman, D.
An assessment of alternative agricultural strategies for
tobacco development in Iringa district, Tanzania. 29pp.
ill. T.shs.12.00 ($3.00) (Research pap., 68.21)
Econ Res Bur - Tanz 1968 TZ

Feldman, D.
Decreasing costs in peasant agriculture: an application of
separable programming. 20pp. T.shs12.00 ($3.00)
(Research pap., 68.20) Econ Res Bur - Tanz 1968 TZ

Feldman, R.
Customs and capitalism: a study of land tenure in Ismani.
45pp. T.shs.12.00 ($3.00) (Research pap., 71.14)
Econ Res Bur - Tanz 1971 TZ

Feldmann-Laschin, G.R.
Income and expenditure patterns of urban Bantu
households (Port Elizabeth/Uitenhage survey) 218pp.
R5.00 (Bureau of Market Research, Research Reports,
17) Bur Market Research 1967 SA

Feldmann-Laschin, G.R.
Income and expenditure patterns of urban coloured
households (Port Elizabeth/Uitenhage survey) 272pp.
R5.00 (Bureau of Market Research, Research Reports,
16) Bur Market Research 1967 SA

Fellah, S.
Les barbelles de l'existence. 190pp. DA8.00 SNED
1969 AE FRE

Fendri, M.
Basilique chrétienne de la Skhira. 67pp. pl. D1.600
(Série I, Archéologie-Histoire, 8) Univ Tunis 1961 TI FRE

Ferguson-Davie, C.J.
The early history of Indians in Natal. 2nd ed. 23pp.
75c. ($1.60) SA Inst of Race Relations 1977 SA

Ferguson, J.
Christian byways: devisions from the Christian path.
60pp. 40k Daystar 1968 NR

Ferguson, J., ed. Thompson, L., ed.
Africa in classical antiquity. 221pp. maps ill. N3.50
Ibadan UP 1969 NR

Ferguson, J.
Roma Aeterna: the value of classical studies for the
twentieth century. An inaugural lecture. 14pp. 30k
Ibadan UP 1961 NR

Ferguson, J.
Some Nigerian church founders. 84pp. 85k Daystar
1971 NR

Ferhi, Y.
Les grandes recettes de la cuisine Algérienne. 95pp.
DA20.00 SNED 1969 AE FRE

Fernandes, E., comp.
Enumeration methods for chemical isomers. 38pp.
R2.60 Dept Bibliog, Lib & Typo 1974 SA

Ferneyhough, F.
The history of railways in Britain. 288pp. col. ill. hd.
R15.20 SA only Philip 1975 SA

Fernie, L.M., ed. Edwards, S., ed.
Jimma research station, Melko: progress report for the
period April 1973 to March 1974. 98pp. ex. only.
Inst Agric Res - Addis 1974 ET

Ferragne, M., Rev., comp.
A catalogue of 1000 Sesotho books. 157pp. R3.00
($4.25) (Southern Sotho Literature) St. Michael's
Mission 1974 LO

Ferrandi, N.C.H. Kambule, T.W.
Guided mathematics, standard 6. 308pp. cl. R3.75 cl.
Shuter 1976 SA

Ferrandi, N.C.H. Kambula, T.W.
Guided mathematics, standard 7. 372pp. R4.35
Shuter 1977 SA

Ferrari, A. Thoret, J.C.
Atiékwa, un village de Côte d'Ivoire. 95pp. CFA1,000
(F20.00) Inst Ethno-Socio 1970 IV FRE

Ferrari, A.
La situation des jeunes à Lakota. Méthodologie et
recensement. 187pp. ill. maps. CFA1,000 (F20.00)
Inst Ethno-Socio 1970 IV FRE

Ferron, J.
La Tunisie antique. 80pp. D0.400 Maison Tunis
1968 TI FRE

Ffolliott, P. Libersidge, R.
Ludwig Krebs: Cape naturalist to the king of Prussia,
1792-1844. 320pp. pl. hd. fl. 38.25 (South African
biographical and historical studies, 9) Balkema 1971 SA

Field, G.D.
Birds of the Freetown peninsula. 2nd rev. & enl. ed.
96pp. ill. Le2.00 (£1.00) Fourah Bay Bkshp 1974
SL

Finaughty, W.
The recollections of an elephant hunter. [Reprint of ed.
1916]. 244pp. ill. map. cl. R$7.20 (Rhodesiana
Reprint Library, Gold Series, 29) Books of Rhodesia
1973 RH

Findlay, G.H.
Dr. Robert Broom, F.R.S.: palaeontologist and physician,
1866-1951 - a biography, appreciation and bibliography.
175pp. pl. hd. fl. 33.75 (South African biographical
and historical studies, 16) Balkema 1972 SA

Fine, J.C.
A socio-economic study of three villages in the Sokoto
close-settled zone. See: Goddard, A.D.

Fine, J.C.
A socio-economic study of three villages in the Sokoto
close-settled zone: land and people. See: Goddard, A.D.

Finlason, C.E.
A nobody in Mashonaland. Reprint of 1893 ed. 330pp.
ill. R$9.45 (Rhodesiana Reprint Library, Gold Series,
9) Books of Rhodesia 1970 RH

Finn, D.E., ed.
Poetry in Rhodesia. 80pp. cl. R$1.00 College Press
1968 RH

Fischer, H.E.
The textile industry in South Africa 1940-1965. 36pp.
80c. Univ Cape Town Lib 1970 SA

Fischer, L.
The published works of Raymond Arthur Dart. 46pp.
R2.40 Dept Bibliog, Lib & Typo 1969 SA

Fisher, H.A.
The history of astronomy and observatories in South
Africa, with special reference to The Royal Observatory,
Cape of Good Hope. 43pp. 80c. Univ Cape Town
Lib 1970 SA

Fisher, J.
Farming, practical and scientific. R5.00 Juta SA

Fitzjohn, W.H.
Ambassador of Christ and Caesar. photo. cl. & pap.
N2.50 pap N6.00 cl. Daystar 1974 NR

Fitzjohn, W.H.
Chief Gbondo- A Sierra Leone story. 79pp. cl. & pap.
75k pap. N2.50 cl. Daystar 1975 NR

FitzPatrick, P.
Jock of the bushveld. 320pp. pl. R2.20 Longman
SA 1968 SA

FitzPatrick, P.
Through Mashonaland with pick and pen. 2nd ed.
136pp. cl. R3.90 (Africana Library) Donker 1973 SA

Fivaz, D.
Bantu classificatory criteria: towards a critical examination
and comparison of the language taxonomies of Doke and
Guthrie. 50c (Rhodes University, Dept. of African
Languages, Communications series, 3) Dept African
Lang - Rhodes 1973 SA

Fivaz, D., comp. Ratzlaff, J., comp.
Shona language lessons. 169pp. R$4.20 Rhod Lit
Bur 1969 RH

Fivaz, D.
Shona morphophonemics and morphosyntax. 245pp.
R6.00 (Dept. African Languages pub.) Witwatersrand UP
1970 SA

Fivaz, D.
Towards explanation in African linguistics. 25pp. ex.
only (Inaugural lec.) Rhodes Univ Lib 1974 SA

Fix, K.
The blood of Jesus. 24pp. K.shs.1.00 Evangel 1968
KE

Flather, H.
The way of an editor. cl. R7.50 Purnell 1977 SA

Fletcher, B.
The educated man. 18pp. 30c Univ Rhodesia Lib
1956 RH

Fletcher, E. Hartshorne, K.B.
English for standard five. R1.75 Maskew Miller 1976
SA

Fletcher, E. Hartshorne, K.B.
English for standard four. R1.50 Maskew Miller 1976
SA

Fletcher, E. Hartshorne, K.B.
English for standard three. R1.50 Maskew Miller 1976
SA

Fletcher, J.E.
Enjoying mathematics in the primary school- a handbook
of teaching methods for primary school teachers. 220pp.
ill. N2.00 Heinemann Educ - Nig 1975 NR

Fletcher, J.E.
Progressive mathematics: pupils bk. 1, 6 bks
See: Akinola, O.

Fletcher, J.E.
Progressive mathematics: pupils bk. 2, 6 bks
See: Akinola, O.

Fletcher, J.E.
Progressive mathematics: pupils bk. 3, 6 bks
See: Akinola, O.

Fletcher, J.E.
Progressive mathematics: pupils bk. 4, 6 bks
See: Akinola, O.

Fletcher, J.E.
Progressive mathematics: teachers bk. 1, 6 bks
See: Akinola, O.

Fletcher, J.E.
Progressive mathematics: teachers bk. 2, 6 bks
See: Akinola, O.

Fletcher, J.E.
Progressive mathematics: teachers bk. 3, 6 bks
See: Akinola, O.

Fletcher, N.G.
Guided English. 1 240pp. R1.40 Shuter 1972 SA

Fletcher, N.G. Stone, S.
Post primary arithmetic, Form 1. 204pp. ill. 75c.
Shuter 1957 SA

Fletcher, N.G.
Post primary English: Forms II & III. 392pp. R1.05
Shuter 1960 SA

Flici, L.
La demesure et le royaume. 108pp. DA4.00 SNED
1969 AE FRE

Flici, L.
Les mercenaires. 48pp. DA4.80 SNED 1973 AE
FRE

Flior, M.
Heralds of the east wind. R6.95 Aegis 1975 SA

Floyd, B.N.
Changing patterns of African land use in Southern
Rhodesia. 2 v. 410pp. maps. K4.00 (£2.34) Inst
Afr Stud - Lusaka ZA

Floyd, B.N.
Junior atlas for Nigeria. See: Menakaya, J.C.

Floyd, T.B.
More about town planning in South Africa. 256pp. ill.
photos. cl. R6.30 Shuter 1966 SA

Floyd, T.B.
Town planning in South Africa. 216pp. ill. cl. R4.50
Shuter 1960 SA

Floyer, E.
The bird that swallowed the stool. ill. 15k (New
Oxford supp. reader grade 3, 1) OUP-Nig NR

Floyer, E.
Going out in the car. 16pp. ill. 15k (New Oxford
supp. reader grade 3, 4) OUP-Nig 1970 NR

Floyer, E.
Lively English reading course: pupil's bk. 1, 6 bks.
40pp. col. ill. 60k OUP - Nig 1967 NR

Floyer, E.
Lively English reading course: pupil's bk. 2, 6 bks.
81pp. ill. 65k OUP - Nig 1968 NR

Floyer, E.
Lively English reading course: pupil's bk. 3, 6 bks.
128pp. ill. 90k OUP - Nig 1969 NR

Floyer, E.
Lively English reading course: teacher's bk. 1, 6 bks.
255pp. ill. N1.50 OUP - Nig 1967 NR

Floyer, E.
Lively English reading course: teacher's bk. 2, 6 bks.
291pp. ill. N2.10 OUP - Nig 1968 NR

Floyer, E.
Lively English reading course: teacher's bk. 3, 6 bks.
235pp. ill. N2.10 OUP - Nig 1969 NR

Floyer, E.
Lively English reading course: workbk. 1, 6 bks. 32pp.
ill. 45k OUP - Nig 1971 NR

Floyer, E.
Lively English reading course: workbk. 2, 6 bks. 49pp.
ill. 50k OUP - Nig 1968 NR

Floyer, E.
Lively English reading course: workbk. 3, 6 bks 64pp.
ill. 60k OUP - Nig 1971 NR

Floyer, E.
Tom's big fish. 16pp. ill. 15k (New Oxford supp.
reader grade 3 6) OUP - Nig 1970 NR

Floyer, E.
The tortoise in the stream. 16pp. ill. 15k (New
Oxford supp. reader grade 3, 6) OUP-Nig 1970 NR

Folivi, L.E. Godman, A.
New certificate physics. 640pp. ill. pl. N4.63
Longman - Nig 1977 NR

Folorunsho, C.O.
Critical notes on Shakespeare's "Henry IV", Part One ('O'
level) 120pp. 75k Publ Int 1973 NR

Folorunso, C.
Model questions/answers on "Julius Caesar". 140pp.
75k Publ Int 1973 NR

Folorunso, C.
Notes on "The African child". 100pp. N1.00
Armolaran 1970 NR

Folorunso, C.O.
Notes on "Richard II". 110pp. N1.70 Armolaran 1970
NR

Fomum, Z.T.
God's love and forgiveness. 46pp. ill. 40k Daystar
1976 NR

Fontaine, I.
Futurité de l'Islam. 46pp. D0.150 Maison Tunis 1972
TI FRE

Fontvieille, J.
Guide bibliographique du monde noir. 2 v. 1175pp.
maps. CFA6000 Univ Cameroun 1971 CM FRE

Foran, R.W.
The Kenya police 1887-1960. 237pp. ill. cl.
K.shs.30.00 ($6.25/£2.50) EALB 1962 KE

Forbes, V.S.
Early visitors to the Eastern Cape. ex. only (Inaugural
lec.) Rhodes Univ Lib 1967 SA

Forbes-Watson, R.
Charles New: Methodist missionary and explorer. 2
2nded. 76pp. ill. K.shs2.50 ($1.50/60p.) EALB
1960 KE

Forde, S.H.M.
An experimental study of secondary school pupils'
attitudes towards certain school subjects. 20pp.
Le1.30 (Dept. of Education, Fourah Bay College,
Research bull., 4) Fourah Bay Bkshp 1971 SL

Forde, W.
Air Force cadet. 125pp. ill. 53k (African Reader's
Library, 18) Pilgrim 1971 NR

Forde, W.
The run away. 112pp. 53k (African Reader's Library,
23) Pilgrim 1973 NR

Fordham, P. Kinyangui, P.
The geography of Kenya. 78pp. ill. K.shs.2.80
($1.50/60p.) EALB 1967 KE

Forestier, J.
Analyse des sucs de l'arachide. 52pp. ill. CFA500
Inst Sciences Hum - Cam 1973 CM FRE

Forestier, J.
Bibliographie commentée de l'arachide. 171pp. ill.
CFA1,000 Inst Sciences Hum - Cam 1972 CM FRE

Forestier, J.
Caracteres vegétatifs. Croissance et rendement de
l'archide hâtive. 41pp. ill. CFA500 Inst Sciences
Hum - Cam 1972 CM FRE

Forestry Research Institute of Malawi.
Research records. [full details and prices upon request
from publisher.]. Forestry Res Inst MW

Forland, K. S.
Analytical chemistry: a lecture course for second year
students in the Department of Chemistry, University of Dar
es Salaam. 62pp. T.shs.7.50 Univ Bkshop - Dar;
distr. 1973 TZ

Forland, K. S.
Practicals in analytical and inorganic chemistry for first
year chemistry students. 155pp. T.shs.12.00 Univ
Bkshop - Dar; distr. 1974 TZ

Forland, K.S.
Elementary chemical calculations. See: Desai, N.C.

Fornacciari, M.F. Kane, M. Mercier.
Thèmes et travaux. Littérature française (1750-1850)
CFA2100 Nouv Ed Afric 1975 SG FRE

Foroma, J.
Penga udzoke. [Mend your ways.] 99pp. pl. 57c
Mambo 1976 RH SHO

Author Index

Forster, E.F.B.
The basic psychology and psychopathology of the Africa peoples. 21pp. C1.00 (50p./$1.00) (Inaugural lecture) Ghana UP 1975 GH

Forster, J.R.
Natural history and description of the tyger-cat of the Cape of Good Hope. [Reprint of ed. London, 1780] 63pp. ill. 50c. (Reprints, 52) State-Lib-SA 1969 SA

Forsyth, J.
Agricultural insects of Ghana. 163pp. cl. C3.50 (£1.50/$3.50) Ghana UP 1966 GH

Fortes, M.
The family: bane or blessing? 27pp. C1.00 ($1.00/50p.) (Inaugural lecture) Ghana UP 1971 GH

Fortier, J., ed.
Contes ngambaye. 254pp. ex. only Inst Nat Tchad 1972 CD FRE

Fortman, S.G., ed.
After Mulungushi. 183pp. K.shs.35.00 cl. K.shs13.50 pap. ($7.80 cl.) ($4.00 pap.) EAPH 1969 KE

Fortune, G., ed.
Selected papers from the 1962 and 1963 conferences held at the college on the teaching of African language in schools. 145pp. 50c pap. (Dept. of African languages, Univ. of Rhodesia, 1) Univ Rhodesia Lib 1964 RH

Fortune, G.
Elements of Shona. 242pp. R$5.00 Longman - Rhod 1957 RH

Fortune, G.
Guide to Shona spelling. 64pp. 75c. Longman - Rhod 1972 RH

Fortune, G.
Ideophones in Shona. 43pp. 30c Univ Rhodesia Lib 1962 RH

Fortune, G.
A preliminary study of the Bantu languages of the federation. 45n. (23p.) (Rhodes-Livingstone communications, 14) Inst Afr Stud - Lusaka 1959 ZA

Fortune, G.   Hodza, A.
Shona. Grade 6: Natsai kudzidza. 148pp. 75c. Longman - Rhod 1969 RH SHO

Fortune, G.   Hodza, A.
Shona. Grade 7: Budirirai. 136pp. 75c. Longman - Rhod 1972 RH SHO

Fortune, G.   Hodza, A.
Shona. Teacher's bk. grade 6. 64pp. 50c. Longman - Rhod 1972 RH SHO

Fortune, G.   Hodza, A.
Shona. Teacher's bk. grade 7. 36pp. 60c. Longman - Rhod 1972 RH SHO

Fosbrooke, H.A.
Maisha ya ole kirasis yaani Justin Lemenye. [The life of Justin Lemenye] ill. K.shs.1.75 ($1.25/50p.) EALB 1953 KE SWA

Fosbrooke, H.A.
Ngorongoro's first visitor. 2nd ed. 25pp. K.shs.2.50 ($1.50/60p.) EALB 1966 KE

Fossberg, P.E.
The treatment of gravel roads with waste sulphite lye. 36pp. ill. (CSIR research reports, 243) CSIR 1966 SA

Foster, W.D.
The early history of scientific medicine in Uganda. 112pp. ill. K.shs.13.15 ($3.25/£1.70) EALB 1970 KE

Fouche, R.   Selkirk, D.K.
Domestic science textbook. 328pp. ill. $3.10 Longman SA 1971 SA

Foucher, L.
La maison de la procession dionysiaque à El Jem. 173pp. ill. pl. D2.130 (Série I, Archéologie-Histoire, 11) Univ Tunis 1964 TI FRE

Fouet, F.   Renaudeau, R.
Littérature africaine. L'engagement. 406pp. CFA2,350 (F47.00) Nouv Ed Afric 1976 SG FRE

Fougeyrollas, P.
L'enseignement du français au service de la nation sénégalaise. 33pp. CFA125 (C.L.A.D. Etude, 24) CLAD 1967 SG FRE

Foulkes, F.
Fight the good fight. 96pp. C1.20 (50p.) Africa Christian 1971 GH

Foulkes, F.
Happy in trouble. 104pp. C1.00 (30p.) Africa Christian 1973 GH

Foulkes, F.
You could be rich! 144pp. 90pes. (30p.) Africa Christian 1968 GH

Fourah Bay College, University of Sierra Leone, Celebrations Committee.
One hundred years of university education in Sierra Leone, 1876-1976. 82pp. pl. Le4.00 (£2.00) Fourah Bay College Lib; distr 1976 SL

Fourcade, H.G.
Check-list of the flowering plants of the division of George, Knysna, Humansdorp, and Uniondale. 25c. (Memoirs of the Botanical Survey of South Africa, 20) Botanical Res Inst 1941 SA

Fourie, G.
Source guide for music 1970. 455pp. ill. R5.95 Human Science Res Council 1973 SA

Fourie, G.
Source guide for music, 1971. 469pp. hd. R7.15 cl. Human Science Res Council 1975 SA

Fourie, H.P.
Communication: introductory essays. [Also available in Afrikaans]. See: Blignaut, F.W.

Fouries, S.
The cranial morphology of sturnis vulgaris vulgaris linnacus; A contribution to the cranial morphology of Nyctisyrigmus pectoralis pectoralis with special reference to the palate and cranial kinesis. See: de Kock, J.M.

Fowler, A.M.   Heathcote, R.G.
A seedling disorder of groundnuts associated with imbalanced mineral nutrition. 4pp. (Samaru misc. pap., 47) Inst Agric Res-Zaria 1974 NR

Fowowe, O.
Who has blood? Poems. 39pp. 60k (Pan-African pocket poets, 5) Univ Ife Bkshop 1972 NR

Fox, H.E.   Botha, J.
Modern revision exercises in biology for standard 8. 90pp. ill. R2.70 Nasou 1975 SA

Fox, H.E.   de Villiers, G.
Modern revision exercises in general science for standard 6. 89pp. ill. photos. R2.40 Nasou 1975 SA

Fox, H.E.   de Villiers, G.
Modern revision exercises in physical science for standard 8. 98pp. ill. R2.50 Nasou 1974 SA

Fox, H.E.
Modern revision exercises in physical science for standards 9-10. See: Villiers, G.

Fox, H.E.
Modern revision exercises in senior biology for standards 9-10. 113pp. ill. R2.90 Nasou 1976 SA

Fox, J.
What is socialism? See: Thomas, M.

Fox, L.K.
East African childhood: Three versions. 154pp. photos. K.shs11.75 OUP-Nairobi 1967 KE

Fox, M.
Your mending. 48pp. ill. 50c. OUP-SA 1966 SA

Fox, M.
Your washing and ironing. 80pp. ill. 50c. OUP-SA 1966 SA

Franck, B.   Hatfield, D.   Manuel, G.
District six. 120pp. ill. hd.   R9.50 Longman SA 1967
SA

Frank, B.
Liberia: a new spirit in the old republic. 91pp.
U.S.$1.50 Cole & Yancy 1972 LB

Frank, C.
The life of Bishop Steere. 55pp. ill.   K.shs1.75
($1.25/50p.) EALB 1953 KE

Frank, C.R.
Economic accounting and development planning.
See: Van Arkadie, B.

Frank, D.   Vorster, O.C.   Low, C.
Investigations into coatings for the protection of structural
metal in southwest Africa. 20pp. (CSIR research
reports, 308) CSIR 1971 SA

Frank, D.   Vorster, O.C.   Low, C.
Investigations into coatings for timber in Southwest Africa.
28pp. (CSIR research reports, 304) CSIR 1971 SA

Frank, D.   Vorster, O.C.   Low, C.
Investigations into the painting of wire-brushed steel.
35pp. (CSIR research reports, 301) CSIR 1971 SA

Frank, G.H.
Contributions to the cranial morphology of Ambystoma
macrodactylum Baird; The development of the
chondrocranium of the ostrich. See: Papendieck,
H.I.C.M.

Frank, S.   Meyer, R.
Basic genetics for schools and colleges. 144pp.
K.shs.18.50 (£1.10) Heinemann Educ - Nair 1975 KE

Frank, W.
Juma mtoto yatima. [Juma the orphan] 80pp.
K.shs.6.50 ($2.80/£2.10) EALB 1974 KE SWA

Frankl, P.
Venereal diseases: a guide for African students and
medical assistants. 43pp. ill.   K.shs.3.50
($1.50/60p.) EALB 1958 KE

Franklin, M.
The story of Greak Brak river. 248pp. cl.   R10.50
Struik 1975 SA

Franzsen, P.J.J.   Wessels, J.A.
A first course in woodwork. 180pp. ill.   R3.50 Nasou
1976 SA

Fraser, B.D.
John William Colenso. 26pp.   60c. Univ Cape Town
Lib 1970 SA

Fraser Ross, W.
New lamps for old: the advance to social medicine.
23pp.   30c pap. Univ Rhodesia Lib 1968 RH

Fraser, T.H.
Comparative osteology of the shallow water cardinal fishes
(Perciformes : Apogonidae) with reference to the
systematics and evolution of the family. 110pp. ill. pl.
R4.00 (Ichthyological bull., 34) Inst of Ichthyology 1972
SA

Fraser, T.H.
The deepwater fish "Scombrosphyraena Oceanica" from
the Caribbean sea with comments on its possible
relationships. 7pp. ill.   R1.00 (Special publ., 8) Inst
Ichthyology 1971 SA

Fraser, T.H.
Evolutionary significance of "Holapogon" a new genus of
Cardinal fishes (Apogonidae) with a redescription of its
type-species "Apogon maximus.". 7pp. ill.   R1.00
(Special publ., 10) Inst Ichthyology 1973 SA

Fraser, T.H.
The fish "Elops machnata" in South Africa. 6pp.   50c.
(Special publ., 11) Inst Ichthyology 1973 SA

Fraser, T.H.
A new species of the Klipfish genus "Springeratus"
(Clinidae) from the Indian Ocean. 14pp. ill.   R1.00
(Special publ., 9) Inst Ichthyology 1972 SA

Freed, L.F.
Crime in South Africa.   R6.00   Juta 1963 SA

Freedom from Hunger Campaign.
Food for your family. 96pp. pl.   45c Rhod Lit Bur
1974 RH

Freemann, R.A.D.
Okoyai aumogbomo. [Seeds of poetry, poems in Ijo]
62pp. pap. & hd.   N1.05 pap.   N1.85 hd. (Inst. of
African Stud., Univ. of Ibadan, Bi-lingual literary works, 5)
Inst Afr Stud-Ibadan 1972 NR IJO

Freeme, C.R.
Dynamic techniques for testing pavement structures.
See: Szendrei, M.E.

Freer, D. J.
Pre-school opportunity and sex differences as factors
affecting educational progress. See: Orbell, S. F. W.

Freeth, S.J., ed.
Stratigraphy: an interdisciplinary symposium.
See: Daniels, S.G.H., ed.

Freire, P.
Research methods. 17pp.   T.shs.1.70 (Studies in
Adult Education, 7) Inst Adult Educ - Dar 1973 TZ

Fremont, I.V.
Stories and plays from Africa. 48pp. ill.   K.shs3.00
OUP-Nairobi 1968 KE

French, S.   Boyd, T.A.
An enquiry concerning employment opportunities for
secondary school leavers in Ghana. 54pp.   C1.00
(Univ. of Cape Coast, Centre for Development Studies,
Research Report Series, 6) Centre Dev Stud 1971 GH

French, S.   Boyd, T.A.
An enquiry concerning employment opportunities for
secondary school leavers in Ghana. 54pp. (University
of Cape Coast, social studies project, research report, 6)
Cape Coast Bkshp 1971 GH

Frend, W.H.C.
Liberty and unity.   50c. (Peter Ainslie Memorial lec.,
15) Rhodes Univ Lib 1964 SA

Frere, B.
Afghanistan and South Africa; letters to the right hon. W.E.
Gladstone, regarding portions of his Midlothian speeches,
and a letter to the late Sir John Kaye, and other papers.
[Reprint of ed. London, 1881] 5th ed. 76pp.   R3.70
(Reprints, 41) State-Lib-SA 1969 SA

Fretz, D.
Cape Town: city between sea and mountain. 128pp.
photos. hd.   R5.00 Longman SA 1973 SA

Friedman, B.
From isolation to detente: 1976 presidential address.
18pp.   60c ($1.25) SA Inst of Race Relations 1976
SA

Friedman, B.
Parliament in a caste society. 1975 Presidential address.
14pp.   45c ($1.30/55p) SA Inst of Race Relations
1975 SA

Friedman, S., comp.
Coats of arms of the municipalities of the Transvaal.
24pp.   R1.60 Dept Bibliog, Lib & Typo 1973 SA

Friend, A.L.
Companies: how to form and manage them.   K.shs0.30
EALB 1969 KE

Friends of the South African Library.
Bibliophilia Africana II, 1971. Proceedings of the second
conference of South African Bibliophiles. 175pp.
R3.00 South African Lib 1975 SA

Froelich, J.C.
La tribu Konkomba du nord-Togo. 255pp. pl. maps.
CFA1600 (Mémoires de l'IFAN, 37) IFAN 1954 SG
FRE

Gallez, L.
La science et la foi. Scientisme, athéisme scientifique, humanisme chrétien. 47pp. 40k St. Paul 1976 ZR FRE

Galloway, A.
The skeletal remains of Bambandyanalo. 154pp. ill. pl. cl. R6.00 Witwatersrand UP 1959 SA

Galloway, A.D.
The useless disciplines. 8pp. 20k Ibadan UP 1957 NR

Galloway, M.H.
Zululand and the Zulus. 16pp. 40c. Univ Cape Town Lib 1963 SA

Galpin, E.E.
Botanical survey of the Springbok Flats (Transvaal) 25c. (Memoirs of the Botanical Survey of South Africa, 12) Botanical Res Inst SA

Galpin, E.E.
The native timber trees of the Springbok Flats. 25c. (Memoirs of the Botanical Survey of South Africa, 7) Botanical Res Inst 1925 SA

Galthung, G.
Sociological theory and social development. 31pp. U.shs2.50 (M.I.S.R. Nkanga ed., 2) Mak Inst Soc Res 1968 UG

Galtimer, U.
Coordinating, planning and budgeting in native authority. 53pp. 55k (40p./$1.00) Inst Admin - Zaria NR

Galvin, P.
The formation of Christian communities in the rural area. 47pp. 40c. (Mambo Missio-Pastoral Series, 1) Mambo 1972 RH

Gambanga, J.N.
Tichaona. [We shall see.] 11pp. pl. 10c. Rhod Lit Bur 1976 RH SHO

Game Division, Tanzania.
Kutumbua wanyama wa porini. [Recognize wild animals] 20pp. ill. Nat Print Co 1972 TZ SWA

Gandari, J.O.
Ane chake anotakura. [Every one carries his own property.] 12pp. pl. 3c. Rhod Lit Bur 1975 RH SHO

Gandari, J.O.
Ane chake anotakura. [You are responsible for your property.] 12pp. pl. 3c Rhod Lit Bur 1975 RH SHO

Gane, P.C., ed.
The selective Voet, being the commentary on the pandects. 7 v. R100.00 Butterworths 1972 SA

Gane, P.C.
Huber's jurisprudence of my time. tr. fr. Afrikaans 2 v. R22.00 Butterworths 1939 SA

Ganiage, J.
Une entreprise Italienne de Tunisie au milieu du XIXe siècle, correspondance commerciale de la thonaire de Sidi Daoud. 173pp. D1.065 (Série V, Sources de l'Histoire Tunisienne, 2) Univ Tunis 1960 TI FRE

Ganiage, J.
Les origines du protectorat français en Tunisie, 1861-1881. 620pp. photos. D1,300 Maison Tunis 1968 TI FRE

Ganiage, J.
La population européenne de Tunis au milieu du XIXe siècle. 97pp. ill. D1.065 (Série IV, Histoire, 2) Univ Tunis 1960 TI FRE

Gann, L.H.
The birth of a plural society: The development of Northern Rhodesia under the British South Africa Company, 1894-1914. 250pp. ill. hd. K3.60 (£1.80/$6.00) Inst Afr Stud - Lusaka 1958 ZA

Ganzei, E.
Ndoto ya mwemdawazimu. [The dream of a madman] 100pp. ill. K.shs10.00 ($2.10/80p.) EALB 1972 KE SWA

Garach, R.B. Moodley, V.
Technical drawing for standard 6 and 7. 112pp. ill. R2.75 OUP-SA 1977 SA

Garagnon, J. Rousset, M.
Droit administratif Marocain. Dir42.00 Ed La Porte 1975 MR FRE

Gardiner, J.
Some aspects of the establishment of towns in Zambia during the nineteen-twenties and -thirties. 20pp. K1.00 (58p.) (Zambian Urban stud., 3) Inst Afr Stud - Lusaka 1970 ZA

Gardner, A.
Aselemi: Adibel adinya itugha onu Abuan. See: Gardner, I.

Gardner, A.
Teachers' notes on aselemi: adibel adinya itugha onu abuan. See: Gardner, I.

Gardner, C.O.
The sole function. See: Berthoud, J.A.

Gardner, G.M.
The parable of the cross. 29pp. 10k Daystar 1972 NR

Gardner, I. Gardner, A.
Aselemi: Adibel adinya itugha onu Abuan. [Abua reader, 1] 128pp. ill. 40k (Inst. of African Stud., Univ. of Ibadan, Rivers readers project, 12) Inst Afr Stud-Ibadan 1971 NR ABU

Gardner, I. Gardner, A.
Teachers' notes on aselemi: adibel adinya itugha onu abuan. 55pp. 40k (Inst. of African Stud., Univ. of Ibadan, Rivers readers project, 13) Inst Afr Stud-Ibadan 1971 NR ABU

Gardner, R.
A primary history of Botswana. 60pp. ill. maps. R1.25 Longman SA 1971 SA

Garelik, J. Depuydt, G.
Fiscalité Algérienne: 1973. 197pp. DA10.00 SNED 1973 AE FRE

Gargett, E.
The administration of transition. African urban settlement in Rhodesia. 104pp. R$1.65 (Mambo Socio-economic Series, 5) Mambo 1977 RH

Garlake, P.S.
The ruins of Zimbabwe. 52pp. pl. 60n. (Haz pamphlets, 4) Neczam 1974 ZA

Garrard, P.
Major zones of transcurrent dislocation and superposition of orogenic belts in part of central Africa. See: de Swardt, A.M.J.

Garriock, L.H.
Omulumu gw'omukazi mu maka. [The work of women in the home] 40pp. K.shs.0.50 EALB 1954 KE LUG

Garrison, W.E.
Liberty and unity. 50c. (Peter Ainslie Memorial lec., 12) Rhodes Univ Lib 1961 SA

Garson, M.S.
The carbonatites and agglomerate vents of the Western Shire valley. 167pp. pl. maps. hd. K1.75 (Geological Survey of Malawi, Memoir, 3) Geol Survey - Mal 1965 MW

Garson, M.S.
Carbonatites of Southern Malawi. 128pp. pl. hd. K2.00 (Geological Survey of Malawi, Bull. 15) Geol Survey - Mal 1965 MW

Garson, M.S. Smith, W.C.
Chilwa Island. 127pp. maps pl. hd. K1.55 (Geological Survey of Malawi, Memoir 1) Geol Survey - Mal 1958 MW

Garson, M.S.
The geology of the Kirk Range-Lisungwe Valley area. See: Bloomfield, K.

Garson, M.S.
    The geology of the Lake Chilwa area. 67pp. maps pl.
    hd.   K1.05   (Geological Survey of Malawi, Bull. 12)
    Geol Survey - Mal 1960 MW

Garson, M.S.   Walshaw, R.D.
    The geology of the Mulanje area. 157pp. pl. map. hd.
    K5.00 (Geological Survey of Malawi, Bull. 21) Geol
    Survey - Mal 1969 MW

Garson, M.W.
    The Tundulu carbonatite ring complex in Southern
    Nyasaland. 248pp. pl. maps. hd.   K1.75
    (Geological Survey of Malawi, Memoir 2) Geol Survey -
    Mal 1962 MW

Gaskell, J.L.
    The geology of the Mzimba area. 30pp. map.   K4.00
    (Geological Survey of Malawi, Bull. 37) Geol Survey -
    Mal 1973 MW

Gaston, S.D.
    Commissaire K contre Dragosc. 58pp.   CFA200
    (F4.00) Nouv Ed Afric 1976 SG FRE

Gatabaki, N.
    The crisis of student power: an African case.
    K.shs.36.00 Pan-african 1977 KE

Gatanyu, J.
    The battlefield. 61pp. ill.   K.shs3.50 ($1.50) EAPH
    1968 KE

Gatarayima.   Delannoy.
    La formation des agents de l'etat au Zaïre.   Z3.00
    ($2.40) (Cahiers du CRIDE, Nouvelle série, I, 5) CRIDE
    1977 ZR FRE

Gathigira, S.K.
    Miikarire ya Agikuyu. [Kikuyu customs] 88pp.
    K.shs.3.60 Equatorial 1973 KE KIK

Gattrall, P.
    Learn to sketch. 14pp. ill.   K.shs2.00 ($1.00) EAPH
    1968 KE

Gauthier, B.
    Analyse phonologique de l'abouré. 61pp.   CFA400
    pap. (Documents linguistiques, 29) Inst Ling Appliquée
    1971 IV FRE

Gavin, R.J., comp.   Betley, J.A., comp.
    The scramble for Africa: documents on the Berlin West
    African conference and related subjects, 1884-1885.
    429pp. map.   N9.00 Ibadan UP 1973 NR

Gawaine, J.
    The diamond seeker. 184pp. pl. maps. cl.   R8.95
    Macmillan - SA 1976 SA

Gawaine, J.
    The diamond seeker. 184pp. pl. cl.   R8.50 (£3.95)
    Macmillan - SA 1976 SA

Gay, J.   Welmers, W.
    Mathematics and logic in the Kpelle language and a first
    course in Kpelle. 184pp.   N3.00 (Inst. of African
    Stud., Univ. of Ibadan, occas. pub., 21) Inst Afr
    Stud-Ibadan 1971 NR

Gazio, J.
    Langage et textes. Méthode complète d'enseignement du
    français en Afrique, classe de 6e, livre de l'élève.
    See: Calvet, L.

Gazio, J.
    Langage et textes. Méthode complète d'enseignement du
    français en Afrique, classe de 6e, livre du professeur.
    See: Calvet, L.J.

Gbadamosi, B.
    Oro peelu idi re. [Words and their meanings] 64pp.
    40k Univ Ife Bkshop 1965 NR YOR

Gbadamosi, R.
    Echoes from the lagoon: a play. 95pp.   85k (African
    Literature series, 5) Onibonoje 1973 NR

Gebeda, C.Z.   Lalendle, C.H.T.   Thipa, H.M.
    Imethodi Yesixhosa. [Language text.] 80pp.   R1.90
    Longman - SA 1977 SA XHO

Gecaga, B.M.
    Home life in Kikuyuland. 2nd ed.   K.shs.1.00
    ($2.00/80p.) EALB 1972 KE

Gecaga, B.M.
    Kariuki na muthoni. [A study of childhood and youth
    among the Kikuyu] 3rd. ed.   K.shs.2.00 ($1.25/50p)
    EALB 1971 KE KIK

Gecau, M.K.
    Know yourself: a guide for adolescent girls.
    See: Roberts, H.M.

Gecau, M.K.
    Mother and child.   See: Roberts, H.M.

Gecau, R.M.
    Kikuyu folktales: their nature and value. 152pp. ill.
    K.shs6.25 ($2.00/95p.) EALB 1970 KE

Geddes, C.L. et al.
    Studies in Islamic arts and architecture.   L.E. 8.50
    ($24.50) Am Univ 1965 UA

Gee, E.   Aldrich, V.   Hunter, L.
    The between bale and between lot variation of South
    African grown cottons, part I: micronaire, maturity ration,
    fineness, 2.5% span length, uniformity ratio and trash
    content. 16pp.   R2.50 (SAWTRI Technical Reports,
    319) SAWTRI 1976 SA

Gee, E.
    The between bale and between lot variation of South
    African grown cottons, part II: bundle tenacity and
    extension at 3.2 mm (1/8") gauge. See: Hunter, L.

Gee, E.
    Core yield as a theoretical estimate of bale yield in a
    changing regain situation. 15pp.   R2.50 (SAWTRI
    Technical Reports, 316) SAWTRI 1976 SA

Gee, E.
    Incorporation of leno weave units into lightweight all-wool
    worsted fabric. See: Robinson, G.A.

Gee, E.
    Objective measurement of the South African wool clip, part
    II: sampling by model T coring equipment in Durban, East
    London and Port Elizabeth ports. 8pp.   R2.50
    (SAWTRI Technical Reports, 318) SAWTRI 1976 SA

Gee, E.   Turpie, D.W.F.
    A statistical assessment of the accuracy of the
    measurement of spinning potential by the "MSS at Break"
    technique. 23pp.   R2.50 (SAWTRI Technical Reports,
    317) SAWTRI 1976 SA

Gee, E.
    Studies of the surface chemistry of wool, part II: the critical
    surface tension of wool and polymers. Some results and
    a reinterpretation of the theory on surface interactions.
    See: Weideman, E.

Gee, F.
    The effect of neutral and alkaline scouring on the
    yellowness of wool at the various processing stages.
    See: Turpie, D.W.F.

Geertsema, H.
    Descriptions of the stages of two subspecies of the pine
    tree emperor moth, nudaurelia cytherea (fabr.)
    (lepidoptera: saturniidae) 37pp. pl.   R1.10 (Univ.
    Stellenbosch, Annals, vol. 46, A.3) Univ Stellenbosch, Lib
    1971 SA

Geertsema, H.
    Descriptions of the stages of two subspecies of the pine
    tree Emporer moth, Nudaurella Cytherea (Fabr.)
    (Lepidoptera: Saturniidae) 37pp. photos. ill.   R1.10
    (A v.46, no.1) Univ Stellenbosch, Lib 1971 SA

Geggus, C.
    Awards available for undergraduates at South African
    universities for whites. pt. 2 273pp.   R3.50 Human
    Science Res Council 1976 SA

Geggus, C.
    Tertiary training outside universities and career
    opportunities. See: Coetzee, C.J.S.

Geggus, C.   Stimie, C.M.
 Training after standard ten excluding university training.
 121pp.   90c.   Human Scienc Res Council 1971 SA

Geggus, C.
 University education in the RSA.   See: Stimie, C.M.

Gehring, G.
 Les relations entre la Tunisie et l'Allemagne avant le
 protectorat français.   155pp. pl.   D1.000 (Série IV,
 Histoire, 13)   Univ Tunis 1971 TI FRE

Geldenhuys, A., et al.
 Systematic typing for beginners.   104pp. ill.   R2.95
 Nasou 1976 SA

Geldenhuys, A., et al.
 Systematic typing for standards 9-10.   252pp. ill.
 R3.50   Nasou 1976 SA

Geldenhuys, A., et al.
 Systematic typing, standard 8.   127pp. ill.   R3.20
 Nasou 1976 SA

Geldenhuys, A.   Ebersohn, J. J.   Woolacott, E.
 Systematic typing for the senior secondary course.
 321pp.   R3.65   Nasou 1974 SA

Geldenhuys, J.P.
 Typing for juniors, standard 8.   See: Eksteen, F.R.L.N.

Gelfand, M.
 African background.   R6.00   Juta SA

Gelfand, M.
 African law and custom in Rhodesia.   See: Goldin, B.

Gelfand, M.
 The genuine Shona.   2nd ed.   R$3.70   Mambo 1976
 RH

Gelfand, M.
 Mother Patrick and her nursing sisters.   R4.50   Juta SA

Gelfand, M.
 A service to the sick. A history of the health service for
 Africans in Southern Rhodesia (1890-1953)   187pp. cl. &
 pap.   R$6.50 cl.   R$5.20 pap.   (Zambeziana, 1)
 Mambo 1976 RH

Gelfand, M.
 Shona religion.   R6.00   Juta SA

Gelfand, M.
 The sick African.   3rd ed.   R7.75   Juta SA

Gelfand, M.W.
 Rivers of death in Africa.   100pp.   50c   Univ Rhodesia
 Lib 1964 RH

Genevray, J.
 Eléments d'une monographie d'une division administrative
 Libérienne. (Grand Bassa County)   135pp.   CFA800
 (Mémoires de l'IFAN, 21)   IFAN 1952 SG FRE

Gengoux, J.
 Qu'est-ce que la littérature.   33pp.   40k   Press Univ
 Zaire 1963 ZR FRE

Geological Society of South Africa.
 Upper mantle project.   R18.00   (Special pub., 2)   Geol
 Soc SA 1970 SA

George, E.F.
 An experiment to compare the selection of sugar cane
 varieties from seedlings bunches planted in two different
 ways and from others singly planted.   35pp.   Rs5
 (Mauritius Sugar Industry Research Institute, occas. paps.,
 7)   Sugar Res Inst 1962 MF

George, F.
 The hospital central sterile supply department: a
 background to procedures, organization and planning.
 20pp.   (CSIR research reports, 187)   CSIR 1962 SA

Gerber, J.J.
 New media in education.   ex. only   (Inaugural lec.)
 Rhodes Univ Lib 1964 SA

Gerber, V.
 Evangélisation et croissance de l'Eglise.   96pp. ill.
 CFA350   CPE 1973 IV FRE

Gering, L.
 The law of negotiable instruments in South Africa.
 See: Cowen, B.A.

German Foundation for International Development, Public
 Administration Promotion Centre.
 Management of large cities in Africa.   395pp.   ex. only
 CAFRAD 1973 MR

Germond, R.C.
 Chronicles of Basutoland.   583pp. pl. photos maps. cl.
 R6.00   Morija 1967 L0

Gerrar, J.K.
 Practical banking for beginners.   76pp.   65pes.
 ($1.30)   Ghana Publ Corp 1971 GH

Gerritsen, J.J.
 The development of a small decorticator for "Phormium
 tenax" leaves.   18pp.   R2.50   (SAWTRI Technical
 Reports, 232)   SAWTRI 1974 SA

Gerritsen, J.J.
 The performance of the Mini Mk II decorticator for
 "Phormium tenax".   25pp.   R2.50   (SAWTRI Technical
 Reports, 242)   SAWTRI 1975 SA

Gershenberg, I.
 Commercial banking in Uganda. Prescriptions for
 economic development.   61pp.   U.shs.8.50   ($2.00)
 Mak Inst Soc Res 1973 UG

Gertzel, C., ed.   Rothchild, D., ed.   Goldschmidt, M.,
 ed.
 Government and politics in Kenya.   611pp. maps.
 K.shs.105.00 cl.   K.shs.39.00 pap.   ($20.00) ($10.00)
 EAPH 1969 KE

Gertzel, C., ed.
 The political process in Zambia: documents and readings.
 v.II: The presidential system: government institutions.
 322pp.   K1.50   School Hum Soc Sci - Zam 1975 ZA

Gertzel, C.
 The politics of independent Kenya.   176pp.
 K.shs.15.00   ($4.20)   EAPH 1970 KE

Gervers, J.H.
 An index to the proceedings of the Coker commission of
 inquiry into the affairs of certain statutory corporations in
 Western Nigeria.   91pp.   50k   (75c)   (N.I.S.E.R.
 indexes and bibliographies, 8)   NISER 1963 NR

Getz, W.M.
 Mathematical models: a vital tool for the utilization and
 preservation of the renewable resources of Southern
 Africa.   17pp.   (CSIR Special Report, WISK 164)   CSIR
 1975 SA

Getz, W.M.
 Modelling and control of birth-and-death processes.
 153pp.   (CSIR Special Report, WISK 196)   CSIR 1976
 SA

Getz, W.M.
 A non-linear multiple migration process.   19pp.   (CSIR
 Special Report, WISK 182)   CSIR 1975 SA

Getz, W.M.   Starfield, A.M.
 Sensitivity analysis of a simple linear model of a savanna
 ecosystem at Nylsvley.   18pp.   (SANSP occasional publ.,
 2)   CSIR 1975 SA

Getz, W.S.
 The South African law of insurance.   See: Gordon, G.

Ghai, D.P.
 Economic independence in Africa.   235pp. cl. & pap.
 K.shs.23.00 pap.   K.shs.39.00 cl.   ($4.50/£1.80 pap.)
 ($7.00/£3.60 cl.)   EALB 1973 KE

Ghai, D.P.
 Education, society and development: new perspectives
 from Kenya.   See: Court, D.

Ghai, Y.P.
 Constitutions and the political order in East Africa.   31pp.
 ill.   T.shs. 1.00   (Inaugural lecture, 10)   Univ Dar es
 Salaam 1970 TZ

Ghai, Y.P.   McAuslan, J.P.W.B.
 Public law and political change in Kenya.   564pp. pap.
 K.shs.50.00   OUP-Nairobi 1970 KE

Ghaidan, U., ed.
  Lamu. A study in conservation.   169pp. photos. maps
  col. maps.   K.shs.85.60   ($16.20/£7.80) EALB 1976
  KE
Ghaidan, U.I.
  Lamu: a study of a Swahili town in Kenya. 94pp. ill. cl.
  & pap.   K.shs.50.00 cl.   K.shs.36.00 pap.
  ($9.80/£4.70 cl.) ($7.30/£2.90 pap.) EALB 1975 KE
Ghana Boyscouts Association.
  Ghana Boyscouts handbook. 70pp. ill.   50pes.
  ($.50) Ghana Publ Corp 1969 GH
Ghana Central Bureau of Statistics.
  1970 population census of Ghana. Statistics of localities
  and enumeration areas. v. 2 662pp. maps.   C10.00
  (£5.00 pap.) Ghana Central Bur Stat 1973 GH
Ghana Central Bureau of Statistics.
  1970 Population census of Ghana. The gazetter. v. 1
  662pp. maps.   C10.00 (£5.00 pap.) Ghana Central
  Bur Stat 1973 GH
Ghana Central Bureau of Statistics.
  Annual report on external trade (annual) 731pp.   C7.00
  Ghana Central Bur Stat 1966-68 GH
Ghana Central Bureau of Statistics.
  Civil aviation statistics, 1970. 35pp.   60 pes. pap.
  (30p) (Series II, 13) Ghana Central Bur Stat 1973 GH
Ghana Central Bureau of Statistics.
  Directory of industrial enterprises and establishments
  (annual) 225pp.   C3.50 Ghana Central Bur Stat 1969
  GH
Ghana Central Bureau of Statistics.
  Distributive trade statistics: wholesale and retail trade
  (annual) 120pp.   C3.50 Ghana Central Bur Stat 1971
  GH
Ghana Central Bureau of Statistics.
  Economic survey (annual) 143pp.   C3.50 Ghana
  Central Bur Stat 1969 GH
Ghana Central Bureau of Statistics.
  External trade statistics of Ghana, 1974. C10.50
  (£5.25) Ghana Central Bur Stat 1974 GH
Ghana Central Bureau of Statistics.
  External trade statistics of Ghana (annual) 259pp.
  C15.00 Ghana Central Bur Stat 1970 GH
Ghana Central Bureau of Statistics.
  Industrial statistics (annual) 66pp.   C3.50 Ghana
  Central Bur Stat 1966-68 GH
Ghana Central Bureau of Statistics.
  Input-output table of Ghana: 1968. 19pp.   C1.00
  (50p) Ghana Central Bur Stat 1973 GH
Ghana Central Bureau of Statistics.
  Labour statistics, 1971. 28pp.   60pes. (30p) (Series
  II, 16) Ghana Central Bur Stat 1974 GH
Ghana Central Bureau of Statistics.
  Labour statistics (annual) 28pp.   60pes. (Statistical
  report, III) Ghana Central Bur Stat 1969 GH
Ghana Central Bureau of Statistics.
  Migration statistics, 1970. 31pp.   60pes. (30p)
  (Series VI, 14) Ghana Central Bur Stat 1973 GH
Ghana Central Bureau of Statistics.
  Migration statistics (annual) 31pp.   60pes. (Statistical
  report, VI) Ghana Central Bur Stat 1969 GH
Ghana Central Bureau of Statistics.
  Motor vehicle statistics, 1970. 36pp.   60pes. (30p
  pap.) (Series V, 15) Ghana Central Bur Stat 1973 GH
Ghana Central Bureau of Statistics.
  Motor vehicle statistics (annual) 36pp.   60pes.
  (Statistical report, V) Ghana Central Bur Stat 1969 GH
Ghana Central Bureau of Statistics.
  National income of Ghana at constant prices: 1965-1968.
  28pp.   C1.00 (50p) Ghana Central Bur Stat 1973 GH
Ghana Central Bureau of Statistics.
  Prison statistics (annual) 40pp.   90pes. Ghana Central
  Bur Stat 1969 GH

Ghana Central Bureau of Statistics.
  Reports of 1960 population census: advance report of
  volumes III and IV (based on a 10 percent sample)
  122pp.   C4.20 Ghana Central Bur Stat 1960 GH
Ghana Central Bureau of Statistics.
  Reports of 1960 population census: Census data for new
  regions. var.pp. (Special reports, C) Ghana Central
  Bur Stat 1960 GH
Ghana Central Bureau of Statistics.
  Reports of 1960 population census. I - The gazetteer
  405pp.   C8.40 Ghana Central Bur Stat 1960 GH
Ghana Central Bureau of Statistics.
  Reports of 1960 population census. II - Statistics of
  localities and enumeration areas 707pp.   C16.80
  Ghana Central Bur Stat 1960 GH
Ghana Central Bureau of Statistics.
  Reports of 1960 population census. III - Detailed
  demographic characteristics 160pp.   C4.20 Ghana
  Central Bur Stat 1960 GH
Ghana Central Bureau of Statistics.
  Reports of 1960 population census. IV - Detailed
  economic characteristics 240pp.   C4.20 Ghana
  Central Bur Stat 1960 GH
Ghana Central Bureau of Statistics.
  Reports of 1960 population census: list of localities by
  local authority. var.pp. (Special reports, D) Ghana
  Central Bur Stat 1960 GH
Ghana Central Bureau of Statistics.
  Reports of 1960 population census: plan of enumeration
  areas. maps. Ghana Central Bur Stat 1960 GH
Ghana Central Bureau of Statistics.
  Reports of 1960 population census: Socio-economic
  indices of enumeration areas. var.pp. (Special reports,
  B) Ghana Central Bur Stat 1960 GH
Ghana Central Bureau of Statistics.
  Reports of 1960 population census: statistical maps.
  maps. Ghana Central Bur Stat 1960 GH
Ghana Central Bureau of Statistics.
  Reports of 1960 population census: Statistics of large
  towns. var.pp.   C5.20 (Special reports, A) Ghana
  Central Bur Stat 1960 GH
Ghana Central Bureau of Statistics.
  Reports of 1960 population census: tribes in Ghana.
  var.pp.   C4.20 (Special report, E) Ghana Central Bur
  Stat 1960 GH
Ghana Central Bureau of Statistics.
  Reports of 1960 population census. V - General report
  410pp.   C8.40 Ghana Central Bur Stat 1960 GH
Ghana Central Bureau of Statistics.
  Reports of 1960 population census. VI - The post
  enumeration survey: statistical summary 491pp.   C7.00
  Ghana Central Bur Stat 1960 GH
Ghana Central Bureau of Statistics.
  Reports of 1970 population census: census data for
  socio-economic regions. (Special report, C) Ghana
  Central Bur Stat 1970 GH
Ghana Central Bureau of Statistics.
  Reports of 1970 population census: Central Region.
  158pp.   C1.20 (Special reports, D) Ghana Central Bur
  Stat 1970 GH
Ghana Central Bureau of Statistics.
  Reports of 1970 population census: detailed demographic
  characteristics. v. 3 Ghana Central Bur Stat 1970 GH
Ghana Central Bureau of Statistics.
  Reports of 1970 population census: detailed economic
  characteristics. v. 4 Ghana Central Bur Stat 1970 GH
Ghana Central Bureau of Statistics.
  Reports of 1970 population census: general report. v. 5
  Ghana Central Bur Stat 1970 GH
Ghana Central Bureau of Statistics.
  Reports of 1970 population census: Greater Accra and
  Eastern Regions. 213pp.   C1.20 (Special reports, D)
  Ghana Central Bur Stat 1970 GH

Ghana Central Bureau of Statistics.
Reports of 1970 population census: Northern and Upper Regions. 197pp. C1.20 (Special reports, D) Ghana Central Bur Stat 1970 GH

Ghana Central Bureau of Statistics.
Reports of 1970 population census: Socio-economic indices of enumeration areas. (Special report, B) Ghana Central Bur Stat 1970 GH

Ghana Central Bureau of Statistics.
Reports of 1970 population census: statistics of large towns. (Special reports, A) Ghana Central Bur Stat 1970 GH

Ghana Central Bureau of Statistics.
Reports of 1970 population census: statistics of localities and enumeration areas. v. 2 971pp. C10.00 Ghana Central Bur Stat 1970 GH

Ghana Central Bureau of Statistics.
Reports of 1970 population census: the 1971 supplementary enquiry - a statistical summary. 6 Ghana Central Bur Stat 1970 GH

Ghana Central Bureau of Statistics.
Reports of 1970 population census: the gazetteer. Ghana Central Bur Stat 1970 GH

Ghana Central Bureau of Statistics.
Reports of 1970 population census: Volta region. 197pp. C1.20 (Special report, D) Ghana Central Bur Stat 1970 GH

Ghana Central Bureau of Statistics.
Reports of 1970 population census: Western Region. 183pp. C1.20 (Special reports, D) Ghana Central Bur Stat 1970 GH

Ghana Central Bureau of Statistics.
Sources and methods of estimation of national income at current prices in Ghana. 117pp. C4.00 Ghana Central Bur Stat 1971 GH

Ghana Central Bureau of Statistics.
Statistical handbook (annual) 238pp. C1.75 Ghana Central Bur Stat 1969 GH

Ghana Central Bureau of Statistics.
Statistical reports: civil aviation (annual) 35pp. 60pes. (Statistical report, II) Ghana Central Bur Stat 1969 GH

Ghana Central Bureau of Statistics.
Statistical yearbook, 1969-70. 193pp. maps. C2.10 (£1.05) Ghana Central Bur Stat 1973 GH

Ghana Library Board.
Ghana Library Board: annual report, 1971/72. 46pp. ex. only Ghana Lib Board 1973 GH

Ghana Library Board.
Ghana national bibliography 1965. 51pp. C1.50 (40p.) Ghana Lib Board 1968 GH

Ghana Library Board.
Ghana national bibliography 1966. 80pp. c1.50 (40p.) Ghana Lib Board 1968 GH

Ghana Library Board.
Ghana national bibliography 1967. 100pp. C1.50 (40p.) Ghana Lib Board 1969 GH

Ghana Library Board.
Ghana national bibliography 1968. 87pp. C1.50 (40p.) Ghana Lib Board 1970 GH

Ghana Library Board.
Ghana national bibliography 1969. 74pp. C1.50 (40p.) Ghana Lib Board 1971 GH

Ghana Library Board.
Ghana national bibliography 1970. 86pp. C1.50 (40p.) Ghana Lib Board 1972 GH

Ghana Library Board.
Ghana national bibliography 1971. 71pp. C4.00 ($5.00) Ghana Lib Board 1973 GH

Ghana Library Board.
Ghana national bibliography 1972. 86pp. C4.00 ($5.00) Ghana Lib Board 1974 GH

Ghana Library Board.
Ghana national bibliography 1973. 70pp. C4.00 ($5.00) Ghana Lib Board 1975 GH

Ghana Library Board. Research Library on African Affairs.
Kwame Nkrumah: a select bibliography. 69pp. C3.00 pap. ($4.00 pap.) (Special Subject Bibliography, 7) Ghana Lib Board 1976 GH

Ghana Library Board.
Silver jubilee souvenir 1950-1975. 115pp. pl. C4.00 Ghana Lib Board 1975 GH

Ghana. Ministry of Education.
New Ga spelling. 84pp. 75pes. Bur Ghana Lang 1975 GH GAA

Ghana Museums and Monuments Board.
Clay figures used in funeral ceremonies. 20pp. ill. pl. map. (50p) Ghana Museum 1974 GH

Ghana Museums and Monuments Board.
Museum handbook. 2nd ed. C2.00 (£1.00) Ghana Museums 1974 GH

Ghana Museums & Monuments Board.
Annual museum lectures (1969-1970) 67pp. 60pes. Ghana Museums GH

Ghana Museums & Monuments Board.
National museums handbook: ethnographical, historical and art collections. C1.00 Ghana Museums GH

Ghana Museums & Monuments.
Figurative art in Ghana. 30pp. photos. 60pes. (Occas. pap. 1-5) Ghana Museums GH

Ghana Publishing Corporation.
Matriculation addresses delivered by Vice-Chancellors of the University of Ghana, Legon. 56pp. 75pes. ($.75) Ghana Publ Corp 1973 GH

Ghana Publishing Corporation.
The new Cedi ready reckoner. 116pp. ill. C1.00 ($1.00) Ghana Publ Corp 1965 GH

Ghanem, I.
An outline of Islamic jurisprudence. 86pp. N3.00 ($5.00/£2.80) Inst Admin - Zaria 1975 NR

Ghartey, K.G.
Ao, m'akoma mu. [Oh, in my heart.] 2nd ed. 64pp. 90pes. Bur Ghana Lang 1975 GH FAT

Ghazi, M.F.
Le roman et la nouvelle en Tunisie. 126pp. D0.480 pap. Maison Tunis 1970 TI FRE

Gibbon, G.
Paget of Rhodesia. 164pp. ill. pl. R$7.15 (R$7.65) Books of Rhodesia 1973 RH

Gibbons.
Songs at school. See: McHarg.

Gibbs, E.D.   Ayo, E.B.
Comprehension practice for forms 3-6. 98pp. ($2.50) Ghana Publ Corp 1975 GH

Gibbs, J., ed.
Nine Malawian plays. 172pp. K2.60 (Malawian Writers series, 3) Popular Publ 1976 MW

Gibbs, P.H.   Moody, K.W.
Teaching structures in situations. 40pp. 45k Pilgrim 1967 NR

Gibran, K.
Mtume. [Prophet.] tr. fr. English J.R. Kotta. 58pp. T.shs.5.00 Tanz Publ House 1971 TZ SWA

Gibson, J. T. R.   Comrie, R. G.
South African mercantile and company law. 3rd rev. ed. 600pp. cl. & pap. R17.50 pap. R21.00 cl. Juta 1975 SA

Gibson, J.T.R., ed.
Wille's principles of South African law. 7th ed. hd. & pap. R15.00 pap. R21.00 hd. Juta 1977 SA

Gibson, J.T.R.
Wille's principles of South African law. 7th ed. cl. & pap. R21.00 cl. R15.00 pap. Juta 1977 SA

Gicheru, H.B.N.
Parliamentary practice in Kenya. 256pp. pl. maps.
K.shs.25.00 Transafrica 1975 KE

Gicheru, M.
Ivory merchant. 96pp. K.shs.9.50 pap. Heinemann
Educ - Nair 1976 KE

Gichuru, S.
The fly whisk. 72pp. ill. K.shs2.00 ($1.00) EAPH
1967 KE

Gicoru, N. Hirst, T.
Take me home. 20pp. ill. K.shs.4.50 (Lioncub
books, 5) EAPH 1974 KE

Giddy, C.
Cycads of South Africa. ill. maps. R12.50 Purnell
1976 SA

Gideiri, Y.B.A.
A dissection guide for the common African toad (Bufo
regularis) 50pp. ill. 15 pt. ($1.00) Khartoum UP
1971 SJ

Gildenhuys, J.G., et al.
Naledi ya Masa. pt.1. 23pp. ill. 60c. Nasou 1976
SA SOS

Giles, P.H.
A record of stored product insects associated with
Northern Nigerian foodstuffs. 7pp. 20k (Samaru
misc. pap., 8) Inst Agric Res-Zaria 1965 NR

Gill, L.
A first guide to South African birds. ill. col. ill. R4.25
Maskew Miller 1975 SA

Gilles, H.M.
Akufo: an environmental study of a Nigerian village
community. 80pp. N1.00 Ibadan UP 1965 NR

Gillham, D.G.
The present state of the humanities in South Africa.
14pp. 30c. (U.C.T. Inaugural lec. New series, 12)
Univ Cape Town Lib 1972 SA

Gillomee, J.H.
Morphological and taxonomic studies on the males of
three species of the Genus pseudococcus (Hemiptera:
Coccoidea) 53pp. ill. R1.00 (A v.36 no.6) Univ
Stellenbosch, Lib 1961 SA

Gingrich, V.L.
The church. 152pp. K.shs7.50 Evangel 1971 KE

Gingyera-Pinycwa, A.G.G.
Issues in pre-independence politics in Uganda. 237pp.
K.shs.37.60 ($7.60/£3.60) EALB 1976 KE

Ginindza, T.T.
Siswati sami series: Imbasha. [Language text for primary
schools.] 48pp. ill. R1.05 Longman - SA 1976 SA
SIS

Ginindza, T.T.
Siswati sami series: Ingungu. [Language text for primary
schools.] 48pp. ill. R1.05 Longman - SA 1975 SA
SIS

Ginindza, T.T.
Siswati sami series: Lifa. [Language text for primary
schools.] 64pp. ill. R1.05 Longman - SA 1975 SA
SIS

Ginindza, T.T.
Siswati sami series: Sancoti. [Language text for primary
schools.] 48pp. ill. R1.05 Longman - SA 1976 SA
SIS

Ginn, P.
Bird safari. 64pp. col. ill. hd. & pap. R$11.25 cl.
R$4.85 pap. Longman - Rhod 1974 RH

Ginn, P.
Birds afield. 140pp. col. ill. R$2.75 Longman - Rhod
1973 RH

Ginn, P.
Birds of the highveld. 160pp. col. ill. R$2.75
Longman - Rhod 1972 RH

Ginn, P.
Birds of the lowveld. 103pp. col. ill. R$3.25
Longman - Rhod 1974 RH

Ginn, P.
Birds of Zimbabwe. 32pp. col. ill. 75c Longman
Rhod 1973 RH

Giorgis, K.W.
African Bibliographic Centre. See: Jordan, R.T.

Girard, J.
Dynamique de la société ouobé. Loi des masques et
coutume. 376pp. ill. pl. CFA4000 (Mémoires de
l'IFAN, 78) IFAN 1968 SG FRE

Girard, J.
Genèse du pouvoir charismatique en basse Casamance
(Sénégal) 372pp. photo. CFA2800 (Initiations et
Etudes Africaines, 27) IFAN 1969 SG FRE

Girardin, N.
Plantes ligneuses du Parc National de l'Akagera et des
savanes orientàles du Rwanda. Clés pratique de
determination scientifique. See: Troupin, G.

Giraud, P.
Les roches basiques de la région d'Andriamena et leur
minéralisation chromifère. 95pp. pl. hd. FMG900 cl.
(F18.00 cl.) (Annales Géologiques de Madagascar, 27)
Service Geol - Mad 1960 MG FRE

Giraudon, R.
La série basique de la Rianila et son cadre géologique
dans la région de Tamatave. 130pp. pl. photos.
FMG1361 (F27.22) Service Geol - Mad 1960 MG FRE

Gitelson, S.A.
Multilateral aid for national development. 208pp.
K.shs.35.00 ($7.00/£2.90) EALB 1975 KE

Gitene, N.
Mami hingurira. [Mummy open the door for me] 24pp.
ill. Njogu 1970 KE KIK

Gitene, N.
Muhura umbanaga wi thegi. 64pp. ill. K.shs.5.00
Njogu 1973 KE KIK

Gitene; N.
Wigirie mathori. [Wipe away your tears] 58pp.
K.shs.4.00 Njogu 1970 KE KIK

Gitene, N.
Wuui mwendwa. [Oh, darling] 48pp. ill. K.shs.3.60
Njogu 1973 KE KIK

Givon, T.
The Si-Luyana language: a preliminary linguistic
description. 111pp. K1.00 (60p.) (Communications,
6) Inst Soc Res - Zam 1970 ZA

Glasker, K.
The United States and world strategy. 19pp. 30c. SA
Inst Int Affairs 1971 SA

Glass, H.M.
South African policy towards Basutoland. 36pp. R1.00
(Research paper, 2) SA Inst Int Affairs 1966 SA

Glass, Y.
Industrial man in Southern Africa. 40c. (Isma paps., 1)
Inst Study of Man 1961 SA

Glasser, L.
Order into chaos. ex. only (Inaugural lec.) Rhodes
Univ Lib 1969 SA

Gledhill, J.A.
The threshold of space. ex. only (Inaugural lec.)
Rhodes Univ Lib 1956 SA

Glen, R.M.
Historia ya Ukristo. Kitabu cha 3. [Church history. Book
3.] 268pp. ill. T.shs.16.50 Central Tanganyika 1975
TZ SWA

Glen, R.M.
Historia ya Ukristo. Ramani na nyakati zake. [Church
history atlas.] 62pp. maps. T.shs.13.00 Central
Tanganyika 1971 TZ SWA

Glick, R.
Language in Uganda. See: Ladefoged, P.

Author Index

Glover, M.
Rorke's drift.   R6.75   Purnell 1976 SA

Gluckman, M.
Analysis of a social situation in modern Zululand.   82pp.
K1.30   (65p.)   (Rhodes-Livingstone paps., 28)   Inst Soc
Res - Zam 1958 ZA

Gluckman, M.
An analysis of the sociological theories of Bronislaw
Malinowski.   28pp.   60n.   (30p.)   (Rhodes-Livingstone
paps., 16)   Inst Soc Res - Zam 1949 ZA

Gluckman, M.
Economy of the Central Barotse Plain.   130pp.   K2.50
(£1.25)   (Rhodes-Livingstone paps., 7)   Inst Soc Res -
Zam 1941 ZA

Gluckman, M., ed.
Seven tribes of British Central Africa.   See: Colson, E.,
ed.

Gluckman, M.
Essays on Lozi land and royal property.   99pp.   K2.10
(£1.05)   (Rhodes-Livingstone paps., 10)   Inst Soc Res -
Zam 1943 ZA

Gluckman, M.
The ideas in Barotse jurisprudence.   301pp.   pap. & hd.
K5.50 hd.   K3.20 pap.   (£2.76 hd.)   (£1.56 pap.)
Inst Afr Stud - Lusaka 1965 ZA

Gluckman, M.
The judicial process among the Barotse of Northern
Rhodesia.   383pp.   ill. photos maps.   hd.   K4.80
(£2.40/$7.50)   Inst Afr Stud - Lusaka 1954 ZA

Gobett.
Discovering world geography.   Grade 7.
See: Moorehouse, F.

Gobett.
Discovering world geography.   Teacher's grade 7.
See: Moorehouse, F.

Goble, G.I.   McPherson, I.H.
Your cookery book.   2nd rev. ed.   258pp.   R1.05
Shuter 1949 SA

Godawa, T.O.
The production of tops from seedy Cape mohair with and
without carbonising.   See: Turpie, D.W.F.

Goddard, A.D.   Norman, D.W.   Fine, J.C.
A socio-economic study of three villages in the Sokoto
close-settled zone.   maps.   N1.00   (Samaru misc.
pap., 34)   Inst Agric Res - Zaria 1971 NR

Goddard, A.D.   Norman, D.W.   Fine, J.C.
A socio-economic study of three villages in the Sokoto
close-settled zone: land and people.   82pp.   maps.
N1.00   (Samaru misc. pap., 33)   Inst Agric Res - Zaria
1971 NR

Godfrey, R.
Bird-lore of the Eastern Cape province.   134pp.   R1.00
(Bantu stud. monog., 2)   Witwatersrand UP 1941 SA

Godlonton, R.
A narrative of the irruption of the Kaffir hordes, 1834-1835
[Reprint of 1835 edition].   595pp.   cl.   R9.00   (Africana
collectanea, 13)   Struik 1965 SA

Godman, A.
Chemistry: a New Certificate approach.   See: Bajah, S.

Godman, A.
New certificate physics.   See: Folivi, L.E.

Godowa, T.O.   Turpie, D.W.F.
The use of faulty wools in blends.   12pp.   R2.50
(SAWTRI Technical Reports, 292)   SAWTRI 1976 SA

Godsell, G.
Cross-cultural differences in cognitive flexibility.   pt. 1:
theory and hypotheses for proposed research.   41pp.
(CSIR Special Report, PERS 242)   CSIR 1976 SA

Goedhals, J.B.
The art of communication.   See: Beeton, D.R.

Goedhuys, D.W.
Money and banking.   R10.50   McGraw-Hill SA 1975
SA

Goetzsche, E.C.
Father of a city.   216pp. cl.   R3.50   Shuter 1967 SA

Goldberg, S.
Infant care, stimulation and sensory-motor development in
a high density urban area of Lusaka.   18pp.   free
(Human Development Research Unit Report, 15)   Dept
Psychology - Zam 1970 ZA

Goldberg, S.
Infant development in Zambia: measuring maternal
behavior.   21pp.   free   (Human Development Research
Unit Report, 13)   Dept Psychology - Zam 1970 ZA

Goldblatt, D.
Some Afrikaners photographed.   176pp. pl.   R25.00
Struik 1975 SA

Goldblatt, I.
The history of South West Africa from the beginning of the
nineteenth century.   R9.75   Juta 1971 SA

Goldie, F.
Ostrich country.   col. photos. ill.   R2.00   Bulpin 1968
SA

Goldin, B.   Gelfand, M.
African law and custom in Rhodesia.   R17.50 cl.
R12.50 pap.   Juta 1976 SA

Goldner, M., et al.
Junior geography for standard 7.   280pp. ill. pl. maps.
R3.25   Nasou 1974 SA

Goldschmidt, M., ed.
Government and politics in Kenya.   See: Gertzel, C., ed.

Goldsmid, J.M.
Ternidens deminutus - a parasitological enigma in
Rhodesia.   20pp.   50c pap.   (Fac. of Medicine, Univ.
of Rhodesia, Research Lec. Series, 4)   Univ Rhodesia Lib
1971 RH

Goldstein, G., comp.
Oswald Mbuyseni Mtshali, South African poet.   31pp.
R2.10   Dept Bibliog, Lib & Typo 1974 SA

Golvin, L.
L'artisanat en Afrique du nord.   235pp. pl.   D2.340
(Série II, Géographie, 2)   Univ Tunis 1957 TI FRE

Gombe, S.U.
Rariya Matatar Salla.   [A sieve for purifying prayers]   1,
2 bks.   27pp.   40k   Northern Nig 1969 NR HAU

Gombe, S.U.
Rariya Matatar Salla.   [A sieve for purifying prayers]   2,
2 bks.   33pp.   50k   Northern Nig 1971 NR HAU

Gomes Eanes de Zurara.
Chronique de Guinée.   Tr. fr. Portuguese L. Bourdon.
301pp. maps.   CFA2800   (Mémoires de l'IFAN, 60)
IFAN 1960 SG FRE

Gonin, A.A., et al.
Modern graded mathematics for standards 9-10.   666pp.
ill.   R6.85   Nasou 1975 SA

Gonin, C.P.
The utilization of sugar cane bagasse in the pulp and
paper industry: sulphate pulping.   See: Venter, J.S.M.

Gonin, C.P.
World survey on bagasse pulping.   14pp.   R5.00
(CSIR Special Report, HOUT 82)   CSIR 1974 SA

Gonin, C.R.
A proposed method to evaluate sugar-cane bagasse for
useful fibre.   See: Burger, R.

Gonin, H.L.
English-Afrikaans legal dictionary.   See: Hiemstra, V.G.

Gonin, H.T.
Mortality trends in South Africa.   61pp. ill.   75c.
(R1.25)   Univ South Africa 1960 SA

Gontier, A.
Grammaire gourmantché.   See: Chantoux, A.

Gonzales, J.
Emmanuel: Mfumu Yesu kele na beto.   [Emmanuel: the
Lord Jesus is with us.]   32pp.   15k   CEDI 1974 ZR KIT

Gonzales, J.
Mateyo ya Yesu. [Jesus our Lord.] 31pp. 15k CEDI 1974 ZR LIN

Gonzales, J.
Yesu weti vova. [Jesus our Lord.] 30pp. 15k CEDI 1974 ZR KIO

Goodall, A.A.
Economics and development: an introduction. See: Livingstone, I.

Goodall, B.B.
Revolutionary warfare in Southeast Asia. 103pp. R1.00 (Research paper, 1) SA Inst Int Affairs 1966 SA

Goodfellow, C.F.
Great Britain and South African Confederation, 1870-1881. 324pp. map. R7.50 OUP-SA 1966 SA

Goodman, I.
Judges I have known. 180pp. pl. cl. R6.00 Legal & Financial 1969 SA

Goosen, J.C., ed.
South Africa's navy - a history of the first fifty years. 228pp. photos. hd. R9.00 Flesch 1973 SA

Gordimer, N.
The black interpreters. Notes on African writing. 76pp. R2.00 ($2.40/£1.25) Ravan 1973 SA

Gordon-Brown, A.
Pictorial Africana. 264pp. ill. pl. col. pl. cl. R25.00 ($45.00) Balkema 1975 SA

Gordon-Brown, A.
Pictorial Africana. 264pp. col. pl. cl. R37.50 cl. (Dfl.112.50/$45.00/£21.50 cl.) Balkema 1975 SA

Gordon, G.   Getz, W.S.
The South African law of insurance. 2nd ed. R26.00 Juta 1970 SA

Gordon, I.
World health manpower shortage, 1971-2000. 136pp. R10.00 Butterworths 1971 SA

Gordon, L.
Lesotho. 62pp. R3.20 Dept Bibliog, Lib & Typo 1970 SA

Gordon, M.
Trade unionism in South Africa, 1952-1966. 30pp. R1.60 Dept Bibliog, Lib & Typo 1968 SA

Gordon, R.J.
Mines, masters and migrants: life in a Namibian compound. 276pp. R6.50 ($8.00/£4.25) Ravan 1977 SA

Gorman, T.P.
Language in education in Eastern Africa: papers from the first Eastern Africa conference on language and linguistics. 214pp. K.shs.14.75 OUP-Nairobi 1970 KE

Gosling, B.J.
Rehabilitation of the physically handicapped in South Africa 1950-1960. 68pp. R1.00 Univ Cape Town Lib 1965 SA

Gottneid, A.J.
Church and education in Tanzania. K.shs.40.00 ($12.00) EAPH 1976 KE

Gould, D.J.
Introduction à la théorie de l'organisation. 112pp. (Essais, 10) Ed Mont Noir 1975 ZR FRE

Gould, J.J.
Les réformés administratives au Zaire. See: Mpinga, K.

Gould T.
Répartition des effectifs des I.S.P. par option et par sexe (1975-1976). Les etudiantes universitaires de Lubumbashi. See: Nshamamba Mahano.

Gouldsbury, C.
Rhodesian rhymes. Reprint of 1932 ed. 264pp. ill. R$14.00 (Rhodesiana Reprint Library, Gold Series, 6) Books of Rhodesia 1969 RH

Gourlay, N.
A study of pictorial perception among Bantu and white primary school children in South Africa. See: Duncan, H.F.

Gouws, M.
Report of the committee for differentiated education and guidance in connection with a national system of education for handicapped pupils...etc. pt. 3, v. 5 121pp. R1.60 Human Science Res Council 1975 SA

Gower, R.H.
Mama Ardhi. [Mother Earth] K.shs.0.10 ($1.00/40p.) EALB 1953 KE SWA

Grabherr, H.
The effect of pretreatment on the critical surface tension of wool. See: Weideman, E.

Grabherr, H.
The effect of the temperature and pH of DCCA solutions on the shrinkresistance of woven wool fabrics during continuous application. See: Weideman, E.

Gracie, N.C.
Butterworths index and noter-up to the South African Law Reports, 1973-1976. R11.50 Butterworths 1977 SA

Graham, C.
The slave raid that failed. 55pp. ill. 45k OUP - Nig 1966 NR

Graham, C.K.
The history of education in Ghana. 126pp. C4.00 ($4.00) Ghana Publ Corp 1976 GH

Grandsaigne, J.D.
France-Afrique: a French course for Africa: pupil's bk. 1, 5 bks. 144pp. ill. N1.15 Macmillan 1969 NR

Grandsaigne, J.D.
France-Afrique: a French course for Africa: pupils' bk. 3, 5 bks. 192pp. ill. N1.40 Macmillan 1972 NR

Grandsaigne, J.D.
France-Afrique: a French course for Africa: pupil's bk. 5, 5 bks. 148pp. ill. N1.30 Macmillan 1970 NR

Grandsaigne, J.D.   Brachet, M.L.
France-Afrique: a French course for Africa: pupil's bk. bk. 4, 5 bks. 208pp. ill. N1.80 Macmillan 1975 NR FRE

Grandsaigne, J.D.
France-Afrique: a French course for Africa: work bk. 1, 2 bks. 62pp. ill. 90k Macmillan 1969 NR

Grandsaigne, J.D.
France-Afrique: a French course for Africa: work bk. 2, 2 bks. 160pp. ill. 90k Macmillan 1970 NR

Granger, V.L.
The engineer and tomorrow. 16pp. 30c. (U.C.T. Inaugural lec. New series, 11) Univ Cape Town Lib 1972 SA

Grant, E.W.
Malungana Nebhayibheli. [The Bible: its meaning and purpose.] 146pp. R1.00 Methodist 1974 SA ZUL

Grant, J.
Information for industry: a study in communications. (CSIR research reports, 229) CSIR 1964 SA

Grant, J.P.
South Africa: the next fifteen years: a microcosm of world problems. See: Oppenheimer, H.F.

Grant-Whyte, H.
Between life and death. 135pp. photos. cl. R6.45 Shuter 1976 SA

Graser, R., ed.
Crime and punishment in South Africa. See: Midgley, J., ed.

Grasser, H.S.P.
A monograph on the general theory of second order parameter-invariant problems in the calculus of variations. 86pp. R2.40 (R3.40) Univ South Africa 1967 SA

Gray, J.
The British in Mombasa, 1824-1826. 216pp. ill. K.shs.9.20 ($2.75/£1.10) EALB 1957 KE

Author Index

Gray, S., ed.
On the edge of the world. Southern African stories of the seventies. 196pp. R3.50 Donker 1974 SA

Gray, S., ed.
A world of their own; Southern African poets of the seventies. 176pp. R3.75 pap. Donker 1976 SA

Gray, S.
It's about time. 32pp. R1.80 (Mantis Poets, 4) Philip 1974 SA

Gray, S.
Local colour. 128pp. ill. cl. R4.95 ($2.40/£1.25) Ravan 1975 SA

Gray, S.
Writers' territory English. 240pp. R3.60 Longman - SA 1974 SA

Grayner, J.B.
Akweesi egu nananom pow. [Akweesi has disgraced the fetish grove.] 2nd ed. 108pp. ill. 60pes. Bur Ghana Lang 1974 GA FAT

Greaves, M., et al.
Nigerian personal authors, and the application of the Anglo-American cataloguing rules 1967. A guide for cataloguers. 9pp. 30k Nigerian Lib Assoc 1974 NR

Greaves, M.A.
Librarianship: a faceted classification scheme as a teaching aid. 22pp. 50k (Inst. of Librarianship, occas. pap., 3) Inst Lib-Ib 1970 NR

Green, E.
African tribal sculpture. 64pp. 90c. Univ Cape Town Lib 1967 SA

Green, E.G.
Raiders and rebels in South Africa. [Reprint of ed. 1898]. 209pp. ill. cl. R$10.10 cl. (Rhodesiana Reprint Library, Silver Series, 9) Books of Rhodesia 1976 RH

Green, H.A.
Urban conditions in Nigeria: a preliminary bibliography. 31pp. 50k pap. (35p/$1.00) Inst Admin - Zaria 1972 NR

Green, I.
The effect of the population explosion on Jamaica's international relations. 85pp. R1.00 (Research paper, 3) SA Inst Int Affairs 1966 SA

Green, L.
Population model report no. 3. N2.50 ($3.75) (N.I.S.E.R. research report, 9) NISER NR

Green, L.P.   Fair, T.J.D.
Development in Africa: a study in regional analysis with special reference to Southern Africa. 203pp. maps. cl. R8.00 Witwatersrand UP 1969 SA

Green, L.P.
A history of local government in South Africa. R2.50 Juta 1957 SA

Green, M.M.
Igbo folk stories. See: Onwuamaegbu, M.O.

Green, M.M.
Igbo language course. 1, 3 bks. See: Igwe, G.E.

Green, M.M.
Igbo language course. 2, 3 bks. See: Igwe, G.E.

Green, M.M.
Igbo language course. 3, 3 bks. See: Igwe, G.E.

Green, M.M.
A short Igbo grammar. See: Igwe, G.E.

Green, M.V.
Cockling in fully-fashioned knitwear, part I: a preliminary report. See: Robinson, G.A.

Green, M.V.
Cockling in fully-fashioned knitwear, part II: an investigation into the effect of various fibre, yarn and fabric properties on cockling. See: Robinson, G.A.

Green, M.V.
A proposed method of assessing the knittability of a yarn. See: Robinson, G.A.

Green, R., ed.
Just a moment God: an anthology of prose and verse from East Africa. 212pp. ill. K.shs11.00 ($3.00/£1.50) EALB 1970 KE

Green, R.H.
International economic system and development. Some limitations of a special case. 16pp. T.shs.12.00 ($3.00) (Research pap., 70.4) Econ Res Bur - Tanz 1970 TZ

Green, R.H.
Toward Ujamaa and Kujitegemea: income distribution and absolute poverty eradication aspects of the Tanzania transition to socialism. T.shs.12.00 ($3.00) (Research pap., 74.11) Econ Res Bur - Tanz 1975 TZ

Green, T.
The bystander. 28pp. ill. K.shs2.80 ($1.00) EAPH 1971 KE

Green-Thompson, A.L.
Exploring life. pt.7 See: Thienel, A.

Green-Thomson, A.
Exploring life. pt. 2. See: Thienel, A.

Green, T.L.
Selection, teaching and examining in universities. 24pp. C1.00 ($1.00/50p.) (Inaugural lecture) Ghana UP 1971 GH

Greenfield, M., ed.
Marine ecology field course handbook. 124pp. T.shs.5.00 Dept Zool. - Dar 1969 TZ

Greenwood, H.
Advanced accounting for South African students. 5th ed. R12.50 Juta 1974 SA

Greenwood, M.J.
Angola. 52pp. 80c. Univ Cape Town Lib 1967 SA

Gregg, M.
The story of a simple man. 78pp. ill. K1.20 Neczam 1973 ZA

Grégoire, H.C.
Cours et exercices de prononciation française. Prosadie. 129pp. CFA500 (Enseignement du français, 34) Inst Ling Appliquée 1972 IV FRE

Gregoire, H.C.
Etude acoustique du système vocalique du Bété (région de Guibéroua) 220pp. CFA1,100 (Linquistique Africaine, 37) Inst Ling Appliquée 1972 IV FRE

Gregoire, H.C.
Vocabulaire essentiel de l'enseignement primaire, 5ème et 6ème années. See: Canu, A.

Gregory, R.M.
The teaching of homecraft. 95pp. ill. K.shs.4.50 ($2.00/80p.) EALB 1958 KE

Greindl, L.
Initiation à la méthode historique. 107pp. (Essais, 5) Ed Mont Noir 1973 ZR FRE

Greindl, L.
Initiation à la méthode historique. 65k Ed Mont Noir 1973 ZR FRE

Greindl, L.
Introduction à l'histoire de l'Afrique Noire. 154pp. (Essais, 6) Ed Mont Noir 1974 ZR FRE

Greindl, L.
Introduction à l'histoire de l'Afrique noire. Des origines à 1800. v. 1 151pp. maps. (Essais, 7) Ed Mont Noir 1974 ZR FRE

Grelier
Recherche des principales interférences dans les systèmes verbaux de l'anglais, du wolof et du français. 179pp. CFA625 pap. (C.L.A.D. Etude, 31) CLAD 1969 SG FRE

Grelier, S.
Essai de classification des fautes d'anglais d'éléves wolof avec exercise d'accompagnement. 35pp. CFA125 (C.L.A.D. Etude, 19 bis) CLAD 1966 SG FRE

Grelier, S.
Essai de comparaison morpho-syntaxique de l'anglais du wolof et du français (le nominal) 142pp. CFA375 (C.L.A.D. Etude, 19) CLAD 1966 SG FRE

Greshoff, C.J.
An introduction to the novels of André Malraux. 190pp. R7.50 ($11.00) Balkema 1975 SA

Greyling, J.J.C. Miskin, J.
Bibliography of Indians in South Africa. 51pp. free Univ Durban-Westville 1976 SA

Greyling, J.J.C.
The squatters' market. 27pp. free Univ Durban-Westville 1976 SA

Grice, D.C.
The conflicting "realities" of the South African scene. 15pp. 45c ($1.30) SA Inst of Race Relations 1974 SA

Griesel, P.O. de Waal, J.S. Levinsohn, S.
Mathematics 6 answers/Wiskune 6 antwoorde. [Bilingual in English and Afrikaans.]. 16pp. 75c pap. Longman - SA 1976 SA

Griesel, P.O. de Waal, J.S. Levinsohn, S.
Mathematics 7. 148pp. ill. R2.95 Longman - SA 1976 SA

Grieve, D.W.
Grammatical structure and its teaching. See: Boadi, L.

Griffiths, I.
Organisation of university research in a developing country. T.shs.1.00 (Inaugural lecture, 4) Univ Dar es Salaam 1969 TZ

Grimsdell, J.J. Bell, R.H.V.
Black lechwe research project: final report, ecology of the black lechwe in the Bangweulu Basin of Zambia. 175pp. ill. pl. maps. (Animal productivity research report, 1) Nat Council Scient Res - Zam 1975 ZA

Grimwood, E.F.
Imani na matendo. [Faith and actions] 48pp. ill. K.shs.1.75 OUP-Nairobi 1965 KE SWA

Grivainis, I.
Material published after 1925 on the Great Trek until 1854. 63pp. 90c. Univ Cape Town Lib 1967 SA

Grob, F.
Témoins camerounais de l'évangile. 68pp. CFA280 CLE 1967 CM FRE

Grobbelaar, C.S.
The distribution of and correlation between eye, hair and skin colour in male students at the University of Stellenbosch. 13pp. 15c. (A v. 28, no. 1) Univ Stellenbosch, Lib 1952 SA

Grobbelaar, C.S. Billingham, P.A.
NBRI introductory guide to damp in buildings. 28pp. 75c. (CSIR Building Guide, 5) CSIR 1975 SA

Grobler, A.
Determination of the bundle tenacity and elongation of wool fibres in yarn form. See: Hunter, L.

Groenewald, C.J., ed.
Occupational and social change among Coloured people in South Africa. Proceedings of a workshop of the Centre for Intergroup Studies at the University of Cape Town. See: van der Merwe, H.W., ed.

Groenewald, D.C.
The Chinese community in South Africa, phase 1. Background and attitudes of the white population towards the Chinese minority group. 103pp. R2.55 Human Science Res Council 1976 SA

Groenewald, P.W.J.
Learn to speak Afrikaans. 146pp. 75c. Shuter 1943 SA

Gross, F.A.
Who hangs the hangman? R2.75 Juta 1970 SA

Gross, M.E.
The fairy tales of Hans Christian Andersen and the brothers Grimm. 104pp. R5.30 Dept Bibliog, Lib & Typo 1969 SA

Gross, P.H.
Legal aid and its management. 335pp. cl. & pap. R25.00 cl. R15.00 pap. Juta 1976 SA

Grosse, M.
Recherches géomorphologiques dans la peninsule du Cap Bon. (Tunisie) 358pp. ill. D4.800 (Série III, Mémoires du Centre d'Etudes Humaines, 10) Univ Tunis 1969 TI FRE

Grossert, J.W.
Art and crafts for Africans. ill. R1.00 Shuter 1954 SA

Grossert, J.W.
Art and crafts in education. 2 v. 950pp. ill. R15.00 Shuter 1970 SA

Groupe d'Etudes et de Recherches.
La Palestine en question. v. 1 526pp. maps. DA7.00 SNED 1971 AE FRE

Groupe d'Etudes et de Recherches.
La Palestine en question. v. 2 430pp. maps. DA7.00 SNED 1971 AE FRE

Grove, A.P., ed. Harvey, C.J.D., ed.
Afrikaans poems with English translations. 334pp. R2.40 OUP-SA 1969 SA

Grove, D. Huszar, L.
The towns of Ghana. 99pp. maps. hd. C4.00 (£2.00/$4.00) Ghana UP 1964 GH

Grundmann, H.E.
Framework for regional allocation of industries. 27pp. T.shs12.00 ($3.00) (Research pap., 70.17) Econ Res Bur - Tanz 1970 TZ

Grundmann, H.E.
Some implications of the concept of effective protection. 13pp. T.shs.12.00 ($3.00) (Research pap., 68.19) Econ Res Bur - Tanz 1968 TZ

Grundmann, H.E.
Towards a more rational protection policy. T.shs.12.00 ($3.00) (Research pap., 69.1) Econ Res Bur - Tanz 1969 TZ

Grundy, G.M.F., ed. Edwards, S., ed.
IAR/EPID cooperative research programme, Chencha: progress report for the period April 1974 to March 1975. 24pp. ex. only. Inst Agric Res - Addis 1976 ET

Grundy, K.W.
Conflicting images of the military in Africa. 57pp. K.shs4.00 ($2.00) EAPH 1968 KE

Guadagni, M.
Ethiopian labour law handbook. 166pp. Eth.$3.00 Bible Churchmen Miss Soc 1972 ET

Gudumbagana, K., ed.
Demain la promotion. (Essai) 102pp. 65k Presses Africaines 1975 ZR FRE

Guellouz, S.
La vie simple. 94pp. D0.500 Maison Tunis 1975 TI FRE

Guenane, D.
Les relations franco-allemandes et les affaires marocaines de 1901 à 1911. 334pp. DA20.00 SNED 1975 AE FRE

Guendouz, N.
Amal. 96pp. DA4.00 SNED 1968 AE FRE

Guendouz, N.
La corde. 72pp. DA4.00 SNED 1974 AE FRE

Guermeur, P.
Diatomées de l'A.O.F. (Première liste: Senegal) 137pp. pl. CFA600 (Catalogues et Documents, 12) IFAN 1954 SG FRE

Guerra de Macedo, N.
Rapport de la mission de reconnaissance géomorphologique de la vallee moyenne du Niger. See: Tricart, J.

Guerry, V.
La vie quotidienne dans un village baoulé. 3rd ed. 151pp. CFA700 INADES 1975 IC FRE

Guevara, E.C.
Journal de Bolivie. 156pp. DA6.00 SNED 1968 AE FRE

Guèye, Y.
Les exilés de Goumel. 64pp. CFA600 pap. Nouv Ed Afric 1975 SG FRE

Guèye, Y.
A l'orée du Sahel. 136pp. CFA600 Nouv Ed Afric 1975 SG FRE

Guèye, Y.
Saheliennes. 22pp. CFA300 Nouv Ed Afric 1975 SG FRE

Guèye, Y.
Saheliennes. 24pp. CFA300 Nouv Ed Afric 1975 SG FRE

Gugler, J., ed.
Urban growth in subsaharan Africa. 63pp. U.shs6.00 (M.I.S.R. Nkanga ed., 6) Mak Inst Soc Res 1970 UG

Guilj, J.
Aethiopia inferior vel exterior 1635. See: Blaeu, J.

Guillaume, H.
Les nomades interrompus, introduction à l'étude du canton twareg de l'Imanan. 145pp. maps photos. CFA1250 (F25.00) (Etudes Nigeriennes, 35) Inst Rech Sci Hum 1974 NG FRE

Guite, H.
One man's classics. 16pp. Free Univ Rhodesia Lib 1965 RH

Guite, H.R.
What kind of classics? 27pp. 30c Univ Rhodesia Lib 1965 RH

Gulleth, M. Olambo, L. D.
Experiments with the Freire method of teaching literacy. 53pp. T.shs.5.30 (Studies in Adult Education, 8) Inst Adult Educ - Dar 1973 TZ

Gulleth, M.I.
A comparative study of Aluminium Africa Company and Tanzania Cigarettes Company. 37pp. T.shs.5.00 (Studies in Adult Education, 25) Inst Adult Educ - Dar 1976 TZ

Guma, S.M.
Dikoma. [Traditional poems] 50c. Shuter 1967 SA SOS

Guma, S.M.
The form, content and technique of traditional literature in Southern Sotho. R3.50 Van Schaik SA

Guma, S.M.
Likoma. [Traditional poems] 45c. Shuter 1967 SA SOS

Guma, S.M.
Likoma. [Traditional poems] 45c. Shuter 1967 SA ZUL

Guma, S.M.
Morena Mohlomi mor'a Monyane. [King Mohlomi, son of Monyane] 140pp. 85c. Shuter 1960 SA SOS

Guma, S.M.
Outline structure of Southern Sotho. 260pp. R1.75 Shuter 1971 SA

Guma, S.M.
Tshehlana tseo tsa Basia. [The beauties of the Basia tribe] 101pp. 47c. Shuter 1962 SA SOS

Gurr, A., ed.
Black aesthetics. Papers from a colloquium held at the University of Nairobi, June 1971. See: Zirimu, P., ed.

Gurzynski, Z.S.
Science, sense and nonsense in economics. 16pp. 30c. (U.C.T. Inaugural lec. New series, 4) Univ Cape Town Lib 1970 SA

Gusimana, B.
Dictionnaire Pende-Français. 236pp. (DM29.00) (CEEBA. série III, Travaux linguistiques, 1) CEEBA 1972 ZR FRE

Gusten, R.
Studies in the staple food economy of Western Nigeria. 304pp. maps. N8.40 ($12.00) NISER NR

Gutkind, A.E.
Supplement to linguistic bibliography. U.shs3.50 (M.I.S.R. linguistic stud., 2a) Mak Inst Soc Res 1958 UG

Gutkind, P.J.
Townsmen in the making. See: Southall, A.W.

Gutmann, D.H.
Through other eyes. 38pp. 30n. Neczam 1974 ZA

Gutsche, T.
The changing social pattern of Johannesburg. 40c. (Isma paps., 24) Inst Study of Man 1967 SA

Gutsche, T., comp.
Index to Some South African Recollections by Mrs. Lionel Philips. gratis Johannesburg Public Lib 1964 SA

Gutsche, T., comp.
Philips, 1820 Settler - His Letters, ed. by Arthur Keppel-Jone. Index. gratis Johannesburg Public Lib 1961 SA

Guy, H.A.
The church in the New Testament. 160pp. N1.90 Macmillan 1968 NR

Guyot, A. Wisselmann, R.
Une expérience de télévision scolaire au Sénégal. 130pp. CFA375 (C.L.A.D. Étude, 55) CLAD 1974 SG FRE

Gwala, M.P.
Black review, 1973. Annual survey of events and trends in the Black community in South Africa. 196pp. R3.00 Black Comm Prog 1974 SA

Gwala, M.P.
Jol'iinkomo. 72pp. R2.50 Donker 1977 SA

Gwam, L.O., comp.
Serials in print in Nigeria, 1968. 18pp. N1.00 (N3.00) (National Library pubs, 15) Nat Lib-Nig 1969 NR

Gwan, L.C. Taiwo, C.O.
Henry Carr: lectures and speeches. 79pp. hd. N1.75 OUP - Nig 1969 NR

Gwarzo, M.A., ed.
Proceedings of the meeting of Agricultural engineers, Zaria, 4-5 September, 1973. See: Cromer, C.A., ed.

Gwass, G.C.K.
Kumbukumbu za vita vya maji maji 1905-07. [Swahili history] 40pp. K.shs.2.50 ($1.00) EAPH 1967 KE SWA

Gwassa, G.C. Iliffe, J.
Records of the Maji Maji rising. 1 32pp. Hist Assoc - Tanz 1969 TZ

Gwassa, G.C.K.
Records of the Maji Maji rising. See: Illife, J.

Gwellem, J.F., ed.
Cameroon yearbook 1975. 138pp. ill. maps. United Publ 1975 CM

Gwengwe, J.W.
Cinyanja cina. [Another way of speaking.] 90pp. 65n. Neczam 1973 ZA NYA

Gwynne-Jones, G. Are, L.A.
Cacao in West Africa. 146pp. pl. N3.50 OUP - Nig 1974 NR

Gyamfi, C.K.
Twelve commandments of soccer. 43pp. ill. 30pes. ($.30) Ghana Publ Corp 1971 GH

Gyane, D.   Bamfo, G.
Mr Mee escapes. 28pp. ill. 30pes. (10p.) Africa Christian 1967 GH

Gyane, D.   Bamfo, G.
Mr Mee runs a race. 28pp. ill. 30pes. (10p.) Africa Christian 1967 GH

Gyane, D.   Banfo, G.
Vers la lumière. 30pp. ill. CFA50 CPE 1969 IV FRE

Gyane, D.   Banfo, G.
Vers le but. 30pp. ill. CFA50 CPE 1969 IV FRE

Gyasi, I.K.
Ordinary level English literature. 119pp. C1.00 ($1.00) Ghana Publ Corp 1973 GH

Gyeke-Dako, K.
Economic sanctions under the United Nations. 128pp. hd. C8.50 ($8.50) Ghana Publ Corp 1974 GH

Haag, D.E.
The relation and inter-relation of oral disease to general and systemic disease: a list of references. 18pp. R1.60 Dept Bibliog, Lib & Typo 1967 SA

Haag, H.   Ruckstuhl, E.
Historia ya wokovu. [History of redemption.] 392pp. col. photos. maps. cl. T.shs.9.50 cl. ($1.50 cl.) TMP 1966 TZ SWA

Haarhoff, T.J.
Smuts the humanist: a personal reminiscence. 113pp. SA Inst Int Affairs 1970 SA

Habgood, F.
The geology of the country west of the River Shire between Chikwawa and Chiromo. 60pp. maps pl. hd. K7.00 (Geological Survey of Malawi, Bull. 14) Geol Survey - Mal 1973 MW

Habgood, F.
The geology of the Livingstonia Coalfield. See: Cooper, W.G.G.

Habgood, F.   Walshaw, R.D.   Holt, D.N.
The geology of the Thyolo area. 24pp. map. K4.00 (Geological Survey of Malawi, Bull. 22) Geol Survey - Mal 1973 MW

Habiyambere, A.
Les conditions de la croissance économique. See: Segers, J.

Haciane, M.
A quoi bon fixer le soleil. 120pp. DA6.00 pap. SNED 1974 AE FRE

Hadeja, M.
Wakokin Mu'azu Hadeja. [Poems of Mu'azu Hadeja] 54pp. 55k Northern Nig 1955 NR HAU

Hadfeild, J.
Vegetable gardening in Central Africa. 2nd. ed. 178pp. photos. hd. R5.95 Purnell 1960 SA

Hadjadji, H.
Vie et oeuvre du poète Andalou Ibn Khafadja. 255pp. DA8.00 SNED 1970 AE FRE

Hadley, A.T.
Trends in inter-library lending in South Africa: report of a survey undertaken at the State Library during the period April to September. 56pp. R4.20 (Contributions to Library Science, 12) State-Lib-SA 1969 SA

Hadley, P., ed.
Doctor to Basuto, Boer and Briton 1877-1906: Memoirs of Dr. Henry Taylor. 232pp. ill. R6.90 cl. R18.00 deluxe ed. Philip 1972 SA

Hadman, R.
Biology for East Africa. 204pp. ill. K.shs13.50 OUP-Nairobi 1966 KE

Hadumbavhinu, L.
Waluguru na desturi zao. [Customs and traditions of the Waluguru of Tanzania] 65pp. K.shs.4.00 ($1.50/60p.) EALB 1968 KE SWA

Haffner, A.
Applications à l'hémodynamique de la mécanique des fluides. 136pp. photos. DA22.00 SNED 1969 AE FRE

Haffner, P.
Chansons pour Bamako. 153pp. ill. Z1.15 Presses Africaines 1975 ZR FRE

Haffter, P.
Isabelle de Saint-Aureol. 20pp. 30c. (80c.) Univ South Africa 1961 SA FRE

Haffter, P.
Practical Portuguese. See: Sabina, J.C.B.

Haffter, P.
Romance literature and opera. 31pp. 25c. (75c.) Univ South Africa 1963 SA

Hafsia, J.
Cendres a l'aube. 270pp. D0.980 pap. Maison Tunis 1975 TI FRE

Hagan, G., ed.
Regional family studies. 252pp. C5.00 (Legon Family Research paps. 2) Inst Afr Stud - Univ Ghana 1975 GH

Hagenbucher, F.
Les Arabes dits "Suwa" du Nord-Cameroun. 37pp. ill. pl. CFA1,000 Inst Sciences Hum - Cam 1973 CM FRE

Hagendorens, J.
Dictionnaire Otetela-Français. 419pp. (DM58.00 pap.) (CEEBA. série III, Travaux linguistiques, 5) CEEBA 1976 ZR FRE

Hahlo, H.R.
Company law through the cases. 3rd ed. hd., pap. R21.00 pap. R35.00 hd. Juta 1977 SA

Hahlo, H.R.
South African company law through the cases. 3rd ed. 800pp. cl. & pap. R35.00 cl. R21.00 pap. Juta 1977 SA

Hahlo, H.R.
The South African law of husband and wife. With an appendix on jurisdiction and conflict of laws by E. Kahn. 4th ed. R35.00 cl. R25.00 pap. Juta 1975 SA

Hahlo, H.R.   Kahn, E.
The South African legal system and its background. R17.50 Juta 1968 SA

Hahne, K.   Pistorius, M.C.   Welscheid, H.
Outline of a data bank system for national and regional planning. 65pp. (CSIR Special Report, WISK 181) CSIR 1975 SA

Haile, A., ed.   Edwards, S., ed.
Results of the IAR/DDA field trials and demonstration project in the highlands 1973-1976. 22pp. ill. Inst Agric Res - Addis 1976 ET

Hailu, A.
English-Amharic dictionary. See: Mosback, G.P.

Hake, J.M.
Child-rearing practices in Northern Nigeria. 142pp. pl. N3.50 Ibadan UP 1972 NR

Hakim, J.
Arabic primer. 110pp. ill. 40k Longman-Nig 1971 NR HAU

Hakim, J.
New Arabic course for Nigeria, pupil's bk. 1, 2 bks. 64pp. col. ill. N1.05 Longman - Nig 1968 NR

Hakim, J.
New Arabic course for Nigeria, pupil's bk. 2, 2 bks. 64pp. col. ill. N1.05 Longman - Nig 1971 NR

Hakim, J.
New Arabic course for Nigeria, teacher's bk. 180pp. N1.85 Longman - Nig 1969 NR

Hakim, T.A.
Mutanen kogo. [Play.] 105pp. N2.20 OUP - Nig 1976 NR HAU

Hälbich, I.W. et al.
On the morphology of the Dwyka series in the vicinity of Loeriesfontein, Cape Province. 765pp. photos. maps. R13.00 (A v.37, no.2-10) Univ Stellenbosch, Lib 1962 SA

Haldane, A.
How we escaped from Pretoria. [Reprint of ed. 1900]. 231pp. ill. cl. R17.00 (Africana Reprint Library, 11) Africana Book Soc 1977 SA

Haliburton, G.M. Blake, E.
From stone axe to space age. 400pp. photos. maps. R3.10 Longman SA 1970 SA

Halim, E.C. Osibodu, B.M.
Modern primary mathematics. pupil's bk. 2. 64pp. ill. 85k Longman - Nig 1974 NR

Halim, E.C. Osibodu, B.M.
Modern primary mathematics. pupils bk. 3. 85k. (98k.) Longman - Nig 1975 NR

Halim, E.C. Igboko, P. Adelaja, S.
Modern primary mathematics. pupils bk. 4. 95k. Longman - Nig 1976 NR

Halim, E.C. Osibodu, B.M.
Modern primary mathematics. teacher's bk. 2. 112pp. ill. N2.30 Longman - Nig 1974 NR

Halim, E.C.
Modern school mathematics: pupils' bk. 3rd ed. 1, 3 bks 198pp. ill. N1.15 Longman - Nig 1961 NR

Halim, E.C.
Modern school mathematics: pupils' bk. 2, 3 bks. 184pp. ill. N1.15 Longman - Nig 1963 NR

Halim, E.C.
Modern school mathematics: pupils' bk. 3, 3 bks. 248pp. ill. N1.15 Longman - Nig 1963 NR

Halim, E.C.
Modern school mathematics: teacher's bk. 1, 2 bks. 73pp. ill. 60k Longman - Nig 1961 NR

Halim, E.C.
Modern school mathematics: teacher's bk. 2, 3 bks. 129pp. ill. 50k Longman - Nig 1963 NR

Halim, E.C.
Modern school mathematics: teacher's bk. 3, 3 bks 129pp. ill. 75k Longman - Nig 1963 NR

Halim, E.C.
Primary mathematics: pupils bk. 1, 5 bks. 48pp. col. ill. 80k Longman - Nig 1967 NR

Halim, E.C.
Primary mathematics: pupils' bk. 2, 5 bks. 64pp. col. ill. 85k Longman - Nig 1972 NR

Halim, E.C.
Primary mathematics: pupils' bk. 3, 5 bks. 92pp. col. ill. 98k Longman - Nig 1972 NR

Halim, E.C.
Primary mathematics: pupils' bk. 4, 5 bks. 137pp. col. ill. N1.10 Longman - Nig 1971 NR

Halim, E.C.
Primary mathematics: pupils' bk. 5, 5 bks. 134pp. col. ill. N1.25 Longman - Nig 1972 NR

Halim, E.C.
Primary mathematics: teacher's bk. 1, 5 bks. 78pp. ill. N1.60 Longman - Nig 1965 NR

Halim, E.C.
Primary mathematics: teacher's bk. 2, 5 bks. 66pp. col. ill. N1.60 Longman - Nig 1971 NR

Halim, E.C.
Primary mathematics: teacher's bk. 3, 5 bks. 64pp. col. ill. N1.60 Longman - Nig 1971 NR

Halim, E.C.
Primary mathematics: teacher's bk. 4, 5 bks. 48pp. ill. N1.50 Longman - Nig 1969 NR

Halim, E.C.
Primary mathematics: teacher's bk. 5, 5 bks. 32pp. N1.50 Longman - Nig 1971 NR

Halima, H.B.
Un demi siècle de théâtre arabe en Tunisie (1907-1957) D2.20 (Série VI, Philosophie-Littérature, 7) Univ Tunis 1973 TI FRE

Halimoja, Y.I.
Bunge la Tanzania. [Parliament in Tanzania] 104pp. K.shs.9.00 ($2.25/90p) EALB 1974 KE SWA

Hall, A.
Common plants of the Volta Lake. 123pp. ill. C3.00 (£1.50/$3.00) Ghana UP 1976 GH

Hall, B.L.
Adult education and development of socialism in Tanzania. 160pp. K.shs.15.85 ($3.70/£1.80) EALB 1976 KE

Hall, B.L., eds. Remtulla, K., eds.
Adult education and national development. Proceedings of the Third Conference of the African Adult Association, held at the University of Dar es Salaam, 19-24 April, 1971. 136pp. K.shs.23.00 ($5.00/£2.40) EALB 1973 KE

Hall, C.G. Burger, A.P.
Hall on water rights. 4th ed. R25.00 Juta 1974 SA

Hall, C.G.
The institutes of South African law: the law of contracts. 8th ed. 3, 4 v. R15.00 Juta 1970 SA

Hall, C.G.
The institutes of South African law: the law of persons. 9th ed. 1, 4 v. R9.50 Juta 1968 SA

Hall, C.G.
The institutes of South African law: the law of property. 10th ed. 2, 4 v. R17.50 Juta 1977 SA

Hall, C.G. Kellaway, E.A.
Servitudes. 3rd ed. R12.75 Juta 1973 SA

Hall, D.E.
Sunday school primer. 80pp. 20k SIM 1965 NR

Hall, R.N. Neal, W.G.
The ancient ruins of Rhodesia. [Reprint of ed. 1904]. 404pp. ill. maps. cl. R$9.70 cl. (Rhodesiana Reprint Library, Gold Series, 23) Books of Rhodesia. [Reprint ed. 1904] 1972 RH

Hall, R.S.
An introduction to statistical methods for NIPR staff. 179pp. (CSIR Special Report, PERS 216) CSIR 1974 SA

Hall, S.A., ed.
Uganda atlas of disease. See: Langlands, B.W., ed.

Hall, S.K.P.
The development of a scale to assess modernization among South African Blacks. 27pp. (CSIR Special Report, PERS 251) CSIR 1976 SA

Hall, T.C.
Burglars at Bukhangale. 72pp. ill. K.shs.7.00 ($2.00) EAPH 1975 KE

Halland, C.A.
Programmed social studies, Form I. See: van Zyl, F.J.T.

Halle, N.
Monographie des hippocrateacées d'Afrique occidentale. 245pp. ill. CFA1600 (Mémoires de l'IFAN, 64) IFAN 1962 SG FRE

Hallowes, E.E.
Social studies for junior certificate, Form 1. See: Dent, S.R.

Hallowes, E.E.
Social studies for junior certificate, Forms 2 & 3. See: Dent, S.R.

Halsey, A.H.
Academic freedom and the idea of a university. 16pp. 50c. (Univ. Cape Town. T.B. Davie Memorial lecture, 17) Univ Cape Town Lib 1976 SA

Halstead, L.B.
Ife and biology. 18pp. 30k (Inaugural lec., 4) Univ Ife Press 1973 NR

Hamandishe, J.
Mashiripiti engozi. 96pp. 75c. Longman - Rhod 1970 RH SHO

Hamandishe, N.P.
Sara ugarike. [Now you shall be happy.] 118pp. pl. 80c Longman - Rhod 1975 RH SHO

Hamballi, M.
Kaara karaatuu. See: Waali, N.S.

Hamblyn, S.M.L. Ascough, S.W. Hatton, T.A.
Computation of thermodynamic equilibrium of heterogeneous reaction systems by minimumization of the free energy. R2.50 (CSIR Report, CENG 086) CSIR 1975 SA

Hamdani, H.F.
On the genealogy of the fatimid caliphs. 36pp. £.E.1.000 ($2.95) Am Univ 1958 UA

Hamdun, S.
Arabic reader. v. 1 ill. K.shs2.50 ($1.50/60p.) EALB 1964 KE

Hamdun, S.
Arabic reader. v. 2 ill. K.shs3.00 ($1.50/60p.) EALB 1964 KE

Hamdy, M.
Annotated guide to journals dealing with the Middle East and North Africa. See: Ljunggren, F.

Hamel, L., comp.
English Southern Sotho dictionary. 6 vols. 303, 180, 180, 370, 582, 172pp. vol. V R3.50 vols. I-IV & VI R3.00 Mazenod Inst 1974(?) LO

Hamley, R.
The regiment: the story of the British South Africa police. 126pp. ill. R12.00 Bulpin 1971 SA

Hammond-Tooke, W.D.
Command or consensus: the development of Transkeian local government. 256pp. cl. R8.40 Philip 1975 SA

Hammond-Tooke, W.D., ed.
Agnates and affines: studies in African marriage, manners and land allocation. ['African Studies' special number. v. 34, no. 4]. See: Webster, D., ed.

Hammond-Tooke, W.D., ed.
The journal of William Shaw. 228pp. pl. hd. fl. 22.50 (The Graham's Town, 2) Balkema 1972 SA

Hammond-Tooke, W.D.
In search of the sacred: a problem in the anthropological study of religion. ex. only (Inaugural lec.) Rhodes Univ Lib 1965 SA

Hampathé Bâ, A.
Jaawanbe. 82pp. CFA350 CELTHO 1970 NG FRE

Hampson, R.M.
Islam in South Africa. 55pp. 80c. Univ Cape Town Lib 1964 SA

Hamrioui, M.
L'épargne volontaire et spontanée. Expérience Algérienne. 357pp. DA20.00 SNED 1975 AE FRE

Hamutyinei, M.
Kusasana kunoparira. [Excessive pleasure.] 110pp. pl. 85c Longman - Rhod 1976 RH SHO

Hamutyinei, M.
Maidei. [What, actually, did you want?] 96pp. 85c Longman - Rhod 1972 RH SHO

Hamutyinei, M.A.
Sungai mbabvu. [Tighten your ribs.] 88pp. 40c Mambo 1973 RH SHO

Hamutyinei, M.A. Plangger, A.B.
Tsumo-Shumo. Shona proverbial lore and wisdom. v. 2 500pp. hd. & pap. R$6.50 cl. R$4.75 pap. (Shona Heritage Series, 2) Mambo 1974 RH

Hamza, B. M'Henni, H. Chamakh, N.
La santé mère - enfant. 244pp. D2,000 Maison Tunis 1976 TI FRE

Hamza, M.M.
Care of the newborn baby in Tanzania. See: Segall, M.M.

Hamzaoui, R.
L'academie de langue arabe du Caire: Histoire et oeuvre. D4.00 (Série VI, Philosophie-Littérature, 8) Univ Tunis 1975 TI FRE

Hana, S. Abdelmalek, Z.A.
Standard contemporary Arabic. 364pp. D2.600 Maison Tunis 1973 TI

Hanafi, H.
Renaissance du monde arabe. See: Malek, A.A.

Hancock, F.D. Lucas, A.
Ferns of the Witwatersrand. 94pp. ill. col. ill. cl. R10.00 Witwatersrand UP 1973 SA

Hanekom, E.C. Barkhuysen, F.A.
Liquid ammonia mercerisation of cotton, part I: construction of a pilot plant chainless merceriser. 10pp. R2.50 (SAWTRI Technical Reports, 277) SAWTRI 1975 SA

Hanekom, E.C. van Rensberg, N.J.J. Barkhuysen, F.A.
The SAWTRI continuous shrink-resist treatment of wool tops. 17pp. R2.50 (SAWTRI Technical Reports, 259) SAWTRI 1975 SA

Hanekom, E.C. Barkhuysen, F.A.
Stability of the chlorinating solution used in the SAWTRI chlorination process. 10pp. R2.50 (SAWTRI Technical Reports, 264) SAWTRI 1975 SA

Hanekom, E.C. Bowler, D.
The treatment of cotton fabrics with dimethyloldihydroxyethylene urea and various catalysts. 12pp. R2.50 (SAWTRI Technical Reports, 275) SAWTRI 1975 SA

Hankins, T. et al.
Sukumaland interdisciplinary report. 238pp. map. T.shs.40.00 (Research report, 40) Bur Res Assess - Tanz 1971 TZ

Hannan, M.
Standard Shona dictionary. 2nd ed. 996pp. maps. hd. R$4.50 Rhod Lit Bur 1974 RH

Hannan, P. van Putten, V.
A writing course for junior secondary schools. 68pp. 80n. Neczam 1976 ZA

Hannigan, A.J.J.
Civics for Kenya schools. 3rd ed. 39pp. ill. K.shs.4.80 ($1.80/70p.) EALB 1976 KE

Hannigan, A.J.J.
What is local government?: a study of local government in Kenya and England. 67pp. map. K.shs.4.00 ($1.50/60p.) EALB 1958 KE

Hanno.
Variational properties of direction: dependent metric fields. See: Rund.

Hansen, D.D.
The life and work of Benjamin Tyamzashe: a contemporary Xhosa composer. 50c (Inst. of Social and Economic Research occas. paps., 11) Inst Soc & Econ Res - SA 1968 SA

Haqqi, Y.
Un Egyptien à Paris. 95pp. DA7.00 SNED 1973 AE FRE

Hardie, A.M.
Robert Burns and his myth. 39pp. C1.00 ($1.00/50p.) (Inaugural lecture) Ghana UP 1971 GH

Hardie, G.M. Hartford, G.F.
Commentary on the Immorality Act. R5.75 Juta 1960 SA

Hardy, E., comps.
South African Bantu homeland boundaries according to final consolidation proposals. See: Hattingh, P.S., comps.

Hare, A.P.
Cyprus conflict and its resolution. 11pp. 30c (Univ. Cape Town. Inaugural lec., 25) Univ Cape Town Lib 1974 SA

Hare, J.
Sauna Ya Dawo. See: Whittam, G.

Harel-Biraud.
Le bégaiement chez l'écolier sénégalais. CFA125 (C.L.A.D. Etude, 45) CLAD 1971 SG FRE

Haresnape, G.
The great hunters. ill. R4.50 (Elsa series, 3) Purnell 1976 SA

Hargrave, K.J.
Area studies in East African geography. photos ill. maps. K.shs22.50 (£1.00) Heinemann Educ - Nair 1973 KE

Haring, P.
A taste of salt. R1.80 (Mantis Poets, 10) Philip 1975 SA

Harjula, R.
Mfano wa Mungu. [The image of God.] 100pp. T.shs.10.00 Central Tanganyika 1971 TZ SWA

Harkema, R.C.
The geographical distribution of cattle in Zambia. 18pp. 60n. ($1.50) (Zambia Geographical Assoc., occas. paps., 4) Zambia Geog Assoc 1972(?) ZA

Harlow, R.E.
The Gospel of Mark. 28pp. 20k SIM 1971 NR

Harlow, R.E.
Peter and the Church. 80pp. 20k SIM 1967 NR

Harmon, R.
Hare, baboon and their friends. 36pp. ill. R2.95 OUP-SA 1967 SA

Harms, T.
The Loskop killer. 200pp. pl. R2.75 Shuter 1975 SA

Harper, S.H.
Food for the chemist. 16pp. 30c Univ Rhodesia Lib 1961 RH

Harries, L.
A grammar of Mwera. 128pp. map. cl. R8.00 (Bantu grammatical archives, 1) Witwatersrand UP 1950 SA

Harries, L.
Hatua ya kwanza. [The first steps; account of the life of Dr. Martin Luther King.] 60pp. photos. K.shs.7.50 Transafrica 1974 KE SWA

Harries, L.
The initiation rites of the Makonde tribe. 46pp. 50n. (25p.) (Rhodes-Livingstone communications, 3) Inst Afr Stud - Lusaka 1944 ZA

Harris, B.K.
Foundations of physics. See: Noakes, G.R.

Harris, B.K.
Physics problems. See: Noakes, G.R.

Harris, C.
Teaching geography in Ghana. 113pp. ill. photos. C1.00 ($1.00) Ghana Publ Corp 1969 GH

Harris, C.B.
Details regarding the Diamond Fields Advertiser, 1878-1968. See: Lighton, C.

Harris, D.
Hydroponics: the gardening without soil. 3rd. ed. 184pp. photos. hd. R9.50 Purnell 1966 SA

Harris, F.J.
Social casework: an introduction for students in developing countries. 200pp. K.shs23.50 OUP-Nairobi 1970 KE

Harris, J.
Books about Nigeria: a select reading list. 5th ed. 83pp. 90k Ibadan UP 1969 NR

Harris, J.
Engineering, science and society. 45pp. 30c. Univ Rhodesia 1975 RH

Harris, J.
Ibadan University library. 44pp. pl. N1.00 Ibadan UP 1968 NR

Harris, J.
Karl Weissenberg: 80th birthday celebration essays. 172pp. K.shs.37.00 ($16.00/£6.50) EALB 1973 KE

Harris, J.
Patterns of library growth in English-speaking West Africa. 28pp. 75pes. ($2.00) (Univ. of Ghana, Dept. of Library and Archival Studies, occas. paps., 3) Dept Lib Stud - Univ Ghana 1970 GH

Harris, L.
Utenzi wa mkunumbi. [The Swahili potlach] 2nd ed. 72pp. ill. K.shs.4.40 ($1.75/70p) EALB 1969 KE SWA

Harris, P.B.
Interest groups in South African politics. 105pp. 50c (Univ. Rhodesia, Monographs in Political Science, 1) Univ Rhodesia Lib 1968 RH

Harris, P.B.
Politics in travail. 36pp. 30c Univ Rhodesia Lib 1969 RH

Harris, P.B.
The withdrawal of the major European powers. 26pp. 50c (Univ. Rhodesia, Monographs in Political Science, 2) Univ Rhodesia Lib 1969 RH

Harris, P.S.
Black industrial workers in Rhodesia. The general problems of low pay. 71pp. R$1.00 (Mambo Socio-Economic Series, 2) Mambo 1974 RH

Harris, W.C.
Portraits of the game and wild animals of Southern Africa. 220pp. ill. hd. fl. 67.50 Balkema 1969 SA

Harris, W.T. Sawyerr, H.
The springs of Mende belief and custom. 152pp. map photos. cl. Le3.50 Sierra Leone UP 1968 SL

Harrison, A.
The release of the muses. 28pp. 30c (Inaugural lectures) Univ Rhodesia Lib 1973 RH

Harrison, C.V.
Medical advances and their implications. 10pp. 45k (35p./80c) (Univ. of Ife, Inaugural Lecture Series, 12) Univ Ife Press 1974 NR

Harrison, T.W. Simmon, J.
Aikin mata. 80pp. 50k OUP - Nig 1966 NR YOR

Harrison, W.A. Patterson.
Mathematics for today. bk. 1 R1.45 Longman SA SA

Harrop-Allin, C.
Norman Eaton: architect. 144pp. pl. col. pl. cl. R15.00 Struik 1975 SA

Hart, E.
Soil conservation in South Africa 1946-1959. 80pp. R1.00 Univ Cape Town Lib 1970 SA

Hart, G.P.
Some socio-economic aspects of African entrepreneurship: with particular reference to the Transkei and Ciskei. 204pp. R3.00 (Inst. of Social and Economic Research occas. paps., 16) Inst Soc & Econ Res - SA 1971 SA

Hart, J.T.
Ibani go diri 1. [Ibani reader, 1] 63pp. ill. 30k (Inst. of African Stud., Univ. of Ibadan, Rivers readers project, 14) Inst Afr Stud-Ibadan 1971 NR IBA

Hart, J.T.
Teachers' notes on Ibani go diri 1. 99pp. 50k (Inst. of African Stud., Univ. of Ibadan, Rivers readers project, 15) Inst Afr Stud-Ibadan 1971 NR IBA

Hart, N.
Clear writing: Africa Christian writers' course. v. 4 76pp. 45t. (52c.) Christ Lit Assoc - Mal 1972 MW

Hart, N., ed.
The lively word: Christian publishing and broadcasting in East Africa. 68pp. K1.00 Popular Publ 1975 MW

Hart, N.
La paix au Soudan. 34pp. photos. CFA75 CLE 1972 CM FRE

Hart, S.
In the wild. 186pp. ill. cl. R10.55 Africana Book Soc 1975 SA

Hartford, G.F.
Commentary on the Immorality Act. See: Hardie, G.M.

Hartmann, F.H.
Musical education in the university. 29pp. 60c (Inaugural lec.) Witwatersrand UP 1968 SA

Hartridge, A., comp.
Rhodesia national bibliography, 1890 to 1930. (National Archives of Rhodesia, Bibliographical series, 2) Nat Archives - Rhod 1977 RH

Hartridge, D., comp. Robarts, T., comp.
Directory of Rhodesian libraries. 2nd ed. 28pp. R$1.25 Nat Archives - Rhod 1975 RH

Hartshorne.
English readers: South African Bantu schools (Benny and Betty at home and in town) 2, 6 bks. See: Hemming, J.

Hartshorne.
English readers: South African Bantu schools (Benny, Betty and their friends) 1, 6 bks. See: Hemming, J.

Hartshorne.
English readers: South African Bantu schools (Betty and Benny) See: Hemming, J.

Hartshorne.
English readers: South African Bantu schools (Radio van and other tales) 4, 6 bks. See: Hemming, J.

Hartshorne.
English readers: South African Bantu schools (Tales from town and country) 3, 6 bks. See: Hemming, J.

Hartshorne, K.B.
English for standard five. See: Fletcher, E.

Hartshorne, K.B.
English for standard four. See: Fletcher, E.

Hartshorne, K.B.
English for standard three. See: Fletcher, E.

Hartshorne.
Teachers books to English readers: South African Bantu schools (Benny and Betty at home and in town) 2, 2 bks. See: Hemming, J.

Hartshorne.
Teachers books to English readers: South African Bantu schools (Benny, Betty and their friends) 1, 2 bks. See: Hemming, J.

Hartwell, A., ed. Bennaars, G., ed.
School and community in East Africa. 127pp. U.shs.10.00 (M.I.S.R., Nkanga editions, 9) Mak Inst Soc Res 1975 UG

Harvey, C.J.D., ed.
Afrikaans poems with English translations. See: Grove, A.P., ed.

Harvey, C.J.D., ed.
Poems for discussion: with commentaries and questions. See: Hooper, A.G., ed.

Harvey, C.J.D., ed.
Talking of poetry: teacher's companion. See: Hooper, A.G., ed.

Harvey, C.J.D., ed.
Talking of poetry: with commentaries and questions. See: Hooper, A.G., ed.

Harvey, C.J.D.
Language, literature and criticism. 20pp. 30c. (80c.) Univ South Africa 1961 SA

Harvey, W.B.
An introduction to the legal system of East Africa. 940pp. K.shs.180.00 cl. K.shs.150.00 pap. ($40.00/£19.20 cl.) ($28.00/£12.00 pap.) EALB 1975 KE

Hasan, Y.F., ed.
Sudan in Africa. 318pp. LS.1.50 ($6.00) Khartoum UP 1971 SJ

Haselbarth, H.
Applied ethics. 68pp. 65k (Christian Ethics in the African Context, 2) Daystar 1976 NR

Haselbarth, H.
Basic ethics. 32pp. 65k (Christian Ethics in the African Context, 1) Daystar 1976 NR

Haselbarth, H.
Christian ethics in an African context. N3.50 Daystar 1975 NR

Haselbarth, H.
Loving attention. A course in the theology of the spiritual life. 80pp. 80k Daystar 1976 NR

Haselbarth, H.
Sex, marriage and the family. 100pp. 65k (Christian Ethics in the African Context, 3) Daystar 1976 NR

Hassan, A.
The Gwari, Gade, and Koro tribes; a discussion of the origins and customs of three tribes in Abuja Emirate. See: Naibi, S.

Hassan, C.
Turanci A Saukake, 1. [English made easy] 1, 3 bks. 64pp. N1.25 Northern Nig 1953 NR HAU

Hassan, C.
Turanci A Saukake, 2. [English made easy] 2, 3 bks. 86pp. N1.50 Northern Nig 1953 NR HAU

Hassan, C.
Turanci A Saukake, 3. [English made easy] 3, 3 bks. 148pp. N1.50 Northern Nig 1953 NR HAU

Hassan. Na'ibi, M.S.
A chronicle of Abuja. 96pp. N1.05 Pilgrim 1962 NR

Hassan, H.M.
Illustrated guide to the plants of Erkowit. 106pp. ill. LS3.50 ($14.00 pap.) Khartoum UP 1974 SJ

Hassan, M.A.
Biomedical research in the Sudan. 121pp. Nat Council Res - Sudan 1973 SJ

Hassan, Y.F.
The Arabs and the Sudan. 2nd ed. 300pp. maps. ($4.00) Khartoum UP 1974 SJ

Hassib, A.
Directory of research centres, institutes and related bodies engaged in scientific and technological research. See: Gadir, L.A.

Hassib, M.A.
Biomedical research in the Sudan. v. 7 122pp. 75pt. ($3.00) Khartoum UP 1973 SJ

Hastie, C.
How to organize handcraft competitions in women's groups. 55pp. ill. K.shs2.00 ($1.25/50p.) EALB 1962 KE

Hastings, A.
Christian marriage in Africa. Abridged East African ed. 44pp. T.shs.5.00 Central Tanganyika 1976 TZ

Hastings, A.
Church and ministry. 52pp. K.shs.7.50 (Gaba Pastoral Papers, 25) Gaba 1972 KE

Hastings, A.
Massacre in Mozambique-- Wiriyamu. 134pp. maps. K.shs.18.00 East & Central Africa only Transafrica 1974 KE

Hastings, A.
Ndoa ya Kikristo katika Afrika siku hisi. [Christian marriage in Africa] 44pp. T.shs.5.00 Central Tanganyika 1974 TZ SWA

Hatfield, D.
District six. See: Franck, B.

Hathaway, E.A.A.
A casebook on the South African law of contract. See: Farlam, I.G.

Hathout, S.
Agricultural soil capability of South East Tanzania. T.shs.15.00 ($5.00) (Research pap., 23) Bur Res Assess - Tanz 1973 TZ

Hathout, S.
A new approach to soil mapping in Tanzania. T.shs.15.00 ($5.00) (Research pap., 22) Bur Res Assess - Tanz 1973 TZ

Hathout, S.   Sumra, S.
Rainfall and soil suitability index for maize cropping in Handeni district.   T.shs.20.00 (Research reports, new series, 12) Bur Res Assess - Tanz 1974 TZ

Hathout, S.
Rainfall and soil suitability index for wheat cropping in West Kilimanjaro.   T.shs.20.00 ($7.00) (Research reports, new series, 8) Bur Res Assess - Tanz 1975 TZ

Hathout, S.
Some notes on mobile soil laboratories and procedure for soil analysis.   T.shs.7.00 ($3.00) (Research reports, new series, 2.1) Bur Res Assess - Tanz 1973 TZ

Hatibu, B.M.R.
Mazoezi ya ufahamu wa Kiswahili.   See: Mazula, A.

Hattersley, A.F.
A camera on old Natal.   81pp. pl./photos. cl.   R1.05 Shuter 1960 SA

Hattersley, A.F.
The convict crisis and the growth of unity.   142pp. R2.10 Univ of Natal 1965 SA

Hattersley, A.F.
An illustrated social history of South Africa.   271pp. ill. hd.   fl. 67.50 Balkema 1973 SA

Hattersley, A.F.
Portrait of a city.   R1.50   Shuter SA

Hattingh, D.L.
Programmed instruction.   120pp.   Human Science Res Council 1976 SA

Hattingh, D.L.
The teaching of geography at South African secondary schools: a condensed version of a survey in the year 1966.   39pp.   80c. Human Science Res Council 1971 SA

Hattingh, P.S.
Black homelands in South Africa.   See: Malan, T.

Hattingh, P.S.
Bophuthatswana: a select and annotated bibliography. 30pp. maps.   60c (70c) (Africa Inst. of South Africa, occas. pap., 36) Africa Inst - Pret 1973 SA

Hattingh, P.S., comps.   Hardy, E., comps.
South African Bantu homeland boundaries according to final consolidation proposals.   map.   40c (50c) Africa Inst - Pret SA

Hattle, J.
Wayward winds.   138pp. col. ill. maps.   R$2.50 Longman - Rhod 1972 RH

Hatton, T.A.
Calculation of thermodynamic equilibrium compositions of heterogeneous reaction systems. User's guide to FORTRAN program HTGR.   R2.50 (CSIR Report, CENG 089) CSIR 1975 SA

Hatton, T.A.
Computation of thermodynamic equilibrium of heterogeneous reaction systems by minimumization of the free energy. See: Hamblyn, S.M.L.

Haughton, H.
Geological history of Southern Africa.   544pp. ill. map. R10.50 Geol Soc SA 1969 SA

Hauhouot, A.
Annales de l'université d'Abidjan.   289pp.   CFA2500 (Série G - Géographie, 6) Univ Abidjan 1974 IV FRE

Hauhouot, A. et al.
Annales de l'université d'Abidjan.   329pp.   CFA1400 (F28.00) (Série G-Géographie, 5) Univ Abidjan 1973 IV FRE

Hauptfleisch, T.
Research into the position of the official languages in the educational system of whites in South Africa.   50pp. ill. R2.95 (Human Sciences Research Council, TLK-series, L-4) Human Science Res Council 1975 SA

Havenga, C.M.
The wheel-point method of survey.   See: Tidmarsh, C.E.M.

Hawkes, M.E.
The Nakambaia sugar estate.   10pp.   60n. ($1.50) (Zambia Geographical Assoc, occas. paps., 2) Zambia Geog Assoc 1972(?) ZA

Hawkins, E.
Bible outline maps. [Canaan and the Holy Land.].   2 2nded. 3 sheetspp.   24c. OUP-SA 1972 SA

Hawkins, E.
Bible outline maps. [The lands of the Bible.].   2nd ed.   3 sheetspp.   24c. OUP-SA 1972 SA

Hawkins, E.
Bible outline maps. [The Roman empire in the first century A.D.].   2nd ed. 3 sheetspp.   24c. OUP-SA 1972 SA

Hawkins, E.K.
Road transport in Nigeria.   99pp.   N1.50 ($2.50) NISER 1958 NR

Hawkridge, D.G., ed.
The less successful secondary school child. Papers and proceedings of a conference held at the College in August 1962.   80pp.   50c (Fac. of Education, Univ. of Rhodesia, 1) Univ Rhodesia Lib 1963 RH

Hawkridge, D.G.
Programmed learning in Central African contexts.   88pp. 50c (Fac. of Education, Univ. of Rhodesia, 7) Univ Rhodesia Lib 1967 RH

Hawksworth, W.A.   Thompson, M.E.   Cotton, A.F.
Patterns and principles.   440pp. ill.   R4.50 Shuter 1977 SA

Hay, A.M.   Smith, R.H.T.
Interregional trade and money flows in Nigeria.   245pp. ill.   N3.75 ($6.75) NISER 1964 NR

Hay, D.
A further report on the low fertility of trout eggs at Jonkershoek Trout Hatchery.   16pp. ill.   15c (A v.18, no. 1) Univ Stellenbosch, Lib 1949 SA

Hayes, A.P.N.   Vandal, P.   Roberts, M.B.
Transfer printing of wool with reactive dyes, part I: the use of a transferable film of polyvinyl alcohol.   15pp.   R2.50 (SAWTRI Technical Reports, 276) SAWTRI 1975 SA

Hayes, A.P.N.
Transfer printing of wool with reactive dyes, part II: the use of a polyethylene/paper laminate support.   12pp. R2.50 (SAWTRI Technical Reports, 302) SAWTRI 1976 SA

Hays, H.M.
The marketing and storage of food grains in Northern Nigeria.   N2.00 (Samaru misc. pap., 50) Inst Agric Res - Zaria 1975 NR

Hayward, A.C.
Studies on bacterial pathogens of sugar cane differentiation of isolates Xanthomonas vasculorum, with notes on an undescribed Xanthomonas sp. from sugar cane in Natal and Trinidad.   (Mauritius Sugar Industry Research Institute, Occas. paps., 9) Sugar Res Inst MF

Hayward, A.C.
Studies on bacterial pathogens of sugar cane differentiation, taxonomy and nomenclature of the bacteria causing red stripe and mottled stripe diseases.   27pp. Rs8 (Mauritius Sugar Industry Research Institute, occas. paps., 10) Sugar Res Inst 1962 F

Hayward, R.L.   White, R.   Boorman, B.L.
North America; studies for East African students.   photos. ill. maps.   K.shs.12.50 (60p.) Heinemann Educ - Nair 1972 KE

Hayward, R.L.   White, R.
North America: studies for East African students.   112pp. pl.   K.shs.12.50   Heinemann Educ - Nair 1974 KE

Head, M.E.
Ensi mwe tuli n'abantu nga bwe bagyeyambisa. [The land and how men use it]   K.shs.1.00 ($1.50/50p.) EALB 1948 KE LUG

Healey, J., ed.
Ujamaa and Christian communities. See: Mwoleka, C., ed.

Hearne, B.   Lucas, D.
Celebration. 62pp.   K.shs.9.00 (Gaba Pastoral Papers, 39) Gaba 1975 KE

Hearne, B., ed.   Mijere, N., ed.
Celebration II. 92pp.   K.shs.13.00 (Spearhead series, 42) Gaba 1976 KE

Hearne, B.
Seeds of unity. 82pp.   K.shs.10.00 (Gaba Pastoral Papers, 41) Gaba 1976 KE

Hearne, B.
Seeds of unity. 82pp.   K.shs.10.00 (Spearhead series, 41) Gaba 1976 KE

Heath, E.
Guide to the dissection and study of domestic ruminants.   N7.00 Ibadan UP 1977 NR

Heathcote, R.G.
A seedling disorder of groundnuts associated with imbalanced mineral nutrition. See: Fowler, A.M.

Hebga, M. et al.
Croyances et guerison. 152pp.   CFA450.00 CLE 1973 CM FRE

Hecht, E.D., ed.
The pottery collection. 124pp. ($5.00) Inst Ethiop Stud 1969 ET

Heese, C.H.T.D.
The evolution of palaeolithic technique. 65pp. photos. ill.   30c (B v.11, no.2) Univ Stellenbosch, Lib 1933 SA

Heigham, J.B.
West African Institute of Social and Economic Research: industrial relations in the Gold Coast.   N1.00 ($2.00) (W.A.I.S.E.R. third annual conference paper, 4) NISER 1954 NR

Heijnen, J.D.
The mechanized block cultivation schemes in Mwanza region 1964-1969. 50pp.   T.shs.7.00 (Research paper, 9) Bur Res Assess - Tanz 1969 TZ

Heijnen, J.D.
The river basins in Tanzania: a bibliography. 39pp. map.   T.shs.7.00 (Research notes, 5e) Bur Res Assess - Tanz 1970 TZ

Heine, B.
The Kuliak languages of Eastern Uganda.   K.shs.14.50 ($4.00) EAPH 1976 KE

Heinemann Educational Books.
Progressive colouring kit. [9 wax crayons.].   35k.   Heinemann Educ - Ib 1976 NR

Heinz, H.J.
Conflicts, tensions, and release of tensions in a bushman society. 40c. (Isma paps., 23) Inst Study of Man 1967 SA

Helander, G.
Must we introduce monogamy? 96pp.   50c. Shuter 1958 SA

Held, C.
Hailstorms in 1970/71. See: Carte, A.E.

Helfet, A., ed.
South Africa. [Also available in German]. See: Cubitt, G.S., ed.

Helleiner, G.K.
Agricultural export pricing strategy in Tanzania. 19pp. ill.   T.shs12.00 ($3.00) (Research pap., 66.6) Econ Res Bur - Tanz 1966 TZ

Helleiner, G.K.
Agricultural planning in East Africa. 179pp.   K.shs42.00 cl.   K.shs15.00 pap. ($7.80 cl.) ($4.00 pap.) EAPH 1968 KE

Helleiner, G.K.
Rationalization in the Tanzania sisal industry.   T.shs.12.00 ($3.00) (Research pap., 68.23) Econ Res Bur - Tanz 1974 TZ

Helleiner, G.K.
Socialism, self-reliance and the Second Plan.   T.shs.12.00 ($3.00) (Research pap., 68.9) Econ Res Bur - Tanz 1968 TZ

Hellman, E.
Rooiyard: a sociological study of an urban slum yard.   125pp.   K1.50 (75p.) (Rhodes-Livingstone paps., 13) Inst Soc Res - Zam 1948 ZA

Hellmann, E.
The impact of city life on Africans. 40c. (Isma paps., 11) Inst Study of Man 1963 SA

Helm, B.
The discipline of charity. 14pp.   30c. (U.C.T. Inaugural lec. New series, 3) Univ Cape Town Lib 1970 SA

Helmlinger, P.
Dictionnaire Duala-Français, suivi d'un lexique Français-Duala. 666pp.   CFA7720 Univ Cameroun 1972 CM FRE

Hemans, H.N.
The log of a native commissioner. [Reprint ed. 1935].   224pp. photos. cl.   R$5.50 cl. (Rhodesiana Reprint Library, Gold Series, 15) Books of Rhodesia 1971 RH

Hemedi' Lajjemy, A.W.
The Kilindi. 255pp. ill.   K.shs.20.00 ($4.50/£1.80) EALB 1963 KE

Hemedi'Lajjemy, A.
Habari za wakilindi.   K.shs.15.00 ($3.75/£1.50) EALB 1962 KE SWA

Hemming, J.   Miller, W.
Day-by-day English. First year wall charts.   R$4.65 Longman - Rhod 1959 RH

Hemming, J.   Miller, W.
Day-by-day English. Fun with Benny and Betty. Grade 2.   128pp.   85c. Longman - Rhod 1968 RH

Hemming, J.   Miller, W.
Day-by-day English. Here and there with Benny and Betty.   160pp.   80c. Longman - Rhod 1968 RH

Hemming, J.   Miller, W.
Day-by-day English. My picture and reading book. 48pp.   55c. Longman - Rhod 1967 RH

Hemming, J.   Miller, W.
Day-by-day English. Second year wallcharts.   R$4.65 Longman - Rhod 1960 RH

Hemming, J.   Miller, W.
Day-by-day English. Stories for work and play. Grade 7.   224pp.   R$1.00 Longman - Rhod 1965 RH

Hemming, J.   Miller, W.
Day-by-day English. Stories from many places. Grade 6.   246pp.   R$1.10 Longman - Rhod 1964 RH

Hemming, J.   Miller, W.
Day-by-day English. Stories from town and country.   Grade 4. 160pp. col. ill.   80c. Longman - Rhod 1963 RH

Hemming, J.   Miller, W.
Day-by-day English. Teacher's grade 1. 224pp.   R$1.40 Longman - Rhod 1967 RH

Hemming, J.   Miller, W.
Day-by-day English. Teacher's grade 2. 216pp.   R$1.95 Longman - Rhod 1968 RH

Hemming, J.   Miller, W.
Day-by-day English. 2nd ed. Teacher's grade 3.   184pp.   R$2.50 Longman - Rhod 1974 RH

Hemming, J.
Day-by-day English. New ed. Teacher's grade 4 168pp. R$1.15 Longman - Rhod 1974 RH

Hemming, J.   Miller, W.
Day-by-day English. Teacher's grade 5. R$1.50 Longman - Rhod 1963 RH

Hemming, J.   Miller, W.
Day-by-day English. Teacher's grade 6. 216pp. R$2.50 Longman - Rhod 1964 RH

Hemming, J.   Miller, W.
Day-by-day English. Teacher's grade 7. 216pp. R$2.00 Longman - Rhod 1967 RH

Hemming, J.   Miller, W.
Day-by-day English. The radio van and other stories. Grade 5. 192pp. col. ill. 85c. Longman - Rhod 1964 RH

Hemming, J.   Miller, W.T.
English courses: primary second language (Benny and Betty) bk. 2 104pp. ill. 95c. Longman SA 1965 SA

Hemming, J.   Miller, W.T.
English courses: primary second language (Benny and Betty in town) bk. 2 128pp. ill. R1.05 Longman SA 1963 SA

Hemming, J.   Miller, W.T.
English courses: primary second language (Benny and his friends) bk. 1 128pp. ill. R1.00 Longman SA 1961 SA

Hemming, J.   Miller, W.T.
English courses: primary second language (My picture book - A) 32pp. ill. 45c. Longman SA 1966 SA

Hemming, J.   Miller, W.T.
English courses: primary second language (Stories for work and play) 228pp. ill. R1.40 Longman SA 1966 SA

Hemming, J.   Miller, W.T.
English courses: primary second language (Stories from many places) bk. 5 238pp. ill. R1.40 Longman SA 1966 SA

Hemming, J.   Miller, W.T.
English courses: primary second language (Stories from town and country) bk. 3 168pp. ill. R1.20 Longman SA 1963 SA

Hemming, J.   Miller, W.T.
English courses: primary second language (The radio van and other stories) bk. 4 192pp. ill. R1.30 Longman SA 1964 SA

Hemming, J.   Miller, W.T.
English readers: South African Bantu schools. 6, 6 bks. Longman SA 1973 SA

Hemming, J.   Hartshorne.   Miller, W.T.
English readers: South African Bantu schools (Benny and Betty at home and in town) 2, 6 bks. 128pp. ill. R1.00 Longman SA 1965 SA

Hemming, J.   Hartshorne.   Miller, W.T.
English readers: South African Bantu schools (Benny, Betty and their friends) 1, 6 bks. 112pp. ill. 95c. Longman SA 1965 SA

Hemming, J.   Hartshorne.   Miller, W.T.
English readers: South African Bantu schools (Betty and Benny) 64pp. ill. 65c. Longman SA 1964 SA

Hemming, J.   Hartshorne.   Miller, W.T.
English readers: South African Bantu schools (Radio van and other tales) 4, 6 bks. ill. R1.05 Longman SA SA

Hemming, J.   Miller, W.T.
English readers: South African Bantu schools (Tales from many places) 5, 6 bks. R1.10 Longman SA 1973 SA

Hemming, J.   Hartshorne.   Miller, W.T.
English readers: South African Bantu schools (Tales from town and country) 3, 6 bks. 128pp. ill. R1.00 Longman SA 1970 SA

Hemming, J.   Miller, W.T.
Teachers books to English readers: South African Bantu schools (Benny and Betty) 144pp. ill. R1.10 Longman SA 1965 SA

Hemming, J.   Hartshorne.   Miller, W.T.
Teachers books to English readers: South African Bantu schools (Benny and Betty at home and in town) 2, 2 bks. 200pp. ill. R1.20 Longman SA 1970 SA

Hemming, J.   Hartshorne.   Miller, W.T.
Teachers books to English readers: South African Bantu schools (Benny, Betty and their friends) 1, 2 bks. 140pp. ill. R1.00 Longman SA 1961 SA

Hemming, J.   Miller, W.T.
Teachers' guides to English courses: primary second language (Benny and Betty book - B) 192pp. ill. R1.50 Longman SA 1960 SA

Hemming, J.   Miller, W.T.
Teachers' guides to English courses: primary second language (Benny and Betty in town) 2, 6 bks. 288pp. ill. R1.90 Longman SA 1961 SA

Hemming, J.   Miller, W.T.
Teachers' guides to English courses: primary second language (Benny and his friends) 1, 6 bks. 140pp. ill. R1.30 Longman SA 1961 SA

Hemming, J.   Miller, W.T.
Teachers' guides to English courses: primary second language (My picture book - A) 136pp. ill. R1.20 Longman SA 1960 SA

Hemming, J.   Miller, W.T.
Teachers' guides to English courses: primary second language (Stories from many places) 5, 6 bks. 272pp. ill. R1.80 Longman SA 1966 SA

Hemming, J.   Miller, W.T.
Teachers' guides to English courses: primary second language (Stories from town and country) 3, 6 bks. 272pp. ill. R1.90 Longman SA 1962 SA

Hemming, J.   Miller, W.T.
Teachers' guides to English courses: primary second language (Stories from work and play) 6, 6 bks. 288pp. ill. R1.90 Longman SA 1966 SA

Hemming, J.   Miller, W.T.
Teachers' guides to English courses: primary second language (The radio van and other stories) 4, 6 bks. 288pp. ill. R1.70 Longman SA 1963 SA

Henderson, H.K.
An outline of traditional Onitsha Ibo socialization. See: Henderson, R.N.

Henderson, I.
Imperialism and the British labour movement. Two views considered. 50c. (Local series pamphlets, 12) Central Africa Hist Assoc 1964 RH

Henderson, I.   Warhurst, P.R.
Revisions in Central African history. R$1.30 (Local series pamphlets, 15) Central Africa Hist Assoc 1965 RH

Henderson, M.   Anderson, J.G.
Common weeds of South Africa. R2.40 (R3.55) (Memoirs of the Botanical Survey of South Africa, 37) Botanical Res Inst 1966 SA

Henderson, R.N.   Henderson, H.K.
An outline of traditional Onitsha Ibo socialization. 48pp. 65k (Inst. of Ed. occas. pub., 5) Inst Educ-Ib 1966 NR

Hendrikse, A.P.
Topics in Xhosa relativization. 63pp. R1.00 (Rhodes University, Dept. of African Languages, Communications series, 4) Rhodes Univ Lib 1975 SA

Hendrikz, E.
Pre-school opportunity and sex differences as factors affecting educational progress. See: Orbell, S. F. W.

Henin, R.   Egero, B.
The 1967 population census of Tanzania. A demographic analysis. 57pp. T.shs.15.00 (Research pap., 19) Bur Res Assess - Tanz 1972 TZ

Hocking, A.
South African government. [Also available in Afrikaans.]. ill. photos. maps. cl.   R6.75   (The Macdonald Heritage Library series)   Purnell 1977 SA

Hocking, A.
South African mining.   photos. maps.   R5.60 pap. (Macdonald Heritage Library)   Purnell 1976 SA

Hocking, A.
South African transport.   photos. maps.   R5.60 (Macdonald Heritage Library)   Purnell 1976 SA

Hocking, A.
Yachting in Southern Africa.   240pp. photos. hd. R10.00   Purnell 1972 SA

Hocking, B.D.W.
All what I was taught and other mistakes: a handbook of common errors in English.   288pp.   K.shs.35.00   OUP - Nairobi 1974 KE

Hockly, H.E.
The law of insolvency in South Africa.   See: Mars, W.H.

Hockly, H.E.
The story of the British settlers of 1820 in South Africa. 2nd rev. ed.   300pp. ill.   R4.50   Juta 1971 SA

Hockly, H.E.
Students' guide to the insolvency law.   4th ed.   pap. R6.50   Juta 1969 SA

Hocombe, S.D.   Yates, R.J.
A guide to chemical weed control in East African crops. 84pp. ill.   K.shs3.00   ($1.50/60p.)   EALB 1963 KE

Hodder, B.W.   Ukwu, U.K.
Markets in West Africa.   254pp. ill. maps.   N4.00 Ibadan UP 1969 NR

Hodge, G.M.M.
South African politics 1933-1939.   94pp.   R1.00   Univ Cape Town Lib 1965 SA

Hodgin, R.W.
The law of contract in East Africa.   356pp.   K.shs.43.00 ($7.50/£4.15)   EALB 1976 KE

Hodgson, A.
A survey of race relations in South Africa, 1975. See: Horrell, M.

Hodza, A.
Shona.   Grade 6: Natsai kudzidza.   See: Fortune, G.

Hodza, A.
Shona.   Grade 7: Budirirai.   See: Fortune, G.

Hodza, A.
Shona.   Teacher's bk. grade 6.   See: Fortune, G.

Hodza, A.
Shona.   Teacher's bk. grade 7.   See: Fortune, G.

Hodza, A.C.
Ugo fiwamadzinza ava Shona.   [The wealth of Shona tradition.]   96pp.   R$1.25   Longman - Rhod 1974 RH SHO

Hoek-Smith, M.C.
The future planning of a Majengo-Masaku Swahili village. Recommendation based on a study of socioeconomic, technical and environmental health aspects of the area. 103pp. ill.   K.shs.30.00   Housing Res Dev Unit 1976 KE

Hoffman, L.H.
South African law of evidence.   2nd ed.   527pp. R15.75   Butterworths 1970 SA

Hoffman, R.R.
The ruminant stomach. Stomach structure and feeding habits of East African game ruminants.   cl. K.shs.143.00   ($26.00/£12.50 cl.)   (East African monog. in Biology, 2)   EALB 1973 KE

Hoffman, R.U., comp.
A list of theatre performances in Johannesburg 1887-1897, based on the programme collection in the Strange library of Africana Johannesburg.   gratis   Johannesburg Public Lib 1964 SA

Hofmeir, R.
Land use and livestock husbandry in Sukumaland. T.shs.12.00 ($3.00)   (Research pap., 68.30)   Econ Res Bur - Tanz 1975 TZ

Hofmeir, R.
Trunk road transport and the possibility of a national transport company in Tanzania.   T.shs.12.00 ($3.00) (Research pap., 68.24)   Econ Res Bur - Tanz 1974 TZ

Hofmeyer, J., comp.
Index to pictures of South African interest in The Graphic, 1900-1902.   140pp.   R7.30   Dept Bibliog, Lib & Typo 1974 SA

Hog, J.
Molecular spectroscopy and molecular structure.   60pp. T.shs.10.00   Univ Bkshop - Dar; distr. 1973 TZ

Hogben, S.J.
An introduction to the history of Islamic states of Northern Nigeria.   351pp. mamaps photos. pap., hd.   N1.85 pap.   N2.50 hd.   OUP - Nig 1967 NR

Hogg, V.W.   Roelands, C.M.
Nigerian motor vehicle traffic: an economic forecast. 72pp.   N1.05 ($1.75)   NISER 1962 NR

Hoh, I.K.
Hencwe fe gbe.   See: Kwasikuma, G.W.K.

Hojer, C., comp.
Ethiopian publications, 1941-1963.   146pp.   ($5.00)   Inst Ethiop Stud 1974 ET

Holas, B.
Le culte de Zié. Eléments de la religion kono (Haute Guinée Française)   275pp. pl.   CFA1200   (Mémoires de l'IFAN, 39)   IFAN 1954 SG FRE

Holas, B.
Image de la mère dans l'art invoirien.   128pp. CFA2,000   (F40.00)   Nouv Ed Afric 1976 SG FRE

Holas, B.
Mission dans l'est Libérien.   566pp. pl. maps. CFA2400   (Mémoires de l'IFAN, 14)   IFAN 1952 SG FRE

Holden, W.C.
British rule in South Africa, illustrated in the story of Kama and his tribe and of the war in Zululand.   [Reprint of ed. London, 1879]   218pp. ill.   R4.00   (Reprints, 37) State-Lib-SA 1969 SA

Holden, W.C.
The past and future of the Kaffir races [Reprint of 1866 edition].   588pp. maps pl. cl.   R8.40   (Africana collectanea, 3)   Struik 1963 SA

Holder, F.
The holy spirit.   96pp.   K.shs.6.50   Evangel 1970 KE

Holding, E.M.
Kamincuria metho.   [Meru reading primer for adults]   3rd ed.   30pp. ill.   K.shs.1.40   ($1.25/50p.)   EALB 1969 KE MER

Holding, E.M.
Mucii jumwega.   [The good home]   23pp. ill. K.shs.0.50   ($1.00/40p.)   EALB 1950 KE MER

Holding, E.M.
Utheru thiini wa mucii.   [Cleanliness in the home]   2 2nded.   21pp.   K.shs.0.50   ($1.00/40p.)   EALB 1964 KE KIK

Holdsworth, A.H.
Technical drawings for South African schools, standard 8. 65pp. ill.   R2.25   Nasou 1975 SA

Hole, H.M.
The Jameson raid.   [Reprint of ed. 1930].   306pp. ill. fold. map. cl.   R$8.00   (Rhodesiana Reprint Library, Gold Series, 30)   Books of Rhodesia 1973 RH

Hole, H.M.
Old Rhodesian days.   [Reprint ed. 1928].   140pp. ill. cl. R$10.30 cl.   (Rhodesiana Reprint Library, Silver Series, 8)   Books of Rhodesia 1976 RH

Holgate, A.M.
Ngono cia afya. [Health games and stories in Meru] 4th ed. 9pp. K.shs.1.30 ($1.25/50p.) EALB 1971 KE MER

Holland, D.F.
Steam locomotives of the S.A.R. & H. 1859-1910. 141pp. Photos. hd. R7.50 Purnell 1971 SA

Holland, D.F.
Steam locomotives of the South African Railways. SAR locos 1910-55 and Harbour Board locos 1873-1904. 144pp. photos. hd. R7.50 Purnell 1972 SA

Holland, F.
Talking with God. See: Holland, G.

Holland, F.
Teaching through T.E.E.: help for leaders in Theological Education by Extension in Africa. 48pp. K.shs.9.00 ($1.40) Evangel 1975 KE

Holland, G.
Bringing people to Jesus. See: Moyo, J.

Holland, G.
Comment amener les gens à Jésus. See: Moyo, J.

Holland, G.
Comment prier, parler avec Dieu. 168pp. CFA500 CPE 1975 IV FRE

Holland, G.
How to pray. 32pp. K.shs.2.00 Evangel 1975 KE

Holland, G.
How to talk with God. 32pp. K.shs.2.00 Evangel 1975 KE

Holland, G. Holland, F.
Talking with God. 150pp. K.shs.13.00 Evangel 1973 KE

Holleman, J.F.
Accommodating the spirit amongst some northeastern Shona tribes. 49pp. 75n. (38p.) (Rhodes-Livingstone paps., 22) Inst Soc Res - Zam ZA

Holleman, J.F.
Experiment in Swaziland. 366pp. maps. R6.90 OUP-SA 1964 SA

Holleman, J.F.
The pattern of Hera kinship. 51pp. 60n. (30p.) (Rhodes-Livingstone paps., 17) Inst Soc Res - Zam 1949 ZA

Holleman, J.F.
Shona customary law. 372pp. ill. hd. K4.20 (£2.10/$6.50) Inst Afr Stud - Lusaka 1952 ZA

Holloway, V.
Cecil Higgs. 64pp. photos. cl. & pap. R6.75 pap. R9.00 cl. (South African Art Library, 2) Struik 1974 SA

Holm, E.
Bibliography of South African pre- and proto-historic archaeology. R5.25 Van Schaik SA

Holmes, T. Chipimo, E.M.
Our land and people: summary and comprehension exercises for school certificate. 198pp. K.shs.7.50 OUP-Nairobi 1966 KE

Holmes, T. Chipimo, E.
Our land and peoples: Summary and comprehension exercises for school certificate. 184pp. K1.24 OUP - Lusaka 1966 ZA

Holt, B.
Greatheart of the Border. A life of John Brownlee, pioneer missionary in South Africa. 162pp. ill. pl. maps. R5.00 SA Missionary Museum 1976 SA

Holt, D.N.
The geology of the Thyolo area. See: Habgood, F.

Holt, D.N.
The Kangankunde rare earth prospect. 130pp. pl. hd. K2.00 (Geological Survey of Malawi, Bull. 20) Geol Survey - Mal 1965 MW

Holtzhausen, J., et al.
Modern general mathematics for standard 6. (New Syllabus OFS) 277pp. ill. R4.35 Nasou 1974 SA

Holtzhausen, J. Marais, C.H.J.
Modern general mathematics for standard 7. 249pp. ill. R5.00 Nasou 1974 SA

Holub, E.
Seven years in South Africa. [Reprint of 1881 ed.]. v. 2 400pp. ill. hd. R13.95 (Africana Reprint Library, 5) Africana Book Soc 1976 SA

Holub, E.
Seven years in South Africa. [Reprint of ed. 1881]. v. 7 458pp. ill. hd. R14.70 (Africana Reprint Library, 4) Africana Book Soc 1975 SA

Holy, L.
Zambia traditional art. 48pp. photos. gratis Zambia Cult Serv 1971 ZA

Homaro, F.
Rà Mandriaka tao amin'. [Villa Rayon d'Or du sang à la villa.] 200pp. FMG250 Ed Takariva 1974 MG MLA

Honey, J.R.de S.
Tom Brown in South Africa. ex. only (Inaugural lec.) Rhodes Univ Lib 1972 SA

Hong Cam, T. Le Boul, M.
Le bilinguisme scolaire au Zaire. 83pp. CELTA 1976 ZR FRE

Hong Cam, T. Le Boul, M.
Une enquête sur le plurilinguisme au Zaire. 190pp. CELTA 1976 ZR FRE

Honore, E.J.
Forestry in Kenya. K.shs.3.00 EALB 1968 KE

Honore, T.
South African law of trusts. 2nd rev. ed. 568pp. cl. R44.00 Juta 1976 SA

Hooper, A.G., ed. Harvey, C.J.D., ed.
Poems for discussion: with commentaries and questions. 160pp. R2.50 OUP-SA 1970 SA

Hooper, A.G., ed.
Short stories from Southern Africa. 160pp. R2.60 cl. R2.48 hd. OUP-SA 1970 SA

Hooper, A.G., ed. Harvey, C.J.D., ed.
Talking of poetry: teacher's companion. 12pp. 30c. OUP-SA 1961 SA

Hooper, A.G., ed. Harvey, C.J.D., ed.
Talking of poetry: with commentaries and questions. 200pp. R2.50 OUP-SA 1967 SA

Hooper, C.
Design for climate. Guidelines for the design of low cost houses for the climates of Kenya. 135pp. K.shs.60.00 Housing Res Dev Unit 1975 KE

Hooper, C.
Kariobangi experimental timber houses. 66pp. K.shs.39.60 Housing Res Dev Unit 1974 KE

Hooper, C.
Kenyatta National Hospital, a user-reaction survey of staff quarters for staff nurses/medical registrars. 42pp. K.shs.11.00 Housing Res Dev Unit 1973 KE

Hooper, C.
Kibera new village, Nairobi. 17pp. K.shs.10.20 Housing Res Dev Unit 1974 KE

Hooper, C.
Pilot rural housing schemes. 11pp. K.shs.6.60 Housing Res Dev Unit 1974 KE

Hooper, C.
Survey of kitchens at the Kariobangi timber experimental housing scheme. 11pp. K.shs.6.60 Housing Res Dev Unit 1973 KE

Hopcraft, P.N., et al.
An evaluation of the Kenya diary improvement programme. 221pp. K.shs.25.00 (Inst. Development Studies, occas. paps., 20) Inst Dev Stud 1976 KE

Hope, G.S., et al., eds.
The equatorial glaciers of New Guinea. Results of the 1971-1973 Australian Universities' Expeditions to Irian Jaya: survey, glaciology, meteorology, biology and palaeoenvironments. 280pp. col. photos. maps. cl. ($16.00/£9.50) Balkema 1976 SA

Hopgood, C.R.
Practical introduction to Tonga. 250pp. K1.00 Neczam 1972 ZA

Hopkins, B.   Stanfield, D.P.
A field key to the savanna trees of Nigeria. 39pp. N1.00 Ibadan UP 1966 NR

Hopkins, D.A.S.
The geology of the Rumphi-Nkhata Bay area. 42pp. pl. maps. K4.00 (Geological Survey of Malawi, Bull. 38/39) Geol Survey - Mal 1973 MW

Hopley, M.L.
Electronic distance measurement. 104pp. R5.30 Dept Bibliog, Lib & Typo 1968 SA

Hopwood, D.
The place names of the County of Surrey including London in Surrey. 101pp. 25c. (B v.4, no.2) Univ Stellenbosch, Lib 1926 SA

Horn, P., eds.
It's gettin late, and other poems from "Ophir".
See: Saunders, W., eds.

Horn, P.
Walking through our sleep. 71pp. R1.95 ($2.40/£1.25) Ravan 1974 SA

Horn, P.R.G.
The literary text as an open-ended structure. 14pp. 30c (Univ. Cape Town. Inaugural lec., 29) Univ Cape Town Lib 1975 SA

Horn, R.E.
A novel method for the crease-resist finishing and dyeing of cotton fabrics using phenolic-formaldehyde resins and diazonium salts, part I: a preliminary investigation. 15pp. R2.50 (SAWTRI Technical Reports, 326) SAWTRI 1976 SA

Horn, R.E.
The simultaneous dyeing and crease-resist finishing of cotton fabrics with acid dyes and resin precondensates part II: a study of catelysts for DMDHEU. 14pp. R2.50 (SAWTRI Technical Reports, 304) SAWTRI 1976 SA

Horn, R.E.
The simultaneous dyeing and crease-resist finishing of cotton fabrics with acid dyestuffs and resin precondensates, part 1: a preliminary investigation. 14pp. R2.50 (SAWTRI Technical Reports, 273) SAWTRI 1975 SA

Horn, R.E.
The simultaneous dyeing and crease-resist finishing of cotton with acid dyes and resin precondensates, part III: a study of some resin precondensates. 13pp. R2.50 (SAWTRI Technical Reports, 324) SAWTRI 1976 SA

Horner, D., comp.
Registered trade unions in South Africa. 51pp. 75c ($2.10/90p) SA Inst of Race Relations 1975 SA

Horner, D., comp.
A select bibliography on the poverty datum line in South Africa. See: Edwards, J., comp.

Horner, D., ed.
Labour organisation and the African worker. 77pp. R1.20 ($2.55/£1.15) SA Inst of Race Relations 1975 SA

Horner, D., ed.
A survey of race relations in South Africa, 1974.
See: Horrell, M., ed.

Horner, D.
A survey of race relations in South Africa, 1973.
See: Horrell, M.

Horner, D.B.
Francis Carey Slater, 1876-1958. 50pp.   R2.60 Dept Bibliog, Lib & Typo 1970 SA

Horner, J.H.
Black pay and productivity. 23pp.   60c. ($1.40) SA Inst of Race Relations 1972 SA

Horrell, M.
Action, reaction and counteraction: a brief review of non-white political movements in South Africa. 2nd. ed. 151pp.   R1.50   ($2.60) SA Inst of Race Relations 1971 SA

Horrell, M.
The African homelands of South Africa. 175pp. maps. R2.25   ($3.45) SA Inst of Race Relations 1973 SA

Horrell, M.
Bantu education to 1968. 170pp. hd.   R1.95 ($3.10) SA Inst of Race Relations 1968 SA

Horrell, M., comp.
Brief guide to some laws affecting African women. 10pp. 30c ($1.00/50p) SA Inst of Race Relations 1975 SA

Horrell, M., ed.   Norman, J., ed.   Horner, D., ed.
A survey of race relations in South Africa, 1974. 422pp. R6.00 ($8.05/£4.50) SA Inst of Race Relations 1975 SA

Horrell, M.
The education of the coloured community in South Africa 1652-1970. 190pp.   R1.75   ($2.95) SA Inst of Race Relations 1970 SA

Horrell, M.
Legislation and race relations: a summary of the main South African laws which affect race relationships. 3 3rd.ed. 121pp.   R1.25   ($2.30) SA Inst of Race Relations 1971 SA

Horrell, M.
The rights of African women: some suggested reforms. 2nd ed. 18pp.   45c ($1.10) SA Inst of Race Relations 1975 SA

Horrell, M.
South Africa and the Olympic games. 26pp. photos. 50c. ($1.45) SA Inst of Race Relations 1968 SA

Horrell, M.
South Africa: basic facts and figures. 115pp.   R1.50 ($2.60) SA Inst of Race Relations 1973 SA

Horrell, M.
South West Africa. 94pp. maps. 50c. ($1.45) SA Inst of Race Relations 1967 SA

Horrell, M.
A survey of race relations in South Africa, 1961. 311pp. R1.50 ($2.75) SA Inst of Race Relations 1962 SA

Horrell, M.
A survey of race relations in South Africa, 1962. 254pp. R1.50 ($2.75) SA Inst of Race Relations 1963 SA

Horrell, M.
A survey of race relations in South Africa, 1963. 346pp. R1.50 ($2.75) SA Inst of Race Relations 1964 SA

Horrell, M.
A survey of race relations in South Africa, 1964. 371pp. R1.50 ($2.75) SA Inst of Race Relations 1965 SA

Horrell, M.
A survey of race relations in South Africa, 1967. 334pp. R2.00 ($3.45) SA Inst of Race Relations 1968 SA

Horrell, M.
A survey of race relations in South Africa, 1968. 327pp. R2.00 ($3.45) SA Inst of Race Relations 1969 SA

Horrell, M.
A survey of race relations in South Africa, 1969. 279pp. R2.00 ($3.45) SA Inst of Race Relations 1970 SA

Horrell, M.
A survey of race relations in South Africa, 1970. 299pp. R2.00 ($3.45) SA Inst of Race Relations 1971 SA

Horrell, M.
A survey of race relations in South Africa, 1971. 360pp. R3.00 ($4.60) SA Inst of Race Relations 1972 A

Horrell, M.
A survey of race relations in South Africa, 1972. 360pp. R3.00 ($4.60) SA Inst of Race Relations 1973 SA

Horrell, M.   Horner, D.
A survey of race relations in South Africa, 1973. 411pp. R3.00 ($4.60) SA Inst of Race Relations 1974 SA

Horrell, M.   Hodgson, A.
A survey of race relations in South Africa, 1975. 370pp. R6.00 ($8.05) SA Inst of Race Relations 1976 SA

Horrell, M.
A survey of race relations in South Africa, 1951/52. 82pp. 50c. ($1.50) SA Inst of Race Relations 1952 SA

Horrell, M.
A survey of race relations in South Africa, 1955/56. 265pp. R1.00 ($2.30) SA Inst of Race Relations 1956 SA

Horrell, M.
A survey of race relations in South Africa, 1959/60. 309pp. R1.25 ($2.60) SA Inst of Race Relations 1960 SA

Horrobin, D.F.
Essential biochemistry, endocrinology and nutrition. 111pp. ill. K.shs10.75 ($3.20) EAPH 1971 KE

Horrobin, D.F.
Essential physics, chemistry and biology. 119pp. ill. K.shs10.75 ($3.20) EAPH 1971 KE

Horton, A.E.
A grammar of Luvale. 221pp. map. R15.00 (Bantu grammatical archives, 2) Witwatersrand UP 1949 SA

Horton, R.
Kalabari sculpture. 127pp. ill. N1.25 Dept Antiquities 1965 NR

Hoshino, Y.
Kisa cha kusisimua cha Mito Komon. [Play.] tr. fr. Japanese. 45pp. K.shs.12.00 ($2.70/£1.50) EALB 1977 KE SWA

Hoskyn, M.
From sackbut to symphony. 3rd ed. ill. R3.00 Juta 1968 SA

Hoskyns, C.
Case studies in African diplomacy: 2. Ethiopian-Kenya-Somali dispute, 1960-67. 96pp. map. K.shs16.50 (I.P.A. Study, 9) OUP-Nairobi 1968 KE

Hoskyns, C.
Case studies in African diplomacy: v. 1. the O.A.U. and the Congo crisis 1964-65. 96pp. K.shs14.50 (I.P.A. Study, 8) OUP-Nairobi 1969 KE

Hottin, G.
Bibliographie géologique de Madagascar, 1967-1969. See: Besairie, H.

Hottin, G.
Etude géologique de la feuille Ambatolam. 36pp. pl. map. FMG1070 (F21.40) (Travaux du Bureau Géologique, 121) Service Geol - Mad 1965 MG FRE

Hottin, G.
Etude géologique et prospection des feuilles: Antenina-M. 25pp. pl. map. FMG843 (F16.86) (Travaux du Bureau Géologique, 9) Service Geol - Mad 1960 MG FRE

Hottin, G.
Etude géologique et prospection des feuilles Vohimenakely, Vavatenima-Fenerive. 45pp. pl. maps. FMG1590 (F31.80) (Travaux du Bureau Géologique, 126) Service Geol - Mad 1967 MG FRE

Hottin, G.
Géochronologie et stratigraphie malgaches. Essai d'interprétation. 16pp. pl. FMG275 (F5.50) (Série Documentation, 182) Service Geol - Mad 1970 MG FRE

Hottin, G.   Liandrat, E.
Géologie de la presqu'île Masoala. 32pp. pl. map. FMG742 (F14.84) (Travaux du Bureau Géologique, 118) Service Geol - Mad 1964 MG FRE

Hottin, G.
Recherches du bauxites sur les Tampoketsa de la région centrale. 27pp. pl. photos. FMG1150 (F23.00) (Travaux du Bureau Géologique, 104) Service Geol - Mad 1961 MG FRE

Hottin, G.
Les terrains cristallins du centre-nord et du nord-est de Madagascar. 1, 2v. 192pp. pl. map. FMG1554 (F31.08) Service Geol - Mad 1969 MG FRE

Hottin, G.
Les terrains cristallins du centre-nord et du nord-est de Madagascar. 2, 2v. 188pp. FMG1780 (F35.60) Service Geol - Mad 1969 MG FRE

Houghton, D.H.   Dagut, J.
Source material on the South African economy, 1860-1899. 1, 3 vols. 396pp. R4.65 pap. R8.40 cl. OUP-SA 1972 SA

Houghton, D.H.   Dagut, J.
Source material on the South African economy, 1899-1919. 2, 3 vols. 264pp. R3.50 pap. R6.90 cl. OUP-SA 1972 SA

Houghton, D.H.   Dagut, J.
Source material on the South African economy, 1919-1970. 3, 3vols. 270pp. R6.90 cl. R3.50 pap. OUP-SA 1972 SA

Houghton, D.H.
The South African economy. 4th. ed. 300pp. maps. cl. & pap. R4.75 pap. R8.50 cl. OUP-SA 1976 SA

Houghton-Hawksley, H.S.   Kleyn, B.D.   Pfaff, D.N.
English with ease for Afrikaans-speaking pupils, standard 5. 147pp. ill. pl. R2.15 Nasou 1974 SA

Houghton-Hawksley, H.S.   Kleyn, B.D.   Pfaff, D.N.
English with ease for Afrikaans-speaking pupils, standard 6. 168pp. photos. R2.15 Nasou 1974 SA

Houghton-Hawksley, H.S.   Kleyn, B.D.   Pfaff, D.N.
English with ease for Afrikaans-speaking pupils, standard 7. 185pp. ill. photo. R2.25 Nasou 1975 SA

Houghton-Hawksley, H.S.   Kleyn, B.D.
English with ease for Afrikaans-speaking pupils, standard 8. 163pp. ill. pl. R2.40 Nasou 1974 SA

Houghton-Hawksley, H.S.   Kleyn, B.D.
English with ease for Afrikaans-speaking pupils, standard 9. 181pp. ill. photo. R3.15 Nasou 1975 SA

Houghton-Hawksley, H.S.   Klyen, B.D.
English with ease for Afrikaans-speaking pupils, standard 10. 231pp. ill. photo. R3.95 Nasou 1975 SA

Houghton, J.
Here's how to be a writer. 18pp. 15n Multimedia 1971 ZA

Houghton, J.
Here's how to write a play. 17pp. 15n Multimedia 1971 ZA

Houghton, J.C.
Borrowed time. 78pp. 95n. Neczam 1973 ZA

Houis, M. et al.
Annales de l'université d'Abidjan. Actes du 8e congres de la société de linguistique de l'Afrique occidentale. 2v. 677pp. (Série H-Linguistique) Univ Abidjan 1971 IV FRE

Houis, M.
Etude descriptive de la langue Susu. 183pp. map. (F34.00) (Mémoires de l'IFAN, 67) IFAN 1963 SG FRE

Houis, M.
Les noms individuels chez les Mosi. 137pp. CFA800 (Initiations et Etudes Africaines, 17) IFAN 1963 SG FRE

Houlberg, P.
Dwelling unit in public low-cost housing, interim analysis and report. 1, 2 v. 38pp. Housing Res Dev Unit 1970 KE

Houlberg, P.
Dwelling unit in public low-cost housing, recordings. 2, 2 v. 131pp. Housing Res Dev Unit 1970 KE

Houlberg, P. Steele, R. Jorgensen, N.O.
Site and service schemes, analysis and report. 109pp.
K.shs.64.40 Housing Res Dev Unit 1971 KE

Houlberg, P.
Timber development committee: pilot scheme at
Kariobangi. 15pp. K.shs.9.00 Housing Res Dev Unit
1971 KE

Houyoux, J.
Budgets ménagers, nutrition et mode de vie à Kinshasa.
303pp. Z3.00 Press Univ Zaire 1973 ZR FRE

How, M.W.
The mountain bushmen of Basutoland. R3.75 Van
Schaik SA

Howarth, A.
Kenyatta: a pictorial biography. 160pp. photos.
K.shs.25.00 ($7.20) EAPH 1967 KE

Howat, G.R.
Not by bread alone. 13pp. 30k (Inaugural lec., 1)
Univ Ife Press 1973 NR

Howell, J.
Local government and politics in the Sudan. 125pp.
90pt. ($4.00) Khartoum UP 1974 SJ

Howells, A.W.
Oruka igbeyawo. [The marriage ring] 36pp. 10k
Daystar NR YOR

Howells, A.W.
To omo re. [Guide your children] 16pp. 10k
Daystar 1966 NR YOR

Howels, F.
Annotated bibliography and index of the geology of
Zambia, 1970-1971. See: von Bornemann, J.

Howson, P.J.
A short history of Karonga. 54pp. pl. maps. 75t
(Department of Antiquities, 11) Dept Antiquities - Mal
1972 MW

Hoyle, S.S.
The seaports of East Africa. 133pp. maps.
K.shs17.00 ($4.20) EAPH 1967 KE

Huard, P. et al.
Annales de l'université d'Abidjan. 317pp. CFA1500
(F30.00) (Série B - Médecine, 1) Univ Abidjan 1965 IV
FRE

Hubback, J.C.
Lessons in English in Bantu schools. 113pp. 28c.
Lovedale 1958 SA

Hudson, J.R.
The effects on agriculture of the growth and prosperity of
the South African economy. 30pp. 61c. (A v.41
no.5) Univ Stellenbosch, Lib 1966 SA

Hudson-Reed., ed.
1820 settlers stories. R2.50 Macmillan, SA 1972 SA

Hudson, W.
A study of pictorial perception among Bantu and white
primary school children in South Africa. See: Duncan,
H.F.

Hughes, A.J.
Kin, caste and nation among the Rhodesian Ndebele.
96pp. K1.05 (53p.) (Rhodes-Livingstone paps., 25)
Inst Soc Res - Zam 1956 ZA

Hughes, A.J.B.
Swazi land tenure. Inst Soc Res-Natal 1964 SA

Hughes, C.M.
A careers guide for East Africa. K.shs7.40
($2.25/90p.) EALB 1963 KE

Hughes, G.
Miti ni Mali. [Trees are wealth] 3rd ed. 22pp. ill.
K.shs.1.20 ($1.25/50p.) EALB 1965 KE SWA

Hughes, G.R.
The sea turtles of south-east Africa, 1: status, morphology
and distributions. 144pp. R3.00 (Investigational
Reports, 35) Oceanographic Res Inst 1974 SA

Hughes, G.R.
The sea turtles of south-east Africa, 2: the biology of the
Tongaland loggerhead turtle "Caretta caretta L." with
comments on the leatherback turtle "Dermochelys coriacea
L." and the green turtle "Chelonia mydas L." in the study
region. 96pp. R1.70 (Investigational Reports, 36)
Oceanographic Res Inst 1974 SA

Hughes, L.
Johannesburg. [Also available in German.]. 80pp. ill. col.
ill. R3.95 (Struik's All-colour Southern Africa series)
Struik 1977 SA

Hugo, A.M.
The Cape vernacular. 28pp. 30c. (U.C.T. Inaugural
lec. New series, 2) Univ Cape Town Lib 1970 SA

Hugo, L.H.
Authority, literature and freedom. 16pp. 60c. (R1.10)
Univ South Africa 1970 SA

Huguet, L. Okafor, R.N.
Annales de l'université d'Abidjan. 323pp. CFA2,420
(F48.40) (Série D-Lettres, 8) Univ Abidjan 1975 IV FRE

Hulls, R.H.
Assessment of agricultural extension in Sukumuland.
65pp. T.shs12.00 ($3.00) (Research pap., 71.7)
Econ Res Bur - Tanz 1971 TZ

Human Sciences Research Council.
Dictionary of South African biography. v. 3. R16.00
Tafelberg 1977 SA

Human Sciences Research Council.
Kwic index of completed research 1969-1974. 95pp.
Human Science Res Council 1976 SA

Human Sciences Research Council.
Report of the committee for differentiated education and
guidance in connection with a national system of education
at primary and secondary school level with reference to
school guidance as an integrated service of the system of
education for the Republic of South Africa and South West
Africa, pt 1. 222pp. R3.15 Human Science Res
Council 1972 SA

Humbaraci, A.
Portugal's African wars. 416pp. maps. T.shs.30.00
Africa only Tanz Publ House 1975 TZ

Humphrey, D.
Malawi since 1964; economic development, progress and
prospects. 47pp. map. ex. only (Univ. Malawi, Dept.
of Economics, occas. paps., 1) Univ Malawi Lib; distr.
1974 MW

Humphrey, N.
Je, ng'ombe zako zatunzwa vema? [Are your cattle cared
for properly?] 2nd ed. 13pp. ill. K.shs.0.40
($1.00/40p.) EALB 1954 KE SWA

Humphrey, N.
Matuta ya mashambani katika nchi kavu. [Tie ridging in
dry areas] 8pp. K.shs.0.40 ($1.00/40p.) EALB
1951 KE SWA

Humphrey, N.
Wapenda lipi: kushiba au kuona njaa? [Aims of healthy
living] 8pp. ill. K.shs.0.40 ($1.00/40p.) EALB 1950
KE SWA

Humphrey, R.
Introduction to geography. 1, 2bks 96pp. photos.
maps. N1.65 Pilgrim 1966 NR

Humphrey, R.
Introduction to geography. 2, 2bks 128pp. photos.
maps. N1.85 Pilgrim 1972 NR

Hungu, J.
Uhuru na taifa Tanzania. [Independence and building of
nation in Tanzania] 74pp. photos. T.shs.4.00
Longman - Tanz 1971 TZ SWA

Hunt, D.
Credit for agricultural development. 416pp. maps.
K.shs.75.00 ($16.00) EAPH 1975 KE

Author Index

Hunter L.
The relationship between certain yarn and fibre properties for single wool worsted yarns. Part II: Yarn tensile properties 44pp. R2.50 (SAWTRI Technical Reports, 223) SAWTRI 1974 SA

Hunter, L.
The relationship between certain yarn and fibre properties for single wool worsted yarns, part III: medium and long term irregularity. 13pp. R2.50 (SAWTRI Technical Reports, 239) SAWTRI 1975 SA

Hunter, L.
The relationship between certain yarn and fibre properties for single wool worsted yarns. Pt. I: Short term yarn irregularity 40pp. R2.50 (SAWTRI Technical Reports, 211) SAWTRI 1974 SA

Hunter, L.   Dobson, D.A.   Cawood, M.P.
The relationship between yarn properties and knitting performance for cotton yarns knitted to a constant stitch length on single and double jersey machines. 9pp. R2.50 (SAWTRI Technical Reports, 327) SAWTRI 1976 SA

Hunter, L.   Cawood, M.   Dobson, D.A.
Single jersey knitting performance, part I: a comparison of the knitting performance at different feeders and of various structures. 15pp. R2.50 (SAWTRI Technical Reports, 260) SAWTRI 1975 SA

Hunter, L.   Turpie, D.W.F.
Some comments on the spinning performance and resulting yarn properties of wool and wool/polyester blends. 15pp. R2.50 (SAWTRI Technical Reports, 228) SAWTRI 1974 SA

Hunter, L.
Some double jersey ruck structures in wool, part II: fabric physical properties. 22pp. R2.50 (SAWTRI Technical Reports, 294) SAWTRI 1976 SA

Hunter, L.
Some double jersey tuck structures in wool, part I: knitting performance and dimensional properties. 24pp. R2.50 (SAWTRI Technical Reports, 247) SAWTRI 1975 SA

Hunter, L.
Some technical information and data: 1. 55pp. R2.50 SAWTRI 1975 SA

Hunter, L.
Studies of some wool–acrylic woven fabrics, part I: untreated plain and 2/2 twill weave fabrics from wool blended with regular acrylic. See: Smuts, S.

Hunter, L.
Studies of some wool/polyester woven fabrics, part III: untreated plain weave fabrics from wool blended with a normal and a special low-pilling polyester, respectively. See: Smuts, S.

Hunter, L.
Studies of some wool/polyester woven fabrics, part IV: easy-care finished fabrics from wool blended with normal and special low pilling polyester respectively. See: Smuts, S.

Hunter, L.
The transfer printing of fabrics knitted from cotton-rich blends of cotton and polyester. See: Roberts, M.B.

Hunter, M.
The study of African society. See: Wilson, G.

Huntly, J.
Veld sketchbook. 168pp. ill. col. ill. cl. R$6.75 (R$3.50) Books of Rhodesia 1974 RH

Huntly, J.
The world of the waggon. A portfolio of prints of six paintings in tempera, with accompanying text by Peter Joyce. (305x430mm) boxed set R$40.95 Books of Rhodesia 1974 RH

Hunwick, J.O.
Islam in Africa, Friend or foe. 27pp. C1.00 (50p./$1.00) (Inaugural lecture) Ghana UP 1976 GH

Hunwick, J.O.
Literacy and scholarship in Muslim West Africa in the pre-colonial period. 39pp. 50k Inst Afric Stud - Nig 1974 NR

Hunwick, J.O.
Study of Muslim Africa: retrospect and prospect. 55pp. C1.50 Univ Ghana Bkshop; distr. 1976 GH

Hurais, S.H., ed.   Bell, H., ed.
Directions in Sudanese linguistics and folklore. 178pp. ill. LS1.75 ($8.00) Khartoum UP 1975 SJ

Hurault, J.
Les noirs réfugiés Boni de la Guyane française. 362pp. ill. CFA3000 (Mémoires de l'IFAN, 63) IFAN 1961 SG FRE

Hurley, D.
Catholics and ecunmenism: prospects and problems. 50c. (Peter Ainslie Memorial lec., 17) Rhodes Univ Lib 1966 SA

Hurwitz, J.   Chosack, H.
Irma Stern. Dept Bibliog, Lib & Typo 1973 SA

Hurwitz, N.
Agriculture in Natal, 1860-1950. $3.25 (Natal regional survey pub., 12) Dept Econ--Natal 1957 SA

Hurwitz, N.   Williams, O.
The economic framework of South Africa. 148pp. maps ill. cl. R4.00 Shuter 1963 SA

Hurwitz, N.
The native reserves of Natal. See: Brookes, E.H.

Hurwitz, N.M.   Nevin, B.M.
A first course in economic analysis. 90pp. ill. R1.35 Shuter 1961 SA

Hushie, S.E.
Jen ye gbeyei. [The world is a wonderful place.] 152pp. ill. C1.60 Bur Ghana Lang 1975 GH GAA

Huss, B.
Textbook on agriculture. 176pp. ill. 90c. Longman SA 1968 SA

Hussein, E.N.
Jogoo Kijijini/Ngao ya jadi. [Dramatic poems.] 56pp. K.shs.7.50 OUP - Nairobi 1976 KE

Hussein, E.N.
Kinjeketile. 64pp. K.shs5.25 (New Drama from Africa, 5) OUP-Nairobi 1970 KE

Hussein, E.N.
Mashetani. [The devils] 68pp. K.shs7.00 OUP-Nairobi 1972 KE SWA

Hussein, H.A.   Pellat, C.
Cheherazade. Personnage littéraire. 156pp. DA10.00 SNED 1976 AE FRE

Hussein, N.
Michezo ya Kuigiza. [Swahili plays] 64pp. K.shs4.10 ($1.30) EAPH 1970 KE SWA

Hussein, N.
Wakati ukuta. [Swahili plays] 41pp. K.shs3.00 ($1.00) EAPH 1971 KE SWA

Hussein, T.
Les jours. Tr. fr. Arabic J. Lecerf & G. Wiet 264pp. DA25.00 SNED 1975 AE FRE

Huszar, L.
The towns of Ghana. See: Grove, D.

Hutchinson, P.
A bibliography of the climate of Zambia. 58pp. K1.00 ($2.00) (Zambia Geographical Assoc., Bibliographic series, 2) Zambia Geog Assoc 1975 ZA

Hutchinson, P.
Climate data for architects in Zambia. 81pp. K5.00 ($10.00) (Zambia Geographical Assoc., occas. paps., 8) Zambia Geog Assoc 1976 ZA

Hutchinson, P.
The climate of Zambia. 95pp. K2.50 ($5.00) (Zambia Geographical Assoc., occas. pap., 7) Zambia Geog Assoc 1974 ZA

Author Index

Hutheasing.
Hadithi ya maisha ya Mahatma Gandhi.   tr. J.S. Wanzala
K.shs3.60   Equatorial 1973 KE SWA

Hutton, J.
Urban challenge in East Africa.   285pp. photos.
K.shs42.00   ($12.00)   EAPH 1972 KE

Hutton, S.P.
College English, pupil's.   1   See: Rogers, J.

Hutton, S.P.
College English, pupil's.   2   See: Rogers, J.

Hutton, S.P.
College English, teacher's notes.   1   See: Rogers, J.

Hutton, S.P.
College English, teacher's notes.   2   See: Rogers, J.

Hyatt, S.P.
The old transport road. [Reprint ed. 1914].   301pp.
photos. cl.   R$8.80 cl.   (Rhodesiana Reprint Library,
Gold Series, 3)   Books of Rhodesia 1969 RH

Hyde, R.
The analysis of crop distribution in Uganda.   172pp.
maps fold. maps.   U.shs.20.00   (Makerere Univ., Dept.
of Geog., occas. paps., 65)   Dept Geog - Mak 1975 UG

Hyde, R.J.   Langlands, B.W.
Patterns of food crop production and nutrition in Uganda.
89pp. maps.   U.shs.40.00   (Occas. paps., 58)   Dept
Geog - Mak 1975 UG

Hyden, G.   Mutaha, A.Z., et al.
Cooperatives in Tanzania.   96pp.   T.shs.15.00   ($3.00)
(Tanzania Studies series, 4)   Tanz Publ House 1976 TZ

Hyden, G.
A decade of public administration in Africa.
See: Rweyemamu, A.H.

Hyden, G.   Okumu, J.   Jackson, R.
Development administration: the Kenyan experience.
320pp. pap. & cl.   K.shs.58.50 cl.   K.shs.35.00 pap.
OUP-Nairobi 1971 KE

Hyden, G., ed.
Developing research in African administration. Some
methodological issues.   See: Adedeji, A., ed.

Hyden, G., ed.
Developing research on African administration. Some
methodological issues.   See: Adedeji, A., ed.

Hyden, G.
Efficiency versus distribution in East African cooperatives:
organizational conflicts in cooperatives in East Africa.   hd.
K.shs.65.00   ($12.00/£6.00)   EALB 1972 KE

Hyden, G.
Political development in rural Tanzania.   275pp. maps.
K.shs.56.00 cl.   K.shs.21.00 pap.   ($10.40 cl.)   ($5.80
pap.)   EAPH 1969 KE

Hyder, S.
Recipes from the coast.   80pp. col. ill.   K.shs.9.75
Longman - Ken 1975 KE

Hyland, T.
The castles of Elmina.   27pp. photos.   30pes.
(Ghana Museums & Monuments Board, 3)   Ghana
Museums 1971 GH

Hyman, L.M.   Magaji, D.J.
Essentials of Gwari grammar.   150pp.   N3.00   (Inst. of
African Stud., Univ. of Ibadan, occas pub., 27)   Inst Afr
Stud-Ibadan 1970 NR

Hyman, R.
Evans first dictionary.   128pp. ill. col. ill.   K.shs.18.00
(95p.)   Evans - Nig 1976 NR

Hyman, R.
Universal primary dictionary.   128pp. ill. col. ill.   N1.60
NR only   Evans - Nig 1976 NR

Hyslop, G.
Since singing is so good a thing.   136pp.   K.shs10.00
OUP-Nairobi 1972 KE

Hyslop, G.H.
Afadhali mchawi.   [A witchdoctor is better]   32pp.
K.shs4.00   OUP-Nairobi 1964 KE SWA

Hyslop, G.H.
Mgeni karibu.   [Welcome, stranger]   16pp.   K.shs2.75
OUP-Nairobi 1964 KE SWA

Ibadan Chamber of Commerce.
Commercial directory of Ibadan. 1974 issue.   50pp.
50k   Ibadan Chamber Comm 1974 NR

Ibadan University Library.
Catalogue of serials in the library.   558pp.   N5.00
Ibadan U Lib 1976 NR

Ibadan University Library.
Index to the Herbert Macaulay (1864-1946) collection.
152pp.   N1.00   Ibadan U Lib 1975 SA

Ibadan University Library.
Nigerian periodicals and newspapers, 1950-1970: a list of
those received by Ibadan University Library, April
1950-June 1970.   122pp.   N1.00   Ibadan U Lib 1971
NR

Ibadan University Library.
Nigerian publications, 1958.   N1.00   Ibadan UP 1959
NR

Ibadan University Library.
Nigerian publications, 1959.   N1.00   Ibadan UP 1960
NR

Ibadan University Library.
Nigerian publications, 1960.   N1.00   Ibadan UP 1961
NR

Ibadan University Library.
Nigerian publications, 1961.   N1.00   Ibadan UP 1962
NR

Ibadan University Library.
Nigerian publications, 1962.   N1.00   Ibadan UP 1963
NR

Ibadan University Library.
Nigerian publications, 1963.   N1.00   Ibadan UP 1964
NR

Ibadan University Library.
Nigerian publications, 1964.   N1.00   Ibadan UP 1965
NR

Ibadan University Library.
Nigerian publications, 1965.   N1.00   Ibadan UP 1966
NR

Ibadan University Library.
Nigerian publications, 1966.   N1.00   Ibadan UP 1967
NR

Ibadan University Library.
Nigerian publications, 1967.   N1.00   Ibadan UP 1968
NR

Ibadan University Library.
Nigerian publications, 1968.   N1.00   Ibadan UP 1969
NR

Ibadan University Library.
Nigerian publications, 1969.   N1.00   Ibadan UP 1970
NR

Ibadan University Press.
Foundation and roots. The Fourth Alexander Brown
Memorial lecture.   18pp.   N1.00   Ibadan UP 1975 NR

Ibeziako, E.A.
An outline of the defence of bona fide claim of right.
116pp. hd. & pap.   N3.00 hd.   N2.50 pap.   Univ
Nigeria Bkshop; distr. 1973 NR

Ibikunle, S.
Iwe ijinle Yoruba.   [A book of pure Yoruba]   1, 3 bks.
86pp. maps ill.   N1.00   OUP - Nig 1969 NR YOR

Ibikunle, S.
Iwe ijinle Yoruba.   [A book of pure Yoruba]   2, 3 bks.
103pp. ill.   N1.10   OUP - Nig 1970 NR YOR

Ibikunle, S.
Iwe ijinle Yoruba.   [A book of pure Yoruba]   3, 3 bks.
178pp. ill.   N1.55   OUP - Nig 1972 NR YOR

Ibingira, G.
The forging of an African nation. The political and constitutional evolution of Uganda from colonial rule to independence, 1894-1962. 332pp. ill. cl. U.shs.30.00 East Africa only Uganda Pub House 1973 UG

Ibongia, J.M.
The magic stone. 40pp. ill. K.shs2.50 ($1.00) EAPH 1967 KE

Ibrahim, H.A.
The 1936 Anglo-Egyptian treaty. 178pp. ($6.00) Khartoum UP 1976 SJ

Ibukun, O.
The return. 271pp. K.shs9.50 ($3.20) EAPH 1970 KE

ICEL-Tanzania Mission Press.
The order of Mass for the altar. 2nd ed. 48pp. loose leaves for binder ($2.20) TMP 1971 TZ

ICEL-Tanzania Mission Press.
The peoples' order of Mass. 5th ed. 32pp. ($0.50) TMP 1974 TZ

I.C.I.C. (Directory Publishers) Ltd.
Directory of incorporated (registered) companies in Nigeria. 2nd. ed. 700pp. cl. N15.00 ($30.00) ICIC 1974 NR

Idang, G.J.
Nigeria: internal politics and foreign policy, 1960-1966. 171pp. N5.00 (Ibadan Political and Administrative Studies, 3) Ibadan UP 1974 NR

Idiok, R.
Feed your enemy. See: Nwakama, J.I.

Idowu, E.B.
Job: a meditation on the problems of suffering. 53pp. 75k Daystar 1966 NR

Idowu, E.B.
Obituary: God's or man's? 27pp. N1.00 (Inaugural lecture) Ibadan UP 1977 NR

Idumesaro, C.A.
Opuru ádírí Ogbia. [Ogbia reader, 1] 63pp. ill. 30k (Inst. of African Stud., Univ. of Ibadan, Rivers readers project, 16) Inst Afr Stud-Ibadan 1971 NR OGB

Idumesaro, C.A.
Teachers' notes on Opuru ádírí Ogbia. 91pp. 50k (Inst. of African Stud., Univ. of Ibadan, Rivers readers project, 17) Inst Afr Stud-Ibadan 1971 NR OGB

Ifejika, S.
The new religion. 192pp. N1.80 Nwamife 1973 NR

Ifeka, S.
Onicha kingship institution. 47pp. photos. N1.25 Herald 1973 NR

Ifwanga Wa P., et al.
Kutanga ti kusonika kikongo I. Livre de l'élève. 49pp. CELTA 1976 ZR LIN

Ifwanga Wa P., et al.
Kutanga ti kusonika kikongo I. Livre du maître. 57pp. CELTA 1976 ZR LIN

Igboko, P.
Modern primary mathematics. pupils bk. 4. See: Halim, E.C.

Igbozurilze, U.M.
Across the gap. 76pp. 85k Onibonoje 1977 NR

Igu, T.
The last days of Biafra: a drama. 46pp. 75k Survival 1972 NR

Iguh, T.
The best record songs. 108pp. 50k Gebo 1973 NR

Igun, A.A., ed. Acsadi, G.T., ed.
Demographic statistics in Nigeria: proceedings of the symposium on technical and practical problems in the collection of demographic statistics for reconstructions and development in Nigeria. 272pp. ill. N2.50 ($4.50/£1.60) Univ Ife Bkshop 1972 NR

Igun, A.A., ed.
Surveys of fertility, family and family planning in Nigeria. See: Ascadi, G.T., ed.

Igwe, G.E. Green, M.M.
Igbo language course. 1, 3 bks. 159pp. N1.50 OUP - Nig 1967 NR

Igwe, G.E. Green, M.M.
Igbo language course. 2, 3 bks. 70pp. 65k OUP - Nig 1967 NR

Igwe, G.E. Green, M.M.
Igbo language course. 3, 3 bks. 181pp. N1.45 OUP - Nig 1970 NR

Igwe, G.E. Green, M.M.
A short Igbo grammar. 60pp. 45k OUP - Nig 1964 NR

Ihezue, E.Y., ed.
Mbido Ogugu Igbo. [Igbo first reader.] 43pp. 65k Nwamife 1973 NR IGB

Ijagbemi, A.
Gbanka of Yoni. 100pp. Le1.00 Sierra Leone UP 1972 SL

Ijere, M.O., ed.
Prelude to the green revolution in the East Central state of Nigeria. 230pp. hd. N10.00 Nwamife 1975 NR

Ijimere, O. Ladipo, D.
Eda. [Man] 56pp. 40k Univ Ife Bkshop 1965 NR YOR

Ike, V.C.
University development in Africa: the Nigerian experience. 232pp. cl. N10.00 OUP - Nig 1976 NR

Ikeobi, I.O.
The mole concept. 76pp. N1.50 Ethiope 1975 NR

Ikime, O., ed.
West African chiefs: their changing status under colonial rule and independence. See: Crowder, M., ed.

Ikime, O.
The Isoko people: a historical survey. 166pp. maps. N2.50 Ibadan U.P. 1972 NR

Ikoku, C.
A chemistry laboratory manual. 128pp. ill. N1.50 Nwamife 1973 NR

Ikoku, S.G.
Economic development. Its conditions and strategies. 20pp. 75k (60p./$1.40) (Univ. of Ife, Faculty of Arts Lecture Series, 1) Univ Ife Press 1974 NR

Ikpe, M.S.
Dictionary of Ekpeye names. 2nd ed. 44pp. 40k (Inst. of Africa Stud., Univ. of Ibadan, occas. pub., 1) Inst Afr Stud-Ibadan 1972 NR EKP

Ikpe, M.S.
Teacher's notes on Ukpulawhu unûzú unu Ekpeye. 92pp. 50k (Inst. of African Stud., Univ. of Ibadan, Rivers readers project, 31) Inst Afr Stud-Ibadan 1972 NR

Ikpe, M.S. Udesi, E.D.C. Ogboka, S.N.
Ukpulawhu unûzú unu Ejpeye. [Ekpeye Reader, 1] 63pp. ill. 30k (Inst. of African Stud., Univ. of Ibadan, Rivers readers project, 30) Inst Afr Stud-Ibadan 1971 NR EKP

Ikpong et al.
Friendship between boys and girls. 2nd ed. 24pp. 10k Daystar 1962 NR

Ikunyua, E.K.
E.A.C.E. revision commerce. 124pp. K.shs.12.00 Textbook Ctre 1977 KE

Ikuponiyi, I.A.
An atlas for the Northern states of Nigeria. 25pp. maps. 80k Macmillan 1968 NR

Ilesanmi, G.E.
Arithmetic exercises for Nigerian schools. 1, 3bks 60pp. 40k Ilesanmi 1970 NR

Ilesanmi, G.E.
Arithmetic exercises for Nigerian schools. 2, 3bks 55pp. 45k Ilesanmi 1970 NR

Ilesanmi, G.E.
Arithmetic exercises for Nigerian schools. 3, 3bks
70pp. 50k Ilesanmi 1970 NR

Ilesanmi, G.E.
Civics made easy. 2nd ed. 1, 2bks 70pp. N1.10
Ilesanmi 1972 NR

Ilesanmi, G.E.
Civics made easy. 2nd ed. 2, 2bks 71pp. N1.10
Ilesanmi 1972 NR

Ilesanmi, G.E. Owoeye, J.A. Oloyede, J.A.
History made easy (Western State) 4th ed. 1, 2 bks
67pp. maps ill. N1.35 Ilesanmi 1971 NR

Ilesanmi, G.E. Owoeye, J.A. Oloyede, J.A.
History made easy (Western State) 4th ed. 2, 2 bks.
88pp. maps ill. N1.35 Ilesanmi 1971 NR

Ilesanmi, G.E.
Iwe asayan orin. [Selected hymns.] 48pp. ill. 60k
Ilesanmi 1973 NR YOR

Ilesanmi, G.E.
Mental sums for Nigerian schools. 1, 2bks 76pp.
95k Ilesanmi NR

Ilesanmi, G.E.
Mental sums for Nigerian schools. 2, 2bks 76pp.
95k Ilesanmi NR

Ilesanmi, G.E. Omopariola, J.A.
Modern English for Nigerian schools. 2nd ed. 1, 3bks
76pp. ill. 95k Ilesanmi 1970 NR

Ilesanmi, G.E. Omopariola, J.A.
Modern English for Nigerian schools. 2nd ed. 2, 3bks
91pp. N1.25 Ilesanmi 1968 NR

Ilesanmi, G.E. Omopariola, J.A.
Modern English for Nigerian schools. 2nd ed. 3, 3bks
107pp. N1.35 Ilesanmi 1970 NR

Ilesanmi, G.E.
Nature study and gardening. bk. 1. 88pp. N1.35
Ilesanmi 1964 NR

Ilesanmi, G.E.
Nature study and gardening. bk. 2. 81pp. N1.35
Ilesanmi 1964 NR

Ilesanmi, G.E.
Preparing for examination workbook. 125pp. maps.
N1.25 Ilesanmi 1962 NR

Ilesanmi, G.E.
Pupils' examination course for Nigerian schools. 96pp.
85k Ilesanmi 1968 NR

Ilesanmi, G.E.
Questions and model answers on past primary six
examinations. 224pp. 40k Ilesanmi 1962 NR

Ilesanmi, G.E.
Social studies for Midwest schools. 2nd ed. 1, 2bks
106pp. photos. maps ill. 65k Ilesanmi 1971 NR

Ilesanmi, G.E.
Social studies for Midwest schools. 2nd ed. 2, 2bks
129pp. photos. maps ill. 65k Ilesanmi 1971 NR

Ilesanmi, M.A. Abimbola, O.
Eko nipa eda ati ilera. [Health text.] bk. 1 72pp. ill.
85k Ilesanmi 1974 NR YOR

Ilesanmi, M.A. Abimbola, O.
Eko nipa eda ati ilera. [Health text.] bk. 2. 80pp. ill.
95k Ilesanmi 1974 NR YOR

Ilesanmi, M.A. Abimbola, O.
Eko nipa eda ati ilera. [Health text.] bk. 3. 65pp. ill.
N1.10 Ilesanmi 1974 NR YOR

Ilesanmi, M.A. Abimbola, O.
Eko nipa eda ati ilera. [Health text.] bk. 4. 69pp. ill.
N1.25 Ilesanmi 1974 NR YOR

Iliffe, J.
Agricultural change in modern Tanganyika. 47pp. Hist
Assoc - Tanz 1971 TZ

Iliffe, J., ed.
Modern Tanzanians. 252pp. photos. K.shs.35.00
(Historical Studies, 9) EAPH 1974 KE

Iliffe, J.
Records of the Maji Maji rising. 1 See: Gwassa, G.C.

Illich, I.
Mission and midwifery. Essays on missionary formation.
62pp. 60c. (Mambo Missio-Pastoral Series, 4)
Mambo 1974 RH

Illife, J.
Agricultural change in modern Tanzania. 47pp. maps.
K.shs2.50 ($1.00) EAPH 1971 KE

Illife, J. Gwassa, G.C.K.
Records of the Maji Maji rising. 30pp. maps.
K.shs.2.50 ($1.00) EAPH 1968 KE

Illife, J.
Tanganyika under German rule 1905-1912. 210pp.
maps. K.shs.15.00 ($5.00) EAPH 1971 KE

Iloeje, N.P. Okoro, E.N.
Beginning social studies in Nigeria. bk. 4 76pp. ill.
N1.30 Macmillan 1974 NR

Iloeje, N.P.
A primary school geography for Nigeria. 2, 3bks
152pp. ill. maps. N1.70 Macmillan 1966 NR

Iloeje, N.P.
A primary school geography for Nigeria. 3, 3bks
139pp. maps ill. N1.70 Macmillan 1966 NR

Iloeje, S.O.
Certificate practical biology. 96pp. ill. N1.44
Longman - Nig 1973 NR

Ilomo, C.S., comp.
Directory of libraries in Tanzania. 52pp. T.shs.20.00
Tanz Lib Serv 1972 TZ

Ilomo, C.S.
Library development in mainland Tanzania. 23pp.
(Tanzania Library Service, occas. paps., 3) Tanz Lib
Serv 1976 TZ

Iltis, A.
Poissons de Côte d'Ivoire (eaux douces et saumâtres)
See: Daget, J.

Ilugbuhi, T.
Nigeria's experience in domestic financing of development.
113pp. N1.25 (£1.00/$2.50) Inst Admin - Zaria 1968
NR

Imam, A.
Magana Jari Ce, 1. [Eloquence is profitable] 1, 3 bks.
134pp. N1.10 Northern Nig 1937 NR HAU

Imam, A.
Magana Jari Ce, 2. [Eloquence is profitable] 2, 3 bks.
234pp. N1.35 Northern Nig 1939 NR HAU

Imam, A.
Magana Jari Ce, 3. [Eloquence is profitable] 3, 3 bks.
276pp. N1.50 Northern Nig 1939 NR HAU

Imam, A.
Ruwan Bagaja. [The water of cure] 44pp. ill. 70k
Northern Nig 1966 NR HAU

Imam, A.A.
Ruwan Bagaja: the water of cure. 44pp. ill. 65k
Northern Nig 1971 NR

Imam, F.B.
Industry in the Sudan (Erkowit conference, 1966) 450pp.
ill. LS2.00 ($8.00) Khartoum UP 1973 SJ

Imam, M.M.
The future of man. 21pp. pl. C1.00 ($1.00/50p.)
(Inaugural lecture series) Ghana UP 1974 GH

Imam, M.M.
Homo scientae. A critical appraisal. 20pp. C1.00
(50p) (Inaugural lecture) Ghana UP 1975 GH

Imasiogbe, O.
Studies in Second Corinthians 1-6. 36pp. 50k
Daystar 1975 NR

Imbuga, F.
Game of silence. 56pp. K.shs.9.00 Heinemann Educ
- Nair 1977 KE

Imbuga, F.
The married batchelor. 60pp. K.shs.8.50 (African Theatre, 3) EAPH 1973 KE

Imbuga, F.D.
Betrayal in the city. 76pp. K.shs.15.00 ($5.00) EAPH 1976 KE

Imevbore, A.M.A., eds. Adegoke, O.S., eds.
The ecology of Lake Kainji. 256pp. pl. photos. maps. cl. N7.00 (£5.60/$13.00) Univ Ife Press 1974 NR

Imevbore, A.M.A.
Man and environment: the Nigerian situation. 22pp. 30k (Inaugural lec., 5) Univ Ife Press 1973 NR

Immelman, R.F.M., ed.
Handlist of manuscripts in the University of Cape Town libraries. 1 See: Quinn, G.D., ed.

Immelman, R.F.M.
The foundations of library management: organisation from the administrative angle. 67pp. R2.55 Univ Cape Town Lib 1975 SA

Immelman, R.F.M.
The Kipling collection in the University of Cape Town library. 38pp. ill. ex. only (Univ. Cape Town Libraries, Varia series, 5) Univ Cape Town Lib 1961 SA

I.N.A.D.E.S.
L'Afrique économique: les pays, les productions. 70 showcardspp. map. CFA1,000 INADES 1973 IV FRE

I.N.A.D.E.S.
L'argent. 34pp. ill. CFA200 (Femmes des Villages Aujourd'hui, 7) INADES 1970 IV FRE

I.N.A.D.E.S.
Boeufs et vaches à Agoudou-Manga, R.C.A. 127pp. CFA300 INADES 1966 IV FRE

I.N.A.D.E.S.
Connaître le milieu rural. 44pp. CFA300 (Vulgarisation, 1) INADES 1973 IV FRE

I.N.A.D.E.S.
Cours d'apprentissage agricole. Comment bien vendre ses produits. [Also available in English]. 32pp. CFA300 (Le Metier d'Agriculteur, 3) INADES 1973 IV FRE

I.N.A.D.E.S.
Cours d'apprentissage agricole: Comment choisir son champ? 36pp. ill. CFA250 (Agriculture générale et élevage, 1) INADES 1974 IV FRE

I.N.A.D.E.S.
Cours d'apprentissage agricole. Comment faire des groupements. [Also available in English]. 34pp. CFA300 (Le Metier d'Agriculteur, 8) INADES 1973 IV FRE

I.N.A.D.E.S.
Cours d'apprentissage agricole: Comment faire les travaux d'entretien? 40pp. ill. CFA250 (Agriculture générale et élevage, 5) INADES 1974 IV FRE

I.N.A.D.E.S.
Cours d'apprentissage agricole. Comment faire ses comptes. [Also available in English]. 36pp. CFA300 (Le Metier d'Agriculteur, 5) INADES 1973 IV FRE

I.N.A.D.E.S.
Cours d'apprentissage agricole: Comment labourer? 32pp. ill. CFA250 (Agriculture générale et élevage, 3) INADES 1974 IV FRE

I.N.A.D.E.S.
Cours d'apprentissage agricole: Comment préparer le champ? 32pp. ill. CFA250 (Agriculture générale et élevage, 2) INADES 1974 IV FRE

I.N.A.D.E.S.
Cours d'apprentissage agricole. Comment produire plus. [Also available in English]. 32pp. CFA300 (Le Metier d'Agriculteur, 2) INADES 1973 IV FRE

I.N.A.D.E.S.
Cours d'apprentissage agricole: Comment protéger les plantes? 32pp. ill. CFA250 (Agriculture générale et élevage, 6) INADES 1974 IV FRE

I.N.A.D.E.S.
Cours d'apprentissage agricole: Comment récolter? 32pp. ill. CFA250 (Agriculture générale et élevage, 7) INADES 1974 IV FRE

I.N.A.D.E.S.
Cours d'apprentissage agricole: Comment semer? 40pp. ill. CFA250 (Agriculture générale et élevage, 4) INADES 1974 IV FRE

I.N.A.D.E.S.
Cours d'apprentissage agricole. Comment utiliser le crédit en agriculture. [Also available in English]. 44pp. CFA300 (Le Metier d'Agriculteur, 6) INADES 1973 IV FRE

I.N.A.D.E.S.
Cours d'apprentissage agricole. Cultures: L'arachide. [Also available in English]. 45pp. ill. CFA300 INADES 1967 IV FRE

I.N.A.D.E.S.
Cours d'apprentissage agricole. Cultures: le bananier. [Also available in English]. 31pp. ill. CFA250 INADES 1967 IV FRE

I.N.A.D.E.S.
Cours d'apprentissage agricole. Cultures: le cacaoyer. [Also available in English]. 58pp. ill. CFA300 INADES 1967 IV FRE

I.N.A.D.E.S.
Cours d'apprentissage agricole. Cultures: le caféier. [Also available in English]. 58pp. ill. CFA350 INADES 1967 IV FRE

I.N.A.D.E.S.
Cours d'apprentissage agricole. Cultures: le cotonnier. 51pp. ill. CFA300 INADES 1967 IV FRE

I.N.A.D.E.S.
Cours d'apprentissage agricole. Cultures: le palmier à huile. (Also available in English) 51pp. ill. CFA300 INADES 1967 IV FRE

I.N.A.D.E.S.
Cours d'apprentissage agricole. Cultures: le riz irrigué. [Also available in English]. 50pp. ill. CFA350 INADES 1967 IV FRE

I.N.A.D.E.S.
Cours d'apprentissage agricole. Cultures: le riz pluvial. [Also available in English]. 50pp. ill. CFA350 INADES 1967 IV FRE

I.N.A.D.E.S.
Cours d'apprentissage agricole: Cultures, les céréales: mil, sorgho, maïs. [Also available in English]. 58pp. CFA350 INADES 1967 IV FRE

I.N.A.D.E.S.
Cours d'apprentissage agricole. Cultures: les cultures marâichére maraîchages plus spécialisés. 2, 2v. 64pp. ill. CFA350 INADES 1967 IV FRE

I.N.A.D.E.S.
Cours d'apprentissage agricole. Cultures: les cultures maraîchères: généralités: tomates, gombo, oignons. v. 1, 2v. 64pp. ill. CFA350 INADES 1967 IV FRE

I.N.A.D.E.S.
Cours d'apprentissage agricole. Cultures: les racines et tubercules: igname, manioc, patate, taro, macabo. [Also available in English]. 62pp. ill. CFA350 INADES 1967 IV FRE

I.N.A.D.E.S.
Cours d'apprentissage agricole. Cultures: l'hévéa. 34pp. ill. CFA250 INADES 1967 IV FRE

I.N.A.D.E.S.
Cours d'apprentissage agricole. Cultures: pâturages et cultures fourragères. 60pp. ill. CFA350 INADES 1967 IV FRE

I.N.A.D.E.S.
Cours d'apprentissage agricole. Elévage: élevage des bovins. 63pp. ill. CFA350 INADES 1967 IV FRE

I.N.A.D.E.S.
Cours d'apprentissage agricole. Elevage: élevage des moutons et des chèvres. 63pp. ill. CFA350 INADES 1967 IV FRE

I.N.A.D.E.S.
Cours d'apprentissage agricole. Elevage: élevage des porcs. 63pp. ill. CFA350 INADES 1967 IV FRE

I.N.A.D.E.S.
Cours d'apprentissage agricole. Elevage: élevage familial des poules. 63pp. ill. CFA350 INADES 1967 IV FRE

I.N.A.D.E.S.
Cours d'apprentissage agricole: Introduction. 16pp. CFA250 (Agriculture générale et élevage, 0) INADES 1974 IV FRE

I.N.A.D.E.S.
Cours d'apprentissage agricole. Introduction. [Also available in English]. 32pp. CFA300 (Le Metier d'Agriculteur, 1) INADES 1973 IV FRE

I.N.A.D.E.S.
Cours d'apprentissage agricole: La nourriture et le logement des animaux. 40pp. ill. CFA250 (Agriculture générale et élevage, 8) INADES 1974 IV FRE

I.N.A.D.E.S.
Cours d'apprentissage agricole. Les dépenses de l'agriculteur. [Also available in English]. 32pp. CFA300 (Le Metier d'Agriculteur, 4) INADES 1973 IV FRE

I.N.A.D.E.S.
Cours d'apprentissage agricole: Les maladies et la reproduction des animaux. 36pp. ill. CFA250 (Agriculture générale et élevage, 9) INADES 1974 IV FRE

I.N.A.D.E.S.
Cours d'apprentissage agricole. Pourquoi faire des groupements. [Also available in English]. 34pp. CFA300 (Le Metier d'Agriculteur, 7) INADES 1973 IV FRE

I.N.A.D.E.S.
Cours d'apprentissage agricole. Technique agricole: la culture attelée. 61pp. CFA350 INADES 1967 IV FRE

I.N.A.D.E.S.
Cours d'apprentissage agricole. Vivre mieux au village. 32pp. CFA300 (Le Metier d'Agriculteur, 9) INADES 1973 IV FRE

I.N.A.D.E.S.
Cours d'initiation au développement: Des Africains parlent du développement. 60pp. CFA450 (L'Afrique en mutation, 1) INADES 1974 IV FRE

I.N.A.D.E.S.
Cours d'initiation au développement: Développement et relations internationales. 68pp. CFA450 (L'Afrique en mutation, 8) INADES 1974 IV FRE

I.N.A.D.E.S.
Cours d'initiation au développement: Histoire de l'Afrique. 66pp. CFA450 (L'Afrique en mutation, 2) INADES 1974 IV FRE

I.N.A.D.E.S.
Cours d'initiation au développement: L'Afrique et la technique. 68pp. CFA450 (L'Afrique en mutation, 7) INADES 1974 IV FRE

I.N.A.D.E.S.
Cours d'initiation au développement: L'école en Afrique. 60pp. CFA450 (L'Afrique en mutation, 6) INADES 1974 IV FRE

I.N.A.D.E.S.
Cours d'initiation au développement: Les changements d'aujourd'hui. 52pp. CFA450 (L'Afrique en mutation, 3) INADES 1974 IV FRE

I.N.A.D.E.S.
Cours d'initiation au développement: Mutations politiques. 48pp. CFA450 (L'Afrique en mutation, 9) INADES 1974 IV FRE

I.N.A.D.E.S.
Cours d'initiation au développement: Transformations économiques. pt. 1. 66pp. CFA450 (L'Afrique en mutation, 4) INADES 1974 IV FRE

I.N.A.D.E.S.
Cours d'initiation au développement: Transformations économiques. pt. 2. 72pp. CFA450 (L'Afrique en mutation, 5) INADES 1974 IV FRE

I.N.A.D.E.S.
Des paysans prennent en main leur développement: fédération des groupements villageois de Bouaké. 72pp. ill. CFA450 INADES 1974 IV FRE

I.N.A.D.E.S.
Développement rural en Afrique Noire. [With suppl.] 11 (Suppl. 10pp.)pp. CFA1,000 set INADES 1973 IV FRE

I.N.A.D.E.S.
Dzobégan, Togo: une action de développement. 71pp. CFA250 INADES 1967 IV FRE

I.N.A.D.E.S.
L'eau et la maison. CFA200 (Femmes des Villages Aujourd'hui, 1) INADES 1970 IV FRE

I.N.A.D.E.S.
L'école en Afrique. Quelques références bibliographiques commentees. 15pp. CFA500 INADES 1973 IV FRE

I.N.A.D.E.S.
L'enfant se développe. 26pp. ill. CFA200 (Femmes des Villages Aujourd'hui, 6) INADES 1970 IV FRE

I.N.A.D.E.S.
Les ethnies du Cameroun: bibliographie. CFA1,000 INADES 1973 IV FRE

I.N.A.D.E.S.
Femme et mère. 25pp. ill. CFA200 (Femmes des Villages Aujourd'hui, 5 bis) INADES 1970 IV FRE

I.N.A.D.E.S.
Fignolé, maison rurale du nord-Cameroun. 87pp. CFA250 INADES 1967 IV FRE

I.N.A.D.E.S.
L'homme et la femme. 29pp. ill. CFA200 (Femmes des Villages Aujourd'hui, 8) INADES 1970 IV FRE

I.N.A.D.E.S.
Initiation à l'Afrique Noire, bibliographie commentée. 30pp. CFA650 INADES 1974 IC FRE

I.N.A.D.E.S.
Le marché aujourd'hui. CFA200 (Femmes des Villages Aujourd'hui, 2) INADES 1970 IV FRE

I.N.A.D.E.S.
Méthode de calcul (guide pour les moniteurs): les quatre opérations. 2, 2v. 64pp. CFA400 INADES 1975 IC FRE

I.N.A.D.E.S.
Méthode de calcul (guide pour les moniteurs): lire et écrire les nombres. 1, 2v. 64pp. CFA400 INADES 1975 IC FRE

I.N.A.D.E.S.
Le métier d'agricultrice. 35pp. ill. CFA200 pap. (Femmes des Villages Aujourd'hui, 3) INADES 1970 IV FRE

I.N.A.D.E.S.
La préparation du repas familial. 33pp. ill. CFA200 (Femmes des Villages Aujourd'hui, 4) INADES 1970 IV FRE

I.N.A.D.E.S.
Quand la femme devient mère. 26pp. ill. CFA200 (Femmes des Villages Aujourd'hui, 5) INADES 1970 IV FRE

I.N.A.D.E.S.
La Sonader. Palmier à huile et agriculture moderne au Dahomey. 144pp. CFA600 INADES 1969 IV FRE

I.N.A.D.E.S.
Structure de l'animation rurale au Cameroun. 32pp. CFA125 INADES 1969 IV FRE

I.N.A.D.E.S.
Thesaurus sur le développement rural. 2 v. CFA5000 pap. INADES 1975 IC FRE

I.N.A.D.E.S.
Le village aujourd'hui. 27pp. ill. CFA200 (Femmes des Villages Aujourd'hui, 9) INADES 1970 IV FRE

I.N.A.D.E.S.
La ville en Afrique, bibliographie, INADES-Documentation. CFA1,000 INADES 1977 IV FRE

Inanga, E.L. Osayimwese, I.G.
Mathematics for business. 430pp. ill. N4.00 Onibonoje 1975 NR

Indaru, P.
Man with the lion heart. 108pp. ill. C1.00 (30p.) Africa Christian 1974 GH

Ingawa, A.
The adventures of Iliya Dan Maikarfi. 44pp. ill. 65k Northern Nig 1971 NR

Ingawa, A.
Iliya Dan Maikarfi. [Iliya, son of Maikarfi] 50pp. ill. 70k Northern Nig 1970 NR HAU

Ingawa, M.
Ka Kara Karatu Sabuwar Hanya, 3. 3, 6 bks. See: Aliyu, A.H.

Ingawa, M. Boyd, J.
Ka Koyi Karatu Sabuwar Hanya, 2. [Learn how to read] 1, 6 bks 48pp. ill. 48k Northern Nig 1972 NR HAU

Ingawa, M. Boyd, J.
Ka Yi Ta Karatu Sabuwar Hanya, 4. [And read it again] 4, 6 bks 48pp. ill. 52k Northern Nig 1973 NR HAU

Ingold, C.K.
The education of a scientist. 11pp. 20k Ibadan UP 1963 NR

Inland Publishers.
Bibli ni ya ajabu. [The Bible is wonderful] 76pp. T.shs4.50 Africa Inland Church TZ SWA

Inland Publishers.
Biblia ya Kikatoliki Inatoa majibu. [The Roman Catholic Bible answers] rev. ed. 12pp. T.shs1.00 Africa Inland Church 1973 TZ SWA

Inland Publishers.
Kanuni mpya. [New canon.] 24pp. T.shs.2.00 Africa Inland Church 1973 TZ SWA

Inland Publishers.
Maswali 20 yenye wasiwasi. [20 awkward questions] Reprint of 1969 ed. 24pp. T.shs.2.00 Africa Inland Church 1972 TZ SWA

Inland Publishers.
Mungu. [God] Reprint of 1964 ed. 48pp. T.shs.2.00 Africa Inland Church 1972 TZ SWA

Inland Publishers.
Mwalimu was milimani. [The mountain teacher.] R Reved. 24pp. T.shs.1.50 Africa Inland Church 1971 TZ SWA

Inland Publishers.
Ndoa iliyo bora. [The excellent marriage] 47pp. T.shs.3.50 Africa Inland Church 1970 TZ SWA

Inland Publishers.
Ole Ulimwenguni. [Woe to the world] 52pp. T.shs.2.50 Africa Inland Church 1973 TZ SWA

Inland Publishers.
Roho ya Paku. [The heart of Paku/man.] 3rd ed. 24pp. T.shs.1.50 Africa Inland Church 1970 TZ SWA

Inland Publishers.
Sifuni. [Praise] Reprint of 1962 ed. T.shs.1.50 Africa Inland Church 1968 TZ SWA

Inland Publishers.
Sikilizeni wenye elimu. [Listen you educated] 48pp. T.shs.3.00 Africa Inland Church 1970 TZ SWA

Inland Publishers.
Ukomunisti naukristo. [Communism and Christianity] Reprint of 1963 ed. 26pp. T.shs.1.00 Africa Inland Mission 1972 TZ SWA

Inland Publishers.
Wakati umewadia. [The time has come] 48pp. T.shs.3.50 Africa Inland Church 1972 TZ SWA

Inskeep, R.
The peopling of southern Africa. 128pp. col. ill. cl. R7.50 cl. (The Peoples of Southern Africa, 1) Philip 1976 SA

Inskeep, R.R.
Preliminary investigation of a protohistoric cemetery at Nkudzi Bay, Malawi. ($1.40/60p.) Nat Mon Comm - Zambia 1965 ZA

Institut Africain de Développement Economique et de Planification, Dakar.
Collection d'etudes sur le développement économique et social, v. 1 (Edition francaise) 68pp. CFA500 (F10.00) Nouv Ed Afric 1973 SG FRE

Institut de Linguistique Appliquée.
Vocabulaire essentiel de l'enseignement primaire, 2e année. 195pp. CFA400 (Enseignement du français, 24) Inst Ling Appliquée 1971 IV FRE

Institut de Linguistique Appliquée.
Vocabulaire essentiel de l'enseignement primaire, 3e année. 176pp. CFA500 (Enseignement du français, 30) Inst Ling Appliquée 1972 IV FRE

Institut d'Ethno-Sociologie.
Village-Savane en pays adioukrou. 150pp. maps. CFA750 (F15.00) Inst Ethno-Socio 1969 IV FRE

Institut Fondamental d'Afrique Noire.
Les Afro-Américains. [Reprint of ed. 1953]. 268pp. ill. (D.fl.80.00) (Mémoires de l'IFAN, 27) IFAN 1953 SG FRE

Institut Fondamental d'Afrique Noire.
Contribution à l'étude de l'air. [Reprint of ed. Paris, 1950]. 562pp. ill. pl. map. (D.fl.160.00) (Mémoires de l'IFAN, 10) IFAN 1950 SG FRE

Institut Fondamental d'Afrique Noire.
Le massif des Monts Loma. pt. 1 419pp. maps. CFA6000 (Mémoires de l'IFAN, 86) IFAN 1971 SG FRE

Institut Fondamental d'Afrique Noire.
Mélanges ethnologiques. 408pp. pl. maps. CFA2400 pap. (Mémoires de l'IFAN, 23) IFAN 1953 SG FRE

Institut Fondamental d'Afrique Noire.
Mélanges ichthyologiques, dédiés à la mémoire d'Achille Valenciennes (1794-1865) 485pp. ill. CFA3600 (Mémoires de l'IFAN, 68) IFAN 1963 SG FRE

Institut Fondamental d'Afrique Noire.
Le parc national du Niokolo-Koba. pt. 1 267pp. map photo. CFA2000 (Mémoires de l'IFAN, 48) IFAN 1956 SG FRE

Institut Fondamental d'Afrique Noire.
Le parc national du Niokolo-Koba. pt. 2 379pp. ill. photo. CFA2400 (Mémoires de l'IFAN, 62) IFAN 1961 SG FRE

Institut Fondamental d'Afrique Noire.
Le parc national du Niokolo-Koba. pt. 3 488pp. ill. pl. map. CFA6000 (Mémoires de l'IFAN, 84) IFAN 1969 SG FRE

Institut Fondamental d'Afrique Noire.
Première conférence internationale des africainistes de l'ouest Dakar. 1, 2v. 531pp. CFA2400 (IFAN comptes rendus) IFAN 1945 SG FRE

Institut Fondamental d'Afrique Noire.
Première conférence internationale des africainistes de l'ouest Dakar. 2, 2v. 567pp. photo. CFA2800 (IFAN comptes rendus) IFAN 1951 SG FRE

Institut Fondamental d'Afrique Noire.
La réserve naturelle intégrale du Mont Nimba. 357pp. ill. pl. (F40.00) (Mémoires de l'IFAN, 53) IFAN 1958 SG FRE

Institut Fondamental d'Afrique Noire.
La réserve naturelle intégrale du Mont Nimba. pt. 1 334pp. CFA2000 (Mémoires de l'IFAN, 19) IFAN 1952 SG FRE

Institut Fondamental d'Afrique Noire.
La réserve naturelle intégrale du Mont Nimba. pt. 2 402pp. CFA2400 (Mémoires de l'IFAN, 40) IFAN 1954 SG FRE

Institut Fondamental d'Afrique Noire.
La réserve naturelle intégrale du Mont Nimba. pt. 4 357pp. pl. ill. CFA2000 (Mémoires de l'IFAN, 53) IFAN 1958 SG FRE

Institut Fondamental d'Afrique Noire.
La réserve naturelle intégrale du Mont Nimba. pt. 5 640pp. ill. CFA4400 (Mémoires de l'IFAN, 66) IFAN 1963 SG FRE

Institut National de Recherche Scientifique.
Rapport pour les années 1965 à 1970. 128pp. maps. RF300 (FB225.00/$5.60) Inst Nat - Rwandaise 1971 RW FRE

Institut National des Hydrocarbures et de la Chimie.
Géologie des provinces pétrolifères de l'Algérie. 173pp. maps. DA14.00 pap. SNED 1975 AE FRE

Institut National Tchadien pour les Sciences Humaines.
Documents d'archives: Tchad et pays limitrophes. v.2. 174pp. ex. only (Etudes et Documents Tchadiens, Série B, 2) Inst Nat Tchad 1975 CD FRE

Institut Pedagogique Africain et Malgache.
Afrique mon Afrique. Cours moyen 2e année: livre du maître. CFA1,670 (F33.40) Nouv Ed Afric 1975 SG FRE

Institut Pédagogique Africain et Malgache.
Afrique mon Afrique. Livre de français pour le cours moyen 1ere année. Lecture, langage. Expression. Etude de la langue. Lîvre du maitre. 213pp. CFA1,670 (F33.40) Nouv Ed Afric 1974 SG FRE

Institute for African Studies, University of Zambia.
The occasional papers of the Rhodes-Livingstone Museum, Nos. 1-16. [Reprinted in one volume.] 832pp. K14.00 Inst Afr Stud - Lusaka 1974 ZA

Institute for Industrial Education.
The Durban strikes. 195pp. R2.00 ($4.75/£2.50) Ravan 1975 SA

Institute for the Study of English in Africa.
English as second language in primary schools: Creative verse writing: new voices. (Inst. for study of English in Africa proceedings, 3) Inst Study Engl 1967 SA

Institute for the Study of English in Africa.
Second-language teaching in high schools: An approach to the novel: audio-visual aids. (Inst. for study of English in Africa proceedings, 2) Inst Study Engl 1965 SA

Institute for the Study of English in Africa.
South African writing in English: English Academy of Southern Africa, conference, 7-11 July. R1.00 Inst Study Engl 1969 SA

Institute for the Study of English in Africa.
Towards a dictionary of South African English. 87pp. R1.00 Inst Study Engl 1972 SA

Institute of Administration, Ahmadu Bello University.
Nigerian administration research project, first interim report. 73pp. free Inst Admin - Zaria 1972 NR

Institute of Administration, University of Ife, ed.
The future of local government in Nigeria. 154pp. N1.25 ($1.80/75p.) Univ Ife Press NR

Institute of Administration.
Reflections on public enterprises in Nigeria. 103pp. 75k (60p./$1.50) Inst Admin - Zaria 1970 NR

Institute of Adult Education.
Mtu ni afya. [An evaluation of the 1973 mass health education campaign in Tanzania.] T.shs.3.00 (Studies in Adult Education, 12) Inst Adult Educ - Dar 1974 TZ

Institute of Adult Education.
Some campaign considerations. T.shs.2.00 (Studies in Adult Education, 20) Inst Adult Educ - Dar 1975 TZ

Institute of Adult Education.
A source book of adult education in Tanzania, a structure bibliography of books, papers and speeches on adult education. T.shs.1.00 (Studies in Adult Education, 13) Inst Adult Educ - Dar 1974 TZ

Institute of African Studies, Legon.
Papers in African Studies, 3. 80pp. ill. maps. 65pes. ($.65) Ghana Publ Corp 1968 GH

Institute of African Studies.
Traditional background to medical practice in Nigeria. 99pp. N1.50 (Inst. of African Stud., Univ. of Ibadan, occas. pub., 25) Inst Afr Stud-Ibadan 1966 NR

Institute of Agricultural Research, Addis Ababa.
Proceedings: sixth annual research seminar. S. Edwards, ed. 335pp. ex. only Inst Agric Res - Addis 1976 ET

Institute of Education, Ahmadu Bello University.
Primary science. Pupil's book 1. 8pp. ill. 22k Longman - Nig 1974 NR

Institute of Education, Ahmadu Bello University.
Primary science. Teacher's book 1. 80pp. ill. pl. N1.25 Longman - Nig 1974 NR

Institute of Education, Ahmadu Bello University, Zaria.
A guide for primary teachers of social studies in Nigerian schools. N1.20 Northern Nig 1973 NR

Institute of Education, Ahmadu Bello University, Zaria.
Primary science. Pupils' bk. 3 12pp. ill. 25k Longman Nig 1976 NR

Institute of Education, Ahmadu Bello University, Zaria.
Primary science. Teachers' bk. 3 80pp. ill. N1.85 Longman Nig 1976 NR

Inter-Territorial Language Committee.
Uvumbuzi wa nchi mpya. 4th ed. 116pp. K.shs.5.00 ($1.75/70p.) EALB 1965 KE SWA

Interafrica Publishers Co. Ltd.
Business directory for East and Central Africa. Classified trade index and local manufacturers. K.shs.150.00 Interafrica 1976 KE

Ipasso.
Le père qui ne voulait pas de fille. Mythes nkundu et tere. Langues locales et versions françaises. See: Osantwene.

Ipeko-Etomane, F.A.
Le lac des sorciers. 48pp. CFA200 CLE 1972 CM FRE

Ipking, B., et al.
Urafiki. [Friendship.] 36pp. T.shs.2.50 Central Tanganyika 1968 TZ SWA

Ipkong, B. et al.
Friendship. 36pp. T.shs.2.50 Central Tanganyika 1968 TZ

Ipp, C.
Doris Lessing. 27pp. R1.60 Dept Bibliog, Lib & Typo 1967 SA

Irele, A.
Theatre in Africa. See: Ogunba, O.

Iroaganachi, J.
How the leopard got his claws. See: Achebe, C.

Iroaganachi, J.
Night and day. 32pp. ill. (African Junior Library 10) Pilgrim 1975 NR

Iroaganachi, J.O.
Oka mgba. [The great wrestler] 120pp. col. ill. 80k Longman - Nig 1973 NR IGB

Iroagariachi, J.
How the leopard got its claws. See: Achebe, C.

Irungu, D.
The powerful magician. 40pp. ill. K.shs.3.00 ($1.00) (East African Readers Library) EAPH 1969 KE

Irvine, C.
Telephone to heaven. 24pp. 45pes. (13p.) Africa Christian 1969 GH

Irvine, E., ed.
Five women. 20pp. ill. 10t (Voices from Africa Series) Christ Lit Assoc - Mal 1974 MW

Irvine, S.H.
The Northern Rhodesia mental ability survey 1963. See: MacArthur, R.S.

Irvine, S.H.
Selection for secondary education in southern Rhodesia. 40pp. 50c (Fac. of Education, Univ. of Rhodesia, 4) Univ Rhodesia Lib 1964 RH

Irving, J.
Economic rent and household income among Cape coloureds in Grahamstown. 25c (Inst. of Social and Economic Research, occas. paps., 1) Inst Soc & Econ Res - SA 1958 SA

Irving, J.
Economic rent and household income among the African population of Grahamstown. 25c (Inst. of Social and Economic Research, occas. paps., 2) Inst Soc & Econ Res - SA 1958 SA

Irving, J.
Macleantown - a study of a small South African community. 75c (Inst. of Social and Economic Research occas. paps., 4) Inst Soc & Econ Res - SA 1959 SA

Irving, J.
Man, machines and society: lectures in industrial sociology. R1.20 (Inst. of Social and Economic Research occas. paps., 12) Inst Soc & Econ Res - SA 1968 SA

Irving, J. St. Leger, F.Y.
Report on an investigation into the attitudes of a sample of male residents of the city of East London, C.P., towards the Daily Dispatch and other newspapers in the area. R6.00 (Inst. of Social and Economic Research, occas. paps., 18) Inst Soc & Econ Res - SA 1967 SA

Irving, J.
Slum clearance and the ability of Europeans to pay economic rent in a small South African city. 25c (Inst. of Social and Economic Research, occas. paps., 3) Inst Soc & Econ Res - SA 1959 SA

Irwin, M.P.S.
A contribution to the ornithology of Zambia. See: Benson, C.W.

Isa, Y.
Hausa customs. See: Madauchi, I.

Isaac-Sodeye, W.A.
Sickle cell disease. 61pp. N1.50 Ethiope 1975 NR

Isaacs, H.
Tests in physics: with answers. See: Ryan, O.

Isaacs, H.
Tests in physics: without answers. See: Ryan, O.

Isaacs, I.
Beck's theory and principles of pleading in civil actions. 4th ed. 352pp. pap. R13.50 Butterworths 1973 SA

Isaacs, I.
Beck's theory and principles of pleading in civil actions. [First supplement to 4th ed.] ed. R1.75 Butterworths 1976 SA

Isaacs, I., ed.
Butterworths South African income tax practice. See: Wells, M.J., ed.

Isaacs, I. Leveson, G.
Law of collisions in South Africa. 5th ed. R19.75 cl. Butterworths 1975 SA

Isaacs, N.
Travels and adventures in Eastern Africa (Natal) 412pp. pl. cl. R15.00 Struik 1970 SA

Isemonger, R.M.
Snakes of Africa. 3rd ed. ill./col. photos. R5.00 Bulpin 1968 SA

Ishag, A.H.
The availability of groundwater in Korfofan Province. See: Rodis, N.G.

Ishag, A.H.
Groundwater geology of Kordofan Province. See: Rodis, N.G.

Ishumi, G.M.
Education and development. In theory and practice. 116pp. K.shs.24.75 ($5.30/£2.10) EALB 1976 KE

Iskander, W.
Iron ore deposits at Jebel Abu Tulu, Dar Messeriya Southern Kordofan. See: Mansour, A.O.

Islam, I.K.
Nabii Yusuf. [Prophet Joseph] K.shs3.50 (Visa Vya Mitume (Stories about Prophets), 1) OUP-Nairobi 1973 KE SWA

Isola, A.
Efunsetan aniwura Iyalode Ibadan. [Tragedy of first lady of Ibadan] 82pp. ill. 75k OUP - Nig 1970 NR YOR

Isola, A.
O Le Ku [Novel]. 108pp. ill. N1.00 OUP - Nig 1974 NR YOR

Issa, A. Labatut, R.
Sagesse de peuples nomades. 68pp. CFA450.00 CLE 1974 CM FRE

Istiphan, I.
Directory of social agencies in Cairo. 496pp. map. £.E.O.500 ($4.00) Am Univ 1956 UA

Itote, W.
Mau Mau general. 290pp. photos. K.shs.10.00 ($3.20) EAPH 1967 KE

Itsueli, B.J.E.
Essays in European history - 1715-1939. 490pp. N1.50 Publ Int 1972 NR

Itsueli, B.J.E.
Essays in European history (1715-1939) 489pp. N3.50 Publ Int 1975 NR

Ivens, G.W.
East African weeds and their control. 2nd ed. 264pp. ill. K.shs25.00 OUP-Nairobi 1972 KE

Iwanoski, G.
The white stallions of Kyalami. cl. R7.50 Purnell 1977 SA

Iwe, A.
Akuko ifo kwesiri: anya iwe. 2nd ed. 102pp. N1.00 Univ Publ 1977 NR IGB

Iwe, N.S.S.
Christianity and culture in Africa. 150pp. N3.00 Univ Publ 1975 NR

Iweama, W.E. Chief J.B.O.
Ilesanmi modern mathematics for Nigerian schools: teacher's notes. bk. 1. 81pp. ill. 95k Ilesanmi 1974 NR

Iweama, W.E. Chief J.B.O.
Ilesanmi modern mathematics for Nigerian schools: teacher's notes. bk. 2. 108pp. ill. N1.00 Ilesanmi 1975 NR

Iwobi, C.C. Nwakolo, W.E. Iwobi, L.
General science for primary classes. 1, 3bks ill. N1.00 Macmillan 1965 NR

Iwobi, C.C. Iwobi, L. Nwakolo, W.E.
General science for primary classes. 2, 3bks ill. N1.30 Macmillan 1965 NR

Iwobi, C.C. Nwakolo, W.E. Iwobi, L.
General science for primary classes. 3, 3bks ill. N1.50 Macmillan 1965 NR

Iwobi, C.C. Nwakolo, W.E. Iwobi, L.
General science for primary classes: teacher's bk. 30k Macmillan 1965 NR

Iwobi, L.
General science for primary classes. 1, 3bks See: Iwobi, C.C.

Author Index

Iwobi, L.
General science for primary classes. 2, 3bks
See: Iwobi, C.C.

Iwobi, L.
General science for primary classes. 3, 3bks
See: Iwobi, C.C.

Iwobi, L.
General science for primary classes: teacher's bk.
See: Iwobi, C.C.

Iwuchukwu, B.
Igbo revision course. See: Carnochan, J.

Jabbi, B.-B.
Achebe: "Things Fall Apart". (Notes.) 59pp. Le1.10
(Outline Hints on African Literature, 1) Fourah Bay
Bkshp; distr. 1974 SL

Jabbi, B.-B.
West African poems. Fifteen analyses. 48pp. 85c
(Outline Hints on African Literature, 2) Fourah Bay
Bkshp; distr. 1974 SL

Jabbour, G.
Settler colonialism in Southern Africa and the Middle East.
216pp. LS.1.00 ($4.00) Khartoum UP 1970 SJ

Jack, A.H.E.
The regulation of termination of employment in the
Sudanese private sector. A study of the law and its
application. See: Taha, A.R.A.

Jackson, A.F.
Chemistry in Sierra Leone. (Annual) v. 3. See: Baldry,
P.J.

Jackson, A.P.
Shumba. [The lion.] 29pp. pl. 20c. Rhod Lit Bur
1977 RH SHO

Jackson, G.S.
Music in Durban: an account of musical activities in
Durban from 1850 to the early years of the present
century. 166pp. ill. cl. R10.00 Witwatersrand UP
1970 SA

Jackson, I. M. Papenfus, J. N. Marais, J. F.
Biology from nature and in the laboratory, standard 7.
137pp. ill. photos. R2.25 Nasou 1974 SA

Jackson, I.J.
Rainfall over the Ruvu basin and surrounding area.
11pp. maps. T.shs.7.00 (Research report, 9) Bur
Res Assess - Tanz 1970 TZ

Jackson, I.J.
The spatial correlation of fluctuations in rainfall over
Tanzania: a preliminary analysis. 13pp. map.
T.shs.7.00 (Research report, 45) Bur Res Assess -
Tanz 1971 TZ

Jackson, M.P.A.
High-grade metamorphism and migmatization of the
Namaque Metamorphic Complex around Aus in the
Southern Namib Desert, South West Africa. 299pp.
maps. R11.50 (Univ of Cape Town, Precambrian
Research Unit, Bulletin 18) Precambrian Res Unit 1976
SA

Jackson, P.B.N.
Common and scientific names of the fishes of southern
Africa. Marine and freshwater. 2 pts. See: Smith, M.M.

Jackson, R., comp.
100 years of Chichewa in writing, 1875-1975. A select
bibliography. See: Made, S.M., comp.

Jackson, R., comp.
An annotated bibliography of education in Malawi. 57pp.
K1.00 (Univ. of Malawi Library Publication, 2) Univ
Malawi Lib 1976 MW

Jackson, R.
Development administration: the Kenyan experience.
See: Hyden, G.

Jackson, R.T., ed.
Essays on rural marketing in West Nile district. 122pp.
U.shs.25.00 (Occas. paps., 47) Dept Geog - Mak 1972
UG

Jackson, R.T.
Land use and settlement in Gamu Gofa province of
southern Ethiopia. 35pp. U.shs.15.00 (Occas. paps.,
17) Dept Geog - Mak 1970 UG

Jackson, T.
The law of Kenya: an introduction. 357pp. pap. & cl.
K.shs.77.00 cl. K.shs.50.00 pap. ($9.80/£3.90 pap.)
($14.60/£3.80 cl.) EALB 1970 KE

Jackson, T.H., ed. Edwards, S., ed. Ohlander, L., ed.
National horticultural centre, Nazareth research station:
progress report for the period April 1973 to March 1974.
164pp. ex. only. Inst Agric Res - Addis 1975 ET

Jackson, W.P.U.
Dieting for overweight and diabetes. R1.25 Juta SA

Jacob, R.
Geology and metamorphic petrology of part of the Damara
orogen along the lower Swakop River, South West Africa.
181pp. ill. photos. col. map. hd. ex. only (Univ of
Cape Town, Precambrian Research Unit, Bulletin 17)
Precambrian Res Unit 1974 SA

Jacobs, H.C.F.
Road traffic legislation: ordinance and regulations. 2
2nded. R25.00 [incl. revision services up to 1976] Juta
1967 SA

Jacobs, P.
Leukaemia: the past, the present, the future. 19pp.
30c (Univ. Cape Town. Inaugural lec., 18) Univ Cape
Town Lib 1973 SA

Jacobson, D.H.
Computer system selection. See: van Deventer, E.N.

Jacobson, D.H.
Conditions for the controllability of constrained linear
autonomous systems on time intervals of arbitrary length.
See: Pachter, M.

Jacobson, E.
The Cape coloured. 50pp. 80c. Univ Cape Town Lib
1972 SA

Jacobson, Z.
Enuresis: an epidemiological survey of Enuresis. 127pp.
R1.75 Inst Soc Res-Natal 1967 SA

Jacobz, A.M.
Upendo wa msalaba. [The love of calvary.] 30pp.
T.shs.1.00 Africa Inland Church 1973 TZ SWA

Jacottet, E.
Practical method to learn Sesotho. 3rd. ed. 272pp. cl.
R2.10 Morija 1972 LO

Jacquemin, J.P.
Terre à feu, suivie de l'aveuglette. 30k pap. Ed Mont
Noir 1973 ZR FRE

Jacquet, P.
Abatou Lilié, village Dida. Les jeunes et l'agriculture.
See: Chatenay, D.

Jahadhmy, A.A., ed.
Anthology of Swahili poetry. [in Swahili]. 72pp.
K.shs.11.50 (Waandishi wa Kiafrika, 13) Heinemann
Educ - Nair 1975 KE SWA

Jakande, L.K., ed.
West Africa annual, 1973/74. 416pp. N5.00 West
1974 NR

Jakande, L.K.
Nigerian school directory, 1972-1973. 754pp. N2.20
West 1973 NR

Jakande, L.K.
The role of the mass media in a developing country.
20pp. N1.50 ($2.50/£1.10) (Faculty of Arts Lecture
Series, 4) Univ Ife Press 1975 NR

Jakande, L.K.
The trial of Chief Obafemi Awolowo. 354pp. N4.50
West 1966 NR

Jakuja.
Imagaqo yentetho yesixhosa. See: Makubalo, P.M.

Jakuja.
Uncuthu Lwesixhosa. See: Makubalo, P.M.

Jalla, A.
Litaba za sicaba Samalozi. [History of the Lozi state]
5th ed. 109pp. 50n. (25p.) OUP - Lusaka 1970 ZA
LOZ

Jamal, G.
Studies in the population geography of Uganda and
Tanzania. See: Hirst, M.A.

Jamal, G.I. Tinkler, K.J.
Uganda canonocalised. U.shs.30.00 (Occas. paps.,
25) Dept Geog - Mak 1973 UG

Jamal, G.I.
Uganda squared: a systematic analysis of geographic data
on Uganda arranged by grid-squares. 275pp.
U.shs.30.00 (Occas. paps., 24) Dept Geog - Mak 1972
UG

James, R.W. Kasunmu, A.B.
Alienation of family property in Southern Nigeria. 117pp.
N5.00 cl. Ibadan UP 1966 NR

James, R.W.
Customary land law of Tanzania. hd. & pap.
K.shs.54.00 hd. K.shs.34.00 pap. ($18.50/£9.00 cl.)
EALB 1973 KE

James, R.W., ed. Kassam, F.M., ed.
Law and its administration in a one party state. Selected
speeches of Telford Georges. pap. & hd. K.shs.38.00
hd. K.shs.15.00 pap. ($3.50/£1.40 pap.)
($7.70/£3.70 hd.) EALB 1973 KE

James, R.W.
Land tenure and policy in Tanzania. 431pp. pap. & hd.
K.shs.54.00 hd. K.shs.34.00 pap. ($7.00/£2.80 pap.)
($10.75/£4.30 hd.) EALB 1971 KE

James, R.W.
Modern land law of Nigeria. 285pp. pap. & hd. N6.00
hd. N3.00 pap. (£5.00/$12.00) Univ Ife Press 1973
NR

Jansen, C.
The Cape Malays. See: Whisson, M.

Jansen, C.
Face of South Africa. 120pp. photos. hd. R7.50
Purnell 1972 SA

Janvier, G.
Bibliographie de la Côte d'Ivoire. v.1. Sciences de la vie.
356pp. CFA1700 (F34.00) Univ Abidjan 1972 IV
FRE

Janvier, G., comp.
Bibliographie de la Côte-d'Ivoire. v. 2: Sciences de
l'homme. 2, 3 v. 431pp. CFA2.700 (F54.00) Univ
Abidjan 1973 IV FRE

Janvier, G., comp. Perron, G., comp.
Bibliographie de la Côte d'Ivoire. v. 3: sciences de
physiques et de la terre. 260pp. CFA2,500 (F30.00)
Univ Abidjan 1975 IV FRE

Japaunjo, R.
Mzee Nyachote. 56pp. ill. K.shs2.50 ($1.00) EAPH
1967 KE SWA

Japheth, K. Seaton, E.
The Meru land case. 91pp. photos. maps.
K.shs.12.00 ($3.60) EAPH 1967 KE

Japheth, K. Seaton, E.
Mzozo wa ardhi ya wameru. [Swahili historical studies]
101pp. K.shs.7.95 ($2.60) EAPH 1970 KE SWA

Jaros, G.G. Meyer, B.J.
Elementary medical biophysics. 260pp. R8.75
Butterworths 1973 SA

Jarvis, M.S.
Ebisooka bya geography. See: Musane, E.

Jaspan, C.
A consolidated index of cases discussed in articles, notes
and reviews in the South African Law Journal: 1954-1968.
52pp. R2.70 Dept Bibliog, Lib & Typo 1970 SA

Jay, B.
Introduction au Nouveau Testament. 288pp. CFA660
CLE 1969 CM FRE

Jeanrenaud, R.
Qu'ils sont beaux les pieds du missionnaire. 120pp.
BF90 Lavigerie 1971 BD FRE

Jeboda, F.
Olowolaiyemo. [The world bows to the rich] 142pp. ill.
N1.40 Longman - Nig 1972 NR YOR

Jeboda, F. Dahunsi, A.
Oloyinmomo: Apa kini. 1, 4 bks. 38pp. col. ill. 65k
Longman - Nig 1966 NR YOR

Jeboda, F. Dahunsi, A.
Oloyinmomo: Iwe keji. 2, 4 bks. 64pp. col. ill. 75k
Longman - Nig 1968 NR YOR

Jeboda, F. Dahunsi, A.
Oloyinmomo: pupils' bk. 3, 4bks. 64pp. col. ill. 92k
Longman - Nig 1968 NR YOR

Jeboda, F. Dahunsi, A.
Oloyinmomo: teachers' bk. 4, 4 bks. ill. 40k
Longman - Nig 1966 NR YOR

Jedidi, M.
Jebeniana et sa région - étude géographique. D4.200
(Série II, Géographie, 3) Univ Tunis 1976 TI FRE

Jeffery, R.W. Oyewole, F.
Advanced practical chemistry for tropical schools.
320pp. ill. N1.50 Macmillan 1966 NR

Jeffery, R.W. Oyewole, F.
Elementary organic chemistry for tropical schools.
128pp. ill. N1.00 Macmillan 1969 NR

Jeffreys, M.D.W.
Man and mythology. 40c. (Isma paps., 29) Inst
Study of Man 1970 SA

Jeffreys, M.D.W.
The semitic origins of Hottentot culture. 27pp. R1.60
(Raymond Dart lec., 4) Inst Study of Man 1967 SA

Jeffreys, M.D.W.
Some semitic influences in Hottentot culture. 27pp. map.
R2.00 (Raymond Dart Lectures, 4) Witwatersrand UP
1968 SA

Jekhowsky, B.
Variation létérale en palynologie quantitative et passage du
continental au marin. Le dogger supéieur du sud-ouest de
Madagascar. 19pp. FMG350 (F7.00) (Série
Documentation, 163) Service Geol - Mad 1963 MG FRE

Jemie, O.
Voyage, and other poems. 28pp. 60k (Pan-African
pocket poets, 2) Univ Ife Bkshop 1971 NR

Jenewari, C.E.W.
Teachers' notes on Kálábari tari go diri 1. 91pp. 50k
(Inst. of African Stud., Univ. of Ibadan, Rivers readers
project, 25) Inst Afr Stud-Ibadan 1972 NR KAB

Jenkins, D. Stebbing, D.
They led the way: Christian pioneers of Central Africa.
88pp. ill. 90c. pap. R1.80 cl. OUP-SA 1966 SA

Jenkins, G.
A century of history: the story of Potchefstroom. 120pp.
ill. hd. fl. 22.50 Balkema 1972 SA

Jenkinson, T.B.
Amazulu; the Zulus, their past history, manners, customs,
and language with obervations on the country and its
productions, climate, etc., the Zulu war, and Zululand
since the war. [Reprint of ed. London, 1882] 215pp.
R4.70 (Reprints, 23) State-Lib-SA 1968 SA

Jennings, I.
Demokrasi katika Africa. [Democracy in Africa] 2nd ed.
123pp. K.shs.1.00 ($1.25/50p.) EALB 1961 KE
SWA

Jensma, W.
Sing for our execution. Poems and woodcuts. 123pp. ill.
pl. R2.95 ($4.25/£2.25) Ravan 1973 SA

Jensma, W.
Where white is the colour. pl. R4.20 Ravan 1974
SA

Jeppe, B.
Natal wild flowers. col. pl. R20.00 Purnell 1976 SA

Author Index

Jolly, R., ed.
Planning education for African development. 160pp. maps. K.shs.56.00 cl. K.shs.23.00 pap. ($10.40 cl.) ($5.60 pap.) EAPH 1969 KE

Jolly, R.
Education in Africa: research and action. 307pp. K.shs.21.00 ($5.80) EAPH KE

Jolly, R. et al.
Atindonikab Betusiechu. [Stories of today] 2, 2 bks. ill. K.shs.1.00 ($1.25/50p) EALB 1958 KE KAL

Jolobe, J.J.R.
Amavo. [Xhosa essays.] repr. in new orthography ed. 118pp. R1.20 (Bantu treasury, 5) Witwatersrand UP 1975 SA XHO

Jolobe, J.J.R.
Poems of an African. 15c. Lovedale 1970 SA

Jolobe, J.J.R.
Umyezo. [Xhosa poems] repr. in new orthography ed. 123pp. cl. R1.20 (Bantu treasury, 2) Witwatersrand UP 1972 SA XHO

The Joma Kenyatta Foundation.
Kiswahili syllabus. 36pp. K.shs.4.00 Jomo Kenyatta Found 1975 KE

The Jomo Kenyatta Foundation.
Art and craft syllabus. 24pp. K.shs.3.50 Jomo Kenyatta Found 1976 KE

The Jomo Kenyatta Foundation.
Christian religious education. Teachers guide. 138pp. K.shs.12.00 Jomo Kenyatta Found 1976 KE

The Jomo Kenyatta Foundation.
A course for backward readers. 96pp. K.shs.7.25 Jomo Kenyatta Found 1968 KE

The Jomo Kenyatta Foundation.
Cross reference index for primary religious education textbooks. 20pp. K.shs.3.50 Jomo Kenyatta Found 1975 KE

The Jomo Kenyatta Foundation.
Curriculum guide. 1, 2v. 372pp. hd. & pap. K.shs.34.00 cl. K.shs.22.00 pap. Jomo Kenyatta Found 1975 KE

The Jomo Kenyatta Foundation.
Curriculum guide. 2, 2v. 292pp. hd. & pap. K.shs.34.00 cl. K.shs.22.00 pap. Jomo Kenyatta Found 1975 KE

The Jomo Kenyatta Foundation.
Education celebrates Uhuru. 96pp. K.shs.9.00 Jomo Kenyatta Found 1975 KE

The Jomo Kenyatta Foundation.
Educational structure in Kenya. 56pp. K.shs.5.00 Jomo Kenyatta Found 1975 KE

The Jomo Kenyatta Foundation.
The first Kenya atlas (standards 3 & 4) rev. ed. 36pp. K.shs.11.50 pap. Jomo Kenyatta Found 1966 KE

The Jomo Kenyatta Foundation.
Fundamental concepts of mathematics. Teachers Guide. v.1 280pp. K.shs.25.00 Jomo Kenyatta Found 1975 KE

The Jomo Kenyatta Foundation.
Fundamental concepts of mathematics. v.1 382pp. K.shs.18.50 Jomo Kenyatta Found 1973 KE

The Jomo Kenyatta Foundation.
Fundamental concepts of mathematics. v.2 262pp. K.shs.19.50 Jomo Kenyatta Found 1974 KE

The Jomo Kenyatta Foundation.
Geography for Kenya schools - Australia and New Zealand. 120pp. K.shs.11.50 Jomo Kenyatta Found 1973 KE

The Jomo Kenyatta Foundation.
Geography for Kenya schools - South America. 112pp. K.shs.11.50 Jomo Kenyatta Found 1974 KE

The Jomo Kenyatta Foundation.
God's power in Christ. 188pp. K.shs.27.50 Jomo Kenyatta Found 1976 KE

The Jomo Kenyatta Foundation.
A guide to field work in Kenya. 118pp. K.shs.19.75 Jomo Kenyatta Found 1975 KE

The Jomo Kenyatta Foundation.
Guidelines for teaching science - standard 4 teachers' guide. 26pp. K.shs.7.50 Jomo Kenyatta Found 1975 KE

The Jomo Kenyatta Foundation.
Guidelines for teaching science. (standard 5) 42pp. K.shs.7.50 Jomo Kenyatta Found 1976 KE

The Jomo Kenyatta Foundation.
Guidelines for teaching science. (standard 6) 50pp. K.shs.10.00 Jomo Kenyatta Found 1977 KE

The Jomo Kenyatta Foundation.
Home science syllabus. 12pp. K.shs.3.00 Jomo Kenyatta Found 1975 KE

The Jomo Kenyatta Foundation.
Introducing and running class libraries. 54pp. K.shs.6.25 Jomo Kenyatta Found 1968 KE

The Jomo Kenyatta Foundation.
Kenya advanced mathematics project - option 1. 90pp. K.shs.10.00 Jomo Kenyatta Found 1974 KE

The Jomo Kenyatta Foundation.
Kenya advanced mathematics project - option 2. 136pp. K.shs.10.00 Jomo Kenyatta Found 1974 KE

The Jomo Kenyatta Foundation.
Kenya advanced mathematics project - option 3. 118pp. K.shs.10.00 Jomo Kenyatta Found 1974 KE

The Jomo Kenyatta Foundation.
Kenya advanced mathematics project - option 4. 86pp. K.shs.10.00 Jomo Kenyatta Found 1973 KE

The Jomo Kenyatta Foundation.
Kenya advanced mathematics project - option 5. 100pp. K.shs.10.00 Jomo Kenyatta Found 1973 KE

The Jomo Kenyatta Foundation.
Kenya advanced mathematics project. pt.1 186pp. K.shs.12.50 Jomo Kenyatta Found 1972 KE

The Jomo Kenyatta Foundation.
Kenya advanced mathematics project. pt.2 324pp. K.shs.12.50 Jomo Kenyatta Found 1972 KE

The Jomo Kenyatta Foundation.
Kenya advanced mathematics project. pt.3 176pp. K.shs.12.50 Jomo Kenyatta Found 1973 KE

The Jomo Kenyatta Foundation.
Kenya advanced mathematics project - transitional text. 64pp. K.shs.10.00 Jomo Kenyatta Found 1975 KE

The Jomo Kenyatta Foundation.
Kenya primary mathematics. Pupils' bk.5 166pp. K.shs.11.50 Jomo Kenyatta Found 1974 KE

The Jomo Kenyatta Foundation.
Kenya primary mathematics. Pupils' bk.6 188pp. K.shs.12.00 Jomo Kenyatta Found 1975 KE

The Jomo Kenyatta Foundation.
Kenya primary mathematics. Pupils' bk. 1 64pp. K.shs.4.90 Jomo Kenyatta Found 1970 KE

The Jomo Kenyatta Foundation.
Kenya primary mathematics. Pupils' bk. 2 156pp. K.shs.9.00 Jomo Kenyatta Found 1968 KE

The Jomo Kenyatta Foundation.
Kenya primary mathematics. Pupils' bk. 3 156pp. K.shs.10.50 Jomo Kenyatta Found 1970 KE

The Jomo Kenyatta Foundation.
Kenya primary mathematics. Pupils' bk. 4 152pp. K.shs.11.50 Jomo Kenyatta Found 1973 KE

The Jomo Kenyatta Foundation.
Kenya primary mathematics. Pupils bk. 7 178pp. K.shs.12.00 Jomo Kenyatta Found 1976 KE

The Jomo Kenyatta Foundation.
Kenya primary mathematics. Teachers' bk.4 215pp. K.shs.25.00 Jomo Kenyatta Found 1974 KE

The Jomo Kenyatta Foundation.
Kenya primary mathematics. Teachers' bk.5 154pp. K.shs.25.00 Jomo Kenyatta Found 1975 KE

Author Index

The Jomo Kenyatta Foundation.
Kenya primary mathematics. Teachers' bk.6 227pp.
K.shs.25.00 Jomo Kenyatta Found 1976 KE

The Jomo Kenyatta Foundation.
Kenya primary mathematics. Teachers' bk. 1 160pp.
K.shs.20.00 Jomo Kenyatta Found 1970 KE

The Jomo Kenyatta Foundation.
Kenya primary mathematics. Teachers' bk. 2 188pp.
K.shs.24.00 Jomo Kenyatta Found 1972 KE

The Jomo Kenyatta Foundation.
Kenya primary mathematics. Teachers' bk. 3 228pp.
K.shs.30.00 Jomo Kenyatta Found 1972 KE

The Jomo Kenyatta Foundation.
Kenya primary mathematics. Teachers' bk. 7 176pp.
K.shs.30.00 Jomo Kenyatta Found 1976 KE

The Jomo Kenyatta Foundation.
Kenya primary mathematics - wall charts (standard 1)
22pp. K.shs.47.50 Jomo Kenyatta Found 1970 KE

The Jomo Kenyatta Foundation.
Kenya primary mathematics - wall charts (standard 2)
22pp. K.shs.47.50 Jomo Kenyatta Found 1972 KE

The Jomo Kenyatta Foundation.
Kenya primary mathematics - wall charts (standard 3)
20pp. K.shs.47.50 Jomo Kenyatta Found 1972 KE

The Jomo Kenyatta Foundation.
Kenya primary mathematics. Wall charts (standard 4)
30pp. K.shs.56.00 Jomo Kenyatta Found 1974 KE

The Jomo Kenyatta Foundation.
Kenya primary mathematics. Wall charts (standard 5)
17pp. K.shs.56.00 Jomo Kenyatta Found 1974 KE

The Jomo Kenyatta Foundation.
Kenya primary mathematics. Wall charts (standard 6)
33pp. K.shs.60.00 Jomo Kenyatta Found 1975 KE

The Jomo Kenyatta Foundation.
Kenya primary mathematics - wall charts. (standard 7)
8pp. ill. K.shs.32.00 Jomo Kenyatta Found 1976 KE

The Jomo Kenyatta Foundation.
Kenya primary science - a scientific look at soil. 26pp.
K.shs.6.50 Jomo Kenyatta Found 1974 KE

The Jomo Kenyatta Foundation.
Kenya primary science - arts and crafts. 20pp.
K.shs.4.05 Jomo Kenyatta Found 1971 KE

The Jomo Kenyatta Foundation.
Kenya primary science - ask the ant lion. 32pp.
K.shs.7.05 Jomo Kenyatta Found 1975 KE

The Jomo Kenyatta Foundation.
Kenya primary science - bricks and pots. 46pp.
K.shs.10.00 Jomo Kenyatta Found 1975 KE

The Jomo Kenyatta Foundation.
Kenya primary science - colour, water and paper. 13pp.
K.shs.5.00 Jomo Kenyatta Found 1975 KE

The Jomo Kenyatta Foundation.
Kenya primary science - construction. 12pp.
K.shs.3.50 Jomo Kenyatta Found 1971 KE

The Jomo Kenyatta Foundation.
Kenya primary science - cooking. 10pp. K.shs.2.90
Jomo Kenyatta Found 1971 KE

The Jomo Kenyatta Foundation.
Kenya primary science - dry sand. 10pp. K.shs.2.90
Jomo Kenyatta Found 1971 KE

The Jomo Kenyatta Foundation.
Kenya primary science - exploring nature. 26pp.
K.shs.6.50 Jomo Kenyatta Found 1972 KE

The Jomo Kenyatta Foundation.
Kenya primary science - exploring the local community.
16pp. K.shs.4.00 Jomo Kenyatta Found 1971 KE

The Jomo Kenyatta Foundation.
Kenya primary science - introduction. 38pp.
K.shs.6.05 Jomo Kenyatta Found 1971 KE

The Jomo Kenyatta Foundation.
Kenya primary science - liquid. 26pp. K.shs.6.50
Jomo Kenyatta Found 1974 KE

The Jomo Kenyatta Foundation.
Kenya primary science - making paints. 18pp.
K.shs.6.00 Jomo Kenyatta Found 1975 KE

The Jomo Kenyatta Foundation.
Kenya primary science - mosquitos. 24pp. K.shs.6.00
Jomo Kenyatta Found 1975 KE

The Jomo Kenyatta Foundation.
Kenya primary science - plants in the classroom. 16pp.
K.shs.3.05 Jomo Kenyatta Found 1971 KE

The Jomo Kenyatta Foundation.
Kenya primary science - playground equipment. 66pp.
K.shs.7.50 Jomo Kenyatta Found 1971 KE

The Jomo Kenyatta Foundation.
Kenya primary science - sinking and floating. 26pp.
K.shs.7.05 Jomo Kenyatta Found 1975 KE

The Jomo Kenyatta Foundation.
Kenya primary science - small animals. 39pp.
K.shs.9.55 Jomo Kenyatta Found 1975 KE

The Jomo Kenyatta Foundation.
Kenya primary science - stars over Africa. 24pp.
K.shs.6.50 Jomo Kenyatta Found 1975 KE

The Jomo Kenyatta Foundation.
Kenya primary science - strangers in the sky. 32pp.
K.shs.7.50 Jomo Kenyatta Found 1975 KE

The Jomo Kenyatta Foundation.
Kenya primary science - the moon watchers. 64pp.
K.shs.8.50 Jomo Kenyatta Found 1975 KE

The Jomo Kenyatta Foundation.
Kenya primary science - tools in the classroom. 42pp.
K.shs.6.30 Jomo Kenyatta Found 1971 KE

The Jomo Kenyatta Foundation.
Kenya primary science - water. 18pp. K.shs.3.50
Jomo Kenyatta Found 1971 KE

The Jomo Kenyatta Foundation.
Kenya primary science - wet sand. 8pp. K.shs.2.90
Jomo Kenyatta Found 1971 KE

The Jomo Kenyatta Foundation.
Lesson notes for Christian teaching in Kenya schools
(standard 5) 110pp. K.shs.17.50 Jomo Kenyatta
Found 1971 KE

The Jomo Kenyatta Foundation.
Lesson notes for Christian teaching in Kenya schools
(standard 6) 116pp. K.shs.17.50 Jomo Kenyatta
Found 1971 KE

The Jomo Kenyatta Foundation.
Lesson notes for Christian teaching in Kenya schools
(standard 7) 132pp. K.shs.17.50 Jomo Kenyatta
Found 1971 KE

The Jomo Kenyatta Foundation.
Mambo ni mazuri. 136pp. K.shs.4.50 Jomo Kenyatta
Found 1972 KE SWA

The Jomo Kenyatta Foundation.
Manual for the heads of secondary schools in Kenya.
88pp. K.shs.7.00 Jomo Kenyatta Found 1975 KE

The Jomo Kenyatta Foundation.
Masomo ya kiswahili (standard 4) Pupils' bk. 1 92pp.
K.shs.6.50 Jomo Kenyatta Found 1971 KE SWA

The Jomo Kenyatta Foundation.
Masomo ya kiswahili. (standard 4) Pupils' bk. 1A 28pp.
K.shs.6.50 Jomo Kenyatta Found 1966 KE SWA

The Jomo Kenyatta Foundation.
Masomo ya kiswahili. (standard 4) Pupils' bk. 1B
104pp. K.shs.6.50 Jomo Kenyatta Found 1966 KE
SWA

The Jomo Kenyatta Foundation.
Masomo ya kiswahili (standard 4) Teachers' bk.1
354pp. K.shs.11.50 Jomo Kenyatta Found 1971 KE
SWA

The Jomo Kenyatta Foundation.
Masomo ya kiswahili (standard 5) Pupils' bk. 2 128pp.
K.shs.7.50 Jomo Kenyatta Found 1968 KE SWA

Author Index

The Jomo Kenyatta Foundation.
Masomo ya kiswahili (standard 5) Teachers' bk.2
280pp. K.shs.15.00 Jomo Kenyatta Found 1968 KE
SWA

The Jomo Kenyatta Foundation.
Masomo ya kiswahili (standard 6) Pupils' bk. 3 192pp.
K.shs.11.00 Jomo Kenyatta Found 1969 KE SWA

The Jomo Kenyatta Foundation.
Masomo ya kiswahili (standard 6) Teachers' bk.3
296pp. K.shs.15.00 Jomo Kenyatta Found 1969 KE
SWA

The Jomo Kenyatta Foundation.
Masomo ya kiswahili (standard 7) Pupils' bk.4 160pp.
K.shs.10.00 Jomo Kenyatta Found 1970 KE SWA

The Jomo Kenyatta Foundation.
Masomo ya kiswahili (standard 7) Teachers' bk.4
254pp. K.shs.15.00 Jomo Kenyatta Found 1970 KE
SWA

The Jomo Kenyatta Foundation.
Masomo ya kiswahili - wall charts (standard 4) 12pp.
K.shs.33.00 Jomo Kenyatta Found 1967 KE SWA

The Jomo Kenyatta Foundation.
Methodology in primary schools. 24pp. K.shs.3.75
Jomo Kenyatta Found 1975 KE

The Jomo Kenyatta Foundation.
The metric system. Teachers' guide. 32pp. K.shs.2.00
Jomo Kenyatta Found 1969 KE

The Jomo Kenyatta Foundation.
Mother tongue syllabus. 44pp. K.shs.4.50 Jomo
Kenyatta Found 1975 KE

The Jomo Kenyatta Foundation.
My christian community. (standard 6) 100pp.
K.shs.25.00 Jomo Kenyatta Found 1977 KE

The Jomo Kenyatta Foundation.
Primary history syllabus. 28pp. K.shs.1.30 Jomo
Kenyatta Found 1973 KE

The Jomo Kenyatta Foundation.
Primary school geography syllabus. 24pp. K.shs.3.00
Jomo Kenyatta Found 1975 KE

The Jomo Kenyatta Foundation.
Primary school music syllabus. 12pp. K.shs.2.50
Jomo Kenyatta Found 1975 KE

The Jomo Kenyatta Foundation.
Safari English course. Children's bk. 1 238pp.
K.shs.11.50 Jomo Kenyatta Found 1968 KE

The Jomo Kenyatta Foundation.
Safari English course. Children's bk. 2 256pp.
K.shs.11.50 Jomo Kenyatta Found 1969 KE

The Jomo Kenyatta Foundation.
Safari English course. Children's bk. 3 300pp.
K.shs.11.50 Jomo Kenyatta Found 1971 KE

The Jomo Kenyatta Foundation.
Safari English course. Children's bk. 4 200pp.
K.shs.11.50 Jomo Kenyatta Found 1973 KE

The Jomo Kenyatta Foundation.
Safari English course. Teachers' bk. 1, term 1 142pp.
K.shs.17.35 Jomo Kenyatta Found 1968 KE

The Jomo Kenyatta Foundation.
Safari English course. Teachers' bk. 1, term 2 142pp.
K.shs.17.35 Jomo Kenyatta Found 1968 KE

The Jomo Kenyatta Foundation.
Safari English course. Teachers' bk. 1, term 3 118pp.
K.shs.17.35 Jomo Kenyatta Found 1968 KE

The Jomo Kenyatta Foundation.
Safari English course. Teachers' bk. 2, term 1 110pp.
K.shs.16.00 Jomo Kenyatta Found 1969 KE

The Jomo Kenyatta Foundation.
Safari English course. Teachers' bk. 2, term 2 102pp.
K.shs.16.00 Jomo Kenyatta Found 1969 KE

The Jomo Kenyatta Foundation.
Safari English course. Teachers' bk. 2, term 3 102pp.
K.shs.16.00 Jomo Kenyatta Found 1969 KE

The Jomo Kenyatta Foundation.
Safari English course. Teachers' bk. 3, term 1 100pp.
K.shs.17.35 Jomo Kenyatta Found 1971 KE

The Jomo Kenyatta Foundation.
Safari English course. Teachers' bk. 3, term 2 106pp.
K.shs.17.35 Jomo Kenyatta Found 1971 KE

The Jomo Kenyatta Foundation.
Safari English course. Teachers' bk. 3, term 3 100pp.
K.shs.17.35 Jomo Kenyatta Found 1971 KE

The Jomo Kenyatta Foundation.
Safari English course. Teachers' bk. 4, term 1 96pp.
K.shs.19.00 Jomo Kenyatta Found 1973 KE

The Jomo Kenyatta Foundation.
Safari English course. Teachers' bk. 4, term 2 92pp.
K.shs.19.00 Jomo Kenyatta Found 1973 KE

The Jomo Kenyatta Foundation.
Safari English course. Teachers' bk. 4, term 3 100pp.
K.shs.19.00 Jomo Kenyatta Found 1973 KE

The Jomo Kenyatta Foundation.
Science schemes of work (standard 6) bk.3 64pp.
K.shs.4.00 Jomo Kenyatta Found 1969 KE

The Jomo Kenyatta Foundation.
Science schemes of work (standard 7) bk.4 68pp.
K.shs.4.50 Jomo Kenyatta Found 1970 KE

The Jomo Kenyatta Foundation.
Science schemes of work (standards 1, 2 & 3) bk.1
64pp. K.shs.3.00 Jomo Kenyatta Found 1968 KE

The Jomo Kenyatta Foundation.
Science schemes of work (standards 4 & 5) bk.2 66pp.
K.shs.3.50 Jomo Kenyatta Found 1968 KE

The Jomo Kenyatta Foundation.
Science syllabus. 24pp. K.shs.3.75 Jomo Kenyatta
Found 1976 KE

The Jomo Kenyatta Foundation.
SSP biology - pupils' year 1 and 2. 216pp.
K.shs.12.50 Jomo Kenyatta Found 1973 KE

The Jomo Kenyatta Foundation.
SSP biology - pupil's year 3. 128pp. K.shs.15.00
Jomo Kenyatta Found 1977 KE

The Jomo Kenyatta Foundation.
SSP biology - pupil's year 4. 96pp. K.shs.15.00
Jomo Kenyatta Found 1977 KE

The Jomo Kenyatta Foundation.
SSP chemistry reader - chemical element. 24pp.
K.shs.6.00 Jomo Kenyatta Found 1977 KE

The Jomo Kenyatta Foundation.
SSP chemistry reader - copper in Uganda. 20pp.
K.shs.7.50 Jomo Kenyatta Found 1977 KE

The Jomo Kenyatta Foundation.
SSP chemistry reader - data book. 52pp. K.shs.9.00
Jomo Kenyatta Found 1976 KE

The Jomo Kenyatta Foundation.
SSP chemistry reader - fermentation and distillation.
28pp. K.shs.7.50 Jomo Kenyatta Found 1977 KE

The Jomo Kenyatta Foundation.
SSP chemistry reader - minerals of East Africa. 32pp.
K.shs.4.50 Jomo Kenyatta Found 1977 KE

The Jomo Kenyatta Foundation.
SSP chemistry reader - objective questions. 92pp.
K.shs.9.00 Jomo Kenyatta Found 1976 KE

The Jomo Kenyatta Foundation.
SSP chemistry reader - salt in East Africa. 24pp.
K.shs.6.00 Jomo Kenyatta Found 1976 KE

The Jomo Kenyatta Foundation.
SSP chemistry reader - structured questions. 142pp.
K.shs.9.00 Jomo Kenyatta Found 1976 KE

The Jomo Kenyatta Foundation.
SSP chemistry - year 1 and 2 pupil's manual. 132pp.
K.shs.12.00 Jomo Kenyatta Found 1974 KE

The Jomo Kenyatta Foundation.
SSP chemistry - year 1 teachers' guide. 78pp.
K.shs.15.00 Jomo Kenyatta Found 1975 KE

The Jomo Kenyatta Foundation.
SSP chemistry - year 2 teachers' guide. 122pp.
K.shs.15.00 Jomo Kenyatta Found 1975 KE

The Jomo Kenyatta Foundatio.
SSP chemistry - year 3 and 4 pupils manual. 148pp.
K.shs.15.00 Jomo Kenyatta Found 1976 KE

The Jomo Kenyatt. Foundation.
SSP chemistry - year 3 and 4 teachers' guide. 110pp.
K.shs.15.00 Jc mo Kenyatta Found 1976 KE

The Jomo Kenyatta Foundation.
SSP physics - pupils' manual year 1. 116pp.
K.shs.12.50 Jomo Kenyatta Found 1973 KE

The Jomo Kenyatta Foundation.
SSP physics - pupils' manual year 2. 160pp.
K.shs.11.00 Jomo Kenyatta Found 1974 KE

The Jomo Kenyatta Foundation.
SSP physics - pupils' manual year 3. 160pp.
K.shs.12.50 Jomo Kenyatta Found 1975 KE

The Jomo Kenyatta Foundation.
SSP physics - pupils' manual year 4. 120pp.
K.shs.12.50 Jomo Kenyatta Found 1975 KE

The Jomo Kenyatta Foundation.
SSP physics reader - motor car. 24pp. K.shs.7.00
Jomo Kenyatta Found 1977 KE

The Jomo Kenyatta Foundation.
SSP physics - year 1 teachers' guide. 132pp.
K.shs.15.00 Jomo Kenyatta Found 1975 KE

The Jomo Kenyatta Foundation.
SSP physics - year 2 teachers' guide. 184pp.
K.shs.15.00 Jomo Kenyatta Found 1975 KE

Tl.e Jomo Kenyatta Foundation.
SSP physics - year 3 teachers' guide. 148pp.
K.shs.15.00 Jomo Kenyatta Found 1974 KE

The Jomo Kenyatta Foundation.
SSP physics - year 4 teachers' guide. 168pp.
K.shs.15.00 Jomo Kenyatta Found 1976 KE

The Jomo Kenyatta Foundation.
Starting to read - pupils' book. 32pp. K.shs.7.50
Jomo Kenyatta Found 1968 KE

The Jomo Kenyatta Foundation.
Starting to read - teachers' notes. 46pp. K.shs.11.50
Jomo Kenyatta Found 1970 KE

The Jomo Kenyatta Foundation.
Teaching written English (a method handbook) 140pp.
K.shs.7.50 Jomo Kenyatta Found 1970 KE

The Jomo Kenyatta Foundation.
Teachmaster series of charts (standards 1, 2 & 3) 48pp.
K.shs.75.00 Jomo Kenyatta Found 1968 KE

The Jomo Kenyatta Foundation.
Wasifu wa Kenyatta. 64pp. K.shs.3.00 Jomo
Kenyatta Found 1971 KE SWA

The Jomo Kenyatta Foundation.
Wholeness in Christ. 184pp. K.shs.22.00 Jomo
Kenyatta Found 1975 KE

The Jomo Kenyatta Foundation.
Woodwork. 10pp. K.shs.2.90 Jomo Kenyatta Found
1972 KE

The Jomo Kenyatta Foundation.
Workmaster series of charts (standards 4 - 7) 48pp.
K.shs.75.00 Jomo Kenyatta Found 1971 KE

Jones, A.M.
African hymnody in christian worship. A contribution to the
history of its development. 65c. (Mambo
Missio-Pastoral Series, 8) Mambo 1976 RH

Jones, A.M. Kombe, L.
The Icila dance, old style. 49pp. photos. ill. 85c. Int
Lib Afric Music 1952 SA

Jones, B.
Ui wiji atia. [Meru reader] 61pp. ill. K.shs.1.00
($1.25/50p) EALB 1970 KE MER

Jones, B.M.
Land tenure in South Africa: past, present and future.
193pp. R3.00 Univ of Natal 1965 SA

Jones, E.D., ed.
Freetown: a symposium. See: Fyfe, C., ed.

Jones, E.D.
Othello's countrymen. 158pp. pl. maps. cl. Le4.00
(£2.00) Sierra Leone UP 1968 SL

Jones, E.M.
Roll of the British settlers in South Africa. 184pp. ill. hd.
fl. 22.50 Balkema 1971 SA

Jones, H.M.
Development in Swaziland: a regional analysis.
See: Fair, T.J.D.

Jones, J.J.
The role of hormones in living control systems. 17pp.
30c Univ Rhodesia Lib 1970 RH

Jones, L.J.
Planning in South Africa 1950-1970. 31pp. map.
R1.20 (Univ. Cape Town Libraries. Bibl. ser.) Univ
Cape Town Lib 1974 SA

Jones, M. Sakkut, H.
Taha Hussein. 342pp. £.E.4.000 ($10.00)
(Leaders in Contemporary Egyptian Literature Series, 1)
Am Univ 1975 UA

Jones, M.J.
Observations on dry-season moisture profiles at Samaru,
Nigeria. 20k (Samaru misc. pap., 51) Inst Agric Res
- Zaria 1975 NR

Jones, M.J.
Planting time studies on maize at Samaru, Nigeria,
1970-73. N1.00 (Samaru misc. pap., 58) Inst Agric
Res - Zaria 1976 NR

Jones, N.
My friend Kumalo by 'Mhlagazanhlansi'.[Reprint of ed.
1944]. 122pp. cl. R$3.00 cl. Books of Rhodesia
1972 RH

Jones-Quartey, K.A.B.
Africa: the dynamics of change. See: Passin, H.

Jones-Quartey, K.A.B.
Education and revolution. 30pp. C1.00 ($1.00/50p.)
(Inaugural lecture) Ghana UP 1972 GH

Jones-Quartey, K.A.B.
History, politics and early press in Ghana. The fiction and
the facts. 160pp. ill. C6.00 ($5.00/£2.50) Afram;
distr. 1975 GH

Jones, R.J.M.
The law and practice of conveyancing in South Africa.
2nd ed. R45.00 Juta 1976 SA

Jones, R.T.
Sir Gawain and the Grene Gome. 136pp. R2.10 Univ
of Natal 1965 SA

Jones, S.M.
Personal accounts of visitors to Simon's town 1770-1899.
84pp. R1.00 Univ Cape Town Lib 1964 SA

Joo, J.
Etude géologique et prospection des feuilles
Ambararata-Bepoaka. 32pp. pl. map. FMG781
(F15.62) (Travaux du Bureau Géologique, 119) Service
Geol - Mad 1964 MG FRE

Joo, J. Rakotondrasoa.
Etude géologique et prospection des feuilles
Ambohimiandra, Fenoarivo, Soavinandriana. 58pp. pl.
maps. FMG1635 (F32.70) (Travaux du Bureau
Géologique, 134) Service Geol - Mad 1968 MG FRE

Joo, J.
Idees actuelles sur la structure et les minéralisations du
J.S. mines de Benato. 82pp. pl. FMG1350 (F27.00)
(Série Documentation, 1976) Service Geol - Mad 1968
MG FRE

Joos de ter Beerst, T.
Calcul analogique. 61pp. 80k Press Univ Zaire 1967
ZR FRE

Jordaan, B.
Splintered crucifix. pl. cl. R6.50 Struik 1969 SA

Author Index

Kaberry, P.M.
Western grassfields, linguistic notes (Camerouns)
See: Chilver, E.M.

Kabesh, M.L.   Widatalla, A.   Afia, M.S.
Fodikwan iron ore deposits. 24pp.   50pt.
($1.47/62p.) (Bulletin, 4) Geol and Min Res - Sudan
1958 SJ

Kabesh, M.L.
The geology and economic minerals and rocks of the
Ingessana Hills. 61pp. ill. pl.   70pt. ($2.01/86p.)
(Bulletin, 11) Geol and Min Res - Sudan 1961 SJ

Kabesh, M.L.   Afia, M.S.
Manganese ore deposits of the Sudan. 54pp. pl. photos.
50pt. ($1.47/62p.) (Bulletin, 9) Geol and Min Res -
Sudan 1961 SJ

Kabesh, M.L.
The Mica deposits of Northern Sudan. 55pp. pl. maps.
70pt. ($2.01/86p.) (Bulletin, 7) Geol and Min Res -
Sudan 1960 SJ

Kabesh, M.L.   Afia, M.S.
The Wollastonite deposits of Dirbat well. 31pp. ill.
50pt. ($1.47/62p.) (Bulletin, 5) Geol and Min Res -
Sudan 1959 SJ

Kabetu, M.N.
Kirira kia Ugikuyu. [The traditional customs of the Kikuyu
people] 2nd ed. 108pp.   K.shs.6.00   ($2.00/80p.)
EALB 1966 KE KIK

Kabeya, F.
Mtemi Mirambo. [Biography of one of Tanzania's tribal
chiefs] 2nd ed. 128pp. ill.   K.shs.7.00   ($2.25/90p.)
EALB 1970 KE SWA

Kabui, J.
The coconut girl. 52pp. ill.   K.shs4.90   ($1.50)
EAPH 1971 KE

Kabwegere, T.B.
The politics of state formation. 276pp.   K.shs.30.00
($7.60/£3.60) EALB 1974 KE

Kachaje, G.A.
Kupitiriza chikondi cha m'banja.   [Improving love in
marriage] 24pp.   13t.   (15c.)   Christ Lit Assoc - Mal
1972 MW CHC

Kacharia, S.M.S.   Mbomere, C.O.
Mikasa iliyompata Machomane. [The adventures of
Machomane] 76pp. ill.   T.shs.4.25   Longman - Tanz
1972 TZ SWA

Kachingwe, G.
Bane naatwangale.   [Friends let's play] 26pp.   50n.
(25c.) OUP - Lusaka 1972 ZA LOZ

Kaddache, M.
L'Algérie dans l'antiquité. 226pp. maps.   DA10.00
SNED 1972 AE FRE

Kaddache, M.
La vie politique à Alger de 1919 à 1939.   390pp.
DA18.00   SNED 1970 AE FRE

Kaddu, J.S.
Nkyalira walumbe ettanda.   [Life after death] 80pp.
K.shs.8.00 ($2.00/80p) EALB 1974 KE LUG

Kadima-Nzuji, D.
Préludes à la Terre. 48pp.   20k   (Jeune Littérature, 2)
Ed Mont Noir 1971 ZR FRE

Kadima-Nzuji, D.
Les ressacs. 40pp.   50k Ed Mont Noir 1969 ZR FRE

Kaele, B.
Marabout et fils de marabout. 12pp.   CFA50 CPE
1975 IV FRE

Kaempfe, F.   Van der Meulen, G.J.R.
Investigations into South African raw materials for
manufacturing expanded lightweight aggregates for
concrete. 23pp. (CSIR research reports, 217) CSIR
1966 SA

Kaestner, E.
Emil na wapelelezi. [Emil and the detectives] 102pp.
K.shs.12.00 ($3.00/£1.20) EALB 1974 KE SWA

Kagambirwe, E.
Causes and consequences of land shortage in Kigezi.
175pp.   U.shs.30.00   (Occas. paps., 23) Dept Geog -
Mak 1972 UG

Kagara, M.B.
Gandoki. [Gandoki, the warrior] 48pp. ill.   90k
Northern Nig 1934 NR HAU

Kaggia, B. M.
Roots of freedom.   202pp.   K.shs.30.00   EAPH 1975
KE

Kaggwa, A.
Basekabaka be Bugunda.   332pp.   K.shs.12.00
($3.20) EAPH 1971 KE SWA

Kagia, J.
Your sincerely. 57pp.   K.shs.6.25 Longman - Ken
1974 KE

Kagiri, S.
Leave us alone. 132pp. ill.   K.shs.12.00   ($3.50)
EAPH 1975 KE

Kago, F.
The kings daughter and other stories. 42pp. ill.
K.shs.5.00 Africa Book Serv 1970 KE

Kago, F.K.
Lucky Mtende and other stories. 27pp. ill.   K.shs.4.50
Africa Book Serv 1970 KE

Kago, F.K.
Mango's grass house and other stories. 28pp. ill.
K.shs.4.50 Africa Book Serv 1970 KE

Kago, F.K.
Stories of Konga I. 38pp. col. ill.   K.shs.4.50 Africa
Book Serv 1967 KE

Kagoro, E.D.
Ezimu ha nfumo z'abanyoro n'abatooro.   2nd ed.
Kshs1.20 ($1.25/50p.) EALB 1956 KE RNY

Kagoro, E.D.
Mainaro omusuma kagingo.   [Mainaro the great thief]
35pp.   K.shs2.00   ($1.25/50p) EALB 1963 KE RUY

Kagoro, V.K.K.G.   Mulindwa, Y.R.R.
Katwetegreze eby'arulimi rwaitu.   [Teaching and learning
of the Runyoro/Rutooro language] 82pp.   K.shs2.00
($2.00/80p.) EALB 1969 KE RNY

Kahari, G.
The imaginative writings of Paul Chidyausiku.   175pp. pl.
R$2.25 Mambo 1975 RH

Kahari, G.
The novels of Patrick Chakaipa. A critique in English and
Shona.   110pp.   R$1.75 pap. Longman - Rhod 1972
RH

Kahiga, S.
Lover in the sky. 88pp.   K.shs.8.00   (55p) (Spear
Books, 2) Heinemann Educ - Nair 1975 KE

Kahiga, S.
Potent ash.   See: Kibera, L.

Kahigi, K.K.   Mulokozi, M.M.
Malenga wa bara.   [Collection of verse.] 128pp.
K.shs.17.00   ($4.00/£1.60) EALB 1976 KE SWA

Kahigi, K.K.   Ngemera, A.A.
Mwanzo wa tufani.   [The start of the tempest.] 51pp.
T.shs.8.00 Tanz Publ House 1975 TZ SWA

Kahimbaara, J.A.   Langlands, B.W.
The human factor in the changing ecology of Mwenge.
155pp.   U.shs.20.00   (Occas. paps., 16) Dept Geog -
Mak 1970 UG

Kahn, E.
Contract and mercantile law through the cases.   1,100pp.
R22.00 Juta 1971 SA

Kahn, E., eds.   Zeffertt, D., eds.
Select South African legal problems. Essays in memory of
R.G. McKerron.   R7.50 Juta 1974 SA

Kahn, E.
The South African legal system and its background.
See: Hahlo, H.R.

Kahombo, M., ed.
Jifunze-Yekola. Lingala-Kiswahili. 136pp. ($1.50) IABL 1975 UG LIN

Kahoto, M.
Muntu, animisme et possessions. 70pp. (Essais, 8) Ed Mont Noir 1974 ZR FRE

Kaisi, M.
Ukunga na utunzaji wa watoto vijijini. [Midwifery and child care in the villages.] 216pp. ill. T.shs.20.00 Tanz Publ House 1974 TZ SWA

Kajiga, B.
Untu et son apport à l'universel. 35pp. 30k ($0.40) Lib Les Volcans 1967 ZR FRE

Kajula, S. et al.
The extension of the Kisitwi-Rubeho pipeline: a planning study. 25pp. maps. T.shs.5.00 (Research report, 15) Bur Res Assess- Tanz 1970 TZ

Kaké, I.B.
Amadou Bamba fondateur du mauridisme (Sénégal) 96pp. CFA250 (F5.00) Nouv Ed Afric 1976 SG FRE

Kake, I.B.
Anne Zingha - Reine d'Angola, première résistante à l'invasion portugaise. 112pp. CFA200 (F4.00) (Coll. "Grandes figures africaines") Nouv Ed Afric 1975 SG FRE

Kake, I.B. Comte, G.
Askia Mohamed. L'apogée de l'empire Songhay. 96pp. CFA250 (F5.00) Nouv Ed Afric 1976 SG FRE

Kake, I.B.
Djouder - La fin de l'empire Songhay. 112pp. CFA250 (F5.00) (Coll. "Grandes figures africaines") Nouv Ed Afric 1975 SG FRE

Kake, I.B.
Dona Béatrice. 96pp. CFA250 (F5.00) Nouv Ed Afric 1976 SG FRE

Kaké, I.B.
Kankou Moussa. Empereur du Mali. 96pp. CFA250 Nouv Ed Afric 1976 SG FRE

Kaké, I.B.
Salou Casais. Une idylle franco-songhay au XVème siècle. CFA250 Nouv Ed Afric 1976 SG FRE

Kakoma, G.W.
Four dozen Negro spirituals. K.shs8.00 ($2.50/£1.00) EALB 1973 KE

Kaku, A.K.A.
Nzema edweke edwendole. [Collection of poems.] 25pp. 20pes. Bur Ghana Lang 1974 GH NZE

Kakule, M., et al.
Kusoma na kuandika Kiswahili I. Livre de l'élève. 63pp. CELTA 1976 ZR SWA

Kakule, M., et al.
Kusoma na kuandika Kiswahili I. Livre du maître. 75pp. CELTA 1976 ZR SWA

Kala, J.
The adventures of Musa Kaago. 99pp. ill. K.shs4.00 ($1.50) EAPH 1967 KE

Kala, J.
Valley of flames. col. ill. K.shs.7.50 EAPH 1976 KE

Kalejaiye, A.O.
Thinking about mathematics. Pupils' bk. 3 96pp. 60k Nelson - Nig 1976 NR

Kalejaiye, A.O.
Thinking about mathematics. Teachers' bk. 3 56pp. N1.00 Nelson - Nig 1976 NR

Kaliai, M.H.I.
Nembe-English dictionary. 305pp. N2.00 (Inst. of African Stud., Univ. of Ibadan, occas. pub., 2) Inst Afr Stud-Ibadan 1966 NR NEM

Kalimugogo, C.T.
Pilgrimage to nowhere. 260pp. K.shs.14.10 ($3.40/£1.60) EALB 1975 KE

Kalimugogo, G.
The department. 157pp. K.shs.18.00 ($4.10/£2.00) EALB 1976 KE

Kalimugogo, G.
The pulse of the woods. 162pp. K.shs.15.70 ($3.70/£1.80) EALB 1975 KE

Kalimugogo, G.
Trials and tribulations in Sandu's home. 172pp. K.shs.21.50 ($4.75/£2.30) EALB 1976 KE

Kalindawalo, A. T. M.
M'thengo mdalaka njoka. [Novel.]. 145pp. ill. K1.16 (58p) Longman - Mal 1974 MW CHC

Kalio, T.J.P.
Kirikeni go diri 1. [Okrika reader, 1] 63pp. ill. 30k (Inst. of African Stud., Univ. of Ibadan, Rivers readers project, 27) Inst Afr Stud-Ibadan 1972 NR OKR

Kalitera, A.E.
A taste of business. 112pp. K.shs.9.50 pap. Heinemann Educ - Nair 1976 KE

Kalk, M., ed.
A natural history of Inhaca Island, Mozambique. See: Macnae, W., ed.

Kal'ngo Kinuana-Ngo Wayisa Yebeni.
Lettres sans cendres. Poèmes et prières. 29pp. 50k (CFA250) Centre Africaine Litt 1973 ZR FRE

Kalongo Mbikayi.
Reponsabilité civile et socialisation des risques en droit Zairois et comparé. 364pp. Press Univ Zaire 1976 ZR FRE

Kamal Khan, M.
Kusoma na kufahamu mashairi. Kitabu cha 1. bk. 1. See: Karama, S.

Kamal Khan, M.
Kusoma na kufahamu mashairi. Kitabu cha 2. [Reading and understanding poetry.] bk. 2. 47pp. K.shs.6.90 Longman - Ken 1974 KE SWA

Kamali, L.
Umusilimu. 82pp. RF28 ($0.28) Caritas 1973 RW KIN

Kamau, G.G.
Adventures of Pongo. col. ill. K.shs.7.00 EAPH 1976 KE

Kamau, L.J.
National housing corporation rental schemes. 229pp. K.shs.60.00 Housing Res Dev Unit 1974 KE

Kamau, L.J. Thethy, B.S. Mulili, N.M.
Two housing schemes in Thika, a user reaction survey. 109pp. K.shs.35.00 Housing Res Dev Unit 1972 KE

Kambole, R.M.
Nkobekela tecupo. [Betrothal is not a guarantee for marriage.] 48pp. 75n. Neczam 1975 ZA BEM

Kambula, T.W.
Guided mathematics, standard 7. See: Ferrandi, N.C.H.

Kambule, T.W.
Guided mathematics, standard 6. See: Ferrandi, N.C.H.

Kamel, R.
Le limon rouge. 152pp. D0.700 Maison Tunis 1975 TI FRE

Kamenju, G. Topan, F.
Mashairi ya Azimio la Arusha. [Poems dedicated to the Arusha Declaration] 128pp. ill. T.shs.7.00 Longman - Tanz 1971 TZ SWA

Kamenyi, J.W.
Songs of Kenya, Kikuyu, Meru and Embu. 53pp. K.shs.15.00 Africa Book Serv 1970 KE

Kamera, W.
A guide to the anatomy of the common African earthworm. See: Oxtoby, E.

Kamera, W.D.
Tales of Wairaqw of Tanzania. 108pp. K.shs.14.75 ($3.50/£1.70) EALB 1976 KE

Kamissoko, W.
Les Peuls du Manding. 140pp. CFA350 CELTHO 1975 NG FRE

Kampusu Mayembi.
Il tua son père le python. Mythes ngongo. Textes ngongo-français. 132pp. map. (DM23.00 pap.) (CEEBA. série II, Mémoires et Monographies, 27) CEEBA 1975 ZR FRE

Kamugunga, C.
Impundu kwa makuba. [La chance inesperée d'un éprouvé.] 46pp. RF45 Caritas 1970 RW KIN

Kamugunga, C.
Mafene. [Mafene, je pars en ville.] 2nd ed. 56pp. RF20 ($0.20) Caritas 1974 RW KIN

Kamungunguni, L.
Abagabe b'ankole. v. 1 See: Katate, A.G.

Kamungunguni, L.
Abagabe b'ankole. v. 2 See: Katate, A.G.

Kan, Z.
Longman primary geography. standard 1 48pp. pl. maps. K.shs.8.50 Longman - Ken 1975 KE

Kan, Z.
Longman primary geography. standard 2 96pp. ill. maps. K.shs.8.75 Longman - Ken 1975 KE

Kandil, O.
Théorie fiscale et le développement. 706pp. DA11.00 SNED 1970 AE FRE

Kandoro, S.A.
Mashairi ya Saadani. [Poems of Saadani] 96pp. Nat Print Co 1972 TZ SWA

Kane, B.
A comparative study of the phonological systems of English and Wolof. 100pp. CFA320 (C.L.A.D. Étude, 57) CLAD 1974 SG

Kane, B.
Tééré wolof. 116pp. CFA375 (C.L.A.D. Etude, 43 ter) CLAD 1971 SG FRE

Kane, M., ed.
Littérature africaine. Textes et travaux. See: Falq, J., ed.

Kane, M.
Thèmes et travaux. Littérature française (1750-1850) See: Fornacciari, M.F.

Kâne, O.
Othman Dan Fodio, fondateur de l'empire de Sokoto. 80pp. CFA250 (F5.00) Nouv Ed Afric 1976 SG FRE

Kangafu-Kutumbagana.
Discours sur l'authenticité. Essai sur la problématique idéologique du 'Recours a l'authenticité'. 58pp. 50k (CFA250) Presses Africaines 1973 ZR FRE

Kani, T.Y.
Amoadu. [The story of Amoadu] 119pp. 60pes. Waterville 1950 GH TWI

Kanié A.
Quand les bêtes parlaient aux hommes. 64pp. ill. CFA350 (F7.00) Nouv Ed Afric 1974 SG FRE

Kaniki, H.
Guidelines for writers. See: Omari, I.M.

Kankuenda M'Baya.
Les industries du pôle de Kinshasa. Z3.00 ($2.40) (Cahiers du CRIDE, Nouvelle série, III, 4) CRIDE 1977 ZR FRE

Kano, A.
Rayuwar Marigayi Sa'Adu Zungur. [Biography of Sa'Adu Zungur] 35k Northern Nig 1973 NR HAU

Kano, D.D.
Tabarmar Kunya. [Guilty conscience] 34pp. 80k Northern Nig 1970 NR HAU

Kantor, C.
Lunch with Livingstone. 75c. Shuter 1954 SA

Kanu, S.H.
A world of everlasting conflict. Critical study of the work of Joyce Cary. 300pp. cl. & pap. N3.00 pap. N5.00 cl. Ibadan UP 1974 NR

Kanyama, B.
Kutora mifananidzo. [Photography.] 88pp. pl. 45c Mambo 1970 RH SHO

Kanyama, C.M.W.
Kwacha. 200pp. photos. K.shs.30.00 ($7.50) EAPH 1975 KE SWA

Kanyeihamba, G.W.
Constitutional law and government in Uganda. 524pp. K.shs.32.55 ($6.75/£3.50) EALB 1975 KE

Kanzi, E.M. Mustafa, H.M.
Survey of the studies of the prospects of Gypsum industries in the Sudan. 19pp. Nat Council Res - Sudan 1974 SJ

Ka'Oje, A.
Dare Daya. 85k Northern Nig 1973 NR HAU

Kapferer, B.
Co-operation, leadership and village structure: a preliminary economic and political study of the Bisa villages in the northern province of Zambia. 77pp. maps. K1.25 (63p.) (Zambian paps., 1) Inst Soc Res - Zam 1967 ZA

Kapferer, B.
The population of a Zambian municipal township: a preliminary report of a 1964 social survey of the Broken Hill municipal townships. 67pp. K1.25 (63p.) (Communications, 1) Inst Soc Res - Zam 1966 ZA

Kapila, V.
The rent restriction act. 28pp. K.shs.7.50 ($2.60) EAPH 1975 KE

Kapindula, R.M.
Noko nkalola nkaya nalyo. [Tragic story of revenge.] 44pp. 70n. Neczam 1975 ZA BEM

Kaplan, M.F.
Engineering and the university. 13pp. 30c. (U.C.T. Inaugural lec. New series, 1) Univ Cape Town Lib 1967 SA

Kaplinsky, R.
Accumulation and the transfer of technology: issues of conflict and mechanisms for the exercise of control. 59pp. K.shs.7.00 (Inst. Development Studies, Discussions paps., 224) Inst Dev Stud 1975 KE

Kaplinsky, R.M.
Suspended sentence: a study of Kalk Bay fishermen. See: Whisson, M.G.

Kapwepwe, S.M.
Afrika kuti twabelela uluse lelo tekuti tulabe. [Africa, we can forgive but cannot forget] 178pp. K1.50 Neczam 1970 ZA BEM

Kapwepwe, S.M.
Ubutungwa mu jambojambo. [Freedom in peace] 115pp. 58n. OUP - Lusaka 1967 ZA LOZ

Karama, S. Kamal Khan, M.
Kusoma na kufahamu mashairi. Kitabu cha 1. [Reading and understanding poetry.] bk. 1. 47pp. K.shs.6.90 Longman - Ken 1974 KE SWA

Karanja, R.
The adventures of Ngondo, Mungai and Wangari. 82pp. K.shs2.00 ($1.25/50p.) EALB 1951 KE

Kareithi, P.M.
The banana tree. 27pp. ill. K.shs2.95 ($1.00) EAPH 1968 KE

Kareithi, P.M.
Kaburi bita msalaba. 128pp. ill. K.shs.4.95 ($2.30) EAPH 1969 KE SWA

Kareithi, P.M.
Kigo in England. 77pp. ill. K.shs.5.50 Africa Book Serv 1970 KE

Kareithi, P.M.
Let the child create. Equatorial 1973 KE

Kareithi, P.M.
The maize plant. 51pp. ill. K.shs3.95 ($1.00) EAPH 1969 KE

Kareithi, P.M.
  Mother's chickens. 48pp. ill. K.shs4.95 ($2.00)
  EAPH 1972 KE

Kariara, J., ed.   Kitonga, E., ed.
  An introduction to East African poetry. 144pp. pl.
  K.shs.25.00 OUP - Nairobi 1977 KE

Karimi, M.
  The arrow poisons. 98pp. ill. pl. K.shs.17.75
  ($4.00/£1.90) EALB 1973 KE

Karioki, E.M.
  Sun's daughter. 35pp. K.shs.5.00 ($1.50) EAPH
  1976 KE

Kariuki, J.M.
  'Mau Mau' detainee. (New ed. with postscript by Ngugi wa
  Thiong'o) New ed. K.shs.30.00pp. OUP - Nairobi
  1975 KE

Kariuki, J.M.
  Mau Mau Kizuizini. 157pp. K.shs.5.00 ($2.30)
  EAPH 1965 KE SWA

Kariuki, N.N.
  Karanja mundu muugi. [Follow-up reader on Kikuyu adult
  literacy primer] ill. K.shs.1.50 ($1.25/50p.) EALB
  1960 KE KIK

Karkhanis, P.D.
  Introduction to Accountancy. 384pp. K.shs.40.00
  Textbook Ctre 1974 KE

Karl, E.
  Traditions orales au Dahomey-Benin. 420pp. CFA350
  CELTHO 1974 NG FRE

Karoki, J.
  The land is ours. 255pp. K.shs.10.50 ($3.00/£1.20)
  EALB 1970 KE

Karugire, S.R.
  The story of Uganda. See: Thomas, H.B.

Karwemera, E.
  Shutama nkutekyerereze. 80pp. K.shs.12.35
  ($3.10/£1.50) EALB 1976 KE SWA

Kasaipwalova, J.
  Reluctant flame. 10pp. 30k (Pan-African pocket
  poets, 1) Univ Ife Bkshop 1971 NR

Kaseka, P.A.
  Kilimo cha Mzabibu. [Cultivating grapes.] 64pp.
  T.shs.4.00 (60c) TMP 1973 TZ SWA

Kaser, M.
  Roman law today: two lectures. 33pp. 30c. (80c.)
  Univ South Africa 1965 SA

Kaser, M.
  Roman private law. 402pp. R9.75 Butterworths 1968
  SA

Kashamura, A.
  Les moeurs et les civilisations des peuples des grands
  lacs africains. 254pp. CFA350 CELTHO 1975 NG
  FRE

Kashoki, M.E.
  A phonemic analysis of Bemba: a presentation of Bemba
  syllable structure, phonemic contrasts and their distribution.
  40pp. K1.25 (63p.) (Zambian paps., 3) Inst Soc
  Res - Zam 1968 ZA

Kasirye, J.S.
  Obulamu bwa Stanslaus Mugwanya. [Story of Stanislaus
  Mugwanya] 267pp. ill. pap. & cl. K.shs.1.00 pap.
  ($1.25/50p. pap.) ($4.25/£1.70 cl.) EALB 1965 KE
  LUG

Kasirye, J.W.S.   Lubnama, S.
  Mmere ki gye tusaanira okulya. [What food should we
  eat?] 25pp. ill. K.shs.0.50 ($1.00/40p.) EALB 1951
  KE LUG

Kaslir, N.
  Politics in Africa. 80pp. hd. U.shs5.00 Adult Educ
  Centre 1969 UG

Kasoma, K.
  Fools marry. 41pp. 90n. Neczam 1976 ZA

Kassam, F.M., ed.
  Law and its administration in a one party state. Selected
  speeches of Telford Georges. See: James, R.W., ed.

Kassam, M.M.
  Bwenyenye. [Bata King 1.] 64pp. K.shs.6.75 EALB
  1977 KE SWA

Kassam, Y.O.
  The diploma course in adult education: an evaluation of
  the diploma course in adult education in relation to the
  functions of professional adult education in Tanzania.
  T.shs.1.00 (Studies in Adult Education, 11) Inst Adult
  Educ - Dar 1974 TZ

Kassam, Y.O.
  Political education vis-à-vis adult education in Tanzania:
  the dynamics of their interaction. T.shs.1.00 (Studies
  in Adult Education, 19) Inst Adult Educ - Dar 1975 TZ

Kasunmu, A.B.
  Alienation of family property in Southern Nigeria.
  See: James, R.W.

Kaswa, J.
  Louis Pasteur. K.shs.1.00 ($1.25/50p.) EALB 1962
  KE LUG

Kaswa, J.
  Omunaku kaama. 3rd ed. ill. K.shs.2.65
  ($1.50/60p.) EALB 1960 KE LUG

Kaszner, O.
  Guidelines for room types in low cost housing, with
  reference to the Highlands climatic region. 25pp.
  K.shs.18.00 Housing Research and Dev Unit 1977 KE

Kaszner, O.
  The Kibera experimental self-help scheme. Explanatory
  notes on the planning of a low-cost housing scheme in
  Nairobi. 18pp. K.shs.15.00 Housing Res Dev Unit
  1976 KE

Katalambula, F.
  Simu ya kifo. [Trail of death] 3rd ed. 76pp.
  K.shs.5.50 ($1.75/70p.) EALB 1968 KE SWA

Katalambulla, F.H.H.
  Buriani. 80pp. K.shs.6.55 ($2.10/80p) EALB 1975
  KE SWA

Katalambulla, F.H.H.
  Lawalawa na hadithi nyingine. [Novel.] 100pp.
  K.shs.14.50 ($3.50/£1.40) EALB 1976 KE SWA

Katalambulla, F.H.H.
  Mirathi. [Play.] 56pp. K.shs.8.85 ($2.50/£1.00)
  EALB 1976 KE SWA

Katalambulla, F.H.H.
  Pendo pevu. [Play.] 53pp. K.shs.8.85
  ($2.50/£1.00) EALB 1976 KE SWA

Katate, A.G.   Kamungunguni, L.
  Abagabe b'ankole. [The kings of Bankole] 3rd ed. v.
  1 149pp. K.shs6.40 ($2.45/90p.) EALB 1967 KE
  RNY

Katate, A.G.   Kamungunguni, L.
  Abagabe b'ankole. [The kings of Bankole] 3rd ed. v.
  2 149pp. K.shs5.80 ($2.00/80p.) EALB 1969 KE
  RNY

Kateete, B.M.
  Two studies in land use and land tenure in Kigezi.
  See: Tindituuza, R.

Kategile, J.A., ed.
  Proceedings of the first scientific conference of the
  Tanzania Society of Animal Production, Morogoro, May
  20-22, 1974. 135pp. T.shs.15.00 Tanz Soc Animal
  Prod 1974 TZ

Kategile, J.A., ed.
  Proceedings of the second scientific conference of the
  Tanzania Society of Animal Production, Arusha, May
  19-21, 1975. T.shs.25.00 Tanz Soc Animal Prod 1977
  TZ

Katende, J.W.   Thomas, P.A.   Chesterman, M.R.
The law of business organisations in East and Central Africa. 1200pp.   K.shs.165.00 cl.   K.shs.145.00 pap. ($37.50/£18.00 cl.) ($30.30/£12.15 pap.) EALB 1976 KE

Katigula, B.
Groping in the dark. 132pp.   K.shs.12.50 ($3.10/£1.50) EALB 1975 KE

Katiti, C.B.
Ishe katabaazi. [An adult Luganda literacy primer] 2 2nded. ill.   K.shs.6.30 ($1.75/70p.) EALB 1970 KE LUG

Kato, B. H.
African cultural revolution and the Christian faith. 56pp. Challenge 1976 NR

Kato, B.
Qui suis-je? 16pp.   CFA50 CPE 1975 IV FRE

Kato, B.
Theological pitfalls in Africa. 300pp.   K.shs.28.00 Evangel 1975 KE

Kato, B.H.
African cultural revolution and the Christian faith. 48pp. ill.   60k Challenge 1975 NR

Katoke, I.
Historia fupi ya utamaduni wa Mtanzania. [A short history of Tanzanian culture.] 96pp. ill.   K.shs.10.00 ($4.50) Foundation 1974 KE SWA

Katoke, I. K.
Karagwe Kingdom. 204pp.   K.shs.30.00 EAPH 1975 KE

Katoke, I.K.
The making of the Karagwe kingdom. 30pp. maps. K.shs.2.50 ($1.00) EAPH 1970 KE

Katoke Teachers' Training Centre.
Musa Na Sara. [A primer] 31pp. ill.   K.shs.1.65 ($1.50/60p.) EALB 1967 KE SWA

Katshi.
Muntu et sa pensée. [Philosophie Bantu] 76pp. Z1.50 Press Univ Zaire 1974 ZR FRE

Katsina, B.W.
The adventures of the warrior Gan'doki. 58pp. ill.   65k Northern Nig 1971 NR

Katz, E.N.
A trade union aristocracy: the Transvaal white working class and the general strike of 1913. 610pp.   R7.00 (African Studies Institute, Communications. 3) African Stud Inst - Wit 1976 SA

Katz, M.
Shock wave phenomena with special reference to interactions. 46pp.   R2.40 Dept Bibliog, Lib & Typo 1967 SA

Kaungamno, E.E., ed.
Introduction to librarianship, with special reference to Tanganyika library service. 67pp. ill.   T.shs.25.00 Tanz Lib Serv 1971 TZ

Kaungamno, E.E.
Mass media in Tanzania. 21pp. (Tanzania Library Service, occas. paps., 2) Tanz Lib Serv 1976 TZ

Kaungamno, E.E.
A review of development of library and documentation services in Anglophone countries since the Kampala meeting 1970. 33pp. (Tanzania Library Services, occas. paps., 1) Tanz Lib Serv 1976 TZ

Kavanagh, R.   Qangule, Z.S.
The making of a servant and other poems. tr. fr. Xhosa 19pp.   30c. ($1.50/75p.) Ravan 1972 SA

Kavila, E.
The three sons. 48pp. ill.   K.shs3.50 ($1.00) EAPH 1972 KE

Kaware, E.K.N.
Nketta mu bizinga. 208pp.   K.shs.15.00 ($3.60) EALB 1975 KE LUG

Kawegere, F.-.
Inspector Rajabu investigates. 36pp. ill.   K.shs36.00 ($1.00) EAPH 1968 KE

Kawere, E.K.N.
Bukadde magezi. 142pp.   K.shs.6.30 ($2.25/90p.) EALB 1968 KE LUG

Kawere, K.N.
Zinunula omunaku. 176pp.   K.shs.14.00 ($3.40) EALB 1975 KE LUG

Kay, G.
Chief Kalaba's village: a preliminary survey of economic life in an Ushi village, Northern Rhodesia. 112pp. K1.40 (70p.) (Rhodes-Livingstone paps., 35) Inst Soc Res - Zam 1964 ZA

Kay, G.
The distribution of African population in Southern Rhodesia: some preliminary notes. 30pp. maps.   35n. (18p.) (Rhodes- Livingstone communications, 28) Inst Afr Stud - Lusaka 1964 ZA

Kay, G.
The geographer's task. 22pp.   30c Univ Rhodesia Lib 1970 RH

Kay, G.
Maps of the distribution and density of African population in Zambia. 24pp. maps.   K1.25 (50p.) (Communications, 2) Inst Soc Res - Zam 1967 ZA

Kay, G.
A population map (1:500.000) of the Luapula-Bangweulu region of Northern Rhodesia, with notes on the population. 14pp. maps.   50n. (25p.) (Rhodes- Livingstone communications, 26) Inst Afr Stud - Lusaka 1962 ZA

Kay, G.
A social and economic study of Fort Rosebury.   KO.75 (38p.) (Rhodes-Livingstone Communications, 21) Inst Afr Stud - Lusaka ZA

Kay, G.
Social aspects of village regrouping in Zambia. 99pp. ill./maps.   K1.25 (75p.) Inst Soc Res - Zam 1967 ZA

Kay, W.
Bolou Izua Egberi fun. See: Egberipou, O.A.

Kaya, S.
Les danseuses d'Impé-Eya. Jeunes filles à Abidjan. 130pp.   CFA900 INADES 1976 IV FRE

Kayanja, F.I.B.
Reproduction in antelopes. ill. cl.   K.shs50.00 ($11.00/£5.50 cl.) (East African monog in Biology, 1) EALB 1972 KE

Kayigana, C.
Imigani n'inshoberamahanga bisobanuye. [Proverbes et expressions expliqués.] 169pp.   RF100 ($1.00) Caritas 1976 RW KIN

Kayoya, M.
Entre deux mondes. Sur la route du développement. 152pp. photos.   BF160 Lavigerie 1970 BD FRE

Kayoya, M.
In my father's footprints. 124pp.   K.shs.9.00 (Modern African Library, 25) EAPH 1973 KE

Kayoya, M.
Sur les traces de mon père. Jeunesse du Burundi à la découverte des valeurs. 2nd ed. 144pp. photos. BF160 pap. Lavigerie 1971 BD FRE

Kayper-Mensah, A.
Sankofa. Adinkra poems. 36pp. ill.   C1.20 ($1.20) Ghana Publ Corp 1976 GH

Kayper-Mensah, A.W.
Akwaaba. [A collection of poems.] 80pp.   ($2.00) Ghana Publ Corp 1976 GH TWI

Kazadi, N.   Mutombo, H.   Kempf, B.
Kubala ne kufunda ciluba I. Livre de l'élève. 59pp. CELTA 1976 ZR LIN

Kazadi, N.   Mutombo, H.   Kempf, B.
Kubala ne kufunda ciluba I. Livre du maître. 44pp. CELTA 1976 ZR LIN

Kazembe, P.T.
Danhiko reshona. Pupils' bk. 1. 168pp. R$2.00
Longman - Rhod 1973 RH SHO

Kazembe, P.T.
Danhiko reshóna. Pupils' bk. 2. 144pp. R$2.00
Longman - Rhod 1974 RH SHO

Kazembe, P.T.
Danhiko reshona. Pupil's bk. 3 156pp. ill. R$2.25
Longman - Rhod 1975 RH SHO

Kazembe, P.T.
Danhiko reshona. Teacher's bk. 3 58pp. R$1.95
Longman - Rhod 1975 RH SHO

Kazembe, P.T.
Mwoyochena unobayisa. [A white heart causes death.]
78pp. R$1.20 Longman - Rhod 1975 RH SHO

Kealy, J.P. Shenk, D.W.
The early church and Africa. 368pp. photos.
K.shs.32.50 OUP - Nairobi 1976 KE

Kearney, B.
Architecture in Natal from 1824 to 1893. 271pp. ill. hd.
fl. 112.50 Balkema 1973 SA

Kebe, M. et al.
Annales de l'université d'Abidjan. 203pp. CFA700
(F14.00 pap.) (Série B - Médecine, 4) Univ Abidjan
1970 IV FRE

Kebe, M. G.
Ebéniques. 48pp. CFA300 (F7.80) Nouv Ed Afric
1975 SG FRE

Kebe, M.G.
Kaala Sikkin. 64pp. CFA550 (F11.00) Nouv Ed
Afric 1976 SG FRE

Kedian, P.J. Montgomery, A.N.
Door to poetry. 128pp. 70c. Shuter 1963 SA

Kedian, P.J. Montgomery, A.N.
Invitation to poetry. 6th ed. 220pp. 85c. Shuter
1953 SA

Keegan, J.
Basic physical education for boys. 96pp. photos.
N1.00 Macmillan NR

Keelson, M.P.B.
Story time with the animals. 50pp. ill. (65c.) Ghana
Publ Corp 1976 GH

Keen, E.N.
Anatomy under siege. 30c (Univ. Cape Town.
Inaugural lec., 34) Univ Cape Town Lib 1975 SA

Keen, P.
Western medicine and the witchdoctors. 40c. (Isma
paps., 2) Inst Study of Man 1961 SA

Keeton, A.A.F.
The auditor's manual. See: Strand, D.

Keeton, A.A.F.
Company law and company taxation in South Africa.
See: Shrand, D.

Keita, K.
Un seul sacrifice. 88pp. ill. CFA225 CPE 1973 IV
FRE

Keita, R.
Kayes et le haut Sénégal. v. 1 238pp. MF1275 Ed
Pop - Mali 1972 ML FRE

Kelchner, H.B.
Living now. 76pp. K.shs.5.00 Evangel 1968 KE

Kellaway, E.A.
Servitudes. See: Hall, C.G.

Kellerman, D.
Let's speak English. See: Knoetze, T.

Kelley, P.M.
Eko igbagbo: iwe kerin. [Teaching faith in Christ book]
5, 5 bks. 85pp. ill. 65k Longman - Nig 1970 NR
YOR

Kelley, P.M.
Eko igbagbo: iwe keta. [Teaching faith in Christ] 4, 5
bks. 64pp. ill. 60k Longman - Nig 1972 NR YOR

Kelly, I.W.
A comparison of certain physical properties of plain weave
fabrics from cotton blended with different polyester fibre
types. Part I: Untreated fabrics 25pp. R2.50
(SAWTRI Technical Reports, 220) SAWTRI 1974 SA

Kelly, I.W.
A comparison of certain physical properties of plain weave
fabrics from cotton blended with different polyester fibre
types, part III: easy-care finished fabrics. 16pp. R2.50
(SAWTRI Technical Reports, 252) SAWTRI 1975 SA

Kelly, I.W.
The correlation between certain parameters used to
characterise fabric wrinkling properties. 16pp. R2.50
(SAWTRI Technical Reports, 300) SAWTRI 1976 SA

Kemijumbi, P.
Uganda recipes. See: Angulo, E.

Kemoli, A., ed.
Pulsations. 202pp. K.shs16.00 ($3.75/£1.80) EALB
1971 KE

Kemoli, A.
Notes on Achebe's "Things fall apart". 44pp.
K.shs.6.00 pap. (Heinemann's Student's Guides)
Heinemann Educ - Nair 1975 KE

Kemp, J.
The geology of the Dwangwa area. 34pp. pl. map.
K4.00 (Geological Survey of Malawi, Bull. 31) Geol
Survey - Mal 1974 MW

Kemp, J.T.
A list of books, articles and government publications on
the economy of Nigeria, 1960-62. 45pp. 75k ($1.25)
(N.I.S.E.R. indexes and bibliographies, 1) NISER 1963
NR

Kemp, P.H.
A guide to ionic relationships in natural waters. 127pp.
(CSIR research reports, 329) CSIR 1977 SA

Kempe, M.E., ed. Smith, L.D., ed.
Strategies for improving rural welfare: proceedings of a
workshop held at I.D.S., Nairobi, May, 1971. 562pp.
K.shs25.00 ($3.50/£1.40) (I.D.S. occas. pap., 4) Inst
Dev Stud 1971 KE

Kempf, B. Tashdjian, A. Pierre, M.
Documents de travail, activites pédagogiques. 190pp.
CELTA 1976 ZR FRE

Kempf, B., et al.
Kotanga pe kokoma Lingala I. Livre de élève. 49pp.
CELTA 1976 ZR LIN

Kempf, B., et al.
Kotanga pe kokoma Lingala I. Livre du maître. 47pp.
CELTA 1976 ZR LIN

Kempf, B.
Kubala ne kufunda ciluba I. Livre de l'élève.
See: Kazadi, N.

Kempf, B.
Kubala ne kufunda ciluba I. Livre du maître.
See: Kazadi, N.

Kempff, C.
A bibliography of Calviniana, 1959-1974. 249pp. Inst
Adv Calvinism 1975 SA

Kempis, T.
Kumfuata Kristo. [The imitation of Christ.] 96pp. ill.
T.shs.6.00 Central Tanganyika 1973 TZ SWA

Kendell, B.
Longman primary science. Pupils' book for standard four.
112pp. col. ill. K.shs.11.00 Longman - Ken 1976 KE

Kendell, B.
Longman primary science. Teachers' book for standard
four. 48pp. ill. K.shs.5.00 Longman - Ken 1976 KE

Kenefick, W.
Comprehensive books for junior secondary classes
English. 196pp. K.shs.12.50 Textbook Ctre 1975 KE

Kenmuir, D. Williams, R.
Wild mammals. 176pp. ill. col. pl. R$4.25 (Bundu
series) Longman - Rhod 1975 RH

Kennedy, R.F.
Africana repository.   R4.00   Juta 1965 SA

Kennedy, R.F.
Africana repository.   R4.00   Juta 1971 SA

Kennedy, R.F.
Catalogue of prints in the Africana museum and in books in the Strange collection of Africana in the Johannesburg public library up to 1870.   2 v.   675pp.   ill.   cl.   R50.00 cl.   Johannesburg Public Lib 1976 SA

Kennedy, R.F., comp.
Catalogue of pictures in the Africana museum.   7 v.   ill. photos.   R135.00   Johannesburg Public Lib 1972 SA

Kennedy, R.F.
The heart of a city.   R16.00   Juta 1971 SA

Kennelly, D.H.
Marine shells of Southern Africa.   3rd ed.   ill.   R5.00 Bulpin 1969 SA

Kenya Institute of Administration.
Kiswahili vocabulary development project: First list of recommended term for committee work, with a supplement of special parliamentary terms.   K.shs.2.00   Kenya Inst Admin 1974 KE

Kenya Red Cross.
Simple mother and baby care.   70pp.   ill.   K.shs.2.10 ($1.50/60p)   EALB 1967 KE

Kenyatta, J.
Asili ya Wakikuyu.   [My people of Kikuyu]   80pp. K.shs.4.50   OUP - Nairobi 1973 KE SWA

Kenyatta, J.
The challenge of Uhuru.   52pp.   ill.   K.shs.5.00 ($2.00)   EAPH 1971 KE

Kenyatta, J.
Facing Mount Kenya: school edition.   169pp.   pl.   ill. photos.   K.shs.10.50   (70p.)   Heinemann Educ - Nair 1971 KE

Kenyatta, J.
My people of Kikuyu and the life of Chief Wang'ombe. 68pp.   K.shs.2.25   OUP-Nairobi 1966 KE

Kenyatta, J.
Naushangilia mlima wa Kenya.   297pp.   K.shs.10.00 ($3.20)   EAPH 1966 KE SWA

Kenyatta, J.
Suffering without bitterness.   348pp.   photos. K.shs.45.00 cl.   K.shs.10.00 pap.   ($10.00 cl.)   ($3.20 pap.)   EAPH 1968 KE

Keppel-Jones, A., ed.
Philipps, 1820 settler: his letters.   371pp.   cl.   R4.20 Shuter 1960 SA

Keppens, G.
Verb preposition construction in English.   27pp.   CELTA 1976 ZR

Kerr, A.
Fort Hare 1915-48: the evolution of an African college. 290pp.   cl.   R5.25   Shuter 1968 SA

Kerr, A.J.
The courts and the law.   ex. only   (Inaugural lec.) Rhodes Univ Lib 1969 SA

Kerr, A.J.
The law of lease.   218pp.   cl. & pap.   R17.25 pap. R20.75 cl.   Butterworths 1969 SA

Kerr, A.J.
The principles of the law of contract.   2nd ed.   cl. & pap.   R16.25 pap.   R19.75 cl.   Butterworths 1975 SA

Kershaw, M.
Annotated bibliography and index of the geology of Zambia, 1970-1971.   See: von Bornemann, J.

Kes, E.W.G.
The manufacture of glulam.   15pp.   R5.00   (CSIR Special Report, HOUT 97)   CSIR 1975 SA

Kesse-Adu, K.
The politics of political detention.   226pp.   C2.00 ($2.00)   Ghana Publ Corp GH

Kestell, J.D.
Through shot and flame. [Reprint of ed. 1903].   347pp. ill. cl.   R17.70   (Africana Reprint Library, 8)   Africana Book Soc 1976 SA

Kesteloot, L., ed.
Neuf poetes camerounais.   112pp.   CFA360 pap.   CLE 1971 CM FRE

Kesting, J.G.
The Anglo-Boer war 1899-1902.   44pp.   80c.   Univ Cape Town Lib 1972 SA

Keteku, H.J.
Biographies: Rev. David Asante and Rev. Thoephilus Opoku.   22pp.   13pes.   Waterville 1965 GH

Keteku, H.K.
Biography: Rev. N.V. Asare.   24pp.   13pes.   Waterville 1965 GH

Keto, A.S.
Nitamshtaki kuzima.   [Folktale.]   54pp.   K.shs.8.00 ($2.60)   EAPH 1976 KE SWA

Keto, A.S.
Pole dada.   [Folktale.]   67pp.   K.shs.9.00   ($3.00) EAPH 1976 KE SWA

Kettle, A.
Is literature a luxury?   16pp.   T.shs.1.00   (Inaugural lecture, 6)   Univ Dar es Salaam 1970 TZ

Keyi, S.B.   Seula, P.J.
Ezabancane qha.   [For children only. Nursery rhymes.] 53pp.   pl.   32c   Mambo 1972 RH NDE

Kezilahabi, E.
Dunia uwanja wa fujo.   100pp.   K.shs.16.80   ($6.00) EALB 1975 KE SWA

Kezilahabi, E.
Kichomi [Poetry].   72pp.   K.shs.8.50   Heinemann Educ - Nair 1974 KE SWA

Kezilahabi, E.
Kichwa maji.   218pp.   K.shs.12.00   (Hadithi za kikwetu)   EAPH 1974 KE SWA

Kezilahabi, E.
Rosa mistika.   123pp.   K.shs.7.25   ($2.25/90p.) EALB 1971 KE SWA

Kgasa, M.L.
Thanodi ya Setswana ya dikole.   [Tswana dictionary] 160pp.   R3.00   Longman - SA 1976 SA TSW

Khader, B.
Anatomie du Sionisme et d'Israel. Essai d'analyse socio-historique.   267pp.   12,00 DA   SNED 1974 AE FRE

Khader, B.
Histoire de la Palestine.   v. 1.   208pp.   D1,500 Maison Tunis 1976 TI FRE

Khader, Y.
Les bourreaux meurent aussi.   206pp.   DA3.00 pap. SNED 1972 AE FRE

Khader, Y.
Délivrez la fidayia.   202pp.   DA3.00 pap.   SNED 1970 AE FRE

Khader, Y.
Halte au plan 'terreur.'.   206pp.   DA3.00 pap.   SNED 1970 AE FRE

Khader, Y.
Pas de phantoms pour Tel-Aviv.   204pp.   DA3.00 pap. SNED 1970 AE FRE

Khader, Y.
Quand les panthères attaquent.   203pp.   DA3.00 pap. SNED 1972 AE FRE

Khader, Y.
La vengeance passe par Gaza.   202pp.   DA3.00 pap. SNED 1970 AE FRE

Khaketla, B.
Moshoeshoe le Baruti.   [Moshoeshoe and the missionaries]   96pp.   40c.   Morija 1954 LO SOS

Khaketla, B.M.
Meokho ea thabo. [Tears of joy] 184pp. R.1.80 Morija 1972 LO SOS

Khaketla, B.M.
Mosali a nkhola. [The woman who misled me] 196pp. R1.45 Morija 1972 LO SOS

Khakhetla, N.M.
Mosali eo u'neileng eena. [The wife you gave me] 96pp. 50c. Morija 1972 LO SOS

Khalis, S.
La vie littéraire à Seville au XI siècle. 242pp. DA14.00 SNED 1966 AE FRE

Khamis, I.A.
Impediments to economic growth in developing countries. T.shs.12.00 ($3.00) (Research pap., 74.6) Econ Res Bur - Tanz 1974 TZ

Khammar, A.
Dix ans de production intellectuelle en Algérie: 1962-1972. Les écrits en langue arabe. pt. 1 See: Bouayed, M.

Khammar, A.
Dix ans de production intellectuelle en Algérie, 1962-1972. Première partie: les écrits en langauge arabe. See: Bouayed, M.

Khan, K. Yahya, S.
Mafunzo ya kiswahili. [Learning Swahili.] bk.1 112pp. ill. K.shs.8.50 Longman - Ken 1976 KE SWA

Khan, K. Yahya, S.
Mafunzo ya kiswahili. [Learning Swahili.] bk.2 112pp. ill. K.shs.8.50 Longman - Ken 1977 KE SWA

Khatib, M.S.
Utenzi wa Ukombozi wa Zanzibar. [Epic poem on the liberation of Zanzibar.] 76pp. K.shs.9.50 pap. (Vito vya Kiswahili, 3) OUP - Nairobi 1975 KE SWA

Kheiredine, A.
Poèmes Ahmed Kheiredine. 116pp. D0 Maison Tunis 1975 TI FRE

Khiddu, M.
The newcomer and other stories. 94pp. ill. 53k (African Reader's Library, 19) Pilgrim 1973 NR

Khoapa, B.A., ed.
Black review, 1972. Annual survey of events and trends in the Black community in South Africa. 227pp. R2.50 Black Comm Prog 1973 SA

Khodja, L.A.
La mante religieuse. 117pp. DA7.00 SNED 1976 AE FRE

Khopung, E.
Apartheid. The story of a dispossessed people. 124pp. K1.35 Daystar - Lusaka 1972 ZA

Khumalo, A. Snook, S. Moalusi, E.
New Testament survey. pt. 1 217pp. K.shs.17.00 ($2.15) Evangel 1968 KE

Khumalo, D.
Umuzi kawakhiwa kanye. 80pp. 55c. Longman - Rhod 1970 RH NDE

Khumalo, J.A.M.
Civil practice and procedure in all Bantu courts in southern Africa. 2nd ed. 264pp. hd. R25.00 cl. Juta 1976 SA

Khwela, S.T.Z. Nxumalo, O.E.H.
Amanqampunqampu. [Tit bits] 192pp. R1.10 Shuter 1967 SA ZUL

Khwela, S.T.Z. Nxumalo, O.E.H.
Emhlabeni. [In the world] 232pp. 95c. Shuter 1963 SA ZUL

Kiango, S.D.
Jeraha la moyo. [Wound in the heart.] 86pp. K.shs.7.00 ($3.50) Foundation 1974 KE SWA

Kiango, S.D.
Ndimi zetu. bk. 1. See: Sengo, T.S.Y.

Kiango, S.D.
Ndimi zetu. bk. 2. See: Sengo, T.S.Y.

Kiapi, A.
Civil service law in East Africa. 140pp. K.shs.25.00 ($5.40/£2.75) EALB 1975 KE

Kibao S. A.
Matatu ya thamani. [Three words of wisdom.] 64pp. K.shs.7.00 (60p) Heinemann Educ - Nair 1975 KE SWA

Kibao, S.A.
Utenzi wa uhuru wa Kenya. [Epic poem on Kenya's independence] 84pp. K.shs8.50 (Vito Vya Kiswahili, 2) OUP-Nairobi 1972 KE SWA

Kibel, M., ed.
The animal that hides in the trees. 29pp. ill. 60c. Africa only (Leopard Books) OUP - SA 1977 SA

Kibel, M., ed.
The brave nurse and other stories. 27pp. ill. 60c. Africa only (Leopard Books) OUP - SA 1977 SA

Kibel, M., ed.
Folk tales from Botswana. 40pp. ill. col. ill. 60c Southern Africa only OUP - SA 1976 SA

Kibel, M., ed.
Journey to Tswapong. 40pp. ill. 60c Southern Africa only OUP - SA 1976 SA

Kibel, M., ed.
Mma-Tshenolo and the school-teacher. 30pp. photos. 60c. Africa only (Leopard Books) OUP - SA 1977 SA

Kibel, M., ed.
Mmutle the hare and the baboons. 27pp. ill. 60c. Africa only (Leopard Books) OUP - SA 1977 SA

Kibel, M., ed.
Mokgowja Matlhware's tales. 40pp. ill. 60c Southern Africa only OUP - SA 1976 SA

Kibel, M., ed.
Pheko the herdboy goes to Tshane. 21pp. ill. 60c. Africa only (Leopard Books) OUP - SA 1977 SA

Kibel, M., ed.
Pulenyane's secret. 40pp. ill. 60c Southern Africa only OUP - SA 1976 SA

Kibel, M.
Mr. Lion thatches his roof. 24pp. col. ill. (Leopard Books) OUP - SA 1975 SA

Kibera, L. Kahiga, S.
Potent ash. 223pp. K.shs8.50 ($2.60) EAPH 1968 KE

Kibera, L.
Voices in the dark. 179pp. K.shs8.50 ($2.60) EAPH 1970 KE

Kiberu, E.R.
Nyumirwa engero ennanda. 40pp. K.shs.1.85 ($1.25/50p.) EALB 1968 KE LUG

Kibuka, K.
Obukulu bwa nursery schools. K.shs.1.50 ($1.25/50p.) EALB 1960 KE LUG

Kibulya, H.M.
Folktales from Bwamba Uganda. 87pp. ill. K.shs.13.50 ($3.30/£1.60) EALB 1976 KE

Kibulya, H.M. Langlands, B.W.
Political geography of the Congo border. 57pp. U.shs.24.00 (Occas. paps., 6) Dept Geog - Mak 1967 UG

Kibwana, J.M.
Utisi. 128pp. K.shs.12.50 ($2.50) (Comb Books in English, Drama, 1) Comb Books 1974 KE YOR

Kibwika-Bagenda, M.E.C., comp. Thomson, C.A., comp. Lwanga, T.K., comp.
Directory of East African libraries. 2nd rev. ed. 113pp. U.shs.15.00 Mak Univ Lib 1969 UG

Kidamala, D.
Historia ya Wanyiramba. EAPH 1973 KE SWA

Kidbodya, G., ed.
Aspects of South African history. 179pp. T.shs.15.00 Inst Educ - Dar 1968 TZ

Kidd, M.M.
Wild flowers of the Cape Peninsula. 2nd ed. 192pp. pl. R6.00 OUP-SA 1973 SA

Kiddle, P.
Ufundi wa kutunga hotuba. [Sermon preparation.] 56pp. ill. T.shs.3.00 Central Tanganyika 1967 TZ SWA

Kiema, C.M.
Kamau na mama yake. [Literacy primer.] ill. K.shs.6.50 ($3.50) Foundation 1977 KE SWA

Kieran, J.A., ed.
Zamani: a survey of East African history. See: Ogot, B.A., ed.

Kiggins, T.J.
A serving people. A textbook on the church in East Africa for the East African Certificate of Education. See: Langley, M.S.

Kiimbila, J.K.
Lila na fila. [A novel about a greedy ruler] 57pp. ill. T.shs.4.00 Longman - Tanz 1970 TZ SWA

Kiimbila, J.K.
Mwalimu wa Kiswahili. See: Mhina, G.A.

Kiimbila, J.K.
Ubeberu utashindwa. [Imperialism will be defeated] 133pp. T.shs.7.50 Inst Swahili Res 1971 TZ SWA

Kiimbila, J.K.
Visa vya walimwengu. [Collected short stories] 96pp. photos. T.shs.5.00 Longman - Tanz 1972 TZ SWA

Kiladi Opaa
Les arbres se mirent à danser. Mythes mputu. Textes mputu-français. 163pp. map ill. (DM27.00) (CEEBA. série II, Mémoires et Monographies, 24) CEEBA 1976 ZR FRE

Kilbride, J.E.
The motor development of rural Buganda infants. 59pp. U.shs.8.50 ($2.00) Mak Inst Soc Res 1973 UG

Kilbride, P.L., eds.
Psychocultural change in modern Buganda. See: Robbins, M.C., eds.

Kileff, C., ed.   Kileff, P., ed.
Shona customs. 104pp. pl. 90c Mambo 1970 RH

Kileff, P., ed.
Shona customs. See: Kileff, C., ed.

Kilgour, A.D.
Sir George Grey 1812-1898. 23pp. 50c. Univ Cape Town Lib 1970 SA

Kilima, V.L., eds.
Parasitosis of man and animals in Africa. See: Anderson, C., eds.

Killam, G.D.
Africa in English fiction, 1874-1939. 200pp. cl. & pap. N3.00 pap. N4.00 cl. Ibadan UP 1968 NR

Killick, D.J.B.
An account of the plant ecology of the Cathedral Park area of the Natal Drakensberg. R2.85 (Memoirs of the Botanical Survey of South Africa, 34) Botanical Res Inst 1963 SA

Killick, D.J.B.
An account of the plant ecology of the Table Mountain area of Pietermaritzburg, Natal. R2.00 (Memoirs of the Botanical Survey of South Africa, 32) Botanical Res Inst 1959 SA

Killick, H.J.
Beginning ecology. 192pp. ill. N2.50 Ibadan UP 1971 NR

Killick, M.   Willmer, J.
Objective questions in geography: with answers. 100pp. maps. N1.00 Pilgrim 1967 NR

Killick, M.   Willmer, J.
Objective questions in geography: without answers. 96pp. maps. 95k Pilgrim 1967 NR

Kimambo, I.N.   Temu, A.J.
A history of Tanzania. 257pp. maps. K.shs.12.50 ($3.20) EAPH 1969 KE

Kimambo, I.N.
Mbiru. 27pp. maps. K.shs.2.50 ($1.00) EAPH 1971 KE

Kimambo, I.N.
Miburu: popular protest in colonial Tanzania. 27pp. Hist Assoc - Tanz 1971 TZ

Kimambo, I.N.
A political history of the Pare. 240pp. maps photos. K.shs52.50 cl. K.shs20.00 pap. ($10.00 cl.) ($5.20 pap.) EAPH 1969 KE

Kimble, H.
Price control in Tanzania. 55pp. K.shs.35.00 cl. K.shs.13.50 pap. ($6.40 cl.) ($3.60 pap.) EAPH 1970 KE

Kimenye, B.
Martha the millipede. 16pp. ill. K.shs3.50 OUP-Nairobi 1973 KE

Kimenye, B.
Moses. 88pp. K.shs5.00 OUP-Nairobi KE

Kimenye, B.
Moses and Mildred. 80pp. ill. K.shs5.50 OUP-Nairobi 1968 KE

Kimenye, B.
Moses and the ghost. 88pp. ill. K.shs5.00 OUP-Nairobi 1971 KE

Kimenye, B.
Moses and the kidnappers. 54pp. ill. K.shs4.00 OUP-Nairobi 1968 KE

Kimenye, B.
Moses and the penpal. 80pp. ill. K.shs5.25 OUP-Nairobi 1973 KE

Kimenye, B.
Moses in trouble. 88pp. ill. K.shs5.00 OUP-Nairobi 1968 KE

Kimenye, B.
Moses on the move. 82pp. ill. K.shs5.25 OUP-Nairobi 1972 KE

Kimenye, B.
Moses the camper. 80pp. ill. K.shs4.50 OUP-Nairobi 1973 KE

Kimenye, B.
Paulo's strange adventure. 70pp. ill. K.shs4.75 OUP-Nairobi KE

Kimenye, B.
The runaways. 80pp. ill. K.shs.7.50 OUP - Nairobi 1974 KE

Kimenye, B.
Sarah and the boy. 16pp. ill. K.shs3.00 OUP-Nairobi 1973 KE

Kimenye, B.
The winged adventure. 56pp. ill. K.shs4.75 OUP-Nairobi 1970 KE

Kimilu, D.N.
Mukamba wawo. [Customs and traditions of the Kamba people] 165pp. K.shs.13.00 ($3.25/£1.30) EALB 1962 KE KAM

Kimowi Iyay.   Naaman, E.
Le destin de la littérature négro-Africain ou problematique d'une culture. 270pp. Z6.20 Press Univ Zaire 1975 ZR FRE

Kimpinde, D.
Vitalité des structures matrimoniales africaines bantoues. 126pp. 18k St. Paul 1967 ZR FRE

Kindy, H.
Life and politics in Mombasa. 236pp. photos. K.shs.18.00 ($5.00) EAPH 1972 KE

King, A.
An economic history of Kenya and Uganda, 1800-1970. See: van Zwanenberg, R.A.M.

King, B.   Ogungbesan, K.
   Celebration of black and African writing. 304pp. cl.
   N10.00 OUP - Nig 1975 NR

King, C.E.J.   Vlotman, E.F.
   Cookery book for the young hostess.   R3.00 Van
   Schaik SA

King, K.   Salim, A.
   Kenya historical biographies. 184pp. photos.
   K.shs.35.00 ($13.00) ($8.60) EAPH 1971 KE

King, M. et al.
   Nutrition for developing countries. 240pp. ill.
   K.shs32.00 OUP-Nairobi 1973 KE

King, M.H.
   Medical care in developing countries. 540pp. ill.
   K.shs40.00 OUP-Nairobi 1966 KE

King, V.E.
   The educational and behavioural problems of the young.
   43pp.   30c. Fourah Bay Bkshp 1973 SL

Kingala Ngwabana.
   Tu es méchant, personne ne te mangera! Mythes
   hungana. Textes hungana-français. 226pp. map.
   (DM28.00 pap.) (CEEBA. série II, Mémoires et
   Monographies, 28) CEEBA 1975 ZR FRE

Kingbo, I.
   Le crédit en agriculture. 56pp.   CFA300 INADES
   1968 IV FRE

Kingdon, D.
   Hadithi ya Bakuria. [The story of Bakuria] 24pp. ill.
   K.shs.2.00 OUP-Nairobi 1965 KE SWA

Kingdon, D.
   Hare and hyena. 32pp. ill.   K.shs3.25 OUP-Nairobi
   1968 KE

Kingsbury, P.
   The Kafue Flats: an account of the effects of the Kafue
   Gorge hydro-electric scheme on the geography of the flats.
   See: Bellers, M.

Kingsley Garbett, G.
   Growth and change in a Shona ward. 100pp.   50c
   (Dept. of Sociology, Univ. of Rhodesia, 1) Univ Rhodesia
   Lib 1964 RH

Kingsley, P.
   The development by Zambian children of strategies for
   doing intellectual work. 25pp.   50n (Human
   Development Research Unit Report, 24) Dept Psychology
   - Zam 1974 ZA

Kingston, N.R.
   Encounter with Christ. Form 1. 256pp.   K.shs.15.00
   Evangel 1971 KE

Kingston, N.R.
   Encounter with Christ. Form 2. 249pp.   K.shs.15.00
   Evangel 1971 KE

Kingston, N.R.
   Truth for God's people. 48pp.   K.shs.4.00 Evangel
   1973 KE

Kinnear-Brown, J.A.
   No more leprosy. 20pp. ill.   K.shs.0.50 ($1.00/40p.)
   EALB 1956 KE

Kinyangui, P.
   The geography of Kenya. See: Fordham, P.

Kinyua, D.M., ed.
   The local government regulations 1963. See: Sevareid,
   P., ed.

Kiome, L.N.S.
   Binadamu mwenye heshima? [A respectable human
   being] 70pp.   K.shs.10.75 ($2.80/£1.10) EALB
   1974 KE SWA

Kiome, L.N.S.
   Napenda kujua. [I'd like to know] 36pp. ill.
   K.shs.4.00 OUP-Nairobi 1971 KE SWA

Kiongo, C.   Dougall, I.C.   Welsh, J.O.
   Imani ya mkristo. [What I believe.] 96pp.   K.shs.7.00
   ($1.00) Evangel 1975 KE SWA

Kiongo, C.   Dougall, I.   Welsh, J.
   Life for God's people. 96pp.   K.shs.4.50 Evangel
   1973 KE

Kiongo, C.   Dougall, I.C.   Welsh, J.O.
   What I believe. 84pp.   K.shs.7.00 ($1.00) Evangel
   1975 KE

Kipkoris, B.E.
   The Marakwet of Kenya. See: Welbourn, F.B.

Kirby, P.R.
   Jacob van Reenen and the Grosvenor expedition of
   1790-1791. 142pp. maps pl. cl.   R3.00
   Witwatersrand UP 1958 SA

Kirby, P.R.
   The musical instruments of the native races of South
   Africa. 2nd ed. 293pp. map pl. cl.   R15.00
   Witwatersrand UP 1968 SA

Kirby, P.R.
   Sir Andrew Smith: his life letters and works. 368pp. pl.
   hd.   fl. 22.50 Balkema 1965 SA

Kirby, P.R.
   The true story of the Grosvenor East Indiaman. 280pp.
   maps ill.   R6.80 OUP-SA 1960 SA

Kirima, N.
   The African religious heritage. A textbook based on
   syllabus 224 of the East African Certificate of Education.
   See: Mugambi, J.

Kirk-Greene, A.H.M.
   Hausa ba dabo Bane. [Hausa proverbs] 84pp.   30k
   OUP - Nig 1966 NR HAU

Kirkpatrick, I.M.
   The geology of the Cape Maclear Peninsula and Lower
   Bwanje valley. See: Dawson, A.L.

Kironde, E.C.N.
   Let's make a play. See: Macpherson, M.

Kirumbi, D.P.
   Ufagaji wa kuku. [Poultry keeping.] 120pp. ill.
   T.shs.11.00 Tanz Publ House 1976 TZ SWA

Kirumbi, J.K.
   Upanga wa Mndewa. [The sword of Mndewa] 90pp.
   T.shs.4.50 Inst Swahili Res 1971 TZ SWA

Kirwan, B.E.R.
   A Runyankore grammar. See: Morris, H.F.

Kirwan, B.E.R.
   Yanguya okusoma. See: Allen, C.P.S.

Kirwan, E.R.   Lutu, A.D.
   Paper patterns for dressmaking. ill.   K.shs6.50
   ($2.25/90p.) EALB 1960 KE

Kisasi.
   La fille désobéissante. Mythes mbun. Versions intégrales
   en trois parlers mbun avec traduction française.
   See: Olung.

Kise, M.
   Love and learn. 32pp.   K.shs.2.50 (Afromance series,
   3) Transafrica 1975 KE

Kisia, J.G.
   Kitabu chakaviri chokusoma mu Lulogooli. See: Lwane,
   B.G.

Kisiedu, C.O.
   Manual for cataloguers, Balme Library, University of
   Ghana, Legon. 96pp.   C3.00 (Univ. of Ghana, Dept.
   of Library and Archival Studies, occas. paps., 13) Dept
   Lib Stud - Univ Ghana 1975 GH

Kiss, R.
   Etude hydrobiologiques des lacs de l'Akagera Moyenne.
   167pp. ill. pl. maps. (FB390.00/$10.72) Inst Nat
   Rwandaise 1976 RW FRE

Kistnasamy, N.
   Sharks of the east coast of southern Africa, 1: the genus
   "Carcharhinus" (Carcharhinidae) See: Bass, A.J.

Kistnasamy, N.
   Sharks of the east coast of southern Africa, 2: the families
   Scyliorhinidae and Pseudotriakidae. See: Bass, A.J.

Kodjo, N.G.   Daget, S.
Annales de l'université d'Abidjan. 161pp.   CFA1,465
(F29.30) (Série I-Histoire, 3) Univ Abidjan 1975 IV FRE

Kodwiw, A.M.
Nana Bentum. [Chief Bentum a despotic chief.]   2nd ed.
70pp.   50pes.   Bur Ghana Lang 1974 GH FAT

Koeune, E.
The African housewife and her home.   7th ed.   85pp.   ill.
K.shs.12.50   ($3.50/£1.40) EALB 1975 KE

Koeune, E.
Cooking for the family in East Africa.   4th ed.   99pp.   ill.
K.shs.4.20   ($1.75/70p.) EALB 1970 KE

Koeune, E.
Jinsi ya kufundisha afya. [How to teach hygiene, home
nursing and first aid] 77pp.   K.shs.2.50   ($1.50/60p.)
EALB 1964 KE SWA

Koeune, E.
Mapambo. [Decorating and furnishing]   4th ed.   12pp.
ill.   K.shs.0.65   ($1.00/40p.) EALB 1966 KE SWA

Koeune, E.
Nyumba. [The home and home nursing]   2nd ed.
24pp.   ill.   K.shs.0.65   ($1.00/40p.) EALB 1955 KE
SWA

Koeune, E.
Umanja. [The compound]   2nd ed.   12pp.   ill.
K.shs.0.65   ($1.00/40p.) EALB 1955 KE SWA

Koeune, E.
Upishi. [Cookery]   2nd ed.   ill.   K.shs.0.65
($1.00/40p.) EALB 1967 KE SWA

Koeune, E.
Utunzi wa nyumba. [Cleaning and care of the home]
2nd ed.   34pp.   ill.   K.shs.0.65   ($1.00/40p.) EALB
1955 KE SWA

Kogbe, C.A., ed.
Geology of Nigeria.   436pp.   hd. & pap.   N25.00 cl.
N15.00 pap.   Univ Ife Bkshop; distr. 1976 NR

Kogbe, C.A., ed.
Introduction to geological map interpretation and
description.   71pp.   ill.   N3.00   Univ Ife Bkshop; distr.
1976 NR

Kogbe, C.A.
Introduction to geological maps (for African students)
71pp.   ill.   N5.00   Elizabethan 1976 NR

Kohler, P., ed.   Edwards, S., ed.
Angar-Gutin sub-station progress report for the period
March 1975 to March 1976.   66pp.   ill.   ex. only   Inst
Agric Res - Addis 1976 ET

K'Okiri, O.
The jungle star.   142pp.   K.shs.15.00   ($3.70/£1.80)
EALB 1974 KE

Kokwaro, J.O.
Luo-English botanical dictionary.   199pp.   ill.
K.shs.18.00   EAPH 1973 KE

Kokwaro, J.O.
Medicinal plants of East Africa.   380pp.   ill.   cl. & pap.
K.shs65.00 pap.   K.shs96.50 cl.   ($18.00/£8.70 cl.)
EALB 1976 KE

Kola, P.
East African how? Stories.   40pp.   ill.   K.shs1.70
($1.00) EAPH 1966 KE

Kola, P.
East African when? Stories.   32pp.   ill.   K.shs1.70
($1.00) EAPH 1968 KE

Kola, P.
East African why? Stories.   40pp.   ill.   K.shs1.70
($1.00) EAPH 1966 KE

Kola, P.
Jinsi chui alipata madoadoa. [East Africa how? Stories]
32pp.   ill.   K.shs.2.80   ($1.00) EAPH 1972 KE SWA

Kola, P.
Kwa nini fisi Hucheka. [East Africa why? Stories]   32pp.
ill.   K.shs.2.80   ($1.00) EAPH 1972 KE SWA

Kola, P.
Mauti yalianza lini. [East Africa when? Stories]   36pp.
ill.   K.shs.2.80   ($1.00) EAPH 1971 KE SWA

Kolbe, G.A.
Ezemvelo.   Ibanga, 3   See: Dent, G.R.

Kolbe, G.A.
Ezemvelo.   Ibanga, 4   See: Dent, G.R.

Kolbe, G.A.
Ezemvelo.   Ibanga, 5   See: Dent, G.R.

Kolbe, G.A.
Ezemvelo.   Ibanga, 6   See: Dent, G.R.

Koli, S.E.
A guide to cotton cultivation in Ghana.   ill.   maps.
c1.25   ($1.00) Ghana Publ Corp 1973 GH

Kollbrunner, F.
The splendour and confusion of mission today.   63pp.
60c.   (Mambo Missio-Pastoral Series, 5) Mambo 1974
RH

Kom, E.D.
Civil procedure in the High Court of Ghana.   2nd rev. ed.
188pp.   cl.   ($11.95) Ghana Publ Corp 1976 GH

Komba, S.M.
Uwanja wa washairi. [Swahili poetry.]   48pp.
T.shs.4.50   Longman - Tanz 1975 TZ SWA

Kombe, L.
The Icila dance, old style.   See: Jones, A.M.

Kombo, S.
Ustaarabu na maendeleo ya Mwafrika. [The African's
civilization and progress]   3rd ed.   54pp.   K.shs.2.20
($1.50/60p.) EALB 1966 KE SWA

Komolafe, K.F.   Agbebi, D.A.
School Certificate objective tests in agricultural science.
156pp.   ill.   N1.20   Macmillan 1973 NR

Komolafe, M.F.
Agricultural science: questions and answers.   2nd ed.
155pp.   N1.20   Onibonoje 1972 NR

Komolafe, M.F.
Biology: past questions and answers.   129pp.   ill.
N1.15   Onibonoje 1969 NR

Komolafe, M.F.
Chemistry: past questions and answers.   2nd ed.
113pp.   ill.   N1.05   Onibonoje 1970 NR

Komolafe, M.F.
The first two years of agriculture.   146pp.   ill.   N1.25
Onibonoje 1973 NR

Komolafe, M.F.
Nature study and gardening.   125pp.   ill.   N1.25
Onibonoje 1971 NR

Komolafe, M.F.
Nature study, gardening and health.   bk. 5   82pp.   ill.
85k   Onibonoje 1973 NR

Komolafe, M.F.
Nature study, gardening and health.   bk. 6   95pp.   ill.
85k   Onibonoje 1973 NR

Komora, Y.
Haguruka na ningio.   ill.   K.shs.3.00   ($1.00) EAPH
1972 KE SWA

Komora, Y.
Makombe matupu.   64pp.   ill.   K.shs.3.00   ($1.00)
EAPH 1971 KE SWA

Komora, Y.
Mpopoonena mpopoo teka.   64pp.   ill.   K.shs.3.00
($1.00) EAPH 1972 KE SWA

Konan, M.
Occupations and family patterns among the Hausa in
Northern Nigeria.   60k   (Samaru misc. pap., 52) Inst
Agric Res - Zaria 1975 NR

Kone, M.
Jusqu'au seuil de l'irréal.   144pp.   CFA850   (F17.00)
Nouv Ed Afric 1976 SG FRE

Kone, S.
Le Football et ses lois par l'image.   104pp.   CFA500
(F10.00)   Nouv Ed Afric 1976 SG FRE

Author Index

Kongwa Theological College.
Tumwimbie mungu. [Let's sing to God.] music.
T.shs.1.50 Central Tanganyika TZ SWA

Konrat, G. von.
Passport to truth. True facets of Apartheid. K.shs.34.25
($7.00/£3.40) EALB 1975 KE

Korama, A.
Abe mako ne nkyene ntokwaw bi. 18pp. ill. (65c.)
Ghana Publ Corp 1976 GH TWI

Korama, A.
Nkura bi ne won na. 12pp. ill. (65c.) Ghana Publ
Corp 1976 GH TWI

Korama, A.
Odwumayefo opokua. 10pp. ill. (65c.) Ghana Publ
Corp 1976 GH TWI

Koranteng, E.O.
Guasohantan. [A cultural play.] 2nd ed. 66pp. ill.
55pes. Bur Ghana Lang 1974 GH TWI

Koranteng, E.O.
Mpuansa Ntiamoa. [The story of Kofi Ntiamoa] 51pp.
18pes. Waterville 1950 GH TWI

Korle Bu Hospital.
Korle Bu Hospital, 1923-1973. (Golden Jubilee Souvenir)
144pp. ill. pl. C5.50 Univ Ghana Bkshop; distr. 1975
GH

Kortebi, B.
Méthode de sténographie. 174pp. DA14.00 SNED
1975 AE FRE

Koster, J.R.
Computers-aid to development or part of the problems?
15pp. C1.00 (50p./$1.00) (Inaugural lecture) Ghana
UP 1977 GH

Kotei, S.I.A.
A history of library education in Ghana. 120pp. Dept
Lib Stud - Univ Ghana 1973 GH

Kotei, S.I.A.
Library resources for African studies in Ghana. 76pp.
C1.00 (Univ. of Ghana, Dept. of Library & Archival
Studies, occas. paps. 10) Dept Lib Stud - Univ Ghana
1974 GH

Kotei, S.I.A.
Persistent issues in African bibliography. 2nd rev. ed.
33pp. 80pes. (Univ. of Ghana, Dept. of Library &
Archival Studies, occas. paps., 7) Dept Lib Stud - Univ
Ghana 1974 GH

Kotei, S.I.A.
Persistent issues in African bibliography. 28pp. Dept
Lib Stud - Univ Ghana 1973 GH

Kotey, R.A., ed. Rourke, B.E., ed. Okali, C., ed.
Economics of cocoa production and marketing:
proceedings of economics research conference Legon,
April 1973. 547pp. ill. C9.40 Univ Ghana Bkshop;
distr. 1974 GH

Kothari, R.
Footsteps into the future. Diagnosis of the present world
and a design for an alternative. 174pp. C6.50
($6.50) Ghana Publ Corp 1975 GH

Kouadio Kouakou, M.
Un bon conseil de Koumba. 32pp. col. ill. CFA65
pap. CEDA 1970 IV FRE

Kouki, M.
La cuisine Tunisienne. 334pp. D2.000 Maison Tunis
1972 TI FRE

Kouki, M.
La patisserie Tunisienne. 92pp. pl. DO.600 Maison
Tunis 1972 TI FRE

Koulibaly, M.A.
Cew Sonay. 75pp. CFA250 CELTHO 1970 NG FRE

Kovalsky, S.J.
Mahatma Gandhi and his political influence in South Africa
1893-1914. 33pp. R1.75 Dept Bibliog, Lib & Typo
1971 SA

Kovari, K., ed.
Field measurements in rock mechanics. Proceedings of
the international symposium, Zurich 4-6 April 1977. 2 v.
1,000pp. cl. ($40.00/£21.00) Balkema 1977 SA

Kowal, J.M. Knabe, D.T.
An agroclimatological atlas of the Northern states of
Nigeria: with explanatory notes. 111pp. maps.
N10.00 Inst Agric Res - Zaria 1973 NR

Kpagane, E.K.
Túátúá kpá Khanà. [Khanà reader, 1] 63pp. 30k
(Inst. of African Stud., Univ of Ibadan, Rivers readers
project, 21) Inst Afr Stud-Ibadan 1971 NR KHA

Kpakote, K. G.
Apercu sur l'enseignement et la recherche dans les
domaines des sciences biologiques, agronomiques,
vétérinaire et forestières dans les universités francophones
d'Afrique. 491pp. ($20.00) AAU 1976 GH FRE

Kraayenbrink, E.A.
Earnings and employment in various sectors of the
economy, second quarter, 1976. 8pp. 40c. ($1.15)
SA Inst of Race Relations 1977 SA

Kranendonk, H.C.
Rural changes in the savanna area of the Western State of
Nigeria: with special reference to tobacco production.
50k NISER NR

Krause, R.C.
Understanding public relations. 128pp. ill. cl. & pap.
R6.00 cl. R3.60 pap. Philip 1977 SA

Krauss, F.
Travel journal/Cape to Zululand: observations by a
collector and naturalist, 1838-40. 96pp. ill. hd. fl.
27.00 Balkema 1973 SA

Kravic, V.
Le budget de l'état (Niger) 65pp. Ecole Nat Admin -
Niger 1976 NG FRE

Kreysler, J.
Uhuru namaji: health, water supply and self reliance in
Mayo village. 14pp. T.shs.7.00 Bur Res Asses -
Tanz 1969 TZ

Krige, E.J.
The social system of the Zulus. 5th ed. 420pp. cl.
R5.75 Shuter 1950 SA

Krige, P.R.
The utilization of municipal wastes: report on the
processing of urban wastes in a mechanized composting
plant. 71pp. (CSIR research reports, 211) CSIR 1964
SA

Krige, U., ed.
Olive Schreiner: a selection. 224pp. R3.00 pap.
R5.70 cl. OUP-SA 1968 SA

Krishnamurthy, B.S., comp.
Cha cha cha. Zambia's struggle for independence. ill.
K2.25 (African Archives, File 2) Neczam 1972 ZA

Kritzinger, L.
The principles and practice of auditing. See: Taylor, I.R.

Kritzinger, M.S.B.
English proverbs and expressions. See: Sabbagha, N.G.

Kroener, A., ed.
Contributions to the Precambrian geology of southern
Africa: a volume in honour of John de Villiers. 213pp. ill.
photos. maps col. maps. hd. ex. only (Univ. of Cape
Town, Precambrian Research Unit, Bulletin 15)
Precambrian Res Unit 1974 SA

Kroener, A.
The Gariep group, part I: Late Precambrian formations in
the western Richtersveld, northern Cape Province.
115pp. ill. photos. hd. ex. only (Univ. of Cape Town,
Precambrian Research Unit, Bulletin 13) Precambrian Res
Unit 1974 SA

Krog, E.W.
African literature in Rhodesia. 236pp. 57c pap.
Mambo 1966 RH

Krohn, A.K.
Tobacco farming in South Africa. 45pp. 80c. Univ Cape Town Lib 1964 SA

Krokfors, C.
Agricultural development in selected Ujamaa villages in Sumbawanga district. T.shs.15.00 ($15.00) (Research reports, new series, 4.1) Bur Res Assess - Tanz 1973 TZ

Kruger, D.
Psychology in the 2nd person. ex. only Rhodes Univ Lib 1976 SA

Kruger, H.
The making of a nation. R6.00 Macmillan - SA 1972 SA

Kruger, J.E. Van Rensburg, J.J.J.
Influence of variation in moisture content on dimensional change characteristics of mortar made with a sand coated with organic matter. 9pp. ill. (CSIR research reports, 313) CSIR 1972 SA

Krumback, G.
La longévité chez l'araignée latrodectus C. Koch. See: Bouillon, A.

Kubau, S.
Kiyaye Haduran Hanyoyi. [Driving manual] ill. 75k Northern Nig 1973 NR HAU

Kubemba Kibaka Myumbi.
Elle partit avec une calebasse trouée. Récits de littérature kwese, ngongo et suku. Textes en langues locales et versions françaises. 193pp. map. (DM28.00 pap.) (CEEBA. série II, Mémoires et Monographies, 14) CEEBA 1976 ZR FRE

Kubik, G.
African music codification and textbook project. Practical suggestions for field research. See: Tracey, H.

Kubik, G.
The Kachamba Brothers' Band. A study of neotraditional music in Malawi. K2.50 (£1.75) (Zambian paps., 9) Inst Afr Stud - Lusaka 1975 ZA

Kuboja, N.J.
Mbojo: simba-mtu. 2nd ed. 112pp. ill. K.shs.11.00 ($2.84/80p.) EALB 1972 KE SWA

Kuguru, F.–M.
Kimi the joker. 56pp. ill. K.shs4.00 ($1.00) EAPH 1972 KE

Kuguru,P.
Tales of Wamugumo. 73pp. ill. K.shs4.00 ($1.50) EAPH 1968 KE

Kuhenga, C.
Kovu la pendo. [The problems of love] 65pp. ill. T.shs.4.00 Longman - Tanz 1971 TZ SWA

Kuimba, G.
Gehena harina moto. 116pp. 60c. Longman - Rhod 1965 RH SHO

Kuimba, G.
Rurimi inyoka. [A wagging tongue.] 170pp. pl. R$1.30 Mambo 1976 RH SHO

Kuimba, G.
Tambaoga mwana'ngu. 128pp. 95c. Longman - Rhod 1968 RH SHO

Kulkarni, H.M., comp.
Periodicals in Tanzania libraries, a union list. 226pp. T.shs.40.00 Tanz Lib Serv 1976 TZ

Kumakanga, S. L.
Nzeru za kale. [Collection of traditional folk-tales] 64pp. ill. 75t (37p) Longman - Mal 1975 MW CHC

Kumalo, A.A.
Izingoma zika-Kumalo. [The songs of Kumalo] music. 90c. Shuter 1967 SA ZUL

Kundeya, D.N.
Perembi and the monkey. 8pp. pl. 3c Rhod Lit Bur 1975 RH

Kundeya, D.N.
Why animals live with people. 8pp. pl. 6c Rhod Lit Bur 1974 RH

Kunikina, J.
The new life. 32pp. ill. 45pes. (15p.) Africa Christian 1967 GH

Kunikina, J.
Une vie nouvelle - un homme nouveau. 54pp. ill. CFA100 CPE 1972 IV FRE

Kuper, B.
Native law in South Africa, 1941-1961. 24pp. R1.60 Dept Bibliog, Lib & Typo 1962 SA

Kuper, H.
Inhliziyo ngumthakathi. [The heart is a witch tr. fr. Eng. T. Cope] 74pp. 40c. Shuter 1962 SA ZUL

Kuria, H.
Nakupenda lakini. [I love you but...] 48pp. K.shs.4.00 OUP-Nairobi 1964 KE SWA

Kuromiema, P.E.A.
Teachers' notes on Kirikeni go diri 1. 89pp. 50k (Inst. of African Stud., Univ. of Ibadan, Rivers readers project, 28) Inst Afr Stud-Ibadan 1972 NR OKR

Kutt, H.R.
On the numerical evaluation of finite-part integrals involving an algebraic singularity. 169pp. (CSIR Special Report WISK, 179) CSIR 1975 SA

Kutt, H.R.
Quadrature formulae for finite-part integrals. 156pp. (CSIR Special WISK, 178) CSIR 1975 SA

Kuzwayo, A.W.Z., ed. Ward, M., ed.
Directory of Swaziland libraries. 23pp. E1.00 (Swaziland Libraries Publication, 1) Univ Bots & Swazi 1975 SG

Kuzwayo, Z.
ESezane. [At Sezane] 232pp. R1.05 Shuter 1969 SA ZUL

Kwakwa, B.S.
Anthology of poetry. 160pp. ill. N1.25 ($1.50) Ghana Publ Corp 1974 GH

Kwakwa, B.S., ed.
Ghanaian writing today. v. 1 184pp. C3.00 ($3.00) Ghana Publ Corp 1974 GH

Kwakwa, M.
L'argent ne fait pas le bonheur. ill. C2.00 (Afram Short Plays in French for Schools) Afram 1975 GH FRE

Kwakwa, M.
A handbook for French studies. A guide for 'O'-level French. 80pp. ill. C2.50 Afram 1975 GH

Kwami, T.H.S., ed.
"Gulliver's Travels", simplified and abridged edition. 78pp. ($2.50) Ghana Publ Corp 1976 GH

Kwantagora, S.
Azumin Watan Ramalana. See: Yamula, S.

Kwantagora, S.
Kimiyya Da Fasaha. [Science and art] 64pp. 40k Northern Nig. 1972 NR HAU

Kwapong, K.A.
Higher education and human development in Africa today: African-American relations. 15pp. C1.00 ($1.00/50p.) Ghana UP 1974 GH

Kwapong, M.A.
The role of classical studies in Africa. 16pp. 25k (Lecture, 2) Univ Lagos Bookshop 1969 NR

Kwarteng, J.S.
My sword is my life. 96pp. C1.50 ($1.50) Ghana Publ Corp 1973 GH

Kwasikuma, G.W.K.
Evegbe-'Daganawo. [Ewe idioms.] 108pp. 85pes. Bur Ghana Lang 1973 GH EWE

Kwasikuma, G.W.K. Hinidza, R.K. Hoh, I.K.
Hencwe fe gbe. [The voice of composers.] 2nd ed. 211pp. ill. C1.60 Bur Ghana Lang 1975 GH EWE

Author Index

Kwei, E.
African entrepreneurship and economic growth: a case study of the fishing industry of Ghana. See: Lawson, R.

Kyei, K.G.
The lone voice: a collection of poems. 190pp. C1.50 ($1.50/75p.) Ghana UP 1969 GH

Kyei, K.G. Schreckenbach, H.
No time to die. 80pp. ill. C7.00 Univ Ghana Bkshop; distr. 1976 GH

Kyejo, A.K.
Kanuni za kufunza na kulea watoto. [Principles of child psychology and education] 120pp. K.shs.11.75 (Vitabu Vya Walimu, 1) OUP-Nairobi 1972 KE SWA

Kyesimira, Y.
Agricultural export development. 100pp. maps. K.shs31.60 cl. K.shs10.50 pap. ($3.20 pap.) ($5.80 cl.) EAPH 1969 KE

Kynaston-Snell, H.F.
French for Africa. 1, 2v. 224pp. maps ill. N1.40 Pilgrim 1964 NR

Kynaston-Snell, H.F.
French for Africa. 2, 2v. 184pp. maps ill. N1.40 Pilgrim 1970 NR

La-Anyane, S.
Agricultural fundamentalism: man and national development. 23pp. C1.00 ($1.00/50p.) (Inaugural lecture) Ghana UP 1972 GH

La-Anyane, S.
Background to agricultural policy in Ghana. 167pp. C1.50 ($1.50) (80p.) Ghana UP 1969 GH

Labakila Hokwel.
Ton douzième enfant te tuera! Mythes mbun. Textes mbun-français. 151pp. ill. (DM29.00) (CEEBA. série II, Mémoires et Monographies, 34) CEEBA 1976 ZR FRE

Labatut, R.
Interferences du Fulfude sur le français écrit par les élèves peuls du Nord-Cameroun. CFA200 (C.L.A.D. Étude, 54) CLAD 1974 SG FRE

Labatut, R.
Sagesse de peuples nomades. See: Issa, A.

Labi Tawaba. Tamundel Mubele.
Qui la sortira de cette pierre? Mythes yansi. Versions yansi-françaises. 168pp. map. (DM22.00 pap.) (CEEBA. série II, Mémoires et Monographies, 11) CEEBA 1974 ZR FRE

Labica, G.
Hayy Ibn Yaqzan, le philosophe sans maître Iban Tofail. Tr. fr. Arabic L. Gautier. 159pp. DA7.00 SNED 1970 AE FRE

Labica, G.
Politique et religion chez Ibn Khaldoun. 260pp. DA8.00 SNED 1968 AE FRE

Laborel, J.
Annales de l'université d'Abidjan. Les peuplements de madréporaires des côtes tropicales du Brésil. 260pp. CFA1100 (F22.00) (Série E-Ecologie, 2-3) Univ Abidjan 1969 IV FRE

Labouret, H.
Nouvelles notes sur les tribus du rameau Lobi, leurs migrations, leur évolution, leurs parlers et ceux de leurs voisins. 295pp. maps. CFA2000 (Mémoires de l'IFAN, 54) IFAN 1958 SG FRE

Labrentz, A.
The young Christian and science. 2nd rev. ed. 96pp. K.shs.6.00 Evangel 1975 KE

Laburthe-Tolra, P.
A travers le Cameroun du sud au nord. Voyages et explorations de 1889 à 1891. 2 v. See: Morgen, C.

Labuschagne, G.S.
Moscow, Havana and the MPLA takover of Angola. 8pp. R1.00 (FAA Study Reports, 3) Foreign Affairs Assoc 1976 SA

Lacabe, L.
Pourquoi la foi en Jésus Christ? 62pp. 40k St. Paul 1976 ZR FRE

Lacabe, P.L.
Pourqoui la foi en Jésus Christ? 64pp. 30k St Paul 1975 ZR FRE

Lacasse, A.
Useful phrases English-Swahili. 11th ed. 64pp. TMP 1976 TZ

Lachaise, D. Tsacas, L.
Annales de l'université d'Abidjan. 599pp. CFA2400 (Série E - Ecologie, 7) Univ Abidjan 1974 IV FRE

Ladapo, T.
Aroye akewi: Apa keji. [The poet's yearnings.] pt. 2 280pp. N2.00 Onibonoje 1975 NR YOR

Ladapo, T.
Aroye Akewi. [The poet's yearnings] pt. 1 92pp. 85k Onibonoje 1973 NR YOR

Ladefoged, P. Criper, C. Glick, R.
Language in Uganda. 192pp. map. K.shs.23.50 OUP-Nairobi 1971 KE

Ladele, T.A.
Igba Lo de. [Now is the time] 149pp. N1.10 Onibonoje 1971 NR YOR

Ladele, T.A.A.
Je ng logba temi. [Let me have my time] 96pp. ill. 80k Macmillan NR YOR

Ladipo, D.
Eda. See: Ijimere, O.

Ladipo, D.
Eda: A Yoruba opera. [Yoruba poetic text developed from the European Everyman story] 128pp. (Inst. of African Stud., Univ. of Ibadan, occas. pub., 24) Inst Afr Stud-Ibadan 1970 NR YOR

Ladipo, D.
Itan awon ere ti Duro Ladipo. [Stories of Duro Ladipo's plays] 52pp. ill. 75k Longman - Nig 1970 NR YOR

Ladipo, D.
Morèmi. [Moremi] 64pp. ill. 80k Macmillan 1971 NR YOR

Ladipo, D.
Oba ko so. [A Yoruba opera tr. fr. Yoruba R.G. Armstrong et al.] 117pp. (Inst. of African Stud., Univ. of Ibadan, occas. pub., 10) Inst Afr Stud-Ibadan NR

Ladipo, D.
Oba ko so. [The king did not hang tr. fr. Yoruba R.G. Armstrong et al.] 39pp. 25k (Inst. of African Stud., Univ of Ibadan, occas. pub., 3) Inst Afr Stud-Ibadan 1969 NR YOR

Ladipo, D.
Oba ko so. [The King did not hang] 136pp. ill. N1.25 Macmillan 1970 NR YOR

Laetti, V.I. Verster, M.A.
National Institute for Personnel Research tests for the assessment of blacks. 44pp. 2.00 (CSIR Special Report PERS, 230) CSIR 1975 SA

Lafage, S.
Dictionnaire du Français du Togo. 215pp. CFA1,000 (Enseignement du Français, 53) Inst Ling Appliquée 1975 IV FRE

Lafage, S.
Français écrit et parlé en pays éwé (Sud-Togo): étude d'interférences. 946pp. CFA2,000 (Linguistique Africaine, 58) Inst Ling Appliquée 1976 IV FRE

Lafitte, J.C.
English in Zaire. See: Tashdjian, M.

Lageer, E.
Guilty. 16pp. ill. 25pes. (7p.) Africa Christian 1973 GH

Lahbabi, M.
La bataille arabe du pétrole. 3rd ed. 224pp. Dir15.00 pap. Ed Maghreb 1975 MR

Lahbabi, M.
Les facteurs de base de l'économie mondiale. 256pp.
Dir18.00 Ed Maghreb 1975 MR FRE

Lahbabi, M.
Le gouvernement marocain à l'aube du XXe siècle. 2
2nded. 224pp. Dir18.00 Ed Maghreb 1975 MR FRE

Lahbabi, M.
Technologie et développement. 416pp. Dir21.00 Ed
Maghreb 1975 MR FRE

Lahbabi, M.A.
De l'être à la personne. Essai de personnalisme réaliste.
2nd ed. 366pp. DA12.00 SNED 1975 AE FRE

Lahbabi, M.A.
Douleurs rythmées. 2 vols. 642pp. pl. DA22.00
SNED 1974 AE FRE

Lahbabi, M.A.
Du clos à l'ouvert. 212pp. DA7.00 SNED 1971 AE
FRE

Lahbabi, M.A.
Liberté ou libération (à partir des libertés bergsonniennes)
254pp. DA10.00 SNED 1975 AE FRE

Lahjomri, A.
L'image du Maroc dans la littérature française. 313pp.
SNED 1973 AE FRE

Laing, E.
An introduction to modern genetics. 119pp. ill. pl.
C1.80 ($1.80) Ghana Publ Corp 1972 GH

Lakhani.
International cookery book. 144pp. K.shs.25.00
Heinemann Educ - Nair 1976 KE

Lal, R.T.
Certificate of primary education past paper 1968-1971.
116pp. K.shs.7.50 Textbook Ctre 1972 KE

Lalendle, C.H.T.
Imethodi Yesixhosa. See: Gebeda, C.Z.

Lamb, A.
Mineral exploitation: an historian's view. 14pp. C1.00
($1.00/50p.) (Inaugural lecture) Ghana UP 1972 GH

Lambert, G.
Integrated mathematics. v. 1 252pp. ill. R1.80
Shuter 1968 SA

Lambert, G.
Integrated mathematics. v. 2 252pp. ill. R1.90
Shuter 1971 SA

Lambert, G.
Post primary arithmetic, Forms II & III. See: Stone, S.

Lambert, H.E.
Ameru Baria Bakeeja Nyumene. [The Meru yet to come]
32pp. ill. K.shs.0.50 ($1.25/50p.) EALB 1958 KE
MER

Lambert, H.E.
Chi-Chifundi - a dialect of the southern Kenya coast.
111pp. T.shs.10.00 Inst Swahili Res 1958 TZ

Lambert, H.E.
Studies in Swahili dialect: Chi-Jomvu and Ki-Ngare -
sub-dialect of the Mombassa area. 119pp. T.shs.9.50
Inst Swahili Res 1958 TZ

Lambert, H.E.
Studies in Swahili dialect: Ki-Mumba - dialect of the
southern Kenya coast. 101pp. T. shs 8.50 Inst
Swahili Res 1957 TZ

Lambert, S.
Diwani ya Lambert. [Lambert's poems] K.shs.3.50
($1.75/70p.) EALB 1971 KE SWA

Lamburn, R.P.
Adabu njema. [African manners and customs in
Tanzania] 3rd ed. 37pp. K.shs.3.00 ($1.40/50p.)
EALB 1960 KE SWA

Lamond, N.
A theoretical approach to the study of the hospital as a
social organisation. See: Schlemmer, L.

Lamont Smith, K., comp.
Henochsberg on the companies act. First (Cumulative)
Supplement to third edition. See: Milne, A., comp.

Lamont, V. Barrett, D.
Graines d'evangile. 64pp. CFA300.00 CLE 1973 CM
FRE

Lamplough, R.W.
Matabele folk tales. 48pp. ill. 55c. OUP-SA 1968
SA

Lamula, P.
Isabelo Sikazulu. [The legacy of the Zulus] 214pp. ill.
55c. Shuter 1936 SA ZUL

Lamy, A. et al.
L'interrogation. 86pp. CFA400 (Enseignement du
français, 25) Inst Ling Appliquée 1971 IV FRE

Lamy, A.
Langues négro-africaines et enseignement du français.
Conférences et comptes rendus. See: Canu, G.

Lamy, A.
La négation. 155pp. CFA600 (Enseignement du
français, 26) Inst Ling Appliquée 1971 IV FRE

Lamy, A.
Phrases de base et expansions. 98pp. CFA400
(Enseignement du français, 23) Inst Ling Appliquée 1971
IV FRE

Lamy, E.
Le droit privé Zairois. 200pp. Press Univ Zaire 1976
ZR FRE

Lamy, E.
Le droit privé Zairois. v. 1. 285pp. Z7.04 Press
Univ Zaire 1975 ZR FRE

Lanes, R. Thomas, P.
Vocabulaire administratif et politique du monde rural.
135pp. CFA600 (Enseignement du Français, 56) Inst
Ling Appliquée 1976 IV FRE

Langevad, E.J.
The mines and minerals act, 1969, and the mineral tax act,
1970. See: Drysdall, A.R.

Langlands, B.W.
The demographic conditions of Uganda as a developing
country. 48pp. U.shs.20.00 (Occas. paps., 9) Dept
Geog - Mak 1970 UG

Langlands, B.W., ed.
Micro-studies in the geography of retailing in the Kampala
area. U.shs.45.00 (Occas. paps., 48) Dept Geog -
Mak 1973 UG

Langlands, B.W., ed. Hall, S.A., ed.
Uganda atlas of disease. 180pp. maps. K.shs.45.00
($12.00) EAPH 1975 KE

Langlands, B.W. Obol-Owit, L.E.C.
Essays in the settlement geography of East Acholi. 94pp.
U.shs.20.00 (Occas. paps., 7) Dept Geog - Mak 1968
UG

Langlands, B.W.
Geographical studies on rural markets in East Africa from
Makerere. 269pp. U.shs.50.00 (Occas. paps., 63)
Dept Geog - Mak 1975 UG

Langlands, B.W.
Geography anatomised: incorporating Geography
anaesthetised. 110pp. U.shs.10.00 (Occas. paps., 3)
Dept Geog - Mak 1967 UG

Langlands, B.W.
The human factor in the changing ecology of Mwenge.
See: Kahimbaara, J.A.

Langlands, B.W.
Inventory of research in geography at Makerere,
1947-1972. 200pp. U.shs.20.00 (Occas. paps., 50)
Dept Geog - Mak 1972 UG

Langlands, B.W.
Land tenure in Uganda. U.shs.20.00 (Occas. paps.,
55) Dept Geog - Mak 1975 UG

Author Index

Langlands, B.W.
Notes on the geography of ethnicity in Uganda. 198pp. map. U.shs.22.00 (Occas. paps., 62) Dept Geog - Mak 1975 UG

Langlands, B.W.
Patterns of food crop production and nutrition in Uganda. See: Hyde, R.J.

Langlands, B.W.
Perspectives on urban planning for Uganda. See: Safier, M.

Langlands, B.W.
Political geography of the Congo border. See: Kibulya, H.M.

Langlands, B.W.
The population geography of each district of Uganda: Acholi. 31pp. maps. U.shs.30.00 (Occas. paps., 30) Dept Geog - Mak 1971 UG

Langlands, B.W.
The population geography of each district of Uganda: Ankole. 51pp. maps. U.shs.30.00 (Occas. paps., 42) Dept Geog - Mak 1971 UG

Langlands, B.W.
The population geography of each district of Uganda: Bugisu and Sebei districts. 57pp. maps. U.shs.30.00 (Occas. paps., 28) Dept Geog - Mak 1971 UG

Langlands, B.W.
The population geography of each district of Uganda: Bukedi. 48pp. maps. U.shs.30.00 (Occas. paps., 27) Dept Geog - Mak 1971 UG

Langlands, B.W.
The population geography of each district of Uganda: Bunyoro. 45pp. maps. U.shs.30.00 (Occas. paps., 35) Dept Geog - Mak 1971 UG

Langlands, B.W.
The population geography of each district of Uganda: Busoga. 53pp. maps. U.shs.30.00 (Occas. paps., 40) Dept Geog - Mak 1971 UG

Langlands, B.W.
The population geography of each district of Uganda: East Mengo. 41pp. maps. U.shs.20.00 (Occas. paps., 41) Dept Geog - Mak 1971 UG

Langlands, B.W.
The population geography of each district of Uganda: Karamoja. 47pp. maps. U.shs.30.00 (Occas. paps., 38) Dept Geog - Mak 1971 UG

Langlands, B.W.
The population geography of each district of Uganda: Kigezi. 41pp. maps. U.shs.30.00 (Occas. paps., 26) Dept Geog - Mak 1971 UG

Langlands, B.W.
The population geography of each district of Uganda: Lango. 49pp. maps. U.shs.30.00 (Occas. pap., 37) Dept Geog - Mak 1971 UG

Langlands, B.W.
The population geography of each district of Uganda: Madi. 31pp. maps. U.shs.30.00 (Occas. paps., 31) Dept Geog - Mak 1971 UG

Langlands, B.W.
The population geography of each district of Uganda: Masaka. 53pp. maps. U.shs.30.00 (Occas. paps., 39) Dept Geog - Mak 1971 UG

Langlands, B.W.
The population geography of each district of Uganda: Mubende. 51pp. maps. U.shs.30.00 (Occas. paps., 33) Dept Geog - Mak 1971 UG

Langlands, B.W.
The population geography of each district of Uganda: Teso. 45pp. maps. U.shs.30.00 (Occas. paps., 36) Dept Geog - Mak 1971 UG

Langlands, B.W.
The population geography of each district of Uganda: Toro. 63pp. maps. U.shs.30.00 (Occas. paps., 34) Dept Geog - Mak 1971 UG

Langlands, B.W.
The population geography of each district of Uganda: West Mengo. 47pp. maps. U.shs.30.00 (Occas. paps., 29) Dept Geog - Mak 1971 UG

Langlands, B.W.
The population geography of each district of Uganda: West Nile. 49pp. maps. U.shs.30.00 (Occas. pap.s, 32) Dept Geog - Mak 1971 UG

Langlands, B.W.
A preliminary review of land use in Uganda. rev. ed. 219pp. U.shs.45.00 (Occas. paps., 43) Dept Geog - Mak 1971 UG

Langlands, B.W.
Research in geography at Makerere - 1947-1967. 87pp. U.shs.15.00 (Occas. paps., 2) Dept Geog - Mak 1967 UG

Langlands, B.W.
Sleeping sickness in Uganda 1900-1920. 49pp. U.shs20.00 (Occas. paps., 1) Dept Geog - Mak 1967 UG

Langlands, B.W.
Soil productivity and land availability studies for Uganda. 79pp. U.shs.35.00 (Occas. paps., 53) Dept Geog - Mak 1974 UG

Langlands, B.W. Namirembe, G.
Studies in the geography of religion in Uganda. 65pp. U.shs.20.00 (Occas. paps., 4) Dept Geog - Mak 1967 UG

Langlands, B.W.
Studies in the population geography of Uganda and Tanzania. See: Hirst, M.A.

Langlands, B.W.
Uganda excruciated: analysis of the 1975 exam for course 300. 62pp. U.shs.30.00 (Occas. paps., 61) Dept Geog - Mak 1975 UG

Langlands, B.W.
Uganda in maps. 1020pp. maps. U.shs.250.00 (Occas. paps., 63) Dept Geog - Mak 1975 UG

Langley, M.S. Kiggins, T.J.
A serving people. A textbook on the church in East Africa for the East African Certificate of Education. 316pp. photos. maps. K.shs.22.00 OUP - Nairobi 1974 KE

Lanham, L.W.
English in South Africa: its history, nature and social role. 40c. (Isma paps., 6) Inst Study of Man 1962 SA

Lanham, Traill, L.
Pronounce English correctly. 64pp. ill. R1.20 Longman SA 1965 SA

Lanning, E.C.
Uganda's past. 20pp. ill. K.shs.2.80 ($1.25/50p.) EALB 1963 KE

Lansdown, A.V.
Outlines of South African criminal law and procedure. 2nd ed. 424pp. R12.50 Juta 1961 SA

Lanteri, M.
Le quotient intellectuel et la division scolaire. Z3.00 ($2.40) (Cahiers du CRIDE, Nouvelle série, II, 1 & 2) CRIDE 1977 ZR FRE

Lantum, D., ed.
Tales of Nso. 80pp. ill. 53k (African Reader's Library, 17) Pilgrim 1969 NR

Laoye, J.A.
Principles and practice of health education. 256pp. photos. N2.60 Macmillan 1966 NR

Laoye.
Oriki ati orile. [Attributive words and their origins] 18pp. 20k Univ Ife Bkshop 1963 NR YOR

Lapido, D.
Moremi. [in English and Yoruba]. 230pp. CFA350 CELTHO 1973 NG MUL

Larabi, H.
Opinions sur l'économie algérienne. Suivies de notes de voyages. 269pp. DA14.00 SNED 1974 AE FRE

Larbaoui, D.
Acquisitions récentes sur la tuberculose en Algérie.
See: Chaulet, P.

Larcombe, H.J.   Okunnuga, C.B.A.
Larcombe's primary mathematics. Teacher's lower
standards book. (Decimal ed.) 2nd ed. 142pp. ill.
N2.50 (£1.35) Evans - Nig 1974 NR

Larcombe, H.J.   Okunnuga, C.B.A.
Larcombe's primary mathematics. Teacher's preparatory
book. (Decimal ed.) 2nd ed. bk. 1 78pp. ill. N1.50
(82p) Evans - Nig 1974 NR

Larcombe, H.J.   Okunnuga, C.B.A.
Larcombe's primary mathematics. Teacher's preparatory
book. (Decimal ed.) 2nd ed. bk. 2 72pp. ill. N1.50
(82p) Evans - Nig 1974 NR

Larsen, A.
Variations in income among farming areas in Sukumaland.
21pp. T.shs12.00 ($3.00) (Research pap., 70.6)
Econ Res Bur - Tanz 1970 TZ

Larudee, F.
TEFL in the Middle East. 181pp. L.E.2.000 ($5.00)
Am Univ 1970 UA

Laryea, S.
Agya Abebrese. [Mr. Abebrese.] 108pp. ill. C1.15
Bur Ghana Lang 1975 GH TWI

Lascelles, P.T.   Donaldson, D.
Essential diagnostic tests. 136pp. K.shs.13.25
($3.60) EAPH 1970 KE

Lasebikan, E.L.
Learning Yoruba. 81pp. 65k OUP - Nig 1958 NR

Lasebikan, E.L.
Ojulowo Yoruba. [Pure Yoruba] 1, 3 pts. 84pp. map
photos. 70k OUP - Nig 1954 NR YOR

Lasebikan, E.L.
Ojulowo Yoruba. [Pure Yoruba] 2, 3 pts. 108pp.
photos. 80k OUP - Nig 1955 NR YOR

Lasebikan, E.L.
Ojulowo Yoruba. [Pure Yoruba] 3, 3 pts. 90pp.
photos. 50k OUP - Nig 1958 NR YOR

Lasebikan, E.L.   Lewis, L.J.
Yoruba revision course. 84pp. 45k OUP - Nig 1949
NR

Lassa, P.N., et al.
Oxford modern mathematics for Nigerian teachers'
colleges. Student's bk. 2 160pp. ill. OUP - Nig 1976
NR

Lassa, P.N.   Downes, L.W.
Oxford modern mathematics for Nigerian primary schools.
pupil's bk. 1, 6 bks. 64pp. col. ill. 65k OUP - Nig
1972 NR

Lassa, P.N.   Downes, L.W.
Oxford modern mathematics for Nigerian primary schools.
New ed. pupil's bk. 2, 6 bks. 72pp. col. ill. 75k
OUP - Nig 1972 NR

Lassa, P.N.   Downes, L.W.
Oxford modern mathematics for Nigerian primary schools.
pupil's bk. 3, 6 bks. 96pp. col. ill. 75k OUP - Nig
1972 NR

Lassa, P.N.   Downes, L.W.
Oxford modern mathematics for Nigerian primary schools.
pupil's bk. 4, 6 bks. 96pp. col. ill. 80k OUP - Nig
1973 NR

Lassa, P.N.   Downes, L.W.
Oxford modern mathematics for Nigerian primary schools.
pupil's bk. 5, 6 bks. 136pp. col. ill. N1.00 OUP - Nig
1974 NR

Lassa, P.N.   Downes, L.W.
Oxford modern mathematics for Nigerian primary schools.
pupil's bk. 6, 6 bks. 136pp. col. ill. N1.20 OUP - Nig
1975 NR

Lassa, P.N.   Downes, L.W.
Oxford modern mathematics for Nigerian primary schools.
teacher's bk. 1, 6 bks. 157pp. ill. N1.50 OUP - Nig
1972 NR

Lassa, P.N.   Downes, L.W.
Oxford modern mathematics for Nigerian primary schools.
teacher's bk. 2, 6 bks. 127pp. ill. N1.50 OUP - Nig
1972 NR

Lassa, P.N.   Downes, L.W.
Oxford modern mathematics for Nigerian primary schools.
teacher's bk. 3, 6 bks. ill. N1.50 OUP - Nig 1972
NR

Lassa, P.N.   Downes, L.W.
Oxford modern mathematics for Nigerian primary schools.
teacher's bk. 4, 6 bks. 152pp. ill. N1.50 OUP - Nig
1973 NR

Lassa, P.N.   Downes, L.W.
Oxford modern mathematics for Nigerian primary schools.
teacher's bk. 5, 6 bks. 176pp. ill. N1.75 OUP - Nig
1975 NR

Lassa, P.N.   Downes, L.W.
Oxford modern mathematics for Nigerian primary schools.
teacher's bk. 6, 6 bks. 159pp. ill. N2.00 OUP - Nig
1975 NR

Lassa, P.N.   Downes, L.W.
Oxford modern mathematics for Nigerian primary schools.
workbook 1, 5 bks. 33pp. ill. 40k OUP - Nig 1973
NR

Lassa, P.N.   Downes, L.W.
Oxford modern mathematics for Nigerian primary schools.
workbook 2, 5 bks. 28pp. ill. 40k OUP - Nig 1972
NR

Lassa, P.N.   Downes, L.W.
Oxford modern mathematics for Nigerian primary schools.
workbook 3, 5 bks. 27pp. ill. 40k OUP - Nig 1972
NR

Lassa, P.N.   Downes, L.W.
Oxford modern mathematics for Nigerian primary schools.
workbook 4, 5 bks. 28pp. ill. 40k OUP - Nig 1973
NR

Lassa, P.N.   Downes, L.W.
Oxford modern mathematics for Nigerian primary schools.
workbook 5, 5 bks. 40pp. ill. 40k OUP - Nig 1974
NR

Lassa, P.N.   Paling, D. et al.
Oxford modern mathematics for Nigerian teachers'
colleges. lecturer's guide, 1. 211pp. ill. N3.75
OUP - Nig 1975 NR

Lassa, P.N.   Paling, D. et al.
Oxford modern mathematics for Nigerian teachers'
colleges. student's bk. 1. 160pp. ill. col. N2.50
OUP - Nig 1976 NR

Lassort, P.
La langue guerzé; grammaire guerzé. See: Casthelain, J.

Last, G.   Pankhurst, R.
A history of Ethiopia in pictures. 56pp. ill. B2.75
OUP-Addis 1969 ET

Last, G.   Pankhurst, R.
Ye Ethiopia Tank Besil. [A history of Ethiopia in pictures]
tr. fr. eng. S. Muluneh 56pp. ill. Eth. $2.75
OUP-Addis 1972 ET AMH

Last, M.
Pupil's book. See: Rogers, J.

Last, M.
Pupil's book. 192pp. ill. B1.40 (The New Oxford
English Course, 4) OUP-Addis 1971 ET

Last, M.
Teacher's notes, book five. See: Rogers, J.

Last, M.
Teacher's notes for book four. See: Scott-Forbes, D.

Author Index

Latrobe, C.J.
Journal of a visit to South Africa in 1815 & 1816 [Reprint of 1818 edition].   450pp. pl. cl.   R25.00   Struik 1969 SA

Latscha, J.
Les conflits de lois en matière de sociétés commerciales au Maroc.   Dir35.00   (Coll. Fac. des Sciences juridiques, économiques et sociales, 7)   Ed La Porte 1960 MR FRE

Lätti, V.I.   Breger, R.A.
Job grading procedure for selection and placement of workers at the lower levels.   17pp.   (CSIR Special Report, PERS 237)   CSIR 1976 SA

Laughton, W.H.
Jukia iuku ukathome.   2nd ed.   103pp.   K.shs.2.25 ($1.50/60p.)   EALB 1961 KE MER

Laughton, W.H.
Twiteni tukathome.   [Come and read]   5th ed.   30pp. K.shs.2.25 ($1.50/60p.)   EALB 1969 KE MER

Laurence, P.   van Zyl Slabbert, F.
Towards an open plural society.   55pp.   R1.00 ($1.50/75p.)   (Spro-cas publication)   Ravan 1973 SA

Laurence, P.
The Transkei: South Africa's politics of partition.   180pp. ill.   R4.50   ($5.60/£2.95)   Ravan 1976 SA

Laurie, D.P.
Algorithm for the solution of the general ionospheric reaction-rate equations.   See: Torr, D.G.

Laurie, D.P.
Automatic step-size control in parabolic partial differential equations.   14pp.   (CSIR Special Report, WISK 166) CSIR 1975 SA

Laurie, J.
Hail and its effects on buildings.   12pp.   (CSIR research reports, 176)   CSIR 1960 SA

Lavendhomme, R.
Introduction à la mathématique.   28pp.   45k   Press Univ Zaire 1962 ZR FRE

Lavendhomme, R.
Théorie des ensembles visqueux et des ensembles floux. 72pp.   60k   Press Univ Zaire 1966 ZR FRE

Laver, M.P.H.
Index to the South African edition of the Anglican book of common prayer.   Dept Bibliog, Lib & Typo 1972 SA

Lavergne de Tressan, M.
Inventaire linguistique de l'Afrique occidentale française et du Togo. [Reprint of ed. 1953].   241pp. maps. (D.fl.80.00)   (Mémoires de l'IFAN, 30)   IFAN 1953 SG FRE

Lavoie, J.
Mother and teacher. [Simplified version of "Mater et Magistra"].   32pp.   T.shs.1.20   (20c)   TMP 1974 TZ

Lawal, O.A.
Advanced level economics of West Africa textbook. 243pp.   N3.00   Onibonoje 1971 NR

Lawal, O.A.
Essentials of 'A' level economics of West Africa.   101pp. ill.   85k.   Onibonoje 1977 NR

Lawal, O.A.
Essentials of 'O' level economics of West Africa.   64pp. ill.   70k.   Onibonoje 1977 NR

Lawal, O.A.
'O' level government.   235pp.   N2.50   Onibonoje 1976 NR

Lawal, O.A.
Ordinary level economics of West Africa.   152pp. N1.55   Onibonoje 1969 NR

Lawal, O.A.
Ordinary level economics of West Africa: questions and answers.   152pp.   N1.25   Onibonoje 1971 NR

Lawani, S.M.
The Aslib-Cranfield studies on the evaluation of indexing system.   24pp.   50k   (Inst. of Librarianship, occas. pap., 5)   Inst Lib-Ib 1970 NR

Lawler, R.
Friederich Duerrenmatt.   50pp.   R2.60   Dept Bibliog, Lib & Typo 1968 SA

Lawrance, J.C.D.
An English-Ateso and Ateso-English vocabulary. See: Hilder, J.H.

Lawrance, J.C.D.
An introduction to the Ateso language.   See: Hilders, J.H.

Lawrence, P., et al.
Regional planning in Tanzania: an economic view from the field.   T.shs.12.00   ($3.00)   (Research pap., 68.29) Econ Res Bur - Tanz 1975 TZ

Lawrence, P.R.
Adoption of innovations and research recommendations in the sisal industry of Tanzania.   20pp. ill.   T.shs12.00 ($3.00)   (Research pap., 69.22)   Econ Res Bur - Tanz 1969 TZ

Lawrence, P.R.
Rationalization and diversification in the sisal industry. 20pp. ill.   T.shs12.00   ($3.00)   (Research pap., 69.3) Econ Res Bur - Tanz 1969 TZ

Lawrence, P.R.
Sisal industry in Tanzania.   30pp. ill.   T.shs12.00 ($3.00)   (Research pap., 70.13)   Econ Res Bur - Tanz 1970 TZ

Lawrence, P.R.
Sisal industry of Tanzania - informal commodity agreement and related questions of strategy.   34pp.   T.shs12.00 ($3.00)   (Research pap., 71.9)   Econ Res Bur - Tanz 1971 TZ

Lawrie, G.
New light on South West Africa: some extracts from and comments on the Odendaal report.   15pp.   20c.   SA Inst Int Affairs 1964 SA

Laws, D.H.
How to apply a bonus incentive plan in your business. 29pp. hd.   U.shs2.50   Adult Educ Centre 1967 UG

Lawson, G.W.
Ecology and conservation in Ghana.   21pp.   C1.00 ($1.00/50p.)   (Inaugural lecture)   Ghana UP 1970 GH

Lawson, J.B.
'O' level objective tests in physics.   54pp.   N1.30 Aromolaran 1975(?) NR

Lawson, J.B.
Revision questions/answers on 'O' level chemistry. 163pp.   N2.50   Aromolaran 1975(?) NR

Lawson, J.B.
School certificate organic chemistry.   50pp.   N1.20 Aromolaran 1975(?) NR

Lawson, R.   Kwei, E.
African entrepreneurship and economic growth: a case study of the fishing industry of Ghana.   262pp. photos. hd.   C8.00   (£4.00/$8.00)   Ghana UP 1974 GH

Lawton, O.
Home appliances.   48pp. ill.   50c.   OUP-SA 1965 SA

Lawton, O.
The home handyman.   96pp. ill.   60c.   OUP-SA 1963 SA

Lawton, O.   Walton, J.
Longman primary maths. Fifth steps.   Pupil's bk.   112pp. 85c.   Longman - Rhod 1971 RH

Lawton, O.   Walton, J.
Longman primary maths. Fifth steps.   Teacher's bk. 192pp.   R$1.65   Longman - Rhod 1972 RH

Lawton, O.   Walton, J.
Longman primary maths. First steps: colour cards and shapes.   25c.   Longman - Rhod 1970 RH

Author Index

Leaf, M.
Ferdinand ho asem. [The story of Ferdinand] 80pp. ill.
10pes. Waterville 1936 GH TWI

Leaf, M.
Ferdinard he sane. [The story of Ferdinand] 80pp. ill.
10pes. Waterville 1936 GH GAA

Leakey, L.S.B.
First lessons in Kikuyu. 60pp. K.shs.4.50
($1.70/70p.) EALB 1959 KE

Lebaud, G.
Léopold Sédar Senghor ou la poésie du royaume
d'enfance. 105pp. CFA600 (F12.00) Nouv Ed Afric
1976 SG FRE

Lebon, G.
La civilisation des arabes. 494pp. pap. & hd.
DA26.50 cl. DA19.50 pap. SNED 1970 AE FRE

Leck, N.
South African sport. [Also available in Afrikaans.]. ill.
photos. maps. cl. R6.75 (The Macdonald Heritage
Library series) Purnell 1977 SA

Leclerc et al.
La réserve naturelle intégrale du Mont Nimba: La chaine
du Nimba. Essai géographique. pt. 3 271pp. pl.
CFA2000 (Mémoires de l'IFAN, 43) IFAN 1955 SG
FRE

Leclercq, H.
Principes pour l'orientation d'une politique fiscale au
Congo. 52pp. 45k Press Univ Zaire 1959 ZR FRE

Lee, B.S., ed.
An English miscellany. 218pp. photos. hd. R5.60
OUP - SA 1977 SA

Lee, C., ed.
Elton in the southern highlands of Tanganyika. 2nd ed.
59pp. K.shs3.00 ($1.50/60p.) EALB 1968 KE

Lee, E.C.
Local taxation in Tanzania. 75pp. K.shs.6.00
OUP-Nairobi 1966 KE

Lee, N. Woodhouse, B.
Art on the rocks of Southern Africa. 165pp. photos. hd.
R10.00 Purnell 1970 SA

Lee, S.G.
Manual of a thematic apperception test for African
subjects. 43pp. ill. R1.25 Univ of Natal 1953 SA

Lefebvre, P.P., ed.
Annoncer l'evangile. Exhortation apostolique "Evangelii
nuntiandi" du Pape Paul VI. Notes et commentaires.
94pp. 50k St. Paul 1976 ZR FRE

Legendre, M.
Survivance des mesures traditionnelles en Tunisie. 90pp.
pl. D0.850 (Série III, Mémoires du Centre d'Etudes
Humaines, 4) Univ Tunis 1958 TI FRE

Legg, C.
The tin belt of the Southern Province. K3.00 (Dept. of
Geological Survey. Economic Reports, 29) Geol Survey
- Zam 1972 ZA

Legg, C.A. Cap, M. Maczka, L.
Brick clays in the Mansa area. K2.50 (Dept. of
Geological Survey, Economic Reports, 48) Geol Survey -
Zam 1976 ZA

Legg, C.A.
A reconnaissance survey of the hot and mineralised
springs of Zambia. K3.50 (Dept. of Geological Survey,
Economic Reports, 50) Geol Survey - Zam 1976 ZA

Leguesdron, H. et al.
Annales de l'université d'Abidjan. 300pp. CFA2600
(F52.00) (Série C-Sciences, 5) Univ Abidjan 1969 IV
FRE

Leigh, R.A.
Bleaching of 55/45 wool/cotton blend fabrics, part I: using
hydrogen peroxide. 19pp. R2.50 (SAWTRI Technical
Reports, 282) SAWTRI 1976 SA

Leighton, S.
Notes on a visit to South Africa 1889. 110pp. ill. hd.
R11.65 cl. (Dfl.35.00/$13.50/£6.50 cl.) Balkema 1975
SA

Leistner, G.M.E.
Aid to Africa. 23pp. map. 65c (Commun. of the
Africa Inst., 3) Africa Inst - Pret 1966 SA

Leistner, G.M.E. Breytenbach, W.J.
The black worker. 101pp. cl. R3.00 (R3.50) Africa
Inst - Pret 1975 SA

Leistner, G.M.E.
Co-operation for development in Southern Africa. 30pp.
60c (70c) (Africa Inst. of South Africa, occas. pap., 33)
Africa Inst - Pret 1972 SA

Leistner, G.M.E.
Economic and social forces affecting the urbanization of
the Bantu population of South Africa. 18pp. (Africa Inst.
of South Africa, occas. pap., 32) Africa Inst - Pret 1972
SA

Leistner, G.M.E., ed.
Rhodesia. Economic structure and change. 239pp. ill.
pl. maps. R7.50 (R8.50) (Commun. of the African
Inst., 30) Africa Inst - Pret 1976 SA

Leistner, G.M.E.
European views on the development of poor countries.
37pp. 20c (30c) (Africa Inst. of South Africa, occas.
pap., 22) Africa Inst - Pret 1969 SA

Leistner, G.M.E.
Influx control - economic and social aspects of physical
control over rural urban population movements in South
Africa and elsewhere. 24pp. 20c (30c) (Africa Inst.
of South Africa, occas. pap., 14) Africa Inst - Pret 1968
SA

Leistner, G.M.E.
Lesotho needs aid and gifted leadership. 5pp. 20c
(30c) (Africa Inst. of South Africa, occas. pap., 9) Africa
Inst - Pret 1968 SA

Leistner, G.M.E.
Perspectives on Africa's economic development. 17pp.
20c (30c) (Africa Inst. of South Africa, occas. pap., 10)
Africa Inst - Pret 1968 SA

Leistner, G.M.E.
Population and resources in Southern Africa. 29pp.
(Africa Inst. of South Africa, occas. pap., 31) Africa Inst -
Pret 1972 SA

Leistner, G.M.E.
Problems and patterns of economic development in Africa.
18pp. 20c (30c) (Commun. of the Africa Inst., 2)
Africa Inst - Pret 1965 SA

Leistner, G.M.E. Smith, P.
Swaziland: resources and development. 219pp. maps.
R3.60 (R3.90) (Commun. of the Africa Inst., 8) Africa
Inst - Pret 1969 SA

Leistner, O.A.
The plant ecology of the southern Kalahari. R3.20
(R4.00) (Memoirs of the Botanical Survey of South Africa,
38) Botanical Res Inst 1967 SA

Leith-Ross, S.
Nigerian pottery. 200pp. pl. map. N15.00 Ibadan
UP 1970 NR

Lejri, M.S.
Evolution du mouvement national - des origines a la 2eme
guerre mondiale. vol. 1. 255pp. D1,400 Maison
Tunis 1974 TI FRE

Lelong, F. et al.
Annales de l'université d'Abidjan. 221pp. CFA950
(F19.00) (Série C-Sciences, 8) Univ Abidjan 1972 IV
FRE

Lema, A.A., ed.
Studies in curriculum development. v. 1 143pp.
T.shs.3.00 Inst Educ - Dar 1972 TZ

Lema, A.A., ed.
Studies in curriculum development. v. 2 48pp.
T.shs.2.00 Inst Educ - Dar 1972 TZ

Lemarechal, A.
Inventaire des sources thermominerales de l'Adamaoua.
96pp. ill. pl. CFA1,000 Inst Sciences Hum - Cam
1969 CM FRE

Lemarechal, A.
Les sources thermominerales de l'Adamaoua. Analyses
chimiques et utilisations. 32pp. ill. maps. CFA500
Inst Sciences Hum - Cam 1970 CM FRE

Lemarechal, A.
Les sources thermominérales de l'ouest du Cameroun.
52pp. ill. pl. maps. CFA1,000 Inst Sciences Hum -
Cam 1971 CM FRE

Lemki, M.
Yarabi maskini. [Short stories.] 160pp. K.shs.23.75
($5.00/£2.00) EALB 1976 KE SWA

Lemu, B.A.
Gabatar da addinin Musulun ci. [An introduction to
Islam.] N1.50 Northern Nig 1976 NR HAU

Lemu, B.A.
A student's introduction to Islam. 104pp. ill. N1.05
Macmillan 1972 NR

Lemu, S.A.
Sakon Mallam. [A message from the teacher] 40pp.
60k Northern Nig 1969 NR HAU

Lemu, S.A.
Tarbiyyar 'Yan Musulmi, 1. [Islam for primary schools]
N1.00 Northern Nig 1973 NR HAU

Lemu, S.A.
Tarbiyyar 'Yan Musulmi, 2. [The training of young
muslims] 34pp. N1.75 Northern Nig 1970 NR HAU

Lemu, S.A.
The young Muslim. 111pp. ill. N1.25 Islamic 1972
NR

Leonard, A.G.
How we made Rhodesia. [Reprint of ed. 1896]. 364pp.
ill. map. cl. R$8.75 (Rhodesiana Reprint Library, Gold
Series, 32) Books of Rhodesia 1973 RH

Leonard, D.K., ed.
Rural administration in Kenya. 166pp. K.shs.16.75
($3.90/£2.00) EALB 1973 KE

Leong, G.C.
Certificate physical and human geography. (Nigerian
adaptation) ill. maps. N3.00 OUP - Nig 1975 NR

Lepesme, P.
Coléoptères cérambycides (longicornes) de la Côte
d'Ivoire. 103pp. pl. CFA600 (Catalogues et
Documents, 11) IFAN 1953 SG FRE

LeRiche, H.
A health survey of African children in Alexandra township.
16pp. ill. 50c Witwatersrand UP 1943 SA

Leshoai, B.
Wrath of the ancestors and other plays. 72pp. ($2.00)
EAPH 1972 KE

Leslie, J.A.K.
A survey of Dar es Salaam. 305pp. hd. U.shs.30.00
(M.I.S.R. Individual monog., 8) Mak Inst Soc Res 1963
UG

Lesotho English Teaching Scheme.
English reading work book. 3rd ed. 86pp. 30c
Mazenod Inst 1975 LO

Lesotho National English Panel.
Let's use the dictionary. 3rd ed. 27pp. 20c
Mazenod Inst 1975 LO

Lessedjina Ikwame Ipu'ozia.
La coopération multilaterale interafricaine en aviation civile.
Les institutions Africains relatives à l'aviation civile.
156pp. Z4.50 Press Univ Zaire 1977 ZR FRE

Lessedsina, I.I.
Le droit aérien. 814pp. Z4.80 Press Univ Zaire 1975
ZR FRE

Lessing, H.W.
A practical English course for standard 6. See: van
Rensenburg, R. C. J.

Lessing, H.W.
A practical English course for standard 7. See: van
Rensenburg, R.C.J.

Lessing, H.W.
A practical English course for standard 8. (Second
language.) See: van Rensenburg, R.J.C.

Lesso, Z.H.
Utenzi wa zinduko la Ujamaa. [The awakening of
socialism] ill. K.shs.7.70 ($2.30/80p.) EALB 1972
KE SWA

Lestner, G.M.E.
South Africa's development aid to African states. 34pp.
(Africa Inst. of South Africa, occas. pap., 28) Africa Inst -
Pret 1970 SA

Lestrade, G.P.
Dintshontsho tsa bo-Juliuse Kesara. See: Plaatje, S.T.

Letcher, O.
When life was rusted through. [Reprint of ed. 1934].
54pp. ill. cl. R$2.00 Books of Rhodesia 1973 RH

Letty, C.
Trees of South Africa. ill. R2.95 Tafelberg 1976 SA

Leulmi, K.
L'organisation de l'économie nationale. DA1.00 SNED
1971 AE FRE

Levadoux, L. Douaouri, B. Benabderabou, A.
Ampelographie algérienne. 120pp. DA12.00 SNED
1971 AE FRE

Lever, H.
The South African voter. 230pp. ill. R7.50 Juta
1972 SA

Leverton, B.J.T.
The Natal cotton industry 1845-1875. 38pp. 40c.
(90c.) Univ South Africa 1963 SA

Leveson, G.
Company directors: law and practice. 255pp. hd.
R9.50 Butterworths 1970 SA

Leveson, G.
Law of collisions in South Africa. See: Isaacs, I.

Leveson, M., ed.
Philip Segal essays and lectures. 224pp. photos. pap.
R2.85 Philip 1975 SA

Lévesque, A., ed.
Contribution à la bibliographie nationale du Rwanda,
1965-1970. 542pp. Lib Univ Rwanda, distr. 1974 RW
FRE

Lévi-Strauss, C. et al.
Annales de l'université d'Abidjan. 338pp. CFA1800
(F36.00) (Série F-Ethno-Sociologie, 3) Univ Abidjan
1971 IV FRE

Levieux, J. Trong, Y.
Annales de l'université d'Abidjan. 325pp. (Série
E-Ecologie, 8) Univ Abidjan 1975 IV FRE

Levin, S.
The Saldanha Bay story. See: Burman, J.

LeVine, B.B.
Yoruba students' memories of childhood rewards and
punishments. 18pp. (Inst. of Ed. occas. pub., 2) Inst
Educ-Ib 1962 NR

Levinsohn, J.S. Dreyer, J.J. de Waal, S.
My mathematics books. My sixth mathematics/arithmetics
book. 192pp. R2.50 Longman - SA 1974 SA

Levinsohn, S.
Mathematics 6 answers/Wiskune 6 antwoorde. [Bilingual
in English and Afrikaans.]. See: Griesel, P.O.

Levinsohn, S.
Mathematics 7. See: Griesel, P.O.

Levinsohn, S. Dreyer, J.J. De Waal, J.S.
My mathematics books. My fifth mathematics/arithmetic
book. 184pp. ill. R1.95 Longman SA 1971 SA

Author Index

Levinsohn, S.   Dreyer, J.J.   De Waal, J.S.
My mathematics books. My first mathematics/arithmetic book. 144pp. ill. R1.20 Longman SA 1969 SA

Levinsohn, S.   Dreyer, J.J.   De Waal, J.S.
My mathematics books. My fourth mathematics/arithmetic book. 180pp. ill. R1.75 Longman SA 1970 SA

Levinsohn, S.   Dreyer, J.J.   De Waal, J.S.
My mathematics books. My third mathematics/arithmetic book. 168pp. ill. R1.50 Longman SA 1970 SA

Levinson, B.
From breakfast to madness. 47pp. R2.10 ($1.80/£95p.) Ravan 1974 SA

Levinson, O.
South West Africa. pl. cl. R11.50 Tafelberg 1976 SA

Levitt, S.Z.
Fluoridation of public water supplies: 1957-1963: a list of references. 42pp. R2.20 Dept Bibliog, Lib & Typo 1966 SA

Levy, F.
The works of Sarah Gertrude Millin 1952-1968. 22pp. R1.60 Dept Bibliog, Lib & Typo 1969 SA

Levyns, M.R.
A guide to the flora of the Cape Peninsula. 2nd ed. R6.50 Juta 1966 SA

Lewalle, J.
Arbres du Burundi. Essences autochtones. pt. 1 61pp. Univ Bujumbura 1971 BD FRE

Lewalle, J.
Les étapes de végétation du Burundi occidental. 173pp. photos. (Faculté des Sciences, 20) Univ Bujumbura 1972 BD FRE

Lewalle, J.
Liste floristique et répartition altitudinale de la flore du Burundi occidental. Univ Bujumbura 1970 BD FRE

Lewcock, R.
Early nineteenth century architecture in South Africa: a study of the interaction of two cultures, 1795-1837. 462pp. ill. hd. fl. 90.00 Balkema 1973 SA

Lewicki, T.
Arabic external sources for the history of Africa to the South of the Sahara. 2nd. ed. 102pp. N3.50 Africa only (Academic Reprints Series) Pilgrim 1974 NR

Lewin, A.
The law, procedure and conduct of meetings in South Africa. 4th ed. R12.50 Juta 1975 SA

Lewis, A.
The periodical holdings in the library of the South African Jewish Board of Deputies, Johannesburg. 28pp. R1.60 Dept Bibliog, Lib & Typo 1968 SA

Lewis, C.
The city kid. 96pp. ill. 80pes. (30p.) Africa Christian 1973 GH

Lewis, C.A.
Ghana after Nkrumah. 109pp. pl. C1.50 Waterville 1975 GH

Lewis, G.J.   Barnard, T.T.   Obermeyer, A.A.
Gladiolus: a revision of the South African species. 368pp. ill. hd. R8.50 Purnell 1972 SA

Lewis, G.P., ed.
Approach to Christian doctrine. 256pp. R3.00 pap. Methodist 1976 SA

Lewis, I.M.
Marriage and family in Northern Somaliland. 51pp. U.shs1.00 (East African studies, 15) Mak Inst Soc Res 1962 UG

Lewis, L.J.
Yoruba revision course. See: Lasebikan, E.L.

Lewis, O.A.M.
Plants, protein and people. 15pp. 30c (Univ. Cape Town. Inaugural lec., 31) Univ Cape Town Lib 1975 SA

Lewis, R.A.
La cloche fêlée. 27pp. R$1.50 Univ Rhodesia 1976 RH FRE

Lewis, R.A.
Pollution of the internal environment. 20pp. C1.00 ($1.00/50p.) (Inaugural lecture) Ghana UP 1971 GH

Lewis, R.A.
Sickle states: clinical features in West Africans. 138pp. photos. maps. cl. C5.00 (£2.50/$5.00) Ghana UP 1970 GH

Lewis, W. A.
Some aspects of economic development. 86pp. C1.00 ($1.50) Ghana Publ Corp 1969 GH

Lewis, W.A.
Some aspects of economic development. 86pp. N1.00 (NR only) Ethiope 1972 NR

Lewsen, P.
The Cape liberal tradition- myth or reality? 40c. (Isma paps., 26) Inst Study of Man 1969 SA

Leyland, J.
Adventures in the far interior of South Africa [Reprint of 1866 edition]. 296pp. pl. cl. R7.50 (Africana collectanea, 40) Struik 1972 SA

Leys, C.
Politicians and policies. 105pp. maps. K.shs12.00 ($3.60) EAPH 1967 KE

Lezine, A.
Architecture punique. 132pp. ill. D1.915 (Série I, Archéologie-Histoire, 5) Univ Tunis 1961 TI FRE

Liandrat, E.
Géologie de la presqu'île Masoala. See: Hottin, G.

Libersidge, R.
Ludwig Krebs: Cape naturalist to the king of Prussia, 1792-1844. See: Ffolliott, P.

Lichtenstein, W.H.C.
Foundation of the Cape: about the Bechuanas. 121pp. pl. hd. fl. 27.00 (South African biographical and historical studies, 18) Balkema 1973 SA

Lichtigfield, A.
Aspects of Jasper's philosophy. 119pp. 75c. (R1.25) Univ South Africa 1971 SA

Liebenberg, A.C.
Arch action in concrete slabs. 35pp. ill. (CSIR research reports, 234) CSIR 1966 SA

Liebenberg, C.R.
The teaching of history at South African secondary schools: a condensed version of a survey in the year 1966. 39pp. R1.45 Human Science Res Council 1972 SA

Liebenberg, D.
The Drakensberg of Natal. 2nd ed. 178pp. photos. col. ill. R10.00 Bulpin 1972 SA

Liebenberg, E.C.   Rootman, P.J.
The South African landscape. An exercise manual for map and air photo interpretation. Tr. f. Afrikaans by V. de Boer. ill. photos maps col. maps. R12.75 Butterworth 1976 SA

Liebenow, C.
Colonial rule and political development. 360pp. maps. K.shs.35.00 ($8.40) EAPH 1971 KE

Lieber, J.W., ed.
Human ecology and education: a catalogue of environmental studies, 1957-1970. 46pp. 70k (Inst. of Ed. occas. pub., 10) Inst Educ-Ib 1970 NR

Lieber, J.W.
Effik and Ibibio villages: human ecology and education series South East State. 2, 2 vls. 70pp. 85k (Inst. of Ed. occas. pub., 13) Inst Educ-Ib 1971 NR

Lieber, J.W.
Ibo village communities: human ecology and education series. East Central State. 1, 2 vls. 92pp. N1.05 (Inst. of Ed. occas. pub., 12) Inst Educ-Ib 1971 NR

Lieke Mahoya.
Authenticité: idéologie de l'actualisation ou de l'authentification humaine. 32pp. 45k Press Univ Zaire 1973 ZR FRE

Lieta, P.
Longman graded reading scheme. Reader 1. See: Bracey, D.

Lieta, P.
Longman graded reading scheme. Reader 2. See: Bracey, D.

Lieta, P.
Longman graded reading scheme. Reader 3. See: Bracey, D.

Lieta, P.
Longman graded reading scheme. Reader 4. See: Bracey, D.

Lieta, P.
Longman graded reading scheme. Teachers bk. See: Bracey, D.

Lighton, C.
Cape floral kingdom. 2nd ed. 230pp. ill. col. pl. R4.75 Juta 1973 SA

Lighton, C. Harris, C.B.
Details regarding the Diamond Fields Advertiser, 1878-1968. 32pp. ill. R1.00 (Monog. on printing in S.A., 2) State-Lib-SA 1969 SA

Lijadu, M., ed.
Awon arofo orin Sobo Arobiodu. [Collection of poems written by the Yoruba poet Sobo Arobiodu.] 112pp. ill. N1.25 Macmillan 1974 NR YOR

Likimani, M.
They shall be chastised. 243pp. K.shs.12.50 ($3.10/£1.50) EALB 1975 KE

Likimani, M.
What does a man want. 2nd ed. 220pp. K.shs.18.25 ($4.15/£2.20) EALB 1976 KE

Lillis, K.M., ed.
Four African plays. 80pp. K.shs.7.00 Longman - Ken 1974 KE

Limenh, F.
Yegara Tinsaye. [Traditional verse.] 133pp. ill. Eth.$2.25 Bookshop Supply Org 1974 ET AMH

Lind, E.M. Tallantire, A.C.
Some common flowering plants of Uganda. rev. ed. 264pp. ill. K.shs17.50 OUP-Nairobi 1972 KE

Lindberg, O.
Attitudes towards squatting: a review. T.shs.15.00 (Research reports, new series, 9) Bur Res Assess - Tanz 1975 TZ

Lindfors, B., comp.
A bibliography of literary contributions to Nigerian periodicals 1946-1972. 231pp. N6.00 Ibadan UP 1975 NR

Lindgren, N. Schoffeleers, M.
Rock paintings and Nyau symbols in Malawi. 80pp. pl. maps. K2.00 (Department of Antiquities, 17) Dept Antiquities - Mal 1977 MW

Lindhard, N.
Choosing your career and your higher education. 128pp. hd. R6.00 Philip 1974 SA

Lindstrom, U.B.
Is our teaching good enough? 13pp. free AFAA 1975 KE

Lindstrom, U.B.
Notre enseignement est-il assez bon? Tr. fr. English 13pp. free AFAA 1975 KE FRE

Liniger-Goumaz, M.
L'Eurafrique, utopie ou réalité? 114pp. CFA600 CLE 1972 CM FRE

Linley, K. et al.
Flowers of the veld. 120pp. col. ill. R$2.50 Longman - Rhod 1972 RH

Linnavuori, R.
Studies on African miridae (Heteroptera) 66pp. ill. N2.00 (Entomological Society of Nigeria, occas. pubs., 12) Entomological Soc - Nig 1974 NR

Lintsen, E.
Study guide: African novels. 16pp. T.shs.1.00 (Study Guide Series) TMP 1975 TZ

Lisimba, M.
Ki ze ne ba bata. [These were what they wanted] 56pp. 50n. Neczam 1970 ZA LOZ

Lisimba, M.
Lumenyo. [Collection of jokes.] 65pp. K1.10 Neczam 1974 ZA LOZ

Lissouba, P.
Conscience du développement et démocratie. 80pp. CFA550 (F11.00) Nouv Ed Afric 1976 SG FRE

Lister, L.A.
African landscape studies. 115pp. photos. R$3.00 cl. ($6.00 cl.) M.O. Collins 1969 RH

Lister, L.A., ed.
Symposium on granites, gneisses and related rocks. 509pp. pl. maps. hd. R25.00 cl. (Special pub., 3) Geol Soc - SA 1973 SA

Liswaniso, M., ed.
Voices of Zambia. 152pp. K1.20 Neczam 1971 ZA

Liversedge, T.
Okavango river delta. ill. pl. photos. cl. R15.00 Purnell 1977 SA

Livingstone, D.
Matendo makuu ya mungu. [The saving events.] 48pp. T.shs.3.00 Central Tanganyika 1968 TZ SWA

Livingstone, D.
A rosary of bone. 32pp. R1.80 (Mantis Poets, 7) Philip 1975 SA

Livingstone, I.
Cowboys in Africa: the socio-economics of ranching. 84pp. K.shs.10.00 (Inst. Development Studies, occas. paps., 17) Inst Dev Stud 1976 KE

Livingstone, I. Goodall, A.A.
Economics and development: an introduction. 216pp. ill. K.shs.16.00 OUP-Nairobi 1970 KE

Livingstone, I.
The national small industries corporation of Tanzania: an examination of current plans and prospects. T.shs.12.00 ($3.00) (Research pap., 70.23) Econ Res Bur - Tanz 1974 TZ

Livingstone, I.
Production, price and marketing policy for staple foodstuffs in Tanzania. 42pp. T.shs12.00 ($3.00) (Research pap., 71.16) Econ Res Bur - Tanz 1971 TZ

Livingstone, I.
Results of a rural survey: ownership of durable goods in Tanzanian households. 61pp. ill. T.shs12.00 ($3.00) (Research pap., 70.1) Econ Res Bur - Tanz 1970 TZ

Livingstone, I.
Socialist planning in Tanzania: second five years. 28pp. T.shs.12.00 (Research pap., 69.13) Econ Res Bur - Tanz 1969 TZ

Livingstone, I.
Some requirements for agricultural planning in Tanzania. 29pp. T.shs12.00 ($3.00) (Research pap., 71.15) Econ Res Bur - Tanz 1971 TZ

Ljunggren, F. Hamdy, M.
Annotated guide to journals dealing with the Middle East and North Africa. 106pp. L.E.0.750 ($5.00) Am Univ 1965 UA

Ljunggren, F.
The Arab world index, 1960-1964. 549pp. L.E.2.500 ($6.00) Am Univ 1967 UA

Lloyd, P.C.
Yoruba land law. 378pp. maps/pl. N4.00 ($6.00) NISER 1962 NR

Lo-Liyong, T.
Ballads of under-development. 184pp. K.shs.15.95 pap. (£1.80/$3.70 pap.) EALB 1976 KE

lo Liyong, T.
The last word. 210pp. K.shs30.00 cl. K.shs8.00 pap. ($5.80 cl.) ($2.60 pap.) EAPH 1972 KE SWA

lo Liyong, T.
Thirteen offensives against our enemies. 90pp. K.shs.9.00 ($2.50/£1.20) EALB 1974 KE

lo Liyong, T.
The uniformed man and other stories. 68pp. ($2.00/£1.00) EALB 1971 KE

lo Liyong, T.A.
Meditations in limbo. 72pp. K.shs.6.50 Africa Book Serv 1970 KE

Lochner, J.P.A.
Preliminary investigations on the hearing of sharks. See: Davies, D.H.

Loening, L.S.E.
The status of South West Africa (1919 up to June 1951) 27pp. 60c. Univ Cape Town Lib 1969 SA

Loening, W.
Your child. See: Edge, W.

Loftus, E.A.
Gregory and the Great Rift Valley. 2nd ed. 63pp. K.shs2.50 ($1.50/60p.) EALB 1961 KE

Loftus, E.A.
Speke and the Nile source. 2nd ed. 73pp. ill. K.shs3.00 ($1.50/60p.) EALB 1964 KE

Loftus, E.A.
Thompson through Masailand. 72pp. ill. K.shs2.50 ($1.50/60p.) EALB 1959 KE

Logan, R.F.
Bibliography of South West Africa, geography and related fields. 152pp. R5.00 SWA Scient Soc 1969 SX

Logan, W.E.M.
Forestry in Uganda. K.shs.3.00 EALB 1968 KE

Logchem, J. Th. van.
The focus and concentrate programme in the Bolgatanga district: evaluation of an extension programme. 90pp. C1.00 (Univ. of Cape Coast, Centre for Development Studies, Research Report Series, 7) Centre Dev Stud 1972 GH

Lomami-Tshibamba, P.
La récompense de la cruauté; N'gobila des Mswata. 94pp. 70k pap. (Jeune Littérature, 10) Ed Mont Noir 1972 ZR FRE

Lombaard, S.G.
Report of the committee for differentiated education and guidance in connection with a national system of education for handicapped pupils...etc. pt. 3, v. 6 128pp. R3.20 Human Science Res Council 1976 SA

Lombard, C.S. Tweedie, A.H.C.
Agriculture in Zambia since independence. 106pp. K1.40 Neczam 1974 ZA

Lombard, C.S.
The growth of co-operatives in Zambia, 1914-71. 40pp. K1.50 (75p.) (Zambian paps., 6) Inst Afr Stud - Lusaka 1971 ZA

Lombard, J.A.
Economic policy in South Africa. 2nd ed. 272pp. cl. R7.90 cl. HAUM 1975 SA

Lombard, R.T.J.
Handbook for genealogical research in South Africa. 150pp. R5.00 Human Science Res Council 1977 SA

Lomo-Tettey, W.B.
He ko Jce. [There is no peace elsewhere.] 37pp. ill. 45pes. Bur Ghana Lang 1975 GH DAG

Long, N.
Social change and the individual: a study of the social and religious responses to innovation in a Zambia rural community. 257pp. ill. pap. & hd. K5.50 hd. K4.20 pap. (£2.76) (£2.10 pap.) Inst Afr Stud - Lusaka 1968 ZA

Long, U.
The journals of Elizabeth Lees Price. fl. 33.75 576 Balkema 1956 SA

Longden, H.W.D.
Wanyama na ndege wa Africa. [The animals and birds of Africa] 80pp. ill. K.shs.3.00 OUP-Nairobi 1964 KE SWA

Longe, F.
Modern economics. N1.75 llesanmi 1972 NR

Longman, Nigeria.
Akwukwo igbo nke abuo. [Uzoma and Ada primary Igbo book] 2, 2 bks 60pp. col. ill. 50k Longman - Nig 1971 NR IGB

Longman, Nigeria.
Akwukwo igbo nke mbu. [Uzoma and Ada primary Igbo book] 1, 2 bks 48pp. col. ill. 32k Longman - Nig 1966 NR IGB

Longman, Nigeria.
Day-by-day English. New ed. bk. 4. 106pp. ill. 95k Longman - Nig 1976 NR

Longman, Nigeria.
Day-by-day English. New ed. bk. 5. 153pp. ill. N1.00 Longman - Nig 1976 NR

Longman, Nigeria.
Day-by-day English. New ed. bk. 6. 203pp. ill. N1.20 Longman - Nig 1975 NR

Longman, Nigeria.
Day-by-day English course - Eastern edition: pupil's bk. 1, 6 bks. 31pp. col. ill. 60k Longman - Nig 1976 NR

Longman, Nigeria.
Day-by-day English course - Eastern edition: pupil's bk. 2, 6 bks. 80pp. col. ill. 80k Longman - Nig 1976 NR

Longman, Nigeria.
Day-by-day English course - Eastern edition: pupils' bk. 3, 6 bks. 128pp. col. ill. 90k Longman - Nig 1971 NR

Longman, Nigeria.
Day-by-day English course - Eastern edition: pupils' bk. 4, 6 bks. 108pp. col. ill. 90k Longman - Nig 1966 NR

Longman, Nigeria.
Day-by-day English course - Eastern edition: pupils' bk. 5, 6 bks. 158pp. col. ill. 95k Longman - Nig 1971 NR

Longman, Nigeria.
Day-by-day English course - Eastern edition: pupils' bk. 6, 6 bks. 207pp. col. ill. N1.50 Longman - Nig 1967 NR

Longman, Nigeria.
Day-by-day English course - Eastern edition: teacher's bk. 1, 6 bks. 125pp. ill. N1.50 Longman - Nig 1971 NR

Longman, Nigeria.
Day-by-day English course - Eastern edition: teacher's bk. 2, 6 bks. 121pp. ill. N2.00 Longman - Nig 1975 NR

Longman, Nigeria.
Day-by-day English course - Eastern edition: teacher's bk. 3, 6 bks. 218pp. col. ill. N1.60 Longman - Nig 1972 NR

Longman, Nigeria.
Day-by-day English course - Eastern edition: teacher's bk. 4, 6 bks. 196pp. col. ill. N1.80 Longman - Nig 1972 NR

Longman, Nigeria.
Day-by-day English course - Eastern edition: teacher's bk. 5, 6 bks. 147pp. N1.00 Longman - Nig 1976 NR

Longman, Nigeria.
Day-by-day English course - Eastern edition: teachers bk. 6, 6 bks. 117pp. 80k Longman - Nig 1967 NR

Longman, Nigeria.
Day-by-day English course - Mid-Western Nigeria: pupil's bk. 1, 6 bks. 31pp. col. ill. 60k Longman - Nig 1971 NR

Longman, Nigeria.
Day-by-day English course - Mid-Western Nigeria: pupil's bk. 4, 6 bks. 108pp. col. ill. 95k Longman - Nig 1971 NR

Longman, Nigeria.
Day-by-day English course - Mid-Western Nigeria: pupil's bk. 5, 6 bks. 158pp. col. ill. 95k Longman - Nig 1971 NR

Longman, Nigeria.
Day-by-day English course - Mid-Western Nigeria: pupil's bk. 6, 6 bks. 207pp. col. ill. N1.05 Longman - Nig 1971 NR

Longman, Nigeria.
Day-by-day English course - Mid-Western Nigeria: pupil's bks. 3, 6 bks. 128pp. col. ill. 80k Longman - Nig 1975 NR

Longman, Nigeria.
Day-by-day English course - Mid-Western Nigeria: teacher's bk. 1, 6 bks. 85k Longman - Nig 1971 NR

Longman, Nigeria.
Day-by-day English course - Mid-Western Nigeria: teacher's bk. 4, 6 bks. 196pp. ill. N1.80 Longman - Nig 1969 NR

Longman, Nigeria.
Day-by-day English course - Mid-Western Nigeria: teacher's bk. 5, 6 bks. 129pp. ill. N1.05 Longman - Nig 1970 NR

Longman, Nigeria.
Day-by-day English course - Mid-Western Nigeria: teacher's bk. 6, 6 bks. 117pp. ill. 38k Longman - Nig 1971 NR

Longman, Nigeria.
Day-by-day English course - Mid-Western Nigeria:pupil's bk. 2, 6 bks. 95pp. col. ill. 70k Longman - Nig 1970 NR

Longman, Nigeria.
Day-by-day English course - Mid-Western Nigeria:teacher's bk. 2, 6 bks. 126pp. ill. N1.60 Longman - Nig 1975 NR

Longman, Nigeria.
Day-by-day English course: pupils' bk. 1, 6 bks. 31pp. col. ill. 60k Longman - Nig 1976 NR

Longman, Nigeria.
Day-by-day English course: pupils' bk. 2, 6 bks 80pp. col. ill. 70k Longman - Nig 1976 NR

Longman, Nigeria.
Day-by-day English course: pupils' bk. 3, 6 bks 123pp. col. ill. 80k Longman - Nig 1972 NR

Longman, Nigeria.
Day-by-day English course: pupils' bk. 4, 6 bks. 108pp. col. ill. 90k Longman - Nig 1970 NR

Longman, Nigeria.
Day-by-day English course: pupils' bk. 5, 6 bks 149pp. col. ill. 90k Longman - Nig 1970 NR

Longman, Nigeria.
Day-by-day English course: pupils' bk. 6, 6 bks. 207pp. col. ill. N1.05 Longman - Nig 1970 NR

Longman, Nigeria.
Day-by-day-English course - South Eastern and Rivers States, Nigeria. pupils bk 2, 6 bks. 78pp. col. ill. 92k. Longman - Nig 1976 NR

Longman, Nigeria.
Day-by-day-English course - South Eastern and Rivers States, Nigeria. pupils bk 3, 6 bks. 128pp. col. ill. N1.05 Longman - Nig 1976 NR

Longman, Nigeria.
Day-by-day-English course - South Eastern and Rivers States, Nigeria. teachers bk. 1, 6 bks. 128pp. N1.75 Longman - Nig 1976 NR

Longman, Nigeria.
Day-by-day-English course - South Eastern and Rivers States, Nigeria. teachers bk. 2, 6 bks. 128pp. N2.30 Longman - Nig 1976 NR

Longman, Nigeria.
Day-by-day-English course - South Eastern and Rivers States, Nigeria. teachers bk. 3, 6 bks. 188pp. N1.05 Longman - Nig 1976 NR

Longman, Nigeria.
Day-by-day-English course - South Eastern and Rivers States of Nigeria. pupils bk. 1, 6 bks. col. ill. 70k. Longman - Nig 1976 NR

Longman, Nigeria.
Day-by-day English course: teacher's bk. 1, 6 bks 118pp. col. ill. N1.44 Longman - Nig 1971 NR

Longman, Nigeria.
Day-by-day English course: teacher's bk. 2, 6 bks 171pp. col. ill. N2.00 Longman - Nig 1975 NR

Longman, Nigeria.
Day-by-day English course: teacher's bk., 3. 3, 6 bks 184pp. col. ill. N2.00 Longman - Nig 1975 NR

Longman, Nigeria.
Day-by-day English course: teacher's bk. 4, 6 bks. 256pp. ill. N1.80 Longman - Nig 1972 NR

Longman, Nigeria.
Day-by-day English course: teacher's bk. 5, 6 bks. 106pp. ill. N1.00 Longman - Nig 1970 NR

Longman, Nigeria.
Day-by-day English course: teacher's bk. 6, 6 bks. 117pp. col. ill. N1.10 Longman - Nig 1972 NR

Longman, Nigeria.
Eko Kristi: Iwe akobere. [Beginners primer of Christ's teachings] 1, 5 bks. 30pp. col. ill. 60k Longman - Nig 1971 N YO

Longman, Nigeria.
Eko Kristi: Iwe keji. [Christ's teachings] 3, 5 bks. 72pp. ill. 60k Longman - Nig 1971 NR YOR

Longman, Nigeria.
Eko Kristi: Iwe kini. [Christ's teachings] 2, 5 bks. 32pp. ill. 60k Longman - Nig 1971 NR YOR

Longman, Nigeria.
Longman integrated science: teachers guide 1. 112pp. N1.60 Longman - Nig 1977 NR

Longman, Nigeria.
Longman integrated science: textbook 1. 112pp. col. ill. N1.50 Longman - Nig 1976 NR

Longman, Nigeria.
Longman integrated science: workbook 1. 72pp. ill. 85k. Longman - Nig 1976 NR

Longman, Nigeria.
Straight for English - North: pupils' bk. 1, 6 bks. 49pp. col. ill. 80k Longman - Nig 1975 NR

Longman, Nigeria.
Straight for English - North: pupils' bk. 2, 6 bks. 96pp. col. ill. N1.10 Longman - Nig 1976 NR

Longman, Nigeria.
Straight for English - North: pupils' bk. 3, 6 bks. 123pp. col. ill. N1.40 Longman - Nig 1976 NR

Longman, Nigeria.
Straight for English - North: pupils' bk. 4, 6 bks. 204pp. col. ill. N1.50 Longman - Nig 1976 NR

Longman, Nigeria.
Straight for English - North: pupils' bk. 5, 6 bks. 168pp. col. ill. N1.50 Longman - Nig 1976 NR

Longman, Nigeria.
Straight for English - North: pupils' bk. 6, 6 bks 182pp. col. ill. N1.60 Longman - Nig 1976 NR

Longman, Nigeria.
Straight for English - North: teacher's bk. 1, 6 bks.
175pp. col. ill. N2.60 Longman - Nig 1976 NR

Longman, Nigeria.
Straight for English - North: teacher's bk. 2, 6 bks.
196pp. col. ill. N2.60 Longman - Nig 1976 NR

Longman, Nigeria.
Straight for English - North: teacher's bk. 3, 6 bks.
299pp. col. ill. N3.00 Longman - Nig 1963 NR

Longman, Nigeria.
Straight for English - North: teacher's bk. 4, 6 bks.
112pp. col. ill. N2.30 Longman - Nig 1976 NR

Longman, Nigeria.
Straight for English - North: teacher's bk. 5, 6 bks.
168pp. col. ill. N2.20 Longman - Nig 1976 NR

Longman, Nigeria.
Straight for English - North: teacher's bk. 6, 6 bks.
104pp. col. ill. N1.65 Longman - Nig 1976 NR

Longman Rhodesia.
Alphabet cards. R$1.65 Longman - Rhod 1974 RH

Longman.
R.S.A. atlas (for primary schools) ill. R1.50 Longman
SA 1970 SA

Longman, South Africa.
Atlas for Botswana. 72pp. maps. R1.95 Longman -
SA 1974 SA

Longman, South Africa.
Atlas for Lesotho. 72pp. R1.95 Longman - SA 1974
SA

Longman, South Africa.
Atlas for Swaziland. 72pp. maps. R1.95 Longman -
SA 1974 SA

Longman, South Africa.
Izaci namaqhalo esixhosa. [Xhosa proverbs] 224pp.
R1.80 Longman SA 1954 SA XHO

Longman, South Africa.
Padiso Tswana series: Mpepi. [First primer.]. 48pp. ill.
55c. Longman SA 1961 SA TSW

Longman, South Africa.
Padiso Tswana series, Std. 1: Borathana. 1, 5 vols
72pp. ill. 80c. Longman SA 1964 SA TSW

Longman, South Africa.
Padiso Tswana series, Std. 2: Bofatlhogi. 2, 5 vols
88pp. ill. 90c. Longman SA 1966 SA TSW

Longman, South Africa.
Padiso Tswana series, Std 3: Morongwa. 3, 5 vols
96pp. ill. 90c. Longman SA 1967 SA TSW

Longman, South Africa.
Padiso Tswana series, Std 4: Molatedi. 4, 5 vols
120pp. ill. 95c. Longman SA 1969 SA TSW

Longman, South Africa.
Padiso Tswana series, Std. 5: Mothatlhami. 5, 5 vols
132pp. ill. 95c. Longman SA 1968 SA TSW

Longman, South Africa.
Padiso Tswana Series: Tshipidi. [Second Primer] 72pp.
ill. 70c. Longman SA 1963 SA TSW

Longman, South Africa.
Some famous schools in South Africa. v.1 279pp.
photos. hd. R7.50 Longman SA 1973 SA

Longman, South Africa.
Some South African edible fungi. 48pp. pl. 80c.
Longman SA 1953 SA

Longman, South Africa.
Some South African poisonous and inedible fungi. 48pp.
pl. 90c. Longman SA 1953 SA

Longman, South Africa.
Teachers' apparatus (First year wall charts) 6pp. R5.65
Longman SA 1959 SA

Longman, South Africa.
Teachers' apparatus (Second year wall charts) 6pp.
R5.65 Longman SA 1960 SA

Longman, South Africa.
Teachers guide to primary mathematics. bk. 1. 80pp.
ill. R2.20 Longman - SA 1974 SA

Longman, South Africa.
Teachers guide to primary mathematics. bk. 2. 72pp.
ill. R2.20 Longman - SA 1974 SA

Longman, South Africa.
Teachers guide to primary mathematics. bk. 4. 72pp.
ill. R2.20 Longman - SA 1973 SA

Longman, South Africa.
Teachers guide to primary mathematics. bk. 5. 80pp.
R2.20 Longman - SA 1973 SA

Longman, South Africa.
Ujock wasezindle. [Jock of the bushveld] 160pp.
R1.20 Longman SA 1962 SA XHO

Longman, South Africa.
Umathokomalisa Sikhakhana. [Zulu short stories] 80pp.
80c. Longman SA 1970 SA ZUL

Longman, Tanzania.
English for Tanzanian schools: pupils' book. 1, 7 bks
8pp. T.shs.1.25 Longman Tanz 1970 TZ

Longman, Tanzania.
English for Tanzanian schools: pupils' book. 2, 7 bks.
64pp. T.shs.5.00 Longman Tanz 1971 TZ

Longman, Tanzania.
English for Tanzanian schools: pupils' book. 4, 7 bks.
141pp. Longman Tanz 1972 TZ

Longman, Tanzania.
English for Tanzanian schools: pupils' book. 6, 7 bks.
158pp. T.shs.4.25 Longman Tanz 1971 TZ

Longman, Tanzania.
English for Tanzanian schools: pupils' book. 7, 7 bks
188pp. T.shs.4.75 Longman Tanz 1971 TZ

Longman, Tanzania.
English for Tanzanian schools: pupils' book. 123pp.
T.shs.3.75 Longman Tanz 1971 TZ

Longman, Tanzania.
English for Tanzanian schools: pupils's book. 5, 7 bks.
Longman Tanz 1973 TZ

Longman, Tanzania.
English for Tanzanian schools: teacher's book. 1, 7 bks.
49pp. photos. T.shs.10.00 Longman Tanz 1970 TZ

Longman, Tanzania.
English for Tanzanian schools: teacher's book. 2, 7 bks.
200pp. ill. T.shs.12.50 Longman Tanz 1970 TZ

Longman, Tanzania.
English for Tanzanian schools: teacher's book. 3, 7 bks.
194pp. ill. T.shs.12.50 Longman Tanz 1972 TZ

Longman, Tanzania.
English for Tanzanian schools: teacher's book. 5, 7 bks.
100pp. ill. Longman Tanz 1973 TZ

Longman, Tanzania.
English for Tanzanian schools: teacher's book. 6, 7 bks.
302pp. ill. T.shs.15.00 Longman Tanz 1967 TZ

Longman, Tanzania.
English for Tanzanian schools: teacher's book. 7, 7bks.
262pp. ill. T.shs15.00 Longman Tanz 1970 TZ

Longman, Tanzania.
English for Tanzanian schools: teacher's book. 72pp. ill.
T.shs.8.00 Longman Tanz 1972 TZ

Longman/Penguin - Southern Africa (Pty.) Ltd.
Senior atlas for southern Africa. 160pp. maps. R5.50
cl. Longman - SA 1976 SA

Lonoh Malangi Bokelenge., ed.
La marche du soleil. Poésie militante Zairoise. 40pp.
50k (CFA250) Centre Africain Litt 1974 ZR FRE

Loor, J.L.
Ngakarimojong-English dictionary. 208pp. ill. maps.
($12.00) Author (Kookeris, Matany, P.O. Kaangole,
Central Karamoja district, Uganda) 1976 UG MUL

Author Index

Loosli, J.K.   Babatunde, G.M.   Oyenuga, V.A.
Animal production in the tropics.   402pp. ill. hd. & pap.
N12.00 cl.   N5.00 pap.   Heinemann Educ - Nig 1975
NR

Lopes, H.
La nouvelle romance.   196pp.   CFA900   CLE 1976
CM FRE

Lopes, H.
Tribaliques.   2nd ed.   104pp.   CFA450   CLE 1975
CM FRE

Lord, W.B.   Baines, T.
Shifts and expedients of camp life, travel and exploration.
[Reprint of ed. 1878].   734pp. ill. cl.   R18.90
(Africana Reprint Library, 3)   Africana Book Soc 1975 SA

Loriaux, J.F.
Business economics and office practice.   3rd rev. ed.
R8.50   Juta 1977 SA

Loriaux, J.F.
The perfect private secretary.   R2.10   Juta 1968 SA

Lorimer, E.K.
Panorama of Port Elizabeth.   208pp. ill. hd.   fl. 56.25
Balkema 1971 SA

Lorofi, G.
Les aventures de Leuk-le-lièvre.   48pp.   CFA595   Nouv
Ed Afric 1975 SG FRE

Loseby, E.D.
Repeated conjugation in Closterium pritchardianum, Arch.
6pp.   15c.   (A v.15, no.1)   Univ Stellenbosch, Lib 1937
SA

Lötter, J.M.   van Tonder, J.L.
Aspects of fertility of Indian South Africans.   37pp. ill.
R1.55   (Human Sciences Research Council, S-series, 40)
Human Science Res Council 1975 SA

Lotter, J.M.   Van Tonder, J.L.
Fertility and family planning among blacks in South Africa
1974.   111pp.   R4.25   Human Science Res Council
1976 SA

Lotz, F.J.
The effect of dust on the efficacy of reflective metal foil
used as roof/ceiling insulation.   8pp.   (CSIR research
reports, 212)   CSIR 1964 SA

Lotz, F.J.   Richards, S.J.
The influence of ceiling insulation on indoor thermal
conditions in dwellings of heavy weight construction under
South African conditions.   16pp.   (CSIR research reports,
214)   CSIR 1964 SA

Lotz, F.J.
Thermal performance of lightweight structure.   27pp.
(CSIR research reports, 307)   CSIR 1971 SA

Loubiere, R.   Ette, A.
Annales de l'université d'Abidjan.   249pp.   CFA1100
(Série B - Médecine, 9)   Univ Abidjan 1974 IV FRE

Loubser, M.
Income and expenditure patterns of Bantu living under
other than family conditions in Pretoria.   116pp.   R5.00
(Bureau of Market Research, Research Reports, 18)   Bur
Market Research 1967 SA

Loubser, M.
Income and expenditure patterns of non-white urban
households, Cape Town survey (multiple Bantu
households)   See: Nel, P.A.

Loubser, M.
Income and expenditure patterns of non-white urban
households, Cape Town survey (single Bantu households)
See: Nel, P.A.

Loubser, M.
Income and expenditure patterns of non-white urban
households, Durban survey (multiple Asian households)
See: Nel, P.A.

Loubser, M.
Income and expenditure patterns of non-white urban
households, Durban survey (multiple Bantu households)
See: Nel, P.A.

Loubser, M.
Income and expenditure patterns of non-white urban
households, Durban survey (single Bantu households)
See: Nel, P.A.

Loubser, M.
Income and expenditure patterns of non-white urban
households, East London survey (multiple Bantu
households)   See: Nel, P.A.

Loubser, M.
Income and expenditure patterns of non-white urban
households, East London survey (single Bantu
households)   See: Nel, P.A.

Loubser, M.
Income and expenditure patterns of non-white urban
households, Johannesburg survey (multiple Asian
households)   See: Nel, P.A.

Loubser, M.
Income and expenditure patterns of non-white urban
households, Johannesburg survey (multiple Bantu
households)   See: Nel, P.A.

Loubser, M.
Income and expenditure patterns of non-white urban
households, Johannesburg survey (multiple coloured
households)   See: Nel, P.A.

Loubser, M.
Income and expenditure patterns of non-white urban
households, Johannesburg survey (single Bantu
households)   See: Nel, P.A.

Loubser, M.
Income and expenditure patterns of non-white urban
households, Krugersdorp survey (multiple Bantu
households)   See: Nel, P.A.

Loubser, M.
Income and expenditure patterns of non-white urban
households, Port Elizabeth survey (multiple Bantu
households)   See: Nel, P.A.

Loubser, M.
Income and expenditure patterns of non-white urban
households, Port Elizabeth survey (multiple coloured
households)   See: Nel, P.A.

Loubser, M.
Income and expenditure patterns of non-white urban
households, Port Elizabeth survey (single Bantu
households)   See: Nel, P.A.

Loubser, M.
Income and expenditure patterns of non-white urban
households, Pretoria survey (multiple Bantu households)
See: Nel, P.A.

Loubser, M.
Income and expenditure patterns of non-white urban
households, Pretoria survey (single Bantu households)
See: Nel, P.A.

Loubser, M.
Income and expenditure patterns of non-white urban
households, Tembisa survey (multiple Bantu households)
See: Nel, P.A.

Loubser, M.
Market potentials of consumer goods and services for
non-white population groups in the five main metropolitan
areas of the Republic of South Africa.   See: Moolman,
B.A.

Loubser, M.
Market potentials of consumer goods in the main
metropolitan areas of the Republic of South Africa for 1968
by population group.   294pp.   R5.00   (Bureau of
Market Research, Research Reports, 26)   Bur Market
Research 1971 SA

Loubser, M.
The minimum and supplemented living levels of non-whites
residing in the main and other selected urban areas of the
Republic of South Africa.   83pp.   R50.00   (Bureau of
Market Research, Research Reports, 47)   Bur Market
Research 1975 SA

Loubser, M.M.
Some aspects of railway mechanical engineering.
126pp. R2.00 (A v.36 no.9) Univ Stellenbosch, Lib
1961 SA

Louhoy Tety Gauz, A. et al.
Annales de l'université d'Abidjan. 171pp. CFA900
(F18.00) (Série F-Ethno-Sociologie, 1-1) Univ Abidjan
1969 IV FRE

Louis, D.
The life cycles and immature stages of the Reduviidae
Hemiptera: Heteroptera of the cocoa farms in Ghana.
65pp. pl. N2.00 (Entomological Society of Nigeria,
occas. pubs., 13) Entomological Soc - Nig 1974 NR

Lounes, M.S.
Le calcul rapide. 1, 4 pt. 24pp. DA2.00 SNED
1975 AE FRE

Lounes, M.S.
Le calcul rapide. 2, 4 pts. 32pp. DA2.00 SNED
1975 AE FRE

Lounes, M.S.
Le calcul rapide. 3, 4 pts. 32pp. DA2.00 SNED
1975 AE FRE

Lounes, M.S.
Le calcul rapide. 4, 4 pts. 32pp. DA2.00 SNED
1975 AE FRE

Louw, J.A.
The acquisition, nature and use of language. 14pp.
25c. (75c.) Univ South Africa 1957 SA

Louw, J.A. Ngidi, J. Ziervogel, D.
A handbook of the Zulu language. R3.50 Van Schaik
SA

Louw, J.A.
The nomenclature of cattle in the South-eastern
Bantu-languages. 19pp. ill. 20c. (70c.) Univ South
Africa 1957 SA

Louw, J.T.
Prehistory of the Matjes river rock shelter. 143pp.
R2.50 (Memoirs van die Nasionale Museum, 1)
Nasionale Museum 1960 SA

Louw, M., ed.
International aspects of overpopulation: proceedings of a
conference held at Jan Smuts House, Johannesburg in
1970. See: Barratt, J., ed.

Louw, W.A. Denyssen, A.J.W.
Needlework and clothing manual, standards 9-10. v. 1.
468pp. ill. R7.75 Nasou 1976 SA

Louw, W.J.
An ecological account of the vegetation of the
Potchefstroom area. 50c. (Memoirs of the Botanical
Survey of South Africa, 24) Botanical Res Inst 1951 SA

Love, J.W.
Woodwork, standard 5. See: de Wet, E.P.

Love, J.W.
Woodwork, standards 9-10. See: de Wet, E.P.

Love, R.M.
Agriculture and civilization. 17pp. C1.00
($1.00/50p.) (Inaugural lecture) Ghana UP 1972 GH

Lovedale Press.
Brownlee J. Ross. His ancestry and some writings.
109pp. 75c. Lovedale 1948 SA

Low, C.
Investigations into coatings for the protection of structural
metal in southwest Africa. See: Frank, D.

Low, C.
Investigations into coatings for timber in Southwest Africa.
See: Frank, D.

Low, C.
Investigations into the painting of wire-brushed steel.
See: Frank, D.

Low, D.A. Pratt, R.C.
Buganda and British overrule. 392pp. maps.
K.shs49.25 OUP-Nairobi 1972 KE

Lowe, J. Stanfield, D. P.
The flora of Nigeria: sedges. 144pp. ill. map. N3.00
Ibadan UP 1974 NR

Lowe, S.M.A.
The hungry veld. 181pp. R2.50 Shuter 1967 SA

Loxley, J.
Behaviour of Tanzanian money supply 1966-70 and use of
monetary indicators. 59pp. T.shs.12.00 ($3.00)
(Research pap., 71.3) Econ Res Bur - Tanz 1971 TZ

Loxley, J.
Domestic finance of development projects in Tanzania.
37pp. T.shs.12.00 ($3.00) (Research pap., 71.8)
Econ Res Bur - Tanz 1971 TZ

Loxley, J.
The monetary system of Tanzania since 1967: progress,
problems, proposals. T.shs.12.00 ($3.00) (Research
pap., 69.30) Econ Res Bur - Tanz 1974 TZ

Lubanzim.
La fille désobéissante. Mythes mbun. Versions intégrales
en trois parlers mbun avec traduction française.
See: Olung.

Lubasi, M.
Kamuyongole. [A young man who never took advice.]
44pp. ill. 25n. Neczam 1973 ZA LOZ

Lubbock, R.
Fishes of the family Pseudochromidae (Perciformes) in the
Western Indian ocean. 21pp. pl. (Ichthyological bull.,
35) Inst Ichthyology 1977 SA

Lubega, B.
The burning bush. 96pp. ill. K.shs7.65 ($2.00/95p.)
EALB 1970 KE

Lubega, B.
Cry jungle children. 79pp. ill. K.shs.6.00
($2.00/80p) EALB 1974 KE

Lubega, B.
The great animal land. ill. hd. K.shs18.50
($4.25/£2.00) EALB 1971 KE

Lubega, B.
Pot of honey. 131pp. ill. K.shs.13.00 ($3.20/£1.50)
EALB 1974 KE

Lubembe, C.K.
The inside of labour movement in Kenya. 240pp. maps.
K.shs.20.00 Equatorial KE

Lubnama, S.
Mmere ki gye tusaanira okulya. See: Kasirye, J.W.S.

Lucas, A.
Ferns of the Witwatersrand. See: Hancock, F.D.

Lucas, B.O.
Model answers on "Macbeth". See: Echebima, G.N.

Lucas, D.
Celebration. See: Hearne, B.

Lucas, D.
Dialogue with the African traditional religions. 60pp.
K.shs.9.00 (Gaba Pastoral Papers, 38) Gaba 1975 KE

Lucas, D., ed.
Development projects: church involvement in eastern
Africa. 65pp. map. K.shs.7.00 pap. (Gaba Pastoral
Papers, 18) Gaba 1971 KE

Lucas, D., ed.
Toward adult Christian community. Report on the AMECEA
Catechetical Congress, Nairobi, Kenya, 1973. 62pp. pl.
K.shs.7.50 (Gaba Pastoral Papers, 29) Gaba 1973 KE

Lucas, D.
Occupation, marriage and fertility among Nigerian women
in Lagos. 12pp. 30k (15p) Univ Lagos Bkshop
1974 NR

Lucas, D.J.
A concise 'O' level physics. 160pp. N1.90 Pilgrim
1973 NR

Author Index

Lucas, G.H.G., ed.
Conference: Driessen Report (16 & 17 October 1975). [Bi-lingual in English and Afrikaans.]. 185pp. R15.00 (R16.00) (Miscellanea Congregalia, 1) Univ South Africa 1975 SA

Lucas, J.O.
The religion of the Yorubas. 420pp. map pl. cl. N3.00 cl. CSS 1948 NR

Lucas, J.O.
Religions in West Africa and ancient Egypt. 453pp. N5.00 cl. N3.00 pap. West 1971 NR

Lucas, J.O.
Yoruba language: its structure and relationship to other languages. 168pp. pl. cl. N1.00 cl. CSS 1964 NR

Lucas, P.
Sociologie de Frantz Fanon. 224pp. DA7.00 SNED 1971 AE FRE

Lucas, S.A.
Utani na jamii ukwere. See: Sengo, T.S.Y.

Lucas, T.J.
Camp life and sport in South Africa. Experiences of Kaffir warfare with the Cape Mounted Rifles. [Reprint of ed. 1878]. 258pp. col. pl. cl. R11.85 (Africana Reprint Library series, 2) Africana Book Soc 1975 SA

Luck, A.
Charles Stokes in Africa. 203pp. photos. K.shs.20.00 (Historical Studies, 8) EAPH 1974 KE

Luckhoff, C.A.
The stapelicae of Southern Africa. 283pp. photos. hd. fl. 56.25 (£9.50/$24.00) Balkema 1952 SA

Lückhoff, H.A.
The natural distribution, growth and botanical variation of Pinus caribaea and its cultivation in South Africa. 160pp. photos. R3.50 (A v.39, no. 1) Univ Stellenbosch, Lib 1964 SA

Ludwin, V.
Rene Guillot, 1900-1969. 53pp. R2.75 Dept Bibliog, Lib & Typo 1970 SA

Lufuluabo, Fr.
Mariage coutumier et mariage chrétien indissoluble. 113pp. 40k St. Paul 1969 ZR FRE

Lufuluabo, Fr.
Valeur des religions africaines selon la Bible et Vatican II. 95pp. 25k St. Paul 1968 ZR FRE

Lugg, H.
Life under a Zulu shield. 110pp. pl. R2.25 Shuter 1975 SA

Lukacs, L.E. Vielrose, E.
A tentative projection of the structure of the Nigerian economy in 1975. 24pp. NISER 1968 NR

Lukwago, I.K.K.
Politics of national integration: the evolution of new Uganda. K.shs.36.00 Pan-african 1977 KE

Lumbwe Mudindaambi.
Objets et techniques de la vie quotidienne mbala. v.1 167pp. ill. map. (DM28.00) (CEEBA. série II, Mémoires et Monographies, 32) CEEBA 1976 ZR FRE

Lumbwe Mudindaambi.
Objets et techniques de la vie quotidienne mbala. v.2 169pp. ill. map. (DM29.00) (CEEBA. série II, Mémoires et Monographies, 33) CEEBA 1976 ZR FRE

Lumbwe Mudindaambi, W.
Mange ces dents! Recueil de mythes mbala. Textes mbala-français. 207pp. (DM24.00 pap.) (CEEBA. série II, Mémoires et Monographies, 7) CEEBA 1972 ZR FRE

Lumbwe Mudindaambi, W.
Pourquoi le coq ne chante plus? Mythes mbala. Version intégrale du texte mbala-français. 207pp. map. (DM24.00) (CEEBA. série II, Mémoires et Monographies, 8) CEEBA 1973 ZR FRE

Lurie, A.S.
Urban Africans in the Republic of South Africa, 1950-1966. 60pp. R3.10 Dept Bibliog, Lib & Typo 1969 SA

Lury, D.A.
Elementary quantitative methods. 128pp. ill. K.shs.10.00 ($3.20) EAPH 1967 KE

Lutke-Entrup, J.
Limitations and possibilities of increasing market production of peasant African cattle holders in Western Province, Zambia. 105pp. K1.50 (84p.) (Inst. African Studies, Univ. Zambia, communications, 7) Inst Afr Stud - Lusaka 1971 ZA

Luttrell, W.L.
Villagization. Cooperative prodution and rural cadres. 81pp. T.shs12.00 ($3.00) (Research pap., 71.11) Econ Res Bur - Tanz 1971 TZ

Lutu, A.D.
Paper patterns for dressmaking. See: Kirwan, E.R.

Luyomba-Tebajjanga, E. Ssekamwa, J.C.
Leonardo Da Vinci. 27pp. K.shs.1.00 ($1.25/50p.) EALB 1962 KE LUG

Lwanda, J.
Mudyazvevamwe. [The sucker.] 39pp. pl. 33c. Mambo 1976 RH SHO

Lwane, B.G. Kisia, J.G.
Kitabu chakaviri chokusoma mu Lulogooli. [A reading primer for Lulogooli schools] 3rd ed. 31pp. ill. K.shs.2.00 ($1.25/50p.) EALB l970 L KE

Lwane, B.G.
Teacher's handbook Lulogooli/Kitabu cho Mwegitsi. Vernacular scheme of work for primary I, II, III and IV. 112pp. ill. K.shs.13.25 ($4.00/£1.80) EALB 1976 KE

Lwanga, T.K., comp.
Directory of East African libraries. See: Kibwika-Bagenda, M.E.C., comp.

Lwanga, T.K., ed.
Papers presented at the fourth East African Library Association conference, Makerere University, Kampala, 16-19 September, 1970. 184pp. U.shs.8.00 (E.A.L.A. bull., 13) Mak Univ Lib 1972 UG

Lwoga, A.B., ed.
Proceedings of the third scientific conference of the Tanzania Society of Animal Production, Mwanza, May 20-22, 1976. 128pp. ill./maps. T.shs.25.00 Tanz Soc Animal Prod 1976 TZ

Ly, A.
Un navire de commerce sur la côte sénégambienne en 1635. 68pp. CFA600 (Catalogues et Documents, 17) IFAN 1964 SG FRE

Lyanga, S.K.
Biostatistics for medical students. 268pp. K.shs.135.50 cl. K.shs.65.00 pap. ($25.00/£10.00 cl.) ($15.10/£6.00 pap.) EALB 1976 KE

Lye, W.F., ed.
Andrew Smith's journal of his expedition into the interior of South Africa 1834-1836. 335pp. ill. col. pl. cl. R28.35 cl. (Dfl.85/$32.00/£16.50 cl.) Balkema 1975 SA

Lyle, M.
Photography simplified. 82pp. pl. R4.95 Shuter 1976 SA

Lynam, A.P.
Annotated bibliography and index of the geology of Zambia, 1972-1973. K1.00 Geol Survey - Zam 1977 ZA

Lynch, C.D.
A behavioural study of Blesbok 'Damaliscus dorcas phillipsi' with special reference to territoriality. 84pp. R2.50 (Memoirs van die Nasionale Museum, 8) Nasionale Museum 1974 SA

Author Index

Lyth, N.
Knitting made easy. 31pp. ill. K.shs2.00
($1.25/50p.) EALB 1963 KE

Lyth, N.
Kufuma kumefanywa rahisi. K.shs.1.50 ($1.25/50p.)
EALB 1964 KE SWA

Ma Mpolo, M.
La libération des envoûtés. 160pp. CFA1,710 CLE
1976 CM FRE

Maalu, B.
Contes populaires du Kasai. [Text in Lingala and French.].
110pp. (Littérature classique, 3) Ed Mont Noir 1974 ZR
FRE

Maasdorp, A.F.S.
The institutes of South African law: delicts, and the
dissolution of obligations. 8th ed. 4, 4 v. Juta SA

Maasdorp, G.G.
The attitudes of Indians to heavy manual work (a job
study) 40c. Dept Econ-Natal 1969 SA

Maasdorp, G.G.
Economic development for the Homelands. 41pp. 60c
($1.50) SA Inst of Race Relations 1974 SA

Maasdorp, G.G.
The educational and employment position of Indian women
in a Natal North Coast area. 40c. Dept Econ-Natal
1969 SA

Maasdorp, G.G.
A Natal Indian community. $1.50 Dept Econ-Natal
1968 SA

Maat, S.J.
Report of the committee for differentiated education and
guidance in connection with a national system of education
for handicapped pupils...etc. pt. 3, v. 8 109pp.
R1.80 Human Science Res Council 1975 SA

Mabele, R.
Agricultural credit and the development of Ujamaa villages
in Tanzania. See: Msambichaka, L.A.

Maberly, C.T.A.
The world of big game. See: Miller, P.

Mabille, A.
Southern Sotho-English dictionary. 7th. ed. 496pp. cl.
R3.00 Morija 1966 LO

Mabogunje, A.L.
Cities and social order. 36pp. ill. pl. N1.00
(Inaugural lecture) Ibadan UP 1974 NG

Mabogunje, A.L., ed. Faniran, A., ed.
Regional planning and national development in tropical
Africa. 320pp. cl. & pap. N9.00 cl. N6.00 pap.
Ibadan UP 1977 NR

Mabogunje, A.L. Omer-Cooper, J.D.
Owu in Yoruba history. 123pp. pl. ill. N2.00 Ibadan
UP 1971 NR

MacArthur, R.S. Brimble, A.R. Irvine, S.H.
The Northern Rhodesia mental ability survey 1963. 93pp.
K1.00 (50p.) (Rhodes- Livingstone communications, 27)
Inst Afr Stud - Lusaka 1964 ZA

Macartney, P.
Wildlife on your farm. 64pp. col. ill. R$1.40
Longman - Rhod 1975 RH

Macartney, W.M.
Aggrey we Africa. 86pp. cl. 50c. Shuter SA SHO

Macauley, J.I.
Motherhood and child care. 148pp. photos. N1.25
Ethiope 1972 NR

MacCormack, J., ed. Wilson, P., ed.
Conference on education and training requirements for
engineers and technicians in Sierra Leone. 81pp.
Le1.25 Fourah Bay Bkshp 1969 SL

MacDonald, A.A.M.
A contribution to a bibliography on university apartheid.
29pp. 70c. Univ Cape Town Lib 1959 SA

Macdonald, C. Ryan, O.
Objective questions in physics: with answers. 88pp.
N1.15 Pilgrim 1968 NR

Macdonald, C. Ryan, O.
Objective questions in physics: without answers. 86pp.
N1.05 Pilgrim 1968 NR

MacDonald, J.F.
The war history of southern Rhodesia, 1939-1945.
[Reprint ed. 1950]. 2, 2 v. 319pp. photos. cl.
R$14.10 cl. (Rhodesiana Reprint Library, Silver Series,
11) Books of Rhodesia 1976 RH

MacDonald, J.F.
The war history of southern Rhodesia, 1939-1945.
[Reprint of ed. 1947]. 1, 2 v. 353pp. ill. photos. maps.
cl. R$15.15 cl. (Rhodesiana Repirnt Library, Silver
Series, 10) Books of Rhodesia 1976 RH

Macdonald, R.
Nyasaland to Malawi. 332pp. K.shs.48.00 ($13.00)
EAPH 1975 KE

Macdonald, R.J.
From Nyasaland to Malawi. 316pp. K.shs.48.00
($12.00) EAPH 1976 KE

Macdonald, S.
Sally in Rhodesia. [Reprint ed. 1927]. 207pp. ill. cl.
R$4.95 cl. (Rhodesiana Reprint Library, Gold Series, 11)
Books of Rhodesia 1970 RH

Macdowell, C.
An introduction to the problems of land ownership in
Northern Nigeria. 35pp. 50k (40p./$1.00) Inst
Admin - Zaria 1966 NR

Macgoye, M.O.
Murder in Majengo. 140pp. K.shs13.00 OUP-Nairobi
1972 KE

Macgregor, D.R.
Non-traditional food sources for feeding increasing
populations. 12pp. C1.00 ($1.00/50p.) (Inaugural
lecture) Ghana UP 1972 GH

Machanik, A.
Herbs and spices for all seasoning. 340pp. R4.80 cl.
Haum 1973 SA

Machanik, A.
Nutritious dishes that replace meats and fishes. 111pp.
cl. R5.00 cl. HAUM 1974 SA

Machiavelli, N.
Mtawala. [The Prince] 137pp. K.shs.7.00 ($2.60)
EAPH 1968 KE SWA

Machichi, D.A.
Les immeubles et le droit commercial. 384pp.
Dir34.00 Ed Maghreb 1975 MR FRE

Machichi, D.A.
Manuel de droit pénal général. 648pp. Dir30.00 Ed
Maghreb 1975 MR FRE

Machimbira, T.J.
Gondoharishari. [A hawk picks anything for food.]
84pp. pl. 65c Longman - Rhod 1975 RH SHO

Macintosh, E.K.
A guide to the rocks, minerals and gemstones of Southern
Africa. 80pp. R3.95 Struik 1975 SA

Macintosh, J.C.
The law of agency in South Africa. See: De Villiers, J.E.

Macintosh, J.C.
Negligence in delict. 5th ed. R25.00 Juta 1970 SA

Mackenzie, J.K.
Mwekuru Mwaria. [Hygiene stories] 2nd ed. 51pp. ill.
K.shs.1.00 ($1.25/50p–) EALB 1960 KE MER

Mackenzie, M.K.
Present location and past diffusion of the flue-cured
tobacco industry in West Nile district. 195pp.
U.shs.25.00 (Occas. paps., 21) Dept Geog - Mak 1971
UG

Mackenzie, N.H.
The outlook for English in Central Africa. 31pp. 30c
Univ Rhodesia Lib 1960 RH

Mackin.
Exercises in English patterns and usage. 1, 5 bks 56pp. 60k OUP-Nig 1960 NR

Mackin.
Exercises in English patterns and usage. 2, 5 bks 60pp. 60k OUP-Nig 1961 NR

Mackin.
Exercises in English patterns and usage. 3, 5 bks 60pp. 60k OUP-Nig 1962 NR

Mackin.
Exercises in English patterns and usage. 5, 5 bks 60pp. 60k OUP-Nig 1966 NR

Mackin.
Exercises in English patterns and usage: book 4. 4, 5 bks 68pp. 60k OUP-Nig 1966 NR

Maclean, J.
A compendium of Kafir laws and customs, including genealogical tables of Kafir chiefs and various tribal census returns. [Reprint of ed. Grahamstown, 1906] 171pp. R3.50 (Reprints, 30) State-Lib-SA 1968 SA

Maclean, J.
The guardians. 304pp. ill. pl. cl. R$6.70 Books of Rhodesia 1974 RH

Macleod, G.
Church union and social concern. 50c. (Peter Ainslie Memorial lec., 4) Rhodes Univ Lib 1951 SA

Maclin, A.
Useful Swahili. 164pp. K.shs.10.50 Evangel 1973 KE

Macmillan, M.
Sir Henry Barkly, mediator and moderator, 1815-1898. 310pp. pl. hd. fl. 33.75 (South African biographical and historical studies, 5) Balkema 1970 SA

Macmillan, Nigeria.
Introduction to decimal currency and metric units for teachers and parents. 32pp. ill. 30k Macmillan 1972 NR

Macmillan Nigeria Publishers.
New onward copy books. Teacher's handwriting. bk. 1 46pp. 60k Macmillan 1973 NR

Macmillan Nigeria Publishers.
New onward copy books. Teacher's handwriting. bk. 2 30pp. 60k Macmillan 1973 NR

Macmillan, R.G., ed. Macquarrie, J.W., ed. Hey, P.D., ed.
Education and our expanding horizons. 534pp. photos. cl. R3.25 Univ of Natal 1960 SA

Macmillan, R.G.
Education in South Africa. See: Behr, A.L.

Macmillan, W. M.
My South African years: an autobiography. 272pp. R8.40 Philip 1975 SA

Macmillan, W.H.
The Cape colour question: a historical survey. 320pp. hd. fl. 27.00 No UK, No US (South African biographical and historical studies, 2) Balkema 1968 SA

MacMillan, W.M.
The South African agrarian problem and its historical development. Reprint of 1919 ed. 104pp. R2.30 (Reprints, 68) State Lib - SA 1974 SA

Macnab, R.
The French colonel: Villebois-Mareuil and the Boers 1899-1900. 337pp. photos. maps. cl. R11.70 OUP - Sa 1975 SA

Macnae, W., ed. Kalk, M., ed.
A natural history of Inhaca Island, Mozambique. rev. ed. 163pp. ill. pl. cl. R10.00 Witwatersrand UP 1969 SA

Macnamara, M.
The falls run back. R2.65 ($3.30/£1.75) Ravan 1972 SA

Macnamara, M.
Philosophy, life and meaning. 28pp. R1.50 (R2.00) (Miscellanea, 7) Univ South Africa 1976 SA

MacPherson, F.
Kenneth Kaunda of Zambia: the times and the man. 496pp. photos. cl. & pap. K2.50 pap. K4.00 cl. OUP - Lusaka 1974 ZA

Macpherson, F.
One blood. 176pp. K1.50 Neczam 1970 ZA

Macpherson, F.
One finger. 382pp. K4.00 Neczam 1974 ZA

Macpherson, G.
First steps in village mechanisation. 224pp. ill. T.shs.35.00 ($8.50) Tanz Publ House 1975 TZ

Macpherson, G.A.
Namna ya kujitengenezea gari la gurudumu moja. [How to make a wheel barrow.] 58pp. ill. (Vitabu vya ufundi, 1) Tanz Publ House 1975 TZ SWA

Macpherson, M. Kironde, E.C.N.
Let's make a play. 44pp. ill. K.shs.3.00 ($1.50/60p.) EALB 1960 KE

Macquarrie, J.W., ed.
Education and our expanding horizons. See: Macmillan, R.G., ed.

Maczka, L. Cap, M.
Brick clays in the Kasama area with particular reference to the Lukashya deposit. K2.00 (Dept. of Geological Survey, Economic Reports, 43) Geol Survey - Zam 1976 ZA

Maczka, L.
Brick clays in the Mansa area. See: Legg, C.A.

Maczka, L. Cap, M.
The Mkushi river illite clays. 50n (Dept. of Geological Survey. Economic Reports, 30) Geol Survey - Zam 1972 ZA

Madala, A.
Amavo amafutshane. [Essays] 72pp. 80c OUP-SA 1965 SA XHO

Madala, A.
Okusemgoka ngokufundisa ibhayibheli: standard 3. 48pp. ill. 50c OUP-SA 1965 SA ZUL

Madala, A.
Okusemgoka ngokufundisa ibhayibheli: standard 4. 112pp. ill. 70c OUP-SA 1967 SA ZUL

Madala, A.
Okusemgoka ngokufundisa ibhayibheli: standard 5. 64pp. ill. 50c OUP-SA 1965 SA ZUL

Madala, A.
Okusemgoka ngokufundisa ibhayibheli: standard 6. 64pp. ill. 50c OUP-SA 1965 SA ZUL

Madauchi, I. Isa, Y. Daura, B.
Hausa customs. 108pp. N1.75 Northern Nig 1968 NR

Made, E.H.A.
Indlalife Yaseharrisdale. [The heir of Harrisdale.] 173pp. R1.80 Shuter 1975 SA ZUL

Made, E.H.A.
Isizula senganyama. Ibanga, 5 See: Buthelezi, G.G.N.C.

Made, E.H.A.
Isizulu sengonyama. Ibanga, 1 See: Buthelezi, G.G.N.C.

Made, E.H.A.
Isizulu sengonyama. Ibanga, 2 See: Buthelezi, G.G.N.C.

Made, E.H.A.
Isizulu sengonyama. Ibanga, 3 See: Buthelezi, G.G.N.C.

Made, E.H.A.
Isizulu sengonyama. Ibanga, 4 See: Buthelezi, G.G.N.C.

Made, E.H.A.
Isizulu sengonyama. Ibanga, 6 See: Buthelezi, G.G.N.C.

Author Index

Made, S.M., comp.　Jackson, R., comp.　Mangoche Mbewe, M.V.B., comp.
　100 years of Chichewa in writing, 1875-1975. A select bibliography.　87pp.　(Univ. of Malawi Library Publication, 4)　Univ Malawi Lib 1976 MW

Made, S.M., ed.　Brown, T.M., ed.
　Directory of Malawi libraries.　112pp.　K1.25 (Univ. of Malawi Library Publication, 3)　Univ Malawi Lib 1976 MW

Madge, D.　Sharma, G.
　Soil zoology.　54pp. pl. ill.　N2.05　Ibadan UP 1969 NR

Mading, F.
　Dynamics of identification.　128pp.　70pt.　($3.00) Khartoum UP 1973 SJ

Mado, H.R.M.
　Complaintes d'un forçat.　124pp.　CFA450　CLE 1970 CM FRE

Madongorere S.
　Moto muziso.　[Self inflicted troubles.]　19pp. pl.　12c. Rhod Lit Bur 1976 RH SHO

Madou, H.
　Réserves de quelques gîtes de fondants feldspatiques de Côte d'Ivoire (Baba, Dienou Anombakro) 15pp. CFA800　(SODEMI rapport, 249)　SODEMI 1969 IV FRE

Maduekwe, J.C.
　Dinta.　[Igbo reader.]　107pp.　N1.65　OUP - Nig 1975 NR IGB

Maes, Y.M.　Andes, B.M.
　Agricultural studies for Lesotho.　296pp. ill. cl.　R2.80 Mazenod Inst 1975 LO

Mafeje, A.
　Langa: a study of social groups in an African township. See: Wilson, M.

Magaji, D.J.
　Essentials of Gwari grammar.　See: Hyman, L.M.

Magalli, M., ed.
　A practical guidebook to Cairo.　See: Cowley, D., ed.

Magande, B.K.
　Kilimo cha minazi.　[Coconut planting.]　37pp.　Tanz Publ House 1975 TZ SWA

Magande, B.K.　Chum, H.
　Kilimo cha minazi.　[Coconut cultivation.]　37pp. ill. T.shs.7.00　Tanz Publ House 1975 TZ SWA

Magbagbeola, J.A.O.
　Pain.　N1.00　(Inaugural lecture)　Ibadan UP 1977 NR

Magesa, L.
　The church and liberation in Africa.　55pp.　K.shs.10.00 (Spearhead series, 44)　Gaba 1976 KE

Magesa, S.M.
　Ole Ulimwenguni.　[Woe to the world]　52pp. T.shs.2.50　Africa Inland Church 1973 TZ SWA

Magesa, S.M.
　Usiingie.　[Do not enter.]　16pp.　T.shs.2.00　Africa Inland Church 1975 TZ SWA

Magona, A.
　Objective questions in East African geography.　50pp. K.shs.11.50 pap.　Heinemann Educ - Nair 1976 KE

Magona, J.
　Ulundi lama Phupha.　[Poems]　64pp.　65c　OUP-SA 1965 SA XHO

Magré, P.
　L'ancien testament.　64pp.　CFA150　(Cahier biblique, enseignement secondaire, 2)　CLE 1970 CM FRE

Magré, P.
　Le mariage chrétien.　48pp.　CFA150　CLE 1972 CM FRE

Mahabane, E.E.
　The urgent need for fundamental change in South Africa. 1977 presidential address.　11pp.　60c.　($1.40)　SA Inst of Race Relations 1977 SA

Mahanya, M.
　Rufu runobereka rufu.　56pp.　65c.　Longman - Rhod 1976 RH SHO

Mahanya, M.
　Rufu runobereka rufu.　[Death begets death.]　54pp. pl. 65c.　Longman - Rhod 1976 RH SHO

Maharaj, M.D.
　Socio-economic study of Chatsworth.　See: Du Toit, A.S.

Mahfuz, M.
　Miramar.　tr. Arabic by Fatma Moussa Mahmoud. Rev. and ed. by Magid el Kommos and John Rodenbeck 160pp.　£E3.00　($6.50)　Am Univ 1975 UA

Mahieu, F., comp.
　Guide des bibliothèques et centres de documentation de Yaoundé.　See: Chateh, P., comp

Mahiga, A.P.　Tumbo, N.S., et al.
　Labour in Tanzania.　96pp.　T.shs.15.00　($3.00) (Tanzania Studies series, 5)　Tanz Publ House 1976 TZ

Mahimbi, E.M.
　Usakubimbi wa mganga.　[The tricks of a witch doctor.] 64pp. ill.　T.shs.3.90　Ndanda Mission Press 1975 TZ SWA

Mahlangu, P.
　Ndebele.　Grade 3: Ngena kwezimnandi.　104pp.　70c. Longman - Rhod 1970 RH NDE

Mahlangu, P.
　Ndebele.　Grade 4: Qhubeka ngezimnandi　120pp. 70c.　Longman - Rhod 1970 RH NDE

Mahlangu, P.
　Ndebele.　Grade 5: Phutsha kwezimnandi.　128pp. 70c.　Longman - Rhod 1971 RH NDE

Mahlangu, P.
　Uncagu kambena.　116pp.　90c pap.　Longman - Rhod 1974 RH NDE

Mahlasela, B.E.N.
　A general survey of Xhosa literature from its early beginnings in the 1800's to the present.　25c　(Rhodes University, Dept. of African Languages, Working Papers series, 2)　Dept African Lang - Rhodes 1973 SA

Mahlasela, B.E.N.
　Jolobe - Xhosa poet and writer.　50c　(Rhodes University, Dept. of African Languages, Working Papers series, 3)　Dept African Lang - Rhodes 1973 SA

Mahlasela, B.E.N.
　Some Xhosa idioms and expressions.　50c　(Rhodes University, Dept. of African Languages, Working Papers series, 1)　Dept African Lang - Rhodes 1973 SA

Mahood, M.M.
　The place of English studies in an African university. An inaugural lecture.　8pp.　20k　Ibadan UP 1955 NR

Maillot, D.
　Le régime administratif du cinéma au Maroc.　Dir25.00 (Coll. Fac. des Sciences juridiques, économiques et sociales, 13)　Ed La Porte 1961 MR FRE

Maillu, D.
　Kisalu and his fruit garden.　64pp. ill.　K.shs3.00 ($1.00)　EAPH 1972 KE

Maillu, D.G.
　After 4.30.　220pp.　K.shs.13.00　($3.00)　(Comb Books in English, 2)　Comb Books 1974 KE

Maillu, D.G.
　Chupa, mpenzi!　[Translation of "My dear bottle".] 193pp.　K.shs.12.00　($2.40)　(Comb Books in Kiswahili, 1)　Comb Books 1975 KE SWA

Maillu, D.G.
　Dear daughter.　59pp.　K.shs.6.00 pap.　($1.20 pap.) (Letters, 2)　Comb Books 1976 KE

Maillu, D.G.
　Dear Monika.　64pp.　K.shs.6.00 pap.　($1.20 pap.) (Letters, 1)　Comb Books 1976 KE

Maillu, D.G.
　Kadosa.　190pp.　K.shs.15.00　($3.00)　(Comb Books in English, 12)　Comb Books 1977 KE

Maillu, D.G.
The kommon man. pt. 1 290pp. K.shs.15.00
($3.00) (Comb Books in English, 5) Comb Books 1975
KE

Maillu, D.G.
The kommon man. pt. 2 300pp. K.shs.15.00
($3.00) (Comb Books in English 6) Comb Books 1975
KE

Maillu, D.G.
The kommon man. pt. 3. 259pp. K.shs.15.00
($3.00) (Comb Books in English, 7) Comb Books 1976
KE

Maillu, D.G.
Kujenga na kubomoa. [To build and to destroy.]
154pp. K.shs.12.00 ($2.40) (Comb Books in
Kiswahili, 5) Comb Books 1976 KE SWA

Maillu, D.G.
My dear bottle. 167pp. K.shs.12.00 ($2.40) (Comb
Books in English, 1) Comb Books 1974 KE

Maillu, D.G.
No. 148pp. K.shs.10.00 pap. ($2.00 pap.) (Mini
Novels, 3) Comb Books 1976 KE

Maillu, D.G.
One by one. See: Maina, A.

Maillu, D.G.
Troubles. 187pp. K.shs.10.00 ($2.00) (Mini Novels,
2) Comb Books 1974 KE

Maillu, D.G.
Unfit for human consumption. 93pp. K.shs.6.00
($1.20) (Mini Novels, 1) Comb Books 1973 KE

Maina, A. Maillu, D.G.
One by one. 125pp. K.shs.12.00 pap. ($2.40 pap.)
(Comb Books in English, 3) Comb Books 1975 KE

Maina, C.G., ed.
Report of the third conference of directors of institutes of
public administration in the commonwealth, held at the
Kenya institute of Administration, 13-17th April 1970.
K.shs.25.00 Kenya Inst Admin 1974 KE

Maina, G.
The use and abuse of drugs and chemical in tropical
Africa. Proceedings of the 1973 annual scientific
conference of the East African Medical Research Council,
Nairobi. See: Bagshawe, A.F.

Maini, K.M.
Cooperatives and law: with special emphasis on Kenya.
hd. K.shs.49.00 hd. ($10.00/£4.00) EALB 1972 KE

Maire, C.D.
Connaître Dieu pour mieux le servir. 192pp. CFA300
CPE 1972 IV FRE

Maire, R. Monod, T.
Etudes sur la flore et la végétation du Tibesti. [Reprint of
ed. Paris, 1950]. 141pp. ill. pl. (D.fl.50.00)
(Mémoires de l'IFAN, 8) IFAN 1950 SG FRE

Maison Tunisienne de l'Edition.
Les mosques de Tunisie. 176pp. ill. D1,600 Maison
Tunis 1973 TI FRE

Maison Tunisienne de l'Edition.
Septembre 1934-Repression et resistence. 472pp.
D2.600 Maison Tunis 1973 TI FRE

Maison Tunisienne d'Edition.
Bourguiba raconté aux enfants. 50pp. D1,500
Maison Tunis 1974 TI FRE

Maison Tunisienne d'Edition.
Cendrillon. 16pp. D0.300 Maison Tunis 1975 TI FRE

Maison Tunisienne d'Edition.
Omar el Khayyam. 80pp. D1.000 Maison Tunis 1972
TI FRE

Maison Tunisienne d'Edition.
Le petit chaperon rouge. 16pp. D0.300 Maison Tunis
1975 TI FRE

Maisonneuve, J.
Annales de l'université d'Abidjan. 131pp. CFA1400
pap. (F28.00 pap.) (Série C-Sciences, 8) Univ Abidjan
1972 IV FRE

Maitha, J., ed.
Agricultural development in Kenya: an economic
assessment. See: Heyer, J., ed.

Maitha, J.K.
Coffee in the Kenya economy. An econometric analysis.
88pp. K.shs.15.00 ($3.80/£1.80) EALB 1974 KE

Majasan, J.A., ed.
New dimensions in Nigerian high school geography:
papers presented at the 1969 High School Geography
conference at the University of Ibadan. 206pp. N1.50
Inst Educ-Ib 1971 NR

Majasan, J.A.
Guide map of Ibadan. 54pp. map. 75k (Inst. of Ed.
occas. pub., 8) Inst Educ-Ib 1968 NR

Majasan, J.A. Crowder, M.
A guide map of Ife. 6pp. 10k Univ Ife Press 1969
NR

Majasan, J.A.
Indigenous education and progress in developing
countries. 20pp. N1.00 (Inaugural lecture) Ibadan
UP 1974 NG

Majmundar, J.
Contribution à l'étude minéralogique et géochimique des
pyroxénites à phlogopite et dans les charnockites du
sud-est de Madagascar. 130pp. FMG910 (F18.20)
Service Geol - Mad 1962 MG FRE

Makaba ma Khiedi Nkiama.
Bibliographie sélective sur le Mayombe (Bas-Zaire) 93pp.
Z3.00 ($2.40) (Cahiers du CRIDE, Nouvelle série, IV, 1
& 2)) CRIDE 1976 ZR FRE

Makaidi, E.J.E.
Mbinu za ukatibu mahsusi. [Guide book for personal
secretaries.] 122pp. T.shs.10.00 Longman - Tanz
1975 TZ

Makani, O.
Ndakatongwa ne Nyika mbiri. [I am judged by two
worlds.] 94pp. 90c. Mambo 1976 RH SHO

Makarfi, S.
Jatau Na Kyallu. [Jatau and Kyallu] 52pp. N1.10
Northern Nig 1970 NR HAU

Makarfi, S.
Zamanin Nan Namu. [This World of ours] 88pp. 40k
Northern Nig 1970 NR HAU

Makari, C.S.
Sarura wako. 124pp. 60c. Longman - Rhod 1971
RH SHO

Makashi, J.N.
Inyimbo sha Cibemba. [Bemba songs] 34pp. 45n.
Neczam 1971 ZA BEM

Makaula, D.Z.
Umadzikane okanye imbali yamaBhaca [Novel]. 84pp.
map. 80c OUP-SA 1966 SA XHO

Makerere University Library.
Annotated list of theses submitted to the University of East
Africa and held by Makerere University Library. 52pp.
U.shs10.00 Mak Univ Lib 1970 UG

Makerere University Library.
Serials union list: Makerere University libraries. 351pp.
U.shs.20.00 Mak Univ Lib 1971 UG

Makerere University Library.
Union list of scientific and technical periodicals in East
African libraries. 287pp. U.shs.15.00 Mak Univ Lib
1969 UG

Makhalisa, B.C.
Qilindini. [You crafty person.] 123pp. pl. 70c
Longman - Rhod 1974 RH NDE

Makhaye, N.J.
Isoka lakwaZulu. [Zulu poems] 163pp. cl. R1.60
(Bantu treasury, 18) Witwatersrand U.P. 1972 SA ZUL

Makin, A.E.
The 1820 settlers of Salem.   R7.50   Juta 1971 SA

Makonnen, R.
Pan-Africanism from within as recorded and edited by Kenneth King.   316pp. photos. cl. & pap.   K.shs58.50 cl.   K.shs41.00 pap.   OUP-Nairobi 1972 KE

Makouta, J.P.
En quête de la liberté.   168pp.   CFA510   CLE 1970 CM FRE

Makouta, J.P.
Les initiés.   98pp.   CFA300   CLE 1970 CM FRE

Makouta-Mboukou, J.P.
L'âme bleue.   112pp.   CFA400   CLE 1971 CM FRE

Makubalo, F.Z.
Yakhani isizwe senu [Novel].   128pp.   R1.50   OUP-SA 1971 SA XHO

Makubalo, P.M.   Jakuja.
Imagaqo yentetho yesixhosa.   80pp.   R1.05   Longman SA 1965 SA XHO

Makubalo, P.M.   Jakuja.
Uncuthu Lwesixhosa.   [Xhosa language book]   112pp.   R1.50   Longman SA 1965 SA XHO

Makumbi, A. J.
Maliro ndi miyambo ya Achewa.   [On Chewa burial customs]   60pp. ill.   75t (37p)   Longman - Mal 1975 MW CHC

Makumi, J.
The children of the forest.   40pp. ill.   K.shs2.50 ($1.00)   EAPH 1969 KE

Makumi, J.
End of the beginning.   38pp. ill.   K.shs3.50 ($1.50)   EAPH 1970 KE

Makumi, J.
The feather in the lake.   32pp. ill.   K.shs2.50 ($1.00)   EAPH 1969 KE

Makumi, K.
The good medicine bird.   52pp. ill.   K.shs.7.00 pap.   Longman - Ken 1976 KE

Makunile, E.C., ed.
Christian press in Africa: voice of human concern.   61pp. hd.   70n   Multimedia 1973 ZA

Makura, T.
Vatete vachabvepi.   [The aunt's advice is no longer available.]   55pp. pl.   40c.   Mambo 1976 RH SHO

Malaba, G.
Ndebele. Grade 7: Kholiwe.   96pp.   70c.   Longman - Rhod 1970 RH NDE

Malaba, G.
Ndebele. Teacher's bk. grade 7.   64pp.   R$1.10   Longman - Rhod 1977 RH NDE

Malaba, G.
Ulunguza.   128pp.   65c.   Longman - Rhod 1968 RH NDE

Malagala, E.
Engero zikuwoomera.   4th ed.   35pp. ill.   K.shs.12.80 ($1.50/60p.)   EALB 1977 KE LUG

Malaku, A.   Rogers, J.
Introductory teacher's notes for book one: Section A, English language teaching.   228pp. ill.   B2.80   (The New Oxford English Course, 1)   OUP-Addis 1967 ET

Malaku, A.   Roger, J.
Pupil's book.   36pp. ill.   B.85c.   (The New Oxford English Course, 1)   OUP-Addis 1965 ET

Malaku, A.   Rogers, J.
Pupil's book.   52pp. ill.   B1.50   (The New Oxford English Course, 2)   OUP-Addis 1967 ET

Malaku, A.   Rogers, J.
Teacher's notes for book one: Section B, English activity periods.   208pp. ill.   B2.80   (The New Oxford English Course, 1)   OUP-Addis 1966 ET

Malan, J.E.
The physical anthropology of the Bushmen 1930-1962.   24pp.   60c.   Univ Cape Town Lib 1967 SA

Malan, R.
Drama-teach: drama-in-education, and theatre for young people.   144pp. hd.   R3.60   Philip 1973 SA

Malan, R., ed.
Inscapes: a collection of relevant verse.   224pp.   R2.95   OUP-SA 1972 SA

Malan, R., ed.
Outridings: a collection of verse for the first year in the high school.   135pp.   R2.40   OUP-SA 1972 SA

Malan, R., ed.
Play workshop: 10 one-act plays.   206pp.   R3.95   OUP-SA 1972 SA

Malan, T.   Hattingh, P.S.
Black homelands in South Africa.   255pp. ill. pl. maps col. maps.   R5.00   (R6.00)   Africa Inst 1976 SA

Malan, T.
Source material on labour earnings in African countries.   36pp.   R1.00   (R1.20 pap.)   Africa Inst - Pret 1975 SA

Malanda, D.
Le développement mental des enfants sourds-muets à Bandundu (Zaire)   168pp.   Z3.50   Press Univ Zaire 1974 ZR FRE

Malandra, A.
A new Acholi grammar.   K.shs7.00   ($2.25/90p.)   EALB 1955 KE

Malcolm, D.M., ed.
The diary of Henry Francis Fynn.   See: Stuart, J., ed.

Malcolm, D.M.
English and Zulu dictionary.   1, 2 pts.   See: Doke, C.M.

Malcolm, D.M.
English-Zulu dictionary.   2, 2 pts.   See: Doke, C.M.

Malcolm, D.M.
Zulu-English vocabulary.   See: Doke, C.M.

Malek, A.A.
L'armée dans la nation.   439pp.   DA40.00   SNED 1975 AE FRE

Malek, A.A.   Hanafi, H.   Belal, A.A.
Renaissance du monde arabe.   551pp.   DA23.00   SNED 1972 AE FRE

Maletnlema, T.N.
Are you too fat? [In English and Swahili].   [Je, una kiriba - tumbo?]   112pp.   K.shs.8.45 ($3.40/£1.40)   EALB 1976 KE

Maletnlema, T.N.
Utunzaji wa mama na watoto vijijini.   [Rural mother and child care]   270pp. ill.   K.shs.18.00 ($4.25/£1.70)   EALB 1970 KE SWA

Maley, A.
The chief's counsellors.   48pp. ill.   45k (African Junior Library, 4)   Pilgrim 1971 NR

Malgras, D.
La coopération en secteur rural traditionnel.   3 pts.   140pp.   CFA900   INADES 1968 IV FRE

Malherbe, E.G.
Education in South Africa. [Reprint of ed. 1925].   2 v.   R15.00 set   Juta 1973 SA

Malherbe, I. de V.
Soil fertility.   5th ed.   316pp. photos.   R3.90   OUP-SA 1964 SA

Malherbe, P.N.
Multistan: a way out of the South African dilemma.   184pp. cl.   R4.95   Philip 1974 SA

Malherbe, V.C.
Eminent Victorians in South Africa.   R7.50   Juta 1972 SA

Malherbe, W.A.
Chronological bibliography of hockey.   rev. ed.   gratis   Johannesburg Public Lib 1965 SA

Malima, K.A.
Cotton, agricultural and general economic growth.   34pp.   T.shs12.00   ($3.00)   (Research pap., 71.10)   Econ Res Bur - Tanz 1971 TZ

Malima, K.A.
Determinants of cotton supply in Tanzania. 30pp.
T.shs.12.00 ($3.00) (Research pap., 71.4) Econ Res
Bur - Tanz 1971 TZ

Malima, K.A.
Economics of cotton production in Tanzania. 24pp.
T.shs.12.00 ($3.00) (Research pap., 70.20) Econ Res
Bur - Tanz 1970 TZ

Malima, K.A.
Self-reliance, East African Community and trade policy.
10pp. T.shs.12.00 ($3.00) (Research pap., 70.21)
Econ Res Bur - Tanz 1970 TZ

Malima, K.A.
Subsistence accounting and development planning in
Africa. 19pp. ill. T.shs.12.00 ($3.00) (Research
pap., 70.14) Econ Res Bur - Tanz 1970 TZ

Malimoto, P.G.
Bless the wicked. 86pp. K.shs.7.00 ($3.25)
(African Leisure Library, 1) Foundation 1974 KE

Maliti, S.
Tanzania treaty practice. See: Seaton, E.

Mallows, E.W.N.
Pre-European settlement patterns in Africa south of the
Sahara. 40c. (Isma paps., 13) Inst Study of Man
1963 SA

Mallows, E.W.N.
Teaching a technology. 94pp. cl. R5.00
Witwatersrand UP 1971 SA

Malmberg, B.
Linguistic barriers to communication in the modern world.
52pp. 20k Ibadan UP 1960 NR

Malone, R.L.
The sounds of English. 65pp. ill. K.shs.6.00 ($2.30)
EAPH 1970 KE

Malong, R.
Ah big yaws? 2nd ed. 64pp. hd. R2.40 Philip 1975
SA

Malu Wa Kalenga.
Les utilisations de l'energie nucléaire. Cas de l'Afrique.
217pp. Z18.00 Press Univ Zaire 1977 ZR FRE

Maluba, G.
Ndebele. Grade G: Sekusile. 112pp. 70c. Longman
- Rhod 1969 RH NDE

Malula, J.A.
L'église de Dieu qui est à Kinshasa vous parle. 31pp.
30k St. Paul 1976 ZR FRE

Malula, J.A.
Je crois en Jésus Christ. Qu'est-ce cette foi change à ma
vie? 47pp. 40k St. Paul 1976 ZR FRE

Malulu, S.M.
Maana ya namba saba. [The meaning of number 7.]
23pp. T.shs.2.00 Africa Inland church 1973 TZ SWA

Malumfashi, G.D.
Amfanin Abinci. [The usefulness of food] 20pp. 10k
Northern Nig 1970 NR HAU

Malumo, J.M., ed.
University of Zambia handbook on research for the year
1974. 110pp. K1.75 Univ Zambia Bkshop 1975 ZA

Malumo, J.M., ed.
University of Zambia. Report on research for the years
1973-1974. 73pp. K1.00 Univ Zambia Bkshop 1975
ZA

Malusi, M., ed.
Black viewpoint 2: Detente. 150pp. R1.50 Black
Comm. Prog 1975 SA

Malya, S.
Babu Simulia. [Grandfather Simulia.] 50pp. ill. Tanz
Publ House 1975 TZ SWA

Malya, S.
Traditional oral literature: procuring post-literacy reading
materials and capturing culture. 16pp. T.shs.1.60
(Studies in Adult Education, 10) Inst Adult Educ - Dar
1974 TZ

Malya, S.
What will our literacy graduates read: a case study.
T.shs.1.00 (Studies in Adult Education, 17) Inst Adult
Educ - Dar 1975 TZ

Mambwe, A.K.
Manzo mwanyike wa Kikaonde. [Manzo, a Kaonde boy]
32pp. ill. 45n. Neczam 1971 ZA KAO

Mameri, K.
Citations du président Boumediene. 424pp. DA8.00
pap. SNED 1975 AE FRE

Mammeri, K.
Les Nations Unies face à la question algérienne. 222pp.
DA8.00 SNED 1970 AE FRE

Mamuya, S.J.
Jando na unyago. [Sex education] 242pp. ill.
K.shs.12.50 ($3.60) EAPH 1972 KE SWA

Mamuya, S.J.
Maarifa mapya ya kuelemisha afya. [New methods of
teaching health] 2nd ed. 232pp. ill. K.shs.6.15
($2.00/80p.) EALB 1971 KE SWA

Mamuya, S.J.
Ujana. [Youth.] 116pp. K.shs.12.50 Transafrica
1974 KE SWA

Mamuya, S.J.
Utu uzima. [Adulthood.] 96pp. K.shs.12.50
Transafrica 1975 KE SWA

Mamuya, S.J.
Uzazi wa majira. [Family planning.] 36pp. ill. Nat
Print Co 1975 TZ SWA

Manda Kizabi.
Contribution à l'étude psycho-pédagogique de
l'arithmétique au niveau de la 6ème année primaire à
Kinshasa. Z3.00 ($2.40) CRIDE 1977 ZR FRE

Mandao, M.
Alone in the city. 24pp. ill. 50pes. (16p.) Africa
Christian 1969 GH

Mandao, M.
Ani afungua mkoba wake. [Ani opens her purse.] 30pp.
ill. T.shs.2.00 Central Tanganyika TZ SWA

Mandao, M.
Ani opens her purse. 28pp. ill. 45pes. (15p.)
Africa Christian 1971 GH

Mandao, M.
Musa. [Children's book.] ill. T.shs.2.00 Central
Tanganyika 1969 TZ SWA

Mandao, M.
Peke yangu mjini. [Alone in the city.] 29pp. ill.
T.shs.2.50 Central Tanganyika 1969 TZ SWA

Mandao, M.
Seule dans la ville. 60pp. ill. CFA300 CPE 1975 IV
FRE

Mandao, M.
Tupigane na safura. [Let us fight against hookworms]
17pp. ill. K.shs.1.50 ($1.25/50p.) EALB 1967 KE
SWA

Mandao, M.
Zowawa za m'tauni. [The evils of city life.] 32pp. 10t.
Christ Lit Assoc - Mal 1973 MW CHC

Mandao, M.
Zowawa za ndalama. [Money and its evils.] 48pp. ill.
15t. Christ Lit Assoc - Mal 1973 MW CHC

Mandebvu, S.
Ndochema naani. [It's all my fault.] 118pp. pl. 70c
Longman - Rhod 1974 RH SHO

Mandelbrote, J.C.
The Cape press 1838-1850. 73pp. 90c. Univ Cape
Town Lib 1950 SA

Mandersloot, W.G.B.
The CSIR mark 3 electrodialysis unit. See: Hicks, R.E.

Mandery, G.
La radio scolaire au service de l'enseignement du français
au Sénégal. 13pp. CFA125 (C.L.A.D. Etude, 39 bis)
CLAD 1969 SG FRE

Martins, J.H.
Income and expenditure patterns of urban Indian households in Johannesburg. 120pp. R80.00 (Bureau of Market Research, Research Reports, 50.7) Bur Market Research 1976 SA

Martins, J.H.
Income and expenditure patterns of urban Indian households in Johannesburg. 130pp. R50.00 (Bureau of Market Research, Research Reports, 50.6) Bur Market Res 1976 SA

Martins, J.H.
Regional population estimates for 1974. 52pp. R50.00 (Bureau of Market Research, Research Reports, 46) Bur Market Research 1975 SA

Martins, J.H.
Regional population estimates for 1975. 53pp. R50.00 (Bureau of Market Research, Research Reports, 51) Bur Market Res 1976 SA

Martinson, A.P.A.
Adwowa dwontofo. [Adwowa, the singer] 27pp. ill. 25pes. Waterville 1964 GH TWI

Martinson, A.P.A.
Afoofi bere nhoma. [Stories for leisure hours] 137pp. 42pes. Waterville 1966 GH TWI

Martinson, A.P.A.
Biography: Rev.B.A. Martinson. 31pp. 10pes. Waterville 1965 GH

Martinson, A.P.A.
Ehwene a eye ha (Akwapim) [The nose that hunts (Akwapim version)] 19pp. ill. 30pes. Waterville 1964 GH TWI

Marwick, M.G.
The modern family in social-anthropological perspective. 22pp. 50c (Inaugural lec.) Witwatersrand UP 1958 SA

Marx, B.
She shall have music. 224pp. photos. hd. R2.00 Flesch 1961 SA

Masamba ma Mpolo.
Sexe et mariage: la perspective chrétienne. 80pp. Z1.15 CEDI 1974 ZR FRE

Mascarenhas, A. C.
Health facilities and population in Tanzania. pt. I: hospitals. See: Thomas, I. D.

Mascarenhas, A. C.
Health facilities and population in Tanzania. pt. II: rural health centres. See: Thomas, I. D.

Mascarenhas, A. C.
Health facilities and population in Tanzania. pt. III: dispensaries. See: Thomas, I. E.

Mascarenhas, O.C.
A preliminary guide to the study of traditional medicine in Tanzania. T.shs.20.00 pap. (Research reports, new series, 13) Bur Res Assess - Tanz 1975 TZ

Mascarhenas, A.C.
Research on subsidiary staple food marketing in Dar es Salaam. See: Mbilinyi, S.M.

Mascarhenhas, A.
Rationalizing the orange trade. See: Mbilinyi, S.M.

Mascarhenhas, A.
Sources and marketing of cooking bananas in Tanzania. See: Mbilinyi, S.M.

Masey, F., comp.
Cecil John Rhodes: a chronicle of the funeral ceremonies from Muizenburg to the Matopos. March-April 1902. [Reprint ed. 1902]. 176pp. pl. cl. R$43.15 cl. Books of Rhodesia 1972 RH

Mashembo, A.K.J., comp.
Tanganyika library service publications, 1963-1972. 16pp. T.shs.20.00 Tanz Lib Serv 1973 TZ

Mashiri, P.
Chakafukidza dzimba matenga. 88pp. 95c. Longman - Rhod 1977 RH SHO

Mashua, J. M.
Masimulizi juu ya Wasukuma. [History, customs and traditions of the Sukuma] 2nd ed. 71pp. K.shs.2.50 EALB 1973 KE SWA

Masiba, A.E.
Kufa na kupona. [Life and death] 117pp. K.shs.11.50 ($3.50/£1.40) EALB 1974 KE SWA

Masiye, A.
You and the church. 32pp. ill. 40pes. (12p.) Africa Christian 1972 GH

Masiye, A.S.
Before dawn. 144pp. K1.50 Neczam 1971 ZA

Masiye, A.S.
Kabvulumvulu. [Talks on the African way of life.] 44pp. 18n. Neczam 1975 ZA NYA

Masiye, A.S.
The lands of Kazembe. 56pp. 75n. Neczam 1974 ZA

Masiye, A.V.
Koze kukufice lawe. 96pp. 55c. Longman - Rhod 1970 RH NDE

Masiye, A.V.
Wangithengisela umntanakhe. [He sold his daughter to me.] 71pp. pl. 35c pap. Mambo 1972 RH NDE

Maske, S.
The petrography of the Ingeli mountain range. 109pp. photos. R3.45 (A v41, no. 1) Univ Stellenbosch, Lib 1966 SA

Maskil, D.
Guided general science. Standard 5. See: Pellew, V.

Mason, C.
The waters of Africa. 136pp. K1.50 Neczam 1972 ZA

Mason, H. Young, B. Yoder, P.
Twende tusome: kitabu cha kusoma. [Teach yourself to write] bk. 1 ill. K.shs.1.00 ($1.00/40p.) EALB 1957 KE SWA

Mason, H.D.
Western Cape Sandveld flowers. 224pp. ill. R10.00 Struik 1972 SA

Mason, J.
Rental survey. See: Anderson, W.W.

Mason, J.
A socio-economic study of a site and service scheme in Durban. free (Chatsworth Community and Research Centre. Research Report, 4) Univ Durban-Westville 1975 SA

Mason, M.P.
Let's write. A composition book for standard six. See: Kitonga, E.

Mason, M.P.
Write on. A composition book for standard seven. See: Kitonga, E.

Mason, R.
Prehistory of the Transvaal: a record of human activity. 498pp. col. ill. cl. R16.00 Witwatersrand UP repr. 1969 SA

Masondo, C.J.A.
Amaculo angcwele ezikole. [Hymns for schools] music. 25c. Shuter 1970 SA ZUL

Masondo, C.J.A.
Amashuni amaculo angcwele. [Music for hymns] music. 40c. Shuter 1970 SA ZUL

Massaki, N.
De quelle race Dieu est-il? 44pp. 25k CEDI 1974 ZR FRE

Massaki, N.
Je suis une femme mariée. 50pp. 30k CEDI 1974 ZR FRE

Massaki, N.
L'orphelin au coeur blesse. 58pp. 30k CEDI 1974 ZR FRE

Author Index

Massamba Mpolo.
Sexe et mariage. 275pp. CEDI 1973 ZR FRE

Massek, A.O.   Sidai, J.O.
Wisdom of Maasai. 52pp. K.shs.7.50 Transafrica 1974 KE

Massih, A.E.
Au seuil de l'Islam. 3rd ed. 56pp. CFA190 CLE 1971 CM FRE

Masson, A.
La verrue. 224pp. CFA1,400 (F28.00) Nouv Ed Afric 1976 SG FRE

Masubu, M.
Ndebele. Teacher's bk. grade 6. 52pp. 65c. Longman - Rhod 1972 RH NDE

Mataamu, B.
The beautiful Nyakiemo. [The origin of the Kikuyu and the Masaai] 39pp. ill. K.shs.1.00 ($1.25/50p.) EALB 1951 KE

Matango, R.R.
The role of agencies for rural development in Tanzania. A case study of the Lushoto integrated development project. 59pp. T.shs.12.00 ($3.00) (Research pap., 76.3) Econ Res Bur - Tanz 1976 TZ

Matano, H.M.
Watoto wetu. [Our children] K.shs.12.50 ($2.75/£1.10) EALB 1973 KE SWA

Matata, B.
Free love. 130pp. K.shs.10.00 ($2.00) Textbook Ctre; distr. 1975 KE

Matata, B.
Love for sale. 216pp. K.shs.12.50 ($2.50) Textbook Ctre; distr. 1975 KE

Matcher, J.L.
Index to pictures of South African interest in The Graphic, 1902-1914. 97pp. R4.95 Dept Bibliog, Lib & Typo 1968 SA

Matemba, C.M.
Mapishi ya kwetu. [Our recipes.] 112pp. T.shs.8.00 Tanz Publ House 1972 TW SWA

Mathe, G.
Abatou Lilié, village Dida. Les jeunes et l'agriculture. See: Chatenay, D.

Mathers, E.P.
The gold fields revisited, being further glimpses of the gold fields of South Africa. [Reprint of ed. Durban, 1887] 352pp. ill. R4.80 (Reprints, 53) State-Lib-SA 1970 SA

Matheson, E.
An enterprise so perilous. 128pp. cl. K.shs.15.00 ($3.75/£1.50) EALB KE

Matheson, G.D.
The economic potential of limestones near Lusaka. See: Newman, D.

Mathews, A.S.
Law, order, and liberty in South Africa. R12.50 Juta 1971 SA

Mathews, A.S.
Law, order and liberty in South Africa. R12.50 Juta 1971 SA

Mathews, J.P.
Contributions to the cranial morphology of the Asiatic Urodele Onychodactylus japonicus; The cranial musculature of the Asiatic Orodele Onychodactylus japonicus. See: Ryke, P.A.J.

Matier, K.O.
Horace: selected odes. A commentary. 231pp. R2.00 Rhodes Univ Lib 1971 SA

Matindi, A.
Jua na upepo. 24pp. ill. K.shs.1.80 ($1.00) EAPH 1968 KE SWA

Matindi, A.
The sun and the wind. 24pp. ill. K.shs1.65 ($1.00) EAPH KE

Matindi, A.   Hunter, G.
The sun men and other plays. 80pp. ill. $1.00 K.shs4.95 EAPH 1971 KE

Matondo Kwa Nzambi.
A l'assaut de l'Himalaya. 59pp. ill. 40k St. Paul 1976 ZR FRE

Matsebuala, J.S.M.
Std. 2: Insika. 4, 7 bks 48pp. ill. R1.05 Longman SA 1972 SA SIS

Matsebula, J.S.M.
A history of Swaziland. 2nd ed. 232pp. photos. maps. R4.75 Longman - SA 1976 SA

Matsebula, J.S.M.
Iqoqo lezinkondlo. [Collection of poems] 136pp. 65c. Shuter 1957 SA ZUL

Matsebula, J.S.M.
Std. 1: Insika. 3, 7 bks 48pp. ill. R1.00 Longman SA 1971 SA SIS

Matsebula, J.S.M.
Std. 3: Insika. 5, 7 bks 48pp. ill. R1.10 Longman SA 1972 SA SIS

Matsebula, J.S.M.
Std. 4: Insika. 6, 7 bks R1.20 Longman SA SA SIS

Matsebula, J.S.M.
Std. 5: Insika. 7, 7 bks R1.25 Longman SA SA SIS

Matsebula, J.S.M.
Sub. A: Insika. 1, 7 bks 48pp. ill. 90c. Longman SA 1968 SA SIS

Matsebula, J.S.M.
Sub. B: Insika. 2, 7 bks 52pp. ill. 95c. Longman SA 1969 SA SIS

Matson, A.T.
The Nandi campaign against the British, 1895-1906. 20pp. map. K.shs.3.50 (Transafrica Historical papers, 1) Transafrica 1974 KE

Matson, A.T.
Nandi resistance to British rule. 391pp. maps. K.shs.40.00 ($12.00) EAPH 1972 KE

Matthews, D., ed.   Apthorpe, R.J., ed.
Social relations in Central African industry. 134pp. K1.20 (70p.) (Rhodes-Livingstone Institute conf. proc., 12) Inst Afr Stud - Lusaka 1958 ZA

Matthews, J., ed.
Black voices shout. 69pp. R1.95 BLAC 1974 SA

Matthews, J.
The park, and other stories. 102pp. R1.75 BLAC 1974 SA

Matthews, J.W.
Incwadi Yami. [Reprint of ed. 1887]. 542pp. ill. cl. R30.40 (Africana Reprint Library, 9) Africana Book Soc 1976 SA

Matthews, V.L.
The importance of the weather and weather services to the South African agricultural sector. A Delphi survey. See: Theron, M.J.

Matthews, Z.K.
African awakening and the universities. 20pp. 25c. (University of Cape Town T.B. Davie memorial lecture, 3) Univ Cape Town Lib 1961 SA

Matton, C.A.
Index to pictures of South African interest in The Graphic, 1896-1899. 93pp. R4.75 Dept Bibliog, Lib & Typo 1967 SA

Matuga, G.S.
Ng'ombe akivunjika mguu. [A cow falling into mishap returns to the herd.] 32pp. K.shs.3.75 Longman - Ken 1975 KE SWA

Matundu Nzita.   Courtejoie, J.   Rotsart de Hertaing, I.
La santé de vos enfants: comment protéger la santé des enfants depuis la naissance jusqu'à leur entrée à l'école. 52pp. photos. Z1.00 ($1.20) (Protection maternelle et infantile, 14) BERPS 1975 ZR FRE

Maubert, J.
Littérature française, classe de lere.   See: Blachère, J.C.

Maududi, A.A.
Guide to Islam.   179pp.   N1.00   West 1969 NR

Mauma, R.
Elimu ya siasa utangulizi.   See: Ericsson, E.

Maunick, E.
Africain du temps jadis.   48pp.   CFA350   (F7.00)
Nouv Ed Afric 1976 SG FRE

Maunik, E.F.
Ensoleillé vif.   120pp.   CFA1,500   (F30.00)   Nouv Ed
Afric 1976 SG FRE

Mauny, R. et al.
Annales de l'université d'Abidjan.   149pp.   CFA500
pap.   (F10.00 pap.)   (Série I-Histoire, 1)   Univ Abidjan
1972 IV FRE

Mauny, R.
Gravures, peintures et inscriptions rupestres de l'Ouest
africain.   93pp.   ill. maps.   CFA600   (Initiations et
Etudes Africaines, 11)   IFAN 1954 SG FRE

Mauny, R.
Tableau géographique de l'Ouest africain au moyen age,
d'aprés les sources écrites, la tradition et l'archéologie.
[Reprint of ed. 1961].   587pp.   ill.   (D.fl.175.00)
(Mémoires de l'IFAN, 61)   IFAN 1961 SG FRE

Maura, M.
Kijanja's lucky escape.   30pp.   K.shs3.60   Equatorial
1972 KE

Maurach, G., ed.
Wilhelm von Conches, Philosophia mundi.   77pp.
R4.50   (R5.50)   (Studia, 15)   Univ South Africa 1974
SA LAT

Maury, P.
Christian witness among intellectuals.   50c.   (Peter
Ainslie Memorial lec., 6)   Rhodes Univ Lib 1954 SA

Mave Mbey.
Tradition et changements: les Basakata.   109pp.   ill.
maps.   (DM19.00)   (CEEBA. serie II, memoires et
Monographies, 25)   CEEBA 1975 ZR FRE

Mavengere, E.P.
Vakafa vakazorora.   [The dead are at rest.]   91pp.
65c   Longman - Rhod 1973 RH SHO

Mavinga Panzu.
Cours d'Algèbre. Première partie.   120pp.   Z1.20
Press Univ Zaire 1974 ZR FRE

Mavumilusa, M.
Kundu dia bandoki.   [Secrets of witchcraft.]   115pp.
45k   CEDI 1974 ZR KIO

Mawa Nkwenambwa.
Pour te marier, coupe une de tes pattes! Mythes yansi.
Textes yansi-français et kongo véhiculaire.   203pp.   ill.
map.   (DM29.00 pap.)   (CEEBA. série II, Mémoires et
Monographies, 29)   CEEBA 1975 ZR FRE

Maxwell, B.
Ecology for tropical schools.   132pp.   ill.   N1.70
Onibonoje 1971 NR

Maxwell, B.
Practical biology for school certificate.   184pp.   ill.
N2.00   Onibonoje 1971 NR

Maxwell, D.A. et al.
Integrated science.   bk. 2   92pp.   ill.   N1.30
Macmillan 1974 NR

Maxwell, D.A.   Shoewu, O.   Adenuga, I.J.
Integrated science.   96pp.   ill.   N1.10   Macmillan 1973
NR

Maxwell, D.E.S., ed.   Bushrui, S.B., ed.
W.B. Yeats 1865-1965: centenary essays on the art of
W.B. Yeats.   252pp.   pl.   N4.00   Ibadan UP 1965 NR

Maxwell, E.
Looking at the Old Testament.   pt. 4   See: Baturi, S.

Maxwell, F.
You da gobe.   [Hausa grammar.]   192pp.   Challenge
1976 NR HAU

Maxwell-Mahon, W.D.
The art of communication.   See: Beeton, D.R.

Maxwell-Mahon, W.D.
New approaches to literature 1920-1976.   18pp.   R1.50
(R2.00)   (Miscellanea, 6)   Univ South Africa 1976 SA

Maxwell-Mahon, W.D.
South African poetry: a critical anthology.   See: Beeton,
D.R.

Maxwell, W.D.
The resurrection.   ex. only   (Inaugural lec.)   Rhodes
Univ Lib 1958 SA

May, A.F.
Beekeeping in southern Africa.   2nd ed.   210pp.   ill. cl.
R5.00 cl.   HAUM 1975 SA

May, A.N.
The atomic nature of matter.   19pp.   C1.00
($1.00/50p.)   (Inaugural lecture)   Ghana UP 1971 GH

May, H.J.
South African cases and statutes on evidence.   4th r
rev.ed.   R9.50   Juta 1962 SA

May, I.R.
The locust threat to Africa.   18pp.   60c (70c)   (Africa
Inst. of South Africa, occas. pap., 34)   Africa Inst - Pret
1973 SA

May, J.
Drinking in a Rhodesian African township.   94pp.
R$1.00   (Dept. of Sociology, Univ. of Rhodesia, paps., 8)
Univ Rhodesia Lib 1973 RH

May, J.
Drinking patterns in Rhodesia: Highfield African township.
See: Reader, D.H.

May, R.
A concise encyclopedia of the theatre.   212pp.   R9.30
S.A. only   Philip 1975 SA

Mayengo, F.M.
Mon coeur de saisons.   36pp.   20k pap.   (Jeune
Littérature, 8)   Ed Mont Noir 1972 ZR FRE

Mayer, I.
The nature of kinship relations: the significance of the use
of kinship terms among the Gusii.   80pp.   K1.05
(53p.)   (Rhodes-Livingstone paps., 37)   Inst Soc Res -
Zam 1965 ZA

Mayer, I.
Gussi bridewealth law and custom.   67pp.   65n.   (35p.)
(Rhodes-Livingstone paps., 18)   Inst Soc Res - Zam 1950
ZA

Mayer, P.
Townsmen or tribesmen: conservatism and the process of
urbanization in a South African city.   2nd ed.   340pp.
R3.90   OUP-SA 1971 SA

Mayer, P.
Witches.   ex. only   (Inaugural lec.)   Rhodes Univ Lib
1954 SA

Mayer, T.
Lectures expliquées à l'usage des lycées, collèges et
cours complémentaires de la Côte d'Ivoire. Classe de 6è
et 5è. Livre de l'élève.   191pp.   ill.   CFA635   CEDA
1965 IV FRE

Mayo-Smith, I.
Case studies: thirty-one problem case studies.   316pp.
K.shs15.00   Kenya Inst Admin 1972 KE

Mayo-Smith, I.
K.I.A. case studies: administration and management in
Africa, thirty-one problem case studies.   K.shs.15.00
Kenya Inst Admin 1973 KE

Mayo-Smith, I.
K.I.A. case studies: notes for case leaders.   62pp.
K.shs.15.00   Kenya Inst Admin 1972 KE

Mayo-Smith, I.
Notes for case leaders (companion volume to "Local
government regulations 1963")   K.shs.15.00   Kenya Inst
Admin 1973 KE

Mayr, R.
The nonsense of music. 25pp. 50c (Inaugural lectures) Rhodes Univ Lib 1973 SA

Mayson, J.S.
The Malays of Capetown. [Reprint of ed. Manchester, 1861] 39pp. R2.20 (Reprints, 58) State-Lib-SA 1970 SA

Mazac, O.
Reconnaissance gravity survey of Zambia. K3.50 pap. (Dept. of Geological Survey, Technical Reports, 76) Geol Survey - Zam 1976 ZA

Mazenod Institute.
History course for Lesotho primary schools. 3rd ed. vol. 1: Lesotho mehleng ea khale/Lesotho in the olden days. (Standard 4). 115pp. ill. 85c Mazenod Inst 1975 LO

Mazenod Institute.
History course for Lesotho primary schools. 3rd ed. vol. 2: From slavery to colonization. (Standard 5). 117pp. ill. 90c Mazenod Inst 1975 LO

Mazenod Institute.
History course for Lesotho primary schools. 3rd ed. vol. 3: From colonization to full nationhood. (Standard 6). 126pp. ill. 95c Mazenod Inst 1975 LO

Mazenod Institute.
History course for Lesotho primary schools. 3rd ed. vol. 4: From foreign rule to self-government. (Standard 7). 134pp. ill. R1.00 Mazenod Inst 1975 LO

Mazri, H.
Les hydrocarbures dans l'économie de l'Algérie. 263pp. DA30.00 SNED 1975 AE FRE

Mazrui, A.
Ancient Greece in African political thought. 34pp. K.shs3.00 ($1.00) EAPH 1966 KE

Mazrui, A.A. Tandon, Y.
Horizons of African diplomacy. K.shs.41.75 ($8.35/£4.00) EALB 1975 KE

Mazula, A. Hatibu, B.M.R.
Mazoezi ya ufahamu wa Kiswahili. [Swahili comprehension exercises] 64pp. K.shs.4.50 OUP-Nairobi 1966 KE SWA

Mba Evina, J.
Politicos. 62pp. CFA360 (Coll. Théâtre) CLE 1974 CM FRE

Mbakwe, C.N.
Model question/answers on school certificate mathematics. 200pp. N2.50 Aromolaran 1975(?) NR

Mbakwe, C.N.
New revision objective tests in mathematics. 200pp. N2.50 Aromolaran 1975(?) NR

Mbamalu, N.C.
School certificate geography for West Africa: Regional geography of West Africa. 2, 2bks 176pp. maps ill. photos. N2.00 Macmillan 1971 NR

Mbanjwa, T.
Black review, 1974-1975. Annual survey of events and trends in the Black community in South Africa. 350pp. R3.85 Black Comm Prog 1975 SA

Mbanjwa, T., ed.
Black perspectives: Bantustans. 230pp. R2.00 Black Comm Prog 1976 SA

Mbatha, S.B.L.
Nawe Mbopha kasithayi. [Even you Mbopha son of Sithayi] 64pp. 60c. Shuter 1972 SA ZUL

Mbaye d'Erneville, A.
Chansons pour Laîty. 16pp. CFA325 (F6.50) Nouv Ed Afric 1976 SG FRE

M'Bayiwa, C.
Zvirevo ZvavaShona. [Proverbs.] 68pp. pl. 48c Mambo 1976 RH SHO

Mbaziira, F.X.
Tuula tuwaye. 56pp. K.shs.4.70 ($1.75/70p.) EALB 1970 KE LUG

Mbeba, D.A.
Ku harare. [Adventures of a journey to Southern Rhodesia.] 36pp. 18n. Neczam 1976 ZA TUM

Mbelwa, H.C.
Donda ndugu. [Gangrene.] 81pp. T.shs.9.00 Tanz Publ House 1973 TZ SWA

Mbelwa, H.C.M.
Mapenzi na shetani. [In love with the devil.] 72pp. T.shs.6.50 Longman - Tanz 1975 TZ SWA

Mbelwa, H.C.M.
Mfu aluyefufuka. [Dead man resurrected] 69pp. K.shs.13.50 ($3.35/£1.35) EALB 1974 KE SWA

Mbengue, I. Diallo, A.W.
Maxureja Gey. 40pp. ill. CFA600 (F12.00) Nouv Ed Afric 1976 SG FRE

Mbengue, M.S.
Le Royaume de Sable. 240pp. CFA850 (F17.00) Nouv Ed Afric 1976 SG FRE

Mbenna, I.C.
Kuchagua. [Folktale.] 38pp. K.shs.12.50 ($3.20) EAPH 1976 KE SWA

Mbenna, I.C.
Sitaki. [Folktale.] 66pp. K.shs.8.00 ($2.60) EAPH 1976 KE SWA

Mbenna, I.C.
Siuwezi Ujamaa. 23pp. K.shs.5.50 ($1.50) EAPH 1976 KE SWA

Mbenna, I.C.
Uandishi wa vitabu. [Writing books] 90pp. T.shs.5.25 Tanz Publ House 1970 TZ SWA

Mbiango Kekese.
La confession du sergent Wanga. 95pp. (Jeune littérature, 16) Ed Mont Noir 1973 ZR FRE

Mbilinyi, J.
Agricultural research for rural development. 248pp. cl. & pap. K.shs.75.00 cl. K.shs.29.00 pap. ($14.80/£6.75 cl.) ($8.40/£3.40 pap.) ($14.80 cl.) ($8.40 pap.) EALB 1975 KE

Mbilinyi, M.
Bendera Yetu. [Civics text.] 16pp. col. ill. K.shs.4.20 ($1.50) EAPH 1975 KE SWA

Mbilinyi, M.I.
The education of girls in Tanzania: a study of attitudes of Tanzanian girls and their fathers towards education. 82pp. T.shs. 8.75 Inst Educ - Dar 1969 TZ

Mbilinyi, M.J.
Participation of women in African economies. 34pp. ill. T.shs12.00 ($3.00) (Research pap., 71.12) Econ Res Bur - Tanz 1971 TZ

Mbilinyi, M.J.
The transition to capitalization in rural Tanzania. T.shs.12.00 ($3.00) (Research pap., 74.7) Econ Res Bur - Tanz 1975 TZ

Mbilinyi, S. M.
Attitudes, expectations and the decision to educate in rural Tanzania. T.shs.15.00 ($15.00) (Research reports, new series, 3.1) Bur Res Assess - Tanz 1973 TZ

Mbilinyi, S.M.
Coffee diversification studies. T.shs.12.00 ($3.00) (Research pap., 68.33) Econ Res Bur - Tanz 1975 TZ

Mbilinyi, S.M.
Economics of central coffee pulperies in Tanzania. 15pp. ill. T.shs12.00 ($3.00) (Research pap., 68.6) Econ Res Bur - Tanz 1968 TZ

Mbilinyi, S.M.
Estimation of peasant farmers' costs of production: the case of Bukoba Robusta coffee. 13pp. ill. T.shs12.00 ($3.00) (Research pap., 68.1) Econ Res Bur - Tanz 1968 TZ

Mbilinyi, S.M.
Problems and possibilities of crop diversification in the robusta areas of Tanzania: the case of West Lake region. T.shs.12.00 ($3.00) (Research pap., 69.26) Econ Res Bur - Tanz 1974 TZ

Mbilinyi, S.M.   Mascarhenhas, A.
Rationalizing the orange trade. 28pp. ill. T.shs12.00 ($3.00) (Research pap., 69.15) Econ Res Bur - Tanz 1969 TZ

Mbilinyi, S.M.   Mascarhenas, A.C.
Research on subsidiary staple food marketing in Dar es Salaam. 16pp. maps ill. T.shs12.00 ($3.00) (Research pap., 68.16) Econ Res Bur - Tanz 1968 TZ

Mbilinyi, S.M.   Mascarhenas, A.
Sources and marketing of cooking bananas in Tanzania. 28pp. ill. T.shs12.00 ($3.00) (Research pap., 69.14) Econ Res Bur - Tanz 1969 TZ

Mbise, I.R.
Blood on our land. 135pp. T.shs.10.50 ($3.00) Tanz Publ House TZ

Mbithi, P.
Rural sociology and rural development. 225pp. K.shs.36.75 ($7.20/£3.45) EALB 1975 KE

Mbithi, P.   Barnes, C.
Spontaneous settlement problems in Kenya. 204pp. ill. K.shs.24.50 ($5.30/£2.60 pap.) EALB 1975 KE

Mbiti, D.M.
Foundations of school administration. 152pp. K.shs.20.00 OUP - Nairobi 1975 KE

Mbiti, J.
Poems of nature and faith. 62pp. K.shs24.00 cl. K.shs4.00 pap. ($4.00 cl.) ($2.00 pap.) EAPH 1969 KE

Mbiti, J.
Religions et philosophie africaines. Tr. fr. English 300pp. CFA1200 CLE 1972 CM FRE

Mbiti, J.S.
English-Kamba vocabulary. 52pp. K.shs.3.00 ($1.50/60p.) EALB 1959 KE

Mbiti, J.S.
Mutanga na ngewa yake. [Mutunga and history] 2 2nded. 59pp. K.shs.2.00 ($1.25/50p.) EALB 1967 KE KAM

Mbokolo, E.
Affonso premier. Le roi chrétien de l'ancien Congo. 96pp. CFA250 Nouv Ed Afric 1976 SG FRE

M'bokolo, E.
Mirambo de l'Afrique Centrale. 96pp. CFA250 (F5.00) Nouv Ed Afric 1976 SG FRE

M'Bokolo, E.
M'Siri du Zaïtre. 96pp. CFA250 (F5.00) Nouv Ed Afric 1976 SG FRE

M'Bokolo, E.
Le Roi Denis du Gabon. 96pp. CFA150 (F5.00) Nouv Ed Afric 1976 SG FRE

Mbomere, C.O.
Mikasa iliyompata Machomane. See: Kacharia, S.M.S.

Mbonde, J.M.
Uandishi wa Tanzania. Bk.1: Insha. 168pp. K.shs.22.80 ($5.35/£2.20) EALB 1976 KE SWA

Mbonde, J.M.
Uandishi wa Tanzania. Bk.2: Michezo ya kuigiza. 200pp. K.shs.26.65 ($5.50/£2.20) EALB 1976 KE SWA

Mbonde, J.P.
Bwana mkubwa. [The big man.] 56pp. K.shs.7.50 Transafrica 1974 KE SWA

Mbonde, J.P.
Hadithi za kiboko Hugo. [Stories of Hugo the hippo] 64pp. T.shs.3.25 Tanz Publ House 1968 TZ SWA

Mbonde, J.P.
Seti Benjamin Mpinga. 64pp. photos. K.shs.7.00 Transafrica 1975 KE SWA

Mbouyom, F.X.
Recueil des grands arrêts de la jurisprudence administrative de la cour suprême du Cameroun. v.2 360pp. CFA2500 pap. SKEA 1976 CM FRE

Mboya, P.
Luo kitgi gi timbegi. [Luo customs] 212pp. K.shs.6.00 Equatorial 1973 KE LUO

Mboya, P.
Utawala na maendeleo ya local government South Nyanza. [The work and progress of Local Government in South Naza, Kenya, 1926-1957] 48pp. K.shs.1.50 ($1.25/50p.) EALB 1959 KE SWA

Mboya, T.
Uhuru ni Mwanzo. [Freedom and after] 229pp. K.shs.6.00 ($2.40) EAPH 1963 KE SWA

Mbugua, E.S.   Schonherr, S.
Bean production in Kenya's central and eastern provinces. 69pp. K.shs.10.00 (Inst. Development Studies, Occas. paps., 23) Inst Dev Stud 1976 KE

Mbulawa, L.M.
Mamfene. [At mamfene] 169pp. 65c. Shuter 1962 SA XHO

Mbunda, D.
Education mass campaigns: The Tanzania experience Chakula ni uhai. 30pp. T.shs.5.00 (Studies in Adult Education, 24) Inst Adult Educ - Dar 1976 TZ

Mbunda, F.L.
Kufundisha kusoma: taratibu na matatizo yake. [Teaching children to read: problems and methods.] 120pp. K.shs.12.50 OUP - Nairobi 1975 KE SWA

Mbunda, F.L.
Mwalimu wa lugha. [The language teacher] 148pp. K.shs.13.50 OUP - Nairobi 1976 KE SWA

M'Buze-Nsomi Lobwanabi.
Révolution et humanisme. Essais. 62pp. 62k Presses Africaines 1974 ZR FRE

McArdell, A.M.
Cataloguing for school library science. 2nd ed. 180pp. R6.00 (R7.00) (Miscellanea, 4) Univ South Africa 1976 SA

McAuslan, J.P.W.B.
Public law and political change in Kenya. See: Ghai, Y.P.

McBain, F.C.A.
Beginning geography in Kenya. See: Anderson, M.P.

McBride, A.
The Zulu war. 40pp. ill. photos. R3.80 (SA only) Shuter 1976 SA

McClain, W.T., ed.
African conference on local courts and customary law. 143pp. T.shs.7.00 Fac Law - Dar 1963 TZ

McCleery, C.S.
The works of Theodore Johannes Haarhoff: 1922-1957. 78pp. R4.00 Dept Bibliog, Lib & Typo 1968 SA

McCormick, D., eds.   Towes, P.J., eds.
University chemistry teaching. Proceedings of the international conference on University Chemistry Teaching held at the University of Nairobi, Kenya, from 14th-18th December, 1971. 164pp. cl. & pap. K.shs.43.00 pap. K.shs.65.00 cl. ($8.60/£4.20 pap.) ($12.60/£6.00 cl.) EALB 1974 KE

McCready, M.S.
How educate for living? 18pp. C1.00 ($1.00/50p.) (Inaugural lecture) Ghana UP 1971 GH

McCree, H.
From controlled to creative writing. 80pp. 77k Pilgrim 1969 NR

McCrystal, L.P. et al.
The Indian South African: papers presented at a conference held under the auspices of the South African Institute of race relations (Natal region) in Durban on 14 October 1966. 55pp. 60c. ($1.50) SA Inst of Race Relations 1967 SA

Author Index

McCulloch, M.
A social survey of the African population of Livingstone. 96pp. K1.50 (75p.) (Rhodes-Livingstone paps., 26) Inst Soc Res - Zam 1956 ZA

McDonald, D.
Aflatoxins: poisonous substances that can be present in Nigerian groundnuts. 50k (Samaru misc. pap., 53) Inst Agric Res - Zaria 1976 NR

McDonald, D.
Research on the aflatoxin problem in groundnuts in Northern Nigeria. 34pp. map. 20k (Samaru misc. pap., 14) Inst Agric Res-Zaria 1966 NR

McDonald, D.
Soil fungi and the fruit of the groundnut: Arachis hypogaea. 31pp. 20k (Samaru misc. pap., 28) Inst Agric Res - Zaria 1968 NR

McDonald, F.
Forming young Christians. Catechetical updating for primary school teachers. 58pp. ill. K.shs.8.50 (Gaba Pastoral Papers, 24) Gaba 1972 KE

McGee, E.P., comp.
National policies of Tanzania: a bibliography. See: Sumar, M., comp.

McGillivray, G.
Organometallic compounds: intermediates in organic synthesis. 22pp. R2.10 (R3.10) (Studia, 11) Univ South Africa 1972 SA

McGowan, W.H.K.
Dibaji ya mahubiri kwa kizaki hiki. See: Thomas, M.

Mchangamwe, A.B., ed.
Utendi wa mikidadi na mayasa. K.shs.4.50 (50p.) (Sanaa ya Utungo, 3) Heinemann Educ - Nair 1972 KE SWA

McHardy, C.
Akosua in Brazil. See: Olympio, A.

McHarg. Gibbons.
Songs at school. 64pp. 45c. Longman - Rhod 1960 RH

McIntosh, B.C.
Ngano. 168pp. maps photos. K.shs.42.00 cl. K.shs12.50 pap. ($8.00 cl.) ($3.60 pap.) EAPH 1969 KE

McIntosh, B.C. Mungeam, G.H.
Primary Kenya documents. EAPH 1973 KE

McIntosh, J.V.
Mosquitoes of the genus Aedes occurring in Southern Africa. 40pp. R2.10 Dept Bibliog, Lib & Typo 1968 SA

McIver, B.A.
Solvent dyeing of wool with a reactive dye/surfactant complex. See: Meissner, H.D.

McIver, B.A.
Solvent dyeing of wool with a reactive dye/surfactant complex. See: Meissner, H.D.

Mckay, J. et al.
A note on a traffic census taken on the Mombo-Lushoto road. 7pp. map. T.shs.5.00 (Research report, 25) Bur Res Assess - Tanz 1971 TZ

McKay, J. et al.
Road feasibility studies in Tanzania. 110pp. maps. T.shs.15.00 (Research pap., 16) Bur Res Assess Tanz 1971 TZ

Mckay, J.
A guide to basic data on road transport in Tanzania. 44pp. maps. T.shs.7.00 (Research notes, 5f) Bur Res Assess - Tanz 1972 TZ

McKay, J.
Kharumwa water supply: final report. See: Berry, L.

McKenzie, H.S. Shapiro, G.B.
The law of building contracts and arbitration in South Africa. 3rd ed. cl. R27.50 Juta 1977 SA

McKenzie, J.C.
Art teaching for primary schools in Africa. 64pp. ill. K.shs13.00 OUP-Nairobi 1966 KE

McKenzie, J.C.
Creative activities: art and craftwork for primary I and II. 19pp. ill. K.shs1.50 ($1.25/50p.) EALB 1962 KE

McKerron, R.G.
The law of delict in South Africa. 7th ed. hd. & pap R13.50 hd. R10.50 pap. Juta 1971 SA

McKilliam, K.R.
Gavumenti kye ki? [What is government?] 24pp. ill. K.shs.0.50 ($1.00/40p.) EALB 1956 KE LUG

McKilliam, K.R.
A handbook for literacy teachers. 62pp. ill. K.shs.4.00 ($1.75/70p.) EALB 1964 KE

McLaren, J.
A new concise Xhosa dictionary. R1.95 Longman SA 1964 SA

McLean, E.
Publishing in Africa in the seventies. Proceedings of an international conference, held at the University of Ife, Ile-Ife, Nigeria, 16-20 December, 1973. See: Oluwasanmi, E.

McLeod, S.
Animal stories. 80pp. ill. col. ill. R$2.00 (Dyker series, 3) Vision 1976 RH

McLoughlin, T.O., ed.
New writing in Rhodesia. 146pp. R$1.15 (Mambo Writers Series, English section, 2) Mambo 1976 RH

McLoughlin, T.O.
Edmund Burke and the first ten years of the 'Annual Register', 1758-1767. 53pp. R$2.00 (Univ. of Rhodesia, Series in Humanities, 1) Univ Rhodesia Lib 1975 RH

McMaster, V.
Stories of the African jungle. col. ill. R$1.50 (Dyker series, 1) Vision 1976 RH

McNab, A.P.
Ukufuywa kwengulube. [Pig keeping.] 49pp. pl. 35c Mambo 1971 RH NDE

McNaughton, D.
An unconventional method of producing a mohair pile fabric on a sinker wheel knitting machine to obtain improved fibre retention. See: Robinson, G.A.

McNown, J.
Technical education in Africa. 147pp. maps. K.shs.56.00 cl. K.shs.22.00 pap. ($10.40 cl.) ($5.20 pap.) EAPH 1970 KE

McPherson, I.H.
Your cookery book. See: Goble, G.I.

Mdoe, J.
Hila za mzee kobe. 40pp. ill. K.shs.1.95 ($1.00) EAPH 1969 KE SWA

Mdoe, J.
Nze mmanyi okusoma. [I know how to read] 2nd ed. 60pp. ill. K.shs.3.20 ($1.75/70p.) EALB 1965 KE LUG

Mdoe, J.N.
Awo Olwatuuka. 3rd. ed. 35pp. ill. K.shs.10.00 ($2.80/70p.) EALB 1970 E LUG

Mdoe, J.N.
Ebipande. [Reading cards] K.shs.3.00 ($1.50/60p.) EALB 1962 KE LUG

Mears, C.
Music for today. 144pp. music. hd. R7.50 OUP - SA 1977 SA

Mears, W.G.
Methodism in the Cape: an outline. 194pp. R2.10 cl. R1.55 pap. Methodist 1974 SA

Mears, W.G.
Mission to Clarkebury. 78pp. R1.85 cl. R1.10 pap. Methodist 1973 SA

Mears, W.G.A.
Wesleyan Baralong mission in Trans-Orangia 1821-1882. 44pp. R1.50 Struik 1970 SA

Mears, W.G.A.
Wesleyan missionaries in Great Namaqualand 1820-1867. 26pp. cl. R1.50 Struik 1970 SA

M'Eboutou, M.M.
Les aventures de Koulou-la-tortue. 64pp. CFA200 pap. CLE 1972 CM FRE

Medhin, T.
Macbeth. [in Amharic]. 92pp. Eth.$2.75 OUP-Addis 1972 ET AMH

Medhin, T.G.
Hamlet [in Amharic]. 148pp. photos. Eth.$3.50 OUP-Addis 1972 ET AMH

Medical Headquarters, Entebbe, Uganda.
The laws that protect your health: a book of village hygiene. 3rd ed. 57pp. ill. K.shs3.50 ($1.50/60p.) EALB 1965 KE

Medical Headquarters, Entebbe, Uganda.
Obulamu bugenda na kweyonja. [A book of village hygiene] 2nd ed. 58pp. ill. K.shs.3.00 ($1.50/60p.) EALB 1959 KE LUG

Meebelo, H.
Reaction to colonialism: a prelude to the politics of independence in northern Zambia 1893-1939. 304pp. pap. & hd. K4.80 hd. K2.40 pap. (£2.40 hd.) (£1.20 pap.) Inst Afr Stud Lusaka 1971 ZA

Meebelo, H.S.
Main currents of Zambia's humanist thought. 176pp. K1.18 (59p.) OUP - Lusaka 1973 ZA

Meena, E.
Misemo. [Sayings.] bk. I, A-E. 64pp. K.shs.5.50 Transafrica 1975 KE SWA

Meena, E.K.
Vitendawili. [Riddles] 32pp. K.shs.3.00 OUP-Nairobi 1964 KE SWA

Mefana, N.
Le secret de la source. 64pp. CFA200 CLE 1972 CM FRE

Megerlin, N.
Etude et réevaluation du gisement de fer de Ambatolaona-Marorangotra. 23pp. pl. photos. FMG2314 (F46.28) (Travaux du Bureau Géologique, 131) Service Geol - Mad 1969 MG FRE

Megherbi, A.
Ibn Khaldoun, sa vie, son oeuvre. DA1.00 SNED 1971 AE FRE

Megherbi, A.
La pensée sociologique d'Ibn Khaldoun. 256pp. DA7.00 SNED 1971 AE FRE

Mehretu, A.
Regional integration for economic development of greater East Africa: a quantified analysis of possibilities. 150pp. ill. U.shs.15.00 Uganda Pub House 1974 UG

Meienberg, H.
Tanzanian citizen. 364pp. K.shs.12.25 OUP-Nairobi 1966 KE

Meikle, J.
Tommy Duiker. 16pp. col. ill. R$1.65 ($3.30) M.O. Collins 1972 RH

Meillassoux, C. Simagha, D. Doucoure, L.
Légende de la dispersion des Kusa (épopée soninke) 133pp. CFA1000 (Initiations et Etudes Africaines, 22) IFAN 1967 SG FRE

Meimang, S.T.
Kusadliwa ngolundala. [On Zulu social customs and beliefs.] 437pp. photos. hd. R6.00 cl. Shuter 1976 SA ZUL

Mein, P.J.
An autonomous housing prototype for low income families. 29pp. K.shs.18.00 Housing Research and Dev Unit 1977 KE

Mein, P.J. Jorgensen, T.
Design for medical buildings. A manual for the planning and building of health care facilities under conditions of limited resources. 146pp. K.shs.60.00 Housing Res Dev Unit 1975 KE

Meinardus, O.
Christian Egypt: ancient and modern. 2nd ed. 680pp. £6.00 ($22.00 pap.) Am Univ 1976 UA

Meinardus, O.
Christian Egypt, ancient and modern. 2nd rev. ed. 680pp. £E6.00 ($22.00) Am Univ 1974 UA

Meinardus, O.
Christian Egypt faith and life. 514pp. £.E.4.500 ($20.00) Am Univ 1970 UA

Meinardus, O.F.
Christian Egypt, faith and life. v.2 513pp. L.E.4.000 ($10.00) Am Univ 1971 UA

Meintjes, J.
The Anglo-Boer war - a pictorial history. 198pp. photos. maps. cl. R9.95 Struik 1976 SA

Meintjes, J.
Sandile: the fall of the Xhosa nation. 312pp. col. ill. R10.00 Bulpin 1971 SA

Meintjes, J.
Sasol: 1950-1975. photos. R7.50 Tafelberg 1976 SA

Meiring, A.M.
Christian unity: a Dutch reformed view. 50c. (Peter Ainslie Memorial lec., 5) Rhodes Univ Lib 1953 SA

Meiring, J., et al.
Modern general science for standard 6. 286pp. ill. R2.80 Nasou 1974 SA

Meiring, J., et al.
Modern general science for the diff. course, standard 7. 234pp. ill. R2.70 Nasou 1974 SA

Meiring, J., et al.
Physical science for South African schools, standard 8. 251pp. ill. R2.40 Nasou 1974 SA

Meiring, J.A., et al.
Physical science for South African schools, standard 9. 370pp. ill. photo. R4.85 Nasou 1975 SA

Meiring, J.A., et al.
Physical science for South African schools, standard 10. 247pp. ill. photo. R4.40 Nasou 1975 SA

Meiring, J.M.
Thomas Pringle. 196pp. pl. hd. fl.22.50 Balkema 1968 SA

Meiring, P.
Smuts the patriot. photos. R6.50 Tafelberg 1976 SA

Meissner, H.D. McIver, B.A.
Solvent dyeing of wool with a reactive dye/surfactant complex. 12pp. R2.50 (SAWTRI Technical Reports, 231) SAWTRI 1974 SA

Meissner, H.D. McIver, B.A.
Solvent dyeing of wool with a reactive dye/surfactant complex. 12pp. R2.50 (SAWTRI Technical Reports, 231) SAWTRI 1974 SA

Mellah, M.F.
L'association du Maroc à la C.E.E.: aspects politiques. 320pp. Dir22.00 Ed Maghreb 1974 MR FRE

Mellanby, K.
The birth of Nigeria's university. 263pp. pl. N4.00 Ibadan UP 1974 NR

Melone, S.
La parenté et la terre dans la stratégie du développement. (L'expérience camerounaise. Etude critique) 203pp. CFA2000 Univ Cameroun 1972 CM FRE

Mémel-Fote, H. et al.
Annales de l'université d'Abidjan. Situation et perspectives de la littérature négro-africaine. Actes du colloque Abidjan, 16-25 avril 1969. 145pp. CFA400 pap. (F8.00 pap.) (Série D-Lettres, 3) Univ Abidjan 1970 IV FRE

Author Index

Menakaya, J.C., ed.
Nigeria school atlas. See: Duze, M., ed.

Menakaya, J.C.   Floyd, B.N.
Junior atlas for Nigeria. 64pp. maps.   N1.30
Macmillan 1965 NR

Menard, A.
Tanger.   Dir15.00 (Collection "Découverte", 4) Ed La
Porte 1974(?) MR FRE

Menga, G.
Les aventures de Moni-Mambou. v.3 62pp.   CFA180
(Coll. Pour Tous) CLE 1974 CM FRE

Menga, G.
Kotawali. 288pp.   CFA140 (F28.00) Nouv Ed Afric
1976 SG FRE

Menga, G.
La marmite de Koka-Mbala, suivi de l'Oracle. 96pp.
CFA450 CLE 1976 CM FRE

Menga, G.
La palabre stérile. 3rd. ed. 140pp.   CFA450.00 CLE
1973 CM FRE

Mengual, A.
La vignette (les taxes sur la possession des véhicules
automobiles au Maroc et en France)   Dir25.00 (Coll.
Fac. des Sciences Juridiques, économiques et sociales,
15) Ed La Porte 1962 MR FRE

Mensah, A.A.
Folk songs for schools. 76pp. ill.   95pes. ($.95)
Ghana Publ Corp 1972 GH

Mensah, A.A.
Music and dance in Zambia. 42pp. photos.   gratis
Zambia Cult Serv 1972 ZA

Mensah, A.A.
Music and dance in Zambia. 40pp. pl.   75n. Neczam
1974 ZA

Mensah-Brown, A.K.
Introduction to law in contemporary Africa. 100pp.
N2.50 ($3.00) (Conch African Monographs, 5) Conch
1975 NR

Mensah, I.D.
Citizenship education for schools. bk. 1. 48pp. ill.
maps.   C3.00 Afram 1975 GH

Mensah, I.D.
Citizenship education for schools. bk. 2. 48pp. ill.
maps.   C3.50 Afram 1975 GH

Mensah, I.D.
Citizenship education for schools. bk. 3. 60pp. ill.
maps.   C3.50 Afram 1975 GH

Mensah, I.D.
Citizenship education for schools. bk. 4. 64pp. ill.
maps.   C3.50 Afram 1975 GH

Mensah, I.D.
Citizenship education for schools. bk. 5. ill. maps.
C3.00 Afram 1975 GH

Mensah, I.D.
Citizenship education for schools. bk. 5 80pp. ill.
C3.50 Afram 1976 GH

Mensah, I.D.
Citizenship education for schools. Teacher's bk. 80pp.
C3.00 Afram 1975 GH

Mensah, J.E., ed.
Woto aduro a. [You reap what you sow.] 2nd ed.
19pp.   50pes. Bur Ghana Lang 1976 GH ASA

Mensah, J.S.
Nimbo the driver. 58pp. ill.   65pes. ($.65) Ghana
Publ Corp 1974 GH

Mensah, J.S.
Osei goes to school. 58pp. ill.   65pes. ($.55)
Ghana Publ Corp 1974 GH

Mensah, R.
The Bible and politics. 52pp.   85pes. ($.85) Ghana
Publ Corp 1973 GH

Mensah, R.
The Bible and sex. 68pp.   85pes. ($.85) Ghana
Publ Corp 1973 GH

Mensah, R.
A guide to the study of the Bible. 75pp. ($1.25)
Ghana Publ Corp 1975 GH

Mensah, R.
Masterpieces of Christian philosophy. 200pp.   C2.50
($2.50) Ghana Publ Corp 1975 GH

Mensah, R.A.
Price reckoner and metric conversion tables. 120pp.
C4.00 Afram 1977 GH

Mercier, H.
Dictionnaire français-arabe.   Dir50.00 Ed La Porte
1970[?] MR FRE

Mercier, P.
Les Asé du musée d'Abomey. 77pp. pl.   CFA400
(Catalogues et Documents, 7) IFAN 1952 SG FRE

Mercier, P.
Les tâches de la sociologie. 93pp.   CFA600
(Initiations et Etudes Africaines, 6) IFAN 1951 SG FRE

Mercier.
Thèmes et travaux. Littérature française (1750-1850)
See: Fornacciari, M.F.

Mertens, A.
Kavango. photos.   R10.00 Purnell 1976 SA

Meskin, P.M., ed.
South African encyclopaedia of forms and precedents.
14 v. 153pp.   R24.00 per v. cl. Butterworths 1972
SA

Metrowich, F.C.
Scotty Smith.   R3.75 Bulpin 1970 SA

Metrowich, F.R., ed.
Nigeria: the Biafran war. 148pp. ill. maps.   R2.25
(60c) Africa Inst - Pret 1969 SA

Metrowich, F.R.
Towards dialogue and détente. 139pp. hd.   R6.00
Valiant 1975 SA

Metrowich, R.
Africa survey. 184pp. photos. hd.   R6.00 Valiant
1975 SA

Metson, J.
A base line survey for the evaluation of the foot and mouth
disease control programme in Narok and Kajiado districts.
67pp.   K.shs.7.00 Inst Dev Stud 1975 KE

Metter, L. et al.
Wage determinations current in South Africa as at
December 31, 1974. 380pp. hd.   R8.00 ($10.95)
SA Inst of Race Relations 1975 SA

Meyburgh, J.C.
Rainfall at the Jonkershoek Forest hydrological research
station. See: Wicht, C.L.

Meyer, A.
Hominids of the lower and middle pleistocene the
Australopithecinae and Homo habilis. 58pp.   R3.00
Dept Bibliog, Lib & Typo 1968 SA

Meyer, A.J.
A histological study of the alimentary canal and associated
structures in the larva of Coryphodema tristis Drury.
26pp. pl.   83c. (A v.41, no. 4) Univ Stellenbosch, Lib
1966 SA

Meyer, B.J.
Elementary medical biophysics. See: Jaros, G.G.

Meyer, F.B.
Help in time of sorrow. 28pp. (4k) SIM 1966 NR

Meyer, P.
Some aspects of the sociology of apartheid.   40c.
(Isma paps., 21) Inst Study of Man 1964 SA

Meyer, R.
Basic genetics for schools and colleges. See: Frank, S.

Meyer, R.S.
Body, mind and perception. 28pp.   55c. (R1.05)
Univ South Africa 1969 SA

Author Index

Meyerowitz, D.
The law and practice of administration of estates. 5th rev. ed. 700pp. cl. R38.00 Juta 1976 SA

Mfodwo, B.
Folk tales and stories from around the world. 30pp. ill. 25pes. ($.25) Ghana Publ Corp 1971 GH

Mgawi, K.
Ndingasankhe bwanji mnzanga wa chikwati. [How can I choose my marriage partner?] 16pp. 13t. (12c.) Christ Lit Assoc - Mal 1971 MW CHC

Mgawi, K.
Safunsa adadya phula. [A guide to courtship and marriage for boys and girls] 16pp. 10t. (12c.) Christ Lit Assoc - Mal 1970 MW CHC

M'Hamsadji, K.
Fleurs de novembre. 129pp. DA5.00 SNED 1970 AE FRE

Mhando, P.
Hatia. 41pp. K.shs5.00 ($2.00) EAPH 1972 KE

M'Henni, H.
La santé mère - enfant. See: Hamza, B.

Mhina, F.E.F.
Mashujaa wa Tanzania. [Heroes of Tanzania] 55pp. photos. T.shs.4.75 Longman - Tanz 1972 TZ SWA

Mhina, G.A. Kiimbila, J.K.
Mwalimu wa Kiswahili. [The Swahili teacher] 105pp. T.shs.8.50 Inst Swahili Res 1971 TZ SWA

Mhina, G.A.
Vifungu vya ufahamu. [Comprehension passages] 72pp. K.shs.8.50 OUP-Nairobi 1971 KE SWA

M'Hiri, A.
Les théories grammaticales d'Ibn Jinni. D2.20 (Série VI, Philosophie-Littérature, 5) Univ Tunis 1973 TI FRE

Mhoya, E.
Here's how to choose a Christian name. 24pp. 15n Multimedia 1972 ZA

Miano, R.
A girl asks why. 28pp. ill. 45pes. (15p.) Africa Christian 1973 GH

Michaelides, G.G. Coetzee, C.
Candid Cape Town. 192pp. R4.95 Struik 1977 SA

Michau, M.
An evaluation of various methods of reducing the degradation of cotton by light. See: van Rensburg, N.J.J.

Michie, W.
Lands and peoples of Central Africa. 208pp. R$3.50 Longman - Rhod 1973 RH

Michuki, D.
Mawaidha ya wamuchuthe. 40pp. photos. K.shs3.50 ($1.30) EAPH 1969 KE SWA

Michuki, D.N.
Bururi wa Embu. [The story of the people of Embu] 119pp. K.shs.4.50 ($1.70/75p.) EALB 1962 KE KIK

Middleton, C.
Bechuanaland. 37pp. 80c. Univ Cape Town Lib 1965 SA

Middleton, I.S.
Mercantile law for standard 10. See: Swanepoel, D.J.

Midgley, J., ed. Graser, R., ed. Steyn, J.H., ed.
Crime and punishment in South Africa. 265pp. hd. R10.50 McGraw-Hill - SA 1975 SA

Mijere, N., ed.
Celebration II. See: Hearne, B., ed.

Mijindadi, N.B., ed.
Lectures on agricultural planning. Report of a course held at Zaria, 17-29 September, 1973. 142pp. free Inst Agric Res-Zaria 1974 NR

Milimo, J.
Kwacha ngwee tuye kuli baama. [Tonga traditional practices of heritage.] 52pp. 60n. Neczam 1972 ZA TON

Milingo, E.
Amake-Joni. [The mother of John] 56pp. 70n. Neczam 1972 ZA NYA

Millais, J.G.
A breath from the Veldt. [Reprint of ed. 1895.]. 236pp. ill. cl. R$57.75 limited ed. Books of Rhodesia 1974 RH

Millar, A.K.
Plantagent in South Africa: Lord Charles Somerset. 304pp. ill. R6.70 OUP-SA 1965 SA

Millar, D.J.T.
A four year course in physical education for primary schools. 3rd ed. 124pp. ill. K.shs6.25 ($2.00/70p.) EALB 1970 KE

Miller, A.
Mamisa, the Swazi warrior. 269pp. cl. R1.05 Shuter 1954 SA

Miller, A.
Umamisa iqhawe Leswazi. [Mamisa the Swazi warrior tr. fr. Eng. J.A.W. Nxumalo, S.W. Zulu] 192pp. 65c. Shuter 1957 SA ZUL

Miller, C.
Battle for the Bundu. R7.50 Purnell 1976 SA

Miller, D. C. et al.
New Oxford secondary English course. pupil's bk. 3, 5 bks. 232pp. ill. N2.00 OUP - Nig 1975 NR

Miller, D.C., et al.
New Oxford English course, Nigeria: pupils bk. 3rd ed. 1, 6 bks. 60pp. col. ill. 60k OUP - Nig 1966 NR

Miller, D.C., et al.
New Oxford English course Nigeria: pupils bk. 3rd ed. 2, 6 bks, 119pp. ill. 80k OUP - Nig 1968 NR

Miller, D.C., et al.
New Oxford English course Nigeria: pupils bk. 3rd ed. 3, 6 bks. 139pp. ill. 90k OUP - Nig 1969 NR

Miller, D.C., et al.
New Oxford English course Nigeria: pupils bk. 3rd ed. 4, 6 bks. 179pp. ill. 95k OUP - Nig 1969 NR

Miller, D.C., et al.
New Oxford English course Nigeria: pupils bk. 3rd ed. 5, 6 bks. 180pp. ill. N1.00 OUP - Nig 1970 NR

Miller, D.C., et al.
New Oxford English course Nigeria: pupils bk. 3rd ed. 6, 6 bks. 220pp. ill. N1.20 OUP - Nig 1972 NR

Miller, D.C., et al.
New Oxford English course Nigeria: teacher's bk. 1. 3rd ed. 1, 6 bks. 369pp. N3.00 OUP - Nig 1972 NR

Miller, D.C., et al.
New Oxford English course Nigeria: teacher's bk. 3 3rded. 2, 6 bks. 523pp. N3.00 OUP - Nig 1968 NR

Miller, D.C., et al.
New Oxford English course Nigeria: teacher's bk. 3 3rded. 3, 6 bks. 366pp. N3.00 OUP - Nig 1969 NR

Miller, D.C., et al.
New Oxford English course Nigeria: teacher's bk. 3 3rded. 4, 6 bks. N3.00 OUP - Nig NR

Miller, D.C., et al.
New Oxford English course Nigeria: teacher's bk. 3 3rded. 5, 6 bks. 347pp. N3.00 OUP - Nig 1971 NR

Miller, D.C., et al.
New Oxford English course Nigeria: teacher's bk. 3 3rded. 6, 6 bks. 332pp. N3.00 OUP - Nig NR

Miller, D.C., et al.
New Oxford English course Nigeria: wall pictures. 3 3rded. ill. N3.00 OUP - Nig NR

Miller, D.C. et al.
New Oxford Secondary English course, pupil's bk. 1, 5 bks. 262pp. ill. N1.55 OUP - Nig 1973 NR

Miller, D.C. et al.
New Oxford secondary English course, pupil's bk. 2, 5 bks. 236pp. ill. N1.75 OUP - Nig 1973 NR

Miller, D.C. et al.
New Oxford secondary English course. pupil's, bk. 4.
339pp. ill. N2.50 OUP - Nig 1976 NR

Miller, D.C. et al.
New Oxford secondary English course, teacher's bk. 1, 5
bks. 382pp. ill. N2.00 OUP - Nig 1973 NR

Miller, D.C. et al.
New Oxford secondary English course, teacher's bk. 2, 5
bks. 412pp. ill. N3.55 OUP - Nig 1973 NR

Miller, D.C., et al.
New Oxford secondary English course. Teacher's bk. 3
390pp. N4.80 OUP - Nig 1976 NR

Miller, F.
Kujua kuishi. [Le savoir vivre en société.] 63pp. ill.
photos. 28k St. Paul 1972 ZR SWA

Miller, J.C.
The town of Springs, Transvaal, Republic of South Africa.
37pp. R1.95 Dept Bibliog, Lib & Typo 1969 SA

Miller, P.
Equipping for ministry in East Africa. 231pp.
T.shs.6.00 Central Tanganyika 1969 TZ

Miller, P.
The great trek. See: Bulpin, T.V.

Miller, P.
The story of Rory. col. ill. R1.00 Bulpin 1965 SA

Miller, P. Maberly, C.T.A.
The world of big game. ill. R1.00 Bulpin 1969 SA

Miller, S.
Measuring absence and labour turnover. See: van der
Merwe, R.

Miller, S.J.
New Oxford English course: link bk. 1, 2 bks 32pp.
45k OUP - Nig 1970 NR

Miller, S.J.
New Oxford English course: link bk. (A dress for Fatma)
2, 2 bks. 47pp. ill. 55k OUP - Nig 1969 NR

Miller, S.J.
Objective comprehension exercises: with answers. 50k
OUP - Nig NR

Miller, S.J.
Teaching the reading passage. 142pp. N1.30 OUP -
Nig 1966 NR

Miller, W.
Day-by-day English. First year wall charts.
See: Hemming, J.

Miller, W.
Day-by-day English. Fun with Benny and Betty. Grade 2.
See: Hemming, J.

Miller, W.
Day-by-day English. Here and there with Benny and Betty.
See: Hemming, J.

Miller, W.
Day-by-day English. My picture and reading book.
See: Hemming, J.

Miller, W.
Day-by-day English. Second year wallcharts.
See: Hemming, J.

Miller, W.
Day-by-day English. Stories for work and play. Grade 7.
See: Hemming, J.

Miller, W.
Day-by-day English. Stories from many places. Grade 6.
See: Hemming, J.

Miller, W.
Day-by-day English. Stories from town and country.
Grade 4. See: Hemming, J.

Miller, W.
Day-by-day English. Teacher's grade 1. See: Hemming,
J.

Miller, W.
Day-by-day English. Teacher's grade 2. See: Hemming,
J.

Miller, W.
Day-by-day English. Teacher's grade 3. See: Hemming,
J.

Miller, W.
Day-by-day English. Teacher's grade 5. See: Hemming,
J.

Miller, W.
Day-by-day English. Teacher's grade 6. See: Hemming,
J.

Miller, W.
Day-by-day English. Teacher's grade 7. See: Hemming,
J.

Miller, W.
Day-by-day English. The radio van and other stories.
Grade 5. See: Hemming, J.

Miller, W.T.
English courses: primary second language (Benny and
Betty) bk. 2 See: Hemming, J.

Miller, W.T.
English courses: primary second language (Benny and
Betty in town) bk. 2 See: Hemming, J.

Miller, W.T.
English courses: primary second language (Benny and his
friends) bk. 1 See: Hemming, J.

Miller, W.T.
English courses: primary second language (My picture
book - A) See: Hemming, J.

Miller, W.T.
English courses: primary second language (Stories for
work and play) See: Hemming, J.

Miller, W.T.
English courses: primary second language (Stories from
many places) bk. 5 See: Hemming, J.

Miller, W.T.
English courses: primary second language (Stories from
town and country) bk. 3 See: Hemming, J.

Miller, W.T.
English courses: primary second language (The radio van
and other stories) bk. 4 See: Hemming, J.

Miller, W.T.
English readers: South African Bantu schools. 6, 6 bks.
See: Hemming, J.

Miller, W.T.
English readers: South African Bantu schools (Benny and
Betty at home and in town) 2, 6 bks. See: Hemming, J.

Miller, W.T.
English readers: South African Bantu schools (Benny,
Betty and their friends) 1, 6 bks. See: Hemming, J.

Miller, W.T.
English readers: South African Bantu schools (Betty and
Benny) See: Hemming, J.

Miller, W.T.
English readers: South African Bantu schools (Radio van
and other tales) 4, 6 bks. See: Hemming, J.

Miller, W.T.
English readers: South African Bantu schools (Tales from
many places) 5, 6 bks. See: Hemming, J.

Miller, W.T.
English readers: South African Bantu schools (Tales from
town and country) 3, 6 bks. See: Hemming, J.

Miller, W.T.
The flesh-eaters: a guide to the carnivorous animals in
Southern Africa. 100pp. photos. maps. hd. R7.50
Purnell 1972 SA

Miller, W.T.
Teachers books to English readers: South African Bantu
schools (Benny and Betty) See: Hemming, J.

Miller, W.T.
Teachers books to English readers: South African Bantu
schools (Benny and Betty at home and in town) 2, 2 bks.
See: Hemming, J.

Miller, W.T.
Teachers books to English readers: South African Bantu schools (Benny, Betty and their friends) 1, 2 bks. See: Hemming, J.

Miller, W.T.
Teachers' guides to English courses: primary second language (Benny and Betty book - B) See: Hemming, J.

Miller, W.T.
Teachers' guides to English courses: primary second language (Benny and Betty in town) 2, 6 bks. See: Hemming, J.

Miller, W.T.
Teachers' guides to English courses: primary second language (Benny and his friends) 1, 6 bks. See: Hemming, J.

Miller, W.T.
Teachers' guides to English courses: primary second language (My picture book - A) See: Hemming, J.

Miller, W.T.
Teachers' guides to English courses: primary second language (Stories from many places) 5, 6 bks. See: Hemming, J.

Miller, W.T.
Teachers' guides to English courses: primary second language (Stories from town and country) 3, 6 bks. See: Hemming, J.

Miller, W.T.
Teachers' guides to English courses: primary second language (Stories from work and play) 6, 6 bks. See: Hemming, J.

Miller, W.T.
Teachers' guides to English courses: primary second language (The radio van and other stories) 4, 6 bks. See: Hemming, J.

Mills, H.D.
The African mudfish: clarias lazera. 4th ed. 42pp. pl. ill. N2.50 Ibadan UP 1966 NR

Mills, J.C.
Price responses of Malawi smallholder farmers; fast, slow or none? 44pp. ex. only (Univ. Malawi, Dept. of Economics, occas. paps., 2) Univ Malawi Lib; distr. 1975 MW

Mills, M.G.
Social services. 49pp. ill. col. ill. maps. ($1.20) (The Environment of the Rhodesian People, 6) M.O. Collins 1974 RH

Mills, P.
Notes on Chinua Achebe's "No longer at ease". 36pp. K.shs.6.00 (Heinemann's Student's Guides) Heinemann Educ - Nair 1974 KE

Mills, R.W.
Basic principles of technical drawing for standard 6. 92pp. ill. R2.45 Nasou 1975 SA

Mills, R.W.
Basic principles of technical drawing for standard 7. 94pp. ill. R3.25 Nasou 1975 SA

Mills, R.W.
Technical drawing and sketching (Practical course), standard 10. 61pp. ill. R2.50 Nasou 1974 SA

Mills, R.W.
Technical drawing and sketching, Standard 7. (Practical course) 86pp. ill. R2.50 Nasou 1974 SA

Mills, S.J.
Autspan: a computer program for the automatic analysis of gamma-ray spectra. 40pp. (CSIR research reports, 289) CSIR 1969 SA

Mills, S.J.
Evap: a computer programme for the calculation of angular momentum distributions in neutron-evaporation reactions. 36pp. (CSIR research reports, 282) CSIR 1968 ZA

Milne, A., comp. Lamont Smith, K., comp. Nathan, C., comp.
Henochsberg on the companies act. First (Cumulative) Supplement to third edition. [Main work together with first cumulative supplement, price R47.50] R6.50 Butterworths 1977 SA

Milsome, J.E.
El Kanemi. 60pp. maps ill. 40k (Makers of Nigeria, 4) OUP - Nig 1968 NR

Milsome, J.E.
Samuel Ajayi Crowther. 60pp. maps ill. 40k (Makers of Nigeria, 3) OUP - Nig 1968 NR

Milsome, J.E.
Usman Dan Fodio. ill. 60k (Makers of Nigeria, 5) OUP - Nig NR

Milton, A.
Teachers outside the walls. 25pp. 30c Univ Rhodesia Lib 1964 RH

Milton, J.R.L.
South African criminal law and procedure: statutory offences. 3, 4v. hd. R30.00 Juta SA

M'Imanyara, A.
Agony on a hide. 116pp. K.shs.9.50 (Modern African Library, 24) EAPH 1973 KE

Minchin, N.C.
English for you and me. 1, 6 bks. 76pp. 40c. Shuter 1961 SA

Minchin, N.C.
English for you and me. 2, 6 bks. 76pp. 40c. Shuter 1961 SA

Minchin, N.C.
English for you and me. 3, 6 bks. 76pp. 45c. Shuter 1961 SA

Minchin, N.C.
English for you and me. 4, 6 bks. 94pp. 45c. Shuter 1961 SA

Minchin, N.C.
English for you and me. 5, 6 bks. 108pp. 50c. Shuter 1961 SA

Minchin, N.C.
English for you and me. 6, 6 bks. 100pp. 50c. Shuter 1961 SA

Mindolo Ecumenical Centre.
You and your baby. 38pp. ill. 40n. Neczam 1970 ZA

Miners, T.W.
Mechanization in the building industry. See: De Vos, T.J.

Ministère de la Culture du Sénégal.
Le Sénégal présente Malcolm de Chazal. 32pp. ill. CFA450 (F9.00) Nouv Ed Afric 1973 SG FRE

Ministère de l'Education Nationale.
Gusoma. Manuel scolaire d'alphabétisation. v. 1 86pp. ill. cl. RF150 cl. ($1.50 cl.) Caritas 1972 RW KIN

Ministère de l'Information et de la Culture, Alger.
Alger. 100pp. DA10.00 SNED 1975 AE FRE

Ministère de l'Information et de la Culture, Alger.
Cinema - Production Cinématographique, 1957-1973. 280pp. pl. col. pl. 20,00 DH SNED 1974 AE FRE

Ministère de l'Information et de la Culture, Alger.
El-Djazair. 112pp. DA25.00 SNED 1975 AE FRE

Ministère de l'Information et de la Culture, Alger.
El-Moudjahid. 3v. 599, 684, 721pp. DA120.00 SNED 1975 AE FRE

Ministère de l'Information et de la Culture, Alger.
L'Emir Abdelkader. 106pp. ill. col. ill. 25,00 DA (Coll. Art et Culture) SNED 1974 AE FRE

Ministère de l'Information et de la Culture, Alger.
Les mosquées. 100pp. DA25.00 SNED 1975 AE FRE

Ministry of Education. Bendel State of Nigeria.
Science is discovering: Pupil's book for year four. 72pp. ill. pl. N1.40 Longman - Nig 1974 NR

Ministry of Education, Bendel State of Nigeria.
Science is discovering. teachers bk. 6. 80pp. ill.
N1.70 Longman - Nig 1977 NR

Ministry of Education. Bendel State of Nigeria.
Science is discovering. Teacher's guide for year four.
104pp. ill. pl. N2.10 Longman - Nig 1974 NR

Ministry of Education, Bendel State of Nigeria.
Science is discovering. teachers guide for years 1-3.
72pp. ill. N1.50 Longman - Nig 1976 NR

Ministry of Education, Tanzania.
Jifunze kusoma. 1, 4 bks. 64pp. ill. Nat Print Co
1972 TZ SWA

Ministry of Education, Tanzania.
Jifunze kusoma. 2, 4bks. 56pp. ill. Nat Print Co
1972 TZ SWA

Ministry of Education, Tanzania.
Jifunze kusoma. 3, 4 bks. 48pp. ill. Nat Print Co
1972 TZ SWA

Ministry of Education, Tanzania.
Jifunze kusoma. ill. Nat Print Co 1972 TZ SWA

Ministry of Finance and Economic Planning.
Kenya 1963-1973. 144pp. ill. col. ill. maps.
K.shs.42.00 EAPH 1974 KE

Ministry of Rural Development, Tanzania.
Jifunze ushirika. [Lessons on co-operatives] 57pp. ill.
($1.25/50p.) EALB 1968 KE SWA

Minnaar, G.G.
The influence of westernization on the personality of a
group of Zulu men. 275pp. R10.30 Human Science
Res Council 1976 SA

Mircea, R.
Gastroentérologie. 347pp. Z5.60 Press Univ Zaire
1976 ZR FRE

Miskin, J.
Bibliography of Indians in South Africa. See: Greyling,
J.J.C.

Mitande, P.K.
Kalikalanje. [Folk tales] 32pp. ill. T.shs.3.30
Longman - Tanz 1971 TZ SWA

Mitande, P.K.
Masimulizi ya kazi katika kijiji Chetu. [Socialism and
village activities] 75pp. ill. T.shs.5.00 Longman -
Tanz 1971 TZ SWA

Mitchell, H.F.
Aspects of urbanisation and age structure in Lourenco
Marques, 1957. K1.50 (£1.25) (Inst. African Studies.
Univ. Zambia, communications, 11) Inst Afr Stud -
Lusaka 1975 ZA

Mitchell-Innes, B.A.
Primary production studies in the south-west Indian Ocean,
1961-1963. 20pp. R1.10 (Investigational Reports,
14) Oceanographic Res Inst 1967 SA

Mitchell, J.
Women and equality. 21pp. 25c (Univ. Cape Town.
T.B. Davie Memorial lec., 16) Univ Cape Town Lib 1975
SA

Mitchell, J.C.
African urbanisation in Ndola and Luanshya. 25pp. ill.
maps. 30n (15p.) (Rhodes-Livingstone
communications, 6) Inst Afr Stud - Lusaka 1954 ZA

Mitchell, J.C., ed.
Social networks in urban situations: an analysis of
personal relationships in Central African towns. 378pp.
£1.56 K2.90 Inst Afr Stud - Lusaka 1969 ZA

Mitchell, J.C.
The Kalela dance: aspects of social relationships among
urban Africans in Northern Rhodesia. 82pp. K1.05
(54p.) (Rhodes-Livingstone paps., 27) Inst Soc Res -
Zam 1956 ZA

Mitchell, J.C.
Tribalism and the plural society. 36pp. 30c Univ
Rhodesia Lib 1960 RH

Mitchell, J.C.
The Yao village: a study in the social structure of a
Nyasaland tribe. 371pp. ill. photos maps. pap. & hd.
K5.40 hd. K3.20 pap. (£2.64 hd.) (£1.56 pap.)
Inst Afr Stud - Lusaka 1956 ZA

Mitchell, M.T.
Source book of parliamentary elections and referenda in
southern Rhodesia, 1898-1962. See: Passmore, G.C.

Mitford-Barberton, I. White, V.
Some frontier families. Biographical sketches of 100
Eastern Province families before 1840. 303pp. R8.50
cl. Human and Rousseau 1968 SA

Mkabarah, J.
Michezo ya kuigiza na hadithi. See: Nyasulu, G.

Mkabarah, J.R.R.
Salum Abdallah: mwanamuziki wa Tanzania. [Salim
Abdallah: musician of Tanzania] 91pp. photos.
T.shs.6.00 Inst Swahili Res 1971 TZ SWA

Mkangi, K.G.C.
Ukiwa. [Isolation] 108pp. K.shs.15 OUP - Nairobi
1975 KE SWA

Mkele, N.
The African middle class. 40c (Isma paps., 4) Inst
Study of Man 1961 SA

Mkelle, M.B.
Utenzi wa Kadhi Kassim bin Jaffar by Sheikh Hemed
Abdallah bin Said. [The epic of the Judge Kassim bin
Haafer] T.shs.5.00 Inst Swahili Res 1972 TZ SWA

Mkhize, D.
Ngavele ngasho. [I told you so] 128pp. 75c Shuter
1965 SA ZUL

Mlagala, M.
Yasin's nightmare. 42pp. ill. K.shs.5.00 ($1.50)
EAPH 1976 KE

Mlekwa, V.
Mass education and functional literacy programmes in
Tanzania: searching for a model. T.shs.1.00 (Studies
in Adult Education, 21) Inst Adult Educ - Dar 1975 TZ

Mlilo, S.O.
Lifile. [The old order has changed.] 144pp. 76c
Mambo 1975 RH NDE

Mlingwa, F.E.
Diwani Yetu. [Primary poetry book] 33pp. T.shs.2.75
Longman - Tanz 1971 TZ SWA

Mlingwa, F.E.
Haki itatawala dunia. [Justice shall prevail] 70pp. ill.
T.shs.5.00 Longman - Tanz 1972 TZ SWA

Mlingwa, F.E.
Kua ukayaone ya dunia. [Growing up] 71pp. ill.
T.shs.3.00 Longman - Tanz 1972 TZ SWA

Mmadu, C.
Guide to African poetry. 95pp. N1.50 Univ Publ
1977 NR

Mmari, J.
Mafunzo ya muziki. [Music primer] ill. music.
Longman Tanz 1973 TZ SWA

Mncwango, L.L.J.
Ngenzeni. [What have I done?] 130pp. 50c Shuter
1959 SA ZUL

Mngola, E.N.
The use and abuse of drugs and chemical in tropical
Africa. Proceedings of the 1973 annual scientific
conference of the East African Medical Research Council,
Nairobi. See: Bagshawe, A.F.

Mnkandla, P.N.
Abaseguswini lesothamlilo. [People and animals.] 76pp.
60c Longman - Rhod 1974 RH NDE

Mnyampala, M.E.
Diwani ya Mnyampala. [Mnyampala's poems] 4th ed.
4, 10 bks. K.shs.14.00 ($3.40/£1.40) (Johari za
Kiswahili, 4) EALB 1976 KE SWA

Mnyampala, M.E.
Historia ya Kiswahili. See: Chiraghdin, S.

Author Index

Mnyampala, M.E.
Kisa cha Bahati na wazazi wake. [The tale of Bahati and his parents] 60pp. ill. T.shs..1.40 Ndanda Mission Press TZ SWA

Mnyampala, M.E.
Kisa cha Mrina Asali na Wenzake Wawili. [The adventures of a honey-gatherer and his two friends] 3 3rded. 65pp. K.shs.3.75 ($1.50/60p) EALB 1975 KE SWA

Mnyampala, M.E.
Mbinu za ujamaa. [Routes of relationship] 50pp. ill. T.shs.1.80 Ndanda Mission Press TZ SWA

Mnyampala, M.E.
Ngonjera za Ukuta. [Ukuta's poems] bk. 1 100pp. K.shs.10.00 OUP-Nairobi 1970 KE SWA

Mnyampala M.E.
Ngonjera za Ukuta. [Ukuta's poems] bk. 2 56pp. K.shs.3.50 OUP-Nairobi 1971 KE SWA

Mnyampala, M.E.
Sikilizeni hekima. [Listen to wisdom] 32pp. T.shs.1.00 Ndanda Mission Press TZ SWA

Mnyampala, M.E.
Utenzi wa Enjili. [Epic of the Gospels] 120pp. ill. T.shs.4.40 Ndanda Mission Press TZ SWA

Mnyampala, M.E.
Utenzi wa Zaburi. [Epic of psalms] 105pp. ill. T.shs.4.20 Ndanda Mission Press TZ SWA

Mnyampala, M.E.
Waadhi wa ushairi. [Poetry] 2nd ed. K.shs.5.75 ($2.00/80p.) (Johari za Kiswahili, 7) EALB 1971 KE SWA

Moalusi, E.
New Testament survey. pt. 1 See: Khumalo, A.

Moalusi, E. Jordahl, R. Snook, S.
New Testament survey, pt. 2. 226pp. K.shs.20.00 ($2.50) Evangel 1977 KE

Moâtamri, C.
De Gafsa à Munich. 112pp. pl. D0.450 Maison Tunis 1974 TI FRE

Mobior, J.G.
Cooperative marketing of non-traditional cooperative commodities in Tanzania. T.shs.12.00 ($3.00) (Research pap., 70.25) Econ Res Bur - Tanz 1975 TZ

Mocoancoeng, J.G.
Tseleng ya bophelo le dithothokiso tse ntjha. [The way of life: a play, and poems] repr. in new orthography ed. 76pp. cl. R1.00 (Bantu treasury, 10) Witwatersrand UP 1972 SA SOS

Modupe, O. Omotoso, M.
Housing in Ibadan. 80pp. maps pl. hd. N8.00 cl. Dept Town Poly - Ib 1976 NR

Moerane, M.T.
Southern Africa fifty years hence. 40c (ISMA paps., 33) Inst Study of Man 1972 SA

Mofokeng, S.M.
Pelong ya ka. [Southern Sotho essays.] repr. in new orthography ed. 118pp. R1.20 (Bantu treasury, 15) Witwatersrand UP 1975 SA SOS

Mofokeng, S.M.
Senkatana. [A play] repr. in new orthography ed. 119pp. cl. R1.20 (Bantu treasury, 12) Witwatersrand UP 1972 SA SOS

Mofolo, T.
Chaka. 166pp. ill. 75c. Morija 1973 LO SOS

Mofolo, T.
Chaka mtemi wa Wazulu. [Chaka: Chief of the Zulus] Tr. from Sesuto by M.S. Attas 108pp. K.shs.12.50 OUP - Nairobi 1975 KE SWA

Mofolo, T.
Moeti oa Bochabela. [The traveller to the east] 74pp. 35c. Morija 1968 LO SOS

Mohamed, M.S.
Nyota ya Rehema. [Novel.] 180pp. K.shs.17.50 OUP - Nairobi 1977 KE SWA

Mohamed, S.A.
Vito vya hekima, simo na maneno ya mshangao. 43pp. K.shs.6.00 Longman - Ken 1974 KE SWA

Mohammadu, E.
Maroua et pette. 482pp. CELTHO 1970 NG FRE

Mohapeloa, J.M.
Government by proxy. cl. ed. pl. photos. maps. R1.80 Morija 1971 LO

Mohapeloa, J.M.
A primary history course. pt. 1 64pp. ill. maps. 70c. Longman SA 1958 SA

Mohapeloa, J.M.
A primary history course. pt. 2 96pp. ill. maps. 75c. Longman SA 1958 SA

Mohapeloa, J.P.
Meluluetsa. [Tonic solfa of 25 Lesotho songs.] 120pp. photo. music. R3.00 OUP - SA 1977 SA

Mohr, E.
To the Victoria Falls of the Zambesi. [Reprint of ed. 1876]. 462pp. ill. map. cl. R$9.50 (Rhodesiana Reprint Library, Gold Series, 28) Books of Rhodesia 1973 RH

Mohr, R.
No homage unto the sun. 12pp. 30c (Univ. Cape Town. Inaugural lec., 16) Univ Cape Town Lib 1973 SA

Mohrlang, R.
Higi phonology. 106pp. N1.50 ($2.60/£1.00) (Studies in Nigerian languages, 2) Inst Ling-ABU 1972 NR

Moine, B.
Etude géologique et prospection de la feuille Ambositra. 28pp. pl. map. FMG950 (F18.00) (Travaux du Bureau Géologique, 122) Service Geol - Mad 1965 MG FRE

Moine, B.
Etude géologique et prospection de la feuille Fianarantso. 31pp. pl. map. FMG770 (F15.40) (Travaux du Bureau Géologique, 116) Service Geol - Mad 1963 MG FRE

Mokgogong, P.C.
Pu Kuntsu ye kogolo ya Sesotho sa leboa/Groot Noord-Sotho woordeboek/Comprehensive Northern Sotho dictionary. [Trilingual in Northern Sotho, Afrikaans and English.]. See: Ziervogel, D.

Mokto, J.J.
Ramitou mon étrangère. 140pp. CFA510 CLE 1971 CM FRE

Mol, H.
Antibiotics and milk. 220pp. R10.50 ($15.00) Balkema 1975 SA

Molema, S.M.
Montshiwa, Barolong chief and patriot 1815-1895. 250pp. pl. cl. R4.75 Struik 1966 SA

Moliere, J.B.P. de.
Mchuuzi mwungwana. [Le bourgeois gentilhomme] tr. fr. French A. Morrison. 3rd ed. 80pp. K.shs3.50 ($1.75) EALB KE SWA

Moliere, J.B.P. de.
Mnafiki. [Tartuffe.] tr. fr. English L. Taguaba. 62pp. T.shs.6.50 Tanz Publ House 1973 TZ SWA

Moll, A.
The flying Sikh. See: Moll, B.

Moll, B. Moll, A.
The flying Sikh. 112pp. photos. K.shs.30.00 Transafrica 1975 KE

Moll, E.J., ed.
Trees of southern Africa. See: Palgrave, C.K., ed.

Moll, F.
Xylophages et pétricoles ouest-africains. See: Monod, T.

Moll, P.
Mzee Jomo Kenyatta. See: Amin, M.

Moll, P.
One man one vote.   See: Amin, M.

Mollard, P.J.
Le régime juridique de la presse au Maroc.   Dir25.00
(Coll. Fac. des Sciences juridiques, éonomiques et
sociales, 17)   Ed La Porte 1963 MR FRE

Moller, J.P.
Journey in Africa through Angola, Ovampoland and
Damaraland.   See: Rudner, I.

Mollison, S.
Kenya's coast.   154pp. photos.   K.shs.15.00   ($4.00)
EAPH 1971 KE

Molteno, R.
The Zambian community and its government.   232pp. ill.
K2.00   Neczam 1974 ZA

Momodu, A.G.S.
The course of justice, and other stories.   98pp.   85k
(African Literature series, 1)   Onibonoje 1973 NR

Mondjannagni, A.
Contribution à l'étude des paysages végétaux du bas
Dahomey.   186pp.   CFA1000   (F20.00)   (Série
G-Géographie, 1-2)   Univ Abidjan 1969 IV FRE

Monekosso, G.L.
Report of a survey on African medical schools,
July-December 1974/75.   238pp.   ($10.00)   AAU 1976
GH

Money, N.J.
The coal resources of the Zambezi valley.   v.5:
Siankondobo - the northeastern area - a preliminary report
See: Denman, P.D.

Money, N.J.
Some aspects of the geology of the Siankondobo coalfield.
See: Drysdall, A.R.

Monfils, G.   Verlhac, A.
Evaluation de la méthode 'Pour Parler Français' au niveau
du C.E.2.   102pp.   CFA320   (C.L.A.D. Étude, 56)
CLAD 1974 SG FRE

Monfils, G.
Evaluation de la méthode 'Pour Parler Français.'
Comparaison entre la méthode traditionnelle et la méthode
CLAD.   CFA320   CLAD 1974 SG FRE

Mongo, P.
Un enfant comme les autres.   64pp.   CFA200   CLE
1972 CM FRE

Monk, O.
Bookbinding projects, standard 2.   See: de Wet, E. P.

Monk, O.
Bookbinding projects, standard 3.   See: de Wet, E. P.

Monk, O.
Bookbinding projects, standard 4.   See: de Wet, E. P.

Monnier, Y.
Annales de l'université d'Abidjan. Il était une fois, à
Ayérémou... un village du sud-baoulé.   136pp.   CFA800
(F16.00)   (Série G-Géographie, 1-1)   Univ Abidjan 1969
IV FRE

Mönnig, H.O.   Veldman, F.J.
Handbook on stock diseases.   cl.   R10.25   Tafelberg
1976 SA

Monod, T.
Le complexe urophore des poissons téléostéens.   705pp.
ill.   CFA6000   (Mémoires de l'IFAN, 81)   IFAN 1968
SG FRE

Monod, T.
Contribution à l'établissement d'une liste d'accidents
circulaires d'origine météorique (reconnue, possible ou
supposée), crypto-explosive, etc.   93pp. map.
CFA600   (Catalogues et Documents, 18)   IFAN 1965 SG
FRE

Monod, T.
Etudes sur la flore et la végétation du Tibesti. [Reprint of
ed. Paris, 1950].   See: Maire, R.

Monod, T.
Hippidea et Brachyura ouest-africains.   674pp. ill.
CFA3000   (Mémoires de l'IFAN, 45)   IFAN 1956 SG
FRE

Monod, T.   Schnell, R.
Mélanges botaniques.   334pp. pl.   CFA2400
(Mémoires de l'IFAN, 18)   IFAN 1952 SG FRE

Monod, T.   Moll, F.   Nickles, M.
Xylophages et pétricoles ouest-africains.   145pp. pl.
CFA600   (Catalogues et Documents, 8)   IFAN 1952 SG
FRE

Monsengo Osantwene.
Il ressuscita sa soeur. Mythes sakata. Textes
sakata-français.   124pp. map.   (DM21.00 pap.)
(CEEBA. série II, Mémoires et Monographies, 31)   CEEBA
1975 ZR FRE

Monteil, V.
Esquisses Sénégalaises (Wâlo, Kayor, Dyolof, Mourides,
un visionnaire)   243pp. ill.   CFA2000   (Initiations et
Etudes Africaines, 21)   IFAN 1966 SG FRE

Montgomery, A.N.
Door to poetry.   See: Kedian, P.J.

Montgomery, A.N.
Invitation to poetry.   See: Kedian, P.J.

Moodie, D., ed.
The Record: a series of official papers relative to the
condition and treatment of the native tribes of South Africa.
672pp. hd.   fl. 112.50   Balkema 1960 SA

Moodley, V.
Technical drawing for standard 6 and 7.   See: Garach,
R.B.

Moody, A.A.
Report on the farm economic survey of tea smallholders in
Bukoba district.   24pp.   T.shs.12.00   ($3.00)
(Research pap., 70.8)   Econ Res Bur - Tanz 1970 TZ

Moody, E.
Growth centres in Lesotho.   118pp. maps.   R3.00
(R3.50 pap.)   Africa Inst - Pret 1975 SA

Moody, K.W., ed.
Organised English.   1, 5 bks.   168pp. ill.   N1.15
Pilgrim 1971 NR

Moody, K.W., ed.
Organised English.   2, 5 bks.   152pp. ill.   N1.15
Pilgrim 1971 NR

Moody, K.W., ed.
Organised English.   3, 5 bks.   186pp. ill.   N1.15
Pilgrim 1971 NR

Moody, K.W., ed.
Organised English.   5, 5 bks.   186pp.   N1.75   Pilgrim
1974 NR

Moody, K.W., ed.
Organised English: teacher's bk.   1, 3 bks.   88pp. ill.
N1.70   Pilgrim 1971 NR

Moody, K.W., ed.
Organised English: teacher's bk.   2, 3 bks.   80pp. ill.
N1.70   Pilgrim 1971 NR

Moody, K.W., ed.
Organised English: teacher's bk.   3, 3 bks.   74pp. ill.
N1.70   Pilgrim 1971 NR

Moody, K.W., ed.
Organised English: teacher's book.   bk. 5   74pp.
N2.00   Pilgrim 1974 NR

Moody, K.W.
Jingles with patterns.   60pp.   75k   OUP - Nig 1970 NR

Moody, K.W.
Pictorial drills in English language.   64pp. ill.   50k
Pilgrim 1967 NR

Moody, K.W.
Teaching structures in situations.   See: Gibbs, P.H.

Moody, K.W.
Written English under control.   147pp.   N2.00   OUP -
Nig 1966 NR

Moody, M.   Odugbose, A.
Common entrance mathematics: without answers. 46pp.
55k Pilgrim 1971 NR

Moody, M.
Objective questions in mathematics: with answers.
See: Potts, H.

Moody, M.
Objective questions in mathematics: without answers.
See: Potts, H.

Moolman, B.A.
Income and expenditure patterns of Coloureds in Beaufort
West and Upington. 135pp.   R30.00 (Bureau of
Market Research, Research Reports, 45.2) Bur Market
Research 1975 SA

Moolman, B.A.   Martins, J.H.
Income and expenditure patterns of Coloureds in George
and Moorreesburg. 135pp.   R30.00 (Bureau of
Market Research, Research Reports, 45.1) Bur Market
Research 1975 SA

Moolman, B.A.
Income and expenditure patterns of Coloureds in Paarl and
Kimberley. 135pp.   R30.00 (Bureau of Market
Research, Research Reports, 45.3) Bur Market Research
1975 SA

Moolman, B.A.
Income and expenditure patterns of rural Coloureds in
Malmesbury and Calvinia. 132pp.   R30.00 (Bureau of
Market Research, Research Reports, 45.4) Bur Market
Research 1975 SA

Moolman, B.A.
Income and expenditure patterns of urban Black
households in East London. 130pp.   R50.00 (Bureau
of Market Research, Research Report, 50.4) Bur Market
Res 1976 SA

Moolman, B.A.   Loubser, M.
Market potentials of consumer goods and services for
non-white population groups in the five main metropolitan
areas of the Republic of South Africa. 269pp.   R25.00
(Bureau of Market Research, Research Reports, 34) Bur
Market Research 1973 SA

Moolman, J.H., et al., eds.
The future of the Homelands. Papers delivered at the 44th
Annual Council Meeting of the South African Institute of
Race Relations. 67pp.   R2.00 ($3.20) SA Inst of
Race Relations 1974 SA

Moolman, J.H., et al.
Key issues in homeland development.   R2.00 (R2.50)
(Africa Inst. of South Africa, occas. paps., 40) Africa Inst
1975 SA MUL

Moor, S.
The published works of Keppel Harcourt Barnard. 54pp.
90c. Univ Cape Town Lib 1964 SA

Moore, B.
Merry-making. See: Waciuma, C.

Moore, B.
Peoples of East Africa; a film strip with teachers' notes.
See: Osogo, J.

Moore, G., ed.
African literature and the universities. 148pp.   N3.50
Ibadan UP 1965 NR

Moore, G.H.
Is God in history. 9pp.   C1.00 ($1.00/50p.) (25p.)
(Inaugural lecture) Ghana UP 1971 GH

Moore, J.E.
Rural population carrying capacities for the districts of
Tanzania. 46pp.   T.shs.7.00 (Research pap., 18)
Bur Res Assess Tanz 1971 TZ

Moore, J.H.
Sanitation in South Africa.   R4.50 Juta 1969 SA

Moorehouse, F.
Discovering African geography. Pupil's grade 6. 128pp.
R$1.00 Longman - Rhod 1972 RH

Moorehouse, F.
Discovering African geography. Teacher's grade 6.
64pp.   50c. Longman - Rhod 1971 RH

Moorehouse, F.   Gobett.
Discovering world geography. Grade 7. 144pp.
R$1.10 Longman - Rhod 1972 RH

Moorehouse, F.   Gobett.
Discovering world geography. Teacher's grade 7. 60c.
Longman - Rhod 1972 RH

Mopilla.
L'enfance. Tr. fr. Spanish J. Castro-Segovia and J.
Lanotte. 78pp.   50k (Jeune Littérature, 11) Ed Mont
Noir 1972 ZR FRE

Morafa, A.
A manual on land use survey, analysis and presentation.
50pp. maps. hd.   N6.00 cl. Dept Town Poly - Ib 1976
NR

Morel, S.W.
The geology and minerals of Sierra Leone. 21pp. map.
Le1.50 (75p.) Fourah Bay Bkshp 1976 SL

Morel, S.W.
The geology of the Middle Shire area. 66pp. map pl.
hd.   K1.05 (Geological Survey of Malawi, Bull. 10)
Geol Survey - Mal 1958 MW

Morgan, K.
How the tortoise captured the elephant. 43pp. ill.   27k
(New Oxford suppl reader grade 3, 8) OUP-Nig 1966
NR

Morgan, K.
The ungrateful hen and other stories. 45pp. ill.   40k
(New Oxford suppl reader grade 3, 6) OUP-Nig 1966
NR

Morgan, W.T.W.
East Africa: its peoples and resources. rev. ed. 328pp.
maps photos. pap.   K.shs150.00 pap. OUP-Nairobi
1972 KE

Morgen, C.   Laburthe-Tolra, P.
A travers le Cameroun du sud au nord. Voyages et
explorations de 1889 à 1891. 2 v. 374pp. ill.
CFA2,400 set CLE; distr 1975 CM FRE

Moriarty, A.
Wild flowers of Malawi. 176pp. col. ill.   R12.50
Purnell 1976 SA

Morija Sesuto Book Depot.
Puisano ea Sesotho le Senyesemane. [Sesotho-English
phrase book] 80pp.   R.35c. Morija 1971 LO

Morin, F.
L'environnment psycho-sociologique de l'élève sénégalais
à l'école primaire. 143pp.   CFA625 (C.L.A.D. Etude,
27) CLAD 1968 SG FRE

Moris, J.
Rural development in Kenya. See: Heyer, J.

Moriseau-Leroy, F.
Kasamansa. 40pp.   CFA300 (F6.00) Nouv Ed Afric
1976 SG FRE

Morley, C.L.
Xerography. 135pp.   R6.85 Dept Bibliog, Lib & Typo
1970 SA

Morris, E.
Technique in litigation. 2nd ed. 384pp. cl. & pap.
R18.00 cl.   R12.50 pap. Juta 1975 SA

Morris, H.F.
A history of Ankole. 60pp. ill.   K.shs4.00
($1.75/70p.) EALB 1961 KE

Morris, H.F.   Kirwan, B.E.R.
A Runyankore grammar. 253pp. cl.   K.shs7.50
($2.50/£1.00) EALB 1957 KE

Morris, J.   West, M.
Abantu. An introduction to the black people of South
Africa. 192pp. ill. col. ill. cl.   R9.95 Struik 1976 SA

Morris, J., ed.   Sailor, G., ed.
Technical innovation and farm development in East Africa.
507pp.   U.shs.60.00 ($10.00) Mak Inst Soc Res 1975
UG

Morris, J.
Scenic South Africa. 128pp. col. pl.   R7.50 Juta
1975 SA

Morris, J.
South Africa. 160pp. pl. hd.   R7.50 Purnell 1971
SA

Morris, L.
Mungu aliyetoka mbinguni. [Lord from heaven.] 96pp.
T.shs.5.00 Central Tanganyika 1968 TZ SWA

Morrow, A.
God, the devil and you. 84pp.   K.shs.4.50 Evangel
1975 KE

Morse, S.J.   Orpen, C.
Contemporary South Africa. Social psychological
perspectives.   R15.00 Juta 1975 SA

Morton, J.G.
Man's environment - Africa. See: Nicholson, J.M.

Morton, J.G.
Man's environment: Africa. pt.2 See: Nicholson, J.M.

Morton, J.G.
Man's environment. Standard 9. See: Nicholson, J.M.

Morton, J.G.
Man's environment. Standard 9. See: Nicholson, J.M.

Morton, J.G.
Man's environment. Standard 10. See: Nicholson, J.M.

Morton, J.G.
Man's environment standard 10. See: Nicholson, J.M.

Morton, J.G.
Man's environment: the northern hemisphere, mapwork,
geomorphology and trade routes. pt.3 See: Nicholson,
J.M.

Morton, J.G.
Primary school geographies, std.III: east of the
Drakensberg. See: Nicholson, J.M.

Morton, J.G.
Primary school geographies, std.IV: Africa far and wide.
See: Nicholson, J.M.

Morton, J.G.
Primary school geographies, std.V: South Africans abroad.
See: Nicholson, J.M.

Morton, J.G.
Primary school geographies, std.VI: from old world to new.
See: Nicholson, J.M.

Morton, J.G.
Working with maps: an introduction to topographical map
interpretation. See: Nicholson, J.M.

Morton, J.M.
Man's environment: the natural regions of the world,
mathematical geography, weather and climate, the oceans,
South America, Australasia. pt.1 See: Nicholson, J.M.

Morton-Williams, P.
Museum of the Institute of African Studies, University of Ife:
a short illustrated guide. See: Ojo, J.R.O.

Mosback, G.P.   Hailu, A.
English-Amharic dictionary. 304pp. Eth.$5.00
OUP-Addis 1972 ET

Moses, L.
The East African transport study: a preliminary appraisal.
T.shs.12.00 ($3.00) (Research pap., 68.27) Econ Res
Bur - Tanz 1974 TZ

Mostert, J.W.C.
Studies of the vegetation of parts of the Bloemfontein and
Brandfort districts. R1.95 (Memoirs of the Botanical
Survey of South Africa, 31) Botanical Res Inst 1958 SA

Mosugu, S.E.
Abandoned properties edict in the Northern states of
Nigeria. 42pp. N1.00 (80c./$2.00) Inst Admin -
Zaria 1972 NR

Mote, J.
The flesh. pt. 1 361pp.   K.shs.25.00 pap. ($5.00)
(Comb Books in English, 9) Comb Books 1975 KE

Mott, F.L.   Fapohunda, O.J.
The population of Nigeria. 100pp.   60k Univ Lagos
Bkshop 1975 NR

Mott, F.L.
Some aspects of health care in rural Nigeria. 31pp.
60k (Univ. Lagos, Human Resources Research Unit
Series, 7) Univ Lagos Bkshop 1975 NR

Motte, S.A.
Mia denyigba. [Our homeland.] 2nd ed. 115pp. ill.
C1.20 Bur Ghana Lang 1976 GH EWE

Mouali, M.
La sédition permanente en Tunisie. 2, 2v. 244pp.
D0.800 Maison Tunis 1972 TI FRE

Mounir, T.
Le prix de la liberté. 162pp.   DA5.50 SNED 1968 AE
FRE

Mountain, E.
Geology of Southern Africa. 2nd ed. col. pl. ill.
R5.00 Bulpin 1968 SA

Mountain, E.D.   Rennie, J.V.L.
The border region: natural environment and land use in
the Eastern Cape. v. 1 Maps photos. maps.   R8.70
OUP-SA 1962 SA

Mountain, E.D., ed.   Rennie, J.V.L., ed.
The border region: natural environment and land use in
the Eastern Cape. v. 2 Text 254pp. photos. maps.
R8.70 OUP-SA 1962 SA

Mountain, F.
The dyeing of wool with some reactive dyes by a
pad/bake method. See: Strydom, M.A.

Mountain, F.
The transfer printing of cotton, part I: an investigation into
the application of reactive dyes by the west transfer
technique. See: Roberts, M.B.

Mouralis, B.
Annales de l'université d'Abidjan. Individu et collectivité
dans le roman négro-africain d'expression française.
169pp. CFA800 pap. (F16.00 pap.) (Série D-Lettres,
2) Univ Abidjan 1969 IV FRE

Moussa, A.
La condition juridique du mineur au Maroc.   Dir40.00
(Coll. Fac. des Sciences juridiques, économiques et
sociales, 21) Ed La Porte 1968 MR FRE

Moyer, R.A.
Coko. Reminiscences of Joseph Scotch Coko - a
Grahamstown resident. 182pp.   R3.00 (Inst. of Social
and Economic Research occas. paps., 18) Inst Soc &
Econ Res - SA 1973 SA

Moyo, A.C.
Uchandifungawo. [You will think of me.] 150pp. pl.
R$1.10 Mambo 1975 RH SHO

Moyo, C.M.M.
Babukhwa bubili. [Double betrothal.] 79pp. pl.   38c
Mambo 1975 RH NDE

Moyo, E.E.E.
Tswana settlement structures. 92pp. maps.
U.shs.30.00 (Occas. paps., 60) Dept Geog - Mak 1975
UG

Moyo, J.   Holland, G.
Bringing people to Jesus. 218pp.   K.shs.13.00
($1.70) Evangel 1967 KE

Moyo, J.   Holland, G.
Comment amener les gens à Jésus. 225pp. ill.
CFA400 CPE 1974 IV FRE

Moyo, J.
Ndebele. Grade 1: Ekhaya lesikolo. See: Childs, J.

Moyo, J.
Ndebele. Grade 2: Zifundele izindaba. See: Childs, J.

Moyo, J.
Ndebele. Teacher's bk. grade 1. See: Childs, J.

Msweli, S.   Crider, D.
Mchungaji na kazi yake. [The shepherd and his work] (Mafundisho ya Thiologia Kwa Enezi, 4) Evangel 1974 KE SWA

Msweli, S.   Crider, D.
The shepherd and his work. 248pp. K.shs.13.00 ($1.70) Evangel 1971 KE

Mtara, S.J.
Mau okuluwika M'cinyanja. [Idiomatic words in Cinyanja.] 82pp. 75n. Neczam 1967 ZA NYA

Mtingane, A.
Inene nasi isibhoza [Drama]. 80pp. 75c OUP-SA 1968 SA XHO

Mtulia, I.A.T.
Pharmacology and therapeutics. A manual for medical assistants and other health workers. 240pp. ill. K.shs.15.00 (Rural Health Series, 5) African Med Res Found 1976 KE

Mubangizi, B.K.
Nkutebeze. 1, 4 bks. 26pp. K.shs.2.45 ($1.50/60p.) EALB 1958 KE LUG

Mubangizi, B.K.
Nkutebeze. 2, 4 bks. 38pp. K.shs.3.20 ($1.50/60p.) EALB 1958 KE LUG

Mubangizi, B.K.
Nkutebeze. 3, 4 bks. 34pp. K.shs.2.45 ($1.50/60p.) EALB 1968 KE LUG

Mubangizi, B.K.
Nkutebeze. 4, 4 bks. 36pp. K.shs.3.20 ($1.50/60p.) EALB 1968 KE LUG

Mubenga Kampotu.
Elements d'analyse infinitesimale. v. 1. 384pp. Z7.33 Press Univ Zaire 1976 ZR FRE

Mubeya, D.
Wanawake vijijini. [Women in villages] 41pp. T.shs.2.50 Inst Swahili Res 1971 TZ SWA

Mubiana, G.S.
Kayama-simangulungwa. [He who lives by deceit.] 96pp. ill. K1.00 Neczam 1973 ZA LOZ

Mubiana, G.S.
Nakaywe u shandauzwi kini? [What destroyed Nakaywe] 66pp. 60n. Neczam 1972 ZA LOZ

Mudimbe-Boyi, M.
L'oeuvre romanesque de Jacques-Stephen Alexis. Ecrivain haitien. 128pp. (Essais, 9) Ed Mont Noir 1975 ZR FRE

Mudimbe, V.Y.
Autour de la 'Nation'. 60k Ed Mont Noir 1973 ZR FRE

Mudimbe, V.Y.
Autour de 'La Nation.' Leçons de civisme. 95pp. (Essais, 4) Ed Mont Noir 1972 ZR FRE

Mudimbe, V.Y.
Contribution à l'étude des variations du genre grammatical des mots français d'origine Latine. pt. 1: mots a initiale vocalique. 144pp. CELTA 1976 ZR FRE

Mudimbe, V.Y.
Déchirures. 48pp. 20k pap. (Jeune Littérature, 3) Ed Mont Noir 1971 ZR FRE

Mudimbe, V.Y., et al.
Français 3e année. Les structures fondamentales. 2 2nded. 223pp. CELTA 1976 ZR FRE

Mudimbe, V.Y.
Poésie vivante. Recueil collectif. 36pp. 20k (Jeune Littérature, 7) Ed Mont Noir 1972 ZR FRE

Mudimbe, V.Y.
Poésie vivante. v. 2 47pp. (Jeune littérature, 13) Ed Mont Noir 1972 ZR FRE

Mudimbe, V.Y.
Réflexions sur la vie quotidienne. 72pp. 20k pap. (Essais, 1) Ed Mont Noir 1972 ZR FRE

Mudimbe, V.Y.
Le vocabulaire politique Zairois. 118pp. CELTA 1976 ZR FRE

Muepa Muamba-di-Mbuyi Kalala.
Ventres creux. Nouvelles. 40pp. 50k (CFA250) Centre Africain Litt 1974 ZR FRE

Muffett, D.J.M.
The story of Sultan Attahiru. 124pp. ill. 53k (African Reader's Library) Pilgrim 1964 NR

Muga, E.
African response to western Christian religion. 228pp. K.shs.26.75 ($5.70/£2.80) EALB KE

Muga, E.
Crime and delinquency in Kenya. 177pp. K.shs.34.55 ($7.00/£3.40) EALB 1975 KE

Mugabe, D.
Rugare tange nhams. [Trouble comes before happiness.] 77pp. 35c Mambo 1972 RH SHO

Mugambi, J.   Kirima, N.
The African religious heritage. A textbook based on syllabus 224 of the East African Certificate of Education. 152pp. K.shs.15.00 OUP - Nairobi 1976 KE

Mugambi, J., ed.
African and Black theology. See: Appiah-Kubi, K., ed.

Mugambi, J.N.K.
Carry it home. 89pp. K.shs.15.50 ($3.85/£1.80) EALB 1974 KE

Mugambi, M.   Thairu, K.
Human and social biology for secondary schools. 103pp. ill. pl. maps. K.shs.26.75 ($5.70/£2.75) EALB 1975 KE

Mugo, M.G.
Daughter of my people sing. 75pp. K.shs.8.40 ($2.40/£1.20) EALB 1976 KE

Mugo, M.G.
The long illness of ex-chief Kiti. 82pp. K.shs.13.30 ($3.30/£1.60) EALB 1976 KE

Mugo, M.G.
The trial of Dedan Kimathi. See: Thiong'o, N.

Mugot, H.
Black night of Quiloa. 90pp. K.shs7.50 ($2.60) EAPH 1971 KE

Muhammad, A.B.
Tazyin-al waraqat. tr. fr. Arabic M. Hiskett 144pp. map pl. N5.00 Ibadan UP 1963 NR

Muhammad, L.
Mu fara karatu. 1, 3 bks. 47pp. ill. 83k Longman - Nig 1971 NR HAU

Muhammad, L.
Mu fara karatu. [Language text]. 2, 3 bks. 46pp. ill. 90k Longman - Nig 1973 NR HAU

Muhammad, S.
Utenzi wa jengo lenye itifaki. [Structure of harmony] 69pp. K.shs.11.00 ($2.90/£1.20) EALB 1974 KE SWA

Muhammadu, A.
Risala. [Message] 173pp. N3.40 Northern Nig 1970 NR HAU

Muhando, P.
Heshima yangu. [Play.]. 20pp. K.shs.3.00 EAPH 1974 KE SWA

Muhando, P.
Pambo. [Drama.] 64pp. K.shs.6.50 ($3.25) Foundation 1976 KE SWA

Muhando, P.
Tambueni haki zetu. [Give us our rights.] 42pp. T.shs.5.00 Tanz Publ House 1972 TZ SWA

Muhire, E.
Wake up and open your eyes. K.shs.9.00 ($3.00) EAPH 1976 KE

Muir, J.
The vegetation of the Riversdale area, Cape Province.
25c. (Memoirs of the Botanical Survey of South Africa,
13) Botanical Res Inst 1929 SA

Mujuru, C.G.
Seka urema wafa. [Don't ridicule others for their
deformities.] 29pp. pl. 18c Rhod Lit Bur 1976 RH
SHO

Mujwahuzi, M.
Impact of rural water supply: eight self-help schemes in
Arumeru, Masai, and Lushoto districts. See: Tschannerl,
G.

Mujwahuzi, M.R.
Impact of rural water supply: eight self-help schemes in
Arumeru, Masai and Lushoto districts. See: Tschannerl,
G.

Mukala, K.N.
Bibliographie littéraire de la Republique du Zaire,
1931-1972. 60pp. Z150.00 CELRIA 1973 ZR FRE

Mukoro, J.K.
Uvuvi wa samaki. [Fishing.] ill. K.shs.6.50 ($3.50)
Foundation 1977 KE SWA

Mukula, P.M.
Calenders of the district notebook. 1 ex. only Nat
Archives - Zambia 1973 ZA

Mukula, P.M., comp.
Calendar of the district notebook, Luapula province,
1798-1963. v. 1. 46pp. 50n Nat Archives - Zam
1973 ZA

Mukuni, R.M.
Linako li fetuhile. [Times have changed] 56pp. ill.
24n. Neczam 1969 ZA LOZ

Mukuni, R.M.
Tukuluho ya luna. [Our freedom] 64pp. pl. 40n.
Neczam 1972 ZA LOZ

Mukuni, R.M.
U zibe mutu. [Story about Bishop Sibimbi.] 54pp.
80n. Neczam 1976 ZA

Mukunyi, D.
The pet snake. 40pp. ill. K.shs2.50 ($1.00) EAPH
1968 KE

Mukwaya, A.B.
Land tenure in Buganda. 79pp. U.shs5.00 (M.I.S.R.
East African stud., 1) Mak Inst Soc Res 1953 UG

Mulago, G.C.
La religion traditionelle des Bantu et leur vision du monde.
182pp. Z1.28 Press Univ Zaire 1974 ZR FRE

Mulendo, R.
Icumfwano ca nganda. [Preparation for marriage] 82pp.
30n Multimedia 1971 ZA BEM

Mulenga, C.J.
Mulenga ne misango yakwe. [Mulengo and his habits]
60pp. 55n. Neczam 1971 ZA BEM

Mulier, F.
Etude des motivations des future instituteurs de l'ex-réseau
protestant à Kinshasa. See: Mulier-Vandamme, S.S.

Mulier-Vandamme, S.S. Mulier, F.
Etude des motivations des future instituteurs de l'ex-réseau
protestant à Kinshasa. 47pp. ill. Z3.00 ($2.40)
(Cahiers du CRIDE, Nouvelle série,I, 1) CRIDE 1976 ZR
FRE

Mulikita, F.M.
A point of no return. 112pp. 60n. Neczam 1968 ZA

Mulila, V.D.
English punctuation. 117pp. K.shs.12.00 ($2.40)
Comb Books 1977 KE

Mulila, V.D.
English spelling and words frequently confused. 85pp.
K.shs.10.00 ($2.00) Comb Books 1977 KE

Mulili, N.M.
Two housing schemes in Thika, a user reaction survey.
See: Kamau, L.J.

Mulindwa, Y.R.R.
Katwetegreze eby'arulimi rwaitu. See: Kagoro, V.K.K.G.

Mulira, E.E.K.
Adult literacy and development. 198pp. K.shs.22.50
($4.90/£2.40 pap.) EALB 1975 KE

Muller, A.L.
Minority interests: the political economy of the coloured
and Indian communities in South Africa. 62pp. R1.50
($2.75) SA Inst of Race Relations 1968 SA

Muller, A.S. et al., eds.
A bibliography of health and disease in East Africa.
700pp. cl. & pap. K.shs.268.00 pap. K.shs.327.00
cl. ($59.00/£26.00 cl.) ($48.80 pap.) EALB 1977 KE

Muller, C.F.J., ed.
Five hundred years: a history of South Africa. 2nd r
rev.ed. 548pp. ill. hd. R10.50 Human & Rousseau
1975 SA

Muller, C.F.J., ed. van Wijk, T., ed. van Jaarsveld,
F.A., ed.
Supplement to 'A Select Bibliography of South African
History. A guide for historical research'. 166pp. hd.
R6.75 (R7.75) (Documenta 13) Univ South Africa
1974 SA

Muller, D.
Whitey. 160pp. R4.75 ($5.00/£2.95) Ravan 1977
SA

Muller, G.
Poetical works by G. Butler, A.Delius, R. Macnab, as
published in anthologies, and South African periodicals.
47pp. R2.45 Dept Bibliog, Lib & Typo 1962 SA

Muller, G.J.
New physical science for standard 7. See: Myburgh,
M.C.

Muller, G.J.
New physical science for standard 8. See: Myburgh,
M.C.

Muller, M.W.
A comparison of some clustering techniques. 186pp.
(CSIR Special Report, PERS 224) CSIR 1975 SA

Mulligan, G.A.
Pothier's thesis on letting and hiring. tr. fr. French
195pp. R5.50 cl. Butterworths 1953 SA

Mullins, T.M., ed.
Municipal law in the Cape of Good Hope. R38.7 cl.
Butterworths 1977 SA

Muloiwa, T.W.
Trilingual elementary dictionary: Venda/Afrikaans/English.
See: Wentzel, P.J.

Mulokozi, M.M.
Malenga wa bara. See: Kahigi, K.K.

Multimedia Publications.
Cotton growing brings more money. 27pp. ill. 20n
Multimedia 1973 ZA

Multimedia Publications.
Credit union. 60pp. ill. 15n Multimedia 1972 ZA

Multimedia Publications.
Credit union [in Cewa]. 56pp. ill. 20n Multimedia
1973 ZA CEW

Multimedia Publications.
First steps in blackboard drawing. 16pp. ill. 30n
Multimedia 1972 ZA

Multimedia Publications.
First steps in book-keeping. 19pp. ill. 30n
Multimedia 1972 ZA

Multimedia Publications.
First steps in dress-making. 20pp. ill. 30n
Multimedia 1973 ZA

Multimedia Publications.
Grade I agreed syllabus. 120pp. ill. K1.00
Multimedia 1972 ZA

Multimedia Publications.
Junior secondary school R.E. education syllabus. K2.00
Multimedia 1972 ZA

Multimedia Publications.
Kamilima nyemu. [Grow more groundnuts] 57pp. ill.
20n Multimedia 1973 ZA TON

Multimedia Publications.
Uses of Kraal manure [in Tonga]. 22pp. ill. N1.00
15n Multimedia 1973 ZA TON

Mulugala, N.E.
Nyungu Ya Mawe. See: Shorter, A.

Mulusa, T.
Our government. 81pp. ill. K.shs6.00 ($2.00/70p.)
EALB 1970 KE

Mumbala, N.
Les reflexes du Proto Bantu en Tetela. See: Omatete, A.

Mumbala.
Les réflexes du proto-bantou en tetela. Approche
générative. See: Omatetete.

Munday, J.T.
Central Bantu historical texts, I. pt. 1, Kankomba
137pp. K1.50 (75p.) (Rhodes- Livingstone
communications, 22) Inst Afr Stud - Lusaka 1961 ZA

Mungai, J.D.
Hadithi za Mfalme Sinsin. [Stories of King Sinsin] 2
2nded. 40pp. ill. Nat Print Co 1972 TZ SWA

Mungeam, G.H.
Primary Kenya documents. See: McIntosh, B.C.

Mungoshi, C.
Coming of the dry season. 68pp. K.shs7.50
OUP-Nairobi 1972 KE

Mungoshi, C.
Ndiko kupindana kwamazuva. [How time passes.]
158pp. pl. R$1.20 Mambo 1975 RH SHO

Munisi, S.A.
Kama ndoto. 118pp. K.shs.15.50 ($3.70/£1.50)
EALB 1976 KE SWA

Munjanja, A.
Rina manyanga hariputirwi. [Evil will out.] 192pp. pl.
50c Mambo 1971 RH SHO

Munjanja, A.
Tsumo nemadimikira. bk. 1. 40pp. 35c. Longman -
Rhod 1965 RH SHO

Munjanja, A.
Tsumo nemadimikira. bk. 2. 48pp. 35c. Longman -
Rhod 1970 RH SHO

Munjanja, A.
Zvirahwe. [Riddles.] 38pp. 22c Mambo 1972 RH
SHO

Munkonge, L.C.
Imfwa shonse. [Examination of the causes of death and
funeral practices in traditional Bemba society.] 58pp.
75n. Neczam 1973 ZA BEM

Munonye, J.
Drills and practice in English language: pupil's bk.
See: Cairns, J.

Munonye, J.
Drills and practice in English language: teacher's bk.
See: Cairns, J.

Munoyne, C.
Aghiriigha. [Novel] 200pp. N2.00 Univ Publ 1975
NR IGB

Munro, G.
Pre-school environment and intellectual development: a
selective survey of the literature, with particular reference
to Africa. 22pp. free (Human Development Research
Unit Report, 5) Dept Psychology - Zam 1967 ZA

Munro, D.
A survey of pre-school children's environments in a Lusaka
suburb. 48pp. free (Human Development Research
Unit Report, 9) Dept Psychology - Zam 1968 ZA

Munro, D.
Three exploratory studies of reinforcement effects with
Zambian children. 30pp. free (Human Development
Research Unit Report, 17) Dept Psychology - Zam 1971
ZA

Munro, D.A.
English-Edo wordlist, an index to Melzian's Bini-English
dictionary. 89pp. N1.50 (Inst. of African Stud., Univ.
of Ibadan, occas. pub., 7) Inst Afr Stud-Ibadan 1967 NR

Munyi, S.
Can dreams come true? 24pp. ill. 40pes. (16p.)
Africa Christian 1971 GH

Munyi, S.
Go tell the news. 48pp. 40pes. (10p.) Africa
Christian 1970 GH

Mupatu, Y.W.
Bulozi sapili [Novel]. 60pp. ill. 40c OUP-SA 1959
SA LOZ

Murdoch, B.D.
Ethyl alcohol and the electroencephalogram: immediate
and longer term effects. 18pp. (CSIR Contract Report
C/PERS, 230) CSIR 1975 SA

Murdoch, B.D.
The Reitan-Indiana neuropsychological test battery for
children (5-8 years) and the Halstead neuropsychological
test battery for children (9-14 years): normative data.
See: Painter, A.

Murdoch, G.
Development in Swaziland: a regional analysis.
See: Fair, T.J.D.

Mureithi, C.M.
The adventures of Thiga. 69pp. ills. K.shs4.80
($1.50) EAPH 1971 KE

Mureithi, K. Ndoria, P.
War in the forest. 126pp. photos. K.shs.10.00
($3.20) EAPH 1971 KE

Mureithi, L.P.
Elasticity of substitution, returns to scale and firm size: an
analysis of Kenya data. 16pp. K.shs.3.00 (Inst.
Development Studies, Discussion paps., 221) Inst Dev
Stud 1975 KE

Murimi, E.
Mwandikire wa marua mega. See: Murrey, J.

Murison-Bowie, S.C.
Contact 1 pupil's book. 408pp. photos ill. maps.
B5.60 (The Oxford Secondary English Course, 1)
OUP-Addis 1970 ET

Murison-Bowie, S.C. Relton, H.
Contact 1 teacher's book. 156pp. Eth. $4.90 (The
Oxford Secondary English Course, 1) OUP-Addis 1970
ET

Murison-Bowie, S.C.
Contact 2 pupil's book. 1 192pp. photos. ill. maps.
Eth. $2.75 (The Oxford Secondary English Course, 2)
OUP-Addis 1971 ET

Murison-Bowie, S.C.
Contact 2 pupil's book. bk. 2 192pp. photos ill. maps.
B2.75 (The Oxford Secondary English Course, 2)
OUP-Addis 1972 ET

Murison-Bowie, S.C. et al.
Contact 2 teacher's book. 176pp. B5.00 (The Oxford
Secondary English Course, 2) OUP-Addis 1972 ET

Muriuki, G.
A history of the Kikuyu, 1500-1900. 200pp. maps. cl. &
pap. K.shs.30.00 pap. K.shs.45.00 cl. OUP -
Nairobi 1974 KE

Murphree, M. W.
The study of race and ethnic relations in Southern Africa.
24pp. 30c (Inaugural lectures) Univ Rhodesia Lib
1973 RH

Murphree, W.M.
Education, development and change in Africa. 25pp.
80c ($1.60) SA Inst of Race Relations 1976 SA

Murphy, M.
Designing multiple-choice items for testing English
language. 72pp. 77k Pilgrim 1969 NR

Murphy, M.   Onadipe, K.
The forest is our playground. 48pp. ill. 45k (African Junior Library, 7) Pilgrim 1971 NR

Murray-Rust, H.
Soil erosion and sedimentation in Kisongo catchment, Arusha region. 83pp. maps. T.shs 10.00 (Research pap., 17) Bur Res Assess Tanz 1971 TZ

Murray, W.H.
Choipa chitsata mwini ndi mbiri zine. [Evil to him who thinks evil and other stories] 49pp. 30t. (29c.) Christ Lit Assoc - Mal 1972 08 CHC

Murrey, J.   Murimi, E.
Mwandikire wa marua mega. [How to write good letters] 22pp. K.shs.1.25 ($1.25/50p.) EALB 1963 KE KIK

Murtagh, D.D.
Education for librarianship in Africa. 41pp. R2.15 Dept Bibliog, Lib & Typo 1968 SA

Muruah, G.K.
Never forgive father. 318pp. pap. & cl. K.shs30.00 cl. K.shs15.00 pap. ($6.00/£3.00) EALB 1973 KE

Murunga, A.S., comp.
East Africana collection: a select booklist. 46pp. Tanz Lib Serv 1972 TZ

Musa, A.
Chinotomba neshumba. [Chinotomba and the lion.] 16pp. pl. 6c Rhod Lit Bur 1975 RH SHO

Musa, H.
Chinotomba. 16pp. pl. 5c Rhod Lit Bur 1973 RH SHO

Musa, H.
Handitauri kuna ani kana ani zvake. [A top secret.] 12pp. pl. 3c. Rhod Lit Bur 1969 RH SHO

Musa, H.
Kangitsheli ngitsho loba ngubani. [A top secret - I will not tell anyone.] 2nd ed. 12pp. pl. 3c Rhod Lit Bur 1974 RH NDE

Musa, H.
Kudzoka Kwachamakanda. [The return of the Chamakanda.] 12pp. pl. 3c. (Children's comic series) Rhod Lit Bur 1969 RH SHO

Musa, H.
Kurangawa kwavatenzi. [Punishment given to the master.] 16pp. pl. 6c Rhod Lit Bur 1976 RH SHO

Musa, H.
Kuregererwa Kwakamba. [The tortoise is pardoned.] 12pp. pl. 3c. Rhod Lit Bur 1969 RH SHO

Musa, H.
Mambo ano unyope. [A slothful king.] 16pp. pl. 6c Rhod Lit Bur 1975 RH SHO

Musa, H.
Tsoko nadhadha. [The monkey and the duck.] 12pp. pl. 3c Rhod Lit Bur 1974 RH SHO

Musa, H.
Tsuro namakarwe. [The hare and the crocodiles.] 12pp. pl. 3c Rhod Lit Bur 1974 RH SHO

Musa, H.
Ubuthutha bukafudu. [Tortoise's stupidity.] 12pp. pl. 3c. Rhod Lit Bur 1969 RH NDE

Musa, H.
Ufuza hwakamba. [Tortoise's stupidity.] 12pp. pl. 3c. Rhod Lit Bur 1969 RH SHO

Musa, H.
Ukubuya kukaZigogo. [The return of Zigogo.] 12pp. pl. 3c Rhod Lit Bur 1973 RH NDE

Musa, H.
Ukuzolelewa kukafudu. [The tortoise is pardoned.] 12pp. pl. 3c. Rhod Lit Bur 1969 RH NDE

Musa, H.
Umvundla lengwenya. [The hare and the baboon.] 2 2nded. 12pp. pl. 3c Rhod Lit Bur 1969 RH NDE

Musa, H.
Unkawu lodada. [The monkey and the duck.] 12pp. pl. 3c Rhod Lit Bur 1969 RH NDE

Musa, H.
Uzenzo. [Mr. artist.] 16pp. pl. 5c Rhod Lit Bur 1974 RH NDE

Musa, H.
Uzenzo lesilwane. [Mr. artist and the lion.] 16pp. pl. 6c Rhod Lit Bur 1975 RH NDE

Musa, H.A.
Inkosi eyayilivila. [A lazy king.] 16pp. pl. 6c. Rhod Lit Bur 1976 RH NDE

Musa, H.A.
Okwakho ngokuthweleyo. [What is in your hand belongs to you.] 12pp. ill. 3c. Rhod Lit Bur 1976 RH NDE

Musane, E.   Jarvis, M.S.
Ebisooka bya geography. [Introductory geography] 2nd ed. 24pp. ill. K.shs.2.00 ($1.25/50p) EALB 1962 KE LUG

Mushang, M.T.
Folk tales from Ankole. 143pp. hd. U.shs5.00 Adult Educ Centre 1970 UG

Mushanga, T.M.
Crime and deviance. An introduction to criminology. 282pp. K.shs.41.20 ($8.25/£3.30) EALB 1976 KE

Mushi, S.S.
Mfalme Edipode. [King Oedipus] 80pp. K.shs7.50 OUP-Nairobi 1972 KE SWA

Mushindo, P.M.B.
Imilumbe ne nshimi bashimika Mulubemba. [Fables and stories in Bemba] 84pp. OUP - Lusaka 1966 ZA BEM

Mushinyi, T.
Mouse and the red locusts. 12pp. pl. 4c. Rhod Lit Bur 1977 RH

Mushinyi, T.
N'anga inobata mai. [Don't ridicule other people's misfortune.] 12pp. pl. 4c. Rhod Lit Bur 1976 RH SHO

Musiker, R.
The Africana collections of the University of Witwatersrand library. 21pp. ill. R1.50 (Occas. paps., 1) Univ of the Witwatersrand Lib 1977 SA

Musiker, R.
The Australopithecinae. 49pp. 80c. Univ Cape Town Lib 1969 SA

Musiker, R.
Guide to South African reference books. Supplement 1970-1974. 3rd supp. to 5th ed. 71pp. R1.50 Univ Witwatersrand Lib 1975 SA

Musiker, R.
Library science literature 1965/1969. 75c (Dept. of Librarianship, occas. paps., 1) Rhodes Univ Lib 1970 SA

Musiker, R.
Library science literature, 1970/1971. 75c (Dept of Librarianship, occas. paps., 5) Rhodes Univ Lib 1972 SA

Musiker, R.
Purchasing guide for South African libraries. 2nd r rev.ed. 15pp. R1.50 (Occas. paps., 2) Univ of the Witwatersrand Lib 1977 SA

Musiker, R.
South African bibliography. Supplement 1970-1974. 32pp. R1.50 Univ Witwatersrand Lib 1975 SA

Musiker, R.
South African reference books of 1970/1971. 75c (Dept. of Librarianship, bibliographical series, 2) Rhodes Univ Lib 1972 SA

Musili, F.P.   Were, C.P.
Essential English for C.P.E. with answers. 118pp. K.shs.15.00 ($3.00) Africa Book Serv 1969 KE

Musis, C.G.K.
Kikonyogo. [Detective story] 69pp. K.shs.4.25 ($1.75/70p.) EALB 1970 KE LUG

Mvuezolo Bagwanga.   Rotsart de Hertaing, I.
Courtejoie, J.
L'éducateur sanitaire! Un enseignant ou un infirmier peut-il
devenir un bon éducateur sanitaire? 64pp. photos.
Z1.20 ($1.44) (Orientation nouvelle de l'action médicale,
27) BERPS 1975 ZR FRE

Mvula, A.D.
Malangizo pa ukwati. [Marriage guide lines.] 46pp.
30n. Neczam 1973 ZA NYA

Mvula, A.D.
Nthanozi Tisaziiwale. 56pp. Nat Print Co TZ SWA

Mvula, A.D.
Nthanozi tisaziiwale. [We shall not forget these stories]
48pp. Neczam 1972 ZA NYA

Mwajombe, R.Z.
Seti ni nini. [A book of sets.] 64pp. T.shs.6.50
Longman - Tanz 1975 TZ SWA

Mwakalukwa, N.G.K.
Mistari na Maumbo. [Elementary geometry] 46pp. ill.
T. shs 3.00 Longman Tanz 1969 TZ SWA

Mwakapi, J.M.
Njia ya kweli. [The true way.] 48pp.   T.shs.4.00
Africa Inland Church 1975 TZ SWA

Mwakasungula, N.E.R.
Jifunze sheria. [Teach yourself the law of Tanzania.] 7th
ed. 96pp. T.shs.5.50 ($1.00) TMP 1975 TZ SWA

Mwakasungula, N.E.R.
Sheria za ndoa na talaka. [Laws of marriage and divorce
in Tanzania.] 2nd ed. 100pp. T.shs.7.00 ($1.00)
TMP 1975 TZ SWA

Mwale, A.U.
Cimwendom'mphako. [A big leg in a branch of the tree.]
94pp.   K1.20 Neczam 1975 ZA NYA

Mwale, J.S.
Umoyo na nchito za mulala wa mpingo. [The life and
duties of a church elder] 36pp. 20t. (23c.) Christ Lit
Assoc - Mal 1970 MW CHM

Mwambungu, O.
Veneer of love. 160pp. K.shs.16.50 ($3.80/£1.80)
EALB 1975 KE

Mwanakatwe, J.M.
The growth of education in Zambia since independence.
260pp. K3.00 (£1.50) OUP - Lusaka 1968 ZA

Mwanga, A.K.
Mastering 40 English structures. 60pp. T.shs.9.00
($3.00) Tanz Publ House 1975 TZ

Mwanga, A.K.
Nyangeta. 98pp. ill. K.shs.15.75 ($3.75/£1.80)
EALB 1976 KE

Mwangi, C.
The secret of the water fall. 130pp. K.shs.10.00
($3.20) EAPH 1976 KE

Mwangi, J.
Kushirikiana husaidia biashara. [Co-operation is a help to
trading] 2nd ed. 70pp. ill. K.shs.1.85 EALB 1965
KE SWA

Mwangi, M.
Taste of death. 260pp. K.shs.10.00 (African
Secondary Readers) EAPH 1975 KE

Mwangi, R.
What a husband! 207pp. K.shs.13.75 Longman - Ken
1974 KE

Mwangudza, J.A.
Thamani yangu. [Play.] 48pp.   K.shs.6.00 OUP -
Nairobi 1976 KE

Mwaniki, H.S.K.
Embu historical texts. 333pp. K.shs.36.00
($7.30/£3.80) EALB 1975 KE

Mwaniki, H.S.K.
Kiembu folklore.   K.shs11.70 ($3.00/£1.20) EALB
1971 KE KIK

Mwaniki, H.S.K.
The living history of Embu and Mbeere. 178pp. ill. maps.
cl. & pap.   K.shs.41.00 cl.   K.shs.16.15 pap.
($8.20/£4.00 cl.) ($3.80/£2.00 pap.) EALB 1973 KE

Mwanje, J.W.
Florence Nightingale. ill.   K.shs.1.00 ($1.25/50p.)
EALB 1962 KE LUG

Mwanjisi, R.K.
Sheikh Abeid Amani Karome. 68pp. photos.
K.shs.2.80 ($1.00) EAPH 1967 KE SWA

Mwansasu, B.U., eds.
Planning in Tanzania. Background to decentralisation.
See: Rweyemamu, A.H., eds.

Mwaruka, R.
Utenzi wa jamhuri ya Tanzania. [The epic of the Republic
of Tanzania] 64pp. K.shs.3.55 ($1.75/70p.) EALB
1968 KE SWA

Mwasada, E.
Wajilipa wenyewe. [They pay themselves.] 13pp. ill.
Tanz Publ House 1975 TZ SWA

Mwata Kazembe XIV.
Central Bantu historical texts II Ifikolwe fyandi na Bantu
Bandi. [Historical traditions of the eastern Luanda] tr. fr.
Bemba I. Cunnison 137pp. 75n. (38p.)
(Rhodes-Livingstone communications, 23) Inst Afr Stud -
Lusaka 1962 ZA

Mwaura, J.N.
Sky is the limit. 253pp. K.shs.16.50 ($5.00/£2.40)
EALB 1974 KE

Mwaura, M.
The renegade. 176pp. K.shs10.00 ($4.20/£1.70)
EALB 1972 KE

Mwaurah, D.M.
Circle of revenge. col. ill. K.shs.9.00 EAPH 1976
KE

Mweemba, J.B.
Mubekwabekwa. 104pp. K1.00 Neczam 1959 ZA
TON

Mwenegoha, H.A.K.
Kifo cha furaha. [Death in happiness.] 108pp. col. ill.
K.shs.10.00 Transafrica 1974 KE SWA

Mwenegoha, H.A.K.
Mwalimu Julius Kambarage Nyerere. [A
bio-bibliography.] 120pp. K.shs.40.00 ($20.00[?])
Foundation 1977 KE

Mwenegoha, H.A.K.
Mwalimu Julius Kambarage Nyerere, a bio-bibliography.
108pp. T.shs.40.00 Tanz Lib Serv 1976 TZ

Mwenegoha, H.A.K.
Mwalimu Julius Kambarage Nyerere. Huduma za Maktaba
Transafrica, Dar-es-Salaam. [Biography of President
Nyerere.] T.shs.20.00 Tanz Lib Serv 1977 TZ SWA

Mwenegoha, H.A.K.
Shujaa wa vijana. 44pp. ill. K.shs.9.00 ($5.00)
Foundation 1977 KE SWA

Mwenegoha, H.A.K.
Shujaa wa vijana. Kwa biaba ya Shirika la Huduma za
Maktaba. 44pp. T.shs.15.00 Tanz Lib Serv 1977 TZ
SWA

Mwewa, M.L., comp.
Descriptive list of the records of the British South Africa
Company, 1887-1924. 2nd rev. ed. v. 1. 97pp.
K1.00 Nat Archives - Zam 1973 ZA

Mweya, E.F.
Remous de feuilles. 46pp.   20k (Jeune Littérature, 9)
Ed Mont Noir 1972 ZR FRE

Mwiinga, B.
Chibuye tapi. [Tonga sayings and idioms.] 24pp.
35n. Neczam 1971 ZA TON

Mwiinga, B.
Maanu a sulwe. [The wisdom of the hare.] 134pp. ill.
K1.20 Neczam 1975 ZA TON

Nassir, A.
Malenga wa Mvita. [The great poet of Mvita] 204pp.
K.shs.25.00 OUP-Nairobi 1972 KE SWA

Nassir, A.
Tamrini za Kiswahili: sarufi na matumizi. [Kiswahili exercises: grammar and usage] 1,2 bks. 60pp.
K.shs.4.00 OUP - Nairobi 1974 KE SWA

Nassir, A.
Tamrini za Kiswahili: sarufi na matumizi (Pamoja na majibu) [Kiswahili exercises: grammar and usage (with answers)] 2, 2 bks. 44pp. K.shs.5.00 OUP - Nairobi 1974 KE SWA

Nasution, A.H.
Functional literacy: a method of vocational training for farmers-workers. 72pp. 30k Inst Adult Educ-Ibadan 1972 NR

Natali, A.
Problems encountered by characters in children's fiction: 1945-1965: an annotated bibliography. 93pp. R4.75 Dept Bibliog, Lib & Typo 1967 SA

Nates, D.H.
Shipwrecks on and off the coasts of Southern Africa: a supplement to R.F. Kennedy's bibliography. Dept Bibliog, Lib & Typo SA

Nathan, C., comp.
Henochsberg on the companies act. First (Cumulative) Supplement to third edition. See: Milne, A., comp.

Nathan, C.J.M.
Handbook on the Compulsory Motor Vehicle Insurance Act, 1972. 188pp. cl. R12.00 Butterworths 1973 SA 3NG

Nathan, C.J.M.
South African divorce handbook. 178pp. R11.75 cl. Butterworths 1970 SA

Nathan, C.J.M. Barnett, A.M.
Uniform rules of court. [Text in Afrikaans and English.]. 2nd ed. 800pp. cl. R45.00 Juta 1977 SA

National Archives of Rhodesia, in conjunction with Centro de Estudos Historicos Ultramarinos, Lisbon.
Documents on the Portuguese in Mozambique and Central Africa, 1497-1840. Vol. XIII (1560-1600) 600pp. hd. R$4.00 Nat Archives - Rhod 1975 RH

National Archives of Rhodesia.
List of publications deposited in the National Archives, 1963. 16pp. Nat Archives - Rhod 1964 RH

National Archives of Rhodesia.
List of publications deposited in the National Archives, 1965. 11pp. Nat Archives - Rhod 1966 RH

National Archives of Rhodesia.
List of publications deposited in the National Archives, 1966. 11pp. Nat Archives - Rhod 1967 RH

National Archives of Rhodesia.
List of publications deposited in the National Archives, 1967. 10pp. Nat Archives - Rhod 1968 RH

National Archives of Rhodesia.
List of publications deposited in the National Archives, 1968. 14pp. Nat Archives - Rhod 1969 RH

National Archives of Rhodesia.
Rhodesia National Bibliography, 1971. 36pp. Nat Archives - Rhod 1971 RH

National Archives of Rhodesia.
Rhodesia national bibliography, 1973. 28pp. Nat Archives - Rhod 1974 RH

National Archives of Rhodesia.
Rhodesia national bibliography, 1974. 30pp. Nat Archives - Rhod 1975 RH

National Archives of Rhodesia.
Rhodesia national bibliography, 1975. 40pp. Nat Archives - Rhod 1976 RH

The National Bank of Commerce, Dar es Salaam.
Tanzania import export directory. T.shs.35.00 ($5.00) Nat Bank Commerce 1977 TZ

National Central Library, Dar es Salaam.
Printed in Tanzania, 1969 A list of publications printed in mainland Tanzania during 1969 and deposited with the Tanganiyka Library Service, etc. 79pp. T.shs.40.00 Tanz Lib Serv 1970 TZ

National Central Library, Dar es Salaam.
Printed in Tanzania, 1970 A list of publications printed in mainland Tanzania during 1970 and deposited with the Legal Deposit Libraries in the country. 61pp. T.shs.40.00 Tanz Lib Serv 1971 TZ

National Central Library, Dar es Salaam.
Printed in Tanzania, 1972: a list of publications printed in mainland Tanzania during 1972 and deposited with the legal deposit libraries in the country. 36pp. T.shs.40.00 Tanz Lib Serv 1974 TZ

National Christian Council of Kenya.
Let's talk about us - sex education. 86pp. K.shs.10.50 ($1.35) Evangel 1977 KE

National Council for Research.
Desert encroachment control project proposed by Sudan government 1975-1980. 68pp. Nat Council Res - Sudan 1974 SJ

National Council for Research.
Horizontal transfer of technology as a tool for development. 44pp. Nat Council Res - Sudan 1974 SJ

National Council for Research.
Science policy and annual report for 1973-1974. 155pp. Nat Council Res - Sudan 1974 SJ

National Council for Scientific Research.
Directory of scientific research organizations in Zambia. 78pp. Nat Council Scient Res - Zam 1975 ZA

National Educational Company of Zambia.
Kapelwa Musonda. [Newspaper articles] Neczam 1973 ZA BEM

National Educational Company of Zambia Ltd.
Mind of the young - What the UN means to me. 84pp. 80n. Neczam 1976 ZA

National Housing Authority, Zambia.
Self help in action. A study of site and service schemes in Zambia. 180pp. K5.00 ($10.00) (Nat. Housing Authority res. study, 2) Nat Housing Author - Zam 1975 ZA

National Housing Corporation.
Homes for Kenya. ill. K.shs.20.00 Africa Book Serv 1969 KE

National Library of Nigeria.
The 4th National Festival of the Arts. Exhibition of Nigeriana, Lagos, 28 December, 1974 - 4 January, 1975. 30pp. free Nat Lib - Nig 1975 NR

National Library of Nigeria.
Annual Report, 1969/70. 16pp. N1.00 (N3.00) NatLib-Nig 1972 NR

National Library of Nigeria.
A bibliography of biographies and memoirs on Nigeria. 11pp. 50k (N1.00) (National Library pubs, 9) Nat Lib-Nig 1968 NR

National Library of Nigeria.
Books on Nigerian languages: a bibliography. 12pp. 50k (N1.00) (National Library Pubs, 10) Nat Lib-Nig 1968 NR

National Library of Nigeria.
Library cooperation in Nigeria. Phase I: interlibrary lending programme handbook. 19pp. N3.00 (National Library pubs, 36) Nat Lib - Nig 1976 NR

National Library of Nigeria.
Meeting of the working group on interlibrary lending, Ile-Ife, April 24-25, 1974. 47pp. N1.50 (N3.00) (National Library pubs., 30) Nat Lib - Nig 1974 NR

National Library of Nigeria.
The national bibliography of Nigeria, 1973. [supersedes 'Nigerian publications', 1958 -]. 131pp. N4.00 (N5.00) Nat Lib - Nig 1975 NR

National Library of Nigeria.
The national bibliography of Nigeria, 1974. 117pp.
N4.00 (N5.00) Nat Lib - Nig 1976 NR

National Library of Nigeria.
National conference on library statistics, Lagos, July 31 -
August 3, 1973. 167pp. N3.00 (N6.00) (National
Library pubs., 31) Nat Lib - Nig 1974 NR

National Library of Nigeria.
National digest of library statistics, 1972. 80pp. N4.00
(N5.00) Nat Lib - Nig 1975 NR

National Library of Nigeria.
National Library of Nigeria: annual Report, 1968/69.
28pp. ill. N1.00 (N3.00) Nat Lib-Nig 1971 NR

National Library of Nigeria.
National Library of Nigeria: annual report 1970/71.
34pp. ex. only Nat Lib - Nig 1975 NR

National Library of Nigeria.
National Library of Nigeria: annual report 1971/72.
42pp. pl. ex. only Nat Lib - Nig 1974 NR

National Library of Nigeria.
Nigerian publications: current national bibliography, 1971.
94pp. N2.00 (N5.00) Nat Lib - Nig 1973 NR

National Library of Nigeria.
Nigerian publications: current national bibliography, 1972.
99pp. N2.00 (N5.00) Nat Lib - Nig 1974 NR

National Library of Nigeria.
Nominal list of practising librarians in Nigeria, 1975.
29pp. N1.50 (N3.00) (National Library pubs, 34)
Nat Lib - Nig 1976 NR

National Library of Nigeria.
Serials in print in Nigeria, 1967. 40pp. 50k (N1.00)
(National Library pubs, 5) Nat Lib-Nig 1967 NR

National Library of Nigeria.
Technical journals for industry, Nigeria FID-415. 12pp.
50k (N1.00) (National Library pubs, 20) Nat Lib-Nig
1970 NR

National Library of Nigeria.
Theses and dissertations accepted for higher degrees in
Nigerian universities, 1970-71. 37pp. 50k (N1.00)
(National Library pubs, 27) Nat Lib - Nig 1972 NR

National Monuments Commission.
Digging up history. 10pp. pl. 17n. Neczam 1971
ZA

National Monuments Commission.
Digging up history. [also available in Bemba, Lozi, Nyanja,
Lunda, Luvale and Tonga.]. 17n. (27c./11p.) Nat
Mon Comm - Zambia 1967 ZA

Native Language Bureau.
Ehi keyuva kokumoho. [Primary readers, A-B, and
standards 1-5; full details from publisher.]. Native Lang
Bur SX HER

Native Language Bureau.
Eraka lyetu. [Primary school grammars, standards 1-5; full
details from publisher.]. Native Lang Bur SX KWA

Native Language Bureau.
Eraka ndi tu hungira. [Primary school grammars,
standards 1-5; full details from publisher.]. Native Lang
Bur SX HER

Native Language Bureau.
Herero arithmatic terminology. 91c. Native Lang Bur
1974[?] SX HER

Native Language Bureau.
Herero linguistic terminology. 41c. Native Lang Bur
1974[?] SX HER

Native Language Bureau.
Herero orthography no.2: handbook for teachers. 96pp.
95c. R1.66 Native Lang Bur 1975 SX HER

Native Language Bureau.
Ila tu leshe. [Primary readers, A-!, and standards 1-5; full
details from publisher.]. Native Lang Bur SX KWY

Native Language Bureau.
Ila tu leshe. [Primary readers, A-B, and standards 1-5; full
details from publisher.]. Native Lang Bur SX NDO

Native Language Bureau.
Kha khasen da ge ra Namakowaba. [Primary school
grammars, standards 1-5; full details from publisher.].
Native Lang Bur SX NAM

Native Language Bureau.
Khomai da ge ra. [Primary readers, A-B, and standards
1-5, full details from publisher.]. Native Lang Bur SX
NAM

Native Language Bureau.
Kwangali linguistic and arithmatic terminology. R1.13
Native Lang Bur 1974[?] SX KWA

Native Language Bureau.
Kwangali orthography no. 2: handbook for teachers.
96pp. 95c. Native Lang Bur 1974 SX KWA

Native Language Bureau.
Kwanyama orthography no.2. 52pp. R1.40 Native
Lang Bur 1973 SX KWG

Native Language Bureau.
Lihongeni. [Primary school grammars, standards 1-5; full
details from publisher]. Native Lang Bur SX KWY

Native Language Bureau.
Mashani. [Primary readers, A-B, and standards 1-5; full
details from publisher.]. Native Lang Bur SX MBU

Native Language Bureau.
Mbukushu linguistic and arithmatic terminology. 91c.
Native Lang Bur 1974[?] SX MBU

Native Language Bureau.
Mbukushu orthography no. 2, handbook for teachers.
48pp. Native Lang Bur 1968 SX MBU

Native Language Bureau.
Nama arithmatic terminology. 25c. Native Lang Bur
1977 SX NAM

Native Language Bureau.
Nama linguistic terminology. 25c. Native Lang Bur
1974? SX NAM

Native Language Bureau.
Nama/Drama orthography no. 2: handbook for teachers.
93pp. R1.12 Native Lang Bur 1970 SX NAM

Native Language Bureau.
Ndimi dhetu. [Primary school grammars, standards 1-5;
full details from publisher.]. Native Lang Bur SX MBU

Native Language Bureau.
Ndonga orthography no.2: handbook for teachers and
secondary pupils. 50pp. R1.01 Native Lang Bur
1973 SX NDO

Native Language Bureau.
Ndonga/Kwanyama terminology. R1.53 Native Lang
Bur 1974[?] SX NDO

Native Language Bureau.
Neg ma Naara. [Reader: sub-standard B] 88pp.
Native Lang Bur 1969 SX XU

Native Language Bureau.
Neng ma Naara. [Reader: sub-standard A] 84pp.
Native Lang Bur 1969 SX XU

Native Language Bureau.
Ntunguru. [Primary readers, A-B, and standards 1-5; full
details from publisher.]. Native Lang Bur SX KWA

Native Language Bureau.
Okwiilonga elaka. [Primary school grammars, standards
1-5; full details from publisher.]. Native Lang Bur SX
NDO

Native Language Bureau.
Xu Bushman orthography, no. 1. 55pp. Native Lang
Bur 1969 SX XU

Naude, A.
Hugo Naude. 64pp. photos. cl. & pap. R6.75 pap.
R9.00 cl. (South African Art Library, 1) Struik 1974 SA

Naudé, A.
Rondebosch and round about. 112pp. photos. cl.
R20.00 deluxe ed. Philip 1973 SA

Naude, C.H.B.
Business methods for standard 8 (Practical course)
See: Eksteen, F.R.L.N.

Author Index

Naudé, G.
Introduction to category theory in automata and systems. 159pp. (CSIR Special Report, WISK 202) CSIR 1976 SA

Naude, G.
On the adjoint situations between behaviour and realization. 22pp. (CSIR Special Report, WISK 221) CSIR 1976 SA

Nawankiti, B.
A short history of the Christian church. 74pp. 75k Daystar 1965 NR

Nazareth, P.
In a brown mantle. 162pp. K.shs19.60 ($4.70/£2.20) EALB 1972 KE

Nazareth, P.
Literature and society in modern Africa. 236pp. pap. & cl. K.shs45.00 cl. K.shs19.60 pap. ($4.50/£1.80 pap.) ($9.00/£4.20 cl.) EALB 1972 KE

Nazareth, P.
Two radio plays. 48pp. K.shs.7.40 ($2.20/95p.) EALB 1976 KE

Nchete, D.C.
Banyama besu mu Zambia. [Our wildlife in Zambia.] 74pp. ill. 60n. Neczam 1972 ZA TON

Nchimbi, B.R.
Penzi la dawa. [Healing love.] 82pp. T.shs.10.00 Tanz Publ House 1974 TZ SWA

Nchimbi, K.
Kaburi la Ukristu. [The tomb of Christianity.] 54pp. T.shs.3.00 (Wananchi wanachambua teolojia, 2) Ndanda Mission Press 1976 TZ SWA

N.C.P.
True? 16pp. 3k SIM 1966 NR

Ncube, N.M.
Ukungazi kufana lokufa. [Ignorance is like death.] 78pp. pl. 38c Mambo 1973 RH NDE

Ndambi Munamuhega.
Les masques pende de Ngudi (Rép. du Zaire) 341pp. map. (DM38.00) (CEEBA publications, I, 23) CEEBA 1976 ZR FRE

Ndanda Mission Press.
Tusali na kanisa. [Let's pray with the Church] 1306pp. hd. T.shs.44.00 Ndanda Mission Press 1972 TZ SWA

N'Dao, M.
Fréquences des graphes et des structures syllabiques en Wolof. See: Doneux, J.L.

Ndebele, J.P.
Akusimulandu wami. [It is not my fault.] 104pp. pl. 60c Mambo 1974 RH NDE

Ndebele, N.N.T.
Ugubudele namazimuzimu. [Gubudele and the cannibals.] repr. in new orthography ed. 96pp. R1.20 (Bantu treasury, 6) Witwatersrand UP 1976 SA ZUL

Ndedi-Penda, P.
La nasse. 156pp. CFA510 CLE 1972 CM FRE

Ndegwa, P.
The common market and development in East Africa. 228pp. maps. K.shs48.00 cl. K.shs20.00 pap. ($7.80 cl.) ($5.20 pap.) EAPH 1965 KE

Ndelu, B.B.
Mageba lazihlonza. [Mageba it has proved itself] 207pp. 70c. Shuter 1962 SA ZUL

Ndeti, J.S.
Kuishi kwingi ni kuona mengi. 137pp. K.shs.6.00 ($2.40) EAPH 1968 KE SWA

N'Diaye, B.
Les castes au Mali. 128pp. MF700 Ed Pop - Mali 1970 ML FRE

N'Diaye, B.
Les groupes ethniques au Mali. 480pp. MF2070 Ed Pop - Mali 1970 ML FRE

N'Diaye, B.
Veillées au Mali. 224pp. MF700 Ed Pop - Mali 1970 ML FRE

Ndiaye, G.
Ethiopiques. (Edition critique) 112pp. CFA500 (F10.00) Nouv Ed Afric 1974 SG FRE

N'Diaye, G.
Initiation à la linguistique générale. Aspect et problèmes du bilinguisme. 29pp. CFA250 (C.L.A.D. Etude, 26 bis) CLAD 1968 SG FRE

Ndiaye, J.P.
Monde noire et destin politique. 91pp. CFA1,800 (F36.00) Nouv Ed Afric 1976 SG FRE

Ndiaye, M.
Assoka, ou les derniers jours de Koumbi. 181pp. CFA850 (F17.00) Nouv Ed Afric 1973 SG FRE

Ndiaye, N.
Histoire du Sénégal et de l'Afrique cours moyen. See: Thiam, I.B.

N'Diaye, N.T.
Si j'étais. 16pp. ill. CFA200 (F4.00) Nouv Ed Afric 1975 SG FRE

Ndiaye, S.W.
La fille des eaux. 64pp. CFA500 Nouv Ed Afric 1975 SG FRE

Ndiaye, T.N.
Le beau voyage de Biram à travers le Sénégal. 24pp. CFA400 Nouv Ed Afric 1976 SG FRE

Ndiaye, T.N.
Si j'étais. 16pp. ill. CFA200.00 (F5.20) Nouv Ed Afric 1975 SG FRE

Ndibalema, C.
Fimbo ya Ulimwengu [Novel]. 84pp. K.shs.8.00 Heinemann Educ - Nair 1974 KE SWA

Ndibalema, C.M.
Nimeponzeka. [I have been deceived] 55pp. ill. T.shs.3.60 Longman Tanz 1970 TZ SWA

Ndibalema, C.M.
Nimeponzeka. [Suckered.] 55pp. ill. T.shs.4.50 Longman - Tanz 1975 TZ SWA

Ndii, A.
A brief assignment. 88pp. K.shs.9.50 pap. Heinemann Educ - Nair 1976 KE

Ndimbo, D.M.
Misingi ya kufundisha sanaa. [Principles of teaching arts and crafts] 128pp. ill. K.shs.10.50 OUP-Nairobi 1973 KE SWA

Ndirangu, E.
Island of Yo. 24pp. col. ill. K.shs.6.00 ($2.00) EAPH 1975 KE

Ndirangu, S.
Temptations of a nurse. 40pp. ill. 60pes. (18p.) Africa Christian 1967 GH

Ndirangu, S.
Tentation à l'hopital. 49pp. 20k CEDI 1974 ZR FRE

Ndlovu, E.M.
Umdengosiba. 127pp. pl. 40c Mambo 1972 RH NDE

Ndlovu, K. et al.
Umgodi wolwazi. Pupil's bk. 144pp. R$2.00 Longman - Rhod 1977 RH NDE

Ndlovu, K. et al.
Umgodi wolwazi. Teacher's guide. 52pp. 35c. Longman - Rhod 1977 RH NDE

Ndlovu, R.S. Shange, O.L. Buthelezi, G.
Isizulu a incwadi yesibili. [Zulu A, bk. 1] 264pp. R1.20 Shuter 1964 SA ZUL

Ndlovu, R.S. Shange, O.L. Buthelezi, G.
Isizulu a incwadi yokuqala. [Zulu A, bk. 2] 152pp. 70c. Shuter 1961 SA ZUL

Ndlovu, T.M.
Ithemba kalibulali. [Hope does not kill.] 142pp. pl. 65c Mambo 1973 RH NDE

Ndoda, D.E.
Omahlakanipheni. [Clever ones.] 21pp. pl. 15c
Rhod Lit Bur 1976 RH NDE

Ndoria, P.
War in the forest. See: Mureithi, K.

Ndoro, J.
The hare's horns. 36pp. ill. K.shs2.00 ($1.00)
EAPH 1968 KE

Ndoumbe-Manga, S.
Le barrage réservoir du Noun et les populations installées
en amont de la cuvette. 145pp. ill. CFA1,500 Inst
Sciences Hum - Cam 1972 CM FRE

Ndu, P.
Golgotha. 34pp. 60k (Pan-African pocket poets, 4)
Univ Ife Bkshop 1971 NR

Nduka, O.
Western education and Nigerian cultural background.
168pp. N1.80 hd. OUP - Nig 1964 NR

Ndungu, F.
Beautiful Nyakio. 32pp. ill. K.shs2.00 ($1.00)
EAPH 1968 KE

Ndungu, S.J.
Hadithi Zetu. 2 bks. K.shs.3.00 ea. Equatorial 1971
KE SWA

Ndunguru, E.
Historia mila na desturi za Wamatengo. [History,
customs and traditions of the Wamalengo tribe] ill.
K.shs.6.25 ($2.00/80p.) EALB 1972 KE SWA

Ndunguru, E.A.
Walowezi hawana siri. [Settlers are not to be trusted.]
60pp. T.shs.6.00 Tanz Publ House 1974 TZ SWA

Ndunguru, S.
Educational essays for teachers. 150pp. K.shs.30.00
($5.80/£3.20) EALB 1976 KE

Ndunguru, S.
Urithi wetu. Jiographia ya Tanzania. bk. 1. 88pp.
K.shs.17.70 ($4.00/£1.60) EALB 1976 KE SWA

Ndupu, A.O.
A short cultural history of Oguta. 159pp. N2.00 Univ
Publ 1973 NR

Nduru, C.T.   Hjekshus, H., et al.
The party: essays on TANU. 80pp. T.shs.15.00
($3.00) (Tanzania Studies series, 6) Tanz Publ House
1976 TZ

Neal, W.G.
The ancient ruins of Rhodesia. [Reprint of ed. 1904].
See: Hall, R.N.

Neckebrouck, V.
L'Afrique noire et la crise religieuse de l'occident. 270pp.
T.shs.15.00 ($2.20 pap.) TMP 1971 TZ FRE

Neethling, P.J.
The importance of the weather and weather services to the
South African agricultural sector. A Delphi survey.
See: Theron, M.J.

Neild, M.
Feathers and floods. 139pp. ill. R$3.00 cl. M.O.
Collins 1969 RH

Neild, M.
Feathers in the mountains. 163pp. ill. R$3.00 cl.
M.O. Collins 1971 RH

Neill, S.
Rome and the ecumenical movement. 50c. (Peter
Ainslie Memorial lec., 18) Rhodes Univ Lib 1967 SA

Neirynck, J.
La génération des harmoniques impairs par les circuits de
redresseurs. 52pp. ill. 60k Press Univ Zaire 1959
ZR FRE

Neirynck, J.
La génération des harmoniques pairs par les circuits de
redresseurs. 55pp. ill. 60k Press Univ Zaire 1958
ZR FRE

Neirynck, J.
Introduction à l'électronique. 15pp. 23k Press Univ
Zaire 1962 ZR FRE

Nel, A.
Report of the committee for differentiated education and
guidance in connection with a national system for
handicapped pupils...etc. pt. 3, v. 2 79pp. R2.10
Human Science Res Council 1976 SA

Nel, A.
Report of the committee for differentiated education and
guidance in connection with a national system of education
for handicapped pupils...etc. pt. 3, v. 9 142pp.
R2.30 Human Science Res Council 1975 SA

Nel, J.A.
Genetic studies in Karakul sheep. 163pp. photos.
R2.95 (A v.42, no.3) Univ Stellenbosch, Lib 1967 SA

Nel, N.E.
The anatomy of the heart of the Plethodontid salamander
Ensatina eschscholtzii eschscholtzii. 18pp. ill. 60c.
(A v.45, no.2) Univ Stellenbosch, Lib 1970 SA

Nel, P.A.
Calculation of market potentials of consumer goods and
development of regional general market potential indices.
145pp. R5.00 (Bureau of Market Research, Research
Reports, 23) Bur Market Research 1969 SA

Nel, P.A.
A comparison of the income and expenditure patterns of
multiple urban Black, Coloured and Indian households.
45pp. R10.00 (Bureau of Market Research, Research
Reports, 43) Bur Market Research 1974 SA

Nel, P.A.   Steenekamp, J.J.A.   Loubser, M.
Income and expenditure patterns of non-white urban
households, Cape Town survey (multiple Bantu
households) 118pp. R5.00 (Bureau of Market
Research, Research Reports, 27.11) Bur Market
Research 1972 SA

Nel, P.A.   Steenekamp, J.J.A.   Loubser, M.
Income and expenditure patterns of non-white urban
households, Cape Town survey (single Bantu households)
77pp. R5.00 (Bureau of Market Research, Research
Reports, 27.19) Bur Market Research 1972 SA

Nel, P.A.   Steenekamp, J.J.A.   Loubser, M.
Income and expenditure patterns of non-white urban
households, Durban survey (multiple Asian households)
118pp. R5.00 (Bureau of Market Research, Research
Reports, 27.3) Bur Market Research 1971 SA

Nel, P.A.   Steenekamp, J.J.A.   Loubser, M.
Income and expenditure patterns of non-white urban
households, Durban survey (multiple Bantu households)
118pp. R5.00 (Bureau of Market Research, Research
Reports, 27.4) Bur Market Research 1971 SA

Nel, P.A.   Steenekamp, J.J.A.   Loubser, M.
Income and expenditure patterns of non-white urban
households, Durban survey (single Bantu households)
77pp. R5.00 (Bureau of Market Research, Research
Reports, 27.16) Bur Market Research 1972 SA

Nel, P.A.   Steenekamp, J.J.A.   Loubser, M.
Income and expenditure patterns of non-white urban
households, East London survey (multiple Bantu
households) 118pp. R5.00 (Bureau of Market
Research, Research Reports, 27.10) Bur Market
Research 1972 SA

Nel, P.A.   Steenekamp, J.J.A.   Loubser, M.
Income and expenditure patterns of non-white urban
households, East London survey (single Bantu
households) 77pp. R5.00 (Bureau of Market
Research, Research Reports, 27.17) Bur Market
Research 1972 SA

Nel, P.A.   Steenekamp, J.J.A.   Loubser, M.
Income and expenditure patterns of non-white urban households, Johannesburg survey (multiple Asian households) 118pp.   R5.00 (Bureau of Market Research, Research Reports, 27.5) Bur Market Research 1972 SA

Nel, P.A.   Steenekamp, J.J.A.   Loubser, M.
Income and expenditure patterns of non-white urban households, Johannesburg survey (multiple Bantu households) 118pp.   R5.00 (Bureau of Market Research, Research Reports, 27.2) Bur Market Research 1971 SA

Nel, P.A.   Steenekamp, J.J.A.   Loubser, M.
Income and expenditure patterns of non-white urban households, Johannesburg survey (multiple coloured households) 118pp.   R5.00 (Bureau of Market Research, Research Reports, 27.8) Bur Market Research 1972 SA

Nel, P.A.   Steenekamp, J.J.A.   Loubser, M.
Income and expenditure patterns of non-white urban households, Johannesburg survey (single Bantu households) 77pp.   R5.00 (Bureau of Market Research, Research Reports, 27.15) Bur Market Research 1972 SA

Nel, P.A.   Steenekamp, J.J.A.   Loubser, M.
Income and expenditure patterns of non-white urban households, Krugersdorp survey (multiple Bantu households) 118pp.   R5.00 (Bureau of Market Research, Research Reports, 27.12) Bur Market Research 1972 SA

Nel, P.A.   Steenekamp, J.J.A.   Loubser, M.
Income and expenditure patterns of non-white urban households, Port Elizabeth survey (multiple Bantu households) 118pp.   R5.00 (Bureau of Market Research, Research Reports, 27.7) Bur Market Research 1972 SA

Nel, P.A.   Steenekamp, J.J.A.   Loubser, M.
Income and expenditure patterns of non-white urban households, Port Elizabeth survey (multiple coloured households) 115pp.   R5.00 (Bureau of Market Research, Research Reports, 27.9) Bur Market Research 1972 SA

Nel, P.A.   Steenekamp, J.J.A.   Loubser, M.
Income and expenditure patterns of non-white urban households, Port Elizabeth survey (single Bantu households) 77pp.   R5.00 (Bureau of Market Research, Research Reports, 27.18) Bur Market Research 1972 SA

Nel, P.A.   Steenekamp, J.J.A.   Loubser, M.
Income and expenditure patterns of non-white urban households, Pretoria survey (multiple Bantu households) 118pp.   R5.00 (Bureau of Market Research, Research Reports, 27.1) Bur Market Research 1971 SA

Nel, P.A.   Steenekamp, J.J.A.   Loubser, M.
Income and expenditure patterns of non-white urban households, Pretoria survey (single Bantu households) 77pp.   R5.00 (Bureau of Market Research, Research Reports, 27.14) Bur Market Research 1972 SA

Nel, P.A.   Steenekamp, J.J.A.   Loubser, M.
Income and expenditure patterns of non-white urban households, Tembisa survey (multiple Bantu households) 118pp.   R5.00 (Bureau of Market Research, Research Reports, 27.13) Bur Market Research 1972 SA

Nel, P.A.
The minimum and supplemented living levels of non-whites residing in the main and other selected urban areas of the Republic of South Africa. 101pp.   R10.00 (Bureau of Market Research, Research Reports, 44) Bur Market Research 1975 SA

Nel, P.A.
The minimum and supplemented living levels of non-whites residing in the main and other selected urban areas of the Republic of South Africa. 87pp.   R50.00 (Bureau of Market Research, Research Reports, 49) Bur Market Research 1976 SA

Nel, P.A.
The minimum subsistence level of Blacks living in black homelands and other rural areas.   R30.00 (Bureau of Market Research, Research Reports, 42) Bur Market Research 1974 SA

Nel, P.A.
The minimum subsistence level of non-whites living in the main urban areas of the Republic of South Africa. 110pp.   R10.00 (Bureau of Market Research, Research Reports, 41) Bur Market Research 1974 SA

Nel, P.A.
Regional indices for marketing purposes. 2 v. See: van Tonder, J.J.

Nel, P.S.
Some aspects of the thigh musculature of certain microranid genera. 15pp. ill.   30c. (A v.19, no. 1) Univ Stellenbosch, Lib 1941 SA

Nelemans, C.J.
Research and development aspects of the CSIR's 'in house' microcircuit manufacturing facility (thin film technology) of interest to designers of thin film circuits. 51pp. ill.   gratis (CSIR research report, 318) CSIR 1973 SA

Nell, R.J.
Nadine Gordimer: novelist and short story writer. 43pp.   R2.25 Dept Bibliog, Lib & Typo 1964 SA

Nellis, J.R.
A theory of ideology: the Tanzanian example. 228pp. pap. & cl. K.shs.40.00 cl.   K.shs.29.25 pap. OUP-Nairobi KE

Nelson, A.
The freemen of Meru. 224pp. maps pl.   K.shs.23.75 OUP-Nairobi 1968 KE

Nelson, G.K.
Race, culture and brain function. 40c. (Isma paps., 20) Inst Study of Man 1964 SA

Nelvig, M.
Machengeterwo emazino. [How to look after your teeth.] 15pp. pl.   18c Mambo 1976 RH SHO

Nencu, E.
Elements de calcul des probabilités. See: Mangalo, N.

Nenquin, J.
Contribution to the study of the prehistoric cultures of Rwanda and Burundi. 301pp. pl. photos maps. RF1050 (FB865.00/$21.60) Inst Nat - Rwandaise 1967 RW

Nero, R.L.
Graphical work. See: Camdem, K.R.

Nesbitt, R.
East African certificate English. See: Singh, A.M.

Nesbitt, R.
Notes on Elechi Amadi's "The Concubine". 44pp. K.shs.6.00 (35p) (Heinemann's Student's Guides) Heinemann Educ - Nair 1974 KE

Nesbitt, R.
Notes on Peter Abraham's "Mine boy". 50pp. K.shs.6.00 pap. (Heinemann's Student's Guides) Heinemann Educ - Nair 1975 KE

Nesbitt, R.
Practical English for the East African certificate. Teacher's handbook 160pp.   K.shs.18.50 Heinemann Educ - Nair 1976 KE

Neto, A.
Sacred hope. 124pp.   T.shs.17.00 ($3.00) Tanz Publ House 1974 TZ

Ngubiah, S.N.
A curse from God. 224pp. K.shs9.00 ($2.50/£1.00)
EALB 1970 KE

Ngugi wa Thiong'o, J.
Hadithi za Zadig. tr. fr. French 2nd ed. 57pp.
K.shs.2.20 ($1.50/60p.) EALB 1966 KE SWA

Ngugi wa Thiong'o, J.
Mtawa mweusi. [Black hermit tr. fr. English J. D.
Mganga] 84pp. K.shs7.50 (60p.) (Waandishi wa
KiAfrika, 2.) Heinemann Educ - Nair 1970 KE SWA

Ngugi wa Thiong'o, J.
Usilie mpenzi wangu. [Weep not child tr. fr. English J.N.
Somba] 135pp. K.shs.10.75 (85p.) (Waandishi Wa
KiAfrika, 3.) Heinemann Educ - Nair 1971 KE SWA

Nguwo, A.B.
Chants intérieurs. 32pp. 20k (Jeune Littérature, 6)
Ed Mont Noir 1972 ZR FRE

Nguya, L.M.
The first seed. 269pp. K.shs.16.50 ($3.80/£1.80)
EALB 1975 KE

Nguya Ndila.
Indépendance de la République Démocratique du Congo
et les engagements internationaux antérieurs. 240pp.
Z2.50 Press Univ Zaire 1971 ZR FRE

Nguyen Chanh, T. Simon, C. Dar Tois, P.
Lexique de droit des affaires zairoises. 293pp. Z3.50
Press Univ Zaire 1972 ZR FRE

Nguyen Van Chi-Bonnardel, R.
L'économie maritime et rurale de Kayar, village sénégalais,
problèmes de développement. [Reprint of ed. 1967].
261pp. ill. pl. (D.fl.120.00) (Mémoires de l'IFAN) IFAN
1967 SG FRE

Ng'wandu, P.Y.
Ujamaa villages: Tanzania's strategy versus rural
underdevelopment, and the role of adult education.
(Studies in Adult Education, 15) Inst Adult Educ - Dar
1974 TZ

Ng'weno, H.
Let's find out about: atoms. 47pp. ill. K.shs8.00 New
ed. K.shs5.00 ($2.30 New ed.) ($2.00/80p.) EALB
1970 KE

Ng'weno, H.
Let's find out about: energy and machines. 47pp. ill.
K.shs8.00 New ed. K.shs5.00 ($2.30 New ed.)
($2.00/80p.) EALB 1969 KE

Ng'weno, H.
Let's find out about: heat. 37pp. ill. K.shs8.00 New
ed. K.shs5.00 ($2.30 New ed.) ($2.00/80p.) EALB
1968 KE

Ng'weno, H.
Let's find out about: light. 34pp. ill. K.shs8.00 New
ed. K.shs5.00 ($2.30 New ed.) ($2.00/80p.) EALB
1968 KE

Ng'weno, H.
Let's find out about: sound. 27pp. ill. K.shs8.00 New
ed. K.shs5.00 ($2.30 New ed.) ($2.00/80p.) EALB
1968 KE

Ng'weno, H.
Let's find out about: the universe. 44pp. ill. K.shs8.00
New ed. K.shs5.00 ($2.30 New ed.) ($2.00/80p.)
EALB 1968 KE

Ng'weno, H.
The men from Pretoria. 172pp. K.shs.12.50 pap.
(Longman Crime Series) Longman - Ken 1975 KE

Nhonoli, A.M., ed.
Degenerative disorders in the African environment.
See: Bennett, F.J., ed.

Nhonoli, A.M., ed.
Degenerative disorders in the African environment.
Epidemiology and consequences. See: Bennett, F.J.,
ed.

Nhonoli, A.M.
Health services and society in mainland Tanzania. A
historical overview - Tumetoka Mbali. See: Nsekela, A.J.

Niane, B.
Le régime huridique et fiscal du code des investissements
au Sénégal. 224pp. CFA1,600 (F32.00) Nouv Ed
Afric 1976 SG FRE

Niane, D. T.
Méry. 88pp. CFA500 (F13.00) Nouv Ed Afric 1975
SG FRE

Nicholson, G.
German settlers in South Africa. 52pp. 70c. Univ
Cape Town Lib 1962 SA

Nicholson, J.M. et al.
Guided social studies. Standard 6. 189pp. pl. maps.
R1.65 Shuter 1975 SA

Nicholson, J.M., et al.
Guided social studies, standard 7. 300pp. photos. cl.
R2.25 cl. Shuter 1976 SA

Nicholson, J.M. Morton, J.G.
Man's environment - Africa. 296pp. pl. maps. R2.85
Shuter 1974 SA

Nicholson, J.M. Morton, J.G.
Man's environment: Africa. 5th rev. ed. pt.2 272pp.
pl. maps ill. R2.10 Shuter 1954 SA

Nicholson, J.M. Morton, J.G.
Man's environment. Standard 9. 395pp. pl. maps.
R3.85 Shuter 1974 SA

Nicholson, J.M. Morton, J.G.
Man's environment. Standard 9. 382pp. ill. maps.
R3.85 Shuter 1974 SA

Nicholson, J.M. Morton, J.G.
Man's environment. Standard 10. 400pp. ill. maps.
R4.50 Shuter 1975 SA

Nicholson, J.M. Morton, J.G.
Man's environment standard 10. 383pp. photos. maps.
cl. R4.50 cl. Shuter 1975 SA

Nicholson, J.M. Morton, J.M.
Man's environment: the natural regions of the world,
mathematical geography, weather and climate, the oceans,
South America, Australasia. 3rd rev. ed. pt.1 200pp.
ill. pl. maps. R1.50 Shuter 1954 SA

Nicholson, J.M. Morton, J.G.
Man's environment: the northern hemisphere, mapwork,
geomorphology and trade routes. 2nd rev. ed. pt.3
354pp. ill. pl. maps. R3.00 Shuter 1955 SA

Nicholson, J.M. Morton, J.G.
Primary school geographies, std.III: east of the
Drakensberg. rev. ed. 98pp. ill. 95c. Shuter 1954
SA

Nicholson, J.M. Morton, J.G.
Primary school geographies, std.IV: Africa far and wide.
rev. ed. 112pp. ill. R1.05 Shuter 1956 SA

Nicholson, J.M. Morton, J.G.
Primary school geographies, std.V: South Africans abroad.
rev. ed. 96pp. ill. R1.10 Shuter 1957 SA

Nicholson, J.M. Morton, J.G.
Primary school geographies, std.VI: from old world to new.
rev. ed. 104pp. ill. 95c. Shuter 1959 SA

Nicholson, J.M. Morton, J.G.
Working with maps: an introduction to topographical map
interpretation. 48pp. maps. 90c. Shuter 1967 SA

Nickles, M.
Xylophages et pétricoles ouest-africains. See: Monod, T.

Nicol, D.
The inaugural lectures of the University of Zambia.
See: Nyerere, J.

Nicolas, F.
La langue berbère de Mauritanie. 476pp. CFA2400
pap. (Mémoires de l'IFAN, 33) IFAN 1953 SG FRE

Nicolas, F.
Tamesna: Les loullemmeden de l'est ou Touareg 'Kel Dinnik, 'cercle de T'awa. Colonie du Niger. 279pp. pl. CFA1200 IFAN 1950 SG FRE

Nicolas, F.J.
Grammaire l'élé; glossaire l'élé-français. See: Bon, G.

Nicolas, J.P.
Bioclimatologie humaine de Saint Louis du Sénégal. 340pp. ill. CFA2400 (Mémoires de l'IFAN, 57) IFAN 1959 SG FRE

Nicoll, I.M.
Mining and industry. 34pp. ill. col. ill. maps. ($1.00) (The Environment of the Rhodesian People, 5) M.O. Collins 1974 RH

Niederberger, O.
The African clergy in the Catholic Church in Rhodesia. 45pp. 50c. (Mambo Missio-Pastoral Series, 2) Mambo 1973 RH

Nienaber, P.J.
National documentation centre for music. 10pp. photos. free Human Science Res Council 1971 SA

Nieuwolt, S.
The climate of Zambia. 26pp. 75n. ($1.50) (Zambia Geographical Assoc., occas. pap., 3) Zambia Geog Assoc 1972 ZA

Nieuwolt, S.
Rainfall and evaporation in Tanzania. T.shs.15.00 ($5.00) (Research pap., 24) Bur Res Assess - Tanz 1973 TZ

The Nigerian Academy of Arts, Sciences and Technology.
The way ahead. The Nigerian People's Manifesto. 117pp. N1.00 Nig Acad Arts Sci 1975 NR

Nigerian Institute of Social and Economic Research.
Eighth annual conference proceedings. N1.25 ($2.00) NISER 1962 NR

Nigerian Institute of Social and Economic Research.
Fifth annual conference proceedings. 50k ($1.00) NISER 1956 NR

Nigerian Institute of Social and Economic Research.
Fourth annual conference proceedings. N1.00 ($2.00) NISER 1955 NR

Nigerian Institute of Social and Economic Research.
Research for national development: a survey of research on problems relating to Nigerian economic and social development, volume II. 212pp. N1.00 ($1.75) (N.I.S.E.R. research report, 3) NISER 1967 NR

Nigerian Institute of Social and Economic Research.
Seventh annual conference proceedings. N1.00 ($2.00) NISER 1960 NR

Nikiema, R.
Ceux adorables rivales. 52pp. CFA200 pap. CLE 1971 CM FRE

Nikoi, K.A.
The very first step in arithmetic. 83pp. ill. 70pes. Waterville 1967 GH

Nimeiri, S.
Taxation and economic development: a case study of the Sudan. 228pp. £S1.45 ($6.00) Khartoum UP 1974 SJ

Nimmo, A.
The Knysna story. ill. col. pl. maps. R7.50 Juta 1976 SA

N.I.S.E.R.
A survey of resources for each of the 12 states of Nigeria. 82pp. 50k each NISER 1973 NR

Nissim, G.
Banjun: étude phonologique du parler de Jo. 116pp. CFA500 Univ Cameroun 1972 CM FRE

Nitecki, A.
Authority files for African libraries. 70pp. 60pes. ($1.50) (Dept. of Library Stud. occas. paps., 5) Dept Lib Stud - Univ Ghana 1972 GH

Nitecki, A., ed.
African studies in the seventies. 119pp. C2.00 (C3.00) (Univ. of Ghana, Dept. of Library & Archival Studies, occas. paps., 8) Dept Lib Stud - Univ Ghana 1974 GH

Nitecki, A., ed.
The Dewey decimal classification and African studies. Selected papers presented at a conference on problems of classification for Africana, held at the University of Ghana, 22-24 November, 1973. 73pp. C1.50 (C2.50) (Univ. of Ghana, Dept. of Library & Archival Studies, occas. paps., 9) Dept Lib Stud - Univ Ghana 1974 GH

Nitecki, A., ed.
Directory of libraries in Ghana. 62pp. C1.00 (Univ. of Ghana, Dept. of Library & Archival Studies, occas. paps., 11) Dept Lib Stud - Univ Ghana 1974 GH

Niven, C.
Jock and Fitz. 128pp. maps pl. R2.50 Longman SA 1968 SA

Niven, C.R.
Short history of Nigeria. 3rd ed. 294pp. N1.25 Longman - Nig 1971 NR

Nixon, J.
The complete story of the Transvaal [Reprint of 1885 edition]. R8.40 (Africana collectanea, 42) Struik 1972 SA

Njai, M.W.
Mapenzi gani haya? [What kind of love is this?] 64pp. ill. K.shs6.00 Njogu 1972 KE SWA

Njau, R.
Ripples in the pool. 168pp. K.shs.20.00 Transafrica 1975 KE

Njoh-Mouelle, E.
De la médiocrité à l'excellence. Essai sur la signification humaine du développement. 158pp. CFA800 CLE 1970 CM FRE

Njoh-Mouelle, E.
Jalons II - l'Africanisme aujourd'hui. 80pp. CFA420 (Coll. Point de Vue, 16) CLE 1976 CM FRE

Njoh-Mouelle, E.
Jalons - recherche d'une mentalité neuve. 92pp. CFA360 (Point de vue, 5) CLE 1970 CM FRE

Njoku, N.O.
How to marry a good girl and live in peace with her. 50k Survival NR

Njoku, N.O.
How to write better letters, applications and business letters. 64pp. 50k Survival 1971 NR

Njoku, N.O.
Life turns man up and down. 52pp. 50k Survival 1970 NR

Njoku, N.O.
No condition is permanent. 48pp. 45k Survival 1970 NR

Njoku, N.O.
Why boys and girls of nowadays don't marry in time. 50k Survival NR

Njoku, P.A.
Certificate human biology and health education. 256pp. pl. N3.25 Africana Educ 1976 NR

Njoroge, J.K.
The greedy host. 32pp. ill. K.shs2.00 ($1.00) EAPH 1967 KE

Njoroge, J.K.
Pestle and mortar. K.shs5.00 (Senior readers) Equatorial 1973 KE

Njoroge, J.K.
Pestle and mortar. Cultural themes from East Africa. 74pp. K.shs.8.00 Africa Book Serv 1969 KE

Njoroge, J.K.
The proud ostrich. 48pp. ill. K.shs2.00 ($1.00) EAPH 1967 KE

Njoroge, J.K.
Spectrum. 182pp. K.shs20.00 cl. K.shs8.50 pap.
Equatorial 1973 KE

Njoroge, J.K.
Tit for tat. 106pp. ill. K.shs4.50 ($2.00) EAPH
1966 KE

Njoroge, L.N.
Kiria gitumaga hiti itheke. [Folktales.] 44pp.
K.shs.5.00 ($1.50) EAPH 1976 KE KIK

Njoroge, L.N.
Mburi yetagwo njiru. [Folktales.] 32pp. K.shs.5.00
($1.50) EAPH 1976 KE KIK

Njoroge, L.N.
Wakonyo. [Folktales.] 40pp. K.shs.5.00 ($1.50)
EAPH 1976 KE KIK

Njue, P.N.
My lovely mother. 97pp. K.shs.10.00 ($2.00 pap.)
(Comb Books in English, 11) Comb Books 1976 KE

Njururi, N.
Tales from Mount Kenya. 128pp. ill. K.shs.12.50
Transafrica 1975 KE

Nkabinde, A.C., ed.
Inkwazi. [White-headed fish-eagle] 168pp. 90c.
Shuter 1972 SA ZUL

Nkabinde, A.C.
Some aspects of foreign words in Zulu. 24pp. 30c.
(80c.) Univ South Africa 1968 SA

Nkanga Kalemba Vita.
L'apprentissage de la conjonction et de la disjonction par
les enfants Zairois et Belges. Etude psychologique de la
pensée logique. 112pp. Z2.30 Press Univ Zaire
1974 ZR FRE

Nketia, J.H.
Akwansosem bi. 48pp. 30pes. Ghana Publ Corp
1967 GH TWI

Nketia, J.H., ed.
Kookoo ho mpanisem. [History of the cocoa industry.]
2nd ed. 53pp. ill. 85pes. Bur Ghana Lang 1976 GH
ASA

Nketia, J.H.
Ethnomusicology in Ghana. 23pp. C1.00
($1.00/50p.) (Inaugural Lecture) Ghana UP 1970 GH

Nketia, J.H.
The folk songs of Ghana. New ed. 205pp. C8.00
(£4.00) Ghana UP 1974 GH

Nketia, J.H.
Kwabena Amoa. 36pp. 30pes. ($.30) Ghana Publ
Corp 1969 GH TWI

Nketia, J.H.
Our drums and drummers. 48pp. photos. 35pes.
($1.00) Ghana Publ Corp 1968 GH

Nketia, J.H.
Semcde. [Sweet sayings] 38pp. ill. 25pes.
Waterville 1953 GH TWI

Nketia, J.H.K.
Anwonsem. [Poems in Asante Twi.] 50pp. C1.20
Afram 1975 GH TWI

Nketia, J.H.K.
Mframa mu akwantuo. [The story of flying] 24pp. ill.
20pes. Waterville 1969 GH TWI

Nketia, J.H.K.
Nsase horow so anansesem. [Tales from other lands]
58pp. ill. 30pes. Waterville 1972 GH TWI

Nkiko, M.
Esquisse grammaticale de la langue Luba Shaba. (Parler
de Kasongo Nyembo) 95pp. CELTA 1975 ZR FRE

Nkiko, M.R.
Esquise grammaticale de la langue Luba-Shaba: parler de
Kasongo Nyembo. 95pp. 79k CELTA 1975 ZR FRE

Nkomo, N.P.
Isi Ndebele esiphezulu. [Advanced Ndebele language.]
279pp. R$1.70 Mambo 1974 RH NDE

Nkomo, P., tr.
Imigodi yenkosi usolomon. 96pp. 85c. Longman -
Rhod 1977 RH NDE

Nkondo, G.M., ed.
Turfloop testimony: the dilemma of a black university in
South Africa. 104pp. R2.40 ($3.30/£1.75) Ravan
1976 SA

Nkongo, J.
Sheria za michezo yetu. [The rules of our sports.]
120pp. ill. T.shs.15.00 Tanz Publ House 1976 TZ
SWA

Nkongolo, M.N.B.
My little picture book. 15n Multimedia 1973 ZA

Nkosi, C.P.
Imithi ephundliwe. See: Hlela, M.

Nkosi, L.
The transplanted heart. 161pp. cl. & pap. N5.00 cl.
N3.00 pap. Ethiope 1976 NR

Nkrumah, K.
Harakati ya kitabaka katika Afrika. [Class struggle in
Africa.] tr. fr. English M.W.K. Chiume. 79pp. ill.
T.shs.9.00 Tanz Publ House 1974 TZ SWA

Nkule, T.
Hadithi za kisasa za Kijerumani. [Modern German
stories.] 208pp. K.shs.15.50 ($3.70) EALB 1975 KE
SWA

Nkwera, F.
Jifunge Utumikie. [Gird yourself for service.] 46pp.
T.shs.3.00 (Wananchi wanachambua teolojia, 3)
Ndanda Mission Press 1976 TZ SWA

Nkwera, F.V.
Mzishi wa baba ana radhi. [Fortune smiles on the dutiful
child] 119pp. K.shs.4.60 ($1.75/70p.) EALB 1967
KE SWA

Noakes, G.R.   Harris, B.K.
Foundations of physics. 672pp. cl. & pap. N2.55 pap.
N4.70 cl. Macmillan NR

Noakes, G.R.
New intermediate physics. 1,012pp. N8.40
Macmillan NR

Noakes, G.R.   Harris, B.K.
Physics problems. 96pp. N1.50 Macmillan NR

Noble, A.
Teacher training: objectives and objections. ex. only
(Inaugural lec.) Rhodes Univ Lib 1972 SA

Noble, A.E.
Constructive English. 65c Van Schaik SA

Noble, A.E.
Grade exercises in comprehension. 70c. Van Schaik
SA

Noble, A.E.
Matriculation English course. R1.60 Van Schaik SA

Noble, A.E.
Steps to fluent English. 75c Van Schaik SA

Noble, F.V.
South African numismatics 1652-1965. 89pp. R1.00
Univ Cape Town Lib 1967 SA

Noble, R.G.
Solid wastes research in South Africa. 13pp. (NSPU
Report, 4) CSIR 1976 SA

Noizet, G.   Dottin, O.
Bibliographie géologique de Madagascar: 1958-1959.
9pp. FMG80 (F1.60) (Série Documentation, 150)
Service Geol - Mad 1960 MG FRE

Noizet, G.
Bibliographie géologique de Madagascar, 1960-1962.
14pp. FMG105 (F2.10) (Série Documentation, 162)
Service Geol - Mad 1963 MG FRE

Noizet, G.
Etude géologique des feuilles: Anosibe-Antanambao
Manampotsy-Vatomandry. 52pp. pl. maps.
FMG1620 (F32.40) (Travaux du Bureau Géologique,
108) Service Geol - Mad 1961 MG FRE

Noizet, G.
Premier inventaire des matières prémières pour céram.
89pp. pl. photos. FMG1745 (F34.90) (Série
Documentation, 155) Service Geol - Mad 1961 MG FRE

Nolan, A.
Jesus before Christianity: the gospel of liberation.
R3.60 SA only Philip 1976 SA

Nomenyo, S.
Tout l'évangile à tout l'homme. 68pp. CFA150 CLE
1967 CM FRE

Nonsenguve, P.
La notion des Nomos dans le pantateuque Grec. 246pp.
Z4.30 Press Univ Zaire 1976 ZR FRE

Norman, D. W. et al.
The feasibility of improved sole crop sorghum production
technology for the small-scale farmer in the northern
Guinea savanna zone of Nigeria. N1.00 (Samaru
misc. pap., 60) Inst Agric Res - Zaria 1976 NR

Norman, D.W.
An economic study of three villages in Zaria province:
land and labour relationships. 2nd ed. 84pp. maps.
N1.00 (Samaru misc. pap., 19) Inst Agric Res-Zaria
1973 NR

Norman, D.W.
An economic survey of three villages in Zaria province:
input-output study. 1, 2v. 191pp. N2.00 (Samaru
misc. pap., 37) Inst Agric Res-Zaria 1972 NR

Norman, D.W.
An economic survey of three villages in Zaria province:
input-output study. 2, 2v. 147pp. N2.00 (Samaru
misc. pap., 38) Inst Agric Res-Zaria 1972 NR

Norman, D.W. et al.
The feasibility of improved sole crop maize production
technology for the small-scale farmer in the northern
Guinea savanna zone in Nigeria. N1.00 (Samaru misc.
pap., 59) Inst Agric Res - Zaria 1976 NR

Norman, D.W.
A socio-economic study of three villages in the Sokoto
close-settled zone. See: Goddard, A.D.

Norman, D.W.
A socio-economic study of three villages in the Sokoto
close-settled zone: land and people. See: Goddard, A.D.

Norman, J., ed.
A survey of race relations in South Africa, 1974.
See: Horrell, M., ed.

Noronha, F.
Kipchoge of Kenya. 162pp. photos. K.shs.8.00
Textbook Ctre 1970 KE

Norris-Newman, C.
With the Boers in the Transvaal and Orange Free State
1880-1881. [Reprint of ed. 1882]. 394pp. ill. cl.
R18.75 cl. (Africana Reprint Library, 6) Africana Book
Soc 1976 SA

Northedge, F.S.
East-west relations, detente and after. 160pp. N4.25
(£3.50) ($8.25) (Univ. of Ife, Inst. of Administration
Monograph Series, 4) Univ Ife Press 1975 NR

Northern Nigerian Publishing Company.
Gangar Wa'azu. [The warning drum] 17pp. 45k
Northern Nig 1969 NR HAU

Northern Nigerian Publishing Company.
Hanyar Karatu Sabuwa. [The new way of reading]
38pp. 20k Northern Nig 1971 NR HAU

Northern Nigerian Publishing Company.
Hanyar Lissafi Sabuwa. [The new way of arithmetic]
17pp. 20k Northern Nig 1971 NR HAU

Northern Nigerian Publishing Company.
Jagorar Fuloti: Raskwana Naira Da Kobo. [A guide to
buyers: naira and kobo ready reckoner] 24pp. 20k
Northern Nig 1972 NR HAU

Northern Nigerian Publishing Company.
Jagorar Malamai Na Yaki Da Jahilci. [Adult education
teacher's guide] 40pp. 80k Northern Nig 1971 NR
HAU

Northern Nigerian Publishing Company.
Ka Koya Wa Kanka Karatun Ajami Da Boko. [Teach
yourself to read Ajami and Boko] 30pp. 35k Northern
Nig 1971 NR HAU

Northern Nigerian Publishing Company.
Karamin Sani. 1, 2 bks. 56pp. ill. 60k Northern
Nig 1944 NR HAU

Northern Nigerian Publishing Company.
Karamin Sani. 2, 2 bks. 62pp. ill. 70k Northern
Nig 1944 NR HAU

Northern Nigerian Publishing Company.
Key to Hausa: a book for learning Hausa idioms and
phrases for all occasions. 28pp. 45k Northern Nig
1966 NR

Northern Nigerian Publishing Company.
Koyad da lissafi. [Modern mathematics.] N1.00
Northern Nig 1976 NR HAU

Northern Nigerian Publishing Company.
Labaru Na Da Da Na Yanzu. [Stories, ancient and
modern] 230pp. N1.75 Northern Nig 1966 NR HAU

Northern Nigerian Publishing Company.
Northern States local government yearbook 1973/73.
N1.50 Northern Nig 1973 NR

Northern Nigerian Publishing Company.
Rubutun Wasika. [Letter writing] 31pp. 20k
Northern Nig 1969 NR HAU

Northern Nigerian Publishing Company.
Saiful Muluki. [Sword of Rulers] 33pp. 30k
Northern Nig 1966 NR HAU

Northern Nigerian Publishing Company.
Wakar Bagauda Ta Kano. [Songs of Bagauda of Kano]
25pp. 55k Northern Nig 1969 NR HAU

Northey, M.
General Joaquim Josè Machada. 36pp. R1.90 Dept
Bibliog, Lib & Typo 1970 SA

Les Nouvelles Editions Africaines.
Abdou Lernt Deutsch. pt. 1. CFA600 (F12.00) Nouv
Ed Afric 1976 SG DEU

Les Nouvelles Editions Africaines.
Abdou Lernt Deutsch. pt. 2. 54pp. CFA600
(F12.00) Nouv Ed Afric 1976 SG DEU

Les Nouvelles Editions Africaines.
Afrique, mon Afrique. Cours moyen deuxième année.
352pp. ill. CFA1380 (F20.00) Nouv Ed Afric 1973
SG FRE

Les Nouvelles Editions Africaines.
L'avion. 64pp. CFA250 (F5.00) (Coll. Notre Monde)
Nouv Ed Afric 1976 SG FRE

Les Nouvelles Editions Africaines.
Le cinéma. 64pp. CFA250 (F5.00) (Coll. Notre
Monde) Nouv Ed Afric 1976 SG FRE

Les Nouvelles Editions Africaines.
Colloque international sur le développement industriel
africain: République du Sénégal et CEDIMOM. 356pp.
CFA1900 (F38.00 pap.) Nouv Ed Afric 1973 SG FRE

Les Nouvelles Editions Africaines.
La désertification au sud du Sahara. Colloque de
Nouakchott (17-19 décembre 1973) 200pp. CFA2,000
(F40.00) Nouv Ed Afric 1976 SG FRE

Les Nouvelles Editions Africaines.
Littérature africaine. 449pp. CFA900 pap. (F18.00
pap.) Nouv Ed Afric 1973 SG FRE

Les Nouvelles Editions Africaines.
Littérature française. 409pp. CFA900 (F8.00 pap.)
Nouv Ed Afric 1973 SG FRE

Les Nouvelles Editions Africaines.
La vie avant la naissance. 64pp. CFA250 (F5.00)
(Coll. Notre Monde) Nouv Ed Afric 1976 SG FRE

Author Index

Les Nouvelles Editions Africaines.
Les volcans. 64pp. CFA250 (F5.00) (Coll. Notre Monde) Nouv Ed Afric 1975 SG FRE

Les Nouvelles Editions Africaines/La Sonapress/Les Editions des Trois Fleuves.
Blaise Diagne. Sa vie son oeuvre. 144pp. pl. cl. CFA2,500 Nouv Ed Afric 1974 SG FRE

Noyce, A.G.
The morphology and histology of the genital system of Theba Pisana (Mueller) (Pulmonata: Helicidae) 40pp. pl. R1.65 (Univ. Stellenbosch, Annals, vol. 48, A.3) Univ Stellenbosch Lib 1973 SA

Nsabimana, J.C.
Aho mbikenge. 88pp. RF26 ($0.26) Caritas 1973 RW KIN

N'Sanda, W.
Organisation interne d'un texte ecrit d'origine traditionelle orale. 50pp. CELTA 1975 ZR FRE

N'Sanda Wamenka.
Rehema. Mnara ya baba na mama. [Histoire et aventures de la belle Rehema.] 40k Ed Mont Noir 1973 ZR MUL

Nsanzubuhoro, V.
Nta byera. [Rien n'est parfait.] 94pp. RF20 Caritas 1972 RW KIN

Nsanzumuhire, H., ed.
Degenerative disorders in the African environment. Epidemiology and consequences. See: Bennett, F.J., ed.

Nsanzumuhite, H., ed.
Degenerative disorders in the African environment. See: Bennett, F.J., ed.

Nsekela, A.J.
Demokrasi Tanzania. [Democracy in Tanzania] photos. maps. Longman Tanz 1973 TZ SWA

Nsekela, A.J. Nhonoli, A.M.
Health services and society in mainland Tanzania. A historical overview - Tumetoka Mbali. 124pp. photos. K.shs.18.50 ($4.20/£2.10) EALB 1976 KE

Nsekela, A.J.
Minara ya historia ya Tanganyika. [Landmarks of Tanzanian history] 234pp. photos. maps. T.shs.10.00 Longman Tanz 1971 TZ SWA

Nshamamba Mahano. Gould T.
Répartition des effectifs des I.S.P. par option et par sexe (1975-1976). Les etudiantes universitaires de Lubumbashi. Z3.00 ($2.40) (Cahiers du CRIDE, Nouvelle série, I, 6) CRIDE 1977 ZR FRE

Nsimba Mumbamuna.
Lettres kinoises. Roman épistolaire. 31pp. 50k (CFA250) Centre Africain Litt 1974 ZR FRE

Nsubuga, H.S.
Livestock farming in Uganda. 31pp. hd. U.shs.3.00 Adult Educ Centre 1967 UG

Ntiru, R.C.
Tensions. 111pp. K.shs7.50 ($2.60) EAPH 1971 KE

Ntloko, P.M.
Iqhazu [Children's Poems]. 36pp. 35c OUP-SA 1954 SA XHO

Ntloko, P.M.
Isiqhelo siyayoyisa ingqondo. R1.50 Maskew Miller 1976 SA XHO

Ntloko, P.M.
Isitha [Poems]. 40pp. 35c OUP-SA 1961 SA XHO

Ntloko, P.M.
Ungodongwana [Drama]. 40pp. 45c OUP-SA 1970 SA XHO

Ntloko, P.M.
Zonwabise [Poems]. 64pp. 50c OUP-SA 1962 SA XHO

Ntogwisangu, W.H.
Asiyesikia la mkuu. [He who never listens to the elders.] 60pp. T.shs.3.00 Africa Inland church 1973 TZ SWA

Ntuli, D.B.Z.
Imicibisholo. [Bows and arrows] 190pp. R1.00 Shuter 1970 SA ZUL

Ntuli, D.B.Z.
Ubheka. [Bheka] 160pp. 50c. Shuter 1962 SA ZUL

Ntumba, K., et al.
Notice explicative de la carte géologique de Buma. 32pp. Z4.80 Press Univ Zaire 1976 ZR FRE

Ntungweriisho, Y.
Ruhondeza mwene busaasi. [An adaption of Rip van Winkle] tr. fr. English W. Irving. 33pp. K.shs2.50 ($1.50/60p.) EALB 1966 KE RNY

Nuhu, A.R.
Labarun musulunci guda goma. [Hausa story book for upper primary schools.] 62pp. ill. 80k OUP - Nig 1974 NR HAU

Nupen, E.M.
The effectiveness of various techniques for the removal of bacteria and viruses. (CSIR reports, RW559) CSIR 1975 SA

Nurse, G.T.
The origins of the Northern Cape Griqua. 19pp. 40c. (Isma paps., 34) Inst Study of Man 1975 SA

Nurse, R.H., et al.
Recycling and disposal of plastics waste in South Africa. 35pp. (NSPU Report, 6) CSIR 1976 SA

Nursey-Bray, P.F., ed.
Aspects of Africa's identity. Five essays. 98pp. U.shs.10.50 ($3.00) Mak Inst Soc Res 1973 UG

Nwabueze, B.
Constitutionalism in emergent states. hd. N9.00 Nwamife 1973 NR

Nwabueze, B.
Judicialism in Commonwealth Africa. hd. N16.80 NR only Nwamife 1977 NR

Nwabueze, B.O.
Nigerian land law. 662pp. cl. N12.00 Nwamife 1974 NR

Nwabueze, B.O.
Presidentialism in Commonwealth Africa. 442pp. hd. N16.80 (Africa only) Nwamife 1975 NR

Nwadialo, F.
The criminal procedure of the southern states of Nigeria. 255pp. cl. & pap. N16.00 cl. N10.00 pap. Ethiope 1976 NR

Nwakama, J.I. Idiok, R.
Feed your enemy. 28pp. 10k Daystar NR

Nwakolo, W.E.
General science for primary classes. 1, 3bks See: Iwobi, C.C.

Nwakolo, W.E.
General science for primary classes. 2, 3bks See: Iwobi, C.C.

Nwakolo, W.E.
General science for primary classes. 3, 3bks See: Iwobi, C.C.

Nwakolo, W.E.
General science for primary classes: teacher's bk. See: Iwobi, C.C.

Nwala, T.U.
Justice on trial. 163pp. N1.10 (African Literature series, 3) Onibonoje 1973 NR

Nwametu, O.C.
Okwu Igbo nke mbu. [Igbo language course for primary schools.] 48pp. ill. 75k Longman Nig 1976 NR

Nwana, O.C.
Comprehensive objective questions in school certificate biology. ill. N2.50 Nwamife NR

Nwana, O.C.
Comprehensive objective test of school certificate biology.
192pp. ill. N2.00 Nwamife 1973 NR

Nwana, P.
Omenuko. 94pp. col. ill. 40k Longman - Nig 1972
NR IGB

Nwanevu, S.S.I. Anokwu, C.C.
Health science objective tests. 120pp. N1.60
Armolaran 1970 NR

Nwangu, N.A.
Continuous education for school drop-outs, a task for adult
education institutions. T.shs.1.00 (Studies in Adult
Education, 14) Inst Adult Educ - Dar 1974 TZ

Nwangwu, G.A.C.
Obi na-aku eze. 88pp. 75k. Univ Publ 1977 NR IGB

Nwankwo, A.
Nigeria: the challenge of Biafra. 112pp. N1.30 (NR
only) Nwamife 1972 NR

Nwankwo, B.
Grammatical structure and its teaching. See: Boadi, L.

Nwankwo, N.
More tales out of school. 80pp. ill. 53k (African
Reader's Library, 7) Pilgrim 1965 NR

Nwankwo, N.
Tales out of school. 80pp. ill. 53k (African Reader's
Library, 2) Pilgrim 1963 NR

Nwanwene, O., comp.
The progress of Nigerian public administration: a report on
research. 2nd ed. 332pp. N2.50 ($3.00/£1.40)
Inst Admin Ife 1970 NR

Nwapa, F.
Never again. 80pp. N1.20 Nwamife 1975 NR

Nwapa, F.
This is Lagos and other stories. 2nd ed. 117pp. 85k
Nwamife 1972 NR

Nwegbu, G.C.
Akara aka. 86pp. N1.00 Univ Publ 1977 NR IGB

Nwoga, D.
Poetic heritage: Igbo traditional verse. See: Egudu, R.

Nwoga, D.I.
Ogogo Igbo 4. pupils bk. 4. See: Ahamba, S.M.

Nwoga, D.I.
Ogogo Igbo. pupil's bk. 3. See: Ahamba, S.M.

Nwoga, D.I.
Ogugu Igbo. pupil's bk. 1 See: Ahamba, S.M.

Nwoga, D.I.
Ogugu Igbo. Pupil's bk. 2 See: Ahamba, S.M.

Nwoga, D.I.
Ogugu Igbo. pupil's bk. 5. See: Ahamba, S.M.

Nwogugu, E.I.
Family law in Nigeria. 412pp. cl & pap. N8.00 pap.
N13.00 cl. (£5.50 pap.) (£7.00 cl.) (Heinemann
Studies in Nigerian Law, 2) Heinemann Educ - Nig 1974
NR

Nwosu, E.J.
Issues in economic development. 200pp. N10.00
Cross Continent 1976 NR

Nwosu, S. Corbin, H.
Handbook for teachers of social studies. 72pp. ill.
N1.25 Longman Nig 1976 NR

Nwosu, S.N. Oboli, H.O.N.
Primary social studies, year 4. 72pp. ill. 85k
Longman Nig 1976 NR

Nwosu, T.C.
And the heavens wept. 50pp. ill. N2.00 Cross
Continent 1976 NR

Nwosu, T.C.
Arrows in a thunderstorm. 144pp. ill. N2.50 Cross
Continent 1976 NR

Nwosu, T.C.
Ashes and sparks. 120pp. ill. N2.00 Cross
Continent 1977 NR

Nwosu, T.C.
The blind spots of God. 60pp. ill. N2.00
(Step-to-Success Readers Series) Cross Continent 1976
NR

Nwosu, T.C.
Born to raise hell. 144pp. ill. N2.50
(Step-to-Success Readers Series) Cross Continent 1977
NR

Nwosu, T.C.
Certificate summary and comprehension pieces for
practice. 160pp. ill. N2.50 Cross Continent 1977
NR

Nwosu, T.C.
Common entrance success tests: English and verbal
attitude. 96pp. ill. N2.00 Cross Continent 1977 NR

Nwosu, T.C.
Controlled composition exercises for primaries five and six.
See: Ajayi, E.O.

Nwosu, T.C.
Controlled composition exercises for primary four.
See: Ajayi, E.O.

Nwosu, T.C.
English through folk-tales. 120pp. ill. N2.50
(Step-to-Success Readers series) Cross Continent 1976
NR

Nwosu, T.C.
Examination guide: university entrance English. 148pp.
N2.50 Cross Continent 1977 NR

Nwosu, T.C.
Examination guide: West African poetry. 160pp. N4.00
Cross Continent 1976 NR

Nwosu, T.C.
Flowers for fatherland. 96pp. ill. N1.50 Cross
Continent 1977 NR

Nwosu, T.C.
Fresh first African reader. 96pp. ill. N1.00 Cross
Continent 1977 NR

Nwosu, T.C.
A game of blood and other plays. 145pp. ill. N2.50
Cross Continent 1976 NR

Nwosu, T.C.
Hot road. 145pp. ill. N2.50 (Step-to-Success
Readers Series) Cross Continent 1977 NR

Nwosu, T.C.
How to murder a rich man! 140pp. ill. N2.50 Cross
Continent 1977 NR

Nwosu, T.C.
Nigerian traditional literature. 160pp. ill. N4.00
(Black Bow series) Cross Continent 1976 NR

Nwosu, T.C.
Objective tests in English lexis and structure. 76pp.
55k Pilgrim 1967 NR

Nwosu, T.C.
Other faces, other places. 116pp. ill. N2.00 Cross
Continent 1977 NR

Nwosu, T.C.
Poems about love and women. 120pp. ill. N3.00
Cross Continent 1976 NR

Nwosu, T.C.
Poems for the African young. bk. 1, 3 bks. 56pp. ill.
N1.00 Cross Continent 1977 NR

Nwosu, T.C.
Poems for the African young. bk. 2, 3 bks. 56pp. ill.
N1.00 Cross Continent 1977 NR

Nwosu, T.C.
Poems for the African Young. bk. 3, 3 bks. 80pp. ill.
N1.50 Cross Continent 1977 NR

Nwosu, T.C.
Primary English through experiment and observation.
96pp. ill. N1.00 Cross Continent 1977 NR

Nwosu, T.C.
Revision certificate essays and letter writing. 160pp.
N4.00 Cross Continent 1976 NR

Nwosu, T.C.
A ride on the back. 120pp. ill. N2.50
(Step-to-Success Readers series) Cross Continent 1976
NR

Nwosu, T.C.
Sirens of the spirit. 136pp. ill. N2.50 Cross
Continent 1976 NR

Nwosu, T.C.
Stories from an African city. 120pp. ill. N2.50
(Step-to-Success Readers series) Cross Continent 1976
NR

Nwosu, T.C.
Voices from the hills. 124pp. ill. N2.50 Cross
Continent 1977 NR

Nwosu, T.C.
The women of Shomolu and other stories. 96pp. ill.
N2.00 (Step-to-Success Readers Series) Cross
Continent 1976 NR

Nxumalo, E.H.
Inqolobane yesizwe. See: Nyembezi, S.

Nxumalo, J.A.W.
Igugu Likazulu. [Treasure of the Zulus] rev. ed.
180pp. 75c. Shuter 1953 SA ZUL

Nxumalo, J.A.W.
Umcebo wolimi Lwesizulu. [Wealth of Zulu language]
160pp. 60c. Shuter 1951 SA ZUL

Nxumalo, J.A.W.
Uzwelonke. [Zwelonke] 170pp. photos. 80c.
Shuter 1950 SA ZUL

Nxumalo, O.E.H.
Amanqampunqampu. See: Khwela, S.T.Z.

Nxumalo, O.E.H.
Emhlabeni. See: Khwela, S.T.Z.

Nxumalo, O.E.H.
Ikhwezi [Poems]. 80pp. 95c OUP-SA 1969 SA ZUL

Nxumalo, O.E.H.
Ngisinga empumalanga. [I look] 180pp. 85c.
Shuter 1969 SA ZUL

Nxumalo, O.E.H.
UmZwangedwa [Poems]. 96pp. 75c OUP-SA 1972
SA ZUL

Nxumalo, S.S.
Our way of life. 24pp. ill. E1.10 Webster's; distr.
1976 SQ

Nyabongo, A.
Ebirembero. [Nursery rhymes] K.shs4.60
($1.75/70p.) EALB 1969 KE RNY

Nyabongo, A.L.
Upepo na mwangaza. [Wind and light.] 56pp.
K.shs.5.75 ($1.90) EALB 1975 KE SWA

Nyagah, S.
The ombudsman, constitutional and legal processes for the
protection of the citizen from administrative abuses.
39pp. K.shs6.50 Kenya Inst Admin 1970 KE

Nyagah, S.
The politicalization of administration in East Africa. 38pp.
K.shs6.50 Kenya Inst Admin 1968 KE

Nyahoza, F.
The eco-physiology of the loss of potential crop in upland
cotton. 47pp. T.shs.8.50 Dept Botany - Dar 1973 TZ

Nyahoza, F.
The eco-physiology of the loss of potential crop in Upland
Cotton. 47pp. T.shs.8.50 Univ Bkshop - Dar; distr.
1975 TZ

Nyakatura, J.
Aspects of Bunyoro; customs and traditions. 152pp.
K.shs10.00 ($2.75/£1.30) EALB 1971 KE

Nyalali, F.L.
Aspects of industrial conflicts. 288pp. ill. K.shs.28.65
($6.00/£2.90) EALB 1976 KE

Nyambe, M.
Ba bulailwe kini? 64pp. ill. 90n. Neczam 1974 ZA
LOZ

Nyambo, J.
Imanueli. [Christ's life.] 32pp. ill. T.shs.1.00 Central
Tanganyika 1968 TZ SWA

Nyambo, J.
Mhubiri Mkuu. [Preaching of Christ.] 32pp. ill.
T.shs.1.00 Central Tanganyika TZ SWA

Nyambo, J.
Yesu Kristo yu mshindi. [Easter story.] 32pp. ill.
T.shs.1.00 Central Tanganyika 1969 TZ SWA

Nyamu, H.J.
The civil service: service training, induction, administrative
change and attitudes. K.shs.2.00 Kenya Inst Admin
1973 KE

Nyamu, H.J.
Constraints on administrative productivity in the civil
service. K.shs.2.00 Kenya Inst Admin 1974 KE

Nyamu, H.J.
Management by objectives or the staff meeting for the
public service. K.shs.2.00 Kenya Inst Admin 1974 KE

Nyamu, H.J.
The state of the civil service today. A critical appraisal.
K.shs.2.00 Kenya Inst Admin 1975 KE

Nyanga, M.C.
Twaambo tumana mate. [Tales that exhaust saliva.]
50pp. 60n. Neczam 1975 ZA TON

Nyangira, N.
Relative modernization and public resource allocation in
Kenya. 184pp. K.shs.32.65 ($6.40/£3.10) EALB
1975 KE

Nyasulu, G.
Laana ya Pandu. [The curse of Pandu] 80pp.
K.shs.6.75 ($2.70/£1.10) EALB 1975 KE SWA

Nyasulu, G. Mkabarah, A.
Michezo ya kuigiza na hadithi. [Plays and a story]
256pp. K.shs7.50 ($2.25/90p.) EALB 1971 KE SWA

Nyembezi, C.L.S.
Compact Zulu dictionary (English/Zulu, Zulu/English)
See: Dent, G.R.

Nyembezi, C.L.S.
Learn more Zulu. 548pp. cl. R2.85 Shuter 1971 SA

Nyembezi, C.L.S.
Learn Zulu. 4th rev. ed. 247pp. R1.05 Shuter 1957
SA

Nyembezi, C.L.S. Dent, G.R.
Scholar's Zulu dictionary (English and Zulu) 620pp. cl.
R2.75 Shuter 1969 SA

Nyembezi, C.L.S.
Uhlelo lwesizulu. [Zulu grammar] 282pp. R1.10
Shuter 1956 SA ZUL

Nyembezi, C.L.S.
Zulu proverbs. rev. ed. 238pp. cl. R6.00
Witwatersrand UP 1974 SA

Nyembezi, L.S.
Izincwadi ezintsha zezempilo. Ibanga, 3 See: Dent,
S.R.

Nyembezi, L.S.
Izincwadi ezintsha zezempilo. Ibanga, 4 See: Dent,
S.R.

Nyembezi, L.S.
Izincwadi ezintsha zezempilo. Ibanga, 5 See: Dent,
S.R.

Nyembezi, L.S.
Izincwadi ezintsha zezempilo. Ibanga, 6 See: Dent,
S.R.

Nyembezi, S., ed.
Amahlungu aluhlaza. [Green pastures] 104pp. 50c.
Shuter 1963 SA ZUL

Nyembezi, S., ed.
Izimpophoma zompherumulo. [The waterfalls of the soul]
144pp. 75c. Shuter 1963 SA ZUL

Nyembezi, S.
Igoda. [The rope] Ibanga, 1 148pp. ill. 50c.
Shuter 1962 SA ZUL

Nyembezi, S.
Igoda. [The rope] Ibanga, 2 160pp. ill. 55c. Shuter 1962 SA ZUL

Nyembezi, S.
Igoda. [The rope] Ibanga, 3 192pp. ill. 60c. Shuter 1962 SA ZUL

Nyembezi, S.
Igoda. [The rope] Ibanga, 4 160pp. ill. 65c. Shuter 1962 SA ZUL

Nyembezi, S.
Igoda. [The rope] Ibanga, 5 180pp. ill. 75c. Shuter 1962 SA ZUL

Nyembezi, S.
Igoda. [The rope] Ibanga, 6 232pp. 80c. Shuter 1962 SA ZUL

Nyembezi, S.
Igoda. [The rope] Isigaba, A 66pp. ill. 40c. Shuter 1962 SA ZUL

Nyembezi, S.
Igoda. [The rope] Isigaba, B. 112pp. ill. 45c. Shuter 1962 SA ZUL

Nyembezi, S.
Imikhemezelo. [Light drizzle] 72pp. 70c Shuter 1963 SA ZUL

Nyembezi, S.
Inkinsela Yasemgungundlovu. [The V.I.P. of Pietermaritzburg] 224pp. R1.15 Shuter 1961 SA ZUL

Nyembezi, S. Nxumalo, E.H.
Inqolobane yesizwe. [The storyhouse of the nation] 300pp. ill. R1.60 Shuter 1966 SA ZUL

Nyembezi, S.
Izibongo zamakhosi. [The praises of kings] 158pp. ill. 75c. Shuter 1958 SA ZUL

Nyembezi, S.
Ubudoda abukhulelwa. [One does not have to be old to do manly deeds] 232pp. 65c. Shuter 1966 SA ZUL

Nyembezi, S.
Ulutya. [The rope] Ibanga, 1 148pp. ill. 50c. Shuter 1964 SA XHO

Nyembezi, S.
Ulutya. [The rope] Ibanga, 2 160pp. ill. 55c. Shuter 1964 SA XHO

Nyembezi, S.
Ulutya. [The rope] Ibanga, 3 192pp. ill. 60c. Shuter 1964 SA XHO

Nyembezi, S.
Ulutya. [The rope] Ibanga, 4 160pp. ill. 65c. Shuter 1964 SA XHO

Nyembezi, S.
Ulutya. [The rope] Ibanga, 5 180pp. ill. 75c. Shuter 1964 SA XHO

Nyembezi, S.
Ulutya. [The rope] Ibanga, 6 232pp. ill. 80c. Shuter 1964 SA XHO

Nyembezi, S.
Ulutya. [The rope] Isigaba, A. 66pp. ill. 40c. Shuter 1964 SA XHO

Nyembezi, S.
Ulutya. [The rope] Isigaba, B 112pp. ill. 45c. Shuter 1964 SA XHO

Nyerere, J.
Freedom and development. [Uhuru na Maendeleo] 420pp. photos. cl. & pap. K.shs.30.00 pap. K.shs.45.00 cl. OUP - Nairobi 1974 KE

Nyerere, J. Pratt, R.C. Nicol, D.
The inaugural lectures of the University of Zambia. 30pp. K1.25 (63p.) (Zambian paps., 2) Inst Soc Res - Zam 1967 ZA

Nyerere, J. K.
Education for liberation. 15pp. T.shs.1.20 (Documents on Adult Education, 1) Inst Adult Educ - Dar 1974 TZ

Nyerere, J.
Man and development. 133pp. K.shs.7.50 OUP - Nairobi 1974 KE

Nyerere, J.K.
Binadamu na maendeleo. [Man and development.] 146pp. K.shs.6.00 OUP - Nairobi 1974 KE SWA

Nyerere, J.K.
Freedom and socialism. 424pp. pap. & cl. K.shs50.00 cl. K.shs35.00 pap. OUP-Nairobi 1966 KE

Nyerere, J.K.
Freedom and unity. 384pp. pap. & cl. K.shs42.50 cl. K.shs27.50 pap. OUP-Nairobi 1966 KE

Nyerere, J.K.
Indépendance et éducation. Tr. fr. English. 104pp. CFA390 (Point de vue, 10) CLE 1972 CM FRE

Nyerere, J.K.
Liberté et socialisme. Tr. fr. English. 152pp. CFA480 (Point de vue, 11) CLE 1972 CM FRE

Nyerere, J.K.
Nyerere on socialism. 64pp. K.shs6.00 OUP-Nairobi 1969 KE

Nyerere, J.K.
Ujamaa. [Socialism] 196pp. K.shs.4.50 OUP-Nairobi 1968 KE SWA

Nygologoza, P.
Kigezi and its people. 140pp. ill. K.shs.8.40 ($2.50/£1.00) EALB 1969 KE

Nyokabi, S.
The chameleon who couldn't stop changing his mind. 24pp. col. ill. K.shs.6.00 (Bushbabes, 1) Transafrica 1975 KE

Nyomi, C.K.
Nunyala enelia. [The fourth wise man.] 3rd ed. 47pp. 50pes. Bur Ghana Lang 1976 GH EWE

Nyoni, C., et al.
Imbongi zalamhla layizolo. [Poets of today and yesterday.] 44pp. 60c Longman - Rhod 1976 RH NDE

Nzamba Mundende.
Gandanda. Initiation et mythes pende. Texte pende, sans traduction. 118pp. map. (DM19.00 pap.) (CEEBA. série II, Mémoires et Monographies, 4) CEEBA 1974 ZR FRE

Nzeako, J.U.T.
Aka ji aku. [A wealthy man.] 72pp. ill. N1.00 Longman - Nig 1975 NR IGB

Nzeako, J.U.T.
Nkoli. [Language text.] ill. 90k Longman - Nig 1973 NR IGB

Nzeako, T.
Chi ewere ehihie Jie. 72pp. ill. 75k Univ Publ 1971 NR IGB

Nzeako, T.
Omenala ndi igbo. 125pp. 65k Longman - Nig 1972 NR IGB

Nzekwu, O. Crowder, M.
Eze goes to school. 76pp. ill. 53k (African Reader's Library, 4) Pilgrim 1963 NR

Nzema Literature and Cultural Association.
Nzema orthography. 3rd ed. 17pp. 25pes. Bur Ghana Lang 1976 GH

Nziata Mulenge.
Pour la guérir, il faut ton coeur! Mythes pende. Texte pende-français. 105pp. map. (DM18.00 pap.) (CEEBA. série II, Mémoires et Monographies, 9) CEEBA 1974 ZR FRE

Nzongola.
Introduction à la science politique. 50k (Essais, 3) Ed Mont Noir 1972 ZR FRE

Nzouankeu, J.M.
Le souffle des ancêtres. 2nd ed. 112pp. CFA300 pap. CLE 1971 CM FRE

Oceanographic Research Institute.
Bulletin: South African Association for marine biological research (annual) photos. Oceanographic Res Inst 1960 SA

Ochai, A., comp.
Ahmadu Bello University. Kashim Ibrahim Library. Catalogue of Africana. 196pp. ABU Lib 1974 NR

Ochecha, A.O.
Synthesis of modern economics for West African secondary schools. 197pp. N3.50 Ethiope 1975 NR

Ochieng, N.A.O.
Education and culture change in Kenya 1844-1925. 107pp. K.shs.10.00 ($2.00) Africa Book Serv 1968 KE

Ochieng, N.A.O.
Luo social system, with a special analysis of marriage rituals. 34pp. K.shs.4.50 Africa Book Serv 1968 KE

Ochieng', W.R.
The first word: essays on Kenyan history. 208pp. K.shs.18.95 ($4.30/£2.00) EALB 1975 KE

Ochieng, W.R.
A history of the Kadino chiefdom of Yimbo western Kenya. K.shs.11.00 ($2.90/£1.50 pap.) EALB 1975 KE

Ochieng', W.R.
An outline history of Nyanza up to 1914. 104pp. K.shs.16.50 (£1.80) ($3.80) EALB 1975 KE

Ochieng', W.R.
An outline history of the Rift Valley of Kenya. 144pp. maps. K.shs.12.85 ($3.20/£1.60) EALB 1975 KE

Ochieng, W.R.
A pre-history of Gusii of Western Kenya. 267pp. K.shs.26.00 ($5.50) EALB 1975 KE

Ochtman, L.H.J. Berhanu Debele.
Detailed soil survey and irrigability land classification of Gode agricultural research station. 112pp. maps. ex. only. Inst Agric Res - Addis 1975 ET

Ochu, T.
The squirrel and his mother. 16pp. ill. 22k OUP - Nig 1966 NR

Ocitii, J.P.
African indigenous education, as practised by the Acholi of Uganda. 280pp. K.shs.16.00 ($3.80/£1.70) EALB 1973 KE

Ocitti, J.P.
Acam toona. 78pp. ill. K.shs.4.00 ($1.75/70p.) EALB 1970 KE LUO

Ocitti, J.P.
Lacan ma kwo pe kinyero. [Every dog has its day] 91pp. ill. K.shs.2.50 ($1.50/60p.) EALB 1961 KE LUO

Ocitti, J.P.
Urban geography of Gulu. 226pp. U.shs.25.00 (Occas. paps., 49) Dept Geog - Mak 1973 UG

O'Connell, J.
Nigeria 1965: crisis and criticism. See: Aboyade, T.

O'Connor, A.M. Semuggoma, S.
The peripheral zone of Kampala. 47pp. U.shs.21.00 (Occas. paps., 8) Dept Geog - Mak 1968 UG

O'Connor, S.
Here's how to be a football referee. 26pp. ill. 15n Multimedia 1972 ZA

Oculi, O.
Kanta Riti. 45pp. ill. U.shs.3.00 Uganda Pub House 1974 UG

Oculi, O.
Orphan. 101pp. ill. K.shs6.00 ($5.80) EAPH KE

Oculi, O.
Prostitute. 132pp. ill. K.shs30.00 cl. K.shs7.00 pap. ($5.80 cl.) ($2.60 pap.) EAPH 1968 KE

Odaga, A.
The angry flames. 48pp. ill. K.shs2.50 ($1.00) EAPH 1968 KE

Odaga, A.
The diamond ring. 32pp. ill. K.shs2.00 ($1.00) EAPH 1967 KE

Odaga, A.
The hare's blanket. 28pp. ill. K.shs1.70 ($1.00) EAPH 1967 KE

Odaga, A.
Jande's ambition. 72pp. ill. K.shs3.50 ($1.00) EAPH 1966 KE

Odaga, A.
Kip on the farm. 15pp. ill. K.shs3.50 ($1.00) EAPH 1969 KE

Odaga, A.
Sweets and sugar cane. 24pp. ill. K.shs1.60 ($1.00) EAPH 1969 KE

Odeleye, A.O.
Ayo: a popular Yoruba game. 64pp. ill. N1.20 OUP - Nig 1976 NR

Odendaal, W.A.
The effect of continued injections of large doses of oestradiol benzoate on the gonads, endocrine glands and growth of mature female rats. 26pp. photos. 30c. (A v.19, no.2) Univ Stellenbosch, Lib 1941 SA

Odenigwe, G., ed.
New system of local government: government by the community in the East Central State of Nigeria. 410pp. hd. N20.00 Nwamife 1977 NR

Odera Oruka, H.
Punishment and terrorism in Africa. Problems in the philosophy and practice of punishment. 116pp. K.shs.13.50 ($3.30/£1.60) EALB 1976 KE

Odetoyinbo, H.A., comp.
Education in Nigeria: a bibliographical guide. See: Oshin, N.R.O., tr.

Odeyemi, J.O.
Comprehensive modern mathematics. v. 1 159pp. ill. N1.50 Onibonoje 1976 NR

Odeyemi, O.
Worked examples in A/L pure & applied mathematics. 178pp. ill. N1.53 Heinemann Educ - Nig 1970 NR

Odhiambo, T.R.
Crawling life. 24pp. ill. K.shs.2.50 ($1.00) EAPH 1970 KE

Odhiambo, T.R.
Life in water. 23pp. ill. K.shs.2.50 ($1.00) EAPH 1970 KE

Odhiambo, T.R.
Our food. 27pp. ill. K.shs2.50 ($1.00) EAPH 1968 KE

Odhiambo, T.R.
Our garden. 24pp. ill. K.shs.2.50 ($1.00) EAPH 1969 KE

Odhiambo, T.R.
Our pets. 24pp. ill. K.shs.2.50 ($1.00) EAPH 1969 KE

Odhiambo, T.R.
Wild animals. 23pp. ill. K.shs.2.50 ($1.00) EAPH 1970 KE

Odiaka, M.O.
Mastering English. 233pp. N2.00 Macmillan 1974 NR

Odiaka, M.O.
Revision notes and workbook on general knowledge. 107pp. 75k. Univ Publ 1975 NR

Odilera, V.
Okpa aku eri eri. 129pp. N2.00 Univ Publ 1975 NR IGB

Odingo, R.S.
The Kenya highlands. 248pp. maps/photos. K.shs.49.00 ($11.00) EAPH 1971 KE

Odjidja, E.H.L.
Mustard seed [Growth of the church in Kroboland]. 162pp. photos. C1.50 Waterville 1974 GH

Author Index

Odjidja, E.M.L.
Biography: Paulo Mohenu. 26pp. 10pes. Waterville 1965 GH

Odjidja, E.M.L.
Sakramentoi enyc le. [The two sacraments] 21pp. 10pes. Waterville 1963 GH GAA

Odjidja, J.R.
Adventures of Yaw Kantinka. 43pp. ill. 35pes. Waterville 1972 GH

Odjidja, J.R.
Ata ke Lawee. [Ata and Lawee] 87pp. ill. 40pes. Waterville 1971 GH DAG

Odjidja, J.R.
Comprehension without tears. 70pp. ill. 55pes. Waterville 1964 GH

Odjidja, J.R.
Ga for beginners. 207pp. ill. C1.00 Waterville 1968 GH

Odjidja, J.R.
Ga wiemc le heususumc. [Thinking about Ga] 68pp. 40pes. Waterville 1961 GH GAA

Odoi-Atsem, K.
Mansaamc onia. [Development tax] 44pp. 18pes. Waterville 1964 GH GAA

Odoi, N.A.
Facts to remember. 7th rev. ed. 157pp. C1.50 Waterville 1976 GH

Odokara, E.O.
Igbo as an effective vehicle for promoting work oriented functional literacy among adults. T.shs.1.00 (Studies in Adult Education, 18) Inst Adult Educ - Dar 1975 TZ

Odokara, E.O.
A study of the differential continuing education interests of young and older homemakers in urban communities, a Nigerian experience as a basis for planning continuing education programmes for women. T.shs.1.00 (Studies in Adult Education, 16) Inst Adult Educ - Dar 1975 TZ

Odoma, M.S.A.
Otakada ukoche alu Igala. pupils bk. 1. See: Okwoli, P.E.

Odoma, M.S.A.
Otakada ukoche alu Igala. pupils bk. 2. See: Okwoli, P.E.

Odongo, T.E.
Asabun nuka Iteso. 125pp. K.shs.6.50 ($2.25/90p) EALB 1971 KE TES

O'Donohue, J.
Magic and witchcraft in Southern Uganda. 50pp. K.shs.6.50 (Gaba Pastoral Papers, 36) Gaba 1975 KE

O'Donovan, B.
The law of sale of goods in South Africa. 4th ed. Juta 1972 SA

O'Donovan, P.B., comp. Alemu, G.W., comp. Galal, E.S.E., comp.
Results of experiments in animal production (from 1966/67 to 1975). S. Edwards, ed. 56pp. map. ex. only Inst Agric Res - Addis 1976 ET

Odoom, A.K.
Some short fireside stories. 40pp. ill. 35pes. Waterville 1975 GH

O'Dowd, A.P.
The law of evidence in South Africa. R7.00 Juta 1963 SA

O'Dowd, E.T.
Hermetic storage in Nigeria using weldmesh silos lined with butyl rubber. 21pp. ill. 60k (Samaru misc. pap., 30) Inst Agric Res - Zaria 1971 NR

O'Dowd, E.T.
Hermetic storage of cowpea: (vigna unguiculata walp), in small granaries, silos and pits in Northern Nigeria. 37pp. ill. 60k (Samaru misc. pap., 31) Inst Agric Res - Zaria 1971 NR

Odu, M.A.C.
Tears of the fathers. 160pp. ill. N3.00 Cross Continent 1977 NR

Odubitan, A.
Oriki awon Timi Ede. [Attributive names of kings of Ede] 16pp. 20k Univ Ife Bkshop 1964 NR YOR

Odugbose, A.
Common entrance mathematics: without answers. See: Moody, M.

Odunaike, S.O.
Jesus is coming. 32pp. K.shs.2.00 Evangel 1974 KE

Odunaike, S.O.
The young Christian and money. 84pp. K.shs.5.00 Evangel 1972 KE

Odunjo, J.F.
Akojopo ewi aladun. [Collection of delightful poems] 59pp. ill. 60k Longman - Nig 1961 NR YOR

Odunjo, J.F.
Alawiye: Iwe karun. [Yoruba primary course] 5, 6 bks. 126pp. ill. N1.30 Longman - Nig. 1971 NR YOR

Odunjo, J.F.
Alawiye: Iwe kefa. [Yoruba primary course] 6, 6 bks. 125pp. ill. N1.30 Longman - Nig 1972 NR YOR

Odunjo, J.F.
Alawiye: Iwe keji. [Yoruba primary course] 2, 6 bks. 63pp. col. ill. 86k Longman - Nig 1971 NR YOR

Odunjo, J.F.
Alawiye: Iwe kerin. [Yoruba primary course] 4, 6 bks. 107pp. N1.15 Longman - Nig 1972 NR YOR

Odunjo, J.F.
Alawiye: Iwe keta. [Yoruba primary course] 3, 6 bks. 79pp. ill. 98k Longman - Nig 1971 NR YOR

Odunjo, J.F.
Alawiye: Iwe kini. [Yoruba primary course] 1, 6 bks. 48pp. col. ill. 75k Longman - Nig 1971 NR YOR

Odunjo, J.F.
Eko ijinle Yoruba: Alawiye: Apa keji. [Advanced Yoruba course] 2, 2 bks. 181pp. ill. N1.95 Longman - Nig 1969 NR YOR

Odunjo, J.F.
Eko ijinle Yoruba: Alawiye: Apa kini. [Advanced Yoruba course] 1, 2 bks. 186pp. ill. N1.95 Longman - Nig 1972 NR YOR

Odunjo, J.F. et al.
Kadara ati egbon re. [Kadara and his brother] 131pp. photos. N1.05 Onibonoje 1967 NR YOR

Odunjo, J.F.
Kuye. 124pp. 65k Pilgrim 1964 NR YOR

Odunjo, J.F.
Omo oku orun. 54pp. 40k Pilgrim 1964 NR YOR

Odunsi, A.T.O.
Mungo Park ati Odo Oya. [Mungo Park and the River Niger] 70pp. photos. ill. 80k Macmillan 1970 NR YOR

Oduyale, T.
Pan-African university sports. (An exhortation) 51pp. pl. N1.00 Univ Lagos Bkshop; distr. 1974 NR

Oduyoye, A.
Youths without jobs. 64pp. ill. 40k Daystar 1972 NR

Oduyoye, M.
The planting of Christianity in Yorubaland. 77pp. maps photos. 85k Daystar 1969 NR

Oduyoye, M.
The vocabulary of Yoruba religious discourse. 138pp. map photo. N2.25 Daystar 1972 NR

Oduyoye, M.
Yoruba names - their structure and their meanings. 108pp. map. pap. & hd. N4.75 hd. N1.25 pap. Daystar 1972 NR

Oduyoye, M.
Yoruba numeration system. 24pp. 50k Daystar 1969 NR

Oedeyi, M.B.
Ìtan 'Robinson Crusoe' ní èdè Yoruba. [Yoruba translation of Robinson Crusoe] 128pp. ill. N1.25 Macmillan 1970 NR YOR

Oettle, A.G.
Cancer research in Africa: illustrated by a recent epidemic of cancer of the gullet. 17pp. hd. R1.00 (Raymond Dart lec., 3) Inst Study of Man 1966 SA

Offei-Darko.
Bedanagya. [You will leave it] 89pp. ill. 50pes. Waterville 1970 GH TWI

Office National de la Recherche Scientifique et Technique.
Dictionnaire des villages des de[Jpartements de Wouri. 15pp. ill. map. CFA1,000 Inst Sciences Hum - Cam 1970 CM FRE

Office National de la Recherche Scientifique et Technique.
Dictionnaire des villages des départements de Adamaoua. 107pp. ill. maps. CFA1,000 Inst Sciences Hum - Cam 1974 CM FRE

Office National de la Recherche Scientifique et Technique.
Dictionnaire des villages des départements de Bui. 39pp. ill. map. CFA1,000 Inst Sciences Hum - Cam 1973 CM FRE

Office National de la Recherche Scientifique et Technique.
Dictionnaire des villages des départements de Donga-Mantung. 40pp. ill. maps. CFA1,000 Inst Sciences Hum - Cam 1973 CM FRE

Office National de la Recherche Scientifique et Technique.
Dictionnaire des villages des départements de Fako. 71pp. ill. maps. CFA1,000 Inst Sciences Hum - Cam 1974 CM FRE

Office National de la Recherche Scientifique et Technique.
Dictionnaire des villages des départements de Lekie. 50pp. ill. maps. CFA1,000 Inst Sciences Hum - Cam 1971 CM FRE

Office National de la Recherche Scientifique et Technique.
Dictionnaire des villages des départements de Manyu. 78pp. ill. maps. CFA1,000 Inst Sciences Hum - Cam 1973 CM FRE

Office National de la Recherche Scientifique et Technique.
Dictionnaire des villages des départements de Margui-Wandala. 89pp. ill. maps. CFA1,000 Inst Sciences Hum - Cam 1972 CM FRE

Office National de la Recherche Scientifique et Technique.
Dictionnaire des villages des départements de Mayo-Danai. 40pp. ill. maps. CFA1,000 Inst Sciences Hum - Cam 1972 CM FRE

Office National de la Recherche Scientifique et Technique.
Dictionnaire des villages des départements de Meme. 88pp. ill. maps. CFA1,000 Inst Sciences Hum - Cam 1973 CM FRE

Office National de la Recherche Scientifique et Technique.
Dictionnaire des villages des départements de Nde. 82pp. ill. maps. CFA1,000 Inst Sciences Hum - Cam 1974 CM FRE

Office National de la Recherche Scientifique et Technique.
Dictionnaire des villages des départements de Nkam. 26pp. ill. maps. CFA1,000 Inst Sciences Hum - Cam 1970 CM FRE

Office National de la Recherche Scientifique et Technique.
Dictionnaire des villages des départements des Moungo. 33pp. ill. maps. CFA1,000 Inst Sciences Hum - Cam 1971 CM FRE

Office National de la Recherche Scientifique et Technique.
Différénciation régionale et régionalisation en Afrique Francophone et à Madagascar. 146pp. ill. CFA1,000 Inst Sciences Hum - Cam 1972 CM FRE

Office National de la Recherche Scientifique et Technique.
Liste bibliographique des travaux de l'ORSTOM au Cameroun. 79pp. CFA1,000 Inst Sciences Hum - Cam 1972 CM FRE

Office National de la Recherche Scientifique et Technique.
Tableau de population du Cameroun. 3rd ed. 117pp. CFA1,000 Inst Sciences Hum - Cam 1971 CM FRE

Ofomata, G.E.C.
Nigeria in maps: Eastern states. 152pp. maps. N5.00 Ethiope 1975 NR

Ofosu-Amaah, P.K.
Objective questions in school certificate geography. 176pp. ill. N1.15 Macmillan NR

Ofosu-Appiah, L.H.
Joseph Ephraim Casely Hayford. The man of vision and faith. 31pp. C1.00 (The J.B. Danquah Memorial Lectures, 8) Univ Ghana Bkshop; distr. 1975 GH

Ofosu-Appiah, L.H.
The life and times of J.B. Danquah. 285pp. photos. cl. & pap. 2.00 pap. C4.00 cl. Waterville 1974 GH

Ofosu-Appiah, L.H.
The life of Dr. J.E.K. Aggrey. 128pp. pl. cl. & pap. C2.00 cl. C1.25 pap. Waterville 1975 GH

Ofosu-Appiah, L.H.
The life of Lt. General Kotoka. 156pp. C1.50 Waterville 1972 GH

Ofosu-Appiah, L.H.
Slavery: a brief survey. 113pp. ill. 60pes. Waterville 1969 GH

Ofosu-Appiah, L.H., tr.
Odusseus. [Homer's Odysseus.] 351pp. C3.50 Bur Ghana Lang 1974 GH TWI

Ofosu-Appiah, L.H., tr.
Sokrates Anoyi. [Twi translation of Plato's apology.] 62pp. 70pes. Waterville 1976 GH TWI

Ofosu-Appiah, L.H., tr.
Sophocles' Antigone. [Twi translation of Antigone.] 65pp. C1.00 Waterville 1976 GH TWI

Ogana, B.W.
Days of glamour. 109pp. K.shs.15.80 ($3.70/£1.80) EALB 1976 KE

Ogana, B.W.
Hand of chance. 244pp. K.shs12.00 ($3.25/£1.30) EALB 1970 KE

Ogbalu, F.C.
Akwukwo ogugu Igbo mbu1. 1, 6 bks. 74pp. ill. 75k Univ Publ 1970 NR IGB

Ogbalu, F.C.
Akwukwo ogugu Igbo mbu2. 2, 6 bks. 74pp. ill. 75k Univ Publ 1970 NR IGB

Ogbalu, F.C.
Akwukwo ogugu Igbo mbu3. 3, 6 bks. 84pp. ill. 75k Univ Publ 1970 NR IGB

Ogbalu, F.C.
Akwukwo ogugu Igbo mbu4. 4, 6 bks. 63pp. ill. 75k Univ Publ 1970 NR IGB

Ogbalu, F.C.
Akwukwo ogugu Igbo mbu5. 5, 6 bks. 66pp. ill. 75k Univ Publ 1970 NR IGB

Ogbalu, F.C.
Akwukwo ogugu Igbo mbu6. 6, 6 bks. 84pp. ill. 75k Univ Publ 1970 NR IGB

Ogbalu, F.C.
British constitution: questions and answers. 143pp. 75k Univ Publ 1971 NR

Ogbalu, F.C.
Complete course in Igbo. 197pp. N1.75 Univ Publ 1971 NR

Ogbalu, F.C.
The correct way to write Igbo. 67pp. 75k Univ Publ 1977 NR

Ogbalu, F.C.
Ebubedike. 150pp. N2.00 Univ Publ 1977 NR IGB

Ogbalu, F.C., ed.
Igbo language and culture. See: Emenanjo, E.N., ed.

Ogbalu, F.C.
Edemede Igbo. 96pp. N1.00 Univ Publ 1976 NR IGB

Ogbalu, F.C.
Higher elementary arithmetic. 118pp. ill. 50k Univ Publ 1970 NR IGB

Ogbalu, F.C.
Igbo dictionary (Okowa Okwu) 166pp. ill. 75k Univ Publ 1971 NR

Ogbalu, F.C.
Igbo etiquette. 36pp. 5k Univ Publ 1975 NR

Ogbalu, F.C.
Igbo institutions and customs. 75pp. N1.50 Univ Publ 1973 NR

Ogbalu, F.C.
Igbo work book for secondary 1-5. 80pp. Univ Publ 1973 NR IGB

Ogbalu, F.C.
Ila oso uzuakoli. 41pp. ill. 50k Univ Publ 1971 NR IGB

Ogbalu, F.C.
Ilu Igbo. 161pp. N1.50 Univ Publ 1971 NR IGB

Ogbalu, F.C.
Improved Igbo numeral system, counting in tens. 161pp. N2.00 Univ Publ 1974 NR

Ogbalu, F.C.
Junior Igbo course. 155pp. N2.00 Univ Publ 1977 NR

Ogbalu, F.C.
Key to success. 200pp. 75k Univ Publ 1977 NR

Ogbalu, F.C.
Mbediogu. 103pp. ill. 55k Univ Publ 1971 NR IGB

Ogbalu, F.C.
Mmoo mmoo. 47pp. 50k Univ Publ 1971 NR IGB

Ogbalu, F.C.
New entrance scholarship success workbook with past questions and answers. 100pp. 65k Univ Publ 1970 NR

Ogbalu, F.C.
New model English. 212pp. 75k Univ Publ 1971 NR

Ogbalu, F.C.
New model essays. 189pp. 75k Univ Publ 1971 NR

Ogbalu, F.C.
Nmoo nmoo. 86pp. N1.00 Univ Publ 1966 NR IGB

Ogbalu, F.C.
Nza na Obu. 100pp. ill. N1.00 Univ Publ 1971 NR IGB

Ogbalu, F.C.
Obiefula. [Novel.] 150pp. N2.00 Univ Publ 1977 NR IGB

Ogbalu, F.C.
Okeu ntuhi. [Book of Igbo riddles.] 56pp. 50k. Univ Publ 1974 NR IGB

Ogbalu, F.C.
Omenala Igbo. 185pp. ill. N2.00 Univ Publ 1971 NR IGB

Ogbalu, F.C.
Ota akara. [Infant Igbo primer.] 2nd ed. 98pp. N1.00 Univ Publ 1977 NR IGB

Ogbalu, F.C.
Questions and answers in West African history. 176pp. 75k Univ Publ 1971 NR

Ogbalu, F.C.
School certificate Igbo. 132pp. 75k Univ Publ 1971 NR

Ogbalu, F.C.
Standard Igbo: path to its development. 96pp. N1.00 Univ Publ 1974 NR

Ogbalu, F.C.
Uwaezuoke. [Novel] 150pp. ill. N2.00 Univ Publ 1975 NR IGB

Ogboka, S.N.
Ukpulawhu unûzu unu Ejpeye. See: Ikpe, M.S.

Ogejo, C.
Mwindaji hodari. [Novel.] 72pp. K.shs.8.50 (60p) Heinemann Educ - Nair 1975 KE SWA

Ogejo, S.C.
Kifunze kuandika barua. [A guide to Swahili letter-writing.] 128pp. K.shs.15.00 Heinemann Educ - Nair 1977 KE

Ogendo, R.
An industrial geography of Kenya. 326pp. maps photos. K.shs.65.00 ($14.00) EAPH 1972 KE

Ogendo, R.B.
Kenya: a study in physical and human geography. See: Ojanyi, F.F.

Oghah Language Translation Committee.
Teachers' notes on Ekwoh Olu Oghah nka mbuh. 50k (Inst. of African Stud., Univ. of Ibadan, Rivers readers project, 35) Inst Afr Stud-Ibadan 1973 NR OGB

Ogidan, O.
The lawyer. 44pp. 50k Univ Lagos Bookshop 1971 NR

Ogieiriaixi, E.
Edo literature. 33pp. ill. 60k (Edo Literature series, monograph 2) Univ Lagos Bkshop; distr. 1973 NR

Ogieiriaixi, E.
Edo phonology. 25pp. 50k Univ Lagos Bkshop; distr. 1973 NR

Ogieiriaixi, E.
Imaguero. 57pp. 70k Emotan 1973 NR

Ogilvie, P.R.
In the bag. 104pp. ill. cl. R7.95 Macmillan - SA 1975 SA

Ogilvie Thompson, N. Cavvadas, J., ed.
South African tax cases. 32v. R20.00 (annually) Juta SA

Oginga-Odinga, J.
Two months in India. 96pp. photos. K.shs.7.50 (50p.) New Kenya 1965 KE

Oginni, A.A. Ojo, J.O.
Ede e Yoruba kiko ati kika ni otun. [Language text.] bk. 1. 44pp. ill. 85k Ilesanmi 1973 NR YOR

Oginni, A.A. Ojo, J.O.
Ede e Yoruba kiko ati kika ni otun. [Language text.] bk. 2. 90pp. ill. 90k Ilesanmi 1973 NR YOR

Oginni, A.A. Ojo, J.O.
Ede e Yoruba kiko ati kika ni otun. [Language text.] bk. 3. 132pp. ill. N1.05 Ilesanmi 1974 NR YOR

Oginni, A.A. Ojo, J.O.
Ede e Yoruba kiko ati kika ni otun. [Language text.] bk. 4. 116pp. ill. N1.20 Ilesanmi 1974 NR YOR

Oginni, F.G.
An outline history of West Africa. 192pp. ill. maps. N1.80 Macmillan 1973 NR

Oginnin, J.B.
Ideas, capital and management for Nigerian businesses. 100pp. N2.50 Bosede NR

Ogot, B.A., ed.
Hadith 5: economic and social history of East Africa. 272pp. K.shs.34.50 ($7.00/£3.35 pap.) EALB 1975 KE

Ogot, B.A., ed.
Hadith 6: History and social change in East Africa. 248pp. K.shs.33.40 ($7.00/£3.30) EALB 1976 KE

Ogot, B.A., ed.
Hadith v.4, politics and nationalism in Kenya. 269pp. K.shs.35.00 EAPH 1974 KE

Ogot, B.A., ed.
Hadith. v. 1 166pp. maps photos. K.shs30.00 cl. K.shs10.00 pap. ($6.40 cl.) ($3.20 pap.) EAPH 1968 KE

Ogot, B.A., ed.
Hadith. v. 2 258pp. maps. K.shs54.50 cl. K.shs22.50 pap. ($10.00 cl.) ($5.80 pap.) EAPH 1970 KE

Ogot, B.A., ed.
Hadith. v. 3 203pp. K.shs22.50 ($5.80) EAPH 1971 KE

Ogot, B.A., ed.
Kenya before 1900. K.shs.55.00 ($13.00) EAPH 1977 KE

Ogot, B.A., ed.
Zamani. 406pp. maps. K.shs.35.10 Longman - Ken 1974 KE

Ogot, B.A., ed. Kieran, J.A., ed.
Zamani: a survey of East African history. 391pp. maps. K.shs52.50 cl. K.shs21.00 pap. ($10.00 cl.) ($5.80 pap.) EAPH 1968 KE

Ogot, B.A.
History of the southern Luo. v. 1 239pp. maps photos. K.shs.36.00 cl. K.shs.20.00 pap. ($8.00 cl.) ($5.20 pap.) EAPH 1967 KE

Ogot, G.
Land without thunder. 204pp. ill. K.shs30.00 cl. K.shs8.50 pap. ($5.80 cl.) ($2.60 pap.) EAPH 1968 KE

Ogot, G.
The other woman and other stories. 150pp. K.shs.15.00 Transafrica 1976 KE

Ogot, G.
The promised land. 193pp. ill. K.shs7.50 ($2.60) EAPH 1966 KE

Ogujawa, S.B.
Akwukwo ogugu nke mbu. [Ibo language text.] bk. 1. 51pp. ill. 95k Ilesanmi 1973 NR IGB

Ogujawa, S.B.
Akwukwo ogugu nke mbu. [Ibo language text.] bk. 2. 40pp. ill. N1.05 Ilesanmi 1973 NR IGB

Ogunba, O.
The movement of transition: a study of the plays of Wole Soyinka. 235pp. cl. & pap. N5.90 cl. N3.50 pap. Ibadan UP 1975 NR

Ogunba, O. Irele, A.
Theatre in Africa. N6.00 Ibadan UP 1977 NR

Ogunbiyi, O.
Laundry work. 67pp. ill. N2.00 Heinemann Educ - Nig 1969 NR

Ogunbowale, P.O.
Asa ibile Yoruba. [Yoruba customs] 88pp. photos. ill. 90k OUP-Nig 1966 NR YOR

Ogunde, R.A.
An outline history of Israel. 128pp. ill. N1.20 Macmillan 1972 NR

Ogunde, R.O.
O'level essays in Old Testament: monarchy to fall of Samaria. 2nd ed. 84pp. 90k Onibonoje 1968 NR

Ogundele, O.
Oju osupa. 1, 2 bks See: Yemitan, O.O.

Ogundele, O.
Oju osupa. 2, 2bks See: Yemitan, O.O.

Ogundimu, D.
"Far from the Madding Crowd": notes. 92pp. 85k Onibonoje 1968 NR

Ogundimu, D.
Fragments. 52pp. N1.00 Onibonoje 1976 NR

Ogundimu, D.
"Great Expectations": notes. 110pp. 85k Onibonoje 1968 NR

Ogundimu, D.
"Northanger Abbey": notes. 85k Onibonoje 1969 NR

Ogundimu, D.
"She Stoops to Conquer": notes. 52pp. 70k Onibonoje 1969 NR

Ogundipe, P.A. Tregidgo, P.S.
Practical English. New ed. bk. 2, 5. 272pp. ill. N1.78 Longman - Nig 1976 NR

Ogundipe, P.A. Tregidgo, P.S.
Practical English. New ed. bk. 3, 5. 260pp. ill. N1.78 Longman - Nig 1976 NR

Ogundipe, P.A. Tregidgo, P.S.
Practical English. New ed. bk. 4, 5. 224pp. ill. N1.87 Longman - Nig 1974 NR

Ogundipe, P.A.
Practical English course. bk. 1, 5 bks. See: Tregidgo, P.S.

Ogundipe, P.A.
Practical English course. bk. 5, 5 bks. See: Tregidgo, P.S.

Ogundipe, P.A.
Practical English. teachers bk. 1 See: Tregidgo, P.S.

Ogunfodunrin, E.O.
Accounts: elementary accounting. bk. 3 222pp. N1.65 Onibonoje 1967 NR

Ogungbesan, K.
Celebration of black and African writing. See: King, B.

Ogunkoya, L.
Introductory organic chemistry. See: Bamkole, T.O.

Ogunlesi, J.S.
English for Africans: workbook. 1, 3 bks. See: Ridout, R.

Ogunlesi, J.S.
English for Africans: workbook. 2, 3 bks. See: Ridout, R.

Ogunlesi, J.S.
English for Africans: workbook. 3, 3 bks. See: Ridout, R.

Ogunmola, E.K.
Ife owo. [Love of money] 24pp. 20k Univ Ife Bkshop 1965 NR YOR

Ogunmola, K.
The palmwine drinkard (A yoruba opera) tr. fr. Yoruba R. G. Armstrong et al 118pp. (Inst. of African Stud., Univ. of Ibadan, occas. pub., 12) Inst Afr Stud-Ibadan NR

Ogunmola, K.
The palmwine drinkard (Omuti) tr. fr. Yoruba R.G. Armstrong et al. 153pp. N1.25 (Inst. of African Stud., Univ. of Ibadan, Bi-lingual literary works, 2) Inst Afr Stud-Ibadan 1972 NR

Ogunmola, M.O.
English language registers. 186pp. photos. N1.90 Onibonoje 1967 NR

Ogunmola, M.O.
A groundwork of English literature. 123pp. 80k Alliance 1971 NR

Ogunmola, M.O.
Study notes on Chinua Achebe's Things Fall Apart. 41pp. 40k Alliance 1970 NR

Ogunniran, L.
Eégun aláaré. [The entertaining masquerade] ill. N1.15 Macmillan 1972 NR YOR

Ogunniyi, D.
New poetry book. 2, 2 bks. 84pp. photos. 85k Onibonoje 1971 NR

Ogunniyi, D.
A new poetry book for primary schools. 122pp. ill. 85k Onibonoje 1975 NR

Ogunniyi, D.
New poetry book. I, 2 bks. 84pp. photos. 85k Onibonoje 1971 NR

Ogunniyi, D.
Teaching of poetry. 94pp. photos. N1.05 Onibonoje 1971 NR

Ogunniyi, L.
Fateful eclipse. 87pp. N1.00 (African Literature Series, 8) Onibonoje 1975 NR

Ogunniyi, L.
Riders on the storm. 71pp. N1.10 (African Literature Series, 10) Onibonoje 1975 NR

Ogunseitan, T.O.
Modern textbook on 'O' level commerce. 150pp.
N2.50 Aromolaran 1975(?) NR

Ogunseitan, T.O.
Questions/answers on School Certificate commerce.
100pp. N2.00 Armolaran 1970 NR

Ogunsheye, F.A.
Nigerian library resources in science and technology.
44pp. N1.00 (Inst. of Librarianship, occas. pap., 2)
Inst Lib-Ib 1970 NR

Ogunsheye, F.A.
The records of civilizations. 40pp. N1.00 (Inaugural
lecture) Ibadan UP 1976 NR

Ogunsola, A.F.
Legislation and education in Northern Nigeria. 112pp. cl.
& pap. N2.50 cl. N1.75 pap. OUP - Nig 1974 NR

Ogunsola, J.B.
West African history, 1,000 A.D. - present day. 193pp.
N3.50 Armolaran 1970 NR

Oguntoye, O.A., comps.
Small-scale industries: Midwestern State, Kwara State, and
Lagos State of Nigeria. See: Aluko, S., comps.

Oguntoye, O.A.
Occupational survey of Old Bussa. 59pp. 75k
($1.25) (N.I.S.E.R. research report, 4) N.I.S.E.R. 1968
NR

Ogunyemi, M.A.
Objective texts for school certificate geography: pupils.
57pp. ill. 64k Heinemann Educ - Nig 1969 NR

Ogunyemi, M.A.
Objective texts for school certificate geography: with
answers. 57pp. ill. 72k Heinemann Educ - Nig 1969
NR

Ogunyemi, O.
"Animal Farm": notes. 84pp. 85k Onibonoje 1970
NR

Ogunyemi, O.
Introducing literature: unseen poetry and prose. 119pp.
N1.20 Onibonoje 1972 NR

Ogunyemi, O.
Notes, Q/A on "Persuasion". 118pp. N1.10
Onibonoje 1974 NR

Ogunyemi, O.
Notes, Q/A on "The Mayor of Casterbridge". 124pp.
N1.10 Onibonoje 1974 NR

Ogunyemi, O.
"Silas Marner": notes. 92pp. 85k Onibonoje 1970
NR

Ogunyemi, W.
Kiriji: an historic drama on Ekiti Parapo war in the
nineteenth century. 76pp. N1.50 Pilgrim 1976 NR

Ogunyemi, W.
Obaluaye. [King, the owner-of-the-world tr. fr. Yoruba W.
Ogunyemi] 83pp. pap. & hd. N1.05 pap. N1.95 hd.
(Inst. of African Stud., Univ. of Ibadan, Bi-lingual literary
works, 4) Inst Afr Stud-Ibadan 1972 NR

Ogwal-Otim, W.
Ojuk - the runaway. 38pp. hd. U.shs2.50 Adult Educ
Centre 1966 UG

Ogwe, S.O.
"Julius Caesar". Questions and answers. 76pp. N1.00
Ilesanmi 1972 NR

Ogwu, S.
The gods are silent. 228pp. N1.50 (African Literature
Series, 7) Onibonoje 1975 NR

Ohadike, P.O.
Development and factors in the employment of African
migrants on the copper mines of Zambia, 1940-66.
24pp. K1.25 (63p.) (Zambian paps., 4) Inst Soc
Res - Zam 1969 ZA

Ohadike, P.O.
Some demographic measurements for Africans in Zambia:
an appraisal of the 1963 census administration and results.
71pp. K1.25 (63p.) (Communications, 5) Inst Soc
Res - Zam 1969 ZA

Ohene-Asante, G.
God's plan for your life. See: Ashton, M.

Ohia, G.
Practical biology for secondary schools. v. 1 100pp.
N1.80 Armolaran 1970 NR

Ohlander, L., ed.
National horticultural centre, Nazareth research station:
progress report for the period April 1973 to March 1974.
See: Jackson, T.H., ed.

Ohonbamu, O.
Introduction to Nigerian law of mortgages. 208pp. hd.
N6.50 Univ Lagos Bookshop 1972 NR

Ojanyi, F.F. Ogendo, R.B.
Kenya: a study in physical and human geography.
229pp. pl. maps. cl. & pap. K.shs.35.00 pap.
K.shs.80.00 cl. Longman - Ken 1974 KE

Ojehomon, A.A.
Catalogue of recorded sound. 39pp. 50k (Inst. of
African Stud., Univ. of Ibadan, occas. pub., 20) Inst Afr
Stud-Ibadan 1969 NR

Ojelabi, A.
One hundred questions and answers on Government of
West Africa. See: Oyebola, A.

Ojelabi, A.
A textbook of government for West Africa. See: Oyebola,
A.

Ojelabi, A.
A textbook of West African history. 2nd ed. 375pp.
maps. N2.00 Educ Res Inst 1971 NR

Oji, N.O.
Modern mathematics for schools. 88pp. N1.50
Nwamife 1973 NR

Ojiako, J., ed.
Nigeria yearbook 1975. A record of events and
developments in 1974. 24th ed. 440pp. ill. photos.
maps. Daily Times - Nig 1975 NR

Ojienda, F.
The native. 176pp. K.shs.15.00 pap. ($3.00 pap.)
(Comb Books in English, 4) Comb Books 1975 KE

Ojo, A.
The cultural dimension in geography. 23pp. 30k
(Inaugural lec., 10) Univ Ife Press 1973 NR

Ojo, A.
A geography course for secondary schools: elements of
physical and world human geography. 3, 5bks 312pp.
ill. N2.50 Macmillan 1969 NR

Ojo, A. Ola, K.
A geography course for secondary schools: geography for
us. 1, 5bks 120pp. ill. N1.40 Macmillan 1969 NR

Ojo, A.
A geography course for secondary schools: North America
and Monsoon Asia. 4, 5bks 192pp. ill. N1.80
Macmillan 1969 NR

Ojo, A.
A geography course for secondary schools: North-West
Europe and the U.S.S.R. 5, 5bks 192pp. ill. N2.60
Macmillan NR

Ojo, A. Ola, K.
A geography course for secondary schools: our homeland
2, 5bks 128pp. ill. N2.10 Macmillan 1969 NR

Ojo, A.
Objective questions in school certificate and G.C.E.
Ordinary level geography. 1, 2 bks 160pp. ill. N1.60
Macmillan NR

Ojo, A.
Objective questions in school certificate and G.C.E.
ordinary level geography. 2, 2bks 196pp. ill. N1.70
Macmillan NR

Ojo, A.O.
Political science. Government of Nigeria. 285pp. N3.00 Ilesanmi 1973 NR

Ojo, E.O.
English language for certificate examinations. 160pp. N3.00 Armolaran 1970 NR

Ojo, E.O.
Essentials of 'O' level English. N3.00 Armolaran 1970 NR

Ojo, E.O.
Notes on "Pageant of longer poems". 70pp. N1.20 Armolaran 1970 NR

Ojo, J.B.O. Adelakun, A.A. Fakuade, R.A.
Onibonoje modern mathematics for secondary schools. bk. 2 257pp. ill. N2.10 Onibonoje 1974 NR

Ojo, J.B.O. Adelakun, A.A. Fakuade, R.A.
Onibonoje modern mathematics for secondary schools. bk. 3 206pp. ill. N2.45 Onibonoje 1975 NR

Ojo, J.B.O. Adelakun, A.A. Fakuade, R.A.
Onibonoje modern mathematics for secondary schools. bk. 4 N2.65 Onibonoje 1975 NR

Ojo, J.O.
Ede e Yoruba kiko ati kika ni otun. bk. 1. See: Oginni, A.A.

Ojo, J.O.
Ede e Yoruba kiko ati kika ni otun. bk. 2. See: Oginni, A.A.

Ojo, J.O.
Ede e Yoruba kiko ati kika ni otun. bk. 3. See: Oginni, A.A.

Ojo, J.O.
Ede e Yoruba kiko ati kika ni otun. bk. 4. See: Oginni, A.A.

Ojo, J.R.O. Morton-Williams, P.
Museum of the Institute of African Studies, University of Ife: a short illustrated guide. 13pp. 55k Univ Ife Press 1969 NR

Ojo, O.
Government for O'level: questions and answers. See: Taiwo, O.

Ojo, O.
Government for 'O'level: textbook. See: Taiwo, O.

Ojo, O.
Ijapa tiroko. [Tortoise stories] 120pp. ill. 95k Longman - Nig 1973 NR YOR

Ojo, O.
Ijapa Tiroko, oko Yanibo. [The tortoise and his wife.] 122pp. ill. 95k Longman - Nig 1973 NR YOR

Ojo, O.
Water balance in Uganda. 70pp. U.shs.30.00 (Occas. paps. 53) Dept Geog - Mak 1974 UG

Ojomo, O.A.
Agricultural science objective tests. 153pp. ill. 90k Onibonoje 1974 NR

Ojomo, O.A.
Essentials of agricultural science. 81pp. ill. 90k Onibonoje 1975 NR

Ojomo, O.A.
Model Q/A in agricultural science. 199pp. N1.60 Onibonoje 1973 NR

Ojomo, O.A.
Practical handbook in agricultural science. 175pp. ill. N1.65 Onibonoje 1974 NR

Okafor, J.M.
Onye oma Emeka. 91pp. ill. 55k Univ Publ 1972 NR IGB

Okafor, R.N.
Annales de l'université d'Abidjan. See: Huguet, L.

Okai, A.
Lorgorligi lorgarithms. 146pp. cl. C5.00 ($5.00) Ghana Publ Corp 1974 GH

Okali, C. Addy, P.L.N.A.
Economics of cocoa production and marketing with special reference to Ghana. 150pp. C3.60 Univ Ghana Bkshop; distr. 1974 GH

Okali, C., ed.
Economics of cocoa production and marketing: proceedings of economics research conference Legon, April 1973. See: Kotey, R.A., ed.

Okanu, D.C.
School certificate accounts. N3.25 Africana Educ 1973 NR

Okara, J.
Busara wa mzee kibiriti. [Primer on agriculture.] K.shs.6.50 ($3.50) Foundation 1977 KE SWA

Okedara, J.T.
Nigerian adult education directory, 1970-1971. 145pp. N1.25 Dept Adult Educ-Ibadan 1972 NR

Okedare, J.T.
Comparative study of adult education programmes of some universities and colleges in Europe, North America and Africa, 1970-1971. 19pp. 60k Dept Adult Educ-Ibadan 1972 NR

Okediji, F.O., ed.
The rehabilitation of beggars in Nigeria: proceedings of a national conference. 74pp. 80k Univ Ibadan Bkshop 1972 NR

Okediji, O.
Agbalagba akan. [The big fool] 192pp. col. ill. N1.90 Longman - Nig 1971 NR YOR

Okediji, O.
Aja l'o l'eru. [The big head carries the big load] 156pp. ill. N1.30 Longman - Nig 1969 NR YOR

Okediji, O.
Ògá ni Bùkólá. [Bukola is boss] 48pp. ill. 45k Macmillan 1972 NR YOR

Okediji, O.
Rere run. [Disaster!] 100pp. N1.10 Onibonoje 1973 NR YOR

Okeke, E.
Veronica the girl. 86pp. 65k Univ Publ 1977 NR

Okello, J.
Revolution in Zanzibar. 222pp. photos. K.shs.8.00 ($2.60) EAPH 1967 KE

Okelo, A.
Kyrie from Missa Maleng for choir and African instruments. 15pp. music. N2.00 ($4.00/£1.75) (Ife Music Editions, 4) Univ Ife Press 1976 NR

Okereke, O.
The economic impact of the Uganda co-operatives. 135pp. cl. & pap. K.shs.21.00 pap. K.shs.38.00 cl. ($4.60/£1.80 pap.) ($9.60/£4.50 cl.) EALB 1974 KE

Okereke, O.
The old woman and the mushroom. 16pp. ill. 18k OUP - Nig 1966 NR

Okiri, K.
So they say. 164pp. ill. K.shs9.00 ($2.50/£1.00) EALB 1970 KE

Okojie, O.
Oziegbe Docteur. 54pp. ill. K.shs4.75 OUP-Nairobi 1970 KE FRE

Okoko, E.U.
How to overcome temptation. 28pp. 10k Daystar 1967 NR

Okoko, E.U.
How to succeed in life. 20pp. 10k Daystar 1961 NR

Okoko, E.U.
Mufano wa kushinda majaribu. 38pp. 30k CEDI 1974 ZR SWA

Okola, L., ed.
Drum beat. 149pp. K.shs7.00 ($2.60) EAPH 1967 KE

Okon, E.E.
School certificate geography for West Africa: general geography. 1, 2bks 160pp. maps ill. photos. N2.20 Macmillan 1971 NR

Okon, F.
A handbook for needlework teachers. 48pp. ill. 50k Macmillan 1966 NR

Okonji, M.O.
The development of logical thinking in pre-school Zambian children: classification. 16pp. free (Human Development Research Unit Report, 23) Dept Psychology - Zam 1972 ZA

Okonkwo, M.N.
A complete course in Igbo grammar. 198pp. N2.30 Macmillan 1974 NR

Okoro, A.
Dr. Amadi's postings. 171pp. N1.00 Ethiope 1975 NR

Okoro, A.
Febechi down the Niger. 116pp. ill. N1.45 Nwamife 1975 NR

Okoro, A.
Febechi in cave adventure. 94pp. ill. N1.50 Nwamife 1971 NR

Okoro, A.
New broom at Amanzu. 96pp. ill. 53k (African Reader's Library, 14) Pilgrim 1967 NR

Okoro, A.
One week one trouble. 112pp. 53k (African Reader's Library, 21) Pilgrim 1973 NR

Okoro, A.
The village school. 124pp. ill. 53k (African Reader's Library, 13) Pilgrim 1966 NR

Okoro, E.N.
Beginning social studies in Nigeria. bk. 4 See: Iloeje, N.P.

Okoro, E.N.
A primary history for Nigeria. 1, 3 bks ill. N1.20 Macmillan NR

Okoro, E.N.
A primary history for Nigeria. 2, 3 bks ill. N1.20 Macmillan NR

Okoro, E.N.
A primary history for Nigeria. 3, 3 bks ill. N1.20 Macmillan NR

Okoth-Ogendo, H.W.O.
The adjudication process and the special rural development programme. 15pp. K.shs.3.00 (Inst. Development Studies, Discussions paps., 227) Inst Dev Stud 1975 KE

Okotonkwo-Eze, E. et al.
The verdict and other stories. photos. 20k Daystar 1965 NR

Okoye, M.
Politics and problems of the first Republic of Nigeria. 30pp. N2.00 ($3.50/£1.75) Univ Ife Press 1975 NR

Okoye, M.
Sketches in the sun. 140pp. N1.60 Nwamife 1975 NR

Okoye, T.O.
Map reading exercises for secondary schools. See: Willmer, J.

Okparocha, T.
Mbari. Art as sacrifice. 66pp. ill. N1.25 Daystar 1976 NR

Okui, E.
Akonye-Auni. [A tale of three eyes] 2nd ed. 23pp. ill. K.shs.1.50 ($1.25/50p) EALB 1966 KE LUO

Okumu, J.
Development administration: the Kenyan experience. See: Hyden, G.

Okunnuga, C.B.A.
Larcombe's primary mathematics. Teacher's lower standards book. (Decimal ed.) See: Larcombe, H.J.

Okunnuga, C.B.A.
Larcombe's primary mathematics. Teacher's preparatory book. (Decimal ed.) bk. 1 See: Larcombe, H.J.

Okunnuga, C.B.A.
Larcombe's primary mathematics. Teacher's preparatory book. (Decimal ed.) bk. 2 See: Larcombe, H.J.

Okunrotifa, P.O.
Evaluation in geography. 138pp. ill. N2.50 OUP - Nig 1977 NR

Okwoli, P.E. Etubi, S.U. Odoma, M.S.A.
Otakada ukoche alu Igala. [Primary Igala course.] pupils bk. 1. 48pp. ill. 75k. Macmillan 1976 NR IGA

Okwoli, P.E. Etubi, S.U. Odoma, M.S.A.
Otakada ukoche alu Igala. [Primary Igala course.] pupils bk. 2. ill. 90k. Macmillan 1976 NR IGA

Okyne, E.S.
A guided English composition. 96pp. C1.00 Advance 1970 GH

Ola, C.S.
Book-keeping for the layman. 49pp. ill. 70k Onibonoje 1974 NR

Ola, C.S.
A guide to accountancy and taxation law for business and government. 175pp. hd. N10.50 OUP - Nig 1977 NR

Ola, C.S.
Income tax and practice in Nigeria. 309pp. cl. N13.00 cl. (£6.00 cl.) (Heinemann Studies in Nigerian Law, 1) Heinemann Educ - Nig 1974 NR

Ola, K.
A geography course for secondary schools: geography for us. 1, 5bks See: Ojo, A.

Ola, K.
A geography course for secondary schools: our homeland. 2, 5bks See: Ojo, A.

Olabimitan, A.
Ewi orisirisi. [An anthology of poems.] 62pp. N1.00 Longman - Nig 1974 NR YOR

Olabimtan, A.
Aadota arofo pelu alaye ati ibeere. [Fifty poems with questions and answers] 80pp. N1.10 Macmillan 1969 NR YOR

Olabimtan, A.
Ayanmo. [Destiny] 128pp. ill. N1.30 Macmillan 1973 NR YOR

Olabimtan, A.
Ewi orisirisi. [Collection of poems] N1.00 Longman - Nig 1973 NR YOR

Olabimtan, A.
Kékeré ekùn. [The cub] 164pp. ill. N1.25 Macmillan 1967 NR YOR

Olabimtan, A.
Olaore afotejoye. [Olaore: the usurping king] 64pp. 90k Macmillan 1970 NR YOR

Oladapo, E.O.
Physical and health education: questions and answers. N151pp. N1.55 Onibonoje 1966 NR

Oladapo, I. O.
The limit state of cracking and deflexion in prestressed concrete design. 98pp. ill. 26k Univ Lagos Bookshop 1971 NR

Oladapo, I.O.
Concrete and structures. 17pp. 25k (13p) Univ Lagos Bkshop NR

Oladapo, I.O.
Survey of facilities in engineering, architecture and the physical sciences in universities in middle Africa. 356pp. ($15.00) AAU 1976 GH

Oladapo, O.
  Arofo awon omode, apa keji. [Yoruba poems for primary school, pt. 2.] 72pp. 75k OUP - Nig 1975 NR YOR

Oladiji, A.
  Akomolede Yoruba. bk. 1. See: Aromolaran, A.

Oladiji, A.
  Akomolede Yoruba. bk. 4 See: Aromolaran, A.

Oladiji, A.
  Akomolede Yoruba: Iwe atona fun oluko. Bks 1-3 See: Aromolaran, A.

Oladiji, A.
  Akomolede Yoruba: Iwe ise-sise ekerin. See: Aromolaran, A.

Oladiji, A.
  Akomolede Yoruba: Iwe ise-sise eketa. See: Aromolaran, A.

Oladiji, A.
  Akomolede Yoruba: Iwe ise-sise ekinni. See: Aromolaran, A.

Oladiji, A.
  Akomolede Yoruba: Iwe kika ekarun. See: Aromolaran, A.

Oladiji, A.
  Akomolede Yoruba: Iwe kika ekefa. See: Aromolaran, A.

Oladiji, A.
  Akomolede Yoruba: Iwe kika ekeji. See: Aromolaran, A.

Oladiji, A.
  Akomolede Yoruba: Iwe kika eketa. See: Aromolaran, A.

Oladiji, A.
  Akómólédè Yorùbá: Ìwé sísé ise èkejì. See: Aromolaran, A.

Oladipo, E.
  Why did Christ come? 32pp. ill. 40pes. (12p.) Africa Christian 1973 GH

Oladipo, O.
  Questions and answers on chemistry. Rev ed. 131pp. N2.00 Ilesanmi 1972 NR

Olafioye, A.O., comp.
  Social life and customs in Nigeria: a selective bibliography. 25pp. 50k (N1.00) (National Library pubs, 12) Nat Lib-Nig 1969 NR

Olagbaiye, A.
  Ile-Ife: guide maps. See: Adejuyigbe, O.

Olagundoye, A.F.
  Questions and answers on physical geography. 131pp. ill. N1.75 Ilesanmi 1975 NR

Olagundoye, M.O.
  My life - so far. 23pp. 10k Daystar 1967 NR

Olagunju, T., ed.
  Nigeria in search of a viable polity. See: Tukur, M., ed.

Olajubu, O.
  Akojopo iwi egungun. [Collection of 'masquerade' songs] N1.50 Longman - Nig 1973 NR YOR

Olajubu, O.
  Akojopo iwi Egungun. [A collection of masqueraders' chants.] 142pp. N1.50 Longman - Nig 1973 NR YOR

Olambo, L. D.
  Experiments with the Freire method of teaching literacy. See: Gulleth, M.

Olaniyan, B.
  Economic history of West Africa. 266pp. maps. N1.50 Educ Res Inst 1971 NR

Olaniyan, B.
  Groundwork of government for West African students ('A' level) See: Taiwo, B.

Olaniyan, B.
  Model questions and answers on school certificate government of West Africa 'O' level. 138pp. N1.50 pap. Publ Int 1975 NR

Olaniyan, B.
  School certificate government for West African students ('O' level) 272pp. N2.50 pap. Publ Int 1975 NR

Olaniyan, C.I.O.
  An introduction to West African animal ecology. 167pp. ill. N1.53 Heinemann Educ - Nig 1968 NR

Olanlokun, S.O.
  West African school certificate history: questions and answers. 152pp. N1.75 Ilesanmi 1972 NR

Olaoba, B.A.
  New school certificate English. 170pp. N1.35 Onibonoje 1968 NR

Olaoye, A.
  Old testament. 152pp. N1.75 Ilesanmi 1976 NR

Olatunbosun, D.
  Nigeria's neglected rural majority. hd. N6.00 OUP - Nig 1975 NR

Olatunbosun, P.O.
  Essentials of B/K: monarchy to fall. 96pp. ill. 90k. Onibonoje 1977 NR

Olayemi, V., comp.
  Orin Ibeji. [Songs in praise of twins] 68pp. 75k (Inst. of African Stud., Univ. of Ibadan, occas. pub., 26) Inst Afr Stud-Ibadan 1971 NR YOR

Olayide, S.
  Intermediate economics analysis. See: Essang, S.

Olayide, S.O., ed.
  Economic survey of Nigeria (1960-1975) 203pp. N5.00 Aromolaran 1976 NR

Olayide, S.O.
  The food problem: tractable or the mere chase of the mirage? 22pp. N1.00 (Inaugural lecture) Ibadan UP 1975 NR

Olayomi, A.
  Itumo oruko ati öriki Yoruba. [Origin of Yoruba names] 54pp. 45k Pilgrim 1968 NR YOR

Olembo, R.J., ed.
  Human adaptation in tropical Africa. 153pp. K.shs.15.00 ($4.00) EAPH 1968 KE

Oliff, W.D.
  South African marine pollution survey report 1974-1975. See: Cloete, C.E.

Oliphant, M.L.
  Science and mankind. 77pp. 95pes. ($.95) Ghana Publ Corp 1970 GH

Oliver, E.G.H.
  Ericas in Southern Africa. See: Baker, H.A.

Oliver, J.
  A guide to writing scientific papers. 24pp. 50c (Dept. of Agriculture, Univ. of Rhodesia, 2) Univ Rhodesia Lib 1968 RH

Oliver, J.
  Introduction to dairying in Rhodesia. 152pp. R$1.00 (Dept. of Agriculture, Univ. of Rhodesia, 3) Univ Rhodesia Lib 1971 RH

Olivier de Sardan, J.P.
  Les voleurs d'hommes. Notes sur l'histoire des Kurtey. 68pp. maps. CFA1000 (F20.00) (Etudes Nigeriennes, 25) Inst Rech Sci Hum 1969 NG FRE

Olivier, F.G.
  General methods of modern education. See: Allsopp, A.H.

Olivier, H.
  Damit. 192pp. ill. pl. cl. R9.90 Macmillan - SA 1975 SA

Olivier, H.
  The large dams of Southern Africa. ill. cl. R12.50 Purnell 1977 SA

Olivier, P.
  Atout coeur. 96pp. photos. D600 Maison Tunis 1972 TI FRE

Olivier, P.
  Gadour et les étoiles. 14pp. D0.350 Maison Tunis 1975 TI FRE

Olivier, P.
Tunisie ma vie. 116pp. D0.800 Maison Tunis 1968 TI FRE

Olivier, P.J.J.
The law of persons and family law. tr. fr. Afrikaans C. Nathan. R16.25 Butterworths 1976 SA

Olivier, R.
Legislation ivoirienne. Index chronologique 1958-1972. 181pp. CFA2000 (F40.00) Univ Abidjan 1974 IV FRE

Olivier, S.P.
Many treks make Rhodesia. (Reprint of ed. 1957) 174pp. photos. hd. R$8.40 (Rhodesiana Reprint Library, Silver Series, 6) Books of Rhodesia 1975 RH

Ollivier, M.
The war in Angola. See: Andrade, M. de.

Olojugba, K.
Economics questions and answers. rev. ed. 175pp. ill. N2.00 Ilesanmi 1973 NR

Olojuigba, K.
Revision questions and answers on economics. 159pp. N2.00 Ilesanmi 1972 NR

Olomu, M.
The antelope that hurried. See: Ukoli, N.M.

Olori, P.S.
Ekwoh Olu Oghah nka mbuh. [Oghah readers, 1] 63pp. ill. 30k (Inst. of African Stud., Univ. of Ibadan, Rivers readers project, 34) Inst Afr Stud-Ibadan 1972 NR OGH

Olorunmodimu, J.A.
Nigerian decided criminal cases: in a nutshell. 175pp. N4.50 Aowa 1973 NR

Oloruntimehin, B.O.
History and society. 20pp. 45k (£0.35/$0.80 pap.) (Inaugural lec., 18) Univ Ife Press 1976 NR

Olowoyo, S.O.
Objective tests in school certificate chemistry (with solutions) See: Sheikh, M.A.

Oloya, J.J.
Coffee, cotton, sisan and tea in the East African economy. 87pp. ill. K.shs7.10 ($2.25/90p.) EALB 1969 KE

Oloya, J.J.
The food supply of Kampala. See: Poleman, T.T.

Oloya, J.J.
Some aspects of economic development. 151pp. ill. K.shs.12.25 ($3.25/£1.30) EALB 1968 KE

Oloye, B.
Tani mola. [Who knows the future] 70pp. ill. 55k Ilesanmi 1971 NR YOR

Oloyede, J.A.
History made easy (Western State) 1, 2 bks See: Ilesanmi, G.E.

Oloyede, J.A.
History made easy (Western State) 2, 2 bks. See: Ilesanmi, G.E.

Olsen, H.
Héros africains. 80pp. pl. CFA200 CPE 1976 IV FRE

Olsen, H.S.
Jifunze kiyunani. [Teach yourself New Testament Greek.] 173pp. T.shs.15.00 Central Tanganyika 1972 TZ SWA

Olson, J.
Histoire de l'église. Vingt siècles et six continents. 232pp. ill. CFA540 pap. CLE 1972 CM FRE

Oludhe-Macgoye, M.
Growing up at Lina School. 77pp. ill. K.shs5.25 ($2.00) EAPH 1971 KE

Olufosoye, T.O.
Egbogi fun ibanuje. [Antedote for unhappiness] 2 2nded. 28pp. 15k Daystar 1969 NR YOR

Oluguna, D.
Introducing geography for class five. 1, 2 bks 96pp. ill. pl. 68k Longman - Nig 1971 NR

Oluguna, D.
Introducing geography for class six. 2, 2 bks 96pp. ill. pl. 90k Longman - Nig 1971 NR

Olukanpo, O.A.
Indigenous enterprise in distributive trades in Nigeria. 104pp. 75k NISER NR

Olukosi, J.O.
Kwara State Farm Institute programme. 50k (Samaru misc. pap., 57) Inst Agric Res - Zaria 1976 NR

Olung. Kisasi. Lubanzim.
La fille désobéissante. Mythes mbun. Versions intégrales en trois parlers mbun avec traduction française. 251pp. map. (DM32.00 pap.) (CEEBA. série II, Mémoires et Monographies, 17) CEEBA 1976 ZR FRE

Olurin, E.O.
The fire of life: the thyroid gland. 29pp. ill. pls. map. N1.00 (Inaugural lecture) Ibadan UP 1975 NR

Olurin, E.O.
Surgical note-taking: a guide for beginners in clinical surgery. 93pp. N1.50 Ibadan UP 1971 NR

Olusanya, G.O.
The evolution of the Nigerian civil service 1861 - 1960: the problems of Nigerianization. 102pp. 50k (Humanities Monograph series, 2) Univ Lagos Bkshop; distr. 1975 NR

Olusanya, G.O.
A history of the West African students' union, 1925-58. 116pp. ill. N3.00 Cross Continent 1977 NR

Olusanya, G.O.
The Second World War and politics in Nigeria, 1939-1953. 181pp. pap. & cl. N5.00 cl. N2.50 pap. Univ Lagos Press 1973 NR

Olusanya, P.O.
Acceptability of modern family planning methods among the Yorubas: some cultural barriers. 13pp. 10k NISER 1968 NR

Olusanya, P.O.
Comments on some social psychological aspects of fertility among married women in an African city. 9pp. 10k NISER 1969 NR

Olusanya, P.O.
A note on estimates of mortiality from the reproductive histories of women in two Nigerian communities. 12pp. 10k NISER NR

Olusanya, P.O.
Polygamy and fertility: a contribution from Yoruba society. 13pp. 10k NISER 1968 NR

Olusanya, P.O.
Social change and marital stability among the Yoruba society. 20pp. 10k NISER 1968 NR

Olusanya, P.O.
Socio-economic aspects of rural-urban migration in Western Nigeria. 164pp. pl. N1.50 ($2.50) (N.I.S.E.R. research report, 5) NISER 1969 NR

Olusanya, P.O.
A study in the beginnings of demographic modernization: status differentials in the fertility attitudes of married women in two communities in Western Nigeria. 19pp. 19k NISER 1968 NR

Olusola, J.A.
A wi bee a se bee: Awon ileri solorun fun ojojumo. [Words and actions: God's promises from day-to-day] 35pp. 10k Daystar 1967 NR YOR

Oluwasanmi, E. Zell, H.M. McLean, E.
Publishing in Africa in the seventies. Proceedings of an international conference, held at the University of Ife, Ile-Ife, Nigeria, 16-20 December, 1973. 412pp. cl. & pap. N5.50 pap. N8.50 cl. (£7.00/$16.50 cl.) (£4.50/$10.50 pap.) Univ Ife Press 1974 NR

Oluyeba, F.
Geographical essays on Africa. See: Oni, O.

Oluyeba, N.F.
Geography questions and answers. See: Oni, O.

Oluyede, P.A.
    Administrative law in East Africa. 255pp. cl. & pap.
    K.shs.42.00 pap.   K.shs.65.00 cl.   ($8.25/£3.30 pap.)
    ($12.50/£6.00 cl.) EALB 1974 KE

Oluyede, P.A.
    Nigerian law of conveyancing. cl. & pap.   N11.00 cl.
    N9.00 pap. Ibadan UP 1977 NR

Oluyi, E.O.
    Geography objective tests. See: Omole, S.E.

Oluyi, E.O.
    Nigerian and West African geography: questions and
    answers. See: Omole, S.A.

Olympio, A.   McHardy, C.
    Akosua in Brazil. 48pp. ill.   30pes. ($.30) Ghana
    Publ Corp 1970 GH

Omanga, C.
    The girl who couldn't keep a secret. 34pp. ill.
    K.shs1.75 ($1.00) EAPH 1969 KE

Omar, S.
    Hadithi ya Hazina Binti Sultani. [The story of Hazina Binti
    Sultani] 52pp. ill.   K.shs.2.00 OUP-Nairobi 1965 KE
    SWA

Omar, S.
    Kisa cha Hasan-li-Basir. [The story of Hasan-li-Basir]
    52pp. ill.   K.shs.3.75 OUP-Nairobi 1964 KE SWA

Omari, C.K.
    Hadithi za Bibi. [Bible stories] 3rd ed. 1 52pp. ill.
    Nat Print Co 1972 TZ SWA

Omari, C.K.
    Kuanguliwa kwa kifaranga. [Novel.] 96pp.
    K.shs.10.00 Heinemann Educ - Nair 1976 KE SWA

Omari, C.K.
    Mimi ni nani. [Who am I.] 48pp.   T.shs.4.50
    Longman - Tanz 1975 TZ SWA

Omari, C.K.
    Mwenda kwao. [Returning home] 157pp.   T.shs.8.50
    Inst Swahili Res 1971 TZ SWA

Omari, C.K.
    Strategy for rural development. The Tanzania experience.
    168pp.   K.shs.27.75 ($5.85/£2.85) EALB 1976 KE

Omari, C.K.
    Usawa wa binadamu. [Poetry.] 48pp.   K.shs.7.50
    ($2.20/90p.) EALB 1976 KE SWA

Omari, I.M.   Kaniki, H.
    Guidelines for writers. 64pp.   T.shs.9.50 ($4.00)
    Tanz Publ House 1976 TZ

Omatete, A.   Mumbala, N.
    Les reflexes du Proto Bantu en Tetela. 37pp. CELTA
    1975 ZR FRE

Omatetete.   Mumbala.
    Les réflexes du proto-bantou en tetela. Approche
    générative. 37pp.   30k CELTA 1975 ZR FRE

Ombu, J.A.
    Niger Delta studies, 1627-1967: a bibliography. 138pp.
    N2.50 Ibadan UP 1970 NR

Ombudo, O.
    Harambee, its origin and use. 2nd ed. 67pp. pl.
    K.shs.8.00 Africa Book Serv 1975 KE

Omer-Cooper, J.D.
    Owu in Yoruba history. See: Mabogunje, A.L.

Ominde, M.
    African cookery book. 160pp. ill.   K.shs.22.50
    (£1.80) Heinemann Educ - Nair 1975 KE

Ominde, S.
    Population in Kenya, Tanzania, Uganda. 144pp.
    K.shs.25.00 (£1.80) Heinemann Educ - Nair 1975 KE

Ominde, S.H.
    The Luo girl: from infancy to marriage. 3rd ed.
    K.shs.5.80 ($2.10/70p.) EALB 1952 KE

Omiyale, O.
    Notes on "Twelth Night.". 55pp.   N1.00 Ilesanmi 1976
    NR

Omiyale, T.A.
    Key (answer book) to Path to common examination I & II.
    See: Adedun, J.

Omiyale, T.A.
    Path to common entrance examination. 1, 2 pts
    See: Adedun, J.A.

Omiyale, T.A.
    Path to common entrance examination. 2, 2pts.
    See: Adedun, J.A.

Omodara.   Dare.
    Ilesanmi health course. 1, 6 bks. 34pp.   85k.
    Ilesanmi 1976 NR

Omodara.   Dare.
    Ilesanmi health course. 2, 6 bks. 41pp.   95k.
    Ilesanmi 1976 NR

Omodara.   Dare.
    Ilesanmi health course. 3, 6 bks. 41pp.   N1.10
    Ilesanmi 1976 NR

Omodara.   Dare.
    Ilesanmi health course. 4, 6 bks. 49pp.   N1.20
    Ilesanmi 1976 NR

Omodara.   Dare.
    Ilesanmi health course. 5, 6 bks. 53pp.   N1.30
    Ilesanmi 1976 NR

Omodara.   Dare.
    Ilesanmi health course. 6, 6 bks. 60pp.   N1.35
    Ilesanmi 1976 NR

Omode, A. et al.
    Organic chemistry. 73pp. ill.   80k Onibonoje 1967
    NR

Omokolo, H.
    Essai de catalogue des noms camerounais. 9pp.
    CFA200 Univ Cameroun 1976 CM FRE

Omole, S.A.   Oluyi, E.O.
    Nigerian and West African geography: questions and
    answers. 81pp. maps.   N1.05 Onibonoje 1967 NR

Omole, S.E.   Oluyi, E.O.
    Geography objective tests. 92pp. maps ill.   90k
    Onibonoje 1966 KE

Omolewa, M.A.
    Essays in European history: the French revolution,
    1774-1799. 155pp.   N1.20 Onibonoje 1968 NR

Omolewa Okoye.
    Geography [course]. bk. 1. 64pp.   85k Ilesanmi
    1972 NR

Omolewa Okoye.
    Geography [course]. bk. 2. 115pp.   N1.00 Ilesanmi
    1972 NR

Omolewa Okoye.
    Geography [course]. bk. 3. 102pp.   N1.25 Ilesanmi
    1972 NR

Omololu, A.
    Food, famine and health. 15pp.   N1.00 (Inaugural
    lecture) Ibadan UP 1974 NG

Omopariola, J.A.
    Modern English for Nigerian schools. 1, 3bks
    See: Ilesanmi, G.E.

Omopariola, J.A.
    Modern English for Nigerian schools. 2, 3bks
    See: Ilesanmi, G.E.

Omopariola, J.A.
    Modern English for Nigerian schools. 3, 3bks
    See: Ilesanmi, G.E.

Omotoso, K.
    The curse. A play. 32pp.   75k New Horn 1976 NR

Omotoso, K.
    Fella's choice. 111pp.   80k Ethiope 1974 NR

Omotoso, K.
    Miracles and other stories. 95pp.   85k (African
    Literature series, 2) Onibonoje 1973 NR

Omotoso, K.
    Sacrifice. 103pp.   N1.20 (African Literature Series, 6)
    Onibonoje 1974 NR

Author Index

Omotoso, K.
The scales. 104pp. N1.00 (African Literature Series, 11) Onibonoje 1976 NR

Omotoso, K.
"West African Narrative": notes. 52pp. 70k Onibonoje 1968 NR

Omotoso, M.
Housing in Ibadan. See: Modupe, O.

Omoyajowo, A.
Witches? 44pp. 20k Daystar 1965 NR

Omoyajowo, J.A.
Iwe adura ojojumo. [The daily prayer book] 35pp. 20k Daystar 1966 NR YOR

Onadipe, K.
The adventures of Souza. 80pp. ill. 53k (African Reader's Library, 5) Pilgrim 1963 NR

Onadipe, K.
The boy slave. 128pp. ill. 53k (African Reader's Library, 12) Pilgrim 1966 NR

Onadipe, K.
The forest is our playground. See: Murphy, M.

Onadipe, K.
Koku Baboni. 80pp. ill. 45k (African Junior Library, 3) Pilgrim 1965 NR

Onadipe, K.
Magic land of the shadows. 64pp. ill. 45k (African Junior Library, 6) Pilgrim 1971 NR

Onadipe, K.
The return of Shettima. 94pp. ill. 53k (African Reader's Library, 22) Pilgrim 1973 NR

Onadipe, K.
Sugar girl. 80pp. ill. 45k (African Junior Library, 1) Pilgrim 1964 NR

Onambele, R.
Le Cameroun en 1914: bilan de la colonisation allemande. 120pp. photos. maps. Univ Cameroun 1973 CM FRE

Onambele, R., ed.
La chefferie traditionnelle. 100pp. Univ Cameroun 1973 CM FRE

Onambele, R., ed.
Textes d'histoire du Cameroun. 200pp. maps photos. CFA500 Univ Cameroun 1973 CM FRE

Onambele, R.
Mrg. Vogt: circulaire à ses missionnaires. 250pp. Univ Cameroun 1973 CM FRE

Onambele, R.
La vie quotidienne dans une mission entre les deux guerres. 80pp. maps photos. Univ Cameroun 1973 CM FRE

Oni, A.
Notes, questions/answers on "Macbeth". 108pp. N1.60 Aromolaran 1975[?] NR

Oni, O. Onimode, B.
Economic development of Nigeria: the socialist alternative. 262pp. N4.00 Nig Acad Arts Sci 1975 NR

Oni, O. Oluyeba, F.
Geographical essays on Africa. 214pp. ill. N2.00 Ilesanmi 1974 NR

Oni, O. Oluyeba, N.F.
Geography questions and answers. 190pp. maps. N1.40 Ilesanmi 1971 NR

Oni, S.O.
Awon itan imulokanle. [Stories on endurance] 32pp. 10k Daystar 1968 NR YOR

Oni, T.A.
Notes, questions/answers on "Tobias and the angel". 56pp. N1.20 Aromolaran 1975(?) NR

Oni, T.A.
Tobias and the Angel. 47pp. 80k Ilesanmi 1971 NR

Onibokun, E.A.
Comprehension exercises for Nigerian schools. See: Adedun, J.A.

Onibon-Okuta, A.
Ilepa dudu Aiye. [Black laterites of the earth] 32pp. 20k Univ Ife Bkshop 1965 NR YOR

Onibonoje, B.
"Houseboy": notes, Q/A. 68pp. N1.00 (Examination Aid Series) Onibonoje 1976 NR

Onibonoje, B.
Notes, Q/A on "The Lion and the Jewel". 141pp. N1.10 Onibonoje 1974 NR

Onibonoje, B.
'O' level business methods. 237pp. ill. N2.50 Onibonoje 1975 NR

Onibonoje, B.
Objective tests in 'O' level business methods. 165pp. ill. N2.00 Onibonoje 1976 NR

Onibonoje, B.
Onibonoje primary social studies; bk. IV: Living in our State. 122pp. ill. N1.50 Onibonoje 1976 NR

Onibonoje, B.
Onibonoje primary social studies; bk. V: Nigeria: unity in diversity. Problems of nation building. 135pp. ill. N1.75 Onibonoje 1976 NR

Onibonoje, B.
Onibonoje primary social studies; bk. VI: Nigeria and the world community. 152pp. ill. N2.00 Onibonoje 1977 NR

Onibonoje, B.
Onibonoje primary social studies: growing up at home and at school. 2nd ed. bk. 1. 57pp. ill. 85k. Onibonoje NR

Onibonoje, B.
Onibonoje primary social studies: living in urban and non-urban community. bk. 2. 119pp. ill. N1.05 Onibonoje 1976 NR

Onibonoje, B.
Onibonoje primary social studies: our immediate neighbours. bk. 3. 60pp. ill. N1.10 Onibonoje 1976 NR

Onibonoje, B.
"The Rhythm of Violence": notes, Q/A. 79pp. N1.10 (Examination Aid Series) Onibonoje 1976 NR

Onibonoje, E.A.
Onibonoje primary social studies. bk. 1 36pp. ill. 85k Onibonoje 1974 NR

Onibonoje, G.O.
Africa in the ancient world. 1, 3 bks. 167pp. ill. maps. N1.10 Onibonoje 1965 NR

Onibonoje, G.O.
Africa in the modern world. 3, 3 bks. 148pp. N1.10 Onibonoje 1966 NR

Onibonoje, G.O.
Africa: rise of Islam to the end of the slave trade. 2, 3 bks. 150pp. N1.10 Onibonoje 1965 NR

Onibonoje, G.O.
Civics for Nigerians. 229pp. photos. N1.30 Onibonoje 1968 NR

Onibonoje, G.O., et al.
The indigenous for national development. 172pp. N2.10 Onibonoje 1976 NR

Onibonoje, G.O.
Nigerians in their environment. 1, 3 bks. 162pp. maps. N1.10 Onibonoje 1964 NR

Onibonoje, J.O.
"Anthology of longer poems": questions and answers. 66pp. 85k Onibonoje 1969 NR

Onibonoje, J.O.
"A Christmas Carol": notes, questions and answers. 84pp. 85k Onibonoje 1972 NR

Onibonoje, J.O., ed.
"A Tale of Two Cities": notes. 154pp. 95k Onibonoje 1975 NR

Onibonoje, J.O.
Lectures on "Julius Caesar". 180pp. N1.20
Onibonoje 1967 NR

Onibonoje, J.O.
Lectures on "Richard II". 176pp. N1.25 Onibonoje
1970 NR

Onibonoje, J.O.
"Macbeth": notes, Q/A. 182pp. N1.25 (Examination
Aid Series) Onibonoje 1976 NR

Onibonoje, J.O.
"Merchant of Venice": notes, Q/A. 141pp. N1.10
(Examination Aid Series) Onibonoje 1976 NR

Onibonoje, J.O.
"A Pageant of Longer Poems": notes. 144pp. N1.35
Onibonoje 1969 NR

Onibonoje, J.O.
"Pageant": questions and answers. 80pp. 85k
Onibonoje 1970 NR

Onibonoje, J.O.
"Richard II": questions and answers. 104pp. N1.10
Onibonoje 1970 NR

Onibonoje, J.O.
"Taming of the Shrew": lectures. 138pp. N1.25
Onibonoje 1972 NR

Onibonoje, J.O.
"Tobias and the Angel": notes. 88pp. 85k Onibonoje
1970 NR

Onibonoje, J.O.
"Twentieth Century Narrative Poems": notes. 171pp.
85k Onibonoje 1969 NR

Onimode, B.
Economic development of Nigeria: the socialist alternative.
See: Oni, O.

Onitiri, H.M.A., ed. Ayida, A.A., ed.
Reconstruction and development in Nigeria. N7.00
($10.50) NISER 1971 NR

Onitiri, H.M.A.
The possibilities of price control in Nigeria. 69pp. 75
NISER 1966 NR

Onwuamaegbu, M.O. Green, M.M.
Igbo folk stories. 16pp. 23k OUP - Nig 1962 NR

Onwubiko, K.B.C.
School certificate history of West Africa AD 1000-1800.
1, 2 bks. 234pp. N2.85 Africana Educ 1972 NR

Onwubiko, K.B.C.
School certificate history of West Africa, AD 1800 to
present day. 2nd rev. ed. 2, 2 bks. 500pp. pl. maps.
N4.60 Africana Educ 1976 NR

Onwudiegwu, J.K.
How to write good letters, business letters and
applications. 64pp. 25k Gebo 1965 NR

Onwudiofu, S.N.
Common entrance examinations. (main book) 132pp.
N2.00 Paico 1967 NR

Onwudiofu, S.N.
School certificate examinations as they are set: Religious
knowledge. 86pp. N1.50 Paico 1975 NR

Onwuka, S.C.O.
I was a juju priest. 20pp. 10k Daystar 1967 NR

Onwuka, W., ed.
Selected speeches of Odumegwu Ojukwu, General Gowon
and Asika. 54pp. 50k Survival 1972 NR

Onwuteaka, J.O.
Gaa n'ime uwa nile. 71pp. 75k. Univ Publ 1977 NR
IGB

Onyango-Abuje, J.C.
Fire and vengeance. 132pp. K.shs.10.00 ($3.20)
EAPH 1975 KE

Onyango-ku-Odongo, J.M. Webster, J.B.
The central Lwo during Achonya. 413pp. K.shs.55.20
($10.75/£5.20) EALB 1976 KE

Onyango-Ogutu, B. P. Roscoe, A. A.
Keep my words: Luo oral literature. 160pp.
K.shs.15.00 (Traditional African Library) EAPH 1974 KE

Onyekwere, A. Creaser, H.
Beginning science in Eastern Nigeria. 2, 2 bks 91pp.
col. ill. 92k Longman - Nig 1970 NR

Onyekwere, A.O. Creaser, H.
Beginning science in Eastern Nigeria. 1, 2 bks. 94pp.
ill. 92k Longman - Nig 1970 NR

Oolabimtan, A.
Oluwa lo mejo da. [God only can judge] rev. ed.
90k Macmillan 1966 NR YOR

Oosthuizen, D.C.S.
The ethics of illegal action, and other essays. 95pp.
R.2.00 ($2.95/£1.50) Ravan 1973 SA

Oosthuizen, D.C.S.
The representative theory of perception. R1.00
(Rhodes University, Dept. of Philosophy, Monograph
series, 1) Dept Philosophy - Rhodes 1973 SA

Oosthuizen, D.C.S.
The sceptical chemist and the unwise philosopher. ex.
only (Inaugural lec.) Rhodes Univ Lib 1960 SA

Oosthuizen, G.C.
Pentecostal penetration into the Indian community in
Metropolitan Durban, South Africa. 355pp. R9.00
(R18.00) (Human Sciences Research Council, Pretoria,
South Africa. Publication series, 52) Univ
Durban-Westville 1975 SA

Oosthuizen, J.H.C.
Report of the committee for differentiated education and
guidance with regard to a national pre-primary educational
programme for the Republic of South Africa and South
West Africa, pt. 2. 62pp. 75c. Human Science Res
Council 1971 SA

Oosthuizen, M.J.
New physical science for standard 7. See: Myburgh,
M.C.

Oosthuizen, M.J.
New physical science for standard 8. See: Myburgh,
M.C.

Oosthuizen, M.J. Schlemmer, L.
A study of community development needs and morale
among Africans in a non-farm rural employee community
in Natal. 171pp. R2.50 (Institute for Social Research,
Research Reports) Inst Soc Res - Natal 1974 SA

Oosthuizen, M.J.
A study of employee morale among Africans in a rural
non-farm employment situation. See: Schlemmer, L.

Opadotun, T.
Arofo Opadotun. [Poems with traditional, philosophical
and contemporary themes.] 136pp. N1.60 Longman
Nig 1976 NR YOR

Opadotun, T.
Eni solorun yan. [The anointed one] 41pp. 20k
Daystar 1972 NR YOR

Opadotun, T.
Ija orogun. [Fighting between co-wives] 35pp. 20k
Daystar 1969 NR YOR

Opare, A.
Abofra bi ne ckraman. [A child and the dog] 24pp. ill.
30pes. Waterville 1971 GH TWI

Opher, A.
The Bible and evolution. 40c. (Isma pap., 16) Inst
Study of Man 1964 SA

Opoku, A.A., ed.
Mo ahenewa. [Congratulations.] 2nd ed. 82pp. ill.
C1.00 Bur Ghana Lang 1976 GH TWI

Opoku, A.A.
Festivals of Ghana. 79pp. photos. C1.00 ($1.50)
Ghana Publ Corp 1971 GH

Opoku, A.A.
Mpanyinsem. [Stories from Ghanaian history] 86pp. ill.
65pes. Waterville 1969 GH TWI

Organisation for African Unity: Scientific, Technical and Research Commission.
Fourth symposium: hydrobiology and inland fisheries (Fort Lamy, 1961) $3.00 (Publication, 76) OAU 1962 ET

Organisation for African Unity: Scientific, Technical and Research Commission.
Geological bibliography: Karroo. 3 (Supplement 1) $3.00 (Publication, 48) OAU 1963 ET

Organisation for African Unity: Scientific, Technical and Research Commission.
Geological bibliography: The Jurassic and Cretaceous systems. 2 $3.00 (Publication, 48) OAU 1959 ET

Organisation for African Unity: Scientific, Technical and Research Commission.
Geological bibliography The Karroo system. 1 $3.00 (Publication, 48) OAU 1959 ET

Organisation for African Unity: Scientific, Technical and Research Commission.
Guinean trawling survey. 3 v. $35.00 (Publication, 99) OAU ET

Organisation for African Unity: Scientific, Technical and Research Commission.
Handbook for phytosanitary inspectors in Africa. $10.00 (Publication, 101) OAU 1970 ET

Organisation for African Unity: Scientific, Technical and Research Commission.
Handbook of harmful aquatic plants (Africa and Madagascar) (Joint project no.14) $3.00 (Publication, 73) OAU 1962 ET

Organisation for African Unity: Scientific, Technical and Research Commission.
The human factors of productivity in Africa: a preliminary survey by ILI. 2nd ed. $3.00 (Publication, 56) OAU 1960 ET

Organisation for African Unity: Scientific, Technical and Research Commission.
Inter-African conference on hydrology (Nairobi, 1961) $5.00 (Publication, 66) OAU 1962 ET

Organisation for African Unity: Scientific, Technical and Research Commission.
Joint meeting of the three regional committees for geology Leopoldville, 1958. $4.00 (Publication, 44) OAU 1960 ET

Organisation for African Unity: Scientific, Technical and Research Commission.
Mapping of vectors of disease. $3.00 (Publication, 29) OAU 1958 ET

Organisation for African Unity: Scientific, Technical and Research Commission.
Meeting of specialists on open forests in tropical Africa (N'Dola, 1959) $3.00 (Publication, 52) OAU 1960 ET

Organisation for African Unity: Scientific, Technical and Research Commission.
Meeting of specialists on the adaptation of education to African conditions (Lagos, 1960) $3.00 (Publication, 59) OAU 1962 ET

Organisation for African Unity: Scientific, Technical and Research Commission.
Meeting of specialists on the basic psychology of African and Madagascan populations (Tananarive, 1959) $3.00 (Publication, 51) OAU 1960 ET

Organisation for African Unity: Scientific, Technical and Research Commission.
Meeting of specialists on the treatment of water (Pretoria, 1960) $4.00 (Publication, 64) OAU 1961 ET

Organisation for African Unity: Scientific, Technical and Research Commission.
A memorandum for phytosanitary procedure in Africa. $4.00 (Publication, 82) OAU 1962 ET

Organisation for African Unity: Scientific, Technical and Research Commission.
Mental disorders and mental health in Africa south of the Sahara CCTA/CSA-WFMH/WHO. (Publication, 35) OAU 1960 ET

Organisation for African Unity: Scientific, Technical and Research Commission.
Methodology of family budget surveys (Joint project no. 9) $4.00 (Publication, 95) OAU 1965 ET

Organisation for African Unity: Scientific, Technical and Research Commission.
Migrant labour in Africa south of the Sahara (Abidjan, 1961) $4.00 (Publication, 79) OAU 1963 ET

Organisation for African Unity: Scientific, Technical and Research Commission.
Ninth meeting of ISCTR (Conakry, 1962) $5.00 (Publication, 88) OAU 1963 ET

Organisation for African Unity: Scientific, Technical and Research Commission.
OAU symposium on schistosomiasis (Addis Ababa, 1969) $10.00 OAU ET

Organisation for African Unity: Scientific, Technical and Research Commission.
OAU/STRC joint rinderpest campaign in Central and West Africa. $5.00 (Publication, 103) OAU 1971 ET

Organisation for African Unity: Scientific, Technical and Research Commission.
Pedological map of Africa (Joint project no. 11) $30.00 (Publication, 93) OAU 1965 ET

Organisation for African Unity: Scientific, Technical and Research Commission.
Physical hydrology (Bukavu, 1958) $2.00 (Publication, 33) OAU 1959 ET

Organisation for African Unity: Scientific, Technical and Research Commission.
Phytogeography (Yangambi, 1956) $2.00 (Publication, 53) OAU 1961 ET

Organisation for African Unity: Scientific, Technical and Research Commission.
Road research (Lourenco Marques, 1958) $2.00 (Publication, 34) OAU 1959 ET

Organisation for African Unity: Scientific, Technical and Research Commission.
Second inter-African conference on housing and urbanisation Nairobi, 1959. $4.00 (Publication, 47) OAU 1960 ET

Organisation for African Unity: Scientific, Technical and Research Commission.
Second inter-African forestry conference Pointe-Noire, 1958. $8.00 (Publication, 43) OAU 1962 ET

Organisation for African Unity: Scientific, Technical and Research Commission.
Second meeting of the inter-African rural welfare conference Tananarive, 1957. (Publication, 42) OAU 1959 ET

Organisation for African Unity: Scientific, Technical and Research Commission.
Seventh meeting of ISCTR Brussels, 1958. $4.00 (Publication, 41) OAU 1960 ET

Organisation for African Unity: Scientific, Technical and Research Commission.
Sixth inter-African labour conference (Abidjan, 1961) $4.00 (Publication, 68) OAU 1962 ET

Organisation for African Unity: Scientific, Technical and Research Commission.
Stored food products. $4.00 (Publication, 31) OAU 1958 ET

Organisation for African Unity: Scientific, Technical and Research Commission.
Symposium on child welfare Lagos, 1959. $3.00 (Publication, 46) OAU 1959 ET

Author Index

Osae, S.K.
The tears of a jealous wife. 47pp. 50pes. Advance 1968 GH

Osahon, N.
Black power. The African predicament. 94pp. N1.00 di Nigro 1976 NR

Osahon, N.
The climate of darkness. 2nd ed. 110pp. 50k Di Nigro 1971 NR

Osahon, N.
Fires of Africa: poems and essays. 88pp. 75k Di Nigro 1973 NR

Osahon, N.
Fringes of my mind. 112pp. 50k Di Nigro 1973 NR

Osahon, N.
God is a racist. 110pp. 50k Di Nigro 1973 NR

Osahon, N.
No answer from the oracle. 100pp. 50k Di Nigro 1974 NR

Osahon, N.
Poems for young lovers. 85pp. 35k Di Nigro 1974 NR

Osahon, N.
Sex is a nigger. 2nd ed. 188pp. 65k Di Nigro 1972 NR

Osahon, N.
Shadows. 94pp. N1.00 Di Nigro 1976 NR

Osahon, N.
We need a dream. 110pp. 50k Di Nigro 1973 NR

Osantwene. Ipasso.
Le père qui ne voulait pas de fille. Mythes nkundu et tere. Langues locales et versions françaises. 203pp. map. (DM27.00 pap.) (CEEBA. série II, Mémoires et Monographies, 18) CEEBA 1976 ZR FRE

Osayimwese, I.G.
Mathematics for business. See: Inanga, E.L.

Osborne, D. Osbourne, D.
Dear Mudlick. 45pes. (15p.) Africa Christian 1973 GH

Osborne, D.
Dear Mudlick, series 1. 32pp. 45pes. (20p.) Africa Christian 1976 GH

Osborne, D.
Dear Mudlick, series 2. 40pp. (30p.) Africa Christian 1977 GH

Osborne, D.G.
A rift across the equator. 15pp. ill. T.shs.1.00 (Inaugural lecture, 5) Univ Dar es Salaam 1969 TZ

Osbourne, D.
Dear Mudlick. See: Osborne, D.

Oscroft, E.B. Allison, A.A. Dent, A.G.
Izibalo zanamuhla. [Modern arithmetic] Ibanga, 1 158pp. ill. 70c. Shuter 1961 SA ZUL

Oscroft, E.B. Allison, A.A. Dent, A.G.
Izibalo zanamuhla. [Modern arithmetic] Ibanga, 2 183pp. ill. 75c. Shuter 1961 SA ZUL

Oscroft, E.B. Alisson, A.A. Dent, A.G.
Izibalo zanamuhla. [Modern arithmetic] Ibanga, 3 ill. 85c. Shuter 1961 SA ZUL

Oscroft, E.B. Allison, A.A. Dent, A.G.
Izibalo zanamuhla. [Modern arithmetic] Ibanga, 4 ill. 90c. Shuter 1961 SA ZUL

Oscroft, E.B. Allison, A.A. Dent, A.G.
Izibalo zanamuhla. [Modern arithmetic] Ibanga, 5 ill.pp. 95c. Shuter 1961 SA ZUL·

Oscroft, E.B. Allison, A.A. Dent, A.G.
Izibalo zanamuhla. [Modern arithmetic] Ibanga, 6 ill. R1.10 Shuter 1961 SA ZUL

Osemwegie, I.
Poems in Bini. 58pp. 30k Macmillan NR BIN

Oser, J.
Promoting economic development. 235pp. K.shs.15.00 ($4.20) EAPH 1967 KE

Osevbegie, I.
Ynunozedo, Ebe okaro. pupils bk. 1. See: Uwaifo.

Oshin, N.R.O., comp.
Education in West Africa: a bibliography. 55pp. 35k (Tedro Library occas. pubs, 1) Tedro 1969 NR

Oshin, N.R.O., tr. Odetoyinbo, H.A., comp.
Education in Nigeria: a bibliographical guide. 452pp. N2.50 Tedro 1972 NR

Osibodu, B.M.
Modern primary mathematics. pupil's bk. 2. See: Halim, E.C.

Osibodu, B.M.
Modern primary mathematics. pupils bk. 3. See: Halim, E.C.

Osibodu, B.M.
Modern primary mathematics. teacher's bk. 2. See: Halim, E.C.

Osiboye, S.
Notes, questions/answers on "A tale of two cities". 98pp. N1.30 Aromolaran 1975[?] NR

Osiboye, S.
Notes, questions/answers on "The lion and the jewel". 64pp. N1.20 Aromolaran 1975[?] NR

Osifo, D.E.
Economics of the rice industry of the Western State of Nigeria. 82pp. 75k NISER 1971 NR

Osin, T.A.
The dates of annual Muslim festivals. 20pp. 50k Daystar 1974 NR

Osinowo, O.
Notes, questions/answers on "Things fall apart". 80pp. N1.30 Armolaran 1970 NR

Osinsanya, E.O.
Nigerian traditional and cultural hairstyles. 16pp. pl. N1.50 Elizabethan 1977 NR

Osiyale, A.
Doing science for primary schools: book I. 32pp. photos. ill. 45k OUP-Nig 1972 NR

Osofisan, F.
The chattering and the song. A play. 75k. New Horn 1976 NR

Osofisan, F.
Kolera kolej. 113pp. 80k ($2.00) New Horn 1975 NR

Osofisan, F.
A restless run of locusts. 51pp. 85k (African Literature Series, 9) Onibonoje 1975 NR

Osogo, J.
Bi arusi aliyetaka zawadi maalum. 66pp. ill. K.shs.8.95 ($2.50/£1.00) EALB 1976 KE SWA

Osogo, J.
The bride who wanted a special present. 2nd ed. 63pp. ill. K.shs3.00 ($1.50/60p.) EALB 1966 KE

Osogo, J.
A history of the Baluyia. 172pp. K.shs14.75 OUP-Nairobi 1966 KE

Osogo, J.
Life in Kenya in the olden days: the Baluyia. 90pp. ill. K.shs9.25 OUP-Nairobi 1965 KE

Osogo, J.
Nabongo Mumia of the Baluyia. 3rd ed. 46pp. map. K.shs.3.65 ($1.50/60p.) EALB 1970 KE

Osogo, J.
Nations of Eastern Africa. bk. 1 115pp. maps photos. K.shs8.50 (Nations of Africa) Equatorial KE

Osogo, J. Moore, B.
Peoples of East Africa; a film strip with teachers' notes. ill. K.shs100.00 (£8.50) Heinemann Educ - Nair 1972 KE

Osogo, J.N.B.
Kenya history wallcharts, including descriptive notes. New ed. maps. K.shs.39.50 Longman - Ken 1974 KE

Osogo, J.N.B.
Kenya's peoples in the past. Pupil's book for standard three. New ed. 46pp. ill. pl. K.shs.5.30 Longman - Ken 1974 KE

Osogo, J.N.B.
Kenya's peoples in the past. Teachers' handbook for standards three and four. 165pp. ill. pl. K.shs.14.10 Longman - Ken 1974 KE

Osuagwu, B.I.N.
Ogogo Igbo 4. pupils bk. 4. See: Ahamba, S.M.

Osuagwu, B.I.N.
Ogogo Igbo. pupil's bk. 3. See: Ahamba, S.M.

Osuagwu, B.I.N.
Ogugu Igbo. pupil's bk. 5. See: Ahamba, S.M.

Osuku, E.D.
Nembe bibi titari go diri. [Nembe reader, 1] 63pp. ill. 30k (Inst. of African Stud., Univ. of Ibadan, Rivers readers project, 3) Inst Afr Stud-Ibadan 1970 NR NEM

Osunkalu, V.O.
Essentials of practical chemistry, 'O' level. 51pp. 60k pap. Publ Int 1973 NR

Oti, S.
The old masters. 95pp. N1.60 (Three Crowns Books) OUP - Nig 1977 NR

Otieno, G.
Kisa cha binti Mambo. [Advice on child-care.] K.shs.6.50 ($3.50) Foundation 1977 KE SWA

Otieno, L.
Our alphabet. (Ill. by Mara Onditi) 28pp. col. ill. K.shs.6.50 ($3.75) (Beginners Library, 1) Foundation 1973 KE

Otoo, S.K.
Ewudsifo whyiamu. [The conspiracy of the animal pests.] 2nd ed. 38pp. ill. 75pes. Bur Ghana Lang 1976 GH FAT

Otoo, S.K.
Prama. [Community living.] 2nd ed. 61pp. ill. 65pes. Bur Ghana Lang 1975 GH FAT

Ottenberg, S.
Anthropology and African aesthetics. 22pp. C1.00 ($1.00/50p.) (Inaugural lecture) Ghana UP 1971 GH

Otto, D.
Niger: a traveller's handbook. (English version) See: Otto, J.

Otto, D.
Niger: guide du voyageur. (Version francaise) See: Otto, J.

Otto, J. Otto, D.
Niger: a traveller's handbook. (English version) 122pp. ill. maps. CFA500.00 Church World 1973 NG

Otto, J. Otto, D.
Niger: guide du voyageur. (Version francaise) 132pp. ill. maps. CFA800.00 Church World 1973 NG FRE

Otuko, J.B.B.
Welo okelo yengo. 240pp. K.shs.26.95 ($5.70/£2.30) EALB 1976 KE SWA

Ouahes, R. Davellex, B.
Chimie générale. 480pp. ill. 68,00 DA SNED 1974 AE FRE

Oualalou, F.
Le tiers monde et la 3e phase de domination. 2nd ed. 224pp. Dir19.00 Ed Maghreb 1975 MR FRE

Ouko, J. et al.
Seven letters to all churches. 250pp. K.shs.16.50 ($2.10) Evangel 1973 KE

Ouko, J.J.
Bribery. It kills you and your nation. 48pp. K.shs.4.50 ($0.55 pap.) Evangel 1976 KE

Ouma, J.
Evolution of tourism in East Africa. ill. K.shs30.00 ($6.25/£3.00) EALB 1970 KE

Owen, J.
Directory of voluntary organisations in Mid-Western Nigeria. 62pp. 50k (75c) (N.I.S.E.R. research reports, 6) NISER 1967 NR

Owen, J.
Directory of voluntary organisations in Western Nigeria. 30k (50c) (N.I.S.E.R. research report, 6) NISER NR

Owen, W.
Lesson notes for Christian teaching. Standard 1. See: Bethel, M.

Owen, W.
Lesson notes for Christian teaching. Standard 2. See: Bethel, M.

Owen, W.
Lesson notes for Christian teaching: standard 3. See: Bethel, M.

Owen, W.
Lesson notes for Christian teaching. Standard 4. See: Bethel, M.

Owino, R.
Sugar Daddy's lover. 80pp. K.shs.8.00 (55p) (Spear Books, 3) Heinemann Educ - Nair 1975 KE

Owne, W.
Mafundisho ya Kikristo. K.shs.6.00 ($2.00/80p.) EALB 1962 E SWA

Owoeye, J.A.
History made easy (Western State) 1, 2 bks See: Ilesanmi, G.E.

Owoeye, J.A.
History made easy (Western State) 2, 2 bks. See: Ilesanmi, G.E.

Owolabi, E.O.
Economic history of West Africa. 334pp. photos. N3.00 Onibonoje 1972 NR

Owolabi, O.
Ori ade kii sun ta. [Novel.] 128pp. ill. N1.20 Macmillan 1974 NR YOR

Owudiofu, S.N.
Common entrance examinations. Solutions and answers. 50pp. 65k Paico 1967 NR

Owuoh, E.F.
Certificate essay. 108pp. C1.50 ($1.50) Ghana Publ Corp 1975 GH

Owusu, J.N.
Ckrabiri. [An unlucky person.] 93pp. ill. 65pes. Bur Ghana Lang 1973 GH TWI

Owusu, M.
Adventure of Sasa and Esi. 23pp. ill. 30pes. ($.30) Ghana Publ Corp 1968 GH

Oxford University Press. Daystar Press.
Together in God's family. bk. 5. 119pp. ill. N1.50 OUP - Nig 1977 NR

Oxford University Press. Daystar Press.
Together in God's family. Teacher's bk. 1 194pp. ill. N1.60 OUP - Nig 1975 NR

Oxford University Press. Daystar Press.
Together in God's family. Teacher's bk. 2 209pp. ill. N1.85 OUP - Nig 1975 NR

Oxford University Press. Daystar Press.
Together in God's family. Teacher's bk. 3 170pp. ill. N1.60 OUP - Nig 1975 NR

Oxford University Press. Daystar Press.
Together in God's family. Teacher's bk. 4 165pp. ill. N1.60 OUP - Nig 1975 NR

Oxford University Press, Nigeria.
A dictionary of Yoruba language. 243pp. N1.60 OUP - Nig 1963 NR YOR

Oxford University Press, South Africa.
Oxford English course - higher primary: pupils' readers, standard 3. 144pp. ill. 82c. OUP-SA 1972 SA

Oxford University Press, South Africa.
Oxford English course - higher primary: pupils' readers standard 4. 2nd ed. 148pp. ill. 82c. OUP-SA 1972 SA

Oxford University Press, South Africa.
Oxford English course - higher primary: pupils' readers standard 5. 2nd ed. 160pp. photos. ill. 85c. OUP-SA 1972 SA

Oxford University Press, South Africa.
Oxford English course - higher primary: pupils' readers standard 6. 2nd ed. 192pp. ill. 85c. OUP-SA 1972 SA

Oxford University Press, South Africa.
Oxford English course - higher primary: teachers' books, standard 3. 108pp. 62c. OUP-SA 1962 SA

Oxford University Press, South Africa.
Oxford English course - higher primary: teachers' books, standard 4. 108pp. 62c. OUP-SA 1962 SA

Oxford University Press, South Africa.
Oxford English course - higher primary: teachers' books, standard 5. 92pp. 66c. OUP-SA 1962 SA

Oxford University Press, South Africa.
Oxford English course - higher primary: teachers' books, standard 6. 96pp. 66c. OUP SA 1962 SA

Oxford University Press, South Africa.
Oxford English course - lower primary: standard 1. 104pp. ill. 70c. OUP-SA 1972 SA

Oxford University Press, South Africa.
Oxford English course - lower primary: standard 2. 112pp. ill. 70c. OUP-SA 1971 SA

Oxford University Press, South Africa.
Oxford English course - lower primary: sub-standard B. 64pp. ill. 55c. OUP-SA 1972 SA

Oxford University Press, South Africa.
Oxford English course - lower primary: teachers' companion, standard 2. 98pp. ill. 55c. OUP-SA 1959 S

Oxford University Press, South Africa.
Oxford English course - lower primary: teachers' companions, standard 1. 80pp. ill. 45c. OUP-SA 1959 SA

Oxford University Press, South Africa.
Oxford English course - lower primary: teachers' companions, sub-standard A. 88pp. ill. 45c. OUP-SA 1959 SA

Oxford University Press, South Africa.
Oxford English course - lower primary: teachers' companions, sub-standard B. 138pp. ill. 60c. OUP-SA 1959 SA

Oxford University Press Southern Africa.
Cattle in Swaziland. 68pp. ill. 45c. (Swaziland Modern Agriculture 4, 7 units) OUP - SA 1977 SA

Oxford University Press Southern Africa.
Crops in Swaziland. 41pp. ill. 45c. (Swaziland Modern Agriculture 7, 7 units) OUP - SA 1977 SA

Oxford University Press Southern Africa.
Farm records. 22pp. ill. 45c. (Swaziland Modern Agriculture 3, 7 units) OUP - SA 1977 SA

Oxford University Press Southern Africa.
Forestry. 37pp. ill. 45c. (Swaziland Modern Agriculture 6, 7 units) OUP - SA 1977 SA

Oxford University Press Southern Africa.
Plants and man. 18pp. ill. 45c. (Swaziland Modern Agriculture 1, 7 units) OUP - SA 1977 SA

Oxford University Press Southern Africa.
Soil and conservation. 59pp. ill. 45c. (Swaziland Modern Agriculture 5, 7 units) OUP - SA 1977 SA

Oxford University Press Southern Africa.
Vegetable production. 85pp. ill. 45c. (Swaziland Modern Agriculture 2, 7 units) OUP - SA 1977 SA

Oxtoby, E. Kamera, W.
A guide to the anatomy of the common African earthworm. 48pp. ill. K.shs.7.05 ($2.15/£1.10 pap.) EALB 1976 KE

Oyawoye, M.O.
Politics and economics of mineral resources in developing countries. 25pp. N1.00 (Inaugural lecture) Ibadan UP 1973 NG

Oyebola, A.
Economic theory for West African students.
See: Aromolaran, A.

Oyebola, A.
A modern approach to economics of West Africa. 2 2nded. 429pp. maps. N2.50 Educ Res Inst 1972 NR

Oyebola, A.
One hundred questions and answers on economics of West Africa. 2nd ed. 183pp. ill. N1.25 Educ Res Inst 1972 NR

Oyebola, A. Ojelabi, A.
One hundred questions and answers on Government of West Africa. 2nd ed. 193pp. N1.25 Educ Res Inst 1972 NR

Oyebola, A. Ojelabi, A.
A textbook of government for West Africa. 4th ed. 436pp. ill. N2.00 Educ Res Inst 1971 NR

Oyedeji, O.O.
Practical management know-how: a checklist, pt. 1. 43pp. N1.25 (Modern management, 2) Univ Lagos Bkshop 1973 NR

Oyedele, A.
Ìwo ni. [You are the one] 128pp. ill. N1.30 Macmillan 1970 NR YOR

Oyejide, T.A.
Tariff policy and industrialization in Nigeria. 118pp. ill. N3.50 (Ibadan Social Science Studies, 3) Ibadan UP 1974 NR

Oyelese, J.O.
Common entrance and scholarship tests. 180pp. ill. N2.20 Macmillan 1974 NR

Oyelese, J.O.
Common entrance arithmetic: decimal currency and metric edition. N1.60 Macmillan 1966 NR

Oyelese, J.O.
Introduction to graphs: arithmetical graphs.
See: Setidisho, N.O.H.

Oyemakinde, A., comp.
Transportation in Nigeria: a bibliography. 57pp. N3.00 (N5.00) Nat Lib - Nig 1975 NR

Oyende, J.P.
Para moko kuom dohini e Kenya. [Some thoughts on native tribunals in Kenya] K.shs.0.75 ($1.25/50p.) EALB 1950 KE LUO

Oyenuga, V.A.
Animal production in the tropics. See: Loosli, J.K.

Oyenuga, V.A.
Nigeria's foods and feeding-stuffs: their chemistry and nutritive value. 3rd ed. 99pp. N2.00 Ibadan UP 1968 NR

Oyetunji, N.O.
Notes on "Julius Caesar". 133pp. N1.25 Ilesanmi 1972 NR

Oyetunji, N.O.
Notes on "Richard II". 116pp. N1.25 Ilesanmi 1972 NR

Oyetunji, N.O.
Old Testament: earliest times to the judges. 1, 2 bks. 83pp. maps. 90k Onibonoje 1971 NR

Oyetunji, N.O.
Old Testament: monarchy to fall of Samaria. 2, 2 bks. 146pp. maps. N1.35 Onibonoje 1971 NR

Oyewole, D.
New physics for 'O' level. bk. 2 249pp. ill. N1.80
Macmillan 1974 NR

Oyewole, D.
New physics for 'O' level. bk. 3,3 240pp. ill. N2.90
Macmillan 1975 NR

Oyewole, D.
Seven short stories. 54pp. ill. 40k Northern Nig
1969 NR

Oyewole, F.
Advanced practical chemistry for tropical schools.
See: Jeffery, R.W.

Oyewole, F.
Elementary organic chemistry for tropical schools.
See: Jeffery, R.W.

Oyewole, F.
Introduction to chemistry. 440pp. photos. N2.90
Macmillan 1964 NR

Oyewole, F.
Introduction to physics. 460pp. photos. N2.90
Macmillan 1964 NR

Oyewole, F.   Faturoti, A.
New chemistry for 'O' level. 144pp. ill. N1.30
Macmillan 1972 NR

Oyewole, F.
Practical physics for secondary schools. 1, 3bks
136pp. ill. N1.35 Macmillan 1970 NR

Oyewole, F.
Practical physics for secondary schools. 2, 3bks
136pp. ill. N1.35 Macmillan 1970 NR

Oyewole, F.
Practical physics for secondary schools. 3, 3bks
128pp. ill. N1.35 Macmillan 1970 NR

Oyinloye, T.
The changing role of the district officer in Northern Nigeria.
90pp. N1.25 (£1.00/$2.50) Inst Admin - Zaria 1966
NR

Oyono, F.
Boi. [Houseboy.] 120pp. K.shs.12.50 (£1.10)
Heinemann Educ - Nair 1975 KE SWA

Oyono-Mbia, G.
Chroniques de Mvoutessi, 1. 64pp. CFA200 CLE
1971 CM FRE

Oyono-Mbia, G.
Chroniques de Mvoutessi, 2. 64pp. CFA200 CLE
1971 CM FRE

Oyono-Mbia, G.
Chroniques de Mvoutessi, 3. 48pp. CFA200 CLE
1972 CM FRE

Oyono-Mbia, G.
Jusqu'à nouvel avis. 3rd ed. CFA240pp. CLE 1975
CM FRE

Oyono-Mbia, G.
Trois prétendants...un mari. 6th ed. 128pp. CFA450
CLE 1975 CM FRE

Paap, E.J.
Cookery in South Africa 1952-1962. 190pp. R1.50
Univ Cape Town Lib 1965 SA

Pacha, N.
Le commerce au Maghreb du XIe au XIVe siècles.
177pp. D900 (Série IV, Histoire, 17) Univ Tunis 1976
TI FRE

Pachai, B., ed.
Malawi past and present: selected papers from the
University of Malawi history conference, 1967.
See: Smith, G.W., ed.

Pachai, B., ed.
Memoirs of a Malawian: the life and reminiscences of
Lewis Bandawe, M.B.E. 160pp. photos. ill. hd. 70t
($3.00) Christ Lit Assoc - Mal 1971 MW

Pachai, B.
The international aspects of the South African Indian
question 1860-1971. 420pp. cl. R9.60 Struik 1971
SA

Pachai, B.
Mahatma Ghandi in South Africa. 21pp. photos. 45c.
($1.26) SA Inst of Race Relations 1969 SA

Pachai, B.
The Malawi diaspora and elements of Clements Kadalie.
60c. (Local series pamphlets, 24) Central Africa Hist
Assoc 1969 RH

Pachai, B.
Mbiri ya pfuko la Malawi. [History of Malawi] 301pp.
pl. K2.80 (£1.40) Longman - Mal 1974 MW CHC

Pachter, M.   Jacobson, D.H.
Conditions for the controllability of constrained linear
autonomous systems on time intervals of arbitrary length.
23pp. (CSIR Special Report, WISK 210) CSIR 1976 SA

Pagden, B.
The warriors. See: Summers, R.

Page, B.A.
South African law of trade marks. See: Webster, G.C.

Pagella, J.F.
Asbestos occurrences of the Eastern Province. 40n
(Dept. of Geological Survey. Economic Reports, 22)
Geol Survey - Zam 1970 ZA

Pahl, H.W.   Dazana, S.
Oxford Xhosa grammars/Ulwimi lwakowethu: standard 3
(Sisagaga) and 4 (Sesigingaa) 2nd ed. 80pp. 80c
OUP-SA 1972 SA XHO

Pahl, H.W.   Dazana, S.
Oxford Xhosa grammars/Ulwimi lwakowethu: standard 5
(Masisus' Unyawo) 2nd ed. 48pp. 70c OUP-SA
1972 SA XHO

Pahl, H.W.   Dazana, S.
Oxford Xhosa grammars/Ulwimi lwakowethu: standard 6
(Phambili) 2nd ed. 56pp. 65c OUP-SA 1972 SA
XHO

Pahl, H.W.
Oxford Xhosa readers/lincwadi zesiXhosa zaseOxford:
standard 1 (Ukuhamba Yin Fundo) 3, 9 bks. 88pp.
55c OUP-SA 1972 SA XHO

Pahl, H.W.
Oxford Xhosa readers/lincwadi zesiXhosa zaseOxford:
standard 2 (Kwathi ke kaloku ngantsomi) 4, 9 bks.
88pp. 55c OUP-SA 1972 SA XHO

Pahl, H.W.
Oxford Xhosa readers/lincwadi zesiXhosa zaseOxford:
standard 3. 2nd ed. 5, 9 bks. 96pp. 55c OUP-SA
1972 SA XHO

Pahl, H.W.
Oxford Xhosa readers/lincwadi zesiXhosa zaseOxford:
standard 4. 2nd ed. 6, 9 bks. 100pp. 60c
OUP-SA 1972 SA XHO

Pahl, H.W.
Oxford Xhosa readers/lincwadi zesiXhosa zaseOxford:
standard 5. 7, 9 bks. 104pp. 65c OUP-SA 1971
SA XHO

Pahl, H.W.
Oxford Xhosa readers/lincwadi zesiXhosa zaseOxford:
standard 6. 8, 9 bks. 104pp. 65c OUP-SA 1972
SA XHO

Pahl, H.W.
Oxford Xhosa readers/lincwadi zesiXhosa zaseOxford:
sub-standard A/Primer. 6th ed. 1, 9 bks. 44pp.
48c OUP-SA SA XHO

Pahl, H.W.
Oxford Xhosa readers/lincwadi zesiXhosa zaseOxford:
sub-standard B and standard 1 supplementary reader
(UnJovana NonJozana lincwadi yesibini) 9, 9 bks 32pp.
25c OUP-SA 1954 SA XHO

Author Index

Pahl, H.W.
Oxford Xhosa readers/lincwadi zesiXhosa zaseOxford:
sub-standard B (UnJovana NonJozana) 2nd ed. 2, 9
bks. 64pp. 50c OUP-SA 1972 SA XHO

Pahl, H.W.
Oxford Xhosa readers/lincwadi zesiXhosa zaseOxford,
teacher's guide (For sub-standard A & B) 2nd ed. 8pp.
06c OUP-SA 1953 SA XHO

Paico Ltd.
New way copy book for Nigeria. pupil's bk. 1, 5 bks.
20pp. 80k Paico 1966 NR

Paico Ltd.
New way copy book for Nigeria. pupil's bk. 2, 5 bks.
20pp. 80k Paico 1966 NR

Paico Ltd.
New way copy book for Nigeria. pupil's bk. 3, 5 bks.
20pp. 80k Paico 1966 NR

Paico Ltd.
New way copy book for Nigeria. pupil's bk. 4, 5 bks.
32pp. 80k Paico 1966 NR

Paico Ltd.
New way copy book for Nigeria: teacher's bk. 5, 5 bks.
28pp. 40k Paico 1966 NR

Paine, R.
Guided general science. Standard 6. See: Pellew, V.

Painter, A.   Murdoch, B.D.
The Reitan-Indiana neuropsychological test battery for
children (5-8 years) and the Halstead neuropsychological
test battery for children (9-14 years): normative data.
27pp. (CSIR Special Report, PERS 243) CSIR 1976 SA

Pairault, C. et al.
Annales de l'université d'Abidjan. See: Diarrassouba, M.

Pairault, C. et al.
Annales de l'université d'Abidjan. See: Bar-David, Y.

Pakshong, J.S.
Industrial property. 43pp. R2.25 Dept Bibliog, Lib &
Typo 1966 SA

Paku, E.K.
Fransegbe srcgbale na Eveawo. [A French reader for
Ewes] 20pp. ill. 90pes. Waterville 1968 GH EWE

Pala, A.O.
A preliminary survey of the avenues for and constraints on
women in the development process in Kenya. 33pp.
K.shs.7.00 (Inst. Development Studies, Discussion paps.,
218) Inst Dev Stud 1975 KE

Palangyo, P.
Kivuli cha mauti. [Dying in the sun tr. fr. English J.D.
Mganga] K.shs.11.75 (80p.) (Waandishi Wa KiAfrika,
4.) Heinemann Educ - Nair 1972 KE SWA

Palayer, P.
Les langues du groupe Boua. Etudes phonologiques.
See: Boyeldieu, P.

Palgrave, C.K., ed.   Moll, E.J., ed.   Drummond, R.B.,
ed.
Trees of southern Africa. 1152pp. pl. col. pl. R15.00
Struik 1977 SA

Paliani, R.H.S.
Cikondi saumiriza. [Love is never forced.] 60pp. 25n.
Neczam 1975 ZA NYA

Paling, D. et al.
Oxford modern mathematics for Nigerian teachers'
colleges. lecturer's guide, 1. See: Lassa, P.N.

Paling, D. et al.
Oxford modern mathematics for Nigerian teachers'
colleges. student's bk. 1. See: Lassa, P.N.

Paling, D.
Oxford arithmetic course (Nig): pupils bk. 6, 6 bks.
See: Downes, L.W.

Paling, D.
Oxford arithmetic course (Nig.): teacher's bk. 1, 6 bks.
See: Downes, L.W.

Paling, D.
Oxford arithmetic course (Nig.): teacher's bk. 2, 6 bks.
See: Downes, L.W.

Paling, D.
Oxford arithmetic course (Nig.): teacher's bk. 3, 6 bks.
See: Downes, L.W.

Paling, D.
Oxford arithmetic course (Nig.): teacher's bk. 4, 6 bks.
See: Downes, L.W.

Paling, D.
Oxford arithmetic course (Nig.): teacher's bk. 5, 6 bks.
See: Downes, L.W.

Paling, D.
Oxford arithmetic course (Nig.): teacher's bk. 6, 6 bks.
See: Downes, L.W.

Paling, D.
Revision, objective and aptitude tests for Oxford primary
mathematics course. See: Downes, L.W.

Palmer, E.   Pitman, N.
Trees of Southern Africa. 288pp. ill. hd. fl. 337.50
(£56.00/$135.00) Balkema 1973 SA

Palmer, J.L.
A list of field experiments involving crop mixtures in the
northern states of Nigeria, 1924-71. 17pp. 40k
(Samaru misc. pap., 29) Inst Agric Res-Zaria 1971 NR

Palmer, M.
The history of the Indians in Natal. $3.75 (Natal
regional survey pub., 10) Dept Econ-Natal 1957 SA

Palmer, R., ed.
Zambia land and labour studies. v. 1, 2. 66pp. 40n
(Nat. Archives of Zambia, occas. paps., 1) Nat Archives
- Zam 1974 ZA

Palmer, R., ed.
Zambia land and labour studies. v. 2, 2. 100pp. 40n
(Nat. Archives of Zambia, occas. paps., 2) Nat Archives
- Zam 1974 ZA

Palmer, R.H.
Aspects of Rhodesian land policy, 1890-1936. R$1.70
(Local series pamphlets, 22) Central Africa Hist Assoc
1968 RH

Palmer, S.
Mingled trails. 68pp. pl. 85c Mambo 1975 RH

Pama, C., ed.
The South African Library. 226pp. pl. hd. fl. 22.50
Balkema 1968 SA

Pama, C.
Heraldry of South African families. 375pp. ill. hd. fl.
67.50 Balkema 1972 SA

Pama, C.
Regency Cape Town. ill. hd. R17.50 cl. Tafelberg
1976 SA

Pankhurst, R., comp.
Register of current research on Ethiopia and the Horn of
Africa. (annual) See: Chojnacki, S., comp.

Pankhurst, R., ed.
The dictionary of Ethiopian biography. v. I.
See: Belaynesh, M., ed.

Pankhurst, R.
A history of Ethiopia in pictures. See: Last, G.

Pankhurst, R.
Ye Ethiopia Tank Besil. See: Last, G.

Pannall, R.
Forensic pharmacy. 168pp. R9.75 Butterworths
1976 SA

Panniers, B.J.
Objective tests in physics. See: Robinson, R.

Papendieck, H.I.C.M.   Frank, G.H.
Contributions to the cranial morphology of Ambystoma
macrodactylum Baird; The development of the
chondrocranium of the ostrich. 98pp. ill. R1.35 (A
v.30, no. 3-4) Univ Stellenbosch, Lib 1954 SA

Papenfus, J. N.
Biology from nature and in the laboratory, standard 7.
See: Jackson, I. M.

Papworth, J.
Economic aspects of the humanist revolution of our time.
126pp. K2.10 Neczam 1973 ZA

Paquet, J.
Salaires et préhendres des professeurs de l'université de
Louvain au XVe siècle. 38pp. 30k pap. Press Univ
Zaire 1958 ZR FRE

Parish, D.H.
Scientists, salesmen and sugar cane planters. 31pp.
K.shs2.00 ($1.00) EAPH 1969 KE

Parkar, A. Buyu, J.
Certificate Kiswahili digest. 152pp. K.shs.13.00 Elimu
(Textbook Ctre) 1974 KE

Parkash, A.
Certificate health science digest. See: Aggarwall, V.P.

Parker, C.
Willing workers and other stories. 90pp. ill. 55k
OUP-Nig 1970 NR

Parker, H.M.
Teaching of class singing. 124pp. R1.10 Lovedale
1973 SA

Parker, R.B. Sabin, R.
A practical guide to Islamic monuments in Cairo. 91pp.
pl. maps. £E1.75 ($6.95) Am Univ 1974 UA

Parkes, M. E.
The use of windmills in Tanzania. T.shs.15.00 ($5.00)
(Research pap., 33) Bur Res Assess - Tanz 1974 TZ

Parkinson, B.M.
The African Railway Workers Union, Ndola, Northern
Rhodesia. 16pp. 20n. (10p.) (Rhodes-Livingstone
communications, 10) Inst Afr Stud - Lusaka 1958 ZA

Parks, S.M.
A guide to Cape Town for African people. 24pp. ill.
40c. ($1.15) SA Inst of Race Relations 1970 SA

Parks, S.M.
A guide to Cape Town for coloured people. 51pp. ill.
40c. ($1.15) SA Inst of Race Relations 1969 SA

Parnis, R.
Focus on health; essays on matters of personal health and
hygiene. 88pp. ill. 85k Daystar 1971 NR

Parnwell, E.C.
Maisha ya nyuki wa asali. [The life of the honey bee]
48pp. ill. K.shs.3.25 OUP-Nairobi 1964 KE SWA

Paroz, R.A.
Southern Sotho-English dictionary. 464pp. cl. R6.00
Morija 1961 LO

Parr, H.H.
A sketch of the Kafir and Zulu wars. [Reprint of ed.
London, 1880] 283pp. ill. R4.10 (Reprints, 56)
State-Lib-SA 1970 SA

Parrinder, E.G.S.
The story of Ketu. 2nd ed. 106pp. map. N2.00
Ibadan UP 1967 NR

Parrot, D.
Jardins tropicaux. 80pp. pl. col. pl. CFA900.00 CLE
1974 CM FRE

Parsons, Q.N.
The High Commission territories, 1900-1964: a
bibliography. 18pp. E1.00 (Swaziland Libraries
Publication, 3) Univ Bots & Swazi 1976 SG

Parsons, Q.N.
The world of Khama. 36pp. 45n. (Haz pamphlets, 2)
Neczam 1972 ZA

Partridge, A.C., ed.
Elisa series: folk tales of Southern Africa. v. 2 Purnell
1973 SA

Partridge, A.C., ed.
Elisa series: lives, letters and diaries. v. 1 199pp.
photos. hd. R4.50 Purnell 1971 SA

Partridge, A.C., ed.
Readings in South African English prose. R1.45 Van
Schaik SA

Pasquall, J.A.
Geometrical and technical drawing course for African
secondary schools. 1, 4 pts. 228pp. ill. K2.15
Neczam 1973 ZA

Pasquill, J.A.
Geometrical and technical drawing course for African
secondary schools. 2, 4 pts. 192pp. ill. K2.15
Neczam 1970 ZA

Pasquill, J.A.
Geometrical and technical drawing course for African
secondary schools. 3, 4 pts. ill. Neczam 1973 ZA

Passin, H. Jones-Quartey, K.A.B.
Africa: the dynamics of change. 262pp. N3.50
Ibadan UP 1963 NR

Passmore, G.C.
Holders of administrative and ministerial office 1894-1964
and members of the legislative council 1899-1923 and the
legislative assembly 1924-1964. See: Willson, R.M.G.

Passmore, G.C.
Local government legislation in southern Rhodesia up to
30th September 1963. 75pp. 50c (Dept. of Political
Science, Univ. Rhodesia, 4) Univ Rhodesia Lib 1966 RH

Passmore, G.C. Mitchell, M.T.
Source book of parliamentary elections and referenda in
southern Rhodesia, 1898-1962. 255pp. R$2.00
(Dept. of Political Science, Univ. of Rhodesia, 1) Univ
Rhodesia Lib 1963 RH

Passmore, G.C.
Theoretical aspects of community action and local
government. 96pp. R$1.00 (Univ. Rhodesia,
Monographs in Political Science, 3) Univ Rhodesia Lib
1971 RH

Patel, A.H.
Independent Kenya's first Martyr-Pio Gama Pinto. 36pp.
photos. K.shs2.50 (15p.) New Kenya 1966 KE

Patel, I.S. Patel, M.R.
C.P.E. text book. 458pp. K.shs.25.00 Textbook Ctre
1977 KE

Patel, M.R.
C.P.E. text book. See: Patel, I.S.

Patel, M.R.
Junior physical science. See: Patel, N.M.

Patel, M.S.
Progress in English. 104pp. K.shs.10.50 Textbook
Ctre 1976 KE

Patel, M.S.
Progress in English, answer book. 36pp. K.shs.4.00
Textbook Ctre 1976 KE

Patel, N.M.
E.A.C.E. physical science. 218pp. K.shs18.00
Textbook Ctre 1970 KE

Patel, N.M.
E.A.C.E. physical science. 252pp. K.shs.18.00
Textbook Ctre 1975 KE

Patel, N.M. Patel, M.R.
Junior physical science. 176pp. K.shs.15.00
Textbook Ctre 1976 KE

Patel, R.B.
The complete CPE guidebook with answers. 343pp. ill.
K.shs.25.00 Textbook Ctre 1977 KE

Paternostre, B.
Le Rwanda, son effort de développement. 413pp. maps
photos. RF300 (FB300) Caritas 1972 RW FRE

Paterson, D., et al.
Applied agriculture, standard 5. 120pp. ill. pl. R1.50
Shuter 1977 SA

Patience, K.
Steam in East Africa, a photo-history of East African
railways. 128pp. photos. cl. K.shs.78.00 cl.
Heinemann Educ - Nair 1976 KE

Author Index

Paton, A.
Apartheid and the archbishop: the life and times of Geoffrey Clayton, archbishop of Cape Town. 328pp. photos. cl. R20.00 deluxe ed. R9.60 cl. Philip 1973 SA

Paton, A.
Christian unity: a South African view. 50c. (Peter Ainslie Memorial lec., 3) Rhodes Univ Lib 1950 SA

Paton, A.
Hofmeyr (abridged) 424pp. R3.30 OUP-SA 1971 SA

Paton, A.
Knocking on the door: shorter writings by Alan Paton, edited by Colin Gardner. 272pp. cl. R9.60 Philip 1975 SA

Paton, A.
Lafa elihle kakhulu. [Cry the beloved country tr. fr. Eng. S. Nyembezi] 247pp. 65c. Shuter 1958 SA ZUL

Paton, J.S., ed.
The grey ones. Essays on censorship. 75c. ($1.50/75p.) Ravan 1973 SA

Pattern, M.D.
Ghanaian imaginative writing in English, 1950-1969: an annotated bibliography. 60pp. C1.00 ($3.25) (Dept of Library Stud. occas. paps., 4) Dept Lib Stud - Univ Ghana 1971 GH

Patterson, C.L.
Africa and the world. See: Robert, K.A.

Patterson.
Mathematics for today. bk. 1 See: Harrison, W.A.

Paula, F.
Words I know. bk. 1 12pp. 6c. Shuter 1952 SA

Paula, F.
Words I know. bk. 2 12pp. 6c. Shuter 1952 SA

Paula, F.
Words I know. bk. 3 16pp. 8c. Shuter 1952 SA

Paula, F.
Words I know. bk. 4 22pp. 9c. Shuter 1952 SA

Paula, F.
Words I know. bk. 5 20pp. 9c. Shuter 1952 SA

Pauling, G.
The chronicles of a contractor [Reprint ed. 1926]. 264pp. ill. photos. map. cl. R$6.75 cl. (Rodesiana Reprint Library, Gold Series, 4) Books of Rhodesia 1969 RH

Pauw, B.
Christianity and Xhosa tradition. R14.50 OUP - SA 1974 SA

Pauw, B.
The second generation: a study of the family among urbanized Bantu in East London. 2nd rev. ed. 256pp. R4.75 OUP - SA 1973 SA

Paynter, B.E. Coetzee, A.G.
Junior secondary history for standard 6. 235pp. ill. pl. maps. R2.90 Nasou 1974 SA

Paynter, B.E. Coetzee, A.G.
Junior secondary history for standard 7. 161pp. ill. pl. maps. R2.25 Nasou 1974 SA

Paynter, B.E. Coetzee, A.G.
Senior secondary history for standard 8. 157pp. R3.40 Nasou 1974 SA

p'Bitek, J.O.
Lak tar miyo kinyero wi lobo. [Are your teeth white? Then laugh] ill. K.shs.2.50 ($2.25/90p.) EALB 1968 KE LGB

p'Bitek, O.
African religion in Western scholarship. pap. & cl. K.shs16.50 cl. K.shs7.50 pap. ($4.00/£1.00 cl.) ($2.50/£1.00 pap.) EALB 1971 KE

p'Bitek, O.
Africa's cultural revolution. 108pp. K.shs.15.00 Books for Africa 1975 KE

P'Bitek, O.
Religion of the Central Luo. pap. & cl. K.shs.24.00 cl. K.shs14.50 pap. ($5.25/£2.50 cl.) ($5.00/£2.00 pap.) EALB 1971 KE

p'Bitek, O.
Song of Lawino. 216pp. ill. K.shs30.00 cl. K.shs8.50 pap. ($5.80 cl.) ($3.00 pap.) EAPH 1966 KE

p'Bitek, O.
Song of Lawino. [in Swahili]. 151pp. ill. K.shs.7.50 ($2.60) EAPH 1969 KE SWA

p'Bitek, O.
Song of Ocol. 86pp. ill. K.shs8.50 ($1.50) EAPH 1970 KE

p'Bitek, O.
Songs of Lawino and Ocol. 255pp. ill. K.shs10.00 ($2.60) EAPH 1972 KE

p'Bitek, O.
Two songs. 184pp. ill. K.shs8.50 ($3.00) EAPH 1970 KE

p'Bitek, O.
Wimbo wa lawino. [Poetry.] 216pp. ill. K.shs.12.00 ($3.50) EAPH 1975 KE SWA

P'Chong, C.C.
Generosity kills, and The last Safari (Two plays) 64pp. K.shs.6.75 Longman - Ken 1975 KE

P'chong, C.L.
Words of my groaning. 68pp. K.shs.10.60 ($3.00/£1.75) EALB 1977 KE

Pearce, I.
Letters of health. 146pp. ill. B4.50 OUP-Addis 1972 ET

Pearse, G.E.
The Cape of Good Hope. R5.00 Van Schaik SA

Pearse, G.E.
Eighteenth century architecture in South Africa. 68pp. pl. hd. fl. 90.00 Balkema 1968 SA

Pearse, G.E.
Eighteenth century furniture. R12.60 Van Schaik SA

Pearson, J.
Wildlife and safari in Kenya. 385pp. photos. K.shs.49.00 ($13.00) EAPH KE

Pedraza, L.
Borriobola-Gha. N1.05 OUP-Nig 1969[?] NR HAU

Peeters, G.
Essai sur l'économie de l'élevage du bovidé au Congo. 28pp. 30k Press Univ Zaire 1960 ZR FRE

Peeters, L.
Introduction à l'étude litteraire. 352pp. R3.20 (R4.20) Univ South Africa 1975 SA FRE

Pelende.
Il mit du poison dans le vin de ses frères. Mythes suku. Textes suku-Français. See: Bulundu.

Pellat, C.
Cheherazade. Personnage littéraire. See: Hussein, H.A.

Pellew, V.
Exploring life. pt.7 See: Thienel, A.

Pellew, V.
Exploring life. pt. 2. See: Thienel, A.

Pellew, V. Maskil, D. Castle, M.
Guided general science. Standard 5. 208pp. ill. R1.60 Shuter 1975 SA

Pellew, V. Paine, R. Castle, M.
Guided general science. Standard 6. 172pp. ill. R1.60 Shuter 1975 SA

Pelling, J.N.
Lessons in Ndebele. 216pp. R$3.20 Longman - Rhod 1974 RH

Pelling J.N.
Ndebele work book. 198pp. R$2.40 Rhod Christ Press 1975 RH

Pelling, J.N.
Practical Ndebele dictionary. 2nd ed. 152pp. R$2.60
Longman - Rhod 1971 RH

Pellow, G.S.
Mapwork for Central Africa. 64pp. maps. 84n.
(23p.) OUP - Lusaka 1969 ZA

Pells, P.J.N. Robertson, A.M.G.
Soil mechanics and foundation engineering. Proceedings
of the sixth regional conference for Africa, Durban, 1975.
2 vols. 450pp. ill. pl. cl. R30.00 ($54.00) Balkema
1975 SA

Penda, G.
La corbeille d'ignames. 64pp. CFA200 pap. CLE
1971 CM FRE

Pendleton, W.
The peoples of South West Africa. 128pp. cl. R7.50
cl. (The Peoples of Southern Africa, 8) Philip 1976 SA

Pendleton, W.C.
Marriage and urban tribalism among Africans. 40c.
(Isma paps., 30) Inst Study of Man 1971 SA

Pene, P. Arziari, A. et al.
Annales de l'université d'Abidjan. 209pp. CFA1500
(F30.00 pap.) (Série B - Médecine, 2) Univ Abidjan
1968 IV FRE

Pene, P. et al.
Annales de l'université d'Abidjan. 209pp. CFA1500
(F30.00) (Série B - Médecine, 3) Univ Abidjan 1969 IV
FRE

Penner, R.G.
Financing local government in Tanzania. 102pp.
K.shs.45.00 cl. K.shs.12.50 pap. ($8.40 cl.) ($3.60
pap.) EAPH KE

Penner, R.G.
Local government revenue, Tanzania. T.shs.12.00
($3.00) (Research pap., 68.22) Econ Res Bur - Tanz
1974 TZ

Penny, P.
Economic and legal aspects of real estate in South Africa.
R7.50 Juta SA

Penrose, C.K.
Education. 101pp. 65pes. Waterville 1965 GH

Penrose, C.K.
Notes on child study. 4th rev. ed. 42pp. 45pes.
Waterville 1964 GH

Penrose, C.K.
Teachers legal guide for Africa. 28pp. 50pes.
Waterville 1976 GH

Pepler, J.
The cause and elimination of odours from kraft mill
operations. 29pp. R1.60 Dept Bibliog, Lib & Typo
1966 SA

Pereira, E., ed.
Contemporary South African plays. 360pp. R7.50
($9.00/£4.95) Ravan 1977 SA

Pereira, E.
John Keats, the poet as critic. 16pp. 60c. (R1.10)
Univ South Africa 1969 SA

Perkins, W.A. Stembridge, J.H.
Nigeria: a descriptive geography. 184pp. photos. maps.
N1.20 OUP-Nig 1966 NR

Perrin, J. Hill, M.V.
Mambila, description phonologique du parler d'Atta.
70pp. CFA500 Univ Cameroun 1969 CM FRE

Perrin Jassy, M. F.
Leadership. 100pp. K.shs.10.50 (Gaba Pastoral
Papers, 32) Gaba 1974 KE

Perrin Jassy, M.F.
La communauté de base dans les églises africaines.
231pp. map. (DM24.00) (CEEBA. série II, Mémoires et
Monographies, 3) CEEBA 1970 ZR FRE

Perrin Jassy, M.F.
Forming Christian communities. Evaluation of pastoral
experimentation based on sociological research in northern
Tanzania. 76pp. K.shs.7.50 (Gaba Pastoral Papers,
12) Gaba 1970 KE

Perron, G., comp.
Bibliographie de la Côte d'Ivoire. v. 3: sciences de
physiques et de la terre. See: Janvier, G., comp.

Perrot, C.H.
Annales de l'université d'Abidjan. Les Sotho et les
missionnaires européens au 19e siècle. 190pp. ill.
CFA1200 (F24.00) (Série F-Ethno-Sociologie, 2-1)
Univ Abidjan 1970 IV FRE ·

Perrot, D., ed.
Outlook on a century. See: Wilson, F., ed.

Perrott, D.V.
Krapf na Rebmann katika uchaga, vuga na ukambani.
[Journeys of early travellers in East Africa] 4th ed.
18pp. ill. K.shs.1.00 ($1.25/50p.) (Safari za
Watangulizi, 1) EALB 1966 KE SWA

Perrott, D.V.
Livingstone avumbua ziwa nyasa mto ruvuma safari na
ugala. 4th ed. 20pp. ill. K.shs.1.00 EALB 1966
KE SWA

Perrott, D.V.
Speke avumbua Nile, bagamoy mpaka Uganda.
[Journeys of early travellers in East Africa] 4th ed.
21pp. ill. K.shs.1.00 ($1.25/50p.) (Safari za
Watangulizi, 2) EALB 1969 KE SWA

Perrott, D.V.
Thomson ukikuyuni, umasaini na Nyanza. [Journeys of
early travellers in East Africa] 5th ed. 18pp. ill.
K.shs.1.00 ($1.25/50p.) (Safari za Watanguluzi) EALB
1972 KE SWA

Perrott, D.V.
Uvumbuzi wa Ziwa Nyasa na mto Ruvuma ma Safari za
Ugala na Umasai. [Exploring Lake Nysa and the Ruvuma
River; Journey among the Galla and Masai] 4th ed. ill.
K.shs.1.00 ($1.25/50p.) (Safari za Watangulizi) EALB
1965 KE SWA

Perrott, D.V.
Wavumbuzi vijana. [Young explorers] ill. K.shs.4.00
($2.50/£1.00) EALB 1958 KE SWA

Person, Y.
Samori, fondateur de l'empire mandinque. 172pp.
CFA250 (F5.00) Nouv Ed Afric 1976 SG FRE

Person, Y.
Samori. Une révolution dyula. 1, 3v. 600pp.
CFA2400 (Mémoires de l'IFAN, 80) IFAN 1968 SG
FRE

Person, Y.
Samori. Une révolution dyula. 2, 3v. 672pp.
CFA3000 (Mémoires de l'IFAN, 80) IFAN 1970 SG
FRE

Person, Y.
Samori. Une révolution dyula. v.3 1107pp.
CFA12.000 (Mémoires de l'IFAN, 89) IFAN 1975 SG
FRE

Petch, G.A.
West African Institute of Social and Economic Research:
Economic planning in Sierra Leone 1945-1953. [2nd
annual conference] N1.00 ($2.00) (W.A.I.S.E.R., 2nd
annual conference pap., 2) NISER 1953 NR

Peteni, R.L.
Hill of fools: a novel of the Ciskei. 160pp. cl. R4.00
cl. Philip 1976 SA

Peters, D.U.
Land usage in Barotseland. 79pp. maps. K1.25
(63p.) (Rhodes-Livingstone communications, 19) Inst Afr
Stud - Lusaka 1960 ZA

Peters, D.U.
Land usage in Serenje district. 100pp. K1.05 (53p.) (Rhodes-Livingstone paps., 19) Inst Soc Res - Zam 1950 ZA

Peters, E.R.
The geology of the Kasungu area. 55pp. pl. maps. hd. K2.00 (Geological Survey of Malawi, Bull. 25) Geol Survey - Mal 1969 MW

Peters, E.R.
The geology of the South Vipya area. 44pp. pl. maps. K6.00 (Geological Survey of Malawi, Bull. 36) Geol Survey - Mal 1975 MW

Peters, J.M.
Pictorial communication. tr. f. Dutch by Murray Coombes. 144pp. ill. pap. R4.95 Philip 1977 SA

Peters, M.A.
The contribution of the Carnegie non-European library service, Transvaal, to the development of library services for Africans in South Africa. 227pp. photos. maps. cl. R6.00 cl. (Contributions to Library Science, 17) State Lib - SA 1975 SA

Peterside, P.D.
Objective questions in English language. See: Cairns, J.

Peterson, A.
Historia ya Ukristo. Kitabu cha pili. [Swahili theological textbook.] 190pp. ill. T.shs.15.00 Central Tanganyika 1972 TZ SWA

Peterson, A.
Historia ya Ukristo. [Church history] rev. ed. v. 1 154pp. cl. & pap. T.shs.10.50 pap. T.shs.20.00 cl. Central Tanganyika 1974 TZ SWA

Petrescu, G.
Zootechnie générale. See: Tudorascu Radu.

Pfaff, D.N.
English with ease for Afrikaans-speaking pupils, standard 5. See: Houghton-Hawksley, H.S.

Pfaff, D.N.
English with ease for Afrikaans-speaking pupils, standard 6. See: Houghton-Hawksley, H.S.

Pfaff, D.N.
English with ease for Afrikaans-speaking pupils, standard 7. See: Houghton-Hawksley, H.S.

Pfouma, O.
Siang. 44pp. CFA200 pap. CLE 1971 CM FRE

Phakathi, A.B.
Isizulu sethu. [Our Zulu] I banga, 5 114pp. ill. 55c. Shuter 1970 SA ZUL

Phakathi, A.B.
Isizulu sethu. [Our Zulu] Ibanga, 1 52pp. ill. 30c. Shuter 1970 SA ZUL

Phakathi, A.B.
Isizulu sethu. [Our Zulu] Ibanga, 2 52pp. ill. 35c. Shuter 1970 SA ZUL

Phakathi, A.B.
Isizulu sethu. [Our Zulu] Ibanga, 3 96pp. ill. 45c. Shuter 1970 SA ZUL

Phakathi, A.B.
Isizulu sethu. [Our Zulu] Ibanga, 4 114pp. ill. 50c. Shuter 1970 SA ZUL

Phakathi, A.B.
Isizulu sethu. [Our Zulu] Ibanga, 6 156pp. ill. 65c. Shuter 1970 SA ZUL

Pheko, S.E.M.
African religion rediscovered. 47pp. 40n Daystar - Lusaka 1972 ZA

Pheko, S.E.M.
Christianity through African eyes. 133pp. 75n Daystar - Lusaka 1969 ZA

Pheko, S.E.M.
A dream that was true. 35pp. 40n Daystar - Lusaks 1973 ZA

Pheko, S.E.M.
My ups and downs. A black Christian in Southern Africa. 94pp. K1.60 Daystar--Lusaka 1976 ZA

Philip, A., et al.
Session d'études administratives, diplomatiques (Rabat, 1958) Dir25.00 (Coll. Fac. des Sciences juridiques, économiques et sociales, 4) Ed La Porte 1959 MR FRE

Philip, M.
Caravan caravel. 144pp. ill. cl. R2.85 SA only Philip 1973 SA

Philips, M.A.
Handy at home. Home economics for standard 8. See: van Niekerk, M.S.E.

Phillips, B.D.
Scientific research innovation and economic growth: a possible relationship. R2.40 (Inst. of Social and Economic Research occas. paps., 10) Inst Soc & Econ Res - SA 1968 SA

Phillips, C.M. Symon, S.A.
Blindness in the Kawambwa district, Northern Rhodesia. African medicine in the Mankoya district, Northern Rhodesia. 77pp. 50n. (25p.) (Rhodes-Livingstone communications, 15) Inst Afr Stud - Lusaka 1959 ZA

Phillips, D.
Industrialization in Tanzania small scale production, decentralization and a multi-technology program for industrial development. 170pp. T.shs.12.00 ($3.00) (Research pap., 76.5) Econ Res Bur - Tanz 1976 TZ

Phillips, M.A.
On with the apron. Housecraft for standard 7. See: van Niekerk, M.S.E.

Phillips, S.
A bibliography of African law with special reference to Rhodesia. See: Bennett, T.

Phillipson, D.W.
An annotated bibliography of Zambian prehistory. 50n. (80c./35p.) Nat Mon Comm - Zambia 1968 ZA

Phillipson, D.W., ed.
Mosi-oa-tunya: a handbook to the Victoria falls region. 222pp. col. ill. maps. R$7.50 Longman - Rhod 1976 RH

Phillipson, D.W.
Historical notes on political development in Zambia. 11pp. 15n. (25c./10p.) Nat Mon Comm - Zambia 1972 ZA

Phillipson, D.W.
The iron age in Zambia. 32pp. ill. 90n. (Haz pamphlets, 5) Neczam 1976 ZA

Phillipson, D.W.
National monuments of Zambia. 71pp. 75n. Nat Mon Comm - Zambia 1972 ZA

Phillipson, D.W.
National monuments of Zambia: an illustrated guide. 50pp. ill. 75n ($1.20/50p.) Nat Mon Comm - Zambia 1973 ZA

Phillipson, D.W.
Prehistoric rock paintings and engravings of Zambia. 60n. (95c./40p.) Nat Mon Comm - Zambia 1972 ZA

Phillipson, D.W.
The prehistory of eastern Zambia. 218pp. pl. maps. K.shs140.00 ($17.50/£9.50) (Memoirs of the British Institute in Eastern Africa, 6) Brit Inst EA 1976 KE

Philological Society, London.
The word "Hottentot". [Reprint of ed. London, 1868]. 21pp. ill. R1.25 (Reprints, 61) State-Lib-SA 1971 SA

Philombe, R.
Histoires queue-de-chat. 112pp. CFA450 CLE 1971 CM FRE

Philombe, R.
Un sorcier blanc à Zangali. 198pp. CFA480 CLE 1969 CM FRE

Author Index

Philpott, R.H.
  Motives and methods in population control. 31pp. 30c pap. Univ Rhodesia Lib 1969 RH

Phiri, D. D.
  Charles C. Chinula. 74pp. photos. maps. K1.16 (58p) (Malawians to Remember) Longman - Mal 1975 MW

Phiri, D. D.
  Dunduzu K. Chisiza. 72pp. photos. K1.16 (58p) (Malawians to Remember) Longman - Mal 1974 MW

Phiri, D. D.
  Inkosi Gomani II. 62pp. photos. maps. K1.00 (50p) (Malawians to Remember) Longman - Mal 1973 MW

Phiri, D. D.
  James F. Sangala. 64pp. photos. maps. K1.00 (50p) (Malawians to Remember) Longman - Mal 1974 MW

Phiri, D.
  Here's how to pass a driving test. 18pp. 15n Multimedia 1971 SA

Phiri, D.D.
  Hints to private students. 2nd ed. 70pp. K.shs3.00 ($1.50/60p.) EALB 1966 KE

Phiri, D.D.
  Kanakazi kayaya. [Novel.] 18pp. 8n. Neczam 1973 ZA TUM

Phiri, D.D.
  Rev. John Chilembwe. photos. K1.40 (70p) (Malawians to Remember) Longman - Mal 1976 MW

Phiri, G.
  Victims of fate. 152pp. K2.20 Neczam 1974 ZA

Phiri, J.E.
  Kalenga ndi mnzace. [Kalenga and his friend] 72pp. 45n. Neczam 1958 ZA NYA

Phiti, G.
  Ticklish sensation. 140pp. K1.20 Neczam 1974 ZA

Photivoire, Abidjan.
  Découverte aèrienne de la Côte d'Ivoire. 220pp. pl. col. pl. cl. CFA8950.00 CEDA 1974 IV FRE

Phythian, J.E.
  Scientific programming on the 1900 series computers. 105pp. T.shs.7.50 Dept Math - Dar 1971 TZ

Piault, C.
  Contribution à l'étude de la vie quotidienne de la femme Mawri. 2nd rev. ed. ed. 133pp. maps photos. CFA1250 pap. (F25.00) (Etudes Nigeriennes, 10) Inst Rech Sci Hum 1971 NG FRE

Picard, G.G.
  Catalogue du musée Alaoui (collection punique) 299pp. pl. D1.000 Univ Tunis TI FRE

Picard, H.M.J.
  Lords of Stalplein. Biographical miniatures of the British governors of the Cape of Good Hope. 175pp. ill. cl. R6.30 cl. Haum 1974 SA

Picard, H.W.J.
  Gentleman's walk. maps pl. photos. ill. cl. R9.60 Struik 1968 SA

Picard, H.W.J.
  Masters of the castle. 244pp. R5.25 Struik 1972 SA

Picard, H.W.J.
  Peter Stuyvesant, builder of New York. 250pp. cl. R6.90 cl. HAUM 1975 SA

Pichon, M.
  Monographie des landolphiées. (Classification des apocynacées, XXXV) 437pp. pl. maps. CFA2000 pap. (Mémoires de l'IFAN, 35) IFAN 1953 SG FRE

Picton-Seymour, D.
  Victorian buildings in South Africa including Edwardian and Transvaal Republican styles, 1850-1910. photos. cl. ($42.00/£26.00) Balkema 1977 SA

Pienaar, J.J.
  Fundamental pedagogics. See: Viljoen, T.A.

Pienaar, P.T.
  Developmental reading programme. R1.00 Inst Study Eng 1968 SA

Pienaar, P.T.
  Double-up. R1.00 Inst Study Engl 1968 SA

Pienaar, P.T.
  Double up. bk. 1 90c. Shuter 1972 SA

Pienaar, P.T.
  Double up. bk. 2 80c. Shuter 1972 SA

Pienaar, P.T.
  Double up. bk. 3 80c. Shuter 1972 SA

Pienaar, U. de V.
  Haematology of some South African reptiles. 298pp. pl. cl. R12.00 Witwatersrand UP 1962 SA

Pierce, J.
  Bamanga. 168pp. K.shs.10.00 (Modern African Library, 28) EAPH 1974 KE

Pierce, J.
  Leopard in a cage. 232pp. K.shs.20.00 ($6.00) EAPH 1976 KE

Pierre, M.
  Documents de base. Enseignement du Français à l'ecole primaire et au cycle d'orientation. 32pp. CELTA 1975 ZR FRE

Pierre, M.
  Documents de travail, activites pédagogiques. See: Kempf, B.

Pierre, M.   Rosse, R.   Le Boul, M.
  Français I. Livre du maître. 150pp. CELTA 1976 ZR FRE

Pieters, A.
  Quelques notions sur les parasoleraies de la région de Lodja (nord Sankuru), République Démocratique du Congo. 51pp. 60k Press Univ Zaire 1968 ZR FRE

Pieterse, J.J.   Schmidt, E.R.
  The relationship between compressive strength and modulus of rupture of fired clay products. 10pp. (CSIR research reports, 213) CSIR 1964 SA

Pifer, A.
  The higher education of Blacks in the United States. 42pp. 75c ($1.60) (Hoernle Memorial Lecture) SA Inst of Race Relations 1973 SA

Pignon, J.
  Khereddine. Homme d'etat. Mémoires. See: Mzali, M.S.

Pigot, S.
  The journal of Sophia Pigot. 200pp. pl. hd. fl. 25.00 (The Graham's Town, 3) Balkema 1974 SA

Pilditch, R.G.
  Agriculture for J.C. Forms I, II and III. 4th ed. 152pp. ill. 65c. Shuter 1958 SA

Pilgrim Books Limited.
  Proceedings of the conference on high level teacher training. 148pp. N1.40 Pilgrim 1969 NR

Pillay, P.N.   Ellison, P.A.
  The Indian domestic budget. $4.00 Dept Econ-Natal 1969 SA

Pim, J.
  Beauty is necessary: creation or preservation of the landscape. 185pp. photos. hd. R10.00 Purnell 1971 SA

Pinhey, E.
  African moths. 152pp. col. pl. R$3.75 (Bundu series) Longman - Rhod 1975 RH

Pinhey, E.
  The emperor moths of South and South Central Africa. 208pp. ill. R9.75 Struik 1972 SA

Pinhey, E.
  Hawk moths of Central and Southern Africa: standard edition. 152pp. pl. hd. R5.00 Longman SA 1962 SA

Pinhey, E.
  The moths of southern Africa. col. ill. hd. R30.00 cl. Tafelberg 1976 SA

Pinhey, E.
Some well-known African moths. 116pp. col. ill. R$3.75 Longman - Rhod 1975 RH

Pinn, F.M.J.
A first guide to the Indian Ocean seashore. 72pp. ill. K.shs.8.50 OUP - Nairobi 1973 KE

Pinto, F.F., comp. Edwards, S., ed.
Preliminary findings of integrated research in field crops at Kobo, 1973-1975. 48pp. map. ex. only Inst Agric Res - Addis 1976 ET

Pinto, F.F., ed. Edwards, S., ed.
IAR/EPID cooperative programme Woretta (Begemdir) progress report 1974-1975. 23pp. ill./map. Inst Agric Res - Addis 1976 ET

Pistorius, A.W.I.
Accounting: an introduction. See: Faul, M.A.

Pistorius, M.C.
Outline of a data bank system for national and regional planning. See: Hahne, K.

Pitblado, J.R.
A review of agricultural land use and land tenure in Tanzania. 44pp. T.shs.7.00 (Research notes, 7) Bur Res Assess - Tanz 1970 TZ

Pitman, N.
Trees of Southern Africa. See: Palmer, E.

Pitot, A.
Récolte et préparations des collections botaniques. 43pp. CFA200 pap. (Instructions Sommaires, 2) IFAN 1950 SG FRE

Pittman, G.A.
Teaching structural English. 220pp. N1.40 Pilgrim 1967 NR

Plaatje, S.T. Lestrade, G.P.
Dintshontsho tsa bo-Juliuse Kesara. [Shakespeare's Julius Caesar.] repr. in new orthography ed. 122pp. R1.00 (Bantu treasury, 3) Witwatersrand UP 1975 SA TSW

Plaatje, S.T.
Mhudi. 225pp. 95c. Lovedale 1957 SA

Plaatje, S.T.
Mhudi. New ed. with an introduction by Tim Couzens. 165pp. ill. cl. R9.00 (African Fiction Library, 1) Quagga 1975 SA

Plangger, A., ed. Diethelm, M., ed.
Serima. On African christian art in Rhodesia. 100pp. R$4.95 Mambo 1974 RH

Plangger, A.B.
Tsumo-Shumo. Shona proverbial lore and wisdom. v. 2 See: Hamutyinei, M.A.

Plessis, I.D.
The Cape Malays: history, religion, traditions, folk tales and the Malay Quarter. 109pp. pl. hd. fl. 33.75 Balkema 1972 SA

Pliya, J.
L'arbre fétiche. 2nd ed. 92pp. CFA420 CLE 1975 CM FRE

Pliya, J.
La secrétaire particuliére. 96pp. CFA350 (Coll. Théâtre) CLE 1973 CM FRE

Plowes, D., et al.
Wild flowers of Rhodesia. 168pp. col. ill. R$16.00 cased R$8.00 pap. Longman - Rhod 1976 RH

Pogson, A.
Sources of finance for African businessmen. 86pp. hd. U.shs.5.00 Adult Educ Centre 1969 UG

Pohl, V.
Farewell the little people. 160pp. ill. cl. & pap. R1.80 pap. R2.50 cl. OUP-SA 1972 SA

Pohl, V.
Savage hinterland. 140pp. ill. R1.60 OUP-SA 1956 SA

Pohl, V.
Their secret ways. 168pp. ill. R1.65 OUP-SA 1970 SA

Poinssot, M.
Inscriptions arabes de Kairouan. 1, 2v. See: Roy, B.

Poinssot, M.
Inscriptions arabes de Kairouan. 2, 2v. See: Roy, B.

Pole Evans, I.B.
A reconnaissance trip through the eastern portion of the Bechuanaland protectorate and an expedition to Ngamiland, June-July, 1937. 75c. (Memoirs of the Botanical Survey of South Africa, 21) Botanical Res Inst 1938 SA

Pole Evans, I.B.
Roadside observations on the vegetation of East and Central Africa. R1.00 (Memoirs of the Botanical Survey of South Africa, 22) Botanical Res Inst 1948 SA

Poleman, T.T. Oloya, J.J.
The food supply of Kampala. 58pp. U.shs8.50 Mak Inst Soc Res 1972 UG

Pollak, H.
Education for progress: a report of the proceedings at the 1971 South African Institute of Race Relations conference on education with special reference to the needs of the coloured community, together with the findings and recommendations. 44pp. 60c. ($1.45) SA Inst of Race Relations 1971 SA

Pollard, G.
Catalogue of the Greek coins in the Courtauld collection. 92pp. R$7.50 cl. Univ Rhodesia Lib 1971 RH

Poller, R.M.
Swakopmund and Walvis Bay. 29pp. 70c. Univ Cape Town Lib 1964 SA

Polley, J., ed.
Poetry South Africa. Selected papers from poetry '74. See: Wilhelm, P., ed.

Pomel, R. et al.
Annales de l'université d'Abidjan. See: Hinschberger, F.

Poncet, Y.
Cartes ethno-démographiques du Niger. 14pp. maps. CFA1250 (F25.00) (Etudes Nigeriennes, 32) Inst Rech Sci Hum 1973 NG FRE

Porter, D.
Scientific English: a comprehension course. 1, 2 pts. See: Crewe, W.

Porter, D.
Scientific English: a comprehension course. 2, 2 pt. See: Crewe, W.

Porter, D.
Scientific English: a comprehension course. Answer book, pt. 1. See: Crewe, W.

Porter, D.
Scientific English: a comprehension course. Answer book, pt. 2. See: Crewe, W.

Porter, P.
A pilot study to determine the feasibility of creating a new vegetation map of Tanzania. T.shs.15.00 ($5.00) (Research reports, new series, 4.2) Bur Res Assess - Tanz 1973 TZ

Porter, P.
Potential photosynthesis and agriculture in Tanzania. T.shs.20.00 ($7.00) (Research pap., 29) Bur Res Assess - Tanz 1974 TZ

Porter, P.
Potential photosynthesis and agriculture in Tanzania. Appendices. T.shs.20.00 ($7.00) (Research pap., 29.1) Bur Res Assess - Tanz 1974 TZ

Posnansky, M.
Myth and methodology: the archaeological contribution to African history. 24pp. C1.00 ($1.00/50p.) (Inaugural lecture) Ghana UP 1969 GH

Posnansky, M.
The Nile quest. 26pp. ill. K.shs2.50 ($1.50/60p.)
EALB 1962 KE

Posnansky, M.
The origins of West Africa trade. 13pp. 50
($1.00/50c.) (Inaugural lecture) Ghana UP 1971 GH

Posnansky, M.
Prelude to East African history. 186pp. K.shs9.50
($1.20/50p.) Brit Inst EA 1966 KE

Post-Graduate Medical Education Committee.
Missile injuries. 46pp. 50c pap. (Fac. of Medicine,
Univ. of Rhodesia, Symposia Series, 1) Univ Rhodesia
Lib 1968 RH

Post, K.W.J.
The Nigerian federal election of 1959: politics and
administration in a developing political system. 518pp.
maps pl. N4.50 ($6.75) NISER 1963 NR

Potel, M.
Connaissance des structures orales en milieu enseignant.
Etude statistique d'un sondage. 50pp. CFA2000 Inst
Ling Appliquée 1972 IV FRE

Potgieter, D.J., ed.
Standard encyclopaedia of Southern Africa. v.12. [The
encyclopaedia consisting of 12 volumes is now complete.]
647pp. cl. R25.00 per vol. R300.00 set Nasou 1976
SA

Potgieter, E.F.
The disappearing bushmen of Lake Chrissie. R1.25
Van Schaik SA

Potgieter, J.T. Durr, H.J.R.
A host plant index of South African plant lice (Aphididae)
20pp. 50c. (A v.36, no.5) Univ Stellenbosch, Lib
1961 SA

Potgieter, L.
Bantu education in the Union 1949-1959. 24pp. 60c.
Univ Cape Town Lib 1965 SA

Potter, E.M.
Obituaries appearing in the Johannesburg Star 1925-1927.
39pp. R2.05 Dept Bibliog, Lib & Typo 1969 SA

Potts, H. Moody, M.
Objective questions in mathematics: with answers. 72pp.
ill. 94k Pilgrim 1967 NR

Potts, H. Moody, M.
Objective questions in mathematics: without answers.
70pp. ill. 82k Pilgrim 1967 NR

Potts, H. Asebiomo, A.J.
Tests in mathematics: with answers. 64pp. 77k
Pilgrim 1971 NR

Potts, H. Asebiomo, A.J.
Tests in mathematics: without answers. 56pp. 72k
Pilgrim 1971 NR

Poulton. Danso.
Okristoni abrabc ho akwankyere. [Teaching concerning
Christian conduct] 75pp. 15pes. Waterville 1955 GH
TWI

Prah, J.H.
Introductory electromagnetics (for West African students
preparing for Advanced Level Physics examination)
334pp. C3.50 Univ Cape Coast Lib (distr.) 1973 GH

Prance, C.R.
Tante Rebella and her friends. 25c. Shuter 1951 SA

Prather, R.
A colouring book of Kenya. ill. K.shs.5.60
($2.00/95p.) EALB 1976 KE

Prather, R.
A is for Africa. A colouring book of Africa. ill.
K.shs.5.80 ($2.00/95p.) EALB 1976 KE

Pratt, R.C.
Buganda and British overrule. See: Low, D.A.

Pratt, R.C.
The inaugural lectures of the University of Zambia.
See: Nyerere, J.

Pratt, S.
The Rhodesian book of the road. col. ill. hd. R$6.00
($12.00) M.O. Collins 1974 RH

Precheur-Ganonge, T.
La vie rurale en Afrique romaine d'après les mosaiques.
98pp. pl. D1.330 (Série I, Archéologie-Histoire, 6)
Univ Tunis 1961 TI FRE

Preen, G.
Adventure across Africa. See: Radford, W.

Preen, G.
Flying doctor. See: Radford, W.

Presbyterian Church.
Sunday worship. 70pp. 25pes. Waterville 1962 GH

Press, Z.
The prospects of a regional organisation in the Middle
East. 110pp. R1.00 (Research paper, 4) SA Inst Int
Affairs 1966 SA

Presses Universitaires du Zaire.
Industrie minière et développement au Zaire. 200pp.
Z6.40 Press Univ Zaire 1973 ZR FRE

Presses Universitaires du Zaire.
Le mariage chrétien en Afrique. Ve semaine théologique
Kinshasa organisee par la faculté de théologie de
l'université Lovanium, 20-25 juillet 1970. 201pp. Z1.50
Press Univ Zaire 1971 ZR FRE

Presses Universitaires du Zaire.
Organisation des études à l'Université Nationale du Zaire.
50pp. Z1.00 Press Univ Zaire 1977 ZR FRE

Presses Universitaires du Zaire.
Recherche et publications scientifiques à l'Université
Nationale de Zaire. 39pp. 20k Press Univ Zaire
1972 ZR FRE

Presses Universitaires du Zaire.
Renouveau de l'église et nouvelles églises. Colloque sur la
théologie africaine, IVe semaine théologique de Kinshasa
organisee par la faculté de théologie de l'université
Lovanium, 22-27 juillet 1968. 30pp. Z1.00 Press
Univ Zaire 1968 ZR FRE

Presses Universitaires du Zaire.
L'Université nationale du Zaire. 47pp. 20k Press Univ
Zaire 1972 ZR FRE

Presses Universitaires du Zaire.
Vade-mecum des responables de la gestion financère et
du patrimoine de l'UNALA. 45pp. Z90.00 Press Univ
Zaire 1973 ZR FRE

Preston-White, E.M., ed.
Social system and tradition in Southern Africa.
See: Argyle, W.J., ed.

Pretoria State Library.
Bibliography of reprography. 142pp. R3.00
(Bibliographies, 15) State-Lib-SA 1970 SA

Pretoria State Library.
Current South African periodicals: a classified list.
167pp. R5.00 [Annual supplements 1-6, 50c. each]
(Bibliographies, 8) State-Lib-SA 1966 SA

Pretorius, J.L.
Thupi la munthu. See: Pretorius, P.V.

Pretorius, P.V. Pretorius, J.L. Retief, R.L.
Thupi la munthu. [The human body] 74pp. ill. 23t.
(26c.) Christ Lit Assoc - Mal 1969 MW CHC

Prewitt, K.
Education and political values. 249pp. K.shs.63.00 cl.
K.shs.28.50 pap. ($7.00) EAPH 1971 KE

Price, C.H.
Pharmacy - yesterday, to-day and to-morrow. ex. only
(Inaugural lec.) Rhodes Univ Lib 1962 SA

Price, C.H.
So you're going to university. 95c. Butterworths 1973
SA

Price, G.N.
Port Elizabeth. 21pp. 70c. Univ Cape Town Lib 1950
SA

Price, T.
English grammar for African schools. 97pp. 70t. (35c.) Christ Lit Assoc - Mal 1972 MW

Price, T.
Short English-Nyanja vocabulary. 128pp. 95n Neczam 1972 ZA

Price, T.W. Beinart, B.
Butterworths South African law review 1954-1957. 229pp. R4.00 Butterworths 1956 SA

Prickett, B.
Island base: a history of the Methodist Church in the Gambia, 1821-1969. 242pp. photo. maps. D3.12 (62 1/2p.) Gambia Meth Bkshp 1971 GM

Priddy, B.
Christiansborg Castle: Osu. 19pp. photos. 30pes. (Ghana Museums & Monuments Board, 1) Ghana Museums 1969 GH

Priddy, B.
A short history of the forts and castles of Ghana. See: Van-Dantzig, A.

Priestley, M.
Ghana's financial bureaucracy: a historical approach. 19pp. C1.00 (50p./$1.00) (Inaugural lecture) Ghana UP 1976 GH

Priestley, M.
Public financial administration in Ghana and its historical sources. 23pp. C1.80 (Univ. of Ghana, Dept. of Library & Archival Studies, occas paps., 14) Dept Lib Stud - Univ Ghana 1977 GH

Prins, A.H.J.
A Swahili-Nautical dictionary. 95pp. T.shs.10.00 Inst Swahili Res 1970 TZ

Prinsloo, D.S.
China and the liberation of Portuguese Africa. 14pp. (FAA Study Report, 2) Foreign Affairs Assoc - SA 1976 SA

Prinsloo, D.S.
Lesotho's expensive border hoax. 14pp. R1.00 (FAA Focus, 6) Foreign Affairs Assoc - SA 1977 SA

Prinsloo, D.S.
SWA: the turnhalle and independence. 35pp. photos. R1.00 (FAA Study Reports, 4) Foreign Affairs Assoc 1976 SA

Prior, A.
Revolution and philosophy: the significance of the French revolution for Hegel and Marx. 144pp. cl. R4.20 cl. Philip 1972 SA

Proctor, J.H., ed.
Building Ujamaa villages in Tanzania. 69pp. T.shs.5.00 (Univ. Dar es Salaam, Studies in political science, 2) Tanz Publ House 1971 TZ

Proctor, J.H., ed.
The cell system of the Tanganyika African National Union. 66pp. T.shs.5.00 (Univ. Dar es Salaam, Studies in political science, 1) Tanz Publ House 1971 TZ

Proehl, L.
Foreign enterprises in Nigeria. N4.80 OUP-Nig NR

Progresso Publishers.
Notes on "Modern poetry from Africa" (with hints on examination requirements) 37pp. N1.30 Armolaran 1970 NR

Prosser, R.
Adult education for developing countries. 140pp. K.shs.14.50 ($4.00) EAPH 1967 KE

Prosser, R., eds. Clarke, R., eds.
Teaching adults. K.shs.7.50 ($2.25/90p.) EALB 1972 KE

Prost, A.
Grammaire gourmantché. See: Chantoux, A.

Prost, A.
Les langues mandé-sud du groupe mana-busa. 182pp. maps. CFA1600 (Mémoires de l'IFAN, 26) IFAN 1953 SG FRE

Prost, R.P.A.
Contribution à l'étude de quelques langues voltaiques. 461pp. map. (F64.00) (Mémoires de l'IFAN, 70) IFAN 1964 SG FRE

Prost, R.P.A.
Contribution à l'étude des langues voltaiques. 461pp. map. CFA3200 pap. (Mémoires de l'IFAN, 70) IFAN 1964 SG FRE

Prost, R.P.A.
La langue Sonay et ses dialectes. 627pp. (F60.00) (Mémoires de l'IFAN, 47) IFAN 1956 SG FRE

Proutière A. Baudet, J.B.
Annales de l'université d'Abidjan. 173pp. CFA1,170 (F23.40) (Série C-Sciences, 11) Univ Abidjan 1975 IV FRE

Proutière, A. et al.
Annales de l'université d'Abidjan. 258pp. CFA1500 (F30.00) (Série C-Sciences, 4) Univ Abidjan 1968 IV FRE

Pryse, B.E.
Let's look at literature. 200pp. 62k Pilgrim 1964 NR

Publications (Central Africa)
Bulawayo directory, 1975. 14th ed. 187pp. R$5.00 Publ Central Africa 1975 RH

Publications (Central Africa)
City of Umtali directory. 45pp. R$2.00 Publ Central Africa annual RH

Publications (Central Africa)
Copperbelt directory. 4th ed. 112pp. K2.00 Publ Central Africa (annual) RH

Publications (Central Africa)
Gwelo directory, 1974/75. 3rd ed. 32pp. fold. map. R$3.00 Publ Central Africa 1975 RH

Publications (Central Africa)
Lusaka directory. 4th ed. 84pp. K2.00 Publ Central Africa annual RH

Publications (Central Africa)
Malawi directory. 7th ed. 98pp. K2.00 Publ Central Africa (annual) RH

Publications (Central Africa)
Ndola directory. 4th ed. 36pp. K2.00 Publ Central Africa annual RH

Publications (Central Africa)
Rhodesia-Zambia-Malawi directory. 63rd ed. 1378pp. R$10.00 Publ Central Africa annual RH

Publications (Central Africa)
Salisbury directory, 1975. 14th ed. 458pp. R$7.00 Publ Central Africa 1975 RH

Publications (Central Africa)
Zambia directory. 9th ed. 354pp. K3.00 Publ Central Africa annual H

Pullen, V.L.
The Holy Spirit. 2nd ed. 40pp. 20k SIM 1969 NR

Pullen, V.L.
How to win souls. 54pp. 20k SIM 1967 NR

Pullybank, E., ed.
Visitors guide to Lagos. See: Seriki, E., ed.

Purdie, J.E.
Five hundred and sixty seven Christian answers. 96pp. K.shs.6.50 Evangel 1969 KE

Purnell & Sons.
This is South Africa. 144pp. col. pl. cl. R6.95 Purnell 1977 SA

Qangule, Z.S.
The making of a servant and other poems. See: Kavanagh, R.

Qoudous, I.A.
Le voleur d'autobus. Tr. fr. Arabic A. Mazouni 264pp. DA9.60 SNED 1971 AE FRE

Quarcoopome, T.N.O.
The Acts of apostles: comprehensive studies. 116pp. C3.00 Afram 1975 GH

Quarcoopome, T.N.O.
History and religion of Israel. From Samuel to the fall of the northern kingdom. 204pp. C4.25 Afram 1975 GH

Quarcoopome, T.N.O.
St. Luke's gospel: comprehensive studies. 116pp. C2.85 Afram 1975 GH

Quarcoopome, T.N.O.
St Mark's gospel: comprehensive studies. 64pp. C2.25 Afram 1975 GH

Quartey, J.A.K.
The role of science in national development. 21pp. C1.00 ($1.00/50p.) (Inaugural lecture) Ghana UP 1972 GH

Quartey, J.K.   Arku Mensha, D.
Onyifurafo n'awar mu. [A blind man's marriage problems.] 47pp. 35pes. Bur Ghana Lang 1973 GH FAT

Quin, P.J.
Foods and feeding habits of the Pedi: with special reference to identification, classification, preparation and nutritive value of the respective foods. 278pp. pl. cl. R15.00 Witwatersrand UP 1959 SA

Quinn, G.D., ed.   Immelman, R.F.M., ed.   Spohr, O.H., ed.
Handlist of manuscripts in the University of Cape Town libraries. 1 81pp. photos. R1.50 (U.C.T. libraries Varia series, 10) Univ Cape Town Lib 1968 SA

Quinn, G.D., ed.
Index to William Ritchie's 'The history of the South African College' and Eric A. Walker's 'The South African College and the University of Cape Town'. 22pp. R1.00 (U.C.T. libraries, Varia series, 7) Univ Cape Town Lib 1964 SA

Quinn, G.D.
The rebellion of 1914-15. 22pp. R1.20 (Univ. Cape Town Libraries. Bibl. ser.) Univ Cape Town Lib 1974 SA

Quinn-Young, C.T.   White, J.E.H.
Geography for Nigerian schools. 2nd ed. bk. 3: Africa. 94pp. ill. maps. N1.50 (82p) Evans - Nig 1973 NR

Rabie, A.
South African environmental legislation. R8.00 Inst For and Comp Law 1976 SA

Radford, W.   Preen, G.
Adventure across Africa. 103pp. ill. K.shs4.95 ($2.00) EAPH 1968 KE

Radford, W.
The elephant's heart. 32pp. ill. K.shs1.65 ($1.00) EAPH 1969 KE

Radford, W.   Preen, G.
Flying doctor. 96pp. ill. K.shs4.95 ($2.00) EAPH 1970 KE

Radford, W.
Game park holiday. 38pp. ill. K.shs2.00 ($1.00) EAPH 1967 KE

Raditladi, L.D.
Motswasele II: [Historical drama]. repr. in new orthography ed. 108pp. cl. R1.00 (Bantu treasury, 9) Witwatersrand UP 1970 SA TSW

Radosevic, B.
The coal resources of the Zambezi valley. v.6: Mulungwa coalfield - a preliminary report. 55n (Dept. of Geological Survey. Economic Reports, 20) Geol Survey - Zam 1969 ZA

Radu, G.
Algèbre homologique. v. 1: Les modules sur un anneau commutatif. See: Mangalo, C.

Rafig, B.A.
The Muslim prayer book. 64pp. photos. ($1.50) Ghana Publ Corp 1975 GH

Raikes, P., ed.   Amann, V.F., ed.
Project appraisal and evaluation in agriculture. 306pp. U.shs.50.00 ($8.50) Mak Inst Soc Res 1974 UG

Raikes, P. L.
Fertilizer projections for Tanzania up to 1974. T.shs.12.00 ($3.00) (Research pap., 74.2) Econ Res Bur - Tanz 1974 TZ

Raikes, P.L.
Historical development of wheat production in N.Mbulu district. 35pp. maps. T.shs12.00 ($3.00) (Research pap., 70.3) Econ Res Bur - Tanz 1970 TZ

Raikes, P.L.
Prospects for exporting agricultural produce to Zambia. 43pp. T.shs12.00 ($3.00) (Research pap., 68.12) Econ Res Bur - Tanz 1968 TZ

Rajih, S.A.
The complete story of Nigeria civil war. 56pp. 50k Survival 1971 NR

Rakoto-Arison, W.
Etude géologique et prospection de la feuille Tsiroanoman-mandidy. 22pp. pl. map. FMG794 (F15.88) (Travaux du Bureau Géologique, 103) Service Geol - Mad 1960 MG FRE

Rakotoarison, W.
Etude géologique et prospection des feuilles Kiranomena-Mahasambo-Analabe. See: Delubac, C.

Rakotoarison, W.
Etude géologique et prospection des feuilles Tananarive-Manjakandriana. See: Delubac, C.

Rakotoarison, W.
Etue géologique et prospection des feuilles: Miarinarivo-Arivonimamo. See: Delubac, C.

Rakotoarivelo, H.
Etude palynologique de quelques échantillons de Houille du bassin de la Sokoa (Madagascar) 49pp. pl. FMG500 (F10.00) Service Geol - Mad 1960 MG FRE

Rakotonanahary, et al.
Etude géologique et prospection de la région d'Ampangabe-Jaba (coupure spéciale d'Ambohimanga). Le gisement de périodotite nickelifère d'Ampangabe-Jaba. 14pp. pl. map photos. FMG235 (F4.70) (Série Documentation, 148) Service Geol - Mad 1960 MG FRE

Rakotonanahary.
Etude géologique et prospection de la feuille Ambohimahas. 17pp. pl. map. FMG590 (F11.80) (Travaux du Bureau Géologique, 115) Service Geol - Mad 1963 MG FRE

Rakotonanahary.
Etue géologique et prospection des feuilles: Miarinarivo-Arivonimamo. See: Delubac, C.

Rakotondranaivo, A.
Fiaraha-monina: fanabeazana fototra. [Coexistence: basis for study.] 178pp. TPL 1976 MG MLA

Rakotondrasoa.
Etude géologique et prospection des feuilles Ambohimiandra, Fenoarivo, Soavinandriana. See: Joo, J.

Ralaitafika, P.S.
Tahirin'antsihanaka 47. [Receuils 1947.] 500pp. FMG500 Ed Takariva 1975 MG MLA

Rald, J.
Ujamaa: problems of implementation (Experiences from West Lake) 33pp. maps. T.shs.7.00 (Research report, 10) Bur Res Assess Tanz 1971 TZ

Ralebitso, A.
Grade A: Motataisi. 64pp. ill. 70c. Longman SA 1963 SA SOS

Ralebitso, A.
Grade B: Itataise. 48pp. ill. 70c. Longman SA 1968 SA SOS

Ralebitso, A.
Teacher's guide to grade A: Mothusi da motataisi. 80pp. ill. 60c. Longman SA 1964 SA SOS

Ralebitso, A.
Teacher's guide to grade B: Mothusi da mitataisi. 48pp. ill. 80c. Longman SA 1968 SA SOS

Ralls, A.
Glory which was yours. 50c. Shuter 1949 SA

Ram Das, M.
Junior history. 144pp. K.shs.11.00 Textbook Ctre 1968 KE

Ram, K.
A guide to the Co-operative Societies Act. See: Craw, W.

Ramarolahy.
Tajirin'ny ntaolo. [Receuil ancien.] 104pp. FMG200 Ed Takariva 1974 MG MLA

Ramsaran, J.
New approaches to African literature: a guide to Negro-African writing and related studies. 2nd ed. 168pp. N3.00 Ibadan UP 1970 NR

Ranc, O.
Mathématique. Collection I.R.E.M. Dakar, classe de 4e. See: Branton, M.

Randall, I. Randall, P.
Cross, castle and compass. 112pp. ill. 95c. Shuter 1968 SA

Randall, I. Randall, P.
Junior verse series: field and fountain. bk. 2 80pp. ill. 40c. Shuter 1966 SA

Randall, I. Randall, P.
Junior verse series: happy hours. bk. 1 64pp. ill. 35c. Shuter 1963 SA

Randall, I. Randall, P.
Junior verse series: sunshine and shadow. bk. 3 70pp. ill. 55c. Shuter 1962 SA

Randall, I. Randall, P.
Junior verse series: winding trails. 4 74pp. ill. 55c. Shuter 1963 SA

Randall, P.
Cross, castle and compass. See: Randall, I.

Randall, P., ed.
Power, privilege and poverty. 127pp. R1.00 ($2.95/£1.50 pap.) (Spro-cas occas. pub., 7) Ravan 1972 SA

Randall, P., ed.
Some implications of inequality. 64pp. 75c (Spro-cas occas. pub., 4) Ravan 1971 SA

Randall, P., ed.
South Africa'a political alternatives. Report of the Political Commission of the Study Project on Christianity in Apartheid Society. 252pp. R2.00 ($6.25/£3.25) Ravan 1973 SA

Randall, P., ed.
Towards social change. 2nd ed. 197pp. R1.50 ($3.75/£1.95) (Spro-cas occas. pub., 6) Ravan 1972 SA

Randall, P. Desai, Yunus.
From 'coolie location' to group area: a brief account of Johannesburg's Indian community. 19pp. photos. 35c. ($1.25) SA Inst of Race Relations 1967 SA

Randall, P. Burrow, P.C.
Johannesburg's coloured community with especial reference to Riverlea. 49pp. photos. 50c. ($1.30) SA Inst of Race Relations 1968 SA

Randall, P.
Junior verse series: field and fountain. bk. 2 See: Randall, I.

Randall, P.
Junior verse series: happy hours. bk. 1 See: Randall, I.

Randall, P.
Junior verse series: sunshine and shadow. bk. 3 See: Randall, I.

Randall, P.
Junior verse series: winding trails. 4 See: Randall, I.

Randall, P.
South Africa's minorities. 77pp. 75c (Spro-cas occas. pub., 2) Ravan 1971 SA

Randall, P.
A taste of power. 2nd. ed. 225pp. ill. R.2.50 Ravan 1973 SA

Randell, G.H. van Niekirk, J.P. Bax, K.C.
South African attorneys handbook. 310pp. hd. R11.75 Butterworths 1968 SA

Randolph, R.H.
Aspects of Catholic life in Rhodesia. 56pp. 55c. (Mambo Missio-Pastoral Series, 3) Mambo 1974 RH

Randolph, R.H.
Statistics of the Roman Catholic church in Rhodesia. 38pp. 50c. (Mambo Missio-Pastoral Series, 6) Mambo 1976 RH

Ranger, T.O.
The African churches of Tanzania. 27pp. K.shs2.50 ($1.00) EAPH 1970 KE

Ranger, T.O.
The African voice in Southern Rhodesia. 242pp. K.shs.18.50 ($5.80) EAPH 1970 KE

Ranger, T.O.
The agricultural history of Zambia. 32pp. 45n. (Haz pamphlets, 1) Neczam 1972 ZA

Ranger, T.O.
Emerging themes of African history. 222pp. K.shs.40.00 cl. K.shs20.00 pap. ($8.00 cl.) ($5.20 pap.) EAPH 1968 KE

Ranger, T.O.
The recovery of African initiative in Tanzanian history. 15pp. ill. T.shs.1.00 (Inaugural lecture, 2) Univ Dar es Salaam 1969 TZ

Ranger, T.O.
State and church in Southern Rhodesia, 1919-1939. R$1.00 (Local series pamphlets, 4) Central Africa Hist Assoc 1962 RH

Ransford, O.
Bulawayo: historic battleground of Rhodesia. 192pp. pl. hd. fl. 38.25 Balkema 1968 SA

Ransford, O. Steyn, P.
Historic Rhodesia. 96pp. col. pl. R$2.95 (Bundu series) Longman - Rhod 1975 RH

Ransford, O.
Rhodesian tapestry. A history in needlework from the embroideries of the Women's institutes of Rhodesia. 96pp. col. ill. 750. Books of Rhodesia 1971 RH

Ranson, B.
A sociological study of Moyamba town. 110pp. N1.25 (1.00/$2.50) Inst Admin - Zaria 1968 NR

Rantoanina, M.
Etude géologique et prospection des feuilles Ambakireny-Andilanatoby. 21pp. dess. map. FMG983 (F19.66) (Travaux du Bureau Géologique, 129) Service Geol - Mad 1968 MG FRE

Rantoanina, M.
Etude géologique et prospection des feuilles: Beanana-Rantabe. 22pp. pl. photo. map. FMG901 (F18.02) (Travaux du Bureau Géologique, 99) Service Geol - Mad 1960 MG FRE

Rantoanina, M.
Etude géologique et prospection des feuilles: Itermo-Ambatofinandrahana. See: Delubac, C.

Rantoanina, M.
Etude géologique et prospection des feuilles Maevatanana-Andriba, Antsitabe. 25pp. pl. maps. FMG2385 (F47.70) (Travaux du Bureau Géologique, 125) Service Geol - Mad 1967 MG FRE

Rantoanina, M.
Etude géologique et prospection des feuilles: Ranomafana-Brickaville. 19pp. pl. map. FMG825 (F16.50) (Travaux du Bureau Géologique, 98) Service Geol - Mad 1960 MG FRE

Rantoanina, M.
Etude géologique et prospection des feuilles Tananarive-Manjakandriana. See: Delubac, C.

Rantoanina, M.
Géologie et prospection des feuilles: Moramanga-Lakato. 27pp. pl. map. FMG850 (F17.00) (Travaux du Bureau Géologique, 111) Service Geol - Mad 1962 MG FRE

Rantoanina, M.
Les gisements fer-nickel des environs de Moramanga. See: Delbos, L.

Rapatsalahy, Z.
Hiteraka aho. [Accoucher.] 70pp. FMG200 Ed Takariva 1975 MG MLA

Raper, P.E.
Onomastic source guide. pt. 1. 40pp. R2.00 Human Science Res Council 1970 SA

Raper, P.E.
Source guide for toponymy and topology. 478pp. R15.00 ($17.50) (Onomastics series, 5) Human Science Res Council 1975 SA

Raper, P.E.
South African Centre of onomastic sciences. 16pp. photos. free Human Science Res Council 1972 SA

Raper, P.E.
Toponymical practice. 64pp. R2.85 (Onomastics series, 4) Human Science Res Council 1975 SA

Rapp, A., ed. Temple, P., ed. Berry, L., ed.
Studies in soil erosion and sedimentation in Tanzania. pl. T.shs.125.00 (Monograph series, 1) Bur Res Assess - Tanz 1973 TZ

Rasik, A.
Divorce before marriage. 146pp. K.shs.12.00 Africa Book Serv 1968 KE

Rasmussen, B.H.
The transition from manuscript to printed book. 25pp. 30c Univ Rhodesia Lib 1962 RH

Rasoamahenina, J.A.
Etude géologique et prospection de la feuille: Ambatomanoina. 27pp. pl. map. FMG988 (F19.76) (Travaux du Bureau Géologique, 128) Service Geol - Mad 1968 MG FRE

Rasoamahenina, J.A.
Etude géologique et prospection des bassins de la Sambao, de la Manigoza et de la Ranobe (N.O. Madagascar) 59pp. pl. map. FMG1160 (F23.20) (Travaux du Bureau Géologique, 133) Service Geol - Mad 1970 MG FRE

Rasoanasy, Jeanne.
Menalamba sy tanindrazana: ny lasan'i Madagasikara. [Rebels and the fatherland.] 316pp. TPL 1976 MG MLA

Ratismbazafy, J.R.
Contribution au projet d'aménagement de la plaine de Tananarive. Etude de 3 sites de barrages) 166pp. pl. FMG1790 (F35.80) Service Geol - Mad 1970 MG FRE

Rattigan, T.
The Winslow boy. 160pp. R1.70 Longman - SA 1976 SA

Ratz, C.C.
God's will for you. 32pp. K.shs.2.00 Evangel 1972 KE

Ratz, C.C.
Light for God's people. 70pp. K.shs.4.00 Evangel 1973 KE

Ratz, C.C.
Sermons for Africa. bk.1 32pp. K.shs.2.50 Evangel 1972 KE

Ratz, C.C.
What do you think? 32pp. K.shs.2.00 Evangel 1975 KE

Ratz, C.C.
Words make a man. 32pp. K.shs.2.00 Evangel 1975 KE

Ratz, C.C.
The young Christian and witnessing. 112pp. K.shs.4.00 Evangel 1973 KE

Ratzlaff, J., comp.
Shona language lessons. See: Fivaz, D., comp.

Rauche, G.A.
The problem of truth and reality in Grisebach's thought. R3.50 Van Schaik SA

Rauf, M.A.
Islam faith and devotion. 133pp. N3.50 Islamic 1974 NR

Rauf, M.A.
The sacred texts of Islam. (Al Qur'an and Al Hadith) 97pp. N3.50 Islamic 1974 NR

Ravan Press (Pty.) Ltd.
The making of a servant. Xhosa poems. 75c. ($1.50/75p.) Ravan 1972 SA

Raven-Hart, R.
Cape Good Hope 1652-1702: the first fifty years of Dutch colonisation as seen by callers. 553pp. ill. hd. fl. 135.00 Balkema 1971 SA

Raven-Hart, R., ed.
Before Van Riebeeck. 240pp. ill. maps. cl. R4.75 Struik 1967 SA

Raymaekers, P. Van Moorsel, H.
Dessins rupestres du Bas-Congo (Lovo) pl. map. 80k Press Univ Zaire 1964 ZR FRE

Raymond, Abbe.
Je t'aimerai d'un amour éternel. Manuel et guide pour le sacrement de mariage. See: Brisbois, P.R.

Raynaut, C.
Quelques données de l'horticulture dans la vallée de Maradi. 164pp. map. CFA1250 (F25.00) (Etudes Nigeriennes, 26) Inst Rech Sci Hum 1969 NG FRE

Rayner, A.A.
A first course in biometry for agriculture students. 626pp. R15.00 Univ of Natal 1969 SA

Razafiniparany, A.
Les charnockites du socle précambrien de Madagascar. 289pp. pl. FMG3800 (F76.00) (Série Documentation, 179) Service Geol - Mad 1969 MG FRE

Razafiniparany, A.
Les charnockites du socle précambrien de Madagascar. 209pp. pl. FMG3800 (F76.00) Service Geol - Mad 1969 MG FRE

Rea, F.B.
Chapel dedication ceremony address. 8pp. Free Univ Rhodesia Lib 1968 RH

Rea, K.
A few thoughts on leadership. 26pp. pl. 15c Rhod Lit Bur 1963 RH

Rea, W.F.
The Bemba's white chief. 75c. (Local series pamphlets, 13) Central Africa Hist Assoc 1964 RH

Rea, W.F.
George Westbeech and the Barostseland missionaries 1878-1888. 75c. (Local series pamphlets, 21) Central Africa Hist Assoc 1968 RH

Rea, W.F.
The missionary factor in Southern Rhodesia. 60c. (Local series pamphlets, 7) Central Africa Hist Assoc 1962 RH

Rea, W.F.
Rhodesian history in 1960. 50c. (Local series pamphlets, 3) Central Africa Hist Assoc 1961 RH

Read, A.K.
Programmed instruction and teaching machines in the pure and applied sciences to 1964. 21pp. R1.60 Dept Bibliog, Lib & Typo 1965 SA

Read, J.H.
Quelea. 40pp. R2.10 Dept Bibliog, Lib & Typo 1966 SA

Reader, D.H. May, J.
Drinking patterns in Rhodesia: Highfield African township. 50pp. R$1.00 (Dept. of Sociology, Univ. of Rhodesia, 5) Univ Rhodesia Lib 1971 RH

Reader, D.H.
Social distortion - an approach to race relations. 30pp.
30c Univ Rhodesia Lib 1969 RH

Red Cross Society, Tanzania.
Njira ya kugiriria mirimu ya maitho na utumumu.
[Prevention of eye troubles and blindness] K.shs0.50
EALB KE KIK

Redcliffe-Maud, Lord.
National progress and the university. 16pp. 25c.
(University of Cape Town T.B. Davie memorial lecture, 13)
Univ Cape Town Lib 1972 SA

Reed, D.
The battle of Rhodesia. 7th ed. ed. 172pp. R2.10 cl.
Haum 1966 SA

Reed, D.
The siege of Southern Africa. 264pp. photos. cl.
R6.50 No U.S. Macmillan - SA 1974 SA

Rees, E.
Pathway to music reading. v. 1 24pp. music. 25c.
Shuter 1956 SA

Rees, E.
Pathway to music reading. v. 2 32pp. music. 30c.
Shuter 1956 SA

Rees, E.
Pathway to music reading. v. 3 40pp. music. 40c.
Shuter 1958 SA

Rees, E.
Rudiments of music. 48pp. music. 55c. Shuter
1958 SA

Rees, W.
Colenso letters from Natal. 440pp. photos. cl. R4.20
Shuter 1958 SA

Reeve, W.H.
The geology and mineral resources of Northern Rhodesia.
K10.50 (Dept. of Geological Survey, Bulletins, 3) Geol
Survey - Zam 1963 ZA

Reeves, D.
Your prayers. 32pp. 60pes. (20p.) Africa Christian
1970 GH

Regan, A.
From school to city. 48pp. K.shs.6.50 (Gaba Pastoral
Papers, 27) Gaba 1973 KE

Rehfisch, F.
Social structure of a Mambila village. 197pp. N2.00
(Dept. of Sociology, Occas. pap., 2) Dept Soc - ABU
1972 NR

Rehman, K.A.
The national bibliography of Zambia 1970-71. 128pp.
ex. only Nat Archives - Zambia 1973 ZA

Rehman, K.A.
The national bibliography of Zambia, 1972. 60pp. 45n
Nat Archives - Zam 1973 ZA

Reichwalder, P.
Brick-clay deposits at Kasondi Dambo, Ngwerere river and
other localities near Lusaka. K2.00 (Dept. of
Geological Survey, Economic Reports, 42) Geol Survey -
Zam 1976 ZA

Reid, A.M.
Earth, moon and planets: a contemporary geological view
of the solar system. 10pp. 30c. (Univ. Cape Town.
Inaugural lec. new series, 40) Univ Cape Town Lib 1976
SA

Reid, J.V.O., ed. Wilmot, A.J., eds.
Medical education in South Africa. 391pp. cl. R10.50
Univ of Natal 1965 SA

Reimers, J.H.W.
The change of form during growth of the dairy cow.
42pp. 20c. (A v.4, no. 1) Univ Stellenbosch, Lib
1928 SA

Reimers, J.H.W.
Correlations in the exterior of milk cattle. 20pp. 15c.
(A v.3, no. 2) Univ Stellenbosch, Lib 1925 SA

Reimers, J.H.W. Swart, J.C.
Relation between the diameter, the extensibility and the
carrying capacity of wool fibers. 33pp. 20c. (A v.8,
no. 3) Univ Stellenbosch, Lib 1939 SA

Reinach, S.G.
The effects of existing methods of property valuation and
taxation on the ratepayers. R2.00 (Inst. for Planning
Research, series B, 4) Inst Planning Res 1974 SA

Reininga, W.
Accounts: record keeping. bk. 1 205pp. N1.50
Onibonoje 1966 NR

Reitz, C.H.
The Reitz family. 38pp. 80c. Univ Cape Town Lib
1964 SA

Relton, H.
Contact 1 teacher's book. See: Murison-Bowie, S.C.

Remili, A.
Les institutions administratives algériennes. 296pp.
DA10.50 SNED 1967 AE FRE

Remnant, G.
Gardening in East and Central Africa. 256pp. ill. col. ill.
pl. K.shs.30.00 Transafrica 1975 KE

Remnant, G.
A guide to gardening in Eastern Africa. 128pp.
K.shs.35.00 Heinemann Educ - Nair 1977 KE

Remtulla, K., eds.
Adult education and national development. Proceedings of
the Third Conference of the African Adult Association, held
at the University of Dar es Salaam, 19-24 April, 1971.
See: Hall, B.L., eds.

Renaud, P., ed.
Pour bien parler français, méthode de langage à l'usage
des sections d'initiation au langage. 2, 6 v. 126pp.
CFA500 Univ Cameroun 1970 CM FRE

Renaud, P., ed.
Pour bien parler français, méthode de langage à l'usage
des sections d'initiation au langage. 3, 6 v. 136pp.
CFA500 Univ Cameroun 1970 CM FRE

Renaud, P., ed.
Pour bien parler français, méthode de langage à l'usage
des sections d'initiation au langage. 4, 6 v. 144pp.
CFA500 Univ Cameroun 1971 CM FRE

Renaud, P., ed.
Pour bien parler français, méthode de langage à l'usage
des sections d'initiation au langage. 5, 6 v. 140pp.
CFA500 Univ Cameroun 1971 CM FRE

Renaud, P., ed.
Pour bien parler français, méthode de langage à l'usage
des sections d'initiation au langage. 6, 6 v. 139pp.
CFA500 Univ Cameroun 1971 CM FRE

Renaud, P., ed.
Pour bien parler français, méthode de langage à l'usage
des sections d'initiation au language. 1, 6 v. 139pp.
CFA500 Univ Cameroun 1970 CM FRE

Renaud, P.
Initiation à l'enquête linguistique. See: Canu, G.

Renaud, P.
Pour bien parler français en CM2, étude typologique et
statistique. 58pp. CFA500 Univ Cameroun 1969 CM
FRE

Renaud, P.
La réalité scolaire au Cameroun oriental. 55pp.
CFA500 Univ Cameroun 1968 CM FRE

Renaudeau, M.
Musée de Dakar - Témoin de l'art Nègre. 146pp. ill. pl.
col. ill. CFA3000 Africa only Nouv Ed Afric 1973 SG
FRE

Renaudeau, R.
Littérature africaine. L'engagement. See: Fouet, F.

Renault, F
Libération d'esclaves et nouvelle servitude. 240pp.
CFA1,800 (F36.00) Nouv Ed Afric 1976 SG FRE

Author Index

Rennhackkamp, W.M.H.
School lighting. 47pp. ill. (CSIR research reports, 209)
CSIR 1964 SA

Rennie, J.V.L.
The border region: natural environment and land use in the Eastern Cape. v. 1 Maps See: Mountain, E.D.

Rennie, J.V.L., ed.
The border region: natural environment and land use in the Eastern Cape. v. 2 Text See: Mountain, E.D., ed.

Rennie, K.J., ed.   Robins, K., ed.
Social problems in Zambia, readings. 111pp. K1.35 (Studies in Zambian Society, 1) Univ Zambia Bkshop; distr. 1976 ZA

Retief, R.L.
Thupi la munthu. See: Pretorius, P.V.

Retord, G.
Annales de l'université d'Abidjan. L'agni, variété dialectale sanwi: phonologie, analyses tomographiques, documents. 212pp. CFA1050 (F21.00) (Série H-Linguistique, 5) Univ Abidjan 1972 IV FRE

Retord, G.
Kó di? Cours de Dioula. See: Dumestre, G.

Reyment, M.A.
The future of geology in Nigeria. 2nd ed. 13pp. map. 30k Ibadan UP 1964 NR

Reynal, R.
Les particularités du droit fiscal par rapport au droit privé en matière d'enregistrement au Maroc. Dir35.00 (Coll. Fac. des Sciences juridiques, économiques et sociales, 14) Ed La Porte 1962 MR FRE

Reynolds, B.
Grahamstown from cottage to village. See: Reynolds, R.

Reynolds, R.   Reynolds, B.
Grahamstown from cottage to village. 112pp. photos. cl. R20.00 R7.50 (South African Yesterdays, 5) Philip 1974 SA

Rhodes University, Department of Geography.
South African Universities Geographical Conference. Proceedings of the 4th conference, Grahamstown. R2.00 Rhodes Univ Lib 1972 SA

Rhodesia Literature Bureau.
Detembai vadiki tinzwe. [Recite children, let us hear.] 69pp. 39c Mambo 1976 RH SHO

Rhodesia Literature Bureau.
Mabvumira enhetembo. [The unison of poetry.] 139pp. 70c Mambo 1969 RH SHO

Rhodesia Literature Bureau.
Musha unofadza. [A happy home.] 24pp. pl. 10c. Rhod Lit Bur 1958 RH SHO

Rhodesia Literature Bureau.
Nhetembo. [Poetry.] 228pp. pl. R$1.20 Mambo 1972 RH SHO

Rhodesia Literature Bureau.
Ugqozi lwezimbongi. [The poet's inspiration.] 156pp. 90c Mambo 1973 RH NDE

Rhodesia Literature Bureau.
Zvamazuva ano. [Ourselves and the boys today.] tr. fr. English. 20pp. pl. 15c Rhod Lit Bur 1962 RH SHO

Rhoodie, E.M.
Penal systems of the Commonwealth. 258pp. R8.50 cl. Human and Rousseau 1966 SA

Ribeiro, E.
Muchadura. [You shall confess.] 128pp. 40c Mambo 1967 RH SHO

Ribeiro, E.F.
Ndakaitei. [What a mess.] 121pp. pl. 70c Longman - Rhod 1974 RH SHO

Rice, R.C.
The Tanzania price control system. Theory, practice and some possible improvement. 47pp. T.shs.12.00 ($3.00) (Research pap., 76.4) Econ Res Bur - Tanz 1976 TZ

Richard, M.
Histoire, tradition et promotion de la femme chez les Batanga. 154pp. (DM22.00) (CEEBA. série II, Mémoires et Monographies, 2) CEEBA 1970 ZR FRE

Richards, A.I.
Bemba marriage and present economic conditions. 123pp. K1.75 (88p.) (Rhodes-Livingstone paps., 4) Inst Soc Res - Zam 1940 ZA

Richards, A.I.
Economic development and tribal change. 360pp. maps. K.shs.60.00 OUP - Nairobi 1974 KE

Richards, C.
Apwoyo jaoledhi kod johana mofuwo. See: Wortington, F.W.

Richards, C.G., ed.
Burton and Lake Tanganyika. 2nd ed. 72pp. K.shs2.50 ($1.50/60p.) EALB 1965 KE

Richards, C.G., ed.
Count Teleki and the discovery of Lakes Rudolf and Stefanie. 85pp. map. K.shs3.30 ($1.50/60p.) EALB 1960 KE

Richards, C.G.
Kagituju kajigi na Johana muritu. See: Worthington, F.

Richards, C.G.
Kisa cha Yohana mjinga. [The tale of simple John] 20pp. ill. K.shs.1.75 OUP-Nairobi 1963 KE SWA

Richards, C.G.
Ludwig Krapf [in Swahili]. 2nd ed. 126pp. ill. K.shs.3.00 ($1.50/60p.) EALB 1963 KE SWA

Richards, C.G.R.
Some historic journeys in East Africa. 144pp. ills. K.shs12.50 OUP-Nairobi 1968 KE

Richards, D.   Walker, C.
Walk through the wilderness. ill. col. photos. R11.25 Purnell 1975 SA

Richards, H.
False dawn. 230pp. ill. maps. cl. R$5.50 R$6.75 Books of Rhodesia 1974 RH

Richards, H.M.
Next year will be better; and the verse of 'T.' [Reprint of ed. 1952]. 262pp. ill. hd. R$8.80 (Rhodesiana Reprint Library, Silver Series, 5) Books of Rhodesia 1975 RH

Richards, M.P., comp.
Bygone Days by W.H. Somerset Bell. An index. gratis Johannesburg Public Lib 1969 SA

Richards, M.P.
Mountaineering in Southern Africa. 28pp. R1.60 Dept Bibliog, Lib & Typo 1966 SA

Richards, S.J.
The influence of ceiling insulation on indoor thermal conditions in dwellings of heavy weight construction under South African conditions. See: Lotz, F.J.

Richardson, E.M.
Aushi village structure in the Fort Rosebery district of Northern Rhodesia. 36pp. 35n. (18p.) (Rhodes-Livingstone communications, 13) Inst Afr Stud - Lusaka 1959 ZA

Richman, C.
Ramblers, riddles and jokes. 40pp. 20k Gebo 1972 NR

Richter, J.
South West. [Also available in German]. See: Cubitt, G.

Ridout, R.   Ogunlesi, J.S.
English for Africans: workbook. 1, 3 bks. 32pp. 25k Pilgrim 1971 NR

Ridout, R.   Ogunlesi, J.S.
English for Africans: workbook. 2, 3 bks. 32pp. 25k Pilgrim 1971 NR

Ridout, R.   Ogunlesi, J.S.
English for Africans: workbook. 3, 3 bks. 32pp. 25k Pilgrim 1971 NR

Ridout, R.
   The facts of English.   See: Witting C.
Ridout, R.
   Structural English workbooks.   1, 8 bks.   32pp.   25k
   Pilgrim 1967 NR
Ridout, R.
   Structural English workbooks.   2, 8 bks.   32pp.   25k
   Pilgrim 1967 NR
Ridout, R.
   Structural English workbooks.   3, 8 bks.   32pp.   25k
   Pilgrim 1967 NR
Ridout, R.
   Structural English workbooks.   4, 8 bks.   32pp.   25k
   Pilgrim 1967 NR
Ridout, R.
   Structural English workbooks.   5, 8 bks.   48pp.   33k
   Pilgrim 1967 NR
Ridout, R.
   Structural English workbooks.   6, 8 bks.   48pp.   33k
   Pilgrim 1967 NR
Ridout, R.
   Structural English workbooks.   7, 8 bks.   48pp.   33k
   Pilgrim 1967 NR
Ridout, R.
   Structural English workbooks.   8, 8 bks.   48pp.   33k
   Pilgrim 1967 NR
Riebeeck, J. van.
   Journal of Jan van Riebeeck, 1651-1662.   3 vols.
   1414pp. pl. hd.   fl. 112.50   Balkema 1952-58 SA
Riekert, H.
   Waste paper recovery. Additional quantities still available
   for collection.   pt.2   See: White, M.D.
Riekert, H.
   Waste paper recovery: an introductory survey.
   See: White, M.D.
Rigby, P.
   Cattle and kinship among the Gogo.   355pp. hd.
   U.shs.77.00   (M.I.S.R. individual monog., 16)   Mak Inst
   Soc Res 1969 UG
Rigby, P., ed.
   Society and social change in Eastern Africa.   56pp.
   U.shs4.00   (M.I.S.R. Nkanga ed., 4)   Mak Inst Soc Res
   1969 UG
Rigby, P.J.
   Patterns of income and expenditure, Blantyre-Limbe,
   Nyasaland.   See: Bettison, D.G.
Riise, U.
   Flood control: Mkondoa river system - hydrological
   records.   10pp. map.   T.shs.7.00   (Research report,
   17)   Bur Res Assess - Tanz 1970 TZ
Riise, U.
   Statistical characteristics of four Tanzanian rivers.   19pp.
   T.shs.7.00   (Research report, 1)   Bur Res Assess- Tanz
   1972 TZ
Rimmer, E.M., et al.
   Zaman Mutum Da Sana'Arsa.   [Man and his occupation]
   199pp.   N1.50   Northern Nig 1948 NR HAU
Rimmer, E.M.
   Mu Koyi Hausa.   [Let's learn Hausa]   32pp.   50k
   Northern Nig 1954 NR HAU
Rinchon, R.P.D.
   Pierre Ignace-Liévin van Alstein, capitaine négrier. Gand,
   1733, Nantes, 1793.   452pp. ill. maps pl.   CFA4000
   (Mémoires de l'IFAN, 71)   IFAN 1964 SG FRE
Ringrose, H.G.
   Trade unions in Natal. $1.25   (Natal regional survey
   pub., 4)   Dept Econ, Natal 1951 SA
Riordan, J., et al.
   Lumko Xhosa self-instruction course.   R3.50   Lumko
   Inst 1968 SA
Rip, C.M.
   Contemporary social pathology.   4th ed.   157pp. hd.
   R3.95   Human & Rousseau 1976 SA

Ririani, R.
   The burning house.   28pp. ill.   K.shs6.00   Njogu KE
Ririani, R.
   The lazy hyena.   20pp. ill.   K.shs4.00   Njogu KE
Ririani, R.
   The naughty hyena.   20pp. ill.   K.shs4.00   Njogu KE
Ririani, R.
   The sisters who were afraid.   28pp. ill.   K.shs6.00
   Njogu KE
Risbec, J.
   Les Chalcidoides d'A.O.F.; II. Les microgasterinae d'A.O.F.
   [Reprint of ed. 1951].   473pp. ill.   (D.fl.140.00)
   (Mémoires de l'IFAN, 13)   IFAN 1951 SG FRE
Ritchie, J.F.
   The African as suckling and as adult: a psychological
   study.   K1.50   (75p.)   (Rhodes-Livingstone paps., 9)
   Inst Soc Res - Zam 1943 ZA
Rive, R.
   Selected writings. Stories, essays, plays.   188pp. cl.
   R6.90   Donker 1977 SA
Rivers, F.
   Your small farm in South Africa.   131pp. pl. cl.   95c.
   Shuter 1954 SA
Riwa, N.L.
   Hadithi za rafiki saba.   [The story of the seven friends]
   64pp. ill.   K.shs.4.00   OUP-Nairobi 1964 KE SWA
Riwa, N.L.
   Kisa cha Sultani Hatibu.   [The story of Sultan Hatibu]
   96pp. ill.   K.shs.2.25   OUP-Nairobi 1964 KE SWA
Rix, L.B.
   Arthur Shearly Cripps. A selection of his prose and verse.
   See: Brown, G.R.
Robarts, T., comp.
   Directory of Rhodesian libraries.   See: Hartridge, D.,
   comp.
Robb, F.
   Fishermen of the Cape.   88pp. ill.   R8.50 cl.
   Longman - SA 1975 SA
Robbins, M.C., eds.   Kilbride, P.L., eds.
   Psychocultural change in modern Buganda.   69pp.
   U.shs.10.00   ($2.50)   (M.I.S.R. Nkanga ed., 8)   Mak Inst
   Soc Res 1973 UG
Robert, J.M.
   Croyances et coutumes des wafipa payens.   256pp. cl.
   T.shs.15.00 cl.   ($2.20 cl.)   TMP 1949 TZ FRE
Robert, K.A.   Patterson, C.L.   Anstee, M.J.
   Africa and the world.   260pp. maps. pap. & hd.   Eth.
   $4.75   Eth. $7.00   OUP-Addis 1970 ET
Robert, S.
   Kieleze cha insha.   [How to write essays]   120pp.
   K.shs.8.50   OUP-Nairobi 1967 KE SWA
Robert, S.
   Koja la lugha.   [The garland of language]   88pp.
   K.shs.5.00   OUP-Nairobi 1969 KE SWA
Robert, S.
   Kufikirika.   [To be thinkable]   68pp.   K.shs.4.50
   OUP-Nairobi 1967 KE SWA
Robert, S.
   Pambo la lugha.   [An ornament of language]   56pp.
   K.shs.4.75   OUP-Nairobi 1967 KE SWA
Robert, S.
   Utenzi wa vita vya uhuru.   [Epic poem on war for
   freedom - World War II]   256pp.   K.shs.15.00
   OUP-Nairobi 1968 KE SWA
Roberts, A., ed.
   Tanzania before 1900: seven area histories.   153pp.
   maps.   K.shs.35.00 cl.   K.shs.10.00 pap.   ($6.50 cl.)
   ($3.20 pap.)   EAPH 1968 KE
Roberts, A.
   The Lumpa Church.   64pp.   45n.   (23p.)   OUP -
   Lusaka 1973 ZA

Roberts, A.
Safari, African archives file: records of East Africa's past. K1.95 (98p.) OUP - Lusaka ZA

Roberts, B.
How to write good letters. 4th ed. 48pp. 80c Longman - SA 1976 SA

Roberts, B.
Kimberley: turbulent city. An illustrated history. 560pp. ill. cl. R18.00 cl. Philip 1976 SA

Roberts, C. M. P.
Cookery and home management. (Practical course). Standard 6. 113pp. ill. pl. R1.75 Nasou 1974 SA

Roberts, C.M.P.
Cookery and home management. (Practical course). Standard 7. 238pp. ill. R3.85 Nasou 1974 SA

Roberts, C.M.P.
Cookery and home management. (Practical course). Standard 8. 251pp. ill. photo. R5.25 Nasou 1976 SA

Roberts, C.M.P.
Handy at home. Home economics for standard 8. See: van Niekerk, M.S.E.

Roberts, C.M.P.
On with the apron. Housecraft for standard 7. See: van Niekerk, M.S.E.

Roberts, C.M.P.
On with the apron. Housecraft for standard 8. See: Schmidt, M.M.

Roberts, E.S.
Preliminary finding-list of Southern African pamphlets in the University of Cape Town libraries. 203pp. R1.00 (U.C.T. libraries, Varia series, 1) Univ Cape Town Lib 1959 SA

Roberts, H.
In the beginning. 42pp. ill. K.shs2.00 ($1.25/50p.) EALB 1962 KE

Roberts, H.M.
Kitabu cha kuandika na kuanza kusoma. [First lessons in calligraphy] 2nd ed. 48pp. K.shs.1.50 ($1.25/50p.) EALB 1962 KE SWA

Roberts, H.M. Gecau, M.K.
Know yourself: a guide for adolescent girls. 48pp. ill. K.shs2.00 ($1.25/50p.) EALB 1963 KE

Roberts, H.M.
Kuanza kusoma: kitabu cha 2. 4th ed. bk.2 40pp. ill. K.shs.1.50 ($1.25/50p.) EALB 1969 KE SWA

Roberts, H.M.
Kuanza kusoma kitabu cha 3: kijana na mbwa mwitu na hadithi nyingine. bk.3 24pp. ill. K.shs.3.60 ($1.25/50p.) EALB 1966 KE SWA

Roberts, H.M. Gecau, M.K.
Mother and child. 42pp. ill. K.shs.2.00 ($1.25/50p.) EALB 1963 KE

Roberts, H.M.
Njia za afya. [Ways of health] 41pp. ill. K.shs.2.00 ($1.25/50p.) EALB 1959 KE SWA

Roberts, H.M.
A review of company financial reports. ex. only (Inaugural lec.) Rhodes Univ Lib 1960 SA

Roberts, H.W.
Education and training in industry. 29pp. 50c (Fac. of Education, Univ. of Rhodesia, 5) Univ Rhodesia Lib 1965 RH

Roberts, J.M.E. Smith, L.E.W.
Common entrance: English language: with answers. 60pp. 55k Pilgrim 1971 NR

Roberts, J.M.E. Smith, L.E.W.
Common entrance: English language: without answers. 58pp. 50k Pilgrim 1971 NR

Roberts, J.M.E.
Teaching English through drama. 84pp. 77k Pilgrim 1972 NR

Roberts, J.M.E. Smith, L.E.W.
Tests in English language: with answers. 144pp. 88k Pilgrim 1967 NR

Roberts, J.M.E. Smith, L.E.W.
Tests in English language: without answers. 128pp. 82k Pilgrim 1967 NR

Roberts, M.B.
A laboratory process for dyeing wool-orlon 42 blends from a charged solvent system. 11pp. R2.50 (SAWTRI Technical Reports, 313) SAWTRI 1976 SA

Roberts, M.B. Botha, C.
A laboratory process for dyeing wool with reactive dyes from a charged solvent system using a single emulsifier. 14pp. R2.50 (SAWTRI Technical Reports, 265) SAWTRI 1975 SA

Roberts, M.B.
A method for the removal of chromium from chrome dyeing effluent. 19pp. R2.50 (SAWTRI Technical Reports, 321) SAWTRI 1976 SA

Roberts, M.B. Mountain, F.
The transfer printing of cotton, part I: an investigation into the application of reactive dyes by the west transfer technique. 14pp. R2.50 (SAWTRI Technical Reports, 285) SAWTRI 1976 SA

Roberts, M.B. Robinson, G.A. Hunter, L.
The transfer printing of fabrics knitted from cotton-rich blends of cotton and polyester. 6pp. R2.50 (SAWTRI Technical Reports, 271) SAWTRI 1975 SA

Roberts, M.B.
The transfer printing of fabrics woven from cotton-rich blends of cotton and polyester. See: Robinson, G.A.

Roberts, M.B.
Transfer printing of wool with reactive dyes, part I: the use of a transferable film of polyvinyl alcohol. See: Hayes, A.P.N.

Roberts, R.
The social laws of the quaran, considered and compared with those of the Hebrew and other ancient codes. 2 2nd.ed. 136pp. N4.00 Africa only (Academic Reprints Series) Pilgrim 1974 NR

Roberts, R.
Tenzi za marudi mema na Omar Khayyam. 127pp. T.shs.8.50 Tanz Publ House 1973 TZ SWA

Roberts, S.
Outside life's feast: short stories. 116pp. R3.50 Donker 1974 SA

Robertson, A.M.G.
Soil mechanics and foundation engineering. Proceedings of the sixth regional conference for Africa, Durban, 1975. 2 vols. See: Pells, P.J.N.

Robertson, G.
What fish is that? (Ocean) 70pp. pl. ill. hd. R1.00 Purnell 1972 SA

Robertson, J.H.
Science and development. 11pp. T.shs 1.00 (Inaugural lecture, 1) Univ Dar es Salaam 1968 TZ

Robertson, M.
Using time for prayer. 20pp. 50c Methodist 1975 SA

Robins, C.
Acting. 65k Daystar 1977 NR

Robins, C.
Play making. A handbook of drama for schools. 85k Daystar 1977 NR

Robins, C.
Producing plays. 85k Daystar 1977 NR

Robins, D.J., comp. Taylor, L.E., ed. Stevens, P.E., ed.
Handlist of manuscripts in the University of Cape Town libraries. Supplement no. 1. 7pp. 50c (U.C.T. Varia ser., 13) Univ Cape Town Lib 1974 SA

Robins, K., ed.
Social problems in Zambia, readings. See: Rennie, K.J., ed.

Robinson, G.A.   Hunter, L.   Green, M.V.
Cockling in fully-fashioned knitwear, part I: a preliminary
report.   18pp.   R2.50   (SAWTRI Technical Reports,
279)   SAWTRI 1976 SA

Robinson, G.A.   Green, M.V.
Cockling in fully-fashioned knitwear, part II: an
investigation into the effect of various fibre, yarn and fabric
properties on cockling.   20pp.   R2.50   (SAWTRI
Technical Reports, 334)   SAWTRI 1976 SA

Robinson, G.A.   Dobson, D.A.   Cawood, M.
Cotton in fine gauge single jersey, part I: plied yarns.
18pp.   R2.50   (SAWTRI Technical Report, 269)
SAWTRI 1975 SA

Robinson, G.A.   Gee, E.   Ellis, R.
Incorporation of leno weave units into lightweight all-wool
worsted fabric.   14pp.   R2.50   (SAWTRI Technical
Reports, 214)   SAWTRI 1974 SA

Robinson, G.A.   Ellis, R.
Incorporation of small percentage of leno using continuous
filament yarns in lightweight wool worsted fabrics.   18pp.
R2.50   (SAWTRI Technical Reports, 255)   SAWTRI 1975
SA

Robinson, G.A.   Dye, N.
Knit-de-Knit in a polyester/cotton blend.   10pp. photo.
R2.50   (SAWTRI Technical Reports, 218)   SAWTRI 1974
SA

Robinson, G.A.   Dobson, D.A.   Cawood, M.P.
Knittability of all-wool yarns on a 28 gauge single jersey
machine.   17pp.   R2.50   (SAWTRI Technical Reports,
291)   SAWTRI 1976 SA

Robinson, G.A.   Hunter, L.
The processing characteristics of South African wools, part
VIII: the influence of style, length and class description on
the properties of knitted and woven fabrics from mixtures
of South African wools.   22pp.   R2.50   (SAWTRI
Technical Reports, 270)   SAWTRI 1975 SA

Robinson, G.A.
Production of mohair yarns on the Repco spinner, part I:
some preliminary spinning trials.   See: Turpie, D.W.F.

Robinson, G.A.   Ellis, R.   Marsland, S.G.
Production of mohair yarns on the repco spinner, part II:
the spinning of wrapped core-spun mohair yarns and their
use in lightweight mohair suiting fabrics.   13pp.   R2.50
(SAWTRI Technical Reports, 335)   SAWTRI 1977 SA

Robinson, G.A.   Green, M.V.   Dobson, D.A.
A proposed method of assessing the knittability of a yarn.
12pp.   R2.50   (SAWTRI Technical Reports, 235)
SAWTRI 1974 SA

Robinson, G.A.
Single jersey knitting performance, part II: the influence of
machine speed, yarn input tension and yarn linear density
on the knitting performance of fine worsted yarns knitted
on a 28 gg single jersey machine.   See: Cawood, M.P.

Robinson, G.A.   Ellis, R.   Layton, L.
Some novel methods for producing mohair blankets.
17pp.   R2.50   (SAWTRI Technical Reports, 230)
SAWTRI 1974 SA

Robinson, G.A.   Ellis, R.   Layton, L.
Some novel methods for producing mohair blankets.
17pp. photo.   R2.50   (SAWTRI Technical Reports, 230)
SAWTRI 1974 SA

Robinson, G.A.
The transfer printing of fabrics knitted from cotton-rich
blends of cotton and polyester.   See: Roberts, M.B.

Robinson, G.A.   Roberts, M.B.
The transfer printing of fabrics woven from cotton-rich
blends of cotton and polyester.   4pp.   R2.50
(SAWTRI Technical Reports, 280)   SAWTRI 1976 SA

Robinson, G.A.   McNaughton, D.
An unconventional method of producing a mohair pile
fabric on a sinker wheel knitting machine to obtain
improved fibre retention.   7pp.   R2.50   (SAWTRI
Technical Reports, 216)   SAWTRI 1974 SA

Robinson, G.A.   Biggs, P.A.
Use of cotton in raschel outerwear.   14pp.   R2.50
(SAWTRI Technical Reports, 263)   SAWTRI 1975 SA

Robinson, G.A.   Ellis, R.
The use of leno in all-wool lightweight shirting and safari
suiting fabrics.   12pp.   R2.50   (SAWTRI Technical
Reports, 281)   SAWTRI 1976 SA

Robinson, K.R.
The iron age of Dedza district, Malawi.   50pp. pl. maps.
K4.00   (Department of Antiquities, 16)   Dept Antiquities -
Mal 1975 MW

Robinson, K.R.
The iron age of Mulanje.   60pp. pl. maps.   K5.00
(Department of Antiquities, 18)   Dept Antiquities - Mal
1976 MW

Robinson, N.H.G.
Theology and the personal.   ex. only   (Inaugural lec.)
Rhodes Univ Lib 1954 SA

Robinson, R.
Objective tests in health science.   96pp.   77k   Pilgrim
1968 NR

Robinson, R.   Panniers, B.J.
Objective tests in physics.   192pp.   94k   Pilgrim 1969
NR

Robinson, R.
School certificate chemistry.   400pp.   N1.85   Pilgrim
1969 NR

Robinson, R.
School certificate chemistry questions.   100pp.   88k
Pilgrim 1969 NR

Robinson, R.L.
Modern mathematics. Multiple choice questions.   bk. 1.
153pp. ill.   80c   Mazenod Inst 1975 LO

Robinson, W.J.R.
Objective tests in chemistry.   144pp.   82k   Pilgrim
1967 NR

Robson, C.
The big house and the little house.   13pp. ill.   12k
Pilgrim 1971 NR

Robson, C.
The big lizard and the little lizard.   13pp. ill.   12k
Pilgrim 1971 NR

Robson, C.
The old monkey and the young monkey.   13pp. ill.
12k   Pilgrim 1971 NR

Robson, C.
Threading beads.   13pp. ill.   12k   Pilgrim 1971 NR

Robson, M.
Children of Africa.   Pupils' grade 3.   96pp.   R$1.00
Longman - Rhod 1971 RH

Robson, M.
Children of the world.   Pupils' grade 4.   64pp.   R$1.40
Longman - Rhod 1972 RH

Robson, M.
Children of the world.   Teacher's bk.   144pp.   R$1.40
Longman - Rhod 1972 RH

Robson, M.
Discovery science.   Teachers' bk, grade 1.   112pp.
R$1.25   Longman - Rhod 1968 RH

Robson, M.
Discovery science.   Teacher's bk. grade 2.   136pp.
R$1.95   Longman - Rhod 1969 RH

Robson, M.
Discovery science.   Teacher's bk. grade 3.   96pp.
R$1.80   Longman - Rhod 1970 RH

Robson, M.
Discovery science.   Teacher's bk. grade 4.   116pp.
R$1.70   Longman - Rhod 1972 RH

Robson, M.
Discovery science.   Teacher's bk. grade 5.   136pp.
R$2.50   Longman - Rhod 1974 RH

Robson, P.
  Mountains of Kenya. 73pp. photos. K.shs.30.00 cl. K.shs10.00 pap. ($5.80 cl.) ($3.20 pap.) EAPH 1969 KE.

Roche, C.
  Conquêtes et résistance des peuples de Casamance. 400pp. CFA1,800 (F36.00) Nouv Ed Afric 1976 SG FRE

Roche, P.
  The Nigerian butterflies: an atlas of plates with notes: nymphalidae, 1. 3, 9 pts See: Boorman, J.

Roche, P.
  The Nigerian butterflies: an atlas of plates with notes: nymphalidae, 3. 5, 9 pts See: Boorman, J.

Roche, P.
  The Nigerian butterflies: an atlas of plates with notes: papilionidae. 1, 9 pts. See: Boorman, J.

Roche, P.
  The Nigerian butterflies: an atlas of plates with notes: pieridae and danaidae. 2, 9 pts See: Boorman, J.

Roche, P.
  The Nigerian butterlfies: an atlas of plates with notes: acraeidae. 6, 9 pts See: Boorman, J.

Rochecouste, E.
  Botanical and agricultural characters of sugar cane varieties of Mauritius. 7pp. Rs10 (Mauritius Sugar Industry Research Institute, occas. paps., 5) Sugar Res Inst 1961 MF

Rochecouste, E.
  Botanical and agricultural characters of sugar cane varieties of Mauritius. 18pp. (Mauritius Sugar Industry Research Institute, occas. paps., 11) Sugar Res Inst 1964 MF

Rodegem, F.M.
  Précis de grammaire Rundi. 198pp. (Faculté de Philosophie et Lettres, 10) Univ Bujumbura 1967 BD FRE

Rodegem, F.M.
  Structures judiciaires traditionnelles au Burundi. 27pp. (Faculté de Philosophie et Lettres, 8) Univ Bujumbura 1966 BD FRE

Roden, D., ed.
  Readings in historical geography. v. 1 304pp. maps. U.shs.56.00 (Occas. paps., 59) Dept Geog - Mak 1975 UG

Rodière, R.
  La tutelle des mineurs. Etude de droit comparé. 393pp. D1.000 Univ Tunis 1950 TI FRE

Rodis, N.G. Wahdan, L. Ishag, A.H.
  The availability of groundwater in Korfofan Province. 15pt. (43c./18p.) (Bulletin, 12) Geol and Min Res - Sudan 1963 SJ

Rodis, N.G. Wahadan, L. Ishag, A.H.
  Groundwater geology of Kordofan Province. 50pt. (Bulletin, 14) Geol and Min Res - Sudan 1963 SJ

Rodney, C.M.
  Jameson's ride to Johannesburg. [Reprint of ed. Johannesburg, 1896] 77pp. R3.95 (Reprints, 54) State-Lib-SA 1970 SA

Rodney, W.
  Biashara ya utumwa katika Afrika ya magharibi. [West Africa and the Atlantic slave trade.] 32pp. K.shs.6.50 ($3.00) Foundation 1974 KE SWA

Rodney, W.
  How Europe underdeveloped Africa. 316pp. T.shs.10.00 Tanz Publ House 1972 TZ

Rodney, W.
  West Africa and the Atlantic slave trade. 27pp. K.shs2.50 ($1.00) EAPH 1967 KE

Rodney, W.
  West Africa and the Atlantic slave trade. 28pp. Hist Assoc - Tanz 1970 TZ

Rodwell, E.
  Coast causerie. v. 1 K.shs.25.00 cl. K.shs.15.00 pap. (£1.90 cl.) (£1.15 pap.) Heinemann Educ - Nair 1972 KE

Rodwell, E.
  Coast causerie, v. 2. 128pp. cl. & pap. K.shs.15.00 pap. K.shs.30.00 cl. Heinemann Educ - Nair 1973 KE

Rodwell, E.
  Coast causerie. v. 3 128pp. cl. & pap. K.shs.40.00 cl. K.shs.20.00 pap. Heinemann Educ - Nair 1977 KE

Roe, A.R.
  Professor Turner's report on incomes policy and its critics. T.shs.12.00 ($3.00) (Research pap., 67.18) Econ Res Bur - Tanz 1974 TZ

Roe, A.R.
  Terms of trade and transfer tax effects in East African Common Market. 21pp. T.shs12.00 ($3.00) (Research pap., 68.10) Econ Res Bur - Tanz 1968 TZ

Roelands, C.M.
  Nigerian motor vehicle traffic: an economic forecast. See: Hogg, V.W.

Roesel, R.
  Basic concepts of rational continuum mechanics. 20pp. (CSIR Special Report, WISK 190) CSIR 1975 SA

Roger, J.
  Pupil's book. See: Malaku, A.

Rogers, E.G., et al.
  Two ears, two eyes and a tongue. (Practical English). Standard 6: first language. 131pp. ill. pl. R2.70 Nasou 1974 SA

Rogers, J. Hutton, S.P. Tan, J.C.
  College English, pupil's. 1 204pp. Eth. $3.25 OUP-Addis 1967 ET

Rogers, J. Hutton, S.P. Tan, J.C.
  College English, pupil's. 2 156pp. Eth. $3.00 OUP-Addis 1967 ET

Rogers, J. Hutton, S.P. Tan, J.C.
  College English, teacher's notes. 1 148pp. Eth. $5.00 OUP-Addis 1967 ET

Rogers, J. Hutton, S.P. Tan, J.C.
  College English, teacher's notes. 2 104pp. Eth. $5.00 OUP-Addis 1967 ET

Rogers, J.
  Introductory teacher's notes for book one: Section A, English language teaching. See: Malaku, A.

Rogers, J.
  The lion's whiskers. 176pp. ill. Eth. $3.10 OUP-Addis 1971 ET

Rogers, J.
  Pupil's book. See: Malaku, A.

Rogers, J. Zerihun, G. Last, M.
  Pupil's book. 168pp. ill. B1.70 (The New Oxford English Course, 5) OUP-Addis 1967 ET

Rogers, J. Eteffa, M. Asrat, T.
  Pupil's book. 172pp. B1.40 (The New Oxford English Course, 3) OUP-Addis 1970 ET

Rogers, J. Zerihun, G. Last, M.
  Teacher's notes, book five. 156pp. B4.50 (The New Oxford English Course, 5) OUP-Addis 1967 ET

Rogers, J.
  Teacher's notes for book one: Section B, English activity periods. See: Malaku, A.

Rogers, J.
  Teacher's notes: section A, English language teaching. 264pp. ill. B4.00 (The New Oxford English Course, 2) OUP-Addis 1967 ET

Rogers, J.
  Teacher's notes: section B, English activity periods. 184pp. ill. B4.00 (The New Oxford English Course, 2) OUP-Addis 1967 ET

Rogers, J.A.
  Commensense about company reports. 48pp. ill. R1.00 Flesch 1967 SA

Author Index

Rotsart de Hertaing, I.   Courtejoie, J.
La tuberculose aujourd'hui! Conceptions récentes de la lutte contre la tuberculose. 36pp. photos. 90k ($1.08) (Protection de la santé, 9) BERPS 1975 ZR FRE

Rotsart de Hertaing, I.   Courtejoie, J.
La tuberculose: l'évolution de la maladie et sa prévention par l'éducation sanitaire. 240pp. ill. photos. Z3.00 ($3.60) BERPS 1976 ZR FRE

Rotsart de Hertaing, I.
Les vers intestinaux à l'école: prise de conscience par la jeunesse. See: Nzungu Mavinga.

Rotsart de Hertaing, I.
Les vers intestinaux: cycles évolutifs des vers intestinaux et moyens de prévention. See: van der Herden, A.

Rotsart de Hertaing, I.
Vers un éclairage nouveau de quelques problèmes de santé: l'attitude des techniciens de la santé en face de leurs nouvelles responsabilités. See: Courtejoie, J.

Rougeot, P.C.
Les lepidoptères de l'Afrique noire occidentale: les attacides. 4, 4pts. 214pp. ill. CFA1200 (Initiations et Etudes Africaines, 14) IFAN 1962 SG FRE

Rouillard, N., ed.
Matabele Thompson. (Reprint of ed. 1936) 293pp. ill. cl. R$13.50 (Silver series, 13) Books of Rhodesia 1977 RH

Roukens de Lange, E.J.
South West Africa 1946-1960. 51pp. 80c. Univ Cape Town Lib 1965 SA

Rourke, B.E., ed.
Economics of cocoa production and marketing: proceedings of economics research conference Legon, April 1973. See: Kotey, R.A., ed.

Rousseau, F.
The porteaceae of South Africa. 110pp. pl. hd. R10.00 Purnell 1970 SA

Rousseau, H.J.
The university in Africa. 29pp. 30c Univ Rhodesia Lib 1957 RH

Rousseau, M.H.
African education in the Federation of Rhodesia and Nyasaland 1890-1958. 29pp. 70c. Univ Cape Town Lib 1969 SA

Rousseaux, R.
Le franc du Rwanda et du Burundi. 24pp. (Faculté des Sciences Sociales, 3) Univ Bujumbura 1964 BD FRE

Rousseaux, R.
La thésaurisation en milieu paysan au Burundi. 14pp. (Faculté des Sciences Sociales, 7) Univ Bujumbura 1966 BD FRE

Rousset, M.
Droit administratif Marocain. See: Garagnon, J.

Rousson, M.
Prestige et connaissance des professions au Burundi. See: Cart, H.P.

Roux, E.
Grass: a story of Frankenwald. 240pp. ill./photos. R6.60 OUP-SA 1969 SA

Roux, G.
La presse ivoirienne: miroir d'une société. Essai sur les changements socio-culturels en Côte d'Ivoire. 2 v. 537pp. CFA7,5000 set INADES 1975 IV FRE

Roux, M.   St. Leger, M.
Grahamstown: Fingo village: an investigation in to the socio-economic conditions of the inhabitants of the Fingo village and their attitude to removal. 31pp. 50c. ($1.30) SA Inst of Race Relations 1971 SA

Roux-Snyman, C.
A practical English course for standard 8. (Second language.) See: van Rensenburg, R.J.C.

Rowe, M.
They came from the sea. 64pp. photos. pl. R1.00 Longman SA 1968 SA

Rowland, L., ed.
Local government finance in Nigeria - problems and prospects: the report of the third national conference on local government, held in Benin City, 9-11 December, 1970. See: Adedeji, A., ed.

Rowland, L., ed.
Management problems of rapid urbanization in Nigeria: the challenge to governments and local authorities. See: Adedeji, A., ed.

Rowley, H.H.
Nchi ya biblia. [Bible atlas.] 52pp. maps. T.shs.12.00 Central Tanganyika 1966 TZ SWA

Rowny, K.
West African contribution to the law of international watercourses. 18pp. 45k (35p./80c.) (Univ. of Ife, Inaugural Lecture Series, 14) Univ Ife Press 197j NR

Rowse, D.E., comp.
Current Rhodesian periodicals. See: Thomas, A., comp.

Roy, B.   Poinssot, M.
Inscriptions arabes de Kairouan. 1, 2v. 429pp. pl. D3.000 (Série I, Archéologie-Histoire, 2) Univ Tunis 1950 TI FRE

Roy, B.   Poinssot, M.
Inscriptions arabes de Kairouan. 2, 2v. 423pp. pl. D2.000 (Série I, Archéologie-Histoire, 2) Univ Tunis 1950 TI FRE

Royston, E.
One hundred and three poems. 72pp. R1.75 ($2.40/£1.25) (Renoster Books) Ravan; distr. 1972 SA

Royston, E.
One hundred and three poems. 72pp. R1.75 ($2.40/£1.25) (Renoster Books) Ravan 1973 SA

Royston, R., ed.
To whom it may concern. An anthology of Black South African poetry. 3rd ed. 96pp. R2.50 Donker 1973 SA

Ruanda, H.M.
Utawala wa wananchi. [Government of the people.] 97pp. T.shs.12.00 Tanz Publ House 1973 TZ SWA

Rubadiri, D.
No bride price. 180pp. ill. K.shs7.00 ($2.60) EAPH 1967 KE

Rubbens, A.
Le droit judiciaire Zairois. 250pp. Press Univ Zaire 1976 ZR FRE

Rubongonya, L.T.
Kibbaate kya kaseegu n'enganikyo ezindi. [Kibbaate, son of Kaseegu and other stories] 2nd ed. 65pp. K.shs2.80 ($1.50/60p.) EALB 1965 KE RNY

Ruch, E.A.
Space and time: a comparative study of the theories of Aristotle and A. Einstein. 62pp. 30c. (80c.) Univ South Africa 1958 SA

Ruckstuhl, E.
Historia ya wokovu. See: Haag, H.

Rudden, P.
The story of Zambia. 68pp. 50n. (25p.) OUP - Lusaka 1968 ZA

Rudengren, J.
1973 socio-economic survey of Kahe Ward, Moshi district. 50pp. hd. & pap. T.shs.20.00 pap. T.shs.35.00 hd. ($7.00 pap.) ($12.00 hd.) (Research reports, new series, 14) Bur Res Assess - Tanz 1975 TZ

Rudengren, J.
1973 socio-economic survey of Kahe ward, Moshi district. T.shs.20.00 (Research reports, new series, 14) Bur Res Assess - Tanz 1975 TZ

Author Index

Rudengren, J.
A methodological study of population density and distribution - a case study of the West-Lake region. T.shs.15.00 ($5.00) (Research reports, new series, 7) Bur Res Assess - Tanz 1974 TZ

Rudengren, J.
Retail service and consumer behaviour in Kahe-Msarange-Mandaka area, Kilimanjaro region. T.shs.20.00 (Research reports, new series, 17) Bur Res Assess - Tanz 1975 TZ

Rudigoz, C.
L'enseignement de la prononciation (anglais) 29pp. CFA125 (C.L.A.D. Etude, 16 bis) CLAD 1966 SG FRE

Rudigoz, C.
Fondements théoriques d'une méthode d'anglais pour le Sénégal. 117pp. CFA320 (C.L.A.D. Etude, 16) CLAD 1966 SG FRE

Rudigoz, C.
Méthode d'anglais pour le Sénégal. Compte rendu de l'enquête sur l'africanisation du contexte. 41pp. CFA250 (C.L.A.D. Etude, 37 bis) CLAD 1969 SG FRE

Rudigoz, C.
Phonétique corrective anglaise à l'usage des wolofs. 141pp. CFA375 (C.L.A.D. Etude, 38) CLAD 1969 SG FRE

Rudigoz, C.
Le plurilinguisme hier, aujourd'hui, demain. 38pp. CFA125 (C.L.A.D. Etude, 24 bis) CLAD 1967 SG FRE

Rudner, I.
The hunter and his art. See: Rudner, J.

Rudner, I.   Moller, J.P.
Journey in Africa through Angola, Ovampoland and Damaraland. Tr. from Swedish and annotated. 256pp. ill. cl. R10.50 Struik 1974 SA

Rudner, J.   Rudner, I.
The hunter and his art. 292pp. pl. ill. cl. R15.00 Struik 1970 SA

Rudolph.
Guide for Zulu court interpreter. 50c. Shuter 1948 SA

Ruganda, J.
Black mamba. 120pp. K.shs.9.00 (African Theatre, 2) EAPH 1973 KE

Ruganda, J.
The burdens. 88pp. K.shs8.25 (New Drama from Africa, 8) OUP-Nairobi 1972 KE

Ruheni, M.
The love root. 104pp. K.shs.9.50 pap. Heinemann Educ - Nair 1976 KE

Ruheni, M.
The mystery smugglers. 120pp. K.shs.8.00 (55p) (Spear Books, 1) Heinemann Educ - Nair 1975 KE

Ruhiu, W.
Mole, rat and the mountain. 18pp. ill. K.shs.4.00 (Lioncub books, 6) EAPH 1974 KE

Ruhumbika, G., ed.
Towards Ujamaa. Twenty years of Tanu leadership. 318pp. K.shs.32.00 ($8.00/£3.80) EALB KE

Ruhumbika, G.
Parapanda [Novel]. 75pp. K.shs.5.00 ($2.50/£1.00) EALB 1974 KE SWA

Ruhumbika, G.
Village in Uhuru. T.shs 9.50 Longman Tanz 1973 TZ

Rulka, C.
An English course for West African secondary schools. 1, 2bks 282pp. N1.55 Macmillan 1959 NR

Rulka, C.
An English course for West African secondary schools. 2, 2bks 320pp. N1.65 Macmillan 1959 NR

Rulka, K.
Objective questions and answers in geography: Africa. 1, 2bks 64pp. maps. 50k macmillan NR

Rulka, K.
Objective questions and answers in geography: the world. 2,2bks 48pp. maps. 40k Macmillan NR

Rund, H.
The world view of modern theoretical physics. 12pp. 20c. (70c.) Univ South Africa 1962 SA

Rund.   Hanno.   Beare, J.H.
Variational properties of direction: dependent metric fields. 65pp. R5.00 (R6.00) (Studia, 3) Univ South Africa 1972 SA

Rundle, M., comp.   Winter, J.S., comp.
R.F. Kennedy - a list of publications.   gratis Johannesburg Public Lib 1971 SA

Runyowa, G.T.
Kurumwa nechokuchera. [Making a rod for one's back.] 76pp. pl. 50c Longman - Rhod 1974 RH SHO

Ruparelia, P.M.
A geography for K.J.S.E. 166pp. maps. K.shs.18.00 Textbook Ctre 1971 KE

Ruperti, R.M.
Organogram of the south and south west African education system. [also available in Afrikaans]. 38pp. 45c. (R1.00) Univ South Africa 1973 SA

Rural Development Research Committee.
Rural corporation in Tanzania. 564pp. T.shs.55.00 ($13.00) Tanz Publ House 1975 TZ

Rushdoony, R.J.
The politics of pornography. 163pp. hd. R8.70 Africa only Valiant 1975 SA

Rushton, A.
Centrifugal recovery of coal from South African fine-coal slurries. 2.00 (CSIR reports, CENG 083) CSIR 1975 SA

Rushton, A.   Dyson, R.H.
Reproducibility of measurements of solute recovery in pilot scale rotary vaccum filtration using a tritium tracer. (CSIR Report, CEWG 132) CSIR 1976 SA

Russel, E.C.M.
Subject index to illustrations in South African periodicals, 1800-1875. 81pp. R1.00 Univ Cape Town Lib 1964 SA

Russel, M.
Notes on teaching reading and writing: supplement to New Oxford English Course, bk. 1. 10k OUP - Nig NR

Russell, M.J.
Study of a South African interracial neighbourhood. 260pp. R2.00 Inst Soc Res-Natal 1961 SA

Rutaro, A.B.
Tebere: emigane omu Runyankore-Rukiga. [Short stories and folk tales] 87pp. K.shs3.65 ($1.75/70p.) EALB 1966 KE RNY

Rutesiya, E.
Mbese uwera uralizwa n'iki? [Roman pour jeunesse.] 47pp. RF30 ($0.20) Caritas 1976 RW KIN

Rwakaikara, D.B.
Ebyokulya byaitu. [Introduction to our food] 78pp. K.shs.6.00 ($2.00/80p.) EALB 1971 KE LUG

Rwechungura, G.R.
Ufahamu wa lugha ya Kiswahili. 90pp. K.shs.7.00 Heinemann Educ - Nair 1974 KE SWA

Rwelengera, J.B.K.
The Nyarubanja system and Ujamaa villages development in West Lake region - Tanzania. See: Bugengo, J.

Rweyemamu, A.
Nation-building in Tanzania. 109pp. maps. K.shs.10.00 ($3.20) EAPH 1970 KE

Rweyemamu, A.H.   Hyden, G.
A decade of public administration in Africa. 371pp. K.shs.100.00 cl. K.shs.65.25 pap. ($18.75/£9.00) ($12.50/£5.00 pap.) EALB 1975 KE

Rweyemamu, A.H., eds.   Mwansasu, B.U., eds.
Planning in Tanzania. Background to decentralisation.
134pp. cl. & pap.   K.shs.16.50 pap.   K.shs.23.00 cl.
($4.10/£1.65 pap.) ($5.70/£2.80 cl.) (Management
and Administration Series, 3)   EALB 1974 KE

Rweyemamu, J.F. et al., ed.
Towards socialist planning. v. 1. 200pp.   T.shs8.00
(Tanzania Studies series, 1)   Tanz Publ House 1972 TZ

Rweyemamu, J.F.
Historical and institutional setting of Tanzanian industry.
104pp. ill.   T.shs.12.00   ($3.00) (Research pap.,
71.6)   Econ Res Bur - Tanz 1971 TZ

Rweyemamu, J.F.
Structure of Tanzanian industry. 80pp.   T.shs.12.00
($3.00) (Research pap., 71.2)   Econ Res Bur - Tanz
1971 TZ

Rweyemamu, J.F.
Underdevelopment and industrialization in Tanzania: a
study of perverse capitalist industrial development.
304pp. pap. & cl.   K.shs.64.25 cl.   K.shs.47.00 pap.
OUP-Nairobi 1972 KE

Ryan, J.O.
Integrated science for tropical schools. Pupil's bk. 1. 2
bks. See: Bajah, S.T.

Ryan, J.O.
Integrated science for tropical schools. Pupil's book 2,
2bks. See: Bajah, S.T.

Ryan, J.O.
Integrated science for tropical schools. Teacher's book
1, 2bks. See: Bajah, S.T.

Ryan, J.O.
Integrated science for tropical schools. Teacher's book
2, 2 bks. See: Bajah, H.S.T.

Ryan, J.O.
Integrated science for tropical schools: workbk. 1, 2 bks.
See: Bajah, S.T.

Ryan, J.O.
Integrated science for tropical schools, workbk. 2, 2 bks.
See: Bajah, S.T.

Ryan, O.
Objective questions in physics: with answers.
See: Macdonald, C.

Ryan, O.
Objective questions in physics: without answers.
See: Macdonald, C.

Ryan, O.   Ashworth, A.E.
School certificate revision course: Physics. 112pp.
N1.05 Macmillan 1975 NR

Ryan, O.   Isaacs, H.   Akande, S.
Tests in physics: with answers. N1.00 Pilgrim 1972
NR

Ryan, O.   Isaacs, H.   Akande, S.
Tests in physics: without answers.   94k Pilgrim NR

Ryan, T.C.I.   Waters, A.R.
Planning for profit and prosperity. 157pp. ill.
K.shs.10.00 ($3.20) EAPH 1967 KE

Rycroft, H.B.
What protea is that? 78pp. ill. hd.   R1.00 Purnell
1970 SA

Ryke, P.A.J.   Mathews, J.P.
Contributions to the cranial morphology of the Asiatic
Urodele Onychodactylus japonicus; The cranial
musculature of the Asiatic Orodele Onychodactylus
japonicus. 41pp. ill.   50c. (A v. 26, no. 1-2) Univ
Stellenbosch, Lib 1959 SA

Sabbagha, N.G.   Kritzinger, M.S.B.
English proverbs and expressions.   R2.75 Van Schaik
SA

Saberwal, S.
The traditional political system of Embu of central Kenya.
106pp. maps.   K.shs.18.50 ($7.80 cl.) ($4.80 pap.)
EAPH 1970 KE

Sabin, R.
A practical guide to Islamic monuments in Cairo.
See: Parker, R.B.

Sabina, J.C.B.   Haffter, P.
Practical Portuguese. Rev. ed. 299pp.   R6.70 pap.
(R7.70) (Manualia, 11) Univ South Africa 1975 SA

Sabot, R. H.
Open unemployment and the employed compound of
urban surplus labour.   T.shs.12.00 ($3.00) (Research
pap., 74.4) Econ Res Bur - Tanz 1974 TZ

Sabot, R.H.
The national urban mobility: employment and income
survey of Tanzania. v.1 See: Bienefeld, M.A.

Sack, P.
Aperçu du phénomène de la déperdition scolaire chez les
adolescents de Kisangani. 63pp.   Z3.00 ($2.40)
(Cahiers du CRIDE, Nouvelle série I, 3) CRIDE 1976 ZR
FRE

Sack, P.
La langue d'instruction et ses incidences sur les écoliers
zairois, cas du Nord-Kivu. 69pp.   Z3.00 ($2.40)
(Cahiers du CRIDE, Nouvelle série, I, 3) CRIDE 1976 ZR
FRE

Sada, M.
Uwar Gulma. [Chief of mischief] 16pp.   75k
Northern Nig 1968 NR HAU

Sadiq, A.
Perspectives d'union douanière maghrébine (Maroc,
Algérie, Tunisie) 160pp.   Dir10.00 Ed Maghreb 1974
MR FRE

Sadiq, M.
Cambridge school certificate essays 1945-1966. 140pp.
K.shs.10.00 Africa Book Serv 1966 KE

Sadler, C.
Never a young man. Letters and journals of the Rev.
William Shaw. 189pp. pl.   R2.10 cl. Haum 1967 SA

Sadler, W.
Mukuua uria muthome. [Mukuua the literate] 40pp. ill.
K.shs1.00 ($1.25/5 p.) EALB 1957 KE KIK

Sadler, W.
Uhoro wa Jesu. [The story of Jesus] 56pp.
K.shs1.50 ($1.25/50p.) EALB 1958 KE KIK

Sadowski, Z.L.
Population growth and the strategy of economic
development. 22pp.   C1.00 ($1.00/50p.) (Inaugural
lecture) Ghana UP 1969 GH

Saeed, O.H.
The industrial bank of Sudan 1962-1968: an experiment in
development banking. 60pp.   15 pt. ($1.00)
Khartoum UP 1971 SJ

Safier, M.   Langlands, B.W.
Perspectives on urban planning for Uganda. 238pp.
U.shs.40.00 (Occas. paps., 10) Dept Geog - Mak 1970
UG

Safier, M.
The role of urban and regional planning in national
development of East Africa. 229pp. hd.   U.shs12.00
Adult Educ Centre UG

Safo, D.B.
The search. 76pp.   N1.25 Onibonoje 1977 NR

Safo, E.N., ed.
Afrakoma. [Afrakoma.] 4th ed. 97pp.   C1.50 Bur
Ghana Lang 1976 GH TWI

Sagay, I.
Case law under the matrimonial causes decree. 147pp.
N3.00 Univ Ife Bkshop; distr. 1976 NR

Sagay, I.
The legal aspects of the Namibian dispute. 464pp. cl.
N10.00 (£8.50) ($19.00) Univ Ife Press 1975 NR

Saglio, C.
Guide de Dakar et du Sénégal. (Edition 1977) 2nd ed.
142pp. ill. col. ill. maps.   CFA1,5000.00 Soc Africaine
1975 SG FRE

Author Index

Sahli, A.
Carthage la prestigieuse cité d'Elissa. 86pp. D0.400 Maison Tunis 1970 TI FRE

Sahli, A.
Esquisse pour une préhistoire Tunisienne. 96pp. pl. D0.400 Maison Tunis 1970 TI FRE

Sahly, A.
Les mains mutilées dans l'art préhistorique. 320pp. photos. D2,500 Maison Tunis 1970 TI FRE

Said Abdulla, M.
Siri ya sifuri. 120pp. K.shs.10.00 EAPH 1974 KE SWA

Saidi, M.
Fani mbali mbali za kiswahili. [First aid in Swahili.] 96pp. ill. K.shs.8.00 Longman - Ken 1976 KE SWA

Saidi, M.
Fani za Kiswahili. [Kiswahili idioms.] 64pp. T.shs.6.50 Longman - Tanz 1975 TZ SWA

Sailor, G., ed.
Technical innovation and farm development in East Africa. See: Morris, J., ed.

Sakara, A.H.
Jizoeze kiswahili. 1, 2 bks. See: Sospate, S.K.

Sakara, A.H.
Jizoeze kiswahili. 2, 2 bks. See: Sospate, S.K.

Sakkut, H.
The Egyptian novel and its main trends from 1913-1952. 165pp. L.E.2.000 cl. L.E.2.500 hd. ($5.00 cl.) ($5.50 hd.) Am Univ 1971 UA

Sakkut, H.
Taha Hussein. See: Jones, M.

Salacuse, J.
A selective survey of the Nigerian family law. 113pp. N1.25 (£1.00/$2.50) Inst Admin - Zaria 1965 NR

Salami, A.
Yoruba personal names: a socio-linguistic study of the significance and use of personal names in Yoruba. 200pp. ill. N5.00 Cross Continent 1977 NR

Salami, R.A.
Learn to speak the four Nigerian main languages. See: Orji, G.

Sales, J.
The development of a coloured Christian community in the Eastern Cape 1800-1852. 184pp. pl. Fl.43.25 Balkema 1974 SA

Sales, J.
Mission stations and the Coloured communities of the Eastern Cape 1800-1852. 184pp. pl. cl. R9.50 ($17.25) (South African Biographical and Historical Studies, 21) Balkema 1975 SA

Salifou, A.
Le Damagaram ou sultanat de Zinder au 19e siècle. 321pp. maps photos. CFA1500 (F30.00) (Etudes Nigeriennes, 27) Inst Rech Sci Hum 1971 NG FRE

Salifou, A.
Kaoussan ou la révolte sénoussiste. 229pp. maps photos. CFA2000 (F40.00) (Etudes Nigeriennes, 33) Inst Rech Sci Hum 1973 NG FRE

Salim, A.
Kenya historical biographies. See: King, K.

Salim A.
The Swahili speaking peoples of Kenya's coast 1890-1965. 261pp. ill. K.shs.35.00 (Peoples of East Africa, 4) EAPH 1974 KE

Sall, I.
La génération spontanée. 40pp. CFA300 Nouv Ed Afric 1975 SG FRE

Sall, K.
Les possibilités d'enseignement et de recherches dans les domaines des sciences de l'architecture dans les universités Africaines. v. 2 195pp. ($9.00) AAU 1975 GH FRE

Sall, M.
Le Sénégal, Géographie. See: Chamard, P.C.

Salmon, E.M.
Beyond the call of duty: African deeds of bravery in World War II. 49pp. ill. K.shs.1.60 ($1.25/50p.) EALB 1952 KE

Samb, A.
Essai sur la contribution du Sénégal à la littérature d'expression arabe. 534pp. maps photos. CFA4000 (Mémoires de l'IFAN, 87) IFAN 1972 SG FRE

Samb, A.
Matraqué par le destin, ou la vie d'un talibé. 200pp. CFA850 (F17.00) Nouv Ed Afric 1973 SG FRE

Sambo, B.
Islamic religious knowledge for West African School Certificate: Fiqh. 2, 3 bks. 168pp. N1.50 Islamic 1974 NR

Sambo, B.
Islamic religious knowledge for West African School Certificate: Hadith. 3, 3 bks. 150pp. N1.50 Islamic 1974 NR

Sambo, B.
Islamic religious knowledge for West African School Certificate: Qur'an and Tafsir. 1, 3 bks. 89pp. N1.50 Islamic 1974 NR

Sambou, K.
Recueil des traditions orales des Mandingues de Gambie et de Casamance. See: Cissoko, S.M.

Sammani, A. Agabani, F. Agabani, Y.
Scientific and technical potential "STP" in the Sudan. Summary of results. 64pp. pl. Nat Council Res - Sudan 1974 SJ

Sampson, G.
Middle stone industries of the Orange river scheme area. 111pp. R3.00 (Memoirs van die Nasionale Museum, 4) Nasionale Museum 1969 SA

Sampson, G.
The Smithfield industrial complex: further field results. 179pp. R3.50 (Memoirs van die Nasionale Museum, 5) Nasionale Museum 1970 SA

Sampson, G.
The stone age industries of the Orange River scheme and South Africa. 288pp. R3.90 (Memoirs van die Nasionale Museum, 6) Nasionale Museum 1973 SA

Sampson, R.
So this was Lusakaas. 108pp. photos. hd. K1.50 Multimedia 1972 ZA

Sampson, R.
A toothbrush in his hat. 158pp. hd. K2.00 Multimedia 1972 ZA

Samson, M.
Notre beau pays. Livre de lecture à l'usage des élèves de C.P. 2 de Côte d'Ivoire. 160pp. photos. cl. CFA695 cl. CEDA 1967 IV FRE

Samuel, J.
I remember. 36pp. 25n. Neczam 1973 ZA

Samuel, J.M.
Notes on ordinary level poetry. 68pp. 65pes. ($.65) Ghana Publ Corp 1971 GH

Samuel, J.M.
Notes on ordinary level poetry - a guide to poetry appreciation for school certificate candidates. 67pp. 75k NR only Ethiope 1972 NR

Samuel, P.S.
Integrated science for tropical schools. Pupil's bk. 1. 2 bks. See: Bajah, S.T.

Samuel, P.S.
Integrated science for tropical schools. Pupil's book 2, 2bks. See: Bajah, S.T.

Samuel, P.S.
Integrated science for tropical schools. Teacher's book 1, 2bks. See: Bajah, S.T.

Author Index

Samuel, P.S.
Integrated science for tropical schools. Teacher's book 2, 2 bks. See: Bajah, H.S.T.

Samuel, P.S.
Integrated science for tropical schools: workbk. 1, 2 bks. See: Bajah, S.T.

Samuel, P.S.
Integrated science for tropical schools, workbk. 2, 2 bks. See: Bajah, S.T.

Samuel, P.S.
New biology for 'O' level. bk. 1 See: Esuruoso, O.F.

Sandberg, A.
Socio-economic survey of Lower Rufiji Flood plain. pt. 1: Rufiji Delta agricultural system. T.shs.15.00 ($5.00) (Research pap., 34) Bur Res Assess - Tanz 1974 TZ

Sandeman, E.F.
Eight months in an ox-waggon. Reminiscences of Boer life. [Reprint of ed. 1880]. 402pp. ill. map. cl. R11.85 (Africana Reprint Library series, 1) Africana Book Soc 1975 SA

Sanders, P.
Moshoeshoe, chief of the Sotho. 368pp. ill. cl. R18.00 SA only Philip 1975 SA

Sanderson, P.
Nandi atlas. 30pp. K.shs.2.00 ($2.00/60p.) EALB 1955 KE

Sandhu, A.S.
English language for E.AC E. 228pp. K.shs.14.00 Textbook Ctre 1976 KE

Sandhu, A.S.
Key English for C.P.E. 148pp. K.shs.11.50 Textbook Ctre 1967 KE

Sandhu, A.S.
Key junior secondary school. 192pp. K.shs.12.00 Textbook Ctre 1969 KE

Sandilands, A., ed.
One hundred and twenty Negro spirituals. 2nd rev. ed. 158pp. cl. R1.50 Morija 1964 LO

Sanford, W.W.
The role of the impractical. 18pp. 30k 30k (Inaugural lec., 7) Univ Ife Press 1973 NR

Sanga, M.B.
Mashujaa wa Afrika. [Heroes of Africa] photos. Longman Tanz 1973 TZ SWA

Sangaré, Y.
Naissa. 160pp. MF685 pap. Ed Pop - Mali 1972 ML FRE

Sangija, D.
Bado mmoja. [One more.] 131pp. T.shs.6.50 Ndanda Mission Press 1975 TZ SWA

Sangree, W.H.
Age, prayer and politics in Tiriki, Kenya. 312pp. U.shs.50.00 (M.I.S.R. Individual monog., 12) Mak Inst Soc Res 1966 UG

Sangster, E.G., ed.
To know my own. 101pp. ill. 85pes. ($.85) Ghana Publ Corp 1971 GH

Sangster, R.G.
Forestry in Tanzania. K.shs.3.00 EALB 1968 KE

Sangster, W.E.
Re ruta ho rapela. [Teach us to pray.] 32pp. 30c. Methodist 1977 SA SOS

Sangster, W.E.
Sifundise ukuthandaza. [Teach us to pray.] 32pp. 30c. Methodist 1977 SA ZUL

Sankai, S.S.
The Maasai. 3rd ed. K.shs.14.00 ($3.25/£1.60) EALB 5971 KE

Sankawulo, W.G.S.
Liberian folktales. 106pp. $2.00 Liberian Lit 1974 LB

Santos, R.
Deux lexiques tenda: Lexique wey (konagi) 92pp. (C.L.A.D. Étude, 61) CLAD 1975 SG FRE

Sar, M.
Louga et sa région (Sénégal) 308pp. pl. CFA2400.00 (Initiations et etudes Africaines, 30) IFAN 1973 SG FRE

Sarazin, S.
Jeune fille prépare. See: Duteil, P.A.

Sari, D.
La dépossession des fellahs. 147pp. DA9.00 SNED 1975 AE FRE

Sari, D.
L'insurrection de 1871. DA1.00 SNED 1971 AE FRE

Sari, D.
Le reboisement. DA1.00 SNED 1971 AE FRE

Sari, D.
Les villes pré-coloniales dans l'Algérie occidentale. 246pp. photos. maps. DA20.00 SNED 1971 AE FRE

Sarpong, P.
Ghana in retrospect. 142pp. ill. hd. C8.50 ($8.50) Ghana Publ Corp 1974 GH

Sarpong, P.
Girls' nubility rites among the Akans of Ghana. 104pp. ill. hd. C5.40 ($5.40) Ghana Publ Corp 1974 GH

Sarpong, P.
The sacred stools of the Akan. 83pp. ill. photos. 25 pes. ($.25) Ghana Publ Corp 1971 GH

Sauer, H.
Ex Africa. [Reprint of ed. 1937]. 335pp. ill. map. cl. R$7.45 (Rhodesiana Reprint Library, Gold Series, 27) Books of Rhodesia 1973 RH

Saukila, W.S.
Mankhwala opezera chuma. [How tô get rich quick] 36pp. ill. 22t. (17c.) Christ Lit Assoc - Mal 1970 MW CHC

Saukila, W.S.
Money! 48pp. ill. 18t (Voices from Africa Series) Christ Lit Assoc - Mal 1974 MW

Saul, J., ed.
Essays on the political economy of Africa. See: Arrighi, G., ed.

Saul, J., eds.
Socialism in Tanzania, v. 2. See: Cliffe, L., eds.

Saumagne, C.
La Numidie et Rome (Massinissa et Jugurtha) 262pp. D2.130 (Série IV, Histoire, 4) Univ Tunis 1967 TI FRE

Saunders, C.   Derricourt, R.
Beyond the Cape frontier. 240pp. photos. maps. cl. & pap. R4.50 pap. R7.50 cl. Longman - SA 1974 SA

Saunders, C., ed.
The Kitchingman papers. [Limited edition of missionary correspondence from unpublished manuscripts in the collection of H.F. Oppenheimer, Esq.]. See: Le Cordeur, B., ed.

Saunders, J.H., ed.   Edwards, S., ed.
Annual report April 1973 to March 1974, Institute of Agricultural Research. 174pp. ex. only Inst Agric Res - Addis 1976 ET

Saunders, J.H., ed.   Edwards, S., ed.
Gambella experiment station: progress report for the period April 1973 to March 1974 and April 1974 to March 1975 and April 1975 to March 1976. 25pp. ex. only. Inst Agric Res - Addis 1976 ET

Saunders, J.H., ed.   Edwards, S., ed.
Melka Werer research station: progress report for the period April 1973 to March 1974. 225pp. ex. only. Inst Agric Res - Addis 1975 ET

Saunders, J.H., ed.   Edwards, S., ed.
Melka Werer research station progress report for the period April 1974 to March 1975. 172pp. ill. ex. only Inst Agric Res - Addis 1976 ET

Saunders, W., eds.   Horn, P., eds.
It's gettin late, and other poems from "Ophir". 52pp. R1.10 Ravan 1974 SA

Author Index

Saungweme, E.
Banga rehove. [The fishes knife.] 16pp. pl. 5c.
Rhod Lit Bur 1974 RH SHO

Savage, E.B.
The rose and the vine. 197pp. L.E.2.000 cl.
L.E.1.500 pap. ($5.75 cl.) ($5.00 pap.) Am Univ
1961 UA

Savage, G.A.R.
The essentials of Luo (Acholi) 99pp. K.shs.2.00
($1.25/50p.) EALB 1956 KE

Savage, G.A.R.
A short Acholi-English and English-Acholi vocabulary. cl.
K.shs2.50 ($1.50/65p.) EALB 1955 KE

Sawyerr, H.
The springs of Mende belief and custom. See: Harris,
W.T.

Sayadi, M.
Al Jam'iyya al Khalduniyya 1896-1958. 272pp. photos.
D1,400 Maison Tunis 1975 TI FRE

Saylor, R.G.
Administration of innovations. 22pp. T.shs12.00
($3.00) (Research pap., 69.18) Econ Res Bur - Tanz
1969 TZ

Saylor, R.G.
An economic evaluation of farmer education in Tanzania.
T.shs.12.00 ($3.00) (Research pap., 68.32) Econ Res
Bur - Tanz 1975 TZ

Saylor, R.G.
An opinion survey of Bwana Shambas in Tanzania.
52pp. ill. T.shs12.00 ($3.00) (Research pap., 70.15)
Econ Res Bur - Tanz 1970 TZ

Saylor, R.G.
A social cost/benefit analysis of the agricultural extension
and research services in selected cotton growing areas of
western Tanzania. T.shs.12.00 ($3.00) (Research
pap., 70.24) Econ Res Bur - Tanz 1974 TZ

Saylor, R.G.
Variations in Sukumaland cotton yields and the extension
service. 37pp. ill. T.shs12.00 ($3.00) (Research
pap., 70.5) Econ Res Bur - Tanz 1970 TZ

Scammaca del Murgo, E., ed.
Afewerk Teklé. Text in English and Italian. ill. col. ill. cl.
$20.00 cl. Bookshop Supply Org (distr.) 1973 ET

Schaeffer, M. Heyne, J.F.
Industrial law in South Africa. R6.50 Van Schaik SA

Schattil, A.
Index to the South African tax cases (v.1-20) R6.00
Juta SA

Schatz, S.P.
Economics, politics and administration in government
lending: the regional loans board. N3.50 ($5.25)
NISER 1970 NR

Schatzl, L.
The Nigerian coal industry. 78pp. N2.00 ($3.00)
(N.I.S.E.R. research report, 8) NISER 1969 NR

Schatzl, L.H.
Petroleum in Nigeria. 257pp. maps. N4.20 OUP-Nig
1969 NR

Schieffelin, H.M.
The people of Africa. A series of papers on their
character, condition and future prospects. (Reprint of ed.
New York, 1871; with a new introduction by K. Mahmud)
164pp. pl. cl. & pap. N3.50 pap. N5.00 cl. Ibadan
UP 1975 NR

Schipper-de Leeuw, M.
Le blanc vu d'Afrique. 262pp. CFA1,500 CLE 1974
CM FRE

Schlemmer, L., ed. Webster, E., ed.
Change, reform and economic growth in South Africa.
250pp. R6.50 ($9.00/£4.25) Ravan 1977 SA

Schlemmer, L. Stopforth, P.
Poverty, family patterns and material aspirations among
Africans in a border industry township. 89pp. R3.00
(Institute for Social Research, Research Reports) Inst Soc
Res - Natal 1974 SA

Schlemmer, L.
Priviledge, prejudice and parties. (A study of political
motivation among White voters in Durban) 85pp. R1.50
($2.75) SA Inst of Race Relations 1973 SA

Schlemmer, L.
Student protest and the white public in Durban.
See: Smith, A.

Schlemmer, L.
A study of community development needs and morale
among Africans in a non-farm rural employee community
in Natal. See: Oosthuizen, M.J.

Schlemmer, L. Oosthuizen, M.J.
A study of employee morale among Africans in a rural
non-farm employment situation. .101pp. R2.00
(Institute for Social Research, Research Reports) Inst Soc
Res - Natal 1974 SA

Schlemmer, L. Weaver, C.
A study of labour turnover in a process industry. 127pp.
R2.00 (Institute for Social Research, Research Reports)
Inst Soc Res - Natal 1974 SA

Schlemmer, L. Stopforth, P.
A study of malnutrition in the Nqutu district of KwaZulu.
58pp. R2.00 (Institute for Social Research, Fact
Papers, 2) Inst Soc Res - Natal 1974 SA

Schlemmer, L. Lamond, N.
A theoretical approach to the study of the hospital as a
social organisation. 43pp. 75c Inst Soc Res-Natal
1968 SA

Schmidt, C.A.
Hydro-electric services, with particular reference to the
Kafue Gorge hydro-electric project. 14pp. 60n.
($1.50) (Zambia Geographical Assoc., occas. paps., 1)
Zambia Geog Assoc 1972(?) ZA

Schmidt, E.R.
The relationship between compressive strength and
modulus of rupture of fired clay products. See: Pieterse,
J.J.

Schmidt, H.E. Turpie, D.W.F.
The processing of wool/cotton blends on the worsted
system, part II: the effect of various carding conditions.
16pp. R2.50 (SAWTRI Technical Reports, 306)
SAWTRI 1976 SA

Schmidt-Ihms, M.
Companion to the study of the German language. 452pp.
R4.50 Univ of Natal 1968 SA

Schmidt, J. Dumont, P.
Eléments de phonétique corrective. v. 3: cahier
d'exercices de phonétique pour les élèves de 6ème.
40pp. CFA320 (C.L.A.D. Etude, 26) CLAD 1968 SG
FRE

Schmidt, J. Dumont, P.
Le film de l'action verbale. 45pp. CFA250 (C.L.A.D.
Etude, 25) CLAD 1968 SG FRE

Schmidt, M.M.
Needlework and clothing, standard 8. See: Walt,
W.A.v.d.

Schmidt, M.M. Roberts, C.M.P.
On with the apron. Housecraft for standard 8. 404pp. ill.
photo. R7.00 Nasou 1976 SA

Schmitz, M.
Flowering plants of Lesotho. 123pp. ill. R7.00
Mazenod Inst 1976 LO

Schneider, B.A.T.
The study of German literature. 13pp. 20c. (70c.)
Univ South Africa 1963 SA

Schnell, B.
Ukunga. [Handbook of midwifery.] 2nd ed. 300pp. ill.
hd. T.shs.30.00 Ndanda Mission Press 1976 TZ SWA

Schnell, C.J.W.
   Junior secondary mathematics for standard 5.
   See: Ahlers, H.J.
Schnell, R. et al.
   Mélanges botaniques. 290pp. ill. CFA2800
   (Mémoires de l'IFAN, 75) IFAN 1966 SG FRE
Schnell, R.
   Mélanges botaniques. See: Monod, T.
Schnell, R.
   Végétation et flore de la région montagneuse du Nimba
   (Afrique occidentale française) 604pp. pl. CFA2800
   (Mémoires de l'IFAN, 22) IFAN 1952 SG FRE
Schnell, W.J.
   What are the Jehovah's witnesses? 13pp. K.shs.1.00
   Evangel 1970 KE
Schnetz-McGreavey, M.
   Language for life. R2.25 Van Schaik SA
Schoeman, E., ed.
   Periodicals on classical antiquity and related subjects.
   29pp. 50c. (Bibliographies, 5) State-Lib-SA 1963 SA
Schoeman, T.
   Guide to the Companies Act and regulations. Revision
   service no. 4. R7.50 Juta 1976 SA
Schoffeleers, M.
   Rock paintings and Nyau symbols in Malawi.
   See: Lindgren, N.
Scholtz, J. du P.
   Moses Kottler - His Cape years. ill. pl. cl. R25.00
   Tafelberg 1976 SA
Scholtz, J.C.
   Stocklam market survey. See: White, M.D.
Schomberg, A.C.B.
   Guide for teachers of English. See: de Turville, J.R.P.D.
Schonau, A.P.G.
   A site evaluation study in black wattle (Acacia mearnsii, De
   wild) 148pp. pl. R4.00 (A v.44, no.2) Univ
   Stellenbosch, Lib 1969 SA
Schonfrucht, R.M.
   The Cape press 1851-1855. 44pp. 50c. Univ Cape
   Town Lib 1955 SA
Schonherr, S.
   Bean production in Kenya's central and eastern provinces.
   See: Mbugua, E.S.
Schonland, S.
   Phanerogamic flora of the division of Uitenhage and Port
   Elizabeth. 25c. (Memoirs of the Botanical Survey of
   South Africa, 1) Botanical Res Inst 1919 SA
Schonseck, P.
   Le privilege des impôts directs au Maroc dans ses
   rapports avec les autres sûretés mobilières. Dir25.00
   (Coll. Fac. des Sciences juridiques, économiques et
   sociales, 12) Ed La Porte 1961 MR FRE
Schoonraad, M.
   Walter Battiss. 64pp. ill. col. ill. cl. R9.75 (South
   African Art Library, 5) Struik 1976 SA
Schoroeder, M. Beissner, R.D.
   Yao lernt Deutsch. Deuxième année. Cahiers d'exercices.
   CFA100 Nouv Ed Afric 1975 SG FRE
Schoroeder, M. Beissner, R.D.
   Yao lernt Deutsch. Deuxième année. Livre de l'élève.
   CFA500 Nouv Ed Afric 1975 SG FRE
Schouteden, H.
   La faune ornithologique du Rwanda. 130pp. map.
   RF140 (FB105.00/$2.60) (Institut National de
   Recherche Scientifique, 1) Inst Nat - Rwandaise 1966
   RW FRE
Schouten, P.
   The simultaneous shrinkproofing and dyeing of wool
   fabrics with the bisulphire adducts of a polyurethane
   resine, a polyacrylate resin and reactive dyes.
   See: Silver, H.M.

Schram, R.
   A history of the Nigerian health services. 480pp. pl.
   maps. N10.00 cl. Ibadan UP 1971 NR
Schreckenbach, H.
   No time to die. See: Kyei, K.G.
Schreiner, O.
   The story of an African farm. (New ed. with an introduction
   by Richard Rive) New ed. 282pp. cl. R6.90 (£4.95)
   (Africana Library) Donker 1975 SA
Schreiner, O.
   Thoughts on South Africa. (Reprint of ed. 1923) 398pp.
   ill. cl. R17.00 (Africana Reprint Library, 10) Africana
   Book Soc 1977 SA
Schreiner, O.
   Trooper Peter Halket of Mashonaland. 126pp. cl.
   R4.90 (£3.50) (Africana Library) Donker 1974 SA
Schreiner, O.D.
   The nettle: political power and race relations in South
   Africa. 95pp. 50c. ($1.45) SA Inst of Race
   Relations 1964 SA
Schrodeder, M.
   Yao Lernt Deutsch. Classe de 4e, livre de l'élève.
   See: Beissner, R.D.
Schroeder, J.
   Isihlaziyo sevangeli Likamathewu. [Commentary on St.
   Mathew's gospel] 95pp. 30c. Shuter 1966 SA ZUL
Schroeder, M. Beisner, R.D.
   Yao lernt Deutsch. Cahier d'exercices. 32pp. CFA140
   Nouv Ed Afric 1974 SG FRE
Schroeder, M. Beisner, R.D.
   Yao lernt Deutsch. Première année. 64pp. CFA600.00
   Nouv Ed Afric 1974 SG FRE
Schutte, A.G., ed.
   Black religion in South Africa, ['African Studies' special
   number, v. 33, no. 2]. See: Dubb, A.A., ed.
Schutte, H.J.
   A course in linear algebra and geometry. R7.50
   Rhodes Univ Lib 1972 SA
Schutte, H.J.
   Ontological commitment and mathematics. ex. only
   (Inaugural lec.) Rhodes Univ Lib 1969 SA
Schwager, C.
   Lesotho. See: Schwager, D.
Schwager, D. Schwager, C.
   Lesotho. 2nd rev. ed. 110pp. cl. R9.95 Struik
   1974 SA
Schwartz, A.
   La vie quotidienne dans un village guéré. 178pp. ill.
   CFA950 pap. INADES 1975 IC FRE
Schyff, P.J.v.d.
   Senior secondary mathematics for standard 9.
   See: Ahle-s, H.J.
Schyff, P.J.v.d.
   Senior secondary mathematics, standard 10.
   See: Ahlers, H.J.
Science Teachers Association of Nigeria (STAN)
   Nigerian integrated science project: teachers guide. 1, 2
   bks 95pp. ill. N1.35 Heinemann Educ - Nig 1972
   NR
Science Teachers Association of Nigeria (STAN)
   Nigerian integrated science project: teachers guide. 2, 2
   bks 60pp. ill. N1.35 Heinemann Educ - Nig 1972
   NR
Science Teachers Association of Nigeria (STAN)
   Nigerian integrated science project: textbk. 1, 2bks
   112pp. ill. N1.10 Heinemann Educ - Nig 1971 NR
Science Teachers Association of Nigeria (STAN)
   Nigerian integrated science project: textbk. 2, 2 bks
   102pp. ill. N1.10 Heinemann Educ - Nig 1972 NR
Science Teachers Association of Nigeria (STAN)
   Nigerian integrated science project: workbk. 2, 2 bks
   62pp. ill. 90k Heinemann Educ - Nig 1972 NR

Science Teachers Association of Nigeria (STAN)
Nigerian integrated science project: workbk. 98pp. ill.
80k Heinemann Educ - Nig 1972 NR

Scoble, C.N.
The law of master and servant in South Africa. 463pp.
hd. R9.50 Butterworths 1956 SA

Scotney, N.
Health education. A manual for medical assistants and
other rural health workers. 141pp. ill. K.shs.10.50
(Rural Health Series, 3) African Med Res Found 1976
KE

Scott, A.
Middle forms objective questions in English language: with
answers. See: Cairns, J.

Scott, A.
Middle forms objective questions in English language:
without answers. See: Cairns, J.

Scott, A.
Objective questions in English language. See: Cairns, J.

Scott, D.B.
The genus eupenicillium ludwig. 150pp. ill. (CSIR
research reports, 272) CSIR 1968 SA

Scott-Forbes, D. Last, M.
Teacher's notes for book four. 196pp. ill. Eth. $3.25
(The New Oxford English Course, 4) OUP-Addis 1972
ET

Scott, J.E.
Etienne LeRoux. 21pp. R1.60 Dept Bibliog, Lib &
Typo 1971 SA

Scott, P.E.
Cataloguing monographs. A manual illustrating the
Anglo-American cataloguing rules, British text, 1975. 2nd
ed. 103pp. R2.00 (Dept. of Librarianship, special
pub., 4) Rhodes Univ Lib 1976 SA

Scott, P.E., ed.
Mqhayi in translation: a short autobiography of Samuel
Krune Mqhayi; the death of Hintsa and the dismissal of Sir
Benjamin D'Urban. 47pp. R1.00 (Rhodes Univ. Dept.
of African Languages. Communications series, 6) Dept.
African Lang - Rhodes 1976 SA

Scott, P.E.
Facsimile title pages; to accompany Cataloguing
monographs, a manual...etc. 88pp. R1.50 Rhodes
Univ Lib 1976 SA

Scott, P.E.
James James Ranisi Jolobe: an annotated bibliography.
50c (Rhodes University, Dept. of African Languages,
Communications series, 1) Dept African Lang - Rhodes
1973 SA

Scott, P.E.
Samuel Edward Krune Mqhayi, 1875-1945: a bibliographic
survey. 49pp. R1.00 (Rhodes Univ. Dept. of African
Languages. Communications series, 5) Dept. of African
Lang - Rhodes 1976 SA

Scott, R.
Computers for developing countries. 86pp. photos.
K.shs.15.95 ($4.00) EAPH 1971 KE

Scott, R.
The development of trade unions in Uganda. 195pp.
maps. K.shs.27.50 ($5.80) EAPH 1966 KE

Scott, T.W. Fairbairn, D.G.
Brick veneer construction for South Africa. 12pp. ill.
(CSIR research reports, 255) CSIR 1968 SA

Scott, T.W.
Cooler houses in a warm climate. A South West African
experiment. 10pp. gratis (CSIR research report, 311)
CSIR 1973 SA

Scott, T.W.
A guide to the design, selection of materials, construction,
and performance of timber-frame brick veneer houses in
South Africa. [Also available in Afrikaans.]. See: Kitcher,
J.S.

Scudder, T.
The ecology of the Gwembe Tonga. 296pp. ill. photos.
maps. K5.25 (£4.00) Inst Afr Stud - Lusaka 1962
ZA

Scudder, T.
Gathering among African woodland savannah cultivators.
A case study: the Gwembe Tonga. 50pp. K1.50
(75p.) (Zambian paps., 5) Inst Afr Stud - Lusaka 1971
ZA

Seagrief, S.C.
Reading the signs. ex. only Rhodes Univ Lib 1976 SA

Searle, C.
Illustrations in the Cape Times Annual 1896-1923. 43pp.
Dept Bibliog, Lib & Typo 1971 SA

Seary, E.R., ed.
South African short stories. 232pp. R2.65 OUP-SA
1970 SA

Seaton, E.
The Meru land case. See: Japheth, K.

Seaton, E.
Mzozo wa ardhi ya wameru. See: Japheth, K.

Seaton, E. Maliti, S.
Tanzania treaty practice. 196pp. K.shs.52.75
OUP-Nairobi 1973 KE

Sebag, P.
Un faubourg de Tunis (Saïda Manoubia) 90pp. photos.
D1.275 (Série III, Mémoires du Centre d'Etudes
Humaines, 6) Univ Tunis 1960 TI FRE

Sebag, P.
La hara de Tunis: l'évolution d'un ghetto. 92pp. photos.
D1.275 (Série III, Mémoires du Centre d'Etudes
Humaines, 5) Univ Tunis 1959 TI FRE

Sebag, P.
Une relation inédite sur la prise de Tunis par les Turcs en
1574. 248pp. pl. D2.000 (Série V, Sources de
l'Histoire Tunisienne, 4) Univ Tunis 1971 TI FRE

Sebukima, D.
Growing up. 2nd ed. 132pp. K.shs.12.00
($3.30/£1.60) EALB 1976 KE

Sebukima, D.
The half-brothers. 280pp. K.shs.12.50 (Modern
African Library) EAPH 1974 KE

Sebukima, D.
A son of Kabira. 2nd. ed. 124pp. K.shs9.25
OUP-Nairobi 1972 KE

Seck, A.
Dakar métropole ouest africaine. 517pp. CFA5000
(Mémoires de l'IFAN, 85) IFAN 1970 SG FRE

Seck, C. A.
Njangaan. 40pp. ill. CFA500 (F13.00) Nouv Ed
Afric 1975 SG FRE

Seck, I.
Jean le fou. 96pp. CFA600 (F12.00) Nouv Ed Afric
1976 SG FRE

Secretariat d'Etat à la culture de Côte d'Ivoire.
Le President Houphouët-Boigny et la nation ivoirienne.
328pp. CFA2000 Nouv Ed Afric 1975 SG FRE

Seddon, D.
Pre-history in perspective: a comment on archaeology in
South Africa. 40c. (Isma paps., 22) Inst Study of
Man 1966 SA

Sefrioui, A.
La maison de servitude. 126pp. DA8.00 SNED 1973
AE FRE

Segal, M.D.
Revenue effects of East African transfer taxes. 13pp. ill.
T.shs.12.00 ($3.00) (Research pap., 71.18) Econ Res
Bur - Tanz 1971 TZ

Segal, M.D.
A survey of firms protected by transfer taxes.
T.shs.12.00 ($3.00) (Research pap., 71.18) Econ Res
Bur - Tanz 1975 TZ

Segal, M.D.
Transfer taxes and East African cooperation: a survey of some issues.   T.shs.12.00   ($3.00)   (Research pap., 70.26)   Econ Res Bur - Tanz   1975 TZ

Segall, M.M.   Hamza, M.M.
Care of the newborn baby in Tanzania.   48pp.   ill.   T.shs.5.00   ($2.35)   Tanz Publ House   1973 TZ

Segers, J.
Actions pour le développement, animées par des responsables de la communauté catholique en République du Zaire.   62pp.   Z2.00   CEPAS   1972 ZR FRE

Segers, J.
Actions pour le développement au niveau des communautés locales.   54pp.   Z1.50   CEPAS   1976 ZR FRE

Segers, J.   Habiyambere, A.
Les conditions de la croissance économique.   2nd ed.   327pp.   Z4.00   CEPAS   1973 ZA FRE

Segganyi, E.A.K. et al.
Ssebato bafuma.   [Short stories and folklore]   2nd ed.   16pp.   ill.   K.shs.6.15   ($1.75/70p.)   EALB   1965 KE LUG

Segun, A.O.
Dissection guides of common tropical animals: v. 1 earthworm.   45pp.   ill.   N1.00   Ethiope   1973 NR

Segun, F.O.
Cry justice: interviews with Old Testament prophets about a nation in crisis.   40pp.   40k   Daystar   1967 NR

Segun, M.
Friends, Nigerians, countrymen.   74pp.   ill.   N1.20   OUP - Nig   1977 NR

Segun, M.
My father's daughter.   80pp.   ill.   53k   (African Reader's Library, 8)   Pilgrim   1965 NR

Sehlke, K.H.L.
A study of the thermal behaviour of blast-furnace slag by means of a heating microscope.   40pp.   ill.   (CSIR research reports, 239)   CSIR   1966 SA

Seidman, A.
Comparative development strategies in East Africa.   294pp.   ill.   K.shs.45.00   ($12.00)   EAPH   1972 KE

Seidman, A.
Planning for development in Sub-Saharan Africa.   382pp.   pl. maps.   T.shs.36.00 (Africa only)   Tanz Publ House   1974 TZ

Seidmann, A.
Ghana's development experience.   312pp.   K.shs.48.00 ($12.00)   EAPH   1976 KE

Seidner, M.
Les nouveaux lotophages.   116pp.   D0.300   Maison Tunis   1968 TI FRE

Sekalala, A.
Guide lines for businessmen and women.   38pp.   hd.   U.shs4.00   Adult Educ Centre   UG

Sekalala, A.
What is a newspaper?   52pp.   hd.   U.shs3.00   Adult Educ Centre   1967 UG

Sekelli, Z.
L'art culinaire à travers l'Algérie.   456pp.   ill. col. ill. cl.   45,00 DA   SNED   1973 AE FRE

Selkirk, D.K.
Domestic science textbook.   See: Fouche, R.

Selous, F.C.
A hunter's wanderings in Africa.   [Reprint ed. 1881].   455pp.   ill. cl.   R$13.15 cl.   (Rhodesiana Repirnt Library, Gold Series, 14)   Books of Rhodesia   1970 RH

Selous, F.C.
Sunshine and storm in Rhodesia.   (Reprint ed. 1896) ed.   299pp.   ill. photos. cl.   R$9.55 cl.   (Gold Series, 2)   Books of Rhodesia   1968 RH

Selous, F.C.
Travel and adventure in south-east Africa.   [Reprint of ed. 1893].   503pp.   ill. map. cl.   R$7.80 cl.   (Rhodesiana Reprint Library, Gold Series, 25)   Books of Rhodesia   1972 RH

Sembajwe, I.
Rural urban differentials in fertility and child mortality in Tanzania.   T.shs.15.00   ($5.00)   (Research pap., 28)   Bur Res Assess - Tanz   1975 TZ

Sembera, F.
Maisha nuksi.   [Troubled life.]   112pp.   T.shs.8.00   Longman - Tanz   1975 TZ SWA

Seme, W.B.N.
Njozi za usiku.   [Night dreams]   Longman Tanz   1973 TZ SWA

Semghanga, F.H.J.
Teuzi za nafsi.   [Poems about personal sentiments]   68pp.   T.shs.3.50   Inst Swahili Res   1971 TZ SWA

Semkiwa, D.
Mazungumzo ya babu zetu.   [Our forefathers' talks]   bk. 1   64pp.   K.shs.4.75   OUP-Nairobi   1971 KE SWA

Semkiwa, D.
Mazungumzo ya babu zetu.   [Our forefather's talks.]   bk. 2   92pp.   K.shs.10.00   OUP - Nairobi   1974 KE SWA

Semple, D.W.
A Scots missionary in the Transkei.   74pp.   35c.   Lovedale   1965 SA

Semple, H.
Encounter with age...or how to avoid a nervous breakdown while growing old.   See: Borowitz, A.

Semuggoma, S.
The peripheral zone of Kampala.   See: O'Connor, A.M.

Sender, J.
Some preliminary notes on the politics of rural development in Tanzania, based on a case study in the western Usambaras.   T.shs.12.00   ($3.00)   (Research pap., 74.5)   Econ Res Bur - Tanz   1974 TZ

Senga, W., ed.
Agricultural development in Kenya: an economic assessment.   See: Heyer, J., ed.

Sengat-Kuo, F.
Fleurs de latérite.   56pp.   CFA270   CLE   1971 CM FRE

Senghor, L.S.
Lettres d'Hivernage.   [With illustrations by Marc Chagall.].   80pp.   ill. col. ill.   CFA4,200 Africa only   (F84.00)   Nouv Ed Afric   1973 SG FRE

Senghor, L.S.
La parole chez Paul Claudel et chez les Négro-Africains.   40pp.   CFA500   (F10.00)   Nouv Ed Afric   1973 SG FRE

Senghor, L.S.
Paroles.   80pp.   CFA300   (F6.00)   Nouv Ed Afric   1975 SG FRE

Senghor, L.S.
Pour une relecture africaine de Marx et d'Engels.   72pp.   CFA600   (F12.00)   Nouv Ed Afric   1976 SG FRE

Sengo, T.S.Y.   Kiango, S.D.
Ndimi zetu.   [Our spoken tongue. Critical essays on Swahili literature.]   bk. 1.   62pp.   T.shs.9.00   Longman - Tanz   1973 TZ SWA

Sengo, T.S.Y.   Kiango, S.D.
Ndimi zetu.   [Our spoken tongue. Critical essays on Swahili literature.]   bk. 2.   80pp.   T.shs.6.50   Longman - Tanz   1975 TZ SWA

Sengo, T.S.Y.
Shaaban Robert.   [Critical survey of the writings by Shaaban Robert.].   80pp.   T.shs.6.50   Longman - Tanz   1975 TZ SWA

Sengo, T.S.Y.   Lucas, S.A.
Utani na jamii ukwere.   [Joking relationship among the Ukwere people: a sociological study.]   107pp.   K.shs.15.00   ($6.00)   Foundation   1975 KE SWA

Sepamla, S.
The blues is you in me. 72pp. R2.50 Donker 1976 SA

Sepamla, S.
Hurry up to it. 72pp. R2.50 Donker 1975 SA

Seriki, E., ed. Pullybank, E., ed.
Visitors guide to Lagos. 2nd ed. 160pp. ill. col. ill. maps col. maps. N1.50 West African Book 1977 NR

Serote, M. W.
Yakhal'inkomo. Poems. 52pp. R1.80 ($2.40/£1.25) (Renoster Books) Ravan 1972 SA

Serote, M.W.
Yakhal' inkomo. Poems. 52pp. R1.80 ($2.40/£1.25) (Renoster Books) Ravan; distr. 1973 SA

Serour, A.
Cairo: A practical guide. [revised entry]. See: Cowley, D.

Serpell, R.
Chi-Nyanja comprehension by Lusaka school children: a field experiment in second language learning. 57pp. free (Human Development Research Unit Report, 16) Dept Psychology - Zam 1970 ZA

Serpell, R.
Cross-cultural differences in the difficulty of copying orientation: a response organization hypothesis. 44pp. free (Human Development Research Unit Report, 12) Dept Psychology - Zam 1969 ZA

Serpell, R.
Culture's influence on behaviour. 144pp. ill. (80p.) School of Hum and Soc Sci - Zam 1976 ZA

Serpell, R.
Estimates of intelligence in a rural community of eastern Zambia. 41pp. 50n (Human Development Research Unit Report, 25) Dept Psychology - Zam 1974 ZA

Serpell, R. Deregowski, J.B.
Frames of reference for copying orientation: a cross-cultural study. 19pp. free (Human Development Research Unit Report, 19) Dept Psychology - Zam 1971 ZA

Serpell, R.
Selective attention: a mediating process in discrimination learning by children. 57pp. free (Human Development Research Unit Report, 14) Dept Psychology - Zam 1970 ZA

Serpell, R.
Selective attention and interference between first and second languages. 105pp. K1.50 (75p.) (Communications, 4) Inst Soc Res - Zam 1968 ZA

Serpell, R.
Selective attention in matching from sample by children. 15pp. free (Human Development Research Unit Report, 2) Dept Psychology - Zam 1966 ZA

Serpell, R. Deregowski, J.B.
Teaching pictorial depth perception: a classroom experiment. 21pp. free (Human Development Research Unit Report, 21) Dept Psychology - Zam 1972 ZA

Seruma, E.
The experience. 165pp. K.shs8.50 ($2.60) EAPH 1970 KE

Seruma, E.
Girl of God. 120pp. K.shs.10.00 Transafrica 1975 KE

Seruma, E.
The heart seller. 165pp. K.shs8.50 ($2.60) EAPH 1971 KE

Seruma, E.
The king hunts. EAPH 1973 NG

Serumaga, R.
The elephants. 68pp. K.shs7.00 (New Drama from Africa, 6) OUP-Nairobi 1972 KE

Serumaga, R.
Majangwa: a promise of rains, and, a play. 100pp. K.shs.9.50 (African Theatre, 5) EAPH 1974 KE

Serunkuma, J.N.B.
George Stephenson. K.shs.1.00 ($1.25/50p.) EALB 1962 UG KE

Service Géologique de Madagascar.
Atlas des fossiles caractéristiques de Madagascar. v.7: Index. 25pp. FMG182 (F3.64) Service Geol - Mad 1962 MG FRE

Service Géologique de Madagascar.
Comptes rendus de la semaine géologique, 1963. 300pp. pl. maps. cl. FMG1500 cl. (F30.00 cl.) (Annales Géologiques de Madagascar, 33) Service Geol - Mad 1963 MG FRE

Service Géologique de Madagascar.
Comptes rendus de la semaine géologique. 150pp. pl. photos. cl. (F30.00 cl.) Service Geol - Mad 1964 MG FRE

Service Géologique de Madagascar.
Comptes rendus de la semaine géologique. 146pp. pl. photos. cl. FMG1500 cl. (F30.00 cl.) Service Geol - Mad 1965 MG FRE

Service Géologique de Madagascar.
Comptes rendus de la semaine géologique. 100pp. pl. photos. cl. FMG1500 cl. (F30.00 cl.) Service Geol - Mad 1967 MG FRE

Service Géologique de Madagascar.
Comptes rendus de la semaine géologique. 184pp. pl. photos. cl. FMG1500 cl. (F30.00 cl.) Service Geol - Mad 1969 MG FRE

Service Géologique de Madagascar.
Comptes rendus de la semaine géologique. 122pp. pl. cl. FMG1500 cl. (F30.00 cl.) Service Geol - Mad 1970 MG FRE

Service Géologique de Madagascar.
La géochronologie à Madagascar en 1962. 10pp. pl. FMG77 (F1.45) (Série Documentation, 158) Service Geol - Mad 1963 MG FRE

Service Géologique de Madagascar.
Géologie de Madagascar. Les terrains sedimentaires. 463pp. pl. cl. FMG3000 cl. (F60.00 cl.) (Annales Géologiques de Madagascar, 35) Service Geol - Mad 1971 MG FRE

Service Géologique de Madagascar.
Rapports annuels du service géologique de Madagascar. 173pp. pl. photos. FMG2233 (F44.66) Service Geol - Mad 1961 MG FRE

Service Géologique de Madagascar.
Rapports annuels du service géologique de Madagascar. 273pp. pl. photos. FMG2814 (F56.28) Service Geol - Mad 1962 MG FRE

Service Géologique de Madagascar.
Rapports annuels du service géologique de Madagascar. 267pp. pl. FMG2261 (F45.22) Service Geol - Mad 1963 MG FRE

Service Géologique de Madagascar.
Rapports annuels du service géologique de Madagascar. 253pp. pl. FMG2163 (F43.26) Service Geol - Mad 1964 MG FRE

Service Géologique de Madagascar.
Rapports annuels du service géologique de Madagascar. 239pp. pl. photo. FMG2.123 (F42.46) Service Geol - Mad 1965 MG FRE

Service Géologique de Madagascar.
Rapports annuels du service géologique de Madagascar. 160pp. pl. FMG1500 (F30.00) Service Geol - Mad 1969 MG FRE

Service Géologique de Madagascar.
Rapports annuels du service géologique de Madagascar. 184pp. pl. FMG1780 pap. (F35.60 pap.) Service Geol - Mad 1970 MG FRE

Service Géologique de Madagascar.
Rapports annuels du service géologique de Madagascar.
197pp. pl. FMG1950 (F39.00) Service Geol - Mad
1971 MG FRE

Seshie M.
Akpalu fe hawo. See: Klutse, L.

Setidisho, E.
Induku ayinamzi [Novel]. 112pp. ill. 80c OUP-SA
1965 SA XHO

Setidisho, N.O.H. Oyelese, J.O.
Introduction to graphs: arithmetical graphs. 112pp.
72k Macmillan 1963 NR

Setiloane, G.M.
The image of God among the Sotho-Tswana. 300pp.
R7.00 ($10.00) Balkema 1975 SA

Setse, T.K.
Current issues in Ghanaian education. 29pp. C1.00
Univ Ghana Bkshop 1974 GH

Setse, T.K.
Foundations of nation-building: the case of Achimota
School. 53pp. map. C1.00 (C1.50) Univ Ghana
Bkshop 1974 GH

Seula, P.J.
Ezabancane qha. See: Keyi, S.B.

Sevareid, P., ed.
Local government councillors' seminar. (Conference
Papers) K.shs.13.00 Kenya Inst Admin 1971 KE

Sevareid, P., ed. Kinyua, D.M., ed.
The local government regulations 1963. 2nd ed.
134pp. K.shs.30.00 Kenya Inst Admin 1977 KE

Sevareid, P.
An introduction to administrative law in Kenya. 2nd ed.
80pp. K.shs10.00 Kenya Inst Admin 1971 KE

Sevareid, P.
Readings in administrative law. 260pp. K.shs20.00
Kenya Inst Admin 1971 KE

Sewitz, M.
Children's books in English in an African setting
1914-1964. 97pp. R4.95 Dept Bibliog, Lib & Typo
1965 SA

Sey, K.A., ed.
Aphra Behn's oroonoko. [The royal slave.] 84pp.
($3.00) Ghana Publ Corp 1977 GH TWI

Seymour, L.F.
The law and you. 79pp. pl. 48c Mambo 1964 RH

Seymour, S.M.
Bantu law in South Africa. 3rd ed. 486pp. hd., pap.
R16.00 hd. R12.50 pap. Juta 1970 SA

Seyoum, Y., ed.
Ninth annual meeting - National Crop Improvement
Committee, 1976. 385pp. Inst Agric Res - Addis 1977
ET

Shabangu, S.S.
Imvu yolahleko. [The lost sheep] 176pp. 80c.
Shuter 1966 SA ZUL

Shagari, S.
Wakar Nijeriya. [Geography and history of Nigeria in
verse] ill. 85k Northern Nig 1973 NR HAU

Shakespeare, W.
Juliasi Kaizari. [Julius Caesar] tr. fr. Eng..J.K. Nyerere
100pp. K.shs.6.50 OUP-Nairobi 1969 KE SWA

Shakespeare, W.
Mabepari wa Venisi. [The Merchant of Venice] tr. fr.
Eng. J.K. Nyerere 96pp. K.shs.6.50 OUP-Nairobi
1969 KE SWA

Shakespeare, W.
Macbeth [in Tigrinya]. 122pp. Eth$2.00 Bible
Churmen's Miss Soc 1972 ET TIG

Shakespeare, W.
Makbeth. [Macbeth tr. fr. Eng. S.S. Mushi] 84pp.
T.shs.5.00 Tanz Publ House 1968 TZ SWA

Shakespeare, W.
Mantse Lear. [King Lear tr. fr. Engl. E.A. Engmann]
151pp. 45pes. Waterville 1960 GH GAA

Shakespeare, W.
Tufani. [The tempest.] tr. fr. English S.S. Mushi.
100pp. T.shs.5.00 Tanz Publ House 1969 TZ SWA

Shakespeare, W.
Venice dzrayelc le. [The Merchant of Venice tr. fr. Engl.
E.A. Engmann] 108pp. 40pes. Waterville 1950 GH
GAA

Shamuyarira, N.M.
Essays on the liberation of Southern Africa. 2nd ed.
95pp. T.shs.6.00 ($2.85) (Univ. Dar es Salaam,
Studies in Political Science, 3) Tanz Publ House 1975
TZ

Shandling, E.R.
Vocational guidance in South Africa 1920-1965. 68pp.
80c. Univ Cape Town Lib 1967 SA

Shange, O.L.
Injula nokujiya Kwesizulu. [Depth and beauty of Zulu]
214pp. 85c Shuter 1953 SA ZUL

Shange, O.L.
Isizulu a incwadi yesibili. See: Ndlovu, R.S.

Shange, O.L.
Isizulu a incwadi yokuqala. See: Ndlovu, R.S.

Shanks, I.P.
School gardening and agriculture. 180pp. ill.
K.shs17.50 OUP-Nairobi 1964 KE

Shanks, I.P.
Simple science and nature study. 224pp. ill.
K.shs15.50 OUP-Nairobi 1965 KE NEG

Shannon, B.A.
Investigation of the suitability of the Rothwell-Miller Interest
Blank for a black population. 23pp. (CSIR Special
Report, PERS 233) CSIR 1975 SA

Shanwa, A.
Mtu asiye na uso. [A man without a face] 80pp. ill.
K.shs.3.50 OUP-Nairobi 1968 KE SWA

Shanwa.
Mtu mamba. [The crocodile man] 60pp. maps.
K.shs.7.50 OUP-Nairobi 1971 KE SWA

Shapire, K.H.
Efficiency and progressiveness in peasant agriculture: a
research proposal for Geita district. T.shs.12.00
($3.00) (Research pap., 69.33) Econ Res Bur - Tanz
1975 TZ

Shapiro, G.B.
The law of building contracts and arbitration in South
Africa. See: McKenzie, H.S.

Shapiro, H.A.
Pneumoconiosis: Proceedings of the international
conference, Johannesburg, 1969. 672pp. photo ill.
R16.00 OUP-SA 1970 SA

Shariff, I.N., ed.
Utendi ya qiyama. K.shs.2.75 (30p.) (Sanaa Ya
Utungo, 5) Heinemann Educ - Nair 1972 KE SWA

Sharma, G.
Soil zoology. See: Madge, D.

Sharma, R.L.
Class room essays. See: Sharma, R.R.

Sharma, R.R. Sharma, R.L.
Class room essays. 89pp. K.shs.6.50 Africa Book
Serv 1961 KE

Sharp, P.S.
Pilot. 280pp. ill. R6.75 Bulpin 1972 SA

Sharp, P.S.
Tales of Table Bay. 230pp. ill. R10.50 Bulpin 1975
SA

Sharpe, M.R.I.
Everyday Sesotho reader. 96pp. Morija 1952 LO

Sharpe, M.R.L.
Every day Sesotho grammar. 164pp. cl. R.85c.
Morija 1970 L0

Shaw, B.
Memorials of South Africa [Reprint of 1840 edition].
371pp. pl. cl.   R8.90   (Africana collectanea, 34)
Struik 1970 SA

Shaw, G.
Some beginnings: The Cape Times (1876-1910)   198pp.
pl. hd.   R12.00   OUP - SA 1975 SA

Shaw, M., comp.
Geobotany and biogeochemistry in prospecting,
1962-1972. 26pp.   R1.75   Dept Bibliog, Lib & Typo
1973 SA

Shaw, R.C.
Graaff-Reinet. 44pp.   80c.   Univ Cape Town Lib 1964
SA

Shaw, T.
Africa and the origins of man: a memorial lecture in
honour of Dr. L.S.B. Leakey, delivered at the University of
Ibadan, on December 7, 1972. 23pp. photog.   N1.00
Ibadan UP 1973 NR

Shaw, T.   Vanderburg, J.
A bibliography of Nigerian archaeology. 68pp.   N1.25
Ibadan UP 1969 NR

Shaw, T.
Discovering Nigeria's past. 130pp. pl.   N2.50   OUP -
Nig 1975 NR

Shaw, T., ed.
Lectures on Nigerian prehistory and archaeology. 61pp.
N1.20   Ibadan UP 1969 NR

Shaw, T.
Why "darkest" Africa? 77pp. ill.   N1.50   Ibadan UP
1975 NR

Shaw, Thurstan.
Unearthing Igbo-Ukwu. 136pp. ill.   N4.00   OUP - Nig
1976 NR

Shaw, T.M.
The foreign policy of Tanzania, 1961-69.   EAPH 1973 KE

Shaw, W.
A defence of the Wesleyan Missionaries in Southern
Africa. 80pp.   R3.70   (Reprints, 79)   State Lib - SA
1976 SA

Shearing, C.D.
Blood donation (The attitudes and motivation of urban
Bantu in Durban)   See: Watts, H.L.

Sheffield, J.R., ed.
Education, employment and rural development. 492pp.
K.shs.70.00 cl.   K.shs.27.50 pap.   ($13.00 cl.) ($7.80
pap.)   EAPH 1967 KE

Sheikh, A.A., ed.   Nabhany, A.S., ed.
Utendi wa mwana kupona. 36pp.   K.shs.3.50   (35p.)
(Sanaa Ya Utungo, 1)   Heinemann Educ - Nair 1972 KE
SWA

Sheikh, M.A.   Olowoyo, S.O.
Objective tests in school certificate chemistry (with
solutions) 100pp.   N2.00   Armolaran 1970 NR

Shenk, D.W.
The early church and Africa.   See: Kealy, J.P.

Shepherd, D.
The man who loves giants.   R8.75   Purnell 1976 SA

Shepherd, R.H.W.
Bantu literature and life. 198pp.   60c.   Lovedale 1955
SA

Shepherd, R.H.W.
Forerunners of modern Malawi.   See: Ballantyne, M.

Shepherd, R.H.W.
Lovedale and literature of the Bantu. 111pp.   35c.
Lovedale 1945 SA

Shepherd, R.H.W.
Lovedale, South Africa 1841-1955. 163pp.   R1.00
Lovedale 1971 SA

Shepherd, R.H.W.
A South African medical pioneer. 249pp.   R1.05
Lovedale 1952 SA

Sher, M.
Bernard Malamud. A partially annotated bibliography.
R1.65   Dept Bibliog, Lib & Typo 1970 SA

Sherlock, J.
The Zambesi. 20pp.   60c.   Univ Cape Town Lib 1965
SA

Sherrington, R.
Adventure in Addis Ababa. 68pp. ill.   Eth$1.60
OUP-Addis 1970 ET

Sherrington, R.
The treasure of Lebna Dengel. 60pp. ill.   B1.85
OUP-Addis 1970 ET

Sherry, S.P.
The black wattle.   cl.   R13.50   Univ of Natal 1971 SA

Sherza, O.A.
Asili ya chumvi ya bahari. [The origin of sea salt]   18pp.
ill.   K.shs.0.50   ($1.50/40p.)   EALB 1962 KE SWA

Shields, C.
The making of a nation. 168pp. ill.   70c.   Shuter
1963 SA

Shilatu, C.
Children of politics. 56pp.   K.shs4.00   Evangel 1970
KE

Shitaye, G.M.
Crop pest handbook.   See: Crowe, T.J.

Shivji, I.
Class struggles in Tanzania. 192pp.   T.shs.20.00
Africa only   Tanz Publ House 1975 TZ

Shivji, I.G., ed.
Tourism and socialist development. 110pp.
T.shs.10.00   ($3.00)   Tanz Publ House 1973 TZ

Shivji, I.G. et al., eds.
The silent class struggle. 200pp.   T.shs.10.00   ($3.00)
Tanz Publ House 1973 TZ

Shoewu, O.
Integrated science.   See: Maxwell, D.A.

Shonga, G.H.
Matsotsi.   See: Zulu, J.N.

Shore, H.L.
Theatre in a changing world. 10pp. ill.   T.shs.1.00
(Inaugural lecture, 3)   Univ Dar es Salaam 1969 TZ

Shore, S.C.
The Newborn Infant.   Juta 1977 SA

Shorter, A.
The African contribution to world church and other essays.
73pp.   K.shs.9.00   (Gaba Pastoral Paper, 22)   Gaba
1972 KE

Shorter, A.
Nyunga-ya-mawe. 28pp. maps.   K.shs.2.50   ($1.00)
EAPH 1969 KE SWA

Shorter, A.   Mulugala, N.E.
Nyungu Ya Mawe.   K.shs.6.00   ($2.00/£1.20)   EALB
1971 KE SWA

Shorter, A.
Nyungu ya mawe: leadership in 19th century. 29pp.
Hist Assoc - Tanz 1969 TZ

Shorter, A.
Prayer in the religious traditions of Africa. 168pp. cl. &
pap.   K.shs.30.00 pap.   K.shs.45.00 cl.   OUP -
Nairobi 1975 KE

Shrand, D.
The administration of deceased estates in South Africa.
3rd ed. 600pp. cl.   R30.00 incl. supplements   Legal &
Financial 1973 SA

Shrand, D.
The administration of insolvent estates in South Africa.
2nd ed. 528pp.   R12.00   Juta 1959 SA

Shrand, D.
Company formalities and precedents.   2nd ed.   R18.00
incl. supplement   Legal and Financial 1976 SA

Shrand, D.   Keeton, A.A.F.
Company law and company taxation in South Africa.
R25.00 incl. supplement   Legal and Financial 1976 SA

Shrand, D.
Company law and company taxation - statutory amendments: 1974/5. R3.50 Legal and Financial 1976 SA

Shrand, D.
Digest of law and finance in South Africa. R10.50 Legal & Financial 1973 SA

Shrand, D.
How to re-organise your affairs so as to pay the least amount of income tax. R5.25 Legal & Financial 1972 SA

Shrand, D.
Law and finance for the farmer. 423pp. cl. R12.00 Legal & Financial 1971 SA

Shrand, D.
Real estate in South Africa. 2nd ed. 428pp. cl. R10.50 Legal & Financial 1971 SA

Shrand, D.
Shrand on the Sectional Titles Act. 204pp. cl. R15.00 incl. supplements Legal & Financial 1972 SA

Shrand, D.
Studies in income tax. 2nd ed. 279pp. cl. R10.50 incl. supplements Legal & Financial 1971 SA

Shrand, D.
Taxation of companies in South Africa. 258pp. R10.50 incl. supplements Legal & Financial 1968 SA

Shrand, D.
Today and yesterday. 149pp. cl. R6.00 Legal & Financial 1969 SA

Shrand, D.
What every attorney should know about income tax. 122pp. R4.75 Legal & Financial 1972 SA

Shrand, D.
What every company secretary/executive should know about income tax. 154pp. R5.25 Legal & Financial 1972 SA

Shrand, D.
What every farmer should know about income tax. 5 5thed. 125pp. R5.25 Legal & Financial 1967 SA

Shrand, D.
What every hotelier should know about income tax. 105pp. R4.75 Legal & Financial 1972 SA

Shrand, D.
What every medical practioner should know about income tax. 122pp. R4.75 Legal & Financial 1972 SA

Shrand, D.
What every merchant/trader should know about income tax. 126pp. R4.75 Legal & Financial 1972 SA

Shrand, D.
What every professional person should know about income tax. 119pp. R4.75 Legal & Financial 1972 SA

Shrand, D.
What every real estate agent/property owner should know about income tax. 131pp. R4.75 Legal & Financial 1972 SA

Shrand, D.
What every salaried person should know about income tax. 116pp. R4.75 Legal & Financial 1972 SA

Shrand, D.
What every taxpayer should know about income tax. 9th ed. 317pp. R5.25 Legal & Financial 1969 SA

Shreve, G.M.
The genesis of structures in African narrative. Vol. I: Zande trickster tales. See: Arewa, O.

Shropshire, D.T.T.
The Bantu woman under the Natal code of native law. 47pp. 50c. Lovedale 1941 SA

Shulman, A.A.
Professor Petrus Johannes Nienaber: A bibliography of his works 1933-1966. 53pp. R2.75 Dept Bibliog, Lib & Typo 1969 SA

Shumaker, C.R.
Mshindi wa Victoria Nyanza. [The winner of Lake Nyanza] 64pp. T.shs.3.00 Africa Inland Church 1962 TZ SWA

Shuter and Shooter.
Easy Zulu vocabulary. 23rd ed. 60pp. 35c. Shuter 1971 SA

Shuter and Shooter.
Ekhaya epulazini. [At home on the farm] ill. 28c. Shuter 1962 SA ZUL

Shuter and Shooter.
Incwadiyami yezilwane. [My book of animals] unpagedpp. ill. 28c. Shuter 1962 SA ZUL

Shuter and Shooter.
Izilwane ezithandekayo. [Likeable animals] unpagedpp. ill. 28c. Shuter 1962 SA ZUL

Shuter and Shooter.
Mashihambisane. [Let us walk together] Ibanga, 4 114pp. ill. 50c. Shuter 1945 SA ZUL

Shuter and Shooter.
Masihambisane. [Let us walk together] Ibanga, 2 122pp. ill. 40c. Shuter 1945 SA ZUL

Shuter and Shooter.
Masihambisane. [Let us walk together] Ibanga, 3 120pp. ill. 45c. Shuter 1945 SA ZUL

Shuter and Shooter.
Masihambisane. [Let us walk together] Ibanga, 5 142pp. ill. 55c. Shuter 1945 SA ZUL

Shuter and Shooter.
Masihambisane. [Let us walk together] Ibanga, 6 142pp. 60c. Shuter 1945 SA ZUL

Shuter and Shooter.
Masihambisane. [Let us walk together] Isigaba, A 48pp. ill. 25c. Shuter 1945 SA ZUL

Shuter and Shooter.
Masihambisane. [Let us walk together] Isigaba, B. 70pp. ill. 25c. Shuter 1945 SA ZUL

Shuter and Shooter.
Routledge's complete letter writer for ladies and gentlemen. 208pp. 80c. Shuter 1945 SA

Shuter and Shooter.
Umtyhili wamaphupha. [Dream book] ill. 35c. Shuter 1966 SA XHO

Shuter and Shooter.
Ungqeqe wokuchaza amaphupho. [Book for explaining dreams] 96pp. 40c. Shuter 1970 SA ZUL

Sianga, M.
Kamunjoto. [The life of Kamunjoto.] 54pp. 50n. Neczam 1967 ZA LOZ

Sibanda, Q.
Akuqili lazikhotha emhlana. [You can't cheat all the people all the time.] 12pp. pl. 10c. Rhod Lit Bur 1976 RH NDE

Sibeso, L.
Bupilo ki masunda. [Life is a problem.] 52pp. 85n. Neczam 1975 ZA LOZ

Sibetta, O.K.
Fa munanga wa Lyambai. [On the banks of Lyambai Zambezi river.] 36pp. 40n. Neczam 1971 ZA LOZ

Sibetta, O.K.
Ze patezwi ba banca. [Things forbidden to young people.] 36pp. 20n. Neczam 1976 ZA LOZ

Sibson-Walker, S.
History of the development of the fundamental devices for detecting electromagnetic oscillations in the range of frequencies used in radio communication and allied systems. 42pp. R2.20 Dept Bibliog, Lib & Typo 1966 SA

Sidahome, J.E.
Stories of Benin empire. 132pp. ill. 75k OUP-Nig 1967 NR

Sidai, J.O.
Wisdom of Maasai. See: Massek, A.O.

Sidhu, J.S.
An introduction to primary science for C.P.E. 206pp. ill. K.shs13.50 Textbook Ctre 1969 KE

Sidikou, A.H.
Sédentarité et mobilité entre Niger et Zgaret. 250pp. maps photos. CFA2000 (F40.00) (Etudes Nigeriennes, 34) Inst Rech Sci Hum 1974 NG FRE

Sidikou, H.A. Chamard, P.C.
Geographie du Niger. 75pp. CFA815 (F16.30) Nouv Ed Afric 1976 SG FRE

Siegried, W.R., et al.
South African red data book: Aves. 108pp. (NSPU Report, 7) CSIR 1976 SA

Sierra Leone Lbirary Board.
Sierra Leone publications 1967 and 1968. 6pp. 10c. Sierra Leone Lib Board 1969 SL

Sierra Leone Library Board.
Sierra Leone publications 1963 and 1964. 14pp. 25c. Sierra Leone Lib Board 1965 SL

Sierra Leone Library Board.
Sierra Leone publications 1965 and 1966. 15pp. 25c. Sierra Leone Lib Board 1966 SL

Sierra Leone Library Board.
Sierra Leone publications 1966 and 1967. 20pp. 25c. Sierra Leone Lib Board 1968 SL

Sierra Leone Library Board.
Sierra Leone publications 1968 and 1969. 11pp. 10c. Sierra Leone Lib Board 1970 SL

Sierra Leone Library Board.
Sierra Leone publications 1969-1971. 15pp. 10c. Sierra Leone Lib Board 1972 SL

Sierra Leone Library Board.
Sierra Leone publications, 1972-1973. 20pp. 10c. Sierra Leone Lib Board 1974 SL

Sierra Leone Library Board.
Sierra Leone publications 1974 and 1975. 12pp. 10c. Sierra Leone Lib Board 1976 SL

Sierra Leone Library Board.
Sierra Leone publications 1975 and 1976. 8pp. 10c. Sierra Leone Lib Board 1976 SL

Sifuna, D.N.
Revolution in primary education. The new approach in Kenya. 112pp. K.shs.25.00 ($4.80/£2.30) EALB 1975 KE

Sifuna, D.N.
Vocational education in schools. A historical survey of Kenya and Tanzania. 212pp. K.shs.27.95 ($6.00/£2.85) EALB 1976 KE

Sigal, J.
Contribution à l'étude des foraminifères du jurassique supérieur et du néocomien du bassin de Majunga. 2 v. See: Espitalie, J.

Sigogo, N.S.
Akulazulu emhlabeni. [There is no heaven on earth.] 126pp. pl. 55c Mambo 1971 RH NDE

Sigogo, N.S.
Indlalifa ngubani. [Who is the heir?] 112pp. pl. 72c. Mambo 1976 RH NDE

Sikakana, J.M.
Ikhwezi likaZulu. [Zulu poems] 90pp. cl. R1.00 (Bantu treasury, 16) Witwatersrand UP 1972 SA ZUL

Sikakana, J.M.A.
English and Zulu dictionary. 1, 2 pts. See: Doke, C.M.

Sikakana, J.M.A.
English-Zulu dictionary. 2, 2 pts. See: Doke, C.M.

Sikakana, J.M.A.
Zulu-English vocabulary. See: Doke, C.M.

Silberberg, H.
The law of property. hd. & pap. R24.00 cl. R18.75 pap. Butterworths 1975 SA

Silbert, R.
Southern African drama in English 1900-1964 in the Johannesburg Public Library and the Gubbins Collection of Africana in the University of the Witwatersrand Library: An annotated bibliography. 51pp. R2.65 Dept Bibliog, Lib & Typo 1965 SA

Silishebo, L.
Ne mu conezi ni? [Why have you stayed so long in town?] 48pp. 40n. Neczam 1972 ZA LOZ

Silke, A.S.
Juta's South African income tax service. R45.00 (annually) Juta 1962 SA

Silke, A.S.
The Rhodesian income tax service. R55.00 [annually] Juta 1977 SA

Silke, A.S.
Silke on South African income tax. 8th ed. 1,672pp. R38.50 Juta 1976 SA

Silke, A.S. Stein, M.L. Divaris, C.
Silke on South African income tax. 1976/77 supplement. 520pp. R18.00 Juta 1977 SA

Sillery, A.
John Mackenzie of Bechuanaland, 1835-1899: a study in humanitarian imperialism. 248pp. pl. hd. fl.33.75 (South African biographical and historical studies, 8) Balkema 1971 SA

Silumessi, B.B.
Butali bwa balauli. [Black magic at work.] 64pp. 35n. Neczam 1973 ZA LOZ

Silva Rego, A.D.
Portuguese colonization in the sixteenth century. 116pp. cl. R3.00 (Oppenheimer Inst. of Portuguese stud. pub., 1) Witwatersrand UP repr. 1965 SA

Silver, H.M. Creed, P.
The dimensional stability of all-wool single jersey fabric. 14pp. R2.50 (SAWTRI Technical Reports, 290) SAWTRI 1976 SA

Silver, H.M.
The dimensional stability of feeder blended wool/texturised acrylic single jersey fabrics. 9pp. R2.50 (SAWTRI Technical Reports, 295) SAWTRI 1976 SA

Silver, H.M. van Heerden, N.
Dimensional stability of wool/acrylic single jersey fabrics. 14pp. R2.50 (SAWTRI Technical Reports, 244) SAWTRI 1975 SA

Silver, H.M.
Dyeing of cotton from a water-assisted solvent system. Part I: Dyeing with monochlorotriazine dyes 13pp. R2.50 (SAWTRI Technical Reports, 219) SAWTRI 1974 SA

Silver, H.M.
Dyeing of cotton from a water-assisted solvent system. Part II: Dyeing with acryloylamide and trichloropyrimidine dyes 30pp. R2.50 (SAWTRI Technical Reports, 225) SAWTRI 1974 SA

Silver, H.M.
Influence of dyeing wool worsted yarns on knittability. 10pp. R2.50 (SAWTRI Technical Reports, 236) SAWTRI 1974 SA

Silver, H.M. Schouten, P. van Heerden, N.
The simultaneous shrinkproofing and dyeing of wool fabrics with the bisulphire adducts of a polyurethane resine, a polyacrylate resin and reactive dyes. 16pp. R2.50 (SAWTRI Technical Reports, 238) SAWTRI 1974 SA

Silvertand, J.H.
Probation maana yake nini? [The work of the probation officer] K.shs.1.25 ($1.25/50p.) EALB 1955 KE SWA

Silvestre, H.
Les manuscrits de Bède à la Bibliothèque Royale de Bruxelles. 32pp. 30k Press Univ Zaire 1959 ZR FRE

Simagha, D.
Légende de la dispersion des Kusa (épopée soninke)
See: Meillassoux, C.

Simango, J.
Zviuya zviri mberi. [Settlement after a long struggle.]
90pp. pl. 70c Longman - Rhod 1974 RH SHO

Simbmwene, J.M.S.
Mapenzi ya pesa. [Love of money.] 48pp. ill.
T.shs.3.00 Ndanda Mission Press 1975 TZ SWA

Simelane, V.
Siswati sesibayeni, 1. [Siswati Grammar] 64pp. ill.
R1.15 Longman - SA 1974 SA SIS

Simelane, V.M.
Siswati sesibayeni, 2. [Language text for primary
schools.] 80pp. ill. R1.25 Longman - SA 1975 SA
SIS

Simelane, V.M.
Siswati sesibayeni 3. [Language text for primary
schools.] 88pp. ill. R1.25 Longman - SA 1974 SA
SIS

Simmon, J.
Aikin mata. See: Harrison, T.W.

Simmonds, D., ed.
Adire cloth in Nigeria: the preparation, dyeing of indigo
patterned cloths among the Yoruba. See: Barbour, J.,
ed.

Simmons, E.B.
Calorie and protein intakes in three villages of Zaria
Province, May 1970 - July 1971. N2.00 (Samaru misc.
pap., 55) Inst Agric Res - Zaria 1976 NR

Simmons, E.B.
Rural household expenditures in three villages of Zaria
province. N1.50 (Samaru misc. pap., 56) Inst Agric
Res - Zaria 1976 NR

Simoko, P.
Africa is made of clay. 76pp. 50n. Neczam 1977 ZA

Simon, B.
Joburg, Sis! 180pp. cl. R5.85 ($6.50/£3.50)
Bateleur 1974 SA

Simon, C.
Lexique de droit des affaires zairoises. See: Nguyen
Chanh, T.

Simonsson, B.
Feature writing: Africa Christian writers' course. v. 2
34pp. 30t. (35c.) Christ Lit Assoc - Mal 1972 MW

Simpson, G.E.
Yoruba religion and medicine in Ibadan. 272pp.
N14.00 Ibadan UP 1977 NR

Simpson, J.G. Drysdall, A.R.
The alluvial gold of the Msidza river, Lundazi District.
22n (Dept. of Geological Survey. Economic Reports, 5)
Geol Survey - Zam 1964 ZA

Simpson, J.G.
The Kankomo clay deposit, Kitwe District. See: Drysdall,
A.R.

Simpson, J.G.
Major zones of transcurrent dislocation and superposition
of orogenic belts in part of central Africa. See: de
Swardt, A.M.J.

Simpson, J.G.
The Nchoncho bismuth prospect, Central Province. 30n
(Dept. of Geological Survey. Economic Reports, 7) Geol
Survey - Zam 1964 ZA

Simpson, J.G. Drysdall, A.R.
The Njoka graphite deposit, Lundazi District. 45n
(Dept. of Geological Survey. Economic Reports, 4) Geol
Survey - Zam 1965 ZA

Simpson, J.G.
Two talc deposits near Lusaka. 45n (Dept. of
Geological Survey. Economic Reports, 9) Geol Survey -
Zam 1965 ZA

Simpson, K.W. Sweeney, G.M.J.
The land surveyor and the law. 300pp. ill. cl. R6.00
Univ of Natal 1973 SA

Sims, G.
Paladin of empire: Earl Grey and Rhodesia. R$2.00
(Local series pamphlets, 26) Central Africa Hist Assoc
1970 RH

Sims, S.
Called to give an account: an introduction to finance and
accounts for Christian workers. 83pp. Uzima 1976 KE

Simson, P.
Bible reflections. no. 3 69pp. K.shs.10.00
(Spearhead series, 43) Gaba 1976 KE

Simson, P.
Biblical catechesis. v. 1: Gospel miracles 32pp.
K.shs.5.50 (Gaba Pastoral Papers, 34) Gaba 1974 KE

Simson, P.
Biblical catechesis. v. 2: Authority and reconciliation.
38pp. K.shs.5.50 (Gaba Pastoral Papers, 35) Gaba
1974 KE

Sinclair, D.M.
The Orange Free State goldfields. 51pp. 80c. Univ
Cape Town Lib 1967 SA

Sinclair, F.D.
The chronology of Gray's elegy: an essay on the origin of
the poem. 52pp. 35c. (85c.) Univ South Africa
1963 SA

Sinclair, F.D.
Three papers on tragedy. 32pp. 50c. (R1.00) Univ
South Africa 1960 SA

Sinclair, N.
Some South African book illustrators 1946-1966, with
biographical notes and examples of their work. 58pp.
R3.00 Dept Bibliog Lib & Typo 1968 SA

Singano, E. Roscoe, A. A.
Tales of old Malawi. 72pp. ill. 80t. Popular Publ
1974 MW

Singh, A.M. Nesbitt, R.
East African certificate English. 156pp. K.shs.14.00
Textbook Ctre 1970 KE

Singh, M.
The history of Kenya's trade union movement to 1952.
320pp. photos. K.shs.56.00 cl. K.shs.21.00 pap.
($10.40 cl.) ($5.80 pap.) EAPH 1969 KE

Singh, S.
Primary level science, geography, history. 240pp. ill.
K.shs.20.00 Bamran (Textbook Ctre) 1974 KE

Sinxo, G.B.
Imfene kaDebeza neminye imidlalwana [Short plays].
120pp. 95c OUP-SA 1965 SA XHO

Sinxo, G.B.
Umzali wolahleko. 77pp. R1.50 OUP - SA 1976 SA
XHO

Sipikin, M.
Tsofaffi Da Sababbin Wakoki. [Old and new poems]
129pp. N1.50 Northern Nig 1971 NR HAU

Sirgel, W.F.
Contributions to the morphology and histology of the
genital system of the pulmonate agriolimax caruanae
Pollonera. 43pp. pl. R2.10 (Univ. Stellenbosch,
Annals, vol. 48, A.2) Univ Stellenbosch Lib 1973 SA

Siriex, J.P.
Felix Houphouët-Boigny, l'homme de la paix. 376pp.
CFA2500 Africa only Nouv Ed Afric 1975 SG FRE

Sisilana, G.S.G.
Ukuphila. [Poems] 32pp. 35c OUP-SA 1957 SA
XHO

Sithole, E.J.H.
Mataka kumafuro. [Boys mischief when herding cattle.]
25pp. pl. 15c Rhod Lit Bur 1976 RH SHO

Sithole, N.
Letters from Salisbury Prison. 186pp. pl. map.
K.shs.30.00 Transafrica 1976 KE

Smith, C.A.
Common names of South African plants.   R7.25
(R.9.10)   (Memoirs of the Botanical Survey of South
Africa, 35)   Botanical Res Inst 1966 SA

Smith, C.H.
Insolvency law.   cl. & pap.   R20.75 cl.   R16.50 pap.
Butterworths 1974 SA

Smith, C.W.
Introdution to book-keeping.   111pp. ill.   K.shs5.00
($2.20)   EAPH 1966 KE

Smith, E.D.
Preliminary investigations on the hearing of sharks.
See: Davies, D.H.

Smith, G.W., ed.   Tangri, R.K., ed.   Pachai, B., ed.
Malawi past and present: selected papers from the
University of Malawi history conference, 1967.   160pp.
photos. map. hd.   K1.00 ($3.45)   Christ Lit Assoc -
Mal 1971 MW

Smith, H.E.   Turpie, D.W.F.
The effect of atmospheric conditions, regain before carding
and water added during gilling on the processing
performance of faulty wools up to combing.   12pp.
R2.50   (SAWTRI Technical Reports, 322)   SAWTRI 1976
SA

Smith, J.
Road transport in Uganda.   40pp. maps.   U.shs.20.00
(Occas. paps., 18)   Dept Geog - Mak 1970 UG

Smith, J.L.B.   Smith, M.M.
The fishes of Seychelles.   2nd ed.   77pp. col. pl. cl.
R10.00   Inst Ichthyology 1969 SA

Smith, J.L.B.
New and interesting fishes from deepish water off Durban,
Natal and southern Mozambique.   30pp.   R1.10
Oceanographic Res Inst 1968 SA

Smith, J.S.
Aids to scoutmasters in East Africa: the standard
handbook.   49pp. ill.   K.shs.1.50   ($1.25/50p.)   EALB
1951 KE

Smith, L.D., ed.
Strategies for improving rural welfare: proceedings of a
workshop held at I.D.S., Nairobi, May, 1971.
See: Kempe, M.E., ed.

Smith, L.E.W.
Common entrance: English language: with answers.
See: Roberts, J.M.E.

Smith, L.E.W.
Common entrance: English language: without answers.
See: Roberts, J.M.E.

Smith, L.E.W.
Examination guide: English language.   80pp.   75k
Pilgrim 1969 NR

Smith, L.E.W.
Examination guide: English literature.   87pp.   88k
Pilgrim 1972 NR

Smith, L.E.W.
Tests in English language: with answers.   See: Roberts,
J.M.E.

Smith, L.E.W.
Tests in English language: without answers.
See: Roberts, J.M.E.

Smith, M.G.
The social structure of the Northern Kadara.   N2.00
(Dept. of Sociology, Occas. pap., 1)   Dept Soc - ABU
1971 NR

Smith, M.M.   Jackson, P.B.N.
Common and scientific names of the fishes of southern
Africa. Marine and freshwater.   2 pts.   213pp.   R5.50
set pap.   (Special publ. of the Inst. of Ichthyology, 14)
Inst Ichthyology 1975 SA

Smith, M.M., ed.
Ichthyological bulletins, 1-20 of J.L.B. Smith, 1956-61.   ill.
R8.00   Inst Ichthyology 1969 SA

Smith, M.M., ed.
Ichthyological bulletins, 21-32 of J.L.B. Smith, 1961-1966.
ill.   R8.00 cl.   Inst Ichthyology 1973 SA

Smith, M.M., ed.
Ichthyological papers of J.L.B. Smith, 1931-1943.   2v.
R7.65   Inst Ichthyology 1969 SA

Smith, M.M.
The fishes of Seychelles.   See: Smith, J.L.B.

Smith, M.M.
A note on Anisochromis kenyae.   2pp. pl.   R4.00   Inst
Ichthyology 1977 SA

Smith, N.
The Presbyterian Church of Ghana, 1835-1960.   303pp.
maps photos. hd.   C4.50   (£2.25/$4.50)   Ghana UP
1966 GH

Smith.
New general mathematics for West Africa. (Metric ed.)
bk. 1.   See: Channon.

Smith.
New general mathematics for West Africa. (Metric ed.)
bk. 2.   See: Channon.

Smith.
New general mathematics for West Africa. (Metric ed.)
bk. 3.   See: Channon.

Smith.
New general mathematics for West Africa. (Metric ed.)
bk. 4.   See: Channon.

Smith, O.J.
Chagua mwenyewe.   [Choose for yourself.]   58pp.
T.shs.3.00   Africa Inland Church 1972 TZ SWA

Smith, O.J.
Kuna njia moja tu.   [There is only one way.]   40pp.
T.shs.2.00   Africa Inland Church 1972 TZ SWA

Smith, O.J.
Mudzisankhire nokha.   [Choose for yourself - life or
death]   48pp.   22t   Christ Lit Assoc - Mal 1975 MW
CHC

Smith, O.J.
Nipe uzima.   [Give me life.]   38pp.   T.shs.2.00   Africa
Inland Church 1973 TZ SWA

Smith, P.
Le récit populaire au Rwanda.   430pp.
(FB600.00/$15.11)   Inst Nat Rwandaise 1975 RW FRE

Smith, P.
Swaziland: resources and development.   See: Leistner,
G.M.E.

Smith, R.
Flame propagation velocity and some related topics.
121pp.   R6.15   Dept Bibliog, Lib & Typo 1965 SA

Smith, R.A.
His challenge is mankind (a political biography of William
R. Tolbert, Jr. 19th president of Liberia)   268pp. photos.
cl.   U.S.$6.00   Cole & Yancy 1972 LB

Smith, R.H.
Labour resources of Natal.   75c.   (Natal regional survey
reports, 1)   Dept Econ-Natal 1950 SA

Smith, R.H.T.
Interregional trade and money flows in Nigeria.
See: Hay, A.M.

Smith, R.S.
Yoruba warfare in the nineteenth century.   See: Ajayi,
J.F.A.

Smith, W.C.
Chilwa Island.   See: Garson, M.S.

Smith, W.E.
Mwalimu Julius K. Nyerere. Kimetafsiriwa kwa Kiswahili na
Sozigwa, P. Huduma za Maktaba, Transafrica,
Dar-es-Salaam.   [Biography of President Nyerere.]
240pp.   T.shs.22.50   Tanz Lib Serv 1977 TZ SWA

Smith, W.E.
Nyerere of Tanzania.   300pp. pl. map.   K.shs.15.00
No UK & Canada   Transafrica 1974 KE

Smith, W.M.
    Chemical equilibrium. 46pp. ill. R2.00 Technitrain 1975 SA

Smith, W.M.
    Electrochemistry. 48pp. ill. R2.00 Technitrain 1975 SA

Smith, W.M.
    Hybridisation. 35pp. ill. col. ill. pl. [with ballons as models]. R2.00 Technitrain 1974 SA

Smith, W.M.
    An introduction to organic chemistry. 48pp. ill. R2.00 Technitrain 1974 SA

Smith, W.M.
    The island system. 55pp. ill. R2.00 Technitrain 1974 SA

Smithies, A.
    Oxford arithmetic course (Nig.): teacher's bk. 1, 6 bks. See: Downes, L.W.

Smithies, A.
    Oxford arithmetic course (Nig.): teacher's bk. 2, 6 bks. See: Downes, L.W.

Smithies, A.
    Oxford arithmetic course (Nig.): teacher's bk. 3, 6 bks. See: Downes, L.W.

Smithies, A.
    Oxford arithmetic course (Nig.): teacher's bk. 4, 6 bks. See: Downes, L.W.

Smithies, A.
    Oxford arithmetic course (Nig.): teacher's bk. 5, 6 bks. See: Downes, L.W.

Smithies, A.
    Oxford arithmetic course (Nig.): teacher's bk. 6, 6 bks. See: Downes, L.W.

Smuts, J.
    A triangle of forces -- language, religion and politics. 25pp. 50c (Inaugural lectures) Rhodes Univ Lib 1973 SA

Smuts, S.   Hunter, L.
    A comparison of the tenacity and extension of mohair and kemp fibres. 15pp. R2.50 (SAWTRI Technical Reports, 215) SAWTRI 1974 SA

Smuts, S.
    A preliminary report on certain physical properties of some commercial double jersey fabrics produced from textured polyester yards. See: Hunter, L.

Smuts, S.
    A preliminary report on certain physical properties of some commercial double jersey wool fabrics. See: Hunter, L.

Smuts, S.
    A preliminary report on the measurement of the unevenness of plain jersey fabrics. See: Hunter, L.

Smuts, S.   Hunter, L.
    Studies of some wool–acrylic woven fabrics, part I: untreated plain and 2/2 twill weave fabrics from wool blended with regular acrylic. 31pp. R2.50 (SAWTRI Technical Reports, 305) SAWTRI 1976 SA

Smuts, S.   Hunter, L.
    Studies of some wool/polyester woven fabrics, part III: untreated plain weave fabrics from wool blended with a normal and a special low-pilling polyester, respectively. 21pp. R2.50 (SAWTRI Technical Reports, 251) SAWTRI 1975 SA

Smuts, S.   Hunter, L.
    Studies of some wool/polyester woven fabrics, part IV: easy-care finished fabrics from wool blended with normal and special low pilling polyester respectively. 20pp. R2.50 (SAWTRI Technical Reports, 287) SAWTRI 1976 SA

Snell, G.S.
    Nandi customary law. 154pp. K.shs.7.50 ($2.00/80p.) EALB 1954 KE

Snelson, P.D.
    Educational development in Northern Rhodesia, 1883-1945. 326pp. K6.50 Neczam 1974 ZA

Snook, S.
    New Testament survey. pt. 1 See: Khumalo, A.

Snook, S.
    New Testament survey, pt. 2. See: Moalusi, E.

Snowsell, R.E.
    Character. 41pp. 50k OUP-Nig 1969 NR

Snowsell, R.E.
    Leadership. 34pp. 45k OUP-Nig 1966 NR

Snoxall, R.A.
    Concise English-Swahili dictionary. 344pp. K.shs.15.00 OUP-Nairobi 1968 KE

Snyman, J.P.
    The missing link in architectural, engineering and quantity surveying education. 19pp. 30c (Univ. Cape Town. Inaugural lec., 19) Univ Cape Town Lib 1973 SA

Soa, I.
    Dokotera Ravelona. [Docteur Ravelona.] 150pp. FMG300 Ed Takariva 1975 MG MLA

Soa, I.
    Ilay Kintana Mainty. [L'étoile Noire.] 200pp. FMG360 Ed Takariva 1974 MG MLA

Soa, I.
    Ilay tsipika mena. [Barré au rouge.] 100pp. FMG250 Ed Takariva 1975 MG MLA

Soa, I.
    Manja. 250pp. FMG500 Ed Takariva 1975 MG MLA

Soa, I.
    Mantasoa. 80pp. FMG200 Ed Takariva 1974 MG MLA

Soa, I.
    Moara. 70pp. FMG250 Ed Takariva 1975 MG MLA

Soa, I.
    Modelin-tsakafo samihafa. [Recettes culinaires.] 52pp. FMG100 Ed Takariva 1975 MG MLA

Soa, I.
    Raharaha 47. [Affaire 47.] 85pp. FMG250 Ed Takariva 1975 MG MLA

Soa, I.
    Soveniran'ny foko. [Souvenirs.] 150pp. FMG350 Ed Takariva 1975 MG MLA

Société Africaine d'Edition.
    L'année politique Africaine, 1976/77. CFA15,000.00 (F300.00) Soc Africaine 1975 SG FRE

Société Africaine d'Edition.
    La Côte d'Ivoire en chiffres, 1977. CFA10,000 (F200.00) Soc Africaine 1976 SG FRE

Société Africaine d'Edition.
    L'économie Africaine, 1977. 5th ed. 240pp. CFA12,000 (F240.00) Soc Africaine 1976 SG FRE

Société Africaine d'Edition.
    Guide de l'industrie au Sénégal. (Edition 1973-1974) 191pp. pl. CFA6,000.00 Soc Africaine 1973 SG FRE

Société Africaine d'Edition.
    Guide du commerce au Sénégal. (Edition 1974) 168pp. pl. CFA6,000.00 Soc Africaine 1974 SG FRE

Société Africaine d'Edition.
    Le Sénégal en chiffres, 1977. CFA12,500 (F250.00) Soc Africaine 1976 SG FRE

Société Africaine d'Etudes et de Développement.
    Etude de facticibilité pour la création d'une entreprise de transports urbains à Ouaga. 34pp. CFA2,500 SAED 1976 UV FRE

Société Africaine d'Etudes et de Développement.
    Etude d'un programme régional de développement intégré. pt. 1. 157pp. CFA5,000 SAED 1976 UV FRE

Société Africaine d'Etudes et de Développement.
    Etude d'un programme régional de développement intégré. pt. 2. 70pp. CFA5,000 SAED 1976 UV FRE

Soreson, J.
Social medicine in South Africa. 56pp. 50c. Univ Cape Town Lib 1955 SA

Sorrenson, K.
Land reform in the Kikuyu country. 278pp. maps. K.shs.23.50 OUP-Nairobi 1967 KE

Sosanya, O.
Collected poems for primary schools. 1, 2bks 48pp. ill. 60k Macmillan 1965 NR

Sosanya, O.
Collected poems for primary schools. 2, 2bks 64pp. ill. 70k Macmillan 1965 NR

Soskolne, C.L.
A computerised statistical census relating to university education: a group of science and engineering students, University of the Witwatersrand, 1970. 76pp. R1.45 Human Science Res Council 1974 SA

Sospate, S.K.   Sakara, A.H.
Jizoeze kiswahili. [Practice Swahili] 1, 2 bks. T.shs.7.00 (Tanz. Publ. House) Tanz Publ House 1969 TZ SWA

Sospate, S.K.   Sakara, A.H.
Jizoeze kiswahili. [Practice Swahili] 2, 2 bks. 72pp. T.shs.7.00 Tanz Publ House 1970 TZ SWA

Souissi, M.
La langue des mathématiques en arabe. 1969pp. D3.500 (Série VIII, Sciences, 1) Univ Tunis 1969 TI FRE

Soulie, J.
Annales de l'université d'Abidjan. Recueil de 12 articles. 120pp. CFA400 (F8.00 pap.) (Série E-Ecologie, 5-2) Univ Abidjan 1972 IV FRE

Soulié, J. et al.
Annales de l'université d'Abidjan. 388pp. CFA1300 (F2.00) (Série E-Ecologie, 1-2) Univ Abidjan 1968 IV FRE

Sourie, R.
Contribution à l'étude écologique des côtes rocheuses du Sénégal. 342pp. pl. CFA2000 (Mémoires de l'IFAN, 38) IFAN 1954 SG FRE

Sousberghe, L.
Les cousins croisés. Comparaison des systèmes du Burundi et Rwanda avec ceux du Bas-Congo. 120pp. (Faculté des Sciences Sociales, 12) Univ Bujumbura 1968 BD FRE

Sousi, D.
Hesitant love. 32pp. K.shs.2.50 (Afromance series, 1) Transafrica 1974 KE

Sousi, D.
Love music. 32pp. K.shs.2.50 (Afromance series, 2) Transafrica 1974 KE

The South African Academy of Arts and Science.
The South African mathematics Olympiad/die Suid-Afrikaanse wiskunde olimpiade. [in English and Afrikaans]. 74pp. ill. R4.00 Nasou 1976 SA MUL

South African Institute of International Affairs.
The commonwealth heads of government meeting, Singapore, January 1971. 43pp. 30c. SA Inst Int Affairs 1971 SA

South African Institute of International Affairs.
Questions affecting South Africa at the United Nations, 1968. 34pp. 30c. SA Inst Int Affairs 1969 SA

South African Institute of International Affairs.
Questions affecting South Africa at the United Nations, 1969. 38pp. 30c. SA Inst Int Affairs 1970 SA

South African Institute of International Affairs.
Questions affecting South Africa at the United Nations, 1970. 58pp. 30c. SA Inst Int Affairs 1971 SA

South African Institute of International Affairs.
Questions affecting South Africa at the United Nations, 1971. 67pp. 50c. SA Inst Int Affairs 1972 SA

South African Institute of International Affairs.
Resolutions of the third conference of non-aligned states. 46pp. 30c. SA Inst Int Affairs 1971 SA

South African Institute of International Affairs.
United States foreign policy in a regional context. papers presented at a symposium at Jan Smuts House, Johannesburg in 1969. 94pp. R1.75 SA Inst Int Affairs 1970 SA

South African Institute of International Affairs.
The use and protection of natural resources in Southern Africa. Proceedings of a symposium held at Jan Smuts House, Johannesburg in 1971. SA Inst Int Affairs 1973 SA

South African Institute of Race Relations.
Administration of security legislation in South Africa. 42pp. 60c. ($1.50) SA Inst of Race Relations 1976 SA

South African Institute of Race Relations.
Intergroup relations in the common area. Papers delivered at the 45th Council Meeting of the South African Institute of Race Relations, January 1975. 69pp. R1.50 ($2.75/£1.40) SA Inst of Race Relations 1975 SA

South African Institute of Race Relations.
South Africa in Africa: an evaluation of détente. Papers delivered at the 46th annual council meeting of the S.A.I.R.R. 97pp. R1.50 ($2.75) SA Inst of Race Relations 1976 SA

South African Institute of Race Relations.
The State versus the Dean of Johannesburg. 40pp. 90c. ($1.85) SA Inst of Race Relations 1972 SA

South African Institute of Race Relations.
The urgent need for fundamental change in South Africa. Papers given at the 47th Annual council meeting. 113pp. R3.00 ($4.50) SA Inst of Race Relations 1977 SA

South African Law Reports.
Appeal court judgment in coloured voters' case. R1.25 Juta 1952 SA

The South African National Scientific Programmes.
A description of the Savanna eco-system project, Nylsvley, South Africa. 24pp. (SANSP occasional publ., 1) CSIR 1975 SA

Southall, A.W.
Alur society. 416pp. photos. maps. K.shs64.25 OUP-Nairobi 1972 KE

Southall, A.W.   Gutkind, P.J.
Townsmen in the making. 248pp. 60shs (East African studies, 9) Mak Inst Soc Res 1957 UG

Southall, R.
Federalism and higher education in East Africa. 160pp. K.shs.22.50 EAPH 1975 KE

Southall, R.J.
Parties and politics in Bunyoro. 73pp. U.shs8.50 Mak Inst Soc Res 1972 UG

Sow, A.
Le Revenant. 128pp. CFA850 (F17.00) Nouv Ed Afric 1976 SG FRE

Sow, A.I.
Dictionnaire Fulfulde. 166pp. CFA800 CELTHO 1971 NG FRE

Sow, A.I.
Jangen fulfulde. 145pp. CFA250 CELTHO 1970 NG FRE

Sow, F.
Les fonctionnaires de l'administration centrale Sénégalaise. 308pp. CFA1600 (Initiations et Etudes Africaines, 29) IFAN 1972 SG FRE

Sowande, F.   Ajanaku, F.
Oruko amutorunwa. [Name from heaven] 72pp. ill. 60k OUP-Nig 1969 NR YOR

Soyinka, W.
Le lion et la perle. Tr. fr. English. 4th ed. 96pp. CFA450 CLE 1974 CM FRE

Soyinka, W.
Masaibu ya Ndugu Jero. [The trials of Brother Jero]
40pp. K.shs.5.00 OUP - Nairobi 1974 KE SWA

Sozigwa.
Risasi zianzapo kuchanua. [Poetry.] 144pp.
K.shs.12.00 ($3.50) EAPH 1975 KE SWA

Speight, A.
Game reserves and game protection in Africa (with special
reference to South Africa) 32pp. 80c. Univ Cape
Town Lib 1972 SA

Spence, T.
Gardening with birds in southern Africa. ill. R6.50
Purnell 1975 SA

Spencer, I.W.F.
Medical responsibility to patient and community. 14pp.
30c (Univ. Cape Town. Inaugural lec., 33) Univ Cape
Town Lib 1975 SA

Spenser, W.
Language and society. See: Brosnahan, L.F.

Spicer, E.
The peoples of Nigeria. 71pp. ill./pl. 48k Longman -
Nig 1962 NR

Spilhaus, M.W.
South Africa in the making, 1652-1806. R7.50 Juta
1971 SA

Spiro, E.
Conflict of laws. R30.00 Juta 1974 SA

Spiro, E.
The law of parent and child in South Africa. 3rd ed.
R32.00 Juta 1971 SA

Spitzer, L.
The Creoles of Sierra Leone. Responses to colonialism,
1870-1945. 260pp. £4.50 elsewhere in Africa
N6.00 (Africa only) Univ Ife Press 1975 NR

Spohr, O.H., ed.
German Africana: German publications on South and
South West Africa. 332pp. R10.50 (Bibliographies,
14) State-Lib-SA 1968 SA

Spohr, O.H., ed.
Handlist of manuscripts in the University of Cape Town
libraries. 1 See: Quinn, G.D., ed.

Spohr, O.H., ed.
Indexes to Limner (R.W. Murray) 'Pen and Ink Sketches in
Parliament' and R.W. Murray 'South African
reminiscences'. 21pp. 60c. (U.C.T. libraries, Varia
series, 9) Univ Cape Town Lib 1965 SA

Spohr, O.H., ed.
Pictorial material of 'Cecil J. Rhodes, his contemporaries
and later South African personalities' in the C.J. Sibbett
collection of the University of Cape Town libraries.
See: Stubbins, E.O., ed.

Spohr, O.H.
Wilhelm Heinrich Immanuel Bleek: a bio-bibliographical
sketch. 78pp. R1.50 (U.C.T. libraries Varia series, 6)
Univ Cape Town Lib 1962 SA

Spohr, O.H.
Zacharias Wagner second commander of the Cape.
111pp. ill. hd. fl. 20.25 Balkema 1967 SA

Sprenger, D.
Animal distribution in Southern Africa. 37pp. R1.95
Dept Bibliog, Lib & Typo 1968 SA

Springer, S. D'Aubrey, J.D.
Two new scyliorhinid sharks from the east coast of Africa
with notes on related species. 19pp. R1.10
Oceanographic Res Inst 1972 SA

Spry, J.
Civil law of defamation in East Africa. 92pp.
K.shs.12.50 ($3.10/£1.45) EALB 1976 KE

Ssali, E.M.
Abazungu nga bwe Tubalaba. [Europeans as we see
them] K.shs1.50 ($1.25/50p.) EALB 1952 KE LUG

Ssekamwa, J.C.
Ebisoko. [Idioms] 125pp. K.shs.8.50 ($2.50/£1.00)
EALB 1963 KE LUG

Ssekamwa, J.C.
Leonardo Da Vinci. See: Luyomba-Tebajjanga, E.

Ssekamwa, J.C.
Okuwandiika ebbaluwa. [Letter writing] 108pp.
K.shs.3.75 ($1.75/70p.) EALB 1960 KE LUG

St. Andrew's Woman's Guild, Nairobi.
Kenya cookery book and household guide. K.shs.23.00
(£1.15) Heinemann Educ - Nair 1972 KE

St. Leger, F.Y.
Report on an investigation into the attitudes of a sample of
male residents of the city of East London, C.P., towards
the Daily Dispatch and other newspapers in the area.
See: Irving, J.

St. Leger, M.
Grahamstown: Fingo village: an investigation in to the
socio-economic conditions of the inhabitants of the Fingo
village and their attitude to removal. See: Roux, M.

Stade, R.C.
Ninety-nine names of God in Islam. tr. fr. Arabic 138pp.
N1.25 Daystar 1970 NR

Staff of the Rural Economy Research Unit.
Farm income levels in the northern states of Nigeria.
(Samaru misc. pap., 35) Inst Agric Res - Zaria 1972 NR

Stagg, L.E.
The published works of Sir Kenneth Mackenzie Clark.
40pp. R2.10 Dept Bibliog, Lib & Typo 1969 SA

Stander, G.J. et al.
Treatment and disposal of yeast wastes. 69pp. (CSIR
research reports, 305) CSIR 1971 SA

Standing Conference of National Voluntary Youth Organizations
in Rhodesia.
Bundu book five: Mammals, reptiles and bees. 126pp.
col. ill. R$1.50 Longman - Rhod 1972 RH

Standing Conference of National Voluntary Youth Organizations
in Rhodesia.
Bundu book four: Meteorology, rock-climbing and
way-finding. 103pp. col. ill. maps. R$1.25 Longman
- Rhod 1971 RH

Standing Conference of National Voluntary Youth Organizations
in Rhodesia.
Bundu book one: Trees, flowers and grasses. New ed.
136pp. col. ill. R$1.25 Longman - Rhod 1972 RH

Standing Conference of National Voluntary Youth Organizations
in Rhodesia.
Bundu book three: Geology, gemmology, archaeology.
123pp. col. ill. R$1.75 Longman - Rhod 1968 RH

Standing Conference of National Voluntary Youth Organizations
in Rhodesia.
Bundu book two: Birds, insects and snakes. 121pp. col.
ill. R$1.50 Longman - Rhod 1967 RH

Stanfield, D. P.
The flora of Nigeria: sedges. See: Lowe, J.

Stanfield, D.P.
A field key to the savanna trees of Nigeria.
See: Hopkins, B.

Stanfield, D.P.
The flora of Nigeria: grasses. 118pp. pl. N3.00
Ibadan UP 1970 NR

Stanfield, J.P., ed.
Nutrition and food in an African economy. 1, 2 v.
See: Amann, V.F., ed.

Stanfield, J.P.
Nutrition and food in an African economy: bibliography.
2, 2v. See: Amann, V.F.

Stanley, J. L., comp.
Nigerian government publications, 1966-1973. A
bibliography. 204pp. cl. N10.00 (£8.50) ($19.00)
Univ Ife Press 1975 NR

Stanway, A.
Nimekuwa Mkristo - sasa je? [Now I am a Christian.] 36pp. T.shs.1.50 Central Tanganyika 1973 TZ SWA

Stanway, A.
Now I am a Christian. 32pp. T.shs.2.50 Central Tanganyika 1970 TZ

Staples, I.
A narrative of the eighth frontier war of 1851-1853. 59pp. R4.00 (Reprints, 62) State Lib - SA 1974 SA

Starck, D.
Parallel development and specialisation during the evolution of the bird skull; The evolution of the cranium of mammals; Specialisation of the skull of mammals. 38pp. photos. ill. R1.20 (A v.44, no.3-5) Univ Stellenbosch, Lib 1969 SA

Starfield, A.M.
Sensitivity analysis of a simple linear model of a savanna ecosystem at Nylsvley. See: Getz, W.M.

Stassen, D.F.
Economics for standard 10. See: Swanepoel, D.J.

State Library, Pretoria.
The Arabian horse. 36pp. R1.50 (Bibliographies, 17) State Lib - SA 1973 SA

State Library, Pretoria.
The Bosjesmans or Bush People. A lecture on the mental, moral and physical attributes of the Bushmen, or African savages. [Reprint of ed. 1847]. 8pp. 50c. State Lib - SA 1974 SA

State Library, Pretoria.
Conference of loyalists. Paarl, August 29-30, 1902. [Reprint ed. 1902]. 56pp. R2.50 (Reprints, 70) State Lib - SA 1977 SA

State Library, Pretoria.
Current South African newspapers. 17pp. R3.00 (Bibliographies, 10) State-Lib-SA 1970 SA

State Library, Pretoria.
Directory of southern African libraries 1975. 310pp. hd. R15.00 cl. (Contributions to Library Science, 20) State Lib - SA 1975 SA

State Library, Pretoria.
Exchange of official government publications. cl. R4.00 cl. (Contributions to Library Science, 16) State Lib - SA 1974 SA

State Library, Pretoria.
Give the people light: essays in honour of Matthew Miller Stirling. 197pp. photos. R5.50 (Contributions to Library Science, 13) State-Lib-SA 1972 SA

State Library, Pretoria.
Index to South African periodicals, 1960-1969. (on microfiche) 230pp. R35.00 State Lib - SA 1976 SA

State Library, Pretoria.
Seminar on centralization and decentralization of the national bookstock, State Library 1971. Proceedings held at the State Library on the 28th and 29th of October 1971. 228pp. ill. R6.45 (Contributions to Library Science, 14) State Lib - SA 1973 SA

State Library, Pretoria.
South African national bibliography: publications received in terms of the Patents, Designs, Trade Marks and Copyright Act, no. 9 of 1916, as amended by the Copyright Act, no. 63 of 1965. cl. R15.00 State Lib - SA [published annually] SA

State Library, Pretoria.
South African newspapers available on microfilm - catalogue. cl. R4.00 cl. (Bibliographies, 19) State Lib - SA 1975 SA

State Library, Pretoria.
State Library seminar on library co-operation. 92pp. ill. R2.50 (Contributions to Library Science, 8) State-Lib-SA 1967 SA

State Library, Pretoria.
Swaziland official publications, 1880-1972, a bibliography. 190pp. maps. cl. R15.00 cl. (Bibliographies, 18) State Lib - SA 1974 SA

Staub, H.R.
Watakuwa mwili mmoja. [Manual on Christian marriage.] 150pp. ill. T.shs.8.00 Central Tanganyika 1970 TZ SWA

Staub, M.
Msichana Ujifahamu! [Young lady, know about yourself] 37pp. ill. T.shs.2.50 Central Tanganyika 1974 TZ SWA

Stead, B.
Plant it. A companion volume to 'Grow it'. ill. cl. R8.95 Purnell 1977 SA

Stebbing, D.
They led the way: Christian pioneers of Central Africa. See: Jenkins, D.

Steedman, A.
Wanderings and adventures in the interior of southern Africa [Reprint of 1835 edition]. 2 v. 340, 363pp. pl. cl. R16.80 (set) (Africana collectanea, 17 & 18) Struik 1966 SA

Steele, A.
A red spy in my house. 155pp. hd. R6.00 Africa only Valiant 1975 SA

Steele, M. C.
Doris Lessing as historical observer. ($2.50) Central Africa Hist Assoc 1974 RH

Steele, M.C.
'Children of Violence' and Rhodesia: a study of Doris Lessing as historical observer. 28pp. ($2.50) (Central Africa Historical Assoc., Local series pamphlets, 29) Central Africa Hist Assoc 1974 RH

Steele, N.
Take a horse to the wilderness. ill. photos. R7.00 Bulpin 1971 SA

Steele, R.
Site and service schemes, analysis and report. See: Houlberg, P.

Steenekamp, J.J.A.
Changes in the income and expenditure patterns of multiple urban non-white households. 42pp. R10.00 (Bureau of Market Research, Research Reports, 36) Bur Market Research 1973 SA

Steenekamp, J.J.A.
Income and expenditure patterns of multiple Bantu households in white rural areas (Bethal/Viljoenskroon survey) 100pp. R40.00 (Bureau of Market Research, Research Reports, 31) Bur Market Research 1972 SA

Steenekamp, J.J.A.
Income and expenditure patterns of multiple urban Bantu households: an interregional comparison. 80pp. R40.00 (Bureau of Market Research, Research Reports, 32) Bur Market Research 1972 SA

Steenekamp, J.J.A.
Income and expenditure patterns of non-white urban households, Cape Town survey (multiple Bantu households) See: Nel, P.A.

Steenekamp, J.J.A.
Income and expenditure patterns of non-white urban households, Cape Town survey (single Bantu households) See: Nel, P.A.

Steenekamp, J.J.A.
Income and expenditure patterns of non-white urban households, Durban survey (multiple Asian households) See: Nel, P.A.

Steenekamp, J.J.A.
Income and expenditure patterns of non-white urban households, Durban survey (multiple Bantu households) See: Nel, P.A.

Author Index

Stern, M.J.
South African Jewish biography 1900-1966. 28pp. 70c. Univ Cape Town Lib 1972 SA

Steuer, M.D.
After the crisis. Longer-term prospects for the economy of Ghana. 30pp. C1.00 ($1.00/50p.) (Inaugural lecture) Ghana UP 1974 GH

Steven, S.J.H. Viljoen, G.v.N.
Cicero, student and statesman. [Bilingual in English and Afrikaans.]. 34pp. 30c. (80c.) Univ South Africa 1959 SA

Stevens, P.
The stone images of Esie. pl. cl. N20.00 Ibadan UP 1976 NR

Stevens, P.E.
Bechuanaland. 27pp. 60c. Univ Cape Town Lib 1949 SA

Stevens, P.E., ed.
Handlist of manuscripts in the University of Cape Town libraries. Supplement no. 1. See: Robins, D.J., comp.

Stevens, P.M.
Zimbabwe culture. 47pp. 80c. Univ Cape Town Lib 1972 SA

Stevenson, R.L.
Kithamani kya uthwii. [Treasure Island] 2nd ed. 53pp. ill. K.shs.1.50 ($1.25/50p.) EALB 1958 KE KAM

Stewart, A.
Central Africa arithmetic. Exercises in mental arithmetic (metric) grade 7. 40pp. 30c. Longman - Rhod 1961 RH

Stewart, A.
Central African arithmetic. Exercises in mental arithmetic (metric) grade 5. 40pp. 30c. Longman - Rhod 1960 RH

Stewart, M.
Guided social studies. Standard 5. See: Brown, S.

Stewart, T.H.
An introduction to public health. 252pp. R7.75 Butterworths 1971 SA

Stewart, T.J.
Conceptual form of model for town planning policy designs. 15pp. (CSIR Special Report, WISK 175) CSIR 1975 SA

Stewart, T.J.
Criterion for optimality of design of EVOP-type experiments. 57pp. (CSIR Special Report, WISK 207) CSIR 1976 SA

Steyn, J.H., ed.
Crime and punishment in South Africa. See: Midgley, J., ed.

Steyn, P.
Historic Rhodesia. See: Ransford, O.

Steyn, P.
Wankie birds. 57pp. col. ill. R$2.50 Longman - Rhod 1974 RH

Stiles, D.E.
Botswana National Library Service: report on the National Library Service for the period April 1973-March 1976. 34pp. P1.00 Botswana Nat Lib Serv 1977 BS

Stillman, C.J.
Namazambwe amethyst deposits, Kalomo District. 60n (Dept. of Geological Survey. Economic Reports, 17) Geol Survey - Zam 1967 ZA

Stimie, C.M.
The education of whites in the Republic of South Africa. 77pp. ill. R3.00 (Human Sciences Research Council, IN-series, 24) Human Science Res Council 1975 SA

Stimie, C.M.
Training after standard ten excluding university training. See: Geggus, C.

Stimie, C.M. Geggus, C.
University education in the RSA. 302pp. R2.65 Human Science Res Council 1976 SA

Stimie, M.
The cranial anatomy of the Iguanid Anolis carolensis. 29pp. ill. 73c. (A v.41, no. 3) Univ Stellenbosch, Lib 1966 SA

Stitt, J.
Day-by-day revised English course. Benny and Betty (reader) Grade 1. 48pp. 75c. Longman - Rhod 1976 RH

Stitt, J.
Day-by-day revised English course. Classroom reading kit. R$5.50 Longman - Rhod 1976 RH

Stitt, J.
Day-by-day revised English course. Grade 2. 1, 3 bks. 32pp. R$1.05 Longman - Rhod 1977 RH

Stitt, J.
Day-by-day revised English course. Grade 2. 2, 3 bks. 48pp. R$1.05 Longman - Rhod 1977 RH

Stitt, J.
Day-by-day revised English course. Grade 2. 3, 3 bks. 48pp. R$1.05 Longman - Rhod 1977 RH

Stitt, J.
Day-by-day revised English course. Pictures and words (pre-reader) Grade 1. 16pp. 75c. Longman - Rhod 1976 RH

Stitt, J.
Day-by-day revised English course. Reading kit. Grade 2. R$6.00 Longman - Rhod 1977 RH

Stitt, J.
Day-by-day revised English course. Teacher's bk. grade 1. 336pp. R$2.50 Longman - Rhod 1976 RH

Stitt, J.
Day-by-day revised English course. T.L.P. Grade 2. 176pp. R$2.50 Longman - Rhod 1977 RH

Stitt, J. et al.
Day-by-day revised English course. Grade 1. Pictures and words- Benny and Betty. Rev. ed. 2 v. 48pp. col. ill. 75c Longman - Rhod 1976 RH

Stitt, J., et al.
Day-by-day revised English course. Grade 1. Teacher's lesson programme. Rev. ed. 300pp. R$2.50 pap. Longman - Rhod 1976 RH

Stitt, J.
Primary English workbooks. stage 3. See: Agunwa, C.O.

Stitt, J.
Primary English workbooks. stage 4. See: Agunwa, C.O.

Stitt, J.
Primary English workbooks. stage 5. See: Agunwa, C.O.

Stitt, J.
Primary English workbooks. stage 6. See: Agunwa, C.O.

Stockenstrom, A.
The autobiography of the late Sir Andries Stockenstrom [Reprint of 1887 edition]. 2 v. 457, 475pp. cl. R16.80 (set) (Africana collectanea, 8 & 9) Struik 1964 SA

Stokes, E.
Imperialism and the scramble for Africa. The new view. 60c. (Local series pamphlets, 10) Central Africa Hist Assoc 1963 RH

Stokes, E.T., ed. Brown, R., ed.
The Zambesian past: studies in Central African history. 462pp. ill. hd. K5.00 (£2.52/$8.50) Inst Afr Stud - Lusaka 1966 ZA

Stokes, E.T.
The political ideas of English imperialism. 38pp. 30c Univ Rhodesia Lib 1960 RH

Stokes, H.
What bird is that? 2nd. ed. 72pp. pl. hd. R1.00 Purnell 1965 SA

Stokes, H.
What flower is that? summer. 78pp. ill. pl. hd. R1.00
Purnell 1971 SA

Stokes, H.
What tree is that? 2nd. ed. 72pp. pl. hd. R1.00
Purnell 1967 SA

Stone, I.M. Clayton, H.
Sketches. Ed. by A.H. Smith. 208pp. ill. cl. R14.50
Donker 1976 SA

Stone, R.H. Cozens, A.B.
New biology for West African schools. 378pp. ill. pl.
N3.74 Longman - Nig 1975 NR

Stone, R.H.
A survey of science teaching in Nigerian grammar schools.
112pp. 55k (Inst. of Ed. occas. pub., 1) Inst Educ-Ib
1960 NR

Stone, S.
Post primary arithmetic, Form 1. See: Fletcher, N.G.

Stone, S. du Preez, J.L. Lambert, G.
Post primary arithmetic, Forms II & III. 238pp. ill. 75c.
Shuter 1958 SA

Stopes, M.
Birth control today. 35c. Shuter 1948 SA

Stopforth, P.
Poverty, family patterns and material aspirations among
Africans in a border industry township. See: Schlemmer,
L.

Stopforth, P.
A study of malnutrition in the Nqutu district of KwaZulu.
See: Schlemmer, L.

Stopforth, P.
Survey of Highfield African township. 55pp. R$1.00
(Dept. of Sociology, Univ. of Rhodesia, 6) Univ Rhodesia
Lib 1971 RH

Stopforth, P.
Two aspects of social change. 120pp. R$1.00
(Dept. of Sociology, Univ. of Rhodesia, 7) Univ Rhodesia
Lib 1972 RH

Storrar, P.
George Rex. Death of a legend. 232pp. photos. cl.
R9.60 Macmillan - SA 1974 SA

Storrs, A.
Antics. 112pp. ill. K1.20 Neczam 1973 ZA

Storrs, A.
The magic tortoise. 80pp. ill. K1.60 Neczam 1974
ZA

Storrs, A.
The tortoise dreams. 96pp. ill. K1.20 Neczam 1969
ZA

Storrs, A.E.G.
Study of Zambia's natural resources. 131pp. K1.20
(60p.) OUP - Lusaka 1968 ZA

Story, R.
Some plants used by the bushmen in obtaining food and
water. R1.30 (Memoirs of the Botanical Survey of
South Africa, 30) Botanical Res Inst 1958 SA

Stott, J.
Niwezeje kuwa Mkristo? [Becoming a Christian.] 16pp.
T.shs. Central Tanganyika 1969 TZ SWA

Stoutjesdijk, E.J.
Uganda's manufacturing sector. 101pp. ill.
K.shs.15.00 ($4.00) EAPH 1967 KE

Stoy, F.A.
The citrus fruit industry in South Africa 1951-1963. 90pp.
R1.00 Univ Cape Town Lib 1964 SA

Strand, D. Keeton, A.A.F.
The auditor's manual. R4.00 Legal and Financial 1976
SA

Strandes, J.
The Portuguese period in East Africa. 3rd ed. 325pp.
ill. cl. & pap. K.shs35.00 cl. K.shs23.00 pap.
($7.75/£3.80 cl.) ($5.00/£2.00 pap.) EALB 1968 KE

Strassberger, E.
The Rhenish mission society in South Africa, 1830-1950.
110pp. photos. cl. R6.75 Struik 1969 SA

Strassen, H.
Etosha image. R9.50 Purnell 1976 SA

Strassen, H.
Windhoek. [Trilingual text in English, German, Afrikaans.]
48pp. col. ill. R3.75 pap. Purnell 1976 SA MUL

Strassen, H. zur.
Land between two deserts. 160pp. photos. hd. R9.50
Purnell 1971 SA

Strauss, C.B.
Pineapples in the Eastern Cape - a study of the farm
economy and marketing patterns. R1.00 (Inst. of
Social and Economic Research, occas. paps., 5) Inst
Soc & Econ Res - SA 1960 SA

Strauss, P.
Photographs of bushmen. 32pp. R1.45 ($1.80/95p.)
Bateleur 1974 SA

Streak, M.
The Afrikaner as viewed by the English, 1796-1854.
256pp. cl. R8.00 Struik 1974 SA

Strokes, H.
What succulent is that? ill. cl. R1.00 Purnell 1973
SA

Strong, A.C.
Free people: the story of the Old Testament showing the
purpose of God in His chosen people, Israel. 52pp.
25k Daystar NR

Strowbridge, N., comp.
Education in East Africa, 1962-1968: a selected
bibliography. 35pp. U.shs7.00 Mak Univ Lib 1969
UG

Strowbridge, N., comp.
Education in East Africa, 1969: a supplement to Education
in East Africa, 1962-1968. 30pp. U.shs2.00 Mak
Univ Lib 1970 UG

Struben, R.
Taken at the flood. 272pp. pl. R3.95 Longman SA
1968 SA

Strutt, D.H.
Clothing fashions in South Africa. 420pp. ill. col. pl. cl.
R33.50 cl. (Dfl.105/$39.50/£20.50 cl.) Balkema 1975
SA

Strydom, G.S.
The establishment and expansion of a school radio service
in Radio Bantu. 97pp. R2.50 Human Science Res
Council 1976 SA

Strydom, J.
Okayupa komusa. R1.12 Native Lang Bur 1975[?] SX
NDO

Strydom, M.A. Mountain, F.
The dyeing of wool with some reactive dyes by a
pad/bake method. 11pp. R2.50 (SAWTRI Technical
Reports, 234) SAWTRI 1974 SA

Strydom, M.A.
Some aspects of the dyeing of acrylic stable fibre from
organic solvent system. Part I: Dyeing from a
non-homogeneous system 12pp. R2.50 (SAWTRI
Technical Reports, 222) SAWTRI 1974 SA

Strydom, M.A.
Some wet processing factors influencing the yellowing of
mohair. 16pp. R2.50 (SAWTRI Technical Reports,
246) SAWTRI 1975 SA

Strydom, N.
History teaching in simple practice. 60pp. 80c.
Shuter 1969 SA

Stuart, J., ed. Malcolm, D.M., ed.
The diary of Henry Francis Fynn. 341pp. cl. R5.25
Shuter 1951 SA

Stuart, P.A.
Unkosibomvu. [Nkosibomvu] 116pp. 35c. Shuter
1938 SA ZUL

Stubbins, E.O., ed.   Spohr, O.H., ed.
    Pictorial material of 'Cecil J. Rhodes, his contemporaries and later South African personalities' in the C.J. Sibbett collection of the University of Cape Town libraries. 156pp.   R1.75   (U.C.T. libraries Varia series, 8)   Univ Cape Town Lib 1964 SA

Stultz, N. M.
    Who goes to parliament?   106pp.   R2.00   (Inst. of Social and Economic Research, occas. paps., 19)   Inst Soc & Econ Res - SA 1975 SA

Stultz, N.M.
    The nationalists in opposition 1934-1948.   168pp. cl. R4.95 SA only   Human and Rousseau 1975 SA

Suchel, J.B.
    La répartition des pluies et les régimes pluviométriques au Cameroun.   288pp. maps.   CFA2000   Univ Cameroun 1972 CM FRE

Sudan Interior Mission.
    Bible examples for today.   [Bible studies from the Old Testament]   64pp.   35k hd.   SIM 1972 NR

Sudan Ministry of Culture and Information.
    Sudan today.   240pp.   £S2.00   ($8.00)   Khartoum UP 1971 SJ

Sudan Ministry of Foreign Affairs.
    Peace and unity in the Sudan. An African achievement. 192pp.   £S1.00   ($4.00)   Khartoum UP 1973 SJ

Sudden, M.A.
    Socio-economic conditions in Verulam.   18pp.   free Univ Durban-Westville 1975 SA

Sugre, M.
    Dagban ni salim nyaysa.   [Popular stories for children.] 2nd ed.   35pp. ill.   65pes.   Bur Ghana Lang 1976 GH DAB

Suleiman, O.
    Pwagu Na Pwaguzi.   24pp.   K.shs.4.00   ($3.00) Foundation 1973 KE SWA

Suleiman, O.
    Sheikh samragaat miraa. Kitabu cha mairongi.   [The wisdom book of the Mairongi plant.]   47pp.   K.shs.4.00 ($3.00)   (Vitabu vya msingi, 1)   Foundation 1974 KE SWA

Suleiman, Y.
    The hydrogeology of part of Eastern Sudan.   50pt. ($1.47/62p.)   (Bulletin, 16)   Geol and Min Res - Sudan 1968 SJ

Sulemana, T.
    Naa luro mini obihi.   [History about a Dagbani chief.] 60pp. ill.   60pes.   Bur Ghana Lang 1975 GH DAB

Suliman, A.A.
    Issues in the economic development of the Sudan. 192pp.   £S1.10   ($5.00)   Khartoum UP 1975 SJ

Sullivan, R.
    South African environment. [Also available in Afrikaans.]. ill. photos. maps. cl.   R6.75   (The Macdonald Heritage Library series)   Purnell 1977 SA

Sülter, M.M.
    A contribution to the cranial morphology of Causus rhombeatus (Lichtenstein), with special reference to cranial kinesis.   40pp. ill.   80c.   (A v.37, no.1)   Univ Stellenbosch, Lib 1962 SA

Sumaili, G.
    Testament.   48pp.   20k   (Jeune Littérature, 1)   Ed Mont Noir 1971 ZR FRE

Sumaili, N.
    Sur les particularites lexicosemantiques du français au Zaire. Description de documents.   pt. 1: La littérature coloniale Belge.   57pp.   CELTA 1975 ZR FRE

Sumar, M., comp.   McGee, E.P., comp.
    National policies of Tanzania: a bibliography.   66pp. T.shs.30.00   Tanz Lib Serv 1972 TZ

Summer, J.
    Natal 1881-1911.   30pp.   70c.   Univ Cape Town Lib 1965 SA

Summers, R.
    Ancient ruins and vanished civilisations of Southern Africa. 246pp. photos. col. ill. maps.   R18.00   Bulpin 1971 SA

Summers, R.   Pagden, B.
    The warriors.   col. ill.   R6.00   Bulpin 1970 SA

Summers, R.F.H., comp.
    A history of the South African museum 1825-1975. 154pp. ill. cl.   R15.00 cl.   (Dfl.45.00/$17.00/£8.75 cl.) Balkema 1975 SA

Sumner, C.
    Ethiopian philosophy.   v. 2.   352pp.   B17.50 ($10.00/£5.25)   Addis Ababa UP; distr 1976 ET

Sumra, S.
    Rainfall and soil suitability index for maize cropping in Handeni district.   See: Hathout, S.

Sundermeier, T., ed.
    Church and nationalism in South Africa.   160pp.   R2.70 ($3.75/£1.95)   Ravan 1975 SA

Super, C.M.
    Cognitive changes in Zambian children during the late pre-school years.   125pp.   free   (Human Development Research Unit Report, 22)   Dept Psychology - Zam 1972 ZA

Surugue, B.
    Contribution à l'étude de la musique sacrée Zarma-Songhay.   65pp. maps photos.   CFA1250 (F25.00)   (Etudes Nigeriennes, 30)   Inst Rech Sci Hum 1972 NG FRE

Surville, N.
    Quelques types de plantes des principales fouilles camerounaises.   80pp. ill.   CFA400   Inst Sciences Hum - Cam 1959 CM FRE

Survival Book-Shops.
    Complete letter writing made easy.   76pp.   50k Survival 1971 NR

Survival Book-Shops.
    How to write famous love letters, love stories and make friend with girls.   60pp.   50k   Survival 1972 NR

Sutherland, E.
    Anansegoro.   [Story telling drama in Ghana.]   200pp. photo.   C10.00   (Afram African Studies Library series) Afram 1975 GH

Sutherland, E.
    Foriwa.   67pp.   60pes.   ($.65)   Ghana Publ Corp 1967 GH

Sutherland, E.T.
    Vulture, Vulture, and Tahinta.   32pp. photos.   45pes. ($.45)   Ghana Publ Corp 1968 GH

Sutton, A.C.
    Wall Street and the Bolshevik revolution.   228pp. hd. R9.60 Africa only   Valiant 1975 SA

Sutton, H.
    Guided composition and letter writing.   72pp.   75k Pilgrim 1968 NR

Sutton, J.E.G.
    The archaeology of the western highlands of Kenya. 165pp. ill. pl. cl. & pap.   K.shs.70.00   (£6.00 cl.) (£3.50 pap.)   (British Inst. in Eastern Africa, Memoirs, 3) Brit Inst EA 1973 KE

Sutton, J.E.G.
    The East African coast.   28pp. maps.   K.shs2.50 ($1.00)   EAPH 1966 KE

Sutu, S.D.R.
    Mathe a ntsi [Poems].   64pp.   60c   OUP-SA 1963 SA SOS

Suzman, A.
    The law of compulsory motor vehicle insurance in South Africa.   2nd ed.   R17.50   Juta 1970 SA

Suzman, Arthur.
    Law and order and the rule of law in South Africa.   13pp. 25c   ($1.00)   (South African Inst. of Race Relations, Topical Talks, 30)   SA Inst of Race Relations 1973 SA

Svendsen, K.E.
  Decision making in the National Development Corporation.
  T.shs.12.00 ($3.00) (Research pap., 68.25) Econ Res
  Bur - Tanz 1974 TZ

Swaak, I., comp.
  Index to South African military intelligence reports
  (technical) of World War II. 64pp. R3.70 Dept
  Bibliog, Lib & Typo 1973 SA

Swami, V.N.
  Comprehensive books for junior secondary classes
  biology. 94pp. ill. K.shs12.00 Textbook Ctre 1977
  KE

Swanepoel, D.J. Stassen, D.F.
  Economics for standard 10. 246pp. ill. R4.60 Nasou
  1975 SA

Swanepoel, D.J. Middleton, I.S.
  Mercantile law for standard 10. 223pp. R3.20 Nasou
  1975 SA

Swanepoel, J.H.
  Contributions to the cranial morphology of Chiromantis
  xerampelina Peters. 81pp. ill. 60c. (A v.41, no.13)
  Univ Stellenbosch, Lib 1966 SA

Swanepoel, J.H.
  The ontogenesis of the chondrocranium and of the nasal
  sac of the Mycrohylid frog Breviceps Adspersus pentheri
  Werner. 119pp. ill. R3.70 (A v.45, no.1) Univ
  Stellenbosch, Lib 1970 SA

Swanevelder, C.J., et al.
  Senior geography for standard 8. 254pp. ill. pl. maps.
  R4.75 Nasou 1974 SA

Swanevelder, C.J., et al.
  Senior geography for standard 9. 362pp. ill. photo.
  R6.50 Nasou 1975 SA

Swanevelder, C.J., et al.
  Senior geography for standard 10. 381pp. ill. photo.
  R7.95 Nasou 1976 SA

Swank, G.O.
  Step to baptism. 32pp. hd. 12k SIM 1970 NR

Swantz, M. L.
  Youth and development in the coast region of Tanzania.
  T.shs.15.00 ($5.00) (Research reports, new series, 6)
  Bur Res Assess - Tanz 1974 TZ

Swantz, M.L.
  The role of participant research in development. 22pp.
  hd. & pap. T.shs.20.00 pap. T.shs.35.00 hd.
  ($7.00 pap.) ($12.00 hd.) (Research reports, new
  series, 15) Bur Res Assess - Tanz 1975 TZ

Swantz, M.L.
  The role of participant research in development.
  T.shs.20.00 (Research reports, new series, 15) Bur Res
  Assess - Tanz 1975 TZ

Swantz, M.L. Henricson, U.S. Zalla, M.
  Socio-economic causes of malnutrition in Moshi district.
  85pp. hd. & pap. T.shs.50.00 pap. T.shs.60.00 hd.
  ($15.00 pap.) ($18.00 hd.) (Research pap., 38) Bur
  Res Assess - Tanz 1975 TZ

Swantz, M.L.
  Socio-economic causes of malnutrition in Moshi district.
  T.shs.50.00 (Research pap., 38) Bur Res Assess - Tanz
  1975 TZ

Swart, D.J.
  Design and standardization of the aptitude tests for school
  beginners. 51pp. R3.50 Human Science Res Council
  1976 SA

Swart, J.C.
  Relation between the diameter, the extensibility and the
  carrying capacity of wool fibers. See: Reimers, J.H.W.

Swart, P.L.
  Anatomy and histology of the external and internal
  reproductive organs in the male and female false codling
  moth, Argyroploce leucotreta Meyr. 65pp. ill. R1.13
  (A v.41, no.12) Univ Stellenbosch, Lib 1966 SA

Swartenbroeck, P.
  Dictionnaire Kongo/kiTuba-Français. 815pp. map.
  (DM64.00) (CEEBA. série III, Travaux linguistiques, 2)
  CEEBA 1973 ZR FRE

Swartz, W.F. van Wyk, M.J. Aucamp, J.H.
  Fitting and turning for standard 9. 152pp. ill. photo.
  R6.00 Nasou 1975 SA

Swebe, B.S.
  Hifadhi ya wanyama. [Wildlife conservation.] 72pp.
  T.shs.7.50 Tanz Publ House 1972 TZ SWA

Sweeney, G.M.J.
  The land surveyor and the law. See: Simpson, K.W.

Sweeney, J.
  Gemmology. 112pp. col. ill. maps. R$2.25
  Longman - Rhod 1971 RH

Sweeting, A.E.
  Modern developments: the making of the modern world.
  bk. 1 152pp. maps. K.shs.9.00 OUP-Nairobi 1969
  KE

Sweeting, A.E.
  Situational composition. 112pp. K.shs.6.50
  OUP-Nairobi 1967 KE

Sweeting, A.E.
  The United States in the modern world: the making of the
  modern world. bk. 2 156pp. maps. K.shs.9.00
  OUP-Nairobi 1969 KE

Swift, M.
  Treading water. 32pp. R1.80 (Mantis Poets, 6)
  Philip 1974 SA

Swithenbank, M.
  Ashanti fetish houses. 68pp. photos. map ill. cl.
  C3.00 (£1.50/$3.00) Ghana UP 1969 GH

Syabbalo, E.
  Kwaana. [Folk stories] 56pp. 55n. Neczam 1971
  ZA TON

Syabbalo, E.
  Masendelela mungano. [Satirical stories.] 120pp.
  K1.20 Neczam 1975 ZA TON

Syad, W.F.J.
  Harmoniques. 166pp. CFA700 (F14.00) Nouv Ed
  Afric 1976 SG FRE

Syad, W.F.S.
  Cantiques. 176pp. CFA700 (F14.00) Nouv Ed Afric
  1976 SG FRE

Syamupa, A.S.
  Bala umvwe. [Tonga folk stories] 40pp. 20c. Shuter
  SA TON

'Syatakali'.
  Should we drink? 28pp. ill. 65pes. (20p.) Africa
  Christian 1972 GH

Sydow, W.
  Report on some fossil human remains from Otjiseva near
  Windhoek. R3.50 SWA Scient Soc 1970 SX

Sykes, F.W.
  With Plumer in Matabeleland. [Reprint ed. 1897]. 296pp.
  ill. photos. map. cl. R$7.20 cl. (Rhodesiana Reprint
  Library, Gold Series, 21) Books of Rhodesia 1972 RH

Sylvester, N.
  Alive from the dead. 40pp. 50pes. (18p.) Africa
  Christian 1966 GH

Sylvester, N.
  La victoire de pâques. 56pp. ill. CFA75 CPE 1971
  IV FRE

Symon, S.A.
  Blindness in the Kawambwa district, Northern Rhodesia.
  African medicine in the Mankoya district, Northern
  Rhodesia. See: Phillips, C.M.

Syphus, E.
  Man through the ages. pt.1 128pp. ill. 90c. Shuter
  1968 SA

Syphus, E.
  Man through the ages. pt.2 396pp. R2.60 Shuter
  1970 SA

Talbi, M.
Ibn haldun et l'histoire. 132pp. D0.500 Maison Tunis 1973 TI FRE

Talbi, M.
Islam et dialogue. 56pp. D0.200 Maison Tunis 1972 TI FRE

Talbot, J.B. et al.
Swift's law of criminal procedure. 3rd ed. 1108pp. R31.50 cl. Butterworths 1971 SA

Talbot, W.J.
Swartland and sandveld: a survey of land utilization and soil erosion in the Western lowland of the Cape Province. 92pp. maps/photos. hd. 70c OUP-SA 1949 SA

Taleb Ibrahimi, A.
De la decolonisation a la révolution culturelle. (1962-1972) 228pp. 10,00 DA SNED 1973 AE FRE

Tall, C.
Le vade mecum de l'enseignant. 108pp. CFA800 Nouv Ed Afric 1975 SG FRE

Tallantire, A.C.
Some common flowering plants of Uganda. See: Lind, E.M.

Tamsanqa, W.K.
Botsang rhe [Drama]. 96pp. 75c OUP-SA 1965 SA TSW

Tamsanqa, W.K.
Buzani kubawo [Drama]. 112pp. R1.50 OUP-SA 1972 SA XHO

Tamsanqa, W.K.
Imitha yelanga [Essays]. 76pp. 90c OUP-SA 1967 SA XHO

Tamsanqa, W.K.
Ukuba ndandazile. [Xhosa story] 3rd. ed. 224pp. ill. R1.95 OUP - SA 1973 SA XHO

Tamundel Mubele.
Qui la sortira de cette pierre? Mythes yansi. Versions yansi-françaises. See: Labi Tawaba.

Tamuno, O.G.
A bibliography of economic integration in Africa. 23pp. 50k (75c) (N.I.S.E.R. indexes and bibliographies, 11) NISER 1968 NR

Tamuno, O.G.
Co-operation for development: a bibliography on inter-state relations in economic, technical and cultural fields in Africa, 1950-1968. 113pp. N1.25 ($2.00) (N.I.S.E.R. indexes and bibliographies, 12) NISER 1969 NR

Tamuno, O.G., comp. Alabi, G.A., comp.
Nigerian publications 1950-1970. [Cumulative volume.]. 433pp. N10.00 Ibadan UP 1977 NR

Tamuno, O.G.
The EEC and developing nations, 1958-1966: a bibliography. 51pp. 50k (75c) (N.I.S.E.R. indexes and bibliographies, 10) NISER 1967 NR

Tamuno, T.N., ed.
The University of Ibadan 1948-1973: a history of the first twenty-five years. See: Ajayi, J.F.A., ed.

Tamuno, T.N.
The police in modern Nigeria, 1861-1965. 332pp. map ill. cl. & pap. N6.50 cl. N4.00 pap. Ibadan UP 1970 NR

Tan, J.C.
College English, pupil's. 1 See: Rogers, J.

Tan, J.C.
College English, pupil's. 2 See: Rogers, J.

Tan, J.C.
College English, teacher's notes. 1 See: Rogers, J.

Tan, J.C.
College English, teacher's notes. 2 See: Rogers, J.

Tancred, A.J.
Letters to Sir Peregrine Maitland, Governor of the Cape of Good Hope, on the present Kafir war. [Reprint of ed. Cape Town, 1846-7] R4.00 (Reprints, 45) State-Lib-SA 1969 SA

Tandon, Y., ed.
Readings in African international relations. v. 1 hd. K.shs.85.00 ($16.25/£6.50) EALB 1972 KE

Tandon, Y., ed.
Readings in African international relations. v. 2 270pp. K.shs.34.75 ($7.10/£3.40) EALB 1974 KE

Tandon, Y.
Horizons of African diplomacy. See: Mazrui, A.A.

Tanganyika Library Service.
Manual for school libraries. 74pp. ill. Tanz Lib Serv 1970 TZ

Tangri, R.
African reaction and resistance to the early colonial situation in Malawi, 1891-1915. 75c. (Local series pamphlets, 25) Central Africa Hist Assoc 1969 RH

Tangri, R.K., ed.
Malawi past and present: selected papers from the University of Malawi history conference, 1967. See: Smith, G.W., ed.

Tanser, G.H.
Founders of Rhodesia. 92pp. maps photos. 75c. OUP-SA 1959 SA

Tanzania African National Union.
Unyonge wa Mwafrika. 64pp. ill. K.shs.2.00 ($1.00) EAPH 1970 KE SWA

Tanzania African National Union.
Vijiji uya ujamaa. 59pp. ill. K.shs.2.00 ($1.00) EAPH 1971 KE SWA

Tanzania Food & Nutrition Centre.
The Tanzania Food laws review. Report of a national expert committee. 32pp. Nat Print Co 1976 TZ

Tanzania Library Service Board.
Periodicals in the National Central Library, Dar es Salaam. 56pp. ex. only Tanz Lib Serv 1976 TZ

Tanzania Library Service Board.
Printed in Tanzania, 1971. A list of publications printed in mainland Tanzania and deposited with legal deposit libraries in the country. 124pp. T.shs.40.00 Tanz Lib Serv 1973 TZ

Tanzania Library Service Board.
Printed in Tanzania, 1973. A list of publications printed in mainland Tanzania during 1973 and deposited with the Legal Deposit Libraries in the country. 53pp. T.shs.40.00 Tanz Lib Serv 1976 TZ

Tanzania Ministry of Culture & Youth.
Elimu kwa michezo. [Education through sports.] 352pp. ill. T.shs.25.00 Tanz Publ House 1976 TZ SWA

Tanzania Mission Press.
Catholic directory of Eastern Africa, 1977-79. 250pp. T.shs.15.00 ($2.20) TMP 1977 TZ

Tanzania Mission Press.
CFM for happier families. 2nd ed. 60pp. ill. ($1.00) TMP 1975 TZ

Tanzania Mission Press.
Misale ya waamini. [People's missal.] 1170pp. cl. T.shs.18.00 ($3.00) TMP 1975 TZ SWA

Tapson, W.
Timber and tides. 4th ed. ill. R4.75 Juta 1973 SA

Tarantino, A.
Locaden remo ma kongi hum me Uganda. [The Uganda martyrs] 3rd. ed. 53pp. ill. K.shs.1.50 ($1.25/50p.) EALB 1957 KE LUO

Tardieu-Blot et al.
Mélanges biologiques. 169pp. photo. CFA1200 (Mémoires de l'IFAN, 50) IFAN 1957 SG FRE

Tardieu-Blot.
Les ptéridophytes de l'Afrique intertropicale française.
241pp. pl. CFA1800 (Mémoires de l'IFAN, 28) IFAN
1953 SG FRE

Tashdjan, A.
Dictionnaire d'accès à l'information. 626pp. CFA1000
(Enseignement du français, 33) Inst Ling Appliquée 1972
IV FRE

Tashdjian, A.
Documents de travail, activites pédagogiques.
See: Kempf, B.

Tashdjian, M. Lafitte, J.C.
English in Zaire. 148pp. CELTA 1976 ZR

Tati-Loutard, J.B.
Anthologie de la littérature congolaise d'express-française.
256pp. CFA1,500 CLE 1976 CM FRE

Tati-Loutard, J.B.
Les normes du temps. 70pp. (Jeune littérature, 1) Ed
Mont Noir 1974 ZR FRE

Tavener-Smith, R.
The Karroo System and coal resources of the Gwembe
District, south-west section. K3.00 (Dept. of Geological
Survey, Bulletins, 4) Geol Survey - Zam 1960 ZA

Taylor, C.
If courage goes...my 20 years in South African politics.
350pp. ill. R11.50 cl. Macmillan - SA 1976 SA

Taylor, C.
A simplified Runyankore/Rukiga-English and
English-Runyankore-Rukiga dictionary. cl. K.shs11.50
($3.00/£1.20) EALB 1959 KE

Taylor, C.J.
Coloured education. 21pp. 60c. Univ Cape Town Lib
1970 SA

Taylor, C.T.C.
The history of Rhodesian entertainment 1890-1930.
185pp. photos. hd. R$3.50 cl. ($7.00 cl.) M.O.
Collins 1968 RH

Taylor, G.
Marriage cases and the parish priest. Declaration of nullity
cases possession and good faith cases. bk.2 See: de
Bekker, E.

Taylor, I.R.
Cost and management accounting with programmed
instruction. See: Cairns, T.

Taylor, I.R.
Graded questions in cost and management accounting.
See: Cairns, T.

Taylor, I.R. Kritzinger, L.
The principles and practice of auditing. 3rd ed.
R14.50 Juta 1975 SA

Taylor, J.B., ed.
Primal world views 1976. Christian dialogue with traditional
thought forms. 132pp. cl. & pap. N6.00 cl. N3.50
pap. Daystar 1976 NR

Taylor, J.V.
Courts of the Lord's house: a guide to the Holy
Communion. 2nd ed. 69pp. ill. 35k Daystar 1966
NR

Taylor, K.
Nyamekye. [Nyamekye.] 2nd ed. 79pp. 65pes.
Bur Ghana Lang 1974 GH FAT

Taylor, L.E., ed.
Handlist of manuscripts in the University of Cape Town
libraries. Supplement no. 1. See: Robins, D.J., comp.

Taylor, L.E.
The University Library buildings. University of Cape Town.
13pp. R1.00 (Univ. Cape Town Libraries. Varia ser.,
11) Univ Cape Town Lib 1974 SA

Taylor, N., eds. Marais Louw, J., eds.
African sun. 112pp. photos. R1.30 Longman - SA
1974 SA

Taylor, N., eds. Marais Louw, J., eds.
Life is poetry. 168pp. R2.50 Longman - SA 1974
SA

Taylor, N. Marais Loun, J.
People and poetry. 4, 6 bks 64pp. ill. R1.00.
Longman SA 1966 SA

Taylor, N. Marais Louw, J.
A poem today. 1, 6 bks. 40pp. ill. 80c. Longman
SA 1966 SA

Taylor, N. Marais Louw, J.
Poems about people and places. 3, 6 bks 56pp. ill.
95c. Longman SA 1966 SA

Taylor, N. Marais Louw, J.
Poems for a wider world. 6, 6 bks 104pp. ill. R1.05
Longman SA 1971 SA

Taylor, N. Marais Louw, J.
Poetry for everyday. 2, 6 bks 48pp. ill. 90c.
Longman SA 1966 SA

Taylor, N. Marais Louw, J.
This is poetry. 5, 6 bks R1.05 64 ill. Longman SA
1966 SA

Taylor, T.A.
Insects and our enviornment. 28pp. N1.00
(Inaugural lecture) Ibadan UP 1974 NG

Taylor, T.R.
The construction of two scales of managerial style. 28pp.
(CSIR Special Report, PERS 235) CSIR 1976 SA

Taylor, W.L.
Reflections on the economic role of education in
underdeveloped countries. 32pp. 30c Univ Rhodesia
Lib 1964 RH

Tayo, M.S.
Muhammed in the light of the Bible. 2nd rev. ed.
200pp. C1.50 ($1.50) Ghana Publ Corp 1975 GH

Te Groen, J.
Basutoland. 34pp. 80c. Univ Cape Town Lib 1949
SA

Teibo, B.O.
Revision notes on school certificate chemistry. 131pp. ill.
N1.50 Onibonoje 1975 NR

Tejani, B.
Day after tomorrow. 148pp. K.shs6.00 ($2.00/95p.)
EALB 1971 KE

Teka, G.E.
The Public Health College and Training Centre, Gondar,
Ethiopia: Review of its origin and development in twenty
years of national service. 140pp. pl. B$6.50 Author
(c/o Ministry of Public Health, POB 5504, Addis Ababa)
1975 ET

Telford, A.A.
Yesterday's dress: a history of costume in South Africa.
177pp. ill. hd. R10.00 Purnell 1972 SA

Telle, L.
Fate of prodigal. 48pp. K.shs.6.75 Longman - Ken
1977 KE

Teller, W.
The government and administration of Morocco. An
introductory series of readings. 164pp. CAFRAD 1970
MR

Tembo, L.
Poems. 32pp. 20n. Neczam 1972 ZA

Temimi, A.
La politique Ottomane face à l'occupation d'Alger.
125pp. D0.800 (Série IV, Histoire, 9) Univ Tunis
1970 TI FRE

Temmar, H.
Approche structurelle du phénomène du
sous-développment. 150pp. 9,00 DA SNED 1973
AE FRE

Temmar, H.
Structure et modèle de développement de l'économie de
l'Algérie. 318pp. DA20.00 SNED 1975 AE FRE

Tempkin, B.
  Gatsha Buthelezi, Zulu statesman.   R12.50   Purnell
  1976 SA
Temple, M.
  Here's how to become a farmer.   20pp. ill.   15n
  Multimedia 1971 ZA
Temple, P., ed.
  Studies in soil erosion and sedimentation in Tanzania.
  See: Rapp, A., ed.
Temple, R.
  Walks and sketches at the Cape of Good Hope.   236pp.
  hd.   fl. 22.50   Balkema 1968 SA
Temu, A.J.
  British Protestant missions.   184pp. cl. & pap.
  T.shs.28.50 pap.   T.shs.57.00 cl.   Longman - Tanz
  1973 TZ
Temu, A.J.
  A history of Tanzania.   See: Kimambo, I.N.
Temu, P.
  Uchumi bora. [Better economics] 116pp.   K.shs.12.50
  OUP-Nairobi 1967 KE SWA
Temu, P.E.
  Marketing board pricing and black market.   21pp.
  T.shs12.00 ($3.00) (Research pap., 71.1) Econ Res
  Bur - Tanz 1971 TZ
ten Boom, C.
  Kushukuru Gerezani. [Prison to praise.] 76pp.
  K.shs.7.50 (95c.) Evangel 1977 KE SWA
Terblanche, J.
  The surgeon and the farmyard pig: research in surgery.
  12pp.   30c (Univ. Cape Town. Inaugural lec., 24)
  Univ Cape Town Lib 1974 SA
Terpstra, G.
  English-Tiv dictionary (An index to Abraham's Tiv
  Dictionary) 120pp.   N2.00 (Inst. of African Stud., Univ.
  of Ibadan, occas. pub., 13) Inst Afr Stud-Ibadan 1959
  NR
Terray, E.
  Annales de l'université d'Abidjan. L'organisation sociale
  des Dida de Côte d'Ivoire. 274pp.   CFA2000 (F40.00)
  (Série F-Ethno-Sociologie, 1-2) Univ Abidjan 1970 IV
  FRE
Terrien, R.R.F.
  Itan inu iwe mimo. [Stories from the Bible] 28pp. ill.
  N1.60 Longman - Nig 1969 NR YOR
Terry, R.
  Man in Africa. 48pp. col. map col. ill.   R1.00 (ISMA
  pub.) Witwatersrand UP 1963 SA
Tet, M.R., ed.
  Rhodesia and Nyasaland law reports, 1956-1963.
  See: Allen, C.J., ed.
Tetteh, M.N.
  Anatomy of rumour mongering in Ghana. Factors
  contributory to the overthrow of Dr. Kwame Nkrumah.
  60pp. ill.   C3.50   Univ Ghana Bkshop; distr. 1976 GH
Teya, P.K.
  Une victoire indésirable. 72pp.   CFA550   (F11.00)
  Nouv Ed Afric 1976 SG FRE
Thadila Masiala.   Courtejoie, J.   Rotsart de Hertaing, I.
  L'Infirmier face au malade. Comment favoriser la guérison
  par un contact authentique? 48pp. photos.   90k
  ($1.08) (Orientation nouvelle de l'action médicale, 30)
  BERPS 1975 ZR FRE
Thairu, K.
  The African civilization. 238pp. ill.   K.shs.32.00
  ($6.60/£3.10) EALB 1975 KE
Thairu, K.
  Human and social biology for secondary schools.
  See: Mugambi, M.
Thatcher, E.C.
  The geology of the Dedza area. 71pp. pl. map. hd.
  K3.00 (Geological Survey of Malawi, Bull. 29) Geol
  Survey - Mal 1968 MW

Thatcher, E.C.   Wilderspin, K.E.
  The geology of the Mchinji-Upper Bua area. 72pp. pl.
  map. hd.   K3.00 (Geological Survey of Malawi, Bull.
  24) Geol Survey - Mal 1968 MW
Thatcher, E.C.   Walter, M.J.
  The geology of the South Lilongwe Plain and Dzalanyama
  Range. 77pp. pl. map. hd.   K3.00 (Geological
  Survey of Malawi, Bull. 23) Geol Survey - Mal 1968 MW
Theal, G.M.
  Basutoland records [Reprint of 1883 edition] 4 v.
  2,454pp. cl.   R55.00 (set) ($77.00) Struik 1964 SA
Theal, G.M.
  A fragment of Basuto history, 1854-1871. [Reprint of ed.
  Cape Town, 1886]. 188pp.   R4.10 (Reprints, 51)
  State-Lib-SA 1970 SA
Theal, G.M.
  Records of South-Eastern Africa [Reprint of 1898-1903
  edition]. 9 v. 4,500pp. cl.   R75.00 (set) Struik 1965
  SA
Theron, J.G.
  Comparative studies on the morphology of male scale
  insects Hemiptera coccoidea. 71pp. pl.   R1.75 (A
  v.34, no.1) Univ Stellenbosch, Lib 1958 SA
Theron, M.J.   Neethling, P.J.   Matthews, V.L.
  The importance of the weather and weather services to the
  South African agricultural sector. A Delphi survey.
  134pp.   gratis (CSIR research report, 321) CSIR
  1973 SA
Thesen, H.
  Country days: chronicles of Knysna and the Southern
  Cape. 176pp. ill. cl.   R5.70   Philip 1974 SA
Thethy, B.S.
  Two housing schemes in Thika, a user reaction survey.
  See: Kamau, L.J.
Thiam, I.B.   Ndiaye, N.
  Histoire du Sénégal et de l'Afrique cours moyen. 167pp.
  CFA1,050 (F21.00) Nouv Ed Afric 1976 SG FRE
Thibault, J.
  Guide d'Abidjan et de la Côte d'Ivoire. (Edition 1976-77)
  150pp. ill. col. ill. maps.   CFA1,500.00   Soc Africaine
  1975 SG FRE
Thiel, J.F.
  La situation religieuse des Mbiem. 208pp. map photos.
  (DM26.00) (CEEBA. série II, Mémoires et Monographies,
  1) CEEBA 1972 ZR FRE
Thieme, J.G.
  Mining and prospecting activities in the Mansa area.
  20n (Dept. of Geological Survey. Occas. paps., 56)
  Geol Survey - Zam 1972 ZA
Thieme, J.G.
  Outline of the geology in the Mansa area. 20n (Dept.
  of Geological Survey. Occas. paps., 54) Geol Survey -
  Zam 1972 ZA
Thienel, A.   Green-Thompson, A.L.   Pellew, V.
  Exploring life. pt.7 560pp. ill. cl.   R8.95 cl. Shuter
  1975 SA
Thienel, A.   Green-Thomson, A.   Pellew, V.
  Exploring life. pt. 2. 250pp. ill. Shuter 1975 SA
Thiollay, J.M. et al.
  Annales de l'université d'Abidjan. 341pp.   CFA1000
  (F20.00) (Série E-Ecologie, 4) Univ Abidjan 1971 IV
  FRE
Thiong'o, N.   Mugo, M.G.
  The trial of Dedan Kimathi. 86pp.   K.shs.9.50
  Heinemann Educ - Nair 1976 KE
Thipa, H.M.
  Imethodi Yesixhosa. See: Gebeda, C.Z.
Thiriet, A.
  Bien entendre et bien dire. Les mots des classes de CI -
  CP. 118pp.   CFA320 (C.L.A.D. Etude, 15) CLAD
  1965 SG FRE

Thiriet, A.
Conclusions générales. 16pp. CFA125 (C.L.A.D. Etude, 5) CLAD 1964 SG FRE

Thiriet, A.
Débuts de l'apprentissage du français - Cl. 32pp. CFA125 (C.L.A.D. Etude, 17) CLAD 1966 SG FRE

Thiriet, A.
Enquête à l'école d'application de Nouakchott-Mauritanie. 27pp. 125 (C.L.A.D. Etude, 21) CLAD 1966 SG FRE

Thiriet, A.
L'enseignement du langage dans les écoles primaires du Sénégal. Un siècle et demi de pédagogie. 12pp. CFA125 (C.L.A.D. Etude, 23 bis) CLAD 1967 SG FRE

Thiriet, A.
Le français écrit- CE et CM- Etude de cahiers d'élèves. 50pp. CFA125 (C.L.A.D. Etude, 3) CLAD 1964 SG FRE

Thiriet, A.
Le français écrit Cl et CP - Instructions et progressions. 23pp. CFA125 (C.L.A.D. Etude, 2) CLAD 1964 SG FRE

Thiriet, A.
Le français écrit de quelques élèves Bambaras (Mali) 38pp. CFA125 (C.L.A.D. Etude, 23) CLAD 1967 SG FRE

Thiriet, A.
Propositions pédagogiques. Eléments et exercises de grammaire - la négation. 12pp. CFA125 (C.L.A.D. Etude, 7) CLAD 1964 SG FRE

Thiriet, A.
Propositions pédagogiques. Eléments et exercises de prononciation. L'opposition (i/y) 33pp. CFA200 (C.L.A.D. Etude, 6) CLAD 1964 SG FRE

Thiriet, A.
Le Sénégal - population, langues, programmes scolaires. 19pp. CFA125 (C.L.A.D. Etude, 1) CLAD 1964 SG FRE

Thiriet, A.
A travers quelques cahiers d'orthographe d'élèves peul. 27pp. CFA125 (C.L.A.D. Etude, 9) CLAD 1965 SG FRE

Thoahlane, A.B.
Anthology of Sotho poetry: Lemuloana. 96pp. ill. R1.20 Longman SA 1971 SA SOS

Thoahlane, T., ed.
Black renaissance: papers from the black renaissance convention. 75pp. R1.95 Ravan 1976 SA

Thomas, A., comp. Rowse, D.E., comp.
Current Rhodesian periodicals. 30pp. (National Archives of Rhodesia, Bibliographical series, 1) Nat Archives - Rhod 1974 RH

Thomas, C.J.
Elimu ya muziki. [Music education.] 72pp. ill. T.shs.15.00 Tanz Publ House 1976 TZ SWA

Thomas, C.Y.
The transition to socialism: issues of economic strategy in Tanzanian type economics. 90pp. T.shs.12.00 ($3.00) (Research pap., 72) Econ Res Bur - Tanz 1972 TZ

Thomas, E.
Wordlist of Delta Edo: Epie, Engenni, Degema. See: Williamson, K.

Thomas, F.M.
Historical notes on the Bisa tribe, Northern Rhodesia. 59pp. 35n. (18p.) (Rhodes-Livingstone communications, 8) Inst Afr Stud - Lusaka 1958 ZA

Thomas, H.
Practical exercises in Nigerian history. 104pp. 88k OUP-Nig 1966 NR

Thomas, H.B. Karugire, S.R.
The story of Uganda. 84pp. pl. ill. maps. K.shs.8.50 OUP-Nairobi 1973 KE

Thomas, H.G.
Abaana omukaaga abomu nsi ezewala. See: Archer, A.B.

Thomas, I. D. Mascarenhas, A. C.
Health facilities and population in Tanzania. pt. I: hospitals. T.shs.15.00 ($5.00) (Research pap., 21.1) Bur Res Assess - Tanz 1973 TZ

Thomas, I. D. Mascarenhas, A. C.
Health facilities and population in Tanzania. pt. II: rural health centres. T.shs.15.00 ($5.00) (Research pap., 21.2) Bur Res Assess - Tanz 1973 TZ

Thomas, I. E. Mascarenhas, A. C.
Health facilities and population in Tanzania. pt. III: dispensaries. T.shs.40.00 ($12.00) (Research pap., 21.3) Bur Res Assess - Tanz 1975 TZ

Thomas, I.D.
Some notes on population and land use in the more densely populated parts of the Uluguru mountains of Morogoro district. 52pp. maps. T.shs.7.00 (Research notes, 8) Bur Res Assess - Tanz 1970 TZ

Thomas, I.D.
Some notes on population and land use in the North Pare mountains. 62pp. maps. T.shs.7.00 (Research notes, 9) Bur Res Asses - Tanz 1970 TZ

Thomas, J.A.C.
The institutes of Justinian. [Complete text with new translation.] 376pp. cl. & pap. R25.00 cl. R15.00 pap. Juta 1975 SA

Thomas, J.D.
The civil practice of the superior courts in South Africa. See: van Winsen, L. de V.

Thomas, K. ed.
Co-ordination of engineering activity for progress in a developing country: the Sierra Leone experience. 29pp. Le1.00 Fourah Bay Bkshp 1968 SL

Thomas, M. McGowan, W.H.K.
Dibaji ya mahubiri kwa kizaki hiki. [Sermon outlines for today] 40pp. K.shs.6.00 (75c.) Evangel 1976 KE SWA

Thomas, M. Fox, J.
What is socialism? 2nd ed. K.shs6.00 ($2.00/80p.) EALB 1977 KE

Thomas, P.
Codage informatique du contenu lexical des programmes télévisuels de français (CP1 - CP2) See: Armand, E.

Thomas, P., ed.
Revealer of secrets. See: Bordinat, P., ed.

Thomas, P.
Vocabulaire administratif et politique du monde rural. See: Lanes, R.

Thomas, P.A.
The law of business organisations in East and Central Africa. See: Katende, J.W.

Thomas, P.P., et al.
Vocabulaire de la technologie simple et de l'agriculture. 30pp. CFA200 (Enseignement du Français, 49) Inst Ling Appliquée 1975 IV FRE

Thomas, W.H., ed.
Labour perspectives on South Africa. 272pp. pap. R3.60 pap. Philip 1974 SA

Thomas, W.H., ed.
Management responsibility and African employment in South Africa. Report of a panel investigation. 142pp. R2.50 Ravan 1973 SA

Thomassery, M.
Catalogue des périodiques d'Afrique Noire francophone (1858-1962) conservés à l'IFAN. 117pp. CFA1000 (Catalogues et Documents, 19) IFAN 1965 SG FRE

Thompson, B.W.
Climate of Africa. 152pp. maps. hd. K.shs.175.00 OUP-Nairobi 1965 KE

Thompson, B.W.
Studies in the development of African resources: The climatic background. 72pp. pl. N1.95 (Studies in the Development of African Resources, 1) OUP - Nig 1975 NR

Thompson, C.G., ed.
The Johannesburg stock exchange handbook. v.1, 1977 320pp. R3.00 Flesch 1977 SA

Thompson, C.G.
The stock exchange handbook. [annual]. v. 1, 1976 384pp. R3.00 Flesch 1976 SA

Thompson, C.G.
The stock exchange handbook. [annual]. v. 2, 1977 344pp. R3.00 Flesch 1977 SA

Thompson, E.
Ngiri's tale. 48pp. pl. 65c College Press 1975 RH

Thompson, J.
Livingstonia centenary: 100th anniversary of the Livingstonia Mission of the Church of Central African Presbyterian - CCAP - in Malawi. 16pp. 20t Christ Lit Assoc - Mal 1975 MW

Thompson, J.S.T., ed.
Sierra Leone's past: Books, periodicals, pamphlets and microfilms in Fourah Bay College library. 131pp. 75c. Fourah Bay Bkshp 1971 SL

Thompson, L., ed.
Africa in classical antiquity. See: Ferguson, J., ed.

Thompson, M.D.
Call the wind. 2nd ed. 112pp. ill. R18.00 deluxe ed. (South African Yesterdays, 1) Philip 1973 SA

Thompson, M.E.
Patterns and principles. See: Hawksworth, W.A.

Thomsen, M.W.
Introducing New Testament theology. 2nd ed. 92pp. N1.75 Africa Daystar 1965 NR

Thomson, A.P.D.
The opportunities that a department of anatomy can provide in a new faculty of medicine. 16pp. 30c Univ Rhodesia Lib 1968 RH

Thomson, B.P.
Two studies in African nutrition: an urban and a rural community in Northern Rhodesia. 74pp. K1.50 (75p.) (Rhodes-Livingstone paps., 24) Inst Soc Res - Zam 1954 ZA

Thomson, C.A., comp.
Directory of East African libraries.
See: Kibwika-Bagenda, M.E.C., comp.

Thonya, L.M.
Siasa hapo kale. ill. K.shs.3.90 ($1.50/60p.) EALB KE SWA

Thoret, J.C.
L'artisanat dans la région de Dabakala. 23pp. maps. Inst Ethno-Socio 1971 IV FRE

Thoret, J.C.
Atiékwa, un village de Côte d'Ivoire. See: Ferrari, A.

Thoret, J.C.
Les jeunes Djimini. Essai sur la dynamique des groupes de jeunes. 340pp. CFA1,700 (F34.00) Inst Ethno-Socio 1973 IV FRE

Thorn, G.W.P.
Adventures of Jonathan. 60pp. 25k OUP-Nig 1966 NR

Thorp, E.
Ladder of bones. 2nd ed. 256pp. 75k CSS 1972 NR

Thorpe, C.O.
Awon eewo ile Yoruba. [The taboos of Yorubaland] 218pp. photos. N1.25 Onibonoje 1967 NR YOR

Thorrington-Smith, M.
Phytoplankton studies in the Agulhas Current region off the Natal coast. 24pp. R1.10 Oceanographic Res Inst 1969 SA

Thowsen, A.
On pointwise degeneracy, controllability and minimal time control of linear dynamical systems with delays. 36pp. (CSIR Special Report, WISK 180) CSIR 1975 SA

Threadgold, N. Welbourn, H.
Health in the home. 5th ed. 95pp. ill. K.shs.5.20 ($1.80/70p.) EALB 1975 KE

Thuku, H.
Harry Thuku: an autobiography. 104pp. K.shs9.00 OUP-Nairobi 1973 KE

Thuku, H.
Harry Thuku: maisha yangu. [Harry Thuku: an autobiography] 120pp. K.shs.9.00 OUP-Nairobi 1971 KE SWA

Thunde, D.M.
Kamtigidi. [Humerous novel.] 38pp. 55n. Neczam 1975 ZA NYA

Thunde, D.M.
Kulingalira m'chichewa. [Poems.] 64pp. 50n. Neczam 1976 ZA NYA

Thurgood, M.A.
Mangrove swamp ecology of the Indo-West-Pacific region. 47pp. R2.45 Dept Bibliog, Lib & Typo 1968 SA

Tiar, M.
Recueil de textes juridiques et actes notaires. 185pp. DA7.00 SNED 1971 AE FRE

Tidadini, A.
Les investissements durant le plan quadriennal. DA1.00 SNED 1971 AE FRE

Tidjani, A.
Le plan quadriennal. DA1.00 SNED 1970 AE FRE

Tidmarsh, C.E.M. Havenga, C.M.
The wheel-point method of survey. 75c. (Memoirs of the Botanical Survey of South Africa, 29) Botanical Res Inst 1955 SA

Tiemo, G.O.E.
Ijo customs and traditions. 36pp. 30k (Inst. of African Stud., Univ of Ibadan, ocas. pub., 17) Inst Afr Stud-Ibadan 1968 NR IJO

Tietz, R.M.
Suggestions for the cataloguing of photographs of South African interest in museum and library collections. 75c (Dept. of Librarianship, occas. paps., 2) Rhodes Univ Lib 1970 SA

Tiffen, M.
Changing patterns of farming in Gombe Emirate, North Eastern State, Nigeria. 45pp. 40k (Samaru misc. pap., 32) Inst Agric Res - Zaria 1971 NR

Tijskens, J.P.
Recyclage des directeurs et de quelques instituteurs de l'enseignement primaire du Kasai occidental, Kananga. 37pp. CELTA 1976 ZR FRE

Tilmann, K.
Pour que ton enfant naisse en bonne santé. 2nd ed. 60pp. 25k St. Paul 1967 ZR FRE

Tilmann, K.
Veux-tu le savoir? 2nd ed. 45pp. photos. 15k St. Paul 1968 ZR FRE

Timitimi, A.O.
Ijo cookery book. 113pp. N1.00 (Inst. African Studies, Univ of Ibadan, occas. pubns., 28) Inst Afr Stud - Ib 1973 NR

Timitimi, A.O.
Izon Fiai fun. [Ijo cookery book] 113pp. N1.00 (Inst. of African Stud., Univ. of Ibadan, occas. pub., 28) Inst Afr Stud-Ibadan 1970 NR IJO

Timothy, B.
Missionary shepherds and African sheep: how does Christianity preached and practised by Europe and America appear to Africans? 67pp. 60k Daystar 1971 NR

Tomori, S.H.O.   Wingard, P.
Progressive English: pupils bk. 3, 6 bks 125pp.
photos. 75k Heinemann Educ - Nig 1967 NR

Tomori, S.H.O.   Wingard, P.
Progressive English: pupils bk. 4, 6bks 109pp. photos.
80k Heinemann Educ - Nig 1970 NR

Tomori, S.H.O.   Wingard, P.
Progressive English: pupils bk. 5, 6bks 146pp. photos.
85k Heinemann Educ - Nig 1972 NR

Tomori, S.H.O.   Wingard, P.
Progressive English: pupils bk. 6, 6bks 128pp. 90k
Heinemann Educ - Nig 1973 NR

Tomori, S.H.O.
Progressive English: teachers bk. 1, 6bks
See: Wingard, P.

Tomori, S.H.O.
Progressive English: teachers bk. 2, 6 bks
See: Wingard, P.

Tomori, S.H.O.   Wingard, P.
Progressive English: teachers bk. 3, 6bks 262pp.
N2.00 Heinemann Educ - Nig 1970 NR

Tomori, S.H.O.
Progressive English: teachers bk. 4, 6bks
See: Wingard, P.

Tomori, S.H.O.
Progressive English: teachers bk. 5, 6bks
See: Wingard, P.

Tomori, S.H.O.
Progressive English: teachers bk. 6, 6 bks
See: Wingard, P.

Tomori, S.H.O.
The teaching of composition writing. 175pp. N1.53
Heinemann Educ - Nig 1971 NR

Tonkin, M.
South Africa - A Nation of pill swallowers. 40c. (Isma
paps., 35) Inst Study of Man 1976 SA

Toogood, D.J.
Structural and metamorphic evolution of a Gneiss Terrain
in the Namaqua Belt near Onseepkans, South West Africa.
189pp. map. R8.00 (Univ of Cape Town, Precambrian
Research Unit, Bulletin 19) Precambrian Res Unit 1976
SA

Tooleyo, E.M.
The Kudeti Book of Yoruba cookery. See: Mars, J.A.

Topan, F.
Aliyeonja pepo. [A man who tasted life in heaven.]
44pp. T.shs.5.00 Tanz Publ House 1973 TZ SWA

Topan, F.
Mashairi ya Azimio la Arusha. See: Kamenju, G.

Topan, F.M., ed.
Uchambuzi wa maandishi ya Kiswahili. [Swahili literary
criticisms] 96pp. K.shs.8.50 OUP-Nairobi 1971 KE
SWA

Topan, F.M.
Mfalme juha. [The foolish king] 44pp. K.shs.3.50
OUP-Nairobi 1971 KE SWA

Topps, J.H.
Animal feeds of the Federation. 90pp. 50c (Dept. of
Agriculture, Univ. of Rhodesia, 1) Univ Rhodesia Lib
1971 RH

Torchar, G., ed.
Dadu à Kumasi. See: Bihan, G., ed.

Tordoff, W.
Government and politics in Tanzania. 251pp.
K.shs.56.00 pl.   K.shs.24.00 pap. ($13.00 cl.) ($7.80
pap.) EAPH 1967 KE

Torki, M.
L'an 732. De Kairouan á Poitiers. 152pp. D0.700
Maison Tunis 1972 TI FRE

Torr, D.G.   Torr, M.R.   Laurie, D.P.
Algorithm for the solution of the general ionospheric
reaction-rate equations. 4pp. ill. (CSIR research
reports, 309) CSIR 1971 SA

Torr, D.G.   Torr, M.R.
An investigation into the effect of temperature change on
the F-region electron density distribution in the south
Atlantic geomagnetic anomaly. 15pp. (CSIR research
reports, 263) CSIR 1967 SA

Torr, D.G.
A theoretical investigation of the F-region of the
ionosphere. See: Torr, M.R.

Torr, M.R.
Algorithm for the solution of the general ionospheric
reaction-rate equations. See: Torr, D.G.

Torr, M.R.
An investigation into the effect of temperature change on
the F-region electron density distribution in the south
Atlantic geomagnetic anomaly. See: Torr, D.G.

Torr, M.R.   Torr, D.G.
A theoretical investigation of the F-region of the
ionosphere. 86pp. (CSIR research reports, 271) CSIR
1969 SA

Torres, P.
La gestion du développement de la ville. 90pp. Ecole
Nat Admin - Niger 1976 NG FRE

Totty, A.
Kikorum cho pu Pokot. [Ten Pokot short stories] 18pp.
K.shs1.00 ($1.52/50p.) EALB 1963 KE POK

Totty, A.
Ng'ala Pokot. [Short stories from Pokot] 4th ed. 13pp.
ill. K.shs1.00 ($1.25/50p.) EALB 1963 KE POK

Totty, A.
Sambo nyo munung. [Adventures of Sambo] 3rd ed.
30pp. ill. K.shs1.50 ($1.25/50p.) EALB 1948 KE
POK

Touabi, A.
Le petrole. DA1.00 SNED 1971 AE FRE

Toualbi, N.
La circoncision. Blessure narcissique ou promotion
sociale? 262pp. DA15.00 SNED 1975 AE FRE

Toubkin, M.E., ed.
Ex-Africa: a sequel to the conference on the teaching of
Latin in Africa. See: Whittaker, C.R., ed.

Toupet, C.
Etude du milieu physique du massif de l'Assaba
(Mauritanie). Introduction à la mise en valeur d'une région
sahelienne. 152pp. photos. CFA1800 (Initiations et
Etudes Africaines, 20) IFAN 1966 SG FRE

Tournier, J.L. et al.
Annales de l'Université d'Abidjan. 120pp. CFA2000
(F40.00) (Série C - Sciences, 10) Univ Abidjan 1974 IV
FRE

Towa, M.
Léopold Sedar Senghor: négritude ou servitude? 120pp.
CFA450 pap. (Point de vue, 7) CLE 1971 CM FRE

Towert, A.M.F.
Constitutional development in South Africa, 1949-1959.
36pp. 80c. Univ Cape Town Lib 1963 SA

Towes, P.J., eds.
University chemistry teaching. Proceedings of the
international conference on University Chemistry Teaching
held at the University of Nairobi, Kenya, from 14th-18th
December, 1971. See: McCormick, D., eds.

Towet, T.
Tears over a dead cow, and other stories. 63pp. ill.
K.shs.5.50 Africa Book Serv 1970 KE

Townrow, J.S.
Some grasses of southwestern Nigeria. 42pp. ill. pl.
N3.00 Ibadan UP 1959 NR

Townsend Coles, C.K., et al.
Community development, with special reference to rural
areas. Papers read at a conference organized by the
Institute of Adult Education, August 1962. 51pp. 50c
pap. (Fac. of Education, Univ. of Rhodesia, 3) Univ
Rhodesia Lib 1963 RH

Townsend, E.R.
The official papers of William V.S. Tubman, 18th president of the Republic of Liberia: addresses, messages, speeches and statements 1960-1967. 688pp. photos. maps. cl. U.S.$10.00 Cole & Yancy 1968 LB

Townsend, J. Wisner, B.
Bibliography of Dodoma region. 23pp. T.shs. 15.00 (Research report, 43) Bur Res Asses Tanz 1971 TZ

Toye, B.O., comp.
Bibliography of entomological research in Nigeria: 1900-1973. 133pp. N2.50 (Entomological Society of Nigeria, occas. pubs., 16) Entomological Soc - Nig 1974 NR

Tracey, A.
African music codification and textbook project. Practical suggestions for field research. See: Tracey, H.

Tracey, A.
African music transcription library. Librarian's handbook. 80pp. ill. cl. R1.00 Int Lib Afric Music 1950 SA

Tracey, A., comp.
Catalogue of the "Sound of Africa" series of 210 records. 1, 2 v. Indexes 182pp. cl. Int Lib Afric Music 1973 SA

Tracey, A., comp.
Catalogue of the "Sound of Africa" series of 210 records. 2, 2 v. Record listing 479pp. photos. cl. R35.00 Int Lib Afric Music 1973 SA

Tracey, A. Zantzinger, G.
A companion to the films "Mgodo wa Mbanguzi" and "Mgodo wa Mkandeni". 47pp. music. R4.50 African Music Soc 1976 SA

Tracey, A.
How to play the mbira (dza vadzimu). An instruction booklet for a Rhodesian mbira. 25pp. R1.00 African Music Soc 1970 SA

Tracey, H.
African dances of the Witwatersrand gold mines. 156pp. photos. R1.00 African Music Soc 1952 SA

Tracey, H. Tracey, A. Kubik, G.
African music codification and textbook project. Practical suggestions for field research. 54pp. R2.00 African Music Soc 1969 SA

Tracey, H.
The evolution of African music and its function in the present day. 40c. (Isma paps., 3) Inst Study of Man 1961 SA

Tracey, H.
Lalela Zulu. 100 Zulu lyrics. 121pp. ill. 50c African Music Soc 1948 SA

Tracey, H.
Ngoma. 96pp. ill. R1.25 Longman SA 1948 SA

Tracey, P.
The lost valley. 139pp. cl. R3.95 Human and Rousseau 1975 SA

Traill, A.
The compleat guide to the Koon. 50pp. maps. R1.60 (University of the Witwatersrand, African Studies Institute, Communications, 1) African Stud Inst - Wit 1974 SA

Traill, A., ed.
Bushmen and Hottentot linguistic studies. 102pp. R1.00 (African Studies Institute Communications. 2) African Stud Inst - Wit 1975 SA

Traill, L.
Pronounce English correctly. See: Lanham.

Transafrica Publishers.
The hare and home made horns. 24pp. col. ill. K.shs.6.00 (Bushbabes, 2) Transafrica 1975 KE

Transafrica Publishers Limited.
Picture bible for all ages. v. 1,6: Creation. 168pp. ill. K.shs.10.00 East/Central Africa only Transafrica 1976 KE

Transafrica Publishers Limited.
Picture bible for all ages. v. 2,6: The promised land. 168pp. ill. K.shs.10.00 East/Central Africa only Transafrica 1976 KE

Transafrica Publishers Limited.
Picture bible for all ages. v. 3,6: Kings and prophets. 168pp. ill. K.shs.10.00 East/Central Africa only Transafrica 1976 KE

Transafrica Publishers Limited.
Picture bible for all ages. v. 4,6: Captivity. 168pp. ill. K.shs.10.00 East/Central Africa only Transafrica 1976 KE

Transafrica Publishers Limited.
Picture bible for all ages. v. 5,6: Jesus. 168pp. ill. K.shs.10.00 East/Central Africa only Transafrica 1976 KE

Transafrica Publishers Limited.
Picture bible for all ages. v. 6,6: The church. 168pp. ill. K.shs.10.00 Transafrica 1976 KE

Traore, B.
The black African theatre and its social functions. tr. fr. French D. Adelugba 130pp. N3.00 Ibadan UP 1972 NR

Traoré, I.
Contes et récits du terroir. 224pp. MF1035 pap. Ed Pop - Mali 1970 ML FRE

Traoré, I.B.
Koumi Diossé. 64pp. MF615 pap. Ed Pop - Mali 1972 ML FRE

Traoré, I.B.
Ombre du passé. 152pp. MF695 Ed Pop - Mali 1972 ML FRE

Traoré, S.
A l'écoute des anciens du village. 104pp. MF685 Ed Pop - Mali 1972 ML FRE

Traub, M.
Pourquoi la souffrance. 36pp. CFA160 CPE 1975 IV FRE

Traub, M.
Secrets of suffering. 32pp. ill. 90pes. (30p.) Africa Christian 1976 GH

Trautmann, R.
La divination à la Côte des Escaves et à Madagascar. [Reprint of ed. Paris, 1939]. 155pp. ill. (D.fl.45.00) (Mémoires de l'IFAN, 1) IFAN 1939 SG FRE

Treadaway, J.
East African secondary school atlas. See: Boorman, B.L.

Treadaway, J.
Uganda: studies in development. U.shs.20.00 Uganda Pub House 1974 UG

Tredgold, R.
Ideas, ideologies and idolatries. 12pp. 25c. (University of Cape Town T.B. Davie memorial lecture, 5) Univ Cape Town Lib 1963 SA

Tree Society of Southern Africa.
Trees and shrubs of the Witwatersrand. 3rd ed. 309pp. ill. col. pl. cl. R10.00 Witwatersrand UP 1974 SA

Tregidgo, P.S.
Practical English. bk. 2, 5. See: Ogundipe, P.A.

Tregidgo, P.S.
Practical English. bk. 3, 5. See: Ogundipe, P.A.

Tregidgo, P.S.
Practical English. bk. 4, 5. See: Ogundipe, P.A.

Tregidgo, P.S. Ogundipe, P.A.
Practical English course. New ed. bk. 1, 5 bks. 272pp. ill. N1.70 Longman - Nig 1976 NR

Tregidgo, P.S. Ogundipe, P.A.
Practical English course. New ed. bk. 5, 5 bks. 224pp. ill. N1.87 Longman - Nig 1976 NR

Tregidgo, P.S. Ogundipe, P.A.
Practical English. New ed. teachers bk. 1 104pp. N1.53 Longman - Nig 1975 NR

Tribe, M.
Housing problems in Uganda. 88pp. hd. U.shs.4.00
Adult Educ Centre 1969 UG

Tricart, J.   Guerra de Macedo, N.
Rapport de la mission de reconnaissance
géomorphologique de la vallee moyenne du Niger.
196pp. pl. maps. CFA1800 (Mémoires de l'IFAN, 72)
IFAN 1965 SG FRE

Trimble, W.B.S.
Basic economics for Lesotho. 250pp. R2.50
Mazenod Inst 1976 LO

Trimèche, R.
Macchu Picchu. 324pp. pl. D1.800 pap. Maison
Tunis 1975 TI FRE

Trioche, R. et al.
Annales de l'université d'Abidjan. 135pp. CFA950
(F19.00) (Série C-Sciences, 7) Univ Abidjan 1971 IV
FRE

Trobisch, W.
Nampenda mvulana. [I love a young man.] 80pp.
T.shs.3.50 Central Tanganyika 1973 TZ SWA

Trobisch, W.
Nilimpenda msichana. [I loved a girl.] 48pp.
T.shs.2.50 Central Tanganyika 1964 TZ SWA

Trobisch, W.
Nilimpenda msichana. [I loved a girl] Reprint of 1
1964ed. 48pp. T.shs.1.50 Africa Inland Church 1972
TZ SWA

Trobisch, W.
Pembetatu ya ndoa. [I married you.] 161pp. ill.
T.shs.8.00 Central Tanganyika 1974 TZ SWA

Trochain, J.
Contribution à l'étude de la végétation du Sénégal.[Reprint
of ed. Paris, 1940]. 433pp. pl. (D.fl.130.00)
(Mémoires de l'IFAN, 2) IFAN 1940 SG FRE

Trollope, A.
South Africa. 512pp. hd. fl. 56.25 (South African
biographical and historical studies, 14) Balkema 1973
SA

Trong, Y.
Annales de l'université d'Abidjan. See: Levieux, J.

Troupin, G.
Etude phytocénologique du parc national de l'Akagera et
du Rwanda oriental. Recherche d'une méthode d'analyse
appropriée à la végétation d'Afrique intertropicale.
293pp. ill. maps. RF660 (FB545.00/$13.00) (Institut
National de Recherche Scientifique, 2) Inst Nat -
Rwandaise 1966 RW FRE

Troupin, G.   Girardin, N.
Plantes ligneuses du Parc National de l'Akagera et des
savanes orientales du Rwanda. Clés pratique de
determination scientifique. 96pp. ill. pl.
(FB107.00/$2.70) Inst Nat Rwandaise 1975 RW FRE

Truelove, R.
History of West Africa. 276pp. photos. maps.
K.shs.27.50 ($7.00) EAPH 1975 KE

Trupie, D.W.F.   Musmeci, S.A.
The effect of different detergents on the primary centrifugal
performance of wool scouring liquors. 11pp. R2.50
(SAWTRI Technical Reports, 315) SAWTRI 1976 SA

Trupie, D.W.F.
Treatment of wool scouring liquors, part I: flocculation by
alum and polyelectrolytes, by T.E. Mozes, part II: the effect
of pH on flocculation by anionic, nonionic and cationic
polyelectrolytes. See: Mozes, T.E.

Truswell, J.F.
The geological evolution of South Africa. Rev. ed. ill.
pl. cl. R9.95 Purnell 1977 SA

Truu, M.L.
Economics in the university. ex. only (Inaugural lec.)
Rhodes Univ Lib 1974 SA

Truu, M.L.
Economics in the university. 25pp. 50c (Inaugural
lectures) Rhodes Univ Lib 1974 SA

Truu, M.L., ed.
Public policy and the South African economy. Essays in
honour of Desmond Hobart Houghton. 160pp. photo.
hd. R8.75 cl. OUP - SA 1976 SA

Truu, M.L.
Survey of the Cape Midlands and Karroo regions, vol. 3:
human resources in the Cape Midlands. 269pp. ill. Inst
Soc & Econ Res - SA 1971 SA

Tsacas, L.
Annales de l'université d'Abidjan. See: Lachaise, D.

Tsaro-Wiwa, K.
Tambari. 96pp. col. ill. 70k (English supp. readers,
4) Longman - Nig 1973 NR

Tsaro-Wiwa, K.B.
Tambari in Dukana. 90pp. ill. 60k (Palm Library for
Younger Readers) Longman - Nig 1973 NR

Tschannerl, G.
The cost of rural water supply construction in Tanzania.
T.shs.15.00 ($5.00) (Research pap., 30) Bur Res
Assess - Tanz 1974 TZ

Tschannerl, G., ed.
Proceedings of the conference on rural water supply in
East Africa, 5-8 April 1971. 277pp. maps.
T.shs.40.00 (Research pap., 20) Bur Res Assess Tanz
1971 TZ

Tschannerl, G. et al.
Handeni water supply: preliminary report on design
criteria. 42pp. T.shs.7.00 (Research report, 22) Bur
Res Assess - Tanz 1971 TZ

Tschannerl, G.   Mujwahuzi, M.
Impact of rural water supply: eight self-help schemes in
Arumeru, Masai, and Lushoto districts. 56pp. maps. hd.
& pap. T.shs.40.00 hd. T.shs.25.00 pap. ($12.00
hd.) ($8.00 pap.) (Research pap., 37) Bur Res Assess
- Tanz 1975 TZ

Tschannerl, G.   Mujwahuzi, M.R.
Impact of rural water supply: eight self-help schemes in
Arumeru, Masai and Lushoto districts. T.shs.25.00
(Research pap., 37) Bur Res Assess - Tanz 1975 TZ

Tseayo, J.I.
Conflict and incorporation in Nigeria. The integration of the
Tiv. 265pp. pl. map. N3.00 ABU Bkshop; distr.
1975 NR

Tsedeke, A.A.
An annotated list of insect pests of field crops in Ethiopia.
See: Crowe, T.J.

Tshibangu.
Eglise et nation. 89pp. 50k St. Paul 1973 ZR FRE

Tshibangu, T.
Eglise et nation. 89pp. 50k St. Paul 1973 ZR FRE

Tshibangu, T.
Le propos d'une théologie Africaine. 47pp. 50k
Press Univ Zaire 1974 ZR FRE

Tshimanga Membu Dikenia.
Fleurs de cuivre. Poèmes. 31pp. 50k (CFA250)
Centre Africain Litt 1973 ZR FRE

Tshuma, D.
Indoda elihaga. [An avaricious man.] 12pp. pl. 3c.
Rhod Lit Bur 1976 RH NDE

Tshuma, D.J.N.
Umpisi losilwane. [The hyena and the lion.] 12pp. pl.
3c. Rhod Lit Bur 1976 RH NDE

Tshuma, D.N.
Ukwaliwa kukandwangu. [How baboon was rejected.]
12pp. pl. 3c. Rhod Lit Bur 1976 RH NDE

Tsige, D.
Poems. 31pp. pl. B5.00 Author (P.O. Box 22072,
Addis Ababa, Ethiopia) 1974 ET

Tsige, H.
The scholarship and other stories. See: Birru, D.

Tubiana, J.
The Zaghawa from an ecological perspective.
Food-gathering, the pastoral system, tradition and
development of the Zaghawa of the Sudan and the Chad.
See: Tubiana, M.J.

Tubiana, M.J.   Tubiana, J.
The Zaghawa from an ecological perspective.
Food-gathering, the pastoral system, tradition and
development of the Zaghawa of the Sudan and the Chad.
136pp. photos. map. cl.   ($14.00/£8.50)   Balkema
1977 SA

Tudorascu Radu.
Reproduction normale et l'insémination artificielle des
animaux domestiques.   235pp. pl.   Z1.20   Press Univ
Zaire 1975 ZR FRE

Tudorascu Radu.   Petrescu, G.
Zootechnie générale.   249pp. pl.   Z1.20   Press Univ
Zaire 1974 ZR FRE

Tuitoek, W.
The boy who learnt a lesson, and other stories.   32pp. ill.
K.shs.3.50   Longman - Ken 1975 KE

Tukur, M.
Administrative and political development: prospect for
Nigeria.   237pp.   N2.00   (£1.50/$3.75)   Inst Admin -
Zaria 1970 NR

Tukur, M., ed.   Olagunju, T., ed.
Nigeria in search of a viable polity.   346pp.   N4.00
(£2.80/$7.00)   Inst Admin - Zaria 1972 NR

Tukur, M.
Nigeria's external relations.   90pp.   75k   (60p./$1.50)
Inst Admin - Zaria 1965 NR

Tukur, M.
Reform of the Nigerian public service.   340pp.   N3.00
(£2.00/$5.00)   Inst Admin - Zaria 1971 NR

Tumbo, N.S., et al.
Labour in Tanzania.   See: Mahiga, A.P.

Tumina Kikusa.
Fils, on n'épouse pas sa soeur! Mythes suku. Texte
suku-français.   111pp. map.   (DM18.00 pap.)
(CEEBA. série II, Mémoires et Monographies, 16)   CEEBA
1974 ZR FRE

Tumusiime-Rushedge, E.
The bull's horn.   202pp.   K.shs16.00   OUP-Nairobi
1972 KE

Tunmer, R., ed.
Documents in South African education.   See: Rose, B.,
ed.

Tunmer, R.
Race and education.   40c.   (Isma paps., 19)   Inst
Study of Man 1964 SA

Tuntufye, N.D.
Mazoezi ya Kiswahili.   [Swahili exercises.]   72pp.
T.shs.4.25   Longman - Tanz 1973 TZ SWA

Turbet-Delof, G.
Bibliographie critique du Maghreb dans la littérature
française 1532-1715.   305pp.   DA40.00.   (D80.00)
(Bibliographies et catalogues, 2)   Bibliothèque Nationale
1976 AE FRE

Turkson, A.
Three pieces for flute and piano.   6pp. music.   N2.00
($4.00/£1.75)   (Ife Music Editions, 5)   Univ Ife Press
1975 NR

Turnbull, C.
Mwafrika gumba.   [The lonely African]   205pp.
K.shs.19.00   ($4.30/£1.75)   EALB 1974 KE SWA

Turnbull, C.E.P.
The work of the missionaries of 'Die Nederduts
Gereformeerde Kerk van Suid-Afrika' up to the year 1910.
An annotated bibliography.   90pp.   R4.60   Dept
Bibliog, Lib & Typo 1965 SA

Turnbull, W.H.
How to grow better crops.   128pp. ill.   95c.   Longman
- SA 1973 SA

Turnbull, W.H.   Bishop, J.W.S.
How to grow vegetables.   64pp. ill.   95c.   Longman
SA 1972 SA

Turnbull, W.H.   Bishop, J.W.S.
How to look after cattle.   64pp. pl.   95c.   Longman
SA 1972 SA

Turnbull, W.H.   Bishop, J.W.S.
Sheep, goats, pigs and poultry.   New ed.   80pp. ill.
95c.   Longman SA 1974 SA

Turner, D.
Certificate English digest.   256pp.   K.shs.15.00
Textbook Ctre 1975 KE

Turner, H.P.
Objective tests in geography.   80pp. maps/photos.
94k   Pilgrim 1968 NR

Turner, L.
Office practice and procedures for Africa.   224pp. ill.
N2.20   Macmillan 1973 NR

Turner, N.
The art of the Greek orthodox church.   97pp.   R$2.00
(Univ. Rhodesia, Series in Humanities, 2)   Univ Rhodesia
1976 RH

Turner, V.W.
Chihamba the White Spirit: a ritual drama of the Ndembu.
96pp.   K1.50   (75p.)   (Rhodes-Livingstone paps., 33)
Inst Soc Res - Zam 1962 ZA

Turner, V.W.
Ndembu divination: its symbolism and techniques.   96pp.
K1.75   (88p.)   (Rhodes-Livingstone paps., 31)   Inst Soc
Res - Zam 1961 ZA

Turner, V.W.
Schism and continuity in an African society: a study of
Ndembu village life.   348pp. ill. pap. & hd.   K4.80 hd.
K2.40 pap.   (£2.40 hd.)   (£2.10 pap.)   Inst Afr Stud -
Lusaka 1957 ZA

Turpie, D.W.F.
Application of a cobaltothiocyanate method for the rapid
determination of synthetic non-ionic detergent (ethylene
oxide type) in wool scouring liquors and in recovered wool
grease.   See: Musmeci, S.A.

Turpie, D.W.F.
The effect of atmospheric conditions, regain before carding
and water added during gilling on the processing
performance of faulty wools up to combing.   See: Smith,
H.E.

Turpie, D.W.F.   Hunter, L.
The effect of changes in the CV of fibre length on spinning
performance and certain physical properties of wool yarns.
16pp.   R2.50   (SAWTRI Technical Reports, 253)
SAWTRI 1975 SA

Turpie, D.W.F.   Gee, F.
The effect of neutral and alkaline scouring on the
yellowness of wool at the various processing stages.
15pp.   R2.50   (SAWTRI Technical Reports, 288)
SAWTRI 1976 SA

Turpie, D.W.F.
The influence of backwashing on the combing performance
of overcrimped wool.   12pp.   R2.50   (SAWTRI
Technical Reports, 301)   SAWTRI 1976 SA

Turpie, D.W.F.
The processing characteristics of South African wools: part
IX: the influence of limited variations in both length and
diameter on the processing performance of mixtures of
South African wools up to spinning.   14pp.   R2.50
(SAWTRI Technical Reports, 284)   SAWTRI 1976 SA

Turpie, D.W.F.
The processing characteristics of South African wools, part
VI: influence of style, length and class description.   32pp.
R2.50   (SAWTRI Technical Reports, 250)   SAWTRI 1975
SA

Author Index

Ubesie, T.
Mmiri oku e ji egbu mbe. [Set a thief to catch a thief] 90k Longman-Nig 1973 NR IGB

Ubesie, T.
Ukpaka miiri onye ubiam. 150pp. ill. N1.50 Nwamife 1976 NR IGB

Ubesie, T.
Ukwa ruo oge ya [Novel]. 88pp. 95k OUP - Nig 1973 NR IGB

Ubesie, T.U.
Ukpana Okpoko buuru. [Novel] 94pp. N1.30 OUP - Nig 1975 NR IGB

Uche, E.I.
Uma ako mkpa. 86pp. N1.00 Univ Publ 1977 NR IGB

Uche, U.E., ed.
Law and population change in Africa. 292pp. K.shs.67.50 ($12.95/£6.20) EALB 1976 KE

Uchendu, V.C.   Anthony, K.R.M.
Agricultural change in Geita, Tanzania. A study of economic, cultural and technical determinants of agricultural change in tropical Africa. 92pp. K.shs.20.50 ($4.55/£2.25) EALB 1975 KE

Uchendu, V.C.   Anthony, K.R.M.
Agricultural change in Kisii District Kenya. 102pp. map. K.shs.18.50 ($4.50/£2.25) EALB 1975 KE

Uchendu, V.C.   Anthony, K.R.M.
Agricultural change in Teso district, Uganda. A study of economic, cultural and technical determinants of agricultural change in tropical Africa. 124pp. K.shs.26.75 ($5.70/£2.80) EALB 1975 KE

Ude, N.
History [course]. bk. 1. 70pp. 80k Ilesanmi 1972 NR

Ude, N.
History [course]. bk. 2. 88pp. N1.10 Ilesanmi 1972 NR

Ude, N.
History [course]. bk. 3. 102pp. N1.25 Ilesanmi 1972 NR

Udeman, E.
The published works of Mrs Margaret Livingstone Ballinger. 68pp. R3.50 Dept Bibliog, Lib & Typo 1968 SA

Udesi, E.D.C.
Ukpulawhu unûzú unu Ejpeye. See: Ikpe, M.S.

Udo-Ema, A.J.   Anwan, O.E.E.
Edikot nwed: pupils book I. 51pp. col. ill. 60k OUP-Nig 1972 NR BIN

Udo-Ema, A.J.   Anwan, O.E.E.
Edikot nwed: teacher's book I. 35pp. 35k OUP-Nig 1972 NR BIN

Udo, R.K.
Examination guidelines for school certificate geography. 55pp. ill. N1.20 Heinemann Educ - Nig 1970 NR

Udo, R.K.
Geographical regions of Nigeria. 212pp. photos ill. maps. N5.95 Heinemann Educ - Nig 1970 NR

Udo, R.K.
Migrant tenant farmers of Nigeria. A geographical study of rural migrations in Nigeria. 154pp. N2.50 Pilgrim 1975 NR

Udoeyop, N.J.
Three Nigerian poets. A critical study of the poetry of Soyinka, Clark and Okigbo. 166pp. N2.00 Ibadan UP 1973 NR

Udoh, G.H.
Map reading for secondary schools. 2nd rev. ed. 44pp. maps ill. N1.30 Macmillan NR

Udoh, G.H.
A primary school geography for Nigeria. 1, 3bks 96pp. maps ill. N1.50 Macmillan 1966 NR

U.G. Kerk-Uitgewers.
Human relations and the South Africa scene in the light of scripture. 100pp. R1.80 Kerk 1976 SA

Uguru, O.O.
A guide to practical agricultural science for schools and colleges. 152pp. ill. N1.10 Macmillan 1965 NR

Uiso, G.B.E.
Chuo Kikuu cha Dar es Salaam. Orodha ya machapisho. 1977. University of Dar es Salaam. Publications catalogue. 1977. [In Swahili and English.]. 3rd ed. 172pp. ex. only Univ Dar es Salaam Lib 1977 TZ

Uka, K.
A consumation of fire. 180pp. N2.00 Nwamife 1976 NR

Uka, N.
The development of time concepts in African children of primary school age. 25pp. 35k (Inst. of Ed. occas. pub., 3) Inst Educ-Ib 1962 NR

Ukairo, G.U.
Olu Igbo. [Igbo primary course.] pupil's bk. 1. 48pp. ill. 50k OUP - Nig 1973 NR IGB

Ukairo, G.U.
Olu Igbo. [Igbo primary course.] pupil's bk. 2. 120pp. ill. 75k OUP - Nig 1974 NR IGB

Ukairo, G.U.
Olu Igbo. [Igbo reader.] Pupil's bk. 3 80pp. ill. 90k OUP - Nig 1975 NR IGB

Ukairo, G.U.
Olu Igbo. [Igbo primary course.] teacher's bk. 1 17pp. 20k OUP - Nig 1973 NR IGB

Ukeje, B.O.
Education for social reconstruction. 184pp. hd. N3.00 Macmillan NR

Ukoki, N.M.
The twins of the rain forest. 66pp. 55k (English supp. readers, 1) Longman - Nig 1968 NR

Ukoli, J.M.A.
Order amongst parasites. 42pp. ill. N1.00 (Inaugural lecture) Ibadan UP 1975 NR

Ukoli, N.M.   Olomu, M.
The antelope that hurried. 16pp. 50k. Ethiope 1975 NR

Ukoli, N.M.
Home to the river. N1.20 Ethiope 1975 NR

Ukpabi, S.C.
Command and conflict in West African military history: the West African Frontier Force example. 140pp. N5.00 Cross Continent 1977 NR

Ukwu, U.K.
Markets in West Africa. See: Hodder, B.W.

Ulenge, Y.
Nguzo ya maji. [The pillar of water] 84pp. ill. K.shs.4.00 OUP-Nairobi 1964 KE SWA

Ulotu, A.
Historia ya Tanu. [Tracing the history of Tanu] 432pp. ill. K.shs.20.00 ($4.50/£1.80) EALB 1971 KE SWA

Umaras-Sakuni, A.A.
Uyun al - Munagarat (polémiques célébres) 527pp. D3.750 (Série VI, Philosophie-Litterature, 11) Univ Tunis 1976 TI FRE

Umaru, H.
Nuni cikin nisha'di. [Collection of stories.] N1.75 Northern Nig 1976 NR HAU

Umayi, L.N.S.
Adon Duniya Kar Ya Ja Min Hasara. [The adornment of the world will never put me in danger] 14pp. 40k Northern Nig 1972 NR HAU

Umezinwa, A.W.
La religion dans la littérature Africaine. 186pp. Z4.86 Press Univ Zaire 1975 ZR FRE

Umo, M.G., comp.
Theses and dissertations accepted in Nigerian universities, 1969-1970. 19pp. 50k (N1.00) (National Library pubs, 24) Nat Lib-Nig 1971 NR

Umobuarie, D.O.
Black justice. 195pp. N2.50 (Three Crowns Books) OUP - Nig 1976 NR

Umuro, M.P.
Learn to speak the four Nigerian main languages.
See: Orji, G.

Ungar, A.
The propagation of elastic waves from moving normal point loads in layered media. 31pp. (CSIR Special Report, WISK 211) CSIR 1976 SA

Ungar, A.
Response of an elastic half-space to a moving normal point load. 28pp. (CSIR Special Report, WISK 189) CSIR 1975 SA

Unger, F.W.
With 'Bobs' and Kruger. [Reprint of ed. 1901]. 422pp. ill. cl. R14.50 (Anglo Boer War Reprint Library, 2) Struik 1977 SA

Union des Avocats Arabes.
La question palestinienne. 237pp. DA7.00 SNED 1968 AE FRE

United Nations. Economic Commission Africa.
Ressources attribuées à la CEA en 1974 au titre des programmes d'assistance technique. 28pp. (E/CN.14/627) ECA 1974 ET FRE

United Nations. Economic Commission for Africa.
African household surveys programme. 20pp. (E/CN.14/CAS.9/5) ECA 1975 ET

United Nations. Economic Commission for Africa.
African statistical yearbook 1974: North Africa. pt. 1 151pp. ECA 1975 ET

United Nations. Economic Commission for Africa.
Concepts, definitions and classifications of the external trade statistics in relation to the SNA and the balance of payments. [Also available in French]. 29pp. (E/CN.14/NAC/58) ECA 1975 ET

United Nations. Economic Commission for Africa.
Concepts, definitions, classifications, and accounts and tables of the SNA relating to external transactions. [Also available in French]. 27pp. (E/CN.14/NAC/56) ECA 1975 ET

United Nations. Economic Commission for Africa.
Development education: rural development through mass media. 59pp. (E/CN.14/SWSA/10) ECA 1974 ET

United Nations. Economic Commission for Africa.
Economic Commission for Africa, annual report (24 February 1974 - 28 February 1975). [Also available in French]. v. 1 136pp. ($7.00) (E/CN.14/642) ECA 1975 ET

United Nations. Economic Commission for Africa.
Estimates and projections of agricultural/non-agricultural population and labour force. 19pp. (E/CN.14/POP/133) ECA 1974 ET

United Nations. Economic Commission for Africa.
The food situation in Africa and a programme of action. [Also available in French]. 29pp. (E/CN.14/637) ECA 1975 ET

United Nations. Economic Commission for Africa.
Foreign trade statistics for Africa, Direction of trade, series A no. 22. [Also available in French]. 99pp. ($5.00) (E/CN.14/STAT/Ser.A/22) ECA 1974 ET

United Nations. Economic Commission for Africa.
Foreign trade statistics for Africa, trade by commodity, series B no. 25./ Statistiques africaines du commerce extérieur, échanges par produits serie B no. 25. 229pp. ($7.00) ECA 1975 ET

United Nations. Economic Commission for Africa.
Habitat. United Nations conference on human settlements: institutional arrangements at the global and regional levels. 5pp. (E/CN.14/HUS/17) ECA 1976 ET

United Nations. Economic Commission for Africa.
Implementation of the declaration and the programme of action on the establishment of a new international economic order. 36pp. (E/CN.14/635/Add.1) ECA 1974 ET

United Nations. Economic Commission for Africa.
L'information au service de la planification démographique ou familiale et du développement. 35pp. (E/CN.14/POP/126) ECA 1975 ET FRE

United Nations. Economic Commission for Africa.
Matters arising from the twelfth session of the Economic Commission for Africa (third meeting of the Conference of Ministers) 23pp. (E/CN.14/CAS.9/6) ECA 1975 ET

United Nations. Economic Commission for Africa.
Politiques et programmes: conceptions et méthodes pour la mobilisation et l'orientation de ressources financières en vue d'investissements dans les établissements humains. 40pp. (E/CN.14/HUS/3) ECA 1975 ET FRE

United Nations. Economic Commission for Africa.
Politiques et programmes: facteurs de la planification régionale influant sur les établissements humains en Afrique. 52pp. (E/CN.14/HUS/1) ECA 1975 ET FRE

United Nations. Economic Commission for Africa.
Progress report on the activities of the commission (1 September 1973 - 31 December 1974) 78pp. (E/CN.14/636) ECA 1975 ET

United Nations. Economic Commission for Africa.
Proposals for a population programme of action for Africa following from the recommendations of the 1974 World Population Conference. [Also available in French]. 18pp. (E/CN.14/POP/135) ECA 1975 ET

United Nations. Economic Commission for Africa.
Register of new and planned industrial projects in selected African countries, 1972-1973. 30pp. (E/CN.14/INR/210) ECA 1974 ET

United Nations. Economic Commission for Africa.
Report of the fifth meeting of the technical committee of experts. [Also available in French]. 51pp. (E/CN.14/641; E/CN.14/TECO/30) ECA 1975 ET

United Nations. Economic Commission for Africa.
Report of the fifth session of the conference of African planners. (Addis Ababa, 19-28 June 1974) 56pp. (E/CN.14/626; E/CN.14/CAP.5/11) ECA 1974 ET

United Nations. Economic Commission for Africa.
Report of the meeting of donor agencies interested in the African regional plan (Addis Ababa, 10-11 July 1974) 15pp. (E/CN.14/623) ECA 1974 ET

United Nations. Economic Commission for Africa.
Report of the second meeting of the inter-governmental committee of experts for science and technology development in Africa (Addis Ababa, 17-19 July 1974) 17pp. (E/CN.14/624) ECA 1974 ET

United Nations. Economic Commission for Africa.
Report of the second seminar of the Association of African Central Banks (Addis Ababa, 15-16 August 1974). [Also available in French]. 21pp. (E/CN.14/AMA/51) ECA 1974 ET

United Nations. Economic Commission for Africa.
Report of the second session of the conference of African demographers (Addis Ababa, 6-10 May 1974). [Also available in French]. 34pp. (E/CN.14/625; E/CN.14/POP/120) ECA 1974 ET

United Nations. Economic Commission for Africa.
Report of the seminar on external transactions, Kampala, 28 April - 7 May 1975. 22pp. (E/CN.14/NAC/60; E/CN.14/CAS.9/8) ECA 1975 ET

Author Index

United Nations. Economic Commission for Africa.
Report of the third meeting between the Trans-African highway bureau and industrialized countries. (Addis Ababa, 6-8 November 1974) [Also available in French]. 15pp. (E/CN.14/TRANS/120) ECA 1974 ET

United Nations. Economic Commission for Africa.
Report of the third subregional workshop on international co-operation in rural development in Africa (Accra 22-27 November 1974) 24pp. (E/CN.14/SWCD/66) ECA 1974 ET

United Nations. Economic Commission for Africa.
Report of the twelfth meeting of the executive committee (Addis Ababa, 18-22 November 1974). [Also available in French]. 25pp. (E/CN.14/633; E/CN.14/ECO/78) ECA 1974 ET

United Nations. Economic Commission for Africa.
Route transafricaine: resume de l'étude des barrières juridiques et administratives. 32pp. (E/CN.14/TRANS/116) ECA 1975 ET FRE

United Nations. Economic Commission for Africa.
Santé et planification familiale. 38pp. (E/CN.14/POP/128) ECA 1974 ET FRE

United Nations. Economic Commission for Africa.
Sociological aspects: African migration and human settlements. [Also available in French]. 28pp. (E/CN.14/HUS/8) ECA 1975 ET

United Nations. Economic Commission for Africa.
Sociological aspects of housing in the framework of integrated rural development. 20pp. (E/CN.12/HUS/9) ECA 1975 ET

United Nations. Economic Commission for Africa.
Some sociological aspects of human settlements: the effects of building costs and other financial considerations. [Also available in French]. 27pp. (E/CN.14/HUS/11/Rev.1) ECA 1975 ET

United Nations. Economic Commission for Africa.
Survey of economic conditions in Africa, 1972. pt. 1 306pp. ($10.00) (E/CN.14/595) ECA 1974 ET

United Nations. Economic Commission for Africa.
Survey of economic conditions in Africa, 1973. pt. 1 223pp. ($9.00) (E/CN.14/621) ECA 1974 ET

United Nations. Economic Commission for Africa.
Technical report on the post-enumeration survey for coverage evaluation of African population censuses. 47pp. (E/CN.14/CAS.9/7) ECA 1975 ET

United Nations. Economic Commission for Africa.
Utilization of resources: formulation and implementation of housing and infrastructure policies and programmes. 70pp. (E/CN.14/HUS/4/Summary) ECA 1975 ET

United Nations. Economic Commission for Africa.
Utilization of resources: sanitation and environmental services in selected African cities. [Also available in French]. 15pp. (E/CN.14/HUS/7) ECA 1975 ET

United Nations. Economic Commission for Africa.
Utilization of resources: the role of energy in the development of human settlements in Africa. [Also available in French]. 19pp. (E/CN.14/HUS/6) ECA 1975 ET

United Nations. Economic Commission for Africa.
Vers une compagnie africaine multinationale de transports aériens des marchandises. 36pp. (E/CN.14/TRANS/122) ECA 1975 ET FRE

United Press of Africa ltd.
Industry in East Africa (annual) 500pp. K.shs50.00 (£5.00) United Africa 1973 KE

Univ. of Cape Coast, Centre for Development Studies.
The flow and marketing of agricultural produce in the central region with special reference to Cape Coast (June 1970-August 1971) 89pp. C1.50 (Univ. of Cape Coast, Centre for Development Studies, Research Report Series, 15) Centre Dev Stud 1974 GH

Univ. of Cape Coast, Centre for Development Studies.
Occupational activities of rural youth and their attitudes towards craft training. An exploratory study. C1.00 (Univ. of Cape Coast, Centre for Development Studies, Research Report Series, 16) Centre Dev Stud 1974 GH

Univ of Cape Coast, English Dept.
Workpapers: Burning issues in African literature. v. 1 Cape Coast Bkshp 1971 GH

Univ. of Cape Coast, English Dept. Workpapers.
Critical essays and reviews. 71pp. 45pes. Cape Coast Bkshp 1972 GH

Univ. of Cape Coast, English Dept. Workpapers.
Imaginative writing. 45pp. 25pes Cape Coast Bkshp 1971 GH

Univ. of Cape Coast, English Dept. Workpapers.
Teaching problems. 52pp. 30pes. Cape Caost Bkshp 1971 GH

Univ. of Natal.
The African factory worker. $3.00 (Natal regional survey reports, 2) Dept Econ-Natal 1950 SA

Univ. of Natal.
Agriculture in Natal, recent developments. $4.50 (Natal regional survey pub., 13) Dept Econ--Natal 1957 SA

Univ. of Natal.
Archaeology and natural resources of Natal. $3.00 (Natal regional survey pub., 1) Dept Econ, Natal 1951 SA

Univ. of Natal, Dept. of Economics.
Monopoly and public welfare. $1.25 Dept Econ-Natal 1962 SA

Univ. of Natal.
The Durban-Pietermaritzburg region. v. 1 $5.50 (Natal regional survey pub., 14) Dept Econ - Natal 1968 SA

Univ. of Natal.
The Durban-Pietermaritzburg region. v. 2 $4.00 (Natal regional survey pub., 14) Dept Econ - Natal 1969 SA

Univ. of Natal.
Electricity undertakings in Natal. $2.50 (Natal regional survey pub., 5) Dept Econ, Natal 1953 SA

Univ. of Natal.
Studies of Indian employment in Natal. $3.00 (Natal regional survey pub., 11) Dept Econ-Natal 1961 SA

Université d'Abidjan.
Catalogue des publications, mai 1975. 54pp. free Univ Abidjan 1975 IV FRE

Université d'Abidjan.
Enseignement supérieur en Côte d'Ivoire, annuaire 1973/1974. FF60.00 CEDA 1974 IV FRE

Université de Tunis.
Recherches et documents d'histoire maghrébine: l'Algérie, la Tunisie, la Tripolitaine de 1816 à 1871. 333pp. pl. ex. only (Série IV, Histoire, 10) Univ Tunis 1971 TI FRE

Université de Tunis.
Travaux du colloque international sur les niveaux de vie en Tunisie: Enquête sur les salariés de la région de Tunis. 1, 3v. 79pp. photos. D0.850 (Série III, Mémoires du Centre D'Etudes Humaines, 3) Univ Tunis 1958 TI FRE

Université de Tunis.
Travaux du colloque international sur les niveaux de vie en Tunisie: Niveaux de vie liés à l'agriculture. 2, 3v. 139pp. pl. D0.850 (Série III, Mémoires du Centre d'Etudes Humaines, 3) Univ Tunis 1958 TI FRE

Université de Tunis.
Travaux du colloque international sur les niveaux de vie en Tunisie: Problèmes généraux et conclusions. 3, 3v. 105pp. D0.850 (Série III, Mémoires du Centre d'Etudes Humaines, 3) Univ Tunis 1958 TI FRE

Université de Yaoundé, Bibliothèque.
Rentrée solennelle de l'Université de Yaoundé, discours 1975-1976. 60pp. CFA500 Univ Cameroun 1975 CM FRE

Universite de Yaoundé.
Rentrée solennelle de l'Université de Yaoundé - Discours 1974-1975. 60pp. CFA500 Univ Cameroun 1974 CM FRE

University College of Rhodesia Manpower Sub-Committee.
The requirements and supplies of high-level manpower in northern Rhodesia 1961-1970. 22pp. 50c (Dept. of Economics, Univ. of Rhodesia, 2) Univ Rhodesia Lib 1964 RH

University College of Rhodesia. Manpower Sub-Committee.
The requirements and supplies of high-level manpower in southern Rhodesia 1961-1970. 22pp. 50c (Dept. of Economics, Univ. of Rhodesia, 3) Univ Rhodesia Lib 1964 RH

University of Benin Library.
Library foundation and first year report, 1970/71. 26pp. Ex. only Benin Univ 1972 NR

University of Cape Town Libraries.
Bibliographical series consolidated list 1941-1966 & second (consolidated) supplement. 38pp. 80c. Univ Cape Town Lib 1966 & 70 SA

University of Cape Town Libraries.
Biographical index to 'Men of the times (Old colonists of the Cape Colony and Orange River Colony, Johannesburg, 1906)'. 22pp. 75c. (U.C.T. libraries Varia series, 3) Univ Cape Town Lib 1960 SA

University of Cape Town Libraries.
Original catalogue of the private library of the Ballot family. 28pp. 75c. (U.C.T. libraries Varia series, 2) Univ Cape Town Lib 1961 SA

University of Dar es Salaam, Election Study Committee.
Socialism and participation: Tanzania's 1970 national elections. 464pp. T.shs.55.00 ($13.00) Tanz Publ House 1974 TZ

University of Dar es Salaam, Institute of Adult Education.
Hadithi za Kinyamwezi. [Stories of the Nyamwezi people of Tanzania.] 48pp. K.shs.6.20 ($2.00) EALB 1975 KE SWA

University of Dar es Salaam, Institute of Adult Education.
Hadithi za Kisukuma. [Stories of the Sukuma people of Tanzania.] 28pp. K.shs.6.20 ($2.00) EALB 1975 KE SWA

University of Ife Bookshop Ltd.
Contemporary African literature: catalogue of books and periodicals displayed during an exhibition, held at Ibadan, Ile-Ife and Lagos, November 25th to December 21st, 1971. 96pp. 75k ($1.00) Univ Ife Bkshop 1971 NR

University of Ife, Faculty of Agriculture.
Eighth annual research report. 67pp. N1.50 (£1.10) ($2.50) Univ Ife Press 1974 NR

University of Ife. Student Press Club.
First student press workshop, 16th-18th April, 1973. Proceedings. 48pp. 20k Univ Ife Bkshop; distr. 1974 NR

University of Khartoum, Graduate College.
Dissertation abstracts. 192pp. £S2.00 ($9.00) Khartoum UP 1977 SJ

University of Khartoum Library.
The classified catalogue of the Sudan collection in the University of Khartoum Library. 942pp. LS10.00 ($75.00/£30.00) Khartoum UP 1971 SJ

University of Khartoum.
Philosophical and Ethnic Society 1969-1970. 72pp. 35pt. ($1.50) Khartoum UP 1971 SJ

University of Khartoum Philosophical Society.
Ethics and society. 72pp. 35 pt. ($1.50) Khartoum UP 1971 SJ

University of Lagos, Faculty of Engineering.
Careers in engineering. 20pp. 50k (25p.) Univ Lagos Bkshop 1974 NR

University of Natal, Department of Economics.
The Dunn reserve - Zululand. 4, 6 vols. $1.25 Dept Econ-Natal 1953 SA

University of Natal, Department of Economics.
The Durban housing survey. $3.50 Dept. Econ-Natal 1952 SA

University of Natal, Department of Economics.
Experiment at Edenvale. $3.00 Dept Econ-Natal 1951 SA

University of Natal, Department of Economics.
The port of Durban. $4.00 (Natal regional survey pub., 15) Dept Econ - Natal 1969 SA

University of Natal, Department of Economics.
Small towns of Natal. $1.75 Dept Econ-Natal 1953 SA

University of Rhodesia Library.
Catalogue of the W.A. Godlonton collection of Rhodesiana in the library of the University of Rhodesia. 222pp. R$6.00 cl. (Library Bibliographical Series, 1) Univ Rhodesia Lib 1972 RH

University of Rhodesia Library.
Periodicals in Rhodesian libraries. rev. ed. 394pp. R$1.00 Univ Rhodesia Lib 1968 RH

University of Rhodesia Library.
Report on African studies: 1950-1963 at the university college. 39pp. Free Univ Rhodesia Lib 1966 RH

University of Sierra Leone, Institute of Education, Curriculum Revision Unit.
A syllabus for English at secondary level. 58pp. Le1.00 Fourah Bay Bkshp; distr. 1974 SL

University of South Africa.
Summaries of theses accepted by the University of South Africa 1919-1971, (annually). [Bilingual in English and Afrikaans]. R3.00 per v. (R4.50 per v.) Univ South Africa SA

University of Zambia. Rural Development Studies Bureau.
An analysis of the pattern of income and expenditure of a sample of the farm families of Chiefdom Hamaundu of the Choma District of the Southern Province of Zambia. 41pp. Rur Dev Stud Bur - Zam 1975 ZA

University Press of Africa.
Engineer in East Africa. 272pp. ill. pl. cl. (£2.95) Univ Press Africa 1973 KE

University Press of Africa.
Ethiopia. 328pp. col. ill. maps. cl. (£5.00 cl.) Univ Press Africa 1969 KE

University Press of Africa.
Homes for Kenya. 108pp. ill. (£1.05 pap.) Univ Press Africa 1969 KE

University Press of Africa.
Kampala. 200pp. ill. maps. (£1.05) Univ Press Africa 1970 KE

University Press of Africa.
Mombasa. 168pp. ill. maps. (£0.90) Univ Press Africa 1971 KE

University Press of Africa.
Sudan today. 234pp. photos. cl. (£4.60 cl.) Univ Press Africa 1971 KE

University Press of Africa.
Tanzania today. 316pp. photos. maps. cl. (£4.60 cl.) Univ Press Africa 1968 KE

University Press of Africa.
Zambian farming today. 120pp. ill. (£1.05) Univ Press Africa 1969 KE

University Publ. Co.
Geography of Africa. 95pp. ill. 75k Univ Publ 1971 NR

University Publishing Company, Nigeria.
Tortoise, fantastic winner. 90pp. N1.00 Univ Publ 1975 NR

Author Index

University Publishing Company.
Recommendations of Igbo standardisation committee.
32pp. 50k. Univ Publ 1977 NR

University Publishing Company.
Seminar on Igbo arts and music. N5.00 Univ Publ 1976 NR

University Publishing.
Model answers in Igbo/GCE. 100pp. N2.50 Univ Publ 1977 NR

Unoh, S.O.
Faster reading through practise. 158pp. N1.50 OUP - Nig 1973 NR

Unoh, S.O.
Reading to remember. 65k OUP-Nig 1970 NR

Unoh, S.O.
The study of reading. 37pp. 70k Ibadan UP 1968 NR

Urban, E.K.
Bibliography of the Avifauna of Ethiopia. 28pp. B2.50 (£1.25/£0.45) Addis Ababa UP 1970 ET

Urban, E.K.   Brown, L.H.
A checklist of the birds of Ethiopia. 143pp. maps. B9.50 ($5.00/£1.70) Addis Ababa UP 1971 ET

Urban, E.K.   Brown, L.H.
A checklist of the birds of Ethiopia. 143pp. cl. B12.00 ($6.50/£2.15) Addis Ababa UP 1971 ET

Urugba, M.   Clevenger, J.
Eni va, 1. [Engenni reader, 1] 43pp. ill. 30k (Inst. of African Stud., Univ. of Ibadan, Rivers readers project, 22) Inst Afr Stud-Ibadan 1971 NR ENN

Urugba, M.   Clevenger, J.
Eni va, 2. [Engenni reader, 2] 51pp. ill. 30k (Inst. of African Stud., Univ. of Ibadan, Rivers readers project, 32) Inst Afr Stud-Ibadan 1972 NR ENN

Urvoy, Y.
L'art dans le territoire du Niger. 68pp. ill. (Etudes Nigériennes, 2) Inst Rech Sci Hum 1955 NG FRE

Urvoy, Y.
Les bassins du Niger. [Reprint of ed. Paris, 1942]. 139pp. ill. pl. maps. (D.fl.45.00) (Mémoires de l'IFAN, 4) IFAN 1942 SG FRE

Urvoy, Y.
Histoire du Bornou. [Reprint of ed. Paris, 1949]. 166pp. ill. maps. (D.fl.50.00) (Mémoires de l'IFAN, 7) IFAN 1949 SG FRE

Urvoy, Y.
Petit atlas ethno-démographique du Soudan entre Sénégal et Tchad. [Reprint of ed. Paris, 1942]. 40pp. ill. pl. maps. (D.fl.25.00) (Mémoires de l'IFAN, 5) IFAN 1942 SG FRE

Usman, S.
Addini A Saukake. [Religion made easy] N1.95 Northern Nig 1966 NR HAU

Usman, S.
Mu Kara Kyautata Addinin Mu. [Let us improve our religion] 195pp. 65k Northern Nig 1973 NR HAU

Usoro, E.J.
The Nigerian oil palm industry: a study of government policy and export production. 153pp. ill. pl. cl. & pap. N5.00 pap. N7.00 cl. (Ibadan Social Science Studies, 2) Ibadan UP 1974 NR

Usua, E.J.
Handbook of practical biology. 62pp. ill. 80k OUP-Nig 1970 NR

Usua, E.J.
Plant and animal science for schools and colleges, a biology book for top primary schools and lower secondary schools with local examples of plants and animals. 86pp. ill. pl. N1.50 Paico 1973 NR

Usua, E.J.
Revision course in biology objective tests: with answers. 299pp. ill. N2.30 OUP-Nig 1967 NR

Usua, E.J.
School certificate and G.C.E. examinations as they are set: Biology. 120pp. ill. N2.00 Paico 1977 NR

Usua, E.J.
School Certificate biology for West Africa. 154pp. ill. N3.10 OUP - Nig 1975 NR

Uti, J.O.
A handbook of physical education. See: Ekperigin, N.I.

Utting, J.
Fossils of Zambia. See: Drysdall, A.R.

Uvieghara, E.E.
Trade union law in Nigeria. 248pp. N4.50 Ethiope 1976 NR

Uwaifo.   Amayo, A.   Osevbegie, I.
Ynunozedo, Ebe okaro. [Primary Edo course.] pupils bk. 1. 40pp. ill. 75k. Macmillan 1976 NR EDO

Uwemedimo, R.
Akpan and the smugglers. 80pp. ill. 53k (African Reader's Library, 9) Pilgrim 1965 NR

Uzodinma, O.
Choice of stars. 132pp. col. ill. 77k (English supp. readers, 5) Longman - Nig 1973 NR

Vagale, L.R.
Anatomy of traditional markets in Nigeria. Focus on Ibadan city. 2nd rev. ed. 46pp. pl. maps. hd. N3.50 Dept Town Poly - Ib 1974 NR

Vagale, L.R.
Industrial environment of an African city: case study of Ibadan, Nigeria. See: Adekoya, O.C.

Vagale, L.R.
A suggestive bibliography on town and regional planning. 84pp. N1.00 Dept Town Poly - Ib 1973 NR

Vail, J.R.
Geological reconaissance in the Zalengei Darfur Province, Sudan. 35pt. ($1.00/43p.) (Bulletin, 19) Geol and Min Res - Sudan 1972 SJ

Vail, J.R.
Geological reconnaissance in part of Berber district, Northern Province, Sudan. 35pt. (Bulletin, 18) Geol and Min Res - Sudan 1971 SJ

Vajner, V.
The tectonic development of the Namaqua Mobile Belt and its foreland in parts of the northern Cape. 201pp. photos. ill. ex only (Univ of Cape Town, Precambrian Research Unit, Bulletin 14) Precambrian Res Unit 1974 SA

Valette, J.
The reconnaissance soil survey of the Mokwa-Kontagora Kainji area, North Western and Kwara States, Nigeria. 109pp. ill. maps fold-out maps. 50k (Soil Survey bull., 44) Inst Agric Res-Zaria 1973 NR

Valkhoff, M.
Studies in Portuguese and Creole, with special reference to South Africa. 282pp. R10.00 cl. (Oppenheimer Inst. of Portuguese Studies publ.) Witwatersrand UP 1966 SA

Van Arkadie, B.   Frank, C.R.
Economic accounting and development planning. 408pp. K.shs.30.00 OUP-Nairobi 1966 KE

van Blommestein, F.
Professional practice for attorneys. R9.50 Juta 1965 SA

Van-Dantzig, A.   Priddy, B.
A short history of the forts and castles of Ghana. 58pp. photos. 75pes. Ghana Museums 1971 GH

van de Laar, A.
Towards a manpower development strategy in Tanzania. T.shs.12.00 ($3.00) (Research pap., 69.27) Econ Res Bur - Tanz 1974 TZ

Van de Wall, G.   Alvord, E.D.
A survey of the food and feed resources of the Union of South Africa. R3.00 Van Schaik SA

Author Index

van den Berg, H.C.
A morphological study of the vine snout beetle, Cryptolarynx vitis. 41pp. 85c. (A v.43, no.2) Univ Stellenbosch, Lib 1968 SA

Van den Berg, H.C.
The morphology of eremnus cerealis marshall (coleoptera: curculionidae) 58pp. pl. R2.40 (Univ. Stellenbosch, Annals, Vol. 47, A.1) Univ Stellenbosch, Lib 1972 SA

van den Berghe, P.
Race and ethnicity. 388pp. K.shs.54.00 ($14.00) EAPH 1975 KE

Van den Bogaerde, F.
Collective bargaining and wage formation in Italian industries. 49pp. ill. 35c. (85c.) Univ South Africa 1963 SA

Van den Eynde, K.
Eléments de grammaire Yaka, phonologie flexionnelle. 114pp. Z2.40 Press Univ Zaire 1968 ZR FRE

Van der Berg, D.J.
Aspects of the training of mathematics teachers for primary and secondary schools in the RSA. 35pp. 80c. Human Science Res Council 1976 SA

Van der Bergh, C.
The socio-economic position of Indian blind persons in Natal. 65pp. R2.30 Human Science Res Council 1976 SA

van Der Bijl, J.
Van der Bijl genealogy. 80pp. hd. fl. 22.50 Balkema 1969 SA

van der Herden, A. Rotsart de Hertaing, I. Courtejoie, J.
Les vers intestinaux: cycles évolutifs des vers intestinaux et moyens de prévention. 144pp. ill. photos. Z2.00 ($2.40) BERPS 1974 ZR FRE

van der Heyden, A.
Comment bien se nourrir? Quelques informations sur les meilleurs aliments. See: Rotsart de Hertaing, I.

van der Heyden, A. Courtejoie, J.
Cours de statistique sanitaire, a l'usage des infirmiers et des techniciens d'assainissement. 120pp. ill. Z4.00 ($4.80) BERPS 1977 ZR FRE

van der Heyden, A. Rotsart de Hertaing, I. Courtejoie, J.
La malaria: cycle évolutif du parasite du paludisme et mesures préventives. 128pp. ill. photos. Z2.00 ($2.40) BERPS 1974 ZR FRE

Van der Heyden, A. Courtejoie, J.
Nourriture saine, meilleure santé: Cours de diététique à l'usage des infirmiers et des enseignants des regions tropicales. 200pp. photos. Z4.00 ($4.80) BERPS 1976 ZR FRE

van der Heyden, A.
Santé meilleure, source de progrès! See: Rotsart de Hertaing, I.

van der Horst, S.T., ed.
The Theron commission: a summary of the findings and recommendations of the commission of enquiry into matters relating to the coloured group. 124pp. R2.10 ($2.30) SA Inst of Race Relations 1976 SA

Van der Laan, H.L.
The Sierra Leone diamonds: an economic survey covering the years 1952-1961. 234pp. pl./maps. cl. Le4.00 (£2.00) Sierra Leone UP 1965 SL

van der Merwe, A.
South African marketing strategy. See: van der Merwe, S.

Van Der Merwe, D.H.
Experiments on the stabilization of collapsing sand with sodium silicate. 8pp. ill. (CSIR research reports, 188) CSIR 1962 SA

van der Merwe, H.W., ed.
The future of the university in Southern Africa. See: Welsh, D., ed.

van der Merwe, H.W., ed. Groenewald, C.J., ed.
Occupational and social change among Coloured people in South Africa. Proceedings of a workshop of the Centre for Intergroup Studies at the University of Cape Town. 278pp. banned in SA; UK distr. Rex Collings Ltd. (£4.95) Juta 1977 SA

van der Merwe, H.W., et al.
African perspectives on South Africa. 144pp. cl. & pap. R6.00 cl. SA only R3.90 pap. SA only Philip 1977 SA

van der Merwe, H.W., et al., ed.
White South African elites. R6.00 Juta 1974 SA

van der Merwe, H.W. in assoc. with Centre for Intergroup Studies., eds.
Looking at the Afrikaner today. 123pp. R7.20 Tafelberg 1975 SA

van der Merwe, J.P.
The dimensional stability of single jersey fabrics from woolrich blends. See: Buys, J.G.

Van der Merwe, M.J.
Archaeology: the past in the service of the future. 16pp. 30c (Univ. Cape Town. Inaugural lec., 36) Univ Cape Town Lib 1976 SA

van der Merwe, R. Miller, S.
Measuring absence and labour turnover. R3.95 McGraw-Hill SA 1976 SA

van der Merwe, S. van der Merwe, A.
South African marketing strategy. R15.50 Juta 1975 SA

van der Merwe, W.J.J.
Biology for standard 5. See: Myburgh, M.C.

Van der Meulen, G.J.R.
Investigations into South African raw materials for manufacturing expanded lightweight aggregates for concrete. See: Kaempfe, F.

van der Reis, A.P.
The activities and interests of urban Black men and women. 68pp. R40.00 (Bureau of Market Research, Research Reports, 40) Bur Market Research 1974 SA

van der Reis, A.P.
The interpretation of illustrations in advertisements by the Bantu. 183pp. R35.00 (Bureau of Market Research, Research Reports, 25) Bur Market Research 1969 SA

van der Reis, A.P.
Motivational factors in Bantu buying behaviour. 74pp. R10.00 (Bureau of Market Research, Research Reports, 15) Bur Market Research 1966 SA

van der Reis, A.P.
Some aspects of the acceptability of particular photographic models to the Bantu. 96pp. R50.00 (Bureau of Market Research, Research Reports, 29) Bur Market Research 1972 SA

van der Riet, F.
Grahamstown in early photographs. 112pp. photos. cl. R20.00 R7.50 (South African Yesterdays, 4) Philip 1974 SA

van der Spuy, K.R.
How to grow roses in the southern hemisphere. Rev. ed. ill. pl. col. pl. R7.50 Juta 1975 SA

van der Spuy, U.
Garden planning and construction. 3rd ed. R4.75 Juta SA

van der Spuy, U.
Gardening in Southern Africa. 4th ed. R3.75 Juta SA

van der Spuy, U.
Ornamental trees and shrubs. 3rd ed. R4.75 Juta SA

van der Vyver, J.D.
Seven lectures on human rights. cl. & pap. R14.50 cl. R9.50 pap. Juta 1976 SA

Author Index

van der Walt, J.J.A.
Pelargoniums of South Africa. ill. pl. cl. R12.50
Purnell 1977 SA

van der Walt, P.J.
Crime and society. [Bilingual in English and Afrikaans.].
2 v. 578pp. R6.00 (R7.00 pap.) Univ South Africa
1975 SA

van der Walt, W.A. du Toit, A.J.W.
Needlework and clothing manual for standards 9-10.
vol.2. 213pp. ill. photo. R4.50 Nasou 1975 SA

van der Wel, P.P.
The development of the Ghana sugar industry, 1960-1970.
pt. I: a preliminary exploration. 38pp. C1.00 (Univ. of
Cape Coast, Centre for Development Studies, Research
Report Series, 13) Centre Dev Stud 1973 GH

van der Westhuizen, W., et al.
Metalwork for the junior secondary standards. ill.
R7.20 Juta 1976 SA

van der Westhuizen, W., et al.
Metalwork for the senior secondary standards. ill.
R9.50 Juta 1976 SA

Van der Westhuyzen, G.C.A.
An account of anthropometrical and anthroposcopical
observations carried out on male students at the University
of Stellenbosch. 64pp. pl. 40c. Univ Stellenbosch,
Lib 1929 SA

van der Wiel, A.C.A.
Poverty eats my blanket. A poverty study: the case of
Lesotho. See: Marres, P.J.T.

Van Deventer, E.N.
Climatic and other design data for evaluating heating and
cooling requirements of buildings. 136pp. R5.00 cl.
(CSIR research reports, 300) CSIR 1971 SA

van Deventer, E.N. Jacobson, D.H.
Computer system selection. 17pp. (CSIR Special
Report, WISK 195) CSIR 1976 SA

Van Deventer, E.N.
Tables and alignment charts for sunlight and shade design
of buildings. 317pp. hd. R3.50 (CSIR research
reports, 262) CSIR 1968 SA

Van Dujk, D.E.
A guide to the frogs of South West Africa.
See: Channing, A.

van Dyk, D.E.
The "tail" of Ascaphus. 71pp. ill. 1.35 (A v.31, no.1)
Univ Stellenbosch, Lib 1955 SA

van Eeden, B.I.C.
The grammar of Soli. 51pp. 20c (B v.14, no. 1)
Univ Stellenbosch, Lib 1936 SA

Van Erdelen, M.N.
A bibliography of some Sestigers: Chris Barnard; Breyten
Bretenbach; Abraham de Vries; Jan Rabie; Bartho Smit;
Dolfvan Niekerk. 61pp. R3.15 Dept Bibliog, Lib &
Typo 1970 SA

van Eyken, A.
Write much better essays. 111pp. K.shs.9.00 pap.
($3.00 pap.) EAPH 1976 KE

van Heerden, L.
Man through the ages. Standard 7. See: Syphus, E.

van Heerden, N.
Dimensional stability of wool/acrylic single jersey fabrics.
See: Silver, H.M.

van Heerden, N.
The simultaneous shrinkproofing and dyeing of wool
fabrics with the bisulphire adducts of a polyurethane
resine, a polyacrylate resin and reactive dyes.
See: Silver, H.M.

van Heerden, P.W.
The green stink-bug Nezara viridula Linn. 13pp. ill.
20c. (A v.9 no. 7) Univ Stellenbosch, Lib 1933 SA

Van Heyningen, C.
Clarissa, poetry and morals. 230pp. cl. R2.75 Univ
of Natal 1971 SA

Van Heyningen, C.
Orange days. 104pp. R1.00 Univ of Natal 1965 SA

Van Hoogstraten, A.
Research on boiling. 90pp. R4.60 Dept Bibliog, Lib &
Typo 1963 SA

Van Jaarsveld, F.A.
The awakening of Afrikaner nationalism, 1868-1881.
259pp. R5.25 cl. Human and Rousseau 1961 SA

van Jaarsveld, F.A., ed.
Supplement to 'A Select Bibliography of South African
History. A guide for historical research'. See: Muller,
C.F.J., ed.

Van Logchem, J.T.
The focus and concentrate programme in the Bolgatanga
district: evaluation of an extension programme. 90pp.
(University of Cape Coast, social studies project, research
report, 7) Cape Coast Bkshp 1972 GH

van Meer, W.
Physical education for primary schools. 1, 4 bks. 16pp.
ill. ($1.50 4 bks.) TMP 1966 TZ

van Meer, W.
Physical education for primary schools. 2, 4 bks. 16pp.
ill. ($1.50 4 bks.) TMP 1966 TZ

van Meer, W.
Physical education for primary schools. 3, 4 bks. 16pp.
ill. ($1.50 4 bks.) TMP 1966 TZ

van Meer, W.
Physical education for primary schools. 4, 4 bks. 20pp.
ill. ($1.50 4 bks.) TMP 1966 TZ

Van Moorsel, H.
Atlas de préhistoire de la plaine de Kinshasa. 287pp.
Z3.60 Press Univ Zaire 1968 ZR FRE

Van Moorsel, H.
Dessins rupestres du Bas-Congo (Lovo)
See: Raymaekers, P.

Van Moorsel, H.
Paléolithique ancien à Léopoldville. 24pp. ill. 35k
Press Univ Zaire 1959 ZR FRE

van Niekerk, M.S.E., et al.
On with the apron. Housecraft for standard 6. 206pp. ill.
pl. R2.30 Nasou 1974 SA

van Niekerk, M.S.E. Roberts, C.M.P. Philips, M.A.
Handy at home. Home economics for standard 8.
419pp. ill. photos. R6.20 Nasou 1975 SA

van Niekerk, M.S.E. Roberts, C.M.P. Phillips, M.A.
On with the apron. Housecraft for standard 7. 320pp. ill.
pl. R.3.25 Nasou 1974 SA

van Niekirk, J.P.
South African attorneys handbook. See: Randell, G.H.

Van Noten, F.
Les tombes du roi Dyirima Rujugira et de la reine-mère
Nyirayvhi Kanjogera. Description archéologique. 82pp.
RF1800 (FB785.00/$19.60) (Institut National de
Recherche Scientifique, 11) Inst Nat - Rwandaise 1972
RW FRE

Van Pee, W.
Précis pratique de microbiologie générale. Techniques
générales. 52pp. 90k Press Univ Zaire 1965 ZR
FRE

Van Pelt, P.
Bantu customs. 3rd ed. 220pp. ($3.00) TMP 1977
TZ

van Pletzen, R.
Ontogenesis and morphogenesis of the breast-shoulder
apparatus of Xenopus laevis. 48pp. ill. 70c. (A v.29,
no.4) Univ Stellenbosch, Lib 1953 SA

van Putten, V.
A writing course for junior secondary schools.
See: Hannan, P.

van Reene, T.H.
Land its ownership and occupation in South Africa.
Revision service no.8 (1977) Loose-leaf binder R37.50
Juta 1977 SA

311

Author Index

van Reenen, T.H.
Land- its ownership and occupation in South Africa. 600pp. binder   R27.50 [including seven revision services]   Juta 1962 SA

van Regenmortel, M.H.V.
The boundaries of microbiology.   10pp.   30c.   (Univ. Cape Town. Inaugural lec., 23)   Univ Cape Town Lib 1974 SA

van Rensberg, N.J.J.
Autoclave setting of wool yarn, part I: a study of the effect of setting on the rates of exhaustion of certain dyes. 18pp.   R2.50   (SAWTRI Technical Reports, 272) SAWTRI 1975 SA

van Rensberg, N.J.J.
The SAWTRI continuous shrink-resist treatment of wool tops.   See: Hanekom, E.C.

Van Rensburg, A.P.J.
Contemporary leaders of Africa.   529pp. photos. maps. cl.   R15.00 cl.   HAUM 1975 SA

Van Rensburg, F.A.J.
Trends in education for coloureds in the RSA.   83pp. R3.65   Human Science Res Council 1976 SA

Van Rensburg, J.J.J.
Influence of variation in moisture content on dimensional change characteristics of mortar made with a sand coated with organic matter.   See: Kruger, J.E.

van Rensburg, N.J.
Observations on some flame-retardand treatments of cotton/polyester blended fabrics.   19pp.   R2.50 (SAWTRI Technical Reports, 226)   SAWTRI 1974 SA

van Rensburg, N.J.J.   White, J.
Autoclave setting of wool, part II: the effect of fibre regain and various setting conditions on the rate of dye exhaustion and snarling twist of different yarns.   16pp. R2.50   (SAWTRI Technical Reports, 340)   SAWTRI 1977 SA

van Rensburg, N.J.J.   Michau, M.
An evaluation of various methods of reducing the degradation of cotton by light.   22pp.   R2.50 (SAWTRI Technical Reports, 309)   SAWTRI 1976 SA

van Rensburg, N.J.J.
The flame-retardant treatment of 55/45 wool/cotton fabrics with THPOH-ammonia and a vinyl phosphonate oligomer. 13pp.   R2.50   (SAWTRI Technical Reports, 314) SAWTRI 1976 SA

van Rensburg, N.J.J.
The flame-retardant treatment of mohair fabrics.   14pp. R2.50   (SAWTRI Technical Reports, 243)   SAWTRI 1975 SA

van Rensburg, N.J.J.
A laboratory investigation of the shrinkresist treatment of wool with polyamide epichlorohydrin-polyacrylate polymer dispersions.   12pp.   R2.50   (SAWTRI Technical Reports, 257)   SAWTRI 1975 SA

van Rensburg, N.J.J.
The SAWTRI simultaneous shrink-resist and flame-retardant treatment for all-wool fabrics, part I: preliminary trials with chlorine-hercosett/THPOH and chlorine-THPOH.   16pp. R2.50   (SAWTRI Technical Reports, 332)   SAWTRI 1976 SA

van Rensburg, N.J.J.
Studies of the surface chemistry of wool, part II: the critical surface tension of wool and polymers. Some results and a reinterpretation of the theory on surface interactions. See: Weideman, E.

van Rensburg, N.J.J.
Treatment of cotton fabrics with aminoplast resins and various silicone and polyurethan polymers.   17pp. R2.50   (SAWTRI Technical Reports, 283)   SAWTRI 1976 SA

Van Rensburg, S.W.J.
Breeding problems and artificial insemination.   R2.75 van Schaik SA

van Rensenburg, R. C. J.   le Roux-Snyman, C.   Lessing, H.W.
A practical English course for standard 6.   144pp. ill. R1.95   Nasou 1974 SA

van Rensenburg, R.C.J.   le Roux-Snyman, C.   Lessing, H.W.
A practical English course for standard 7.   165pp. ill. R2.80   Nasou 1974 SA

van Rensenburg, R.J.C.   Roux-Snyman, C.   Lessing, H.W.
A practical English course for standard 8.   (Second language.)   224pp. ill.   R3.80   Nasou 1975 SA

van Rheenen, H.A.
Castor ("Ricinus communis L.") in the northern states of Nigeria.   80k   (Samaru misc. pap., 62)   Inst Agric Res - Zaria 1976 NR

van Rooyen, A.M.
The dimensional stability of single jersey fabrics from woolrich blends.   See: Buys, J.G.

van Rooyen, J.
Maggie Laubser.   64pp. photos. cl. & pap.   R6.75 pap.   R9.00 cl.   (South African Art Library, 4)   Struik 1974 SA

Van Schaik, J.L.
Northern Sotho phrase book.   50c   Van Schaik SA

Van Schaik, J.L.
Our baby book.   R1.50   Van Schaik SA

Van Schaik, J.L.
Van Schaik's modern English dictionary.   65c   Van Schaik SA

Van Schalkwyk, P.B.
The school library and its use.   92pp.   R1.60 Longman - SA 1976 SA

van Schoor, M. C. E., et al.
Senior history for South African schools, standard 8. 129pp. cl.   R2.85   Nasou 1974 SA

van Schoor, M.C.E., et al.
Senior history for South African schools, standard 9. 194pp. ill. photo. hd.   R5.00   Nasou 1975 SA

van Schoor, M.C.E., et al.
Senior history for South African schools, standard 10. 225pp. ill. photo.   R5.50   Nasou 1976 SA

van Selms, A.
Nisibis: the oldest university.   16pp.   25c.   (University of Cape Town T.B. Davie memorial lecture, 8)   Univ Cape Town Lib 1966 SA

Van Slageren, J.
Histoire de l'église en Afrique (Cameroun)   152pp. CFA240   (Cahier biblique, enseignement secondaire, 5) CLE 1969 CM FRE

Van Slageren, J.
Les origines de l'église évangélique du Cameroun. Missions européennes et christianisme autochtone. 300pp. maps.   CFA990   CLE 1972 CM FRE

van Spies, P.G.Z.
Report of the committee for differentiated education and guidance in connection with a national system of education for handicapped pupils...etc.   pt. 3, v. 7   123pp. R2.80   Human Science Res Council 1976 SA

Van Themaat, E.V.
Pranas Domsaitis.   64pp. ill. col. ill. cl.   R9.75 (South African Art Library, 6)   Struik 1976 SA

van Tonder, J.J.   Nel, P.A.
Regional indices for marketing purposes.   2 v.   404pp. R5.00   (Bureau of Market Research, Research Reports, 20)   Bur Market Research 1969 SA

van Tonder, J.L.
Aspects of fertility of Indian South Africans.   See: Lötter, J.M.

Van Tonder, J.L.
Fertility and family planning among blacks in South Africa 1974.   See: Lotter, J.M.

312

Author Index

Van Velson, J.
The politics of kinship: a study in social manipulation among the lakeside Tonga. 357pp. ill. K3.60 (£1.80) Inst Afr Stud - Lusaka 1964 ZA

van Vuuren, L.M.
Accounting: an introduction. See: Faul, M.A.

van Warmelo, N.J., comp.
Anthropology of Southern Africa in periodicals to 1950. 1,484pp. map. cl. R60.50 Witwatersrand UP 1977 SA

Van Warmelo, P.
An introduction to the principles of Roman civil law. cl. R25.00 cl. R16.00 pap. Juta 1976 SA

van Wijk, T., ed.
Supplement to 'A Select Bibliography of South African History. A guide for historical research'. See: Muller, C.F.J., ed.

van Winsen, L. de V. Thomas, J.D.
The civil practice of the superior courts in South Africa. 2nd ed. R25.00 Juta 1966 SA

Van Wyk, A.J.
Lesotho: a political study. 68pp. ill. map. R1.00 (Commun. of the Africa Inst., 7) Africa Inst - Pret 1967 SA

Van Wyk, A.J.
Swaziland: a political study. 75pp. ill. (Commun. of the Africa Inst., 9) Africa Inst - Pret 1969 SA

Van Wyk, G.F.
A preliminary account of the physical anthropology of the "Cape coloured people" (male) 62pp. map. 25c. (A v.17, no. 2) Univ Stellenbosch, Lib 1939 SA

Van Wyk, J.H.
A mathematical expression for the growth of trees in their dependence on time and density of stocking. See: Cilliers, A.C.

van Wyk, J.L.
Mechanization of timber harvesting and timber transport systems, based on an overseas study tour, March - June, 1975. 17pp. R5.00 (CSIR Special Report, HOUT 100) CSIR 1975 SA

van Wyk, J.L.
Review of saw-milling techniques in Europe and North America based on an overseas study tour, March-June 1975. 34pp. R5.00 (CSIR Special Report, HOUT 99) CSIR 1975 SA

van Wyk Louw, N.P.
Oh wide and sad land. tr. f. Afrikaans by Adam Small. R5.45 Maskew Miller 1975 SA

van Wyk, M.J.
Fitting and turning for standard 9. See: Swartz, W.F.

van Wyk, P.
Trees of the Kruger National Park. 2v. 412pp. pl. maps ill. hd. R30.00 Purnell 1973 SA

Van Ypersele de Strihou, J.
Variations des coefficients de fabrication dans une entreprise congolaise et équilibre économique 1931-1958. 50pp. 45k Press Univ Zaire 1961 ZR FRE

van Zinderen Bakker, E.M., ed.
Palaeocology of Africa and the surroundings islands and Antartica. v. 9. 250pp. pl. maps. cl. R7.50 ($13.50) Balkema 1975 SA

van Zinderen Bakker, E.M., ed.
Palaeoecology of Africa and the surrounding islands and Antarctica. v. 3 (vols. 1 & 2 OP) 158pp. maps. fl. 27.00 Balkema 1967 NR

van Zinderen Bakker, E.M., ed.
Palaeoecology of Africa and the surrounding islands and Antarctica. v. 4 288pp. pl. fl. 27.00 Balkema 1969 SA

van Zinderen Bakker, E.M., ed.
Palaeoecology of Africa and the surrounding islands and Antarctica. v. 5 254pp. fl. 27.00 Balkema 1969 SA

van Zinderen Bakker, E.M., ed.
Palaeoecology of Africa and the surrounding islands and Antarctica. v. 6 312pp. maps. fl. 33.75 Balkema 1972 SA

van Zinderen Bakker, E.M., ed.
Palaeoecology of Africa and the surrounding islands and Antarctica. v. 7 222pp. maps. fl. 33.75 Balkema 1972 SA

van Zinderen Bakker, E.M., ed.
Palaeoecology of Africa and the surrounding islands and Antarctica. v. 8 208pp. pl. fl. 33.75 Balkema 1973 SA

van Zinderen Bakker, E.M., et al., ed.
Marion and Prince Edward Islands: report on the South African biological and geological expedition, 1965-66. 438pp. pl. hd. fl. 101.25 Balkema 1971 SA

van Zinderen Bakker, E.M.B.
South African pollen grains and spores. 3, 6 pts. 104pp. map. fl. 22.50 Balkema 1959 SA

Van Zwanenberg, R.
The agricultural history of Kenya. 54pp. K.shs5.00 ($1.50) EAPH 1972 KE

van Zwanenberg, R.
The European invasion of East Africa. 32pp. maps. K.shs.6.00 (Transafrica Historical papers, 2) Transafrica 1975 KE

van Zwanenberg, R.A.M. King, A.
An economic history of Kenya and Uganda, 1800-1970. 326pp. K.shs.45.50 cl. K.shs.26.75 pap. ($8.00/£3.85 cl.) ($2.95/£1.20 pap.) EALB 1976 KE

Van Zwanenberg, R.M.A.
Colonial capitalism and labour in Kenya, 1919-1939. 338pp. K.shs.42.50 ($9.00/£4.30) EALB 1975 KE

van Zyl, A.H.
God's word in human speech. Pt. 1: the origins and message of the first five books of the bible. (Tr. of the 2nd rev ed by B. Johanson) R8.85 Butterworth 1976 SA

van Zyl, D.
The geology of the O'okiep Copper Mine, Namaqualand. 68pp. photos./maps. R2.33 (A v.42, no.1) Univ Stellenbosch, Lib 1967 SA

van Zyl, F.J.T. Halland, C.A.
Programmed social studies, Form I. 74pp. maps. 45c. Shuter 1970 SA

Van Zyl, P. Duminy, P.A.
Theory of education. 128pp. R2.50 Longman - SA 1976 SA

van Zyl Slabbert, F.
Towards an open plural society. See: Laurence, P.

Vancompernolle, G.
Titration des argiles en milieux non-aqueux. 52pp. ill. 65k Press Univ Zaire 1959 ZR FRE

Vandal, P.
Transfer printing of wool with reactive dyes, part I: the use of a transferable film of polyvinyl alcohol. See: Hayes, A.P.N.

Vandame, R.P.
Le Ngambay-Moundou. Phonologie, grammaire et textes. 211pp. map. (F32.00) (Mémoires de l'IFAN, 69) IFAN 1963 SG FRE

Vanderborght, H.
A nutritional survey in the Republic of Rwanda. [Also available in French.]. See: Vis, H.L.

Vanderburg, J.
A bibliography of Nigerian archaeology. See: Shaw, T.

Vanhoutte, M.
La notion de liberté dans 'Gorgias' de Platon. 43pp. 35k Press Univ Zaire 1957 ZR FRE

Vanneste, A.
Introduction à la théologie. 18pp. 30k Press Univ Zaire 1963 ZR FRE

Author Index

Vansina, J.
Les anciens royaumes de la Savane. 256pp. Z9.60
Press Univ Zaire 1976 ZR FRE

Varian, H.F.
Some African milestones. [Reprint of ed. 1953]. 272pp.
ill. maps. cl. R$8.00 (Rhodesiana Reprint Library,
Gold Series, 31) Books of Rhodesia 1973 RH

Varley, D.H.
Role of the librarian in the new Africa. 24pp. 30c
Univ Rhodesia Lib 1963 RH

Varley, V.
Index to 'The growth and government of Cape Town' by
P.W. Laidler. 30pp. 75c. (U.C.T. libraries, Varia
series, 4) Univ Cape Town Lib 1961 SA

Varty, A.E.
English through activity. Fourth year, teacher's manual.
See: Arnold, L.M.

Vatsa, M.J.
Verses for children. 43pp. ill. 70k Onibonoje 1973
NR

Vatsa, M.J.
Verses on Nigerian state capitals. 12pp. ill. 35k
Onibonoje 1973 NR

Vaufrey, R.
Préhistoire de l'Afrique. v. 2 372pp. ill. pl. D4.500
(Série I, Archéologie-Histoire, 4) Univ Tunis 1959 TI FRE

Veldman, F.J.
Handbook on stock diseases. See: Mönnig, H.O.

Vella, J., ed.
Pronunciation teaching. 282pp. T.shs.10.00 Inst Educ
- Dar 1972 TZ

Vellut, J.L.
Guide de l'etudiant en histoire du Zaire. 208pp.
(Essais, 7) Ed Mont Noir 1974 ZR FRE

Vellut, J.L.
Guide de l'etudiant histoire du Zaire. 208pp. Z1.50
Press Univ Zaire 1974 ZR FRE

Venkatraman, T.V. Badawi, A.I.
Agricultural zoology for students in Africa. 174pp. ill.
pap. cl. LS1.25 pap LS2.00 cl. ($5.00 pap.)
($8.00 cl.) Khartoum UP 1969 SJ

Venter, A.J.
Africa today. 304pp. pl. cl. R8.50 Macmillan - SA
1975 SA

Venter, A.J.
Coloured. A profile of two million South Africans. 564pp.
R9.50 cl. Human and Rousseau 1974 SA

Venter, A.J.
Underwater Africa. 164pp. photos. hd. R8.50
Purnell 1971 SA

Venter, H.C.A.
Report of the committee for differentiated education and
guidance in connection with a national system for
handicapped pupils...etc. Pt. 3, v. 3 59pp. R1.05
Human Science Res Council 1976 SA

Venter, J.S.M.
Summary of pulp and paper research at the Timber
Research Unit during the period 1964-1974. 36pp.
R5.00 (CSIR Special Report, HOUT 102) CSIR 1975
SA

Venter, J.S.M. Arbuthnot, A.
The utilization of sugar cane bagasse in the pulp and
paper industry - soda and NSSC pulping. 51pp.
R5.00 (CSIR Special Report, HOUT 88) CSIR 1974 SA

Venter, J.S.M. Arbuthnot, A.
The utilization of sugar cane bagasse in the pulp and
paper industry - soda semi-chemical pulping. 21pp.
R5.00 (CSIR Special Report, HOUT 108) CSIR 1975
SA

Venter, J.S.M. Gonin, C.P.
The utilization of sugar cane bagasse in the pulp and
paper industry: sulphate pulping. 25pp. R5.00
(CSIR Special Report, HOUT 81) CSIR 1974 SA

Venuti, D.
Textbook writing guide. 35pp. K.shs4.50 Equatorial
KE

Vercruijsse, E.V.W. Boakye, J.K.A. Vercruijsse, L.M.
Composition of households in some Fante communities (A
study of the framework of social integration) 21pp.
C1.00 (Univ. of Cape Coast, Centre for Development
Studies, Research Report Series, 10) Centre Dev Stud
1972 GH

Vercruijsse, E.V.W.
The dynamics of fanti domestic organisation. A
comparison with Fortes' Ashanti Survey. 35pp. C1.00
(Univ. of Cape Coast, Centre for Development Studies,
Research Report Series, 12) Centre Dev Stud 1972 GH

Vercruijsse, E.V.W. Boyd, T.A.
Evaluation of an extension programme. Report of a pilot
study into the effects of the focus and concentrate
programme in the Tamale area. 71pp. C1.00 (Univ.
of Cape Coast, Centre for Development Studies, Research
Report Series, 4) Centre Dev Stud 1970 GH

Vercruijsse, E.V.W. Boyd, T.A.
Evaluation of an extension programme: report of a pilot
study into the effects of the focus and concentrate
programme in the Tamale area. 71pp. (University of
Cape Coast, social studies project, research report, 4)
Cape Coast Bkshp 1970 GH

Vercruijsse, E.V.W. Boyd, T.A.
Occupational differentiation in rural areas. A research
design. 29pp. C1.00 (Univ. of Cape Coast, Centre
for Development Studies, Research Report Series 2)
Centre Dev Stud 1970 GH

Vercruijsse, E.V.W. Boyd, T.A.
Occupational differentiation in rural areas: a research
design. 29pp. ill. (University of Cape Coast, social
studies project, research report, 2) Cape Coast Bkshp
1970 GH

Vercruijsse, L.M.
Composition of households in some Fante communities (A
study of the framework of social integration)
See: Vercruijsse, E.V.W.

Verger, P.
Bahia and the West African trade, 1549-1851. 39pp. pl.
map. N1.00 Ibadan UP 1970 NR

Verger, P.
Notes sur le culte des Orisa et Vodun à Bahia, la Baie de
tous les Saints, au Brésil et à l'ancienne Côte des
Esclaves en Afrique. [Reprint of ed. 1957]. 609pp. map.
pl. (D.fl.200.00) (Mémoires de l'IFAN, 51) IFAN 1957
SG FRE

Verger, P.
Trade relations between the Bight of Benin and Bahia
17th-19th century. 629pp. cl. & pap. N20.00 cl.
N15.00 pap. Ibadan UP 1975 NR

Verger, P.F.
Awon we osanyin. [Yoruba medicinal leaves] 70pp.
40k Univ Ife Bkshop 1967 NR YOR

Verhaegen, B., et al.
Kisangani (ex Stanleyville) 1876-1976. 287pp. Z13.00
Press Univ Zaire 1976 ZR FRE

Verheust, T.
Physionomie du corps enseignant des écoles secondaires
au Zaire. Année scolaire 1972-1973, enseignant
catholique. See: Albert, J.

Veridiano, C. M.
Curriculum studies made easy. 80k Dept Educ - ABU
1975 NR

Verlhac, A.
Evaluation de la méthode 'Pour Parler Français' au niveau
du C.E.2. See: Monfils, G.

VerLoren van Themaat Centre for Public International Law.
The South African yearbook of international law, 1975.
v.1 R10.00 Inst For and Comp Law 1976 SA

Author Index

Vermeulen, W.
La grande nocturne. 94pp. (Jeune littérature, 2) Ed Mont Noir 1975 ZR FRE

Verner, B.A.
Huguenots in South Africa. 44pp. 80c. Univ Cape Town Lib 1967 SA

Verron, G.
Céramique de la région Tchadienne. Culture 'Sao' (Tchad, Cameroun, Nigeria) pt. 1 70pp. ill. ex. only Inst Nat Tchad 1969 CD FRE

Verron, G.
Céramique de la région Tchadienne. Culture 'Sao' (Tchad, Cameroun, Nigeria) pt. 2 70pp. ill. ex. only Inst Nat Tchad 1969 CD FRE

Verryn, T. D., ed.
Church and marriage in modern Africa. 497pp. R5.00 Ecumenical Res Unit 1975 SA

Verryn, T.D.
A history of the Order of Ethiopia. 3rd ed. 193pp. pl. 70c Ecumenical Res Unit 1973 SA

Verryn, T.D., joint author. Curran, C., joint author.
New perspectives in moral theology and on the future. 108pp. cl. R1.25 Ecumenical Res Unit 1974 SA

Verryn, T.D.
The vanishing clergyman. A sociological study of the priestly role in South Africa. 208pp. 75c Ecumenical Res Unit 1971 SA

Versfeld, M.
Our selves. 176pp. cl. R4.50 cl. Philip 1976 SA

Versfeld, M.
The Socratic spirit. 11pp. 30c. (U.C.T. Inaugural lec. New series, 7) Univ Cape Town Lib 1971 SA

Verster, E.
Olive Emilie Albertina Schreiner, 1855-1920. 28pp. 70c. Univ Cape Town Lib 1972 SA

Verster, M.A. Breger, R.A.
Installation of general testing programme for the selection and classification of workers. 16pp. (CSIR Special Report, PERS 236) CSIR 1976 SA

Verster, M.A.
National Institute for Personnel Research tests for the assessment of blacks. See: Laetti, V.I.

Verwoerd, L.
The distribution and prevalence of physiologic forms of Puccinia graminis tritici in the Union of South Africa 1930-1934. 7pp. 15c. (A v.8, no.3) Univ Stellenbosch, Lib 1935 SA

Verwoerd, L.
Preliminary report on the occurence in South Africa of black chaff disease in wheat. 4pp. pl. 15c. (A v.8, no.6) Univ Stellenbosch, Lib 1930 SA

Verwoerd, W.J.
South African carbonatites and their probable mode of origin. 119pp. photos./maps. R3.60 (A v.41, no. 2) Univ Stellenbosch, Lib 1966 SA

Vesey-Fitzgerald, D.
East African grasslands. 96pp. pl. K.shs.35.00 EAPH 1975 KE

Vibert, L.
Salaire et équilibre économique. 265pp. D1.000 Univ Tunis 1951 TI FRE

Vice, K.
Pointers 1: "Major Barbara". 64pp. ill. R1.25 Nasou 1976 SA

Vice, K.
Pointers 2: verse for you. bk. 3. 90pp. R1.50 Nasou 1976 SA

Vice, K.
Pointers 3: "Richard III". 109pp. ill. R1.80 Nasou 1976 SA

Vice, K.
Pointers 4: study guide for "Tess of the d'Urbervilles". 61pp. ill. R1.55 Nasou 1976 SA

Vielrose, E.
A tentative projection of the structure of the Nigerian economy in 1975. See: Lukacs, L.E.

Vilakazi, A.
Zulu tranformations: a study of the dynamics of social change. 160pp. R3.00 Univ of Natal 1965 SA

Vilakazi, B.W.
Amal'ezulu. [Poems] repr. in new orthography ed. 68pp. cl. 80c (Bantu treasury, 8) Witwatersrand UP 1970 SA ZUL

Vilakazi, B.W.
Inkondlo kaZulu. [Zulu poems.] repr. in new orthography ed. R1.00 (Bantu treasury, 1) Witwatersrand UP 1976 SA ZUL

Vilakazi, B.W.
Zulu-English dictionary. See: Doke, C.M.

Vilakazi, B.W.
Zulu horizons. Tr. into English verse by F.L. Friedman, from the literal translations of D.M. Malcolm and J.M. Sikakana New ed. 144pp. ill. cl. R25.00 deluxe ed. R10.00 Witwatersrand UP 1973 SA

Viljoen, G.v.N.
Cicero, student and statesman. [Bilingual in English and Afrikaans.]. See: Steven, S.J.H.

Viljoen, T.A. Pienaar, J.J.
Fundamental pedagogics. 218pp. R5.25 Butterworths 1971 SA

Villard, G.
Notions de résistance des matériaux. v. 1 237pp. DA20.00 SNED 1972 AE FRE

Villeneuve, M.
Les obstacles à la mécanisation agricole rationnelle dans les pays en voie de développement. Dir18.00 (Coll. du Centre d'étude du développement économique et social, 6) Ed La Porte 1963 MR FRE

Villiers, A.
La collection de serpents de l'IFAN. 155pp. ill. CFA400 (Catalogues et Documents, 6) IFAN 1950 SG FRE

Villiers, A.
Contribution à l'étude du peuplement de la Mauritanie. Notations écologiques et biogéographiques sur la faune de l'Adrar. See: Dekeyser, P.L.

Villiers, A.
Hemiptères de l'Afrique noire (punaises et cigales) 256pp. ill. CFA1200 (Initiations et Etudes Africaines, 9) IFAN 1952 SG FRE

Villiers, A.
Les lepidoptères de l'Afrique noire occidentale. Introduction: structure, moeurs, récolte, conservation, classification. 1, 4pts. 84pp. ill. CFA400 (Initiations et Etudes Africaines, 14) IFAN 1957 SG FRE

Villiers, A.
Mission P.L. Dekeyser et A. Villiers en Guinée et en Côte d'Ivoire (1946). Insectes. pt. 1 90pp. ill. CFA400 (Catalogues et Documents, 5) IFAN 1949 SG FRE

Villiers, A.
Récolte et préparation des collections zoologiques. See: Dekeyser, P.L.

Villiers, A.
Les serpents de l'Ouest africain. 196pp. pl. CFA30,000 (F60.00) IFAN 1975 SG FRE

Villiers, A.
Les serpents de l'Ouest africain. 176pp. CFA3,000 (F60.00) Nouv Ed Afric 1976 SG FRE

Villiers, G. Fox, H.E.
Modern revision exercises in physical science for standards 9-10. 119pp. ill. R3.20 Nasou 1976 SA

Vincent, A.
Food and nutrition. ill. 45k Macmillan NR

Vincke, J.
Le prix du péché. 54pp. (Essais, 6) Ed Mont Noir 1973 ZR FRE

315

Author Index

Vine, D.
Index of the basic materials used in preparing Nigerian cocoa farmers. 33pp. 30k (45c) (N.I.S.E.R. indexes and bibliographies, 9) NISER 1965 NR

Vinnicombe, P.
People of the Eland. Rock paintings of the Drakensberg bushmen as a reflection of their life and thought. 400pp. ill. cl. R63.00 Univ of Natal 1975 SA

Vis, H.L. Vanderborght, H. Yourassowsky, C.
A nutritional survey in the Republic of Rwanda. [Also available in French.]. 192pp. ill. map. (FB430.00/$10.80) Inst Nat Rwandaise 1975 RW

Visser, D.J.L., ed.
Symposium on the bushveld igneous complex and other layered intrusions. See: Von Gruenewaldt, G., ed.

Visser, G.C.
OB: Traitors or patriots? 209pp. pl. cl. R9.90 Macmillan - SA 1976 SA

Visser, H.W.A.
A responsible university in a responsible society. 17pp. 25c. (University of Cape Town T.B. Davie memorial lecture, 11) Univ Cape Town Lib 1971 SA

Visser, J. Chapman, Dr.
Dangerous snakes and the treatment of snake bites in South Africa. ill. photos. cl. R10.00 Purnell 1977 SA

Visser, J.
A list of books, articles and government publications on the economy of Nigeria, 1963-64. 81pp. 75k ($1.25) (N.I.S.E.R. indexes and bibliographies, 2) NISER 1965 NR

Visser, J.
A list of books, articles and government publications on the economy of Nigeria, 1965. 61pp. 75k ($1.25) (N.I.S.E.R. indexes and bibliographies, 3) NISER 1967 NR

Visser, J.
A list of books, articles and government publications on the economy of Nigeria, 1966. 65pp. 75k ($1.25) (N.I.S.E.R. indexes and bibliographies, 4) NISER 1968 NR

Visser, J.
A list of books, articles and government publications on the economy of Nigeria, 1967. 84pp. 75k ($1.25) (N.I.S.E.R. indexes and bibliographies, 5) NISER 1969 NR

Visser, J.
A list of books, articles and government publications on the economy of Nigeria, 1968. 89pp. N1.25 ($2.00) (N.I.S.E.R. indexes and bibliographies, 6) NISER 1970 NR

Visser, J.G.J.
The cranial morphology of Rhyacotriton olympicus olympicus (Gaige); The cranial anatomy and kinsesis of the bird snake Thelotornis capensis (Smith) See: Cloete, S.E.

Visser, J.G.J.
Ontogeny of the chonrocranium of the chamaeleon, microsaura pumilapumila (daudin) 68pp. pl. R2.40 (Univ. Stellenbosch, Annals, Vol. 47, A.2) Univ Stellenbosch, Lib 1972 SA

Visser, M.H.C.
The ontogeny of the reproductive system of gonaxis gwandaensis (Preston) (Pulmonata: Streptaxidae) with special reference to the phylogeny of the spermatic conduits of the pulmonata. 79pp. pl. R3.10 (Univ. Stellenbosch, Annals, vol. 48, A.4) Univ Stellenbosch Lib 1973 SA

Visser, S.A.
Kainji: a Nigerian man-made lake: Kainji lake studies, vol I: ecology. 126pp. maps/pl. N2.00 ($3.00) NISER 1970 NR

Vittoz, P.
Les évangiles. 56pp. CFA150 (Cahier biblique, enseignement secondaire, 3) CLE 1971 CM FRE

Vittoz, P.
Manuel de l'engagement chrétien. 68pp. CFA180 CLE 1970 CM FRE

Vlachos, G.S.
Institutions administratives et économiques de l'Algérie. 2v. 479pp. DA31.00 pap. SNED 1974 AE FRE

Vlotman, E.F.
Cookery book for the young hostess. See: King, C.E.J.

Voeltzel, R.
Selons les écritures: Nouveau Testament. 820pp. cl. & pap. CFA2500.00 pap. CFA2700.00 cl. (Coll. Théologique CLE) CLE 1973 CM FRE

Vogel, J.O.
Kamangoza: an introduction to the iron age cultures of the Victoria Falls region. 140pp. ill. K3.00 (Zambia Museum paps. 2) Nat Mus Board - Zam 1971 ZA

Vogel, J.O.
Kamangoza: an introduction to the Iron Age cultures of the Victoria Falls region. 145pp. ill. maps. K3.50 (Zambia Museum paps., 1) Nat Mus Zambia 1971 ZA

Vogel, J.O.
Kumadzulo: an early iron age village site in southern Zambia. 119pp. ill. K3.50 (Zambia Museum paps, 3) Nat Mus Board - Zam 1971 ZA

Vogel, J.O.
Simbusenga: the archaeology of the intermediate period of the southern Zambia iron age. 156pp. K5.00 (Zambia Museum paps., 4) Nat Mus Board - Zam 1975 ZA

Vogel, L.C. et al., ed.
Health and disease in Kenya. 529pp. maps. cl. & pap. K.shs.134.00 cl. K.shs.75.50 pap. ($35.00/£16.00 cl.) ($18.00/£8.20 pap.) EALB 1974 KE

Vogler, P. et al.
Annales de l'université d'Abidjan. 114pp. CFA1500 pap. (F30.00 pap.) (Série H-Linguistique, 1) Univ Abidjan 1968 IV FRE

Voigt, J.C.
Fifty years of the history of the republic in South Africa 1795-1845 [Reprint of 1899 edition]. 2 v. 666pp. cl. R18.00 set (Africana collectanea, 31 & 32) Struik 1969 SA

Vollar, M.
E'yo laza. 1st ed. 32pp. K.shs.2.00 ($1.25/50p.) EALB 1971 KE LGB

Von Allmen, D.
L'évangile de Jésus-Christ. Naissance de la théologie dans le Nouveau Testament. 404pp. CFA1500 CLE 1972 CM FRE

von Bornemann, J. Kershaw, M. Howels, F.
Annotated bibliography and index of the geology of Zambia, 1970-1971. 50n Geol Survey Zam 1976 ZA

von Eisenhart, D.
Factors influencing fit and adhesion of glaze to earthenware bodies. 11pp. (CSIR research reports, 276) CSIR 1969 SA

Von Gruenewaldt, G., ed. Visser, D.J.L., ed.
Symposium on the bushveld igneous complex and other layered intrusions. 733pp. ill. R20.00 (Special pub., 1) Geol Soc SA 1970 SA

Von Habsburg, O.
European unity. 11pp. 30c. SA Inst Int Affairs 1971 SA

von Holub, E.
Travels north of the Zambezi, 1885-1886. tr. from German by C. Johns. 325pp. ill. K14.00 hd. K5.00 pap. (£9.00 hd.) (£3.00 pap.) Inst Afr Stud - Lusaka 1975 ZA

316

Vorster, O.C.
Investigations into coatings for the protection of structural metal in southwest Africa. See: Frank, D.

Vorster, O.C.
Investigations into coatings for timber in Southwest Africa. See: Frank, D.

Vorster, O.C.
Investigations into the painting of wire-brushed steel. See: Frank, D.

Vos, K.
The church on the hill. 194pp. R4.75 Struik 1972 SA

Vos, W.J.
Decisions of the water courts, 1946-1970. R32.00 Juta 1971 SA

Vos, W.J.
Elements of South African water law. R12.50 Juta 1968 SA

Vrana, S.
The geology of the area south of the Lukanga swamp: explanation of degree sheet 1427, SE quarter. K2.50 (Dept. of Geological Survey, Reports, 28) Geol Survey Zam 1976 ZA

Vrana, S.
A non-metamict allanite from Zambia. See: Cech, F.

Vrdoljak, M.K.
The history of South African regiments. 31pp. 70c. Univ Cape Town Lib 1970 SA

Vuattoux, R.
Annales de l'université d'Abidjan. Le peuplement du palmier rônier (Borassus aethiopum) d'une savane de Côte d'Ivoire. 138pp. CFA1500 (F30.00) (Série E-Ecologie, 1) Univ Abidjan 1968 IV FRE

Vyas, C.
Flight of the eagle. 58pp. photos. 95n. Neczam 1970 ZA

Vyas, C.L.
A collection of Zambian verse. 32pp. 25n. Zambia Cult Serv 1971 ZA

Vyas, C.L.
A collection of Zambian verse. Bk. 2 34pp. 25n. Zambia Cult Serv 1972 ZA

Vyas, C.L.
The Falls and other poems. K1.00 Zambia Cult Serv 1968 ZA

Vyas, C.L.
Folktales of Zambia. 88pp. K1.20 Neczam 1975 ZA

Vyas, C.L.
I have a point: a collection of essays. 120pp. 55n. Zambia Cult Serv 1972 ZA

Vyas, C.L.
Traditional tales of Zambia. 70pp. 65n. Zambia Cult Serv 1971 ZA

Vyas, C.L.
Two tales of Zambia. 48pp. 70n. Neczam 1974 ZA

Vyas, C.L.
Wind is the messenger: a collection of poems. Zambia Cult Serv 1973 ZA

wa Thiongo, N.
Njia Panda. [Novel.] 240pp. K.shs.12.00 ($3.50) EAPH 1975 KE SWA

Wa Thiongo, N.
This time tomorrow: three plays. 56pp. K.shs5.50 (£1.50/$3.00) EALB 1970 KE

Waali, N.S. Hamballi, M.
Kaara karaatuu. [Manuel de lecture Hawsa.] 100pp. CFA250 CELTHO 1971 NG HAU

Wachanga, H.K.
The swords of Kirinyaga. The fight for land and freedom. 206pp. K.shs.46.00 ($5.80/£2.80) EALB 1975 KE

Wachira, G.
Ordeal in the forest. 288pp. K.shs9.00 ($3.20) EAPH 1968 NG

Waciuma, C.
The daughter of Mumbi. 153pp. ill. K.shs7.00 ($2.60) EAPH 1969 KE

Waciuma, C.
The golden feather. 48pp. ill. K.shs2.50 ($1.00) EAPH 1966 KE

Waciuma, C. Moore, B.
Merry-making. 15pp. ill. K.shs3.50 ($1.00) EAPH 1972 KE

Waciuma, C.
Mweru the ostrich girl. New ed. 22pp. ill. K.shs.6.00 (Lioncub books, 7) EAPH 1974 KE

Waciuma, C.
Who's calling? 15pp. ill. K.shs.4.00 (Lioncub books, 3) EAPH 1973 KE

Wadood, T.A.
African Bibliographic Centre. See: Jordan, R.T.

Wagenbuur, H.T.M.
Labour and development. An analysis of the time-budget and of the production and productivity of lime farmers in southern Ghana. 42pp. C1.00 (Univ. of Cape Coast, Centre for Development Studies, Research Report Series, 11) Centre Dev Stud 1972 GH

Wagenbuur, H.T.M.
Labour and development: an analysis of the time-budget and of the production and productivity of lime farmers in southern Ghana. 42pp. (University of Cape Coast, social studies project, research report, 11) Cape Coast Bkshp 1972 GH

Wagenbuur, H.T.M.
Lime farmers: a case study of a cashcrop subsistence economy. See: Brenner, Y.

Wager, V.
All about tomatoes. 2nd ed. 97pp. photos. hd. R3.50 Purnell 1967 SA

Wager, V.A.
Flower garden diseases and pests. 220pp. pl. hd. R10.00 Purnell 1970 SA

Wagner, L.
Potters of Southern Africa. See: Clark, G.

Wagner, M.C.
The first British occupation of the Cape of Good Hope 1795-1803. 34pp. 70c. Univ Cape Town Lib 1970 SA

Wagner, P.A.
The diamond fields of Southern Africa [Reprint of 1914 edition]. 416pp. maps pl. cl. R12.50 Struik 1971 SA

Wagner, P.A.
The platinum deposits and mines of South Africa. (Reprint of ed. 1929]. 373pp. ill. maps. cl. R12.50 Struik 1973 SA

Wahab, Z.B.A.
Ulimbo. 84pp. K.shs.6.75 ($2.10/85p.) EALB 1976 KE SWA

Wahadan, L.
Groundwater geology of Kordofan Province. See: Rodis, N.G.

Wahdan, L.
The availability of groundwater in Korfofan Province. See: Rodis, N.G.

Wahl, R.
Thomas Pringle in South Africa: deluxe edition. 136pp. maps. hd. R12.50 Longman SA 1970 SA

Wahl, R.
Thomas Pringle in South Africa: school edition. 224pp. maps ill. R1.35 Longman SA 1970 SA

Wainwright, G.
Le baptême, accès à l'église. Tr. fr. English. 156pp. CFA660 CLE 1972 CM FRE

Waititu, S.N. Obasa, Y.G.
Sleepless night. 68pp. K.shs.5.75 pap. ($2.75/£1.30 pap.) EALB 1976 KE

Author Index

Wakerley, I.C.
Les amours de Ronsard (pour Cassandre et Hélène). Etude comparative. 40pp. 50c pap. (Dept. of Modern Languages, Univ. of Rhodesia, 1) Univ Rhodesia Lib 1972 RH FRE

Wako, D.M.
Akabaluyia Bemumbo. [Customs of the western Abaluyia people of the Nyanza province, Kenya] 4th ed. 66pp. ill. K.shs.3.00 ($1.50/60p.) EALB 1965 KE LUG

Wakoli, A.N.
Chiisimo cha babukusu. [Collection of oral literature.] 20pp. K.shs.4.50 ($1.50) EAPH 1975 KE SWA

Walford, A.S.
Mazoezi na mafumbo. [Exercises and puzzles] 64pp. K.shs.4.00 OUP-Nairobi 1964 KE SWA

Wali, N.S. et al.
Wakokin Hausa. [Hausa poems] 32pp. 68k Northern Nig 1957 NR HAU

Wali, N.S.
Mu Koyi Ajami Da Larabci. See: Binji, H.

Wali, N.S.
Tarbiyya Ga Mutum. [The training of man] 24pp. 25k Northern Nig 1959 NR HAU

Walker, C.
Walk through the wilderness. See: Richards, D.

Wallace, C.S.
Swaziland. 94pp. R4.80 Dept Bibliog, Lib & Typo 1967 SA

Wallace, C.T.   Weeks, S.G.
Success or failure in rural Uganda: a study of young people. 94pp. U.shs.20.00 ($4.00) Mak Inst Soc Res 1975 UG

Wallace, F.M.
The district of Wodehouse, Cape Province. 80pp. R4.60 Dept Bibliog Lib & Typo 1975 SA

Wallace, H.
Your child. See: Edge, W.

Wallace, I.R., ed.   Brock, B., ed.   Belshaw, D.G.R., ed.
The Bugisu coffee industry: an economic and technical survey. 387pp. U.shs.35.00 ($8.50) Mak Inst Soc Res 1973 UG

Wallace, J.H.
The batoid fishes of the east coast of southern Africa, 2: Manta, eagle, duckbill, cownose, butterfly and sting rays. 56pp. R1.20 Oceanographic Res Inst 1967 SA

Wallace, J.H.
The batoid fishes of the east coast of southern Africa, 3: skates and electric rays. 62pp. R1.20 Oceanographic Res Inst 1967 SA

Wallace, J.H., ed.
Durban's centenary aquarium: guidebook. See: Wallace, L., ed.

Wallace, J.H.
The estuarine fishes of the east coast of South Africa, 1: Species composition and length distribution in the estuarine and marine environments, 2: seasonal abundance and migrations. 72pp. R2.10 (Investigational Reports, 40) Oceanographic Res Inst 1975 SA

Wallace, J.H.
The estuarine fishes of the east coast of South Africa, 3: Reproduction. 51pp. R1.60 (Investigational Reports, 41) Oceanographic Res Inst 1975 SA

Wallace, J.H.
The estuarine fishes of the east coast of South Africa, 4: Occurrence of juveniles in estuaries, 5: ecology, estuarine dependence and status. 63pp. R1.90 (Investigational Reports, 42) Oceanographic Res Inst 1975 SA

Wallace, L., ed.   Heydorn, A., ed.   Wallace, J.H., ed.
Durban's centenary aquarium: guidebook. 4th. ed. 32pp. photos. 60c. Oceanographic Res Inst 1972 SA

Wallace, L.
Reactions of the sharks "Carcharhinus leucas" (Muller & Henle) and "Odontaspis taurus" (Refinesque) to gill net barriers under experimental conditions. 24pp. R1.20 (Investigational Reports, 30) Oceanographic Res Inst 1972 SA

Walldorf, H.
Clemens Brentano: a bibliography to supplement Mallon, 1926. 66pp. R3.40 Dept Bibliog, Lib & Typo 1971 SA

Waller, H.
The death of David Livingstone. 40pp. ill. 40n. (Haz pamphlets, 3) Neczam 1973 ZA

Wallis, J.P.R., ed.
The Matabele journals of Robert Moffat 1829-1860. (Facsmile reprint) 1, 2 v. 382pp. R$16.50 set (National Archives of Rhodesia, Oppenheimer series, 1) Nat Archives - Rhod 1976 RH

Wallis, J.P.R., ed.
The Matabele journals of Robert Moffat 1829-1860. (Facsmile reprint) 2, 2 v. 295pp. cl. R$16.50 set (National Archives of Rhodesia, Oppenheimer series, 1) Nat Archives - Rhod 1976 RH

Wallis, J.P.R.
One man's hand. (Reprint ed. 1950) ed. 254pp. cl. R$5.35 cl. (Gold Series, 22) Books of Rhodesia 1972 RH

Wallis, J.P.R.
Thomas Baines. His life and explorations in South Africa, Rhodesia and Australia 1820-1875. 2nd ed. 272pp. ill. col. pl. cl. R33.50 cl. (Dfl.105/$39.50/£20.50 cl.) Balkema 1976 SA

Wallis, M.
The Kenya functional literacy programme: an appraisal. See: Gakuru, O.N.

Wallis, N., comp.
The analysis, physiology and effects of fluoride. 48pp. R3.00 Dept Bibliog, Lib & Typo 1973 SA

Walmsley, R.W.
Nairobi: the geography of a new city. 56pp. ill. K.shs.3.25 ($1.50/60p.) EALB 1957 KE

Walpole, V.
Conrad's method: Some formal aspects. 20pp. 20c (B v.8, no.1) Univ Stellenbosch, Lib 1930 SA

Walshaw, R.D.
The geology of the Mulanje area. See: Garson, M.S.

Walshaw, R.D.
The geology of the Ncheu-Balaka area. 96pp. hd. K2.00 (Geological Survey of Malawi, Bull. 19) Geol Survey - Mal 1965 MW

Walshaw, R.D.
The geology of the Thyolo area. See: Habgood, F.

Walshe, P.
Black nationalism in South Africa. A short history. 40pp. photos. R1.00 ($2.40/£1.25) Ravan 1973 SA

Walt, W.A.v.d.   Toit A.J.W.   Schmidt, M.M.
Needlework and clothing, standard 8. 382pp. ill. photo. R5.75 Nasou 1975 SA

Walter, M.J.
The geology of the Lilongwe-Dowa area. 38pp. pl. map. K4.00 (Geological Survey of Malawi, bull. 26) Geol Survey - Mal 1972 MW

Walter, M.J.
The geology of the Salima-Mvera Mission area. 30pp. pl. map. hd. K4.00 (Geological Survey of Malawi, Bull. 30) Geol Survey - Mal 1972 MW

Walter, M.J.
The geology of the South Lilongwe Plain and Dzalanyama Range. See: Thatcher, E.C.

Walter, M.W.
Observations on the rainfall at the Institute for Agricultural research, Samaru, Northern Nigeria. 57pp. 70k (Samaru misc. pap., 15) Inst Agric Res-Zaria 1967 NR

Walters, A.
Progress with practice.   R4.00   Shuter   1955 SA

Walton, J.
African Village: Gewone band.   R6.30   Van Schaik SA

Walton, J.
African Village: Luukse band.   R10.50   Van Schaik SA

Walton, J. et al.
Amanyathelo okuquala: itsethi nemizobomilo.   32pp. ill.
85c.   Longman SA 1968 SA XHO

Walton, J. et al.
First steps: sets and shapes-metric.   32pp. ill.   85c
Longman SA 1968 SA

Walton, J. et al.
Primary mathematics for Botswana, Lesotho and
Swaziland.   1, 5 bks.   128pp. ill.   R1.30   Longman
SA 1971 SA

Walton, J. et al.
Primary mathematics for Botswana, Lesotho and
Swaziland.   2, 5 bks.   160pp. ill.   R1.45   Longman
SA 1971 SA

Walton, J. et al.
Primary mathematics for Botswana, Lesotho and
Swaziland.   5, 5 bks.   168pp. ill.   R1.95   Longman
SA 1971 SA

Walton, J. et al.
Primary mathematics for Botswana, Letsotho, and
Swaziland.   2nd ed.   3, 5 bks.   96pp. ill.   R1.60
Longman SA 1975 SA

Walton, J. et al.
Primary mathematics for Botswana, Letsotho and
Swaziland.   4, 5 bks.   136pp. ill.   R1.80   Longman
SA 1971 SA

Walton, J. et al.
Second steps: numbers and measures.   71pp. ill.
R1.05   Longman SA 1940 SA

Walton, J. et al.
Teacher's guide to primary mathematics, standard 3 -
metric.   2nd ed.   96pp. ill.   R2.20   Longman SA
1975 SA

Walton, J. et al.
Teacher's lesson programme for primary mathematics sub-
A (English/Xhosa/Sotho edition)   120pp. ill.   R2.00
Longman SA 1968 SA

Walton, J. et al.
Teacher's lesson programme for primary mathematics
sub-B metric.   120pp. ill.   R2.00   Longman SA 1968
SA

Walton, J.
Homesteads and villages in South Africa.   R6.50   Van
Schaik SA

Walton, J.
Longman primary maths. Fifth steps.   Pupil's bk.
See: Lawton, O.

Walton, J.
Longman primary maths. Fifth steps.   Teacher's bk.
See: Lawton, O.

Walton, J.
Longman primary maths. First steps: colour cards and
shapes.   See: Lawton, O.

Walton, J.
Longman primary maths. First steps: sets and shapes.
Pupils' bk. grade 1.   See: Lawton, O.

Walton, J.
Longman primary maths. First steps: sets and shapes.
Teacher's bk. grade 1.   See: Lawton, O.

Walton, J.
Longman primary maths. Fourth steps: apparatus cards.
See: Lawton, O.

Walton, J.
Longman primary maths. Fourth steps.   Pupils' bk.
See: Lawton, O.

Walton, J.
Longman primary maths. Fourth steps.   Teacher's bk.
See: Lawton, O.

Walton, J.
Longman primary maths. Second steps: colour cards.
See: Lawton, O.

Walton, J.
Longman primary maths. Second steps: numbers and
measures.   See: Lawton, O.

Walton, J.
Longman primary maths. Second steps: numbers and
measures.   Teacher's bk. grade 2.   See: Lawton, O.

Walton, J.
Longman primary maths. Seventh steps.   Pupil's bk.
See: Lawton, O.

Walton, J.
Longman primary maths. Seventh steps.   Teacher's bk.
See: Lawton, O.

Walton, J.
Longman primary maths. Sixth steps.   Pupils' bk.
See: Lawton, O.

Walton, J.
Longman primary maths. Sixth steps.   Teacher's bk.
See: Lawton, O.

Walton, J.
Longman primary maths. Third steps: abacus cards.
See: Lawton, O.

Walton, J.
Longman primary maths. Third steps: apparatus cards.
See: Lawton, O.

Walton, J.
Longman primary maths. Third steps.   Pupils' bk.
See: Lawton, O.

Walton, J.
Longman primary maths. Third steps.   Teacher's bk.
See: Lawton, O.

Walton, J.
Longman primary maths. Wallcharts.   See: Lawton, O.

Walton, J.
My second number book.   32pp. ill.   60c.   Longman
SA 1965 SA

Walton, J.
My second number book: teacher's guide.   72pp. ill.
75c.   Longman SA 1966 SA

Walton, J.
Water-mills, windmills and horse-mills of South Africa.
216pp. ill. photos. cl.   R12.50   Struik 1974 SA

Walton James.
Early Ghoya settlement in the Orange Free State.   40pp.
R1.95   (Memoirs van die Nasionale Museum, 2)
Nasionale Museum 1965 SA

Wambakha, O.
The way to power.   204pp.   K.shs.10.50 pap.
($4.70/£2.30 pap.)   EALB 1975 KE

Wamenka, N.
Mnara ya baba na ya mama. [Text in Lingala and
French.].   (Littérature classique, 5)   Ed Mont Noir 1974
ZR LIN

Wamweya, J.
Freedom fighter.   199pp. photos.   K.shs.12.50
($3.60)   EAPH 1971 KE

Wane, Y.
Les Toucouleurs du Fouta Toro (Sénégal)   250pp.
CFA1600   (Initiations et Etudes Africaines, 25)   IFAN
1969 SG FRE

Wangora, K.
Ufugaji wa kuku. [Poultry keeping.]   ill.   K.shs.6.50
($3.50)   Foundation 1977 KE SWA

Wangwe, S.M.
The excess capacity in manufacturing. A case study of
selected firms.   26pp.   T.shs.12.00   ($3.00)
(Research pap., 76.2)   Econ Res Bur - Tanz 1976 TZ

Wanjala, C., ed.
Faces at crossroads. 234pp. K.shs14.25 ($3.50/£1.70) EALB 1971 KE

Wanjala, C., ed.
Singing with the night. 86pp. K.shs.13.00 ($3.25/£1.60) EALB KE

Wanjala, C., ed.
Standpoints on African literature. K.shs80.00 K.shs33.50 pap. ($11.60/£5.50 cl.) EALB 1973 KE

Wanjau, G.
Mihiriga ya Agikuyu. [Kikuyu clans] 62pp. K.shs3.00 Equatorial 1973 KE KIK

Wanyoike, E.N.
An African pastor. 256pp. K.shs.55.00 EAPH 1974 KE

Wapnick, S.
The small intestine and the effect of partial resection. 10pp. 50c pap. (Fac. of Medicine, Univ. of Rhodesia, Research Lec. Series, 5) Univ Rhodesia Lib 1972 RH

Warburton, P.G.
Key to junior bookkeeping exercises. R7.50 Van Schaik SA

Warburton, P.G.
Senior bookkeeping exercises. R1.85 Van Schaik SA

Ward, B.
A new history. 28pp. 25c. (University of Cape Town T.B. Davie memorial lecture, 10) Univ Cape Town Lib 1969 SA

Ward, H.
Ces enfants que Dieu donne. See: Osae-Addo, G.

Ward, H., comp.
What is Christian marriage? 40pp. 45pes. (15p.) Africa Christian 1970 GH

Ward, H.
Newtown families. See: Osae-Addo G.

Ward, M., ed.
Directory of Swaziland libraries. See: Kuzwayo, A.W.Z., ed.

Ward, W.E.F.
Fraser of Trinity and Achimota. 328pp. photos. hd. C2.50 (£1.25/$2.50) Ghana UP 1965 GH

Warhurst, P.R.
Revisions in Central African history. See: Henderson, I.

Warmington, W.A.
West African Institute of Social and Economic Research: some aspects of industrial relations in the Cameroons plantations. N1.00 ($2.00) (W.A.I.S.E.R. third annual conference paper, 5) NISER 1954 NR

Warner, A.
About books: some notes on books and reading for the English student and the general reader. 50c. Rhodes Univ Lib 1972 SA

Warner, D.
Design criteria for water supply systems in East Africa. T.shs.15.00 ($5.00) (Research pap., 27) Bur Res Assess - Tanz 1973 TZ

Warner, D.
Economics of rural water supply in Tanzania. 64pp. T.shs.12.00 ($3.00) (Research pap., 70.19) Econ Res Bur - Tanz 1970 TZ

Warner, D.
Preliminary survey of impact of rural water supply upon households and villages. 23pp. ill. T.shs.12.00 ($3.00) (Research pap., 70.12) Econ Res Bur - Tanz 1970 TZ

Warner, D.
Project planning for rural development: a case study of the Manonga plains water supply scheme. T.shs.12.00 ($3.00) (Research pap., 69.29) Econ Res Bur - Tanz 1974 TZ

Warner, D.
Rural water supply and development: comparison of nine villages in Tanzania. 16pp. ill. T.shs12.00 ($3.00) (Research pap., 69.17) Econ Res Bur - Tanz 1969 TZ

Warner, H.W.
A digest of South African native civil case law, 1894-1957. R18.00 Juta 1962 SA

Warottere, S.M.
Jionee maisha yako. 28pp. K.shs.3.00 Equatorial 1972 KE KIK

Warren, D.M.
The Akan of Ghana. An overview of the ethnographic literature. 74pp. C1.20 Univ Ghana Bkshop; distr. 1973 GH

Warren, N.L.
Wewe ni Mkristo? [Adaptation from Journey into life.] 20pp. ill. T.shs.1.50 Central Tanganyika 1967 TZ SWA

Wartemberg, N.K.
The corpse's comedy. 82pp. N1.30 (Three Crowns Books) OUP - Nig 1977 NR

Waruhiu, S.N.
Affiliation law in Kenya. 47pp. K.shs.3.00 ($1.50/60p.) EALB 1962 KE

Wassenaar, A.D.
Assault on private enterprise. R6.50 Tafelberg 1976 SA

Watene, K.
Dedan Kimathi. 98pp. K.shs.8.50 Transafrica 1974 KE

Watene, K.
My son for my freedom. 104pp. K.shs.6.50 (African Theatre, 4) EAPH 1973 KE

Watene, K.
Sunset on the Manyatta. 264pp. K.shs.11.00 (Modern African Library) EAPH 1975 KE

Watergaard, P.
Cashew nuts: the quality problem. 11pp. T.shs12.00 ($3.00) (Research pap., 68.8) Econ Res Bur - Tanz 1968 TZ

Waters, A.R.
Planning for profit and prosperity. See: Ryan, T.C.I.

Waterville Publishing House.
Autobiography of Rev. Peter Hall. 74pp. photos. 20pes. Waterville 1965 GH

Wathika, J.
Kilimo ni mali. [Farming.] K.shs.6.50 ($3.50) Foundation 1977 KE SWA

Watkins, H. M.
Tarihin Bulus manzo. [Story of Paul.] 98pp. Challenge 1976 NR HAU

Watkins, H.M.
Tarihim ikilisiya. [Church history.] 178pp. Challenge 1976 NR HAU

Watkins, M.O.
The university's role in a developing country. 21pp. C1.00 ($1.00/50p.) (Inaugural lecture) Ghana UP 1972 GH

Watkins-Pitchford, H.
Besieged in Ladysmith. 132pp. map ill. R1.80 Shuter 1964 SA

Watkins-Pitchford, H.
In God's good time. 25c. Shuter 1949 SA

Watkinson, E.J.
Star of Africa and other stories. 140pp. 50c. Shuter 1963 SA

Watson, A.
Objective questions in chemistry: with answers. 64pp. ill. 95k Pilgrim 1968 NR

Watson, A.
Objective questions in chemistry: without answers. 62pp. ill. 82k Pilgrim 1968 NR

Weideman, E.   Grabherr, H.
  The effect of the temperature and pH of DCCA solutions on the shrinkresistance of woven wool fabrics during continuous application. 15pp. R2.50 (SAWTRI Technical Reports, 254) SAWTRI 1975 SA

Weideman, E.   van Rensburg, N.J.J.   Gee, E.
  Studies of the surface chemistry of wool, part II: the critical surface tension of wool and polymers. Some results and a reinterpretation of the theory on surface interactions. 32pp. R2.50 (SAWTRI Technical Reports, 331) SAWTRI 1976 SA

Weideman, E.
  Studies on the surface chemistry of wool, part I: the surface free energy of diiodomethane. 10pp. R2.50 (SAWTRI Technical Reports, 320) SAWTRI 1976 SA

Weil, W.
  Domestic servants: a microcosm of 'the race problem'. See: Whisson, M.G.

Weilenmann, J.
  Continuity properties of fractional powers, of the logarithm and of holomorphic semi-groups. 30pp. (CSIR Special Report, WISK 204) CSIR 1976 SA

Weinmann, H.
  Agricultural research and development in Rhodesia, 1924-1950. R$2.00 (Dept. of Agriculture, Univ. of Rhodesia, Series in Science, 2) Univ Rhodesia Lib 1975 RH

Weinmann, H.
  Agricultural research and development in Rhodesia under the rule of the British South Africa Company, 1890-1923. 161pp. R$1.00 (Dept. of Agriculture, Univ. of Rhodesia, 4) Univ Rhodesia Lib 1972 RH

Weinmann, H.
  Agricultural research and development in Southern Africa 1924-1950. 240pp. R$2.00 (Univ. Rhodesia, Series in Science, 2) Univ Rhodesia 1975 RH

Weir, B.M.
  Principal lighthouses on the South African and South West African coasts 1824-1960. 51pp. 90c. Univ Cape Town Lib 1970 SA

Weisner, S.
  Professional social work in Kenya: training and performance. 76pp. K.shs.6.50 Kenya Inst Admin KE

Wekman, W.G.
  South African pollen grains and spores. 6, 6 pts. 120pp. map. fl. 22.50 Balkema 1959 SA

Welbourn, F.B.   Kipkoris, B.E.
  The Marakwet of Kenya. 98pp. pap. & cl. K.shs.34.00 cl. K.shs.14.00 pap. ($7.00/£3.50 cl.) EALB 1973 KE

Welbourn, F.B.
  Religion and politics in Uganda, 1952-1962. 63pp. K.shs.10.00 ($3.20) EAPH 1965 KE

Welbourn, H.
  Endiisa ennungi ey'omwana. [How you should feed your child] 3rd ed. 40pp. ill. K.shs.1.00 EALB 1963 KE LUG

Welbourn, H.
  Health in the home. See: Threadgold, N.

Welch, F.J.
  South West Africa. 41pp. 80c. Univ Cape Town Lib 1967 SA

Weller, J.C.
  Priest from the lakeside: the story of Leonard Kamungu of Malawi and Zambia. 69pp. map. 30t. (35c.) Christ Lit Assoc - Mal 1971 MW

Weller, R.K.
  Karroo sedimentation in Northern Rhodesia. See: Drysdall, A.R.

Wellington, J.H.
  Human evolution now: the significance of South West Africa and Rhodesia. 40c. (Isma paps., 25) Inst Study of Man 1967 SA

Wells, J.
  Construction industry in East Africa. 28pp. T.shs12.00 ($3.00) (Research pap., 72.2) Econ Res Bur - Tanz 1972 TZ

Wells, J.C.
  Agricultural policy and economic growth in Nigeria, 1962-1968. 490pp. N8.00 OUP - Nig 1974 NR

Wells, J.C.
  Government agricultural investment in Nigeria: 1962-67. N2.00 NISER NR

Wells, L. G.
  Health, healing and society. 55pp. R1.95 ($2.40/£1.25) Ravan 1974 SA

Wells, M.J., ed.   Isaacs, I., ed.
  Butterworths South African income tax practice. R28.00 Butterworths SA

Welmers, W.
  Mathematics and logic in the Kpelle language and a first course in Kpelle. See: Gay, J.

Welmers, W.E.
  Efik grammar. 256pp. N2.00 (Inst. of African Stud., Univ. of Ibadan, occas. pub., 11) Inst Afr Stud-Ibadan 1968 NR EFI

Welmers, W.E.
  Jukun of Wukari and Jukun of Takum. 163pp. N2.00 (Inst. of African Stud., Univ. of Ibadan, occas. pub., 16) Inst Afr Stud-Ibadan 1968 NR

Welscheid, H.
  Outline of a data bank system for national and regional planning. See: Hahne, K.

Welsh, D., ed.   van der Merwe, H.W., ed.
  The future of the university in Southern Africa. cl. & pap. R15.00 cl. R9.00 pap. Philip 1977 SA

Welsh, D.
  The roots of segregation: native policy in colonial Natal, 1845-1910. 392pp. R9.50 OUP-SA 1971 SA

Welsh, J.
  Life for God's people. See: Kiongo, C.

Welsh, J.O.
  Imani ya mkristo. See: Kiongo, C.

Welsh, J.O.
  What I believe. See: Kiongo, C.

Welter, C.
  Etude géologique et prospection des feuilles Tsinjoarivo-miarinavaratra. 22pp. pl. maps. FMG928 (F18.56) (Travaux du Bureau Géologique, 101) Service Geol - Mad 1960 MG FRE

Welz, S.
  Cape silver and silversmiths. 184pp. photos. cl. ($37.00/£23.00) Balkema 1976 SA

Wembash-Rashid, J.A.R.
  Social, political and economic organization of the people of Masasi district: ethnographic field research report. 36pp. (National Museum of Tanzania, occas. paps., 2) National Museum - Tanz 1976 TZ

Wembo-Ossako.
  Amour et préjugés. Theatre. 48pp. 50k (CFA250) Centre Africain Litt 1973 ZR FRE

Wentzel, J.
  A view from the ridge. (Parktown, Johannesburg) 112pp. pl. cl. R7.95 cl. (South African Yesterdays series, 6) Philip 1975 SA

Wentzel, P.J.   Muloiwa, T.W.
  Trilingual elementary dictionary: Venda/Afrikaans/English. 525pp. R5.50 (R6.50) (Documenta, 16) Univ South Africa 1976 SA MUL

Were, C.P.
  Essential English for C.P.E. with answers. See: Musili, F.P.

Were, G.S.
  A history of the Abaluyia of western Kenya. 186pp. maps. K.shs30.00 cl. K.shs16.00 pap. ($6.40 cl.) ($4.00 pap.) EAPH 1967 KE

Were, G.S.
The survivors. 53pp. K.shs.7.00 Africa Book Serv 1968 KE

Were, G.S.
Western Kenya historical texts. 196pp. maps. K.shs.10.50 ($3.00/£1.20) EALB 1967 KE

Were, J.M.
The geography of international trade for East Africa. 49pp. U.shs25.00 (Occas. paps., 56) Dept Geog - Mak 1974 UG

Were, M.K.
The boy in between. 108pp. ill. K.shs6.00 OUP-Nairobi 1970 KE

Were, M.K.
The eighth wife. 167pp. ill. K.shs9.75 (African Secondary Readers, 1) EAPH 1974 KE

Were, M.K.
The high school gent. 180pp. K.shs14.00 OUP-Nairobi 1972 KE

Wesley Guild Hospital, Ilesha.
The medical care of children under five. 26pp. 35k Daystar 1973 NR

Wessels, D.M.
The employment potential of graduate housewives in the PWV region - pt. I: part-time employment. 75pp. R2.95 Human Science Res Council 1972 SA

Wessels, D.M.
Manpower requirements and utilization of women: the views of fifty employers in nine major industry groups. 113pp. ill. R1.70 (Human Sciences Research Council, MM-series, 52) Human Science Res Council 1975 SA

Wessels, D.M.
Part-time work for married women. 70pp. R1.50 Human Science Res Council 1971 SA

Wessels, J.A.
A first course in woodwork. See: Franzsen, P.J.J.

Wessels, S. A.
Bookbinding projects, standard 2. See: de Wet, E. P.

Wessels, S. A.
Bookbinding projects, standard 3. See: de Wet, E. P.

Wessels, S. A.
Bookbinding projects, standard 4. See: de Wet, E. P.

West African Book Publishers Ltd.
You and your baby. 7th ed. 84pp. ill. West African Book 1975 NR

West African Book Publishers Ltd.
You and your health. 3rd ed. 100pp. ill. West African Book 1975 NR

West, H.W.
Land policy in Buganda. 244pp. K.shs.42.50 ($13.00) EAPH 1976 KE

West, M.
Abantu. An introduction to the black people of South Africa. See: Morris, J.

West, M.
Bishops and prophets in a black city: African independent churches in Soweto, Johannesburg. 240pp. ill. cl. R.8.40 Philip 1975 SA

West, M., ed.
Religion and social change in Southern Africa: anthropological essays in honour of Monica Wilson. See: Whisson, M., ed.

West, M. Endicott, J.
New method English dictionary. 352pp. hd. R2.10 Longman SA 1945 SA

West, O.
Aloes of Rhodesia. 128pp. R$3.50 Longman - Rhod 1974 RH

West, O.
A field guide to the aloes of Rhodesia. 96pp. col. ill. R$3.50 Longman - Rhod 1974 RH

West, O.
The vegetation of Weenen country, Natal. 75c. (Memoirs of the Botanical Survey of South Africa, 23) Botanical Res Inst 1951 SA

Westergaard, P.
The cashew nut industry in Tanzania: marketing costs. T.shs.12.00 ($3.00) (Research pap., 69.28) Econ Res Bur - Tanz 1974 TZ

Westergaard, P.
Cashew nut industry in Tanzania: quality of raw product. T.shs12.00 ($3.00) (Research pap., 69.28) Econ Res Bur - Tanz 1969 TZ

Westergaard, P.
Farm surveys of cashew products in Mtwara region: preliminary results. 12pp. ill. T.shs12.00 ($3.00) (Research pap., 68.3) Econ Res Bur - Tanz 1968 TZ

Westergaard, P.
Marketing margin: an analysis of cashew nut marketing costs in Tanzania. 25pp. T.shs12.00 ($3.00) (Research pap., 68.13) Econ Res Bur - Tanz 1968 Z

Westergaard, P.
Outline of the joint research project on cooperatives. T.shs.12.00 ($3.00) (Research pap., 69.34) Econ Res Bur - Tanz 1975 TZ

Westergaard, P.
A theoretical framework for the study of foreign assistance to Tanzania. T.shs.12.00 ($3.00) (Research pap., 67.20) Econ Res Bur - Tanz 1975 TZ

Westergaard, P.W.
Cooperatives in Tanzania: their functions as democratic and economic institutions. 31pp. T.shs.12.00 ($3.00) (Research pap., 70.16) Econ Res Bur - Tanz 1970 TZ

Westley, S.B., ed.
Development and the environment in Africa. 290pp. K.shs.25.00 (Inst. Development Studies, occas. paps., 15) Inst Dev Stud 1975 KE

Westley, S.B., ed. Johnston, B.F., ed.
Proceedings of a workshop on farm equipment innovations for agricultural development and rural industrialisation. K.shs.25.00 (Inst. Development Studies, occas. paps., 16) Inst Dev Stud 1975 KE

Westley, S.B., ed. David, M., ed. Johnston, B.F., ed.
Summary report of a workshop on a food and nutrition strategy for Kenya. 40pp. K.shs.7.00 (Inst. Development Studies, occas. paps., 14) Inst Dev Stud 1975 KE

Wheat, J.
An analysis of data on Azaouak and Rahaji cattle at Gumel, Kano state, Nigeria. 14pp. 60k (Samaru misc. pap., 40) Inst Agric Res-Zaria 1972 NR

Wheat, J. Koch, B.A. de Leeuw, P.N.
Bunaji cattle at the Shika research station, North Central State, Nigeria. 12pp. 60k (Samaru misc. pap., 41) Inst Agric Res-Zaria 1972 NR

Wheat, J.D. Broadhurst, J.
An analysis of data on Bunaji cattle at Birnin Kudu and Kabomo, Northern Nigeria. 13pp. 20k (Samaru misc. pap., 25) Inst Agric Res - Zaria 1968 NR

Wheat, J.D. Broadhurst, J.
An analysis of data on Sokoto Gudali cattle at Bulassa and Dogondaji, Northern Nigeria. 11pp. 60k (Samaru misc. pap., 39) Inst Agric Res-Zaria 1972 NR

Wheat, J.D.
An analysis of data on Wadara cattle at Dalori and the Bornu ranch at Maiduguri, North Eastern State of Nigeria. 20k (Samaru misc. pap., 49) Inst Agric Res - Zaria 1975 NR

Wheeler, D.L.
Portuguese expansion in Angola since 1836. 75c. (Local series pamphlets, 20) Central Africa Hist Assoc 1967 RH

Author Index

Whisson, M.   Jansen, C.
The Cape Malays. 152pp. col. pl. cl. R12.50 Struik 1977 SA

Whisson, M., ed.   West, M., ed.
Religion and social change in Southern Africa: anthropological essays in honour of Monica Wilson. 240pp. cl. R9.00 Philip 1975 SA

Whisson, M.G.   Weil, W.
Domestic servants: a microcosm of 'the race problem'. 54pp. 60c. ($1.45) SA Inst of Race Relations 1971 SA

Whisson, M.G.
The fairest cape?: an account of the coloured people of the district of Simonstown. 37pp. 90c. ($1.95) SA Inst of Race Relations 1972 SA

Whisson, M.G.   Kaplinsky, R.M.
Suspended sentence: a study of Kalk Bay fishermen. 46pp. 55c. ($1.45) SA Inst of Race Relations 1969 SA

White, C.M.N.
Elements in Luvale beliefs and rituals. 76pp. K2.75 (£1.38) (Rhodes-Livingstone paps., 32) Inst Soc Res - Zam 1961 ZA

White, C.M.N.
An outline of Luvale social and political organisation. 70pp. K1.05 (53p.) (Rhodes-Livingstone paps., 30) Inst Soc Res - Zam 1960 ZA

White, C.M.N.
A preliminary survey of Luvale rural economy. 78pp. 85n. (43p.) (Rhodes-Livingstone paps., 29) Inst Soc Res -Zam 1959 ZA

White, C.M.N.
Tradition and change in Luvale marriage. 47pp. K1.25 (63p) (Rhodes-Livingstone paps., 34) Inst Soc Res - Zam 1962 ZA

White, E.C.
Chimwemwe cheni cheni. [True happiness.] 115pp. Malamulo 1975 MW CHC

White, J.
Autoclave setting of wool, part II: the effect of fibre regain and various setting conditions on the rate of dye exhaustion and snarling twist of different yarns. See: van Rensburg, N.J.J.

White, J.E.H.
Geography for Nigerian schools. bk. 3: Africa. See: Quinn-Young, C.T.

White, K.D.
Historical Roman coins illustrating the period 44 B.C. to A.D. 55: a selection from the departmental coin collection. 69pp. R1.00 Rhodes Univ Lib 1958 SA

White, M.D.   Scholtz, J.C.   Crawford, C.E.
Stocklam market survey. 24pp. R5.00 (CSIR Special Report, HOUT 90) CSIR 1975 SA

White, M.D.   Riekert, H.
Waste paper recovery. Additional quantities still available for collection. pt.2 45pp. R5.00 (CSIR Special Report, HOUT 91) CSIR 1975 SA

White, M.D.   Riekert, H.
Waste paper recovery: an introductory survey. 100pp. R5.00 (CSIR Special Report, HOUT 83) CSIR 1974 SA

White, P.
Du mauvais coté. 16pp. ill. CFA30 CPE 1976 IV FRE

White, P.
Le grand mur. 16pp. ill. CFA30 CPE 1976 IV FRE

White, P.
The great wall. ill. 30pes. (9p.) (Cartoon Booklets) Africa Christian 1970 GH

White, P.
Les léopards grandissent. 16pp. ill. CFA30 CPE 1976 IV FRE

White, P.
Little leopards become big leopards. ill. 30pes. (9p.) (Cartoon Booklets) Africa Christian 1970 GH

White, P.
Le marais maudit. 16pp. ill. CFA30 CPE 1976 IV FRE

White, P.
Monkey in the bog. ill. 30pes. (9p.) (Cartoon Booklets) Africa Christian 1970 GH

White, P.
The monkey who didn't believe in the crocodile. ill. 30pes. (9p.) (Cartoon Booklets) Africa Christian 1970 GH

White, P.
Out on a limb. ill. 30pes. (9p.) (Cartoon Booklets) Africa Christian 1970 GH

White, P.
Yakobo in slippery places. 96pp. ill. C1.00 (30p.) Africa Christian 1973 GH

White, R.
Africa: studies for East African students. 192pp. pl. K.shs.22.50 Heinemann Educ - Nair 1974 KE

White, R.
North America; studies for East African students. See: Hayward, R.L.

White, R.
North America: studies for East African students. See: Hayward, R.L.

White, V.
Some frontier families. Biographical sketches of 100 Eastern Province families before 1840. See: Mitford-Barberton, I.

Whitehead, D.
Satan our enemy. 37pp. 15k Daystar 1968 NR

Whiteley, F.G.H.
Riding horse types in South Africa 1940-1960. 26pp. 60c. Univ Cape Town Lib 1960 SA

Whiteley, W.H.
The dialects and verse of Pemba: an introduction. 61pp. T. shs 5.50 Inst Swahili Res 1958 TZ

Whiteley, W.H.
A linguistic bibliography of East Africa. U.shs10.50 (M.I.S.R. linguistic stud., 2) Mak Inst Soc Res 1958 UG

Whiteley, W.H.
A short description of item categories in Iraqw. 75pp. U.shs.15.00 (M.I.S.R. linguistic stud., 3) Mak Inst Soc Res 1958 UG

Whiteley, W.H.
Studies in Swahili dialect: Ki-mtang'ata - a dialect of the Mrima coast - Tanganyika. 64pp. T. shs 5.50 Inst Swahili Res 1956 TZ

Whiteley, W.H.
The tense system of Gusii. 67pp. U.shs.16.00 (M.I.S.R. linguistic stud., 4) Mak Inst Soc Res 1960 UG

Whiteley, W.H.
Tippu-Tip. [Autobiography of Tippu-Tip] 4th ed. ill. K.shs.7.50 ($2.25/90p.) (Johari za Kiswahili, 8) EALB 1966 KE SWA

Whitely, W.H.
Language in Kenya. 582pp. ill. col. maps. K.shs.115.00 Africa only OUP - Nairobi 1974 KE

Whiteman, A.J., ed.
African geology: proceedings of the conference on African geology held at the University of Ibadan from 7-14 December 1970, in commemoration of the tenth anniversary of the founding of the geology department. See: Dessauvagie, T.F.J., ed.

Whitfield, G.M.B.
South African native law. 2nd ed. R10.50 Juta 1948 SA

Whitfield, M.
Learning to run. 131pp. photos. K.shs.7.00 ($2.60) EAPH 1968 KE

Williamson, K.
Bolou izon go fun.   See: Egberipou, O.A.

Williamson, K., ed.
Igbo-English dictionary (based on the Onitsha dialect) 568pp. ill. pap., cl.   N7.00 cl.   N3.00 pap.   Ethiope 1972 NR

Williamson, K., ed.
An introduction to Ika and Ukeuani.   55pp.   N1.00 (Inst. of African Stud., Univ. of Ibadan, occas. pub., 14) Inst Afr Stud-Ibadan 1968 NR

Williamson, K.
Reading and writing Epíe.   21pp.   10k   (Inst. of African Stud., Univ. of Ibadan, Rivers readers project, 11)   Inst Afr Stud-Ibadan 1970 NR EPI

Williamson, K.
Reading and writing Etche.   21pp.   10k   (Inst. of African Stud., Univ. of Ibadan, Rivers readers project, 19) Inst Afr Stud-Ibadan 1970 NR

Williamson, K.
Reading and writing Ikwerre.   29pp.   10k   (Inst. of African Stud., Univ. of Ibadan, Rivers readers project, 8) Inst Afr Stud-Ibadan 1970 NR IKW

Williamson, K.
Reading and writing Kálábari.   21pp.   10k   (Inst. of African Stud., Univ. of Ibadan, Rivers readers project, 26) Inst Afr Stud-Ibadan 1971 NR KAB

Williamson, K.
Reading and writing Nembe.   21pp.   10k   (Inst. of African Stud., Univ. of Ibadan, Rivers readers project, 5) Inst Afr Stud-Ibadan 1970 NR NEM

Williamson, K.
Reading and writing Ogbia.   24pp.   10k   (Inst. of African Stud., Univ. of Ibadan, Rivers readers project, 18) Inst Afr Stud-Ibadan 1970 NR

Williamson, K.
Reading and writing Okrika.   12pp.   10k   (Inst. of African Stud., Univ. of Ibadan, Rivers readers project, 29) Inst Afr Stud-Ibadan 1972 NR

Williamson, K.
Teachers' notes Okwukwo ke mbom nu Ikwere.   91pp. 50k   (Inst. of African Stud., Univ. of Ibadan, Rivers readers project, 7)   Inst Afr Stud-Ibadan 1970 NR IKW

Williamson, K.
Teacher's notes on Bolou izon go fun.   See: Egberipou, O.A.

Williamson, K.   Thomas, E.
Wordlist of Delta Edo: Epie, Engenni, Degema.   105pp. N1.50 (Inst. of African Stud., Univ. of Ibadan, occas. pub., 8)   Inst Afr Stud-Ibadan 1967 NR

Williamson, L.
Test your honesty.   24pp. ill.   4k   SIM 1972 NR

Williamson, R.H.
The thermal environment and its effects on road pavements.   75pp. ill. pl.   (CSIR research reports, 320) CSIR 1976 SA

Williamson, S.G.
Akan religion and the Christian faith.   186pp. cl.   C6.00 (£3.00/$6.00)   Ghana UP 1965 GH

Willmer, J.   Okoye, T.O.
Map reading exercises for secondary schools.   48pp. N1.05   Pilgrim 1969 NR

Willmer, J.
Objective questions in geography: with answers. See: Killick, M.

Willmer, J.
Objective questions in geography: without answers. See: Killick, M.

Willot, P.
Complément à la bibliographie rwandaise.   51pp.   RF25 ($0.25)   Caritas 1968 RW FRE

Wills, W.A., ed.   Collingridge, L.T., ed.
The downfall of Lobengula. [Reprint ed. 1894].   354pp. ill. photos. map. cl.   R$7.20 cl.   (Rhodesiana Reprint Library, Gold Series, 17)   Books of Rhodesia 1971 RH

Willson, F.M.G.
Why study government?   28pp.   30c   Univ Rhodesia Lib 1962 RH

Willson, R.M.G.   Passmore, G.C.
Holders of administrative and ministerial office 1894-1964 and members of the legislative council 1899-1923 and the legislative assembly 1924-1964.   75pp.   50c (Dept. of Political Science, Univ. Rhodesia, 3)   Univ Rhodesia Lib 1966 RH

Wilman, M.
The rock-engravings of Griqualand West Bechuanaland South Africa.   89pp. pl. hd.   fl. 56.25   Balkema 1968 SA

Wilmot, A.J., eds.
Medical education in South Africa.   See: Reid, J.V.O., ed.

Wilmot, P.F., ed.
Sociology in Africa.   320pp.   N2.20   Dept Soc-ABU 1973 NR

Wilson, C.J.
Uganda in the days of Bishop Tucker.   K.shs.2.80 ($1.50/60p.)   EALB 1955 KE

Wilson, D.
English for Africans.   cl.   50c.   Shuter 1952 SA

Wilson, Dr.   Wilson, Mrs.
Christian marriage.   32pp.   15pes.   Waterville 1951 GH

Wilson, E.M.
A feedlot profit model.   35pp.   R$1.50   Univ Rhodesia 1976 RH

Wilson, F., ed.   Amann, V.F., ed.
Financing rural development.   277pp.   U.shs.40.00 ($7.50)   Mak Inst Soc Res 1975 UG

Wilson, F., ed.   Perrot, D., ed.
Outlook on a century.   746pp. ill.   R15.00   Lovedale 1973 SA

Wilson, F.
Migrant labour.   281pp. ill.   R1.95   Ravan 1973 SA

Wilson, F.
Migrant labour in South Africa. Report to the South African Council of Churches.   281pp. pl. map.   R3.50 ($5.00/£2.75)   Ravan 1972 SA

Wilson, G.
The constitution of the Ngonde.   36pp.   K1.50   (75p.) (Rhodes-Livingstone paps., 3)   Inst Soc Res - Zam 1939 ZA

Wilson, G.
An essay on the economics of detribalisation in Northern Rhodesia. v. 1 71pp.   K1.50   (75p.) (Rhodes-Livingstone pap, 5)   Inst Soc Res Zam 1941 ZA

Wilson, G.
An essay on the economics of detribalisation in Northern Rhodesia. v. 2 82pp.   (75p.)   (K1.50) (Rhodes-Livingstone paps., 6)   Inst Soc Res - Zam 1942 ZA

Wilson, G.
The land rights of individuals among the Nyakusa.   52pp. K1.50   (75p.)   (Rhodes-Livingstone paps., 1)   Inst Soc Res - Zam 1938 ZA

Wilson, G.
Owen Falls: Electricity in a developing country.   105pp. maps.   K.shs.15.00   ($4.00)   EAPH 1967 KE

Wilson, G.   Hunter, M.
The study of African society.   21pp.   35n.   (18p.) (Rhodes-Livingstone paps., 2)   Inst Soc Res - Zam 1939 ZA

Wilson, J.M.
Health talks.   2nd ed.   49pp.   30pes.   Waterville 1969 GH

Author Index

Wilson, M. Mafeje, A.
Langa: a study of social groups in an African township.
2nd ed. 190pp. R2.75 OUP - SA SA

Wilson, M.
Missionaries: conquerors or servants of God? Address
given on the occasion of the official opening of the South
African Missionary Museum, 30th January 1976. 11pp.
20c. Missionary Museum 1976 SA

Wilson, M.
Python cave. 125pp. ill. R$1.50 (Dyker series, 2)
Vision 1976 RH

Wilson, M.
The thousand years before van Riebeeck: reflections on
early peoples of South Africa. 19pp. R1.00
(Raymond Dart lec., 6) Inst Study of Man 1969 SA

Wilson, Mrs.
Christian marriage. See: Wilson, Dr.

Wilson, P., ed.
Conference on education and training requirements for
engineers and technicians in Sierra Leone.
See: MacCormack, J., ed.

Wilson, P.M.
English-Swahili: classified vocabulary. 3rd ed. 30pp.
K.shs.4.50 ($1.00/60p.) EALB 1976 KE

Wilson, P.M.
Simplified Swahili. 561pp. pap. & cl. K.shs.57.50 cl.
K.shs.45.00 pap. ($9.00/£4.30 pap.) ($11.20/£5.75
cl.) EALB 1970 KE

Wilson, P.M.
Swahili picture vocabulary. 76pp. ill. K.shs.11.00
($3.00/£1.50) EALB 1972 KE

Wiltshire, C., comp.
Tristan da Cunha, 1509-1961. 21pp. R1.60 Dept
Bibliog, Lib & Typo 1973 SA

Wimble, B.J.S.
Consolidated balance sheet values and other contentious
matters. 2nd ed. R4.00 Juta 1972 SA

Wimble, B.J.S. Cairns, T.
Selected questions in accounting, 1 - elementary. 4
4thed. R4.00 Juta 1977 SA

Wimble, B.J.S. Cairns, T.
Selected questions in accounting, 2 - intermediate. 4
4thed. R5.00 Juta 1976 SA

Wimbush, D.
Dangerous exchange. 51pp. 45k (Adventures in
Africa, J3) OUP-Nig 1973 NR

Wimbush, D.
The kidnappers: wisdom of Mallam Faruku. 60pp. ill.
50k OUP-Nig 1968 NR

Wimbush, D.
The land of the crocodile's teeth: Hassan and the spirits.
64pp. ill. 50k OUP-Nig 1968 NR

Wimbush, D.
Professor Q's secret. 90pp. ill. 50k OUP-Nig 1971
NR

Wimbush, D.
A strange adventure and other stories. 68pp. ill. 45k
OUP-Nig 1969 NR

Winful, E.A.
Akan awensem. [Akan poems.] 3rd ed. 32pp.
50pes. Bur Ghana Lang 1975 GH FAT

Wingard, P. Tomori, S.H.O.
Progressive English: pupils bk. 1, 6bks 38pp. photos.
60k Heinemann Educ - Nig 1965 NR

Wingard, P. Tomori, S.H.O.
Progressive English: pupils bk. 2, 6 bks 64pp. photos.
65k Heinemann Educ - Nig 1965 NR

Wingard, P.
Progressive English: pupils bk. 3, 6 bks See: Tomori,
S.H.O.

Wingard, P.
Progressive English: pupils bk. 4, 6bks See: Tomori,
S.H.O.

Wingard, P.
Progressive English: pupils bk. 5, 6bks See: Tomori,
S.H.O.

Wingard, P.
Progressive English: pupils bk. 6, 6bks See: Tomori,
S.H.O.

Wingard, P. Tomori, S.H.O.
Progressive English: teachers bk. 1, 6bks 208pp.
89k. Heinemann Educ - Nig 1965 NR

Wingard, P. Tomori, S.H.O.
Progressive English: teachers bk. 2, 6 bks 228pp.
89k. Heinemann Educ - Nig 1965 NR

Wingard, P.
Progressive English: teachers bk. 3, 6bks See: Tomori,
S.H.O.

Wingard, P. Tomori, S.H.O.
Progressive English: teachers bk. 4, 6bks 131pp.
N1.75 Heinemann Educ - Nig 1971 NR

Wingard, P. Tomori, S.H.O.
Progressive English: teachers bk. 5, 6bks 168pp.
N1.85 Heinemann Educ - Nig 1973 NR

Wingard, P. Tomori, S.H.O.
Progressive English: teachers bk. 6, 6 bks 168pp.
N2.25 Heinemann Educ - Nig 1973 NR

Winks, R.
The roots of American foreign policy. 19pp. 30c. SA
Inst Int Affairs 1972 SA

Winter, J.S., comp.
R.F. Kennedy - a list of publications. See: Rundle, M.,
comp.

Winter, J.S., ed.
Catalogue of books on insurance. rev. ed. gratis
Johannesburg Public Lib 1968 SA

Winter, J.S.
First-hand accounts of Johannesburg in English-language
periodicals, 1886-1895. 42pp. R2.20 Dept Bibliog,
Lib & Typo 1967 SA

Winterbottom, J.M.
A preliminary check list of the birds of South West Africa.
268pp. maps. R5.00 SWA Scient Soc 1971 SX

Winterbottom, R.
Notes on South African gobies possessing free upper
pectoral fin rays (Pisces:Gobiidae) 11pp. ill. R1.00
(Special publ., 16) Inst Ichthyology 1976 SA

Winterbottom, R.
Rediscovery of certain type specimens of fishes from the
collections of the Government Marine Survey made by
J.D.F. Gilchrist and the S.S. Pickle. 10pp. R1.00
(Special publ., 12) Inst Ichthyology 1974 SA

Wioland, F.
Enquête sur les langues parlées au Sénégal par les élèves
de l'enseignement primaire. Etude statistique 1965.
252pp. CFA875 pap. (C.L.A.D. Etude, 11) CLAD
1965 SG FRE

Wioland, F. Calvet, M.J.
L'expansion du wolof au Sénégal. CFA125 (C.L.A.D.
Etude, 11 bis) CLAD 1965 SG FRE

Wioland, F.
Le genre en français parlé et en wolof. 31pp. CFA250
(C.L.A.D. Etude, 18) CLAD 1966 SG FRE

Wiredu, A.
Nii Ayi Bontey. 54pp. ill. 60pes. ($.50) Ghana Publ
Corp 1972 GH TWI

Wiredu, A.
Queen Amina. 32pp. ill. 45pes. ($.50) Ghana Publ
Corp 1972 GH

Wiredu, A.
La reine Amina. 24pp. ill. (60c.) Ghana Publ Corp
1975 GH FRE

Wisner, B.
Bibliography of Dodoma region. See: Townsend, J.

Wisselman, N.
Samba et le guinarou. 16pp. CFA200 Nouv Ed Afric
1976 SG FRE

Wisselman, R.
Langage et textes. Classe de 5e. Livre de l'élève.
See: Calvet, L.J.

Wisselman, R.
Langage et textes. Classe de 5e. Livre du maître.
See: Calvet, L.J.

Wisselmann, R.
Comment définir des objectifs pédagogiques. 35pp.
CFA200 (C.L.A.D. Étude, 53) CLAD 1974 SG FRE

Wisselmann, R.
Une expérience de télévision scolaire au Sénégal.
See: Guyot, A.

Wisselmann, R.
Langage et textes. Méthode complète d'enseignement du
français en Afrique, classe de 4e, livre de l'élève.
See: Calvet, L.J.

Witting C. Ridout, R.
The facts of English. 328pp. N1.40 Pilgrim 1966 NR

Wolf, H.
Architecture south of the Sahara 1963-1965. 42pp.
R2.20 Dept Bibliog, Lib & Typo 1966 SA

Wolf, P.G.
The programmes of the Johannesburg Repertory Players,
1928-1959. 101pp. R5.15 Dept Bibliog, Lib & Typo
1968 SA

Wolff, R.D.
Britain and Kenya 1870-1930. (The economics of
Colonialism) 225pp. map. K.shs.30.00 Africa only
Transafrica 1974 KE

Wolfsdorf, J.
The changing concepts of paediatric care. 20pp. 30c
Univ Rhodesia Lib 1972 RH

Wolfson, J.G.E.
Turmoil at Turfloop: a summary of the reports of the
Snyman and Jackson commissions of inquiry into the
University of the North. 112pp. R2.10 ($3.20) SA
Inst of Race Relations 1976 SA

Wollheim, O.D., ed.
The Theron commission report: an evaluation and early
reactions to the report and its recommendations. 39pp.
75c. ($1.60) SA Inst of Race Relations 1977 SA

Wolpowitz, L.
James and Kate Hyde and the development of music in
Johannesburg up to the First World War. R4.50 Van
Schaik SA

Wolseley, G.
The South African diaries of Sir Garnet Wolseley, 1875.
303pp. pl. hd. fl. 33.75 (South African biographical
and historical studies, 11) Balkema 1971 SA

Wolseley, G.
The South African journal of Sir Garnet Wolseley,
1879-1880. 367pp. hd. fl. 42.75 (South African
biographical and historical studies, 12) Balkema 1973
SA

Woltz, C.C.
Case studies in the management of economic
development. v. 2 64pp. K.shs.11.75 (I.P.A. Study,
7) OUP-Nairobi 1969 KE

Wood, J.G.
Through Matabeleland: ten months in a waggon. [Reprint
of ed. 1893]. 198pp. pl. cl. R$7.90 (Rhodesiana
Reprint Library, Gold Series, 33) Books of Rhodesia
1974 RH

Wood, J.M.
Handbook to the flora of Natal. 197pp. R3.00 Univ of
Natal 1907 SA

Wood, L.J.
Market origins and development in East Africa. 63pp.
map. U.shs.20.00 (Occas. paps., 57) Dept Geog -
Mak 1975 UG

Wood, P.
A comprehensive guide to gardening in Rhodesia. v. 1
184pp. ill. col. ill. map. cl. & pap. R$12.50 cl.
R$9.50 pap. Galaxie 1975 RH

Woodhouse, A.J.
Obituaries appearing in the Johannesburg Star 1902-1903.
71pp. R3.65 Dept Bibliog, Lib & Typo 1969 SA

Woodhouse, B.
Art on the rocks of Southern Africa. See: Lee, N.

Woodhouse, H.C.
Archaeology in Southern Africa. 170pp. ill. hd. R4.50
Purnell 1971 SA

Woodhouse, H.C.
History on the rocks: themes in the rock art of Southern
Africa. ill. 40c. (Isma paps., 28) Inst Study of Man
1976 SA

Woodman, D., ed.
Egyptian one-act plays. [English version; also available in
Arabic]. 224pp. £E1.00 ($6.00) Am Univ 1974 UA

Woodman, G.R., ed.
Essays in Ghanaian law: supreme court centenary
publication 1876-1976. See: Daniel, W.C.E., ed.

Woodruff, A.B.
Psychology: that nasty little subject of the science of
rescue. 16pp. C1.00 ($1.00/50p.) (Inaugural
lecture) Ghana UP 1971 GH

Woods, C.A.
The Indian community in Natal. $2.50 (Natal regional
survey pub., 9) Dept Econ-Natal 1954 SA

Woods, D.R.
Genes, microbes and man. ex. only (Inaugural lec.)
Rhodes Univ Lib 1973 SA

Woods, D.R.
Genes, microbes and man. 25pp. 50c (Inaugural
lectures) Rhodes Univ Lib 1973 SA

Woodward, C.S.
Oriental ceramics at the Cape of Good Hope, 1652-1795.
240pp. ill. pl. col. pl. cl. R25.00 ($45.00) Balkema
1974 SA

Woolacott, E.
Systematic typing for the senior secondary course.
See: Geldenhuys, A.

World Council of Churches.
Jesus Christ frees and unites. Bible studies prepared for
the World Council of Churches for its 5th Assembly
Nairobi, 1975. 50k Daystar 1975 NR

Worrall, D.
The republic of South Africa and detente. 20pp. ($1.60)
(Local series pamphlets, 32) Central Africa Hist Assoc
1976 RH

Worthington, F. Richards, C.G.
Kagituju kajigi na Johana muritu. [The rascal hare and
the simple John] 2nd ed. 32pp. ill. K.shs.1.25
($1.25/50p.) EALB 1970 KE MER

Worthington, F.
Sungura mjanja. [The cunning rabbit] 14pp. ill.
K.shs.1.50 OUP-Nairobi 1964 KE SWA

Worthington, G.D.P.
The private pilot's handbook. 7th ed. 352pp. ill.
R6.60 cl. Flesch 1975 SA

Wortington, F.W. Richards, C.
Apwoyo jaoledhi kod johana mofuwo. 32pp.
K.shs.1.20 EALB 1963 KE LUO

Wright, A.
Grey ghosts at Buffalo Bend. 136pp. ill. R$3.90
Galaxie 1976 RH

Wright, A.
Valley of the ironwoods. 400pp. ill. R10.00 Bulpin
1972 SA

Wright, D.
A South African album. R1.80 (Mantis Poets, 9)
Philip 1975 SA

Wright, E.L.C.
From start to finish. 176pp. photos. cl. R6.50
Macmillan - SA 1974 SA

Wright, H.M.
The burden of the present: Liberal-radical controversy in southern African history. 144pp. cl. & pap. R5.85 cl. R3.90 pap. Philip 1976 SA

Wright, J.B.
Bushman raiders of the Drakensberg, 1840-1970. ill. cl. R9.60 Univ of Natal 1971 SA

Wright, J.B.
The James Stuart archive of recorded oral evidence relating to the history of Zulu and neighbouring peoples. v. 1 See: Webb, C.B.

Wright, M.
Hygiene and sanitation in South Africa. 3rd ed. R5.00 Juta 1971 SA

Wright, M.J.
Buganda in the Heroic Age. 260pp. photos. K.shs35.00 OUP-Nairobi 1971 KE

Wright, M.K.
Fibre systems of the brain and spinal cord. 2nd ed. 103pp. ill. cl. R6.00 Witwatersrand UP 1972 SA

Wright, W.E.
Searching science and scripture. 40pp. 8k SIM 1966 NR

Wright, W.E.
Sex and marriage. 2nd ed. 56pp. 20k SIM 1972 NR

Wright, W.E.
Why one wife? 2nd ed. 12pp. hd. 5k SIM 1966 NR

Wrigley, C.C.
Crops and wealth in Uganda. 96pp. map. K.shs15.25 OUP-Nairobi 1972 KE

Wroblicki, J.
The Kapiri Mposhi glass sand. K1.50 (Dept. of Geological Survey. Economic Reports, 24) Geol Survey - Zam 1970 ZA

Wrogemann, N.
Cheetah. R12.95 McGraw-Hill SA 1975 SA

Wudneh, M.
Yehulet alem sellay. [The spy of two worlds] 318pp. Eth.$3.00 Bible Churmen's Miss Soc 1972 ET AMH

Wugo, S.A.
Okwukwp ke mbom nu ikwere. [Ikwerre reader, 1] 63pp. ill. 30k (Inst. of African Stud., Univ. of Ibadan, Rivers readers project, 6) Inst Afr Stud-Ibadan 1970 NR IKW

Wumbrand, R.
Kuteswa kwa ajili ya Kristo. [Tortured for Christ] Reprint of 1967 ed. 166pp. T.shs.3.00 Africa Inland Church 1968 TZ

Wyatt, J.
Ilinde Amana. Historia ya Biblia. See: Engel, K.F.

Wycherley, K.E.
Practical physical chemistry. 58pp. ill. C4.00 ($4.00) Ghana Publ Corp 1976 GH

Wyllie, R.H.
The role of the virtue of prudence in the ethics of St. Thomas Aquinas. 131pp. R1.95 Univ of Natal 1966 SA

Wyndam Smith, K.
From frontier to midlands. A history of the Graaf-Reinet District, 1786-1910. R6.00 Inst Soc & Econ Res 1976 SA

Yaa, J.D.
A guide to English/Kiswahili translation. 77pp. K.shs.9.00 ($1.80 pap.) (Comb Books in Kiswahili, 3) Comb Books 1975 KE

Yaba College of Technology Library.
Index to West African commercial and technical periodicals, received in the college library covering 1967-1973. 88pp. (Information Series, 8) Yaba 1975 NR

Yaba College of Technology Library.
Index to West African commercial and technical periodicals received in the college library during the year 1967-1969. 79pp. ex. only (Yaba College of Technology Library, Information series, 7) Yaba 1973 NR

Yaffey, M.J.H.
Effect of nationalization on external payments. 11pp. T.shs.12.00 ($3.00) (Research pap., 69.2) Econ Res Bur - Tanz 1969 TZ

Yaffey, M.J.H.
Methods of paying for Tanzania's imports. 12pp. T.shs.12.00 ($3.00) (Research pap., 68.2) Econ Res Bur - Tanz 1968 TZ

Yahaya, I.Y.
Da koya a kan Iya. 3, 3 bks. 83pp. 45k OUP-Nig NR HAU

Yahaya, I.Y.
Da koyo a kan iya. [Oxford Hausa course.]. 1, 3 bks. 49pp. OUP - Nig 1975 NR HAU

Yahaya, I.Y.
Da koyo akan iya. 2, 3 bks ill. 40k OUP-Nig 1971 NR HAU

Yahaya, I.Y.
Daren Sha Biyu. [Twelfth night] 131pp. 50k Northern Nig 1971 NR HAU

Yahaya, I.Y., ed.
Wakokin hikima. [Collection of Hausa poems.] 99pp. N1.70 OUP - Nig 1975 NR HAU

Yahaya, I.Y.
Labarun gargajiya. [Hausa story book for secondary schools.] bk. I. 94pp. ill. N1.30 OUP - Nig 1974 NR HAU

Yahaya, I.Y.
Tatsuniyoyi da wasanni: littafi na biyar. 5, 6 bks 58pp. ill. 65k OUP-Nig 1971 NR HAU

Yahaya, I.Y.
Tatsuniyoyi da wasanni: littafi na biyu. 2, 6 bks 40pp. ill. 55k OUP-Nig 1971 NR HAU

Yahaya, I.Y.
Tatsuniyoyi da wasanni: littafi na daya. 1, 6 bks ill. 45k OUP-Nig NR HAU

Yahaya, I.Y.
Tatsuniyoyi da wasanni: littafi na hudu. 4, 6 bks 55pp. ill. 65k OUP-Nig 1971 NR HAU

Yahaya, I.Y.
Tatsuniyoyi da wasanni: littafi na shida. 6, 6 bks 58pp. ill. 65k OUP-Nig 1972 NR HAU

Yahaya, I.Y.
Tatsuniyoyi da wasanni: littafi na uku. 3, 6 bks 62pp. ill. 65k OUP-Nig 1971 NR HAU

Yahya, A.S.
Alfu lela ulela (au siku elifu na moja). Kitabu cha nne. [The Arabian nights entertainment] bk. 4. 80pp. ill. K.shs.7.25 Longman - Ken 1974 KE SWA

Yahya, A.S.
Alfu lela ulela (au siku elifu na moja). Kitabu cha pili. [The Arabian nights entertainment.] bk. 2. 65pp. ill. K.shs.6.00 Longman - Ken 1974 KE SWA

Yahya, S.
Mafunzo ya kiswahili. bk.1 See: Khan, K.

Yahya, S.
Mafunzo ya kiswahili. bk.2 See: Khan, K.

Yakiah, N.K.
Ibi onu Epíe 1. [Epie-Atissa reader, 1] 63pp. ill. 30k (Inst. of African Stud., Univ. of Ibadan, Rivers readers project, 9) Inst Afr Stud-Ibadan 1971 NR EPI

Zahar, R.
Colonialism and alienation: political thoughts of Frantz Fanon. Tr. fr. German by W. Feuser. 124pp. hd. & pap. N1.25 pap. N3.00 hd. Ethiope 1974 NR

Zaidi, N.H.
Hadithi kutoka nchi mbalimbali. [Stories from other lands] 56pp. ill. K.shs.3.00 OUP-Nairobi 1968 KE SWA

Zaidi, N.H.
J. F. Kennedy. 36pp. photos. K.shs.3.00 OUP-Nairobi 1966 KE

Zajaczowski, A.
Elements of introductory sociology. 37pp. U.shs5.00 (M.I.S.R. Nkanga ed., 5) Mak Inst Soc Res 1969 UG

Zakayo, M.
Siri 10 za ushindi. [Ten secrets of victory.] 60pp. T.shs.3.50 Africa Inland Church 1975 TZ SWA

Zalla, M.
Socio-economic causes of malnutrition in Moshi district. See: Swantz, M.L.

Zalla, T.M.
The herd composition and farm management data on small holder milk producers in Kilimanjaro. T.shs.12.00 ($3.00) (Research pap., 74.8) Econ Res Bur - Tanz 1975 TZ

Zama, J.M.
Ingwe idla ngamabala. [A leopard eats by its spots] 100pp. 45c Shuter 1967 SA ZUL

Zama, J.M.
Isinkwa sethu semihla ngemihla. [Our daily bread] 96pp. 42c. Shuter 1960 SA ZUL

Zambenga Batukezanga
Les hauts et les bas. 62pp. ill. 25k pap. St. Paul 1971 ZR FRE

Zambezi Mission Inc. (rev. by Christian Literature Association in Malawi)
The student's English-Chichewa (Nyanja) dictionary. 173pp. K1.60 ($1.67) Christ Lit Assoc - Mal 1972 MW

Zambia Geographical Association.
Schools supplement 1973. 43pp. K1.00 ($2.00) Zambia Geog Assoc 1973 ZA

Zambia Geographical Association.
Schools supplement 1974. 96pp. K1.50 ($3.00) Zambia Geog Assoc 1974 ZA

Zambia Geographical Association.
Schools supplement 1975. 85pp. K1.50 ($3.00) Zambia Geog Assoc 1974 ZA

Zambia Information Service.
Report of the second national convention. 68pp. photos. gratis Zambia Cult Serv 1970 ZA

Zambia Information Services.
Fourth graduation ceremony. 28pp. gratis Zambia Cult Serv 1972 ZA

Zambia Information Services.
The origin and growth of non-alignment. 16pp. 20n. Neczam 1971 ZA

Zambia Information Services.
Speeches of H.E. President Kaunda: the imperative of human dignity. 16pp. 20n. Neczam 1968 ZA

Zambia Information Services.
Speeches of H.E. President Kaunda: the rich and poor nations. 20pp. 20n. Neczam 1968 ZA

Zambia Information Services.
Speeches of H.E. President Kaunda: towards self-sufficiency through development. 28pp. 20n. Neczam 1971 ZA

Zambia Information Services.
"Take up the challenge" - speeches of President Kaunda to National Council, 1970. 70pp. gratis Zambia Cult Serv 1970 ZA

Zambia Information Services.
Zambia in the security council. 88pp. photo. gratis Zambia Cult Serv 1972 ZA

Zambia Library Association.
A directory of libraries in Zambia. 15pp. 50n. Zambia Lib Assoc 1975 ZA

Zani, K.
Mafarakano na michezo mingine. [Three plays.]. 68pp. K.shs.14.50 (80p) Heinemann Educ - Nair 1975 KE SWA

Zani, Z.M.
Kiswahili kwa shile za sekondari. [Kiswahili for secondary schools.] bk. 1 168pp. K.shs.17.50 Heinemann Educ - Nair 1976 KE SWA

Zani, Z.M.
Mwongozo - Kiswahili kwa shule za sekondari. [Kiswahili for secondary schools, teacher's guide.] bk. 1 66pp. K.shs.9.50 Heinemann Educ - Nair 1976 KE SWA

Zanone, L.
Bibliographie de la géologie et de la recherche minière en Côte d'Ivoire (1885-1970). Documents dactylographiés ou non diffusés. pt. 2 69pp. CFA1000 SODEMI 1972 IV FRE

Zanone, L.
Bibliographie de la géologie et de la recherche minière en Côte d'Ivoire (1885-1970). Ouvrages publiés ou multigraphiés. pt. 1 185pp. CFA1815 SODEMI 1971 IV FRE

Zantzinger, G.
A companion to the films "Mgodo wa Mbanguzi" and "Mgodo wa Mkandeni". See: Tracey, A.

Zeeman, D.A.
Eleanor Farjeon. 1881-1965. 42pp. R2.20 Dept Bibliog, Lib & Typo 1970 SA

Zeffertt, D., eds.
Select South African legal problems. Essays in memory of R.G. McKerron. See: Kahn, E., eds.

Zeiss, C.
The teaching of English in South African schools. 20pp. R1.60 Dept Bibliog, Lib & Typo 1965 SA

Zeleza, P.
Night of darkness and other stories. 217pp. K3.00 (Malawian Writers series, 2) Popular Publ 1976 MW

Zell, H.M. ed.
Writings by West Africans. rev. ed. 31pp. 75c. Fourah Bay Bkshp 1967 SL

Zell, H.M.
Freetown vademecum. 80pp. map. 75c. Fourah Bay Bkshp 1966 SL

Zell, H.M.
Publishing in Africa in the seventies. Proceedings of an international conference, held at the University of Ife, Ile-Ife, Nigeria, 16-20 December, 1973. See: Oluwasanmi, E.

Zerihun, G.
Pupil's book. See: Rogers, J.

Zerihun, G.
Teacher's notes, book five. See: Rogers, J.

Zewi, M.
The lost finger. 102pp. N1.20 Nwamife 1977 NR

Zharare, C.M.
Kudzidzoroya. [Beginning witchcraft.] 109pp. 85c Longman - Rhod 1975 RH SHO

Zielinski, J.G.
On the theory of socialist planning. 170pp. pap., hd. N2.50 ($3.75) NISER 1968 NR

Ziervogel, D.
The Eastern Sotho. R2.50 Van Schaik SA

Ziervogel, D.
A grammar of Northern Transvaal Ndebele. R4.20 Van Schaik SA

Ziervogel, D.
Handbook of the Northern Sotho language. R2.85 Van Schaik SA

Ziervogel, D.
A handbook of the Zulu language. See: Louw, J.A.

Ziervogel, D.   Mokgogong, P.C.
Pu Kuntsu ye kogolo ya Sesotho sa leboa/Groot Noord-Sotho woordeboek/Comprehensive Northern Sotho dictionary. [Trilingual in Northern Sotho, Afrikaans and English.]. 1664pp. R20.00 cl. (R21.00 cl.) Univ South Africa 1975 SA MUL

Ziervogel, D.
Swazi texts. R1.90 Van Schaik SA

Zimerman, Z.
Bilharzia in Africa south of the Sahara 1958-1966. 88pp. R4.50 Dept Bibliog, Lib & Typo 1967 SA

Zimmermann, J.L.
Détermination de l'age de quelques mica de Madagascar par la méthode potassium-argon. 58pp. pl. FMG450 (F9.00) (Série Documentation, 166) Service Geol - Mad 1964 MG FRE

Zirimu, E.N.
When the hunchback made rain, and Snoring strangers. 88pp. K.shs.9.00 ($3.00) EAPH 1975 KE

Zirimu, P., ed.   Gurr, A., ed.
Black aesthetics. Papers from a colloquium held at the University of Nairobi, June 1971. 216pp. cl. & pap. K.shs.42.00 cl. K.shs.17.00 pap. ($8.00/£3.95 cl.) ($4.00/£2.00 pap.) EALB 1973 KE

Zmerli, S.
Espoirs et deceptions, 1942-43. 72pp. photos. D0.450 Maison Tunis 1971 TI FRE

Zmerli, S.
Figures Tunisiennes. Les contemporains et les autres. v.1. 160pp. photos. D600 Maison Tunis 1972 TI FRE

Zmerli, S.
Figures Tunisiennes. v. 2. 130pp. photos. D700 Maison Tunis 1976 TI FRE

Zondi, E.
Ukufa kukaShaka. [The death of Shaka.] repr. in new orthography ed. 53pp. R1.00 (Bantu treasury, 14) Witwatersrand UP 1976 SA ZUL

Zschintzsch, J., ed.   Edwards, S., ed.
Bako research station: progress report for the period April 1973 to March 1974. 171pp. ex. only. Inst Agric Res - Addis 1974 ET

Zulu, A.H.
The dilemma of the black South African. 14pp. 25c. (University of Cape Town T.B. Davie memorial lecture, 12) Univ Cape Town Lib 1972 SA

Zulu, J.B.
Zambian humanism. 96pp. K1.30 Neczam 1970 ZA

Zulu, J.N.
Cibwana ndi ukwati. [Pride and marriage.] 40pp. 40n. Neczam 1973 ZA NYA

Zulu, J.N.   Shonga, G.H.
Matsotsi. [Collection of four short stories about hooligans.] 84pp. 35n. Neczam 1972 ZA NYA

Zulu, J.N.
Mwai wanga. [Story of two brothers and their quest for education.] 70pp. K1.20 Neczam 1973 ZA NYA

Zulu, P.
A sheaf of gold: a collection of poems. 38pp. K1.00 Zambia Cult Serv 1971 ZA

Zungur, S.
Wakokin Sa'adu Zungur. [Poems of Sa'adu Zungur] 22pp. 45k Northern Nig 1968 NR HAU

Zvarevashe, I.
Tsuro nagudo. [The hare and the baboon.] 16pp. pl. 6c Rhod Lit Bur 1973 RH SHO

Zvarevashe, I.
Tsuro nanzou. [The hare and the elephant.] 12pp. pl. 5c Rhod Lit Bur 1972 RH SHO

Zvarevashe, I.M.
Kurauone. [Experience comes with age.] 116pp. pl. 70c. College Press 1976 RH SHO

Zwarenstein, H.   Burgers, A.C.J.
Xenopus Laevis: a supplementary bibliography. 40pp. 50c. Univ Cape Town Lib 1955 SA

Zwilenduna, I.
Umvundla londwangu. [The hare and the baboon.] 16pp. pl. 6c Rhod Lit Bur 1972 RH NDE

Zzizinga, S.M.
The family bumbel bees. 28pp. col. ill. K.shs.3.65 ($2.00/80p.) EALB 1976 KE